Contents

Foreword

Today's changing economy and technology require improved efficiency, additional power, and extended service life in modern on- and off-highway equipment. Because the supply of suitably trained diesel technicians has not kept pace with the demand, more must be trained, and the skills of those already trained must be upgraded. Experienced technicians often have difficulty coping with the technological advancements in their field, because innovations occur so rapidly and new material becomes available in such huge quantities that there is not enough time to properly assimilate it before having to use it.

There has long been a need for a comprehensive approach to the organization of information used in the diagnosis, maintenance, and repair of today's on- and off-highway diesel equipment. This material must also be in a form that both novice and experienced technician will find useful.

The author has written these textbooks with this goal in mind. His many years of experience as a diesel technician, instructor, and author in the area of diesel mechanics and the related fields of on- and off-highway equipment are evident in his systematic approach. His extensive training experience is evident to the users of the workbooks and instructor's guides that accompany the text. His experience has provided him with the background necessary to write a textbook whose philosophy keeps the student foremost while presenting the realities of work in the industry and stressing the instructor's role in the learning process. These texts, along with the author's previous book, *Diesel Mechanics,* fill a vacuum that existed for materials for use in training diesel service technicians.

Thomas L. Lownie
Campus Principal
Burnaby Campus
Pacific Vocational Institute

DIESEL EQUIPMENT II

Design, Electronic Controls, Frames, Suspensions, Steering, Transmissions, Drive Lines, Air Conditioning

ERICH J. SCHULZ

Former Director of Training Programs
Vocational Institute, Burnaby Campus
Burnaby, British Columbia

Gregg Division
McGraw-Hill Book Company
New York • Atlanta • Dallas • St. Louis • San Francisco • Auckland
Bogotá • Guatemala • Hamburg • Johannesburg • Lisbon • London
Madrid • Mexico • Montreal • New Delhi • Panama • Paris • San Juan
São Paulo • Singapore • Sydney • Tokyo • Toronto

Editors: D. Eugene Gilmore, Paul Berk
Design Supervisor: Nancy Axelrod
Production Supervisor: Priscilla Taguer
Art Supervisor: George T. Resch

Manuscript Editors: Ed Millman, Lester Strong
Cover Designer: Infield D'Astolfo Associates
Technical Studio: Vantage Art, Inc.

Library of Congress Cataloging in Publication Data

Schulz, Erich J
Diesel equipment.
Includes index.
CONTENTS: v. 1. Lubrication, hydraulics, brakes, wheels, tires.—v. 2. Design, electronic controls, frames, suspensions, steering, transmissions, drive lines, air conditioning.
1. Motor vehicles. 2. Construction equipment.
I. Title.
TL145.S33 629.2'25 80-15383
ISBN 0-07-055716-0 (v. 1)
ISBN 0-07-055708-x (v. 2)

DIESEL EQUIPMENT II: Design, Electronic Controls, Frames, Suspensions, Steering, Transmissions, Drive Lines, Air Conditioning

1 2 3 4 5 6 7 8 9 0 SMSM 8 9 8 7 6 5 4 3 2 1

ISBN 0-07-055708-X

Preface

Mechanical engineering technology has greatly advanced since the appearance of the first engine-powered motor vehicle and track machine. This progress is particularly apparent when we look at modern motor buses, on-highway motortrucks, truck-tractor trailers, huge off-highway motortrucks, and modern farm and industrial tractors. This equipment has become significantly more efficient, rugged, and customized to its end use. But at the same time it has become so sophisticated that 4.5 million mechanics are employed to keep diesel equipment operating. Moreover, as production continues and new technology makes more equipment obsolete each year, a shortage of trained mechanics is developing. Fifty thousand more mechanics are needed now, and the projected figures for 1990 call for 100,000 more.

Industrial consumers expect a motortruck, truck-tractor, or motor bus to travel at least 300,000 miles [482,700 kilometers] before requiring a major overhaul. Users of off-highway motor vehicles expect the equipment to operate at least 10,000 hours before a major overhaul is necessary. Although these expectations are usually met, improved work performance and durability cannot be credited to a single component, part, or system; it is the combined improvement of all these areas that has resulted in the overall technological success of modern on- and off-highway equipment. Nevertheless, if one area were to be seen as improving the productivity and handling performance of the equipment, it would be the various hydraulic systems. Power plants, transmissions, tires, and tracks have progressed almost simultaneously to improve performance and to decrease fuel consumption, thereby helping to lower operating costs.

Extending the service life of on- and off-highway equipment does not rest entirely with improved engineering design. Credit must also be extended to those responsible for maintaining and servicing the equipment. While it is true that vast sums of money have been spent and will continue to be spent on research to develop equipment that will meet the constantly increasing demands placed upon it, the problem of getting good mechanics, that is, those trained to the degree of competence required to service this sophisticated equipment, must also be solved.

It is the objective of *Diesel Equipment I* and *II* to help solve this problem by expanding the knowledge of all student mechanics so that they will eventually be able to diagnose, repair, and service much of today's on- and off-highway equipment.

Each of these textbooks can be used by the novice or the experienced mechanic, since each unit comprehensively covers the design and purpose of a particular system and its components and concludes with troubleshooting and servicing.

With the exception of the unit entitled "Shop Safety," which is in both textbooks, the units are not repeated. *Diesel Equipment I* covers lubrication, seals, gaskets, filters, bearings, hydraulics, tires, wheel hubs, and the various brake systems. *Diesel Equipment II* covers electricity and electronics, on- and off-highway equipment design, frames and suspensions, steering systems, track-type undercarriages, final drives and steering mechanisms, mechanical clutches, standard transmissions, fluid couplings, torque converters, drive lines, front and rear carriers, winches, wire ropes, and air-conditioning and refrigeration.

The time needed to cover both of these books would be about 30 weeks, with about 40 percent classroom lecture and assignment time, and 60 percent "hands on" shop work projects. The student must first know how to use hand and power tools and measuring instruments and understand the fundamentals of electricity and electronics. It would be helpful, although not essential, to know something of the design, operation, and servicing of the power plant. However, the latter may be taught before or after completing the *Diesel Equipment* program.

The author's engine textbook, *Diesel Mechanics,* may be used along with its accompanying workbook and instructor's guide for instruction in the design, operation, and servicing of diesel engines.

Workbooks have been prepared to complement these texts. They contain questions directly related to the textbook contents and also suggest hands on assignments for shop practice. The textbooks and workbooks have been organized so that the instructor can begin with any unit and then select units thereafter according to the course outline.

Instructor's guides, which give answers to the workbook questions, are available.

Dual dimensioning has been used throughout *Diesel Equipment I* and *II*. Metric measurements are given in brackets following the U.S. Customary measurement, and metric conversion tables are included at the back of the book.

It is hoped that through this program students will achieve sufficient knowledge and practical experience to make them employable in today's ever-growing diesel equipment field.

Erich J. Schulz

Acknowledgments

Many of the illustrations in this textbook were provided by the companies listed below. To these companies, I wish to express my thanks for their cooperation and generosity.

Allis-Chalmers Engine Division

American Hoist and Derrick Company

Bear Manufacturing Company

BLH Austin-Western

Caterpillar Tractor Co.

Chrysler Canada Limited

Clark Equipment of Canada

Columbia Trailer Co. Ltd.

Dana Corporation, Spicer Transmission Division

Deere & Company

Delco-Remy Division of General Motors Corporation

Eaton Corporation

Fiat-Allis

FMC Corporation

Ford Motor Company

Fruehauf Trailer Company of Canada Limited

Gearmatic Co.

General Motors Corporation

GMC Detroit Diesel Allison Division

GMC Truck and Coach Division of General Motors Corporation

Harnischfeger

Hendrickson Mfg. Company

International-Harvester Company

J I Case Company Agricultural Equipment Division

Lipe-Rollway Corporation

Mack Canada Inc.

Northwest Engineering Company

Pacific Car and Foundry Co.

Reyco Industries Inc.

Rockwell International, Automotive Operations

Rockwell-Standard, North American Rockwell Corporation

Schield Bantam Division of Koehring Company

Sundstrand Corporation

Terex Division of General Motors Corporation

Thermo King Corporation

The Trane Company

United States Steel International

WABCO, An American-Standard Company

Wagner Electric Corporation

Wire Rope Industries Ltd.

To my wife, I gratefully acknowledge the never ending hours when she placed her personal projects second in priority to the typing of this manuscript.

Erich J. Schulz

Unit 1
On-Highway Equipment

Trucking, as a mode of transporting, by far exceeds any other form of transportation in North America. An estimated 25.5 million motortrucks, truck-tractors, and tractor trailers travel an aggregate 300 billion mi (miles) [482.7 billion km (kilometers)] per year. They transport anything and everything that is produced, manufactured, grown, mined from the earth, or gathered from the sea; in fact their earnings are about 85 percent of the total revenue received from the transportation of goods. The initial purchase price of this equipment cannot be fully evaluated, but it is estimated to exceed $800 billion. The number of people employed in the truck-transport industry exceeds 10 million.

The off-highway equipment manufactured and operated in North America is highly sophisticated in design. The vehicles range from small farm tractors to giant shovels, some individually valued at over $2 million. The off-highway industry employs over 2.5 million people; the original cost of the equipment is staggering.

It is to on- and off-highway equipment that this textbook addresses itself. It is written to provide the student with sufficient insight and knowledge to qualify him or her for employment in this ever expanding industry—an industry which continuously requires technicians at the career entry level who have already developed the fundamental mechanical skills needed to service its sophisticated equipment. It is no longer sufficient to "turn a wrench." To service today's vehicles, the mechanic must understand the interrelationship of all components in order to logically solve problems by the most expeditious and economical methods, an approach pursued throughout this text.

MOTOR VEHICLES

Vehicles are, for the purposes of this textbook, any type of equipment in or on which something is carried. A *motor vehicle* is one that is operated by a motor or engine.

The motor vehicle outnumbers all other vehicles using the highways. Its chassis consists of the frame, suspension, axles, wheels, engine, transmission, steering control, and brakes (see Fig. 1-1). The standard frame width is 34 in (inches) [0.863 m (meters)]. The frame length of a four- or six-wheel motortruck, measured from the rear of the cab to the center of the rear axle (or to the center between the tandem axle), ranges from 39 in to 156 in [0.99 m to 3.96 m]. If longer frames are required, they are extended by 1-ft (foot) [0.304-m] increments.

Motor Vehicle Cab The motor vehicle cab (Fig. 1-2) consists of a driver or operator enclosure, with the essential controls, structural and mechanical parts, and gauges for the motor vehicle equipment. The overall width of the cab is about 58 in [1.47 m] unless it is a sleeper cab, in which case the width would be 87 in [2.2 m].

A conventional truck, with the cab located behind the engine and over the transmission, is the most economical design, and its overall length lends itself to a more favorable bridge formula. The steering gear, accessories, and engine are more accessible on this design than on others.

When the cab is located over the engine, the vehicle is referred to as a cab-over-engine truck or tractor. The shorter overall length of this design is more attractive to the operator who places a premium on maneuverability. Furthermore, visibility is greater than on a conventional cab.

Dead and Live Axles A motor vehicle may have an axle arrangement of one or more live axles (powered) (Fig. 1-3) or dead axles (nonpowered) (Fig. 1-4). A live axle supports a portion of the vehicle weight and provides the mechanical means of transmitting and multiplying the torque from the transmission to the wheels. A dead axle merely supports a portion of the vehicle weight. The axle is a tube, beam, or iron bar that extends across the vehicle frame and is fastened to the frame with leaf springs, coil springs, air bags, rubber torque bars, or is hydrostatically mounted.

The wheel hub is attached to each end of the axle, to which either a single or a dual disk wheel (or a single or dual demountable rim) is attached. On a live axle the carrier is mounted into the axle housing and the carrier side gears are connected by an axle shaft to the wheel hub.

Steering Axle A steering axle supports a portion of the vehicle weight, provides directional control, and may be of a live axle or dead axle design. Tandem axles are either two live axles or two dead axles, or may be two steering axles attached by some mechanical means one behind the other to the same vehicle frame, so that a specific relation and loading is accomplished. A steering axle may be a tube, beam, or iron bar which extends across the vehicle frame and is mounted with coil springs, leaf springs, torque bars, or hydropneumatically. See Fig. 1-5. The spindle is fastened to each end of the axle with a kingpin or a ball joint. The wheel hub is attached by bearings to the spindle. A single disk wheel or a

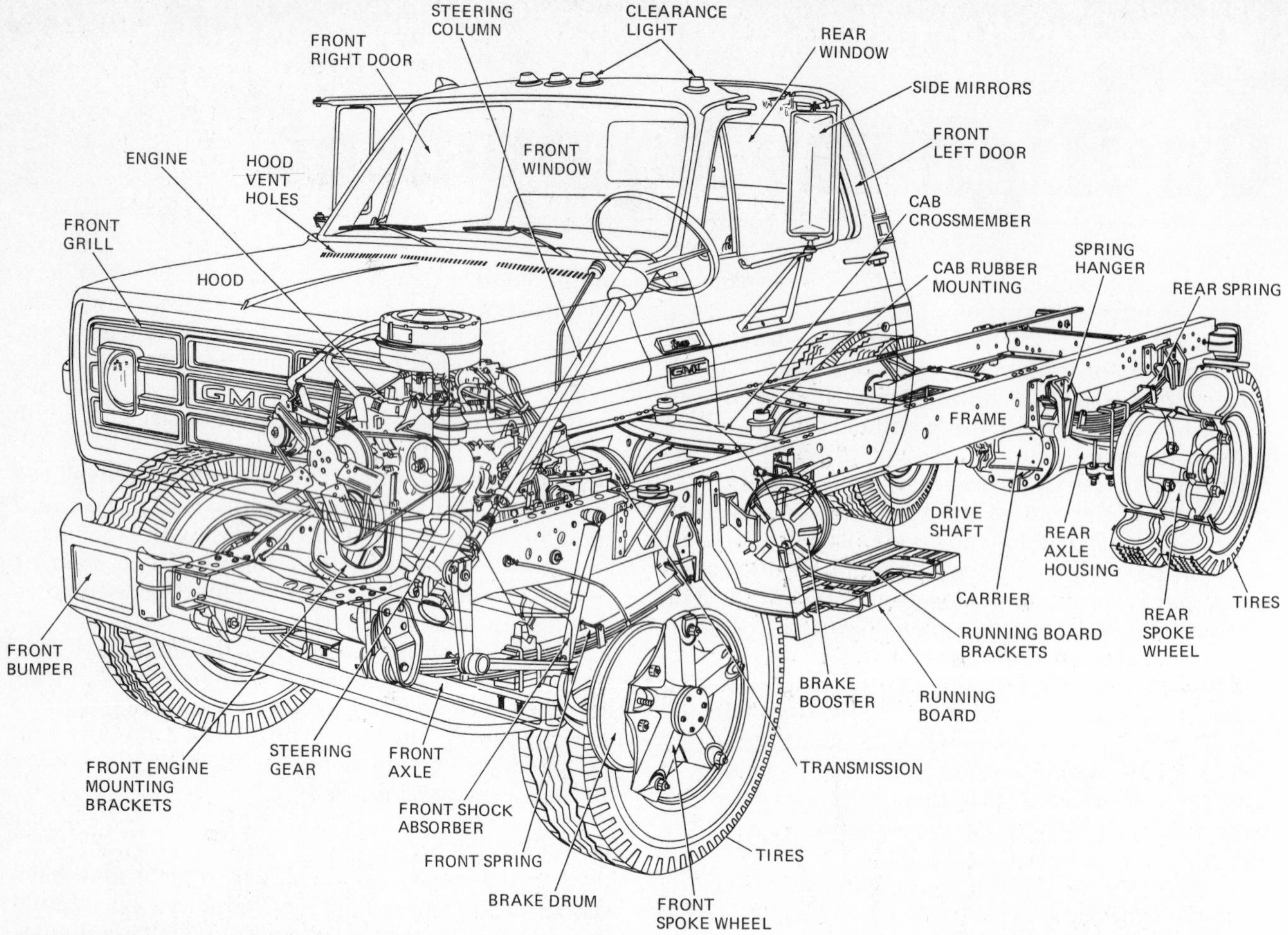

Fig. 1-1 Cutaway of truck components. (*GMC Truck & Coach Division*)

Fig. 1-2 Interior of motor vehicle cab.

single demountable disk wheel is attached to the wheel hub (see the material on wheel hubs).

Motor Vehicle Classification by Number of Wheels In the building trade, a 2 × 4 is clearly understood to be a piece of wood having a standard height and width. Equally clear, in the automotive trade, is a dimension such as 4 × 2; it indicates the total number of live (powered) axles. In other words, the first number is indicative of the total number of wheels and the second number is the number of the wheels which are driven. **NOTE** "Wheels" refers to a single wheel, not to dual wheels.

Motor vehicle	Total wheels	Driven wheels	Total axles	Drive axles
4 × 2	4	2	2	1
4 × 4	4	4	2	2
6 × 2	6	2	3	1
6 × 4	6	4	3	2
6 × 6	6	6	3	3
8 × 4	8	4	4	2
8 × 8	8	8	4	4

NOTE The 6 × 2 motor vehicle has a tandem rear axle but only one drive axle because the second rear axle is an unpowered tag-along axle. Its function is to extend the distance between the first and last axle, thereby increasing the load-carrying capacity of the motortruck or bus.

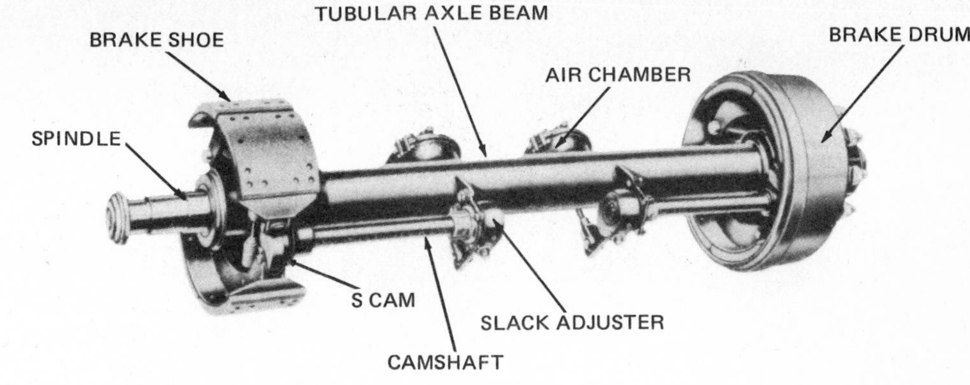

Fig. 1-3 Dead axle. (*Rockwell-Standard, North American Rockwell Corporation*)

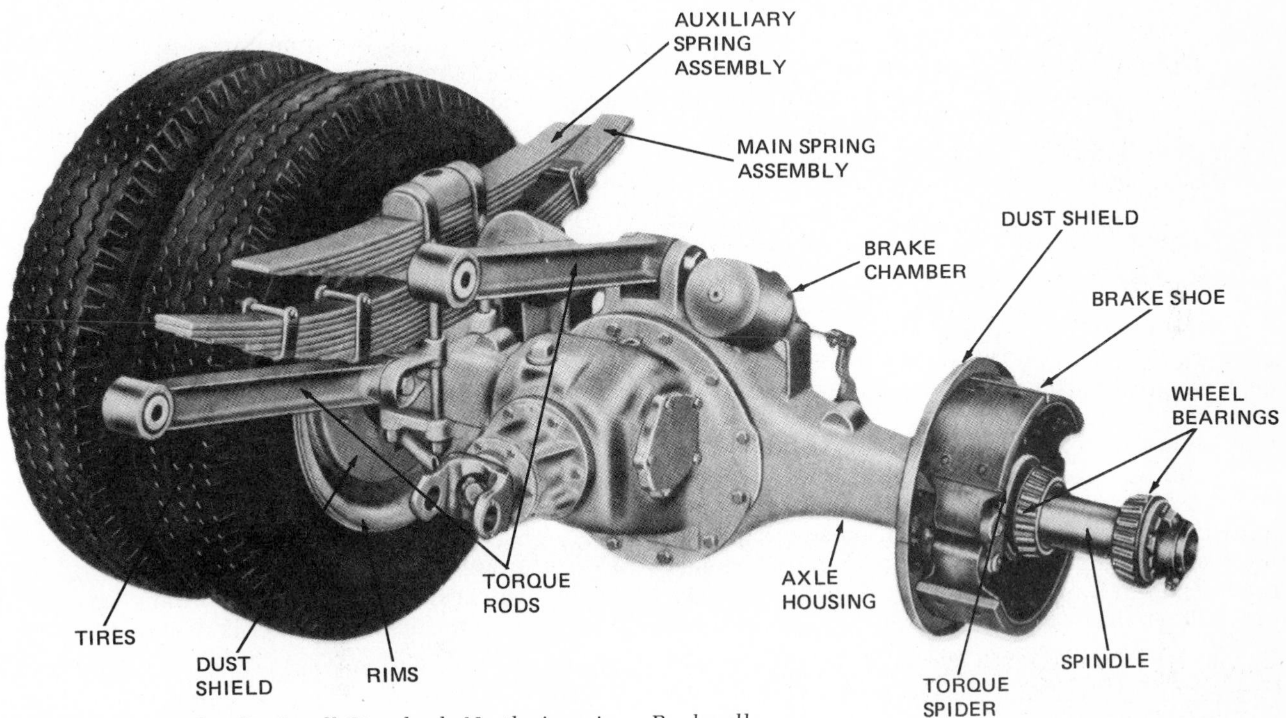

Fig. 1-4 Live axle. (*Rockwell-Standard, North American Rockwell Corporation*)

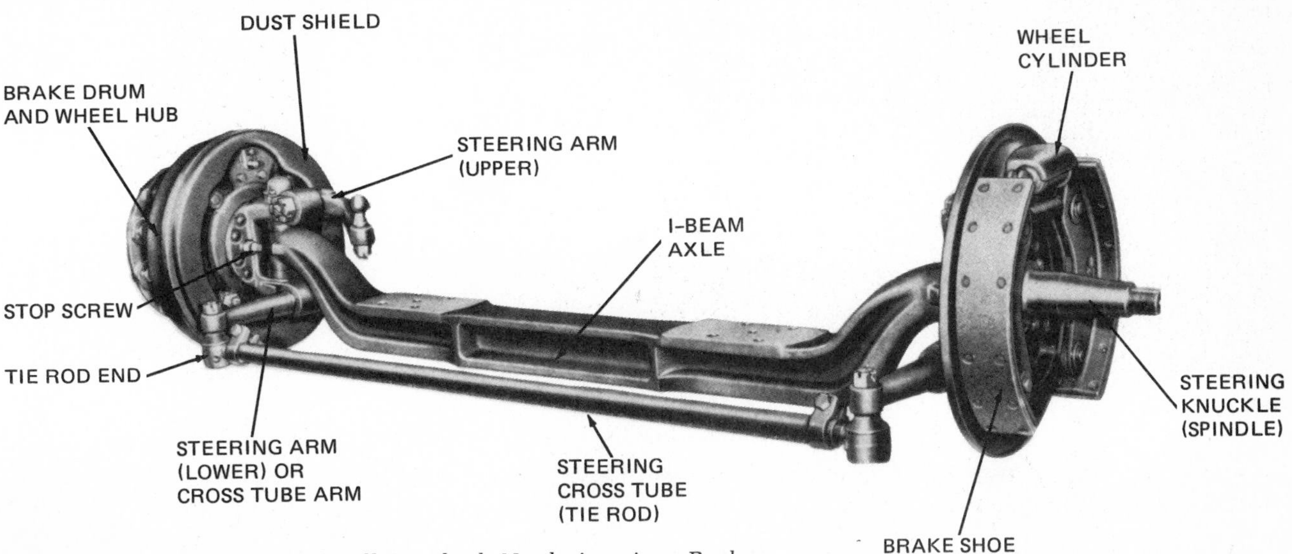

Fig. 1-5 Steering axle. (*Rockwell-Standard, North American Rockwell Corporation*)

Fig. 1-6 Motortruck with grain box.

Motortruck A motortruck is a motor vehicle designed and constructed to carry the weight of its load on its own wheels and/or to draw one or two full trailers. (A truck-tractor is a motor vehicle particularly designed to draw and to carry part of the weight and load of a semitrailer.) As the trucking industry has become more and more specialized, trucks and trailers are now built without bodies. Usually only small trucks are available with bodies.

MOTORTRUCK BODIES The body of a motortruck or truck-trailer is that part which supports or maintains the load and is fastened to the truck or trailer frame.

FLATDECK The simplest body is a flatdeck, the frame of which is iron and the floor (deck) is wooden. Flatdecks are designed to haul goods packed in boxed containers or on pallets (Fig. 1-6). Some are designed with short sides or poles fastened to the body to prevent the load from shifting on the deck. Others have a roof supported by several posts, with side canvas hung from the roof to protect the load against the weather.

Truck-bed crane Some flatdecks have a truckbed crane (mounted behind the cab), used to self-load and unload the material or goods (Fig. 1-7). The cranes may be simple in design—that is, the mast may be located over the mast plate that is fastened to the truck frame, with the boom fixed to the mast. A hand-operated winch is bolted to the mast and the live end of the wire rope is fastened to the winch. The wire rope is guided over two sheaves (pulleys), one on the mast and the other on the boom. The dead end of the wire rope is fastened to a swivel hook.

When the truck-bed crane is of a more sophisticated design, it has the appearance of a boom-man-lift without the platform. The boom may be telescopic and can be raised and lowered hydraulically. The mast, mounted to a turntable, can be rotated through the action of a hydraulic motor and reduction gear, while the winch is hydraulically driven.

Truck-bed cranes are available to suit any number of work situations, and therefore vary in their lift capacity and lift height, swing radius, boom extension (manual or hydraulic), and winch speed range. Some units also have stabilizers or outriggers. (See sections on boom lifts and hydraulic telescopic cranes in Unit 2.)

The lift capacities range from 2400 to 26,400 lb (pounds) [1089.6 to 11,985.6 kg (kilograms)] and have a hook height varying from 19 to 61 ft [5.7 to 18.60 m].

ENCLOSED BODIES Merchandise that must be protected against theft during transport and layover is transported in truck and trailer bodies that are fully

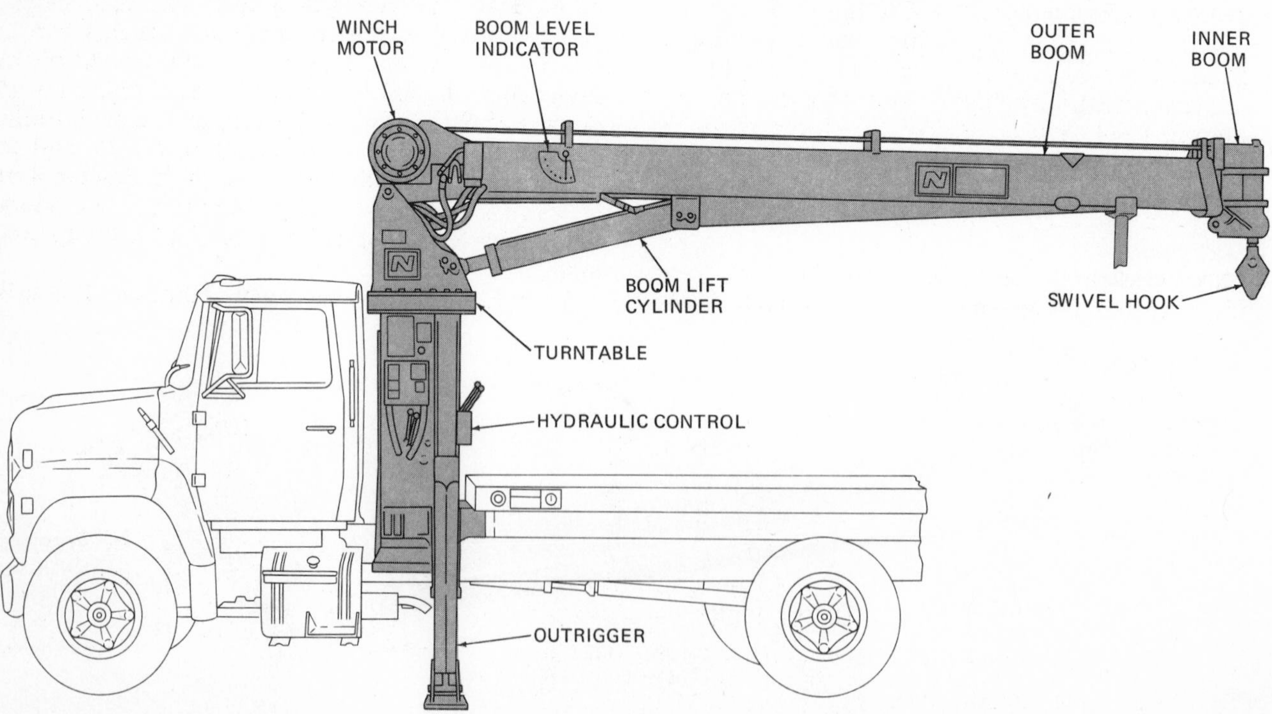

Fig. 1-7 Truck-bed crane.

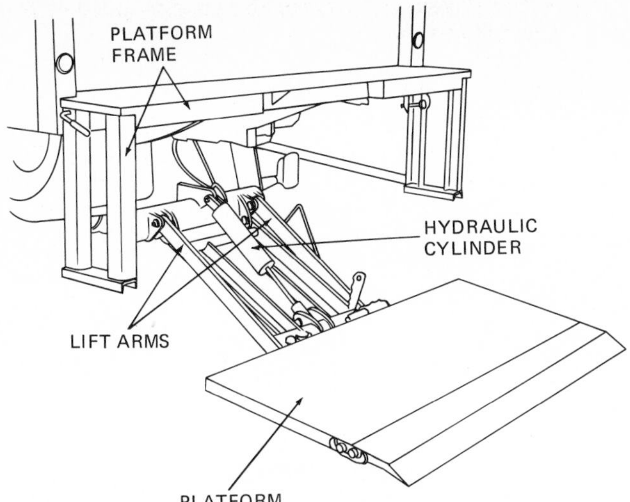

Fig. 1-8 Hydraulic operator platform.

Fig. 1-11 Truck-tractor.

Fig. 1-9 Concrete mixer.

enclosed and have either side or rear doors. Some of these trucks are equipped with an hydraulically operated platform, pivot-fastened to the truck frame to facilitate loading and unloading where docking facilities are inadequate or nonexistent (Fig. 1-8).

To transport perishables or frozen foods, the truck body must not only be enclosed, but it must be especially designed and insulated. To maintain a low temperature within the box, a refrigeration unit is fastened to the front of the body.

OTHER TYPES OF BODIES Other specially designed bodies are those required to carry livestock, heavy machinery, pipes, automobiles, loose agricultural goods, and road construction material.

Even dirt excavation truck bodies are specially designed. The aluminum dump box mounted to the frame is pivot-fastened at the rear frame. Single or dual telescopic hydraulic cylinders are used to raise the box to a dump angle of about 70°. Other specially designed bodies are those which carry fuel, oil, milk, cement, etc. (see Fig. 1-9 for one such example).

TRAILERS

Semitrailers A semitrailer (Fig. 1-10) has one or more rear dead axles; the front end of the trailer is connected to a truck-tractor (Fig. 1-11) through the upper plate and the fifth wheel. The fifth wheel, being attached to the tractor frame, carries part of the weight load and a portion of the weight of the semitrailer. Under ideal load-weight distribution, 20 percent of the total weight would rest on each trailer axle, 20 percent on each tractor rear axle, and 20 percent on the tractor front axle. (If the tractor were of the single drive axle design, 40 percent of the total semitrailer weight would then rest on the tractor rear axle.)

To achieve ideal weight distribution, the fifth

Fig. 1-10 Semitrailer, with fifth wheel shown at the right.

Fig. 1-12 Low-bed loader.

wheel can be repositioned on the tractor, and on some semitrailers the tandem trailer axles can be repositioned on the trailer frame.

The body of a semitrailer may be the same in design as other truck bodies. However, semitrailers that transport large equipment and heavy loads such as track machines, steel bridge structures, large generators, etc., are of a special design, often referred to as *low-bed loaders* or *low loaders*. See Fig. 1-12. Immediately in front of the tandem or triple axle, the trailer frame is lowered so that the frame side rails are about 1 ft [30.48 cm (centimeters)] from the ground. At the end of the long flatdeck, the side rails are fabricated into the shape of a goose neck, to which the fifth wheel upper plate (with kingpin) (see Fig. 1-13) is attached. The circular cast-steel upper plate is 38 in [96.52 cm] in diameter, with a 2-, 2.5-, or 3.5-in [5.08-, 6.35-, or 8.89-cm] kingpin fastened to its center. It is rigidly fastened below, some 36 in [91.44 cm] from the front frame face of the semitrailer.

Fifth Wheel One of several designs is shown in Fig. 1-14. A cast-steel plate, also called an *apron plate*, is rib-reinforced and cast as one piece. The top surface is machined so as to reduce friction and the lower parts are machined to facilitate the mounting of the coupling mechanism. The diameter is the same as that of the upper plate, but it has two nose-end extensions curved slightly downward. A locking mechanism is fastened underneath in the center of the plate. Special steel pins hold the front and rear jaws and the lock plate to the provided supports. When the fifth wheel is of the fixed-mounting design, it is bolted by two brackets to the tractor frame. When it is of the slide-mounting design, the mounting brackets are part of the saddle plate which slide in angle rails or in a base plate which is fastened to the trailer frame. The fifth wheel can be moved by hand or by an air cylinder. Tapered locking devices are used to lock the saddle plate to the angle rails or base plate. The tractor load and trailer weight are borne by the bearing surface of the brackets and fifth wheel plate. However, pins pass through the brackets or saddle plate to secure the fifth wheel plate to the bracket (or saddle plate).

NOTE The distance from the rear of the cab to the center of the clamping jaw varies, depending upon the trailer width and whether or not it has round or square corners. Minimum distances are set to allow a minimum clearance of 4 in [0.101 m] between the cab and the trailer body when the trailer center line is at a 45° angle with the center line of the trailer.

OPERATION To move the fifth wheel either forward or backward, first move the handle to release the safety latch and then pull the handle to eject the tapered lock pins from the elongated holes in the base plate. Position the fifth wheel by moving the

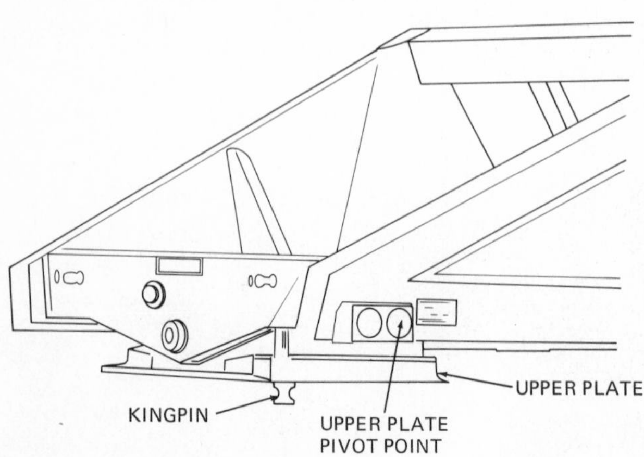

Fig. 1-13 Fifth-wheel upper plate. (*Fruehauf Trailer Company of Canada Limited*)

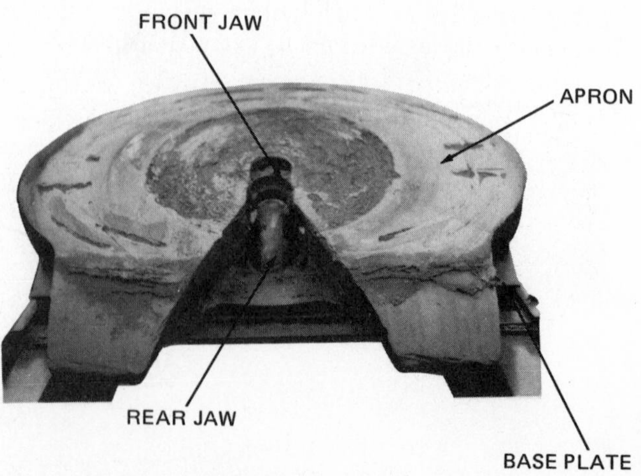

Fig. 1-14 Fifth wheel.

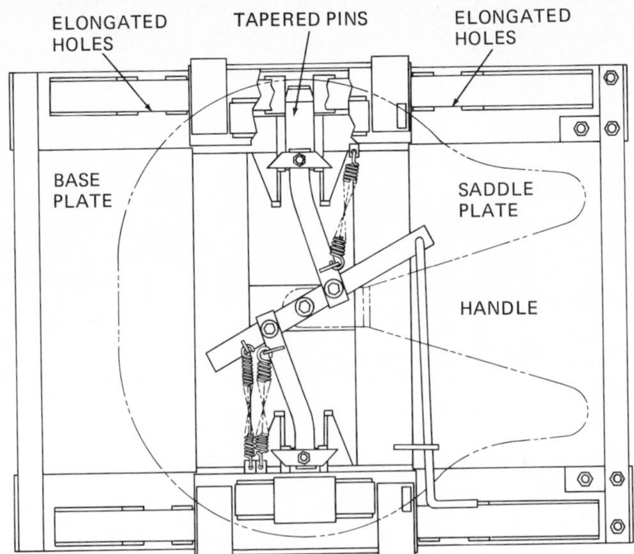

Fig. 1-15 Fifth-wheel adjustment.

saddle plate into place and then lock that plate. To couple the trailer, unlock the operating handle's safety lock and move it backward. This action pivots the lever and cam. The cam releases the lock, allowing the rear jaws to pivot backward sufficiently below the fifth-wheel plate surface to prevent the rear jaw from interfering with the kingpin when the plate slot is guided into it. As the tractor is backed up, the kingpin moves the front and rear jaws against the buffer rubber, compressing it slightly and causing the jaws to clamp around the kingpin. This action allows the lock to fall against the end at the rear jaws at the same time the lock rotates the cam into the locked position. The operating handle then moves below the safety latch and the safety latch enters the locked position. See Fig. 1-15.

Full Trailer A full trailer (Fig. 1-16) is a vehicle which has at least two axles and which bears the full weight and load on its own wheels. The type of trailer coupling used is relative to the trailer's gross vehicle weight (GVW). Trailers with a GVW up to 10,000 lb [4540.0 kg] can use a ball hitch. The ball is mounted to the motor vehicle frame and a hitch clamp is fastened to the trailer draw bar. When coupled, the movable jaw is screwed against the ball, securing the trailer. With all types of trailer couplings, two safety chains connecting the motor vehicle with the trailer must be used as a compulsory additional safety measure. Trailers with a GVW of 10,000 lb to 40,000 lb [4540.0 to 18,160 kg] use a

RUBBER MOUNTED HITCH

TAILGATE PIVOT POINT

TURNTABLE

DRAWBAR PIVOT POINT

CHAIN

Fig. 1-16 Five-axle full trailer. (*Fruehauf Trailer Company of Canada Limited*)

Fig. 1-17 Sliding full trailer.

Fig. 1-19 Pole trailer (loaded).

pivot-mounted drawbar fastened to the trailer, and the drawbar eye is hooked into a safety latch which is fastened to the truck or trailer frame. The coupling is secured by manually actuating a lever, or else it is air-actuated.

To increase the possible load capacity, some trailers of the open box design rest on guide rails which are fastened to the trailer frame. The guide rails extend about 2 ft [0.61 m] beyond the trailer frame. A chain which can be driven by a hydraulic motor is fastened to the trailer box. (See Fig. 1-17.) The trailer box is narrower and slightly shorter than the truck dump box. After the truck is loaded, the truck can be backed onto the trailer so that the two guide rails lock into the truck guide rail pockets. After the hydraulic lines are connected (by quick couplings), the driver operates the directional control valves to actuate the hydraulic motor. The chain then pulls the trailer box onto the truck box. After the load is dumped, the truck is again backed onto the trailer, the hydraulic lines are reconnected, the operator moves the control valve in the opposite direction, and the trailer box is pulled out of the truck box onto the trailer frame.

Balance Trailer A *balance trailer,* whether of a low or high GVW class, is a trailer having only one axle. The load-carrying axle is so positioned to the trailer frame that, when the load is placed onto the trailer, the load is nearly in balance and only a small amount of weight rests on the fixed drawbar.

Fig. 1-18 Converter dolly.

Converter Dolly A trailer *converter dolly* has either a single or a tandem axle and is equipped with a fixed drawbar and a fifth wheel. It is used to convert a semitrailer into a full trailer which can then be hooked to a truck or to another trailer hitch. See Fig. 1-18.

Pole Trailer A *pole trailer* could have either a single axle or a tandem axle to which one end of a reach or pole is attached. The other end is attached to the tractor. The pole trailer is designed to transport long or odd-shaped loads, which are capable of supporting themselves between the pole trailer and the tractor. See Fig. 1-19.

REGULATIONS AND SPECIFICATIONS

The mechanic, per se, has very little to do with formulation of the various regulations and laws regarding motor vehicle height, total length, carrying capacity, tire size, axle arrangement, or the required engine power. It is the responsibility of the vehicle manufacturers to supply users with the vehicles best suited for their particular needs and to achieve maximum load capacity or volume while keeping within the boundaries of governing regulations and legal restrictions. It would not be practical to list all the regulated figures for each state under whose jurisdiction readers of this text might find themselves, but a random sample is given for comparative purposes.

Legal Dimensions and Weights The maximum vehicle height, width, and length, as well as the gross combination weight (GCW), are closely related across North America. The maximum vehicle height, from the ground to the top of the body, is 13.6 ft [4.148 m] and the overall standard width is 96 in [2.44 m]. However, 9 ft or 108 in [2.745 m] is allowed on nearly all highways. The width is measured from the outside of one tire, say, on the left, to the outside of the other tire, here the tire on the right. The overall length of a single motor vehicle is limited to about 36 ft [10.89 m]. The overall length of a semitrailer is limited to 45 ft [13.72 m] and a com-

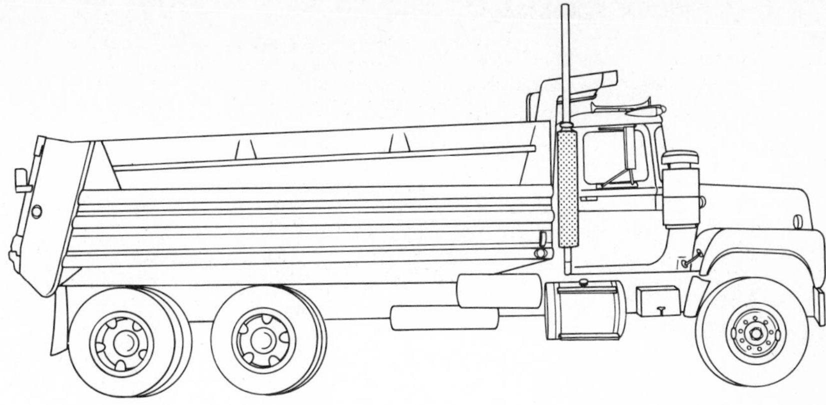

Fig. 1-20 Dump truck.

bination, that is, a tractor and trailer, or a truck trailer, is limited to 65 ft [19.82 m]. In some states laws allow a truck or tractor to pull one semitrailer, and a full trailer or two full trailers, but the overall length must not extend beyond 72 ft [21.96 m]. There are, however, additional limitation regulations regarding the distance from the kingpin of the semitrailer to the extreme end of the full trailer.

As a rule, special road permits can be obtained in nearly every state or province, if so required, to carry a load greater than 80,000 lb [36,320.0 kg] or to operate a vehicle on the highway in excess of the normal vehicle length restrictions. The maximum allowable special load varies between states and provinces, ranging from 110,000 to 140,000 lb [49,940.0 to 63,560.0 kg] and the maximum allowable length varies from 75 to 110 ft [22.87 to 33.55 m].

To be compatible with normal loading and unloading facilities (docking), all manufacturers have their vehicles designed to a floor height of 44 to 56 in [1.11 to 1.42 m], depending on the type of vehicle or tire size.

Axle Spacing and Load Capacity Motortrucks and truck-tractors are manufactured in a variety of sizes to give the user the most efficient service, while minimizing the initial capital outlay.

Motortrucks are grouped by gross vehicle weight (GVW) which is also indicative of their general use. GVW is the total weight of a motor vehicle including its load, fuel, cooling, oil, and the weight of the driver. Trucks grouped at 5000, 14,000, and 24,000 lb [2270.0, 6356.0, and 10,895.0 kg] GVW are two-axle units and are used as pickup trucks and for short-distance hauls. Motortrucks grouped at 30,000, 40,000, and 55,000 lb [13,620.0, 18,160.0, and 24,970.0 kg] GVW are usually three-axle units and are used as line haul or gravel trucks, etc. Motortrucks grouped from 55,000 to 80,000 lb [24,970 to 36,320 kg] GVW are three-axle, four-axle, and five-axle units, used in line hauling to carry maximum load capacities, or are especially designed to transport liquid or, more particularly, heavy equipment. See Fig. 1-20.

Truck-tractor and semitrailer combinations within the 42,000- and 60,000-lb [19,068- and 27,270.0-kg] GCW range are four-axle units with either the trailer having only one axle or the tractor having only one drive axle. These units are used in line haul where lighter-density loads (cubic volume) will not utilize the maximum GCW capacity. These units may increase their GCW range by using an additional full trailer, under which circumstance they could have seven axles. Truck-tractor and semitrailer combinations in the 50,000- to 80,000-lb [22,700.0- to 36,320.0-kg] GCW range are four- and five-axle units where the tractor has two or three axles and the semitrailer has two axles. See Fig. 1-21. These and the seven- and nine-axle units are the most predominant in the trucking industry.

To conform with weight regulations which allow a single axle to carry a load of 20,000 lb [9080.0 kg] and a tandem axle 34,000 lb [15,436.0 kg], the distance between the center of the first axle and the center of the last axle must conform with the axle spacing (bridge formula) and the gross weight on any wheel must not exceed 242.5 lb [110 kg] for every 0.39 in [1 cm] of tire width.

A bridge formula is shown in Table 1-1. It gives the distance in feet [meters] between the center of the first axle and center of the last axle of any group of axles, and the load in pounds [kilograms] that can be carried.

Fig. 1-21 Truck-tractor—semitrailer and full trailer combination.

Table 1-1 BRIDGE FORMULA

Distance		Two axles		Three axles		Four axles		Five axles		Six axles		Seven axles	
ft	[m]	lb	[kg]	lb	[kg]	lb	[kg]	lb	[kg]	lb	[kg]	lb	[kg]
4	1.22	34,000	15,436										
6	1.83	36,000	16,344										
8	2.44	38,000	17,252	42,000	19,068								
10	3.05	40,000	18,160	43,500	19,749								
12	3.66			45,000	20,430	50,000	22,700						
14	4.27			46,500	21,111	51,500	23,381						
16	4.88			48,000	21,792	52,500	23,835	58,000	26,332				
18	5.49			59,500	22,473	54,000	24,516	59,500	27,013				
20	6.01			51,000	23,154	55,500	25,197	60,500	27,467	66,000	29,964		
22	6.71			52,500	23,835	56,500	25,651	62,000	28,148	67,000	30,418		
24	7.32			54,000	24,516	58,000	26,332	63,000	28,602	68,500	31,099	74,000	33,596
26	7.93			55,500	25,197	59,500	27,013	64,500	29,283	69,500	31,553	75,000	34,050
28	8.54			56,000	25,878	60,500	27,467	65,500	29,737	71,000	32,234	76,500	34,731
30	9.15			58,500	26,559	62,000	28,148	67,000	30,418	72,000	32,688	77,500	35,185
32	9.76			60,000	27,240	63,500	28,829	68,000	30,600	73,000	33,142	78,500	35,639
34	10.37					64,500	29,283	69,500	31,553	74,500	33,823	80,000	36,320
36	10.98					66,000	29,964	70,500	32,007	75,500	34,277		
38	11.59					67,500	30,645	72,000	32,688	77,000	34,958		
40	12.20					68,500	31,099	73,000	33,142	78,000	35,412		
42	12.81					70,000	31,780	74,500	33,823	79,000	35,866		
44	13.42					71,500	32,461	75,500	34,277				
46	14.03					72,500	32,915	77,000	34,958				
48	14.64					74,000	33,596	78,000	35,412				
50	15.25					75,000	34,050	79,500	36,093				
52	15.86					76,500	34,731						
54	16.47					78,000	35,412						
56	17.08					79,500	36,093						
or more						80,000	36,320						

It becomes apparent that not only the load capacity of the axle itself governs the GVW or the GCW, but also the tire width and axle spacing. In order to pull its load (or a combined load), a motortruck or a tractor must have an adequate number of drive axles, the required engine power, and the recommended tire size.

Motor Vehicle Dimension Code To refer to certain dimensions on a motor vehicle or vehicle, manufacturers use the following abbreviations (See Fig. 1-22):

- AC— from center line of front axle to back of cab
- AE— rear axle (tandem) to end of chassis
- BA— from front bumper to center line of front axle or of the tandem front axle
- BBC— from front bumper to backup axle (conventional cab), about 105 in [2.66 m] cab over engine 75 in [1.9 m]
- BL— length of body
- BC— distance between tandem axles, which is about 4.0 to 4.2 ft [1.22 to 1.28 m]
- CG— load center, a point within the length and width on a motor vehicle or vehicle
- CL— clearance between cab and body
- CE— from body of cab to end of frame
- CA— from back of cab to center of rear axle or center between the two tandem axles
- D— distance between front and the last axle (see Table 1-1, Bridge Formula)
- FG— from front of body to center of payload
- F/X— weight carried by the front axle
- R/X-1-2-3— weight carried by the rear axles
- H-1-2— front frame height loaded and unloaded
- H-3-4— rear frame height loaded and unloaded
- KP— distance from center axle or center of tandem axle to kingpin
- L— payload plus truck-tractor weight
- LT— payload and trailer weight
- OA— overall length of chassis
- PD— hitchpoint to center of first trailer axle
- TWB— semitrailer wheel base to center of tandem axle
- WB— wheel base, the distance between the center of the front axle to the center of the rear axle, or where tandem axles are used, from the center of the front axle to the midpoint between the two tandem axles.

Engines and Power A single "all-purpose" engine, whether gasoline, liquid petroleum gas, or diesel, cannot be designed to perform satisfactorily under any and all circumstances. When researching and developing an engine, the manufacturers must consider such things as the following: (1) How much will the consumer pay for the power plant? (2) How many miles per year must it operate? (3) What is the

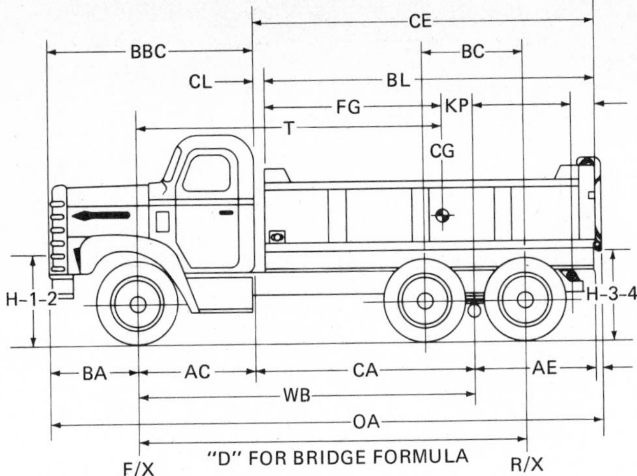

Fig. 1-22 Truck diagram.

nature of the operation—short haul, long haul, or city pickup? Will the load gradually diminish enroute? (4) What is the grade factor on which the load will be hauled? (5) What is the intended payload (weight or cubic volume)? (6) What would be the preferable type of box (in regard to wind resistance)? (7) How would this conform to regulatory weight and length requirements? (8) What is the desired engine performance in regard to torque and engine revolutions per minute (rpm)? In most applications, a flatter torque curve is more desirable as it reduces wear on the drive train and extends the life of the foundation brakes. With a flat torque curve, the engine maintains its maximum torque over a greater engine rpm range. (9) What priority is placed on fuel economy? (10) What is the anticipated engine life and the interim maintenance cost? (11) Under what traffic conditions and altitude will the vehicle operate? (13) What type of transmission carrier, tire size, and rolling resistance must it complement? (14) What degree of importance should be attached to engine weight? (Less engine weight means a greater payload can be carried.)

In view of the myriad of problems that would need to be solved, you can see that an all-purpose engine is obviously impractical. In any event, a gasoline engine is, at times, more suitable for a particular type of operation, a liquid petroleum gas for another, and the diesel engine is preferable for yet others. At present, gasoline engines are used most widely in small motortrucks (pickups and vans), although in the last few years small light-weight diesel engines have become increasingly popular for these kinds of vehicles. This light-weight diesel engine falls within the range of 70 to 160 hp (horsepower) [52.15 to 119.2 kW (kilowatts)] and has a torque range of 113 to 315 lb · ft (pound-feet) [153.11 to 426.82 N · m (newton-meters)].

About 80 percent of motor vehicles within the 5000- to 24,000-lb [2270- to 10,896-kg] GVW range use gasoline engines, whereas only 40 percent of motor vehicles above 24,000- to 50,000-lb [10,896.0- to 22,700.0-kg] GVW use them. Gasoline engines ranging from 160 to 250 hp [119.2 to 186.4 kW] have a torque range of 250 to 360 lb · ft [338.75 to 487.8 N · m]. Trucks and tractors having a GVW or GCW of 50,000 to 80,000 lb [22,700 to 36,320 kg] use diesel engines exclusively. The diesel engines used are either naturally aspirated, turbocharged, or turbocharged and after-cooled. Engines ranging from 140 to 600 hp [104.39 to 447.41 kW] have a torque of 180 to 1600 lb · ft [243.9 to 2168.0 N · m]. The 270- to 350-hp [201.31- to 260.96-kW] engines are used mostly in motor vehicles having a GVW or GCW range of 40,000 to 80,000 lb [18,160 to 36,320 kg].

Transmissions The transmissions used in motor vehicles are automatic, powershift, or manual. Automatic and powershift transmissions have found increasing popularity not only in buses or gravel trucks, but also in line haul trucks and tractors. The automatic transmissions used in lower GVW classes are three speed, whereas the automatic or powershift transmissions used in higher GVW or GCW classes are four and six speed and they usually have a lockup clutch and retarder.

The three- to five-speed transmissions are used in vehicles of a relatively low GVW. Line haul trucks and tractors as well as dump trucks use 6- to 15-speed transmissions. The 16- to 20-speed transmissions are somewhat uncommon and, when used, apply to such industries as logging and oil exploration.

TERMINOLOGY For the student who may have a sparse background with regard to heavy-equipment transmissions, the following short review of some terms as they are used in this field may be helpful:

- *Work.* Work has a technical meaning apart from its common meaning of manual labor. In either case, however, a force is exerted which produces motion. Physicists interpret work as force acting through distance. The work done is expressed in foot-pounds (ft · lb) [newton-meters (N · m)]. The formula for work is force times distance equals work, or $F \times D = W$.
- *Torque.* Torque is the twisting effort applied to a crank at a 90° angle. The twisting effort on the shaft is equal to the force times the distance from the center of the shaft to the point at which the force is applied. The standard unit of measurement for torque is the pound-foot (lb · ft), or newton-meter (N · m).

Torque can only produce work when the applied torque is greater than the resistance. Torque can be increased by increasing the distance of the torque arms, the force, or both.

- *Power (horsepower).* Power is the work done in a given time, or the rate of doing work. It may be expressed in terms of work per minute or work per second. However, in the English system of measurement it is expressed in horsepower (hp). This term was first used by James Watt as he tried to compare the power of a steam engine with the power of a horse. He found that a horse could pull a 150-lb load $3\frac{2}{3}$ feet per second (ft/s) doing 550 ft · lb of work every second, or 33,000 ft · lb of work every minute. In the metric system, power is measured in watts (W); 1 hp = 745.7 W.

- *Transmission.* A transmission is a mechanical or hydraulic device to transmit power and to change torque and speed. Most transmissions can also reverse the output shaft direction.
- *Automatic transmission.* An automatic transmission is a transmission that changes the gear ratio automatically in response to the load or engine rpm and the mph (miles per hour) [km/h (kilometers per hour)].
- *Powershift transmission.* A powershift transmission is a transmission that can be manually shifted without interruption of the power flow.
- *Torque converter.* A torque converter is a hydrodynamic device which doubles as a coupling as well as a transmission.
- *Lockup clutch.* A lockup clutch is a coupling that locks the engine to the input shaft of the transmission, thereby neutralizing the torque converter.
- *Clutch.* A clutch is a mechanical device that connects an output shaft to, or disconnects it from, the input shaft; for example, it connects an engine crankshaft to a transmission input shaft.

Review Questions

1. Name nine major components which are basic to all motor vehicles.
2. Name three gauges, common to all on-highway motor vehicles, which give the operator visual indication of the operating condition of the engine.
3. Very briefly describe the difference between a dead axle and a live axle.
4. What is the main difference (with respect to weight load) between a motortruck and a truck-tractor?
5. State three ways in which a full trailer differs from a semitrailer.
6. Give the maximum (highway) motor vehicle height (in meters and inches).
7. Give the maximum (highway) motor vehicle length (in meters and inches).
8. What are the determining factors governing the GCW and GVW?
9. In your opinion, which is the most important of the 14 textbook points listed on page 11 that manufacturers must consider when selecting the engine for a specific motor vehicle?
10. Personally examine a number of motortrucks and truck-tractors in your shop (or nearby dealership), then record for each vehicle (*a*) the GVW or GCW, and the engine hp; (*b*) the type of engine; (*c*) the type of transmission; (*d*) the number of gear ratios.
11. Convert the torque of a capscrew tightened to 100 lb · ft into metric units of measurement.
12. Convert 600 hp into metric units of measurement (kW).

Unit 2
Off-Highway Equipment

The influence of modern off-highway equipment on our daily lives is seldom thought about—it is taken for granted. How many millions enjoy comforts which would not be available to them without the benefits derived from nature's coal and from crude oil, so capably extracted from the earth by our heavy machinery? And what of the arable farm lands, now abundantly and speedily harvested by off-highway equipment for our ever increasing populations?

Continuing population growth long ago demanded increased productivity as well as the most highly efficient means possible of getting raw products to the market. Our heavy-equipment manufacturers have been meeting both these challenges. In fact, the technological advancements of off-highway equipment have overtaken those of the general trucking industry.

WHEELED MOTOR VEHICLES

Dumpers The number of off-highway dumpers now in operation is infinitely higher than it was a few years ago and, further, their load capacities have increased and their designs improved. Dumpers may be divided into four classes:

- Dump trucks
- Bottom dumpers
- Articulated steering dumpers
- Tractor scrapers

Dump Trucks All dump trucks have a rigidly welded frame structure. To dump the load rearward the dump box is raised by two three-stage hydraulic cylinders, and some specially designed units can dump the load to one side. Dump trucks have either a single drive axle (4 × 2) or tandem drive axle (6 × 4), and the front axle is the steering axle. They are used in the mining industry and for large excavating projects and, although quite similar in design to the on-highway 80,000-lb [36,320.0-kg] GVW dump truck, the components and overall construction are larger and stronger to accommodate a greater load capacity. The modern large dump truck shown in Fig. 2-1 has a GVW of 727,750.0 lb [330,010.0 kg] with an overall length of 50.6 ft [15.39 m], a width of 17.5 ft [5.31 m], and a height of 16.7 ft [5.05 m].

Larger dump trucks usually use hydropneumatic suspensions whereas smaller units, that is, below 60-ton (English ton) [54.42-t (metric tonne)] load capacity, may use a front and rear multileaf spring suspension or an independent coil spring suspension on the steering axle.

The engines are diesel and range from 600 to 1800 hp [447.36 to 1341.54 kW] and have a torque range between 1600 to 11,900 lb · ft [2168.0 to 16,124.4 N · m]. The smaller units use six- or eight-speed powershift transmissions having a hydraulic retarder and lockup clutch. Usually a differential lock and planetary wheel hubs are used. The larger units also use planetary wheel hubs; however, the sungear is driven by a dc wheel motor which is similar to a dc cranking motor. Current is supplied from an ac generator (a large alternator) that is bolted to the engine; the rotor is driven by the engine crankshaft. The alternating current is rectified, through diodes, into direct current in order to power the wheel motors.

The brake system is either full air brakes, or air over hydraulic, and the foundation brake is either wedge, expander tube, or a multidisk brake.

Dynamic brakes (braking achieved through dc motors) are the main braking system of the electrically driven trucks. When the current flow to the drive motors is cut off, the dc motors are driven by the wheels, and the motors become dc generators. The direct current that is produced by the motors is reverse in direction to the current which drives the motors, thus retarding the wheels. The regenerated current from the wheel motion is dissipated as heat.

Hydrostatic steering is a common feature. This type of steering is hydraulically controlled and hydraulically actuated without any mechanical linkage from the steering gear to the spindle.

Bottom Dumpers As the name indicates, bottom dumpers release their load from below, through clamshell doors. Once the load is dumped, the doors hydraulically close.

Bottom dumpers may be 4 × 2 motortrucks with a dump box positioned between the two axles. On this design the engine is located at the rear (the rear axle is the drive axle, and the front axle is the steering axle), or they may be of the bottom dumper design, that is, a truck-tractor with a semitrailer. Here the dump box is located between the fifth wheel and

Fig. 2-1 235-ton rear dump truck.

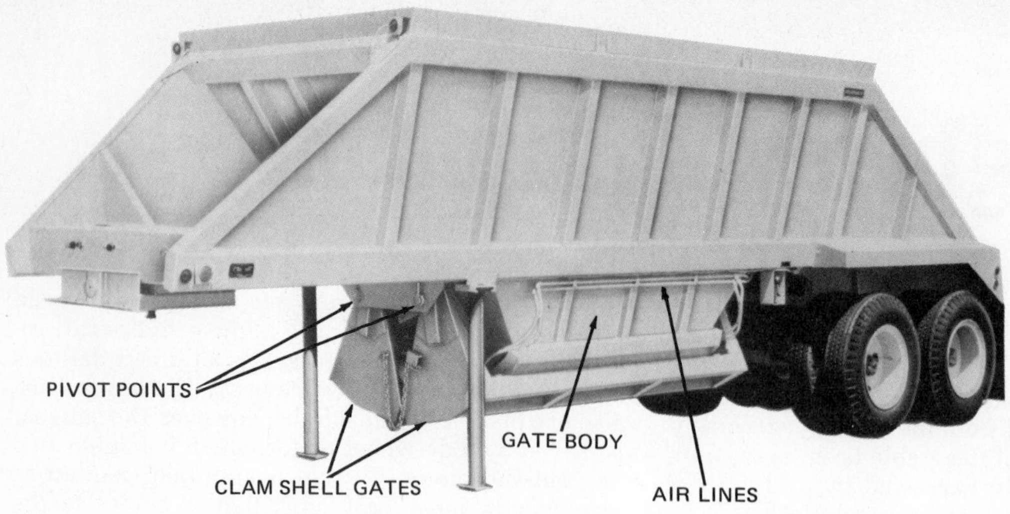

Fig. 2-2 Semitrailer bottom dumper with air-actuated clam shell gates. (*Fruehauf Trailer Company of Canada Limited*)

the tandem trailer axle. A third type of bottom dumper is the tractor and semitrailer (see Fig. 2-2). A tractor is a self-propelled machine whose prime purpose is to pull or push an object through its mounting attachment, (hitch or drawbar). **NOTE** Tractors include farm tractors and wheel-type tractors as well as track-type tractors. The main difference between a semitrailer bottom dumper and a truck-tractor bottom dumper is in the coupling that connects the semitrailer to the tractor. A pin hitch design is often used, and a tractor is used instead of a truck-tractor.

The load capacity of the bottom dumper shown in Fig. 2-3, is 150 ton [136.05 t] or 194 yd^3 (cubic yards) [148.41 m^3] with a GCW of 486,600 lb [220,714 kg]. The overall length is 74.7 ft [22.73 m] and the width is 16.8 ft [5.08 m]. The minimum required engine power is 800 hp [596.4 kW] with a torque of 765 lb · ft [1036.57 N · m]. It uses a six-speed powershift transmission having a hydraulic retarder and lockup clutch with a drive axle of the planetary wheel hub design. This particular bottom dumper tractor has an air over hydraulic brake system and a wedge foundation brake. The steering system is full power (hydrostatic). A hydropneumatic suspension design is used on the tractor and an air ride suspension is used on the semitrailer.

Articulated Steering Dumpers Articulated steering dumpers are commonly three-axle units where the tractor axle and the front trailer axle drive, or all three axles drive. Articulated means "united through a joint," in this case a joint uniting the tractor and trailer (see Fig. 2-4). Articulated steering means that the direction change is made by pivoting the tractor at the joint, moving it to the left or right, through the action of hydraulic cylinders. Two hydraulic cylinders are fastened to the tractor mounting brackets, and the two piston rod ends of the cylinders are fastened to the trailer. When the steering wheel is manipulated to make a left turn, oil is directed to the piston end of the right-hand steering cylinder and to the rod end of the left-hand steering cylinder. This action pulls the tractor to the left. When the steering wheel is manipulated to make a right-hand turn, the oil flow through the steering cylinder is reversed and the tractor is pulled to the right. Although various types of joints are used, most joints only allow a horizontal rotation of about 70° to the left and right. The one illustrated in Fig. 2-5, however, allows full rotary movement. This joint is like a front axle spindle; the towing cylinder is fastened to the trailer frame and the piston forms part of the joint. It is fastened with pins through mounting brackets that are welded to the tractor frame. The joint permits infinite oscillation about its longitudinal axle, thereby making the two drive axles independent of each other. The "bogie" (mounting structure from the trailer frame to the axle) is designed with independently suspended axles to allow each trailer axle to pivot individually, assuring full tire contact with the ground at all times. The dump box has a load volume of 14.4 yd^3 [11 m^3], a GCW of 69,000 lb [31,300 kg], an overall length of 30.2 ft [9.29 m], and a width of 8.2 ft [2.48 m]. A four-speed forward and four-speed reverse powershift

Fig. 2-3 Semitrailer bottom dumper. (*WABCO, An American-Standard Company*)

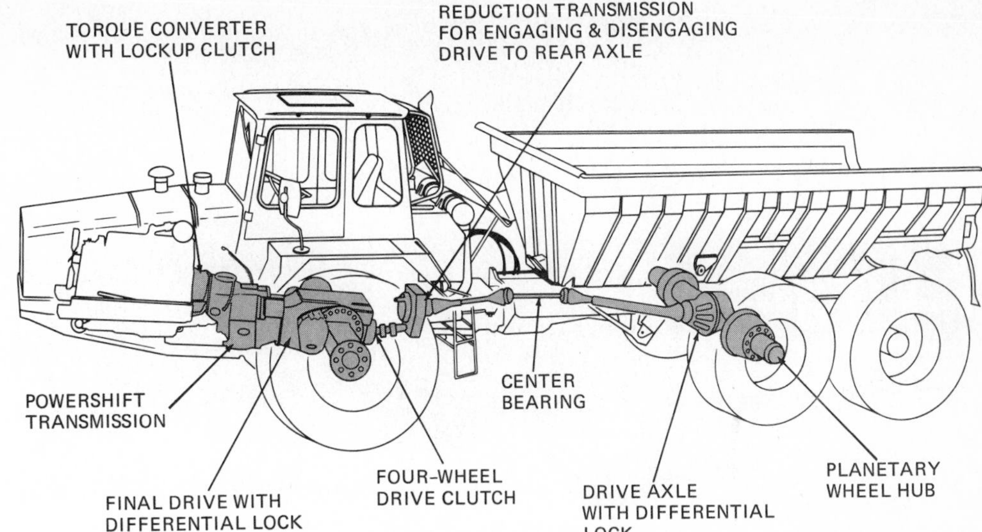

Fig. 2-4 Articulated steering. (*Volvo BM AB Eskilstuna Sweden*)

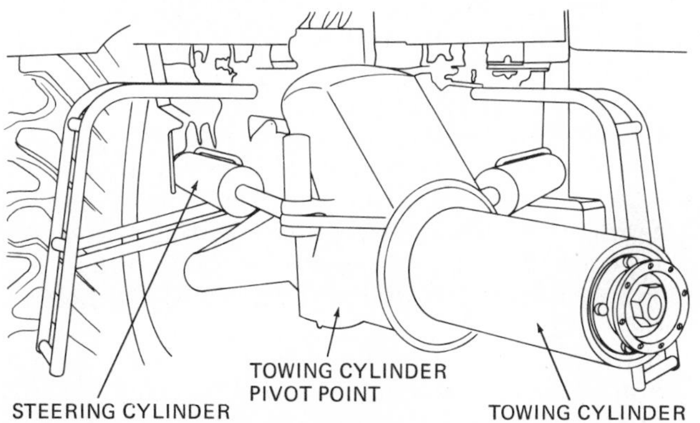

Fig. 2-5 The towing cylinder.

transmission with lockup clutch is mounted directly to the drive axle of the tractor, and the engine is mounted to the transmission. A short drive line connects the reduction gear box with the tractor's drive axle. A long drive line, having two universal joints supported by two center bearings, connects the reduction gear box with the front axle of the trailer. The drive axles have a differential lock while the trailer drive axle is of the planetary wheel hub design. Two three-stage hydraulic cylinders, hinge-mounted at the rear of the trailer frame, are used to pivot the box to a 70° dump angle. Hydrostatic steering is used with a followup link.

Tractor Scrapers Some tractor scrapers have a bowl (the box) positioned between the tractor axle and the scraper axle to load, transport, and discharge the load, while others have a self-powered elevator mounted to the bowl to load the soil into the bowl. They are the workhorses in the earth-moving field and are immensely popular because of their versatility. Other advantages are that they (1) are self-loaders and dumpers, (2) are able to load and dump within a shorter turn-around time than any other dumper, (3) can operate at a higher ground speed, (4) have a greater maneuverability, and (5) are manufactured for use on large or small construction sites. See Fig. 2-6.

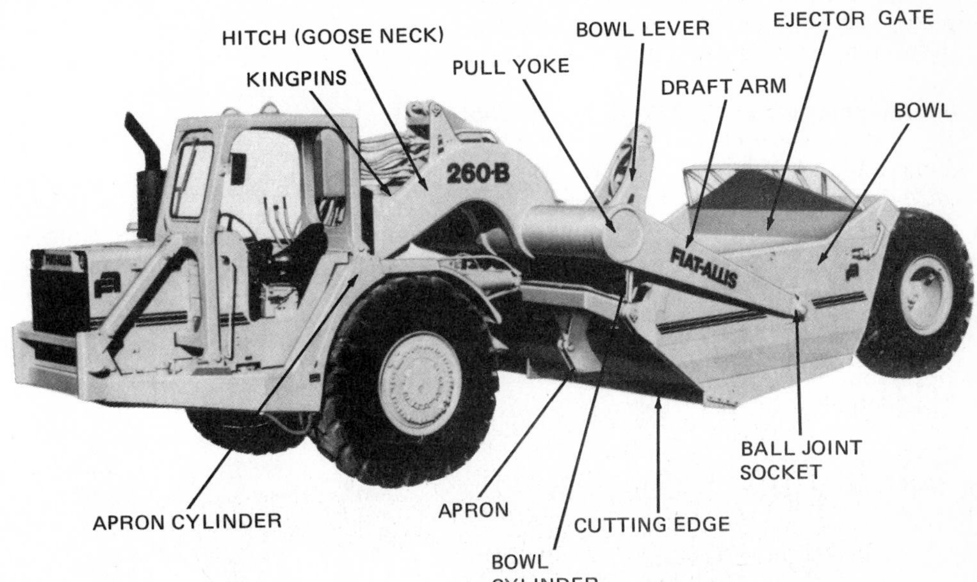

Fig. 2-6 Articulated steer tractor scraper (single-axle drive) (*Allis-Chalmers Engine Division*)

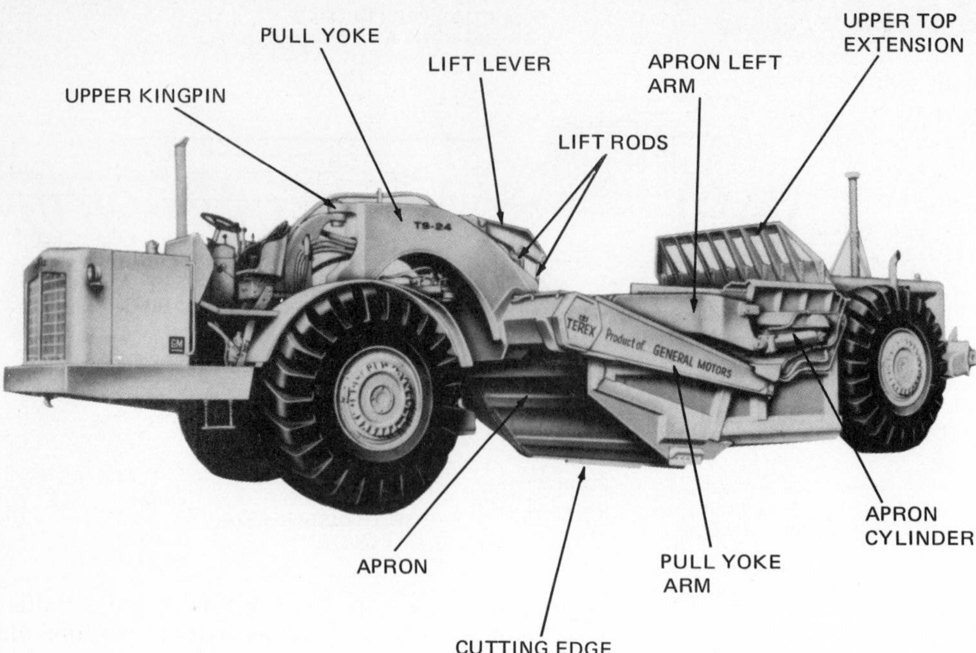

Fig. 2-7 Two-axle drive articulated steering scraper (*Terex Division of General Motors Corporation*)

Overall dimensions of tractor scrapers vary to accommodate load capacity. They may carry a load volume of 9.5 to 54 yd^3 [7.25 to 41.25 m^3] up to the load weight of 11.8 to 64 ton [10 to 58 t]. The overall length can vary from 28.5 to 56.6 ft [8.69 to 17.26 m] and the width from 8 to 14.16 ft [2.44 to 4.31 m]. Tractor scrapers using single engines have a power range of 183 to 550 hp [136.44 to 410.08 kW] and those using two engines have a total power range of 500 to 960 hp [372.8 to 715.77 kW]. Powershift transmissions ranging from four to eight speeds forward and one or two speeds reverse are used almost exclusively on large tractor scrapers, whereas the smaller units use standard four-speed transmissions with one reverse. The larger powershift transmissions have a lockup clutch and hydraulic retarder.

A tractor scraper may be of the articulated steering design or of the tractor semitrailer design. The articulated scraper design may have two axles where the tractor axle drives and steers, or it may be designed with an additional engine mounted at the rear, which drives the rear axle (see Fig. 2-7). Whether or not a hydrostatic steering system with followup linkage or power steering is used, the two steering cylinders are fastened to the pull frame and the piston rod ends to the tractor frame. When the steering wheel is turned, oil is directed into the cylinders and one piston extends as the other retracts, pulling the tractor to the left or to the right by pivoting on the articulated joint (kingpin).

Another type of tractor scraper design is one where the tractor is a 4 × 2 or 4 × 4 unit. When it is a 4 × 4 unit, the wheels are all of equal size and the tractor may be of the articulated steering design. When the tractor is a 4 × 2, the front axle wheels are smaller than the rear axle wheels and the front axle is the steering axle. **NOTE** This unit could also have an additional engine at the rear mounted to the tail structure. The pull yoke of the scraper is fastened to the tractor frame with a joint similar to that used on a bottom dump tractor unit.

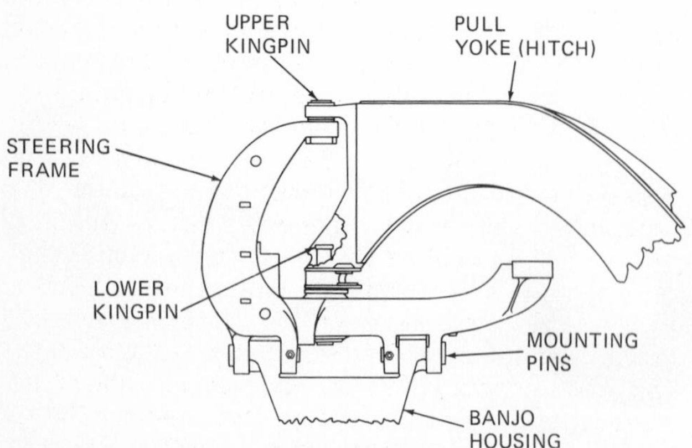

Fig. 2-8 Hitch assembly. (*Terex Division of General Motors Corporation*)

SCRAPER DESIGN AND OPERATION The scraper assembly consists of a fabricated welded hitch and pull yoke, the bowl (with the cutting edge), the ejector (with its cutting edge), the apron, and the tail structure with axle and wheels. The hitch is fastened with two kingpins to the articulated joint (see Fig. 2-8) and the pull yoke is pivot-fastened to the bowl by ball joint sockets. The bowl cylinders are fastened to the pull yoke and the piston rod ends are fastened to the bowl lever. One end of the bowl lever is pivot-fastened to the hitch and the other end to the link rod. When the directional control valve directs oil to the piston ends of the hydraulic cylinders, the piston rods retract, pivoting the bowl levers which raise the bowl, and cause the bowl to pivot on the bowl ball joint sockets. When the pistons are fully retracted, the bowl is raised to its maximum travel height. When the oil flow is reversed, the bowl descends, partly because of its weight but also because of the force of the hydraulic pressure acting on the bowl cylinder pistons.

The apron acts as a door to maintain the load in the bowl during transport, and to vary the bowl opening during unloading (ejecting). The apron and apron cylinders are pivot-mounted to the bowl, and the piston rod ends are fastened to the apron arms. When the piston rods retract, the apron pivots in a circular motion and closes the bowl front opening. When the oil flow is reversed, the apron pivots backwards and opens the front of the bowl. See Fig. 2-9.

The hydraulic ejector cylinder(s) positioned in the tail assembly is (are) double-acting two or three stage. They are attached to the tail frame, and the piston rods are attached to the ejector. The ejector is a reinforced curved steel plate that acts as the rear enclosing wall of the bowl. It is either supported by the front and rear guide rollers and guides, which are attached to the bowl, or it is pivot-mounted to the bowl, near the cutting edge (see Fig. 2-10). When the oil is directed to the piston end of the ejector cylinder(s) (and the apron is open), the piston(s) forces (force) the ejector toward the bowl opening, unloading the bowl; or the ejector cylinder pistons pivot the ejector, which also results in unloading the bowl.

The scraper tail assembly is a structure of welded steel. It is welded to the rear of the bowl and its tail assembly is extended and forms the pusher block. The axle brackets are welded to the tail structure and the wheel hubs are attached to the spindles.

LOADING To load the bowl, the ejector is retracted, the bowl is lowered, the apron is fully open, and the tractor is placed in low gear. The forward motion of the tractor causes the cutting edge of the bowl to cut into the terrain, forcing it into the bowl.

The hydraulic lines from the directional control valves to the bowl, apron, and ejector cylinders and back to the control valves are routed through a swivel joint. This joint not only allows the use of short hoses, but serves as a hose support and prevents the hoses from twisting, kinking, or otherwise being damaged.

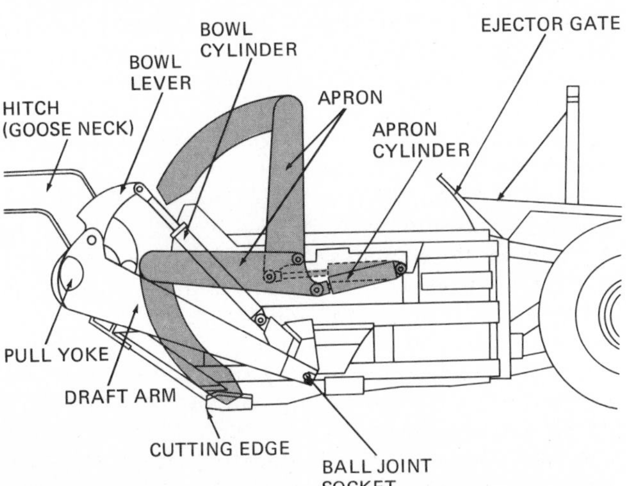

Fig. 2-9 Schematically illustrated unloading mechanism. (*Terex Division of General Motors Corporation*)

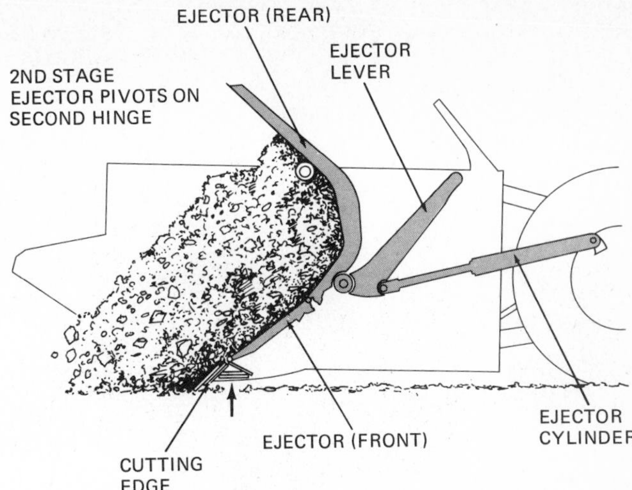

Fig. 2-10 Second stage of unloading. (*Terex Division of General Motors Corporation*)

When the ground is hard or there is insufficient traction, or otherwise to speed up the operation, a tractor with a dozer blade can be placed behind the scraper tractor so that the dozer blade rests against the pusher block.

Elevating Tractor Scrapers There are many similarities between the elevating tractor scraper and the open bowl design (see Figs. 2-11 and 2-12). The bowl of the elevating type also pivots on ball joint sockets fastened to the bowl and pull arm. Raising and lowering is also accomplished by double-acting hydraulic cylinders. However, since this type of scraper does not require a pusher tractor to facilitate loading, the tail assembly requires only a bumper. Ejector action is another similarity to the open bowl scraper design.

Briefly, the main differences in the elevating tractor scraper are that (1) the elevating scraper has no apron, (2) the front bowl opening is partly closed by the elevator, (3) the soil is loosened by the bowl cutting edge or teeth and then elevated into the bowl and (4) the load is dumped through a bottom door.

The elevator serves as a conveyer to lift the earth into the bowl. It is float-mounted to the entrance of the bowl at an angle of about 45°. Rollers mounted to the bottom of the elevator frame are guided in the crescent-shaped arms bolted to each side of the bowl to guide and support the elevator at the bottom. On top, the elevator is supported and guided on channeled frames (fastened to each bowl side) on which it can slide up or down. Two coil springs, one on each side, are attached to the elevator frame and bowl to hold the elevator assembly with a predetermined tension against the lower frame stop. When the bowl contacts a rock or a mound of earth larger than the clearance between the elevator flight and bowl floor, the elevator is forced upward against the coil spring tension, but as soon as the object has passed the opening the spring force returns the elevator back to its lower position. **NOTE** Some elevators are pivot-mounted at the top and are guided to and supported with rollers to the bowl. This type

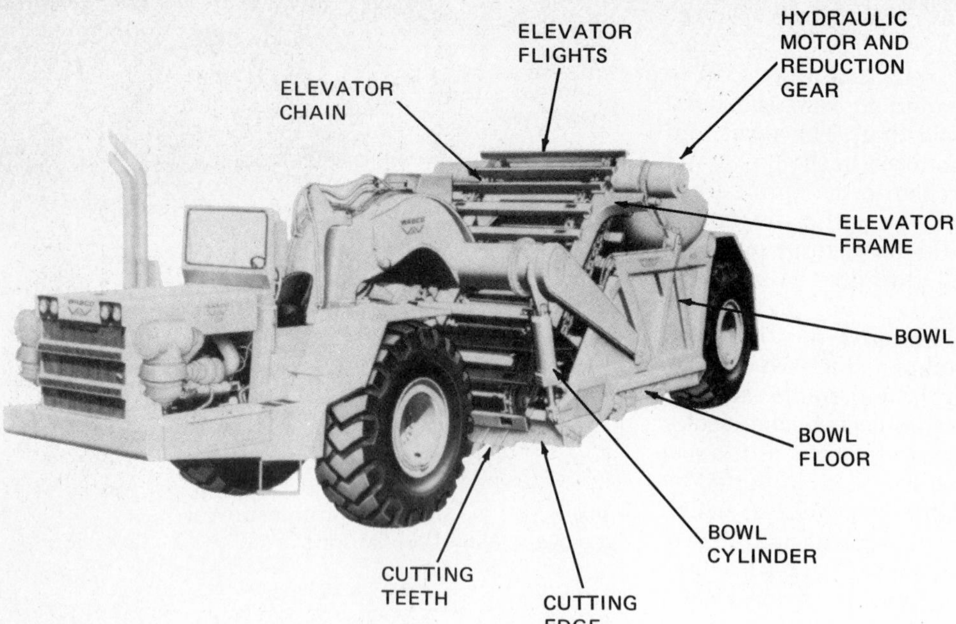

Fig. 2-11 Elevating scraper. (*WABCO, An American-Standard Company*)

has double-acting hydraulic cylinders fastened to the bowl frame, and the rod ends are fastened to the elevator frames.

Tapered roller bearings support the drum shaft against the top of the elevator frame. Two drive sprockets are fastened to the frame position and drive the elevator chain, which is guided and supported at the lower end by traction wheels positioned on the lower shaft. The shaft is supported with tapered roller bearings to the lower elevator frame. The flights are fastened to the chains. The elevator reduction gears used to reduce speed and to gain torque are not all alike; some use a single-reduction gear whereas others use a double-reduction planetary gear set. However, all use a hydraulic motor to drive the elevator and some use a flywheel to reduce the speed fluctuation. When a double-reduction gear box is used, an air shift mechanism is usually incorporated to provide two elevating speeds.

The front half of the bowl floor is supported by roller bearings and guide rails which allow it to slide open and closed. A cutting edge or cutting teeth are fastened to the front edge of the floor. The floor is opened and closed by the ejector movement, linkage, and lever, whereas other tractor elevator scrapers use two double-acting hydraulic cylinders to open and close the floor.

ELEVATING SCRAPER OPERATION To fill the bowl, the operator actuates the ejector directional valve, which retracts the ejector cylinder. Oil then flows through the swivel joint into the rod end of the ejector cylinder, retracts the ejector, and closes the floor. The oil leaving the piston end of the cylinder returns over the swivel joint and the directional valve to the reservoir. The operator must then direct oil to the elevator motor whereupon the elevator rotates in a counterclockwise rotation. The correct elevating speed is then selected by actuating the air valve. This done, the bowl directional valve is placed in the float position (that is, no hydraulic force is used to lower the bowl), after which the transmission is placed into first gear (see Fig. 2-13). If the bowl digs too deeply into the ground, the operator raises the bowl by directing oil into the rod ends of the bowl cylinders, and if it rides over the ground he or she directs oil to the piston ends of the bowl cylinders to force the bowl downward. The cutting edge or ripper teeth then break the earth loose and force it toward the flights, which transport it into the bowl. To dump the load, oil is directed to the piston end of the ejector cylinder. The ejector piston rod is forced out, and through the mechanical linkage and levers the floor opens, whereupon the ejector is pivoted, forcing the earth out of the bottom opening. See Fig. 2-14.

Wheel-Type Tractors Wheel-type tractors (Fig. 2-15) greatly outnumber other off-highway machines simply because they are so versatile. They are used in the farming industry to pull farm implements, compactors, scrapers, etc., or with a loader (shovel), a backhoe, or a dozer attached they can be used for loading, excavating, and grading.

Wheel-type tractors are two-axle machines where the rear axle is commonly the drive axle and the front axle is the steering axle. The larger units are 4 × 4 fixed-frame tractors or 4 × 4 tractors of the articulated steering design. Tractors can be classified by the drive, the engine hp, or the drawbar pull. *Drawbar pull* means the maximum pulling power, measured in pounds [newtons], when the atmospheric pressure is about 29.9 in [75.9 cm] of mercury, without exceeding a wheel slippage of 15 percent.

Small tractors have gasoline, liquid petroleum gas, or diesel engines, whereas about 95 percent of the midrange and large-size tractors have diesel engines and 5 percent have liquid petroleum gas en-

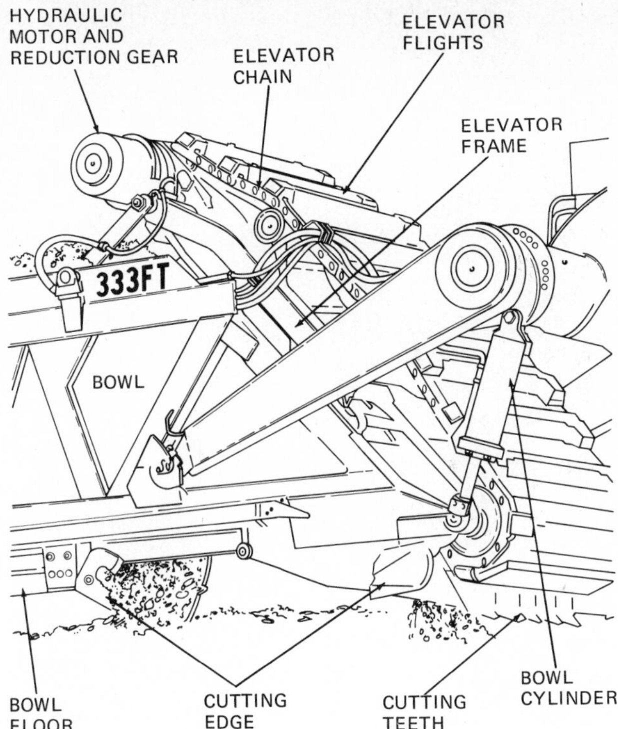

Fig. 2-12 Side view of elevator.

Fig. 2-13 Elevating scraper (loading). (*WABCO, An American-Standard Company*)

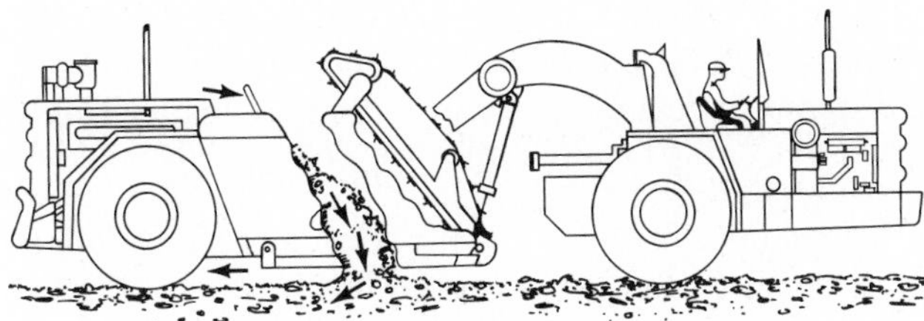

Fig. 2-14 Elevating scraper (unloading). (*WABCO, An American-Standard Company*)

gines. The engine power range is 30 to 635 hp [22.36 to 473.45 kW], the larger tractors having twin engines. Small farm tractors in the 30- to 40-hp [22.36- to 29.82-kW] range use a standard four-speed transmission, whereas the large farm tractors use a powershift transmission or have a torque converter with a standard eight- to twelve-speed transmission behind. Furthermore, the 120- to 210-hp [89.47- to 156.57-kW] range tractors have a planetary wheel hub and may be of the articulated steering design. In the last few years several equipment manufacturers have produced farm tractors with a hydrostatic drive.

Fig. 2-15 Conventional farm tractor.

THREE-POINT HITCH To raise and lower farm implements, a three-point hitch is used. See Fig. 2-16. The draft arms are fastened through brackets to the left- and right-hand lower axle housing, and the upper link is fastened to the mast that is attached to the top center of the axle housing. The draft arms are the pull arms, and the turnbuckles are the leveling devices, the center turnbuckle being used to adjust and level the implement. The hydraulic cylinder is attached to the relay shaft lever, and the shaft is positioned and supported by the bearing stem that is bolted to the axle housing. The upper link arms are keyed or splined to the relay shaft and connected through swivel links and turnbuckles to the draft arm. To accommodate a different type of implement, a hitch coupler could be fastened to the three-point hitch.

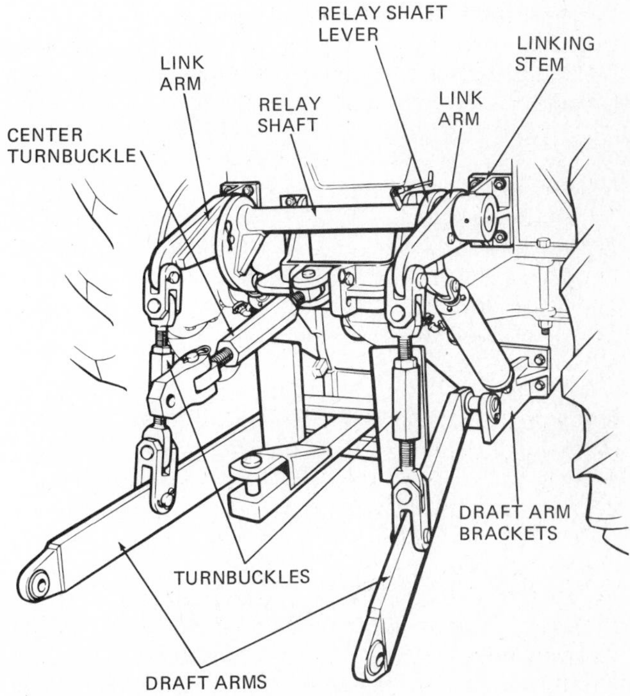

Fig. 2-16 Three-point hitch.

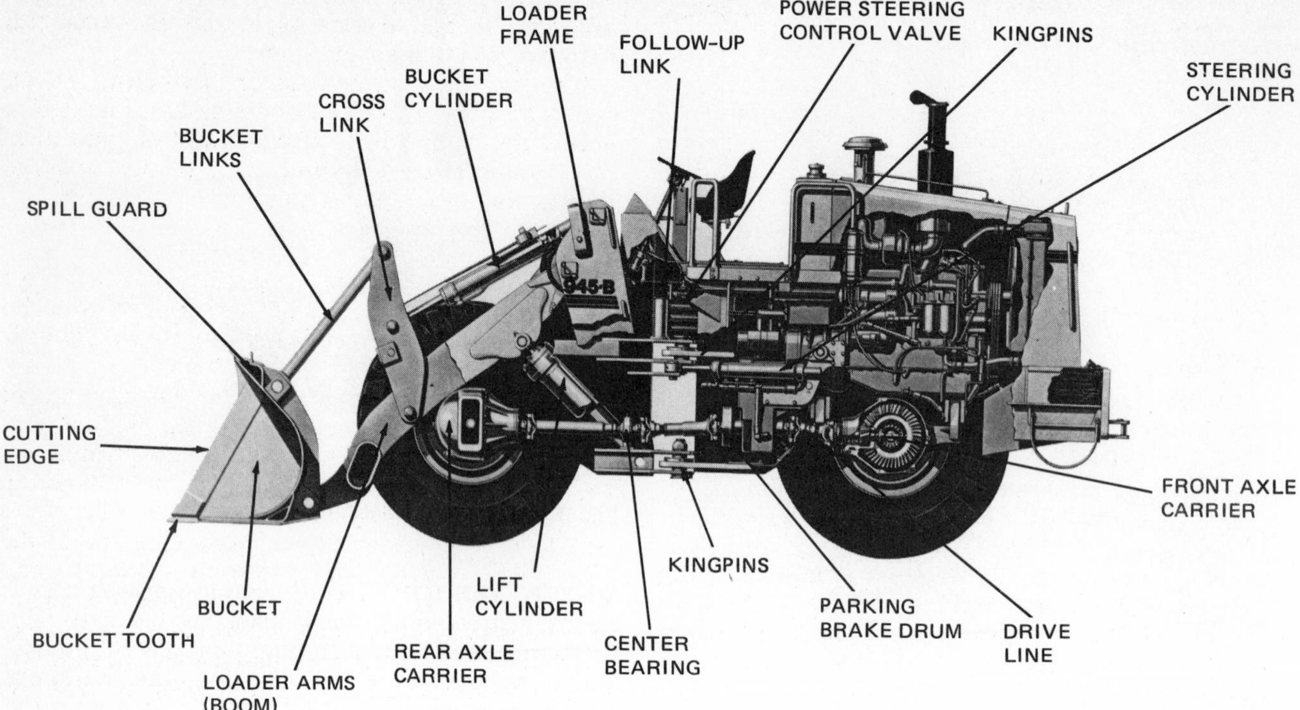

Fig. 2-17 Four-wheel drive articulated steering loader. (*Allis-Chalmers Engine Division*)

POWER TAKEOFF Nearly all farm tractors have a rear live power takeoff (PTO) mounted to the axle housing, that is, a gear box having a set of gears, a clutch, and an output shaft. The input shaft to the PTO gear is taken from the master clutch and, when the engine operates, the shaft rotates. To disconnect and connect the power from the engine to the output shaft, the clutch is used, and the gear set reduces the engine rpm to the recommended PTO speed (which is either 540 or 1000 rpm). The clutch is commonly of the multidisk design and either hydraulically engaged and disengaged, or manually actuated and then engaged or disengaged through an overcenter linkage.

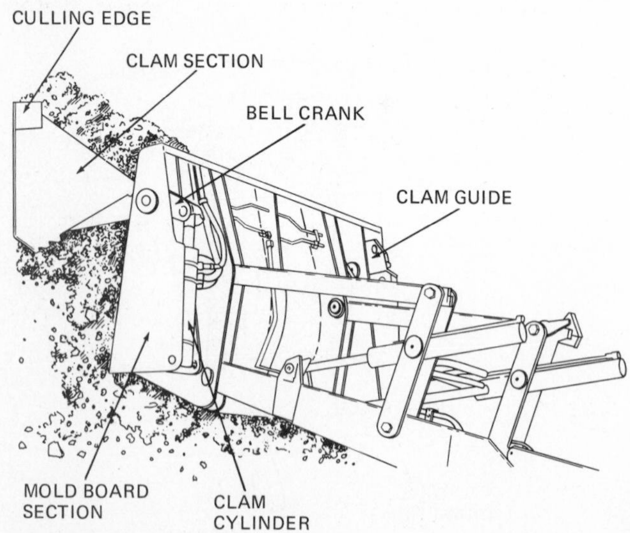

Fig. 2-18 Multipurpose bucket.

Wheel Loaders Wheel loaders are two-axle tractors designed to load the bucket, lift, transport, lower, and dump the load through the action of the wheel tractor, loader, and hydraulic components. Loaders are classified by their driving, steering, lifting, and load-carrying capacity. **NOTE** Over 200 different types and/or sizes are manufactured, varying in their lifting capacity from 1600 to 232,470 lb [726.4 to 105,541.3 kg] and in their load-carrying capacity from 0.20 to 24 yd^3 [0.15 to 18.14 m^3]. See Fig. 2-17.

DESIGN The lift arms are pivot-fastened to the tractor frame or fastened to the one-piece loader frame or to the tractor frame, and the piston rod ends are pivot-attached to the lift arms. The bucket is pivot-attached to the ends of the lift arms, and its cylinders are pivot-attached to the cross beam of the lift arm. The rod ends are pivot-attached to the bucket or to levers which are linked to the bucket. The latter, referred to as "self-leveling," ensures that the bucket remains level regardless of the bucket lift height.

Some buckets attached to the loader arm are designed exclusively to dump the load forward, while others are designed to dump the load sideways, and others use a multipurpose bucket design (see Fig. 2-18).

A multipurpose bucket consists of two halves hinged at the top, the clam section and moldboard section. The clam section can be opened and closed through the action of the clam cylinders and can be used to "grab" an object and to carry it, through the combination of the hydraulic cylinders, bell cranks, and clam guides. When the clam section is moved away from the moldboard section, it can be used as a dozer blade.

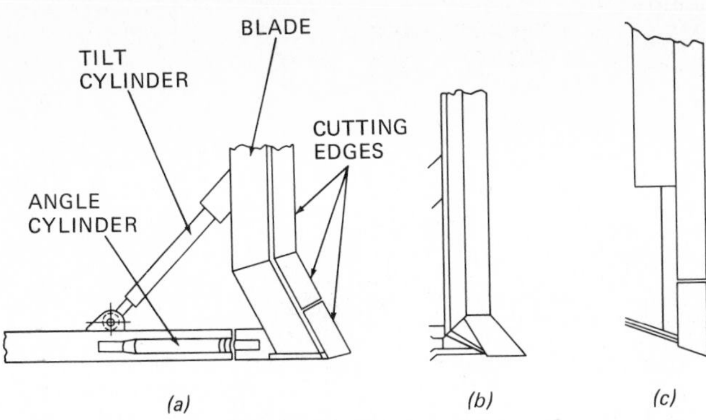

Fig. 2-19 (*a*) U moldboard (blade) dozer. (*b*) Semi-U moldboard. (*c*) Straight moldboard.

Following are some design variations of wheel loaders:

1. When the engine is mounted at the front, the front axle is the steering axle and the rear is the drive axle, or both the front and rear are drive axles. When both are drive axles, the tires on both axles are of equal size.
2. When the engine is at the rear, the front axle is the drive axle and the rear wheels steer. In this case the front wheels are larger in size than the rear wheels.
3. When both axles are drive axles, the rear wheels steer, or both front and rear wheels steer.
4. When the wheel loader is of the articulated steering design, either both or only the rear axle is the drive axle and the operator cab could be at the front or at the rear.

As the loader size varies, so does the required engine hp, thereby necessitating numerous different transmissions and rear axles. Small wheel loaders use gasoline, petroleum gas, or diesel engines; however, the midrange and larger wheel loaders use diesel engines exclusively. They range from 40 to 635 hp [29.82 to 473.45 kW] and may have twin engines.

Manual transmissions are used on only a few loaders, the majority having powershift transmissions ranging between four and six speed, forward and reverse. In the last few years, however, some midrange loader tractors have been manufactured with hydrostatic transmissions.

The braking systems used are hydraulic, power assist, air over hydraulic, or air brakes; foundation brakes are drum, disk, wedge, cam, or multidisk. Most loaders use a hydrostatic steering system, though some have power steering.

Wheel Dozers Unlike a wheel loader, a wheel dozer has a dozer blade to push, dig, or to level the earth. The blade may be of a straight, semi-U, or full-U design. See Fig. 2-19.

The blade is made of steel with a cutting edge, or with individual cutting edge sections bolted to it. The blade may be rigidly attached to the push frame, rigidly fastened by pins and linkage, or mounted to the push frame so that the blade can be tilted (that is, one end of the blade can be raised) and/or the blade can be angled (changed from a straight position to an angle position). The desired tilt and/or angle position can be achieved by changing the mechanical linkage between the blade and push frame or through the action of hydraulic cylinders. See Fig. 2-20. The terms push frame, push beam, C frame, or angle strut indicate the shape of the frame. The push frame is fastened to the tractor using a ball socket or trunnion mounting. The dozer lift cylinders are pivot-fastened to the tractor, and the piston rod ends are pivot-fastened to the push frame or blade. When the blade is power-angled, the angle cylinder is fastened to one side of the push frame and the piston rod end to the blade. When the blade is power tilt, the tilt cylinder is also fastened to the push frame, and the piston rod end is fastened to the blade.

Backhoes A *backhoe* is a hydraulically operated utility excavator designed to dig, scoop, or cut a trench and to move the excavated earth away from the trench or into a truck box. When its frame forms part of the tractor or machine it is referred to as an "excavator," but when the frame is separate it is referred to as a "backhoe."

Backhoes are classified according to their loader

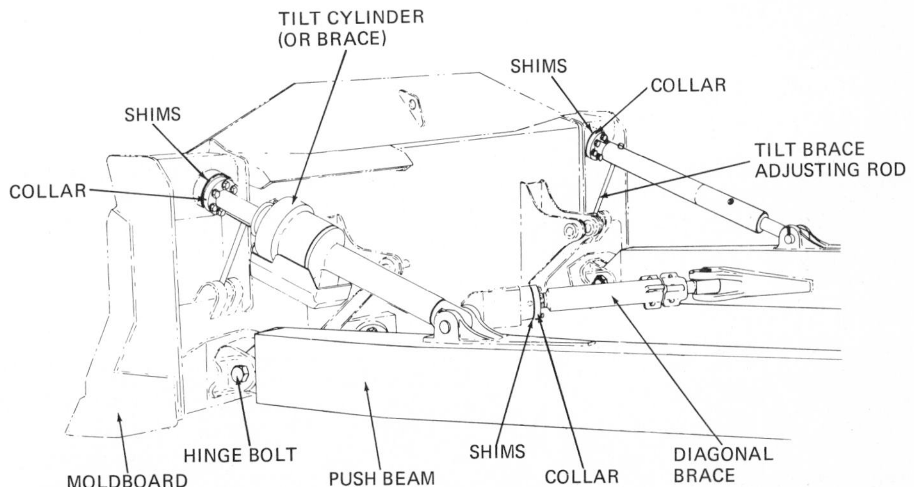

Fig. 2-20 Hydraulic tilt dozer blade. (*Allis-Chalmers Engine Division*)

lift height, load capacity, and their backhoe digging depth and digging force. The digging depth range is about 12 to 20 ft [3.66 to 6.1 m]. Approximately 70 percent use a diesel engine. The power range is between 40 and 90 hp [29.82 and 67.1 kW] whether a gasoline engine or diesel is used. The power train commonly consists of a torque converter, a hydraulically actuated forward and reverse transmission, and a four-speed standard transmission or a full powershift transmission. **NOTE** Some recently designed tractors are of a hydrostatic drive design. On nearly all of the newer backhoes, the tractor utilizes some kind of differential lock and the larger models have planetary wheel hubs. The foundation brakes are of the shoe, single-disk, or multidisk brake design and are actuated hydraulically or through air. The steering system is either power or hydrostatic.

UTILITY BACKHOE DESIGN A backhoe frame is bolted to the loader frame and rear tractor axle housing. Two one-piece stabilizers are pivot-fastened to the backhoe frame, to which the stabilizer foot is pinned. See Fig. 2-21. **NOTE** Some stabilizers are of a two-piece construction so that they can be manually extended to increase the reach. The hydraulic stabilizer cylinders are fastened to the backhoe frame, and the rod ends fastened to the stabilizer. It is the function of the stabilizer to lift the wheels off the ground to place the backhoe in a fixed position.

The swing frame (or boom pivot) is pivot-fastened to the backhoe frame, as are the swing cylinders, and the rod ends are attached to the boom pivot. The backhoe boom and either one or two boom cylinders are fastened to the boom pivot, the rod ends of the boom cylinders being fastened to the upper part of

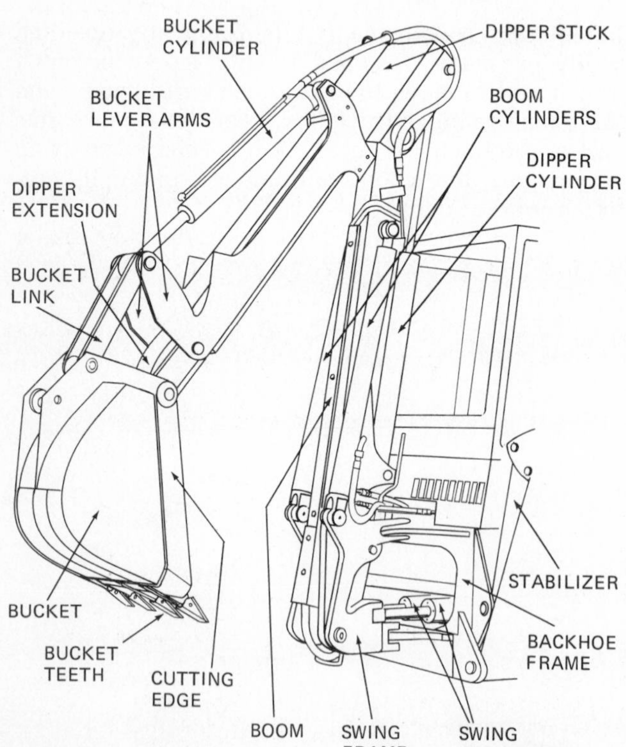

Fig. 2-21 Backhoe attached to side shift main frame.

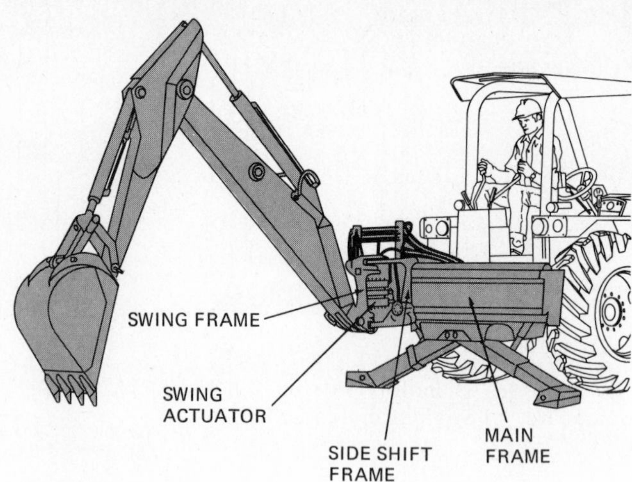

Fig. 2-22 Backhoe attached to side shift main frame. *(Deere & Company)*

the boom. If the backhoe and boom pivot are designed so that they can be moved to any position (far left to far right), the backhoe frame then has a wide rail and the boom pivot is two piece and has a semirotary swing cylinder. See Fig. 2-22. The dipper is attached to the boom end, the dipper cylinder is fastened to the boom, and the rod ends are attached to the end of the dipper stick, to which the bucket is pinned. The dipper stick may be a one-piece construction or of a telescopic design. When it is telescopic, a hydraulic cylinder actuates the dipper extension, forcing it to move within the main dipper section to extend or shorten the overall length of the dipper stick. The rod end of the bucket cylinder is connected with the end of the dipper stick and bucket through guide links and coupler guides, and the cylinder is pivot-fastened to the dipper stick. This lever arrangement multiplies the hydraulic force, increasing the digging force of the bucket.

Special equipment, such as a hydraulically operated grapple (to load logs), a hydraulically rotated post hole digger, or a hydraulically operated hammer to break up the earth or pavement can be mounted to the dipper stick.

Front-End Loaders Front-end loaders used in conjunction with backhoes have a lift capacity ranging from 3000 to 6000 lb [1362 to 2724 kg] and a volume capacity between 0.375 and 1.25 yd^3 [0.19 and 0.96 m^3]. The loader arms are fastened either to a specially designed loader frame, or to a modified tractor frame. (Commonly the loader frames are the reservoirs.) (See Fig. 2-23.) Loader buckets can also be of a multipurpose design. The hydraulic system may be of a split system design where one hydraulic pump supplies oil to the loader and the other pump supplies oil to the backhoe, or both pumps may supply oil to the loader as well as to the backhoe system, or a single hydraulic pump may be used. To direct oil to and from the hydraulic cylinders and back to the reservoir, one directional control valve is used for each hydraulic cylinder (with the exception of swing cylinders and loader lift cylinder). Therefore two or three valve spools are needed to operate the

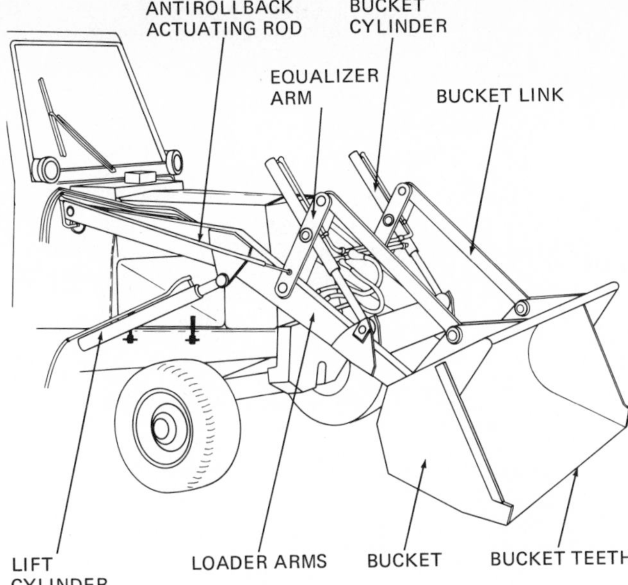

Fig. 2-23 Backhoe loader.

loader, one to raise, lower, hold, and float the loader arms, and one to dump, hold, and roll back the bucket. When a multibucket is used, another spool is needed to open, hold, and close the clam. For backhoes, usually six valve spools are needed, one to raise, lower, and hold the boom, one to hold and pivot the dipper stick up or down, one to hold and roll the bucket in and out, one to hold and to swing the boom to the left or the right, and two control valve spools, one for each stabilizer cylinder, to hold, lower, and raise the stabilizer.

Rubber-Tired Log Skidders and Skidder Grapples Rubber-tired log skidders are self-propelled machines (tractors) which have a dozer blade and a winch with fair leads to lift and to haul logs from the felling site to the loading facilities. See Fig. 2-24.

A winch is a transmission-fastened to a drum and driven by the engine or by a hydraulic motor. Fair leads are rollers which guide the winch cable onto the drum.

Usually the tractors are of 4 × 4 articulated steering design with front and rear drive axles. The dozer blade, used to clear minor obstructions from the haul road, is a one-piece welded structure pivot-fastened to the tractor frame, and the rod ends of the cylinders are pivot-fastened to the dozer blade. The winch is mounted on top and in front of the rear axle, and the primary auxiliary fair lead rollers are mounted to an arch that extends beyond the rear tractor frame.

Diesel engines, as well as powershift transmissions, are used exclusively. The engine used ranges in power from 120 to 250 hp [89.47 to 186.4 kW] and four-speed forward and reverse transmissions are common.

The most obvious difference between a log skidder and a skidder grapple is in the method by which the logs are fastened and transported. On a log skidder, the tow cable which encircles one end of the log (or logs) is then winched to raise the end of the logs off the ground. The tractor pulls the logs to the loading site with one end skidding on the ground. With a skidder grapple, the logs are clamped by the grapple; one end of the log is raised hydraulically and held off the ground during transport. The boom is supported by the boom cylinder and by the arch that is pivot-fastened to the tractor body. The arch cylinder is fastened to the rear of the tractor body. By actuating the boom cylinder control valve, the boom cylinder is raised or lowered; and by actuating the arch cylinder control valve, the boom is moved rearward or forward. The grapple arms are narrow steel curved plates, pivot-fastened to a swivel device, which allows the arms to rotate 360° and to move sideways. **NOTE** Some swivels incorporate a hydraulic motor to rotate the grapple arms in clockwise or counterclockwise directions. A double-end hydraulic cylinder is positioned to the swivel device and the rod ends are fastened to the grapple arm. Some skidder grapples have a different type of lifting mechanism which is similar to a backhoe design but without the bucket and bucket cylinder. The boom and boom cylinders are attached to a turntable, and a jib boom (short boom) and a jib cylinder are fastened to the end of the boom. The swivel device is fastened to the lower center of the jib boom. To raise the log off the ground, the boom is first hydraulically rotated to position the grapple arms in line with the log end, then the boom cylinder and the jib boom cylinder control valves are actuated to bring the grapple arms over the log end. Now the grapple arm cylinders are actuated to clamp the logs and the logs are then raised to the skidding position by the boom and jib boom cylinder. See Fig. 2-25.

Compactors and Roller Compactors A compactor is a self-propelled machine used to compact the earth or the asphalt once it is spread or laid on the

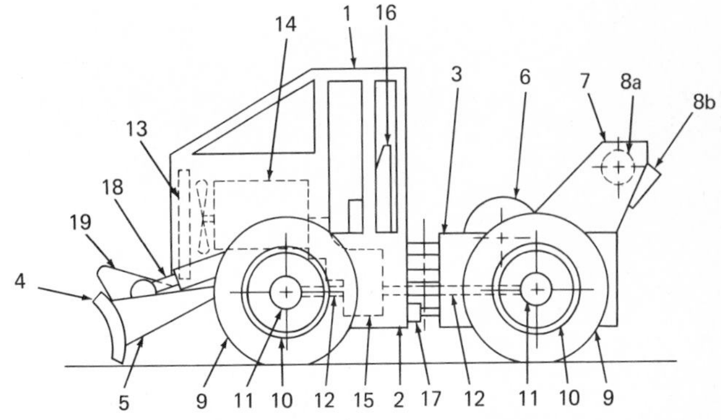

1. Operator protective structure
2. Front frame
3. Rear frame
4. Blade
5. Blade arm
6. Winch
7. Arch
8. Fairlead
   8(a) Main fairlead roller
   8(b) Auxiliary fairlead rollers
9. Tire
10. Rim
11. Axle
12. Drive line
13. Radiator
14. Engine
15. Power transmission system to wheels and/or winch
16. Seat
17. Steering cylinder
18. Blade cylinder
19. Decking lug
20. Log bumper

Fig. 2-24 Log skidder.

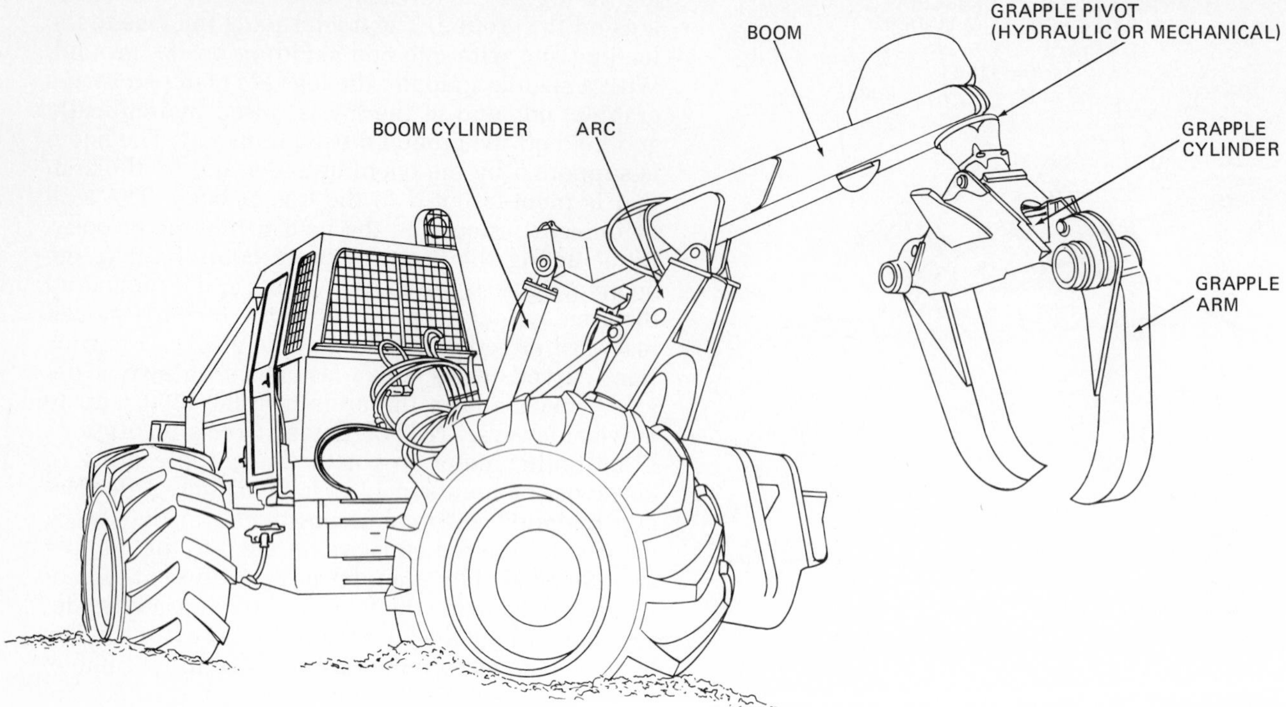

Fig. 2-25 Articulated steering skidder grapple.

road surface. Roller compactors are specially designed equipment which serve the same purpose as a compactor but must be pulled by a tractor. Depending on that equipment's intended usage, the parts that are used to compact the earth or asphalt vary. For road construction the ballast drum is fastened to a one-unit frame and tongue, which is coupled to the pull tractor. The feet are welded to the drums. Cleaning bars are fastened to the frame to keep the spaces between the feet clean. The shape of the feet may vary, depending upon the earth in which they are intended to operate. If a roller compactor is used to compact asphalt, rubber tires having flat treads are mounted to the axle and then the axle is fastened to a pull trailer. The trailer box is ballasted and has a water tank, water being necessary to cool the tires as well as prevent the hot asphalt from sticking to the treads. The roller is a smooth steel drum weighted with ballast and fastened with its axle to a frame or tongue. Roller wipers, assisted by water sprinklers, keep the roller surface clean during operation. See Fig. 2-26.

Tamping foot compactors (Fig. 2-27) vary in design as well as in size, but the complementing tractors are all of the two-axle designs. Most have a four-speed forward and reverse powershift transmission and planetary wheel hubs. The foundation brake is of the air-actuated cam or wedge design, and in most cases includes a parking brake. Diesel engines are used exclusively in a power range of 150 to 400 hp [111.84 to 298.24 kW]. The total weight of these machines ranges from 30,000 to 79,000 lb [13,620 to 35,866 kg], and the diameter of the tamping drums ranges between 34 and 48 in [0.766 and 1.219 m]. The drums are fastened to the rear drum hub, and usually the rear drums drive and the front drum steers. If the tractor is of the articulated steering design, it has two front and two rear tamping drums, and the rear and/or front drums are driven.

When the tractor is moving (in either forward or

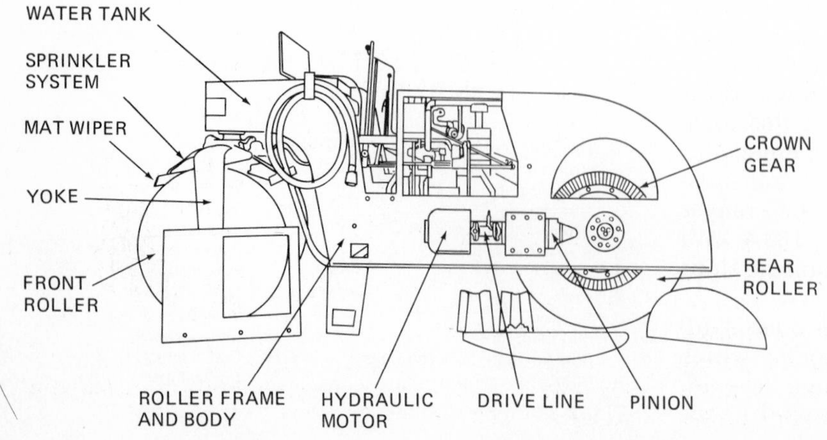

Fig. 2-26 Two-wheel roller. (*BLH Austin-Western*)

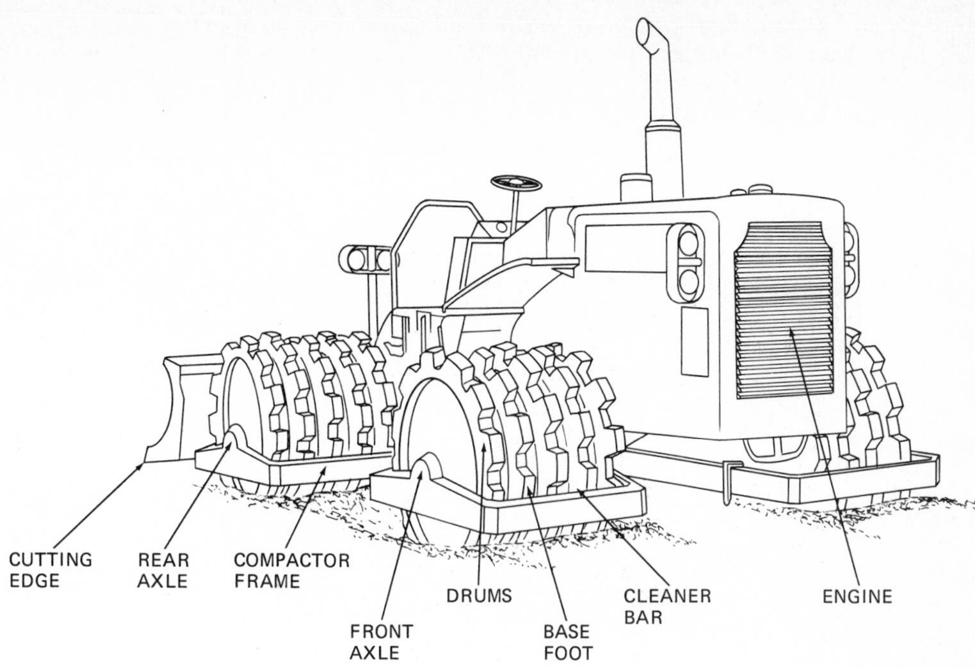

Fig. 2-27 Articulated tamping foot compactor.

reverse direction), the feet first break up the rough terrain and then penetrate into the ground, thereby packing the earth.

There are also some articulated steering compactors with a simple one-piece dozer mounted to the front axle, used for minor road-leveling jobs.

The self-propelled steel roller compactors may have two narrow rollers of large circumference (drive rollers) and one steering roller, or they may be designed with one large drive roller at the rear and a single steering roller at the front. The drive rollers are fastened to the wheel hubs of the rear drive axles. The steering roller axle is fastened to a one-piece cast-iron fork which has a (large-diameter) pivot shaft positioned into the roller frame. Steering is accomplished through a double-acting hydraulic cylinder fastened to the fork arm and roller frame.

The rollers of compactors having a single front roller and a single drive roller are of equal diameter. The drive from the transmission to the drive roller is achieved through a bevel gear set. The self-propelled rollers are classified by weight and range between 3 to 20 ton [2.72 and 18.14 t]. About 75 percent use diesel engines in a power range between 25 to 95 hp [18.64 and 70.83 kW]. The majority have a hydrostatic transmission and the remainder use a torque convertor and a two-speed, forward-reverse transmission. All types of rollers use some kind of hydraulic steering, most of them being hydrostatic.

Fork Lifts and Lift Trucks Fork lifts and lift trucks serve the same purpose in that they transport goods, materials, etc., from one place to another and stack them ready for storage, or load them onto trucks, box cars, etc. On the other hand, a lift truck is designed to operate in rough terrain and has as its power source a conventional wheel tractor. Fork lifts are also self-propelled machines, but they have smaller wheels which are about 10 to 14 in [25.4 to 35.56 cm] in diameter and are of a solid rubber design. The lift capacity and lift height of lift trucks is greater than that of the fork lift. Fork lifts are powered by air-cooled gasoline or petroleum gas en-

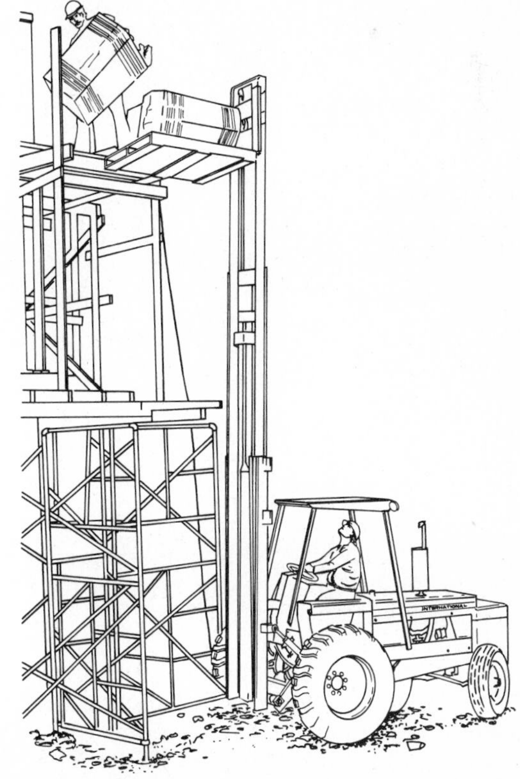

Fig. 2-28 Small lift truck. (*International Harvester Company*)

gines, or some are battery-powered, while the larger lift trucks use diesel engines exclusively. However, when the unit has to operate inside buildings they employ petroleum gas engines or battery power to drive the wheel motor and the hydraulic pump. Fork lifts are commonly driven hydrostatically or by electric wheel motors, whereas lift trucks use standard transmissions, powershift transmissions, or are hydrostatically driven. Four-speed forward and reverse ranges are used in the standard or powershift transmissions. See Fig. 2-28.

The lift trucks are classified by their lift capacity and lift height. Their lift capacity range is between 1400 and 120,000 lb [65.6 and 54,480 kg]. The lift height range is between 9.6 and 42 ft [2.9 and 12.81 m]. Depending on the lift capacity, either a conventional drive axle or a drive axle having planetary wheel hubs is used.

The fork lift uses band brakes which are hydraulically applied, whereas lift trucks use drum brakes which may be applied hydraulically or by oil or air.

The lift of a fork lift and lift truck is similar in design and in turn, in operating principles. The major components are

- The lift frame
- The mast, consisting of the inner and outer mast
- The single-acting lift cylinders
- The double-acting tilt cylinders
- The carriage with the forks

The lift frame is mounted to the tractor, and the outer mast is pivot-fastened at the bottom to the lift frame. The two double-acting tilt cylinders are fastened to the lift frame or tractor and the rod ends of the pistons are pivot-fastened to the outer mast. The inner mast is guided by rollers in the channels of the outer mast. Carriage load rollers and carriage thrust rollers are fastened to the carriage frame to support the carriage and guide it through the inner mast. The lift cylinder is fastened to the lower mast crossmember, and the piston rod end is pivot-fastened to the inner mast crossmember (crosshead shaft). The ends of the two lift chains are fastened to the sides of the lift cylinders and placed over guide rollers which are bearing-supported by the crosshead shaft. The other ends of the lift chains are fastened to the bottom of the carrier frame. The two forks are positioned on the shaft and supported in the bores of the carrier frame, and the lower ends of the forks rest against the lower cross frames. See Fig. 2-29.

LIFT OPERATION Before driving the forks under the pallet or positioning them over the load, the operator must first operate the directional control valve to direct oil to the tilt cylinders, either into the piston ends or into the rod ends of the cylinders, to tilt the mast to a suitable fork position. At the same time the lift cylinder directional control valve must be operated to direct oil into or from the lift cylinders to raise or lower the forks. When raising the load, the piston is forced upward, raising the inner mast. Since the lift chains are fastened to the upper end

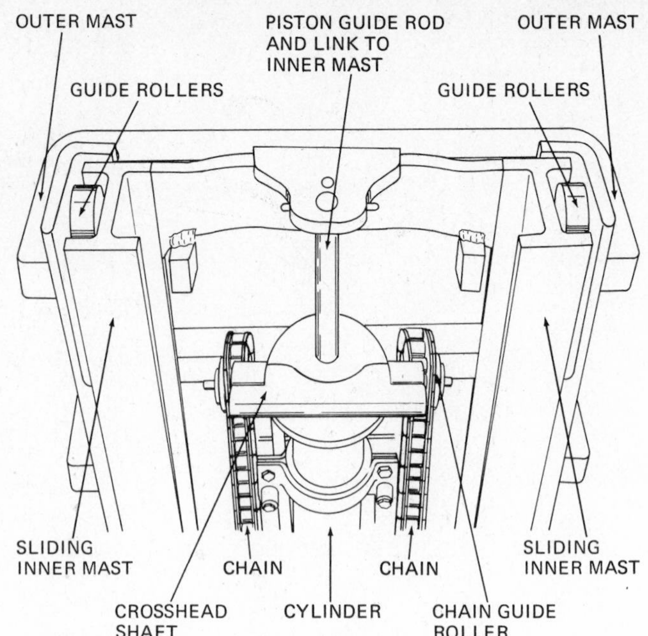

Fig. 2-29 Fork lift or lift truck mast.

of the lift cylinder piston, and on the bottom to the carriage frame, the extension of the inner mast raises the carriage frame by this extended distance because the chain is shortened. To lower the load, the directional control valve position is reversed, allowing the oil to flow from the lift cylinder to the directional control valve and back to the reservoir. This removes the force from the piston and the weight, lowering the piston, the inner mast, and the carriage. See the lift truck carriage illustrated in Fig. 2-30.

Motor Graders Motor graders are self-propelled machines designed to spread and level road material and otherwise maintain the road. They can also cut a ditch, dress or cut a new embankment, and are useful as snow plows. There are about 50 different

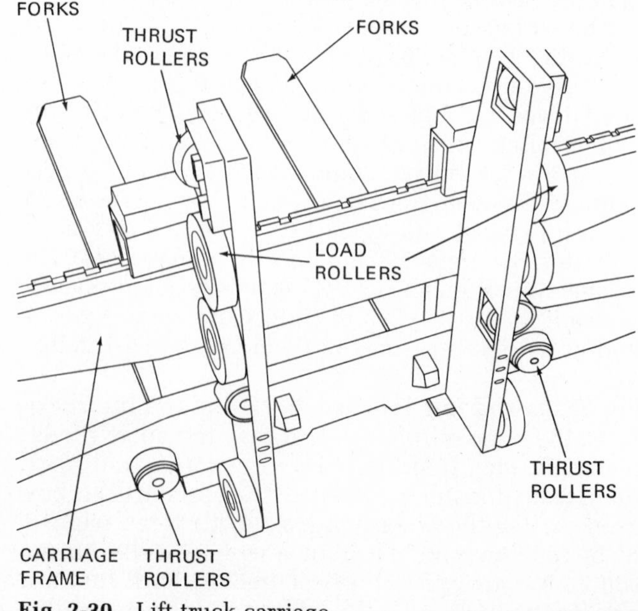

Fig. 2-30 Lift truck carriage.

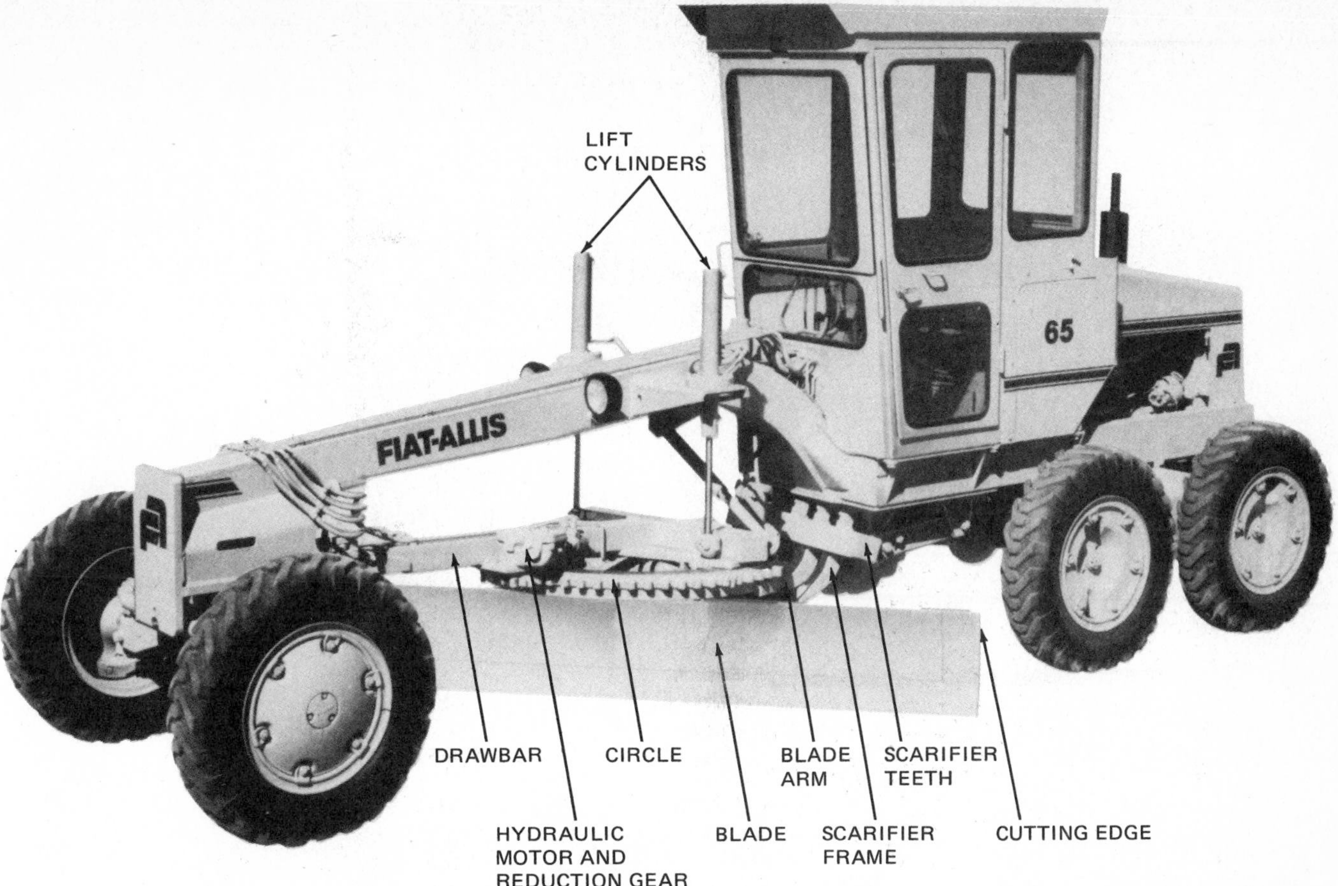

Fig. 2-31 Fixed-frame grader (*Fiat-Allis*)

types and models and they are classified according to drive, steering arrangement, and/or performance complexity.

Motor graders use diesel engines exclusively, ranging from 100 to 150 hp [74.56 to 111.84 kW]. The transmission on the larger units are six- to eight-speed powershift, whereas some midrange and smaller units use a standard four-speed transmission with a shuttle transmission, giving the grader four speeds forward and four speeds reverse. The three largest motor graders built to date have a hydrostatic transmission and a 340-hp [253.5-kW] diesel engine.

Motor graders can be divided into two classes: the fixed-frame design (Fig. 2-31) and the articulated steering design, both frames being of a welded structure. The frame of the fixed-frame design reaches from the front wheels to the rear wheels, and on the articulated steering design the front frame is fastened through an articulated joint, close to the front axle of the tandem rear axle. **NOTE** The frame may be constructed in several sections and then bolted to form the front or to form the entire frame section.

On all designs the engine is positioned over the rear axles and the power to the tandem housing is transmitted from the transmission to the carrier to the final drive housing. Final drive housings vary in design, and in the instance shown in Fig. 2-32 it consists of a planetary reduction gear and two drive sprockets, which are splined to the carrier shaft.

The motor grader shown in Fig. 2-32 has the tandem housing bolted to the spindle drive housing and the front and rear spindle housings bolted to the tandem housing. Each final drive has a multidisk brake and a drive axle to which the drive sprocket is splined. One roller chain links the final drive sprocket with the outside spindle drive sprocket, and the other roller chain links the inside spindle drive sprocket with the rear final drive sprocket. When the transmission is in gear, the spindle drive sprockets are rotated and the chains transmit the rotation at a ratio of 1 to 1 to the final drive sprockets, thereby rotating the drive axle and the wheel.

WHEEL LEAN MECHANISM The front wheels on a motor grader have two functions in addition to carrying part of the grader load: to steer the grader and to prevent side slippage. When the blade is pushed into the ground, a side thrust is developed which would push the front end of the grader to the left or the right, depending on the angle of the blade. To reduce the side slippage, the front wheels can be hydraulically leaned about 18° to either side. To achieve wheel lean, and steering, and to allow the axle to oscillate, the front axle (Fig. 2-33) is pivot-fastened to the front end of the grader frame. The lean arms are pivot-fastened to the axle ends and the top of the lean arms are connected to each other through the wheel lean bar. The lean cylinder is fastened to a mounting bracket attached to the front axle, and the

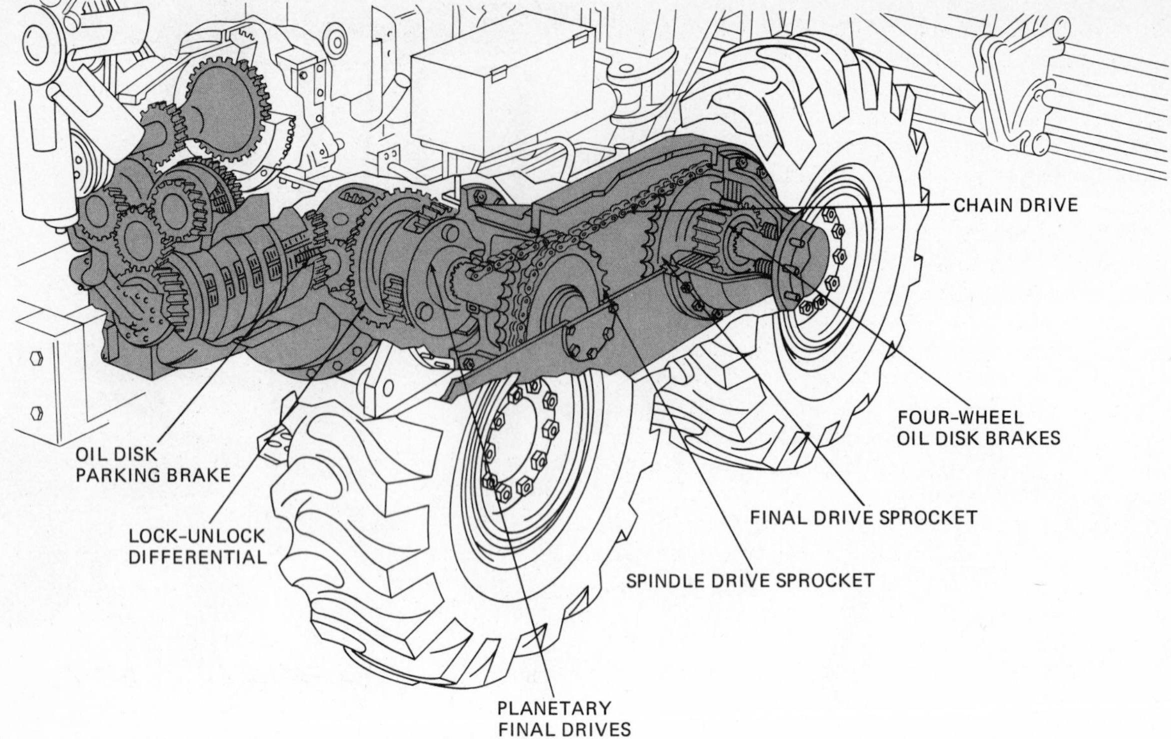

Fig. 2-32 View of a grader transmission and tandem housing.

rod end of the piston is fastened to the lean bar. The wheel hub is supported on bearings on the spindle and the housing is pivot-fastened with two pins to the lean arm. The two steering cylinders are pivot-fastened to the front axle mounting brackets and the piston rod ends are pivot-fastened to the spindle lean arm. A tie-rod links both spindle housings with each other.

When the lean cylinder piston end receives oil, the piston rod extends, moving the lean bar. This pivots the lean arm, wheel spindles, and the wheels on the axle, causing the top of the wheels to move to the right. If the oil flow is reversed (the top of) the wheels move in the opposite direction. **NOTE** The maximum lean on this grader is 18° in either direction.

When the steering wheel is turned, oil flows to the steering cylinders, with one steering cylinder receiving oil at the piston end and the other at the rod end. One piston rod then retracts and the other extends, pivoting the spindle housings on their pins, and the lean arm thereby pivots the wheels.

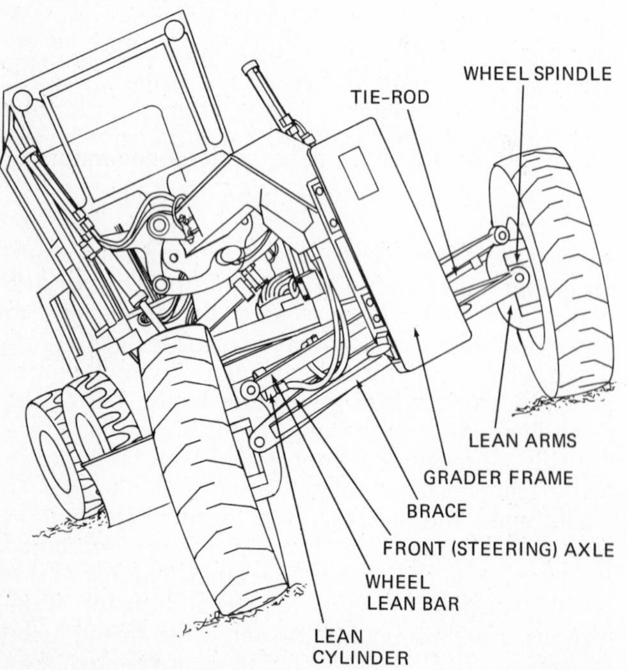

Fig. 2-33 Grader front axle.

BLADE AND DRAWBAR The upper circular drawbar is fastened to the front of the grader frame through a large ball socket joint. The other end of the drawbar is fastened through the blade lift cylinders to the grader frame. Depending on the grader design, the lift cylinders may be swivel-fastened to the frame, or through lift arms and lift bars to the frame. The latter design permits a greater circular drawbar tilt and provides for several lock positions to the lock plate which is welded to the frame.

The center shift cylinder is pivot-fastened to the upper circle, and the rod end of the piston is pivot-fastened to the blade lift bar. The lower circle is held to the upper circle through shoes which have bearings. The circle drive reduction gear consists of a worm drive and a planetary gear set which are so bolted to the upper circle that the drive pinion meshes with the internal ring gear (which is part of the lower circle). The piston hydraulic motor is bolted to the reduction gear. The blade may be pivot-fastened to the extended arms of the lower circle and through pins and brackets, located in several tip positions, or it may be fastened to a bracket having a rail on the top and bottom, the bracket being pivot-fastened to the extended lower circle arms. The tip cylinders are attached to the lower circle, and the rod ends of the pistons are fastened to the rail bracket.

The blade side-shift cylinder is fastened to the rail bracket, and the rod end of the piston is fastened to the blade mounting bracket.

BLADE OPERATION When the operator actuates both lift cylinder directional control valves (to raise the blade), oil is directed over the swivel joint check valves into the rod end of the cylinders, raising the blade evenly. The oil returns from the piston ends of the cylinder via the check valve, the swivel joint, and the directional control valve, to the reservoir. If the operator wishes to lower the blade, he or she reverses both control valves and the blades lower evenly. However, if only the left- or the right-hand side of the blade is to be raised or lowered, only one directional control valve is actuated.

If the motor grader is equipped with a center shift cylinder, and the operator has removed the mechanical lock and raised the blade to its maximum height, and if he or she then actuates the directional control valve to extend the piston rod of the center shift cylinder, the rod end pivots both lift arms (including the lift cylinders), whereupon the upper circle is semirotated, lifting the right- or left-hand side of the blade.

NOTE By using the blade lift cylinders, the blade can be positioned at a 90° angle.

To tip the blade backward or forward, oil is directed either into the piston ends or into the rod ends of the tip cylinder. The piston rod then moves in or out and pivots the bracket as well as the blade.

To side-shift the blade (left or right), oil is directed into the shift cylinder piston end or rod end, extending the piston rod or retracting it and thus forcing the blade to move in the guide rails to the right or left. If the operator desires to rotate the blade in a clockwise or a counterclockwise direction, oil is directed into the piston motor, driving the reduction gear. The pinion then transmits the rotation to the internal ring gear, which causes the lower circle and the blade to rotate.

ARTICULATED STEERING MOTOR GRADERS Articulated steering design motor graders have the pivot joint almost in line with the front axle of the tandem axle. The joint, however, allows the front frame to move only 20° to the left or right without rotating. See Fig. 2-34. The piston rod ends of the steering cylinders are fastened to the tractor-mounting brackets and the cylinders are fastened to the brackets of the grader frame. When oil is directed into the steering cylinders to make a left turn, the piston end of one cylinder and the rod end of one cylinder receive oil under pressure, and as a result the piston rods pull the grader frame to the left. If the directional control valve is reversed in direction, the oil flow into the cylinders is reversed and the front end of the grader is pulled to the right.

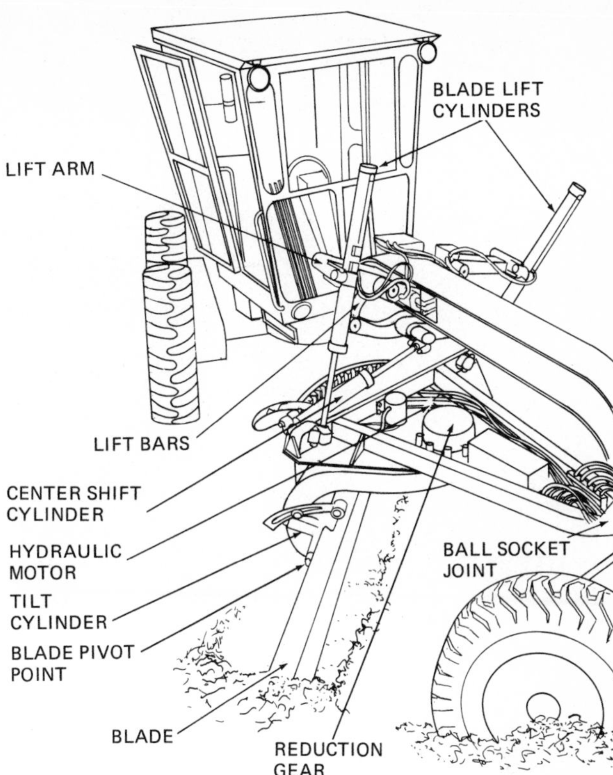

Fig. 2-34 Top view of an articulated grader circular drawbar and blade.

Motortrucks, Truck-tractors, and Trailers Although the majority of motortrucks, truck-tractors, and trailers satisfy the requirements of the on-highway/off-highway industry, to transport special equipment or unusually large loads, some must be manufactured to a much greater size than the conventional types. A specially manufactured motortruck with full trailer is shown in Fig. 2-35. This motortruck with full trailer is capable of hauling a load of logs weighing up to 200 tons [181.4 t] or any heavy utility equipment, such as generators or reactors. When it is used as a logging unit, the bunks on the trailer and the front bunk on the truck are pivot-mounted to the truck or trailer frame and positioned in the center of the frame between the tandem axles. This allows the tandem truck front axle and the two tandem trailer axles to turn for steering while the load remains stationary. This arrangement increases the handling ability and the turning radius. The outside turning radius is 65 ft [19.82 m] and the inside radius is 35.4 ft [10.79 m], which means that this unit requires a maximum roadway of 19.6 ft [5.97 m]. (See Fig. 2-36) The tandem front axle is steered through two steering cylinders, and the tandem trailer axles are also steered through hydraulic cylinders. The steering control to the trailer axles is through a specially designed joint so that the trailer wheels actually track the rear wheels of the truck.

The one-piece box frame is of a bolted structure

Fig. 2-35 Specially designed logging truck.

to maintain high flexibility. Leaf spring suspension is used to give maximum control and stability. The wheel base of the truck and trailer are the same, that is, 24.6 ft [7.503 m], and the overall width is 14 ft [4.27 m]. The cab, which is at the front left, is mounted on air bags to reduce road shock. Minimum required engine power is 1000 hp [745.6 kW]. The engine and the six- or eight-speed powershift transmission are bolted in front of the first steering axle. The transmission has a hydraulic retarder and the drive axles have planetary wheel hubs. The brake system is full air and the foundation brakes are shoe brakes.

Motortrucks and Chassis for Cranes and Excavators Rubber-tired motortrucks and chassis are specially designed for the mounting of a crane or an excavator. They are grouped into five classes. Classes 3, 4, and 5 are chassis only, without an engine, and some are without a cab (driver compartment). The engine is located in the superstructure. They have a road speed of less than 40 mph [64.35 km/h (kilometers per hour)]. They may have two drive axles (4 × 4), or a tandem drive axle and a tandem steering axle (8 × 4), or a tandem rear axle and a single steering axle (6 × 4). See Fig. 2-37 for a view of a steering axle. The excavator shown in Fig. 2-38 has two drive axles and planetary wheel hubs. The wheel base and the overall width are nearly the same. Each axle can move individually, and the front axle can be locked through two hydraulic cylinders. The cylinders are fastened to the frame, and the piston rod ends are fastened to the axle. This arrangement holds the superstructure rigid when the machine is operating.

The *superstructure* is the entire structure above the chassis, including the excavator. It is fastened to the chassis through a turntable and, since it is rotated through a hydraulic motor and a reduction gear, the rotation is not restricted in either direction. The carrier shown in Fig. 2-38 uses an 80-hp [59.64-

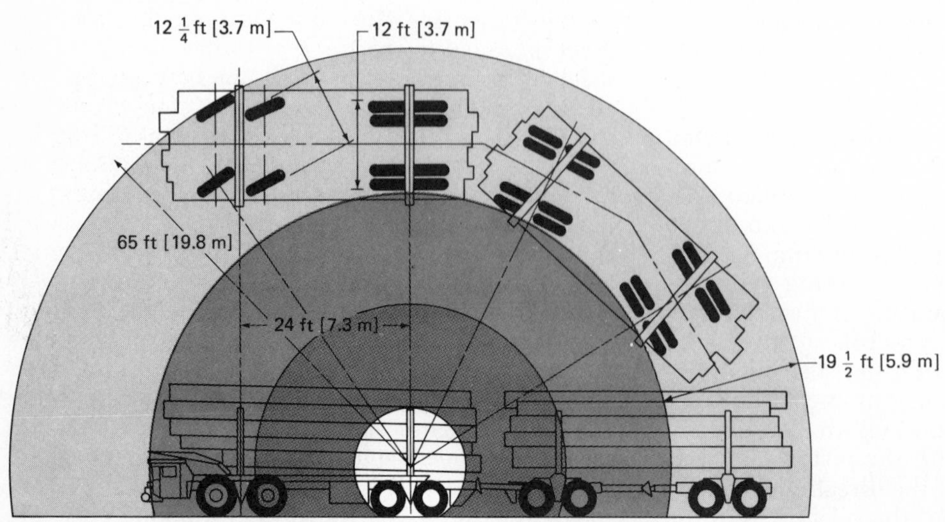

Fig. 2-36 Maximum outside turning radius 65.0 ft [19.82 m]. (*Butler Bros. Supplies Ltd.*)

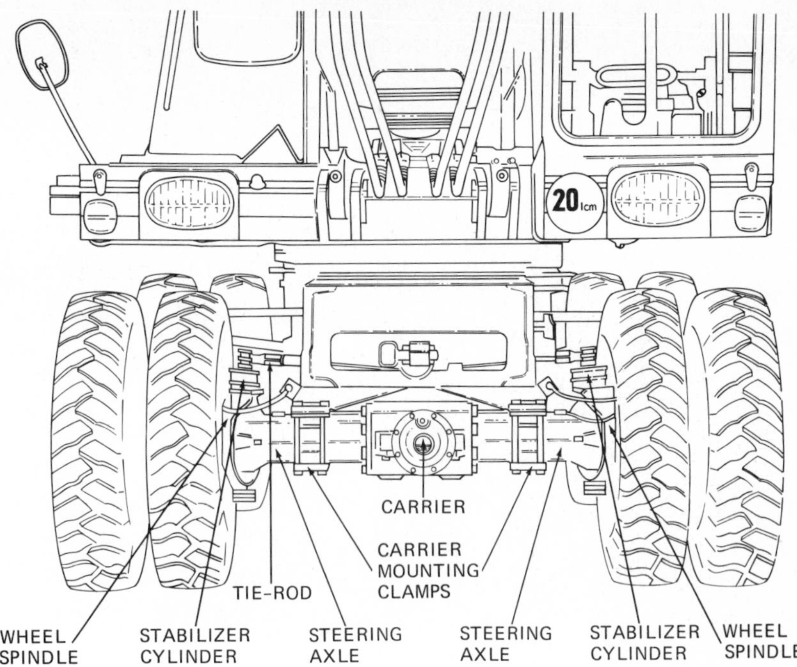

Fig. 2-37 View of steering axle.

kW] air-cooled engine. Its power can be used to excavate or to propel the machine forward or in reverse. The power that drives the front and rear carriers originates from the hydraulic motor and is transmitted to the divider transmission, to the drive lines, and onto the carriers. Steering is hydrostatic.

The excavator is similar in design to a utility backhoe, but its structure and hydraulic cylinders are, of course, larger and stronger. To make this unit more versatile, a log grapple can be attached to the end of the dipper stick to load logs onto a truck or to stockpile the logs. A cradle, a pallet handler, or a multiclaw grab can also be attached. Each of these units is hydraulically actuated to rotate 360°.

Classes 1 and 2 chassis are motortrucks having a chassis especially designed to mount a revolving superstructure such as that used for classes 3, 4, and 5. They have their own engine for propulsion, and are capable of a road speed of at least 40 mph [64.35 km/h]. The engines used are usually diesel, ranging between 115 and 350 hp [85.74 and 260.96 kW]. When the units have two engines (the additional one to operate the hydraulic systems), they are diesel-powered exclusively, and range from 83 to 238 hp [61.88 to 177.45 kW]. The overall width of the small units, class 1, is 8 ft [2.44 m] with an average overall length of 32 ft [9.76 m]. Class 1 units have a tandem drive axle and a single steering axle (6 × 4). The larger units, class 2, have an overall width ranging from 8 to 11 ft [2.44 to 3.35 m] and an overall length

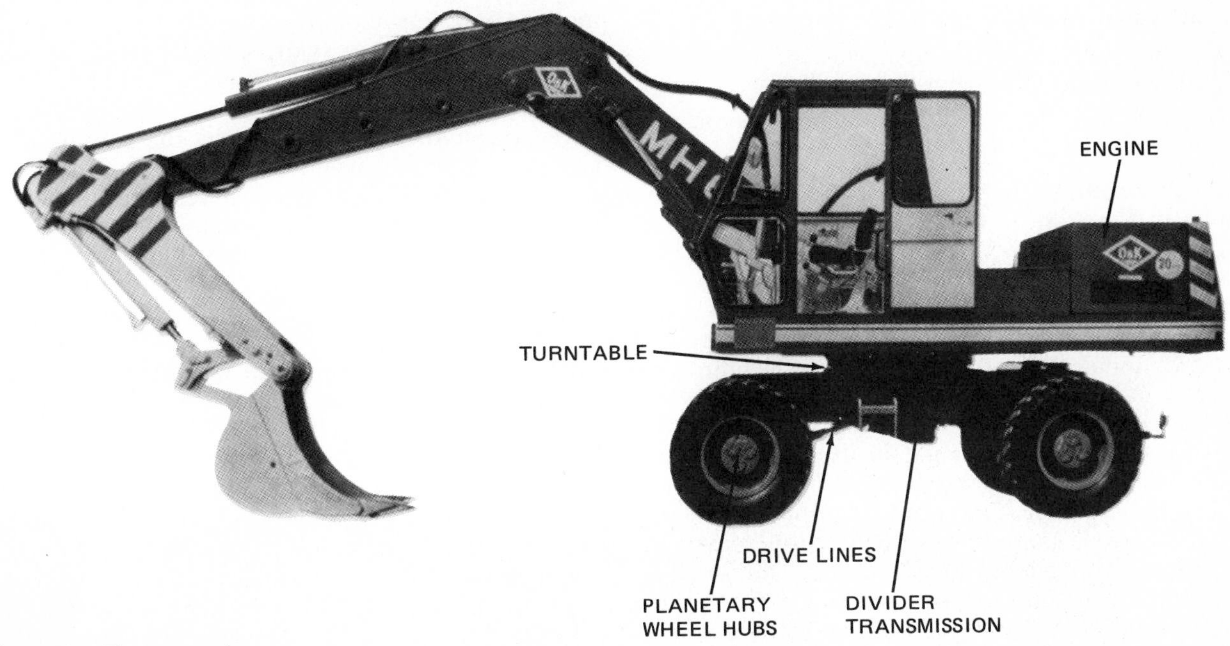

Fig. 2-38 Class 3 carrier excavator.

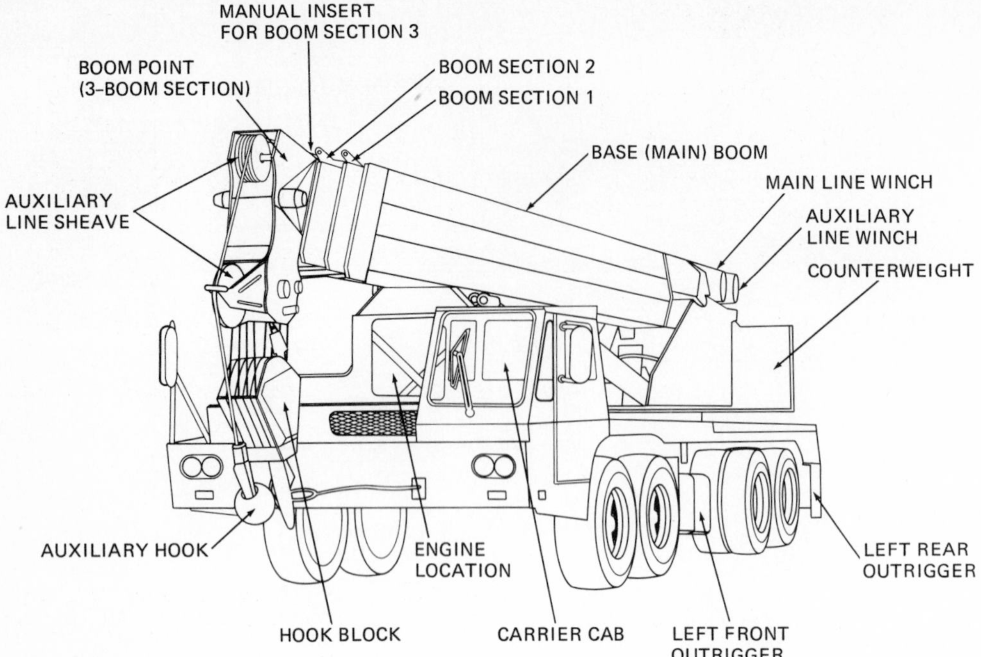

Fig. 2-39 Hydraulic motortruck crane. (*Harnischfeger*)

ranging from 32 to 47 ft [9.76 to 14.33 m]. A class 2 unit could also have a single steering axle and tandem drive axle (6 × 4), but more often it has a tandem steering axle (8 × 4). The largest unit built to date has three steering axles and three drive axles, with a cab mounted in the front of the first steering axle (12 × 6).

Although the chassis carriers are classed in five groups, they are further broken down by

1. The type of working equipment, that is, excavator, crane, or shovel
2. Their load capacity in tons, cubic meters, or cubic yards
3. The digging depth and swing reach and grade level dumping height in meters or feet when it is an excavator or shovel
4. Lift capacity in kilograms or pounds and the standard boom length and the lift capacity at extended boom length when it is a crane

NOTE In both lift capacity ratings, the boom radius in feet or meters is also given.

As an example, the hydraulic motortruck crane shown in Fig. 2-39 has an 8 × 4 chassis and only one 300-hp [223.68-kW] diesel engine and a 12-speed forward and two-speed reverse manual (air shift assist) transmission. The engine speed is controlled through a single-acting, air-applied, spring return cylinder. A hand- and foot-operated throttle air valve is located in the cab of the superstructure, and it is connected over an air swivel with the throttle cylinder. The foot-operated air throttle valve and selector valve in the truck cab are also connected to the throttle cylinder. The engine, equipped with an engine brake, is mounted in the forward center of the chassis; the cab is at the left-hand side of the engine and the hydraulic reservoir is at the right-hand side of the engine. A dual air brake system, including spring brakes, is used. The rear axle is of the walking-beam design and has planetary wheel hubs, whereas the front axles are spring-suspended.

The entire hydraulic system has five hydraulic pumps. The power steering/outrigger pump is mounted at the rear of the engine and supplies oil for the power steering circuit. When the operator flips the outrigger master switch, the solenoid-operated selector closes the oil flow to the power steering circuit, and opens the flow to the outrigger circuit (see below). The other four pumps are attached to a four-stage gear box that is fastened to the carrier frame between the engine and front rear axle. The hydraulic pumps are balanced vane pumps to supply oil to the swing circuit, winch motors, and boom cylinders. The fourth pump is a piston pump (pressure-compensating) used to supply oil to the pilot circuits of the winch brakes, the two-speed winch motors, and the boom-hoist-holding valve control circuits. The gear box is driven through a propeller shaft which is connected to the engine crankshaft pulley. A clutch in the form of a sliding gear is engaged through levers actuated by the single-acting air cylinder, and is disengaged through spring force. The throttle selector valve is used to direct air to the air cylinder to engage the clutch. Two scissor-type outriggers are located at the rear (left and right) of the frame and two are located after the rear steering axle.

OUTRIGGERS The difference between a stabilizer and an outrigger (Fig. 2-40) is that the stabilizer pivots in a semicircle from the top position to the lift position, whereas an outrigger moves in a vertical direction. The outrigger arms or beams are positioned in a hollow tunnel (outrigger box) below the frame and are forced in and out through a single- or a dual-stage double-acting hydraulic cylinder. The outrigger box is pivot-mounted to the carrier frame; the hydraulic cylinder is fastened to the outrigger bracket, the rod ends are fastened to the out-

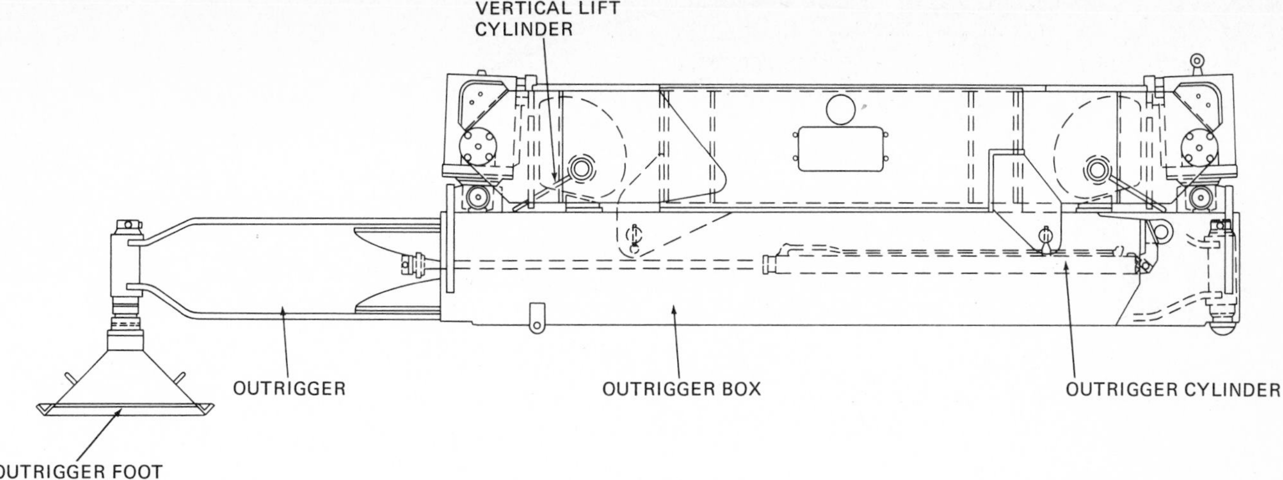

Fig. 2-40 Schematic illustration of an outrigger. (*Harnischfeger*)

rigger beam, and the foot is swivel-fastened to the outrigger beam. The vertical double-acting lift cylinder is pivot-fastened to the outrigger bracket which is welded to the carrier frame, and the rod ends are attached to the outrigger box. **NOTE** Some outriggers have the vertical lift cylinder positioned on the outrigger beam end.

The eight outrigger directional control valves, located at each side of the carrier, are controlled electrically through switches located in the superstructure cab.

OUTRIGGER OPERATION To extend or to retract the outrigger, one solenoid is energized to actuate one directional valve and oil is directed to extend or retract the outrigger beam. To lower or raise one outrigger box, a second solenoid is energized and oil is directed to one vertical lift cylinder. Each outrigger box is automatically mechanically locked, thereby removing the force from the vertical lift cylinder. The safety lock consists of a solenoid-controlled air valve, a single-acting air cylinder, a pivot-mounted safety pawl, and a fixed mounted pawl. To release the safety lock, the solenoid is energized. This shifts the air valve, and air is then directed to the air cylinder; the piston rod extends, pivoting the pawl, thus disengaging the lock. See Fig. 2-41.

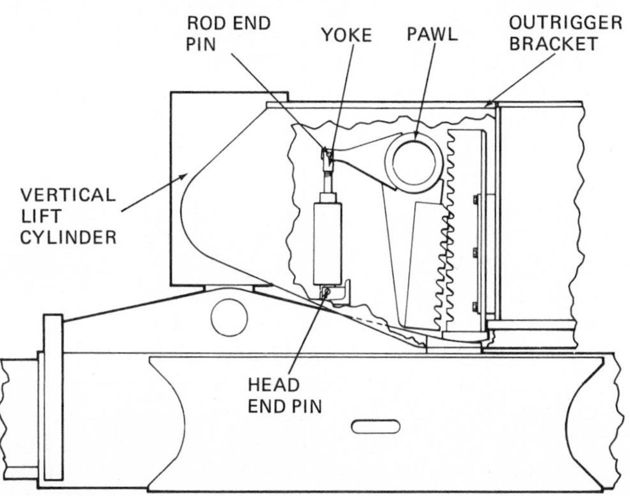

Fig. 2-41 Outrigger safelock cylinder. (*Harnischfeger*)

SUPERSTRUCTURES

All revolving superstructures are fastened to the frame through a turntable to give them a free-wheeling swing rotation. Multiload precision rollers are located between the main outer ring and sleeve ring gear raceways. The bearings and raceways are sealed to protect them from contamination. See Fig. 2-42. The hydraulic motor with the reduction gear and swing brake is fastened to the outer ring so that the drive pinion meshes with the sleeve ring gear. The outer ring is fastened to the carrier frame, whereas the inner ring gear is fastened to the superstructure frame. When oil is directed to the hydraulic motor, the motor is forced to rotate, and its rotation is transmitted to the reduction gear which rotates the pinion gear. The pinion gear revolves around the internal ring gear, causing the superstructure to rotate. The swing brake is of the disk brake design, and is hydraulically applied and spring-released. When the master cylinder pedal is depressed, oil is forced into the disk brake cylinder, applying the brake and holding the input shaft of the reduction gear. When the hydraulic force is removed, the spring force releases the brake. To keep the brake applied, the application pressure can be held by moving the swing lock valve. This valve is a simple ball check valve operated through the swing lock lever and, when the lever is placed in the lock position, the ball check valve holds the applied brake pressure.

Booms The main boom is pivot-fastened to the superstructure frame, as well as to the two boom cylinders. The two rod ends of the cylinders are fastened to the main boom. This mounting arrangement allows the main boom to be lowered about 4.5° below the horizontal position for quick reeving, for

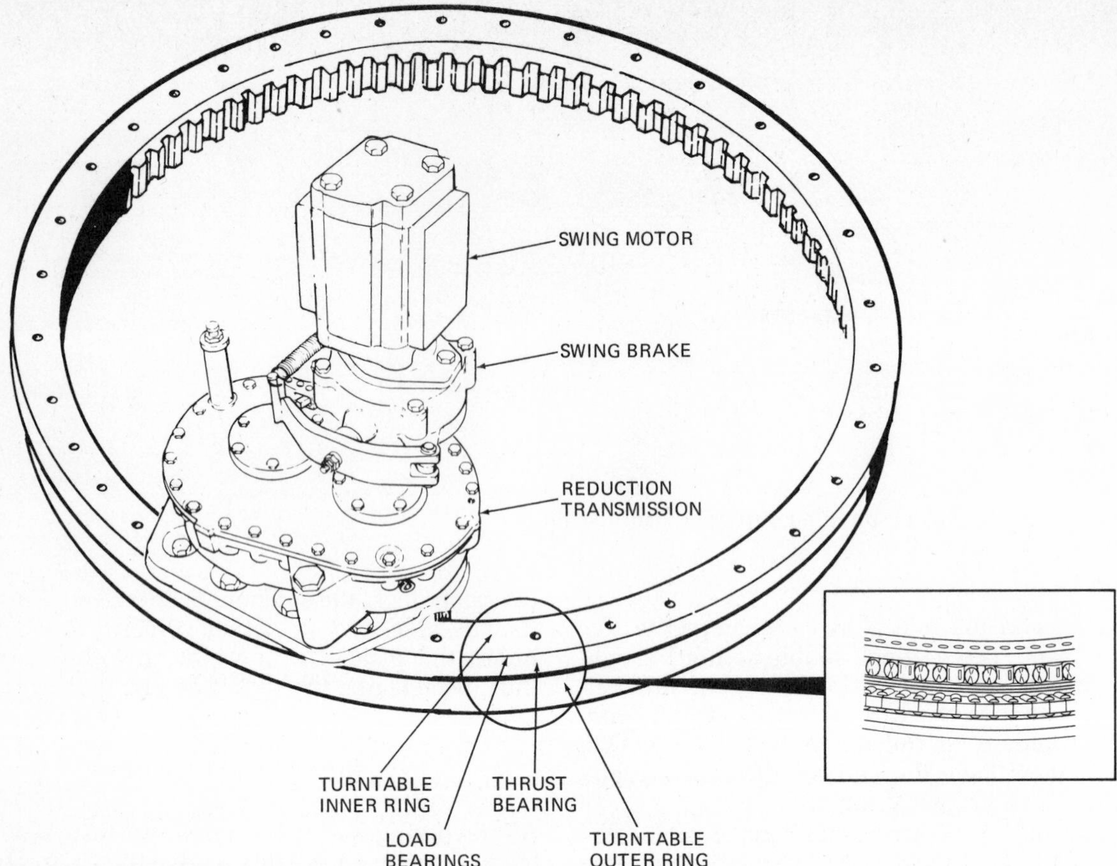

Fig. 2-42 Schematic illustration of a swing assembly from an excavator. (*J I Case Company Agricultural Equipment Division*)

installation of a boom extension or jib, or for maintenance work.

The standard boom has four sections: the main boom section, two sections hydraulically extended and retracted (using telescopic cylinders), and a fly section. The fly section can be extended and retracted through a hydraulic cylinder but must be manually pinned to either one of the two positions. The standard boom length fully extended is 114 ft [34.77 m]. The hoist capacity at the maximum vertical angle of 80° is 30,000 lb [13,608 kg]. If the optional extension is fastened to the fly section, the tip height is extended to 149 ft [45.4 m] (measured from the ground to the tip) and the hoist capacity is then 12,000 lb [5448 kg]. If the offset jib is fastened to the extension, the tip height is 178 ft [54.21 m] and the hoist capacity is reduced to 7500 lb [3405 kg]. When the boom is fully retracted to 39 ft [11.89 m], it can hoist 120,000 lb [54,480 kg]. **NOTE** The hoist capacity declines with (1) an increase in swing radius, (2) an increase in boom length, which also increases the swing radius and the lever arm, and (3) a forward or side positioning of the boom. The hoist capacity is at its maximum when the boom points rearward. The hoist capacity is reduced when the boom points forward or to either side. The reason that the hoist capacity must be reduced is to prevent the crane from overturning because the hoist weight must be in direct proportion to the lever ratio and counterbalance weight of the carrier (see Fig. 2-43).

HYDRAULIC BOOM OPERATION When the operator pulls the control lever back, oil from the pump is directed over the directional control valve and over the boom-hold check valves, to the piston ends of the boom cylinders. The piston rods extend, raising the boom. When the direction of the control valve is reversed, oil is directed to the rod ends of the boom cylinders. As the pressure on the boom-holding valve spool (lockback) increases beyond the piston pressure, the valve shifts and allows oil to flow from the piston ends of the cylinders and return over the directional control valve back to the reservoir. In the event the return oil pressure becomes higher than the oil pump pressure, an anticavitation valve located in the directional control valve will open to allow return oil to be added to the pump oil.

To extend the boom, the operator pushes the control lever forward. This directs oil through the holding valve and onto the lower telescopic cylinder piston. When the telescopic lever is moved, all six of the solenoid valves (two for each holding valve) are electrically shifted. Oil then flows through the solenoid directional valve, over the check valves, and into the cylinder, and the piston rods extend. To retract the boom, the operator reverses the control lever position and all six solenoids are electrically shifted. Oil flows from the control valve, through the holding valve, through the cylinder rod, and into the rod end of the cylinder body. Oil flows from the cylinder body of the lower telescopic cylinder to the

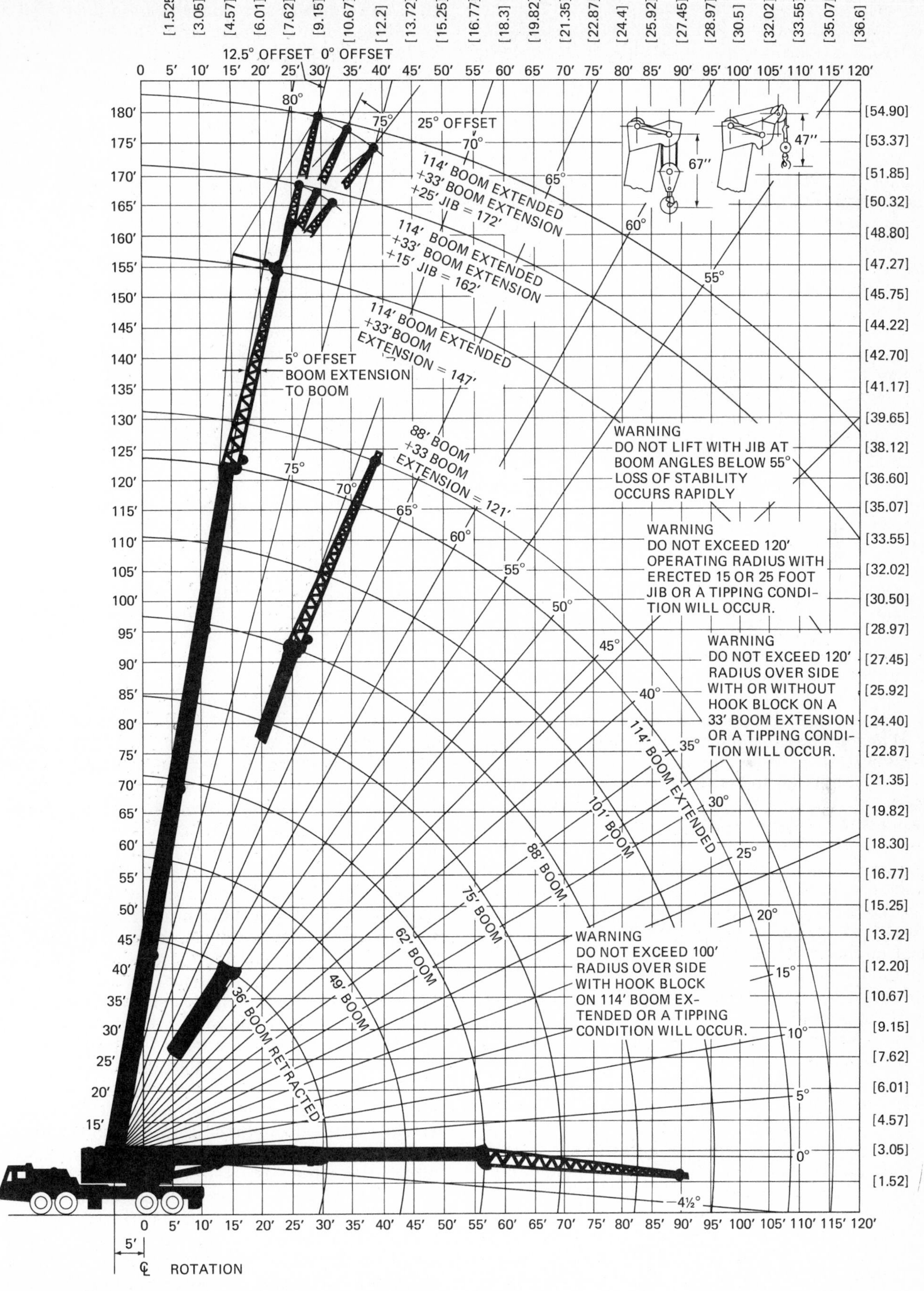

Fig. 2-43 Range diagram (hook distance from center of rotation in feet and meters) (*Harnischfeger*)

adjacent holding valve and cylinder body. Pressure on the rod side of the cylinder builds up and this pressure is sensed at the back side of the holding valve spool. This causes the holding valve spool to shift, allowing the oil from the head of the telescopic cylinder to return through the holding valve spool, through the solenoid valve, and to the reservoir.

Two hydraulically driven winches are located on top of the counterweight; one is the main winch used for the main winch line, and the other the auxiliary winch used when the boom extension is used. Both are identical in construction (see material on winches). Each winch is equipped with a dual-stage fixed-displacement gear motor (Fig. 2-44). A caliper disk brake is fastened to the input shaft of the winch. A double planetary reduction gear within the housing reduces the winch line speed to gain torque. When the main winch control lever is placed into the raised position, both hydraulic motors receive oil and drive the winch drum at low speed (high torque). When the two-speed solenoid valve is shifted electrically into the high-speed position, oil is directed to the motor valve and the valve is shifted. This directs all pump oil to only one gear motor, and therefore the motor is driven at higher speeds (lower torque) because more oil enters the motor. When the control valve is placed in the raise position, the disk brakes are not released but the sprags allow the hydraulic motor shaft to drive the winch input shaft. But as soon as the control valve is brought to the neutral position, or into the lowering position, the sprags on the hub of the disk brake lock up, holding the input shaft against the disk brake and holding the load stationary.

When the main winch control valve is placed into the lowering position, the main winch brake valve shifts to allow oil to be directed to the winch brake cylinder, releasing the brake. Anticavitation valves are positioned within the main control valve, which automatically opens when the pump line pressure is lower than the motor return line pressure. With the main control valve open, oil from the return line is allowed into the pump line. The valve automatically closes as soon as the pump pressure increases beyond the motor return line pressure.

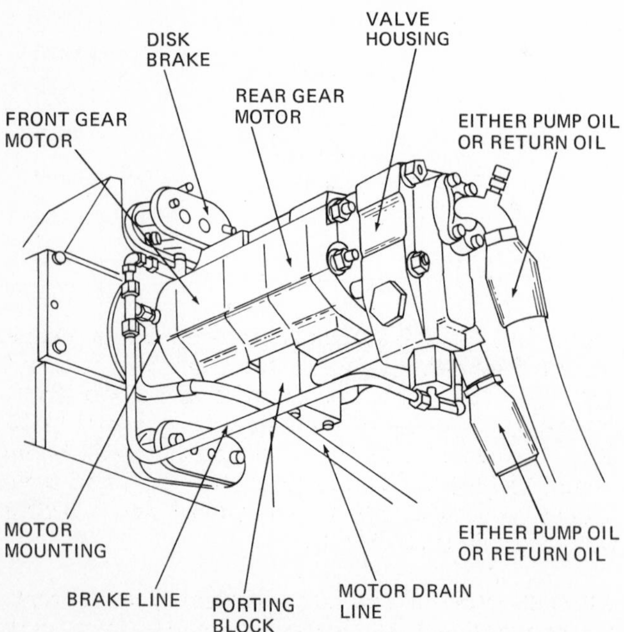

Fig. 2-44 Winch motor. (*Harnischfeger*)

Nontelescopic Boom Crane The main difference between a nontelescopic crane and a hydraulic crane lies in the structure of the main boom. The superstructure—that is, the machine deck and operating components—change also when the crane is mechanically or electrically powered. The carrier used may be any of classes 1 to 5 (see Fig. 2-45), or the boom may be mounted to a track-type machine. The individual boom sections may be tubular or angular welded structures, whereas the supercrane uses I-beam or box-section welded structures. The base section is pivot-fastened to the superstructure frame and the boom inserts are bolted between the point section and base section. **NOTE** These sections are manufactured in lengths of 10, 20, 30, and 50 ft [3.05, 6.1, 9.15, and 15.25 m] to give the boom its required operating height. When a jib is used, the jib section is pivot-fastened to the point section and suspended by the jib suspension (backstay) line and jib strut. The boom backstop is pivot-fastened to the end of the boom base section and to the bottom of the gantry. It is of the telescopic design, which gives the operator a safety and warning device to indicate the maximum horizontal and other boom positions. The gantry is used to lower and raise the boom, to transfer the boom and load weight to the carrier, and to mount and demount the boom from the superstructure. The front gantry frame (compression member) is pivot-fastened to the winch frame. The tension member consists of several links which are fastened to the frame of the superstructure. The gantry lift cylinders, which are used to extend or retract the tension member, are fastened to the winch frame and the rod ends of the pistons to the compression frame. The two members are attached to one another through a shaft. The gantry spreader assembly, which consists of a shaft with several sheaves (pulleys), is pivot-fastened through links to the top of the gantry. The floating boom spreader assembly (handlers or bridles), which also consists of a shaft with several sheaves, is fastened through wire ropes (boom backstay or pendants) to the point section. The reeving, that is, the route which the wire ropes take to raise or lower the boom, or to multiply the lifting power, is shown in Figs. 2-46 and 2-47. The dead end of the wire rope is fastened to the gantry or to the superstructure, and the other (live) end is fastened to the boom hoist drum. When the drum is rotated in a counterclockwise rotation (to raise the boom), the wire rope is wound around the drum, shortening the rope. This reduces the distance between the boom spreader assembly and the gantry assembly, pulling the boom on the backstay wire rope upward. When the drum direction is reversed, the rope is wound off the boom hoist drum, and the distance between the boom spreader and the gantry assembly increases, lowering the boom.

The main hoist line is reeved in a similar fashion; however, the sheaves (some booms have as many as eight) are fastened to the boom point and located in

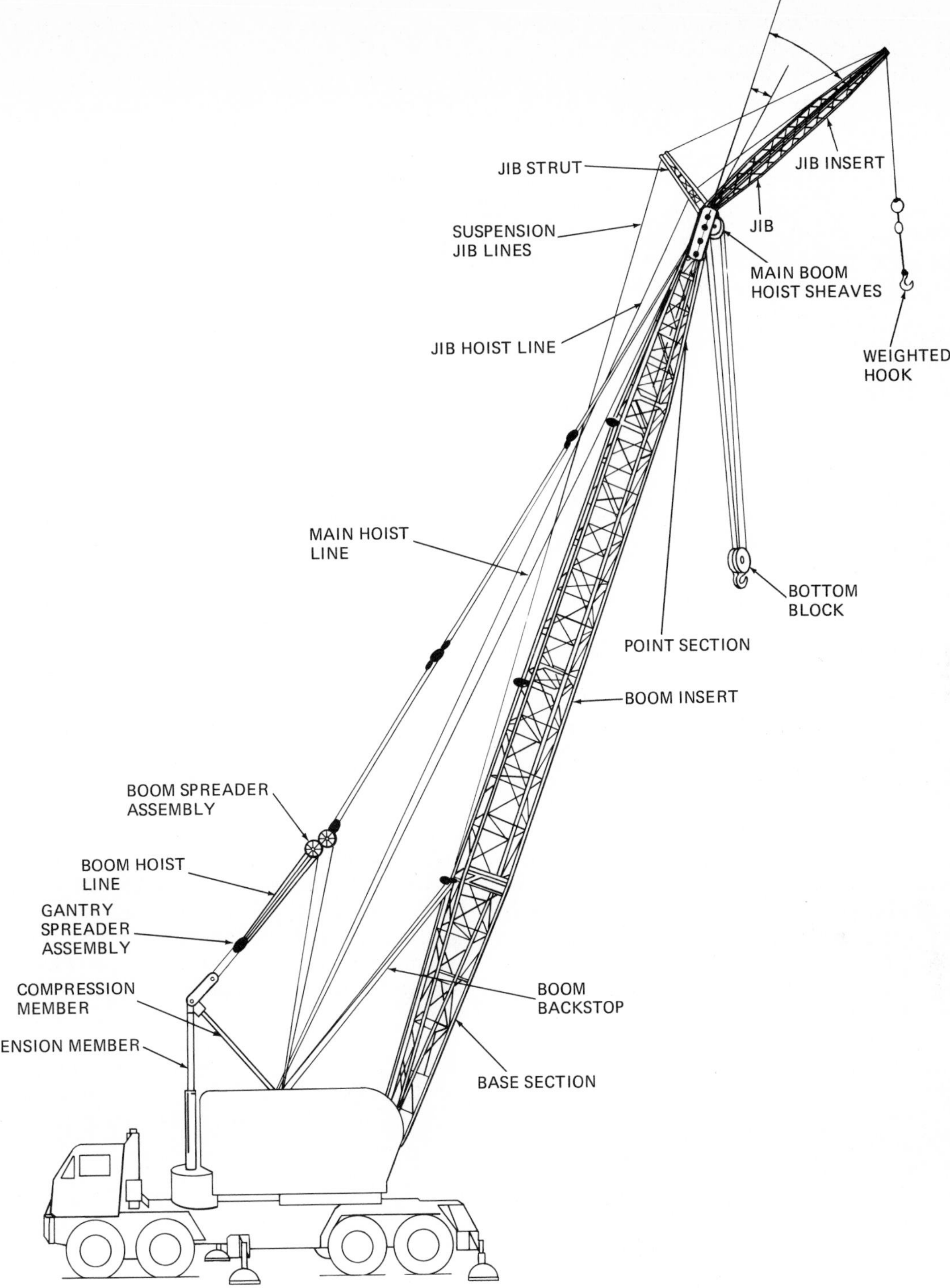

Fig. 2-45 Typical crane boom with jib attached. (*Harnischfeger*)

the main boom block or in the bottom block, which has in addition a swivel-fastened lift hook. The dead end of the wire rope is fastened to the boom point and the live end is fastened to the main hoist drum. The jib line reeving is only 3 or 5 point, that is, the wire rope is threaded only through three or five sheaves because this line is more or less an auxiliary line.

As with the hydraulic crane, the lift capacity of the nontelescopic boom crane is also reduced when the radius from the center of rotation is increased or the boom height increased. The average maximum boom length of the nontelescopic boom crane mounted on carriers or on a track machine is about 140 ft [42.7 m], with an average lift capacity of about 15,000 lb [8100 kg] at a swing radius of 60 ft [18.3 m]. The largest contemporary nontelescopic boom cranes can lift 566,700 lb [257,281.8 kg], and have a boom length of 260 ft [118.04 m] and a swing radius of 100 ft [30.5 m].

ATTACHMENTS To perform different types of work, the conventional lift block is exchanged with any one of several different working attachments. For

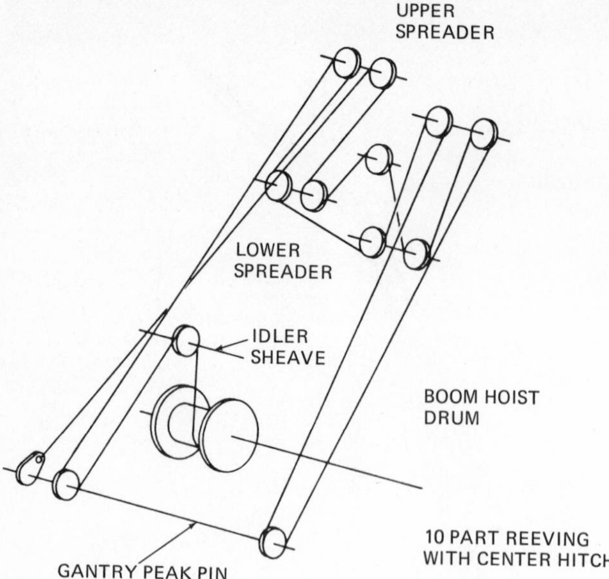

Fig. 2-46 Boom hoist reeving. (*Harnischfeger*)

example, a clamshell can be attached for the excavating of earth or for loading or stockpiling; or a log grapple can be attached to load and stockpile logs. The main hoist line (rear drum) is reeved to the clamshell, and the jib line (front drum) is reeved to close the clamshell bucket or the log grapple. To prevent the grapple from turning, a spring tag line winder is attached to the upper end of the boom section or is mounted to one side so as not to interfere with the operator's vision. The dead end of the wire rope is fastened to the bucket, and the live end is fastened to the drum. The drum is always under spring tension, thereby holding the attachment in one position. (See Fig. 2-48.) A fair lead is fastened close to the tag line winder to guide the wire rope onto the drum. A drag-line bucket can be attached to hoist and drag lines and when the two lines are properly operated it can scoop up the earth.

If a drag-line bucket is attached to the crane, the reeving is as shown in Fig. 2-49. The wire rope of the hoist drum is fastened to a chain and the chain is fastened to the bucket in such a way that the weight of bucket is always pointing downward, ready to cut into the earth. The jib line (pull-in line) from the front drum is fastened over a sheave to the pivot front end and the chain is fastened to each side and clamped to the pull-in line. A fair lead is swivel-fastened to the superstructure frame to guide the pull-in line onto the front drum.

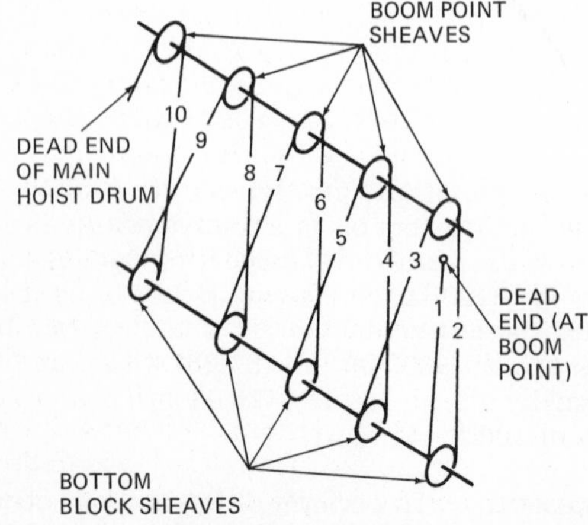

Fig. 2-47 Main hoist line reeving. (*Harnischfeger*)

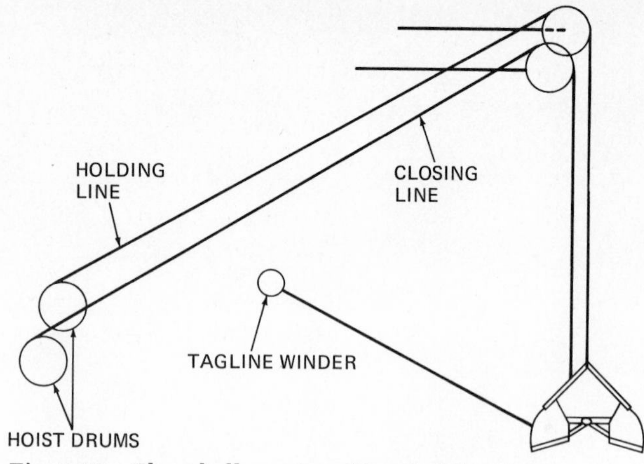

Fig. 2-48 Clamshell reeving. (*Harnischfeger*)

POWER AND GEARING The machine deck consists of the components shown in Fig. 2-50. The engine is mounted at the rear, and either a standard clutch and transmission or a torque converter and power-shift transmission are bolted directly to the engine. The output power is transmitted over a multichain drive and then over a constant-velocity joint onto the swing clutch shaft. The reduction between input and output shaft is about 5:1. An internal clutch band is used or a magnetorque unit is fastened outside of the swing shaft, and the internal swing brake drum is fastened to the left-hand magnetorque inner member. See material in the section on winches. The brake is spring-applied and hydraulically (oil-) released. The two pinions are supported on bearings on the swing shaft but fastened to the inner member of the magnetorque unit, and the sprocket is keyed to the swing shaft. The two pinions are in mesh with the bevel gear on the intermediate swing gear, and

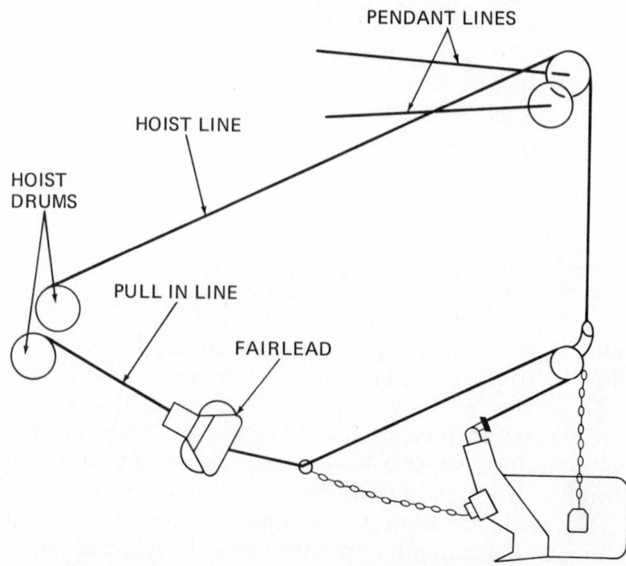

Fig. 2-49 Drag line reeving. (*Harnischfeger*)

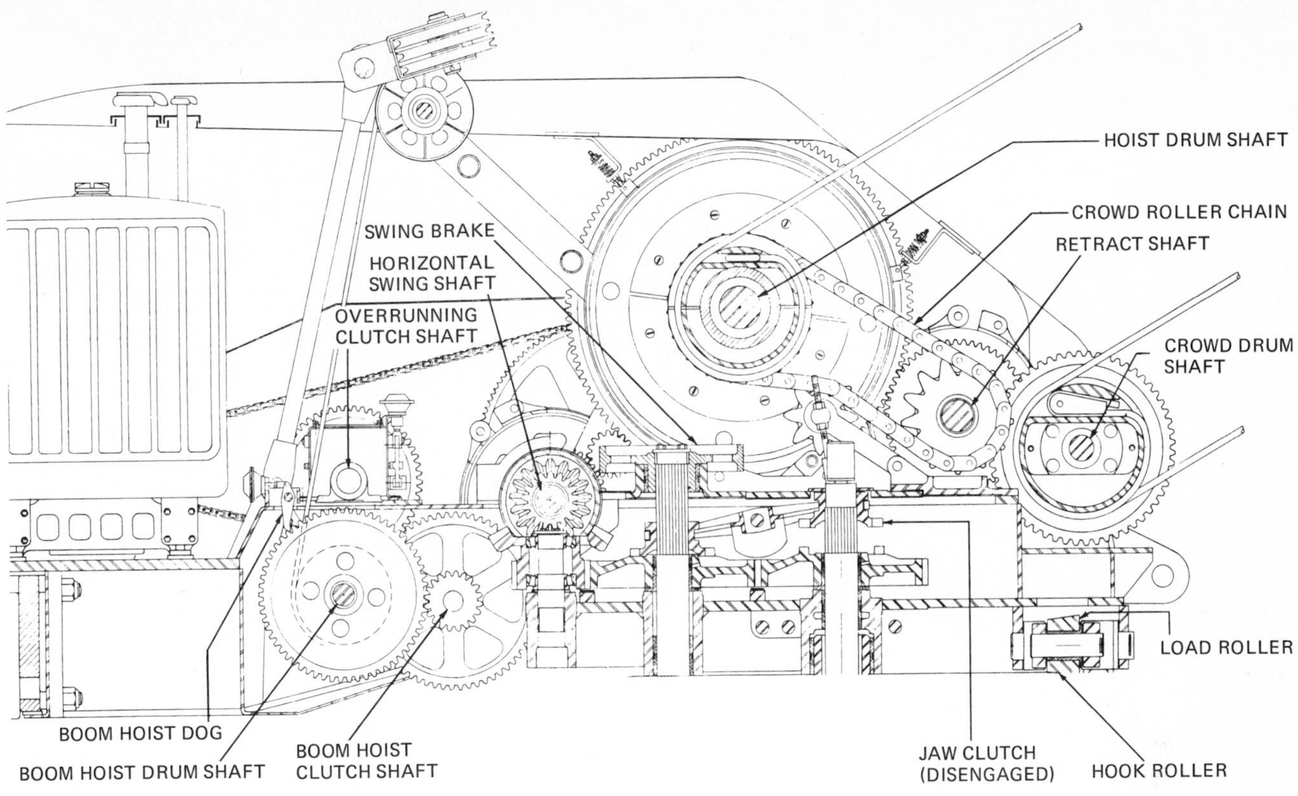

Fig. 2-50 Machine deck. (*Harnischfeger*)

its spur gear is in mesh with the large spur gear of the swing shaft assembly. The swing pinions are in mesh with the internal gear.

NONTELESCOPIC BOOM OPERATION When the operator pulls back on the swing brake lever, oil is directed to the swing brake cylinder, releasing the external swing brake band. When the lever is pushed forward (toward the operator), oil is directed to the set brake valve, holding the swing brake release and thereby allowing the operator to control the swing brake action with the magnetorque couplings.

The power from the intermediate reduction shaft is transmitted through a multichain drive onto the jack shaft at a reduction of about 2:1. The jack shaft pinion drives the front hoist drum shaft gear, which in turn drives the rear hoist drum shaft gear and the boom hoist drum since both drums are on the same shaft. Therefore, whenever the engine is operating and the transmission is in gear, the swing clutch shaft rotates but no power is transmitted until one of the clutches is engaged and the brake is released.

NOTE The brakes are spring-applied and hydraulically (oil-) released. Internal band clutches are used. They are spring-released and hydraulically (oil-) applied, but note that the front and rear drum shaft gears are driven in opposite directions.

To raise the load, the operator first hydraulically releases the brake and then hydraulically applies the front hoist clutch. The power from the drum shaft gear is first transmitted to the clutch drum and then to the winch drum, winding the wire rope onto the drum and raising the load. To lower the load, the operator applies the brakes and at the same time releases the clutch, which holds the load. He or she then partially releases the drum brakes to allow the brakes to slip and lower the load (controlling braking). This is not practical on larger cranes; therefore, a planetary gear set is incorporated into each drum assembly to lower the load under power. See material in the section on winches. **NOTE** The front and rear (crowd) drum assemblies are alike in design and operation, but the boom hoist planetary gear set is connected to different components in order to slow down the lowering speed of the boom.

Shovels A shovel (Fig. 2-51) was considered at one time to be an excavator having a fixed boom and a bucket (dipper) that scooped up the earth. This description has been modified to include hydraulic shovels, which have a boom that can be raised and lowered hydraulically (Fig. 2-52). Basically a hydraulic shovel is designed as a hydraulic backhoe or excavator with the bucket opening pointing forward instead of backward as on a nonhydraulic excavator. The dipper, since it is hydraulically actuated, is similar in design to a multiloader bucket. The rear section of the dipper is pivot-fastened to the end of the dipper stick and the roll back and forward tilt is achieved through the dipper cylinders. The clamp section, pivot-fastened to the top of the rear section, opens and closes through the action of the dipper cylinders.

On an electrical or mechanical shovel, the boom is supported through wire ropes fastened to the gantry spreader and boom point equalizer to hold the boom at an angle of about 45°. The dipper handle is

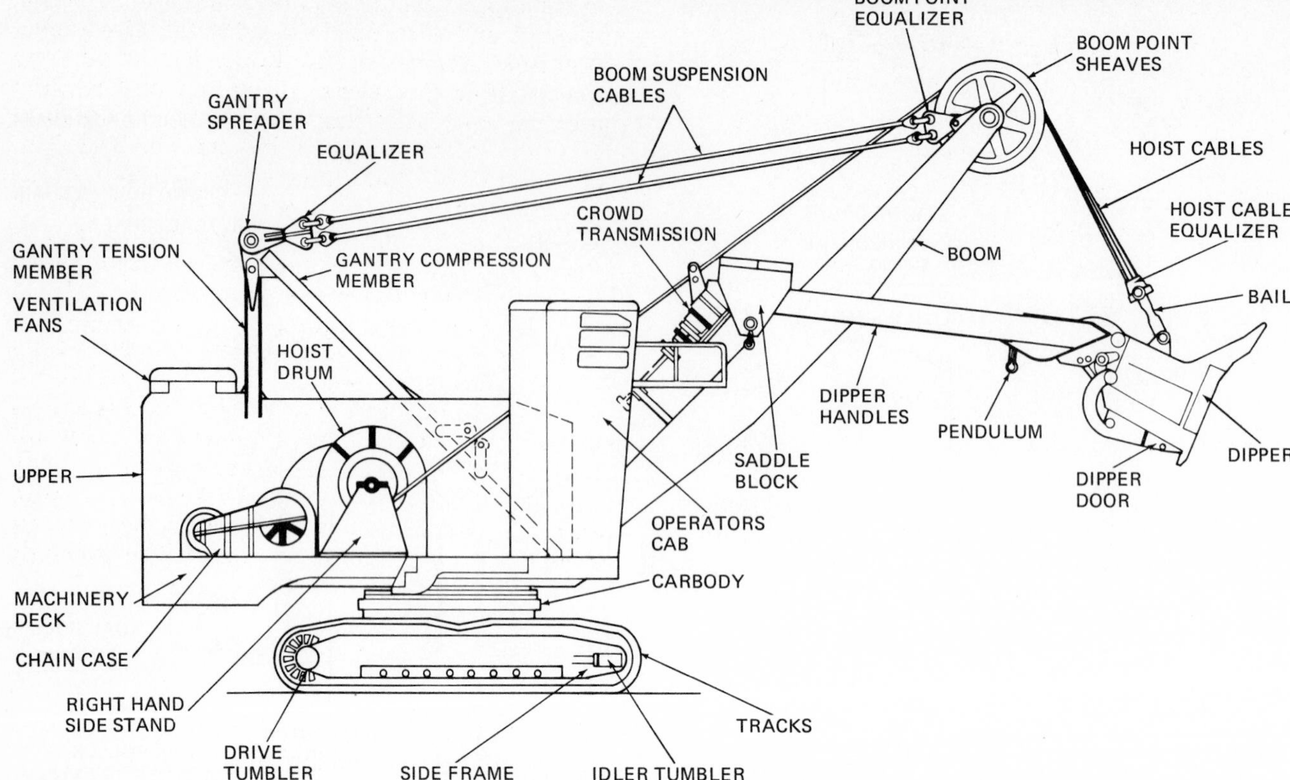

Fig. 2-51 Terminology for a shovel (excavator). (*Harnischfeger*)

pivot-fastened to the boom through the shipper shaft or saddle block. It can be moved forward and backward through a winch and wire rope or through a dc motor and transmission to extend or retract the dipper reach. The reeving of the hoist wire rope to raise or lower the dipper (live end) is commonly fastened to the hoist drum, from there over one boom point sheave, down through the padlock sheave, back over the second boom point sheave, and down to the winch frame where the dead end is fastened.

On large machines two wire ropes, similarly reeved, are used instead of one, or an 8-point reeving is used. In either case, when the main hoist drum is rotated clockwise, the wire rope is wound off the

Fig. 2-52 Hydraulic shovel.

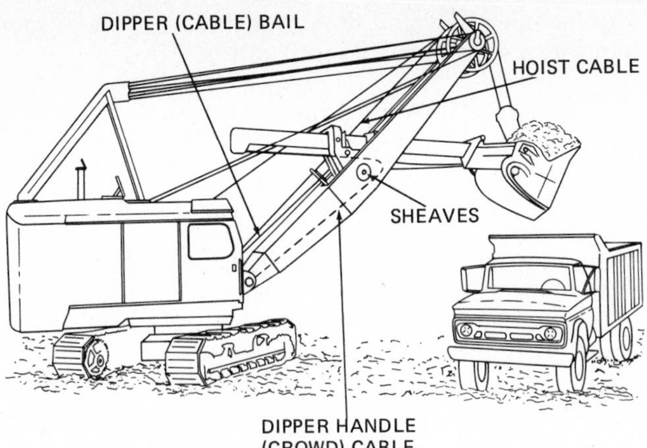

Fig. 2-53 Mechanical shovel.

hoist drum, lowering the dipper. When the drum is driven in a counterclockwise rotation, the wire rope is wound onto the drum, raising the dipper.

If the dipper handle is moved through the action of a winch and wire rope (Fig. 2-53), the wire (crowd cable) rope that moves the dipper handle outward is reeved from the reverse drum and underwound under the sheaves on the dipper shaft to the dead end on the top of the dipper handle. The back haul reeving (to retract the dipper handle) is from (over) the top of the reversing drum, over the sheave on the shipper shaft, and over the dead end, which is fastened to the bottom of the dipper handle. When the reverse drum is rotated clockwise, the dipper handle is pulled outward, sliding in the guide rails as one wire rope is wound onto the reverse drum and the other rope is wound off. If the operator reverses the rotation of the drum, the wire ropes reverse direction, and the handle is pulled backward.

On electric shovels (for example see Fig. 2-54), the dipper handle is moved outward and rearward through a crowd transmission driven by a dc reversible motor and a rack and pinion. The crowd dc

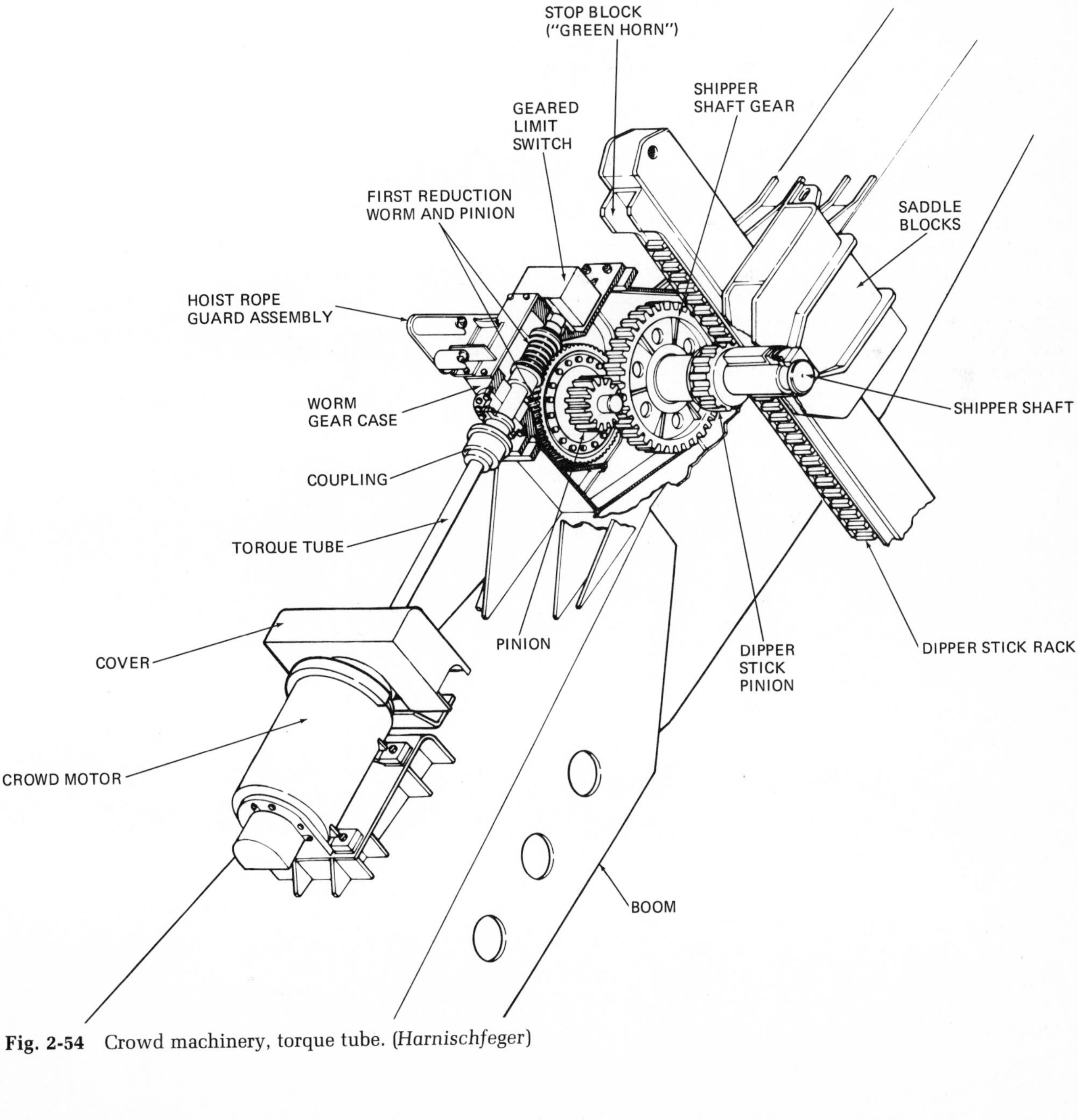

Fig. 2-54 Crowd machinery, torque tube. (*Harnischfeger*)

motor drives the crowd transmission through a torque tube, using a special coupling. The crowd transmission then has a worm drive and the crowd brake is attached to the dc motor. With another type of crowd drive arrangement, the input shaft of the transmission is driven through multibelts and the crowd brake is attached to the other side of the transmission's input shaft. The shipper shaft gear and dipper pinions are splined to the shipper shaft that is supported in the saddle block. The dipper stick is supported and guided within the saddle block so that the dipper stick, rack, and pinion are in mesh.

When the dc motor is energized to extend the dipper handle, so is the crowd brake valve. The valve spool shifts, air is directed to the rotor chamber, and the crowd brake releases. The dc motor drives the crowd transmission over the multibelts or through the torque tube. This, in turn, rotates the dipper stick pinion at a reduced speed in a clockwise direction, causing the dipper handles to move outward.

As the dc motor is de-energized, the crowd brake is also de-energized. The valve then shifts, the air exhausts from the rotor chamber, the spring force applies the brake, and the input shaft and the dipper handles are held in a fixed position.

THE DIPPER The shovel bucket (dipper) (Fig. 2-55) is pivot-fastened to the end of the dipper handle. Because the dipper scoops up the earth, it requires a bottom door to dump the load. The hinge pins of the dipper door are fastened midway on each side of the dipper in such a way that, when the load is dumped and the dipper is lowered, the door automatically closes. To prevent the door from slamming shut too rapidly (which would damage it), dipper door snubbers are employed. The snubbers are multidisk friction plates positioned between the reaction members. One end of the reaction member is connected with a pin to the dipper and the other end to the dipper door. A mechanical locking mechanism holds the door shut. To open the door a trip assembly (consisting of a dc motor and drum fastened to the saddle block or shipper shaft, a trip lever, a wire rope) is used. The trip motor operates always at low torque, holding the trip cable under tension. To trip the door, the motor is fully energized, winding the

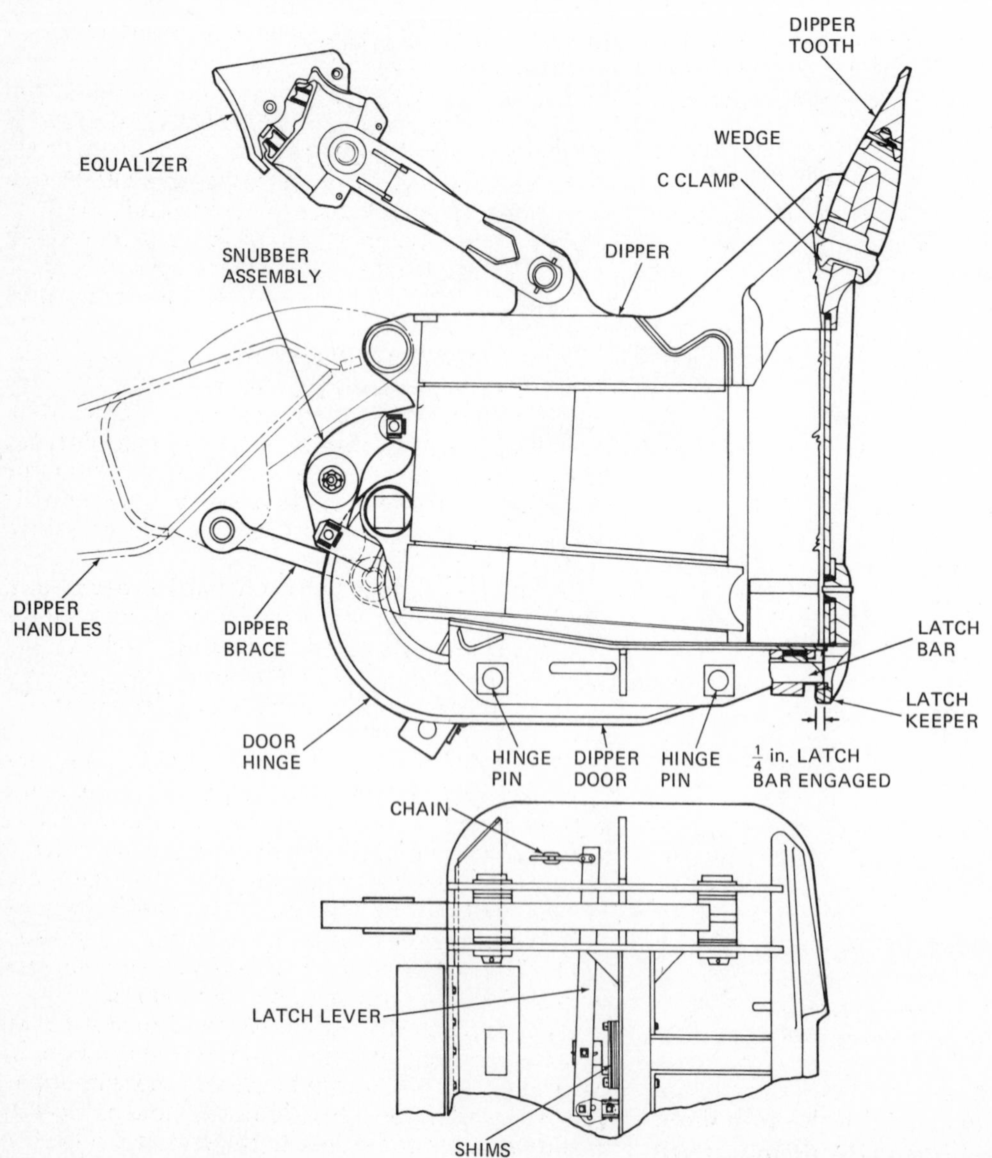

Fig. 2-55 Dipper. (*Harnischfeger*)

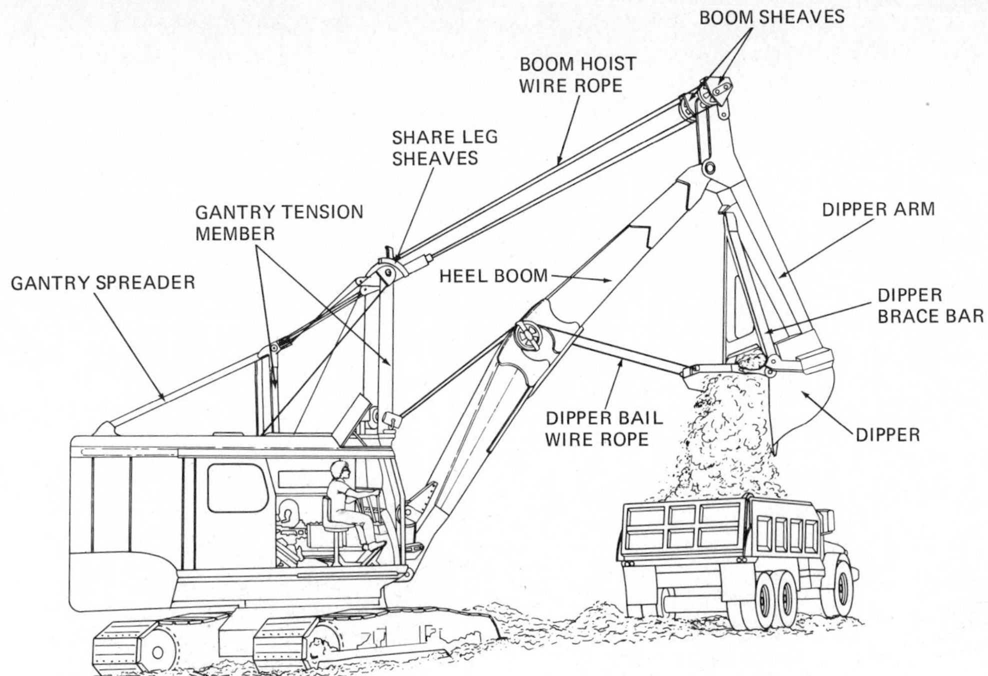

Fig. 2-56 Pull shovel.

wire rope onto the drum. This pivots the dipper trip lever, pulls the dipper trip, and the load opens the door. When the motor is partly de-energized and the dipper is lowered, the door closes.

PULL SHOVELS These shovels (see Fig. 2-56), by means of wire ropes, pull the dipper toward the machine to fill it. In other words, they are excavators, operated through winches and wire ropes which manipulate the dipper stick (arm) and dipper. To accomplish this manipulation, the boom is pivot-fastened to the superstructure frame. The dipper and dipper brace are pivot-fastened to the dipper stick so that the cutting angle of the dipper can be adjusted by repositioning the dipper brace on the dipper stick. The dipper stick is pivot-fastened to the heel boom while the share leg is pivot-fastened to the superstructure frame to absorb twist, strain, and compression load, and to guide the boom hoist wire ropes. The reeving of the dipper is usually from its dead end, on the heel boom, over the dipper bail sheaves, over the sheaves on the heel boom, and overwound on the hoist drum. The other wire cable, also overwound on the hoist drum, is directed over the left-hand inside share leg sheave, over the bail sheave on the dipper stick, and back underwound on the right-hand inside share leg sheave, and the dead end is fastened to the share leg.

The boom hoist wire rope (bail line) is reeved from its dead end, on the winch frame, overwound over the outside share leg sheave, then underwound over the right- and left-hand gantry spreader sheaves, then overwound over the left-hand share leg sheave. From here it is overwound over the inside frame sheave, and the live end is fastened to the boom hoist drum.

When the operator activates the lever to raise the boom, the hoist brake is released and the hoist drum clutch is engaged. This action causes the boom hoist drum to rotate in a counterclockwise rotation, winding the wire rope onto the drum (shortening the wire rope), pulling the share leg rearward, and raising the heel boom. To lower the boom, the hoist lever is moved to the lowering position. Air then exhausts from the clutch chamber, releasing the clutch and slowly releasing the brakes. This unwinds the wire rope from the drum, lowering the boom. **NOTE** Most shovels have a separate boom-hold valve which must first be released before the boom can be lowered.

To pull the dipper inward, the right-hand hoist clutch is engaged and the brakes are released. The hoist drum then rotates counterclockwise, shortening the wire rope pull-in line. During this time, the left-hand hoist brake partially releases, allowing the hoist line to unwind from the drum, lengthening the wire rope, and permitting the dipper to be pulled inward.

To pull the dipper outward, the left-hand hoist clutch is engaged and the brakes are released. At the same time, the right-hand hoist winch brake is partially released to unwind the wire rope from the drum and allow the dipper stick to pivot outward.

Log Loaders A log loader (Fig. 2-57) is a machine that has the capacity to pick up logs, load them onto a tractor trailer, or stockpile them. It can also be used for short-distance log skidding if the operator is competent enough to throw the grapple tongues 200 to 300 ft [61.0 to 91.5 m] on the downhill slope.

A log loader may be a shovel having a grapple rather than a clamp or dipper, or it may be a machine with a specially designed boom and grapple.

This boom is also pivot-fastened to the superstructure and can be raised and lowered through the combined action of a winch, sheave, and wire ropes. The boom is shaped as a long "Z" and is heavily reinforced from the center to the end of the heel. A

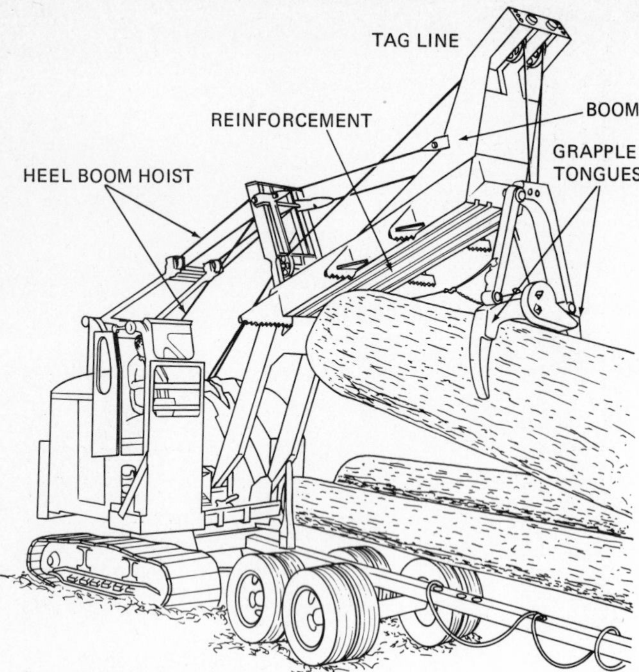

Fig. 2-57 Log loader.

toothlike surface is welded to it so that the log end, as it is raised, sinks into the teeth, holding it to the boom. The grapple is held with a tag line in such a position that the grapple tongues can grab the log. The tag line on some machines also is the line which closes the grapple.

The heel boom hoist is reeved very similarly to a pull-in shovel, as is the pull-in line, used to close the grapple. The only difference is the reeving of the grapple hoist line, which is from the dead end of the boom over the right-hand boom tip sheave, under the grapple sheaves, back up over the left-hand boom tip sheave, and the live end is fastened over and onto the right-hand hoist drum.

Manlifts It is the function of these machines to elevate a maintenance person, a painter, a fruit picker, etc., to a predetermined height and to a working position without the use of a scaffold. A variety of these machines have been designed for mounting to a farm tractor, to a class 1, 3, 4, or 5 carrier, or to a full trailer.

Manlifts may be divided into two types: where the superstructure is fixed to the trailer or a carrier, and where the superstructure is mounted to a self-propelled machine or carrier and the superstructure can be rotated.

Scissor Manlift The scissor model (see Fig. 2-58 for an example) comes under the first classification. It may be mounted to a full trailer or to a self-propelled carrier. In any event, two base legs of the scissor are fastened to the carrier and the other two base legs roll within the frame guide rails. The ends of each scissor section are pivot-fastened to the leg ends of the next section, and the last scissor section ends are fastened to the working platform. On small units only one hydraulic cylinder is used to raise the platform, but on larger units two hydraulic cylinders are used. The hydraulic cylinder is pivot-fastened to the crossmember of the base scissor legs and the rod end of the piston is pivot-fastened to a crossmember of the opposing base scissor legs. The carrier (or the trailer) has four stabilizers or outriggers, depending on the lift height and lift capacity. The smaller units use battery power, or gasoline, or a petroleum gas engine as the power source to drive the hydraulic pump and propel the machine, and the larger units use diesel engines. When the unit is battery-powered, it usually has a 36-volt (V) system having a built-in battery charger, and may have a dc motor, or the engine drives the hydraulic pump to supply oil for the hydraulic system. When the unit is self-propelled, the same hydraulic pump supplies oil to the wheel motors as well as to the steering motor. The lift capacity of scissor lifts ranges from 1500 to 6000 lb [681 to 2724 kg]. The maximum lift height ranges between 25 and 50 ft [7.62 and 15.25 m]. The scissor manlift can be controlled from the control panel on the carrier and from the control panel on the platform. The control valves for the lift cylinder, outrigger cylinder, or stabilizer cylinders, and for propulsion, are commonly electrically controlled. On many models the brakes are also electrically controlled.

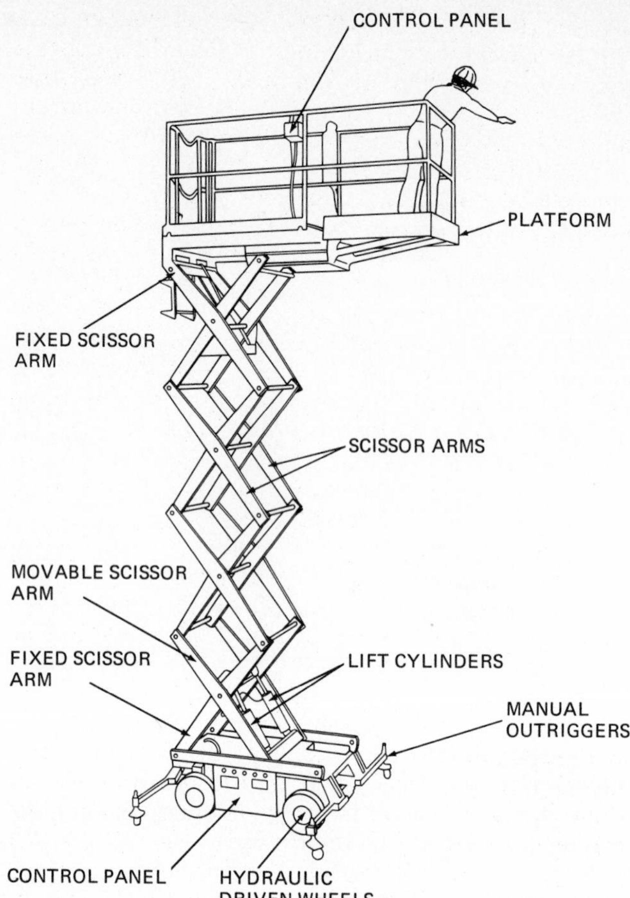

Fig. 2-58 Electrically powered miniscissors lift; lift height 27 ft [8.23 m].

SCISSOR MANLIFT OPERATION When either the control switch to the electric motor or the switch to start the engine is actuated, the motor, or the engine, drives the hydraulic pump. When the operator actuates the switch to raise the platform, current flows to the directional control valve, energizing the solenoid coil and shifting the spool valve. Oil then flows over the safety check valves into the piston end of the lift cylinder(s), forcing the pivot-fastened scissor legs upward and causing the base scissor legs to move on the guide rails toward the pivot-fastened scissor leg. That action is instantly transferred to all scissor sections, thereby raising the platform. If the electric circuit is de-energized, the control valve spring brings the spool valve to the neutral position and the load is held by the safety check valves. To lower the platform, the opposite solenoid coil is energized, the spool valve shifts in the opposite direction, and oil flows to the safety check valve. When the pump pressure is higher than the pressure in the piston end of the lift cylinder, the safety check valve opens and the platform is lowered under controlled pressure.

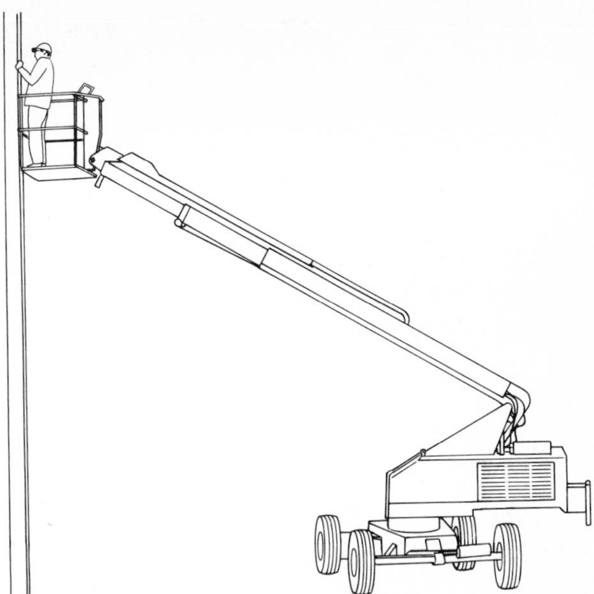

Fig. 2-59 Carrier-mounted hydraulically propelled and operated manlift.

Vehicle- or Carrier-Mounted Boom Manlift These types of manlifts are more mobile than the scissor manlifts because they are all self-propelled and, furthermore, are able to rotate the superstructure. They all have a telescopic boom which is pivot-fastened to the mast. The boom lift cylinders are pivot-fastened to the mast and the piston rod ends are pivot-fastened to the boom. The hydraulic piston that extends and retracts the boom extension is located inside the main boom. The railed platform is pivot-fastened through mechanical linkage or a hydraulic cylinder to the end of the extension to maintain it horizontally. The mast is fastened to a turntable which is secured to the carrier, as shown in Fig. 2-59; or the base of the mast is attached to the turntable and the mast is pivot-fastened to the base. This structure is similar to a backhoe. A hydraulic motor in conjunction with a reduction gear is used to rotate the superstructure. The hydraulic cylinder that raises and lowers the mast is attached to the base of the turntable, and the piston rod end is fastened to the mast.

Boom manlifts may be grouped according to their boom structure, operation, lift height and/or lift capacity, or the carrier. The superstructure may be mounted to a motor truck, or to a specially designed motor vehicle, or to a class 3, 4, or 5 carrier.

Boom manlifts which are mounted to a motortruck use the power takeoff from the transmission or a special drive arrangement from the engine to drive the hydraulic pump. They sometimes use mechanically actuated control valves located on the platform. **NOTE** When the unit is used to maintain or service power lines or electric equipment, the boom and the masts are fiberglass-insulated to safeguard the workers against electrocution.

The boom and mast mounted to motor vehicles, or to a class 3, 4, or 5 carrier, are powered by gasoline engines, petroleum gas, or diesel engines. When powered by batteries, the hydraulic pump is driven by an electric motor and dc wheel motors may be used for propulsion. When the power is supplied from an engine, the unit is hydrostatically propelled and steered, and the control circuit is electrically controlled as is actuation of the brakes. Depending on the design and mounting, the engine may be located in the carrier frame or on the superstructure frame, serving in the latter position also as the counterweight of the boom. When the width is almost the same as the wheel base, the unit usually has no stabilizer or outrigger. However, when the carrier width is narrower, a stabilizer or outrigger is used and occasionally a counterweight is also attached to the mast.

The boom manlifts, due to their design, have a lower lift capacity than a scissor lift. The capacity range is between 450 and 1200 lb [204.35 and 544.8 kg] with the extension fully retracted. The average lift height varies from 25 to 55 ft [7.62 to 16.77 m], with a reach or turning radius between 21 and 38 ft [6.4 and 11.57 m]. Control panels are on the carrier and on the platform.

BOOM MANLIFT OPERATION When the engine is operating and the operator manipulates any one of the electric switches, the solenoid shifts the valve spool and oil is directed to the selected circuit. The cylinder piston rods extend or retract to raise or lower the boom, to extend or retract the boom extension, to level or tilt the platform, to raise or lower one stabilizer or the outrigger, or to steer the manlift to the left or the right. When the operator actuates the switch to drive forward or reverse, oil is directed to the drive motor and the manlift is moved in a forward or reverse direction. **NOTE** The maximum speed is about 1.5 mph [2.41 km/h]. If the operator desires to reswing the boom to the left or to the right, the power switch is actuated and oil flows into the hydraulic motor and the motor drives the reduction gear pinion which rotates the superstructure.

TRACK-TYPE VEHICLES (CRAWLERS)

Track-Type Tractors Although wheel loaders, dozers, pipe layers, or backhoes are gradually replacing track-type tractors (illustrated in Fig. 2-60), the latter are still used in great numbers and in various sizes and designs. In certain circumstances, perhaps because of poor wheel traction, or drawbar pull, or conditions conducive to excessive wear, the track-type tractor will perform more efficiently. They are usually preferred in the following instances:

- To pull farm implements or equipment to clear land
- To build highways and off-highway roads
- To excavate
- For pull or push operations
- To rip the earth
- To lay pipes
- To clear away overburden in the mining field

Wheel-type tractors differ from track-type tractors in the way in which they carry the vehicle weight, in the way the vehicle moves over the ground, and in the way in which the vehicle is steered.

As you know, the weight of a wheel-type vehicle is carried by the tires. When the tires are rotated the vehicle moves forward or backward, and when the wheels are turned to the left or to the right the vehicle almost follows the tire tracks of the steering wheels.

On a track-type tractor or machine, two track chains take the place of the tires, one on each side of the machine. They are placed around the drive sprocket and the front track idler, then joined through a master pin to form an endless chain. The weight of the tractor or machine is therefore carried by the track shoes bolted to the track chain. The forward and reverse motion of the tractor is achieved by rotating the drive sprocket which pulls the chain either in a clockwise or a counterclockwise rotation, bringing the individual track shoes one after the other into contact with the ground. The tractor body, supported and guided by the track rollers and the front track idler roller, is forced to roll on the track rails in a forward or reverse direction.

Various methods can be used to steer the tractor: The left- or the right-hand drive (power) to the drive sprocket is disconnected, or one drive sprocket is held and the other drive sprocket is driven, or one sprocket is driven slower than the other, or one sprocket is driven forward and the other backward.

POWER AND GEARING The engine, transmission, and rear axle housing are attached to the tractor frame. About 95 percent of track-type tractors use diesel engines. The engine power ranges from 40 hp to twin-diesel engines each having 440 hp [29.82 to 328.06 kW]. The powershift transmissions used may have five or six speeds forward and reverse. However, the average track-type tractor has three or four speeds forward and reverse. The smaller track-type tractor may have a standard transmission in conjunction with a torque converter.

The power from the output shaft of the transmission is transmitted to the pinion, and from there onto the crown gear. At the crown gear, the incoming power is diverted to the left and right onto the steering clutches. The steering clutches (multiplate) are spring-applied and hydraulically released, whereas single-plate steering clutches are spring-applied and mechanically released. A brake band encircles the steering clutch drum which is connected, through lever and linkage, to the mechanical brake actuating mechanism or to the hydraulic actuating mechanism. The steering clutch drum is connected to the final drive pinion shaft, and the pinion is splined to it. When the final drive is of the single-reduction design, that is, when it consists of only one set of gears, the final drive gear and sprocket are splined to the final drive shaft which is supported on bearings on the final drive inner and outer housing. If a

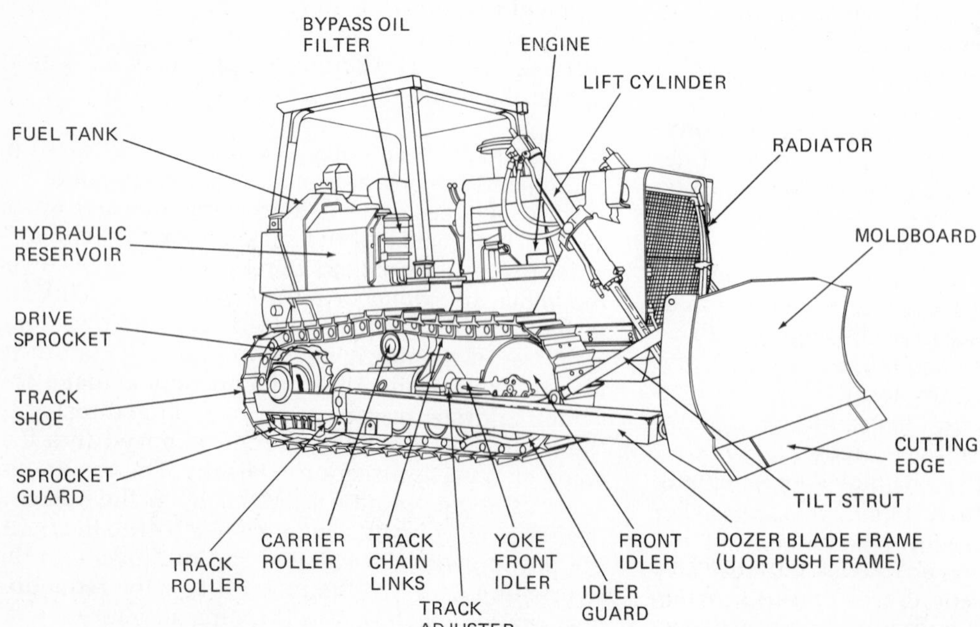

Fig. 2-60 Track-type tractor. (*Fiat-Allis*)

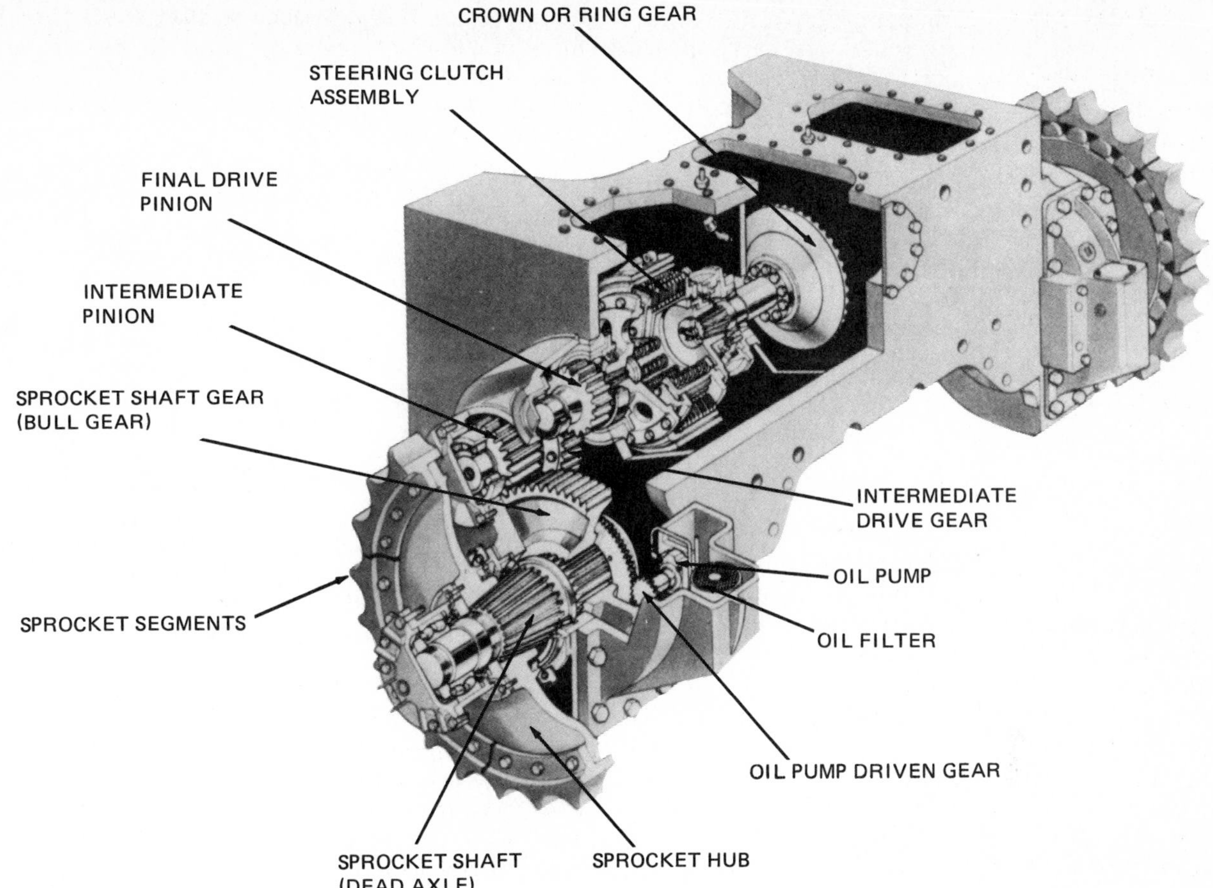

Fig. 2-61 Cutaway view of final drive and steering clutch.

double-reduction final drive is used as shown in Fig. 2-61, that is, if two sets of gears are used, the intermediate gear and intermediate pinion gear are splined to an idler shaft and the sprocket shaft gear and the sprocket are splined to the sprocket shaft which is supported on bearings in the inner and outer final drive housing.

When the steering clutch is engaged, the power is transmitted to the pinion which drives the intermediate gear and pinion gear. The pinion gear drives the final drive gear (sprocket gear) and the sprocket. When the steering clutch is disengaged, no power is transmitted to the sprocket; therefore, it is free to rotate in either direction. However, when the brake is applied, the steering clutch drum is held stationary, stopping the rotation of the sprocket.

MODIFICATION AND ATTACHMENT To increase the drawbar pull and/or the maneuverability of a track-type tractor, two engines are installed to one dozer tractor (see Fig. 2-62). The tractor shown has a gross weight of 104,970 lb [47,656.38 kg]. Each engine and its transmission, carrier, and final drive is positioned in its own tractor frame, but both engine frames are bolted to make a single unit. Not only does each engine drive its own track to increase the drawbar pull and the tractor maneuverability, but each track is always live; therefore, the drawbar pull is not reduced while making a turn. Steering is accomplished as follows:

1. To make a slow turn, select a lower speed range in one transmission.
2. To make a pivot turn, put one transmission in forward position and the other into reverse.

The tractor has conventional multiplate steering clutches to disengage the drive to the final drive and a brake to hold the drive sprocket.

Because of its overall weight, the track frames are bolted to the tractor frame and do not move.

Drawbar pull can be increased by two other methods: by coupling together two tractors, in series,

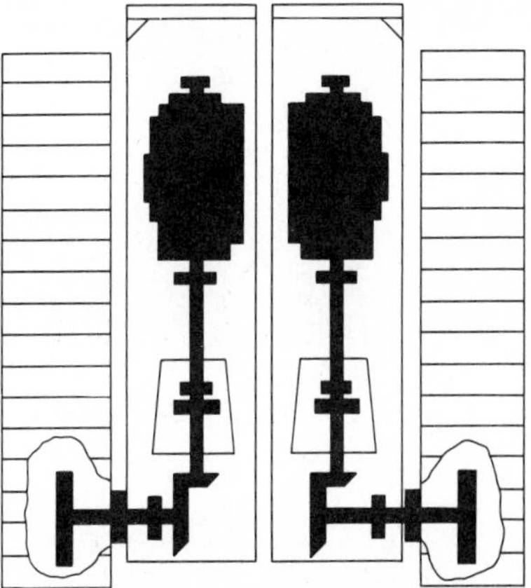

Fig. 2-62 Terex twin engines—live power on both tracks. (*Terex Division of General Motors Corporation*)

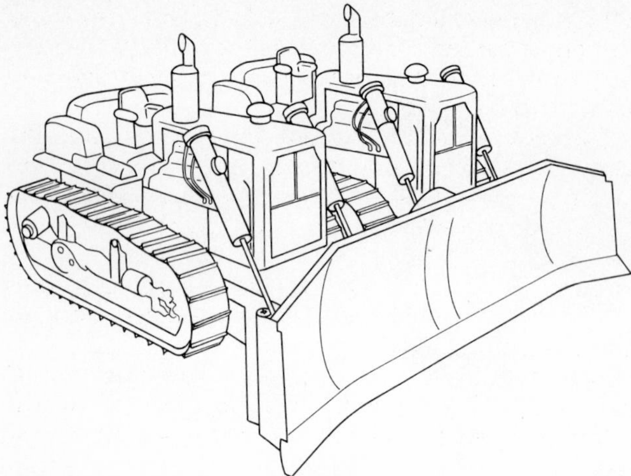
Fig. 2-63 Caterpillar side-by-side D9G tractor.

through a hitch, or by coupling two tractors parallel with each other. The latter type of tractor arrangement has a dozer blade which has an overall length of 26.1 ft [7.95 m] and a height of 7.2 ft [2.18 m], while the gross weight of the tractor is 188,600 lb [85,547.07 kg]; see Fig. 2-63.

A noticeable difference between a wheel dozer and a track-type tractor dozer is in the mount of the C frame. The C frame on the track machine usually is pivot-fastened, with a bearing or ball joint socket to the pivot shaft of the final drive or to a trunion shaft which is fastened to the track frame; otherwise the dozer mounting and hydraulic arrangement are identical. A backhoe and/or a loader or backhoe mounted to a wheel-type or track-type tractor are almost identical.

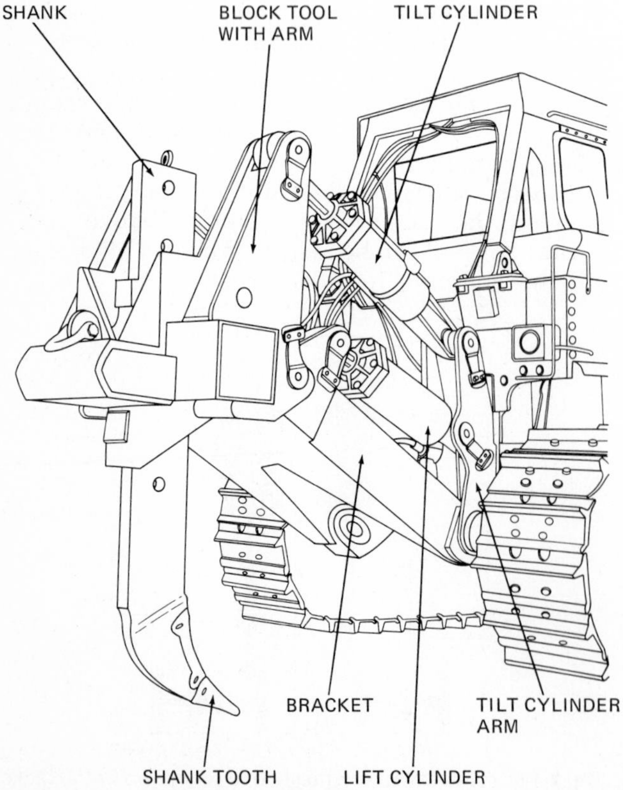

Fig. 2-64 Single-shank adjustable ripper.

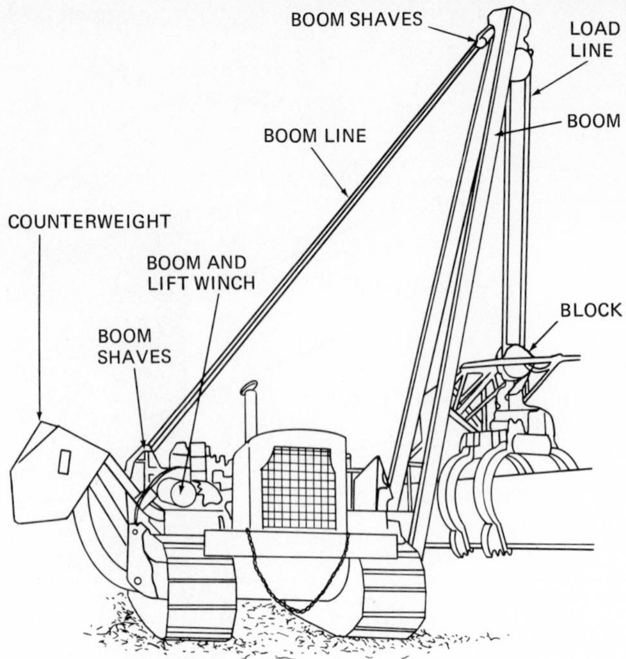

Fig. 2-65 Pipe layer.

Depending upon the type of work for which the tractor will be utilized, either a winch or a ripper (Fig. 2-64) is mounted to the rear of the tractor housing. Naturally, the size of either one depends on the size of the tractor.

Pipe Layers As the name indicates, these machines (Fig. 2-65) are specially designed to lift, transport, and lay pipes. The boom is pivot-fastened to either side of the track-type tractor frame and the winch and counterweight are bolted to the other side. **NOTE** The track frame is rigidly attached to the tractor frame. The winch has two drums, is similar in design to the winch used on the hydraulic crane, and is also driven through a hydraulic motor or is mechanically driven. The boom line has a 3- to 5-point reeving; the dead end of the wire rope is fastened to the winch frame, and the live end is fastened to the winch drum. The load line may have as high as a 7-point reeving, depending upon the lift capacity. The lift capacity at the maximum vertical angle (about 80°) varies from 40,000 to 200,000 lb [18,160 to 90,800 kg] which, of course, decreases as the vertical angle is decreased. The boom length varies between 15 and 24 ft [4.75 and 7.32 m].

Track-Type Carriers The greatest assets of the crawler carriers are their heavy load-carrying capacity, increased stability, maneuverability, and good work performance. The machines used today that are mounted on crawler carriers range in gross weight from about 23,000 to 1,750,000 lb [10,442 to 794,500 kg] and higher. Depending on the gross machine weight, their number of track shoes and their width is increased to reduce the crawler ground pressure and to maintain good ground support.

Track chains, shoes, and drives vary according to operating weight and/or anticipated operating con-

KEEPER PLATE
CENTER ROLLER, NONADJUSTABLE
KEEPER PLATE
ECCENTRIC PIN
ROLLER
ROLLER PATH

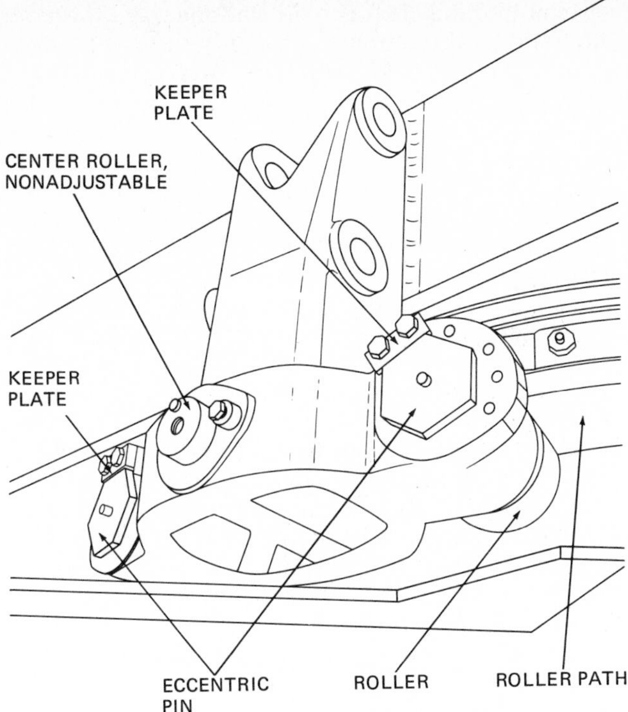

Fig. 2-66 Typical hook roller. (*Harnischfeger*)

ditions. Many machines have identically designed tractor-type track frames, track rollers, drive sprockets, and track adjustment. Also, depending on the type of superstructure, gross weight, and track frame design, some lend themselves more suitably to a hydrostatic drive, whereas others are electrically or mechanically driven.

The power used to operate the transmission, the winches, the hydraulic pumps, and the swing, and to propel the machines, is exclusively by diesel engines, except for the larger units which use dc motors.

There is such a large number of superstructures on the market, and hence such a multitude of variations as to strength of shoes, track length, side frames, turntables, and method of propulsion and swing, etc., that it would be impractical to attempt to cover them in one text. Therefore, we must deal with generalities.

One method of supporting a superstructure is shown in Fig. 2-66 and another in Fig. 2-67. In the latter illustration, four sets of rollers, having three rollers per set, are used, each roller being slightly tapered and positioned on shafts. The center rollers are the hook rollers and the outside ones are the rotating rollers. The assembly is fastened to the upper turntable. The hook rollers take the upward force and the rotating rollers take the downward force. The rollers are positioned in the grooved roller paths of the lower turntable. The center rollers are mounted on the center shaft and are adjustable to maintain proper clearance of all three rollers between the rollers and the roller paths. Some other

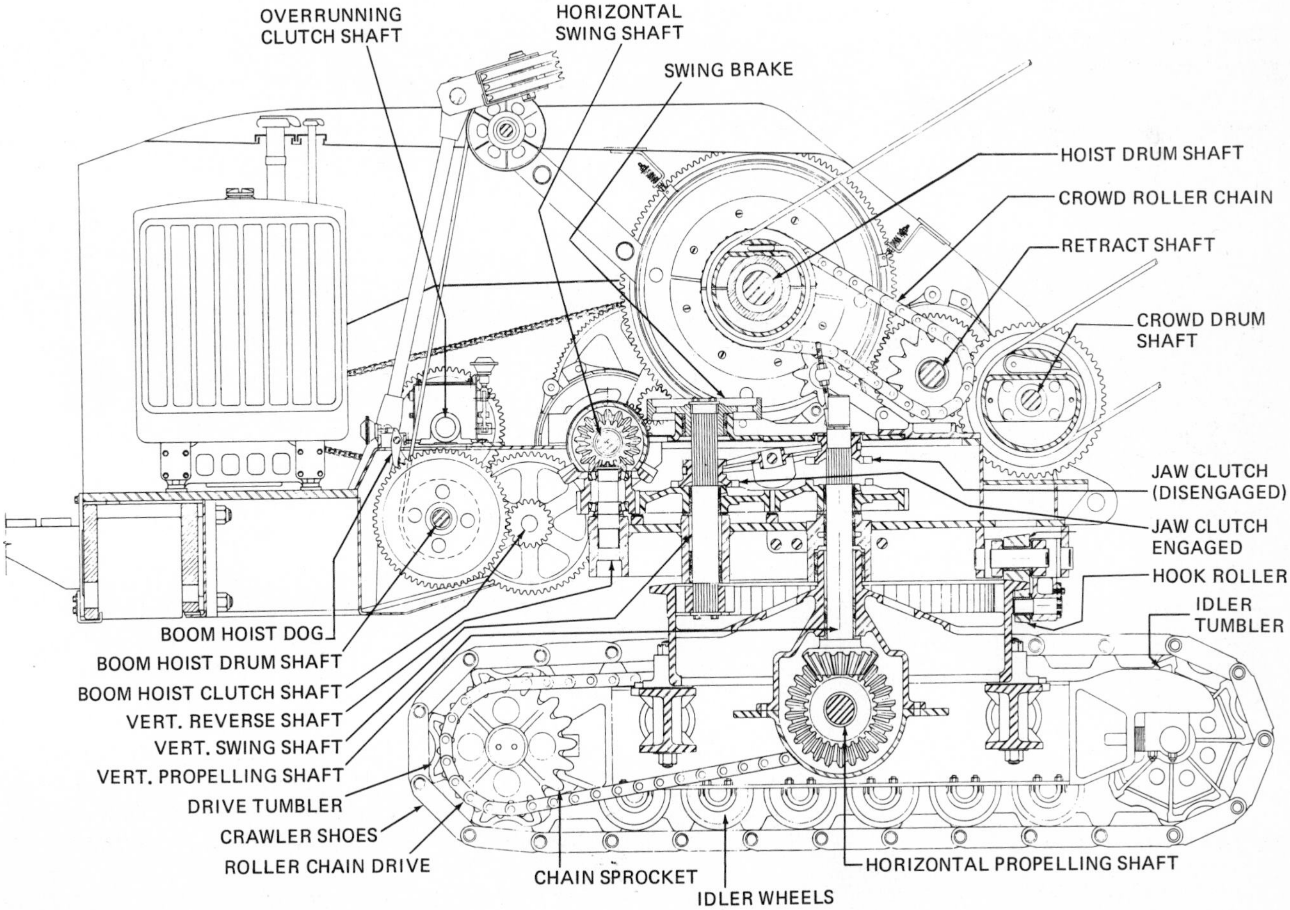

OVERRUNNING CLUTCH SHAFT
HORIZONTAL SWING SHAFT
SWING BRAKE
HOIST DRUM SHAFT
CROWD ROLLER CHAIN
RETRACT SHAFT
CROWD DRUM SHAFT
JAW CLUTCH (DISENGAGED)
JAW CLUTCH ENGAGED
HOOK ROLLER
IDLER TUMBLER
BOOM HOIST DOG
BOOM HOIST DRUM SHAFT
BOOM HOIST CLUTCH SHAFT
VERT. REVERSE SHAFT
VERT. SWING SHAFT
VERT. PROPELLING SHAFT
DRIVE TUMBLER
CRAWLER SHOES
ROLLER CHAIN DRIVE
CHAIN SPROCKET
IDLER WHEELS
HORIZONTAL PROPELLING SHAFT

Fig. 2-67 Track-type carrier crawler.

supports are designed with four hook rollers positioned in the roller path and eight rotating rollers positioned on the flat top surface of the lower turntable. Midsize crawler carriers use only four to six tapered rollers which serve as hook rollers and rotating rollers.

Track chains, shoes, and drives vary according to operating weight and/or anticipated operating conditions. Many machines have identically designed tractor-type track frames, track rollers, track carrier rollers, front idler rollers, drive sprockets, and track adjustment. Most crawler carriers use multidisk brakes, hydraulically applied and spring-released to hold the track(s) for parking and steering.

HYDROSTATIC DRIVE Depending on the type of superstructure, gross weight, and track frame design, some crawler carriers lend themselves more suitably to a hydrostatic drive, whereas others are electrically or mechanically driven. When the carrier is of the hydrostatic drive, the double- or single-reduction gear is bolted to the inside of each final drive housing and the input shaft is connected to the hydraulic motor, or the reduction gear and hydraulic motor are located on the machine deck. (See Fig. 2-68 and "Powershift Transmissions," Unit 12.)

HYDROSTATIC DRIVE OPERATION When the engine is operating the traction (propel) control valve is in neutral, the traction and track brakes are applied, the vertical traction shaft is held stationary are therefore the horizontal traction shaft and both traction drive chains are also held stationary. When the left and right track brakes are released and oil is directed from the traction directional control valve to the traction motor, oil is also directed to the traction brake and releases the brake. The motor is then forced to rotate in either a clockwise or counterclockwise direction (depending on the directional valve position). This drives the vertical traction shaft clockwise or counterclockwise which, in turn, drives the horizontal traction shaft and traction drive chains clockwise or counterclockwise. As a result the crawler carrier moves straight forward or back. If the oil flow to the traction motor is low the track speed is low; if the oil flow is high (at maximum flow) the track speed is high and the carrier travels at its maximum speed, that is, between 1.5 and 2.5 mph [2.41 and 4.02 km/h]. To make a left turn the left steering clutch is disengaged. This disengages the horizontal traction shaft from the left traction chain drive sprocket and consequently the carrier right track propels the carrier into a left turn. When the right steering clutch is disengaged and the left engaged, the carrier is propelled into a right turn. When the traction directional valve is placed in neutral the traction brake automatically applies.

HYDROSTATIC SWING OPERATION When the machine is in operating position and the track brake is ap-

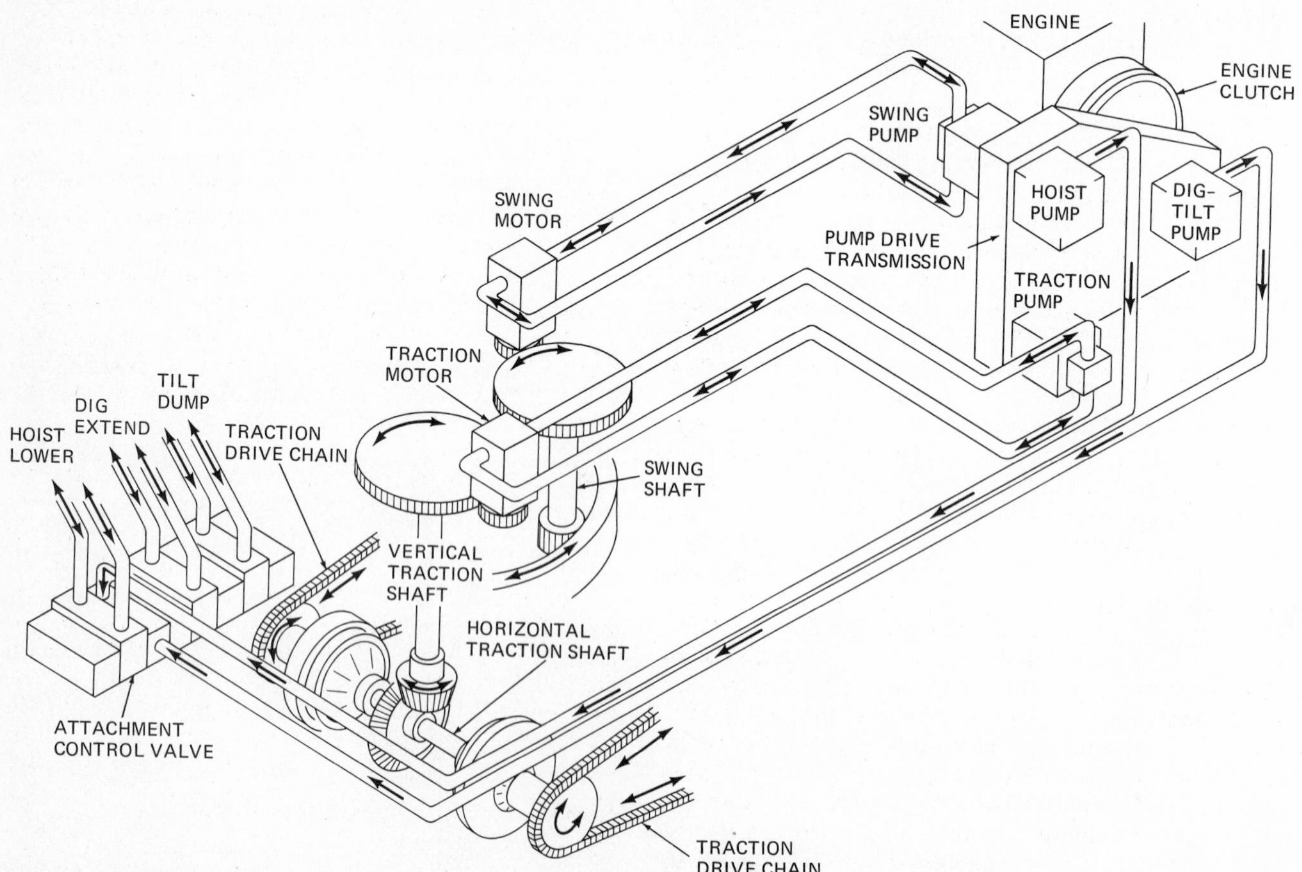

Fig. 2-68 Schematic illustration of track and swing drives without the control system.

plied, owing to the interaction of electricity and hydraulics the swing directional control valve can be operated. When the swing directional control valve is moved, oil is forced to the swing brake and to the hydraulic swing motor. As the oil pressure increases the brake releases and the swing motor is forced to rotate in either a clockwise or counterclockwise rotation. This forces the swing motor pinion to rotate within the internal gear of the turntable, forcing the superstructure to rotate either in a clockwise or counterclockwise rotation. If the oil flow is low the rotation is low. If the oil flow is at its maximum the superstructure turns at its maximum speed. When the swing directional valve is placed in the neutral position and the oil pressure drops to a certain value, the swing brake automatically applies.

MECHANICAL DRIVE AND SWING The power from the engine is transmitted over the clutch to the multichain drive, to a gear set, and to the horizontal swing shaft. A swing clutch is fastened to each end of the horizontal swing shaft and the bevel gear is attached at the center. See Fig. 2-67. The bevel gear is in mesh with the pinion that is fastened to the vertical reverse shaft. The reverse shaft gear is in mesh with the vertical swing shaft drive gear, and the swing shaft gear is in mesh with the vertical propelling shaft drive gear. Both gears are cast with jaws and splined to their shafts, which are bushing-supported in the upper housing. The swing pinion gear is fastened to the bottom end of the vertical swing shaft, and the brake drum is fastened to the top. The jaw clutches are pivot-fastened above the swing and propelling drive gears and are slide-fitted over the shafts.

MECHANICAL DRIVE AND SWING OPERATION Before engaging the swing jaw clutch with the swing drive gear, the propelling drive gear travel lug must first be engaged. Before engaging the propelling jaw clutch with the propelling drive gear, the swing brake must be applied and then the propelling lug must be disengaged. When the engine is operating, the master clutch engages; the swing clutch drum rotates, but no power is transmitted. If air is directed to either one of the swing clutches, the internal band clutch is applied, locking the clutch drum to the horizontal swing shaft. This action causes the bevel gear to drive the vertical reverse shaft (say in a clockwise rotation) which drives the vertical swing shaft, and its pinion rotates within the internal ring gear, rotating the superstructure. When the operator reduces the air pressure to one clutch and at the same time directs air to the other, the swing action comes to a smooth stop. The bevel gear then drives the vertical reverse shaft in the opposite direction (counterclockwise), causing the superstructure to rotate in the other direction. The operator, however, has also another means to stop the rotating (swing) action—that is, by reducing the air pressure to the swing clutch air cylinder and at the same time directing air to the swing brake air cylinder. This action stops the drive to the bevel gear, and the brake band clamps around the brake drum, holding the vertical swing shaft and bringing the superstructure to a stationary position.

To move the machine either forward or backward, the operator must

1. Apply the swing brakes.
2. Engage both jaw clutches with the horizontal propelling shaft by placing the air shift lever in neutral. This releases the air pressure, and the spring force engages both jaw clutches.
3. Shift the swing to travel, which means the operator has to disengage the swing jaws and engage the propel jaw clutch.
4. Release the travel brakes.

The operator then selects forward or reverse by directing air to either swing clutch. This drives the bevel gear (clockwise or counterclockwise) and the rotation is then transmitted both to the vertical reverse shaft gear and to the swing drive gear (which idles on the vertical swing shaft) and drives the vertical propelling shaft drive gear. Since the jaw clutch is engaged, the gear drives the vertical propelling shaft, and its pinion drives the bevel gear on the horizontal propelling shaft as well as the drive chains. The drive chains transmit the motion to the chain sprockets, driving the tumblers, and one crawler shoe after the other reaches the ground, pulling the machine in the desired direction. To turn (left or right), the operator places the air valve either into the left- or right-hand steering position. This action directs air to the steering rotor chamber and the brake rotor chamber. Both pushrods are forced out, causing the left- or right-hand jaw clutch to disengage and the propel brake to apply. With the driving power removed from the chain sprocket and the brake applied, the track belt is stopped and the machine pivots on the stationary track belt. If the air valve is placed in neutral position, the air exhausts from both rotary chambers, releasing the propel brakes, and the spring force engages the propel jaw clutch. As a result, the machine travels in a straight line in the desired direction. **NOTE** Long-distance travel in the idler tumbler direction is not recommended since it increases track belt wear.

ELECTRICAL PROPEL (DRIVE) SYSTEM One of several methods used to propel a crawler carrier electrically is shown in Fig. 2-69. The assembly consists of a dc reversible propel motor, connected through a power takeoff shaft to the triple-reduction propel transmission. The female half of the propel jaw clutch is fastened to the right-hand side of the transmission's output shaft. The horizontal propel shaft is coupled to the other side of the transmission, and the female half of the propel jaw clutch is attached to the outer end.

NOTE Both propel clutches are located within the propel brake area.

The final drive assembly consists of the final drive shafts and pinion, the final drive gear, the shaft, and

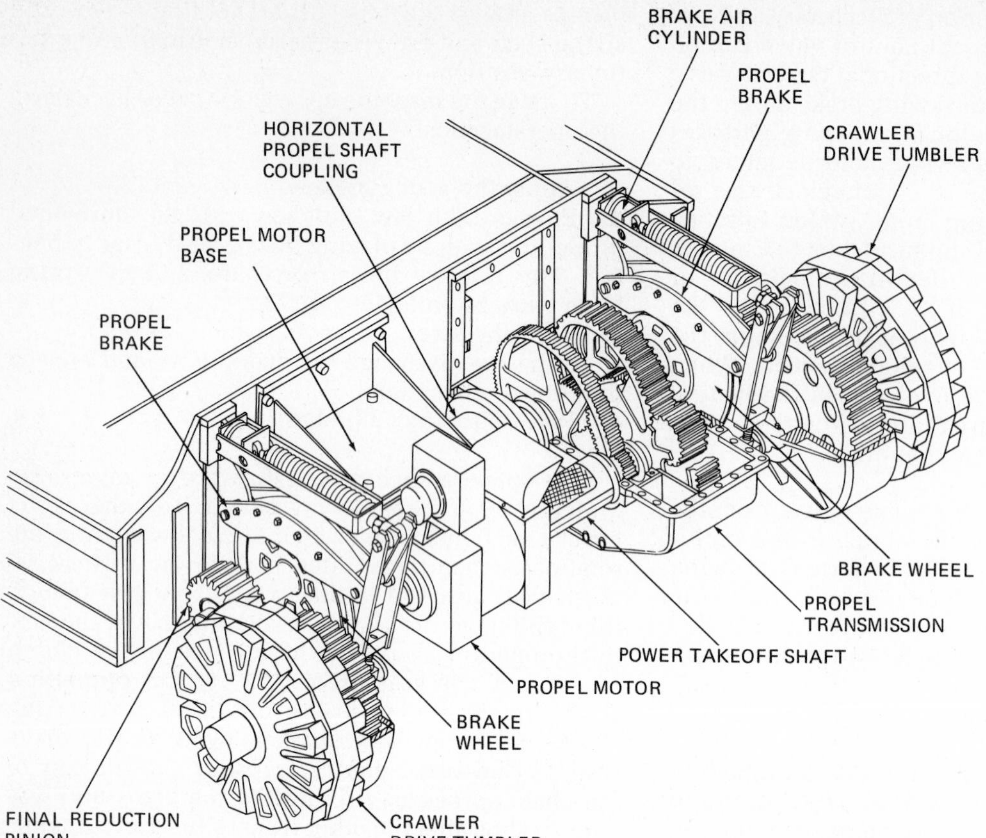

Fig. 2-69 Propel transmission. (*Harnischfeger*)

the drive tumbler. The propel brake wheels (brake drums) are attached to the final drive pinion shafts and are of a V-type design. They are slotted to guide the male jaw clutch members that ride on the brake wheel hubs.

The male jaws protrude through the slots and can be engaged or disengaged with the female jaw members through a lever and yoke arrangement actuated by a double-acting air cylinder. The pivot shafts of the propel steer linkage levers are linked with each other through an interlocking pipe. When the propel jaws are engaged with the female members, the power from the propel transmission output shafts are transmitted over the jaw clutches, onto the brake wheel hubs, and to the final drive shafts, and when disengaged from the female jaw members the power is interrupted.

The propel brake consists of the brake wheel, lower and upper brake arms to which the linings are bolted, a single-acting air cylinder (air-applied, spring-released), and the levers to apply and release the brake. See Fig. 2-70 for an example of a steering clutch assembly.

OPERATION (STEERING) The steering is controlled through toggle switches in the operator cab, but only after the crowd propel switch is placed in the propel position. When any of the toggle switches are placed in a steering position, three systems—electrical, air, and mechanical—interact to achieve the various steering modes. When the operator places the crowd propel switch in the propel position, it energizes the left- and right-hand brake valves; the valve spool shifts and allows air to flow over the quick release valve into the left- and right-hand brake cylinders. This action moves the piston rod out, compressing the spring, and the lever action releases the brakes. Because both left- and right-hand steering switches are open (deenergized), the left- and right-hand steering valves remain in a position which allows the air to pass into the rod ends of the steering cylinders and hold both jaw clutches engaged. When the dc propel motor is energized, it rotates (clockwise or counterclockwise), and the motor rotation (power) is transmitted to the triple-reduction propel transmission and from the transmission output shafts to the female jaw members. The male jaw members then drive the brake hubs which transmit their rotation to the final drive pinions and from there to the final drive gears and tumblers.

When one of the steering toggle switches is placed in the right-hand steering position, first the brake valve and then the right-hand steering valve energize and shift, directing air to the air chambers, applying the right-hand brake and disengaging the right-hand jaw clutch. As a result, the machine pivots on its stationary track belt, making a right-hand turn. When the steering toggle switch is moved from the right- into the left-hand steering position, the right-hand brake is released and the right-hand jaw clutch is engaged. At the same time, the left-hand brake is applied and the left-hand jaw clutch is engaged through the actions of the brake valves and steering valves and air chambers.

ELECTRICAL SWING The superstructure rotating principle is the same regardless of the type of power used. Machines which are electrically propelled use

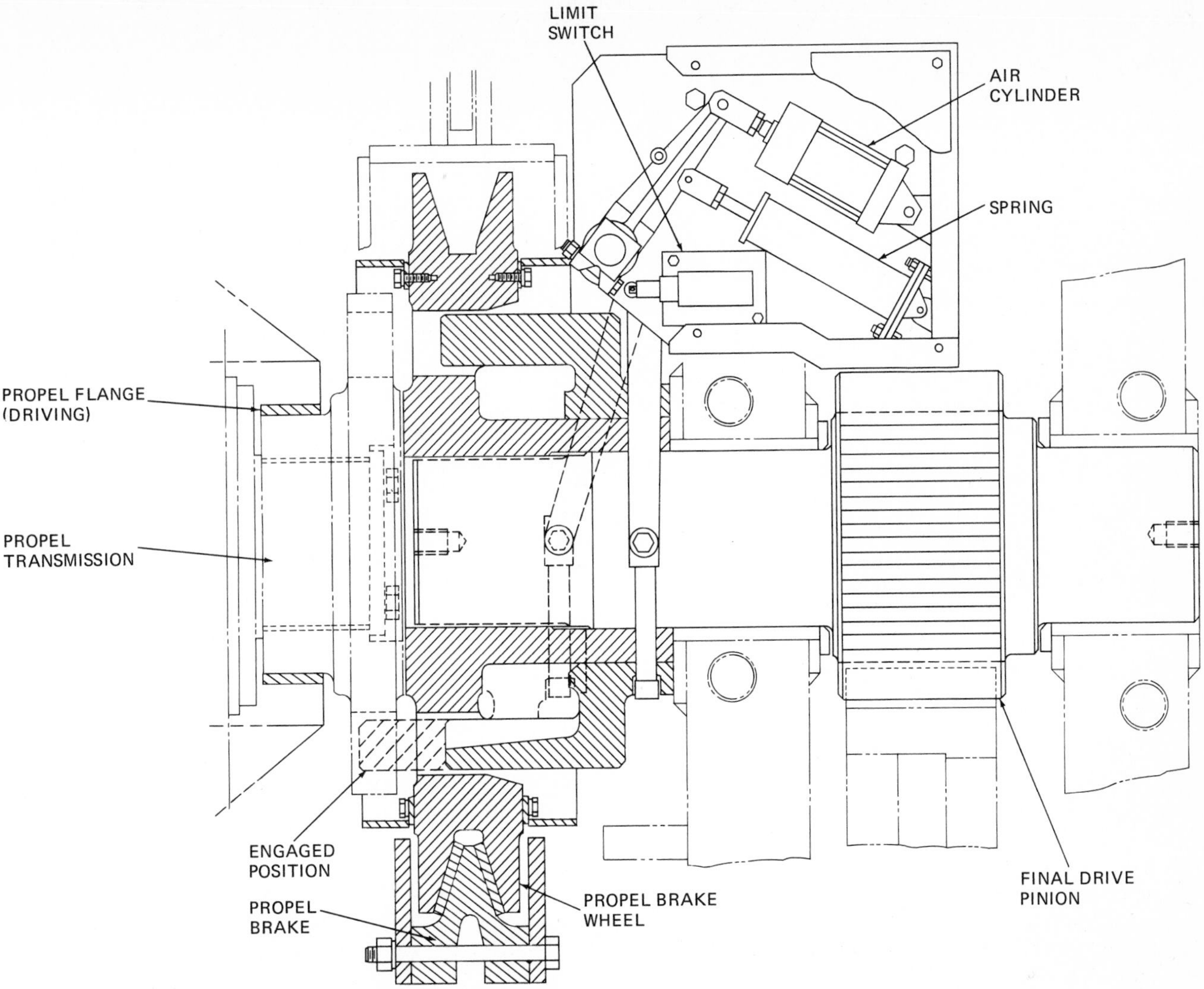

Fig. 2-70 Right-hand steering clutch assembly. (*Harnischfeger*)

one dc reversible motor that drives a double- or triple-reduction swing gear, or (on large electrically propelled machines) two dc propel motors and two swing transmissions are used—one for the left- and the other for the right-hand swing. The pinion that is in mesh with the internal swing gear is splined to the output shaft of the swing transmission. The swing brake is either a disk or external shoe brake and is positioned between the motor output shaft and the transmission input shaft. The swing brake is spring-applied and air-released to assure that the brake will automatically apply in the event the air pressure is lost.

ELECTRICAL SWING OPERATION When the electric circuit is closed to the swing motor, the swing motor and the brake valve energize simultaneously and the valve spool shifts, directing air into the rotor chamber, releasing the brake. As the motor drives the reduction gear, the pinion rotates within the internal ring gear, causing the superstructure to rotate. When the swing motor is de-energized, so is the brake valve. Air then exhausts from the brake chamber and the spring force applies the swing brake. See Fig. 2-71 for a superstructure diagram illustrating electrical swing.

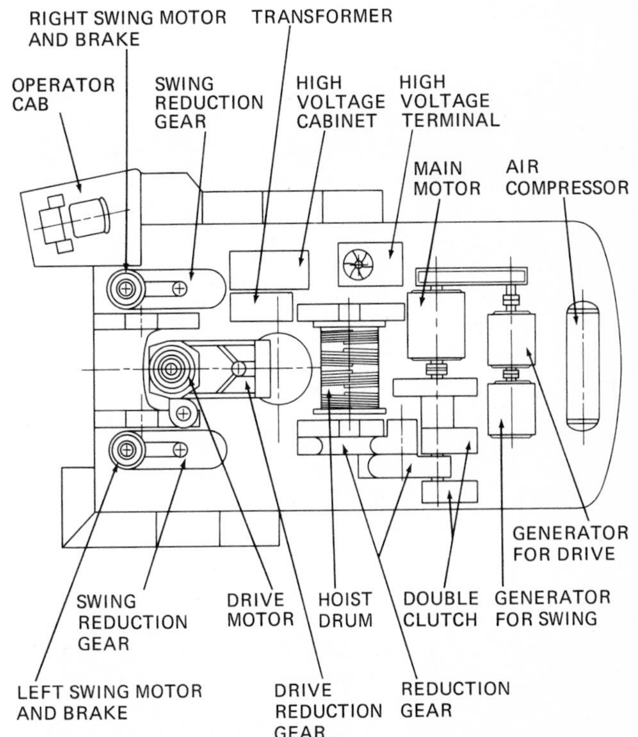

Fig. 2-71 Superstructure diagram of electrical swing.

Review Questions

1. What is the main difference between a dump truck and a bottom dumper?
2. List three differences between a tractor scraper and an elevating tractor scraper.
3. By what mechanical means is the elevator protected against damage in the event a large rock passes between the flights and bowl?
4. List four different instances where wheel-type tractors could be used.
5. What is the major difference between a 4 × 4 fixed-frame wheel-type tractor and a 4 × 4 articulated-frame wheel-type tractor?
6. What is the main purpose of PTO?
7. List four different ways in which an all-purpose bucket can be used.
8. List the four trade names which identify the component to which the dozer blade is attached.
9. To which part of the backhoe is (*a*) the bucket attached? (*b*) the boom attached?
10. What hydraulic movements are incorporated in a skidder grapple?
11. Briefly outline four differences between a fork lift and a lift truck.
12. Why are the front wheels of a motor grader constructed so that they can lean about 18° to either side?
13. What is the main difference between rubber-tired motortruck classes 1 and 2 in relation to rubber-tired chassis classes 3, 4, and 5?
14. Which method is used to (*a*) attach the superstructure to motortrucks or chassis? (*b*) rotate the superstructure?
15. What two purposes do the bunks of a logging truck trailer serve?
16. To perform different types of work, the conventional lift block of a crane can be exchanged with other working attachments. Name three common working attachments.
17. Give two advantages of a boom manlift over a scissor manlift.
18. What is the main function of the steering clutch and of the brake band?
19. Briefly outline three advantages of a crawler having a hydrostatic drive over a crawler having a mechanical drive.
20. Which components prevent the dipper door from closing too quickly?

Unit 3
Shop Safety

Employers and employees alike know the meaning of the word "safety," and each has some concept of the responsibility this one word conveys. The most basic rule of safety can be summed up in three words—use common sense! A number of examples of this elementary rule are as follows:

1. Never take chances or short cuts.
2. Always block the vehicle or equipment before removing a wheel or hydraulic cylinder.
3. Carefully select your blocking material or tool to conform to the weight, size, etc., of the vehicle.
4. Check your service manual for specifications, torque, etc. (do not guess).
5. Upon completion of the job recheck to make certain that you have not forgotten to tighten a cap screw, nut, fitting, etc., and that, where necessary, they have been secured with a cotter pin, lockwire, or lockplate.

Safety Is Up to You There may be times when the urgency of a job causes you to consider breaking one or more safety rules, but stop and THINK—what profit is there in a few minutes when balancing time against the life or limb of the operator, or coworker, or perhaps yourself? And, on the mercenary side, there is the possibility of a lawsuit against you and/or your employer if, for instance, a tire were incorrectly inflated or installed and the operator, as a result, were maimed in a subsequent accident.

To protect the worker, the government has decreed safety rules, but the onus is on the individual to practice good work habits even where governmental laws do not exist. Although today's workshops and equipment carry built-in safety devices, the value of those devices is limited if tools are unclean, if inflammables are left uncovered, and so forth. In the final analysis, it is up to each individual manufacturer, shop owner, service mechanic, operator, and worker to obey all safety rules, use common sense, and practice good work habits whether the job is complicated or extraordinarily simple. And finally, maintain your tools at peak efficiency and conform to the relevant service manual with regard to specifications and other recommendations.

NOTE There are no such things as fail-safe tools, machines, vehicles, or equipment in the hands of the careless. Accidents do not happen, they are caused, primarily from unsafe working conditions or careless work habits, including negligence due to haste. See Fig. 3-1.

General Safety Rules for the Mechanic

1. Keep your mind on your work. If you daydream or allow your personal problems to divide your attention, you become an easy mark for an accident.
2. Keep fit, and do not continue to work when you are overtired.
3. Do not wear an open jacket or shirt when coveralls should be worn. Either one could get caught in the machine or vehicle and cause injury to the wearer.
4. Do not wear unclean coveralls. They should be free of oil, grease, or fuel to prevent skin irritation or severe burns should a spark ignite.
5. Wear safety shoes and make certain they are in good condition.
6. Do not wear any type of jewelry (not even a wedding ring). Neck jewelry can get caught up in machinery, and rings can get hooked on a corner, ledge, bolts, etc.
7. When working on electrical equipment, batteries, starters, etc., use a leather watch band rather than a metal one, but preferably remove the watch temporarily. It is possible, for instance, in removing a battery cable connection, for the metal wrist band or jewelry to cause a connection to ground, resulting in severe skin burning and in some cases in the loss of a hand or finger.
8. Wear a hard hat when recommended. Failure to do so may result in a severe head injury or may even cost you your life.

An endless set of accident prevention rules would be required to cover servicing and operating the myriad of vehicles, machines, and equipment used in the on- and off-highway industry. The precautions you would take, for instance, to manually lift a tire from a light-duty truck would be considerably different from those to lift a tire of a 300-ton dump truck, which in fact would require a 10-ton lifting device. Nevertheless, a number of common precautions, warnings, and safety rules are listed which will prevent minor and/or major accidents or personal injury. See Fig. 3-2.

Fig. 3-1 Accidents do not happen. They are caused.

Fig. 3-2 Accidents do not pay. Ask the person who had one.

Precautions against Explosion and Fire Flammable materials, when heated to their kindling temperatures in the presence of oxygen, will ignite. However, no two materials have the same atomic structure or ignition temperatures; moreover the methods by which they must be extinguished also differ. Fires may be classified into the three categories A, B, and C. Fire extinguishers may be classified into six categories, Nos. 1 to 6 (see Fig. 3-3).

Class A fires are those where the combustible material is wood, fiber, paper, fabric, rubber, etc. Subdue these fires by cooling and quenching, using a fire hose, or using Nos. 1 to 3 fire extinguishers.

Class B fires are those where the combustible material is a liquid, such as gasoline, fuel, or paint. Subdue these fires by smothering or using Nos. 2 to 6 fire extinguishers.

Class C fires are those where the combustible materials are electrical components, such as motors, generators, or switch panels. Subdue these by smothering (use noncombustible material), or by using Nos. 4 to 6 fire extinguishers which have a nonconducting extinguisher agent.

Most explosions and fires could have been prevented from spreading, by having activated the fire alarm before attempting to extinguish the fire. It is therefore important that you

1. Know where the fire alarm switches are located.
2. Know where the different fire extinguishers are located.
3. Know where the fire hoses are located.
4. Know which type of fire extinguisher to use.
5. Know how to operate the different types of fire extinguishers.
6. Regularly check that all fire-fighting equipment is in operating condition and in its proper place and that the fire extinguishers are full.
7. Keep all flammable fluid and material in a safe container and whenever possible store them in a separate area.
8. Keep your workshop clean and immediately discard all rubbish and combustibles. Dispose of oily rags as soon as you are finished with them by placing them in a covered steel container.
9. Keep all solvent tanks tightly covered when they are not being used.
10. Use solvent as a cleaning fluid—do not use gasoline or carbon tetrachloride.
11. Make certain that all electrical equipment is properly connected and grounded.
12. Avoid using an octopus connection when using power tools, as this could overload the extension cable.
13. Make certain that the lamp guard is in place when using an extension light. Lamp breakage near accumulated oil or fuel may cause a fire.
14. Make certain that you have a fire extinguisher within reach when using a torch of any kind, and always keep your attention on the flame.
15. Never point the flame toward yourself or others, and never rest a flaming torch on an object. Shut the torch off immediately after using it.
16. Do not enter a room marked "NO SMOKING" with an open flame or even a smoldering cigarette.
17. Do not flip a match or cigarette in any direction before you are certain it is extinguished. *Do* use an ashtray.
18. Do not block fire doors with any object whatsoever.
19. Do not approach a battery which is being charged with an open flame or lighted cigarette since the charging gases are highly explosive.
20. Do not connect the charger cables to the battery when the charger is switched on, or an explosion may result.
21. Disconnect the battery ground cable first when removing batteries; and when reconnecting the batteries, connect the ground cable last.
22. Connect the ground cable of the booster battery to the engine and not to the vehicle battery when boost-starting an engine.
23. Do not leave a soldering iron or heating device plugged in after you have finished with them. Overheating when unattended could start a fire.

Precautions when Starting, Stopping, and Moving a Vehicle Many accidents occur when starting the engine and moving a vehicle into the shop area or into a safe working area. It is usually because the mechanic is not familiar with the machine or vehicle, or is in a hurry and therefore neglects to follow basic safety rules. See Fig. 3-4.

Again, it must be repeated that, because of the endless variety of equipment, it is impractical to categorize every safety rule; however, some basic safety steps and dos and don'ts are listed below.

Before attempting to start an engine in order to move the equipment to the work area, make certain that

1. No one is working on the machine
2. There are no parts or components removed or missing which would affect the operation of the engine, the brakes, or the movement of the vehicle and working attachments
3. You know the nature of the intended service so that you do not start the engine or move the vehicle if it would cause further damage to the vehicle or those nearby
4. You familiarize yourself with the location of the instruments, brake control, steering system, the starting and stopping control of the engine, and the

	CAPACITY	PROTECT FROM FREEZING	EXTINGUISHING EFFECT	APPROXIMATE STREAM RANGE	METHOD OF DISCHARGE
	Soda-Acid				
1	2½ gal	Yes	Cooling	45-55 ft	Chemically generated gas pressure
	20 gal			65-75 ft	
	40 gal			65-75 ft	
	Clear Water, Pressurized Type				
	2½ gal	Yes	Cooling	40-45 ft	Stored air pressure
	Clear Water, Cartridge Type				
	2½ gal	Yes	Cooling	40-45 ft	Gas pressure from carbon dioxide cartridge
2	**Antifreeze, Cartridge Type**				
	2½ gal	No	Cooling	40-45 ft	Gas pressure from carbon dioxide cartridge
	Pump Tank (Antifreeze or Plain Water)				
	2½ gal	Where clear water is used — Yes Antifreeze Solution — No	Cooling	45–50 ft	Hand pump action
	5 gal				
3	**Loaded Stream, Pressurized Type**				
	2½ gal	No	Cooling	45-60 ft	Stored air pressure
	Foam				
	2½ gal	Yes	Blanketing	30-40 ft	Chemically generated gas pressure
	20 gal			55-65 ft	
	40 gal			55-65 ft	
	VL Pressurized Type				
	1 qt	No	Smothering	25-30 ft	Internally stored air pressure
4	2 qt			25-30 ft	
	1 gal			25-30 ft	
	VL Hand Pump Type				
	1 qt	No	Smothering	25-30 ft	Hand pump action
	1½ qt			25-30 ft	
	Dry Chemical				
	2½ lb	No	Smothering	10-12 ft	Stored air pressure
	5 lb			10-12 ft	
	10 lb			10-12 ft	
	10 lb			10-12 ft	Gas pressure from carbon dioxide cartridge
	20 lb			15-20 ft	
5	30 lb			15-20 ft	
	75 lb			18 ft	Gas pressure from nitrogen cylinder
	150 lb			18 ft	
	Carbon Dioxide				
	2½ lb	No	Smothering	Approx. 8 ft	Carbon dioxide under pressure in extinguisher
	5 lb				
	10 lb				
6	15 lb				
	20 lb				
	50 lb				
	75 lb				
	100 lb				

Fig. 3-3 Fire extinguishers.

Fig. 3-4 Operate that vehicle as though it were your own—with your family in it! Think first!

operation and shift control of the transmission, hydraulics, and winches if the machine is one that you have not previously started, operated, or driven.

START THE ENGINE PROPERLY If you have not been informed about the engine's or machine's present condition, promptly check the coolant, oil level of the engine, and oil level of the machine, the hydraulics, and the transmission.

NOTE When checking the engine coolant level after the engine has been operating, turn the pressure cap slightly before removing it completely. Check or close the air reservoirs.

Next, place the transmission in neutral or in the safety position, or disengage the master clutch. If it is necessary to use a preheater (glowplug), turn it on and after about 15 seconds engage the electric, hydraulic, or air starter. The engine should start after about three full revolutions. **NOTE** Do not run the engine in an enclosed area without proper exhaust piping and ventilation. The lack of oxygen and/or the presence of carbon monoxide is lethal and could kill you without warning.

Once the engine is running, check the lube oil pressure and closely watch the coolant temperature and the rise in the air pressure. If the air pressure is not rising but you have closed the reservoirs, stop the engine and check the air compressor and the drive belts for broken or leaking air hoses. Repair if necessary. Do not move the vehicle on its own power unless you know the brakes are adequate.

Operate the engine at about 1000 rpm until the engine temperature gauge shows about 180°F (degree Fahrenheit) [82°C (degrees Celsius)]. When the engine temperature is at 180°F [82°C], the air pressure is at the cutoff pressure; the vehicle is then ready to move into the work area.

MOVE THE VEHICLE PROPERLY Depending on the type of machine and the location of your work area, you may require an assistant to guide you into the shop or drive the machine into the servicing position. If an assistant is not available, recheck the entire travel area and make certain that there are no obstructions and that the shop doors are fully open. Then raise the working attachment off the ground and position it to a level which gives you good vision and good maneuverability. Release the parking brake, place the transmission into the lowest gear, and then drive the vehicle into the shop or to the desired location. If you use an assistant to guide you into position, follow that individual's hand signals implicitly, as he or she is responsible for your safe maneuvering.

NOTE Operate the vehicle as though it were your own. (Think before taking action.)

SECURE THE VEHICLE After the machine is in position, apply the parking brakes or block the wheels. This, of course, depends on the type of machine as well as the service you have to perform. Next, position the attached equipment—that is, as an example, the loader, excavator, shovel, crane, etc.—in such a way that it will not impede your work, and then block the equipment securely. Reduce the engine temperature by placing the throttle in low idle and when it declines to about 160°F [71°C] turn off the ignition switch or pull the fuel stop. **NOTE** Each manufacturer provides special instructions for moving their equipment or machine. As an example, here are a few safety steps one manufacturer recommends for a crane mounted on a crawler carrier: Do not travel with the swing brakes released. Do not engage the engine clutch until you are sure that everything is clear and in neutral. Do not maintain less than 5 ft [1.525 m] of clearance around high voltage lines. Do not travel on a steep slope without the use of blocking (in case a drive chain fails).

Precautions when Lifting and Blocking Before starting any type of service work except an engine tuneup, disconnect the batteries, remove the hydraulic pressure from the system as well as from the cylinders, and drain the air reservoir.

NOTE Use extreme care if it is necessary to make adjustments on the engine or equipment while the engine is running. Keep your hands away from moving parts.

Clear away any parts from the work area which would obstruct your work. It is statistically proven that a very high percentage of injuries and accidents occur while removing, cleaning, and installing parts or components. When selecting a lifting device, a chain block, a comealong, a crane, a loader, a fork lift, etc., make certain that the lifting capacity of the unit is higher than the load to be lifted. Use, when possible, an adjustable lifting beam, chains, and eye bolts in such fashion that the chains are parallel to each other and as nearly perpendicular as possible to the top of the object to be lifted. This will ensure that each eye bolt and chain carries only half the load. Place the sling eyes or chain rings on the lift hook only when the slings or chains are vertical, and do not lay one eye over the other. Both should lie on the bottom of the hook. When it is necessary to remove components and the slings or chains have to be fastened at an angle to the object to be lifted, note that (1) with an increase in angle the force on the slings or chains increases and may exceed the load capacity (see Fig. 3-5). Therefore, use a shackle and

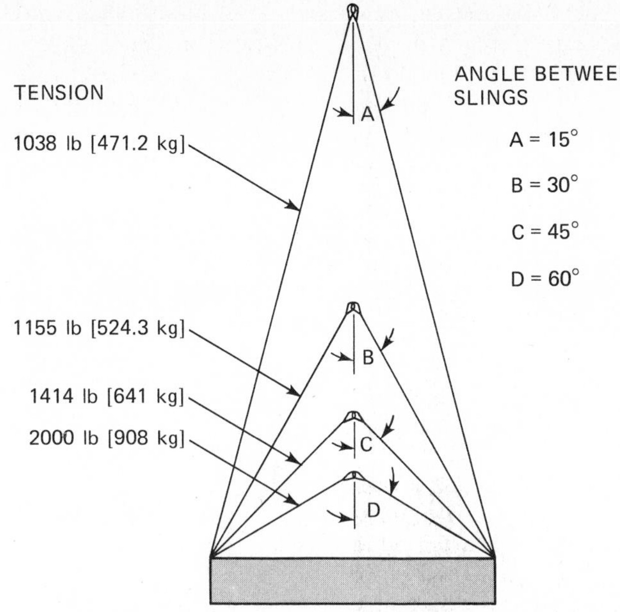

Fig. 3-5 The greater the angle between the slings, chains, or ropes used when lifting a piece of equipment, the greater the strain on them and the stronger they must be.

shackle both sling eyes or chain rings together, then place the shackle on the hook. (2) Bottom the eyebolts against the object to be lifted, or support them as shown in Fig. 3-6, otherwise the eyebolts could bend and break.

When selecting a wire rope sling, make certain the eyes are spliced properly and that there are no wire breaks or sharp kinks. Fiber or synthetic ropes or slings are not as often used to lift an object, but are used as tag lines (guide lines).

When using a rope make certain that it is properly hitched or knotted to the object. Use the common timber hitch, half hitch, the square or reef knot, the bowline knot, all of which are easy to remove (Figs. 3-7 to 3-10).

When lifting, stay clear of the load and lift it only as high as required, then swing it free and lower it to the minimum height. Do not leave the load sus-

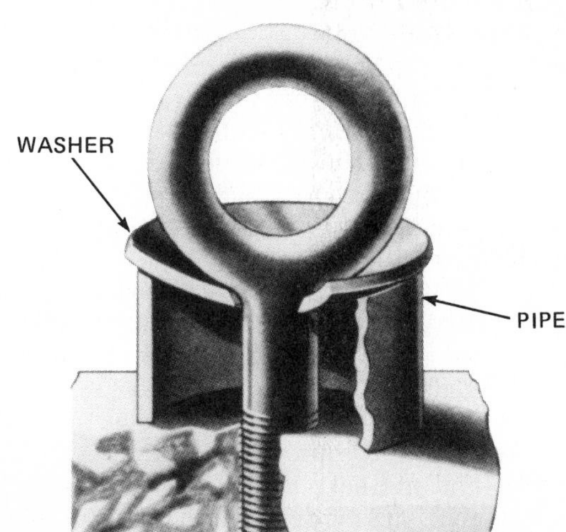

Fig. 3-6 Lifting eye.

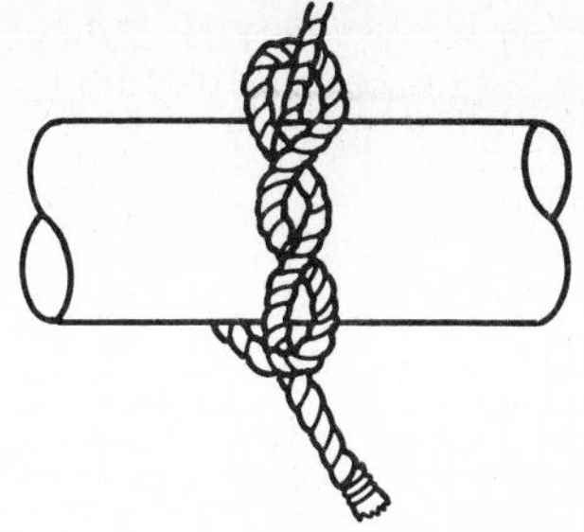

Fig. 3-7 Timber hitch.

Fig. 3-8 Half hitch.

Fig. 3-9 Square or reef knot.

Fig. 3-10 Bowline knot.

pended in the air or travel with the load suspended high in the air, as the lifting device could tip when the load swings back and forth. If it is necessary to have the load suspended up high, use tag lines to prevent it from swinging.

When placing an object on the bench, jack, or floor, make certain it is supported by wooden blocks so that it cannot tip over.

When lifting a vehicle with a hydraulic jack or screw jack, block the wheels and/or apply the parking brakes. Select a jack with adequate lifting capacity and make sure that the jack footing holds firm and is on level ground. If necessary, use wood blocking to increase the area on which the jack will rest. Place the jack square to the components to be lifted and use a suitable saddle, head, or wooden block to ensure safe lifting.

After the object is raised, support it with rigid stands or axle stands or through crossblocking, in case the hydraulic jack should bleed off and gradually lower the vehicle.

Fig. 3-11 Always bend at the knees when lifting a heavy object.

CAUTION When working below a vehicle, wear safety glasses to prevent any fuel, oil, acid, or dirt from dropping into your eyes. Such an acid drop could cause blindness.

When placing a load or a component on a fork lift or lift truck, use (if possible) a pallet. If a pallet is not available, secure the object to the mast with a rope so it cannot fall off the forks. When operating a fork lift or lift truck, be alert for other floor traffic and obstructions especially when passing through doors or beyond blind openings.

Have respect for weight as it applies to your own strength and bear in mind that you may lift or place an object of a particular weight in position when standing upright, but when lying on your back you can maneuver less than half that weight. Never attempt to lift heavy parts—use a lifting device.

Your hands are the most important tools you possess—protect them! Never try to use them as a vise or a hammer, etc., and do not place them or your arm between objects that are to be engaged or moved into mesh. Use a rope, a wire, a pair of pliers, or a prybar, etc.

If you must manually lift an object, lift it from a squat position (Fig. 3-11). Avoid pushing objects—pull them, and always make sure you have a firm grip in each case to prevent muscle and back strain.

Precautions when Using Tools To avoid injury to yourself or to others, always use the tool designed for the job. Do not use a pair of pliers as a jumper cable or your hands will be burned. Do not use a pair of pliers to tighten a nut or fitting. They are inadequate and will cause a leak or a loose fastener, which will eventually lead to an accident. Do not use screwdrivers in place of a chisel or prybar. In such circumstances they have been known to break and cause injury to the user or helper. Do not use blunt chisels or chisels or punches having mushroom heads. Dress them properly to prevent cuts. Do not jump or reach awkwardly for a tool which you have inadvertently dropped or you may find yourself in a precarious and dangerous position. Perform your work carefully without undue haste and make certain that all bolts, nuts, and fittings are tightened properly and, if applicable, locked. Do not use oily or dirty tools as they could slip from your hands and cause injury to yourself or to others. Do not use wrenches that have spread jaws or are defective. They will slip. Do not use a file without a handle as it may pierce your hands. Do not use a hammer on a hardened surface, as knifelike slivers could fly off the hammer or surface and cut you or others. Do not use a drill until the object to be drilled is properly secured. Never use any type of electrical equipment, machine, or tools that is not properly grounded, or cables or tools that are not in good working condition. You could be electrocuted. If you are inexperienced in welding, grinding, chiseling, or any other task that has an element of danger to it, leave it to those who are qualified. If you are doing any of these jobs, place a shield around your work area and wear the correct face shield or goggles. It is a good habit to write "hot" on parts just welded, cut, or grounded, to warn others against the possibility of burns.

When filling the battery with electrolyte, wear a face shield and rubber gloves as protection against skin blisters should you accidentally spill the acid. If any is spilled, use a lot of water and wash it away. If electrolyte is spilled on the vehicle, sprinkle baking soda onto the contacted area and then wash the area thoroughly with water.

Precautions while Cleaning Components A great number of eye injuries and cuts result from a disregard for the simplest of rules when cleaning components. For instance, you should never use compressed air to clean your clothes, hands, or body (Fig. 3-12). The pressure could cause the cleaning fluid or dirt particles to penetrate your skin, resulting in infection and/or blood poisoning. Neither should you spin a bearing (fool around) by com-

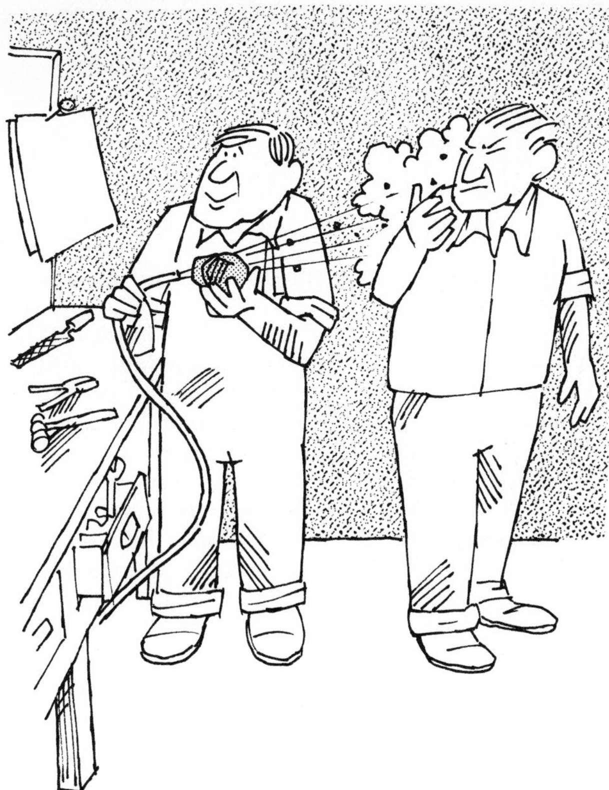

Fig. 3-12 Never be careless with compressed air! Never aim the air stream at yourself or another person.

pressing it with air. It could explode. Do not use compressed air unless you are wearing a face shield—it could cause eye injury. Do not use compressed air to clean an object immediately after it has been removed from a hot cleaning tank. First rinse the cleaning solution away with water. Do not use carbon tetrachloride as a cleaning solution. The fumes, when inhaled, can cause serious internal injury and possibly result in death. Wear a face shield and rubber gloves when inserting or removing components or parts from a hot tank. If the acid solution spills or splashes on you, it could cause skin infection and/or burns. Lower the object slowly into the hot tank to prevent splashing. When using a power wire wheel, always wear a face shield, and also place a shield around the object to protect others from flying wire and particles. When using a putty knife or scraper, keep your free hand behind the tool so that it will not be pierced in the event the scraper should slip. When steam-cleaning, place the object to be cleaned on a pallet and wear a face shield and rubber gloves for protection against rebounding objects.

If a job or cleaning task requires the use of gloves, use the appropriate gloves. Do not, for instance, use welding gloves when removing an object from a hot tank, or rubber gloves when welding. If you have cut, nicked, or burned yourself, or something has gotten into your eyes, report immediately to the first aid person. Procrastination could cause blood poisoning even from a slight cut, or could place your eyesight in jeopardy.

Review Questions

1. Describe acceptable working clothes for a diesel mechanic.
2. Why is it extremely important to ground all electric power tools and motors?
3. Explain why an overloaded electric circuit can cause a fire.
4. Sketch the outside work area of your shop, indicating (*a*) the location of the fire alarm, (*b*) the location of the fire hose outlet and the hose length, and (*c*) the type of fire extinguisher.
5. What precaution must you take before checking the cooling system when the engine temperature is about 158°F [70°C]?
6. If you are required to drive an unfamiliar tractor, machine, etc., to the work area, which controls or instruments would you first learn to utilize?
7. Why is it imperative that the driver follow the hand signals of the assistant when driving the machine into position?
8. What checks should you make before using (*a*) a wire rope sling? (*b*) a fiber rope sling?
9. Practice knotting and hitching using the lumber hitch, the half hitch, the square or reef knot, and the bowline knot.
10. Define the term "crossblocking."
11. What precautionary measures must you take when lifting or transporting an object with a fork lift or lift truck?
12. Why should you use a shackle rather than placing both sling eyes onto the lift hook?

Unit 4
Electricity and Electronics

A great percentage of motor vehicle downtime is attributed to electric system failure as a result of improper maintenance, adjustment, and service of the individual components or circuits. The beginning of this unit will therefore review the fundamental physical properties, laws, and principles governing electricity, magnetism, and electronics and then the electric system proper, its circuits, and its components, will be considered as well as testing, causes of electrical failure, and preventive maintenance.

PHYSICAL PROPERTIES, LAWS, AND PRINCIPLES

All matter is composed of small particles called *molecules.* Each molecule is made up of two or more *atoms.* Atoms are made up of even smaller particles, called *electrons, neutrons,* and *protons.*

Physical Properties and Electricity Electrons revolve in certain orbits or energy levels around the nucleus of the atom. The nucleus normally has the same number of protons as the atom has electrons.

Each atom is assigned an atomic weight which is approximately equal to the number of protons and neutrons in the nucleus. Each atom also is given an atomic number which represents its total number of electrons (or protons). For example, copper has an atomic number of 29. It has 29 electrons that orbit in four rings around a nucleus of 29 protons and 29 neutrons (Fig. 4-1). The nucleus, which has the greatest mass and weight, keeps the electrons in orbit around itself by gravitational pull. The electrons which are closest to the nucleus are more strongly attracted (pulled) to it than the electrons which are farthest away. The electrons in the outer orbit are not as strongly attracted and therefore can sometimes be forced off their orbit. They are called "free" electrons, and those in the inner orbit are called "bonded" electrons.

Normally the atom is electrically balanced—that is, the electric charge on the electrons (conventionally labeled "negative") balances the charge on the protons (labeled "positive"). (Note that neutrons are "neutral," i.e., have neither a positive nor a negative charge, and therefore have no effect on the electric balance of the atom.) If a state of imbalance should develop through the loss of electrons, the atom as a whole becomes positive in charge. It then tends to attract other electrons to regain its electrical balance. Electric imbalance (called *potential difference*) is the basic principle underlying electric current flow because imbalance causes electrons to flow from atom to atom.

ELECTRON FLOW Electrons will flow from atom to atom when there are more electrons present at the negative terminal than at the positive terminal and when there is a path which connects the negative terminal with a positive terminal that lacks electrons.

THEORIES OF CURRENT FLOW The flow of electrons is called *current,* and there are two ways to explain it: the conventional theory and the electron theory. The conventional theory states that current flows from the positive terminal of the power source to its negative terminal, while the electron theory states that free electrons flow from negative to positive (see Fig. 4-2). The rate of this electron flow per second past a given point can be measured by using an instrument called an *ammeter,* in units called *amperes* (A). You can measure the current at the negative or the positive side of a circuit and the reading will always be the same because the electrons that leave the negative terminal post reenter the positive terminal post.

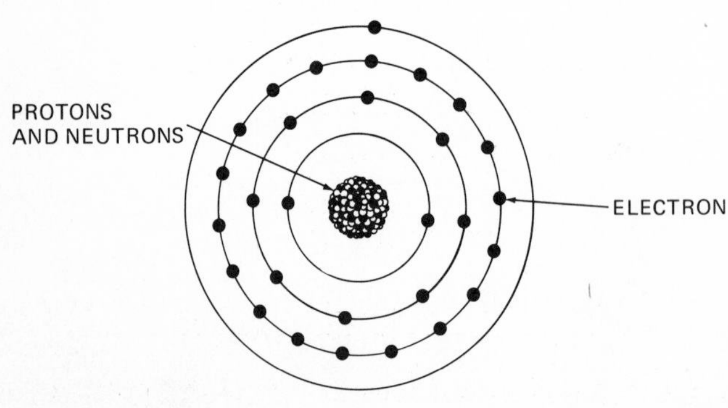

Fig. 4-1 Copper atom.

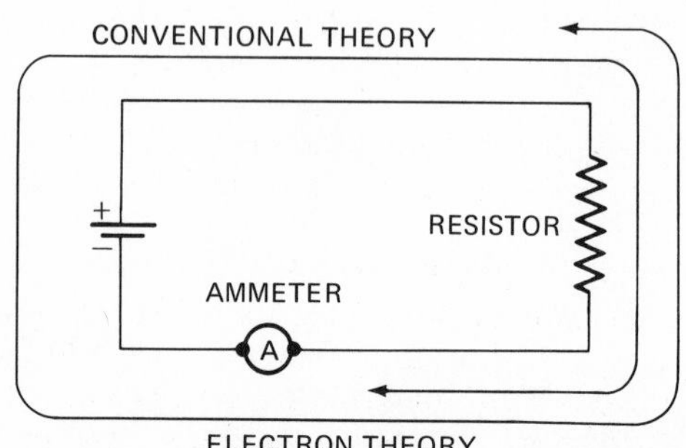

Fig. 4-2 Demonstrating the electron theory and the conventional theory.

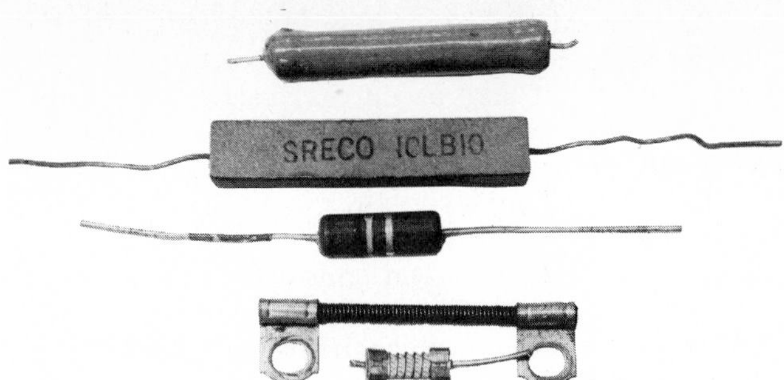

Fig. 4-3 Typical resistor designs.

DIRECT AND ALTERNATING CURRENT *Direct current* (dc) is a flow of electrons in one direction only. When the flow of electrons changes direction continually (cycles), it is called *alternating current* (ac).

RESISTANCE *Resistance* is any force tending to hinder electron flow. Resistance in a conductor, semiconductor, or insulator (see below) is in opposition to the movement of electrons.

Resistors used in the various electric components or circuits vary in material and shape (Fig. 4-3). Their purpose is to reduce current flow [calculable by Ohm's law (discussed below)], stabilize voltage, and reduce voltage (also calculable by Ohm's law). Resistance is measured in ohms (Ω).

VOLTAGE OR ELECTROMOTIVE FORCE Voltage arises from a difference in the concentration of electrons between the negative and the positive terminals. This potential difference is called *voltage* or *electromotive force* (emf), and the unit of measurement is the volt (V).

VOLTAGE SOURCE There are many ways to produce voltage, including friction, heat, light, pressure, chemical energy, and magnetism. This book will be concerned only with voltage produced by heat, chemical energy, and magnetism (discussed below).

CONDUCTORS Electric devices involve conductors, which are made from elements such as copper or aluminum. These metals are good electron carriers because they have one or two free electrons per atom, which are easily dislodged from their atomic orbits, thus allowing easy electron flow from atom to atom. In addition, temperature changes affect their resistance characteristics very little. However, you should remember that the resistance of any conductor decreases when the cross-sectional area is increased, and it increases when the area is reduced. When the conductor is lengthened without increasing its cross-sectional area, the resistance increases.

INSULATORS (NONCONDUCTORS) An insulator is composed of one or more atoms with an atomic structure of more than four electrons bonded in a compact outer orbit. The structure will not allow the movement of electrons because there are no free electrons present.

Insulators are essential to the conductors of any electric device because they prevent electron loss to the environment outside the conductor, and thus can prevent a short or grounded circuit (see definition of term "circuit" below) and can be used to separate two conductors.

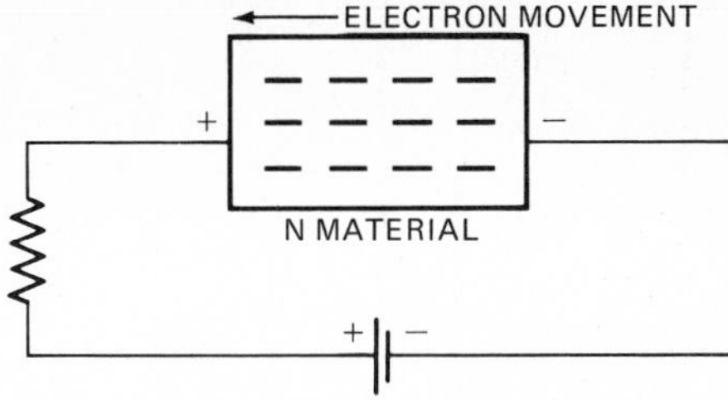

Fig. 4-4 Electron movement through N material. (*Delco-Remy Division of General Motors Corporation*)

SEMICONDUCTORS Semiconductor materials are neither good conductors nor good insulators because they are made up of elements which have an atomic structure of three or five electrons in their outer orbit. However, these elements can be altered to fulfill a useful purpose, that is, can be made into electric devices called *diodes* which act as conductors under certain conditions and as nonconductors under others, and thus are useful in rectifiers, safety switches, and to change circuit resistance.

DIODES Diodes are made up of negative or N type material, which has an excess of electrons (negative polarity), and positive or P type material, which has a deficiency of electrons (positive polarity).

When either material is connected with a power source of sufficient voltage, the N and P materials obey the simple law of opposite polarity attracting and like polarity repelling. Electrons will flow through the N material (as shown in Fig. 4-4) toward the positive terminal to the power source. Additional electrons flow out of the negative terminal to reenter the N material.

Similarly, when the P material is connected to the circuit, as shown in Fig. 4-5, the holes (lack of one electron in an atom) move to the negative terminal. There they will meet with the electrons from the power source and recombine.

Some of the electrons enter the P material, fill the holes, and cause an imbalance within the semiconductor. The electrons are discharged forcibly at the positive terminal, creating new holes which act as

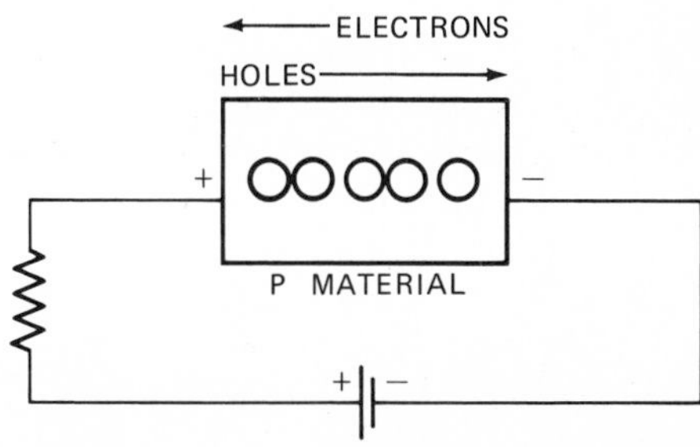

Fig. 4-5 Electron and hole movement through P material. (*Delco-Remy Division of General Motors Corporation*)

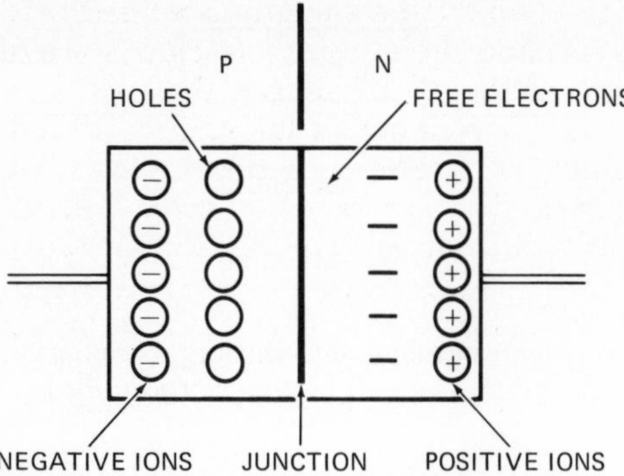

Fig. 4-6 PN material after the fusion process. (*Delco-Remy Division of General Motors Corporation*)

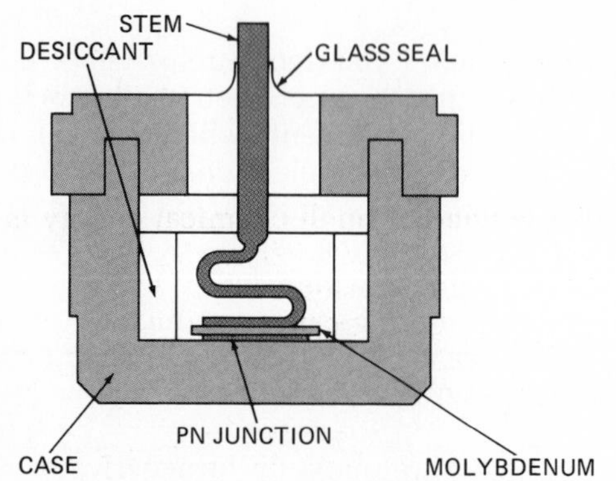

Fig. 4-7 Diode construction (PN). (*Delco-Remy Division of General Motors Corporation*)

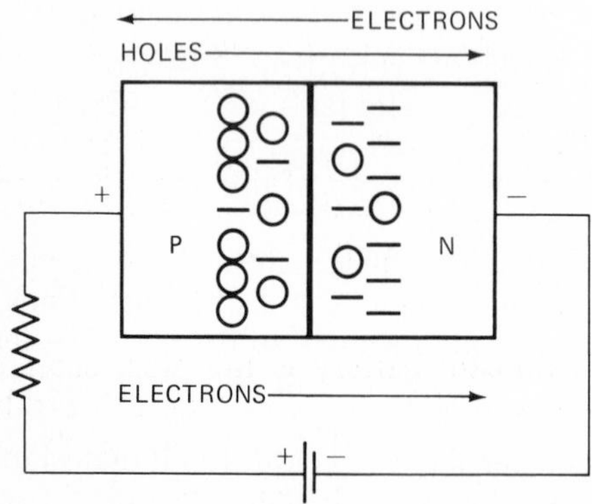

Fig. 4-8 Forward-bias diode connection. (*Delco-Remy Division of General Motors Corporation*)

current carriers. This movement continues until the circuit is opened. **NOTE** The hole movement is only in the semiconductor material. Electrons flow through the entire circuit.

Diode construction By a fusion process, manufacturers join two small slices of N and P material together. The point where they join is called a *junction*. Because unlike charges attract, a few electrons near the junction drift into the P material and fill the holes, thereby nullifying those holes as current carriers. On the other hand, a few holes drift into the N material and combine with the electrons, thus eliminating them also as current carriers. Equilibrium is achieved and no holes or electrons can move across the (PN) junction, as shown in Fig. 4-6, making the diode an open switch.

The junction rests in a copper case (see Fig. 4-7). The stem with its S-shaped conductor is welded to the P or N material. The S-shaped conductor prevents the stem seal as well as the electric connection from breaking when the diode expands and retracts during operation. A dessicant is placed inside the case to absorb any moisture. The stem is glass-sealed, insulated, and its top is bonded to the case. The case makes up the other side of the electric connection to which either the P or N material is connected. In a *PN diode*, the case is connected to the N material, while for an *NP diode*, the P material is connected to the case.

Diode action When a diode is connected in the circuit as shown in Fig. 4-8 (*forward bias*), the positive terminal of the battery connects to the P material and the negative terminal to the N material. The holes in the P material repel and the electrons in the N material repel from their terminals and move toward the junction. Usually only a fraction of the voltage is required (about 0.2 V) to cause the holes and the electrons to move through the junction.

As soon as a hole enters the N material and combines, an electron enters the P material. This forces an electron to leave the P material, creating a new hole, and a new electron to enter from the N material. The diode now conducts current.

When the battery is connected in *reverse bias* (reverse polarity), the negative terminal of the battery connects to the P material and the positive terminal to the N material. The holes move toward the negative terminal and the electrons move toward the positive terminal, causing the junction to void itself of current carriers. The junction becomes a high-resistance area causing an open circuit.

Generators, regulators, and other electrical components use positive and negative diodes. They are

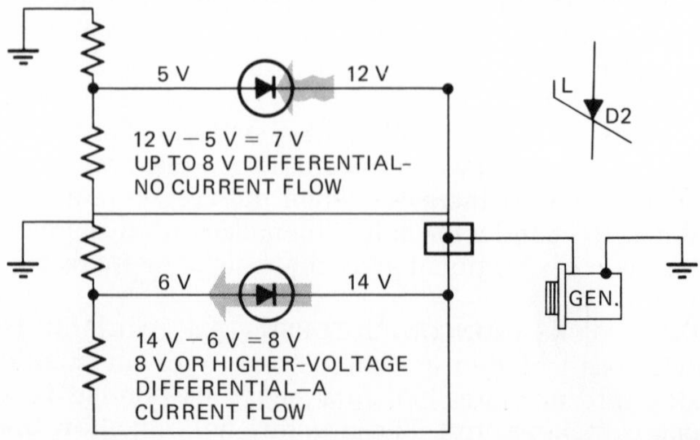

Fig. 4-9 Zener diode symbols and circuit voltage reaction. (*Delco-Remy Division of General Motors Corporation*)

identified according to their polarity: negative diode—black, or right-hand thread; positive diode—red, or left-hand thread.

Zener diodes A zener diode is an electric switch that reacts to a predetermined value of reverse system voltage so as to switch a transistor on and off. The symbols used to identify the zener diode are shown in Fig. 4-9.

Transistors A transistor is made from a PN or NP junction by fusing one additional P or N material section to it. The left-hand P or the left-hand N material is called the *emitter;* the N or P material at the right is called the *collector.* The transistor *base* is usually connected to the transistor case, and the emitter and collector stems form the wire leads. The emitter-to-base diode is always in forward bias; the base-to-collector diode is always in reverse bias; the base and collector are always of the same polarity.

PNP or NPN transistors perform in essentially the same manner, but they differ in their polarity.

A transistor is something like an electric switch and, at the same time, can be used as an amplifier. However, it only allows a larger current flow (from the emitter to collector) when the emitter-to-base circuit is complete.

Transistor operation When a diode is placed in a simplified field circuit, and the circuit is completed by closing the switch, or through a voltage relay or zener diode, field current will flow (see Ohm's law) from the positive terminal of the battery, through the field coil, diode, and switch, to the negative terminal of the battery.

When you replace one diode with a PNP transistor, the current flow remains the same but something rather unexpected happens. Refer to Fig. 4-10. From this illustration you can see that 5 amperes (A) enter the emitter, 4.8 A leave the collector, and a current of only 0.2 A flows in the emitter-to-base circuit.

The holes created in the emitter by the departing electrons travel directly into the collector due to velocity, and some holes at the emitter-to-base junction combine with electrons and become neutralized. However, the number which combine is quite small because of the base potential, which is usually less than 5 percent of the emitter-to-collector circuit. The unusual characteristics of a transistor are due to the potential difference between the base and the collector, and the base and the emitter. When the base potential is closer to the collector potential, the ratio of current flow between the emitter–base and the emitter–collector is higher, and the ratio will decrease by moving the base potential toward the emitter. When the emitter and collector potentials are equal there is no current flow. (See material on semiconductors and diodes for more details.)

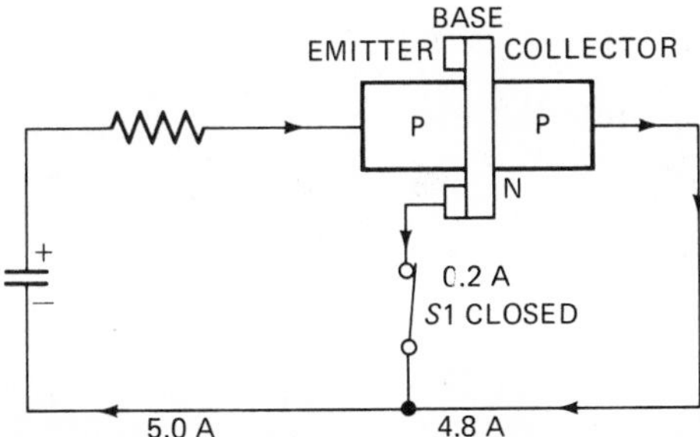

Fig. 4-10 Current flow when the emitter-to-base circuit is completed. (*Delco-Remy Division of General Motors Corporation*)

Voltage through Heat When two wires or plates made of different metals twisted or welded together are heated, the junction transmits the heat to their opposite ends, causing a potential difference, or voltage. The voltage produced in this way is very small, but the current flow is sufficient to energize the coil of a small gauge to trigger a transistor or to activate a relay (see the discussion of relays).

Electricity through Chemical Energy The production of a voltage through chemical energy is important because it is the way batteries work.

BATTERIES A battery is an electrochemical device that stores electric energy in chemical form, which can then be released for use as electricity. There are two major types of batteries—*primary* and *secondary*. Primary batteries (sometimes called *dry batteries*), which are used in test instruments, are irreversible, that is, they can only convert energy stored in chemical form to electricity and cannot be recharged. However, secondary batteries such as lead-acid, nickel-iron, and nickel-cadmium are reversible, that is, they can be recharged. Secondary batteries are used to store electric energy in chemical form, stabilize voltage, and supply electric energy to motor vehicle electrical systems. High charging rate is the high current with which the battery can be charged, and high discharge rate is the current which the battery can supply without being damaged

The lead-acid battery is the most economical of the three secondary battery designs. It produces the highest voltage per cell (2.2 V) and is the lowest in cost per watthour for its capacity. Furthermore, the cells withstand a fairly high charge and discharge rate.

Generally speaking, most lead-acid batteries are alike, notwithstanding the manufacturer. The construction of one is shown in Fig. 4-11.

The main differences between the various types of batteries in (1) the number and area of the negative and positive plates, which govern the amount of energy [measured in ampere-hours (Ah)] which the battery can store, (2) the method used to manufacture the plates or plate groups (see (Fig. 4-12), (3) the number of cells (three, six, or twelve), (4) the design of the battery case cover (one-piece, individual, or sealed cover), (5) the cell cover vents, and (6) the location of the battery terminals and the type of battery terminals.

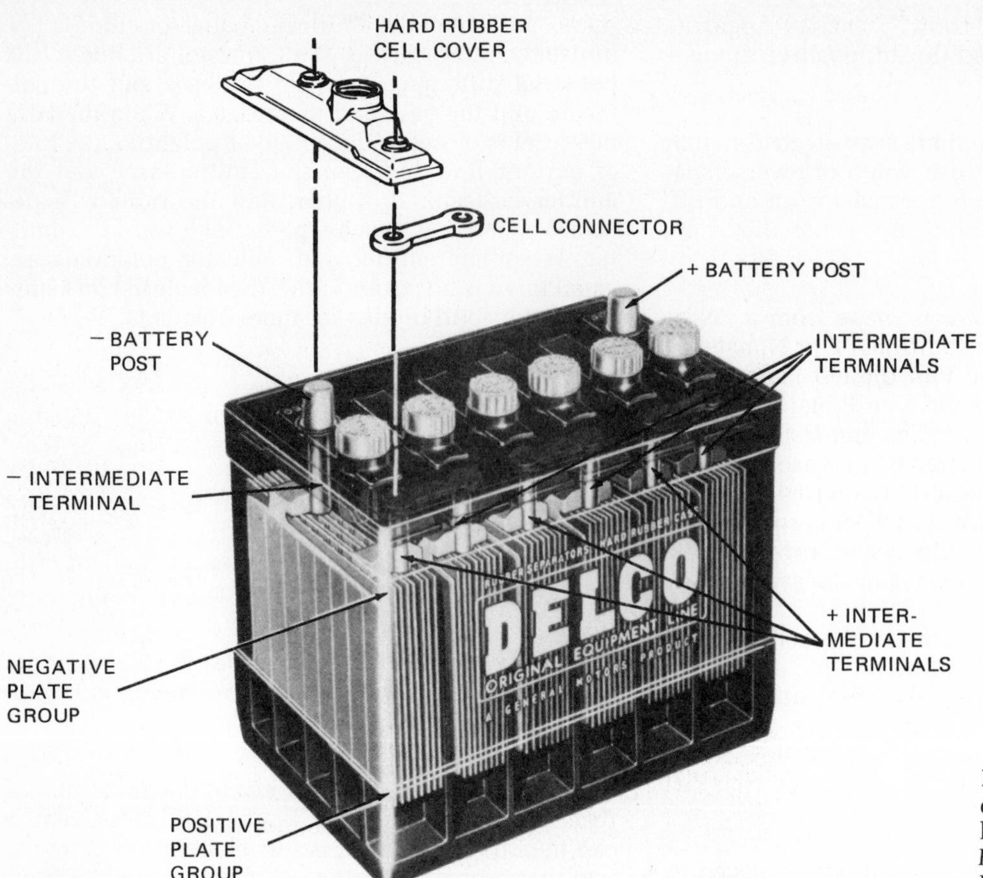

Fig. 4-11 External view of an individual cell cover lead-acid battery. (*Delco-Remy Division of General Motors Corporation*)

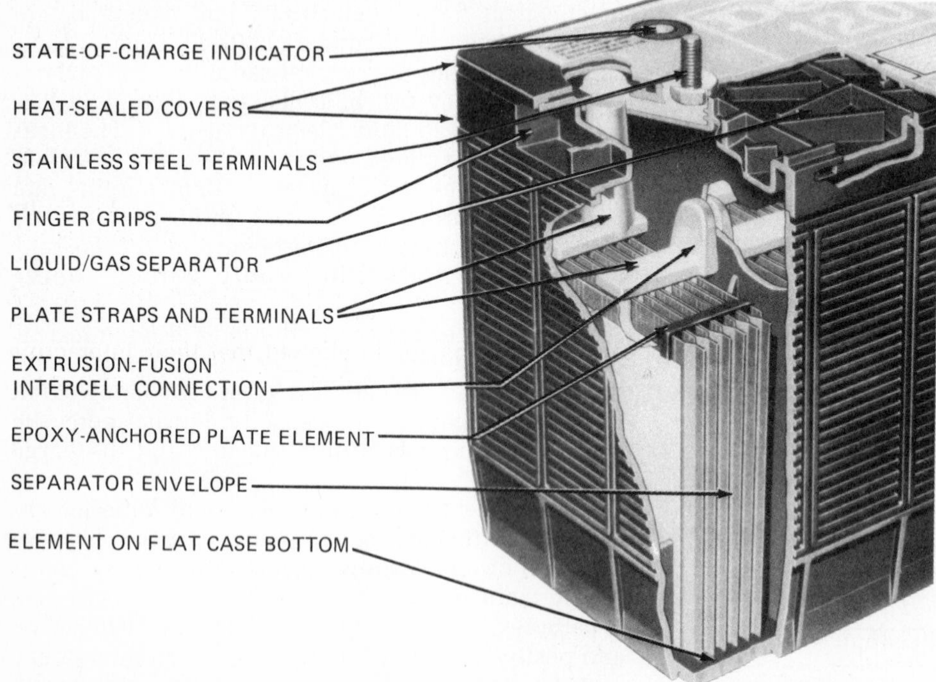

Fig. 4-12 Cutaway view of a Delco 1200 battery. (*Delco-Remy Division of General Motors Corporation*)

BATTERY CLASSIFICATION AND RATINGS The amount of current (capacity) that a battery can deliver depends on the number, size, and weight of its plates, and the volume of acid present. The emf, that is, the open-circuit voltage, of a fully charged cell with a specific gravity of 1.265 is 2.1 to 2.15 V regardless of the number, size, or weight of the plates. But the voltage on discharge is influenced by the size of the cells—the larger the plate area, the longer the cranking voltage remains the same (under any given con-

Table 4-1 ELECTROLYTE STRENGTH AS RELATED TO CELL, VOLTAGE, AND TEMPERATURE

Specific gravity	Opening voltage, V	Freezing temperature, °F [°C]
1.285	2.30—2.40	−100 (−73.3)
1.275	2.20—2.30	− 88 (−66.7)
1.265	2.10—2.20	− 79 (−61.6)
1.250	1.90—2.00	− 62 (−52.2)

Table 4-2 CCA RECOMMENDATIONS

Manufacturer	Engine displacement, in^3	Minimum, A	CCA	Watts
Caterpillar	1674	638	1500	18,000
Mack Maxidyne	675	672	1460	17,520

dition). Cranking voltage is the voltage required to force the current through the cranking motor in order to crank the engine over.

To crank an engine you need electric power. The power demanded from a battery varies with the engine displacement and compression ratio. Engine manufacturers test their engines to establish starting power, that is, the energy [measured in watts (W)] required to crank an engine at 0°F [−17.8°C]. From this test factor, the recommended minimum cold-cranking amperes (CCA) for a given engine are established. For example, suppose that 18,000 W are required to start the engine, and that the cranking-motor voltage is 12 V. To arrive at the cold-cranking amperes, divide 18,000 by 12. The answer is 1500 CCA. If the cranking-motor voltage were 24 V, only 750 CCA would be required. Two engine manufacturers' CCA recommendations are listed in Table 4-2.

To standardize the CCA requirements for the great number of diesel and other internal combustion engines, battery manufacturers in cooperation with the Society of Automotive Engineers (SAE) have classified batteries with a number and letter system. This system distinguishes battery voltage, battery dimension, reserve capacity, cold-cranking amperes at 0 and −20°F [−17.8 and −28.9°C], overcharge, and charge acceptance in amperes.

The classification and ratings for five battery groups recommended for use on diesel engines are listed in Table 4-3.

CHEMICAL ACTION IN BATTERY WHEN DISCHARGING While a battery is discharging, the sulfuric acid within the electrolyte is absorbed by the negative sponge lead plates and the positive lead peroxide plates, so that both plates gradually are changed into lead sulfate. The greater the similarity between the positive and the negative plates, the lower the voltage within the cell, since voltage depends on the potential difference between the two materials of which it is composed.

CHEMICAL ACTION IN BATTERY DURING CHARGING While the battery is being charged by a generator or charger, current passes through the battery in a direction opposite to that of discharge. As the sulfuric acid leaves the plates and returns to the electrolyte, the negative plates change gradually to lead and the positive plates change to lead peroxide. During the charging action, the negative and positive plates give off a hydrogen and oxygen gas. The nearer the battery comes to the fully charged state, the greater the quantity of gas released. **CAUTION** Do not approach the battery area with an open flame. Do not smoke when checking or testing batteries. The gases are highly explosive, so that the possibility of an explosion is always present.

Electricity through Magnetism Before discussing devices involving the use of electromagnetism, the relationship between magnetism and electricity must be explained.

THEORY OF MAGNETISM Each molecule in iron or in iron alloys has north and south magnetic poles. When not "magnetized," the poles of the molecules are oriented randomly within the material. But if an iron bar, for example, is struck by a magnet in the right way, placed in a strong magnetic field, or placed in an electromagnetic field, it can be magnetized by induction—that is, those actions cause the molecules within the bar to align themselves so that all the north poles point in the same direction, as do all the south poles. It is now known that the magnetic lines of force running from north to south poles are essentially electrical in nature, arising from the interaction between the spinning and orbiting electrons. The iron bar, then, is magnetized when these electrons are so aligned that their interacting forces combine rather than cancel each other out.

FACTS ABOUT MAGNETISM

1. A magnet has a north and a south pole, and the magnetic lines of force leave the north pole and enter the south pole. This can be proven by placing a com-

Table 4-3 BATTERIES RECOMMENDED FOR DIESEL ENGINE SERVICE

SAE	Group	Voltage, V	Reserve capacity, min	Cold-cranking amperes, A — At 0°F [−17.8°C]	Cold-cranking amperes, A — At −20°F [−28.9°C]	High discharge 15 s, A
6T3A	7D	6	430	900	650	450
20T4A	4D	12	285	640	450	450
20T6A	6D	12	350	800	555	450
20T8A	8D	12	430	900	650	450
Delco 1200	4D	12	130	475	375	230

pass near a magnetic bar. The compass needle will align itself so that the south pole of the compass needle points to the north pole of the bar.

2. The concentration of magnetic lines of force is heaviest at the pole ends and decreases in density midway between the poles since magnetic lines have "like" polarity and therefore repel each other.

3. Like poles (charges) repel each other, and unlike poles (charges) attract each other.

4. If you cut a piece from one end of a magnet, the result is two shorter magnets, each with its own north and south poles.

5. To date, there is no known insulation against magnetic lines of force. However, magnetic lines can be reduced by placing an iron core near one pole piece. This results in magnetic lines of force splitting in two separate parts, reducing the lines of force of the left-hand magnet.

6. Permanent magnets can be either naturally magnetic iron or alloys with atomic structures similar to iron, such as nickel-iron or aluminum-nickel-cobalt, that have their magnetic fields induced. Alloys with a loose molecular structure allow magnetic lines of force to pass through themselves more easily and are used only as temporary magnets because their magnetic strength does not last.

FACTS ABOUT ELECTROMAGNETISM

1. A straight wire which carries current creates a magnetic field around itself. The lines of force form concentric circles around the wire. The right-hand rule is used to determine the direction of electron flow as well as the north and south poles of the wire when the conventional current theory is applied. The left-hand rule is used when the electron theory is applied (see Fig. 4-13). The magnetic field of a current-carrying conductor behaves in the same manner as the magnetic field of a permanent magnet as long as current is flowing through it.

2. When the direction of current flow is changed, the direction of the lines of force also change.

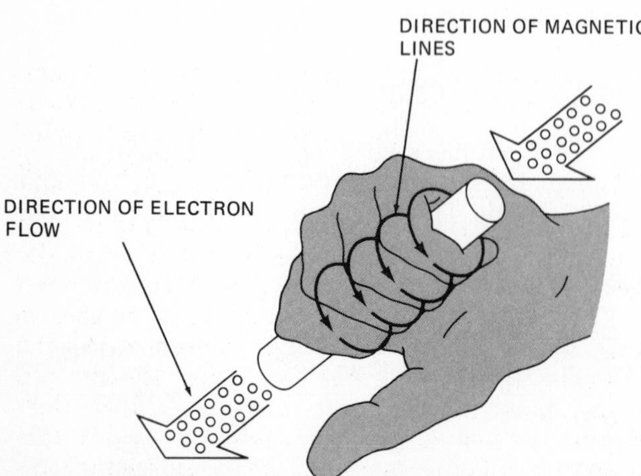

Fig. 4-13 Left-hand rule (electron theory). (*Delco-Remy Division of General Motors Corporation*)

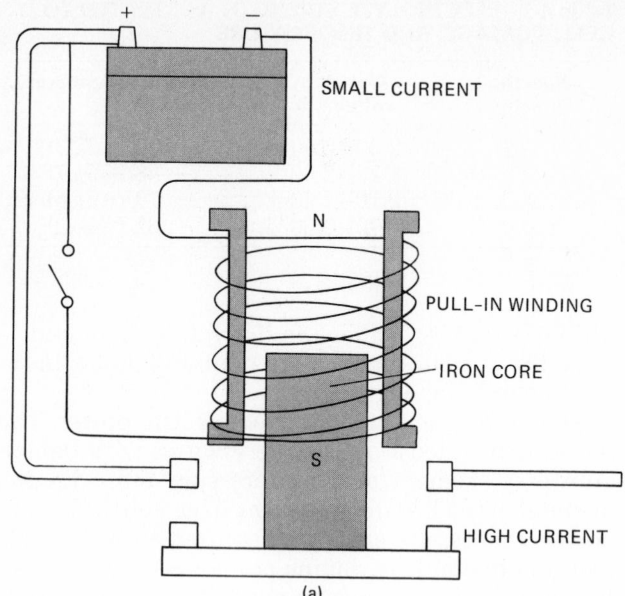

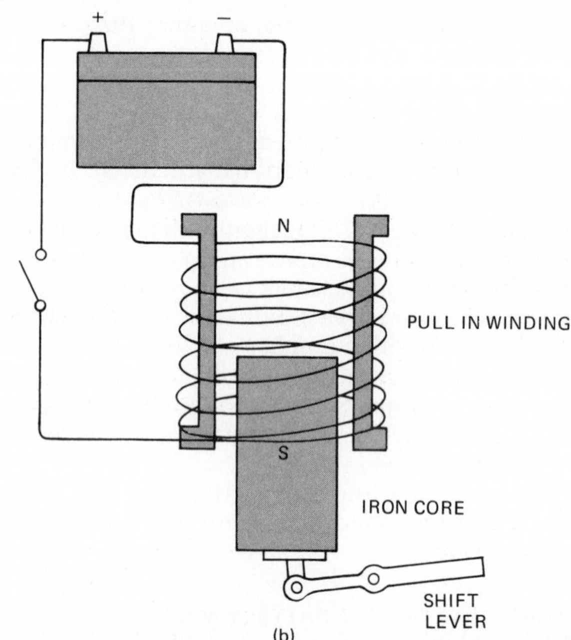

Fig. 4-14 Schematic view of a magnetic switch and circuit connection (*Delco-Remy Division of General Motors Corporation*) and (*b*) a solenoid and circuit connection.

3. When two conductors carrying equal currents flowing in opposite directions are placed side by side, the lines of force are also in opposite directions and are more concentrated between the conductors than on the outside of the two conductors. The current-carrying conductors move apart to relieve the imbalance in the magnetic field.

4. If there is an equal current flow in the same direction through two or more parallel conductors, each conductor alone creates a circular field of magnetic force and all the fields of force move in the same direction. The lines of force between the conductors move in the opposite direction. Because the strength of each field is the same, the total magnetic

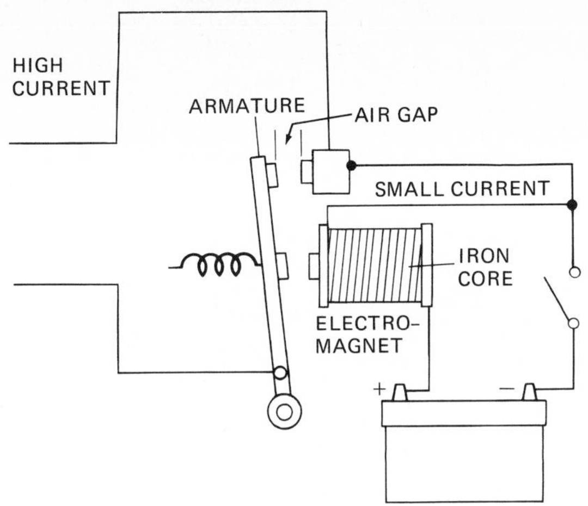

Fig. 4-15 Schematic view of a relay and circuit connection. (*Delco-Remy Division of General Motors Corporation*)

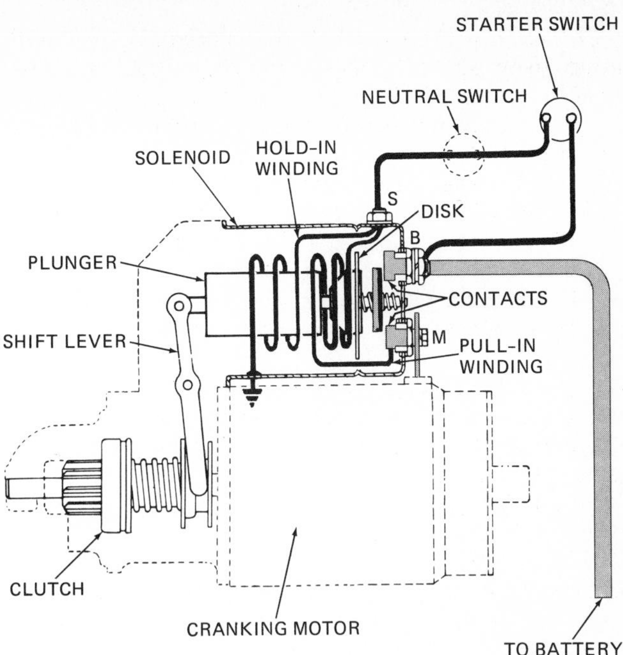

Fig. 4-16 Schematic view of a solenoid switch and circuit connection. (*Delco-Remy Division of General Motors Corporation*)

effect between the conductors is canceled. The conductors will tend to move toward each other, causing the magnetic effect to increase as the lines of force from each conductor join and surround each conductor.

5. An electromagnet is produced when a straight current-carrying conductor is formed into a single loop. All lines of force enter the inside of the loop on one side and leave on the other side.

6. When the number of loops (coils) is increased, the magnetic field of force increases. When using the right-hand rule to determine the polarity of the coil according to the conventional current theory, the lines of force travel from the south pole to the north pole.

7. Air is a very poor conductor of magnetic lines of force. The smaller the air gap between the armature and the magnet, the greater the number of lines of force.

8. When a soft iron core is inserted into the coil, it forms a true electromagnet (see Figs. 4-14 through 4-16). The magnetic field flux (lines of force) will increase as much as several hundred times, because the permeability of rough iron may be 2500 times that of air.

9. When the current flow is increased, say from 10 to 50 A, the magnetic lines of force also increase in the ratio of 1:5.

10. The same magnetic force will be produced by an electromagnet having 1000 turns of wire carrying 10 A as that of an electromagnet having 200 turns of wire carrying 50 A. The number of turns times the amperes equals 10,000 ampere-turns in either case.

ELECTROMAGNETIC INDUCTION In 1831 Michael Faraday proved that voltage (electromotive force or emf) is induced in a conductor when the conductor is moved between the poles of a magnet or when the magnet is moved over the conductor. The electromotive force obtained in this way is said to be an *induced emf* and the process is called *electromagnetic induction.* He also proved that the conductor, when moved from left to right or from right to left through a magnetic field whose poles maintain their same positions, changes its induced emf polarity, that the polarity of the induced voltage changes when the polarity of the magnetic field changes but the current flow in the conductor maintains its direction. **NOTE** When the conductor moves *across* the magnetic field or the magnetic field moves over the conductor, voltage is induced. (However, it must have a complete electric circuit or there is no current flow.) On the other hand, when the conductor is moved *parallel* to the magnetic lines of force no voltage is induced.

GENERATORS A generator is a mechanical device involving the use of magnets that converts mechanical energy supplied by the engine into electric energy. A motor vehicle's generator supplies the batteries and electric systems of motor vehicles with a direct current.

Alternating electromagnetic induction A simple, one-loop generator is shown in Fig. 4-17. When the magnet rotates, the south and the north poles approach the conductor loop, and voltage is induced. Voltage gradually increases to its maximum, which is reached when the south pole is under the conductor and the north pole is over it. With the magnet rotating as shown in Fig. 4-17, the direction of the induced voltage, which causes a current to flow, is determined by the right-hand rule. As the poles move away from the conductor, the induced voltage decreases, and current ceases to flow when they reach the middle of the conductor loop. At this point, the poles again approach the conductor loop in a reverse polarity. The induced voltage reverses and gradually rises to its maximum when the north

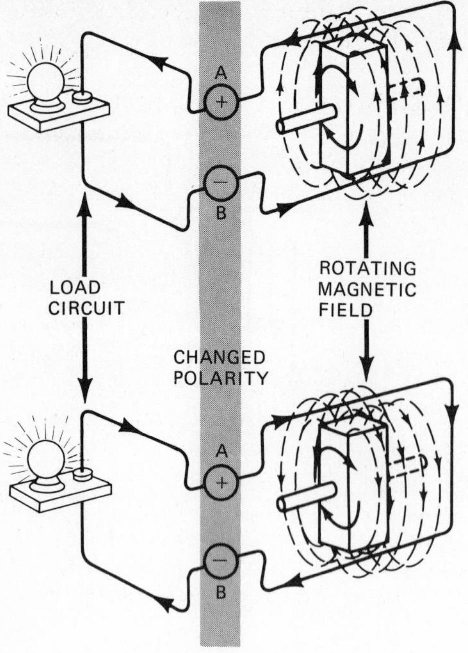

Fig. 4-17 Alternating electromagnetic induction. (*Delco-Remy Division of General Motors Corporation*)

pole is under the conductor loop and the south pole is over it (Fig. 4-18). Further rotation decreases the induced voltage to zero when the poles return to the middle of the conductor loop. Polarity again reverses, and the cycle is repeated.

The induced voltage (emf) which periodically reverses its polarity (direction) is known as *alternating electromotive force*, and the resulting current flow is called *alternating current*.

Phase As the alternator rotor rotates 360°, an alternating voltage is induced in each stator winding. This causes alternating current to flow in each stator winding. The alternating current flow of each stator winding is called a *phase*. Each phase winding is placed in the stator frame electrically 120° apart from the others. The three phase windings are

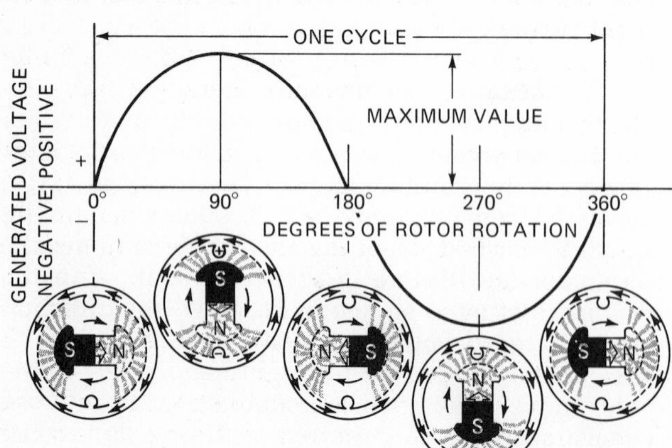

Fig. 4-18 Generated voltage during one cycle (one revolution of the rotor). (*Delco-Remy Division of General Motors Corporation*)

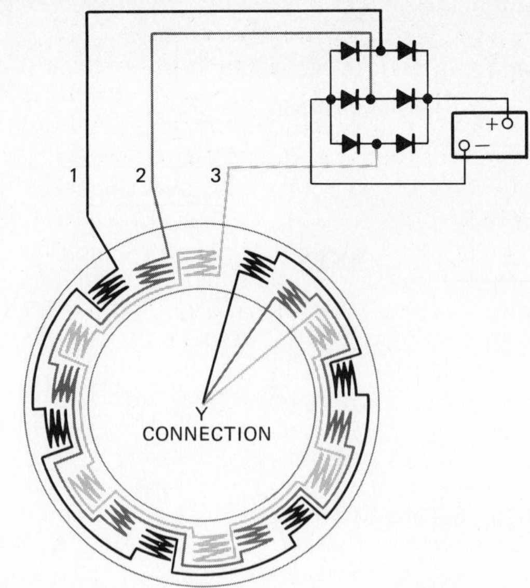

Fig. 4-19 Schematic view of a three-phase stator and diode assembly. (*Delco-Remy Division of General Motors Corporation*)

connected to each other by a Y or delta connection. Each winding is connected to one negative and one positive diode (Figs. 4-19 and 4-20).

Cycle and frequencies When the alternator rotor has rotated 360° (one revolution), it has completed one cycle and has produced one positive and one negative sine wave. One half-cycle (one sine wave) is called an *alternation*. The number of cycles generated per second is called the *frequency*.

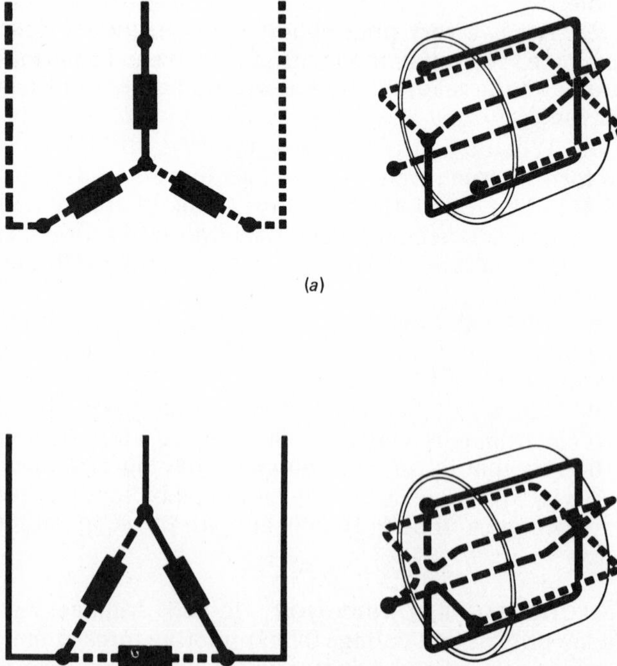

Fig. 4-20 (*a*) Three-phase Y connection. (*b*) Three-phase delta connection. (*Delco-Remy Division of General Motors Corporation*)

Factors affecting output voltage The output voltage of a generator will increase when the speed of the rotor is increased, when the strength of the magnetic field is increased, or when the number of turns of wire in the stator winding are increased.

AC GENERATORS Today's ac generators (called *alternators*) convert alternating current to direct current through rectification, whereas earlier (dc) generators converted alternating current to direct current through brush commutation. The ac generator has replaced the dc generator because (1) it can produce a high current at lower engine speed, (2) it can rotate in either direction, (3) it can rotate safely, without destruction, at high speed, (4) its output voltage and current can be controlled easily, and (5) it has a long service life.

Inductive reactance AC generators are electrically designed so that the maximum current output will not exceed the output rating of the generator. For example, a 12-V 60-A generator will produce approximately 66 A with a maximum voltage of about 19 V. As current flow increases in the stator windings, the magnetic lines of force cut across the adjacent winding. The direction in which the lines of force cut the adjacent conductor induces a voltage opposite to that of the applied voltage, limiting the current flow in the stator winding. That inductive opposition to current flow is called *inductive reactance*.

SOLENOIDS A solenoid is an electromagnet with one or two coil windings wound around an iron tube which also serves as the bushing of the movable iron core (Fig. 4-14*b*). Its purpose is to perform work. When current is passed through the coil windings, the iron core is pulled in or pushed out. This movement can be made to shift a transmission or a cranking-motor drive-in mesh, to shut off the fuel, air, or oil supply, or to move the fuel rack to the shutoff position.

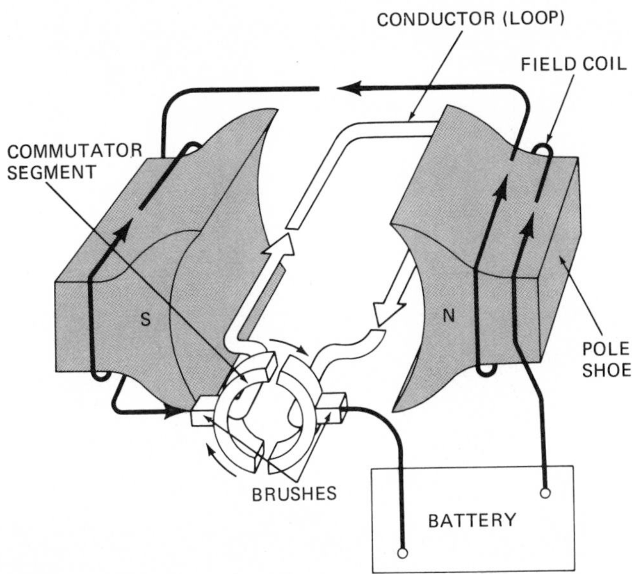

Fig. 4-21 One-loop cranking motor.

MAGNETIC SWITCHES The purpose of a magnetic switch is to open and close an electric circuit through electromagnetic action. It is used on a starting circuit having a cranking motor with an inertia drive. (See Fig. 4-14*a*.)

RELAYS The purpose of a relay is to control, through a small current flow, the flow of a larger current (Fig. 4-15). The small current is controlled by a toggle, push-button, or key switch which closes the electric circuit of the coil winding. The electromagnet pulls the armature toward its core, closes a set of contact points, and thereby closes the electric circuit with the higher current flow. Relays are used to open and close motor circuits, to open and close the generator field circuit, or to act as safety switches—for example, to prevent the cranking-motor circuit from being energized when the engine is running.

SOLENOID SWITCHES The purpose of a solenoid switch is to do work and to close or open an electric circuit. It combines features of the solenoid and the magnetic switch. A solenoid switch is used on cranking motors which employ an overrunning clutch cranking-motor drive. It has two coil windings wound over a hollow cylinder and paired off at the S (starter) terminal (Fig. 4-16). The coil winding with the smaller gauge wire has its own ground and is called the *hold-in winding*. The *pull-in winding* (of heavier gauge copper wire) is connected to the cranking-motor terminal and is in series with the fuel oil, armature, and ground brushes. The iron core plunger is connected at one end to the shift lever and at the other to a spring-loaded copper disk. Two insulated heavy-contact terminals are fastened to the end of the solenoid-switch housing. The terminal marked "battery" is connected to the battery, and the terminal marked "cranking motor" is connected to the cranking motor.

CRANKING MOTOR The operating principle of a cranking motor (starter) involves the effect of a current-carrying conductor in a magnetic field. A cranking motor receives direct current from the battery and converts it to mechanical energy (rotating motion).

The conductor loops are placed in a magnetic field. When the current flows in the conductor, the lines of force are distorted. A strong field is produced on one side of the conductor and a weaker field on the other. The conductor loop rotates in a clockwise direction (Fig. 4-21) and the rotation will stop when the loop reaches the center position between the north and south poles.

To make a continuous rotation possible, the loop ends are connected to a pair of sliding contacts (the commutator segments). A set of brushes is placed in a fixed position on the commutator to connect the battery with the armature loop. When the circuit is closed, the loop turns in a clockwise rotation and coasts through the static neutral point (commutation). At the same time, the brushes slide onto the other commutator segments, thereby changing the direction of current flow in the loop, resulting in continuous rotation.

Cranking-motor circuits To increase the torque or the speed of a cranking motor, the field coil windings are connected in combinations of series, series-parallel, or parallel circuits. Torque can also be increased by adding more field coils or by increasing the ampere-turns of the field coil.

A straight series circuit is used when high top speed is required. One or two shunt coils limit the top speed to prevent the armature loops from flying out of their grooves.

When the armature is rotating, the cranking motor generates voltage (emf) that cannot be shut off and, as the armature speed increases, the generated voltage increases. The induced voltage, which opposes the battery voltage, is called *counterelectromotive force* (cemf). It is because of the cemf that a cranking motor has a larger current flow when starting than when running at full speed.

Wires and terminals The electric system is probably the most common problem area of all automotive or diesel equipment components or systems. Often the problem results from loose or corroded terminals or incorrectly selected terminals. Sometimes it is simply that the terminals are not properly fastened to the wire (conductor).

Conductor size selection The conductor size (wire number) used to connect the various electric components is governed by the maximum allowable circuit resistance (voltage drop).

The maximum allowable circuit resistance (including connections and switches) must not exceed the values in Table 4-4.

Subtract the following from the total circuit resistance recommended before determining wire sizes for a given length of battery to cranking motor cable.

- Each connection = 0.00001 Ω
- Each contact = 0.0002 Ω

NOTE Make certain when you fasten the battery cable end to the cable that the resistance of each connection is not higher than 0.00001 Ω and that each contact resistance in the circuit is not higher than 0.0002 Ω.

Table 4-4 MAXIMUM ALLOWABLE VOLTAGE DROP AND CIRCUIT RESISTANCE FOR A 12-, 24-, AND 32-V CRANKING-MOTOR CIRCUIT

Circuit voltage, V	Maximum voltage drop, V/100 A	Maximum resistance, Ω
12	0.12	0.0012
12 (High-output starting motor)	0.075	0.00075
24—32	0.2	0.002

Table 4-5 BATTERY-TO-ALTERNATOR WIRE SIZES

12-V system		24- to 32-V system	
Amperes (max)	AWG size*	Amperes (max)	AWG size
53	8	25	14
85	6	40	12
125	4	60	10
205	2	100	8

*AWG = American Wire Gauge.

Cranking-motor circuit wiring and cables The cranking-motor circuit supplies the high current to the motor. The selection chart shown in Fig. 4-22 gives the resistance in ohms of various size battery cables, according to their length. To stay within the maximum allowable voltage drop of the cranking-motor control circuit, that is, the resistance between the battery and the solenoid switch, resistance should not exceed 0.007 Ω for a 12-V starting circuit, or 0.030 Ω for a 24-V starting circuit. The selection chart in Fig. 4-22 shows the wire size required to maintain resistance within these values.

Battery-to-alternator circuits When the total wire length from the battery to the alternator does not exceed 16 ft [4.88 m], the recommended wire sizes are as shown in Table 4-5.

Accessory circuit resistance The wire sizes for all accessory feed circuits should be Nos. 12 or 14 if the total length does not exceed 15 ft [4.62 m]. Most other control circuits should use No. 14 wire, the two exceptions being the glow-plug circuit and insulated ground circuits for which, when they are used, a No. 10 wire is recommended.

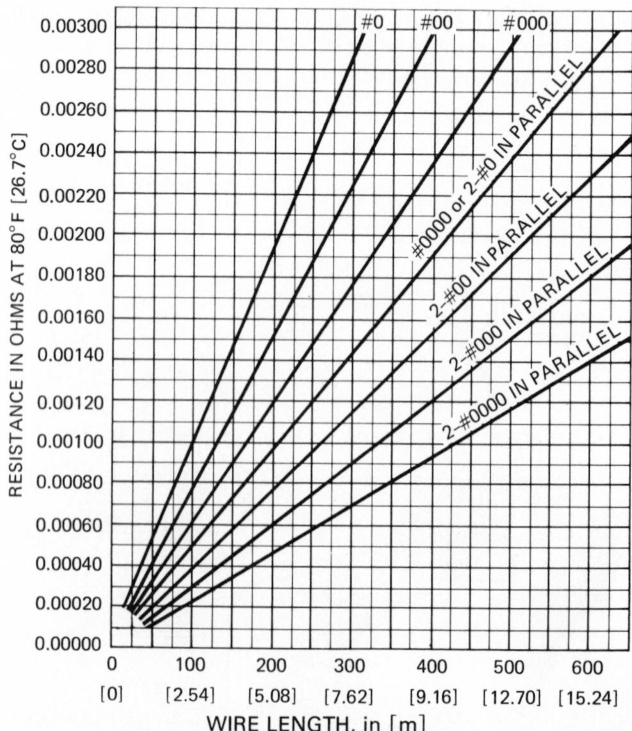

Fig. 4-22 Battery-cable selection chart. (*Delco-Remy Division of General Motors Corporation*)

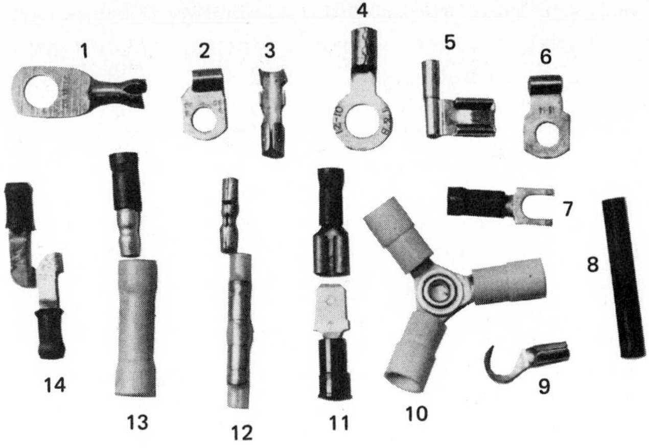

1. Ring type
2. Roll type
3. Female snap-on
4. Lug type
5. Female slide connector
6. Roll type
7. Slotted-flange bay type
8. Insulator
9. Slotted-hook type
10. Three-way connector
11. Male and female slide connector
12. Male and female plug connector (bullet connector)
13. Male and female plug connector (bullet connector)
14. Knife disconnector

Fig. 4-23 Wire terminal ends.

Terminal ends Some terminal ends (wire ends) are shown in Fig. 4-23. Before selecting a terminal end, you must decide where crimping or soldering is to be used. Crimped terminal fastenings are acceptable for some applications, while others require the security of solder. **NOTE** A soldered terminal is more effective than a crimped fastening because the latter may connect only three-quarters of the strands with the terminal. This will reduce the current flow and may cause overheating because of the higher resistance.

Preliminaries to fastening terminal ends Before you crimp or solder the terminal end to the wire, you must remove part of the insulation. Use a wire stripper (to avoid cutting conductor strands) and cut and remove an amount of insulation equal to the length of the terminal barrel.

Fastening through crimping To fasten a terminal end through crimping, first insert the wire into the terminal barrel until it bottoms or is flush with the barrel end. In this position, secure the wire by placing the crimping tool over the barrel (make certain to use the correct crimping opening) and squeeze the barrel by forcing the handles together.

NOTE Do not use a pair of pliers, a side cutter, or a vise to crimp the terminal barrel because they will not produce an adequate connection.

Fastening through soldering When you use solder, insert the stripped wire into the terminal barrel. Apply a small amount of soldering paste to the open end of the barrel and hold the soldering iron and the wire resin solder in contact with the edge of the barrel. Allow sufficient melted solder to flow into the barrel, then remove the soldering iron from the terminal to allow the solder to bond with the barrel and wire. Clean the soldered connection and push the insulation onto the barrel.

When you solder a lip-type terminal to a wire, position the wire so that the insulation is flush with the holding tang, then roll the tang around the insulation. Use a crimping tool to fasten the wire to the terminal. Bend the lips over onto the wire. Hold the soldering iron on the bent lips and hold the wire resin solder in contact with the wire between the bent lips and tang. When the soldering iron reaches a high enough temperature, the solder will melt and draw toward the lips, bonding the wire to the terminal.

Replacing battery terminals Figure 4-24 illustrates five popular battery terminals. Regardless of which terminal is selected as the replacement for the worn one, it must be soldered to the battery cable.

When you replace a battery terminal, cut the cable as closely as possible to the worn terminal. Use a 32-tooth hacksaw blade to ensure that the cable maintains its roundness. Strip away an amount of insulation exactly equal to the length of the terminal barrel. Hold the new battery terminal (with the barrel up) in a vise. With an acetylene or propane torch,

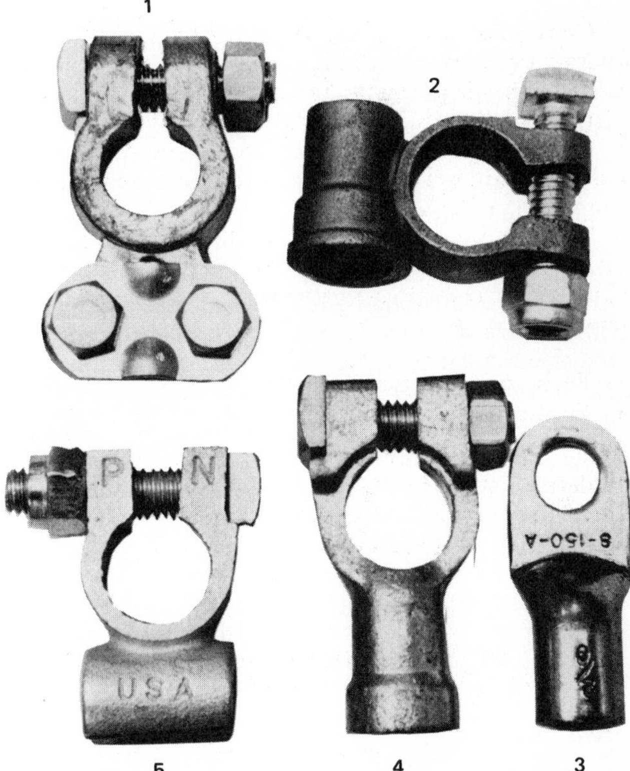

1. Clamp type
2. Close-barrel type (90°)
3. Lug-type close barrel
4. Straight close barrel
5. Flat type

Fig. 4-24 Battery cable terminals.

apply low heat to both the cable end and terminal. Tin the cable end by holding the resin solder against the copper wire until all strands are saturated with the resin. Apply soldering paste to the inside of the barrel and let the solder flow into it. Place the cable end over the terminal opening. Keep applying low heat to the terminal and the cable end until the cable slides into the opening. Solder may run out of the opening at this point; however, continue to apply low heat to ensure a good bond. When all the solder at the edge of the opening has been drawn into the barrel, you can be sure that the joint between the barrel and cable end has been well connected. However, when there is no solder on the edge of the barrel more solder should be applied to the terminals to ensure joint effectiveness. After removing the torch, hold the cable steady until the solder is set. Clean the terminal and tape over part of the barrel and cable insulation to prevent corrosion.

Pointers for connecting wires Keep in mind the following:

1. When you connect a terminal to a component, make certain that the contact surfaces are clean and not pitted.
2. If possible, use an internal-external lock washer. If this is not available, place a plain washer below a plain lock washer.
3. Do not allow the terminal to touch the component.
4. Do not allow the terminal stud bolt (post) to turn as you tighten the nut.
5. When you have a slide or bullet connector, tape the unit to prevent its separation.
6. Be sure the terminal screw is not too long because this may ground out the terminal.
7. Return the wire to the same position in which it was originally routed and clamped.
8. When you install an additional circuit, use the existing wire or cable route, clamps, and grommets.
9. If you are forced to reroute the cable in a new direction, use rubber grommets or short pieces of rubber hose to prevent the wire from being cut by the sheet metal or by the sharp corners of the frame.
10. Secure the wire in enough places so that it does not hang loose.

Electric Circuits An electric circuit is the entire path traversed by an electric current. It includes the voltage (power) source, one or more resistance units (field coil, light bulb, etc.), the flow control device (switch), and the conductors (wires) which form the path for the current. But before discussing types of circuits, something must be said about Ohm's law.

OHM'S LAW Ohm's law states that the intensity of the electric current in a circuit is proportional to the voltage (emf) and inversely proportional to the resistance. In other words, the current can be changed by changing the voltage or by changing the resistance in the circuit. Note that current has no effect on resistance or voltage, but each has an effect on current.

If you know two of the three factors [I (amperes), V (volts), or R (resistance)], you can apply Ohm's law to find the third: $V = I \times R$, $I = V/R$, $R = V/I$.

SERIES CIRCUIT Electric circuits are classified according to the manner in which the electric components are inserted into the circuit. In a series circuit, the current has only one path through which it can flow. Therefore, the total circuit resistance is equal to the sum of all individual resistances.

Figure 4-25 illustrates a 12-V series circuit with four resistors. The total resistance for this circuit is 2 Ω + 5 Ω + 4 Ω + 1 Ω = 12 Ω. The current, calculated according to Ohm's law, is $I = V/R = 12/12 = 1$ A.

When an ammeter is connected into the circuit at any place and it shows a reading lower than 1 A, the lower reading may be due to additional resistance in the circuit (in the form of a loose or poor connection) either on the live or ground side of the circuit, or it may be the result of one or more resistors yielding higher resistance due to a damaged coil. When the current is higher than 1 A, one or more resistors may have short-circuited or grounded. An ohmmeter can be used to detect the components having the higher or the lower resistance, but before doing so you must remove the battery connection.

A more expedient way of identifying a component with a resistance lower or higher than normal is to use a voltmeter. This method is possible because voltage drops when the current has passed through the resistor. When using the voltmeter method you must know the circuit voltage and the value of each resistor in order to calculate the current flow. Take as an example Fig. 4-25, where the voltage is 12 V, the values of the resistors are 2, 5, 4, and 1 Ω, therefore the current flow is 1 A.

To calculate the voltage drop across the resistor R1, multiply the amperes by the resistor value: $1 \times R = 1 \times 2 = 2$-V drop. Subtracting 2 V from 12 V equals 10 V. Therefore, when the voltmeter is connected to point B and to ground, it should read 10 V. When it is connected to points A and B in parallel with resistor R1, it should read 2 V.

When the voltmeter is connected to point C and to ground, it should read 5 V because the resistor R2 has a 5-Ω resistance ($I \times R = 1 \times 5 = 5$ V). When there are 10 V at point B and the voltage drop is equal to 5 V, to find the voltage at point C, you must subtract: 10 V − 5 V = 5 V. When the voltmeter is connected to points C and D, it should read 4 V because the resistor R3 has a 4-Ω resistance ($I \times R$

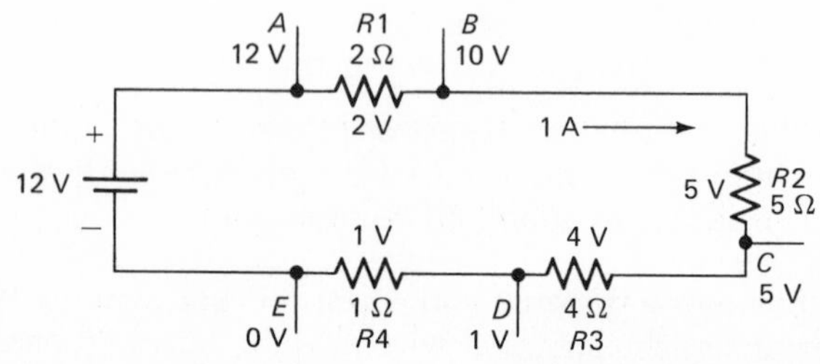

Fig. 4-25 Series current. (*Delco-Remy Division of General Motors Corporation*)

= 1 × 4 = 4 V). To find the voltage at point D, subtract: 5 V − 4 V = 1 V. When the voltmeter is connected to point E and to ground, the voltmeter should read 0 V. When connected to points D and E, it should read 1 V; but after connecting the voltmeter from A to E, it should read 12 V.

PARALLEL CIRCUIT In a parallel circuit, the current has as many paths as there are resistors in parallel. These paths are sometimes called *branch circuits* (Fig. 4-26). The sum of the branch circuits' current is equal to the total current flow in the circuit. Current flow through each branch will differ as the resistance differs. The total current flow in Fig. 4-26 should be 12 A:

$$I = \frac{V}{R} = \frac{12}{6} = 2\ \text{A} \quad \text{in branch one}$$
$$+$$
$$I = \frac{V}{R} = \frac{12}{3} = 4\ \text{A} \quad \text{in branch two}$$
$$+$$
$$I = \frac{V}{R} = \frac{12}{4} = 3\ \text{A} \quad \text{in branch three}$$
$$+$$
$$I = \frac{V}{R} = \frac{12}{4} = 3\ \text{A} \quad \text{in branch four}$$

Another method that can be used to find the total current is to calculate the total resistance R_T of the parallel circuit using the following formula. For Fig. 4-26:

$$R_T = \frac{1}{R1} + \frac{1}{R2} + \frac{1}{R3} + \frac{1}{R4}$$
$$= \frac{1}{6} + \frac{1}{3} + \frac{1}{4} + \frac{1}{4} = 1\ \Omega$$
$$= 0.17 + 0.33 + 0.25 + 0.25 = 1\ \Omega$$

Therefore the total current flow is $I = 12/1 = 12$ A.

To locate the cause of high or low current flow in the parallel circuit shown in Fig. 4-26, you would connect a voltmeter successively to points A and B, points A and C, points A and D, and points A and E. A battery voltage of 12 V would occur each time because the voltage drop across each resistor would be the same. However, if the voltage in any instance were lower, it would be because of the additional resistance between points B and E.

To locate the cause of the additional resistance, connect the voltmeter to point B and to the battery ground terminal, take a reading, and then remove it from B and connect it successively to points C, D,

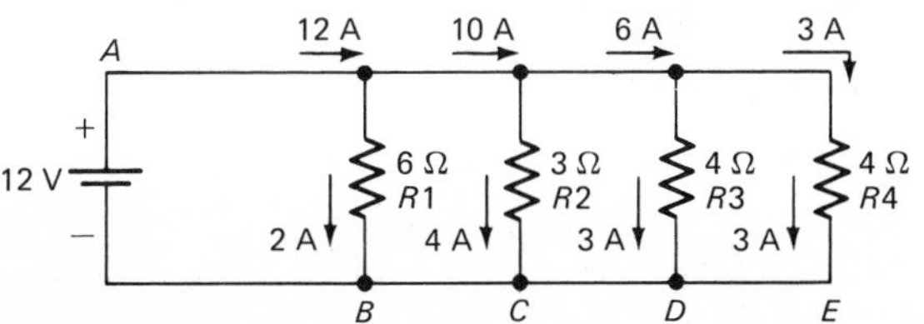

Fig. 4-26 Parallel circuit. (*Delco-Remy Division of General Motors Corporation*)

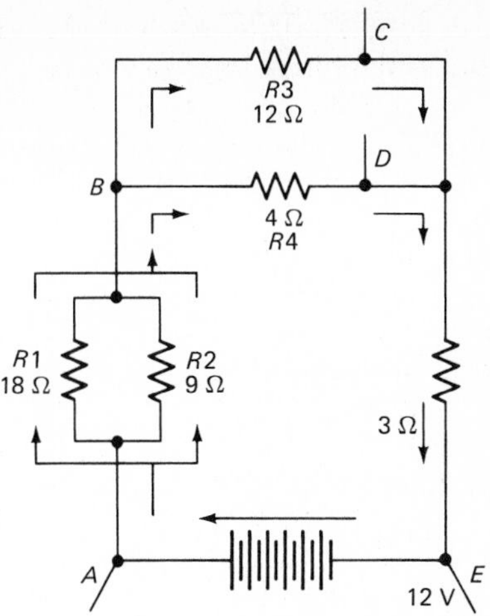

Fig. 4-27 Series–parallel circuit. (*Delco-Remy Division of General Motors Corporation*)

and E. If a voltage reading occurs at any of these four points, loose or poor connections or partly damaged conductors can probably be found there.

SERIES-PARALLEL CIRCUIT A series-parallel circuit is made up of one major path and two or more branches through which current flows (Fig. 4-27). The total current flow of the circuit shown in Fig. 4-27 can also be found from Ohm's law: $I = V/R = 12/12 = 1$ A.

You should notice that the 18- and 9-Ω resistors and the 12- and 4-Ω resistors are in parallel and that the 3-Ω resistor is in series with them. To arrive at the total circuit resistance, the two parallel resistors must be reduced to series resistance, using the following formulas:

$$R_{eq1} = \frac{R1 \times R2}{R1 + R2} = \frac{18 \times 9}{18 + 9} = \frac{162}{27} = 6\ \Omega$$
$$R_{eq2} = \frac{R3 \times R4}{R3 + R4} = \frac{12 \times 4}{12 + 4} = \frac{48}{16} = 3\ \Omega$$
$$R_T = R_{eq1} + R_{eq2} + R5 = 6 + 3 + 3 = 12\ \Omega$$
$$I_T = \frac{V}{R_T} = \frac{12}{12} = 1\ \text{A}$$

where R_{eq1} = equivalent resistance of R1 and R2
R_{eq2} = equivalent resistance of R3 and R4
R_T = total resistance
I_T = total current, A
V = voltage, V

When the ammeter indicates that the current flow in this circuit is more or less than 1 A, use a voltmeter to measure the voltage drop and thereby locate the point of higher or lower resistance.

CAPACITORS *Capacitors,* also called *condensers,* may be used to store electricity and to equalize system voltage which varies when a transistor is switched on or off. They are also used to assist in switching a transistor on and off and to prevent excessive heat from developing.

A capacitor, when placed in a circuit as shown in

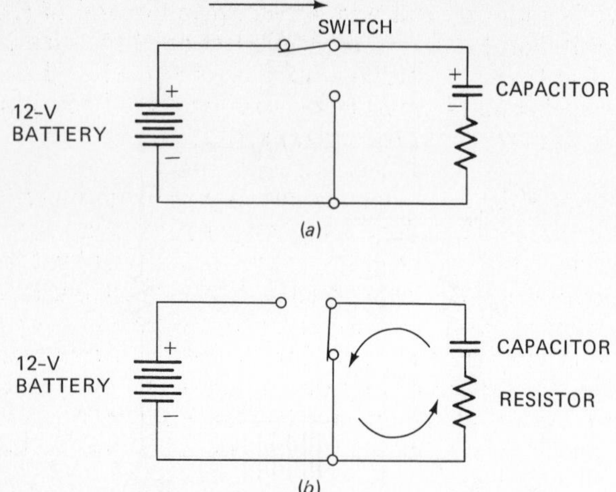

Fig. 4-28 Switching action and current flow of a capacitor when: (*a*) charging, and (*b*) discharging. (*Delco-Remy Division of General Motors Corporation*)

Fig. 4-28*a*, will receive a charge when the switch is closed. The capacitor voltage will increase from zero to battery voltage, at which time the current flow stops. When the switch position is reversed (see Fig. 4-28*b*) the capacitor will discharge until all stored energy is dissipated by the resistor.

ELECTRIC COMPONENT AND SYSTEM TESTING

All motor vehicles and motorized equipment require an electric system to become operative, even if it consists of only one individual (starting) circuit. Some motor vehicles and motorized equipment require as many as 20 individual circuits.

To facilitate servicing and testing of the individual circuits and components in order to determine the cause of electric failure, wire diagrams are provided in each service manual. The manuals also include detailed layouts of individual circuits or parts of a circuit and their components, as well as keys to the color codes of the wires. Consequently, it is relatively easy to trace component connections and therefore determine interconnections of circuits within the entire system.

The basic wire color code recommended by the SAE is

- Black—for hot wire
- White—for ground wire
- Brown—for license and tail light circuit
- Yellow—for stop light and left-hand turn signal light
- Green—for stop light and right-hand turn signal light
- Blue—for auxiliary circuits

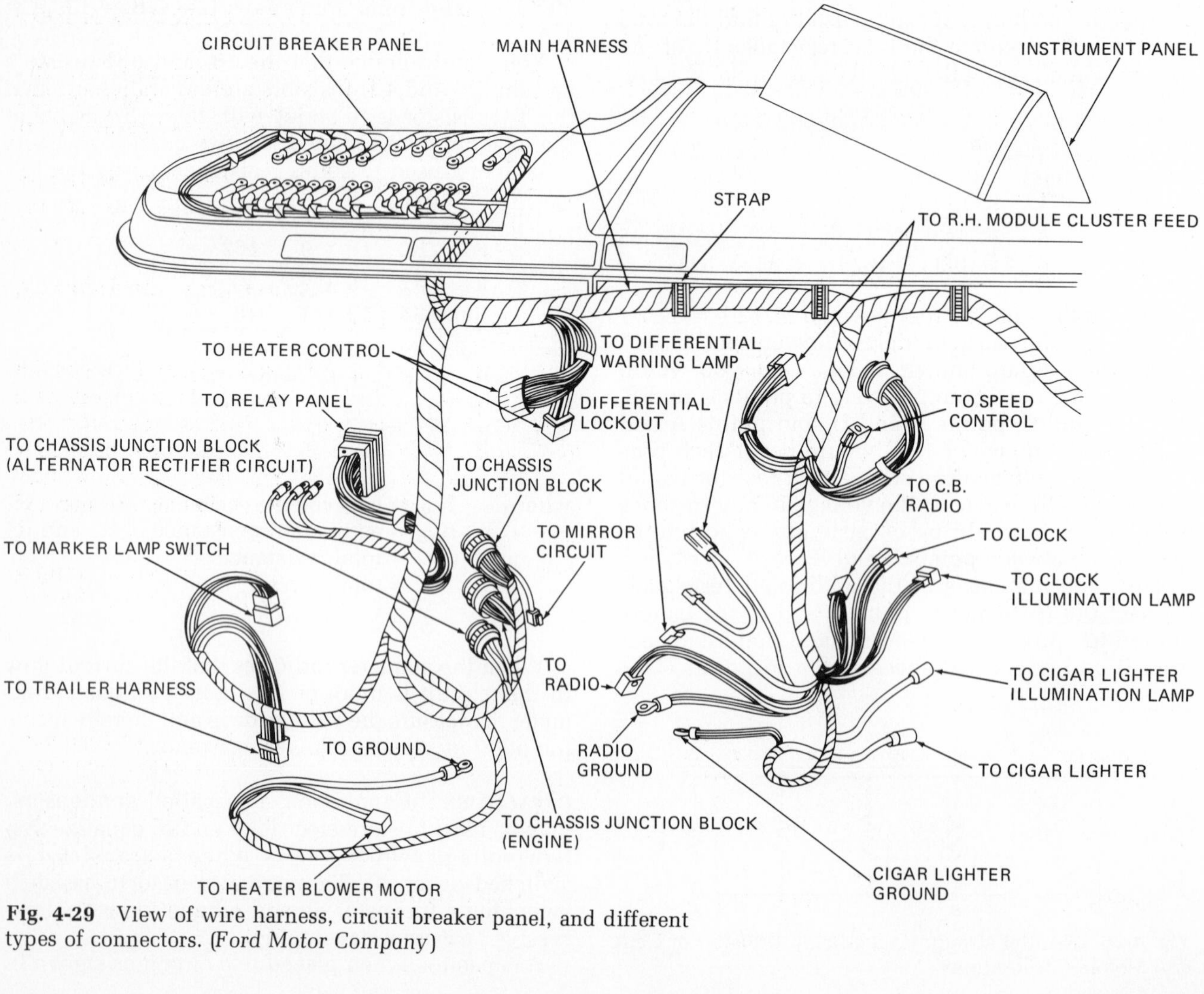

Fig. 4-29 View of wire harness, circuit breaker panel, and different types of connectors. (*Ford Motor Company*)

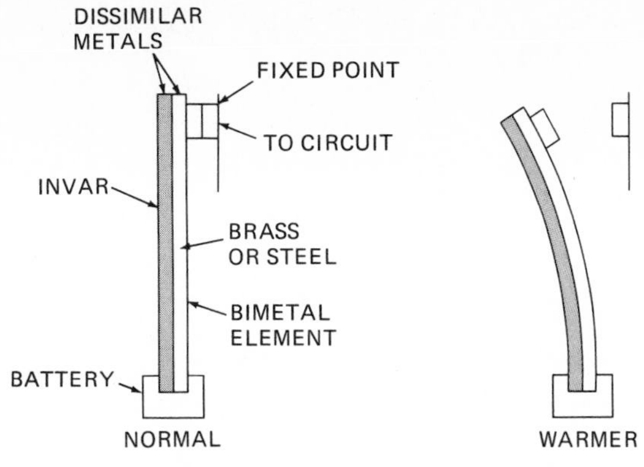

Fig. 4-30 Principle of a circuit breaker.

However, because of the increased number of auxiliary circuits in the electric systems of newer vehicles, additional wire colors are used and/or coded with markings such as stripes, or in the case of conductors' insulation with solid or interrupted lines.

Some wires of individual circuits are grouped and taped together and may be further encased in a convoluted conduit to form a wire harness. The connections between the dashboard, engine, body, and lighting circuits are made through multiplug and receptacle connectors (Fig. 4-29). Each harness wire set or individual wire is held securely in place and out of harm's way by a clip or some such device to prevent any damage to the conductor it encases.

The individual circuits are protected against overload through fuses, circuit breakers, or fusible links.

A *fuse* consists of a fine wire or wire strip placed inside a glass tube. The fuse is placed in series with the circuit it is intended to protect and when the circuit becomes overloaded the wire or strip melts, thereby interrupting the current flow.

NOTE Fuses are rated in amperes and not all circuits have the same current flow. It is therefore essential to replace a blown-out fuse with one of the same rating.

A *circuit breaker* uses a bimetallic strip to open and close the circuit. Under normal temperature, the bimetallic strip is straight and the point-set is closed. When the circuit is overloaded, though, the strip increases in temperature because of the higher current flow and curls (warps), thereby separating the point and opening the circuit (Fig. 4-30).

A fusible link is a wire attached to the end of the circuit conductor. The diameter of this wire is smaller than the diameter of the circuit wire. If the circuit becomes overloaded, the fusible link wire melts, interrupting the current flow.

Electric Failures No matter how well an electric system is built or how well an electric component (resistor unit) is designed, it will not last or operate indefinitely. To diagnose circuit or component failure you must (1) be able to trace the circuit wiring and understand the operation of the circuit components, (2) follow a definite step-by-step test procedure, (3) know how to use the test equipment, and (4) know how to interpret the data provided by the test equipment.

There are four types of electric failure that could reduce efficiency of the electric components or cause a conductor to become ineffective: a short circuit, an open circuit, a grounded circuit, and a circuit having high resistance.

The term "short circuit" indicates that part of the circuit resistance is removed (Fig. 4-31*b*). It can be caused by one coil winding touching the adjacent winding or when one live conductor touches another live conductor.

The term "open circuit" indicates that the circuit is broken either by the conductor or by the resistor unit (Fig. 4-31*a*). This term also is used when the conductor is removed from the terminal or is loose and without conductivity.

The term "grounded circuit" indicates that the circuit is partly isolated because the conductor has found another ground (either accidentally or through design) (Fig. 4-31*c*).

"High resistance" refers to the resultant added resistance of a conductor with a poor, loose, or corroded connection.

Test Instruments You will be using the following to test electric failures:

TEST LIGHT A test light is used to quickly check the continuity of a circuit. It may be in the form of a light bulb with two wires attached that uses the motor vehicle batteries as its power source, or it may have a battery of its own. A test light cannot be used to detect a short circuit, high resistance, or ground circuit resistance.

NOTE A test light having its own power supply unit must be connected only in parallel to the cir-

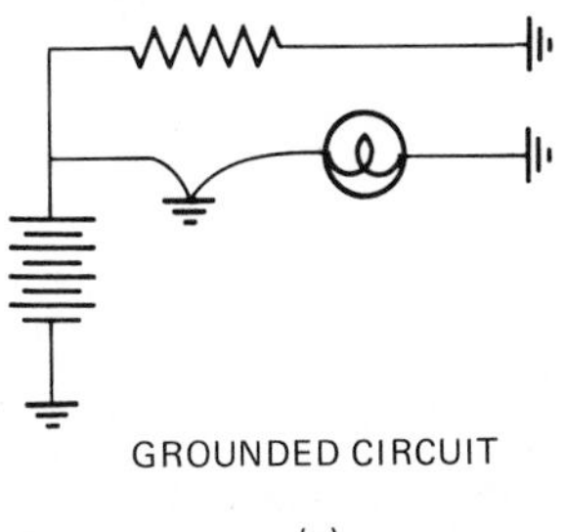

Fig. 4-31 Circuit failure: (*a*) Open circuit—no current flow. (*b*) Short circuit—increased current flow. (*c*) Grounded circuit—no current flow through right resistor. (*GMC Truck and Coach Division*)

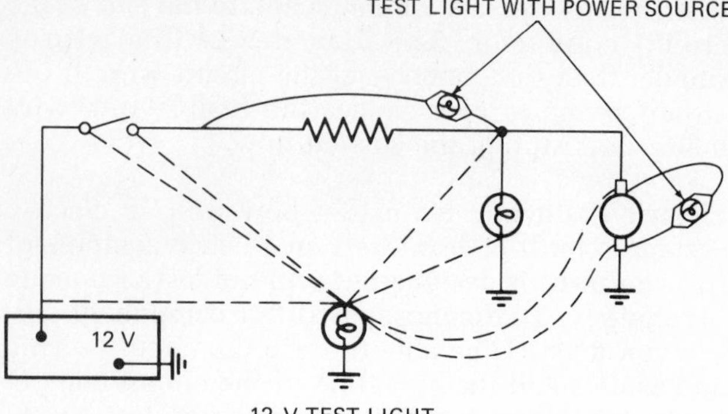

Fig. 4-32 Test light connection to measure continuity. *(GMC Truck and Coach Division)*

cuit, whereas a test light without one can also be placed in series with the circuit (Fig. 4-32).

COMPASS AND INDUCTION AMMETER These instruments are valuable tools to help quickly locate a short or grounded circuit. The usefulness of both is the result of their sensitivity to the magnetic field created by every current-carrying conductor. When you hold a compass or the induction ammeter to a wire which carries a current, the needle will point to the wire as long as current flows; when the current flow is interrupted, however, the ammeter needle moves to zero while the compass needle faces toward the magnetic north.

VOLTMETER A voltmeter is by far the most important of the electric system test instruments because it measures the electric pressure (voltage) and voltage drop. To measure voltage and/or voltage differential (voltage drop), that is, the voltage between two points of a circuit, the voltmeter must always be connected in parallel (across the circuit) because of the higher meter resistance (Fig. 4-33). To be of maximum use, it should have more than one scale and the lowest scale should be calibrated in tenths of a volt.

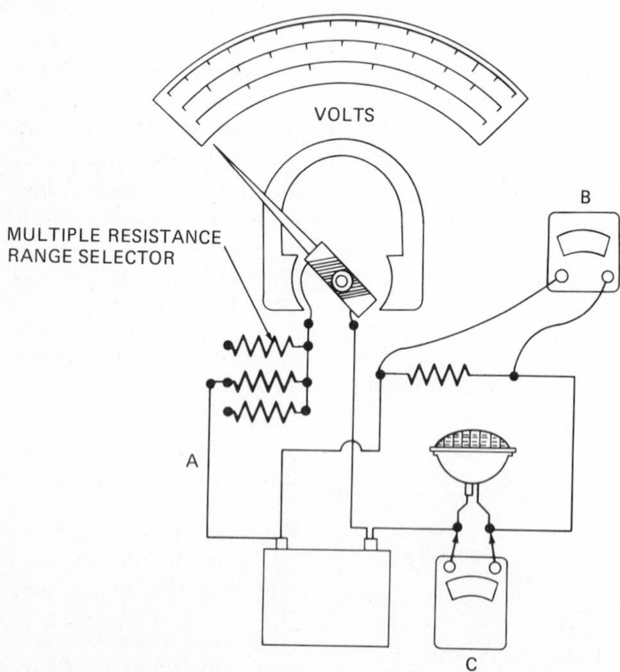

Fig. 4-33 Basic construction of a voltmeter and connections: (*a*) Measuring battery voltage. (*b*), (*c*) Voltage drop. *(GMC Truck and Coach Division)*

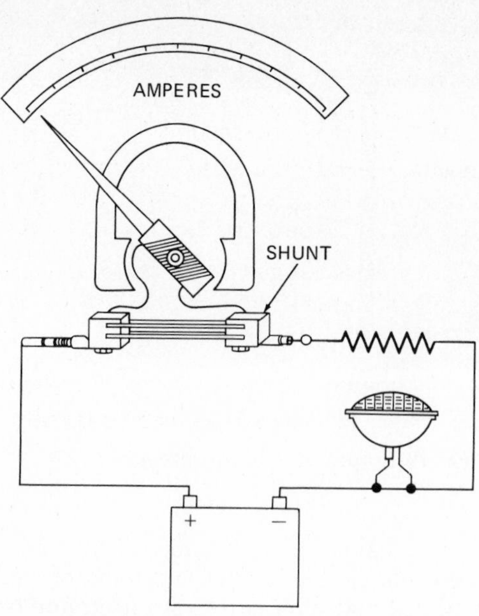

Fig. 4-34 Basic ammeter construction and connections. *(GMC Truck and Coach Division)*

AMMETER An ammeter measures the current flow within a circuit to which it is connected. There are two types—the conventional ammeter (Fig. 4-34) and the induction ammeter.

The conventional ammeter must be placed in series with the circuit being tested because all elec-

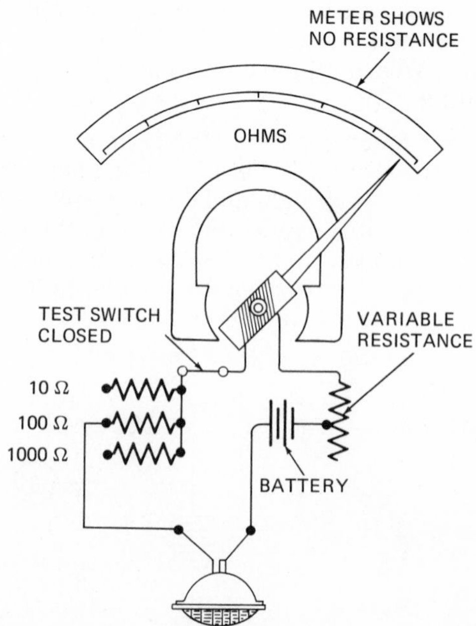

Fig. 4-35 Basic ohmmeter construction and connections. *(GMC Truck and Coach Division)*

trons must flow through the meter in order to indicate the number of amperes passing through it.

The induction ammeter is placed around the conductor, and measures the magnetic field that is created when there is a current flow.

An ammeter should have scales calibrated from 1 A to no less than 100 A, and as a battery starter tester it should be calibrated as high as 1000 A.

NOTE The voltmeter and ammeter must be so connected to circuits that current flows through the movable coil in the intended direction.

OHMMETER An ohmmeter is designed to measure and indicate the direct resistance in ohms. When connected, it supplies its own test voltage, forcing the current through the coil winding (tester) to the electric components or circuit and back to its own voltage source (Fig. 4-35). In order to indicate the circuit or component resistance value in ohms, the ohmmeter scale is directly related to and calibrated to the resistor within the ohmmeter.

Calibration When the ohmmeter probes are connected together, the circuit is completed, causing the meter needle to deflect. The variable resistance is then used to calibrate the meter to zero. Zero is full-scale deflection, indicating no resistance between the test probes. An ohmmeter should have a selection of scales, with the lowest calibrated to 10 Ω and the highest not less than 1000 Ω.

CAUTION Do not connect a voltmeter in series, an ammeter in parallel, or an ohmmeter to a live (hot) circuit. Any one of these procedures could damage the test instruments.

The three test instruments mentioned above have some basic working parts in common, including a permanent horseshoe magnet and a movable coil. Current flowing through the movable coil reacts with the permanent magnetic field, causing the coil to rotate. The relative movement of the coil is in proportion to the amount of current flow through the coil windings. A pointer attached to the coil moves across a calibrated scale, indicating the number of volts, amperes, or ohms. The voltmeter and the ohmmeter, additionally, have one or more resistors which are directly related to the scales.

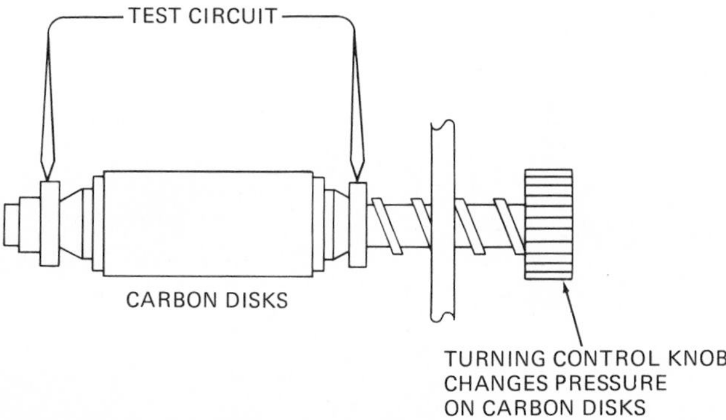

Fig. 4-36 Basic construction of a carbon pile. *(Delco-Remy Division of General Motors Corporation)*

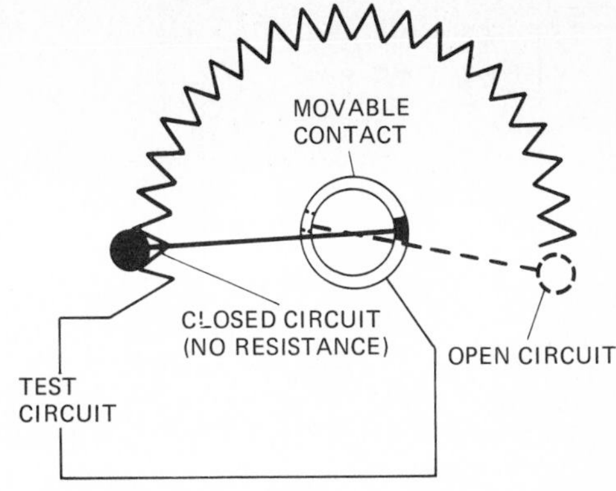

Fig. 4-37 Basic construction of a rheostat. *(Delco-Remy Division of General Motors Corporation)*

CARBON PILE A carbon pile is used to vary the resistance of a circuit. This type of resistor can absorb and dissipate, without damage, reasonably high current flow by converting it into heat. A carbon pile consists of a stack or pile of carbon disks which can be forced together or separated by a screw thread, thereby increasing or decreasing circuit resistance (Fig. 4-36). When the screw separates the disks, no current can flow through the pile, so that, while connected to a circuit, the circuit remains open. A control knob turns the screw and forces the disks together, thereby gradually reducing the resistance. When the disks are forced tightly together, all resistance is removed and a conductorlike effect is produced.

RHEOSTAT A rheostat is used to vary the resistance of a circuit, although it is limited by the amount of current it can absorb and heat it can dissipate. It consists of a resistance wire wound around an insulator, over which a movable contact can slide (Fig. 4-37). The right-hand side of the resistor wire is connected to the movable contact and the contact slip ring is connected to one circuit lead. The left-hand side of the resistor is connected to the other circuit lead.

When the rheostat is connected in series to a circuit and the movable contact is in the position shown in Fig. 4-37, no resistance is produced in the circuit. However, when the contact is moved in a clockwise direction over the resistance wire, the resistance increases. The amount of resistance produced in the circuit depends not only on the position of the movable contact, but on the resistance of the coil wire as well.

Battery Maintenance and Testing To prevent electric circuit and system failure, the batteries must be regularly serviced. This, naturally, also prolongs battery life and circumvents battery failure. **NOTE** Servicing is especially needed when a series-parallel switch is used.

Maintenance should always commence with a

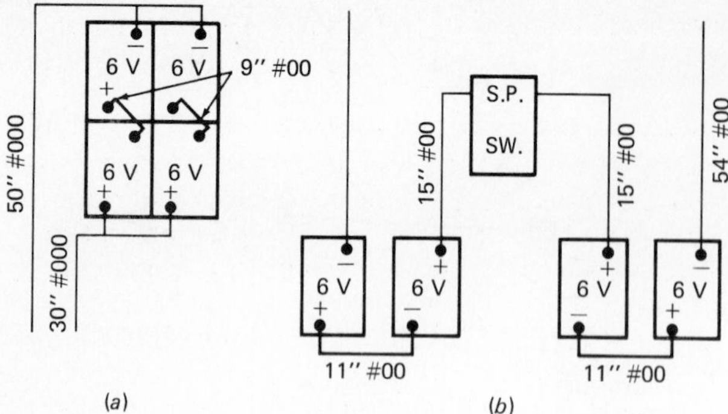

Fig. 4-38 (*a*) Battery connections for a 12-V starting circuit. (*b*) Battery connections for a 24-V starting circuit.

visual inspection of the batteries. Check for cracks caused by overly loose or tight hold-down clamps and inspect the battery compartment for foreign matter.

Check for signs of wetness or leakage on the top of the batteries which might be the result of a missing filler cap or of overfilling or overcharging.

Check the battery terminals for corrosion. Excessive corrosion is an indication of high resistance (poor connections) at the terminals or within the battery itself.

To do any work required on the batteries efficiently, remove them to the service area. This will minimize battery damage during servicing and permit unobstructed access to the battery compartment.

Before removing the batteries, first make a mental note of the position of the terminal posts to simplify reinstallation later (see Fig. 4-38 for examples of such posts). Disconnect the ground cable to prevent a short circuit, which could damage the batteries or other components should the wrench you are using touch the ground. It could also prevent your hands from being burnt, particularly if you are wearing a metal ring.

Remove battery hold-down clamps (covers). When they are damaged or corroded, replace them. If they are in good condition, clean them thoroughly and paint them with acid-resistant paint. Use two wrenches when loosening the terminal bolt nut to prevent loosening or breaking the terminal post from the cell connector. Pull the terminals from the battery posts with a battery puller. Do not use a pair of pliers or a screwdriver because either of these may damage the post connection or cell cover. Use a carrying strap to lift and carry the battery to the service area. Do not use a pair of pliers or a vise grip to lift the batteries from the compartment. Do not carry the batteries in your hands.

Before you clean the battery, tape or block the vent holes. Use a wire brush to remove excessive dirt or oil. Wash away corrosion and electrolyte from the terminals with a baking soda solution, then rinse with clean water. If necessary, use steel wool or a terminal cleaning brush to clean the posts. To dry the batteries, use compressed air. Make sure the sealer has not broken away from the case because this could allow acid to be drawn from the battery.

BATTERY LEAKAGE TEST The first test you should make is the electric leakage test, since such leakage, if present, drains the battery continuously. Use a low-reading voltmeter or adjust the voltmeter to its lowest scale. Rest one prong against the positive post. With the other prong resting lightly over the cell covers (or battery cover), slide it from the positive to the negative side of the battery and watch the voltmeter's reaction. When the prong rests on the last cell cover near the negative post, the voltmeter should not read more than 0.1 V. If the reading is higher, check for cracks, a loose intermediate post, or a loose battery post.

HYDROMETER TEST The battery's charge may be measured with a hydrometer by testing the specific gravity of the battery fluid (electrolyte). As a cell discharges, sulfuric acid from the electrolyte enters the battery plates and the active material gradually changes to lead sulfate, thereby lowering the strength of the electrolyte. The specific gravity of the electrolyte varies directly in proportion to the strength of charge of each individual battery cell.

Before you check the specific gravity, make sure that the gases have escaped, the sediments have settled, and the surface charge is removed. To remove the surface charge, crank the engine over once or twice or turn the headlights on for a few minutes.

NOTE Do not make a hydrometer test if water has just been added to the battery or if the engine has been cranked too long.

To ensure an accurate reading, warm up the hydrometer float to the temperature of the electrolyte by drawing electrolyte in and out of the barrel. Draw up enough so that the float moves to the middle of the barrel. Hold the hydrometer at eye level without tilting it and allow the float to "float." Do not take the fluid level at the float stem or at the barrel since the fluid level is high at both of these points owing to surface tension of the fluid. At the same time, take the temperature reading. **NOTE** To arrive at the correct specific gravity when electrolyte temperatures exceed 80°F [26.7°C], you must add 4 points (0.004 specific gravity) for every 10°F [5.6°C] over 80°F. When the electrolyte temperature drops below 80°F, you must subtract 0.004 points for every 10°F below 80°F (see Fig. 4-39).

Assume the hydrometer reading is 1.240 and the electrolyte temperature is 100°F [37.8°C]. Add 0.008 points to the specific gravity reading to account for the temperature rise above 80°F. The correct specific gravity is 1.240 + 0.008 = 1.248. The cell is then about 90 percent charged and should have a voltage of 2.05 V.

Check all the cells of one battery and compare their specific gravity. A difference of more than 50 points (0.050 specific gravity) between the cells is generally an indication that the plates are deteriorating. However, the difference may be caused by an internal short circuit, a loss of electrolyte due to leakage, or an excessive charging rate. A battery with a high variation should be recharged and retested.

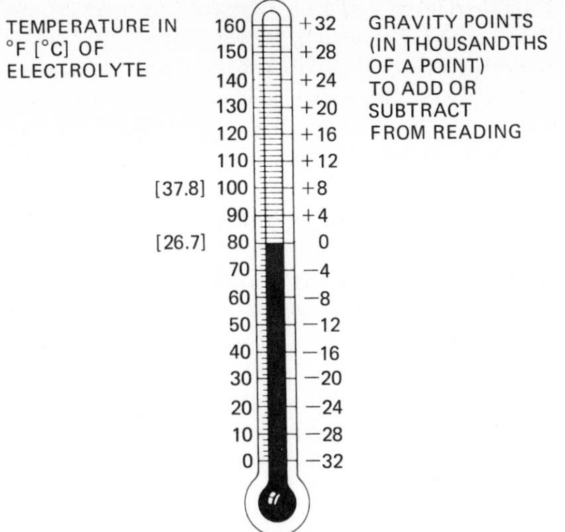

Fig. 4-39 Hydrometer temperature correction scale. (*J I Case Company Agricultural Equipment Division*)

If the variation persists, the battery should be replaced.

When battery cells have a specific gravity of less than 1.215, the length of the battery's remaining service life is questionable. It should be recharged and retested, or replaced.

OPEN CIRCUIT VOLTAGE (EMF VOLTAGE) Another method of determining if a battery is in a fully charged condition, if it requires recharging, or if it is defective is by the use of a low-reading voltmeter with a 2.3-V scale in a 0.10-V division.

Place the test prong of the voltmeter across each battery cell. The individual cell voltages should be within 0.05 V of each other. When there is a greater difference (or when any cell voltage is 1.95 V or less), the battery should be recharged and retested. A high-discharge test (capacity test) should then be made. **NOTE** Batteries with a one-piece cover cannot be tested with a voltmeter. A cadmium probe tester must be used to test their voltage (see Fig. 4-40).

LIGHT-LOAD TEST A light-load test is more reliable than an open circuit voltage or a hydrometer test because it requires the battery to convert chemical energy into current flow. To make this test, either a low-reading voltmeter or a cadmium probe tester may be used.

When using a cadmium probe tester, place a carbon pile across the battery and draw about 15 A from the battery. Alternatively, when the batteries are installed, turn on the headlights or other electric components to equal a 15-A draw. With the current flowing from the battery, insert one cadmium probe into one cell and the other into the adjacent cell. Observe the scale reading (see Fig. 4-40 for an example). To check the next cell, remove the outer probe from the cell, insert it into the third cell, and observe the reading. Continue until all cells have been tested. If the cell voltage is 1.95 V or higher with no voltage variation between cells, the battery is in good condition. When the voltage is lower, but still without variation, the battery requires recharging and retesting. When the voltage variation between cells is more than 0.5 V, also recharge and retest the battery. In addition, perform a high-discharge test to make certain the battery is reusable.

HIGH-DISCHARGE TEST AND COLD-CRANKING TEST The battery tests with which you will be most concerned are the high-discharge test, the cold-cranking test, and the reserve-capacity test. These are the most reliable because, under maximum and minimum strain, they measure the battery capacity to change chemical energy into current flow.

To perform the high-discharge or cold-cranking test, an ammeter, voltmeter, and carbon pile (variable resistor) or battery starter tester are required. Connect the battery starter tester as shown in Fig. 4-41. **NOTE** To perform a true cold-cranking test, the temperature of the battery should be brought to 0°F [−17.8°C], and as this is not always possible, a

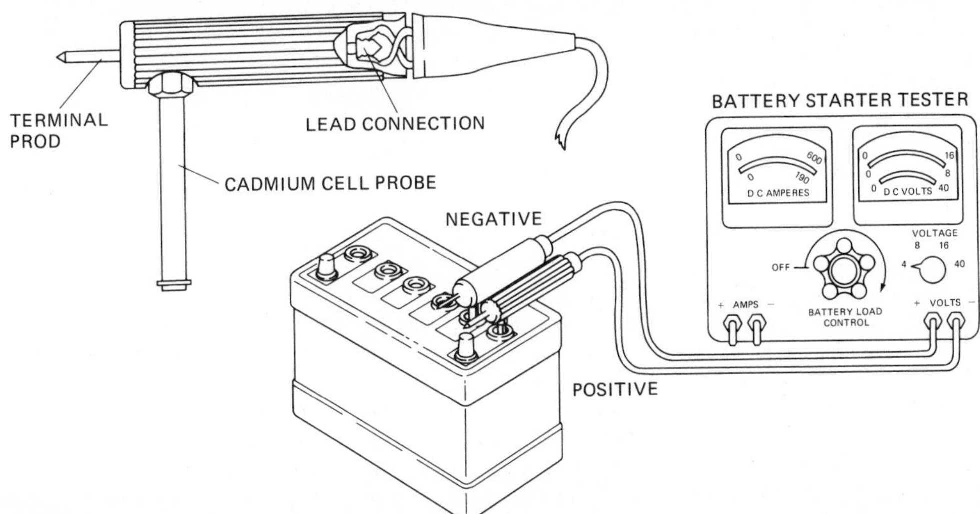

Fig. 4-40 Checking the battery using cadmium cell probe. (*J I Case Company Agricultural Equipment Division*)

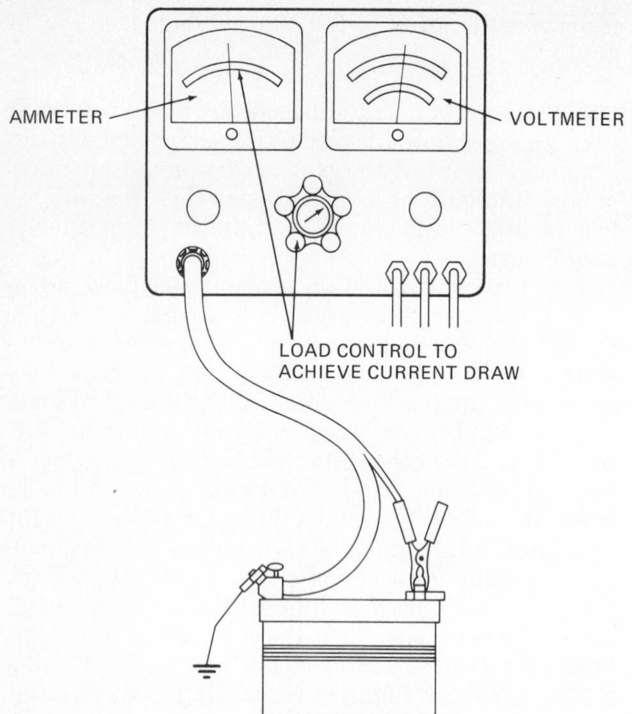

Fig. 4-41 Connections for high-battery discharge test. *(J I Case Company Agricultural Equipment Division)*

high-discharge test can be used to simulate it. When the test instrument is connected (see Fig. 4-41), measure the open circuit voltage. When the open circuit voltage is 6 V or lower for a 6-V battery (12 V or lower for a 12-V battery), or if the specific gravity is lower than 1.220, recharge the battery before testing; otherwise the battery plates could be damaged during testing.

One more requirement before actually making the high-discharge test is that you remove the surface charge so that you will be able to obtain a true battery-capacity reading. This is done with the help of a carbon pile. The amount of current draw from the battery needed to remove the surface charge is fixed for each battery group. For instance, batteries recommended for diesel engines, such as groups 7D, 4D, 6D, 8D, and Delco 1200, would require a current drain of 300 A for 15 seconds (s).

To perform a high-discharge test on groups 7D, 4D, 6D, or 8D batteries, draw 450 A from the battery for 15 s. When testing a Delco 1200 battery, draw 230 A for 15 s. At the conclusion of the test, the voltage in all cases should register not less than 9.6 V for a 12-V battery and not less than 4.8 V for a 6-V battery, assuming that the ambient temperature is 70°F [21.1°C] or more. (If the ambient temperature is less, the minimum acceptable voltage is also less.)

When the load from the battery is removed (the variable resistor is open), the voltmeter reading should be within 0.2 V of the open circuit voltage reading before the test. If the voltage is lower than the 9.6 or 4.8 V referred to above, or if it did not recover to within 0.2 V of the previous reading, the battery is in poor condition and should be replaced.

To perform a true cold-cranking test, place the fully charged battery in a cold room to reduce its temperature to 0°F [−17.8°C]. When that temperature has been achieved, connect the same test instrument you used to perform the high-discharge test to the battery to be tested. Now use the carbon pile and discharge the battery for 30 s at the same rate as its cold cranking rating. At the end of that time, the individual cell voltage must be 1.2 V or greater, that is, the terminal voltage must be 7.2 V for a 12-V battery and 3.6 V for a 6-V battery.

RESERVE-CAPACITY TEST The reserve-capacity test procedure is similar to that of the old 20-ampere-hour (Ah) test. That is, a 100-Ah battery fully charged must deliver 5 A for 20 hours (h) at a temperature of 80°F [26.7°C], and the cell voltage at the end of the test must be 1.7 V or higher. For a reserve capacity test you also test a fully charged battery at 80°F, but you draw 25 A from the battery until the terminal voltage of each cell is 1.75 V. The reserve capacity is defined as the time of discharge in minutes. As an example, a 4D-640 battery has a reserve capacity of 285 min.

BATTERY CHARGING Prepare the batteries for charging, that is, clean, test, and adjust the liquid level. Add only water that is pure enough for drinking. When using a fast charger, all batteries must be of the same voltage and connected in parallel to the charger. When connected, select the voltage and adjust the charging current to 10 percent of the CCA of the smallest battery.

Frequently use the hydrometer to check the temperature of the electrolyte. It must not exceed 125°F [51.6°C], and the charging rate must be reduced when the temperature is near that point. When all cells are gassing freely, the battery is nearing its fully charged state. From this time on, take frequent hydrometer readings, and, when the specific gravity ceases to increase, *stop* charging. Let the battery cool and then, if necessary, adjust the fluid level.

BOOSTER BATTERIES TO AID STARTING When you use booster batteries to assist starting, connect only boosters with the same voltage as the batteries of the truck, tractor, etc., which are supplying the voltage. Follow the steps outlined below to prevent battery explosion.

Connect one booster cable end securely to the tractor battery live post, and the other end of the booster cable to the booster battery post having the same polarity. **CAUTION** Reverse polarity could damage the regulator, generator, radio, and other accessories.

Connect one end of the second booster cable to the booster battery ground post and the other to good ground. Do not connect it to the truck battery because this could cause battery explosion.

After the engine has started, first remove the booster cable from the ground connection, then remove the cable from the live posts of the booster battery.

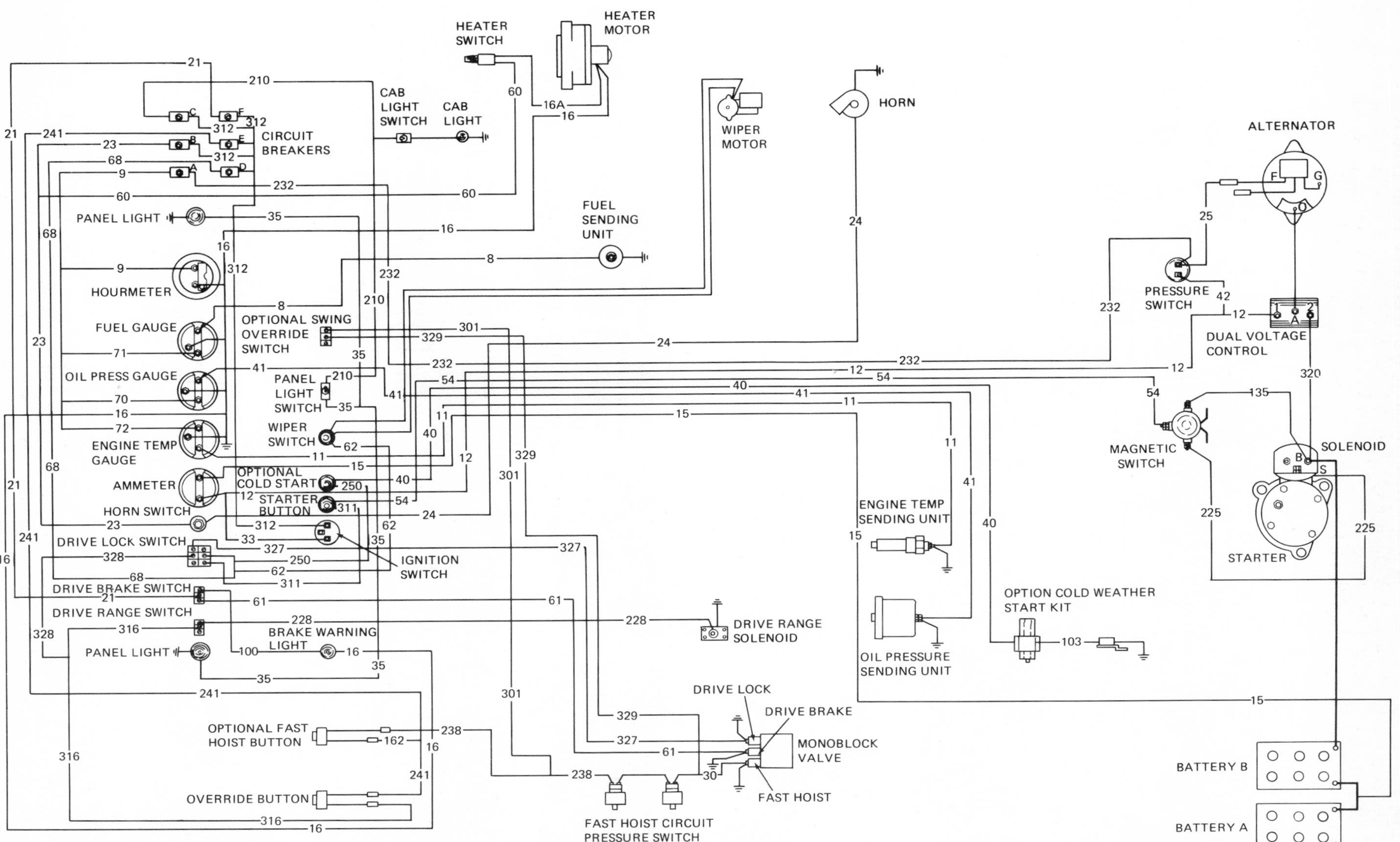

Fig. 4-42 Electric system schematically illustrated. *(J I Case Company Agricultural Equipment Division)*

BATTERY INSTALLATION Before you install a battery, make certain the battery compartment is clean and preferably repainted. Make sure all battery cables and terminals (including the battery terminal bolts and nuts) are in good condition and that the battery hold-down clamps or covers have been repaired or replaced.

NOTE To prevent future electric problems, install only fully charged batteries. When your equipment requires more than one battery, do not install one new battery alongside older batteries, do not install batteries of different capacity, and do not install batteries from different battery manufacturers since the counterelectromotive force of those batteries will differ, along with their capacity or plate area. This last point is especially important when a series-parallel switch is used.

Individual Circuit Operation and Testing A complete electric system of an excavator is schematically illustrated in Fig. 4-42. It has the following circuits: (1) charging, (2) starting, (3) cold-weather starting, (4) oil pressure indicator, (5) engine temperature, (6) horn, (7) wiper motor, (8) heater, (9) fuel level indicator, (10) hour meter, (11) lights (two circuits) (12) drive brake, (13) fast hoist, (14) drive range, and (15) swing override. In addition, although not shown in this figure, it also has an air conditioning circuit

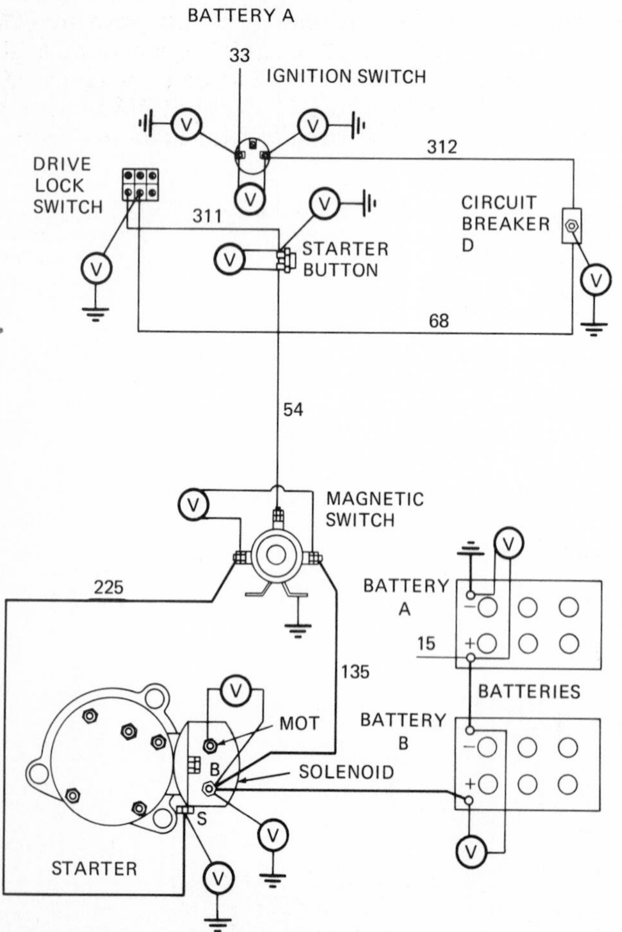

Fig. 4-43 Schematic illustration of a starter circuit. *(J I Case Company Agricultural Equipment Division)*

and the ignition circuit (fuel shutoff switch). Most of these will be discussed later in some detail.

The circuits are protected through six circuit breakers. Two main-wire harness sets are used to deliver power to the system circuits.

The electric system shown is of the dual voltage design—that is, it uses 24 V for starting (two batteries A and B, each 12 V) and a 12-V charging circuit.

NOTE Battery A (12 V) only supplies power to the accessory circuits.

STARTING CIRCUIT The starter controls current to energize the starter-solenoid switch (see Fig. 4-43) coming from battery A, routing it over the ammeter, thence to the ignition switch, and over line 312 to the circuit breaker D. Current is then routed over line 68 to the drive-lock switch (the drive-lock switch is de-energized), and from the switch over line 307 to the starter button. From there it is routed over line 54 to the magnetic switch, energizing the coil and closing the switch. Current from the starter solenoid switch B terminal flows over line 135, over the contacts of the magnetic switch, and over line 225 to the S terminal of the solenoid switch. The solenoid is energized and the disk bridges terminals A and M, and the battery current flows into the starter motor circuit.

If the cranking motor fails to energize, first record from the service manual the cranking motor specifications, and then compare actual measurements against them. An example of these specifications are given below.

Cranking-motor measurements against manual specifications Manual specifications are the following: maximum cranking voltage 18 V. Solenoid switch current draw at 80°F [26.7°C], with a voltage of 18 V both windings (hold-in and pull-in) should draw 70.5 to 77.8 A. Hold-in windings should draw 18 to 20 A; maximum voltage for drop insulated circuits should be 0.5 V, for each cable 0.4 V, for the starter solenoid 0.1 V, and for each connection ground circuit 0.5 V.

To find the actual performance measurements of the cranking motor and solenoid switch, connect the positive lead of the voltmeter to the B terminal of the cranking motor, and the negative voltmeter lead to a good ground. Turn the ignition key to the ON position, push the starter button, and then read the cranking voltage. If the voltage at the B terminal during cranking is lower than 18 V, or the cranking motor turns slowly or does not energize at all, perform an insulated circuit test.

Start by using a voltmeter and check the following: (1) the open voltage at both batteries—if the batteries' voltage is less than 12 V, charge them before proceeding with any other test; (2) the system voltage at the B terminal of the cranking motor; and (3) the system voltage at the ignition switch. Turn the ignition switch to the ON position and measure the voltage at the circuit breaker, drive-lock switch, and starter button. Next, connect the positive lead of the voltmeter to the M terminal of the cranking motor

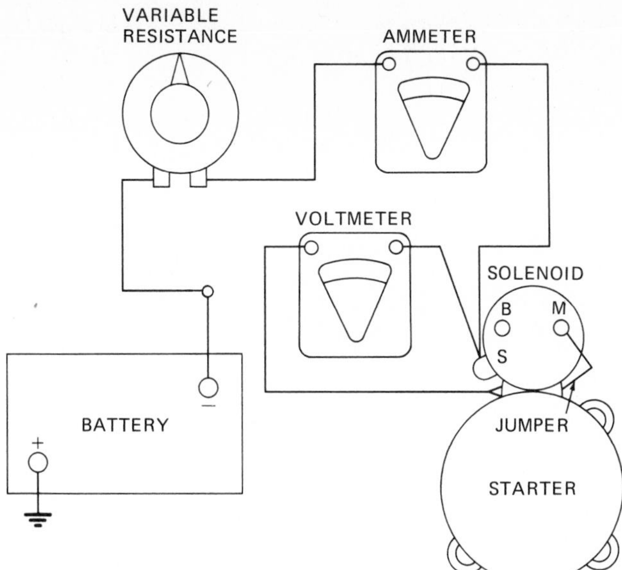

Fig. 4-44 Test instrument connections to check solenoid switch. (*J I Case Company Agricultural Equipment Division*)

and its negative lead to ground. Now push the starter button and measure the voltage drop at the ignition switch, starter button, magnetic switch, and the solenoid switch between the B and M terminals. Also measure the voltage at the S terminal. Record the measured voltages and compare them with the manual specifications. If the voltage drop at either the ignition switch, starter button, drive-lock switch, magnetic switch, or between the B and M terminals of the cranking motor is higher than specified, replace the unit because the electric contacts are pitted or worn.

If the voltage at the S terminal of the cranking motor reads, say, 18.5 V during cranking, but the cranking-motor drive fails to engage, or engages and then disengages, or the cranking speed of the engine is slow, perform a ground circuit test. **NOTE** Excessive resistance in the ground circuit not only causes sluggish cranking speed, but also interferes with the charging system. To check for resistance, connect the positive lead of the voltmeter to the B terminal of the cranking motor and its negative lead to the negative terminal of battery A. **NOTE** Do not connect the negative lead of the voltmeter to any other ground as this would only measure part of the ground circuit. Now, crank the engine. If the voltmeter reading exceeds specification by 0.5 V there is excessive ground circuit resistance between the cranking motor and battery A.

To test the solenoid switch, remove the battery cable from the B terminal, remove the connection between the B and M terminals, remove the wire from the S terminal, and connect a jumper wire from the M terminal to ground. Now connect the test instrument as shown in Fig. 4-44. Next, turn the hand knob of the carbon pile clockwise to obtain a voltmeter reading of 18 V. The ammeter should read between 70.5 and 77.8 A if both windings are not grounded or shorted, or do not have an open circuit.

Series-parallel switch The purpose of this switch is to convert a 12-V electric system into a 24-V cranking circuit. When the switch is energized for cranking, it connects two 12- or four 6-V batteries in series to make 24 V available for cranking. When

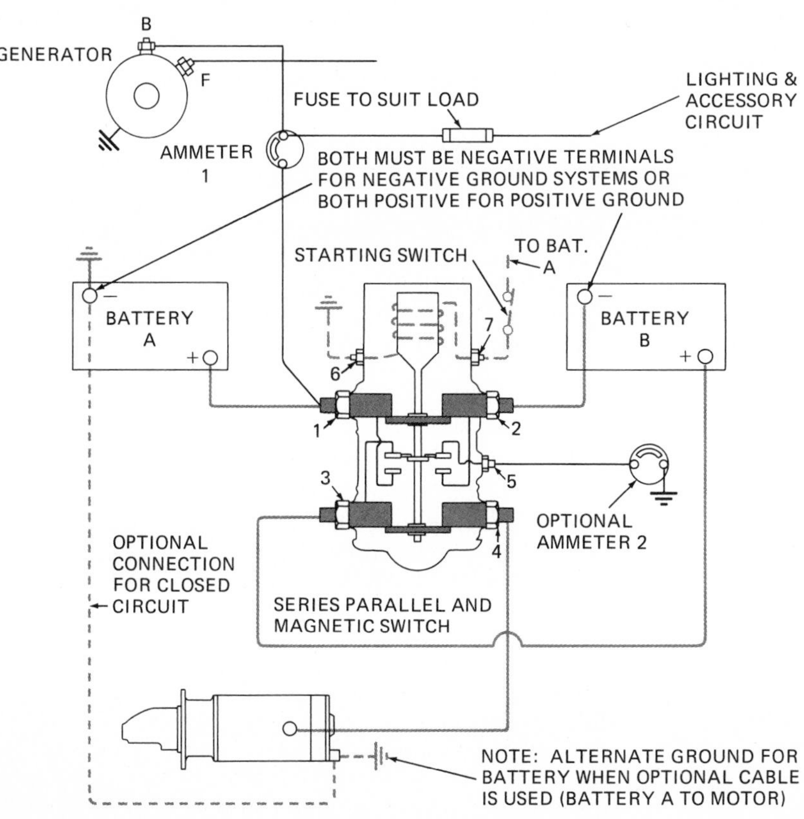

Fig. 4-45 Current flow of a series–parallel switch when cranking. (*Delco-Remy Division of General Motors Corporation*)

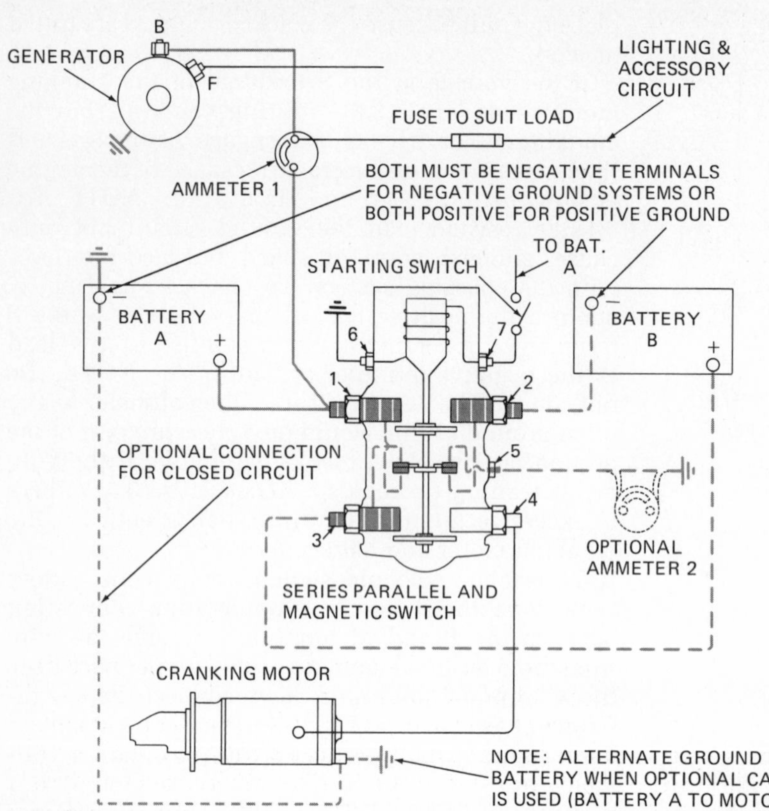

Fig. 4-46 Current flow of a series–parallel switch when charging. (*Delco-Remy Division of General Motors Corporation*)

de-energized, it connects the batteries in parallel to 12 V.

Switch action and current flow when cranking As the operator closes the starting switch, it closes the solenoid coil and energizes and pulls the plunger and rod inward. The two disks bridge the contacts between terminals 1 and 2, and between terminals 3 and 4. This connects the negative terminal of battery B with the positive terminal of battery A and the positive terminal of battery B with the cranking motor. This closes the cranking motor circuit and permits cranking to take place. See Fig. 4-45.

Switch action and current flow when charging As the operator opens the starting circuit, the solenoid coil de-energizes and the return spring forces the disks away from the contacts. Simultaneously, two small contact sets are being closed. This opens the cranking-motor circuits and connects the battery in parallel with the charging circuit.

Current from the generator flows through the first ammeter to the series-parallel switch terminal 1. Here the current flow splits. One flow path is to the positive post of the A battery and then to ground. The other is from terminal 1 over the first small contact sets, on to terminal 3, to the battery B positive terminal, out of the negative battery terminal to terminal 2, over to the second small contact sets, and out of terminal 5 through the second ammeter to ground. See Fig. 4-46.

Troubleshooting and testing the series-parallel switch Ninety percent of all cranking troubles emanate from the parallel switch as a result of the undercharged condition of battery B. Among the ways to prevent this situation are (1) to keep all connections clean and tight, (2) to keep the top of the battery dry, (3) to replace batteries with those of the same make, (4) to choose batteries of the same capacity, age, and chemical and mechanical condition, and (5) to interchange battery A and battery B periodically to avoid undercharging conditions and to prolong battery life.

When the engine cranks slowly, the batteries may be undercharged or the switch may have high resistance. To solve these problems, first check the battery voltage and, if necessary, charge the batteries. Measure the voltage at the ignition switch, the starter button, and terminal 7. The voltage reading at the various points must be equal to that of battery A, minus the allowable circuit resistance. Next, using an ohmmeter, measure the resistance of the solenoid coil, or push the starter button and measure the voltage drop between terminals 6 and 7. At the same time, measure the voltage drop between terminals 1 and 2, and between 3 and 4, to determine the condition of the disk contacts.

To check the parallel-switch charging circuit, operate the engine and measure the charging voltage at the alternator, terminal 1, battery A positive terminal, terminal 3, battery B negative and positive terminals, and terminals 2 and 5. If there is a voltage difference between terminals 1 and 3, and between 2 and 5, measure the voltage drop. If the difference between the charging circuit voltage of battery B and the battery B circuit voltage exceeds 0.5 V, the parallel switch must be serviced.

CHARGING AND OIL PRESSURE SWITCH CIRCUITS The charging circuit is connected to the system as shown

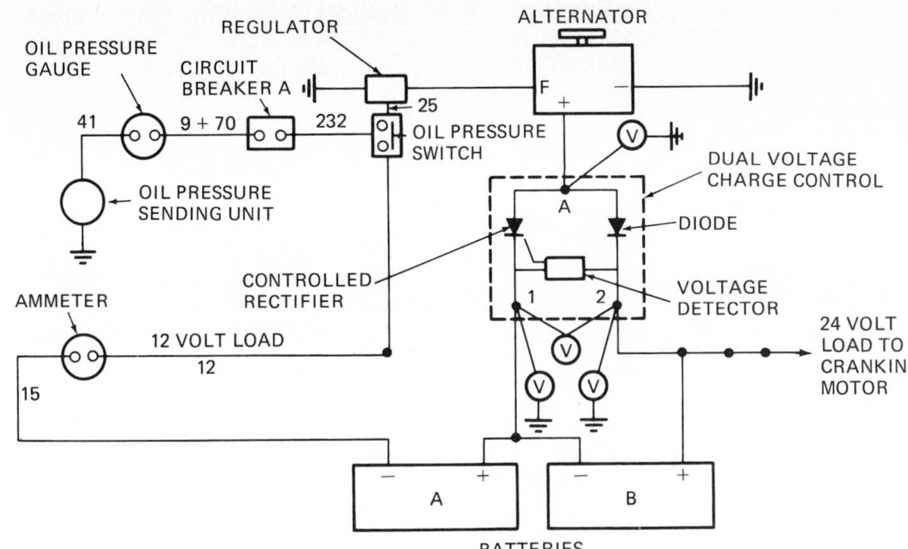

Fig. 4-47 Charging circuit schematically illustrated. *(J I Case Company Agricultural Equipment Division)*

in Fig. 4-47. The oil pressure switch serves two purposes: (1) It prevents current from flowing to the regulator during cranking, and (2) it prevents the batteries from discharging through the field coils, engine oil pressure gauge, or oil pressure sending unit.

The purpose of the dual voltage charging control is to maintain both batteries fully charged. It is an all-electronic (solid state) switching device and is connected in series between the alternator and battery.

When the engine is not operating or during cranking, voltage from the positive post of battery A is present at the oil pressure switch and terminal 1 of the dual voltage charging control, while voltage from battery B is present at terminal 2. See Fig. 4-47.

When the engine starts to operate, the engine oil pressure closes the sending unit contacts. (See Fig. 4-48.) This completes the oil pressure switch circuit, and field current flows into the solid state regulator. It then flows through the resistor R1 in forward bias through the emitter/base of transistor TR1 to ground, and back to the ground rectifier bridge (ground diodes) and to the stator, thus completing the circuit. This turns on transistor TR1 and the current then flows from the diode trio into the field coils, from there to transistor TR1 collector/emitter, to the grounded rectifier bridge, and to the stator winding. At the same time, depending on the voltage of the regulator (fixed adjustment), there is a current flow from the battery terminal to the voltage regulator, through the two parallel resistors R2, and then to R3 and to ground. As the voltage between resistors R2 and R3 increases to the value where the zener diode conducts, that is, 8.1 V, transistor TR2 suddenly conducts current from the emitter/base to ground. This causes transistor TR1 to switch off, stopping the current from flowing into the field coil and thus eliminating the output voltage. As soon as the voltage drops at the battery terminal of the generator, the zener diode acts as an open switch and forces transistor TR2 to switch off and therefore transistor TR1 to switch on again. This cycling could be as high as 5000 times per second.

The rectified output current flows to the dual voltage charging control, terminal A. After the generator output voltage exceeds the cemf of both batteries (24 V), the voltage detector switches on and consequently the control rectifier blocks the current flow to terminal 1. Now all generator output current flows over the diode out of terminal 2 to the positive terminal of battery B. Since the batteries are connected in series, both batteries, A and B, will be charged. The voltage and current output increases until the battery A voltage reaches the value of the voltage regulator setting, say 14.2 V. From this point on, the regulator regulates the voltage in the normal manner. Since the voltage regulator senses the voltage of battery A, battery B becomes fully charged first. As soon as that charge is reached, say at 14.2 V, the voltage detector in the control unit switches the control rectifier on, and the current can now only flow into battery A. Battery B is therefore out of the charging circuit and only charged again after the engine has been restarted. **NOTE** Voltage offers no real problem for an alternator. The alternator is capable of producing 110 V or more for an extended period of time, as long as sufficient cooling is provided and the amp draw is not excessive.

Charging system testing and troubleshooting The first indication that a charging system is not operating properly is when the batteries do not have the power to crank the engine. If such is the case, check the following first:

1. The drive belt tension (adjustment).
2. The drive belts and pulleys for wear.
3. The belts and pulleys for grease and oil, as this will cause belt slippage under load condition.
4. The batteries and their cable connections. If necessary, charge the batteries. Test them and clean the connections.
5. All other terminal connections. They should be

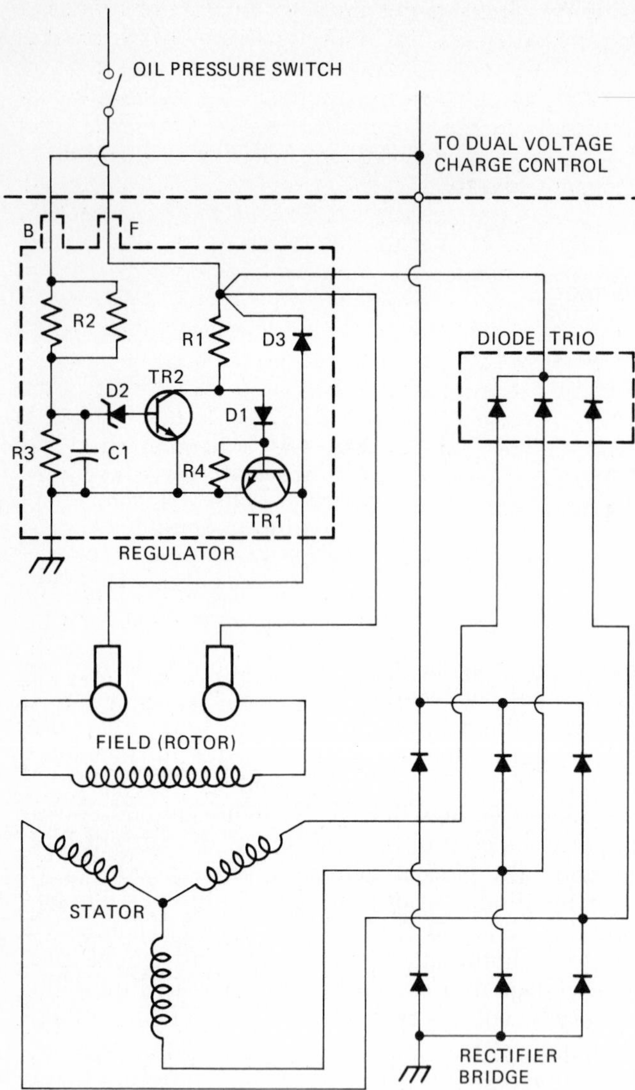

Fig. 4-48 Circuit of the alternator and regulator schematically illustrated. (*J I Case Company Agricultural Equipment Division*)

tight and free of corrosion or any other form of foreign matter that could cause additional resistance.

6. Measure the voltage of battery A with a voltmeter and check the oil pressure switch.

Next, perform an alternator output test. To do this, connect the volt/amp tester as shown in Fig. 4-49. **NOTE** The ammeter is connected in series with the ground, because of the dual voltage charging control. Before connecting the carbon pile, turn it to the OFF (open) position. Disconnect the fuel pressure switch wire and connect to it one field rheostat lead; connect the other lead to the battery terminal of the alternator. Turn the knob clockwise to the direct position. Start the engine and operate it at the recommended rpm. If the test ammeter shows less than 10 A, turn the carbon pile knob clockwise until the ammeter shows 10 A. Now, operate the engine for about 5 minutes (min) to stabilize the temperature of the charging system components. Shut the engine off, and with the fuel injection pump in the OFF position crank the engine, or use the carbon pile to discharge the batteries so that the charging system at startup is into the 24-V mode. Restart the engine and operate it at the recommended rpm. Turn the carbon pile knob clockwise to obtain maximum current output, that is, at the point where the ammeter needle just starts to move toward zero. Take a reading for current and voltage, then turn the carbon pile and field rheostat counterclockwise to the OFF (open) position and stop the engine. If the current output and voltage are below specification (which is about 63 A, 28.8 V), check for high resistance in the alternator ground circuit and check the voltage regulator setting. To do this, start the engine and operate it for about 5 min to bring the charging circuit into the 12-V mode. Turn the field rheostat to the direct position, then read the voltage. If it is below 14.7 V, the regulator is damaged and must be replaced. If it is higher, again check for poor regulator connections. If, after retesting, the voltage remains high, the regulator must be replaced. Next, retest the output voltage and current. If the alternator fails to charge or has a low or unsteady charging rate, check the dual voltage charging control with a voltmeter. With the engine not operating, connect the positive voltmeter lead to terminal 1 and the negative lead to ground. The voltmeter reading should coincide with the voltage of battery A. Next, connect the positive voltmeter lead to terminal 2—the voltage reading

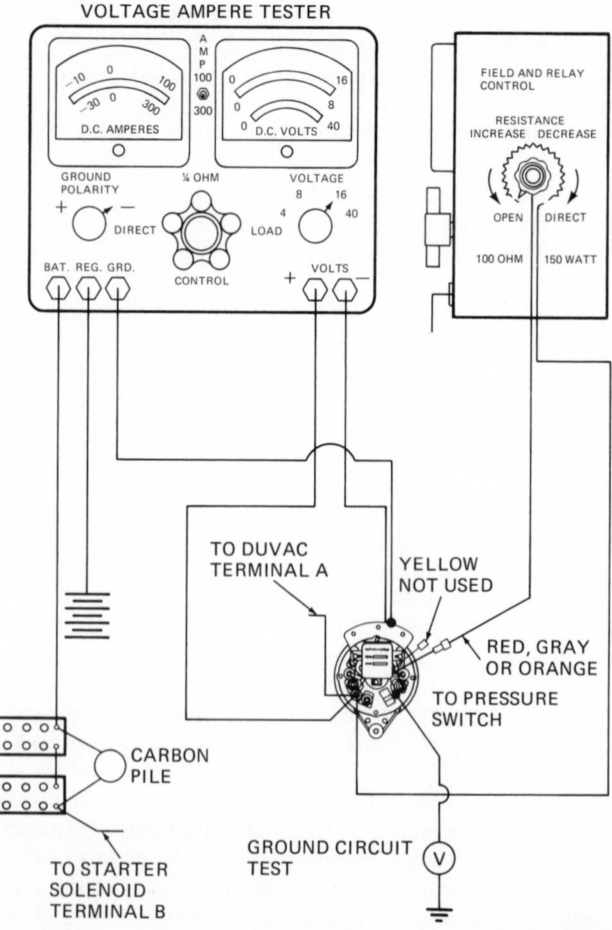

Fig. 4-49 Test instrument connections to perform a generator output test. (*J I Case Company Agricultural Equipment Division*)

should be the combined voltage of batteries A and B. If this is the case, connect the positive lead of the voltmeter to terminal 2 and the negative lead to terminal 1. Start the engine and observe the voltmeter reading. When battery B becomes fully charged, at 14.2 V, the voltage detector should switch on. This will be noticeable by the voltmeter needle reaction.

If the current output remains below specification, you can assume the trouble is within the alternator and is due to (1) an open, grounded, or short stator winding, (2) an open, grounded, or short field winding, (3) a slip ring in dirty condition, (4) brushes worn or damaged, (5) rectifier diodes shorted, (6) pulley or rotor loose, and/or (7) bearings worn. In all of these cases, the alternator must be removed for service.

30 SI-TR series alternator To provide 24 V for the cranking circuit and 12 V for the accessory circuit, the Delco Remy 30 SI-TR is used, which can produce both charging voltages. This is made possible by adding a TR unit (which is a transformer rectifier) to the generator. The unit consists of three transformers and a rectifying bridge. Each stator output phase is electrically connected to the primary coil of the transformer. The secondary transformer windings are connected to the rectifying bridge of the TR unit and from there connected with the 24-V terminal of the generator. See Fig. 4-50.

When the generator is operating, the voltage regulator reacts to the cemf of battery A and regulates it in the normal manner, say to a maximum of 14.4 V. The transformer steps up the maximum regulated voltage to 28.8 V, which produces a current flow of about 5 to 15 A. The current flows to the rectifying bridge, where it is rectified to direct current, and then flows to the 24-V generator terminal.

HEATER CIRCUIT The current required to operate the heater motor comes from the ignition switch over line 312 (Fig. 4-42), flows through circuit breaker B, into line 23, into line 16, to the heater switch, and then to the heater motor. **NOTE** The heater motor ground circuit is over line 16 to ground.

If the heater motor does not operate or rotates at a reduced speed, first make sure the circuit breaker is not tripped and that there are no loose connections. Having done this, connect the voltmeter successively to the ignition switch (terminal 312) and to ground, to the circuit breaker (terminal 23) and to ground, and then to the heater terminal 60 and to ground. The voltage reading at each connection should coincide with that of battery A. If this is so, turn the ignition key and heater switch to ON and measure the available voltage at the heater motor terminal 16A. If the voltage does not equal that of battery A, check the ground circuit resistance. If the voltage at the heater motor is lower, measure the voltage across the heater switch. If the voltage is correct, then you can assume the heater motor has an electric or mechanical high resistance and must be serviced.

ENGINE GAUGE AND HOURMETER CIRCUITS The oil pressure, engine temperature, fuel-indicating, and hourmeter circuits all receive their current from the oil pressure switch (line 232), though only when the switch is closed by the engine oil pressure (see Fig. 4-42). The current then flows from the dual voltage control (lines 12 and 42), over the oil pressure switch into line 332, over the circuit breaker A, and into line 9, where it branches off. One circuit directs current from line 9 to line 71, over the fuel gauge, into line 8, and over the fuel sending unit to ground. The second circuit flows over the hourmeter into line 16, to ground. The third circuit directs current from lines 9 to line 70, over the oil pressure gauge, into line 41, over the oil pressure sending unit, to ground. The fourth circuit directs current from lines 9 to line 72, over the engine temperature gauge, into line 11, over the engine temperature sending unit, to ground.

Operation of oil-pressure-indicating circuit When the engine operates, a fixed current flows through the right-hand and the left-hand coil windings of the pressure gauge to ground. Current also flows to and through the variable resistor (in the

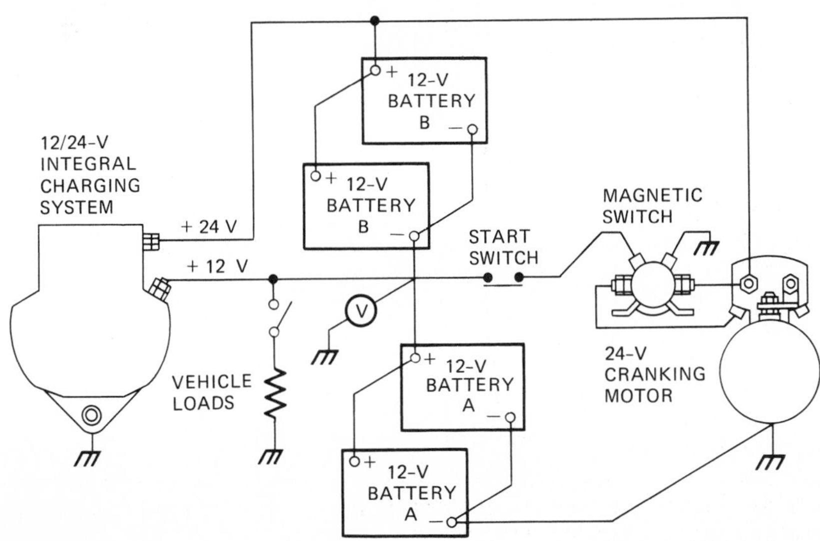

Fig. 4-50 Schematic of 12- and 24-V charging circuits.

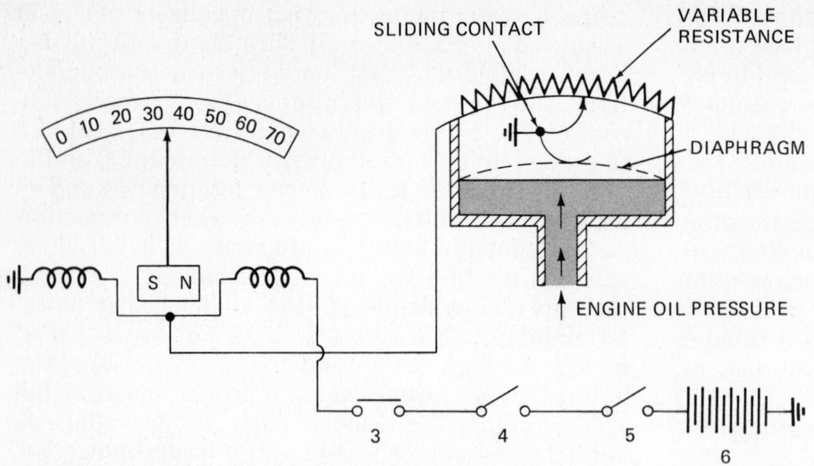

Fig. 4-51 Oil pressure indicating circuits schematically illustrated.

sending unit) over the sliding contact, to ground. When the engine oil pressure is high, the diaphragm curves upward and moves the sliding contact to the left, thereby reducing the resistance, which causes a higher current to flow. This increases the magnetism in the right-hand coil and causes the pressure gauge needle to move to the right, thus indicating the higher oil pressure. When the oil pressure is reduced, the diaphragm straightens and causes the sliding contact to move to the right, thereby increasing the resistance and reducing the current flow. This action reduces the magnetism in the right-hand coil, which in turn causes the gauge needle to move to the left. See Fig. 4-51.

Operation of temperature-indicating circuit Although the temperature gauge is of the same design as the oil pressure gauge, it has different coil windings and scale calibration. The sending unit is a bimetal arm which acts at the same time as the sliding contact on the variable resistor. If the bimetal arm is heated it warps to the right, and when it cools down to ambient temperature it warps to the left. The movement of the bimetal arm, in response to the temperature, increases or decreases the resistance of the temperature circuit, thereby varying the current flow and magnetic strength of the right-hand coil in the temperature gauge. See Fig. 4-52.

Operation of fuel-level-indicating circuit When the engine is operating, current flows through the bimetal heater coil to the variable resistor and over the sliding contact to ground. If the fuel tank is empty (as shown in Fig. 4-53), the sliding contact is moved by the float so that the total resistance of the variable resistor is placed into the fuel-level-indicating circuits. Consequently, the current flow is low, and therefore the bimetal heating coil produces very little heat. As a result, the bimetal warps to the left and mechanically moves the fuel gauge needle to the EMPTY position. If the fuel tank is full, the float has risen, thus moving the sliding contact, and all resistance of the variable resistor is removed. This causes a higher current flow, which produces maximum heat from the heating coil; therefore the bimetal arm warps to its maximum right-hand position, thus moving the gauge needle to FULL.

If one or more circuits do not function, that is, if the engine temperature, oil pressure, or fuel-level-indicating circuits fail or indicate incorrectly, or if the hourmeter does not operate, start the engine and measure the voltage at battery A. Next, measure the voltage and voltage drop at the various sending units and gauges, and at the hourmeter. Do not forget to measure the ground resistance at the fuel sending, temperature sending, and oil pressure sending units.

LIGHT AND BRAKE CIRCUITS The current for the light circuit (see Fig. 4-42) comes from line 12 into line 33 to the ignition switch. From the ignition switch, it flows into line 312, over circuit breaker C, into line 210, and to the panel light and cab light

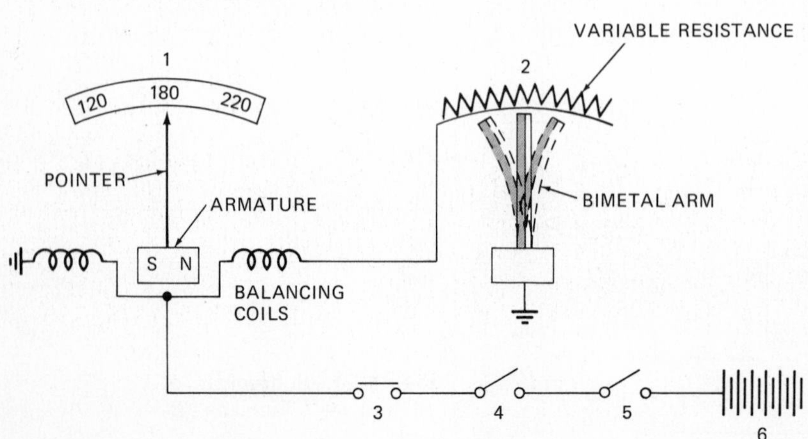

Fig. 4-52 Temperature indicating circuits schematically illustrated.

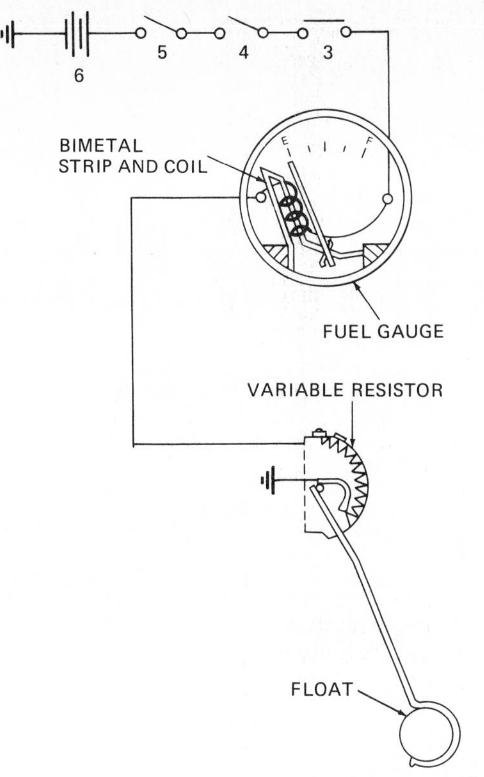

Fig. 4-53 Fuel level indicating circuit schematically illustrated.

switches. When either of the latter two switches is placed in the ON position, the cab or panel light lights.

The brake circuit flows over circuit breaker F, into line 21, and to the brake-drive switch. When the switch is at the OFF position, current flows to line 100, over the brake-warning light switch, and over line 16 to ground. When the switch is at the ON position, the current flows from the switch into line 61, to the monoblock, and to both drive brakes, and hydraulically releases the brakes, thus opening the brake light circuit.

WIPER MOTOR AND WASHER CIRCUIT A wiper and washer circuit is schematically illustrated in Fig. 4-54. When the washer motor switch is closed, current at the ignition switch flows over line 12, through the solenoid coil, to terminal 4, and over the wiper button (switch) to ground. The washer pump piston is pulled out against its spring force, drawing cleaning fluid over the inlet valve into the cylinder area. When the washer button is released, the circuit is open and the spring force pushes the piston forward, forcing the liquid past the outlet valve and into the washer distributor hoses.

When the wiper motor switch is in the low-speed position, current flows from the battery over the fuse into line 10, to terminal 3, and through the series field coil windings, whereupon the current flow is divided. The current in the series field coil circuit flows over the live brush, armature, ground brush, circuit breaker, and park switch to ground. The current in the shunt coil circuit flows through the shunt field coil windings, over line 2, to terminal 3, and over the low-speed switch position to ground.

If the wiper switch is placed in the high-speed position, the switch places a 20-Ω resistance into the circuit between lines 2 and 4. This reduces the shunt field current flow, thereby weakening the magnetic field and increasing the wiper motor speed.

When the wiper motor switch is placed in the OFF position, the switch removes the ground and the motor circuit is open. However, the points of the park switch are still closed because the wiper arms are not in the PARK position. Therefore, the wiper motor continues to operate because the current flows through the park switch to ground. However, as soon as the wiper gear cam mechanically opens the park switch points, the motor stops because the circuit is then open.

If the wiper motor or washer fails to operate, check all connections and make certain they are clean. Next:

1. Check the batteries and their voltage.

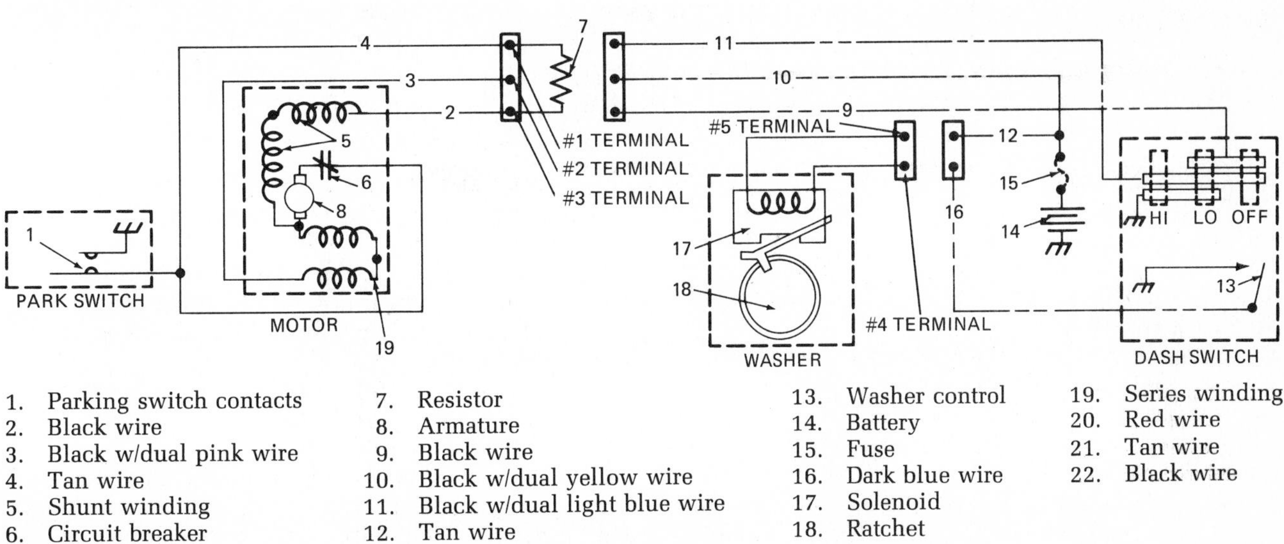

1. Parking switch contacts
2. Black wire
3. Black w/dual pink wire
4. Tan wire
5. Shunt winding
6. Circuit breaker
7. Resistor
8. Armature
9. Black wire
10. Black w/dual yellow wire
11. Black w/dual light blue wire
12. Tan wire
13. Washer control
14. Battery
15. Fuse
16. Dark blue wire
17. Solenoid
18. Ratchet
19. Series winding
20. Red wire
21. Tan wire
22. Black wire

Fig. 4-54 Electric circuit of a washer wiper motor, schematically illustrated. (*GMC Truck and Coach Division*)

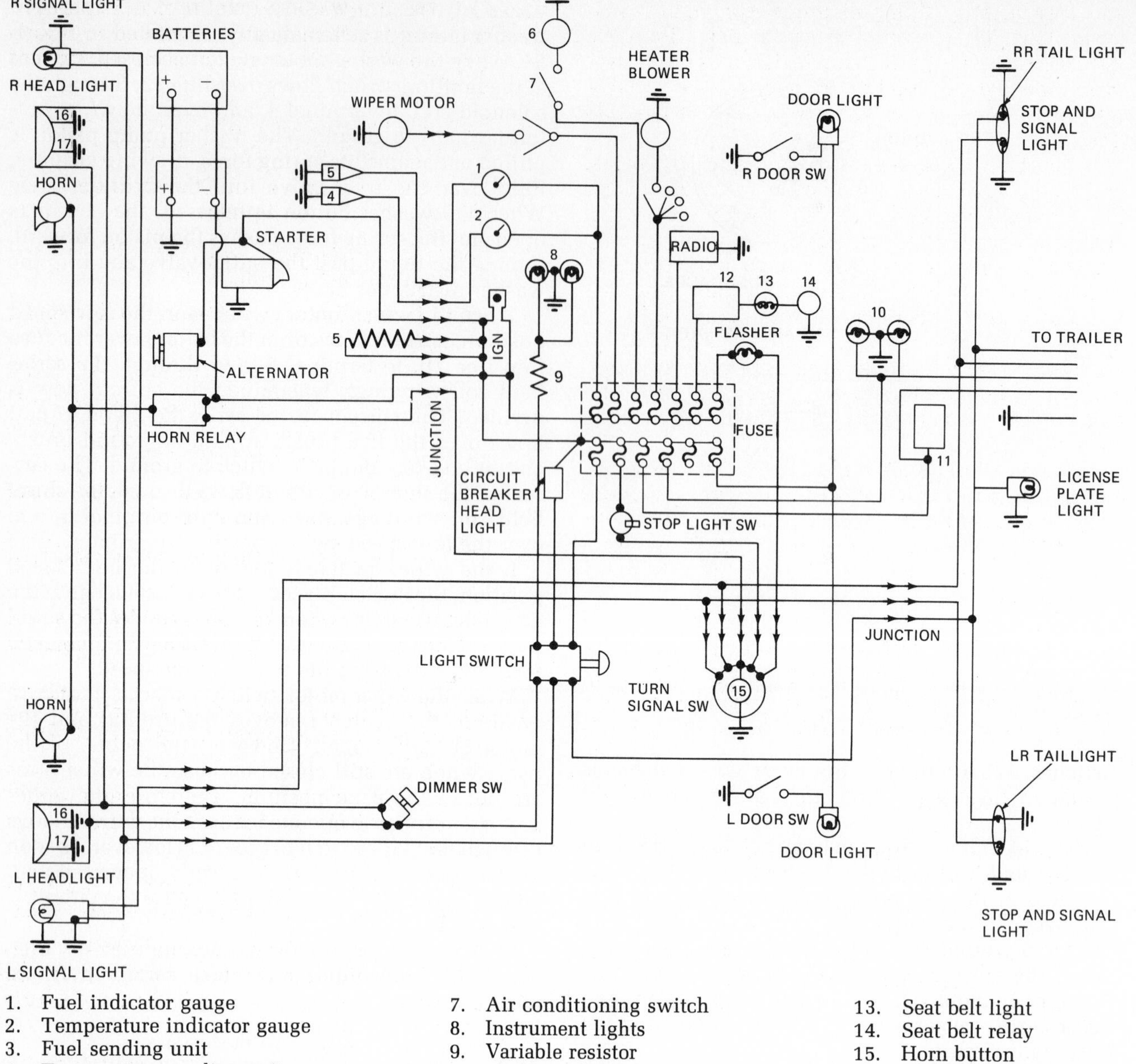

1. Fuel indicator gauge
2. Temperature indicator gauge
3. Fuel sending unit
4. Temperature sending unit
5. Fuel injection shutoff solenoid
6. Air conditioning clutch
7. Air conditioning switch
8. Instrument lights
9. Variable resistor
10. Clearance light (body light)
11. Antilock brake
12. Seat belt buzzer
13. Seat belt light
14. Seat belt relay
15. Horn button
16. Headlight low filament
17. Headlight high filament

Fig. 4-55. Electric system of a motortruck, schematically illustrated.

2. Check the fuse.
3. Turn the ignition switch on and the wiper motor to low-speed position, then measure the voltage at terminals 1, 2, 3, 4, and 5.
4. Measure the voltage drop at the wiper, washer, and park switches.
5. Measure the ground resistance at the wiper, washer, and park switches. If the wiper motor will not operate at low speed, measure the resistance of the shunt coil. If it fails to operate at high speed, check the park switch—the points may be pitted or the ground circuit may have high resistance. Also measure the resistance of resistor No. 7. It may be open, shorted, or grounded.

Electric System for a Motortruck The electric system of a motortruck is schematically illustrated in Fig. 4-55. **NOTE** The light, signal, and brake circuits are all slightly different. Current from the alternator and battery is directed to the ignition switch then to both fuse blocks, and to the headlight switch circuit breaker.

When either the left- or right-hand driver cab door is open, the door switch closes and the door light circuit is completed.

If the light switch is partly pulled out, the front, rear, and trailer parking lights and the dashboard light circuits are completed. Current flows over the circuit breaker, over the light switch, and to the front and rear parking lights of the motor vehicle and trailer parking connection. Current flows from the light switch over the variable resistor, to the instrumentation lights. **NOTE** By varying the variable resistor position, the brightness of the instrumentation lights can be changed.

If the driver actuates the brake pedal (hydraulic brake), the brake switch is released, thereby closing the circuit. On air brakes, it is the air pressure that closes the switch and completes the brake circuit. Current flows from the fuse box to the stop light switch, and over the turn signal switch to the rear tail and trailer stop lights. If the signal switch is moved to the left-hand turn position, the circuit to the left-hand stop light filaments is completed. However, it is constantly opened and closed by the flasher which is actuated by the higher signal light current flow.

If the headlight switch is pulled all the way out, current flows from the switch to the dimmer switch, and, depending on the switch position, either both low- and high-headlight filament circuits are completed or only the circuit to the low (dim) filament is completed.

If any circuit failure occurs, begin service by checking the batteries and the battery voltage, the fuses, and the light bulbs. Use a voltmeter to check the existing voltage at the switches, lamps, and terminals, and do not forget to check the ground circuit resistance.

Review Questions

1. Complete the following sentences by filling in the missing words:
   (*a*) An electron is a unit of an atom which is ______ charged.
   (*b*) A proton is a unit of an atom which is ______ charged.
   (*c*) A neutron is a unit of an atom which is ______ charged.
2. List four reasons why it is essential to insulate a conductor.
3. Is it the P material or the N material that is connected to the negative terminal of the battery when the diode is connected in forward bias?
4. How do manufacturers identify and discern between positive and negative diodes?
5. Why are the elements in a battery chemically separated from one another?
6. Write the formulas for calculating (*a*) voltage, (*b*) amperes, and (*c*) resistance.
7. What is the difference between a relay and a magnetic switch?
8. Why do all cranking motors draw the maximum specified current when the armature is not turning, and why does the current decrease as the armature increases in speed?
9. Outline the procedure to solder a closed-end battery terminal to a battery cable.
10. Outline three methods to protect an electric circuit against overload.
11. Outline the procedure you would follow and the precautions you would take when cleaning a battery.
12. Outline the steps required to perform a high-discharge test on a battery having a CCA rating of 475 A.
13. Explain why battery B, when using a series-parallel switch, is usually less charged than battery A.
14. List four reasons why the output of the alternator may be below specification when tested.
15. If the engine temperature gauge fails to indicate the engine temperature, how would you determine if the trouble lies in the temperature gauge or in the sending unit?
16. Outline two reasons why the headlights may not produce maximum candle power.

Unit 5
Frames

The frame, which is supported by the suspension, is the main part of any motor vehicle structure. It must bear the engine and its accessories, the transmission, the cab, the body, and the working attachments as well as the pay load. In addition it must be able to absorb the full engine torque, the braking effort from the suspension, and the shock load, strain, and stress. It must, therefore, be sturdy but flexible enough to absorb the stress, strain, and shock vibrations that roll like waves throughout the structure.

Each of these desirable features contributes to the necessity for a variety of types and sizes of on- and off-highway equipment frames and, what is more, the varieties increase so as to include such changing characteristics as the intended load-carrying capacity, the type of work to be done, and so forth. Frame structures also vary from one manufacturer to another, even though the equipment may be put to the same use.

ON-HIGHWAY FRAMES

The frames of all on-highway vehicles are very similar in basic design—that is, they consist of two side rails which carry the load and crossmembers which stabilize the rails and may serve as the mounting pads for the accessories. However, since motor vehicles or vehicles in general are specifically designed according to their intended load-carrying capacity, purpose, or operating condition, or are designed to accommodate a particular engine type or cab design, the rail material, dimensions, and length will vary accordingly. The number and types and the strength of the crossmembers must also be designed to complement the rails.

Motor Vehicle Frames A standard frame is one with straight, parallel rails (see Fig. 5-1). A drop-center frame is one where the side rails drop in height immediately behind the cab crossmember, lowering the center of gravity and giving the motortruck or truck-tractor greater stability. It has an additional advantage in that the lower cab floor makes it easier for the operator to get in and out of the vehicle. To accommodate a specific engine and to allow a "cab over mounting," the front section of the frame is widened (right after the cab crossmember) by bulging the left-hand rail slightly outward and offsetting the right-hand rail, or the frame side rails are equally offset but start further back (from approximately the first intermediate crossmember).

Motortrucks and some full railers in the 6000- to 10,000-lb [2724.0- to 4540.0-kg] GVW ranges may use side rails and crossmembers that are press-formed from carbon sheet steel. In this case, the side rails are not straight, they are not parallel to each other, they are not equal in depth, height, or flange width, and the crossmembers as well as the body mounting and suspension are either riveted or welded to the side rails. See Fig. 5-2 for one such example. Rails other than these are hot- or cold-drawn from carbon steel, steel alloy, or aluminum. Each of these frame materials is manufactured to a different yield strength, which is measured in pounds per square inch (psi) or kilopascals (kPa). The yield strength of a material is the maximum pressure it will withstand before it is permanently bent or twisted out of shape. The yield strength of carbon steel frames, rails, and crossmembers varies from 36,000 to 80,000 psi [248,040 to 551,200 kPa]. The yield strength of steel alloy (heat-treated steel) varies from 80,000 to 110,000 psi [551,200 to 757,900 kPa] and is sometimes higher. Aluminum yield strength ranges from 40,000 to 60,000 psi [275,600 to 413,400 kPa].

Standard rails are channel-structured and vary in depth, height, and flange width from about $6 \times 2 \times \frac{3}{16}$ in, to about $14\frac{5}{8} \times 3 \times \frac{5}{16}$ in, or $11 \times 3\frac{1}{2} \times \frac{3}{8}$ in. The channel of the aluminum rails is usually $11 \times 3\frac{1}{2}$ in, having a $2\frac{1}{2}$-in web and a $\frac{3}{4}$-in flange thickness.

To increase resistance to bend and twist, and to increase the load-carrying capacity, various methods of frame rail reinforcement are applied (see Fig. 5-3). Although the strength of the section modulus relates to the frame section length, width, height, and thickness and the shape of the rail, it does not account for the yield strength of the rail material or crossmember. (A section modulus refers to that area between the side rails and two crossmembers). **NOTE** To be fully effective, the reinforcement material must have a yield strength equal to that of the rail. However, in order to avoid a rapid change in strength of one frame section modulus to the one adjoining, the reinforcement should be gradual (tapered).

The rail is reinforced rather than being made wider, higher, and thicker, to retain its flexibility and to increase its longevity.

Fish plating—that is, bolting a steel plate to the outside of the rails—is no longer a common practice by manufacturers; however, it is applied when the truck tractor or motortruck has a standard frame but has to carry a load greater than the standard frame design allows, or when the vehicle has to operate on rough terrain. (It also can be used to mount the body to the frame.) Various types of crossmembers are bolted with special frame bolts to the rails or gussets. A *gusset* is a steel plate or angle iron reinforcement

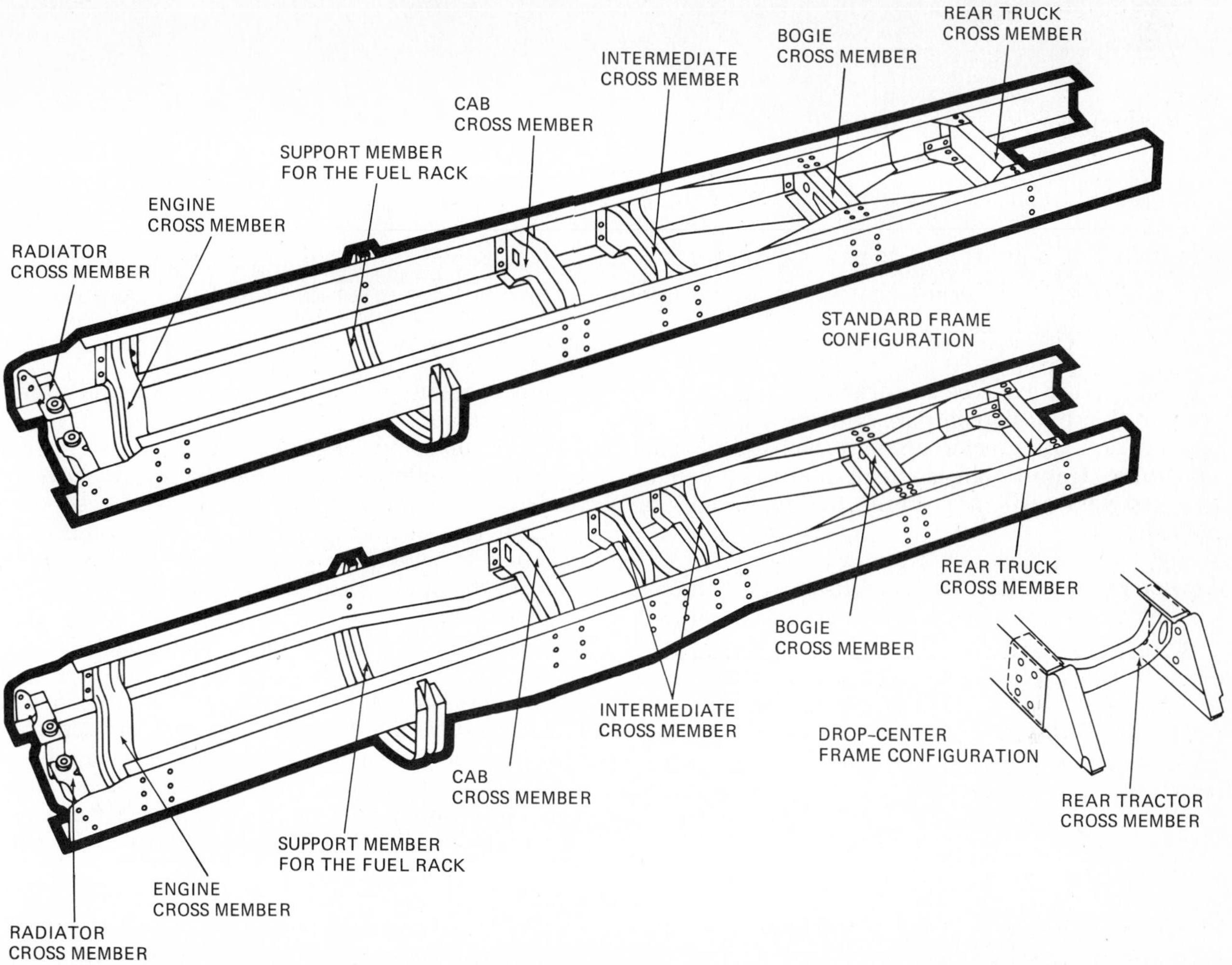

Fig. 5-1 Schematic view of standard (top) and drop-center (lower) frame configurations.

used to strengthen the structure. On smaller frames, the crossmembers and brackets are riveted to the rails.

The crossmember that supports the radiator on two rubber mounting pads is almost identical on all frames. The two brackets and the cab crossmember supporting the cab are also common in design, and usually the same type of special rubber cushion supports are used to help reduce road shocks. The drive shaft support bracket(s) and on some models also the air-tank brackets are usually bolted to this crossmember. Also common to all frames is the fuel tank support member which is bolted in front of the cab mounting bracket. The number and shapes of the intermediate crossmembers vary according to the frame width and/or the frame length. The rear axle (bogie) crossmember is commonly a back-to-back channel, bolted to the left- and right-hand gussets, which in turn are bolted to the rails. The rear crossmember design depends upon whether the vehicle is a motortruck, a dump truck, or a truck-tractor.

Figure 5-4 shows a correctly installed body-bound bolt. Body-bound bolts are manufactured with a shank diameter closely controlled to effect an interference fit with the members which are to be attached. **NOTE** Use only body-bound bolts having the correct shank length, a self-locking nut, and steel washers. When the rail is aluminum, two steel washers are used, one on each side of the rail.

It is obvious that any weight added to a motortruck, truck-tractor, or trailer will reduce the pay load, and therefore increase the operating costs. For this reason, when the vehicle is required to carry bulk loads, the motortruck, truck-tractor, and trailer frame rails are made from an aluminum alloy. When aluminum rails and steel crossmembers are used, or whenever unlike metals are fastened together, the surfaces must be painted or another surface covering must be applied to retard corrosion.

The experimental frame design shown in Fig.

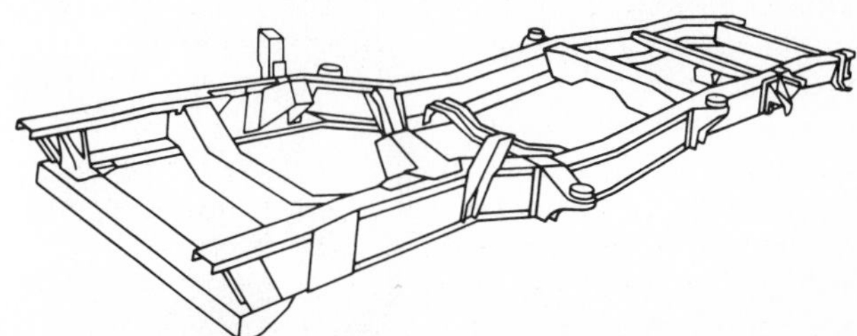

Fig. 5-2 Schematic view of a C frame fabricated from hot-rolled C-1008 steel.

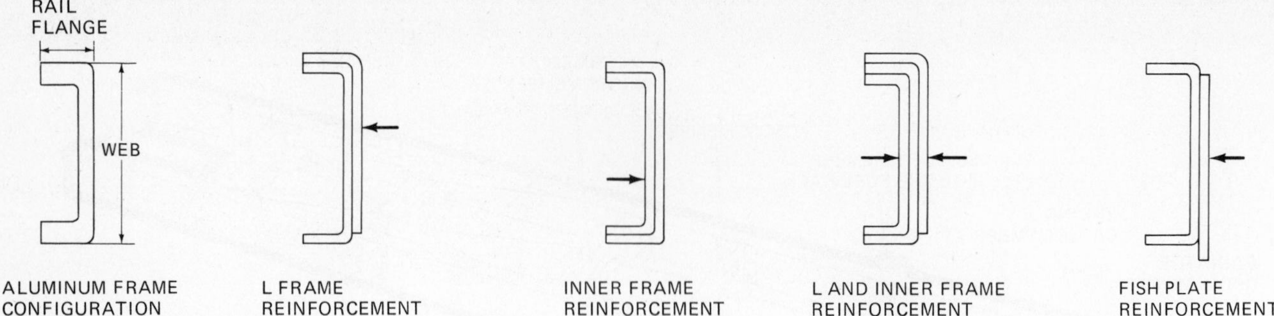

Fig. 5-3 Frame rail reinforcement.

5-5 could very well be the frame of tomorrow. It weighs about 20 percent less and has a greater deflection rate and greater strength than today's conventional frame. The section modulus can be changed very easily by varying the height and the web angles.

Trailer Frames Full trailer and semitrailer frames may have the same frame structure as a motortruck frame, except that additional intermediate crossmembers are used instead of the radiator and engine crossmembers.

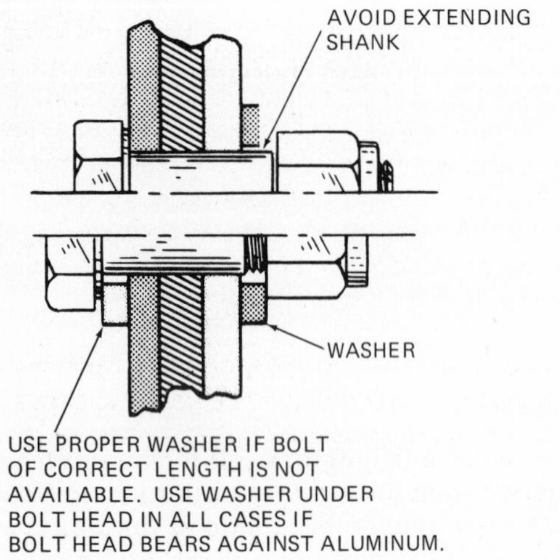

Fig. 5-4 Correct body-bound bolt installation. (*Mack Canada Inc.*)

Full trailers and semitrailers that are designed for capacity by volume rather than by weight have no frames. The flatdeck body floor is reinforced with longitudinal steel or aluminum channels and cross channels to which the suspension, the upper turntable, or the upper plate is welded or bolted. See Fig. 5-6. On some of these trailer structures, the tandem trailer axle can be moved forward and backward on plates welded to the center frame channel.

To increase the load-carrying capacity on this type of trailer, the outside deck irons are replaced with rails of the same material as the frame rails or with I-beam rails manufactured from sheet steel. Some full trailers and semitrailers have either cold- or hot-drawn I-beam frame rails instead of the conventional channel rails, or have rails of a welded structure, in which case the mounting bracket for the suspension, upper plate, and the deck or floor frame members are welded to the frame rails. See Fig. 5-7. On some of the latter type of trailer frame designs, the tandem trailer axle can also be moved. In that case, the mounting brackets for the suspension are welded to a specially designed I-beam frame, and the I-beam rail of the frame rests on the brackets. Two spring-loaded locking pins secure the suspension to the frame rails, and the clamps anchor the suspension to the rail flanges (see Fig. 5-8).

With the ability to shift the tandem rear axle, the

Fig. 5-5 Prototype truss frame using standard crossmembers. (*United States Steel International*)

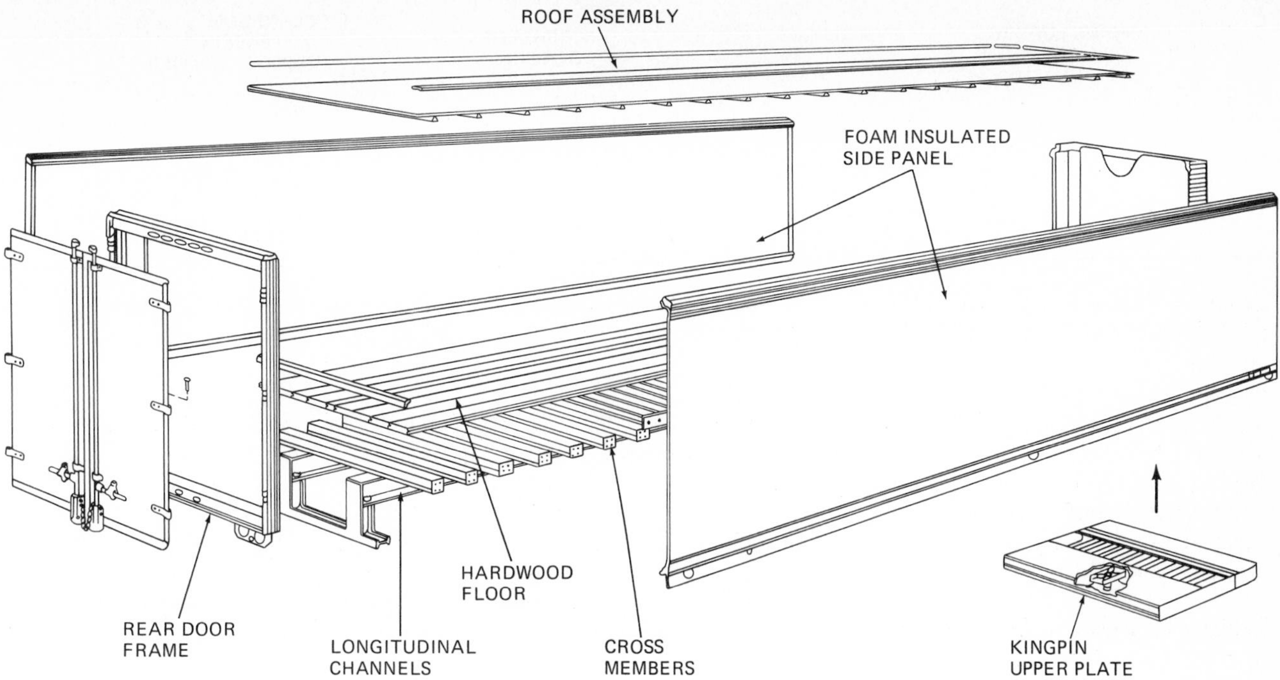

Fig. 5-6 Schematic view of a van semitrailer.

bridge formula is increased and a better utilization of the load distribution is possible. Some of these 45-ft [13.72-m] box-type liquid- or dry-freight bodies use a center lift steering axle.

Full trailers and semitrailers that have a body designed to carry liquid, milk, oil, fuel, etc., or designed to carry road-building material, coal, ore, etc., use the body structure as the frame and crossmember. This gives the motor vehicle, trailer, or semitrailer a greater load-carrying capacity. See Fig. 5-9.

Body Mounting A concentrated stress is inadvertently placed on the frame and body when the body is not mounted correctly, which promotes not only damage to the frame but also to the body. In this regard, a number of common body-mounting methods are outlined and some general dos and don'ts.

It is relatively simple to mount a dump box to the frame, since the body and frame manufacturers have produced the mounting facilities and bored the bolt holes. However, to correctly mount a platform body, or any other type of attachment to the frame requires careful consideration and common sense. Remember that any body mounting will place additional stress on the frame; therefore, you should avoid welding the body to the frame. To weld them together will reduce the flexibility of the frame and permit early frame failure at the welding point.

WELDED BRACKETS AND PLATES If you have to weld the bracket or plate to the frame, or to repair or reinforce the frame by welding, first remove the ground cable from the battery. This step will prevent damage to such electric components as the generator, wheel sensor, etc., or damage to electronic components. Always clamp the ground cable as close as possible to the welded area and never to rotating components, as this could cause pitting on the bear-

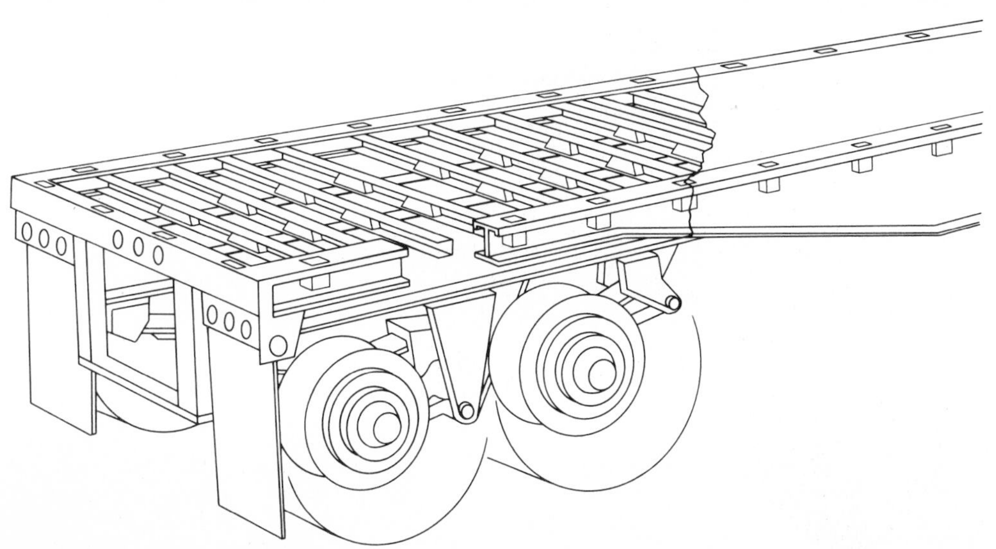

Fig. 5-7 Schematic view of a flat-deck having fabricated I-beam rails.

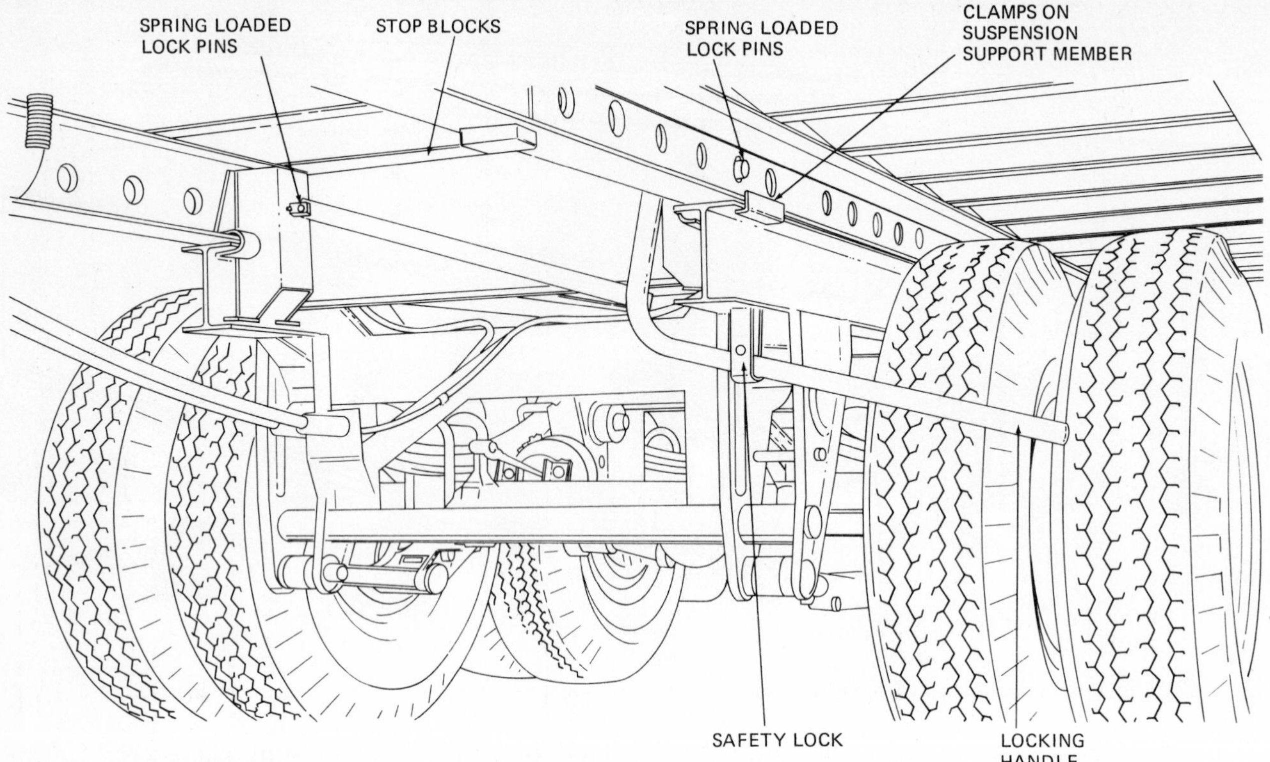

Fig. 5-8 Tandem axle shift. (*Fruehauf Division, Fruehauf Corporation*)

ing races and the rolling elements. Make certain the surfaces to be welded are free of rust and oil. When the components to be welded are near wires, cables, hoses, or fuel lines, protect them with asbestos cloth. Cast brackets should never be welded to the frame because the weld will not hold. Never use the oxygen method of welding or a torch for heating the frame. It will weaken the frame and cause failure. Use the recommended welding rod and size for the rail material and follow the suggested current and voltage specification to ensure good penetration. You may use smaller-diameter electrodes and make several passes to reduce the heat, but do not weld across the rail flange or closer than 0.75 in [2 cm] from the flange face, and stop your weld at least 0.375 in [0.7 cm] from the end of the part to be welded. Always have a fire extinguisher at your work area.

BOLTED BRACKETS AND PLATES If the bracket or plate is to be bolted to the frame, try to use existing holes. If new holes must be drilled, make sure their size does not exceed the size of the crossmember or spring bracket bolt holes. Use cobalt high-speed drills, sharpened to an included angle of 150°, with a lip clearance angle between 7° and 15°. Drill a pilot hole first, and then drill the hole to the desired size. However, do not drill right through. Stop just before the hole becomes full-size. Use a tapered reamer to remove the lip. Do not drill holes closer than 1.75

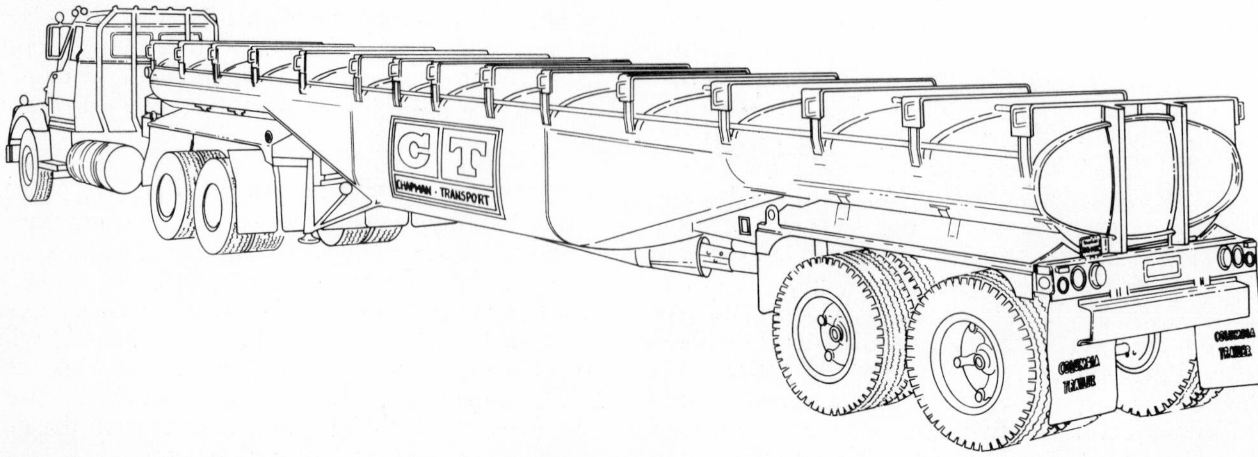

Fig. 5-9 10,900-gallon semitrailer. (*Columbia Trailer Co. Ltd.*)

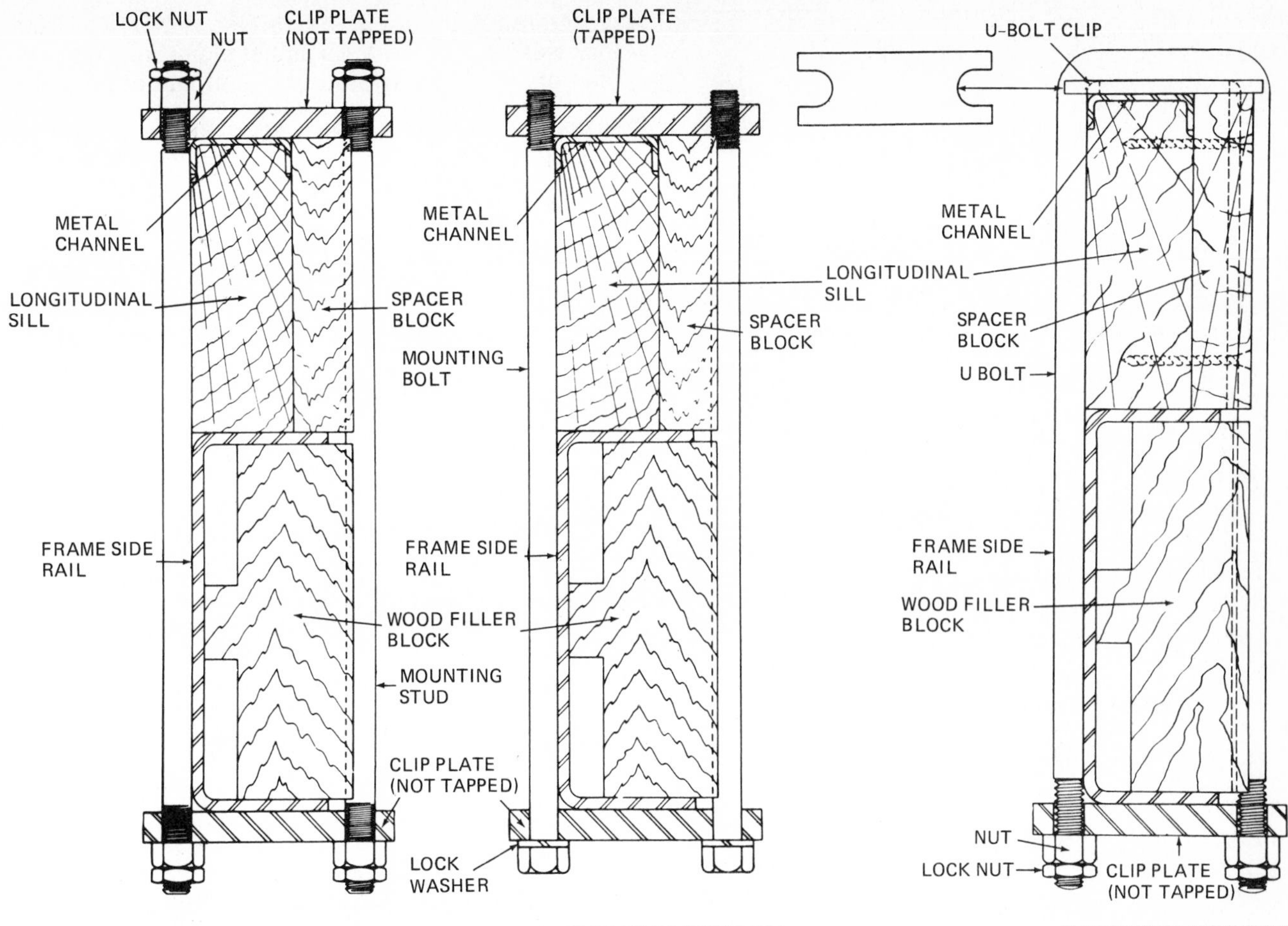

Fig. 5-10 Three types of longitudinal sill mountings. (*GMC Truck and Coach Division*)

in [4.5 cm] from the top or bottom of the rail flange face; do not have the center of the holes less than 3 in [7.5 cm] apart; do not drill more than two holes in a vertical line; do not drill a hole in a frame.

MOUNTING A BODY HAVING LONGITUDINAL SILLS A body having longitudinal sills can be mounted with relative ease (see Fig. 5-10). Longitudinal sills are two beams fastened to the underside of the body, which extend from the front to the rear. This body design provides even weight distribution onto the frame rails, prevents additional localized stress, maintains frame flexibility, and is extremely secure. Nevertheless, several precautionary checks and preliminary steps have to be taken prior to and during the mounting of this type of body to the frame. First, you must decide which method of fastening should be used: stud bolts, mounting bolts, or U bolts, and then you must select the appropriate bolt size. If the appropriate sized bolt is not available it is better to use a bolt which is one size larger rather than one which is too small, and it is important that the bolt grade is not lower than grade 5. Next, you must check and measure the sill height and sill spacing. The width must be the same as that of the rail flanges so that both sills rest, full face, on the top surface of the rail flanges. The sill height must be sufficient to guarantee that under no circumstance will the body come in contact with the tire when it is under maximum spring deflection. The sills must extend as close as possible to the back of the cab but must not interfere with the cab. Next, you must decide how many mounting points are needed and where to place them. **NOTE** Use at least three for each sill and try to space them evenly so as to minimize additional stress. In order for the sills and the frame flanges to have 100 percent contact, the location of the projecting bolts or rivet heads must be marked on the sills and the sills then countersunk. Next, you must taper out approximately 0.5 in [1.27 cm] at the front ends of the sills. The length of the taper should run about 20 in [0.5 m] to allow the frame to deflect without placing a stress on it at the point where the sill ends.

If the sills are channel iron or aluminum, a hardwood strip the width of the rail flange and the length of the sill must be placed between the sill and frame flange to assure secure mounting. Under this circumstance the hardwood strip would, of course, be countersunk to take care of the protruding bolts or rivet heads. If the steel or aluminum channel sills are of a light structure but have the required sill height, a spacer must be fitted inside the body channel. When the body sills are narrower than the rail flanges, a spacer block must be securely fastened to the sills at the points where you intend to fasten the

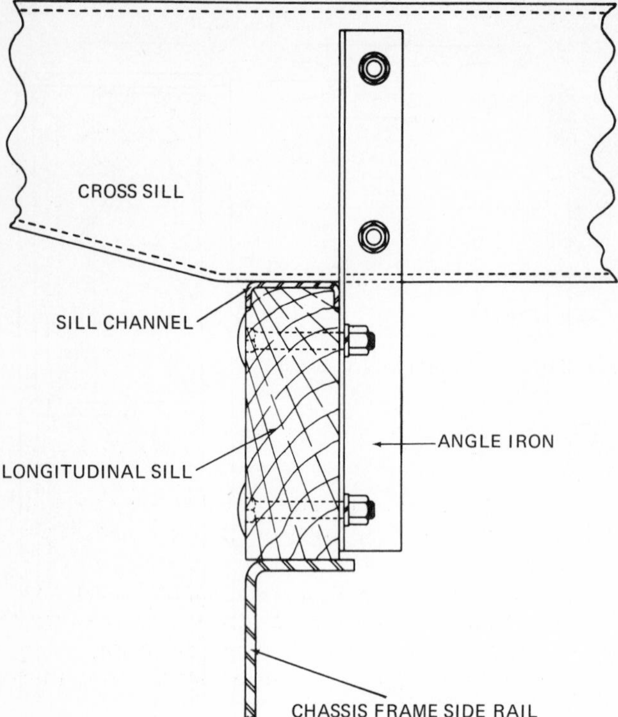

Fig. 5-11 Method used to attach longitudinal still to cross sills. (*GMC Truck and Coach Division*)

sills to the rails. **NOTE** Some manufacturers recommend cutting a clearance groove in the wood spacer for the mounting bolts to further secure the wood to the sill. Next, you must fit a filler block about 12 in [0.3 m] long, and about 0.5 in [1.7 cm] wider than the inside frame rail flange, inside the frame rail at the point where you intend to fasten the sill to the frame. Cut a groove in the filler block to give mounting bolt clearance and to hold the filler block in position. You may have to cut out some corners to provide clearance for the air line and wiring cable, located inside the rail channel. Once this is done, cut six pieces of 6-in [15.24-cm] channel iron having the external width of the sill, or bend six pieces of No. 14 gauge sheet metal to these dimensions. Locate and mark the fastening point and then cut the sill so that the iron channel fits flush over the sill. **NOTE** The two end mountings should be located about 15 in [0.4 m] from the sill ends, and the other mounting(s) should be spaced as equally as possible. If you are required to make the U-bolt clips or the clip plates, they must be at least as thick as the bolts to be used and the holes must be spaced so that the bolts fit snugly against the outside rail and against the filler and spacer block. The width of the clip must be at least three times the diameter of the bolts, and the clip length must allow at least one bolt thickness of material from the hole to the end of the clip. When you use tappet plate mountings, make certain the threads in the clip plates are not damaged.

Upon completion of these steps, lift the body into place, align it to the frame, and recheck the sill to see that it rests firmly on the rail flanges. Next, install the mounting bolts and draw them evenly to the specified torque. Make certain the clip plates are flat on the rail flanges and sill surfaces. **NOTE** Use a lock washer when using a tappet mounting and double nuts when using stud or U-bolt mountings.

MOUNTING A BODY HAVING CROSS SILLS Mounting bodies having cross sills is more time-consuming since you must make two sills to fit the width and length of the body. You must also fasten (with carriage bolts and angle iron) each cross sill to the longitudinal sills (Fig. 5-11) and then fasten the longitudinal sills to the frame rails. Bodies having cross sills are few in number because the weight of the load is concentrated at the intersection of the cross sills and the longitudinal sills. Furthermore, the body floor is higher, therefore raising the center of gravity.

When you are required to mount this type of body, use angle iron of a width at least four times the diameter of the carriage bolt to be used and cut it about 1 in [2.54 cm] shorter than the overall height of the two sills. Mark and then drill the holes in the angle iron so that when the iron is placed into position the holes are about one-quarter distance (of the sill height) from the sill faces. Mount the longitudinal sills to the frame first, and then lift the body into position. Clamp the angle iron into position, using C clamps, and then drill the holes to the longitudinal and cross sills. Use flat washers under the nuts, and tighten the nuts until the carriage bolts begin to bite into the hardwood sills.

FISH-PLATE MOUNTINGS FOR BODIES When the frame is not reinforced and the body is designed to carry a maximum load, the fish-plate mounting method is usually used. It gives the frame additional strength and durability, yet reduces frame flexing. Fish plating is the bolting of a steel plate (which is commonly wider than the web of the rail) to the outside of the frame web. It is recommended that for this type of mounting you use as many of the existing frame holes as possible to preserve frame strength that would be lost by additional holes.

Select one piece of sheet steel of a width and length which will extend beyond the critical stress area (which is immediately after the cab and first rear spring mounting point). Taper the plate ends to an angle of about 45° so that the plate gradually overlaps between frame sections to avoid having an abrupt change in section modulus. Remove all mounting brackets, hangers, and bolts that can be moved (by the thickness of the plate) outward whose removal will not hinder operation of the vehicle. Next, cut the plates so that they fit around the remaining brackets or holders, but avoid sharp internal angles (round off or make angles large). Smooth all sharp edges, nicks, and burrs by grinding. Clamp the plate to the frame web, drill holes in the plate, and reinstall the brackets, holders, or clamps. Make certain you remove the rough edges from the holes before installing the bolts. Although it may be necessary to use longer frame bolts, do not use a lock washer or bolt less than grade 5.

Body-bound bolts If the mounting of the body is in any way precarious, use body-bound bolts. In this case, drill the bolt holes to the recommended shank diameter—for example, a $\frac{5}{8}$-in-18 UNF-2 A bolt requires a drill size of 0.653/0.657, and then the hole must be reamed to the specified size. **CAUTION** Do not turn the reamer in a counterclockwise rotation as this could break the cutting edge. If the plate is fastened and you find you must drill some additional holes, choose carefully the location of the new bolt holes. (Follow the drilling dos and don'ts previously outlined.)

Plug welding Another method recommended by manufacturers to avoid using additional bolts is to attach the plates through plug welding. To plug weld the plate to the frame, you must determine the additional mounting points and drill plug holes before bolting the plate to the web. The size of the plug holes will vary depending on the thickness of the plate material. For example, a 0.25-in [6.35-mm] plate requires a 0.75-in [19.05-mm] hole, whereas a 0.75-in [19.05-mm] plate requires a 1.375-in [34.9-mm] hole. **CAUTION** Drill these holes—do not use a cutting torch.

When the fish plate is bolted to the frame web, use a C clamp to hold the plate tight against the frame at the point where you intend to weld the plate to the frame. Select the correct current, voltage, and the correct electrode size, as well as electroyield strength (check service manual), and make certain any scale is removed from each successive pass to assure good penetration.

After the fish plate is fastened to the frame web, lift the body into place, align it, and then weld the fish plate to the subframe of the body.

Frame Damage and Repair Frame damage may be classified into seven types:

- Cracked rails and/or crossmembers
- Bent rail flanges and crossmembers
- Sag frame
- Twisted frame
- Buckled frame
- Diamond frame
- Sidesway frame

Frame cracks are partial openings which do not divide the frame into separate parts. Bent flanges are distorted surfaces. A sag frame is a frame which has one high or low corner owing to a bent side rail. A twisted frame is one which has side rails that are no longer horizontal although they are not distorted. A buckled frame is one which is bent upward at one point and bent downward at another. A diamond frame is one which has had one rail forced forward or backward so that the rails are no longer squared off. A sidesway frame is one which is no longer straight. Both rails are bent either at the front or the rear, to the left or to the right.

Damage to frame rails and/or crossmembers is caused by high stress resulting from

1. Overloading
2. Uneven load distribution (particularly on dump trucks which localize high stresses on the frame)
3. Using the dump truck to spread the load (which may cause excessive flexing and bending of the frame)
4. Inadequate baffles or uneven separation of livestock (which may cause high stresses to the frame during stopping, acceleration, and cornering)
5. Operating the vehicle on extremely rough terrain
6. Improper or loose body mountings
7. Incorrect bolt pattern or loose bolts
8. Rail flanges that have been welded
9. Holes drilled in the rail flanges
10. Mounting improperly reinforced

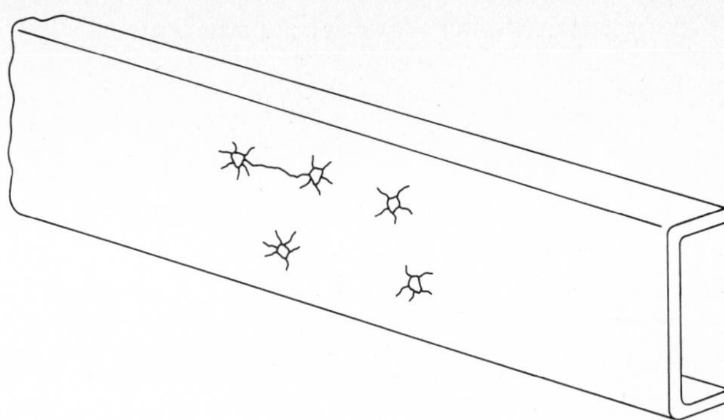

Fig. 5-12 Sunburst cracks.

FRAME REPAIRS Although manufacturers do not recommend repairing damaged side rails, there are several methods by which this can be done, and it is more practical, less expensive, and involves a shorter downtime if they are repaired rather than replaced. On the other hand, it is generally more expedient to replace a damaged crossmember, and less time is lost by doing so.

To replace a loose rivet or a crossmember or bracket that is riveted to the side rail, first remove any component or part that could hamper the replacement process. Where applicable, protect any wire cables, hoses, or pipes. Next, use a center punch to mark the center of the rivet head, then drill a pilot hole through the head and rivet body. Then, using a drill $\frac{1}{32}$ in smaller than the body, drill through the head and body. Hold a pipe having the inside size of the rivet head over the undrilled side of the rivet and then drive the rivet out with a punch and hammer. Do not use a hammer and chisel or a cutting torch to remove the rivet head, as this will damage the frame flange or web and/or elongate the hole.

If the crossmember bracket or gusset bolts are loose, remove them and check the holes, as a loose bolt could cause a crack in the frame or crossmember. If a hole is enlarged or elongated, use a drill and reamer to enlarge it to the next size. If the hole shows sunburst cracks (see Fig. 5-12), manufacturers recommend replacing the rail.

To repair the cracked hole, enlarge it by grinding beyond the cracks, weld a plug into it, grind both surfaces smooth, and place a reinforcement over it as shown in Fig. 5-13. Next, redrill the mounting

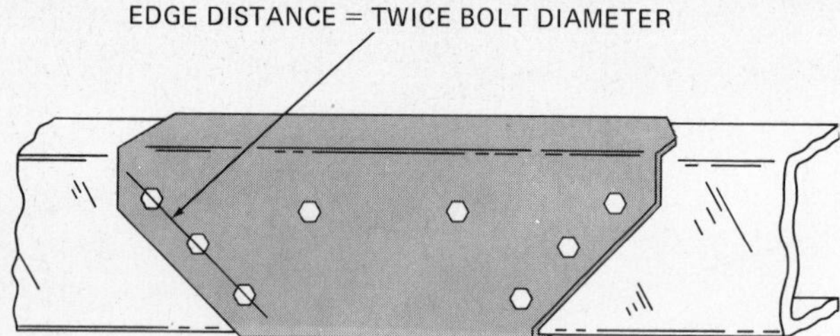

Fig. 5-13 Correct method of reinforcing frame rail. (*Mack Canada Inc.*)

bolt holes. If the crossmember or gusset is welded to the rails, use a grinder to open the weld points and then follow the recommendations of the applicable frame service manual with regard to welding and reinforcement.

If the frame flange(s) is (are) cracked, follow the preliminary steps outlined on p. 101 and then drill a 0.25-in [6-mm] hole at the end of the crack(s). Grind (in a V shape) the entire length of the crack, one side only, from the hole to the end of the flange. The total angle of the V should not be smaller than 60° or larger than 90°. Check the horizontal and longitudinal alignment of the rails by holding a chalk line to one end of the frame rail end and holding the other end as close as possible to the cab. If the frame rail is straight, widen the crack with a hacksaw to provide good penetration of the weld. If the frame is not straight, use jacks and chains to align it and then proceed with the welding. After the crack is welded, grind the inside and outside surfaces smooth. **NOTE** If the frame is reinforced, you must follow the same procedure with the inside rail. Next, you must decide if a reinforcement is necessary and, if so, which method you will use. The most common is the channel reinforcement. This method requires a steel plate which will extend beyond the critical area, then cutting, grinding, and bending it to the desired shape and attaching it to the frame rail with bolts, rivets, or through plug welding (see Figs. 5-14 and 5-15). Fish-plating L reinforcement and strap reinforcement are very seldom used.

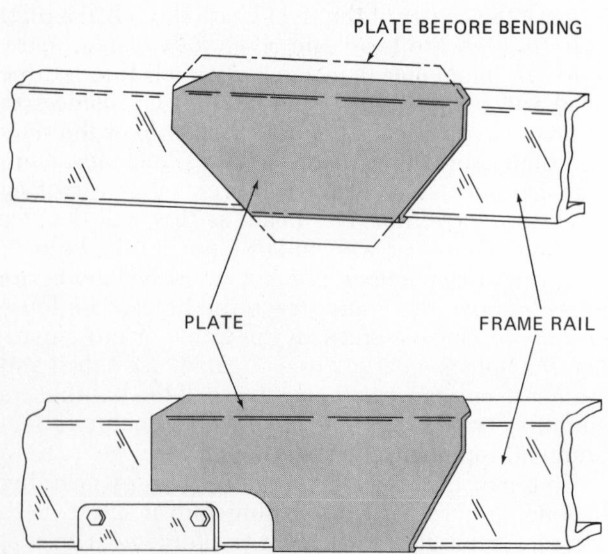

Fig. 5-14 Plate reinforcement. (*Mack Canada Inc.*)

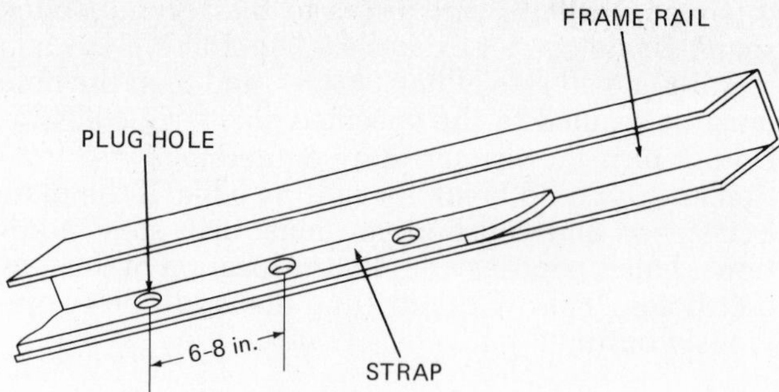

Fig. 5-15 Strap reinforcement using plug welding. (*GMC Truck and Coach Division*)

SPECIALTY SHOP REPAIRS A frame that is sagged, twisted, buckled, sideswayed, or diamond shaped must be repaired in a specialty shop. These wheel and alignment shops have all the necessary equipment—that is, the hydraulic jacks, brackets of various types, and holding dollys with frame hooks, reach beams, hydraulic riveting clamps, and the electronic measuring equipment to measure and force the frame back to its original shape and dimension (see Fig. 5-16 for an example of such equipment).

NOTE A frame that has been exposed to temperatures above 1300°F [687°C] must be checked to determine the yield strength of the rail material before the frame can be placed back in service.

The average service shop does not have the special equipment to determine if the truck or trailer frame needs to be repaired; therefore, the following guide lines are given to check the frame and axle alignment. **NOTE** A frame or axle which is even slightly out of alignment increases the tire wear, the rolling resistance, and may affect handling.

MOTOR VEHICLE FRAME ALIGNMENT CHECKS Before starting the frame and axle alignment measurements, select a clean level area onto which you can position the motor vehicle. Then check, and if necessary, replace any loose mounting bolts or rivets, and visually check for damage on the frame and suspension before proceeding further. If the frame rails and/or crossmember flanges are bent, straighten them with a device similar to that shown in Fig. 5-17. Do not heat the flanges or use a sledge hammer to straighten them out, as this would cause a bend in the rail.

Next, check to determine if the tire sizes correspond and the pressures are equal. Check the kingpins (for wear) and the wheel bearing adjustment, and then measure the height of the two front spindles—they should be even. If the spindle heights vary, the front axle is bent. If they check out unsatisfactorily, measure the camber to determine which side of the axle(s) is (are) bent. See the material on wheel alignment.

To determine if there is variation in the suspension height, measure at each wheel the distance from the bottom of the rail flange to the top of the axle housing. If the left- and right-hand sides are equal

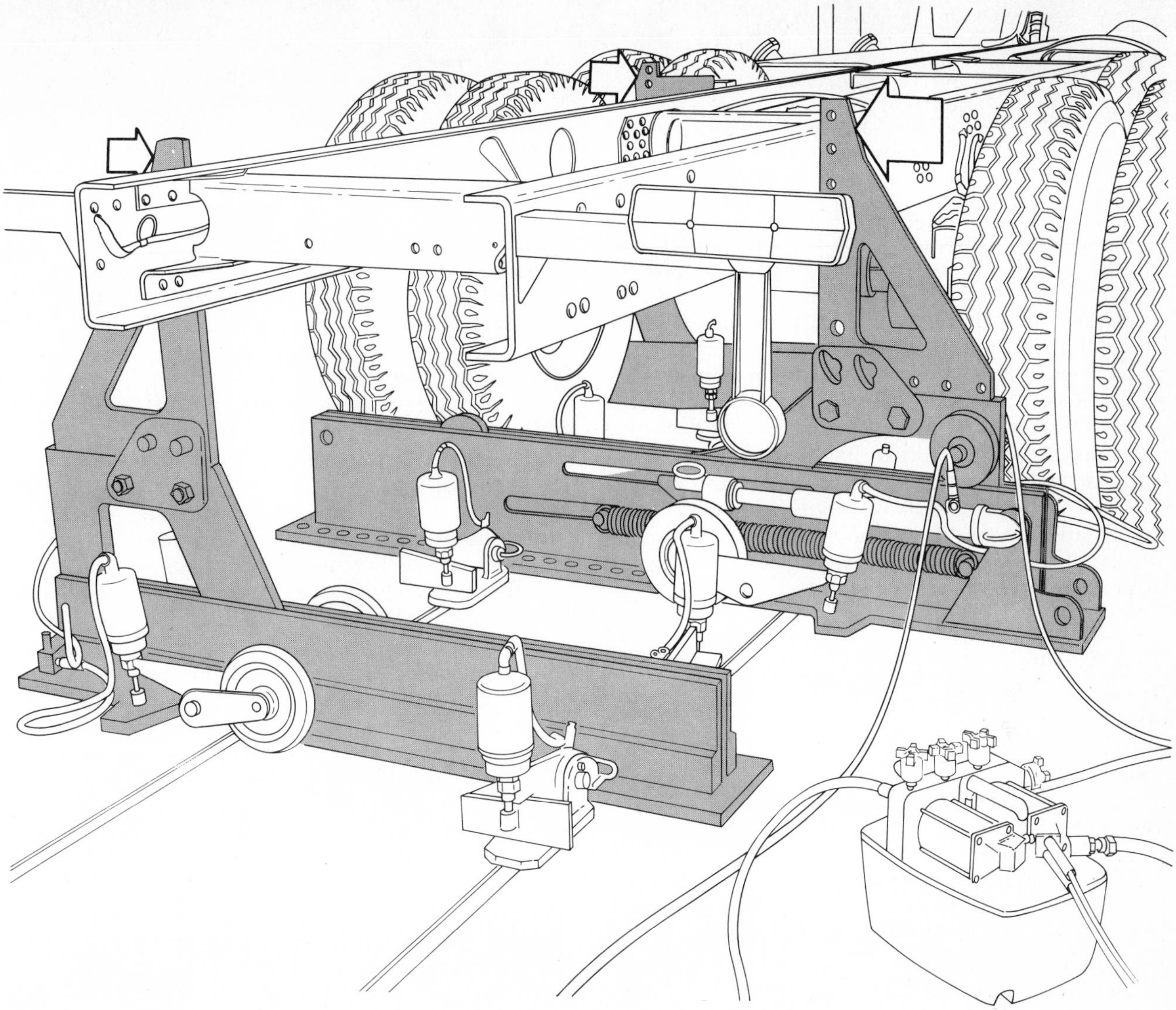

Fig. 5-16 Equipment installed to straighten a sideswayed frame.

or within 0.375 in [0.95 cm], the suspension is satisfactory. A variation in the measurement could indicate a weak suspension, a weak air-leveling device, or that the torque bar is out of adjustment or the rubber parts have deteriorated. It could also indicate a twisted, buckled, or sidesway frame, or a bent axle.

To check the frame height (see Fig. 5-18), first refer to the service manual for the measuring distance and reference points. With a measuring stick, measure the distance from the reference point to the floor at A to G (Fig. 5-18) on both sides of the frame rails. Compare the measurements with those given in the service manual and, if they vary more than allowable, the frame defect is sidesway, swag, buckle, or twist. By comparing the measurements from the left- and right-hand sides, you can establish the points where the damage has occurred.

After all the points mentioned above have been checked and the necessary repairs or adjustments made, refer once more to the service manual for the frame layout (see Fig. 5-19). The reference points given must now be projected onto the floor by means of a plumb bob, with a scriber to accurately mark the points. (Do not use chalk.) Once the points are marked on the floor, move the motor vehicle out of the way and then chalk a line as shown to connect the points. If the frame is straight, the lines crossing at X, Y, and Z will pass over the frame center lines U and V or come within the tolerance given in the service manual. If they do not, you must then measure the distance of each diagonal line to determine which side frame rail is swayed, sagged, or diamond-shaped.

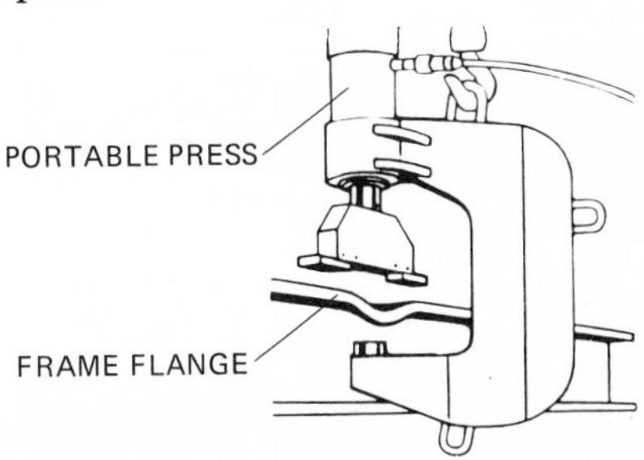

Fig. 5-17 Schematic view of straightening frame rail flange.

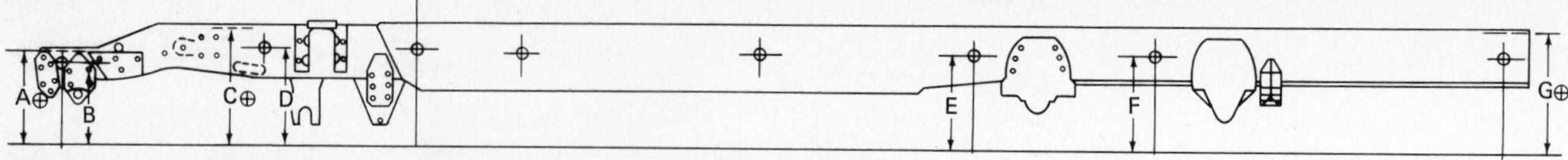

Fig. 5-18 Straight side rail horizontal alignment points. (*Mack Canada Inc.*)

If the frame is straight, measure the distances DL/ER and DR/EL. They should be equal. If not, the front axle is bent. When the motor vehicle is of the single-axle design, measure the distances GR and GL. If the distances are equal, the axle housing is straight and the suspension is not damaged. If they are not equal, the axle housing is bent or the suspension is worn.

When the motor vehicle has a tandem axle you may also have to measure GR and GL, but that will depend on the suspension design. Otherwise measure distances A and B and also C and D. If they are not equal, the axle housing(s) is (are) bent, or the suspension is worn or damaged.

TRAILER ALIGNMENT CHECKS A full trailer or semitrailer that shows any of the following symptoms requires a thorough checkout, including an alignment check: excessive tire wear; the outside left- or right-hand tire does not fully contact the road surface; the vehicle handles poorly; the vehicle does not have the same left- and right-hand steering characteristics, or the trailer is not tracking.

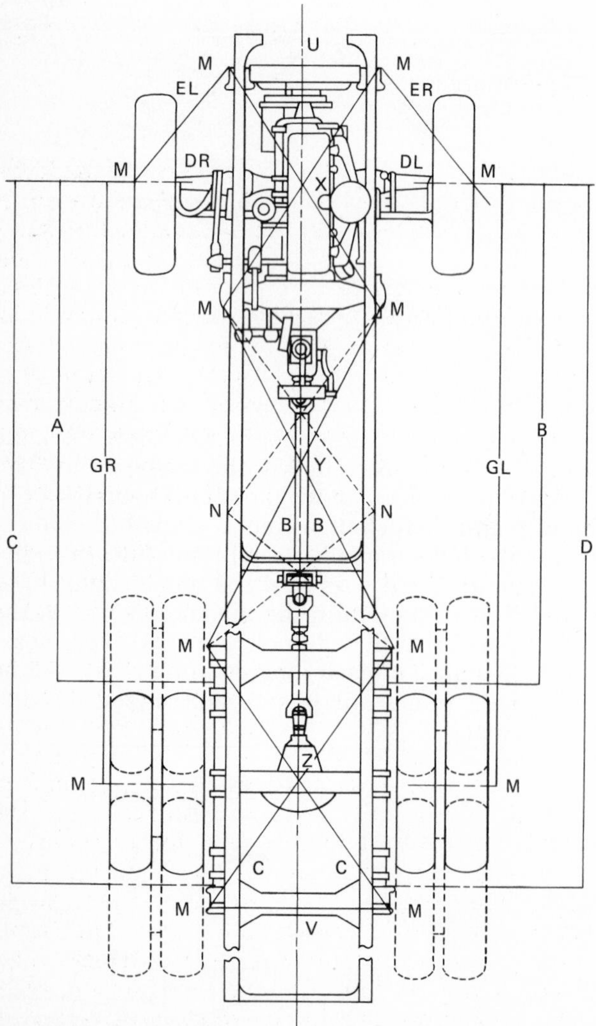

Fig. 5-19 Straight side rail vertical alignment points. (*Mack Canada Inc.*)

To check the trailer frame and axle alignment, perform the same preliminary checks recommended under motor vehicle frame alignment checks. Next, drive the rig onto a clean, level floor and measure the left- and right-hand frame height at the fifth wheel before disconnecting the tractor. Level the trailer frame to the measured trailer frame height, and then measure the spring, axle, and frame height at the manufacturer's specified reference points. With a plumb bob, project the reference points onto the floor, which include the trailer center line and the kingpin center. (If you check the alignment of a full trailer, mark the center of the tongue.)

With the aid of a protractor, measure the spring seat angle and the frame angle before moving the trailer. Both angles should not only be equal but should correspond with the service manual specifications. **NOTE** If the frame angle is ±1°, the fifth wheel is at its proper height and you can proceed with the alignment measurement. If the spring seat angle is greater or less than the frame angle, indications are that the spring or axle installation is incorrect or the suspension parts have broken loose or are worn.

Check the toe-in. (See Unit 9, "Final Drives and Steering Mechanisms.") When the trailer is loaded, it should be zero; when the trailer is not loaded, only a slight toe-in should exist. To change toe-in or toe-out, install a wedge pad (of service manual specification) between the spring and spring seat to rotate the axle. Do not make this adjustment before you have measured the alignment of the axle(s) because a bent axle could either increase or decrease the toe-in and camber. If there is no toe-in and no difference between the spring seat angle and frame angle, the suspension is in good condition and correctly installed. (If the spring seat angle is correct but there is no toe-in, it may indicate the trailer manufacturer has made allowance for axle rotation when under load.) When checkouts have proceeded satisfactorily so far, raise the trailer (at the kingpin), say to about 2°, and once again measure the angles at the spring pads. They should also show an increase of 2°.

If one axle of a tandem axle suspension rotates more than the other, it indicates a worn or loose suspension, but it could also be the result of a bent axle(s). If the camber is less than specified, the axles are bent (usually upward); however, first make certain the tires have the same rolling radius and equal air pressure. (See Unit 9.)

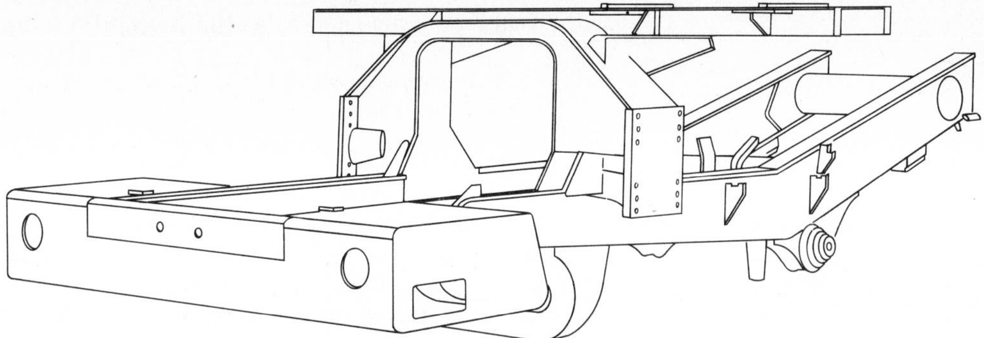

Fig. 5-20 View of a 200-ton dump truck frame.

OFF-HIGHWAY FRAMES

Since innumerable off-highway frames have been designed for the many motortrucks, truck-tractors, trailers, tractors, loaders, and excavators, both of the wheel and track types, they can be covered only generally in this textbook.

Motortrucks, Truck-Tractors, Dump Trucks The frames of the motortrucks, truck-tractors, and dump trucks are all of a one-unit welded structure, made from special alloy steel having a tensile strength as high as 110,000 psi [757,900 kPa]. The single-unit structure design provides excellent section modulus that reduce the areas of stress concentration. Some side rails are modified box section rails with tubular or right-angular crossmembers. The side plates may be as thick as 1 in [25.4 mm] and the top and bottom plates as thick as 1.5 in [38.1 mm]. **NOTE** The individual section modulus on off-highway trucks vary in strength, depending on the load-carrying capacity of the unit. On the dump truck frame illustrated in Fig. 5-20, the height of the rail side plate decreases toward the front and the maximum height of the rail is at or near the pivot point of the dump cylinder and at the pivot point of the dump box.

The front half of some box frame rails are fabricated with 0.5-in [12.7-mm] side plates and the rear with 0.875-in [22.22-mm] side plates, the plates overlapping at the pivot point of the dump cylinders. All mounting brackets, clamps, supports, and pivot points are fabricated with reinforcing plates and then welded to the side rails or crossmembers to give additional strength at these points. In most cases the front bumper, which consists of a tubular structure, is welded to the frame.

Another type of motortruck or truck-tractor frame design is shown in Fig. 5-21. Here, the side rails are of an I-beam structure and are fabricated so that the front and rear of the I beams taper off to a height of approximately 8 in [203.2 mm]. Again, all mounting brackets, including the hitch point, the logging bung plate, and the front and rear axle mountings are fabricated and then welded to the side rails or crossmembers. **NOTE** The full side rails on some motortrucks are parallel, whereas on others the rails are parallel only at the engine area and then both rails taper evenly inward. This design accommodates a large diesel engine at the front and dual wheel mountings at the rear.

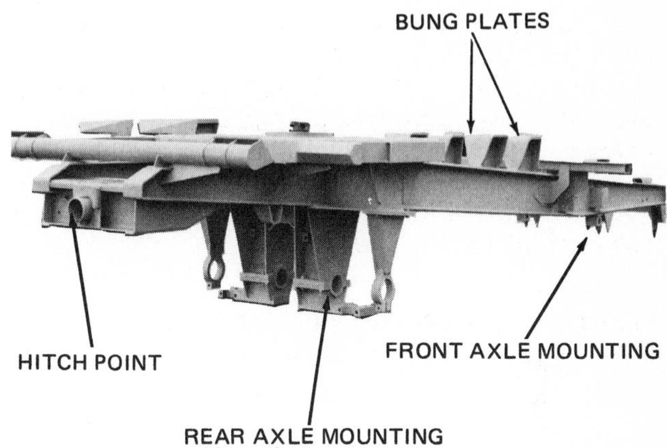

Fig. 5-21 Logging truck-tractor frame.

Other Motorized Vehicles The frames of track and wheel loaders, dozers, backhoes, etc., are all of welded construction. On smaller units, the frame halves or sections are press-formed from sheet steel and then welded to become one unit, and the stress areas are then reinforced. The mounting brackets for the axles, engine, transmission, loader, backhoe, and pivot points are then welded to the main frame. The larger units (of the group of motorized vehicles mentioned above) have a box frame structure. The support brackets (and in some cases the radiator, crankcase guard, etc.) are welded to the main structure. See Fig. 5-22.

The thickness of plate frame material varies with the size of the motorized vehicle. Some use 0.25-in [6.35-mm] while others use 0.75-in [19.05-mm] or thicker plate steel.

Articulated tractors have two individual frames, both halves being of an all-welded steel structure. The frames are fabricated from thick steel plates, some as thick as 2 in [50.8 mm]. The pivot points for the lift arms and cylinders, the front and rear axles, the pivot and/or mounting brackets, and the articulating joint are fabricated to form part of the frame. The pivot points are heavily reinforced to increase their strength and to transfer the stress placed upon them onto a larger frame area. The frame shown in Fig. 5-23 is used for 12-yd^3 [9.16-m^3] electrically driven loaders. The rear axle housing articulates on the two ball joints which are attached to the rear frame, whereas the front axle housing is part of the front frame. **NOTE** In some cases, the front

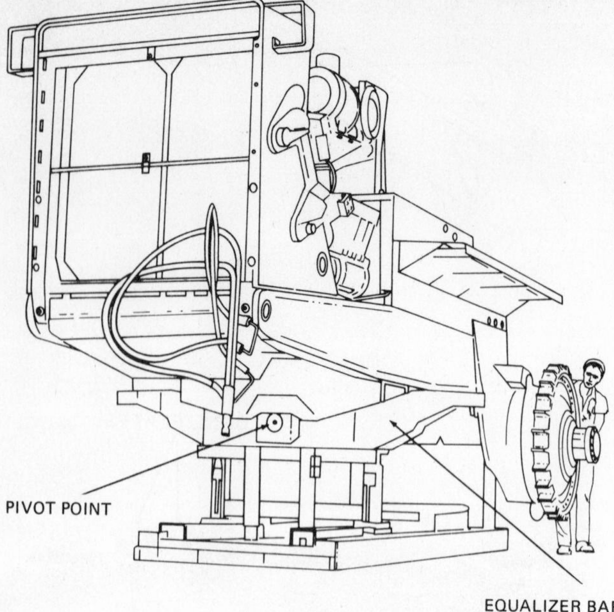

Fig. 5-22 Front view of track frame and equalizer. (*Fiat-Allis*)

or the rear frame also serves as the hydraulic reservoir.

The main frames (machine deck) of smaller revolving machines are also fabricated from plate steel into a single-unit structure which provides the pivot point for the boom, the mounting brackets for the winches, the engine, and the transmission, and the rotating base; or it provides the mounting pads for the turntable (see Fig. 5-24). The lower base frame, to which the track frame and the turntable base are attached, are fabricated from steel plates. The I beams or the box frame extension sections are bolted to the base frame. The main frame as well as the lower frame of large machines are cast alloy steel. See Fig. 5-25.

Trailers The frames of off-highway full trailers or semitrailers, although structured similarly to off-highway motortrucks, have two outside I-beam rails, in addition to the two center rails, to increase the load-carrying capacity. To reduce the overall weight of the trailer, some have longitudinal or round holes cut into the I-beam web and sometimes also into the crossmembers. Trailers or semitrailers up to

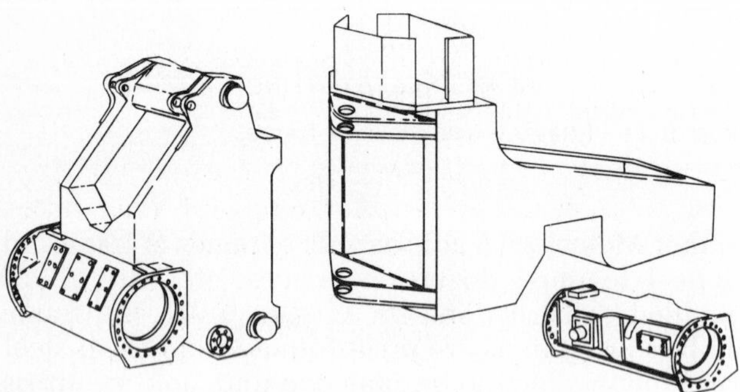

Fig. 5-23 Schematic view of an articulating loader frame.

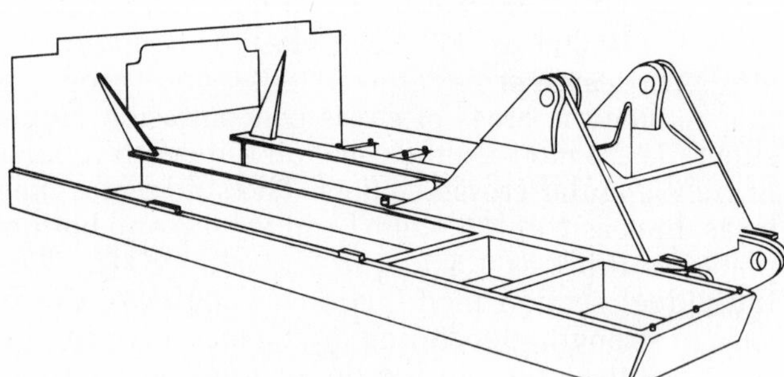

Fig. 5-24 View of main frame end machine deck. (*American Hoist and Derrick Company*)

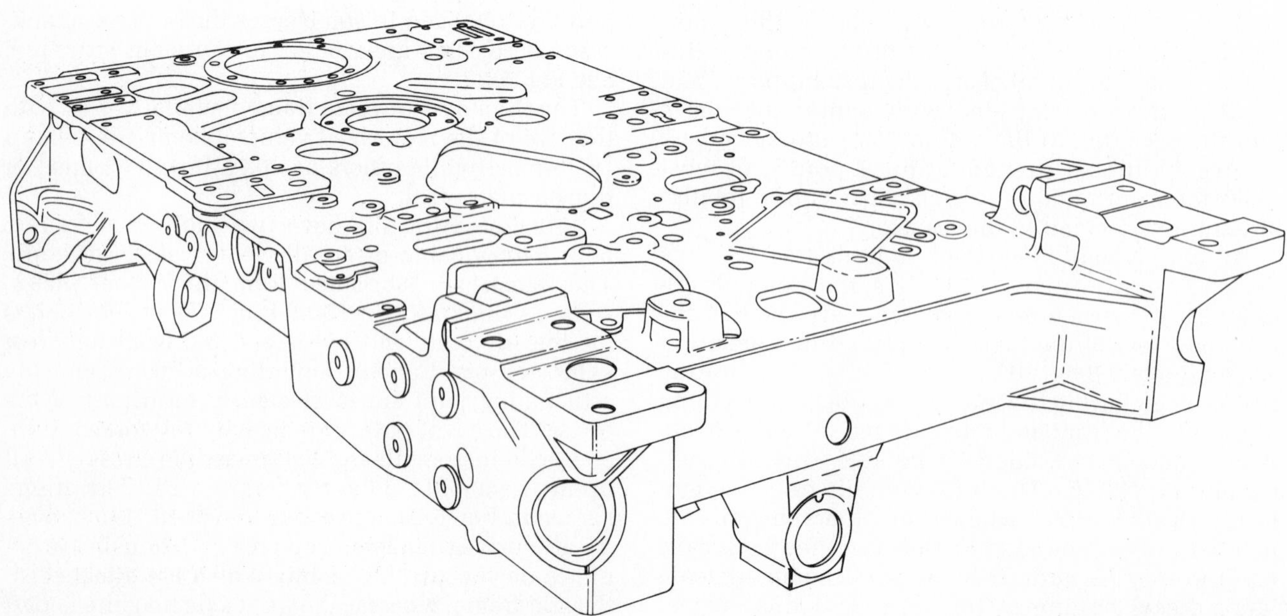

Fig. 5-25 View of a machine deck and main frame.

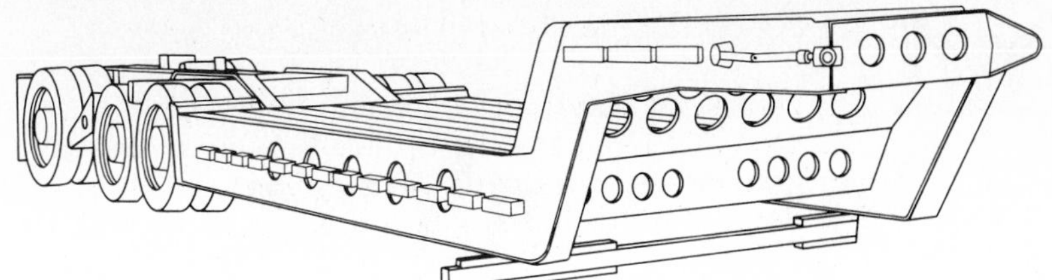

Fig. 5-26 View of a low-bed semitrailer.

100,000-lb [45,400-kg] GVW capacity may have a lower rail height at the front and rear, whereas trailers or semitrailers of a greater load-carrying capacity have side rails of equal height, or rails that gradually increase in height from the front to the end of the turntable or fifth-wheel kingpin and then again gradually increase to the full rail height.

The side and center rails of low-bed semitrailers and specially designed low-bed trailers (see Fig. 5-26) are commonly fabricated from plate steel to form I-beam rails. The crossmembers are of the box frame design or of a tubular structure. The two center rails which form the goose neck are usually thicker at the point where the rail rises, to strengthen the frame modulus at this point. The tail frame modulus is fabricated to a loading ramp or to a hitch so that a tag axle can be fastened to it to increase the bridge formula.

Semi- or full-trailer bottom dumpers or liquid carriers as a rule do not have a separate frame. The body provides the frame to which the fifth wheel or the turntable and the suspension are mounted.

Frame Repairs Although the frames of off-highway motortrucks, truck tractors, or other machines are ruggedly built, they are sometimes subjected to such harsh operating or overload conditions that the frame develops cracks at the pivot points or at the sharp corners. Twist, sag, sidesway, or other frame distortion is usually the result of misadventure, for instance, if an object falls onto the motortruck or the truck or motortruck has rolled over. When so distorted, the frame must be replaced. If the frame is cracked or the pivot points worn, the damaged areas can be repaired through welding and then by reinforcing the weld, or by cutting out the worn pivot point bushings and replacing them with factory replacement bushings (or shop-made bushings).

The preparation for welding a damaged frame, selecting the correct size and type of electrode, and the procedures to weld and reinforce are the same as those outlined earlier in the material on welding and reinforcing an on-highway frame.

CAUTION Improper preparation, poor welding technique, and poor reinforcement will cause repeated frame failure.

Review Questions

1. What are the functions of a frame, whether or not it is designed for a motor vehicle, vehicle, or other equipment?
2. Why are some frames built with one side rail or double-side rails offset?
3. Name the two most common methods used to manufacture on-highway side rails.
4. Define the term "yield strength."
5. Why are special frame (body-bound) bolts used to attach the crossmember or brackets, etc., to the side rails?
6. Why is it not recommended (apart from a few body designs) to weld the body to the motortruck or trailer frame?
7. List seven basic rules pertaining to drilling a hole into the frame.
8. Why should the longitudinal sills have the same width as the rail flange, and why must they rest fully on the rail flange face?
9. Why is it recommended when using U bolts to fasten the sill to the frame to use lock nuts instead of lock washers.
10. Frame damage can occur through numerous circumstances or operating conditions. What can cause (*a*) bent rail flanges? (*b*) cracked rails? (*c*) a sagged frame?
11. If a suspension height measurement indicates a higher suspension variation than allowable, what could have caused the excessive variation?
12. Plumb the motor vehicle frame measuring points onto the floor. Explain what may cause the measurements to show that the rear axle housing at the right-hand side is about 1.5 in [0.59 cm] more toward the rear of the frame than it is toward the left-hand side.
13. List five indications that the frame of a full trailer or semitrailer needs an alignment check.
14. Assume that the rear-axle multileaf suspension is not worn but the rear axle of the semitrailer measured toe-out. How would you change it to toe-in?

Unit 6 On-and Off-Highway Suspensions

On- and off-highway vehicle suspensions are mechanical levers and mounting arrangements with some type of spring to support the vehicle and attach it to the dead or live axles. The weight which the suspension supports is called the *sprung weight* and the weight of the components and parts which are attached to the axles is called the *unsprung weight*. The manufacturers attempt to make these components and parts as light as possible to minimize the unsprung weight. Since this reduces the upward force of the tire, a spring having a higher spring rate (i.e., greater resilience) can be used. If the unsprung weight is low, the tire can follow road irregularities with ease, and the upward force is low when the tire hits a bump. If the unsprung weight is high, a spring of a lower rate (less resilience) must be used to absorb the upward force. As a result, more upward motion is transmitted to the frame, increasing its vibration and adversely affecting handling and steering.

Inherent in a good suspension are the following characteristics and performance capacities:

1. It must have the capacity to support the maximum load with a safety factor of about 1000 lb [454 kg] per axle. **NOTE** For off-highway suspensions, a safety factor of about 1500 lb [681.80 kg] per axle is recommended.
2. It must transmit full drive and brake torque to the vehicle frame and at the same time maintain maximum tire-to-road contact (to maintain good vehicle control.
3. It must have the ability to prevent or reduce wheel hop.
4. It must secure the axle(s) and maintain the proper axle and drive line alignment to provide good handling and steering and to reduce tire wear.
5. It must allow up and down axle movement according to road contour, and the tandem rear axles must be able to articulate sufficiently to maintain tire-to-road contact under all normal road conditions.
6. It must cushion the ride to reduce wear and tear on the vehicle (and load), and give comfort to the operator.
7. The spring rate and oscillation time of the front and rear suspensions must be in balance.
8. It should be sufficiently durable but nevertheless as light as possible, and designed for easy maintenance.

From the few facts set out above, it is obvious that one type of suspension alone could not fulfill the needs of all motor vehicles, vehicles, and machines.

Steering Geometry Terminology Wheel alignment is altered by any of the following: excessively worn, bent, broken, or loose suspension components, weak or broken springs, or broken center bolts. Misalignment accelerates tire wear and adversely effects handling. Tire wear is greater and poor handling is more predominant if the cause originates on the front suspension, since it alters one or more of the following steering geometry angles: (1) camber, (2) caster, (3) toe, (4) toe-out on turns (turning radius), and (5) the steering axle inclination. These angles are precalculated into the front suspension and wheel assembly design of any motor vehicle to provide proper weight distribution on all moving parts as well as good steering. **NOTE** The built-in angles on live and dead rear axles are toe, camber, and caster.

CAMBER Camber (Fig. 6-1) is the inward or outward tilt of the tire (wheel assembly) at the top. It indicates the amount which the center line of the tire is tilted from true vertical, measured in degrees. The outward tilt of the tire at the top, from true vertical, is positive (P) camber, and the inward tilt of the tire is negative (N) camber.

The purposes of camber are (1) to bring the tire in contact with the road as nearly as possible under the point of load and thereby achieve easier steering and

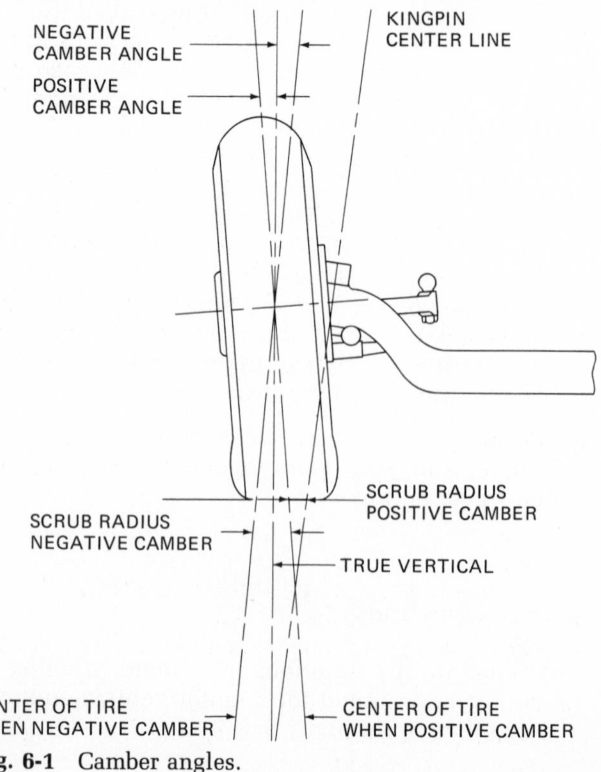

Fig. 6-1 Camber angles.

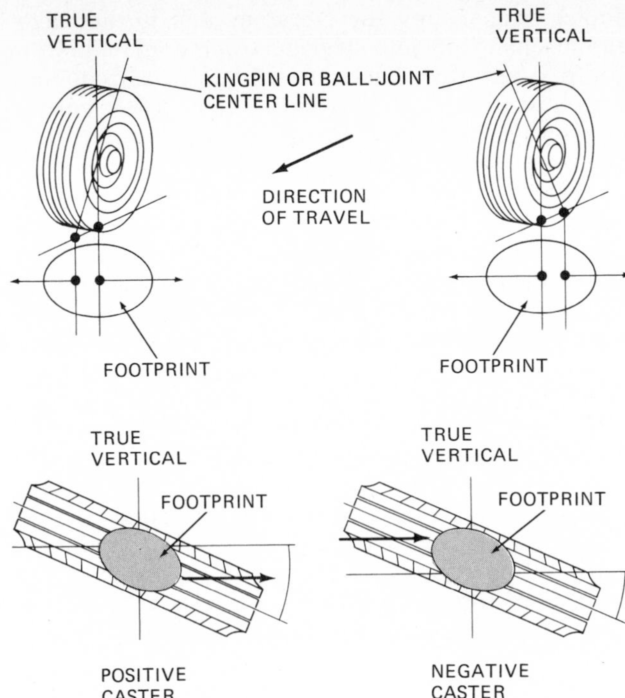

Fig. 6-2 Caster angles and effects of caster on a wheel in turn.

have most of the vehicle weight supported by the inner wheel bearing and spindle, and (2) to increase tire life. **NOTE** Camber will change to some degree under weight, jounce, and rebound because of the flexing of the axles and the independent front wheel suspension.

Incorrect camber causes excessive wear to tires, kingpins, ball joints, and wheel bearings. Unequal camber will cause the vehicle to pull to one side.

However, the suspension alone does not govern the handling, performance, and the overall ride of a motor vehicle. There are many other factors such as the power flow (force) of acceleration, braking, steering, and weight passing from (1) the frame through the suspension to the tires, (2) the drive axles to the wheels and through the suspension to the frame, and (3) the tires to the drive axles, suspension, and frame. Since the tires are included in each of the above three power flows it is evident that tires very highly affect handling and steering.

You probably know from personal experience that your car handles and steers most comfortably when all tires are in full contact with the road and each tire has equal tire-to-road friction, and, conversely, that when the tire-to-road friction is reduced, handling and steering are less efficient. The five foremost causes of reduced tire-to-road friction are the following:

- The tire or tires are out-of-round.
- The tires are out of dynamic balance.
- The tires are unequal in size.
- The steering geometry, especially caster and camber, is not as specified.
- The frame is distorted, or is sidesway-twisted, which may uplift one or more tires or change the steering geometry.

CASTER Caster (Fig. 6-2) is the backward or forward tilt of the kingpin or steering knuckle center line, from the true vertical, measured in degrees. When the top of the center line is tilted backwards it is referred to as positive (P) caster, and when tilted forward it is negative (N) caster.

The purpose of caster is to provide directional stability by maintaining the front wheels in a straight-ahead position or to return to a straight-ahead position after a turn. The steering ability is achieved as follows: (1) For positive caster, the center line on the bottom is projected forward, thereby establishing the lead point of the vehicle weight ahead of the tire-to-road contact point; (2) for negative caster, the center line on the bottom is projected rearward, and the vehicle weight therefore trails the tire-to-road contact. Excessive negative caster could result in road wander and loss of directional stability because the turning forces of the negative caster might be sufficient to overcome the other inherent directional forces.

Caster is not an angle that affects tire wear, but it changes slightly with vehicle weight and each time the suspension oscillates. Too little caster may cause wandering, waving, or instability at high speeds, whereas too much caster may cause hard steering, excessive road shocks, and shimmy. Unequal caster causes the vehicle to pull to the side of the least caster.

TOE Toe, as shown in Fig. 6-3, is the difference in the distance between the front of the tires, *A*, and the distance between the back of the tires, *B*. Toe-in indicates that the distance between the front of the tires is less than the distance between the rear of the tires. Conversely, toe-out indicates that the distance between the front of the tires is greater than the distance between the rear of the tires.

The purpose of toe-in is to compensate for widened tolerances in the steering linkage, and without it the wheel camber would force the front wheels into a slippage condition. Incorrect toe causes the most serious tire wear; the wear appears as a feathered edge scuff across the tread of both front tires (see Fig. 6-13).

STEERING AXIS INCLINATION Steering axis (kingpin) inclination (Fig. 6-4) is the inward tilt of the kingpin

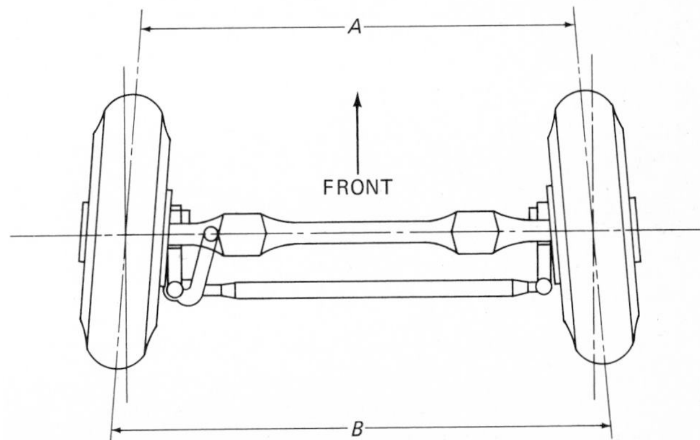

Fig. 6-3 Toe-in. B minus A camber (inches).

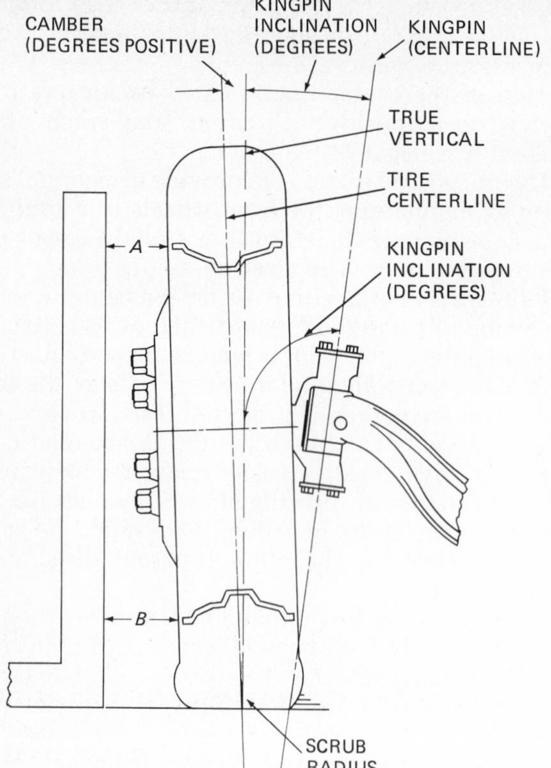

Fig. 6-4 Camber and kingpin inclination. B minus A = camber.

or steering knuckle arm at the top. It is a directional control angle, measured in degrees, and is the amount the center line is tilted from true vertical. This angle is nonadjustable, and its relationship to camber does not change except when the spindle or steering knuckle arm becomes bent.

One purpose of the kingpin inclination is to reduce the distance between its center line and the center line of the tire where both lines meet the road surface, reducing the need for excessive camber. Another is to distribute the vehicle weight more nearly under the road contact of the tire, thereby reducing the distance (called *scrub radius*) to produce easy steering.

NOTE When the scrub radius is outside the center line of the kingpin, the wheel is forced outward, and when it is inside, the wheels are forced inward.

TOE-OUT ON TURNS This is the amount one front wheel turns sharper on a turn than the other. The design of the steering arms in relation to the vehicle's wheel base provides the required degree of angle. (See material on steering system for wheel-type motor vehicles.)

Another factor quite apart from the motor vehicle or vehicle itself, but one which could reduce the tire-to-road friction and therefore affect steering and handling, is improper payload weight distribution. This may also be caused by incorrect fifth-wheel position.

Vibration Vehicle vibration has a negative effect on the life of those components which are causing and/or transmitting the vibration, and further deteriorates handling and steering. Component vibration could cause the chassis to vibrate at a frequency which would convert the entire frame into a spring. The frame, instead of the suspension, would then absorb the load and road shocks, reducing the weight on the tires. Vibration could originate from loose power train mountings, loose crossmembers, loose or damaged cab-mounting pads, misadjusted drive line angle, or a loose or worn suspension.

Suspension Action A tire deflects continuously as it makes its print on the road, and after the print is made the tire expands. When the tire hits a surface variation it deflects further to absorb the shock, but deflection is limited and when its limit is reached the tire is forced upward. In effect, it tries to leave the road surface but the suspension absorbs the upward force and maintains the tire in contact with the road. When the upward force is higher than the downward force, for a fraction of a second, the tire partially or fully loses road contact. See Fig. 6-5.

NOTE The tire-to-road position during the oscillation cycle is a built-in suspension factor comprised

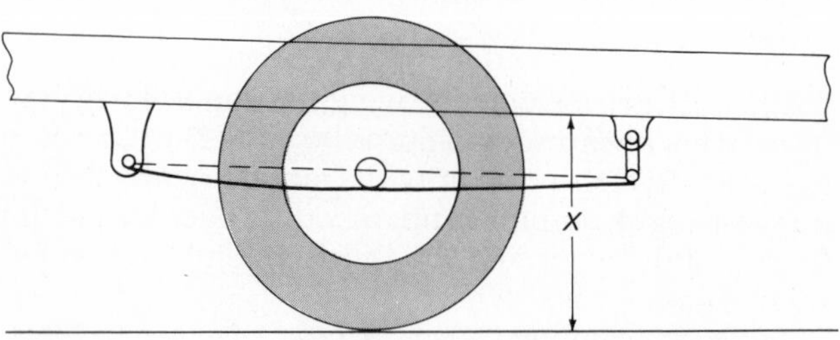

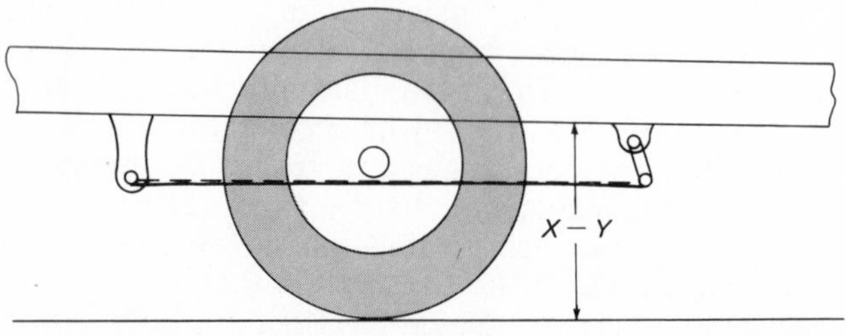

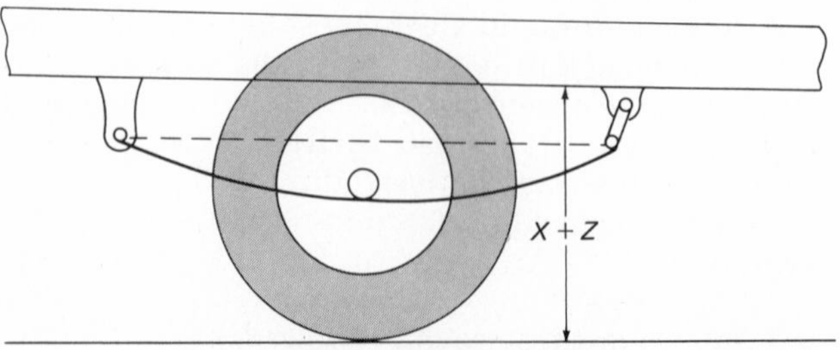

Fig. 6-5 Suspension action during jounce and rebound. (*a*) Static position. (*b*) Jounce position. (*c*) Rebound position.

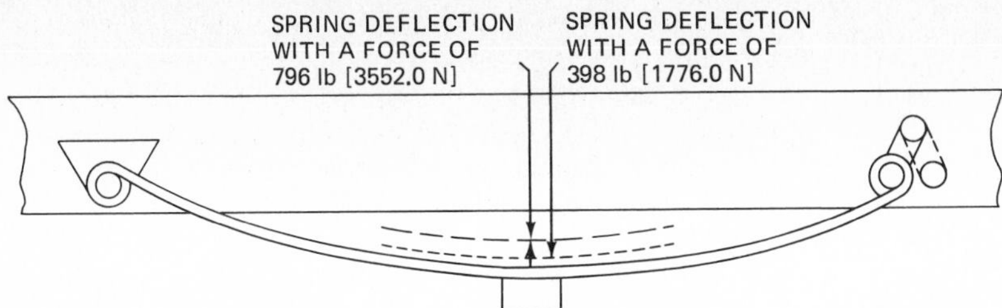

Fig. 6-6 Spring rate.

through levers, linkages, or arms, or by the spring itself.

During the upward motion of the tire(s) (called *jounce*), the spring is compressed and its energy increased. When the upward and downward forces are equal, the upward motion stops, but the additional energy in the spring forces the unsprung weight downward and the spring tries to return to its original energy (static position). However, as the spring expands, it passes the static point and overexpands. The downward motion, or expansion, of the spring is called *rebound*. If during the time the suspension cycles there was no additional upward force, the spring would oscillate and each jounce and rebound would become shorter due to the absorbing energy of the spring and the friction within the suspension. When the tire rolls over a pothole, the static energy of the suspension (spring) forces the tire to follow the contour of the road surface; the tire bounces into the hole, deflects, and rebounds, which deflection is absorbed by the suspension.

SPRING RATE The spring rate (Fig. 6-6) is the deflection of the spring measured 1 in [25.4 mm] above and 1 in below the midpoint of the specified loaded position (load range). The load range (maximum load-carrying capacity) of a spring is expressed in pounds or newtons, and is equal to the deflection (spring rate) in inches or millimeters.

Hooke's law states that within the elastic limit the deformation of a spring is proportional to the load to which it is subjected. A spring which will deflect 0.25 in [6.4 mm] under 400 lb [1776 N] of force will then deflect 0.5 in [12.7 mm] under a force of 800 lb [3552 N]. And if the spring were of the same length but would deflect 0.5 in [12.7 mm] under a force of 400 lb [1776 N], it would be a softer spring with a higher spring rate and a lower load range.

Spring oscillation time is another factor which affects handling and steering. A short spring will generate more up-and-down cycles in a given length of time than will a longer spring. For this reason, longer springs with a higher spring rate are used on the steering axle, and shorter ones with lower spring rate are used on the rear axle(s) to ensure pitch axis location ahead of the center of gravity. This prevents the front suspension and rear suspension of the vehicle from cycling at the same rate.

To reduce the spring rate (increasing the load range), manufacturers make one or more of the following spring design changes:

- Increase the number of spring leaves
- Increase the thickness of the leaves
- Increase the width of the leaves
- Increase the diameter of the coil spring wire
- Reduce the number of coils
- Shorten the overall length of the spring assembly
- Decrease the cam (spring height)

To force the suspension to return to the neutral position in about $2\frac{1}{2}$ cycles, various types of shock absorbers are used (see material on shock absorbers later in this unit).

SPRINGS FOR VEHICLES A spring that could absorb road shocks rapidly and return to its static position slowly without overexpanding would be ideal and most suitable for any suspension; but to date such a spring has not been developed, nor is there a spring that is equally effective under loaded and unloaded conditions. As a compromise, that is, to have a stiff suspension for the loaded condition and a soft suspension for the unloaded condition, numerous types of springs have been designed.

Multi-leaf, staked, or single-leaf springs are the most popular springs for on-highway motor vehicle and vehicle suspensions. Coil springs are common on small on-highway trucks and recreation vehicles, and are found to some extent on the steering axles of large dump trucks and logging truck-tractors (see Fig. 6-7).

COIL SPRING SUSPENSIONS

Two types of coil spring suspension are used—the independent front wheel suspension and the independent I-beam suspension.

Independent Front Wheel Suspension As the name indicates, this suspension (Fig. 6-8) allows each front wheel to move up and down independ-

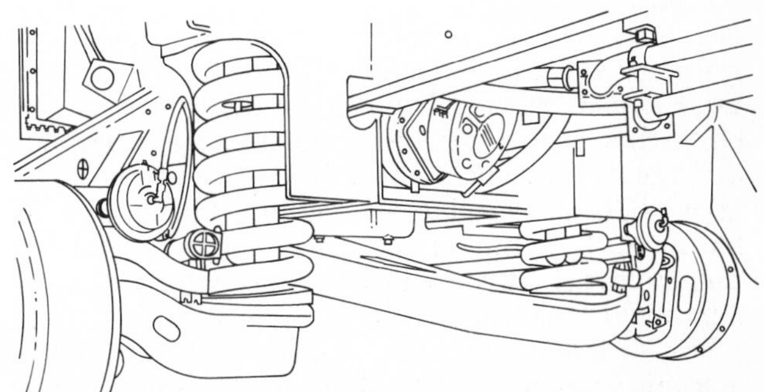

Fig. 6-7 Coil spring suspension of a logging truck tractor.

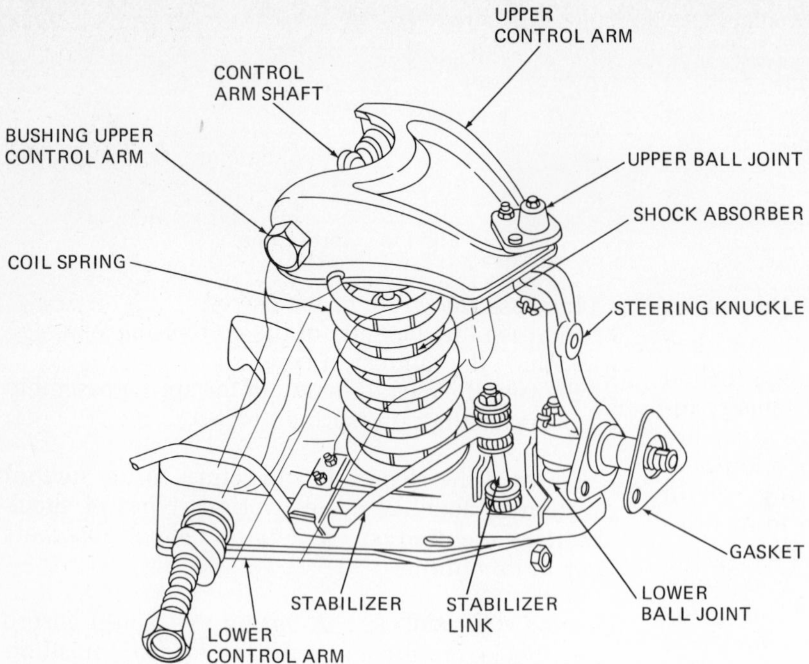

Fig. 6-8 Standard independent front wheel coil suspension. (*Ford Motor Company*)

ently without affecting the other wheel, thereby minimizing the twisting motion imposed on the frame.

COIL SPRING To achieve the independent wheel action, to maintain nearly the same camber angle during jounce and rebound, and to allow the wheels to be semirotated, the coil spring (which carries the sprung weight) is positioned between the lower control arm and the frame, or between the frame and the upper control arm. The coil spring ends rest in the press-formed spring saddles of the lower control arm and frame. To lessen the sprung weight force on the suspension and wheel assembly, and thereby reduce the wear on the pivot points and wheel bearings, the spring is positioned at an angle to the wheel. This angle is not the same for all suspensions—it depends on the intended sprung weight.

The spring steel wire from which coil springs for small vehicles is made varies in thickness from about 0.5 to 0.9 in [12.7 to 22.86 mm] and the spring varies in its number of coils. Both these factors are governed by the intended maximum sprung weight.

CONTROL ARMS The length variation of the two (upper and lower) control arms and the pivot point position in relation to the two control arms are calculated to form precise angles, in order to maintain the camber angle during jounce and rebound. Tire-to-road contact is therefore controlled, reducing tire wear and improving handling and steering ability. On earlier suspensions the two arms were parallel, and later the pivot points were brought closer together. On today's suspensions the pivot points are farther apart so that the center line of the lower and upper control arms cross outside the wheel (see Fig. 6-9*a* and *b*). This suspension permits the top of the wheel to move outward on jounce and to move inward on rebound, giving the tire better road contact and therefore better handling during a turn.

The control arms, which provide the hinge between the steering knuckle and frame, are press-formed from sheet steel. They are attached through the control arm shaft which is bolted to the frame. The pivot between the shaft and the control arms is achieved either through metal-clad rubber torsion bushings or through metal screw bushings.

BALL JOINTS Ball joints which connect the steering knuckle to the two control arms provide (for) the semirotation of the wheel assembly. A ball joint is a metal ball stud mounted in a socket. In this case it is attached to the outer ends of the lower and upper control arms, and acts as a hinge between the arms and steering knuckle. It allows the wheel to turn and to move up and down. There are three methods by which the ball joints can be attached to the arms:

- The socket is pressed into the control arm
- It is screwed into the control arm
- It is riveted or bolted to the arm

The tapered stud of the ball joint fits into the tapered hole in the steering knuckle and is secured with a castle nut. **NOTE** The ball joints are either prelubricated and sealed, or designed to be lubricated. There are two types of ball joints—the load carrier and the follower (see Fig. 6-10*a* and *b*). The load-carrying ball joint (which carries the vehicle load) is attached to the loaded control arm, commonly the lower control arm. There are two basic load-carrying ball joints, the compression and the tension, and either one may be attached to the load-carrying control arm. When the ball joint is attached from below, to the lower control arm, a compression type must be used because the weight of the vehicle forces the ball into its socket. When the ball joint is attached from above, to the lower control arm, a tension type must be used because under this condition

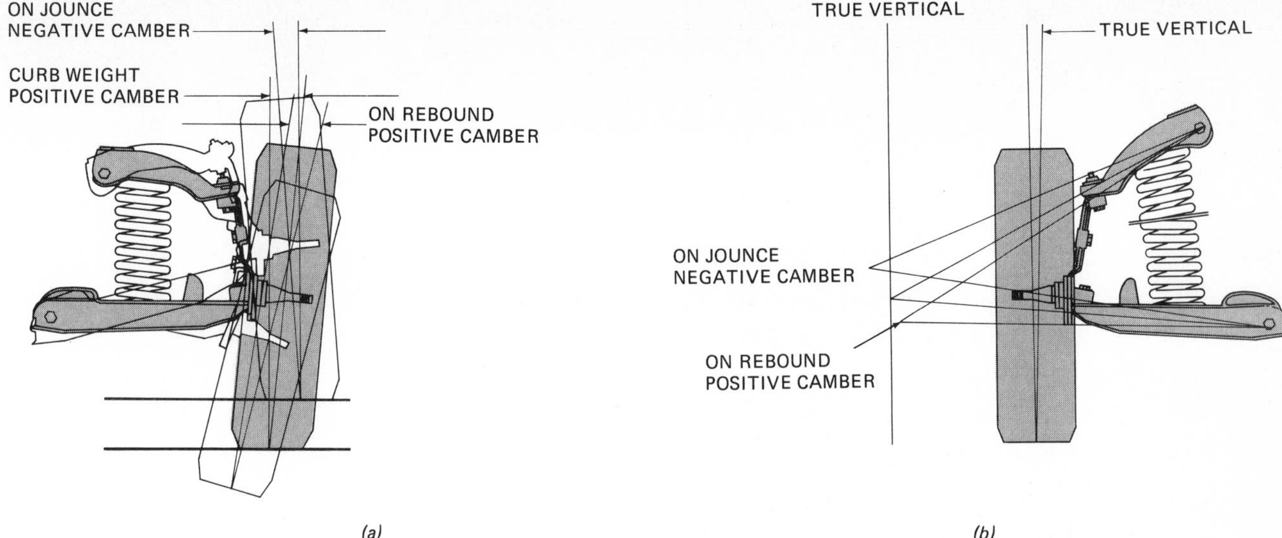

Fig. 6-9 Comparison of (*a*) early and (*b*) more recent suspensions.

the vehicle weight tends to pull the ball out of its socket.

CAUTION Make sure you have the correct ball joint when making a replacement.

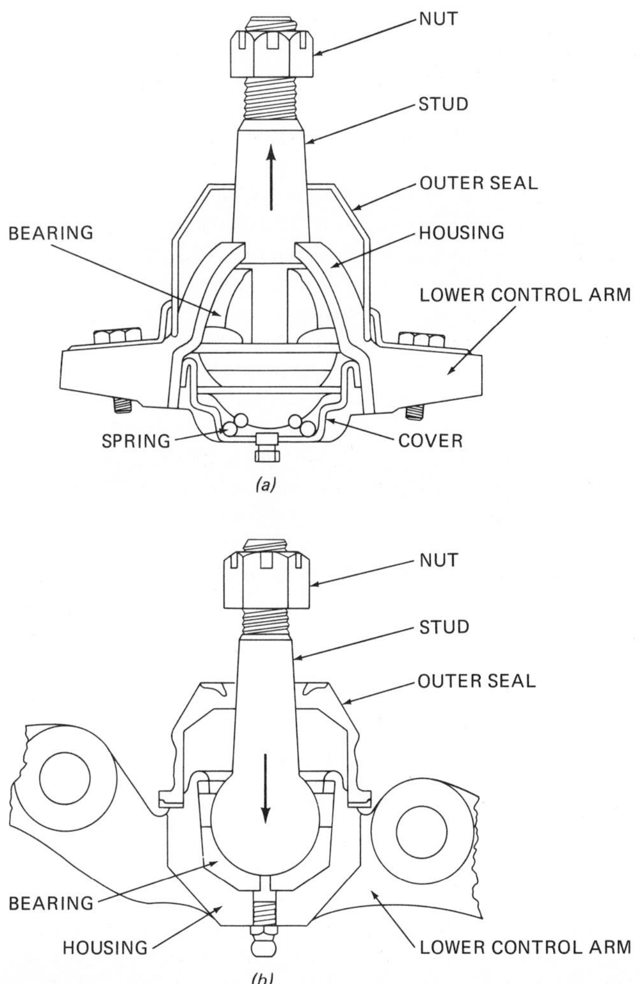

Fig. 6-10 (*a*) Follower ball joint (bolt-on type). (*b*) Load-carrier ball joint (press-in type).

The follower joint is attached to the unloaded control arm, commonly the upper arm. This type is also referred to as a *friction* or *preloaded ball joint* because a steel or rubber spring holds the ball stud firmly in contact with the socket. The primary function of the follower ball joint is to maintain steering knuckle alignment while absorbing road shocks and vibration.

STRUT ROD AND STABILIZER BAR Narrow lower control arms require a strut rod (see Fig. 6-11) to increase the arm rigidity and to reduce wear on the ball joints. The strut is also used to adjust caster setting. A stabilizer bar or sway bar, in the form of a U-shaped steel rod, is attached with rubber insulator bushings to the side rails of the frame or cross-member, and the ends of the rod are attached to the lower control arm. The primary purpose of the sway or stabilizer bar is to reduce vehicle lean on turns. However, when both wheels are forced upward at the same time, the steel rod just rotates in the insulation bushings of the side rails. If one wheel is forced upward, or when the vehicle is in a turn, centrifugal force places an additional weight on the outside wheel and less weight is placed on the inside wheel. When this occurs, the lower control arm is forced upward, and with it the end of the stabilizer rod. The twisting motion is transmitted to the other lower control arm and exerts a downward force on the arm. However, the arm cannot go down; therefore the outside lower control arm resists the upward force and adds spring energy, which raises the outside frame and reduces vehicle lean.

The shock absorber is positioned inside the coil spring and is attached with rubber bushings or grommets to the lower control arm and frame.

Troubleshooting and Inspection Any suspension, during normal service, is constantly flexing. Light trucks and recreational vehicles are often overloaded, loaded improperly, or travel on rough roads, each of which places additional force at the points shown in Fig. 6-12, causing excessive wear. More-

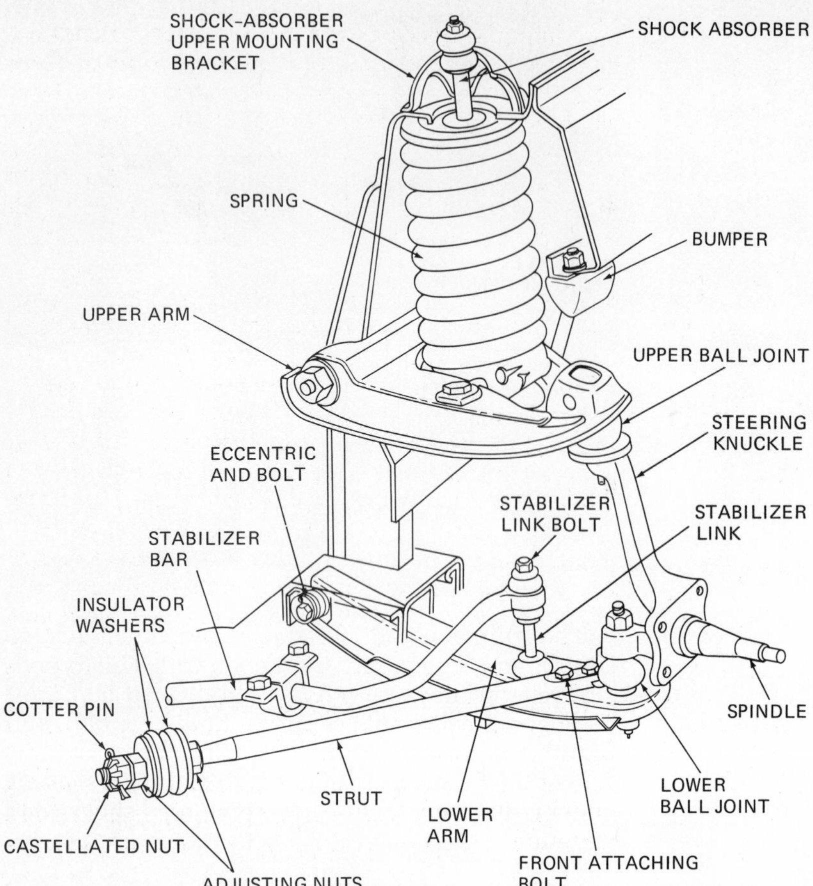

Fig. 6-11 Coil spring suspension with spring positioned above upper control arm. *(Ford Motor Company)*

over, the coil springs gradually weaken, causing a change in the suspension angles. This forces the steering components out of position, alters the toe-in, the camber, the caster, and sometimes the toe-out on turns. The result is excessive tire wear and reduced handling. See material on steering wheel and tire and wheel alignment.

When a vehicle is in for service, or if the operator complains of poor handling, first visually inspect the tires for wear, as most suspension and steering problems will be revealed by the condition of the tire treads. If the tire treads are worn on the inside, it indicates one or more of the following: that the spring has weakened, the ball joints are worn, or that the control arm bushings and shafts or mounting brackets are worn. Inside tread wear can also come from bent or broken suspension components, loose mounting bolts, loose or damaged wheel bearings, or from a bent or cracked frame rail.

If the tire treads are like hacksaw blades, and the edges feathered inward, there is too much toe-in. The tires are therefore contacting the road surface at an angle, so that the outside edge of each tread rib wears away and the inner edge becomes sharp and ragged. If this occurs when the steering linkage is behind the steering knuckle, it indicates a weak spring—the tie-rod has been forced outward because of the drop in suspension height. Worn suspension components and loose or damaged wheel bearings will also change the camber angle, causing increased toe-in. Conversely, if the sharp feather edges are on the outside ribs, the tires are toeing out. If this occurs

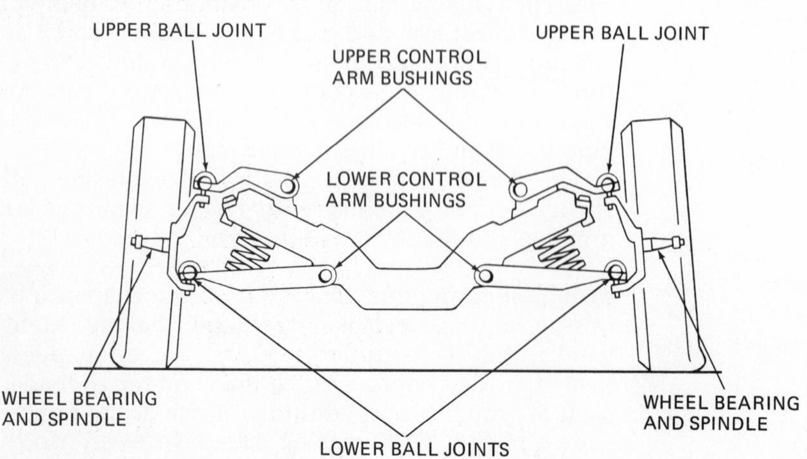

Fig. 6-12 Wear points.

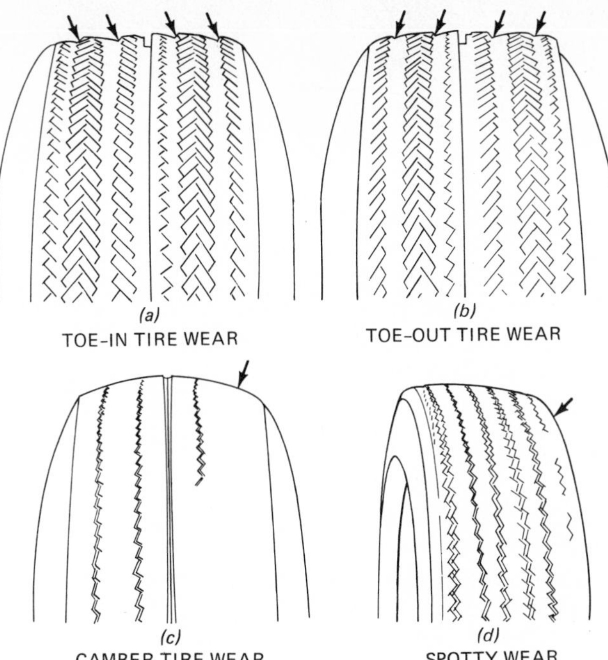

Fig. 6-13 Tire wear. (*a*) Toe-in tire wear; (*b*) toe-out tire wear; (*c*) camber tire wear; (*d*) spotty wear; may be due to imbalanced wheel, badly worn ball joints, worn control arm bushings, weak spring, or bent spindle. (*Bear Manufacturing Company*)

when the steering linkage is in front of the steering knuckle, it indicates that the springs are weak, the suspension worn, loose, damaged, or bent, or that the wheel bearings are loose or worn—the tie-rod or the tire has been forced outward, causing toe-out. Toe-out can also originate from worn tie-rod sockets notwithstanding the location of the steering linkage. When a vehicle with worn tie rods is driven forward, the front tires are forced outward. See Fig. 6-13 for examples of tire wear.

The next step is to visually inspect the vehicle from below for damaged control arms, ball joints, rubber bushings, steering linkage, and tie-rod sockets. Check to determine if both lower control arm ends are equal in height. If one or both of the coil springs show shiny spots, this indicates a bent coil spring. It is usually expedient at this point to raise the front end of the vehicle and block it securely in order to thoroughly scrutinize the bushings and ball joints for wear or damage and for missing or cracked grease boots. Check the bushings of the shock absorbers and stabilizer bar for deterioration. Check the wheel bearing adjustment and note which type of load-carrying ball joint is used.

If some control arm shaft bushings indicate wear, all bushings should be replaced and the shafts that are worn should be replaced also. If one coil spring is bent, replace both (not only one). However, before commencing service, check the ball joints for wear to determine if they could be reused.

MEASURING THE LOAD-CARRYING BALL JOINTS FOR WEAR Before checking these joints for wear, first refer to your service manual and then follow the method it recommends. For instance, service manuals for most vehicles manufactured before 1973 usually recommend that the load-carrying ball joints be checked with the ball joints unloaded, that is, the tire must hang free on the suspension. After 1973 some manufacturers provided wear-indicating ball joints, to facilitate faster and more accurate analysis of ball joint wear.

To check the conventional load-carrying ball joint for radial movement, raise the vehicle until the tires just clear the floor and then block the frame. If the spring rests on the upper control arm, use a C clamp or the special tool designed for this task to hold the upper control arm (and therefore hold the spring compressed) and then raise and block the vehicle so that the tires hang free (clear from the floor). In either case, adjust the wheel bearings to a slight preload to assure correct radial ball joint wear measurement. Place the radial inspection gauge with its roller against the tire sidewall and zero the dial. Now grab the tire on the top and bottom and rock it inward and outward while at the same time noting the dial gauge reading. If the movement exceeds the specification, the ball joint must be replaced. See Fig. 6-14.

To check the vertical wear of the load-carrying ball joint, install the special tool as shown in Fig. 6-15. Hand-tighten the screw. Stop turning it when the ball joint moves and then back off the screw to the point where movement just begins. With a socket wrench, turn the cam until the hook point penetrates through any dirt, grease, and undercoating and makes solid contact. You may have to reset the screw by hand, but do not overtighten it. Mount the dial indicator to the mounting bracket and position the dial spindle. With a socket wrench turn the cam on the tool body to take up the slack in the tool, until

Fig. 6-14 Method of measuring horizontal free play. (*Bear Manufacturing Company*)

Fig. 6-15 Method of measuring vertical free play. (*Bear Manufacturing Company*)

the ball stud joint just begins to move. At this point, zero the dial indicator. Continue to rotate the socket wrench until all movement stops. When you feel the ball bottom in the socket, read the dial indicator. The total movement shown on the indicator is the vertical movement of the load-carrying ball joint. Repeat this procedure to confirm your first reading and then compare the reading with that specified in the service manual (which could vary from 0.020 to 0.125 in [0.508 to 3.17 mm]. If the vertical movement exceeds the maximum specification, the ball joint must be replaced.

On vehicles with wear-indicating ball joints, wear is indicated by the extent the boss (into which the grease fitting is threaded) protrudes past the cover. On a new ball joint, this boss projects 0.050 in [1.27 mm] beyond the ball joint cover. Before inspecting the ball joints for wear, check that the vehicle wheels are at a position where the load-carrying ball joints are in their normal loaded position. Wipe the grease fitting and boss free of dirt and grease, and with a screw driver feel across the socket cover. If the grease fitting boss is flush with (or beneath) the cover surface, the ball joint must be replaced. If the boss protrudes past the cover surface, the ball joint can remain in service.

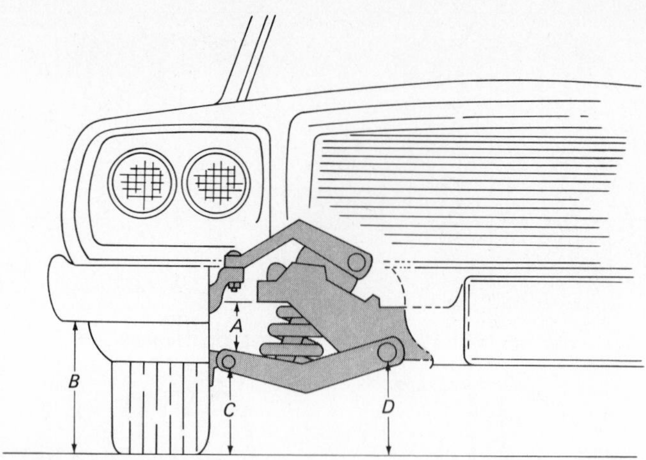

Fig. 6-16 Common reference points to measure suspension height.

CHECKING THE FOLLOWER BALL JOINT FOR WEAR It is difficult to check the follower ball joint accurately because of its construction. If the follower ball joint visually appears in good condition but the load-carrier ball joint indicates excessive wear, the follower should also be replaced.

If visual inspection has shown no evidence of failure but the tire treads are worn (on the inside), drive the vehicle onto a level floor, remove from it any additional weight, and check if necessary bring the tires to the correct inflation pressure. Next, measure the suspension and frame height on each side at the recommended points and compare your measurements with those given in the service manual (see Fig. 6-16). If the measurements reveal a drop in suspension height, you can assume one or both coil springs have lost their energy and should be replaced.

NOTE If the suspension drop on each side is equal (but not excessive), you may realign the front end.

Do *not* use any type of spring insert to raise the suspension height. Although the insert will raise the suspension, it may raise it too high and this would alter the steering linkage geometry and cause reduced handling and reduced ability to absorb shocks. Furthermore, it concentrates stress on the spring at the insert points rather than distributing this force throughout the spring, and will eventually bring about fatigue and spring failure. **CAUTION** Use overload or air shock absorbers only to maintain the suspension height for overload conditions—do not use them to compensate for weak coil springs.

Servicing the Independent Front Wheel Suspension The service of an independent front wheel suspension consists of replacing defective parts or components. The individual parts or components that have to be replaced will vary to some extent between suspensions, and the method of replacement will vary accordingly.

REPLACING A LOAD-CARRYING OR FOLLOWER BALL JOINT Raise the front of the vehicle so that the wheels are

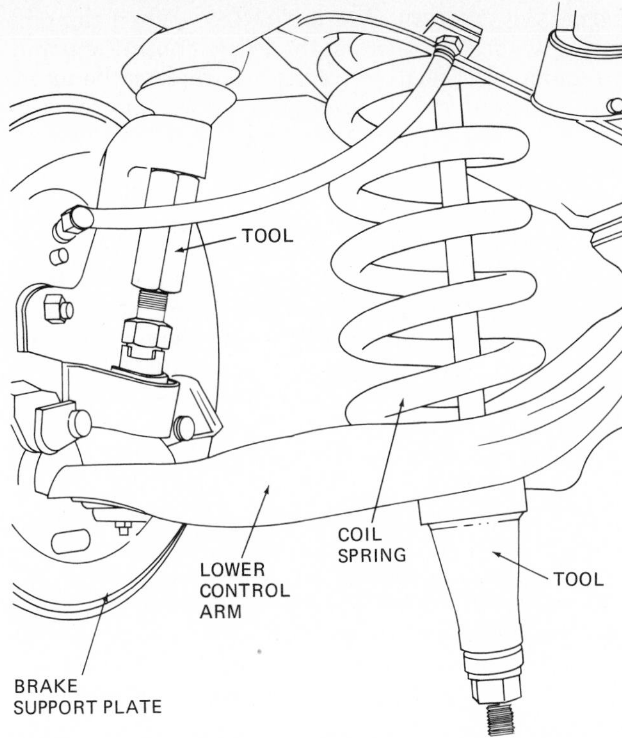

Fig. 6-17 View of ball joint breaker tool installed to free lower ball joint.

off the floor, and then securely block the vehicle under the frame. Remove the wheel hub (or, if practical, only the wheels) to allow more room to work. **NOTE** Neither any steering linkage components or the shock absorber need be removed. Next, remove the cotter pins from both ball stud nuts; then loosen both nuts about three full turns. To break the ball joint stud loose from the steering knuckle, drive a ball joint and pitman arm wedge between the steering knuckle and ball stud. The spring tension will help you to break the taper loose, and the ball stud nut holds the suspension together.

A more appropriate method, and one which does not cause damage to any components or parts, is to use a special puller (Fig. 6-17). Otherwise, use a spreader bolt and place it between the two nuts of the upper and lower ball joints and then turn the screw to force the tapered ball studs from the steering knuckle. When both ball studs are loose, position a C clamp (or the special tool) in such a way that turning the screw compresses the coil spring and takes the force from both ball stud nuts; remove the nuts. Next, turn the screw to increase the distance between the upper and lower control arms while holding the steering knuckle. When the arms are sufficiently separated, lift the steering knuckle from the lower ball joint stud and with a rope or wire, secure it to the frame. Do *not* allow the steering knuckle to hang on the brake hose. It will damage the hose.

The manner in which the ball joint is attached to the control arm will determine the tool and/or the method to be used to remove it. For instance, if the ball joint is screwed into the control arm, the appropriate socket and handle must be used to replace it. If it is bolted to the control arm, simply loosen and remove the two or three nuts, washers, and bolts. If it is riveted to the arm, use a cutting torch to remove the rivet head and after a cooling off period drive the rivet stem out.

CAUTION Have a fire extinguisher at your side while cutting the rivet head off, and support the control arm securely when driving the rivet out.

Use only the bolts which are supplied with the replacement joint to secure the new ball joint to the control arm. You may have to drill holes in the control arms to the size of the bolt shank. If the ball joints are pressed into the control arm, you will require a special puller (Fig. 6-18) to remove (and to install) them. Upon removing them, examine the tapered bores in the steering knuckle for damage and wear and, when necesary, clean the bores. Examine the control arm ends for damage and wear and, if it is a screw-type ball joint, clean the threads and examine them for wear and damage. If it is a press-type ball joint, clean and lubricate the bore. Then start the new ball joint, by hand, into the control arm. Make certain it is straight before installing the puller. Tighten the puller bolts alternately to pull the ball joint straight into the bore. You may have to tap lightly on the bottom with a hammer to ease installation. After the ball joint is replaced, position the steering knuckle onto the lower ball stud and align it with the upper ball joint stud while at the same time reducing the distance of the two control arms by turning the C clamp screw or special tool (see Fig. 6-19). Install the nuts and tighten them to

Fig. 6-18 Removing lower ball joint.

Fig. 6-19 Method used to install steering knuckle.

the specified torque. Install the cotter pin and the wheel hub or wheels.

NOTE Always increase the torque to align the cotter pin holes. Do not back off the nuts.

The last reassembly step is the wheel alignment.

REPLACING CONTROL ARM BUSHINGS When the coil spring is located between the lower control arm and the frame, it is relatively simple to replace the metal or metal-clad rubber torsional upper control arm bushings. First, block the rear wheels, raise the front of the vehicle until the wheels are off the floor, and place jack stands under the lower control arm. Remove the wheels, place a jack under the wheel hub, and disconnect the upper control arm from the frame. Take note of the number of shims and their locations. Swing the upper control arm outward. It will pivot on the follower ball joint. Remove the cap screws and washers from both ends of the control arm shaft. Install the bushing-removing tool around the bushing flange, tighten it, and by turning the puller screw, pull the bushing from the control arm. Repeat this procedure with the other bushing.

After removal check the bushing saddle for damage and wear and remove any burrs, dirt, and corrosion. Select the correct cup size, and position the cup against the bushing flange and then place the tool so that the new bushing rests in the bushing saddle. Now tighten the bolt against the cup until the bushing flange is seated against the control arm. See Fig. 6-20*a* and *b*.

When both bushings are replaced, position and attach the shaft to the frame. If a new shaft and bushing combination is used, lower the front end so that the weight of the vehicle rests on the tires, and then tighten the bolts at the ends of the control arm shaft. This precaution will prevent early bushing failure caused by the bushings twisting when tightening the bolts without a load on the control arm.

In most cases, it is also a simple task to replace the lower control arm bushings, although on some suspensions you have to remove the lower control arm. This means you must compress the spring before lowering the lower control arm. See material on removal of springs earlier in this unit.

When it is necessary to replace the lower control arm bushing, first block the rear wheels and then raise the front of the vehicle until the wheels are off the floor. Block the front of the vehicle by placing

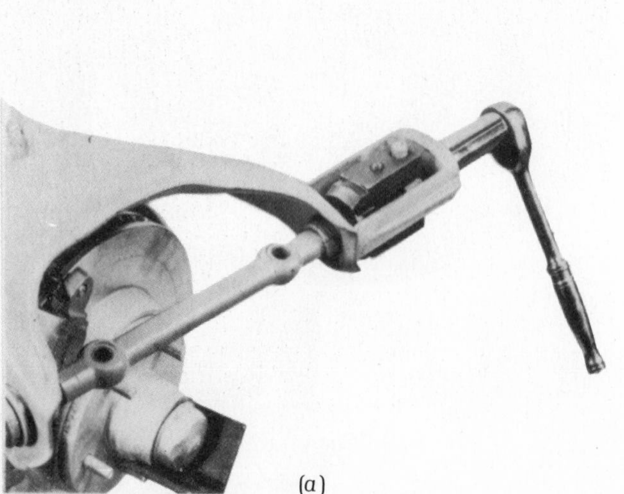

(*a*)

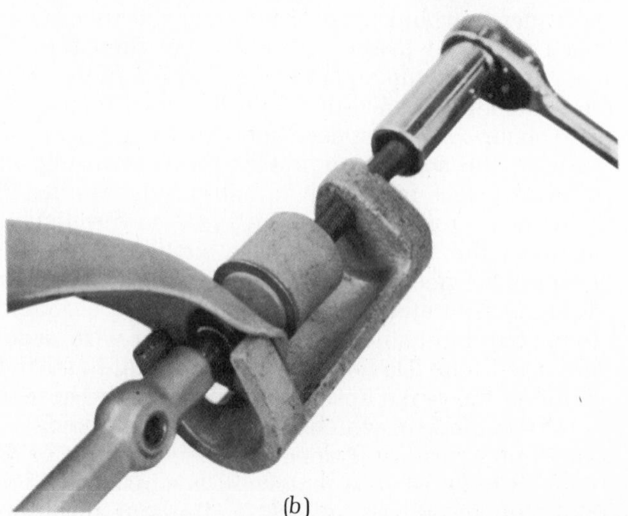

(*b*)

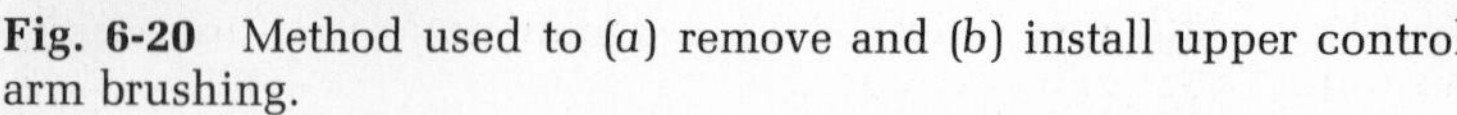

Fig. 6-20 Method used to (*a*) remove and (*b*) install upper control arm brushing.

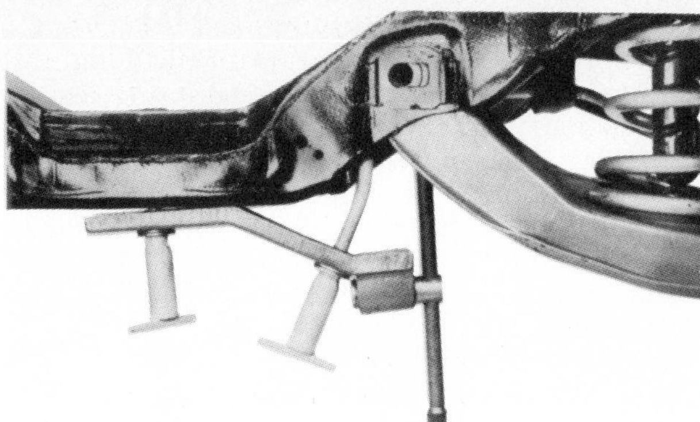

Fig. 6-21 Special cradle—fastened and ready to lower the lower control arm.

jack stands under the frame, and a jack under each lower control arm, to release the force from the lower control arm shaft mounting bolts. Disconnect the control arm shaft from the frame, and lower the control arm just far enough so that you can install the bushing removal and installation tool.

NOTE Some manufacturers have designed a special cradle to support the lower control arm when removing the spring and control arm bushings. See Fig. 6-21.

To replace the upper control arm bushings when the spring rests on the upper control arm, you must first remove the spring. In this instance, raise and block the vehicle as when replacing the lower control arm bushings. Remove, in order, the suspension bumper bracket, the shock absorber tower bolts, and the lower shock absorber mounting bolts, and then lift the assembly out.

There are several spring compression tools available, similar to the one shown (installed) in Fig. 6-22. When using this type of compression tool, insert the bolt from above through the upper opening of the suspension bracket. Position the jaws either on the second or third coil, depending on the coil length, and then insert the fork between the coils so that the convex side of the fork faces toward the thrust washer and the grooves on the fork rest on the coils. Spiral the fork on the spring until it seats against the thrust washer. By using a flat ratchet wrench, turn the bolt to compress the spring to the desired length, so that it can be removed.

CAUTION Make certain the jaws and fork are properly engaged at all times. When the spring is removed, disconnect the upper control arm shaft from the frame, swing the control arm outward, and then replace the bushing.

INSTALLING A COIL SPRING When a new spring is to be installed, lay the removed spring on the floor, place one foot on the spring and turn the bolt to remove the spring tension, and then remove the fork and the jaw assembly. Reinstall the spring compression tool to the new spring, compress it to the required height (Fig. 6-23), and position the spring according to service manual recommendations onto

Fig. 6-22 Method of installing spring compression tool.

the upper control arm before removing the spring tension and the compression tool.

To replace the coil spring when it is located between the lower control arm and frame, block the rear wheels, raise the front of the vehicle, block it under the frame, and place a jack under each lower control arm. Remove the wheels, remove the stabilizer mounting brackets from the frame or crossmember, and remove the through bolts, the washers, and the rubber grommets from the lower control arms. Note the locations of the washers and rubber grommets. Remove the bottom shock absorber attaching nuts or bolts, the washers, and the rubber grommets. Install the spring compression tool precisely according to manufacturer's instructions and

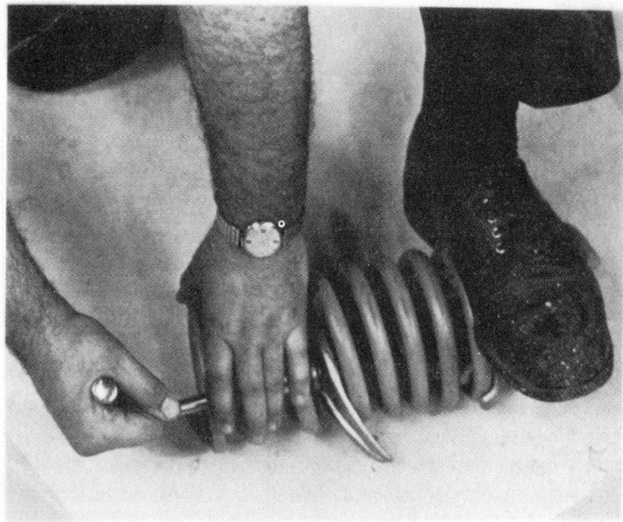

Fig. 6-23 Method of removing and installing spring compression tool.

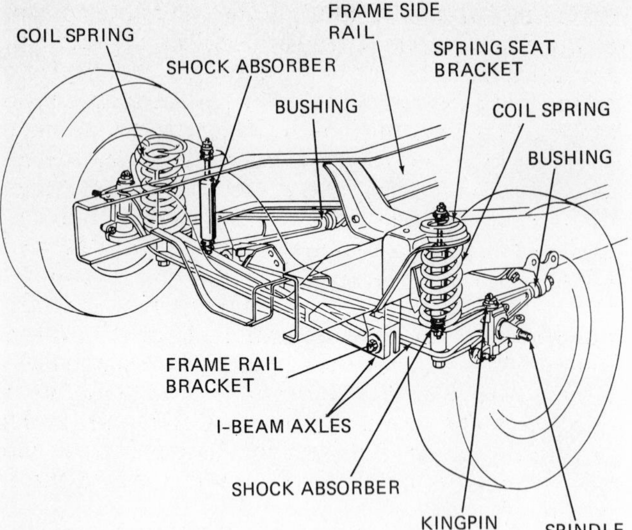

Fig. 6-24 Schematic view of a twin I-beam suspension. *(Ford Motor Company)*

then turn the screw to compress the spring. When the spring force is removed from the lower control arm shaft, remove the control arm shaft mounting nuts and the washers and bolts. Lower the jack while holding the spring upward against the frame spring seat. Swing the control arm out of the way and remove the spring. Remove and reinstall the spring compression tool as previously outlined. Compress the spring to the required height and position it onto the lower control arm precisely as indicated in the service manual before removing the spring tension and the compression tool. **CAUTION** If the spring is not positioned exactly as the manufacturer has specified, the coil spring will bend when installed, causing it to come in contact with the frame, and it may raise the suspension height.

Whenever a suspension has been serviced, the final step is to check the front-end alignment.

Twin I-Beam Suspension This type of suspension (Fig. 6-24) also features independent wheel oscillation. The major difference between it and the independent wheel suspension is that I-beam axles are used as the lower control arm.

The solid tapered forged-steel I beams are mounted through rubber bushings to the opposite frame rail brackets. The steering knuckles are connected through kingpins to the other end of the I beam. Radius arms are used to stabilize the forward and backward force yet allow the individual I-beam axles to move up and down. One end of the radius rod is connected through a fork and through bolt to the I-beam axle, and the other end is connected through rubber insulators to the frame rail bracket. The coil spring that supports the sprung weight and absorbs the road shocks and road surface variations is of a low spring rate design and is located between the I beam and the frame. The upper spring end rests in the upper spring seat bracket, which is bolted to the frame rail; the lower spring end rests against the lower spring seat. The seat is positioned over the through bolt that attaches the radius arm to the I-beam axle. The lower coil spring end is held to the lower spring seat by the lower retainer and nut, and the upper end is held to the upper spring seat by two retainers, which are fastened by bolts to the spring seat bracket. The double-acting shock absorber is attached with a through bolt to the shock absorber's lower bracket (which is bolted to the radius arm), and the upper end of the shock absorber is attached with a nut to the upper spring bracket (see Fig. 6-25).

The suspension arrangement pivots each axle at a point underneath the frame rail opposite the wheel to which it is attached, providing fixed camber and caster angles and good road stability. The camber and caster angles change slightly with changes in the load and acceleration, and during braking.

Troubleshooting and Inspection The cause of poor handling and excessive tire wear in vehicles utilizing a twin I-beam suspension parallels those of an independent front-wheel suspension—in effect: damaged, worn, or deteriorated bushings, weak coil springs, worn kingpin or bushings, loose or damaged wheel bearings.

When inspecting a truck or van, perform the

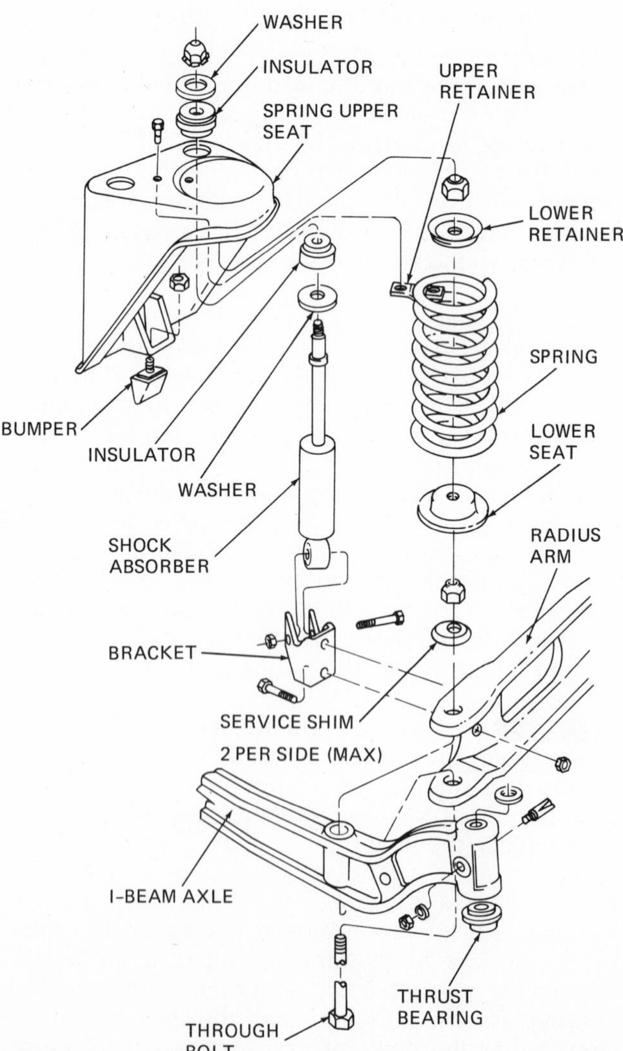

Fig. 6-25 Exploded view of front spring and related parts. *(Ford Motor Company)*

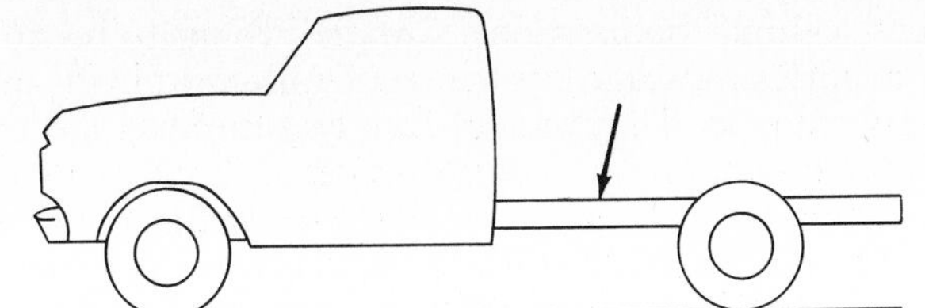

Fig. 6-26 Arrow points to location of the protractor position to measure frame angle.

checks and inspections outlined earlier in the material on independent front wheel suspension. In addition you must check the wear of the kingpin rather than the wear of the ball joints. Always refer to the service manual for wear specifications. Check the wear of the bushings at the I-beam pivot point and of the rubber bushings at the radius arm-to-frame connection. If the rubber insulators show deterioration, they must be replaced. **NOTE** Before performing a front-end alignment, you must measure the frame angle. If the frame is not level, or one frame rail angle varies from the other, the caster angle must be modified. See Fig. 6-26. These variations could arise from the difference between the size of front and rear tires, weak front or rear springs, a damaged frame, or improper payload weight distribution on the truck or van.

Servicing the Twin I-Beam Suspension Such servicing involves the following:

REPLACING THE COIL SPRING If the coil spring is bent or the frame height is below specification, both coil springs should be replaced. To make this replacement, block the rear wheels, raise the front frame so that the tires clear the floor by about 6 in [15.24 cm], and in this position safely block the frame. Next, place a hydraulic jack under each I-beam axle (near the steering knuckle) and slightly compress the coil spring. Remove in order the lower shock absorber nut and bolt from the mounting bracket, the two upper spring retainer bolts and the retainers, and the nut from the through bolt which holds the lower retainer to the lower spring seat. If the suspension is equipped with a stabilizer bar, you need move only the bolt that attaches the stabilizer link to the bracket. This bracket is also fastened with the through bolt that attaches the radius arm to the I-beam axle.

Next, lower the axle and lift the spring from the lower spring seat, taking note of the position of the spring. Some coil spring ends are not both the same—the top end may be bent inward (see Fig. 6-27).

The coil spring is installed in precisely the reverse order in which it was removed. However, check the following for damage and/or deterioration: the spring seat and retainers, the shock absorber, and the radius arm insulators. Replace them if necessary before starting the reassembly.

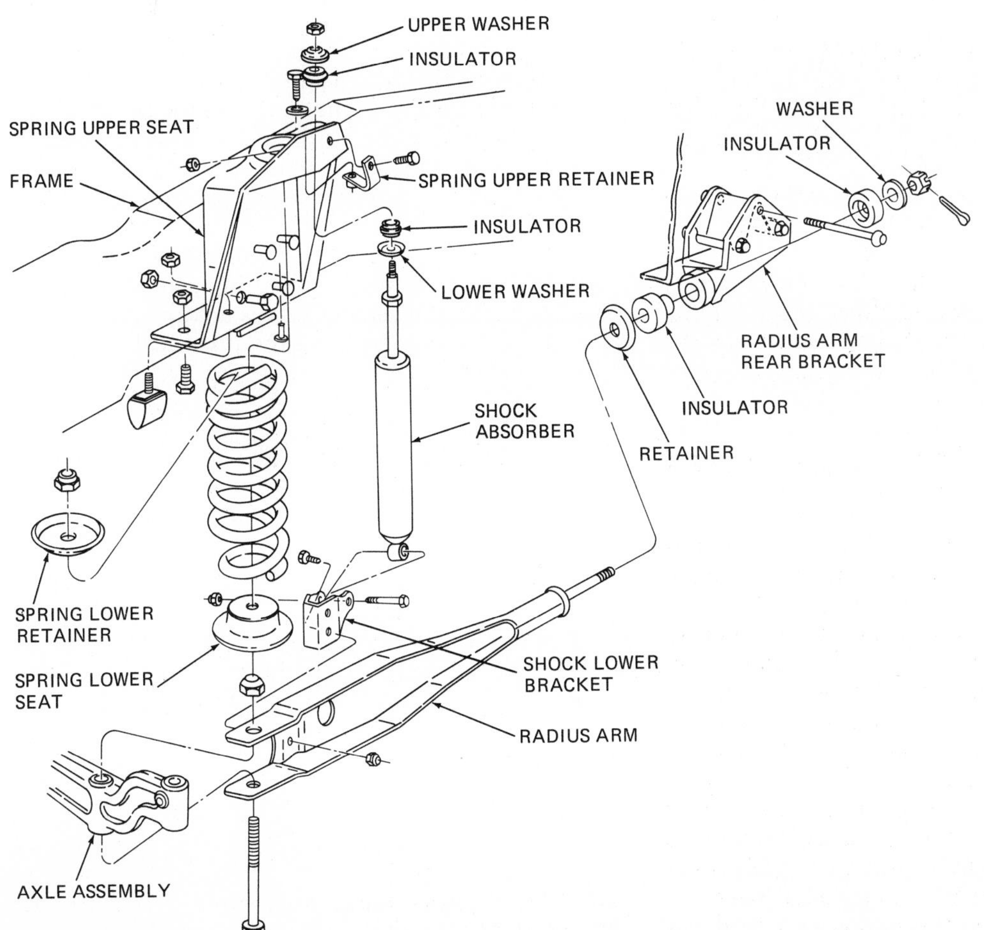

Fig. 6-27 Exploded view of front spring radius arm and related parts. (*Ford Motor Company*)

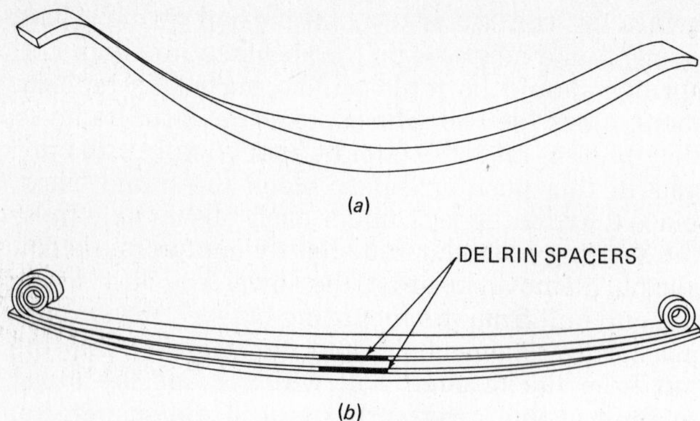

Fig. 6-28 (*a*) Tapered single-leaf spring. (*b*) Tapered triple single-leaf spring.

REPLACING THE RADIUS ARM To replace the radius arm because of a damaged arm frame, bent insulator end, or elongated holes, or to replace the rubber insulators, you must remove the coil spring. When this has been done, remove in order: the lower spring seat from the through bolt, the nut from the through bolt, and the bolt from the radius arm, stabilizer bracket, and I-beam axle, the cotter pin nut, washer, and rear insulator from the radius arm stud and/or bracket. In some cases you must remove the tie-rod in order to move the radius arm forward to slide the stud out of the rear radius arm bracket. When the arm is removed, slide from the radius arm stud the front insulator and retainer.

Replace worn or damaged parts, check the I-beam axle bushing for wear, and make certain the nuts which secure the rear radius bracket to the frame rail are tight. Reinstall the radius arm precisely in the reverse order of removal; tighten the stud nut to the specified torque and secure the nut with a new cotter pin. **NOTE** If the nut is too loose, or overtorqued, the caster angle is changed from that designed into the suspension.

LEAF SPRING SUSPENSIONS

As mentioned previously, leaf springs of various designs are the most commonly used on motor vehicles and vehicle suspensions. This is primarily because the spring rate and cycle can be tailored to any specific vehicle. They are reliable and durable and can be serviced without special tools.

The most common leaf spring designs are the semielliptical types, so named because of their shape. Quarter-elliptical leaf springs are used in conjunction with an air spring suspension. Single-leaf springs or staked single-leaf springs are tapered springs which have one, two, or three leaves (see Fig. 6-28*a* and *b*). Multileaf springs have several single leaves which vary in length but are the same in width and thickness. The ends may be square, trimmed to a shape, tapered, or rolled to a spring eye. The second leaf may be wrapped partly around the main spring eye. Most leaves are formed (cambered), heat-treated, and then coated for protection, although the multileaf springs of off-highway equipment and motor vehicles are not cambered. See Fig. 6-29.

A center bolt (or bolts) holds (hold) the leaves together as a unit and the head of the bolt serves as a locating dowel to position the spring to the axle spring seat. Rebound clips or clamps are used to keep the leaves in alignment. The rebound clips also reduce the rebound. To increase the load range and yet have a softer spring when not loaded, a second multileaf spring (helper spring) may be used, or the first few leaves may be cambered and the remainder left without camber, or a spring arrangement such as the one shown in Fig. 6-30 may be used. In the latter instance, the spring is held in alignment with the frame by means of the radius rod leaf spring, and the main and second leaves rest on a specially contoured spring bracket. When the motor vehicle is not loaded, the spring camber increases, as does the overall spring length. With an increase in load, the spring length and the camber are reduced. This reduces the spring rate, makes the spring stiffer, and increases the load capacity.

Another way to improve handling and steering is with the use of a two-stage spring rate suspension. The main and the second leaves are about one-third longer toward the rear than the third leaf. A second

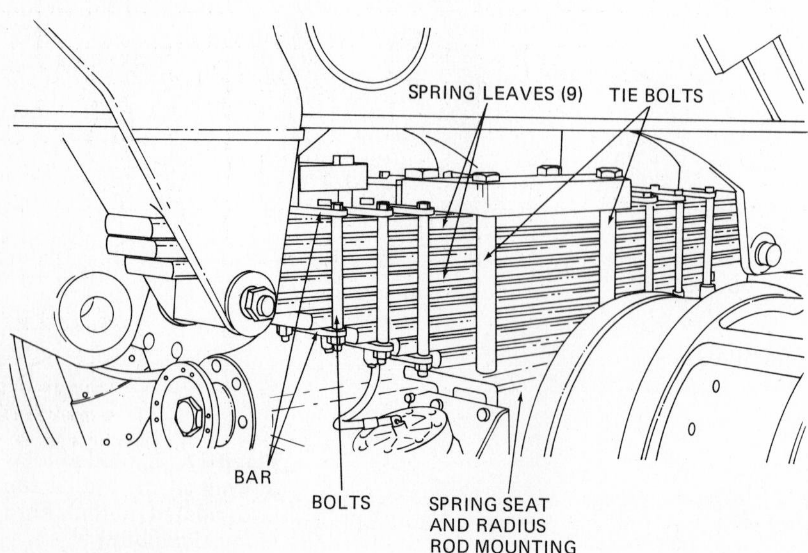

Fig. 6-29 Off-highway front axle spring.

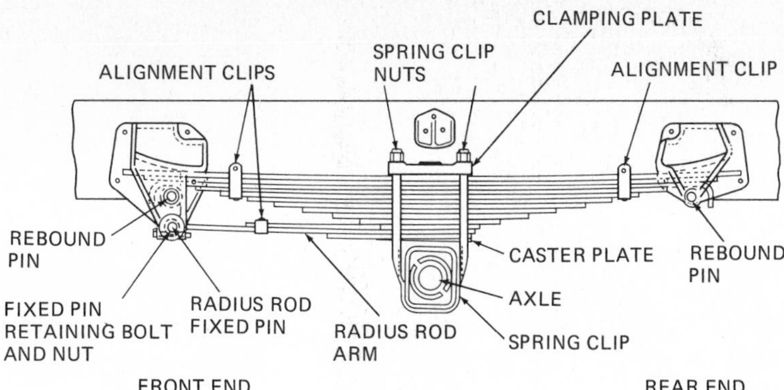

Fig. 6-30 Variable-rate and radius rod spring assembly. (*Mack Canada Inc.*)

spring slipper bracket is bolted above, but close to the end of the third leaf. When the motor vehicle is under light load, or not loaded (see Fig. 6-31), there is a gap between the inside slipper bracket and the main leaf, and the sprung weight is transferred from the frame rail to the spring eye and the outside spring slipper bracket. Nearly all spring deflection is through the main and second leaves. Under a load, the main leaf comes to rest against the inside slipper bracket, thereby reducing the overall length of the spring; the spring weight is now transferred from the frame rail to the spring eye and the two slipper brackets.

Some multileaf, single-, and staked single-leaf springs designed for steering axles may have unequal distances from the center bolt to the spring eye (see Fig. 6-28). As you may assume, this type of spring has a different spring rate on each side of the center bolt. The purpose of this type of spring is to achieve smooth acceleration, maximize efficiency to transmit brake torque to the frame during braking, and thereby prevent wheel hop. A spring of this design must be mounted so that the shorter part faces forward (see Fig. 6-32). Multileaf, single-, or staked single-leaf springs are usually of the positive opening design—that is, when loaded or on jounce, the spring height and camber are reduced and the spring length increased. These springs are either fastened to the top or bottom of the axle seat (overslung or underslung). Oversling or undersling can also be achieved by fastening the axle on top or below the spring ends. See Fig. 6-33.

Some multileaf springs are of the negative opening design and then normally fastened below the axle to the axle seat (underslung). A negative multileaf spring is one which, when loaded or when the spring is on jounce, the spring height and camber increase and the overall length shortens. See Fig. 6-34.

In the last few years, the single- or staked single-leaf springs of the tapered design have become quite popular on steering, trailer, and drive axles. They are highly acceptable because of their variable spring rate design, which provides good handling and steering under nearly all loaded and unloaded conditions. They have proved less subject to breakage and they weigh less than a multileaf spring of the same load range. In addition, their brake torque and weight transfer are about 40 percent better than that of a multileaf spring. In essence, this means that the front end of a three-leaf tapered-leaf spring absorbs about 67 percent and the rear end about 100 percent of the brake torque and weight—the spring will act to resist windup.

On a typical multileaf suspension, only 25 percent of the front end of the spring is available, along with 100 percent of the rear end of the front spring, to resist windup. The single- or staked single-leaf springs are evenly tapered toward the end and then formed to a spring eye or formed to rest on a slipper

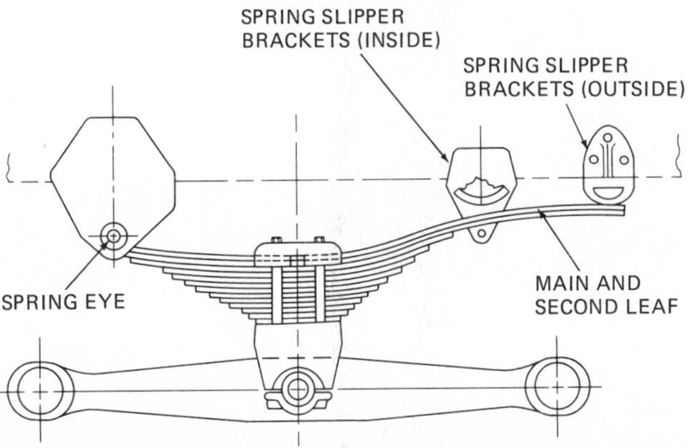

Fig. 6-31 Schematic view of a two-stage multileaf spring in the unloaded stage.

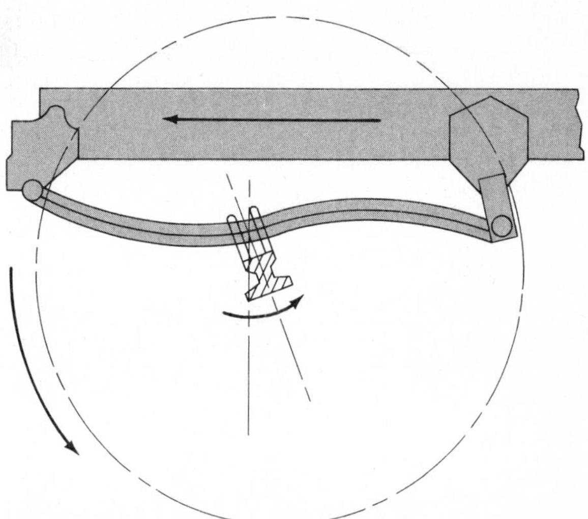

Fig. 6-32 Schematic view of spring reaction (torque and weight transfer). (*Rockwell International, Automobile Operations. Troy, Mich.*)

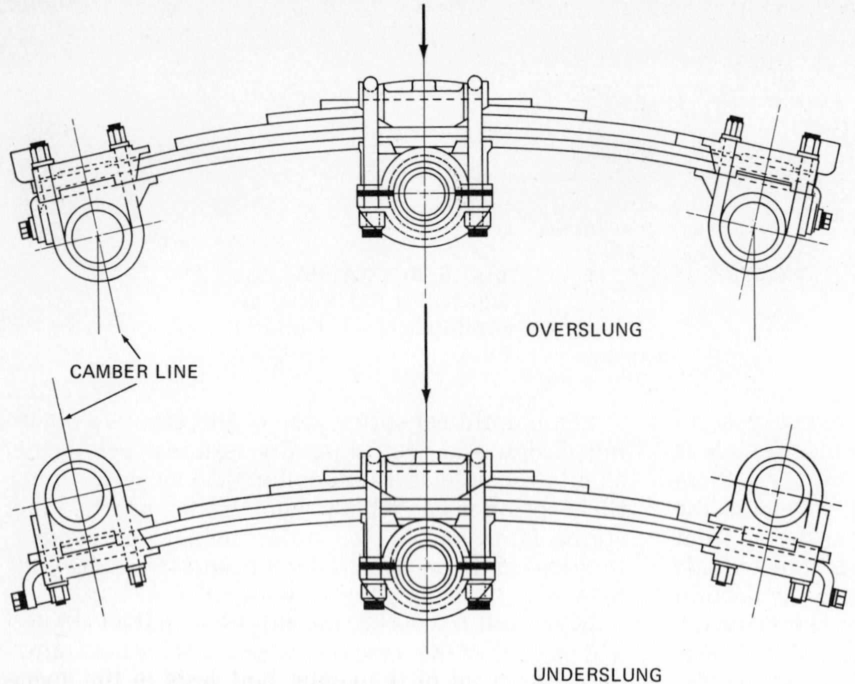

Fig. 6-33 Overslung and underslung trailer suspensions (positive opening). (*Reyco Industries Inc.*)

bracket. The leaves are separated by Delrin liners to alleviate fretting and corrosion and to reduce interleaf friction. When the spring is under low sprung weight only, the ends deflect at a high rate, and when at or below maximum sprung weight the spring length increases until it is almost straight. Under this condition the entire spring deflects, but at a lower spring rate. See Fig. 6-35.

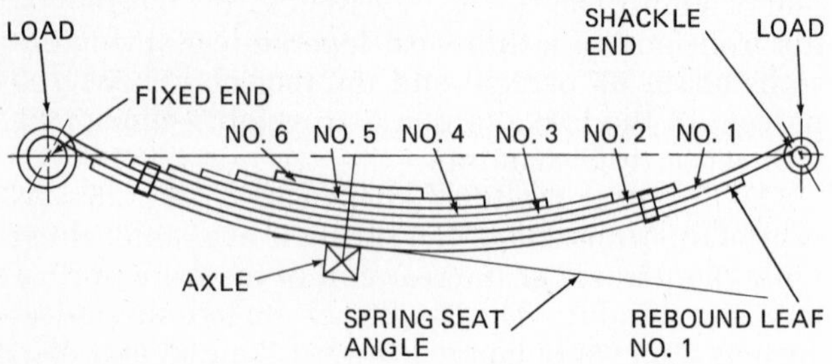

Fig. 6-34 Underslung trailer suspension (negative opening).

Single-Axle Leaf Spring Suspension On motortrucks or truck-tractors with a single or tandem steering axle or having a single drive axle, or on trailers with a single axle, one end (the spring eye) is commonly pivot-fastened to the front spring bracket. The bracket is either riveted or bolted to the frame. The other end of the spring is pivot-fastened to one end of the shackle, and the shackle is pivot-fastened to the spring bracket. A shackle is the coupling link between the spring and the spring bracket, and it compensates for spring length variations during jounce and rebound.

Another mounting, instead of the shackle type, is

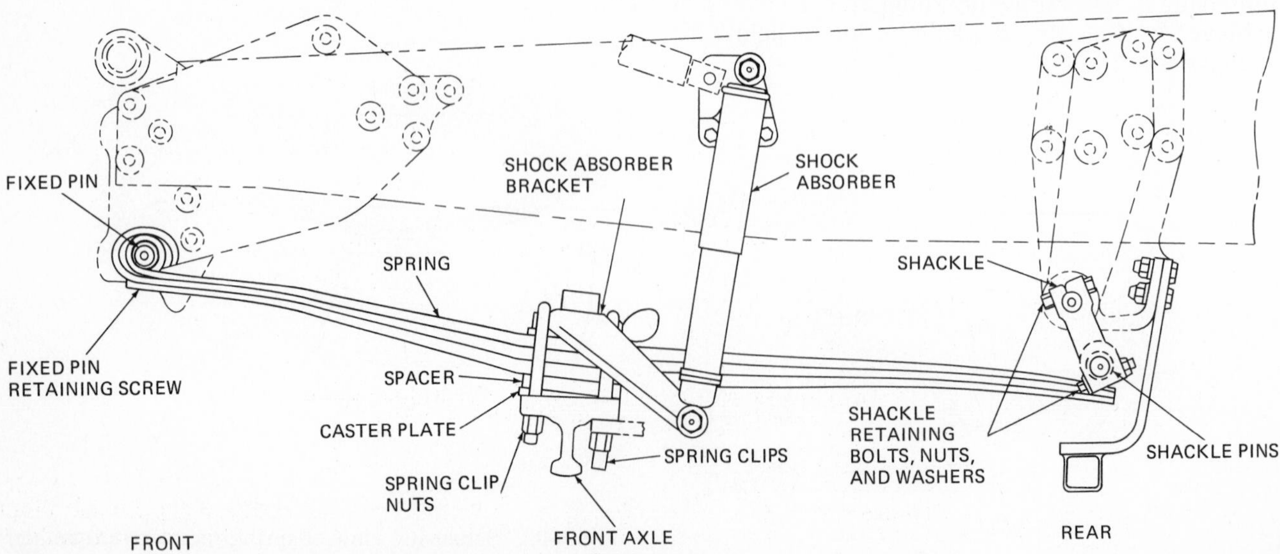

Fig. 6-35 Taper-leaf spring front axle suspension. (*Mack Canada Inc.*)

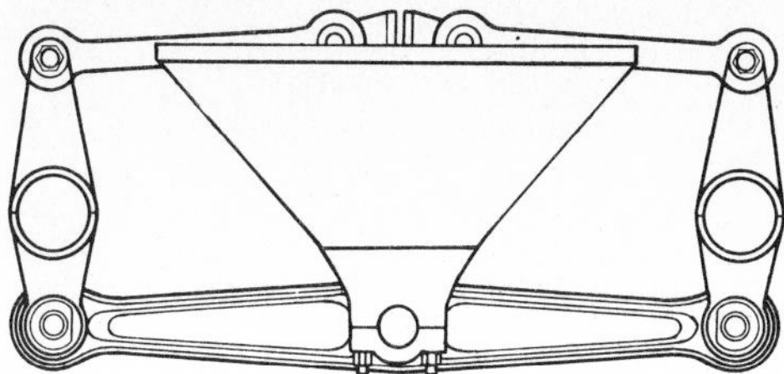

Fig. 6-43 Schematic illustration of a solid mounted suspension.

parallelness of the axles. The aluminum, modular iron, or fabricated steel box beam equalizer bar pivots on the center bushing. The bushing material varies from rubber, to synthetic, to bronze. The two drive axles are fastened to the ends of the equalizer beam bore through a rubber bushing, adapters, and bolt. Bumpers—one at the front and one at the rear—are bolted to the frame rail to limit beam oscillation to about 12 in [30.48 cm]. The torque rod, which absorbs acceleration, brake torque, and road shocks, is fastened at one end to the axle housing and at the other end to the crossmember. Some suspensions have, in addition, two diagonal torque rods to absorb side thrust from the axle. The end of one torque rod is fastened to the left-hand frame rail, and the other end to the front axle housing. One end of the second torque rod is fastened to the right-hand frame rail, and the other end to the second axle housing.

Solid Mounted Equalizer Beam Suspension Since this type of suspension has no spring, it is used exclusively where maximum stabilization is required and/or where the vehicle is designed to carry loads above the maximum on-highway load limits. It is designed for motortrucks or motor tractors, and for carriers intended for the logging industry, for oil field operation, for heavy, large-load transportation, and for excavation and crane applications. See Fig. 6-43.

Adequate cushion for the load or mounting equipment and reasonably good ride is provided through the articulating equalizer beam, torque arm, and the tires. The elimination of the leaf spring makes the load-carrying capacity of this suspension nearly unlimited, and its maintenance is negligible.

Leaf Spring Suspension Checks To prevent suspension failure and reduce wear, the suspension must be checked at regular intervals and, in some cases, greased. When inspecting the suspension, check for

1. Shifted axle and/or broken center bolts.
2. Broken spring leaves.
3. Loose, worn, or broken shackles.
4. Worn spring ends and slipper brackets.
5. Loose U bolts.
6. Missing or loose rebound spring clips.
7. Extent (lack) of lubrication.
8. Worn or loose torque arms.
9. Oil leaks, damaged rods, deteriorated bushings, external dents, cracked pins, or bushing saddles in shock absorbers.
10. Deteriorated rubber bushings. In some cases the frame should be raised (to take the weight from the suspension) in order to determine if the bushings and torque arms are worn.

If the operator complains of excessive axle oscillation, check the shock absorbers even though no external damage is apparent on them. See the section on shock absorbers later in this unit.

If the operator complains of a noisy suspension, the problem may be loose U bolts, lack of lubricant (at shackles or trunnion or between the spring leaves), or damaged shock absorbers.

If the operator complains of a weak or sagging suspension, check for broken leaves and worn or damaged shackles or slipper brackets; also check the effectiveness of the shock absorbers. **NOTE** Broken springs or leaves are the result of loose U bolts, overloading, damaged torque arms, excessive suspension friction, and normal fatigue.

Leaf Spring Suspension Service The initial steps are the same in servicing a front or a rear leaf spring suspension. In each case you must

1. Block the front or rear wheels, depending on which suspension you are working on.
2. Raise the vehicle frame with a jack or hoist, just high enough to remove the force from the springs.
3. Block the frame securely in this position.

From here on the procedure will depend on the service that the suspension requires, the type of suspension, and the additional work you intend to do. For instance, to repack or replace the wheel bearings, replace the tires, service the brakes, or replace the kingpins, it is recommended that you remove the axle assembly.

FRONT AXLE SUSPENSION To service a front axle I-beam suspension, proceed as follows: Apply penetrating oil to all exposed threads and then loosen all nuts or cap screws. Match-mark all parts and components to ensure proper positioning and location when reassembling. Remove the U-bolt nuts, the U bolts, bumper, and spacer (shock absorber bracket) and then swing the shock absorber bracket out of the way or disconnect it from the shock absorber. Slide the caster wedge and/or the axle spacer and shock absorber bracket from between the axle and spring. Remove the fixed-pin-locking device and push the fixed pin from the front bracket and spring bushing. As the assembly requires, remove the rebound pin or bolt, or the insulator cap and the top and bottom insulator, or remove the nuts and bolts from the shackle retainer pin and force the pin from the rear spring bracket, and the shackle bore and the pin from the shackle and spring eye bushing. Next, raise the frame or tilt the spring so that the spring eye clears the bracket, or the center bolt clears the dowel hole in the axle seat, and then remove the spring.

Cleaning and inspection Use a suitable cleaning solution to clean all parts; then dry them with

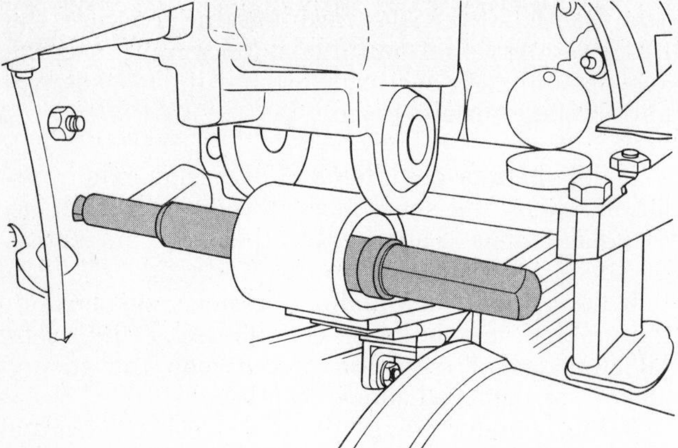

Fig. 6-44 Removing and installing spring eye bushing with tool. *(GMC Truck and Coach Division)*

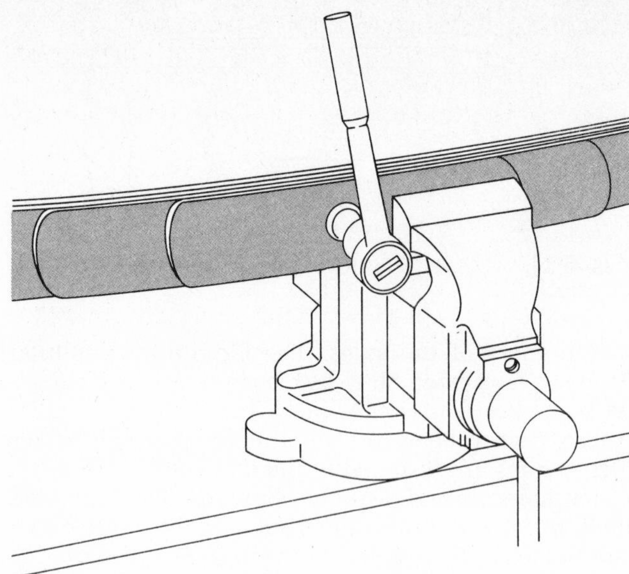

Fig. 6-45 Disassembling spring assembly.

compressed air. *Follow all recommended safety rules.*

Inspect the pins, cap screws, U bolts, bushings, and shackle brackets for excessive wear, distortion, and cracks, and check threads for any damage. Inspect the spring brackets for looseness, wear, cracks, and twists and bends. **NOTE** It is advisable to disassemble the springs, clean and lubricate the leaves, and replace the spring eye bushing(s), the center bolt, and the spring rebound clips and bolts to prevent later suspension trouble. If, for good reason, you are unable to disassemble and service the spring, inspect the spring for broken or fatigued leaves, check the condition of the center bolt, and measure the bushing wear. **NOTE** Always replace rubber bushings. Make certain the rebound clip bolts are tight and that the leaves are aligned.

Repair and replacement To replace a worn bushing while the spring is assembled and fastened to the axle, raise the vehicle frame so that you can use, without interference, the installation and removal tool. See Fig. 6-44.

NOTE Check the relevant service manual with regard to the use of the tools and the bushing position.

If the rebound clips are loose or damaged or the bolts are loose or broken, remove all bolts and install new ones. To prevent spring shifting, leaf breakage, shearing of the center bolt, front axle misalignment (especially caster), and rear axle dog tracking which may damage or break the drive line, tighten the rebound clip precisely as follows: First, tighten the rear spring clip nuts until snug and then tighten the front nuts. Next, use a torque wrench and first tighten the two rear nuts and then the two front nuts to the specified torque, which may range from 100 to 1700 lb · ft [689 to 11,713 N · m] depending on the bolt size.

To disassemble a multileaf spring in order to replace a leaf or to clean and relubricate it, first use a grease pencil and match-mark the assembly to ensure reassembly to its original position. Grind off the peened center bolt. Depending on the size of the spring, either clamp the spring in a vise (Fig. 6-45) or lay it onto the press bed in such a way that you can remove the center bolt and the spring tension without injuring yourself. Remove the rebound nuts, bolts, and spacers, and then remove the center bolt nut. You can now slowly release the spring force. Cut the rivet heads from the rebound clip to remove any damaged or worn clips. With an arbor press or hydraulic press, force out the bushing.

Compare the camber of the main and second leaves with a new leaf. If they are not identical, the leaves must be replaced. **NOTE** If the spring height is below specification, the entire spring assembly must be replaced or recambered in a special spring shop. Use a sandblaster or power wire wheel to clean the leaves.

NOTE Do not sandblast or use a wire brush on single and staked single leaves as they are coated with a zinc-rich material. If when inspecting the leaves you find the surfaces to be rough, pitted, or damaged, they must be replaced.

If the main spring can be reused, install new bushing(s) into the spring eye with the aid of a press. Cold-rivet the new rebound clip to the spring leaf, if required. Clamp the center bolt in the vise, coat the leaf surfaces with the recommended lubricant, and stack them onto the center bolt. Use C clamps to draw the leaves together to start the nut on the center bolt. Tighten the nut firmly, cut the end of the bolt, and then peen the end to secure the nut. **NOTE** While tightening the nut, tap the leaves into alignment with a soft face hammer. Install the rebound spacers, bolts, and nuts, and tighten the nuts as previously explained.

To install the spring, place the components onto the axle seat according to the marking guides made prior to removal. Make certain the parts seat firmly and are in the dowel holes. This is especially important for the caster wedge. Install the spring assembly in precisely the reverse order of removal and torque all bolts and nuts to the specified torque (to prevent repeat suspension failure) before lowering the frame.

REAR AXLE SUSPENSION If any work additional to suspension service is to be performed on the rear axles, say for example the carrier must also be serviced, it is faster and easier to roll out the entire axle assembly. The general procedure is as follows: Block the front wheels, raise the frame to remove the force from the springs, and block it securely in this position. Release the spring brakes, drain the air tanks, and identify all connections before removing the air hoses (which may include a differential lock). Remove all electric wiring. Remove the rebound bolts from the rear spring brackets and the fixed pin or bolt from the front spring bracket. Place a floor jack under the front carrier to raise it up. Remove, if applicable, the torque rod or arms from the axle-housing mounting brackets, and wire up the ends. Disconnect the universal joint from the carrier pinion flange. Now, raise the frame just enough to clear the carrier height so that the assembly can be rolled out.

The service procedure for a single-axle rear spring suspension is very similar to that of a front axle suspension with some exceptions: The rear wheel hub must usually be removed, and when a variable-rate radius rod suspension is used you must use a C clamp to clamp the main leaf and radius rod leaf together in order to remove the tension from the radius leaf and to remove the fixed pin from the front bracket and spring bushings.

In most cases, tapered shims are used for adjusting the drive line angle. Take note of the number of shims and the direction in which the tapered ends are pointing.

Equalizer Beam Suspension Service The general procedure to replace the spring assembly of an equalizer beam suspension is first to block the front wheels, raise the frame with a hoist, and then raise the front rear axle using two jacks under the front end of the equalizer beams. Next, block the frame and axle so that the force from the spring is removed and the front tires just clear the floor. Remove the front axle wheel hub to allow working room when removing the fixed spring pin and spring (see material on wheel hubs). **NOTE** Sometimes you must also remove the rear wheel hub, in which case you must block the rear axle.

Loosen the lower trunnion saddle cap nuts and then the top pad bolts, or the U-bolt nut bolts (see Fig. 6-46). Next, remove the nuts and trunnion cap, the nut from the tapered draw key, and then the key from the front spring bracket. With a soft punch and hammer, drive out the fixed hanger pin. Lower the equalizer beam to clear the spring eye for easier removal of the spring. Attach a hoist cable to the spring, position the hoist and take up the slack, and then lift the spring and spring saddle from the center bushing. Remove either the U bolts or the four bolts that secure the spring to the saddle.

After the spring is serviced, replace the bushing (if the bushing is bronze it must be reamed to specification) and check the spring brackets for wear and damage and the equalizer beam for wear; check the rubber bushings for deterioration, position the saddle and plate to the spring, and snugly tighten the nuts. Next, tighten the spring plate set screws to force the spring firmly against the machined surface of the saddle, and then lock the nuts. While holding the nuts, torque the cap screws in the proper sequence to the specified torque. Lift the assembly onto the center sleeve beam so that the rear of the spring is between the rear hanger flanges, position the lower saddle cap and then install and tighten the nuts to the specified torque. Jack up the equalizer beam, align the bushing bore with the front hanger bore, install the hanger pin and the draw key, and tighten the nut to specification.

Reinstall the rear spring bracket, rebound bolt, and the wheel hub or hubs, readjust the wheel senser and the brakes, and, finally, connect the air lines and wiring.

EQUALIZER BEAM REMOVAL AND ASSEMBLY If the equalizer beam is damaged or worn, or the bushings are worn or deteriorated, the beam must be serviced or replaced. To service the equalizer beam, first raise the frame with a hoist so that the tires clear the floor and then block the frame securely in this position. Remove the wheel hub from the front and rear axles and then remove air hoses, brake chamber brackets, wheel senser wiring, and, if applicable, the brake backing plate. Place hydraulic jacks under both axle housing ends and to support the equalizer beam place a jack underneath the center tube. Next, remove the four stud nuts and the saddle cap. Remove the nuts, washers, and bolts from both axle beam hangers and with two prybars or with the special puller (Fig. 6-47) remove the adapters from the axle beam hanger and bushing. When this has been done, lower the center tube and slide the equalizer beam from it. If the equalizer beam is not aluminum, you may have to use a sling and hoist to lift it off.

Before cleaning the beam, press out the center and the two end bushings, using a hydraulic press or the portable power tool shown in Fig. 6-48. Before pressing the new bushing into place, clean the bores thoroughly using fine emery cloth, lubricate the bore and bushing with the recommended grease, and then press them into place as shown in the illustration.

The equalizer beam is reinstalled in precisely the reverse order of disassembly. However, take care when placing the adapter into position that the flat on the adapter is in the vertical position and the special flat washers are placed onto each side. Always use a new self-locking nut. *Do not forget* to readjust the brakes and the wheel sensor and if applicable to lubricate the bushings. **NOTE** Although some service manuals advocate replacing only the damaged bushing in the equalizer beam, it is usually more profitable in the long run to replace all bushings once one of them has failed.

Torque Arm or Torque Rod Service The torque arms or rods of any suspension must always be in good condition; otherwise the axle will roll and/or come out of alignment. This would cause excessive wear and stress on the entire suspension and increase tire and drive line wear. Regular checks are therefore necessary and, if the arms are bent, or the

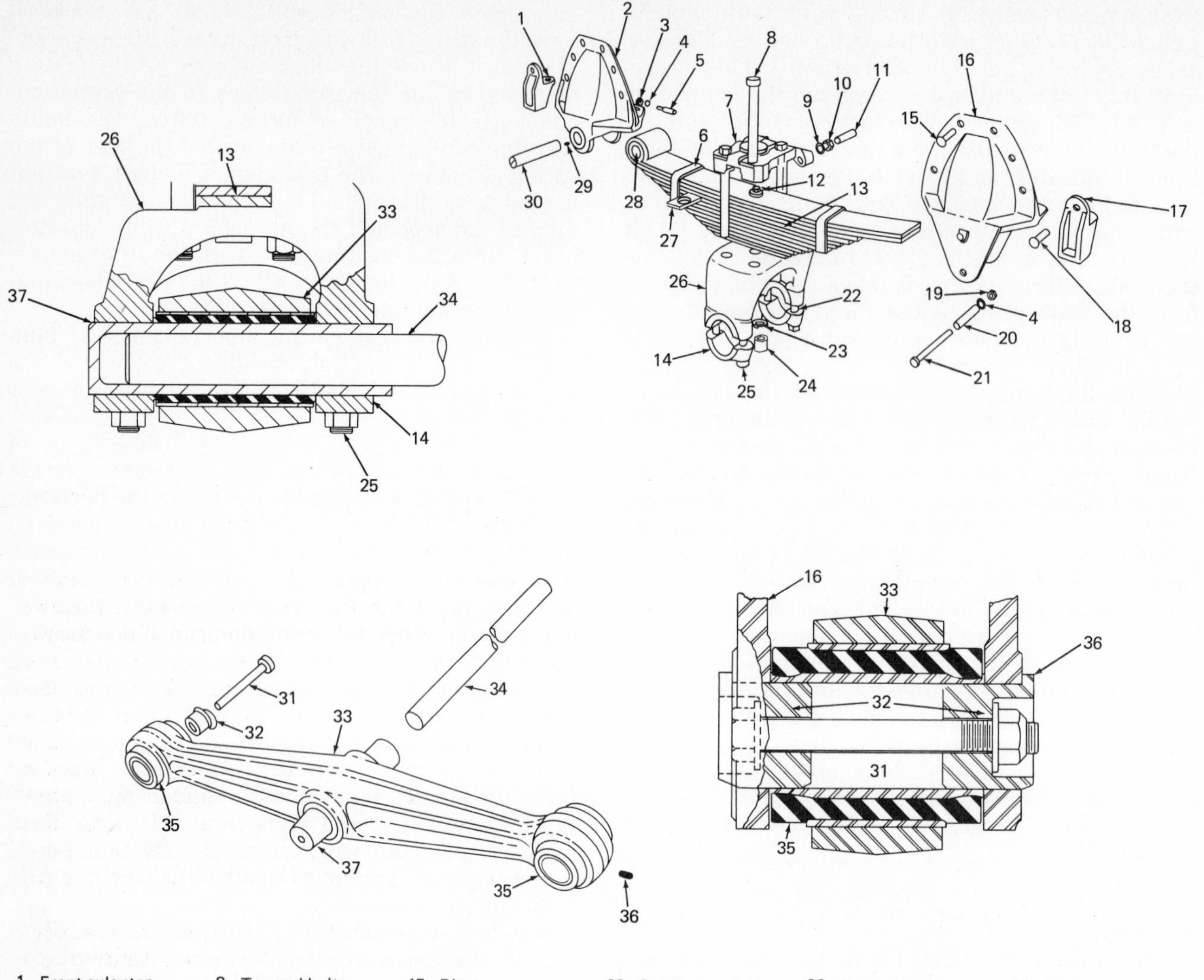

1. Front axle stop
2. Front spring bracket
3. Nut
4. Lock washer
5. Spring pin draw key
6. Spring clip
7. Top spring pad
8. Top pad bolts
9. Lock washers
10. Nuts
11. Set screw
12. Center spring bolt
13. Spring assembly
14. Saddle cap retainer
15. Rivet
16. Spring bracket, rear
17. Axle stop, rear
18. Rivet
19. Nut
20. Spacer
21. Bolt
22. Saddle cap studs
23. Lock washers
24. Nuts
25. Nuts
26. Saddle assembly
27. Top pad
28. Spring eye bushing
29. Grease nipple
30. Front spring pin
31. Bolt
32. Beam end adapter
33. Equalizer beam
34. Center cross tube
35. Beam end bushing
36. Set screw
37. Center beam sleeve

Fig. 6-46 Exploded view of leaf spring suspension.

rubber bushings deteriorated, or the mounting bolts loose or bent, the assembly must be serviced.

This service is relatively simple, as in most cases the torque arms or rods can be serviced without removing any other components and sometimes without a puller or jack. In most instances, however, you have to jack the drive end of the carrier up to remove the force from the torque arm, and to prevent the axle from tipping before removing the mounting bolts or through bolts.

The simplest method to secure the torque arm or the rods to the vehicle frame rail or crossmember, spring saddle, or axle housing, is shown in Figs. 6-49 and 6-50. The torque arm pins are bolted to the frame mounting brackets and to the axle housing, or else through bolts are used to hold the torque arm to the center spring bracket and spring saddle.

TORQUE ROD WITH REPLACEABLE BUSHINGS If the torque arm or rod has replaceable bushings, use a hydraulic press and the recommended adapter to replace them. When the torque rods or arms are pin- or saddle-mounted, you then need a special torque rod or pin puller or a hydraulic jack to prevent damage to the pin and/or the torque rod and/or bushing.

To remove a torque rod of this type, first clean the assembly thoroughly with a wire brush and then apply penetrating oil generously to the tapered shaft and nuts. Tap the nuts and bracket gently to increase penetration and then remove the pin-locking device, which may be a nut, a through bolt, or a tapered lock key.

If the torque rod bracket is fastened to the frame (as shown in Fig. 6-49), screw the puller stud into the pin end, install the puller sleeve over the stud bolt, and screw the nut onto the stud puller bolt. Tighten the puller nut to pull the torque rod pin from the bushing and bracket.

To install the torque rod, align the rod and bracket holes and the pin so that the lock pin hole and

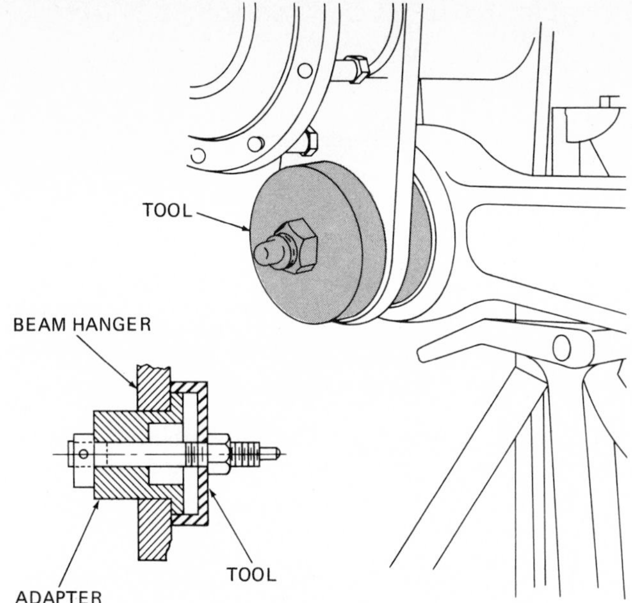

Fig. 6-47 Removing beam adapter.

milled slot on the pin align, and then drive the pin into place. Install the tapered lock pin, lockwasher, and nut.

STUB-MOUNTED TORQUE ROD If the torque rod is stub-mounted (see Fig. 6-50), remove the cotter pin and the nut. Install a two-jaw puller over the torque rod (pin-end side) with the jaws hooked on or into the yoke slots. Center the puller screw and then tighten it. You may have to strike the puller screw with several sharp blows to loosen the rod yoke from

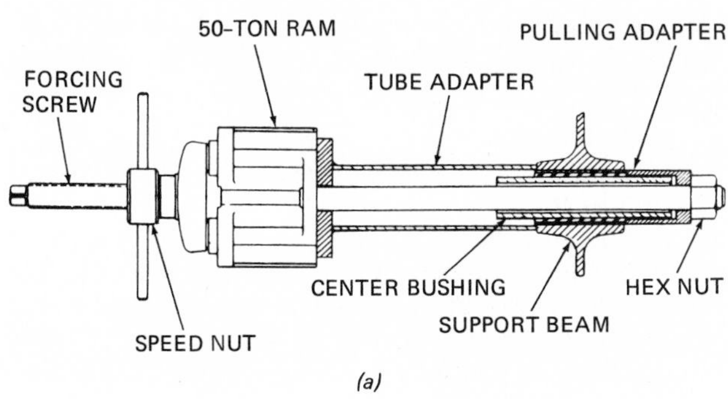

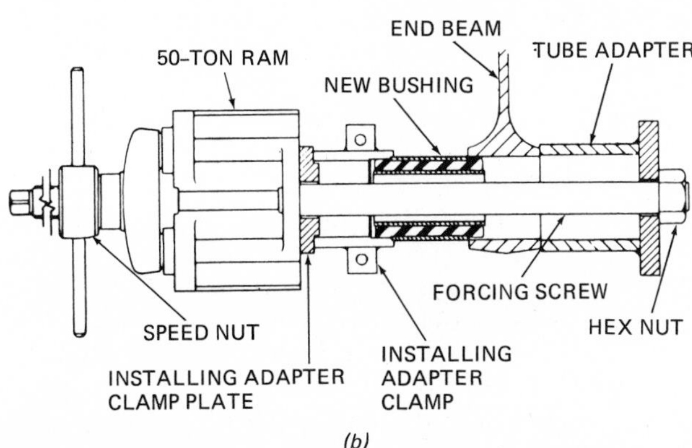

Fig. 6-48 (*a*) Method of removing center beam bushing. (*b*) Method of installing beam end bushing.

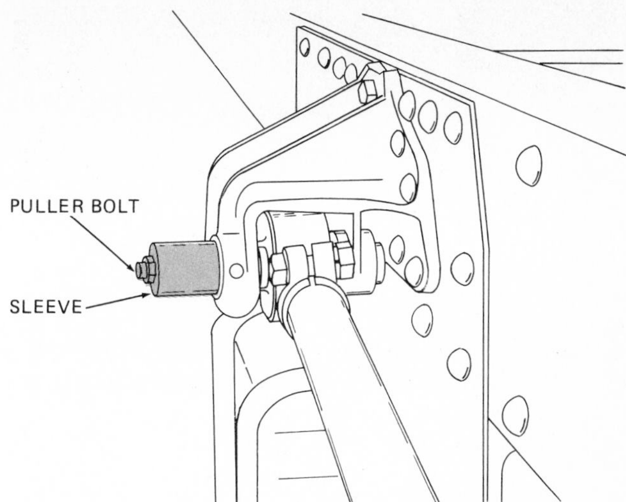

Fig. 6-49 Removing torque rod (*Rockwell International, Automotive Operations, Troy, Mich.*)

the tapered pins. Repeat the same steps to remove the other torque rod end from the bracket. Inspect the pin for wear, bend, or other damage. If necessary, clean the tapered torque rod hole and the pin. Use emery cloth to remove the rust or other contaminants. Wipe the rod hole and the pin clean, and apply a moderate lubricant to the hole surface but not to the pin. Place the pin into the tapered bracket hole, install and tighten the nut to the recommended torque, and then install the cotter pin. Place the torque rod yoke over the pin, install and torque the nut to specification, and then install the cotter pin.

SADDLE-MOUNTED TORQUE ROD To remove a saddle-mounted torque rod (see Fig. 6-51), remove both cotter pins, nuts, and washer. Place the spacer between the torque rod and outer housing brackets. Position the hydraulic jack, and press the pin from the bracket and torque rod end. To install the torque rod, insert the dowel into the bracket bore, align the bores, and insert the pin. Slide the outer dowel onto

Fig. 6-50 Using a two-jaw puller to remove stub-mounted torque rod (*Rockwell International, Automotive Operations, Troy, Mich.*)

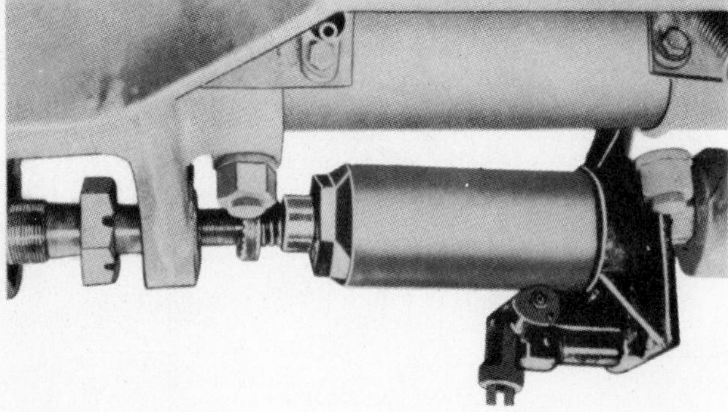

Fig. 6-51 Removing saddle-mounted torque rod. (*Rockwell International, Automotive Operations, Troy, Mich.*)

the pin and into the bracket bore. Place the thicker larger washer onto the inside of the pin, and the other washer onto the outside. Install and tighten the nuts to the specified torque, and install the cotter pins.

On some types of torque rod installations, the only way to remove the pin from the bracket bore is to drive a large tie-rod wedge between the rod end and the bracket.

RUBBER SPRING SUSPENSIONS

Three types of rubber springs are used on single-axle and tandem axle suspensions. All have more or less the same advantages:

1. They weigh less than a leaf spring of comparable capacity.
2. They give the vehicle good stability and traction.
3. They reduce shock vibration.
4. They have longer service life and less maintenance than leaf-type springs because rubber accommodates motion without lubrication, bushings, or shafts.
5. They have good handling and steering ability under nearly all load and road conditions.
6. In some cases no shock absorbers are required.
7. No additional valves or air lines are needed.
8. Some can be used on on- and off-highway suspensions simply by varying the diameter and height of the spring.
9. Some can be used (in addition to the conventional leaf spring suspension) to improve handling and steering at light load, and act as an overload protection when capacity-loaded, thereby increasing the life of the spring and suspension as a whole.

Lastosphere Spring The solid rubber spring shown in Fig. 6-52, called a *lastosphere spring*, has the mounting plates permanently bonded to the top and bottom surfaces. This spring is made of a special compound which maintains flexibility under nearly all ambient temperature conditions. It can be used on light-weight vehicles and on trucks up to 150 tons [136 t]. When used on an equalizer suspension, the single rear axle is supported by four rubber springs and the spring is fastened with two bolts to

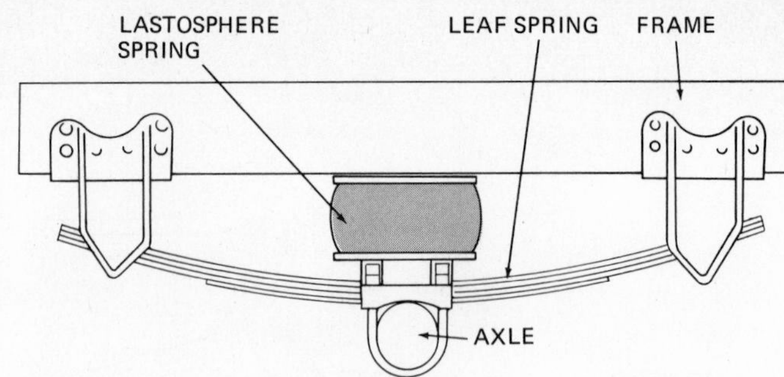

Fig. 6-52 Lastosphere spring used as a booster spring.

the axle seats and with two bolts to the frame or spring saddle. As a rule, this solid rubber spring is usable wherever rubber springs, leaf springs, or air springs are used.

The only maintenance it requires is the occasional check for tightness of the mounting bolts, and care of its external condition. On heavy-duty applications, the life span of the lastosphere spring is reported to be over 10,000 hours (h). The rubber spring of an on-highway motor vehicle or vehicle would last the life of the vehicle.

OPERATION When the vehicle is not loaded, the springs are expanded to nearly their free height and the forward and reverse force from the axles is transmitted through the spring to the frame. As the sprung weight increases, the spring decreases in height and at the same time increases in diameter (see Fig. 6-53). When the tire hits a bump or rolls into a hole, the rubber takes up the additional force or else forces the tire down to follow the road contour.

Rubber Load Cushion Spring This type of spring has many of the advantages of the solid rubber spring, although, as you can see from Fig. 6-54, it is not of solid composition—it has individual rubber load cushions. The rubber load cushion spring is fastened to the spring saddle by means of a bracket and drive pin (which is part of the bracket), and by means of the drive pin bushing that is pressed into the spring saddle bore. The drive pin and bushing transmit the forward and reverse force from the axles onto the frame. The four cushion brackets are bolted to the frame rails, distributing the load equally onto the frame. Since this type of spring is designed in

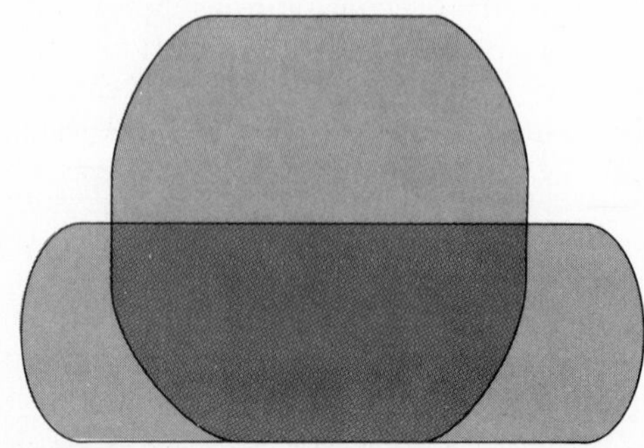

Fig. 6-53 Lastosphere spring in the static and loaded condition.

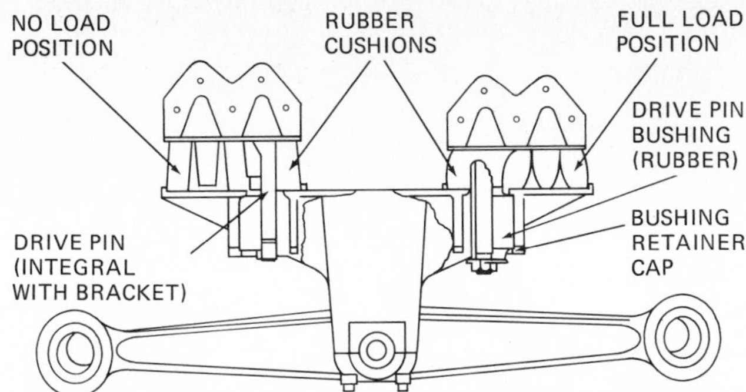

Fig. 6-54 Sectional view of a rubber load cushion suspension.

various load-carrying capacity ranges from 34,000 to 200,000 lb [15,436 to 90,800 kg], it can also be used on on- and off-highway motor vehicles and vehicles.

OPERATION When the vehicle is not loaded, the sprung weight is carried only on the outer load cushions, which rest constantly on the spring saddle surface. When the sprung weight is increased or the tires roll over a bump, the outer cushions are further compressed and the crossbar cushions then come into contact with the saddle surface to absorb the additional load or the upward force of the tire. As the cushions compress or expand during vehicle operation, the drive pin moves up or down in the drive pin bushing, in direct proportion to the movement of the individual load cushions.

INSPECTION The load cushions are also trouble-free over a long period of time, but routine maintenance checks are nevertheless necessary. Measure the load cushion height to determine their energy and at the same time check them for external damage or deterioration, the drive pin nuts for looseness, and the bushings for damage or deterioration. Damaged or deteriorated bushings and loose or bent drive pins will cause suspension misalignment, dog tracking, and excessive wheel hop during acceleration and braking.

SERVICE Service of the equalizer beam, that is, replacing the beam or bushings, has been previously outlined.

To replace the load cushion, the bracket and drive pin, or the drive pin bushing, block the rear wheels and attach a sling and hoist so that you can raise the rear of the frame. Remove the drive pin nuts and the load cushion bracket nuts and bolts. Because the nuts are staked, you may have to use a cold chisel and hammer to split them. Next, raise the rear frame about 8 in [20.3 cm] and block it in this position. Pull the bracket upward to extract the drive pin from the drive bushing, and lift the assembly from the saddle surface. Remove the drive pin bushing cap screws and the retainer cap, and then force the bushing out of the saddle bore. Clean the saddle bore and saddle surfaces and if necessary use emery cloth to remove rust or rubber particles from the surfaces. Apply the recommended lubricant to the bushing bore surface and then push the bushing (from the bottom) into the bore. Install the bushing retainer cap and tighten the cap screws to the specified torque. Position the load cushion, lubricate the drive pin, and push the bracket and pin assembly downward so that the pin slides through the load cushion and into the drive bushing. Lower the frame to align the frame holes with the bracket holes. Install the mounting bolts and nuts and the drive pin washer and nut, tighten them to the specified torque, and then stake the drive pin nut.

Rubber Shear Spring This type of spring also has many of the advantages of the solid rubber spring; however, it is designed to a load-carrying capacity limit of 38,000 lb [17,252 kg]. See Fig. 6-55. The assembly consists of a one-piece mounting bracket and drive pin and a two-stage rubber shear spring. The rubber is bonded to the outer, center, and inner steel bushings, at an angle of about 45°. The spring assembly is positioned in the spring saddle bore and held in place by retainer clamps. When assembled and installed, the flange on the drive pin rests on the upper inner steel bushing, the washer rests on the lower inner steel bushing, and the nut holds the pin in place. When the sprung weight increases, the drive pin flange forces the first-stage shear spring inner bushing downward, absorbing the force, reducing the angle, and providing a high deflection rate. When the sprung weight increases, the drive pin flange comes to rest against the center steel bushing and forces the second-stage shear spring down, increasing the spring rate but reducing the deflection.

INSPECTION To check the energy and condition of the spring, measure the height between the spring saddle and frame rail, and measure the drive pin center. If the spring height is less than specified, or the spring heights vary, or the drive pins are not in

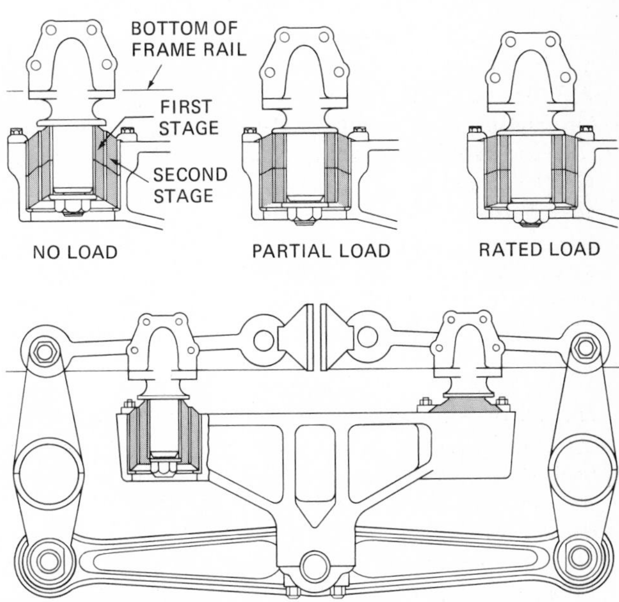

Fig. 6-55 Rubber shear spring suspension. (*Hendrickson Mfg. Company*)

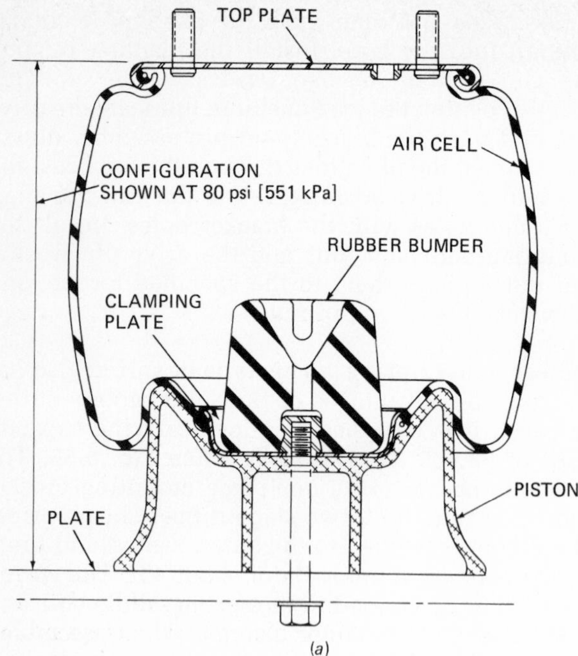

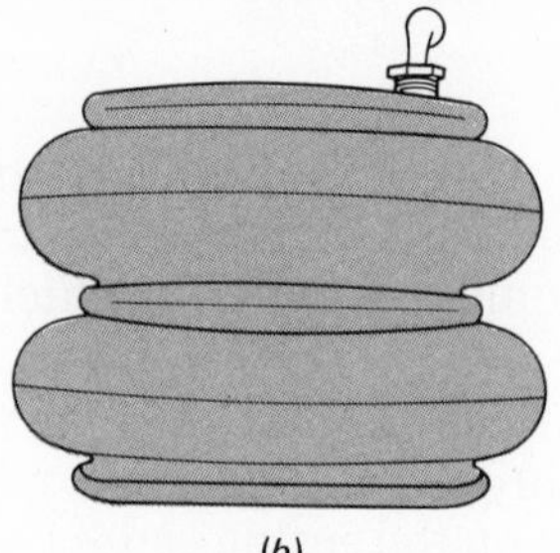

Fig. 6-56 (*a*) Schematic view of a diaphragm air spring assembly. (*b*) Two-convolution air springs.

the center, the shear spring and/or drive pin assemblies must be replaced.

SERVICE To replace a drive pin assembly or a shear spring assembly, prepare the vehicle as you would when replacing the load-cushioning spring. Next, remove the drive pin nut (you may also have to use a cold chisel and hammer to split the nut). Remove the bracket mounting nuts, washers, and bolts, the shear spring clamp bolts, and the clamp. Raise and block the frame so that you can pull the drive pin assembly from the center bushing. Pull the shear spring assembly from the saddle bore. Thoroughly clean the bore, and reassemble the unit in precisely the reverse order of disassembly, but do not forget to stake the drive pin nuts.

AIR SPRING SUSPENSIONS

Air Springs (Pneumatic Springs) A pneumatic spring relies on the energy of compressed air or gas to do the work of a leaf, rubber, coil, or torsion spring. The air or gas is confined by various types of air chambers.

Three main types of air springs are used on on- and off-highway motor vehicles and vehicles. They vary to some extent in design and size to provide for different load-carrying capacities, which range from about 38,000 to 400,000 lb [17,252 to 181,600 kg].

- *Diaphragm air spring.* This type has the air cell or diaphragm clamped to the top plate. The top plate may be designed as shown in Fig. 6-56, or it may extend downward to form a cup, or even further downward partly enclosing the piston. The lower end of the air cell or diaphragm is fastened to the piston through a clamping plate. A rubber bumper placed on top of the clamping plate absorbs and limits maximum deflection. The top plate is bolted to the frame rail, and the piston is bolted to the axle, the spring seat, or the spring saddle.
- *Bellow air spring.* This type has one or two convolute sections which are either round or oblong. The top and bottom plates are bonded or clamped to the self-retaining flexible member. The top plate is fastened to the frame rail, and the lower plate to the spring seat or the spring saddle.
- *Hydropneumatic spring.* This type requires a piston and cylinder and uses both liquid and gas. The spring characteristic is provided by the confined gas and the damping action is provided by the liquid that is restricted through orifices from flowing from one part of the assembly to the other. They are used exclusively on trucks from 50 to 300 tons [45 to 272 t].

These three types of air springs have the same advantageous features as the solid rubber spring, but in addition the diaphragm and bellow types have the ability to automatically vary the spring rate. The variations give the motor vehicle or vehicle a softer ride at lower and higher sprung weights, reducing bogie hop and increasing traction. They also maintain the same frame height regardless of load distribution or centrifugal force when the vehicle is steered into a turn or when it is operated on a crown road surface or grade.

Air Ride Leveling Valve On tractor applications, these springs maintain the fifth wheel at a fixed height, maintaining the trailer deck at a specified level ± 1°. To do this the air pressure within the air chamber is varied. The air ride leveling valve controls the air pressure into one spring assembly and thereby controls the frame height. It is bolted to the frame, and the actuating lever arm is fastened to the axle through an adjustable rod. (See Fig. 6-57.) One air leveling valve is used for each spring assembly,

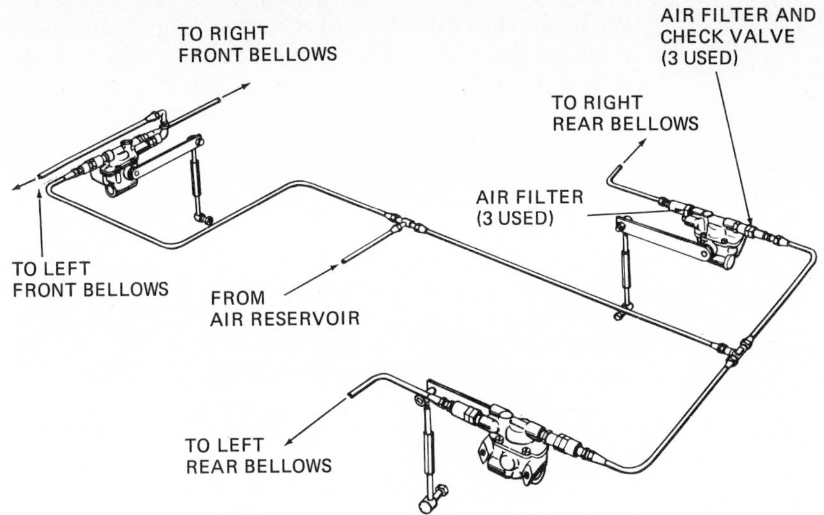

Fig. 6-57 Typical bus or motor-truck air-suspension piping.

or the two left- and the two right-hand spring assemblies (tandem axles) are connected in parallel to one air ride leveling valve. The valve, however, becomes insensitive and will not change the air pressure within the spring chambers when the wheels bounce up and down more than 80 cycles per second.

Air from the air brake primary reservoir is piped in parallel to the inlet ports of the air ride leveling valves. The outlet ports of the valves are connected with hoses to the spring assembly. (One type of valve is shown in Fig. 6-58.) The lower valve body is filled with hydraulic fluid. When the cam follower rests on the flat side of the lever shaft, the actuating arm is in the vertical position and the valve actuating fork has positioned the exhaust stem so that the exhaust valve rests against the exhaust valve seat. The inlet valve is held on its seat by the air pressure and spring force. The damping pistons rest against the actuating arm. Under this condition the air in the air spring(s) is trapped and the reservoir air is blocked by the inlet valve.

If the axle is forced upward, or the frame is forced downward, the actuating lever arm moves upward, pivoting the lever shaft and moving the cam follower upward against the force of the two cam follower springs. If the movement at the end of the actuating lever is less than 0.0625 in [1.5 mm], no action takes place within the valve. If the lever arm moves more than 0.0625 in [1.5 mm], the cam follower then swings the actuating arm to the right. The right-hand damping piston compresses the fluid in the right-hand damping chamber and forces the fluid through a control orifice (needle valve—not shown) to the left-hand damping chamber. If the swing of the actuating arm is sufficient, the actuating fork lifts the exhaust stem and forces the inlet valve off its seat. Reservoir air then passes by the inlet valve, out of the outlet port, and into the air spring chamber. The higher pressure within the chamber raises the frame and brings the actuating lever to its neutral position. This action places the flat of the lever shaft in a horizontal position, allowing the spring force to set the cam follower. The actuating arm then swings to the vertical position, and the left-hand damping piston forces the fluid from the left-hand damping chamber into the right-hand chamber, delaying the valve action.

When the lever shaft cycles more than 80 times

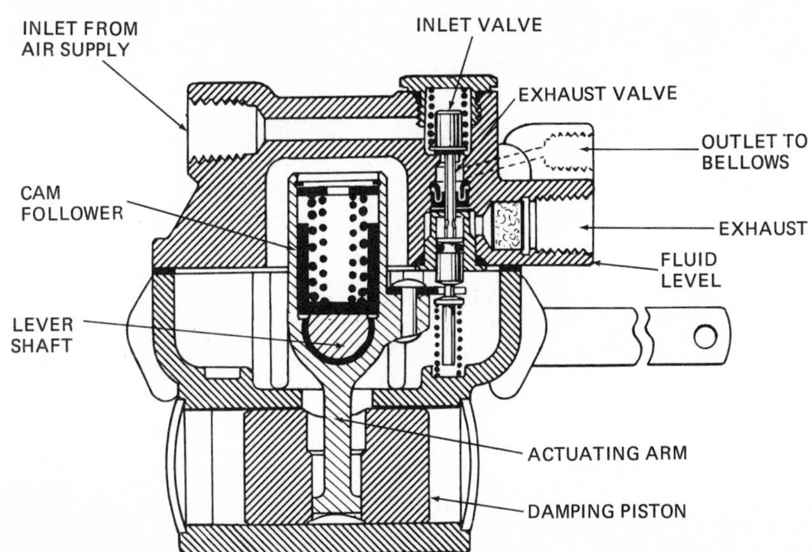

Fig. 6-58 Sectional view of an air ride leveling valve. (*Wagner Electric Corporation*)

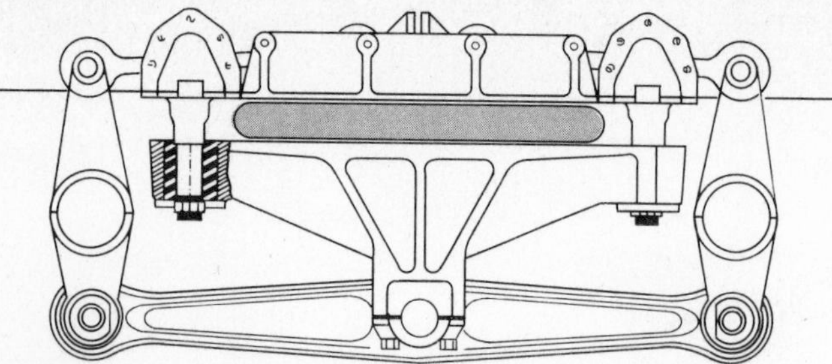

Fig. 6-59 Schematic view of a single-section convolution air spring suspension. (*Hendrickson Mfg. Company*)

per second, clockwise or counterclockwise, the damping piston holds the actuating arm in the vertical position and no valve action takes place.

If the frame rises due to reduced sprung weight, the action within the air ride leveling valve reverses. The actuating arm swings to the left and moves the actuating fork and the exhaust valve stem downward. This action opens the exhaust valve, and the air from the air spring chamber escapes out of the exhaust port through the hollow and cross-drilled exhaust valve. As the air pressure within the air spring chamber is reduced, the frame lowers and the actuating lever comes back to the neutral position. The actuating arm swings back to the vertical position and the exhaust stem spring closes the exhaust valve, trapping the reduced air pressure in the air chambers.

Although the actuating arm is moved downward when the tire(s) rolls (roll) into a hole, the damping piston delays the swing of the actuating arm and thereby delays the opening of the exhaust valve.

Air Suspension Components An air spring of an air spring suspension supports the sprung weight only. It does not and cannot provide lineal stabilization to the axle. Furthermore, all air spring suspensions require strong shock absorbers because of the high rebound action of the air spring. Axle alignment on this suspension is achieved through various means. One of the oldest methods, but still very popular today, is the air suspension shown in Fig. 6-59. The single-section convolute oblong air spring is positioned between two spring saddles, and the drive pins and drive pin bushings maintain axle alignment and also transmit the axle force to the frame rails or vice versa.

In the last few years, air suspensions of the independent axle trailing arm design have greatly increased in number. "Trailing arm" means that the axle is pulled or trails. With this suspension, the vehicle has good axle control during acceleration and braking, and provides good axle alignment.

There are two main designs. On one of these (see Fig. 6-60) the trailing arm is a multileaf spring, pivot-fastened to the spring bracket, and a piston air spring is fastened to the end of the main leaf. The live or dead axle is fastened with specially designed U bolts and brackets (spring saddle) to the multileaf spring. The fastening arrangement between the multileaf spring and axle serves as a strong swag bar and provides excellent stability under nearly all conditions. This air spring suspension can therefore be used for single- or multiaxle (tandem, triple, etc.) vehicles because each suspension is a unit by itself, and can be used on nearly all types of on- and off-highway equipment with various load-carrying capacities. The axle may be either overslung or underslung to the multileaf spring, or the air spring may consist of two round convolute sections, or the multileaf spring may be of the radius rod multileaf spring design.

Another type of trailing arm air spring suspension is shown in Fig. 6-61. Although these two suspensions are basically equal, there are three primary differences:

- The second air suspension illustrated does not

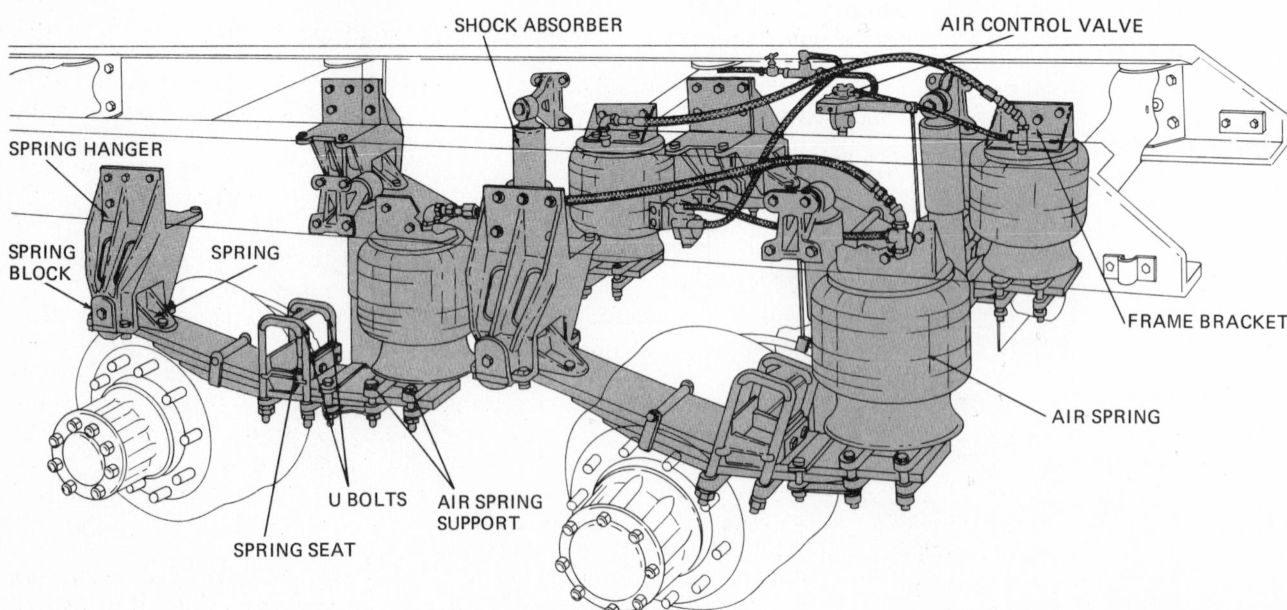

Fig. 6-60 Schematic view of Stabilaire rear axle air suspension.

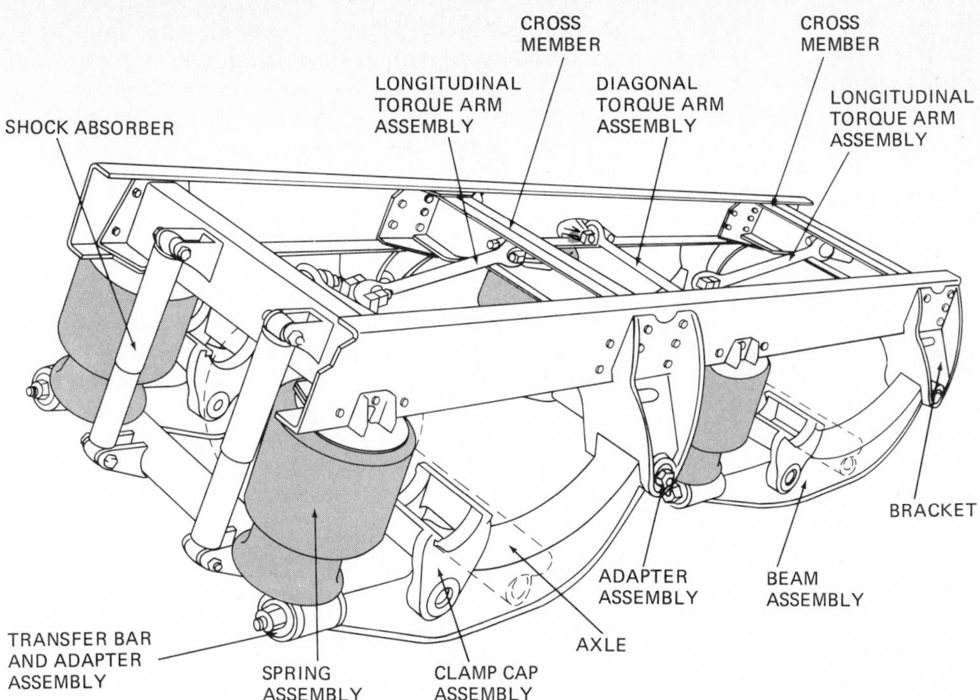

Fig. 6-61 Schematic view of Neway rear axle air suspension.

use a multileaf spring; instead the trailing arm is rigid.

- The axle is pivot-fastened to the trailing arm in Fig. 6-61 whereas on the one shown in Fig. 6-60 it is rigidly fastened.
- For each axle, two torque arm assemblies are used—one to transmit the axle torque to the crossmember and the other to transmit side thrust to the frame rail, stabilizing the axle.

However, both suspensions use rubber bushings at the individual pivot points. The pivot point of the multileaf spring, or of the rigid trailing arm spring, is adjustable for adjusting axle alignment.

Troubleshooting the Air Spring Suspension Since an air spring carries only the sprung weight, tire wear and dog tracking (misalignment between front and rear tires) can only result from damaged or worn unsprung weight components. If the vehicle frame height is lower on one side than the other, or the front axle is lower than the rear, or the motor vehicle or vehicle rides too high or too low, the air springs and/or control valves are more than likely defective. Therefore, if any of these complaints have been registered, first check the general condition of the air springs. They may be punctured, cut, or blown out, or the air hoses may be broken or damaged or the fittings may be leaking.

Check the connecting rod links between the air ride leveling valve and the axle. They may be bent or broken, or the pins and holes may be excessively worn, preventing the valve from correctly controlling the air pressure within the spring. If there is no evidence of external damage, you can assume that the air ride leveling valve is not adjusted properly or, when the vehicle rides high, the inlet valve is leaking, allowing a higher pressure into the air spring chamber. If the air spring chamber is blown out, check to determine if the air chamber has been rubbing on the air brake chamber, the tire, or the rim. Other problems that may contribute to a blown-out air spring chamber are a damaged or broken shock absorber which allows a higher spring rebound, or an incorrectly adjusted air ride leveling valve which allows the frame to rise too high.

If the air spring chamber(s) deflates (deflate) rapidly after the vehicle is parked, check for air leaks from the air ride valve to the air spring, using an air leakage detector or the soap solution method. If air leaks from the air ride leveling valve exhaust port or from the leveling shaft or top cover, the valve must be serviced.

Testing and Adjusting the Air Ride Leveling Valve To adjust the frame height or to check the operation of the valve, first drive the rig onto a level surface. Block the wheels and apply the parking brake. Raise the reservoir pressure to cutout pressure and then stop the engine. Disconnect all linkages between the valves and axles. See Fig. 6-57. Move the lever arm down to exhaust air from the air spring chambers, then connect one valve. In a few seconds the valve should direct air into the air spring chamber, and then the air flow should stop automatically. Next, measure the distance from the axle housing to the frame and compare it with the service manual specification. If the distance is too short, make the adjustment to increase the rod length, or move the lever arm to lengthen the stroke. If the distance is too great, shorten the length. When this adjustment is made, by trial and error, deflate the air spring chamber and then repeat the same procedure with each of the other valves until all are adjusted.

Servicing the Air Spring and Air Ride Leveling Valve To remove the air spring from the suspension shown in Fig. 6-60, raise the rear of the frame

Fig. 6-62 View of front suspension cylinder fastened to truck frame.

until the weight is off the spring, block it in this position, and then place portable jacks under the axle housing. Disconnect the links between the axle and lever arm and manually exhaust all air from the air spring chambers. Remove, identify, and cap all air line connections. Remove the lower spring mounting bolts and remove the nuts from the upper spring plate stud bolts. Lower the axle and remove the spring, but take note of the upper stud bolt positions. Install the new spring in precisely the reverse order of removal.

Hydropneumatic Springs As mentioned previously, this type of spring is used on the front and rear axles of off-highway dump trucks. One reason, among others, is that a hydropneumatic spring can withstand more adverse service conditions than other types of springs. Moreover, in addition to having the same advantages as the rubber load cushion, or shear spring, it also acts as a shock absorber and, when used on the steering axle, it serves as the pivot point of the wheel assembly (kingpin). Several different models, types, and sizes are manufactured to relate to the designed load-carrying capacity, to facilitate the various mountings, or for use on the front or rear axles. (See Fig. 6-62.)

Because it is different from the other types of air springs, we shall discuss it in some detail.

DESIGN Basically, a hydropneumatic spring carries the sprung weight, reduces vehicle oscillation, reduces impact when loading, acts as a shock absorber, and sometimes acts as the kingpin. See Figs. 6-63 and 6-64. It consists, in essence, of the stationary cylinder (housing), which is pinned, bolted, or fastened through a ball stud to a bracket that is welded to the truck frame, and of a movable piston rod or piston pinned or fastened through a ball stud to the axle housing or to the front spindle. About 80 percent of the hydropneumatic spring assembly is filled with engine or hydraulic oil to provide lubrication as well as shock absorber action. The remaining volume is charged with dry nitrogen gas to provide the spring action. Wear rings on the top and bottom support and guide the piston rod or piston on the cylinder wall, and seals and wipers are used to seal them to the cylinder. The location and the size of the lower wear ring and seals, as you can see from Figs. 6-63 and 6-64, vary between the front and the rear Hydrair springs, as do the designs of the pistons. This is because the front piston rod requires a larger bearing surface in order to support its semirotation. Furthermore, the front suspension cylinders require a fixed mounting pad.

The bearing retainer, with wear rings, is bolted to the piston rod or piston. The latter has several orifices and one check valve. The orifices, however, are not in the same plane—they are arranged in a spiral around the piston rod or piston to control the flow rate. When the Hydrair cylinder is installed, filled with oil, and charged with dry nitrogen to about 200 psi [1378 kPa], the piston rod or piston extends to a specified distance.

NOTE Since the nitrogen is lighter than the oil, it always surfaces above the oil.

CAUTION Nitrogen gas is the only gas approved for use in hydropneumatic suspensions because it will not explode when mixed with oil or when subjected to pressure.

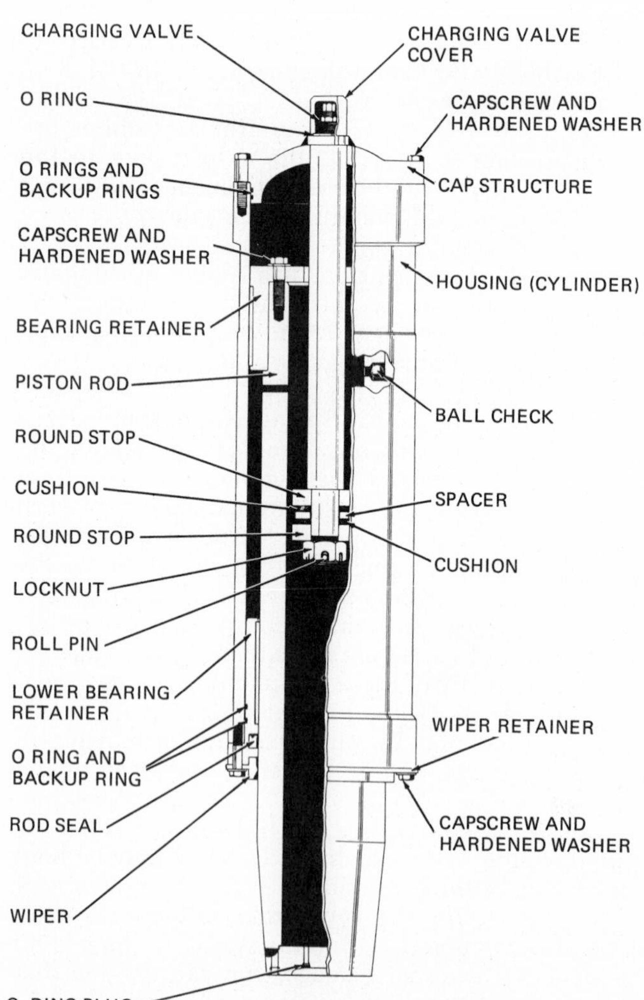

Fig. 6-63 Sectional view of front Hydrair air suspension cylinder construction. (*WABCO, an American Standard Company*)

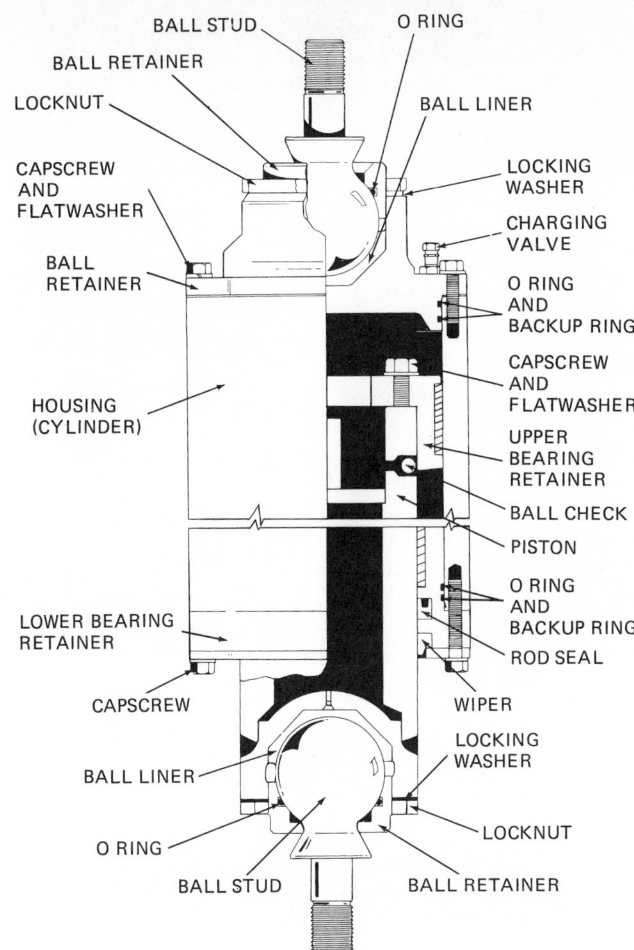

Fig. 6-64 Sectional view of Hydrair rear suspension. (*WABCO, an American Standard Company*)

OPERATION During operation, when a tire rolls over an obstacle, the wheel is forced upward and its motion is directly or indirectly transmitted to the piston rod or piston, forcing it up also. At the same time the pressure between the bearing retainer and cap structure or ball retainer increases, and as a result the oil inside the piston rod or piston is forced through the orifices and check valve and into the low-pressure area, damping the upward movement of the tire. When the upward force ceases, the gas and oil pressure, along with the unsprung weight, forces the piston rod or piston downward. This increases the oil pressure between the piston rod or piston and the cylinder walls; at the same time the oil and nitrogen pressure above the bearing retainer decreases. This dampens the extension of the piston rod or piston because the check valve closes and the oil must pass through several orifices. As the piston rod or piston further extends, the orifices, one after the other, close off.

TROUBLESHOOTING THE SUSPENSION CYLINDER A hydropneumatic suspension is generally trouble-free. However, because trucks sometimes operate under such adverse conditions, they are subjected to external damage which carries through to the piston or piston rod, causing oil leaks. Then again, the ball stud pins and bushings may wear, or the cylinders may be damaged externally, thereby damaging the wear rings. The piston would then tilt and cause an oil leak.

Another cause of suspension failure is nitrogen pressure loss due to a damaged seal or valve. If there is such loss, or if the cylinder is low on oil, you will notice when making your daily maintenance check that, in addition to accumulated dirt on the piston or piston rod and top of the cylinder, the truck is not level. Check the suspension height, drive the empty truck onto a level surface, and measure the extended distance (from the point recommended) of the front and rear piston rod or piston and compare this measurement with that shown in the service manual. You will notice when one piston or piston rod is low that the diagonally opposite piston rod or piston extends further than specified. If the suspension height is less than specified, you may check the oil level and recharge the cylinder, but in most cases it is better to service the cylinder.

OIL CHECKS AND NITROGEN CHARGING To perform these services, drive the empty truck onto a level surface, position jacks, and block the truck so that all weight is taken off the tires. Next, remove the protection cap from the nitrogen-charging valve and open the valve one full turn.

CAUTION The frame comes down very quickly.

With the nitrogen pressure fully removed, you may need to further lower the frame to fully retract the piston rod or piston. Depending on the type of truck you are servicing, either leave the cylinder fully retracted, or raise the frame to extend it to the specified dimension for filling or checking the oil level. When this is done and you find the cylinder requires oil, install a pressure oil gun to the oil filler fitting and fill the cylinder until oil, free of air bubbles, emerges from the leveling device. Then reinstall the plugs. Repeat this procedure with the other hydropneumatic cylinders.

Position the nitrogen gas cylinder and to it connect the nitrogen-charging valve. Check your service manual for the procedure when using the charging equipment. In general, the procedure is to close both shutoff valves leading to the two hydropneumatic cylinders. See Fig. 6-65. Open the nitrogen supply cylinder valve fully, and then adjust the regulator so that the pressure gauge shows about 500 psi [3445 kPa]. Slowly open both shutoff valves to charge both hydropneumatic cylinders simultaneously. You may have to close the valves several times to measure the extension of the piston rods or pistons. It is also recommended to raise the frame with jacks to support it in the event of an accident during the charging procedure. When the piston rods or pistons have extended the specified distance, close both shutoff valves, remove the charging valve connection, replace the valve caps, turn off the nitrogen supply cylinder, and open both shutoff valves to remove the pressure from the gauge.

REPLACING HYDROPNEUMATIC CYLINDERS Although there are some variations in the mounting of front

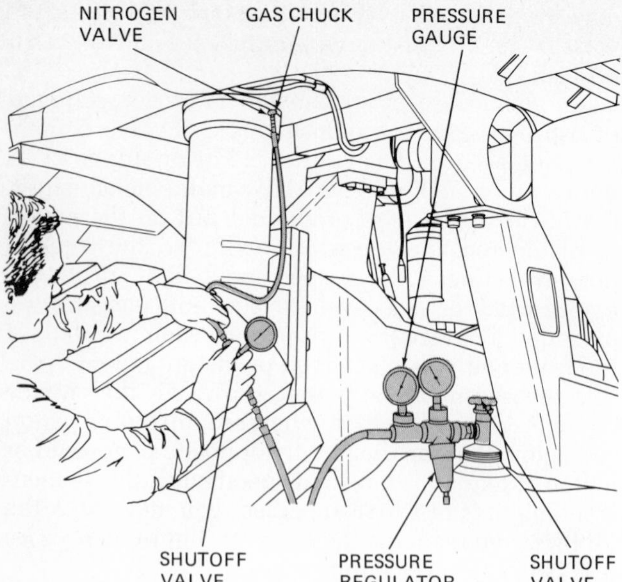

Fig. 6-65 Charging the front suspension cylinder.

and rear axle cylinders, in general the removal procedure is the same for both. However, bear in mind that the trucks are huge, and the weight of the components to be removed are heavy. Therefore you will need at least two 50-ton [45-t] jacks, good blocking material, and a hoist that can lift 10 tons [9 t].

To remove the rear axle hydropneumatic cylinder, raise and block the main truck frame to the recommended height, or place steel blocks of the recommended thickness between the axle housing and truck frame. Release the nitrogen pressure from both cylinders. Attach a sling and hoist to the cylinder, take up the slack, remove first the top mounting device and then the lower one, then lift the cylinder from the axle.

Installation is precisely the reverse procedure. After installation, fill the cylinders to the recommended oil level, and charge both cylinders with dry nitrogen.

The front suspension cylinders are less easily removed or replaced than the rear. The basic steps are as follows: Place jacks under the front main frame or crossmember. Release the nitrogen gas pressure from both cylinders, fully retract the piston or piston rod, and close the valve. Raise and block the truck frame so that the front tire to be serviced just clears the ground. Depending on the wheel and tire size, either remove the wheel assembly or support it with a sling and hoist so that it cannot tip or fall when the spindle is removed from the piston rod or piston.

CAUTION Some tires weigh more than 6 tons [5 t].

Remove and cap the hydraulic brake lines and openings. Remove the steering cylinders and tie-rod from the spindle. Remove the cap screws which secure the spindle through the retainer plate to the piston rod or piston. Attach the puller and pull the spindle from the piston rod or piston. **NOTE** Before proceeding, check the blocking, the sling, the tire, and the hoist.

Attach a sling and hoist to the suspension cylinder and take up the slack. Then remove the mounting nuts, washers, and the cap screws that secure the cylinder to the truck frame and lift the assembly from its dowel pins if so equipped.

Installation is precisely the reverse of removal.

CAUTION Make certain you torque every cap screw, nut, fitting, etc., to precise specification; otherwise a repeat failure will occur.

NOTE The servicing procedure for a hydropneumatic cylinder is very similar to that for a hydraulic cylinder and therefore will not be repeated.

SHOCK ABSORBERS

All types of suspensions need a device, the shock absorber, to reduce suspension spring oscillation. A vehicle without shock absorbers would be most dangerous to drive because of the vibration that would travel throughout the entire vehicle, causing the weight on the tires to alter continuously and the tires to bounce off the road.

Shock absorbers provide a firm, stable ride, resist road impact and vehicle sway, increase tire life, and reduce wheel hop. They also reduce suspension, spring, and steering linkage wear, and slow the transfer of weight from one axle to the other and to the front axle during sudden brake application.

It is apparent, then, that the shock absorbers are extremely useful, and it is equally obvious that one type or design would not serve the needs of all suspensions. Manufacturers, therefore, produce several different types for use on cars, small trucks, linehaul motortrucks, truck-tractors, trailers, buses, and off-highway vehicles. An oversimplified way to classify them is by their operating principle and according to the vehicle's GVW.

On- and off-highway vehicles use shock absorbers which are direct-acting, and of the telescoping design. One end attaches to the frame, and the other to the axle, at or near the spring seat; no levers or linkages are used. A telescoping shock absorber has two sections, one of which slides into and out of the other.

One type of suspension which does not require shock absorbers is the hydropneumatic since it has a built-in shock absorption feature. Nor are shock absorbers required on very large motor vehicles which use a multileaf spring or a solid mounting walking-beam suspension. This is because multileaf springs are so stiff that there is almost no spring deflection, while characteristics inherent in the walking-beam design mean that it smooths out the axle oscillation.

NOTE It is a trend in the trucking industry today to use a softer suspension on truck-tractors and trailers even though this places a greater strain on the shock absorber.

Operating Principles All types of shock absorbers rely on two basic physical principles: Liquids are

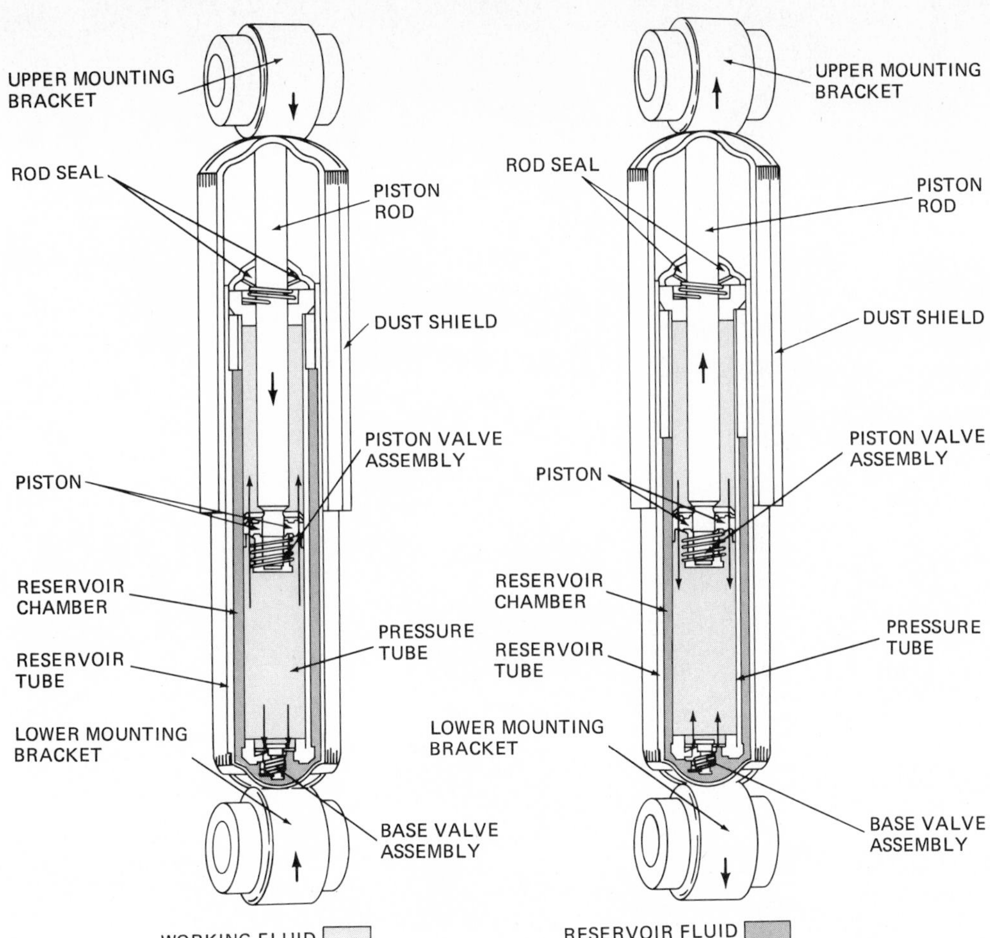

Fig. 6-66 Sectional view of a double-acting shock absorber.

nearly incompressible, and pressure (energy) is required to force the liquid through an orifice. These two principles account for the similarity in the operation and design of shock absorbers, and any differences lie in the size (the diameter and overall length), the valve design, and the size of the orifice that controls the fluid flow on jounce and rebound. They may, however, be classified as to whether they are single- or double-acting shock absorbers. A single-acting shock absorber is one which does not resist extension during rebound, and therefore only resists compression (jounce). A double-acting shock absorber resists both extension (rebound) and compression. The double-action ratio between rebound and jounce varies among shock absorbers to accommodate the suspension design. It may be 20 to 80 percent or 40 to 60 percent, but it is always greater in resistance on rebound.

Design The shock absorbers of medium-size motor vehicles and of large trucks are attached through a mounting stud bolt that passes through the rubber bushing(s). The stud is fastened to either an axle bracket, the lower control arm, or the frame bracket to give the mounting more strength (see Fig. 6-66). The rubber grommet cushions the mounting, and the retainer confines the grommet.

The angle in relation to the true vertical, at which the shock absorber is mounted, depends on the type of suspension. It is angled so that it can help to transfer weight from one axle to the other or reduce vehicle sway and reduce spring windup.

A shock absorber consists of the components shown in Fig. 6-66. The dust shield protects the reservoir tube and the rod seal. The mounting brackets or stud bolts are welded to the dust shield and to the bottom of the reservoir tube. Inside the reservoir tube is the *cylinder tube* (also called the *pressure tube*), and both are sealed to each other through the rod seal assembly (which also serves as the piston rod guide). One end of the piston rod is attached to the dust shield, and the piston with the compression relief and rebound valve is bolted to the other. Attached to the end of the pressure tube is the relief check valve and intake valve with orifice. The piston divides the pressure tube into two pressure chambers, top and bottom. Both chambers are filled with fluid, and the reservoir (which is made up of the reservoir tube and pressure tube) is partly filled. **NOTE** A shock absorber with a high reserve reservoir capacity has a greater cooling capacity; therefore it maintains a lower operating temperature and gives longer efficiency and a longer service life.

Some pressure tubes have external spiral baffles attached to them, and on others the spiral baffles are formed into the reservoir tube. The purpose of the spiral baffles is to control the fluid flow from and into the reservoir, thereby preventing aeration which would develop shock absorber lag without causing damping action. Fluid of a high viscosity index is

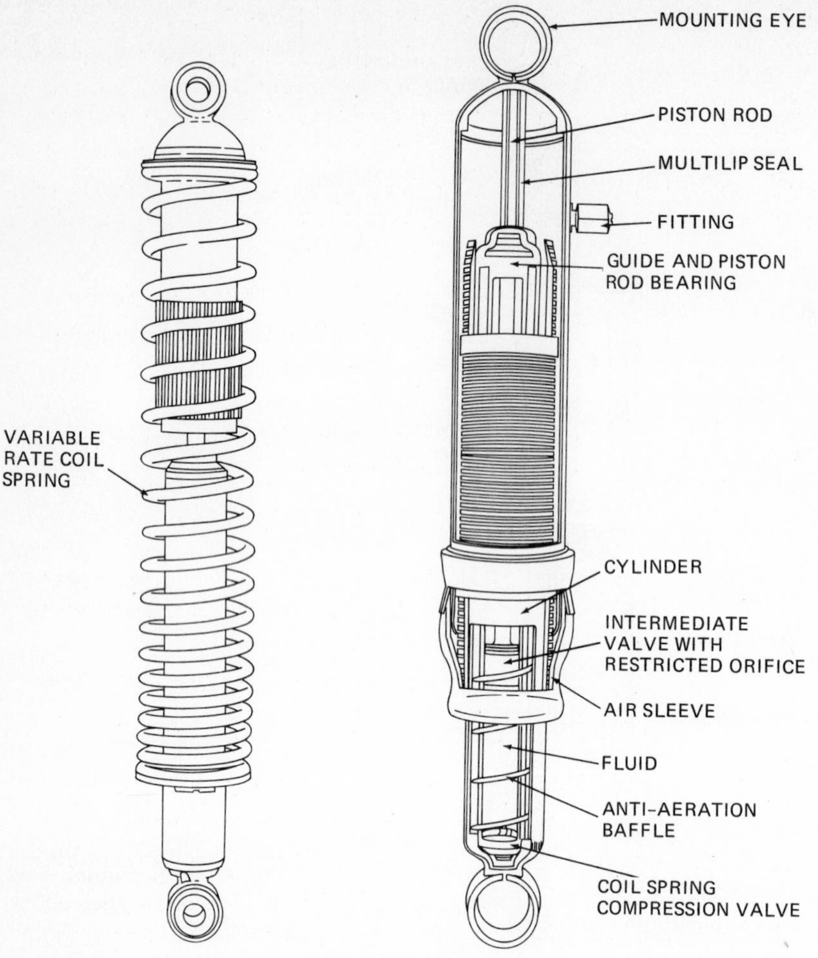

Fig. 6-67 (*a*) Three-phase shock absorber. (*b*) Air shock absorber.

used to maintain a viscosity (fluid thickness) under nearly all ambient temperatures, thereby maintaining positive control.

Operation When the shock absorber is at rest, the compression relief and rebound valves and the rebound check valve and intake valve are closed. On a compression stroke (suspension and jounce), the pressure tube is forced upward. This action moves the piston in the pressure tube downward, increasing the fluid pressure in the lower pressure tube chamber, causing the compression relief valve to open, and allowing the fluid to flow into the lower pressure tube chamber. In a single-acting shock absorber the fluid flows, almost unrestricted, into the upper chamber without causing a damping action. When the shock absorber is double-acting, the fluid flows through the piston orifices and creates a damping action on the compression stroke. By varying the orifice size, the ratio can be varied. Note, however, that the piston rod reduces the volume in the upper pressure chamber and that the fluid volume displaced by the piston is greater; therefore only part of the fluid can enter the upper chamber, and the remaining volume of the fluid flows through the relief check valve (forced open by the higher pressure) and reenters the reservoir.

At the instant of reversal from jounce to rebound, the pressure tube is pulled downward, causing the piston to move up, thereby increasing the pressure in the upper pressure chamber and lowering the pressure in the lower chamber. Two actions take place almost at the same time: (1) The rebound valves open and allow the fluid to flow with high resistance through the orifices in the piston into the lower chamber. The high resistance of the fluid flow causes a high rebound damping action. (2) The displacement of the fluid from the upper chamber into the lower is not great enough to keep the lower chamber filled, and the lower pressure opens the intake valve to allow makeup oil to flow from the reservoir into the lower pressure chamber.

The energy (pressure) that forces the fluid to flow through the orifices and valves on jounce and rebound is converted into heat which enters the atmosphere through conduction and convection.

Three-Phase and Air Shock Absorbers These are used on small trucks and recreational vehicles to increase rear suspension load-carrying capacity. A three-phase shock absorber (Fig. 6-67*a*) is a double-acting type to which a variable-rate steel coil spring is attached. The coil spring rests against the shield and reservoir tube. A rubber cushion acts as a second spring when severe overload occurs.

An air shock absorber (Fig. 6-67*b*) is also a conventional double-acting type, combined with an (air spring) air pressure chamber. It is designed to increase or decrease the air pressure to compensate for the increased load and to maintain the suspension frame height. The bias-ply sleeve air chamber is attached to the shield and reservoir tube. Plastic hoses, using O-ring fittings, are used to connect both air chambers (over a T fitting) with a charging valve. The charging valve is a conventional tire valve. The recommended air pressure ranges from a minimum of 20 to a maximum of 90 psi (137.8 to 620.1 kPa). The charging or depressurizing of the air pressure chamber is as simple as letting the air out of a tire or pressurizing a tire. However, you should load the vehicle first and then adjust the air pressure to achieve the recommended frame height.

Both types of shock absorbers, because of the additional coil or air spring, have a higher resistance on compression, but not on rebound. In addition, the air shock absorber, besides its adjustable feature, increases the operating range, minimizing bottoming, and when correctly adjusted it improves handling by balancing the weight to the front suspension, thereby increasing stability.

Shock Absorber Service Shock absorber service consists of regular checks and of replacing worn or damaged components or parts. Therefore, when performing the routine maintenance checks, do not forget to include the shock absorbers. They are out of sight, but they are very important.

When checking the absorbers, check for fluid leaks, deteriorated or worn rubber bushings or grommets, broken mountings, and external damage to the reservoir tube or shield. Also check the absorber alignment. When uneven tire tread wear is noticeable (cupping or chunking), check the operation of the shock absorbers. The cause of tire wear can often be traced to worn or damaged shock absorbers.

If the driver complains of excessive suspension oscillation or vibration, but the shock absorbers, their rubber bushings, the brackets, and the bolts show no damage, remove one end of the shock absorber from its mounting and then cycle the shock absorber about four times (pull it in and out). If it is in good working order, it will require approximately five times more force to extend it than to compress it.

To determine if the piston rod is bent or the piston or pressure tube damaged, compress the shock absorber within 0.25 in [6 mm] of the end of its stroke. Then turn the rod about one-quarter of a turn. Extend it to within 0.25 in [6 mm] of full extension and rotate it again. If there is excessive resistance to rotation in either position, the piston rod is bent or the piston or pressure tube is damaged, in which case the shock absorbers must be replaced. **NOTE** It is recommended to replace both shock absorbers on a single axle rather than only the one which is worn or damaged.

Review Questions

1. Give six purposes of a suspension.
2. Why do manufacturers attempt to make the unsprung weight as light as possible?
3. Give three purposes of camber.
4. To assure good acceleration, braking, and steering, all tires must have equal and full load contact. List five causes of reduced tire-to-road contact.
5. What are the consequences when a motor vehicle has (*a*) too much caster? (*b*) too little caster? (*c*) unequal caster?
6. How is steering axis inclination achieved?
7. Does a high spring rate classification refer to a soft spring or a hard spring?
8. Why are the upper and lower control arms of unequal length, and the pivot points farther apart than the ball joints?
9. To which control arm is the load-carrying ball joint usually attached?
10. List six defects or malfunctions which could cause the camber to change from positive to negative.
11. When positioning the coil spring, why must the coil spring end rest in the spring saddle groove?
12. Why are leaf springs more suitable for medium and larger motor vehicles or vehicles?
13. List the two purposes of the spring center bolt.
14. Why do some front axle leaf springs have unequal spring halves (different distances from the center bolt)?
15. On a steering axle, what governs the location of the shackle?
16. By what means is a double-slipper multileaf spring held in alignment with the frame to prevent it from rotating?
17. A good maintenance program includes checking the suspension at regular intervals. List six checks which should be made.
18. Why is it so important to precisely follow the manufacturer's recommendations when replacing and retorquing the rebound clip-bolt nuts?
19. State the difference between a torque rod and a radius rod or arm.
20. List the three types of rubber suspension springs.
21. Give the principle by which a rubber shear spring operates.
22. What is the main advantage of a pneumatic suspension over a rubber spring suspension?
23. Which part or component controls the rebound on a hydropneumatic spring?
24. List five malfunctions or defects which would be apparent when visually checking a shock absorber for its serviceability that would suggest component replacement.

Unit 7 **Conventional Steering Systems**

The purpose of any steering system for wheel-type motor vehicles and machines is, of course, to control the directional movement of the front wheels and thereby steer the motor vehicle or machine in the desired direction. **NOTE** Hydrostatic steering systems, which differ from conventional steering systems, will be covered later in this unit. As you know, the steering knuckle (front spindle) is supported with a kingpin to the front axle, or with two kingpins to a front drive axle, or with two ball joints to the lower and upper control arms which are the pivot points of the front wheels. Furthermore, the built-in angles of the front-end suspension—camber, caster, steering axis or kingpin inclination, toe-in and toe-out on turns—and the caster and toe-in of the rear suspension give the motor vehicle or machine steering stability, easy steering, and a natural inclination to steer straight ahead.

A conventional steering system consists of two major components: the steering gear assembly and the steering gear linkages.

Steering Gear Assembly The steering gear assembly transmits and multiplies the steering effort of the operator and converts rotary motion from the steering wheel into semirotation of the pitman arm. The increased torque from the steering wheel to the front wheels is developed mostly by the steering gear and only partly by the steering linkage. The increase in torque is expressed as a ratio, which varies among motor vehicles and machines. The ratio is the relation between the rotation of the steering wheel and front wheels, measured in degrees, and could vary from as low as 15:1 to as high as 41:1. For example—one service manual gives a steering gear ratio of 24:1 and a steering linkage ratio of 13:1. This would give the vehicle an overall ratio of 37:1, and it would require a steering wheel rotation of 37° to move the front wheel 1°. However, some integral power steering gears have a variable ratio, which means that the ratio stays constant, say 20:1 for the first 50° of rotation from the straight-ahead position to either left or right, and then gradually reduces to, say, 15:1 at the end of the full left- or right-hand turn. This variable ratio is accomplished by changing the tooth contour of the sector gear and rack gear.

The steering gear assembly components vary further since some have mechanical steering gears, some have power assist steering gears, and yet others have no steering gears at all—they use a hydrostatic steering system. In addition they vary because of the relation in height and distance between the steering wheel and steering gear, and differ further if a steering column shift mechanism is used.

The steering gear assembly components consist of a steering column which is usually bolted to the cab frame and firewall. It supports the directional switch, and on small units also the transmission shift mechanism. See Fig. 7-1. The *steering shaft*, otherwise called the *steering* or *wheel tube*, is supported through bearings or bushings within the steering column. The steering wheel is splined to one end and the worm shaft (steering gear shaft or stop shaft) is coupled to the other end. In some cases it is coupled to the intermediate shaft or tube, and the intermediate shaft is then coupled to the steering gear shaft. The couplings may be designed as a flexible coupling assembly or may be a universal joint, a constant-velocity joint, or directly splined to the steering gear shaft and held in position with a clamp. See Fig. 7-2. The steering gear is bolted to the left-hand frame side rail and the pitman arm is splined to the *pitman shaft* (also called the *cross shaft, roller shaft,* or *sector shaft*).

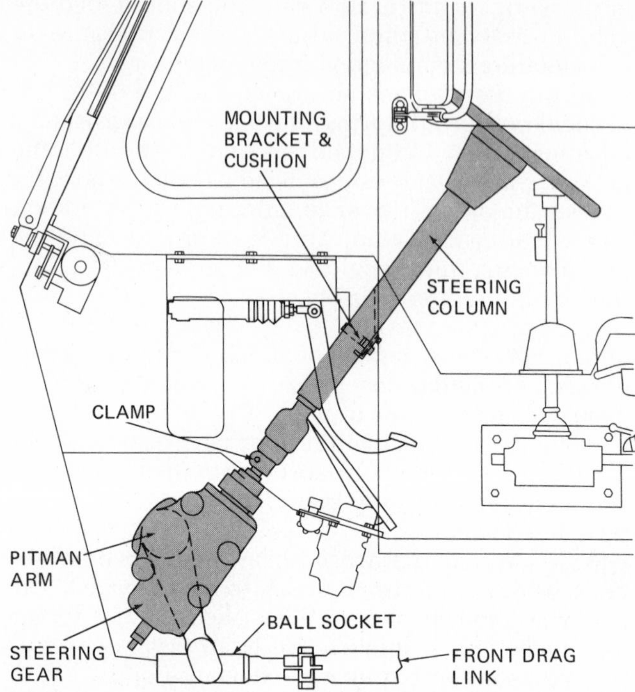

Fig. 7-1 Schematic view of a typical steering assembly mounting.

Steering Gear Linkage The steering linkage assembly transmits the motion from the pitman arm to the left- and right-hand front wheel steering arm. These component assemblies consist of the pitman arm, which is splined or keyed to the pitman shaft, and the drag link, which is attached (at the other end) with a ball socket or ball joint to the upper steering arms. The tie-rod ends are attached (also

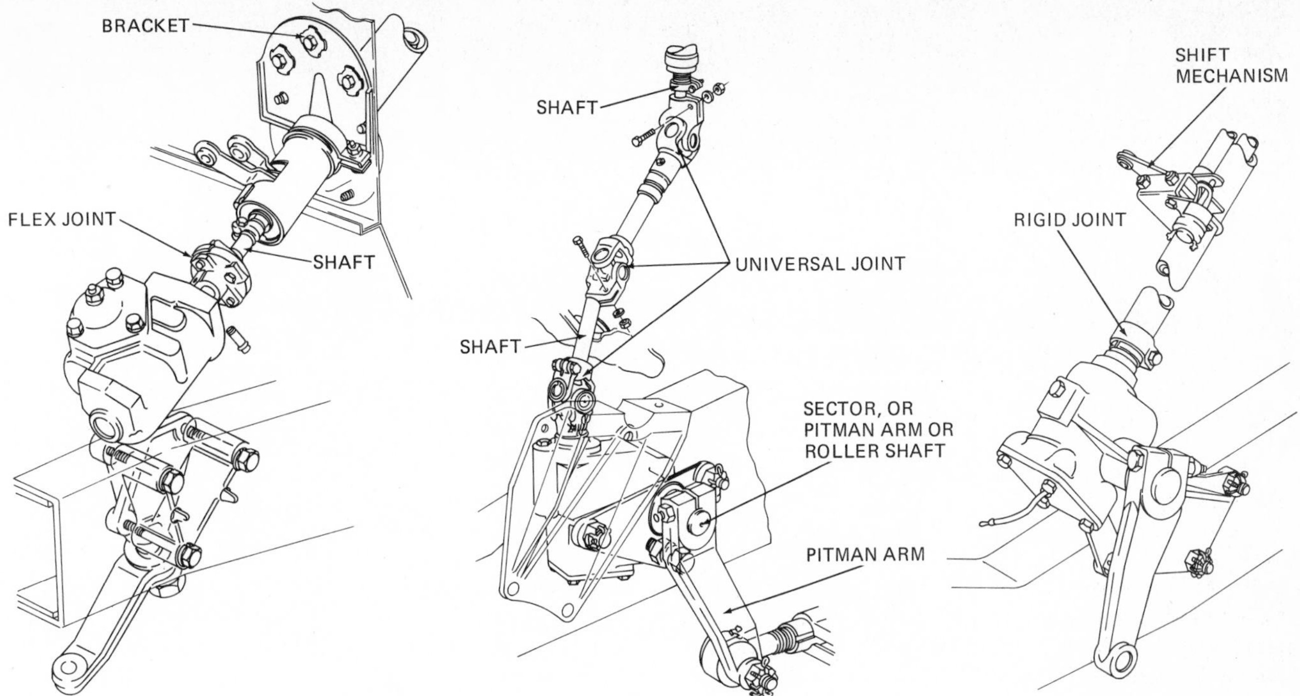

Fig. 7-2 Three methods of connecting the steering shaft. (*Ford Motor Company*)

with a ball joint or ball socket) to the lower steering (spindle) arms. The toe-in can be adjusted through the tie-rod ends. See Fig. 7-3.

Two other methods of linking the steering gear with the steering arms are shown in Figs. 7-4 and 7-5. The pitman arm is attached to a relay rod, to which the tie-rod assembly is attached, and an idler assembly supports the relay rod. Figure 7-5 shows one end of the front drag link attached to the pitman arm and the other end to the front axle steering arm. Also attached to the same steering arm are the rear drag link and the front axle tie-rod ends. The other end of the rear drag link is attached to the rear front axle steering arm, to which the tie-rod end of the front rear axle is attached.

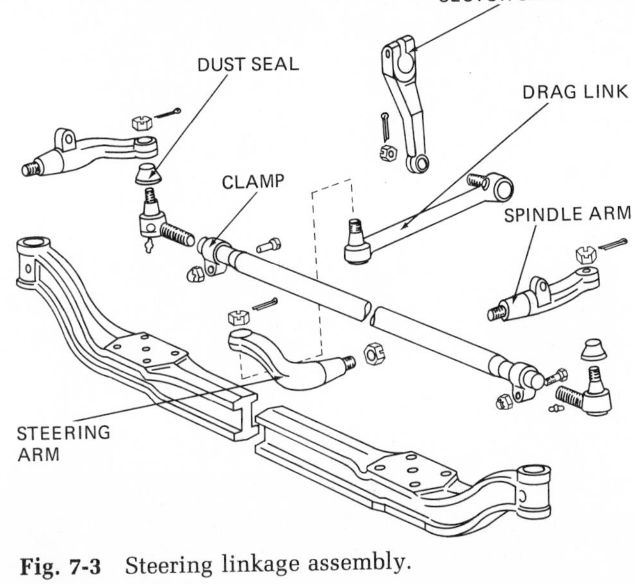

Ball sockets or ball joints link the steering linkages together (see Fig. 7-6) to provide a nearly unlimited motion in all directions without any looseness or slack.

The tie-rod end ball sockets are screwed into the tie-rod tube or sleeve and held in position with a clamp or clamps. The tie-rod end on the driver side of the vehicle is usually right-hand-threaded and the right-hand-side tie-rods are then left-hand-threaded. This is also true when a sleeve is used, as this arrangement provides for a quick toe-in adjustment.

NOTE The ball socket of the drag-link idler arm or relay rods are welded to the arm, rod, or tube (see Fig. 7-7). Because of the design of the steering linkages and location of the pivot points, there are minimal toe-in changes during jounce or rebound of the front suspension.

SECTOR SHAFT ARM
DUST SEAL
DRAG LINK
CLAMP
SPINDLE ARM
STEERING
ARM

Fig. 7-3 Steering linkage assembly.

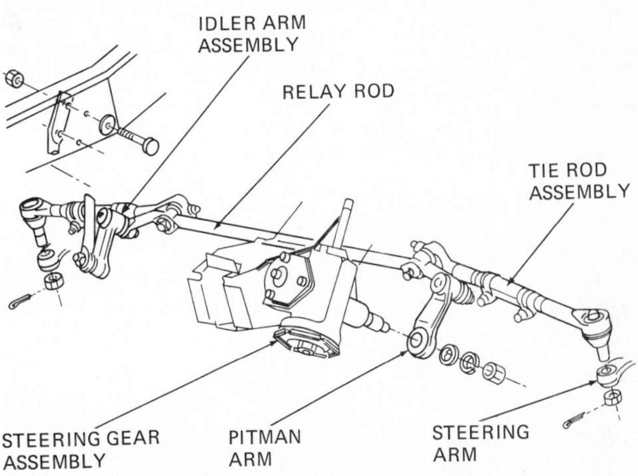

Fig. 7-4 Steering linkage assembly.

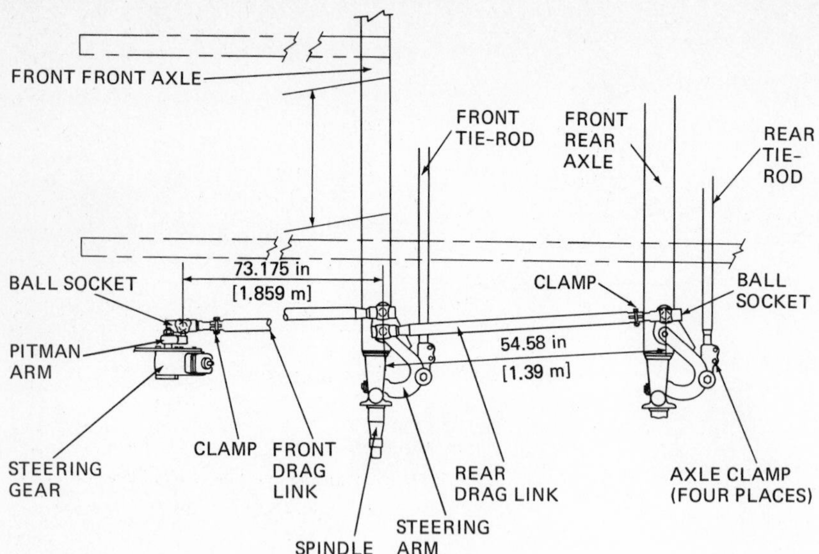

Fig. 7-5 Schematic view of typical steering linkage assembly having tandem steering axles.

Steering System Action In the earlier units on frames and suspensions you were introduced to the terms "steering axis" or "kingpin inclination" and "toe-out on turns," where it was stated that the steering axis inclination is a directional control angle and in addition is used to reduce the scrub radius. Directional control is achieved through tilting the center line of the kingpins or the ball joint center lines, thereby positioning the spindle end so that the motor vehicle's central point of gravity is nearer the road surface and maintained in this position by virtue of its weight. When the front wheels are turned to the left or right, the spindle ends are lowered closer to the road surface. On an impenetrable road surface the front end of the motor vehicle would gradually rise as the front wheels turn from the straight-ahead position into a left- or right-hand turn. However, since caster angle and kingpin inclination are obtained by tilting their center lines from the vertical, any change in caster from zero, in either direction (+ or −), affects the spindle reaction. See Fig. 7-8. If the caster angle is positive and a left- or right-hand turn is made, the *inside* spindle is lowered (raising the motor vehicle) and the outside spindle end is also lowered, but by a lesser amount. If the caster angle is negative and a left- or right-hand turn is made, the *outside* spindle end is lowered (raising the motor vehicle) and the inside spindle end is also lowered, but by a lesser amount. Therefore, whether or not the motor vehicle has negative or positive caster, as soon as the force from the steering wheel is removed, both spindles turn into the straight-ahead position because the motor vehicle responds to gravity and pushes downward, forcing the spindles into the straight-ahead position.

TURNING As previously stated, the steering arm angle and length affect the front wheel angle when the motor vehicle or machine rounds a corner. The front and rear wheels turn about a common center with regard to the turning radius of the motor vehicle. This is necessary to reduce tire wear and improve handling and steering ability.

To ensure that the inside front wheel always has

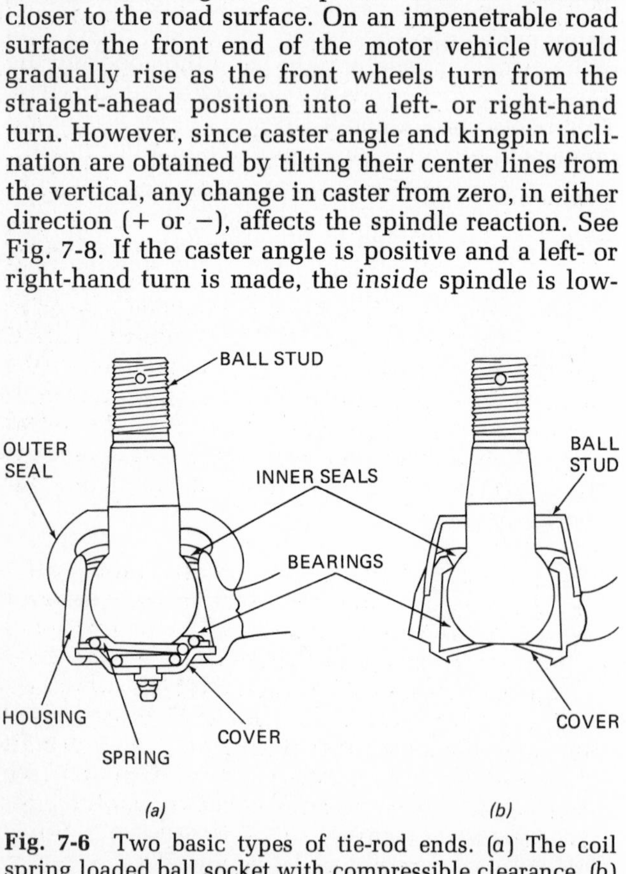

Fig. 7-6 Two basic types of tie-rod ends. (*a*) The coil spring loaded ball socket with compressible clearance. (*b*) One which is preloaded with zero vertical clearance.

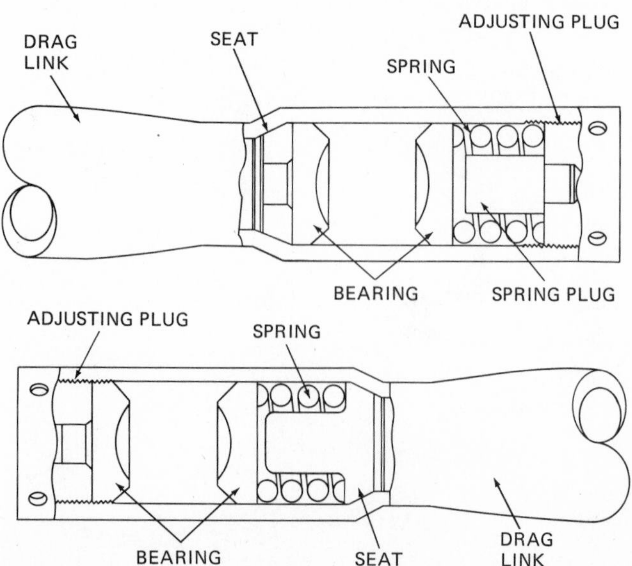

Fig. 7-7 Two basic types of drag-link ends. (*Mack Canada Inc.*)

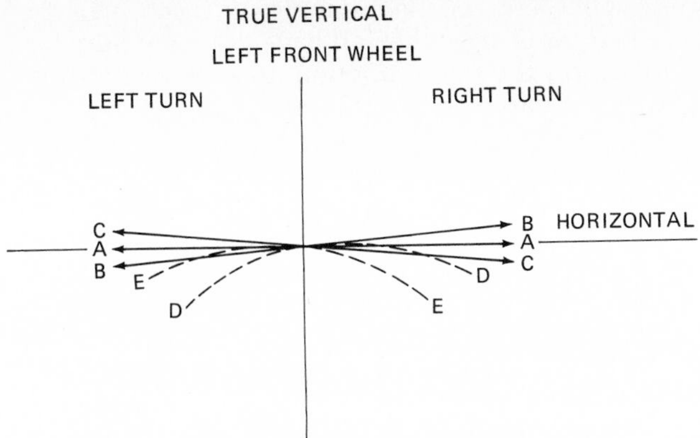

A: With no caster or kingpin inclination
B: With positive caster and no kingpin inclination.
C: With negative caster and no kingpin inclination
D: With positive caster and kingpin inclination
E: With negative caster and kingpin inclination

Fig. 7-8 Spindle travel of left front wheel.

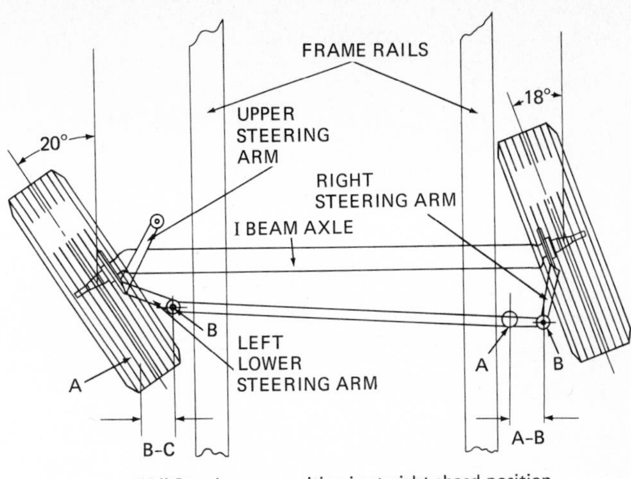

Fig. 7-10 Steering axle design that allows the inner wheel to turn at a greater angle than the outer wheel.

a greater steering angle than the outside front wheel, a simple geometric principle is applied—that is, if you move a lever in a circular motion, from 0° to 15°, the lever travels a fixed distance of 0.413 in [10.5 mm] in the circular and horizontal plane. If the lever is again moved 15° to 30°, or 45°, or 60°, the distance the lever travels in the circular plane remains the same (0.413 in [10.5 mm]). However, the distance in the horizontal plane constantly decreases. See Fig. 7-9. From this example, you can see that by moving the lever toward the horizontal position the arc scribed by the lever increases although the horizontal travel distance constantly decreases. This principle is applied to the front suspension. Each steering arm (the lever) is bent to a calculated angle

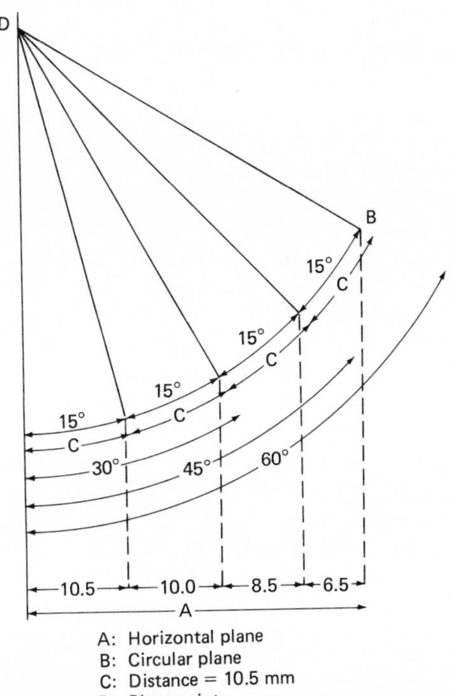

A: Horizontal plane
B: Circular plane
C: Distance = 10.5 mm
D: Pivot point

Fig. 7-9 Geometric principle that allows inside steering wheel to turn at a greater angle than the outside wheel.

and has a calculated arm length, and the ends are attached together through the tie-rod. **NOTE** The angle and length of the steering arm are calculated according to the wheel base, the wheel distance, the tire size and rolling radius, and the anticipated vehicle speed.

In the straight-ahead position both steering arms are at an angle of, say, 15°. When a left-hand turn is made, the drag link moves the upper left-hand steering arm to an angle of, say, 20° to the right. This rotates the left-hand front wheel and causes the left- and right-hand steering arms to travel the same horizontal distance. The left-hand front wheel pivots to an angle of 20° and because the right-hand steering arm moves toward the vertical the right-hand front wheel turns only 18°. See Fig. 7-10. In addition, when the motor vehicle has multileaf or staked single-leaf spring suspensions the front and rear axles shift during a turn, thereby assisting in the steering of the motor vehicle. During a turn, the centrifugal force places more weight on the outside wheels and reduces the weight on the inside wheels. This decreases the spring camber on the outside springs, and the springs lengthen. The spring camber on the inside springs increases, shortening the overall length. As a result the inside axle end is moved in the direction of travel and the outside axle end is moved rearward.

UNDERSTEER AND OVERSTEER Most motor vehicles are designed to understeer, that is, when making a left- or right-hand turn, the motor vehicle will make a greater turning radius than that of the front wheels. Oversteer means that the motor vehicle, when making a left- or right-hand turn, will make a shorter turning radius than that of the front wheel (see Figs. 7-10 and 7-11). Understeer adds to directional control stability, whereas an oversteering motor vehicle is unstable on turns, is susceptible to spin-out, and requires a reverse steering action to come out of a turn.

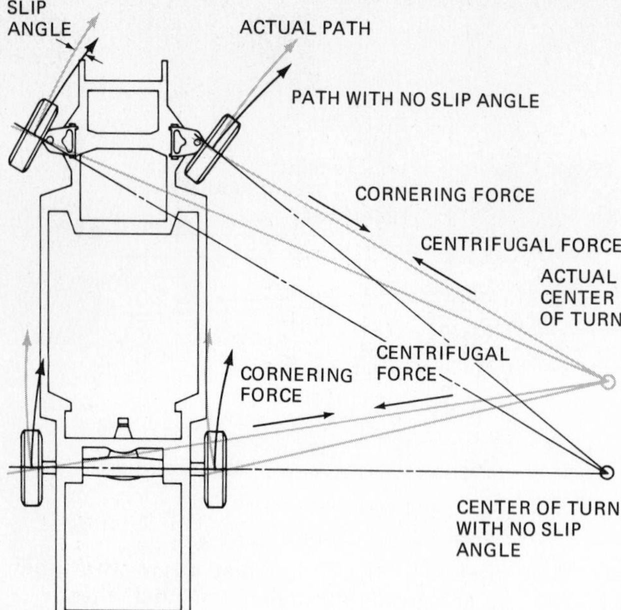

Fig. 7-11 Slip angle. (*Ford Motor Company*)

SLIP ANGLE Any motor vehicle or machine when making a turn (at any speed) is subject to centrifugal force, and with increased speed and/or reduced turning radius the centrifugal force increases. The centrifugal force places a side thrust on the tires which causes all tires more or less to deflect and twist the tire tread. The twist in the tire tread forces the tire to roll in a greater radius than that steered and this creates the slip angle (Fig. 7-11). As a result the actual turning center is moved forward from the calculated turning center, giving the motor vehicle the desired understeer characteristics to achieve good cornering ability. However, if the slip angle is greater at the rear tires than at the front tires, a dangerous oversteer occurs which could lead to a spinout. Conversely, if the front tires have a greater slip angle, this would produce a greater understeer and would force the operator to more forcibly hold the steering wheel into the turn to stay within the driving lane. For these reasons it is obvious why the steering arm length and angle varies among different motor vehicles and machines.

Another factor which affects a slip angle, but which has nothing to do with the design of the motor vehicle suspension or steering linkage, is a strong wind. No doubt you have personally experienced a strong wind push your car in the wind direction, although you did not move the steering wheel. In this case the wind acts as a side force, deflecting the tires and creating a slip angle either on the front or rear tires, or both.

Manual Steering Gears Three types of manual steering gears are used on on- and off-highway equipment:

- Recirculating ball steering gear
- Worm and roller steering gear
- Cam and lever steering gear

Although there are peculiarities to each type of steering gear design, they all have the same purpose and perform the same function, that is, to multiply the applied torque, convert rotary motion into semirotation, provide a 90° change in power direction, reduce internal friction to its minimum, provide preload adjustment, and maintain uninterrupted positive power transmission. Because some are used on small motor vehicles or machines and others on larger ones, the different steering gears vary in size and in torque ratio.

RECIRCULATING BALL STEERING GEAR One of several types of recirculating ball steering gears is shown in Fig. 7-12. The pitman shaft with its sector gear is supported within the steering gear housing either by needle bearings or by bushings and sealed with a lip-type seal. The left-hand side of the pitman shaft is supported by a bushing or needle bearing in the side cover, that is, the enclosure of the gear housing. The adjusting screw is threaded into the side cover and is hooked into the T slot of the pitman arm. The right-hand end of the shaft may be tapered and keyed, or splined, or straight and splined. The ball-grooved worm shaft is supported on the right-hand side by tapered or barrel bearings, either in the housing or in the adjuster plug. The latter is screwed into, and locked with a lock nut to, the housing. The same type of bearings support the left-hand side in the end cap or in the housing. A double lip-type seal is commonly used to keep out contaminants and seal in the lubricant. The ball nut is positioned over the worm shaft, between which the balls act like roller threads. The balls are held and guided by the two ball return guides which are bolted to the ball nut. The teeth on the sector gear and ball nut rack are so machined and positioned that a tighter fit exists between the two when the ball nut is in the center position than when it is in the off-center position.

Operation and preliminary checks When the worm shaft is rotated, the threading action of the balls forces the ball nut either to the left or to the right, and the ball nut rack moves the sector gear and the pitman shaft.

Before making any adjustment to a manual steering gear, raise the front end of the motor vehicle or machine and block it securely. Next, inspect all steering linkages for looseness and wear and to determine if they are bent. Also check the kingpins or ball joints and the wheel bearings. Check the steering gear mounting bolts and the tightness of the steering column and stop clamps. Make sure that the steering linkage and steering gear are adequately lubricated. **NOTE** These checks should be made at regular intervals to prolong steering system service life and to prevent accidents.

After servicing and/or replacing parts as necessary, check the steering gear by turning the steering wheel so that the front wheels are in a straight-ahead position. Next, grab one front wheel and move the wheels from side to side. If excessive end play exists, this motion will be felt at the pitman arm ball socket. If a bearing or backlash adjustment is necessary, turn

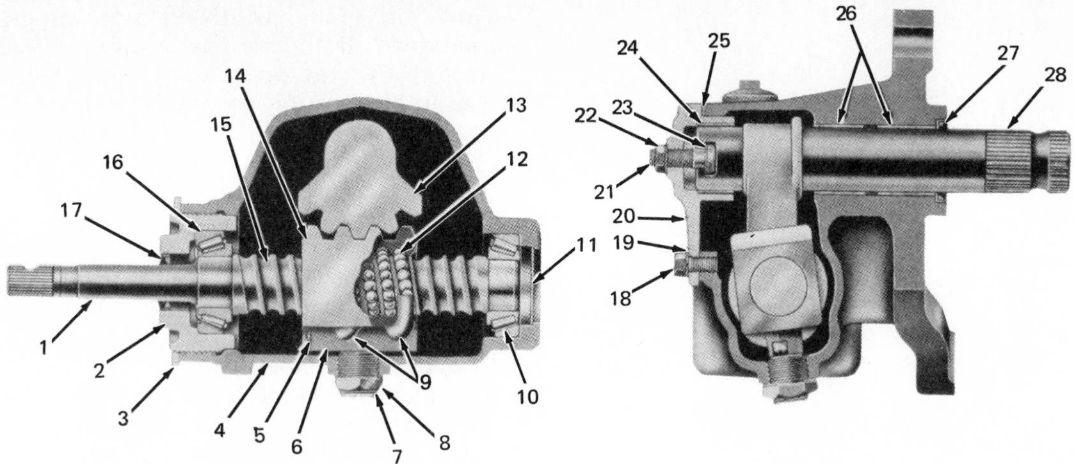

1. Worm shaft
2. Bearing adjuster
3. Adjuster locknut
4. Steering gear housing
5. Clamp retainer screw
6. Ball guide clamp
7. Backup adjuster
8. Backup adjuster locknut
9. Ball guide
10. Lower bearing
11. Expansion plug
12. Worm balls
13. Sector gear
14. Ball nut
15. Worm (integral with shaft)
16. Upper bearing
17. Worm shaft oil seal
18. Side cover bolt
19. Lockwasher
20. Side cover
21. Lash adjuster
22. Lash adjuster locknut
23. Lash adjuster shim
24. Side cover bushing
25. Side cover gasket
26. Housing bushing
27. Sector shaft oil seal
28. Sector shaft

Fig. 7-12 Sectional view of recirculating ball steering gear. (*Mack Canada Inc.*)

the steering wheel to the center position. This is achieved by turning the steering wheel from the left-hand stop position to the right-hand stop, while counting the number of rotations. Next, turn the steering wheel back exactly one-half the number of rotations. This centers the steering gear.

Worm shaft bearing adjustment Remove (with the appropriate puller) the pitman arm from the pitman shaft, or the drag link from the pitman arm. Next, loosen the pitman shaft adjusting screw lock nut, and turn the adjusting screw counterclockwise about two revolutions to increase the backlash between the ball nut and sector gear. Remove the steering wheel shaft cover, or horn ring, and place a socket using a torque wrench as the handle onto the steering shaft nut. While turning the torque wrench, read from the scale the torque that is required to maintain rotation. If the steering column is properly adjusted (aligned) and its bearing and the worm shaft bearing are correctly adjusted, the torque reading on the torque wrench should be as specified in the service manual. If the rotating torque is below specification, but the rotation is not rough or sticky, loosen the adjusting plug jam nut and turn the adjusting nut counterclockwise to remove the existing preload, and then retighten the adjusting plug and the jam nut and recheck the rotating torque. You may have to readjust the adjusting plug to achieve the specified rotating torque, in which case always lock the jam nut before measuring the rotating torque. If, for one reason or another, there is no torque wrench available, you can use a spring scale to measure the rotating torque. When using a spring scale (see Fig. 7-13), hook it onto one spoke, 6 in from the center of the steering wheel, and then pull it sufficiently to cause the steering wheel to rotate. During the rotation read from the scale the required pounds to maintain rotation. Multiply this by 6 in [15.24 cm] to determine the torque. If the spring scale reads 5 lb, then the rotating torque is $5 \times 6 = 30$ lb · in [5253 N · m].

Backlash adjustment Next, center the steering gear and again place the socket onto the steering shaft nut and then turn the adjusting screw clockwise to decrease the backlash and lock the adjusting screw with the lock nut. Next, turn the torque wrench about 60° in either direction, and from the scale read the torque required to turn the steering shaft. To increase the torque to specification, turn the adjusting screw clockwise; to decrease the torque, turn the screw counterclockwise. But always remember before measuring the torque to make certain the adjusting screw is locked. Some service manuals recommend turning the adjusting screw until you feel a light resistance and then to back off about one-eighth to one-quarter turn to achieve the required preload (backlash). After the adjustment is made, reconnect the components previously removed and recheck that all parts are securely tightened and locked.

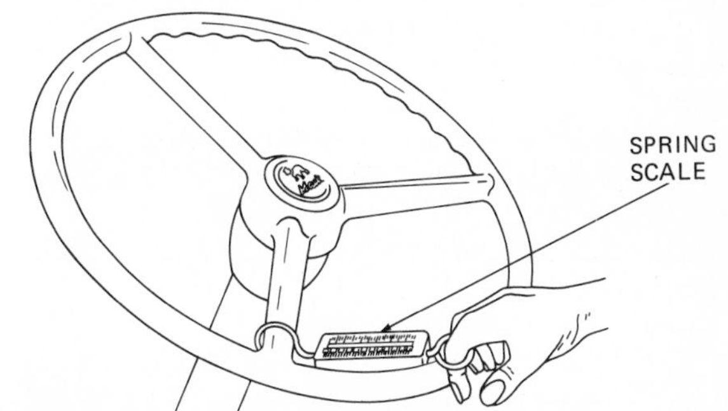

Fig. 7-13 Checking steering wheel rim pull. (*Mack Canada Inc.*)

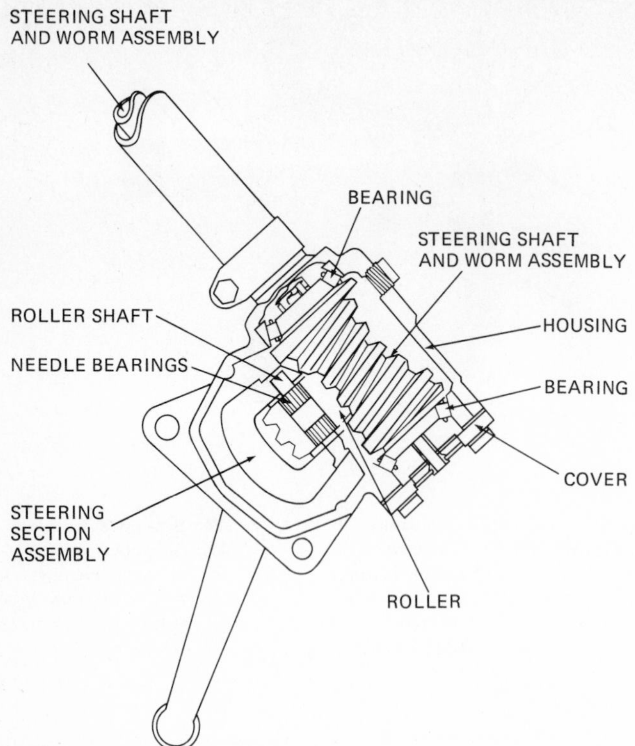

Fig. 7-14 Sectional view of a worm and roller steering gear. (*Ford Motor Company*)

Worm and Roller Steering Gears One of several types of worm and roller steering gears is shown in Fig. 7-14. The steering sector shaft assembly consists of the shaft and support brackets that support the roller shaft on which the roller is free to rotate. As a rule, the roller has three circular teeth which are in mesh with the grooves in the worm gear. The roller shaft assembly is supported on the right-hand side by two needle bearings or by two bushings pressed into the housing. On the left-hand side the roller shaft assembly is supported by the shaft bearing or bushing which is pressed into the shaft (housing) cover. The adjusting screw is threaded into the shaft housing and is hooked into the T slot at the left-hand shaft end. The worm shaft or steering shaft, or input shaft, are each single-machined units. The worm diameter is larger at both ends than in the center, to provide the steering gear with a near equal preload between the worm and roller gears during the semirotation of the roller shaft. The worm shaft assembly is supported by tapered or barrel bearings in the gear housing, and shims are used to adjust the bearing preload.

Adjustment of the Worm and Roller Gear When the steering wheel is turned, the worm shaft rotates, causing the worm to rotate, the roller teeth to move to the left or right in the worm grooves, and the roller shaft to semirotate.

Before the steering gear is tested or adjusted, follow the procedure outlined in the section on operation and preliminary checks. Where necessary, correct the problems.

If during the measurement of the rotating torque the rotation is rough or sticky, the steering gear must be serviced. If the torque is below specification, drain the oil and remove the cover bolts and the cover. With a knife separate the shims and, with scissors, cut to remove one of the required thickness to achieve the specified preload. Shims with thicknesses of 0.002, 0.003, 0.010, and 0.075 in [0.05, 0.076, 0.25, and 1.9 mm] are used. **CAUTION** Take care not to damage the remaining shims and do not remove those which are rubber-coated because the latter not only act as shims but also as gaskets. The thickness of shims you select to remove will depend on the amount by which you must increase the rotating torque.

Reinstall the remaining shims, return the cover to the gear housing, and torque the cap screws to the specified torque.

CAUTION If you remove several shims, you could damage the bearings and/or break the worm cover when tightening the cap screws. Therefore, check the rotation of the steering gear during the tightening procedure. Always recheck the rotating torque.

The procedure for adjusting the worm-to-roller preload (backlash) is the same as that outlined previously in the section on backlash adjustment. After the adjustments are made, relubricate the steering gear and reconnect the parts removed.

Cam and Lever Steering Gear These types of steering gears are used on large motor vehicles and machines because they are designed and built for rough operating conditions and have a high gear ratio. The steering gear consists of a lever shaft and cam. One, two, or three tapered studs are attached (through tapered roller bearings) to the lever shaft. The shaft is supported by bushings in the steering gear housing, and sealed with a lip-type seal. The housing side cover encloses the cam and lever shaft; the adjusting screw is threaded into the cover, and the head is hooked into the T slot at the lever shaft end. The outside diameter of the cam is consistent. However, the diameter of the cam groove becomes gradually smaller toward the midpoint of the cam and consequently the groove becomes narrower. This provides an even contact between the studs and cam groove over the full range of travel. The cam ends are supported through angular ball thrust or tapered roller bearings in the housing, and shims are used to adjust the bearing preload. See Fig. 7-15.

Adjustment of the Cam and Lever Gear When the steering gear is in the center position, each tapered roller stud rests in a cam groove. When the steering wheel is turned, the cam rotates. This forces the studs to follow in the cam groove, thereby semirotating the lever shaft. If the steering wheel is turned to its maximum left- or maximum right-hand position, one of the studs will leave the cam near the end of the turn, and when the steering wheel is turned in the opposite direction the roller stud will again reengage with the cam.

Before making any adjustment to the cam and le-

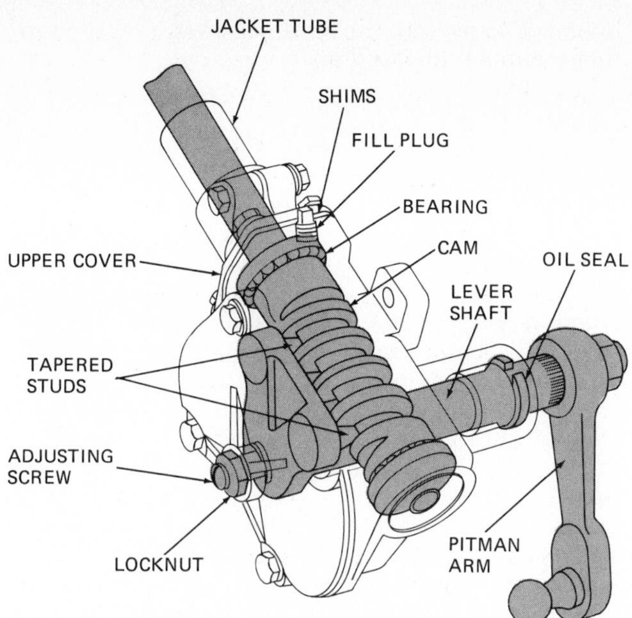

Fig. 7-15 Schematic view of a cam and lever steering gear. (*Terex Division of General Motors Corporation*)

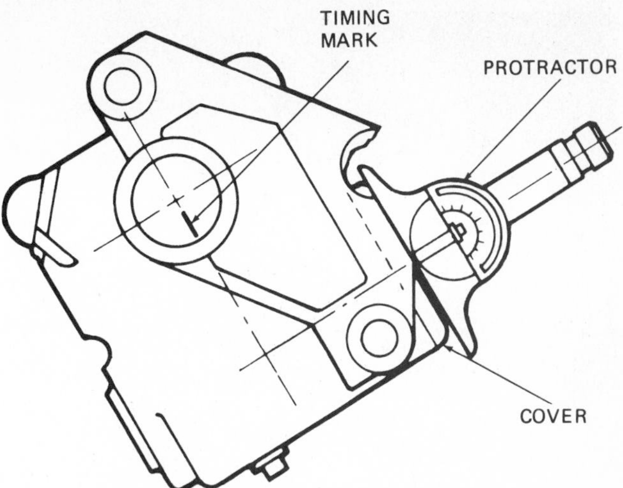

Fig. 7-16 Method used to center steering gear.

ver steering gear, perform the same checks and tests as outlined above in the section on recirculating ball steering gear.

If the rotation is rough or sticky, the steering gear must be serviced. If the rotating torque is below specification, clean, if necessary, the cam shaft before removing the cover cap screws and pushing the cover upward to prevent seal damage. Remove the necessary shim or shims and then place the shims onto the cover and the cover onto the housing. Install and torque the cap screws to the specified torque. Retest the rotating torque.

To check the adjustment of the stud mesh, turn the steering wheel so that the studs are moved through their center position. If the adjustment is correct, a slight drag will be felt. If not, loosen the adjusting lock nut and turn the adjusting screw. Recheck the stud mesh adjustment. Reconnect the removed parts and then check that all parts are secure.

Steering Gear Centering Regardless of the type of steering gear, it must be correctly centered. Otherwise most steering will be done in the off-center position instead of the center (high-spot) position, resulting in hard steering during turns and excessive steering gear wear.

To check the steering gear center position, first turn the steering wheel to the straight-ahead position and disconnect the drag link. When the tires are in the straight-ahead position, the steering wheel spokes should be in the horizontal position and the alignment marks on the steering gear housing and pitman shaft should be in line. If the pitman shaft has only a timing mark, you could visually check to see if it is parallel with the top cover of the steering gear.

However, as these methods lack precision, you should use a protractor (see Fig. 7-16). Position the protractor on the steering gear cover, center the bubble, and then move the protractor to the pitman shaft. Align the base of the protractor with the timing mark and then turn the steering wheel until the bubble is in the center. This action will center the steering gear. When the steering gear is in the center position but the steering wheel spokes are not in the horizontal position, pull the steering wheel and reposition it to bring the spokes horizontal. **NOTE** Use a steering wheel puller to remove it—do not use a hammer to drive it off.

If the steering wheel is centered but the tires do not point in the straight-ahead direction, you must either change the length of the drag link or turn the tie-rod clockwise or counterclockwise to bring the tires into the straight-ahead position.

Manual Steering Gear Service If through testing or visual inspection you find that the steering gear requires service, the general preliminary procedures are as follows: First, steam clean the general work area. Turn the steering wheel to position the front wheels as recommended in the service manual. Mark the position of the drag link to pitman arm, the pitman arm to pitman shaft, and the steering shaft coupling to worm shaft. **NOTE** On some smaller vehicles you may have to raise and block the front end in order to remove the steering gear. Next, remove the cotter pin and the pitman arm shaft nut, and with a puller remove the pitman arm (Fig. 7-17). Otherwise, remove the pitman-arm-attaching nut and bolt, and then, with a chisel, spread the pitman arm open to slide the arm from the shaft. Check the appropriate service manual before loosening and removing the coupling, as procedures differ depending on the type of coupling and mounting. In some cases you may have to loosen the steering wheel, and in others the steering column. Next, remove the steering gear mounting nuts, washers, and bolts and then lift the steering gear assembly from the vehicle. Drain the lubricant from the housing and once again clean the steering gear thoroughly. From this point on the procedure depends on the type of steering gear.

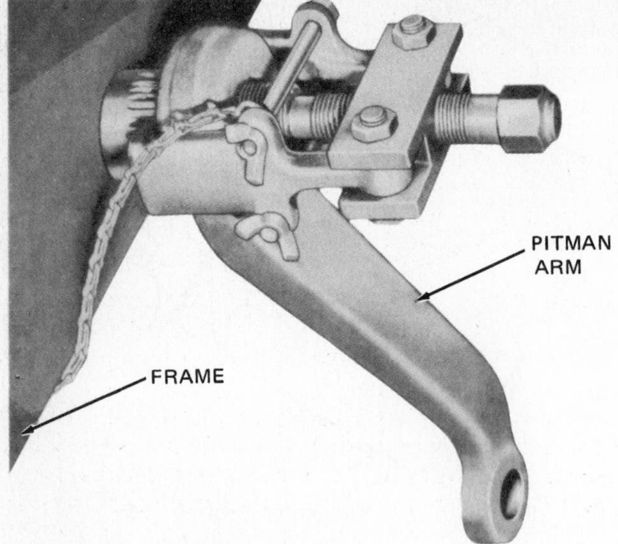

Fig. 7-17 Method of removing the pitman arm. (*GMC Truck and Coach Division*)

SERVICING THE CAM AND LEVER STEERING GEAR To service a cam and lever steering gear, first clean the exposed lever shaft with fine emery cloth to prevent damaging the bore and seal. Loosen the adjusting lock nut and back out the adjusting screw approximately three turns. Remove the side cover cap screws and washers, and slide the cover and the gasket from the housing. Push the lever shaft from the bushing bore, and then remove the upper-cover cap screws and washers. Lift the cover, shims, and then the cam from the housing. Remove the upper and lower cam bearing retainer rings and slide the bearing assembly from the cam (Fig. 7-18). With a hammer puller, remove the shaft seal from the upper cover, and the lever shaft seal from the housing. Thoroughly clean all removed parts and the gear housing, especially the stud bearings, and then dry them with compressed air.

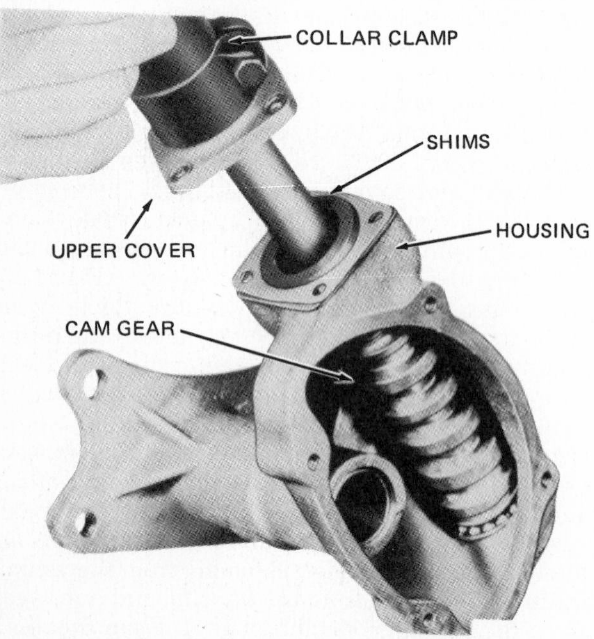

Fig. 7-18 Removal of jacket tube and upper housing cover assembly. (*International Harvester Company*)

NOTE As a general rule, you should replace the upper and lower cam bearings.

Inspect the cam, the bearings, and seal surfaces for wear, pitting, and scoring. Check the lever shaft bushing and seal surfaces for excessive gear and pitting. To check the bushing-to-shaft fit, measure the shaft and the bushing. If the clearance is more than 0.006 in [0.152 mm] but the shaft is not worn, you need only replace the bushing.

To replace the bushing, lay the gear housing onto the press bed, select and position the bushing adapter onto the bushing, align the assembly with the press piston, and press out the bushing(s). When there are two bushings, make certain when pressing the inside bushing into position that it is flush with the inside housing face and that the outside bushing is flush with the seal seat. Next, use a reamer and line-ream the bushing to service manual specification.

Clean the assembly thoroughly and press a new shaft seal into position. Check the tapered stud surfaces. If one stud has a flat spot, both studs must be replaced. This is also true when one set of the stud bearings are damaged or when the stud rotation is rough or sticky.

To replace damaged studs or bearings, clamp the stud in a vise having protected jaws. Straighten out the prong washer (away from the stud nut). Loosen and remove the nut, the stud, and the two tapered roller bearings and then press out the oil bearing cup and insert a new one in its place.

CAUTION When removing the bearings from the studs, note that some steering gears have shims on the right-hand side. Make certain that you place the same number of shims on the right-hand stud when positioning the bearing cup. Lubricate the bearings only with the lubricant recommended for the steering gear, and then insert the stud and bearing assembly. Position the prong lock washer onto the stud; commence tightening the nut, fingertight. Again hold the stud in a vise, tighten the nut snug, and then, using a torque wrench, measure the rotating torque. It should be about 3 lb · in [0.338 N · m]. If it is, bend one prong square against the nut. Repeat this procedure with the other stud.

The reassembly of the steering gear is precisely the reverse of disassembly; however, when reassembling, tighten the upper-cover cap screws only fingertight. Next, adjust the steering gear as previously outlined.

SERVICING THE WORM AND ROLLER AND RECIRCULATING BALL STEERING GEARS The servicing procedure for worm and roller steering gears is very similar except that the bearing cups have to be removed with a puller from the top housing cover and worm shaft, and the roller shaft assembly must be replaced as a unit because no separate parts are available.

Recirculating ball steering gear service procedures will be covered with the material on integral power steering later in this unit because the two steering gears are similar.

REINSTALLING THE STEERING GEAR Before reinstalling the steering gear, check the coupling(s), splines, or keyways for wear and the steering shaft-to-column fit. Then position the steering gear onto its mounting bracket. Secure it firmly with the mounting bolts, washers, and nuts. Whether or not you must align the steering gear with the column, or vice versa, depends on the position or location of the steering gear—refer to your service manual in this regard. Next, align the coupling to the worm shaft or cam shaft and secure the coupling. Torque the steering gear mounting nuts to the recommended torque. Position the pitman arm onto the pitman shaft so that the marks align. Then install and torque the nut to specification and secure it with a cotter pin. If necessary fill the gear housing with the recommended lubricant and torque the filler plug to specification.

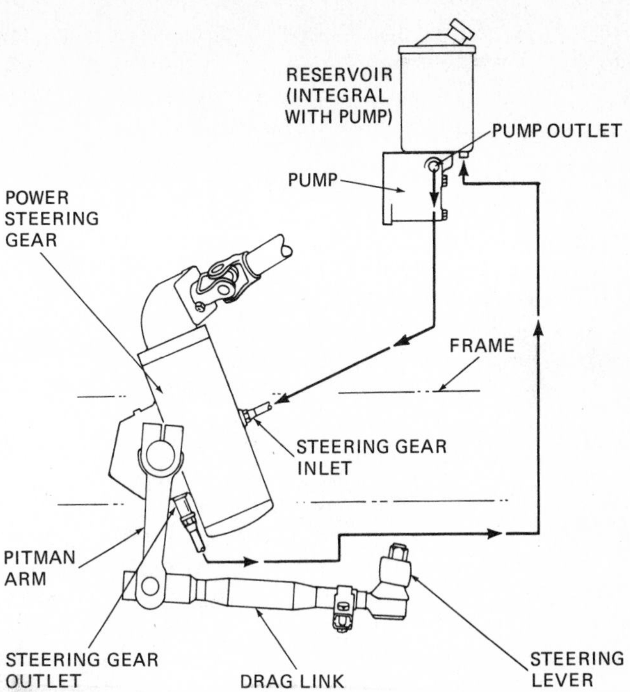

Fig. 7-19 Schematic view of an integral power steering system. (*Mack Canada Inc.*)

Power Steering The purpose of any type of power steering is to minimize the operator's steering effort, to increase steering response, and to increase steering control.

The term "power steering" is only relevant to hydrostatic steering systems since other types are actually power-assist manual steering gear, although they are referred to as "power steering." Basically, all power steering systems use the same components and utilize oil under pressure to assist in the steering effort and control. Nevertheless, there is one major difference between the various power steering systems, and that is the location of the power-assist control unit (steering valve) and the hydraulic cylinder (steering booster). In fact, the position or location of these components defines the power steering system. For instance, when the steering valve and the booster cylinder is located within the steering gear, the power steering is called an *integral power steering (gear) system*. When the control valve is located within the steering linkage it is a *semi-integral* steering system. When the control valve and booster cylinder are positioned within the steering linkage it is a *linkage-type* power steering system.

The components that make up an integral power steering system are shown in Fig. 7-19. On some large motor vehicles or machines two integral steering gears are used, but the right-hand steering gear has no steering valve. Its response is controlled from the left-hand integral steering gear.

As you can see from the illustration, the only external difference between a manual steering gear and an integral steering gear is that the two hydraulic hoses are visibly connected to the latter.

The components of a linkage power steering system are shown in Fig. 7-20. The steering booster cylinder including the control valve is pivot-attached to a bracket that is bolted to the front axle or frame, and the piston rod is pivot-attached to a clamp which is bolted to the tie-rod (cross steering tube). When two booster cylinders are used, the piston rod ends are attached with ball sockets to the left- and right-hand upper steering arms. Another type of linkage power steering system is one in which the control valve and the drag link are a combined unit and the steering booster cylinder is attached as shown in Fig. 7-21. In this illustration, one end of the steering valve is screwed to the drag link, while the ball socket is attached to the pitman arm (steering gear levers). The drag link is attached through a ball socket to the upper steering arm.

The components of a semi-integral power steering are shown in Fig. 7-22. The control valve is bolted to the steering gears, the steering booster piston rod is bolted to the pitman arm, and the cylinder is bolted to the frame. Hydraulic hoses and/or steel tubings are used to connect the power steering pump with the steering valve and the valve with the booster cylinder.

The power source for all power steering systems is the hydraulic pump. As a rule, on small motor vehicles and machines the hydraulic reservoir, the main relief valve, and power steering pump comprise a single unit, driven through one or more V belts, although on some vehicles the main relief valve may be separately mounted. The power steering pump could be any one of the following designs: balance vane, gerotor, roller, slipper, or external gear pump. The average flow rate of these pumps is between 3 to 12 gallons per minute (gal/min) [11.35 to 45.42 liters per minute (l/min)] and the main relief valve setting is 1200 psi [8273 kPa].

On large machines and large dump trucks the hydraulic reservoir and the power steering reservoir are usually one and the same, and the main relief valve is separately mounted. The power steering pump is commonly driven directly by the engine. However, some use a two-stage hydraulic pump—one pump for the hydraulic system and the other for

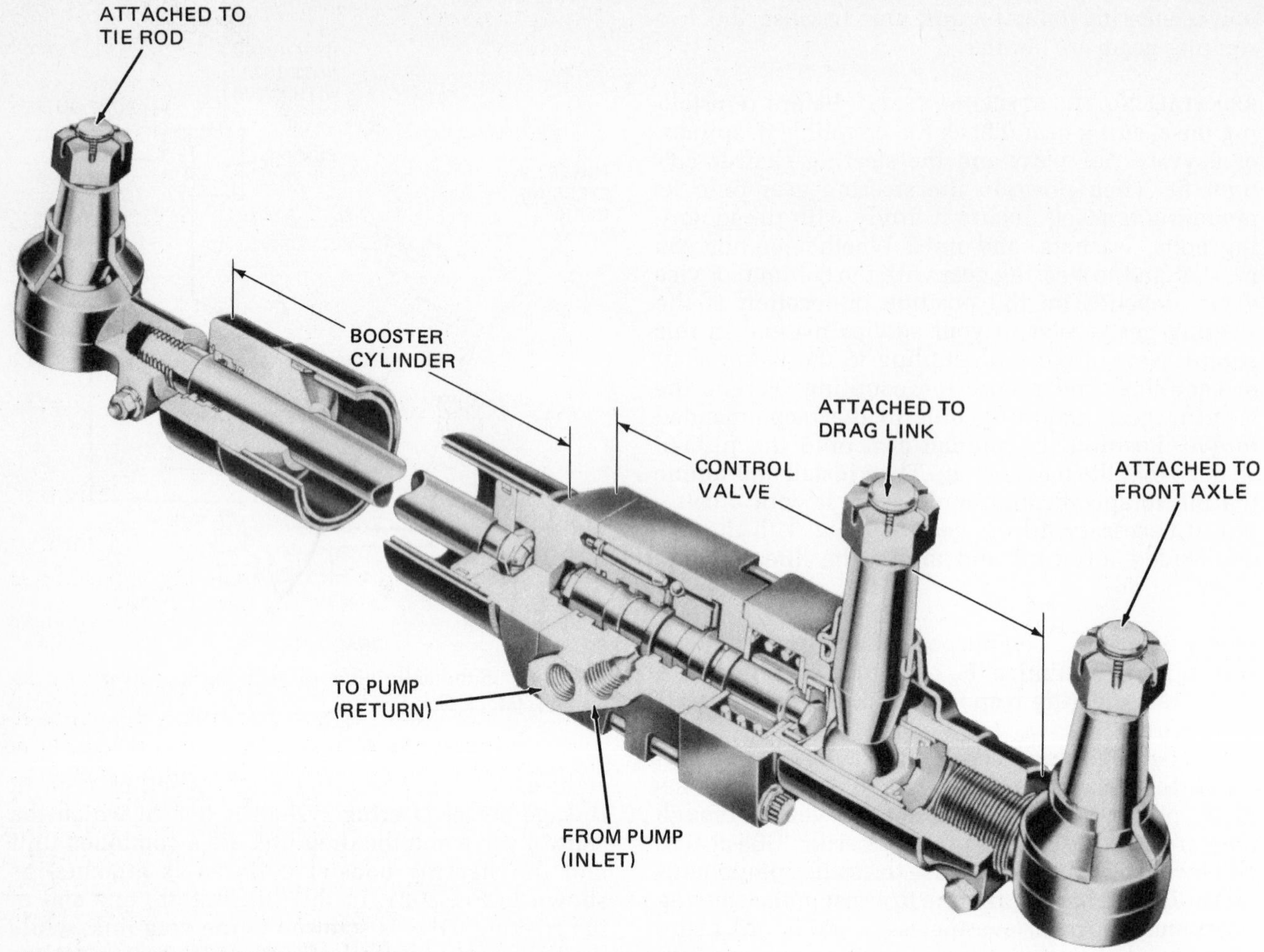

Fig. 7-20 Sectional view of a linkage power steering system. (*Sperry Vickers Division of Sperry Inc.*)

the steering system. External gear or balance vane pumps are used which have a flow rate between 12 to 25 gal/min [45.42 to 94.62 l/min] and operate at a pressure between 1200 to 2100 psi [8273 to 14,479 kPa].

The steering valves for all types of power steering, whether mounted internally or externally, are either of the two- or four-way three-position open center spool valve design, and when the valve spool is in the neutral position the ports to the steering cylinder booster piston are open. In this circumstance, oil from the power steering pump enters the inlet port, passes through the steering valve, and flows out of the outlet port and back to the reservoir. At the same time, the pump oil passes by the spool lands and flows out of the left- and right-hand booster ports onto the left- and right-hand sides of the booster piston. See Fig. 7-23. However, some steering systems use closed center spool valves, in which case the spool land closes the flow to the booster piston.

Semi-Integral Power Steering The schematic drawing of a semi-integral power steering gear is shown in Fig. 7-24. **NOTE** The steering booster cylinder

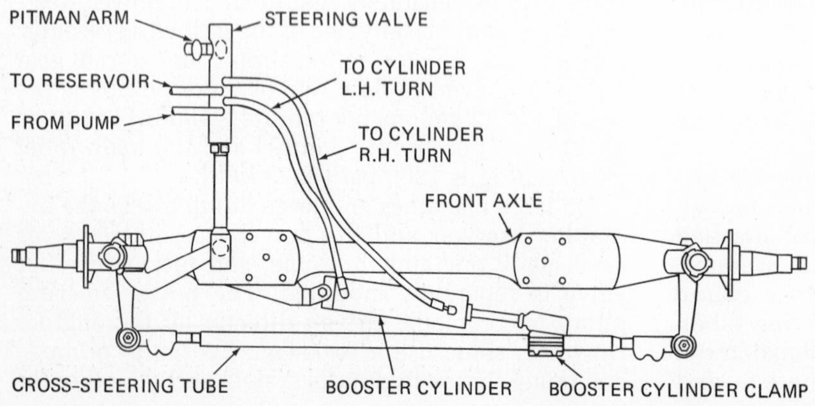

Fig. 7-21 Schematic view of a linkage power steering system. (*Mack Canada Inc.*)

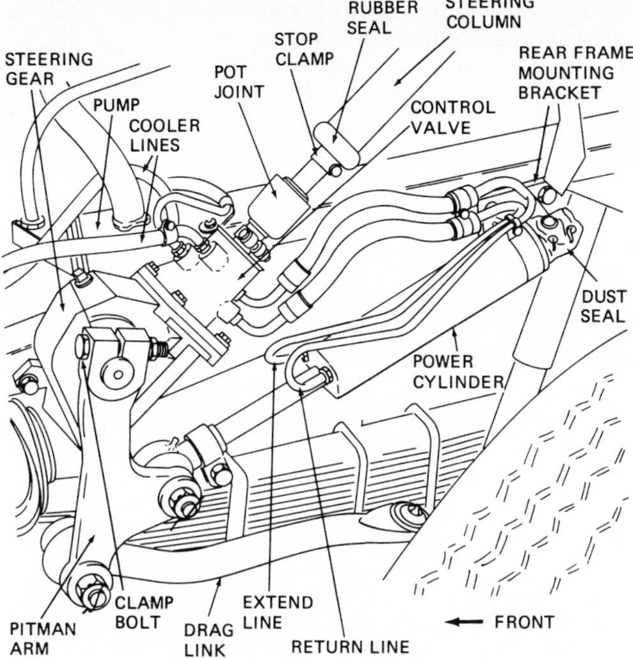

Fig. 7-22 Semi-integral power steering gear installed—conventional cab. (*GMC Truck and Coach Division*)

could be attached, as illustrated, or in any of the positions previously described.

DESIGN AND OPERATION The steering valve spool is located within the spool valve housing, which has four ports—the pump inlet and outlet port, and two ports leading into the left- and right-hand sides of the booster cylinder. The valve spool is centered by a spring (not shown) and by oil pressure acting on the spool ends. A (bypass) ball check valve is located within the control valve housing. The actuator rod passes through the valve spool's center bore and is held to the spool with a nut. O-ring seals are used

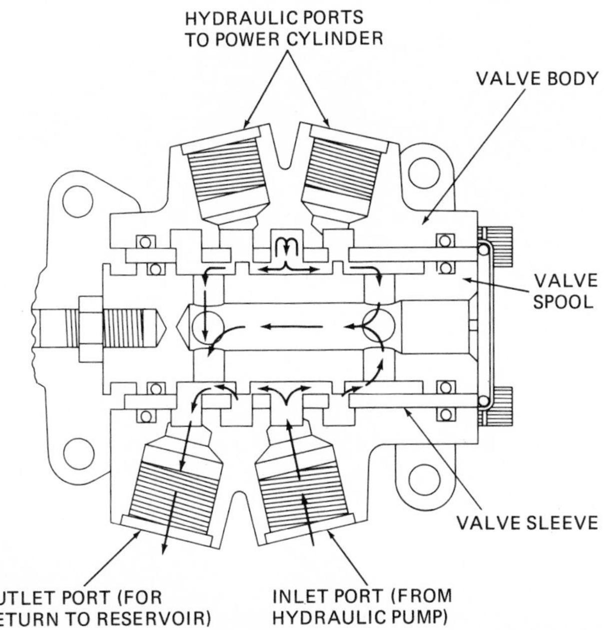

Fig. 7-23 Sectional view of control valve in neutral. (*International Harvester Company*)

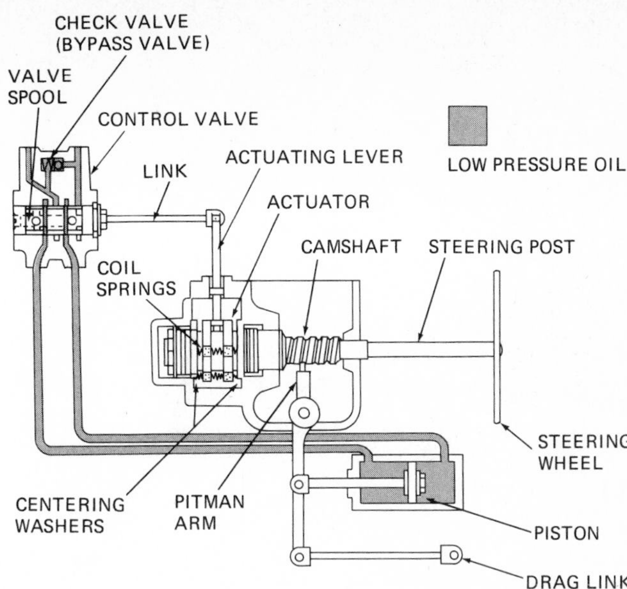

Fig. 7-24 Schematic view of a semi-integral power steering system. (*International Harvester Company*)

to seal the spool and to seal the valve housing with the actuator housing, the latter being bolted to the cam and lever steering housing. The actuator is positioned inside the gear housing bore. Several coil springs are positioned within the actuator assembly, which is located between the left- and right-hand thrust washers. The assembly is held to the end of the cam by the adjusting nut. One end of the adjuster lever ball rests in the actuator (Fig. 7-25), and the other rests in the yoke pin of the flexible rod.

When the engine is operating (assuming the steering gear and steering valve are properly adjusted and in neutral), oil from the steering pump flows into the inlet port, around and through the valve, out of the outlet port, and back to the reservoir. Oil also flows past the left- and right-hand spool lands, out of the left- and right-hand booster cylinder ports, and into the rod end and piston end of the booster cylinder. The booster piston remains stationary.

When the steering wheel is turned with a force of about 5 to 6 lb [22.2 to 26.68 N], say to the left (see Fig. 7-26), the cam rotates and, because of the counterforce of the wheels, the cam is then forced to the right. The cam also moves the actuator, compressing the left-hand coil springs, causing the actuator lever to pivot. As a result, the rod moves the valve spool to the right and its movement results in (1) the left-hand spool land reducing or fully blocking (depending on the steering effort) the pump oil flow to the rod side of the cylinders, (2) increasing the opening of the right-hand spool land, allowing an increased oil flow to the booster cylinder piston end, and (3) reducing or fully blocking the pump oil flow to the reservoir. The oil returning from the rod end of the cylinder is directed into the cross-drilled and center-drilled passage of the valve spool and flows to the outlet port and back to the reservoir. The increased or reduced steering effort is felt by the operator through the combined force of the compressed coil spring, valve spool spring, and hydraulic pressure.

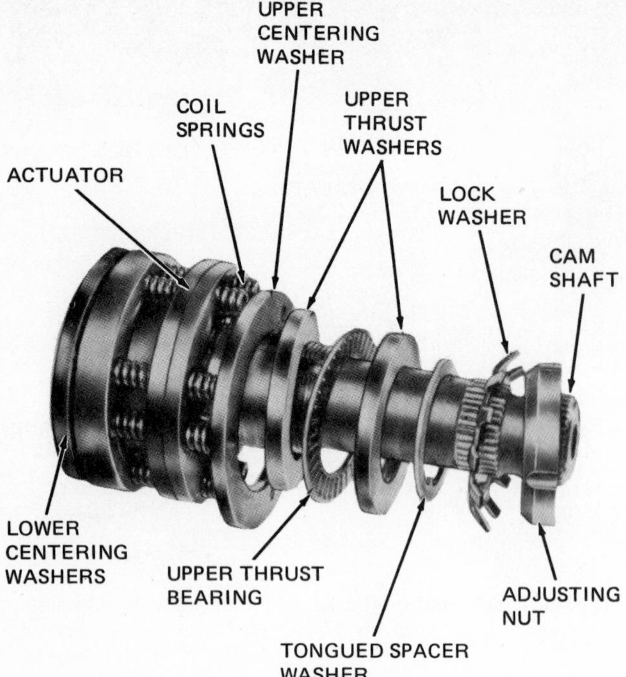

Fig. 7-25 Exploded view of upper thrust bearing and actuator assembly. (*International Harvester Company*)

Since the pump return oil flow is restricted or fully blocked, the pump pressure increases, forcing the booster piston to the low-pressure side and causing the linkage to move the front wheels to the left. When the steering force falls below 5 lb [22.2 N], the centering force is then higher and the centering spring moves the actuator to neutral.

The actuator lever then moves to neutral and centers the valve spool, and again a low pressure is maintained within both sides of the booster cylinder. **NOTE** Some valve spool designs do not allow an oil flow to the booster cylinder when they are in the neutral position.

The valve spool also moves into the neutral position when the steering linkage responds more quickly than the steering wheel rotates. Under this condition, the movement of the steering linkage removes the counterforce from the pitman arm, which causes the cam and actuator to move to neutral, and the operator must again turn the steering wheel in order to maneuver the front wheels into a turn. If, for any reason, the front wheels are forced away from the straight-ahead position, say, for instance, to the left, the force from the left-hand front wheel, or wheels, is then transmitted to the pitman arm. This forces the cam and actuator to the left, and pivots the actuator lever, which in turn moves the valve spool to the left. Oil is then directed into the left-hand side of the booster cylinder, increasing the oil pressure and counteracting the force on the front wheels, thereby stabilizing the steering. Should the power steering pump fail to supply oil to the steering valve, the vehicle reverts to manual steering and a much greater effort is required to steer the vehicle into a turn.

To allow the mechanical steering gear to turn the front wheels, the oil from one side of the booster cylinder must be released and redirected. This is achieved through the bypass valve. As the pump oil flow stops, the bypass valve moves off its seat and, during a turn, redirects the oil displaced by the booster piston to the other side of the piston, maintaining the steering booster full of oil.

ADJUSTMENT The adjustment of the cam thrust bearing is slightly different from the mechanical steering gear. The procedure is as follows:

1. Remove the pitman arm and steering shaft coupling and unscrew the stud-adjusting screw to remove the mesh load from the cam.
2. Remove the actuator cover housing bolts and washers, and then the cover. Be sure to clean the cam shaft first, so that you do not damage the seal.
3. Using the same cap screws, and a 0.375-in [9.525-mm] spacer on each bolt and fasten the actuator to the housing.
4. Unlock the lockwasher prong from the adjusting nut, loosen the nut, and then retorque it to the recommended torque. After the nut is torqued to specification, unscrew it the number of degrees recommended in the service manual. This could be 10° to 25°, depending on the motor vehicle or machine. However, make certain that you do not dislodge the center washers while making the adjustment. Once the adjustment is made, bend the lockwasher prong against the nut, reinstall the upper cover, and readjust the stud roller and cam mesh.

To check the centering position of the spool valve, remove the end cover and hold a straight edge across the valve housing and valve spool end to determine if both surfaces are even. If they are not, the centering washer or spring is worn or damaged or the valve spool is sticking within its bore. In any of these cases, the steering valve must be serviced.

Linkage Power Steering The most pertinent differences between a linkage power steering system and a semi-integral power steering system is that on the linkage type the steering valve is either an integral part of the drag link or the steering valve and booster cylinders are one unit. Although linkage steering valves have much in common with those of the semi-integral power steering gears, they are dissimilar in the actuation of the valve spool, in that some of the linkage steering valves use two reaction-limiting pistons, and some of the valve spools include a pressure relief valve. **NOTE** Some valve spool ends vary in diameter and valve land position.

The ball stud of the linkage power steering system is located within the inner sleeve. The inner sleeve can slide within the outer sleeve as far as the inner-sleeve flange plate bushing. The ball stud is held to the inner sleeve through the spring seat that rests against the inner-sleeve shoulder, the spring, the two ball stud seats, and the plug that is screwed into the inner sleeve. The spool bolt passes through the inner-sleeve bore, spool bore, and spool seal retainer washer. The centering washer, centering spring, and a second centering washer are placed over the

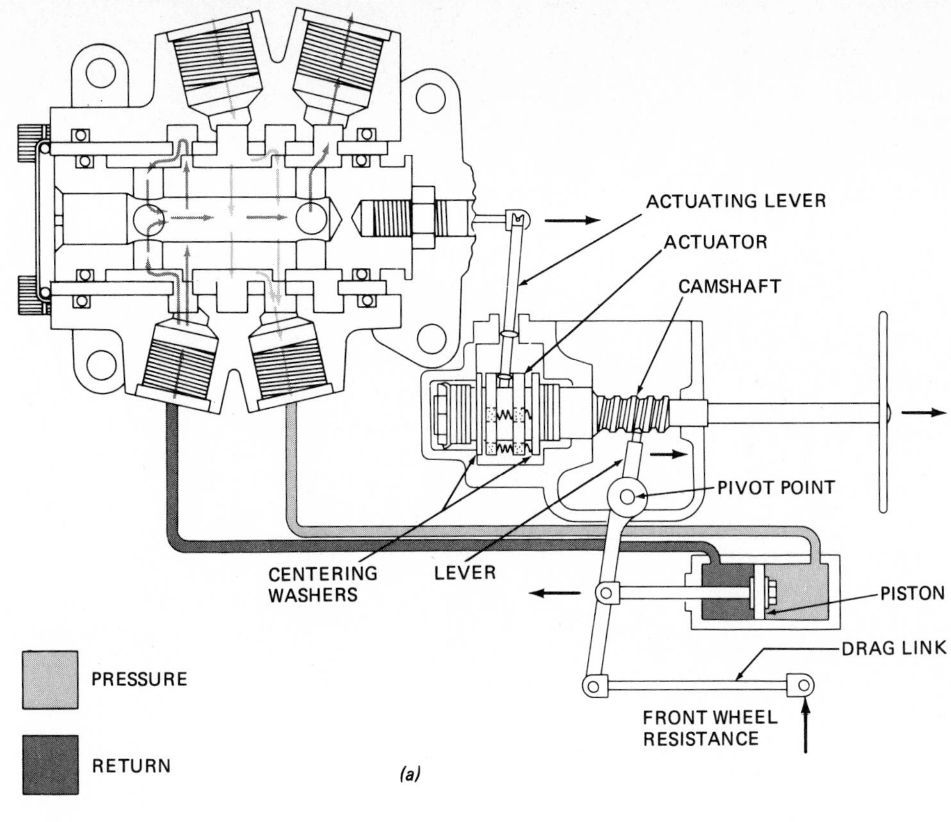

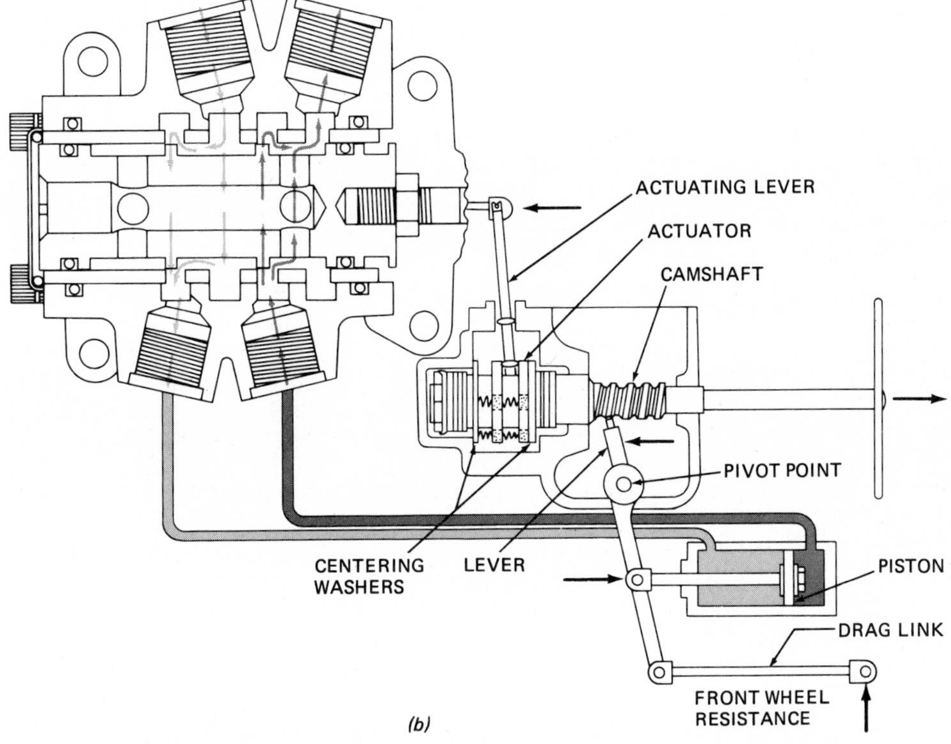

Fig. 7-26 (*a*) Schematic view of steering system and oil flow (left-hand turn). (*b*) Schematic view of steering system and oil flow (right-hand turn). (*International Harvester Company*)

spacer. The assembly is held to the inner sleeve by the self-locking nut. See Fig. 7-27.

OPERATION When the engine is operating and the steering wheel is in a fixed position, oil enters the inlet port, passes through the valve, and leaves the outlet port. At the same time oil also passes by the valve spool lands, and onto and into the left- and right-hand sides of the booster cylinder. With equal pressure on both sides of the piston, it is held stationary. The low oil pressure acting on the reaction-limiting plunger (not shown), in addition to the centering spring force, centers the valve spool.

When the steering wheel is turned with a steering

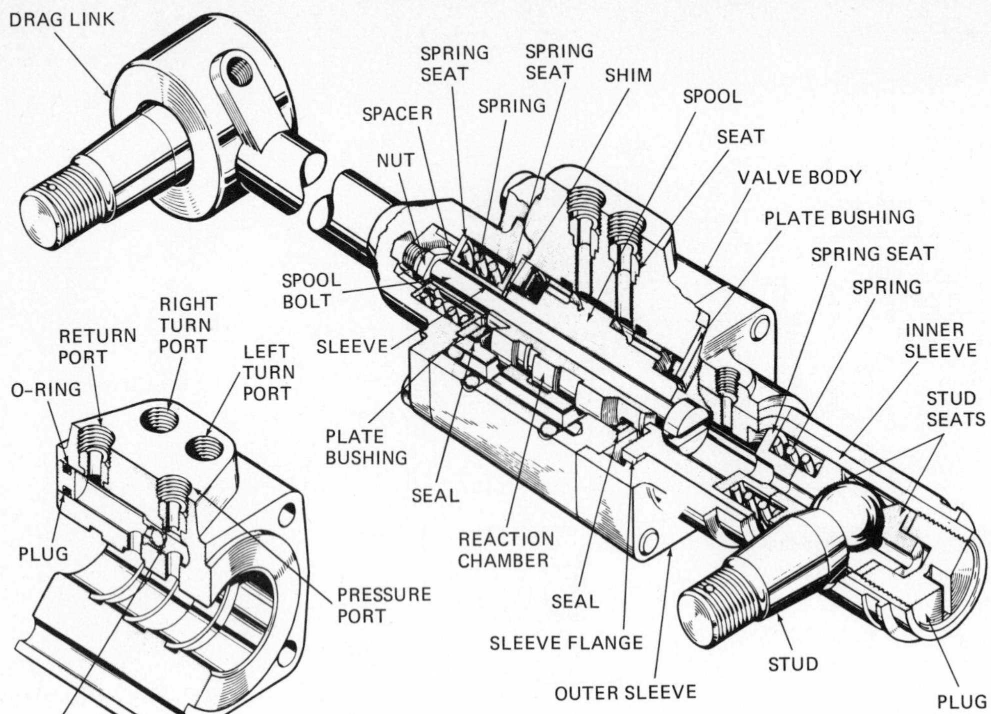

Fig 7-27 Sectional view of a control valve. *(Ford Motor Company)*

effort of more than 4 lb [17.79 N], the ball stud, the inner sleeve, and the valve spool are moved to the left or right. The valve spool is moved against its centering force, and positioned to restrict or block the pump return oil flow. Pump oil is directed to one side of the booster piston and allowed to flow from its other side through the valve and back to the reservoir. The applied pressure moves the booster piston and the reaction-limiting piston; oil then enters the reaction chamber and the oil pressure force is transmitted to the ball stud, giving the operator a proportional feel of the steering effort. If the steering wheel effort is less than 4 lb [17.79 N] or the movement of the front wheels has removed the drag-link force, the spool valve is automatically centered through the combined centering action of hydraulic and spring force.

When the front wheels are externally forced to either side, or when one front wheel momentarily rolls on a softer surface than the other front wheel, the spool valve is moved to counteract the external force, thereby stabilizing the impact.

Should the power steering pump fail to supply an oil flow, the manual steering gear provides the steering control, in which case a greater effort must be exerted by the operator. To allow booster piston movement during a manual steering action, the anticavitation check valve in the steering valve redirects the oil from one side of the booster piston to the other.

Integral Linkage Power Steering System The integral linkage and linkage power steering systems are similar except that, on the integral system, (1) the booster cylinder and steering valve are one unit, (2) internal passages direct the oil from the steering valve to the cylinder rod and piston end, and (3) only two hydraulic lines are used—the oil supply and oil return lines. See Fig. 7-28. These two types of power steering have a bypass check valve and some have in addition a pressure relief valve.

OPERATION When the steering valve is in neutral and the engine is operating, oil flows into and through the steering valve, and out of the return port to the reservoir. On some valve designs, the spool valve lands block the oil flow to the rod and piston end of the booster cylinder, and thereby hold the piston in a fixed position. Others have the spool lands positioned to direct oil to the piston and rod end of the cylinder, and thereby hold the piston in a fixed position.

When the steering wheel is turned, this motion is transmitted to the ball stud, which forces the inner sleeve to slide within the outer sleeve, moving the spool bolt and spool to the left or right against the centering force of the spring and hydraulic pressure. The movement of the spool, say to the right, depending upon the valve spool position, restricts or fully blocks the return flow to the reservoir. At the same time the right-hand spool land opens a passage to the lower internal passage. The oil can then flow to the piston end of the cylinder, forcing the piston to the right. The displaced oil passes between the outer shell and cylinder, by the left-hand open spool land, and returns to the reservoir. The system pressure always seats the check valve, and the force of the application pressure on the valve spool transmits the steering effort to the ball stud, onto the drag-link steering gear, and to the steering wheel, giving the

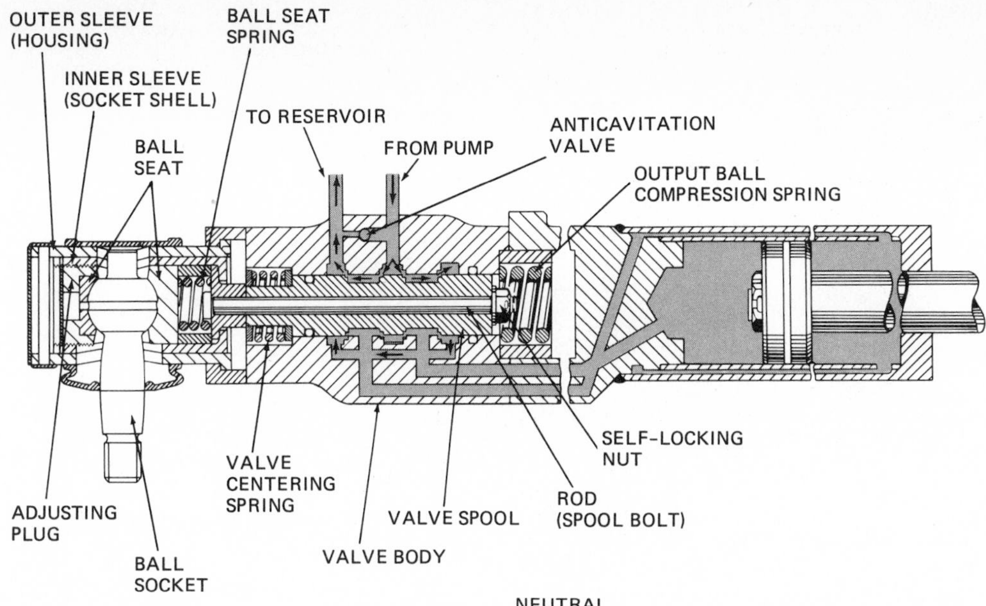

Fig. 7-28 Schematic view of a standard integral steering booster in neutral. (*International Harvester Company*)

operator the "steering feel." **NOTE** Although some steering valves have a built-in relief valve preset by the manufacturer, they can be shim-adjusted.

Integral Power Steering Gears The components that control the oil flow (steering valve) and multiply the steering effort (booster cylinder) are located within the steering gear. Although several different types of integral power steering gears are used on on- and off-highway equipment, their objective is the same and their parts are all similar.

Rotary Valve Power Steering Gear A cross-section view of a rotary valve power steering gear is shown in Fig. 7-29. For a specific truck the steering gear is designed with a ratio of 17.5:1 and a steering linkage ratio of 5.5:1, giving the motortruck a total ratio of 23:1. The manual section of the illustrated steering gear relates closely to a recirculating ball steering gear, but with the following exceptions:

1. The left-hand side of the gear housing is machined to a cylinder bore in which the rack piston can slide.
2. The ball nut is enlarged to the rack piston size and is sealed with an O ring, and two backup washers are used to seal the piston to the cylinder bore.
3. Three internal passages within the housing connect the rotary valve spool ports with the left- and right-hand piston areas (not shown).
4. The gear housing in which the control valve assembly is located is extended at the right-hand side.

The valve assembly consists of the components shown in Fig. 7-29. The valve spool is of the open center four-way three-position design. It is attached by means of pins to the stub shaft and to the left-hand end of the torsion bar. The valve spool has four oil return passages and eight spool lands, four large and four small. The valve body has three Teflon seal rings that seal and separate the inlet oil from the outlet oil. In addition it has four left-turn passages, four right-turn passages, and four inlet passages. See Fig. 7-30.

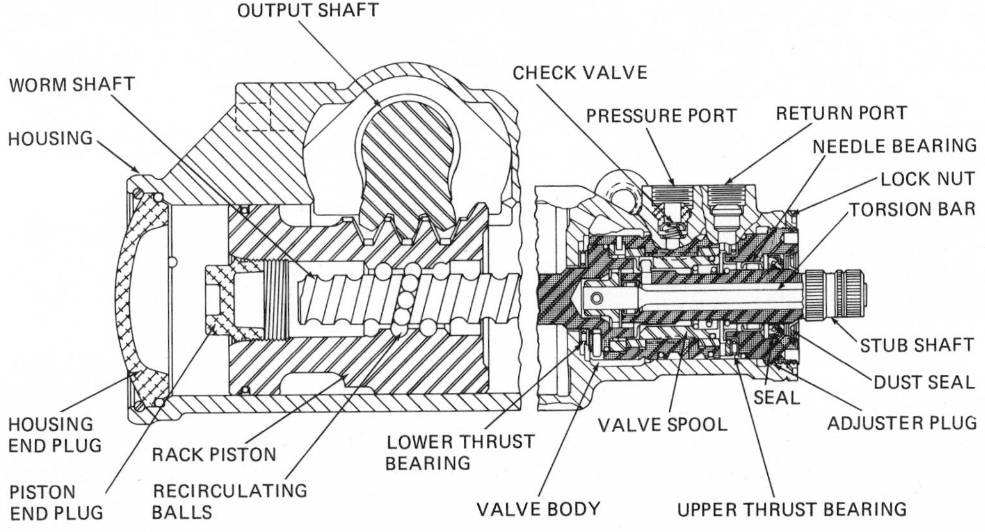

Fig. 7-29 Sectional view of a rotary valve power steering gear. (*International Harvester Company*)

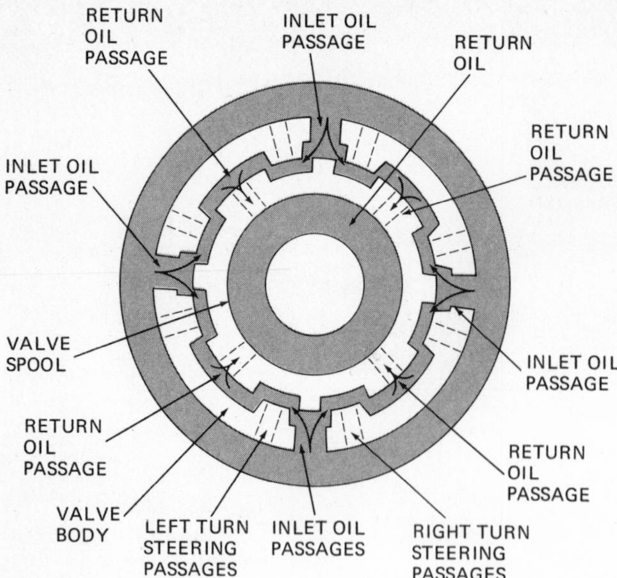

Fig. 7-30 Schematic view of the control valve (neutral).

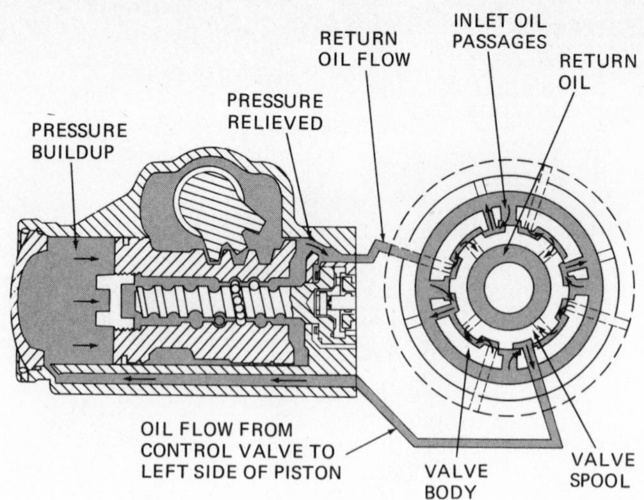

Fig. 7-31 Schematic view of oil flow (right-hand turn).

The worm shaft is linked with the valve body through a drive pin that fits into the valve body and is sealed with an O ring. Its forklike end fits into two oval slots in the valve which is attached to the torsion bar. To reduce friction, a thrust bearing is placed between the worm shaft and the shoulder in the valve housing. At the other end the valve assembly is secured and supported to the gear housing by the thrust bearing, spacer, retainer, thrust-bearing-adjusting plug with O ring, needle bearing, oil and dust seal, and the retainer and adjusting plug locknut.

OPERATION With the engine operating and the steering wheel in a fixed position, oil under low pressure flows from the power steering pump into the inlet port around the valve body, through the four inlet passages, through the left- and right-hand steering passages, and then back through the four oil return passages to the outlet port and then the reservoir. The oil from the left- and right-hand steering passages flows into the left- and right-hand pressure chambers, holding the rack piston in a fixed position. **NOTE** The low oil pressure in the two pressure chambers, in addition to cushioning the road shocks, provides lubrication to the steering gear's mechanical parts.

When the steering wheel is turned to the right, the turning effort is transmitted from the stub shaft to the torsion bar, and then to the worm shaft (Fig. 7-31). The torsion bar is then deflected due to the turning resistance of the front wheels. This changes the relationship between the spool lands and the steering holes in the valve body and restricts or fully closes off the flow to the left-hand steering passage and reservoir. The opening to the right-hand steering passage increases, causing the system pressure in the left-hand pressure chamber to rise, forcing the rack piston to the right. The latter force assists the turning force. The oil displaced by the rack piston from the right-hand pressure chamber flows through the left-hand steering passage, and from there through the four return passages to the outlet port and back to the reservoir. The higher the turning resistance of the front wheels, the higher is the deflection of the torsion bar, thereby reducing the pump return oil flow and resulting in a higher oil pressure.

When the operator reduces the steering effort, the torsion bar untwists and the valve moves to increase the pump return flow, reducing the oil pressure in the left-hand chamber. When the steering effort is fully removed, the valve comes to the neutral position.

NOTE Some manufacturers do not recommend adjusting the steering gear when installed. Others recommend adjusting only the output shaft preload.

Servicing the Rotary Valve Power Steering Gear

If you have found, through testing, any of the following conditions, the steering gear must be removed for service:

- The steering gear has lost power or speed.
- The steering is erratic.
- The steering gear is externally damaged.
- The steering shaft has excessive bearing clearance.
- The steering gear backlash is excessive.

To remove the steering gear for service, first steam clean the area on which you will be working and block the rear wheels. If necessary, raise the front end of the motor vehicle or machine and support it with floor stands and, if applicable, safely support the hydraulic equipment. In order:

1. Remove the battery ground cable.
2. Remove the steering gear coupling from the stub shaft and/or from the column shaft.
3. Remove the pitman arm.
4. Place an oil receptacle under the steering gear and remove the two hydraulic hoses and cap the openings and identify the hose positions.

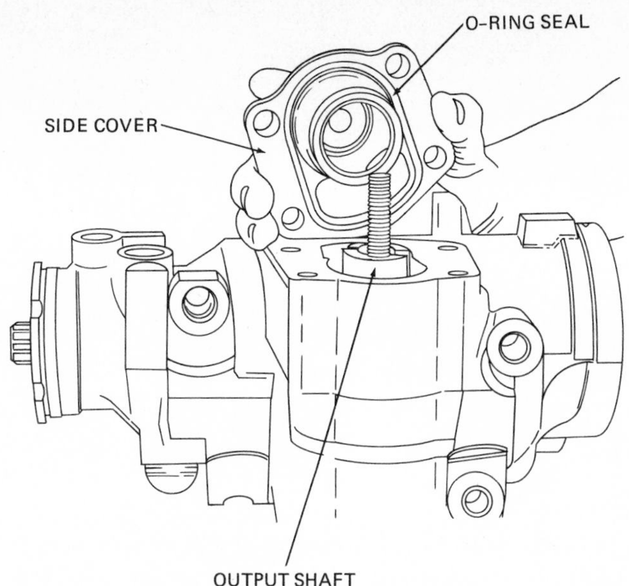

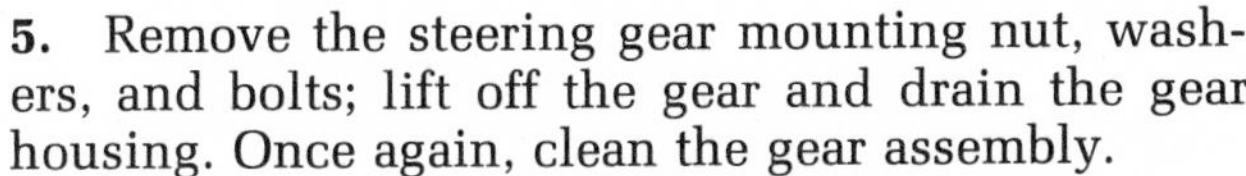

Fig. 7-32 Removing side cover (*International Harvester Company*)

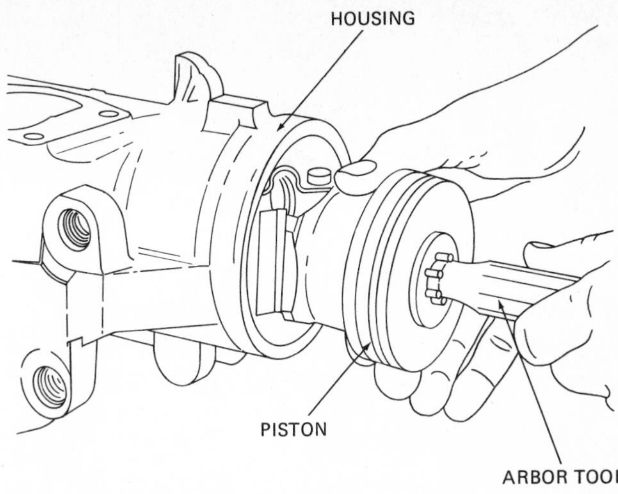

Fig. 7-33 Removing rack piston from gear housing. (*International Harvester Company*)

5. Remove the steering gear mounting nut, washers, and bolts; lift off the gear and drain the gear housing. Once again, clean the gear assembly.

DISASSEMBLY Clamp the gear housing in a vise having protected jaws, but take care not to distort the housing bore. Center the steering by turning the stub shaft, and then remove the side housing cover by first removing the adjusting screw locknut from the adjusting screw and then removing the cap screws and washers. With a hexagon wrench, turn the adjusting screw in order to force the cover from the housing (see Fig. 7-32). When the cover is removed, use a plastic hammer and tap on the output shaft to remove it from the housing. To remove the end cap, first remove the retainer by rotating the retainer ring until the end of the retainer slides under the housing hole. While pushing the ring inward with a punch, place a screwdriver between the ring gear and housing in order to twist the ring from the groove. To force the end cap and O ring from the housing, turn the stub shaft counterclockwise. This will push out the end cap.

CAUTION Do not turn the stub shaft more than necessary; otherwise the balls will fall out of their circuit. Next, remove the rack piston end plug and insert the arbor tool into the hole (see Fig. 7-33). While forcing the arbor tool toward the stub shaft, turn the shaft counterclockwise to force the rack piston onto the arbor tool. Do not remove the tool from the rack piston or the balls will fall out. With a hook wrench, loosen the adjusting plug locknut and with a pin wrench loosen and remove the adjuster plug from the gear housing. Pulling on the stub shaft will lift the control valve assembly from the gear housing (see Fig. 7-34). You can now lift out the housing, the worm shaft, and the lower thrust bearing assembly (Fig. 7-35).

To remove the output shaft needle bearing and

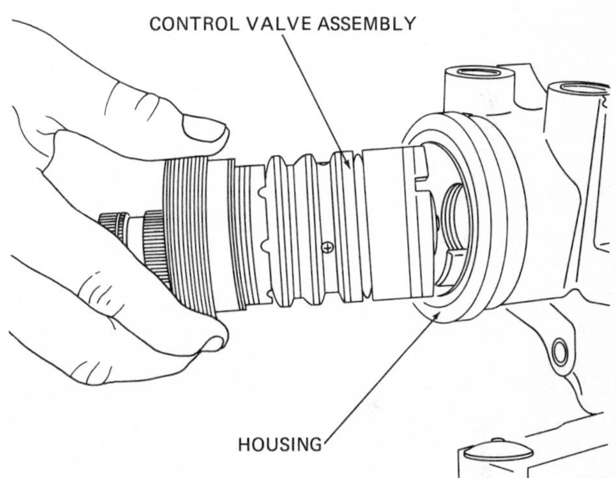

Fig. 7-34 Removing control valve assembly. (*International Harvester Company*)

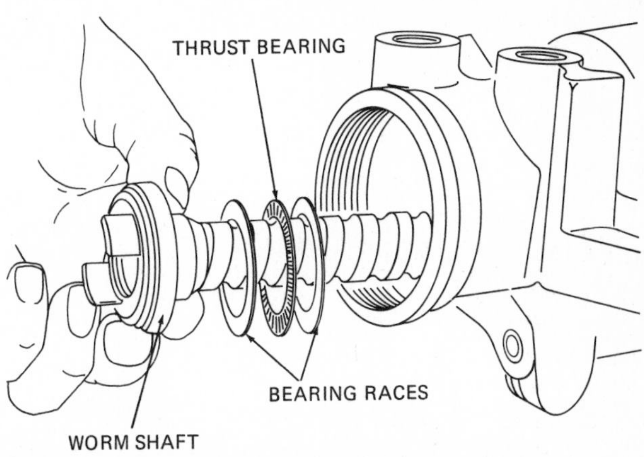

Fig. 7-35 Removing worm shaft thrust bearing and races from housing. (*International Harvester Company*)

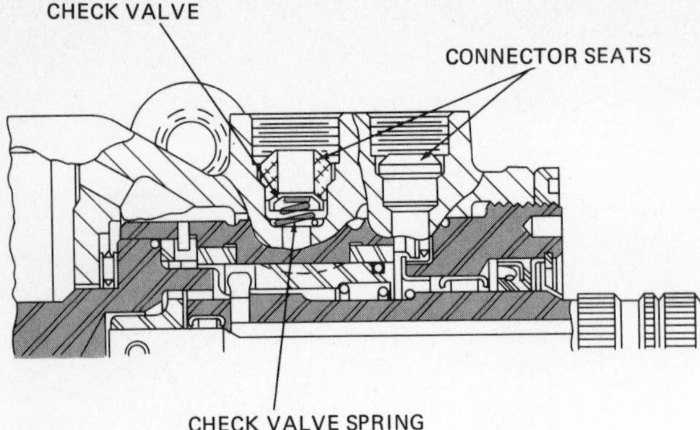

Fig. 7-36 Hose connector seats and check valve. (*International Harvester Company*)

seals, remove the seal retainer ring and outer backup washer and then lay the housing onto a press bed. Position the adapter onto the needle bearing and press from the housing the outer double lip-type seal, the inner backup washer, the inner single lip-type seal, and the needle bearing.

CAUTION Take care not to damage the bore or housing during this procedure.

GEAR HOUSING, SIDE COVER, AND OUTPUT SHAFT Clean and check the gear housing for cracks, damaged surfaces, and threaded bores, and then check the bores of the rack piston and control valve for wear, pitting, or score marks. If the cylinder bores are damaged even slightly, or grooved, use a rigid hone to restore them. Check the hose connector seat and retainer ring grooves for damage. If the connector seats are damaged or you have to replace the check valve, use a $\frac{5}{16}$-in 18 tap, and tap about three to four threads into the connector (see Fig. 7-36). Place a washer over the opening and through the center bore, and insert a $\frac{5}{16}$-in 18 cap screw, having a nut screwed onto it. Next, thread the cap screw into the connector and, while holding the cap screw, turn the nut to pull the connector from its bore. Take note of the location of the check valve and the position of the spring.

Thoroughly clean the housing, blow it dry with compressed air, and then relocate the check valve spring (large end against the counterbore seat). Place the check valve onto the spring and the connector onto the valve, and with a bronze drift tap the connector into position.

Check the output shaft sector teeth, seal, and bearing surface. If you notice wear, pitting, or scoring, the output shaft must be replaced. If necessary, again clean the gear housing and lubricate the output shaft seals, the backup washers, the bearing, and the bores with automatic transmission oil; press the components into place as shown in Fig. 7-37, and then install the seal retainer ring.

Remove the O ring from the side cover, clean and inspect the cover for wear and external damage and the bearing surface for pit and score marks, and then measure the bearing clearance. If any of these defects exist, or there is too much clearance, the side cover must be replaced.

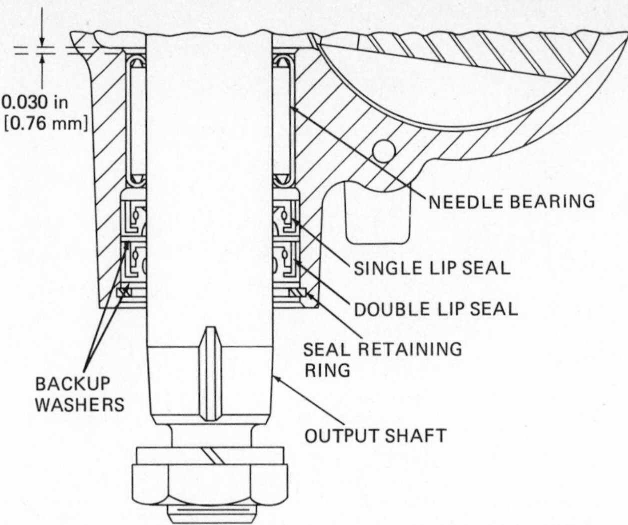

Fig. 7-37 Correct installation or output shaft seals and bearings (cross-sectional view). (*International Harvester Company*)

ADJUSTER PLUG The next component to be serviced is the adjuster plug. Remove the outside O-ring seal from it, and with a screwdriver lift away the upper thrust bearing retainer, the thrust bearing spacer, the upper thrust bearing race, the thrust bearing, and the lower race. Next, remove the stub shaft seal retainer ring, and with an adapter drive or press from the plug the needle bearing, the oil seal, and the dust seal. Discard all seals and the bearing assembly.

If the adjuster plug bore and/or the external threads are damaged or worn, the plug must be replaced. Otherwise, clean it, lubricate all parts, and reinstall them to the bore in precisely the reverse order of removal. **NOTE** All needle bearings must be pressed or driven into position with the manufacturer's identifying inscription facing toward the adapter; otherwise the needle bearing will be damaged during installation. Also make certain that the O ring is well lubricated and not twisted, the needle bearing is positioned as recommended in the service manual, the oil seal lips face inward, and the lips of the dust seal face outward. See Fig. 7-38.

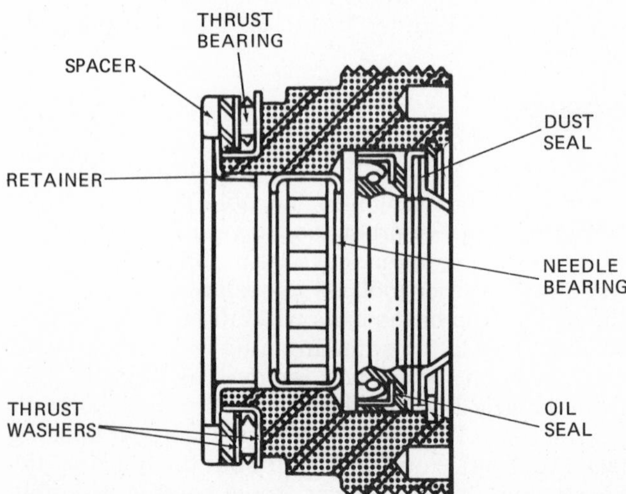

Fig. 7-38 Correct installation of adjuster plug needle bearing, oil seal, and dust seal. (*International Harvester Company*)

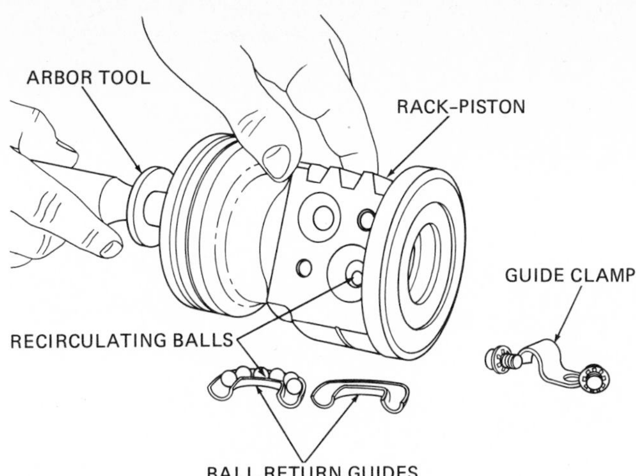

Fig. 7-39 Removing ball return guides and balls. (*International Harvester Company*)

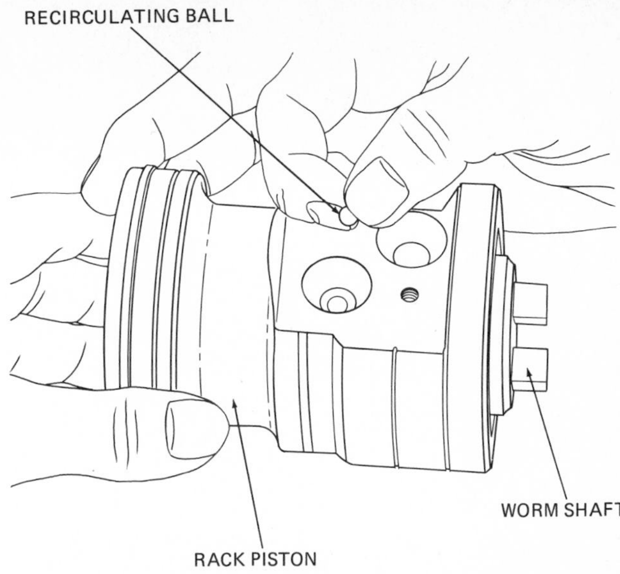

Fig. 7-40 Installing balls and rack piston. (*International Harvester Company*)

STUB SHAFT AND VALVE Because this assembly is a precision-machined hydraulically balanced unit, parts cannot be replaced individually. Therefore when the stub shaft splines or the seal and bearing surfaces are damaged or scored, or the valve body is worn, or the worm end cap drive pin and the valve groove show excessive wear, the assembly must be replaced. If no damage is evident, remove and discard the O rings and backup washer from the valve body, and then thoroughly clean the assembly and dry it with compressed air. Lubricate the valve body, the O rings, and backup washer, and then install them so that the O rings face toward the stub shaft. Next, install the O ring that seals the worm to the valve body.

RACK PISTON AND WORM SHAFT First, examine the grooves on the worm shaft. If they are pitted or scored, both the rack piston and worm shaft must be replaced since they are manufactured as matched sets. Next, check the rack piston teeth for wear and chipping and the outside of the piston for score marks or burrs.

If the assembly is serviceable, proceed as follows: Remove and discard the piston ring and O-ring backup seal from the piston. Remove the screw and lockwasher that hold the ball return guide to the piston. Remove the clamp, and cautiously remove the return guide, the arbor tool, and the 22 steel balls (Fig. 7-39). Count the balls. There should be 11 black and 11 silver. It is good practice to replace the ball return guide and the balls to protect the worm and rack piston grooves, for if the guide ends are slightly damaged or even one ball pitted or scored, the worm or rack piston groove (or both) could be damaged, or the rack piston could stick.

Clean the rack piston thoroughly and dry it with compressed air. Lubricate the worm shaft and rack piston and slide the worm shaft into the piston so that it rests against the bearing shoulder. Align the holes in the piston with the worm shaft grooves, and then alternately insert one silver and one black ball into the hole nearest to the piston ring groove while rotating the worm shaft counterclockwise (Fig. 7-40). This will locate 16 balls (eight black and eight silver) into the circuit. Now hold the two ball return guide halves together; close one opening using vaseline or grease, and place the remaining six balls (three black and three silver) into the other opening. When inserted, close the opening with vaseline or grease to hold them within the guide.

NOTE Make certain the first and last balls in the guide are opposite in color to those of the rack piston balls. Furthermore, when placing the ball guide into the rack piston holes, make certain it slides freely into the holes. Reinstall the return guide clamp, and torque the screw to specification.

To assure that the worm-shaft to piston preload is up to specification, clamp the piston in a vise having protected jaws. Position the valve assembly onto the worm shaft so that the drive pin engages. Place a pound-inch torque wrench with a $\frac{3}{4}$-in 12-point deep socket onto the stub shaft. Before measuring the rotating torque, the piston must be centered, that is about 3 lb · in [525.3 N · m]. If the torque is less, [3.81 cm] from the piston. When in this position, rotate the torque wrench about 90° to the left and then 90° to the right and note the torque reading while it is in motion (see Fig. 7-41). The highest torque reading is achieved as the rack piston passes over the highest point in the worm shaft groove, and this reading should be within specification, which is about 3 lb · in [0.338 N · m]. If the torque is less, remove the 22 balls and the worm shaft, discard the 11 silver balls, and select the next larger size of silver balls; reinstall the worm shaft by inserting the larger silver balls and the removed black balls. Recheck the rotating torque. **NOTE** The black balls can be reinserted because they have no effect on the preload.

REASSEMBLY Install the arbor tool into the rack piston as you remove the worm shaft. If necessary, again clean all components and parts and lubricate them well. Begin the reassembly by positioning the thrust bearing race, the thrust bearing, and the second race onto the worm shaft and then that shaft

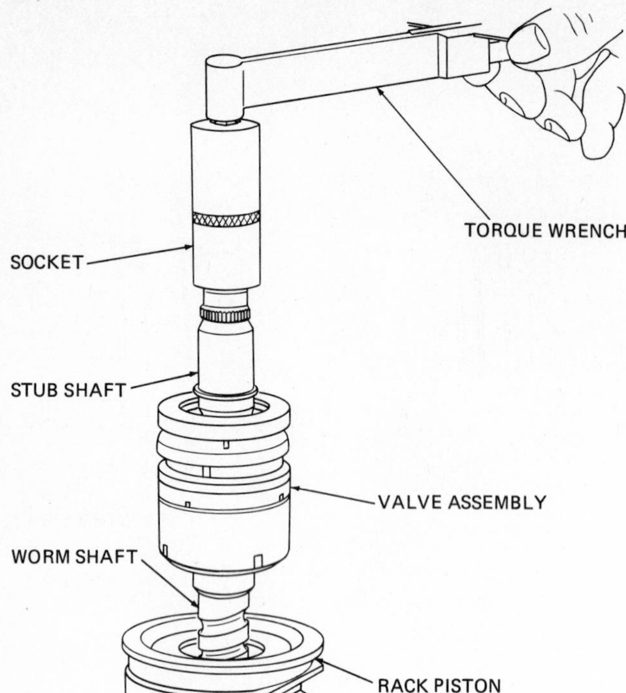

Fig. 7-41 Checking worm-to-piston preload. (*International Harvester Company*)

onto the valve assembly. Make certain the O ring is installed and the drive pin is engaged in the valve body slot. See Fig. 7-42. Next, clamp the gear housing into a horizontal position in a vise. Holding the valve body in your fingers, insert the assembly into the housing.

CAUTION Do not push on the stub shaft, as this will push the spool and worm shaft from the worm body.

Next, place a seal sleeve protector over the stub shaft, screw the adjuster plug into the housing bore, and then tighten it just enough to secure the assembly to the housing. Using a pin wrench, tighten the adjuster plug snugly to preload the thrust bearing,

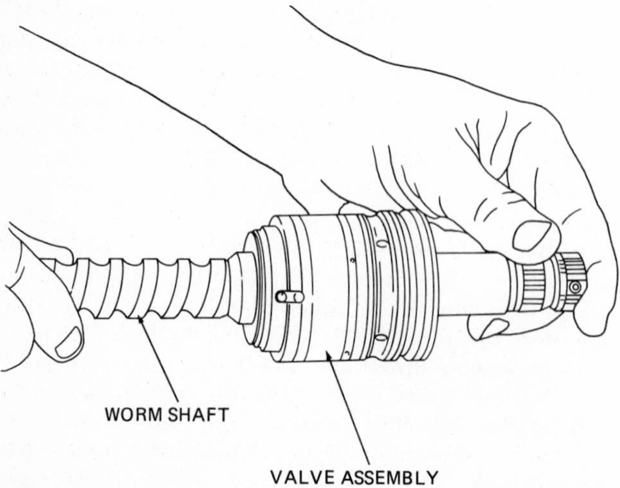

Fig. 7-42 Assembling worm to valve body. (*International Harvester Company*)

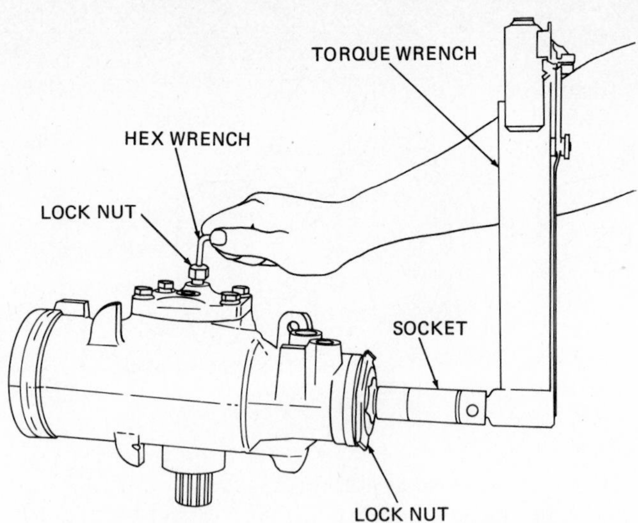

Fig. 7-43 Adjusting output shaft preload. (*International Harvester Company*)

then back off about one-eighth of a turn and screw the locknut onto the adjuster plug. Place the pound-inch torque wrench with the $\frac{3}{4}$-in 12-point socket onto the stub shaft and rotate the wrench about 90° in both directions (see Fig. 7-43). The rotating torque should be about 5 lb · in [876 N · m]. If it is too low, tighten the adjuster plug, if it is too high, loosen the plug. When it is within specification, lock the adjustment with the locknut and then recheck it.

Next, install the rack piston, but make certain you hold the arbor tool firmly and toward the worm shaft while rotating the stub shaft in clockwise rotation. Otherwise you could lose the balls from the piston. Stop just before the piston seal starts to enter the bore, and at this point again lubricate the seal. With your fingers, start the piston ring into the bore. When the piston is drawn in and is flush with the housing, the arbor can be removed. Next, turn the stub shaft to center the middle gear groove with the output shaft bore, then insert the output shaft into the housing so that the center tooth meshes with the center groove of the rack piston. Lubricate the side cover bearing bore and output shaft; and by using vaseline or grease, position the O ring to the cover groove. Position and align the side cover with the housing. Turn the adjuster screw, pushing the side cover toward the housing, and draw the cover into position.

When the remaining parts are reinstalled and torqued to specification, again place the socket onto the stub shaft to measure the output shaft preload. To do this, center the rack piston and then turn the adjusting screw to force the output shaft sector gear against the rack piston. Now rotate the stub shaft in an arc not exceeding 20° and note the rotating torque. It should be about 7 lb · in [1226 N · m]. If it is too low, tighten the adjusting screw, and if too high, loosen the screw. When it is within specification, lock the adjustment and recheck it. See Fig. 7-43.

INSTALLING THE STEERING GEAR Position and bolt the steering gear to the side frame. Center the steering gear, align the steering wheel, position and se-

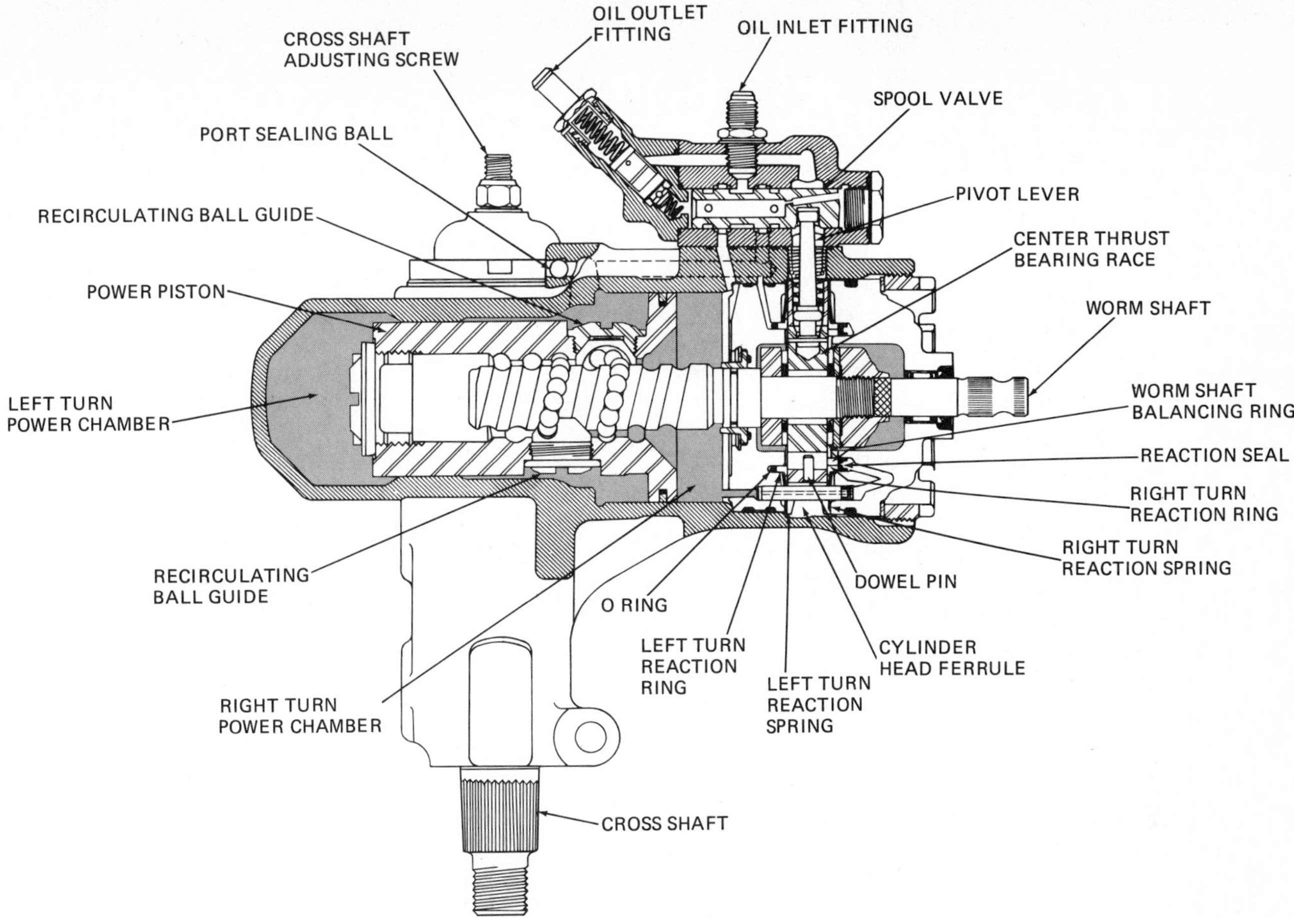

Fig. 7-44 Constant-control integral power steering. (*Chrysler Canada Limited*)

cure the coupling(s), and then torque the steering mounting bolt nut to specification. Again center the steering gear, position the front wheels in the straight-ahead direction, and then install and secure the pitman arm. Remove the caps from the hose ends and the plugs from the gear housing, and reconnect the hoses to the respective ports as previously marked.

Assuming that the power steering was flushed and the filter replaced, fill the reservoir with the recommended oil. Reconnect the battery ground cable, start the engine, and operate it at low idle speed. (You may have to refill the reservoir to the recommended fluid level.) During startup, there will be a pump noise because of the air mixed with the oil (which requires a little while to separate). When the pump noise ceases, increase the engine speed to about 1000 rpm, turn the steering wheel about three or four times throughout its maximum travel, and then recheck the fluid level and the color of the oil. If it is milky, stop the engine and let the oil settle to allow the air to separate from it, then repeat the steps until the oil is clear. Finally, recheck the adjustment of the relief valve setting and the operation of the steering gear.

Constant-Control Integral Power Steering Gear Although the rotary and the constant-control integral power steering gears are much alike, there are some differences to be found in their control sections; also, the gear housing and rack piston (power piston) in the former have a larger diameter at the right- than at the left-hand side. In the constant integral power steering, the cylinder head seals the right-hand pressure chamber against the actuating mechanism, and at the same time supports the worm shaft. The actuating mechanism and the reaction components are positioned over the worm shaft, as shown in Fig. 7-44, and are held there by the worm shaft nut. The housing head, which supports and seals the worm shaft, fits into the gear housing and is secured to the housing with the adjusting nut and locknut. The pivot lever rests in the ball socket located in the gear housing. Its lower end rests in the opening in the center thrust bearing race, and the other in the valve spool slot. The coil spring holds the pivot lever on its seat and the reaction springs hold or bring the pivot lever to the neutral position. The valve body is bolted to the gear housing, and O rings seal the internal passages leading from the valve body to the internal passages of the gear housing. The valve spool is of the open center design and is center- and cross-drilled. A piston and two springs are positioned within the outlet fitting to restrict the return flow and thereby maintain a fixed pressure within the gear housing.

OPERATION When the engine is operating and the steering gear is in a fixed position, oil flows into the inlet port and around the valve spool, passes by the piston in the outlet fitting, and flows back to the reservoir. At the same time the oil from the right-hand valve passage flows into the left- and right-hand reaction areas, applying oil pressure against the left- and right-hand reaction rings and centering the thrust bearing race. Oil also flows through the top internal passage into the left-hand pressure chamber, and from the left-hand valve passage flows through the center passage into the right-hand pressure chamber. The oil flow has then not only centered the valve spool, but also holds the power piston in a fixed position. When the steering wheel is turned to the right, the worm shaft rotates, but the front wheels resist the rotation, thereby forcing the shaft slightly to the right. This action also moves the centering thrust bearing race and compresses the right-hand reaction springs, allowing the operator to sense the steering. It also results in swinging the pivot lever on the top to the left. Because the ratio is about 1:3, the valve spool is moved three times the distance of the worm shaft. The movement of the valve spool increases the left-hand spool land opening, increasing the oil flow to the right-hand pressure chamber. The right-hand spool land then partially or fully blocks the pump oil flow to the left-hand pressure chamber and brings the right-hand cross-drilled passage in the valve spool into line with the port. As the oil pressure builds up in the right-hand pressure chamber and against the right-hand reaction ring, the rack piston is forced to the left. The oil displaced from the left-hand pressure chamber flows through the top passage into the right-hand valve passage, through the center of the valve spool, and out of the outlet fitting back to the reservoir. This maintains a fixed although low pressure in the left-hand pressure chamber and left-hand reaction area.

If the steering effort is reduced to about 5 lb · in [525.3 N · m] or the force from the pitman arm is reduced, the oil pressure in the right-hand reaction area and the right-hand reaction springs centers the thrust bearing race and pivot lever, bringing the valve spool to the neutral position.

When the steering wheel is rotated to the left, the oil flow within the spool valve, steering gear, and pressure chamber is reversed. The low-pressure areas that existed on the right-hand turn now become high-pressure areas. **NOTE** If a shock load or an external force moves the front wheel during a left-hand turn, say to the left, the valve spool automatically positions to neutral because the force from the pitman arm is removed, thereby centering the center thrust bearing race. When the impact is extreme, the pitman arm is forced in the opposite direction, which causes the worm shaft to move to the right. The valve spool is then positioned to direct oil into the right-hand pressure chamber, counteracting the impact and stabilizing the steering gear.

ADJUSTMENT Manufacturers recommend adjusting only the sector-gear-to-power piston rack preload and the valve spool once the steering gear is installed. To adjust the preload, remove the drag link from the pitman arm, operate the engine at low idle speed, and center the steering gear. Next, loosen the adjusting screw locknut and with a screwdriver remove the existing preload by turning the adjusting screw counterclockwise. Now turn the adjusting screw clockwise until no backlash can be felt and then turn the screw an additional three-eighths to one-half of a turn to place a preload between the sector gear and the piston rack. Lock the adjustment with the locknut.

If the steering wheel turns as the engine is cranked over or during startup, or if the front wheels turn to the left or right although the steering wheel is held in a fixed position, the valve spool may be out of adjustment or may be sticking, or part of the actuating mechanism or the worm may be damaged, worn, or sticking.

To adjust a misadjusted valve spool, loosen the valve body mounting cap screws so that the body can be moved with slight force. If the front wheel self-steers to the left, tap the valve at the plug end (using a plastic hammer) to move it to the left. To correct self-steer to the right, tap the valve body to the right. When the adjustment is made, retorque the mounting cap screws to the recommended torque. If this does not correct the self-steer action, the steering gear must be removed for service.

Gear-and-Rack Integral Power Steering Gear Figure 7-45 shows a sectional view of an integral power steering gear of the gear-and-rack design. This type of power steering is used on motor vehicles and truck-tractors in the GVW range of 35,000 to 110,000 lb [15,890 to 49,940 kg] or even higher. Some large motor vehicles use a main steering gear plus a secondary steering gear to ensure safe steering. This precaution is taken because, under severe operating conditions, with only one steering gear the output shaft could break. The cross-sectional view of the secondary gear is shown in Fig. 7-46.

When two power steering gears are used, the output shaft of the main steering gear is connected through the pitman arm and drag link to the upper left-hand steering arm. The output shaft of the secondary gear is connected through the pitman arm and drag link to the right-hand upper steering gear. See Fig. 7-47.

MAIN POWER STEERING GEAR DESIGN The actuating shaft is supported in the housing cover with a double-roller thrust bearing and adjusting nut. Two lip-type seals are used to seal the shaft—one is press-fitted into the left-side housing bore, and the other into the right-side housing bore. If a 90° input drive is desired, a miter gear box consisting of the parts shown in Fig. 7-45 is bolted to the main steering gear housing. Shims used to adjust the miter gear backlash are positioned between the gear box and the housing cover. In this case, one lip-type seal is in the gear box cover and the other is on the inside of the bearing cap.

The output shaft is supported by two bushings—

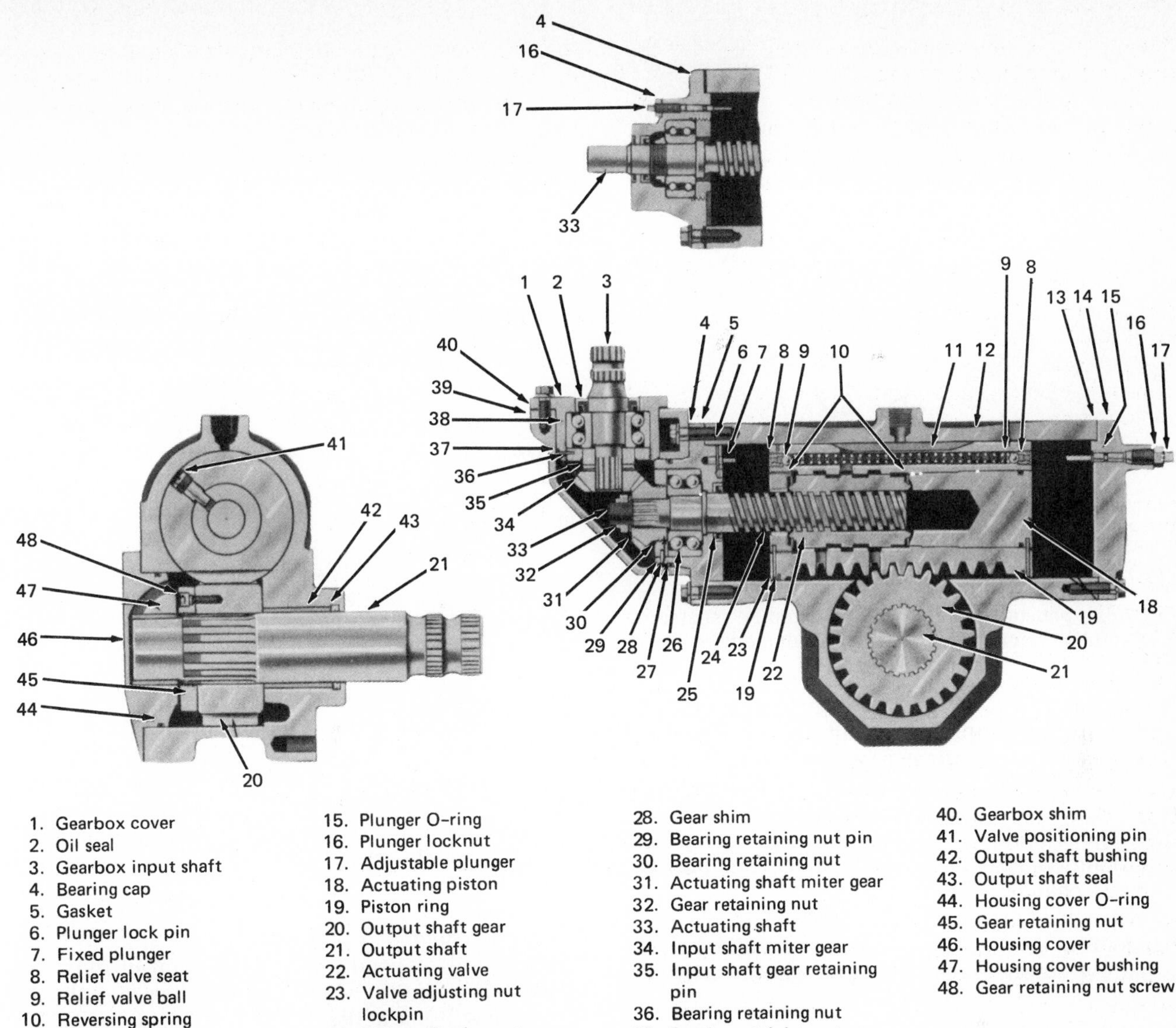

1. Gearbox cover
2. Oil seal
3. Gearbox input shaft
4. Bearing cap
5. Gasket
6. Plunger lock pin
7. Fixed plunger
8. Relief valve seat
9. Relief valve ball
10. Reversing spring
11. Relief valve spring
12. Housing
13. Gasket
14. Cylinder head
15. Plunger O-ring
16. Plunger locknut
17. Adjustable plunger
18. Actuating piston
19. Piston ring
20. Output shaft gear
21. Output shaft
22. Actuating valve
23. Valve adjusting nut lockpin
24. Valve adjusting nut
25. Oil seal
26. Actuating shaft bearing
27. Bearing cap O-ring
28. Gear shim
29. Bearing retaining nut pin
30. Bearing retaining nut
31. Actuating shaft miter gear
32. Gear retaining nut
33. Actuating shaft
34. Input shaft miter gear
35. Input shaft gear retaining pin
36. Bearing retaining nut
37. Bearing retaining nut lockpin
38. Input shaft bearing
39. Gearbox housing
40. Gearbox shim
41. Valve positioning pin
42. Output shaft bushing
43. Output shaft seal
44. Housing cover O-ring
45. Gear retaining nut
46. Housing cover
47. Housing cover bushing
48. Gear retaining nut screw

Fig. 7-45 Sectional view of a gear and rack of an integral power steering gear. (*Mack Canada Inc.*)

one in the steering gear housing and the other in the steering gear housing cover. The output shaft pinion gear is splined to the shaft and held to it by the mounting nut. The nut is secured to the pinion with a screw.

The power piston, which has a piston ring on each end, is equipped with teeth (rack) which engage with the output shaft pinion gear. It is machined in the center to a cylinder bore to accommodate the actuating valve. This valve is retained on the left by the large index locking nut, and on the right by the piston plug. Two reversing springs are used to center the actuating valve within the piston. **NOTE** The actuating valve uses an acme thread. Two relief check valves—one at each end of the piston—are positioned in the top horizontally drilled passage and are held to their seats through the relief valve spring. There are two relief valve adjusting plungers in the bearing housing and one in the cylinder head. Their purpose is to reduce the applied pressure as the front wheels approach the maximum turning angle, thereby protecting the steering gear and linkage from undue stress. Below the horizontally drilled passage are three additional passages: The center passage is used to connect the oil inlet port with the actuating valve; the one to the left connects the left-hand pressure chambers with the actuating valve; and the one to the right connects the right-hand pressure chamber with the actuating valve. The two vertical passages in the lower half of the power piston lead into the pinion gear area, and from there to the return port. See Fig. 7-48.

OPERATION When the engine is operating and the steering wheel is in a fixed position, oil from the power steering pump flows into the inlet port, along the horizontal groove in the piston, into and through the center passage, and into the relief valve spring

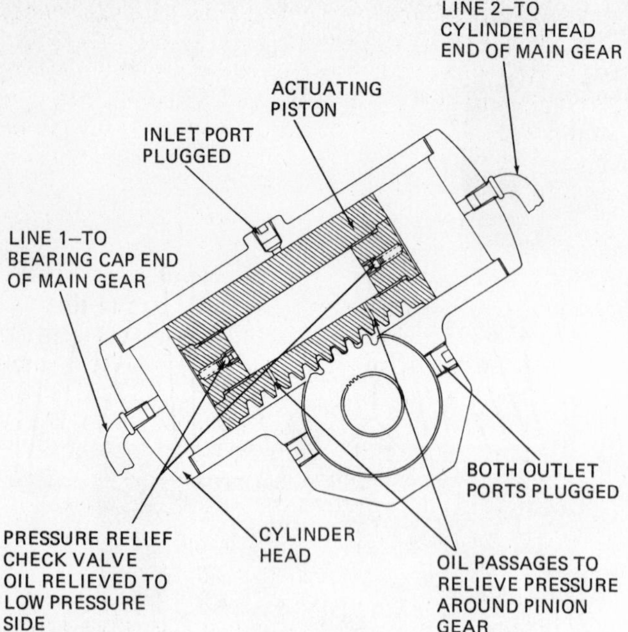

Fig. 7-46 Schematic view of dual integral power steering gear system. (*International Harvester Company*)

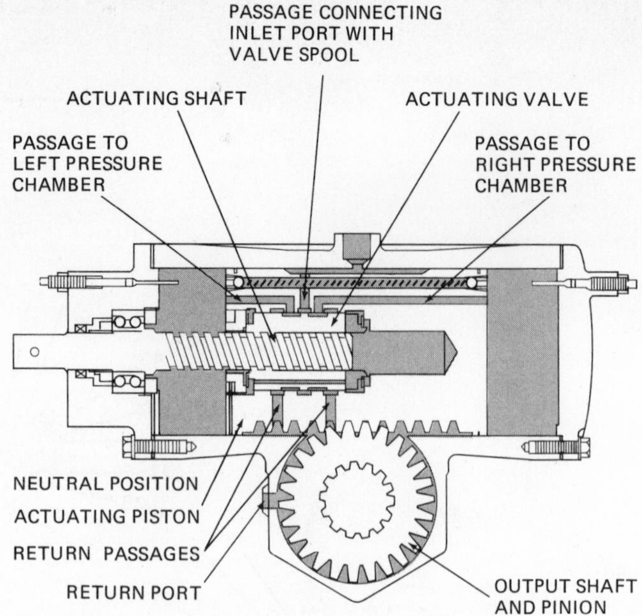

Fig. 7-48 Schematic view of steering gear when in neutral. (*Mack Canada Inc.*)

area. It then flows around the actuating spool, into left- and right-hand reversing spring areas and through the two vertical passages into the pinion gear area, and then out of the outlet port back to the reservoir. The oil also flows past the left- and right-hand spool lands and into and through the left- and right-hand horizontal passages that lead into the pressure chambers.

When the steering wheel is rotated to make a left-hand turn, the twisting force is transmitted to the actuating shaft. Since the front wheels resist the force, the piston remains in a fixed position; however, the actuating valve moves slightly to the left, against the reversing spring. This moves the center spool land also to the left and reduces or fully closes the oil flow into the left-hand passage, but increases the oil flow into the right-hand pressure chamber. Simultaneously, the lower left-hand (return oil) spool land increases its opening and the right-hand spool land reduces or fully closes the (pump oil) opening. The extent by which the spool lands open or close will depend upon the amount of force applied to the steering wheel by the driver, and the oil pressure will rise at the right-hand side of the piston accordingly, thereby forcing the piston to the left.

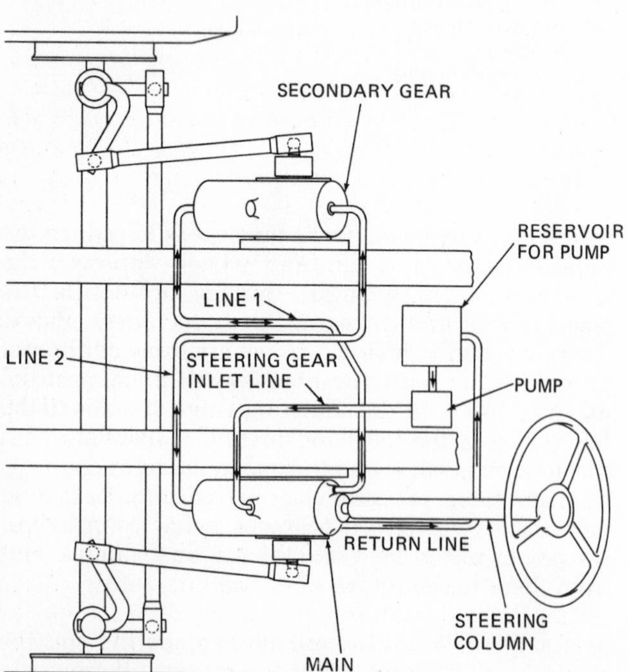

Fig. 7-47 Sectional view of the secondary steering gear. (*International Harvester Company*)

The oil displaced by the piston passes in and through the left-hand horizontal passage and around the valve spool, and flows through the left-hand lower passage, into the pinion gear area, and out of the outlet port. Oil that passes by the valve spool also increases the oil pressure in the area of the right-hand reversing spring, allowing the operator to sense the steering. If the piston approaches the left-hand adjusting plunger, the relief valve is lifted off its seat and oil is allowed to flow into the left-hand pressure chamber. With equal pressure in both chambers, the piston comes to a stop before the front wheels are halted by the wheel stop. When the steering effort is reduced or the force from the pitman arm is removed, the energy of the left-hand reversing spring centers the spool valve. When the steering wheel is turned in the opposite direction, the actuating valve action and oil flow are reversed.

ADJUSTMENT To check or adjust the relief valve plunger of the main and secondary gears, raise the front axle and place the front wheels on a portable turning radius gauge, or drive the vehicle onto a front alignment machine, or use a turning angle gauge as shown in Fig. 7-49. Adjust the degree scale

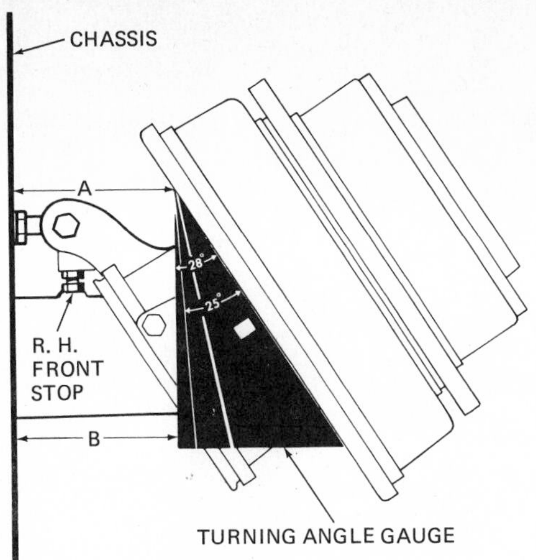

Fig. 7-49 Front axle stop adjustment.

to zero. Next, turn the steering wheel to the left until the scale conforms to the specified angle (which is commonly 28° on a standard front axle and 25° on a front drive axle). Be sure that the tires have at least 0.5-in [12.7-mm] clearance from any part of the steering system, suspension, or frame. If necessary, loosen the locknut and turn the stop screw against its stop, and lock the adjustment. **NOTE** The location of the stop screw varies—it may be on the axle center or the steering knuckle. When both turning angles are adjusted, loosen both plunger locknuts and turn both adjusting plungers clockwise until they bottom. Start the engine and operate it at about 1000 rpm. Next, turn the steering wheel to the left until you feel an increase in steering effort, which is the point when the relief valve unseats. While holding the steering wheel, have your assistant measure the clearance between the stop screw and stop. To reduce the clearance, turn the adjusting plunger in the bearing cap counterclockwise until the clearance is as specified, then lock the adjustment. Repeat this procedure for a right-hand turn and adjust the cylinder head adjusting plunger.

Troubleshooting Power Steering Systems A malfunction in the power steering system generally leads to one or more of the following four symptoms:

- The steering system is noisy.
- The steering speed is reduced.
- The steering force is reduced.
- The steering system does not appear to operate properly.

Apart from these problems, of course, the tires, the suspension, improper front-end adjustment, and a bent frame affect steering.

Power steering system noise will occur if parts or components are improperly secured or partially broken. High return oil pressure will cause a "growling" noise from the pump. Other sources of steering system noise may be a power steering pump which is worn or damaged, an oil filter which is plugged, or a reservoir which is low on oil. Air in the system, or hydraulic lines contacting the frame, would be heard as a chattering noise. If there is a squealing noise when making a turn, it may be coming from the relief valve as oil bypasses the valve and is redirected back to the reservoir, or it may be caused by a loose belt or a worn or damaged drive coupling.

Before proceeding with any tests, first visually check the entire steering system for loose mounting bolts, bent components or parts, or misalignment of the ball sockets, the steering booster, or the steering column. Service or replace any components which are defective and make any necessary repairs if there are external oil leaks, then proceed with testing.

To determine the cause of reduced steering speed and/or power, assuming there is no external damage or wear and no oil leaks are visible, install a flowmeter to the steering system to check the effectiveness of the following: the oil supply system, the power steering pump, the steering system pressure, the control valves, and the accumulator. Before checking the efficiency of the steering valve, check the service manual to find out if the valve is of the open or closed center design. (See material on hydraulic flowmeter testing.)

Reduced steering *speed* could be caused by a slipping drive coupling or belt, a worn or damaged steering pump, restricted inlet filters or lines, high restriction in the return line, or damaged steering cylinder piston seal(s) (which would allow oil to flow from one side of the piston to the other). If the latter is the problem, the operator would also have complained of reduced steering power. Another cause of reduced steering speed may be a damaged spool valve or housing, since in this case some oil bypasses the spool and flows back to the reservoir.

If the operator complains of reduced steering *power*, look for damaged or worn piston packings, damaged or worn spool valves, or a bent part or parts of the steering system (which would increase steering friction). Steering power can also be reduced by a damaged or worn drive coupling or belt(s) (which causes the pump to stall out before the maximum pressure is reached), or by a damaged or worn relief valve, a low relief valve setting, or high internal leakage at the cylinder or valve spool.

If the steering system shimmies or is slow to recover from a turn to the straight-ahead position, check the steering valve adjustment for loose or worn steering linkages and the mechanical steering gear for wear and misadjustment. (Do not overlook the steering column alignment.) These same effects would be noticeable if the spool valve was sticky or the steering components bent.

If the front wheels or front end of the machine veers while the steering gear is held in a fixed position, check for a misadjusted valve spool, which could be directing more oil to one side of the piston than to the other, or for excessively damaged piston packings, which allow oil transfer within the cylinder from one side to the other.

If the operator complains of delayed steering action, check the steering linkages and booster cylinder(s) for looseness and wear, and check the

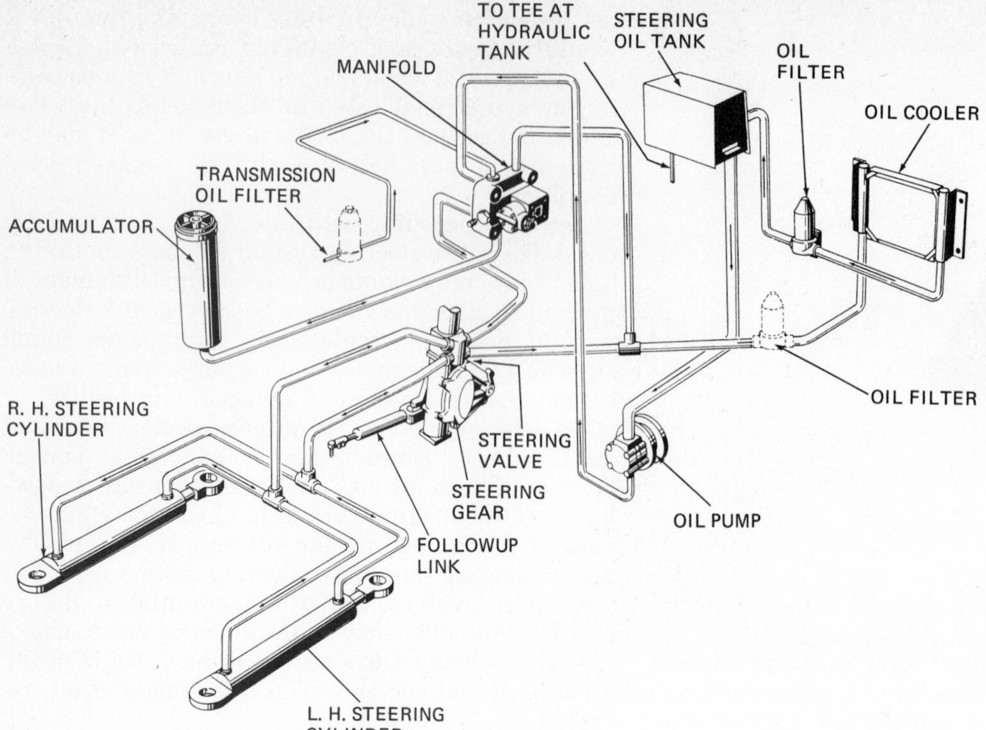

Fig. 7-50 Schematic view of a semihydrostatic steering system. (*Terex Division of General Motors*)

mechanical steering gear adjustment including the centering of the steering gear.

Semihydrostatic Steering for Wheel-Type Tractors and Articulated Machines This steering system differs from others in that it has no mechanical linkage from the steering gear to the front wheels. The linkages are replaced with two hydraulic steering cylinders which are attached on one end to the frame and on the other to the steering arm. On articulated machines, the cylinders are attached to the rear frame, and the piston rods are attached to the front frame.

One semihydrostatic steering system is shown in Fig. 7-50. The steering gear is of the semi-integral cam and lever design (see Figs. 7-51 and 7-24). The hydraulic system is of the constant-pressure closed center spool valve design. In Fig. 7-50 you will see components new to you, such as the accumulator, the manifold, the unloading valve (bolted to the manifold), and the followup link. The manifold and unloading valve are used to unload the power steering pump when the system pressure is at the set pressure, and to again charge the system when the system pressure falls below the set pressure. The accumulator maintains a constant pressure of about 1400 psi [9653 kPa], thereby providing the steering system with a constant oil pressure at all engine speeds (see material on hydraulics).

The followup link relays "steering feel" to the operator and at the same time absorbs road shock, thereby preventing steering gear damage. In addition it centers the valve spool when the force from the steering wheel is removed, thereby holding the steering cylinder piston(s) in a fixed position.

The followup link consists of the parts shown in Fig. 7-52. One end is connected with a universal joint to the pitman arm, and the other is connected by a ball stud to the front frame. Because the followup link centers the steering gear valve spool, no centering spring or washer is used. The yoke link is screwed into the valve spool and secured with a locknut.

The hydraulic lines are so connected that the line which connects the piston end of one cylinder also connects the piston rod end of the other. This hydraulic line connection assures even piston speed of both steering cylinders.

OPERATION When the engine is operating and no turning effort is applied to the steering wheel, the oil from the hydraulic pump flows into and through the manifold and into the unloading valve, from the manifold over a one-way check valve to the accumulator, and also from the manifold to the steering valve. Because the valve spool is of the closed center design, it blocks the oil flow and at the same time blocks the ports leading to the steering cylinder. As the oil pressure rises it charges the accumulator, and as the set pressure of the unloading valve is reached the valve responds by redirecting the pump oil into the common return line. The oil then flows through the oil cooler back to the reservoir. This action closes the check valve and maintains the system pressure. As the steering action causes the system pressure to drop to about 200 psi [1378 kPa] below that of the unloading valve setting, the unloading valve responds and again directs oil to the accumulator and steering valve to raise the oil pressure to the set pressure.

When the engine is shut off and the transmission oil pressure drops to zero, the transmission check valve within the manifold is forced open by the steering system pressure, and the oil from the steer-

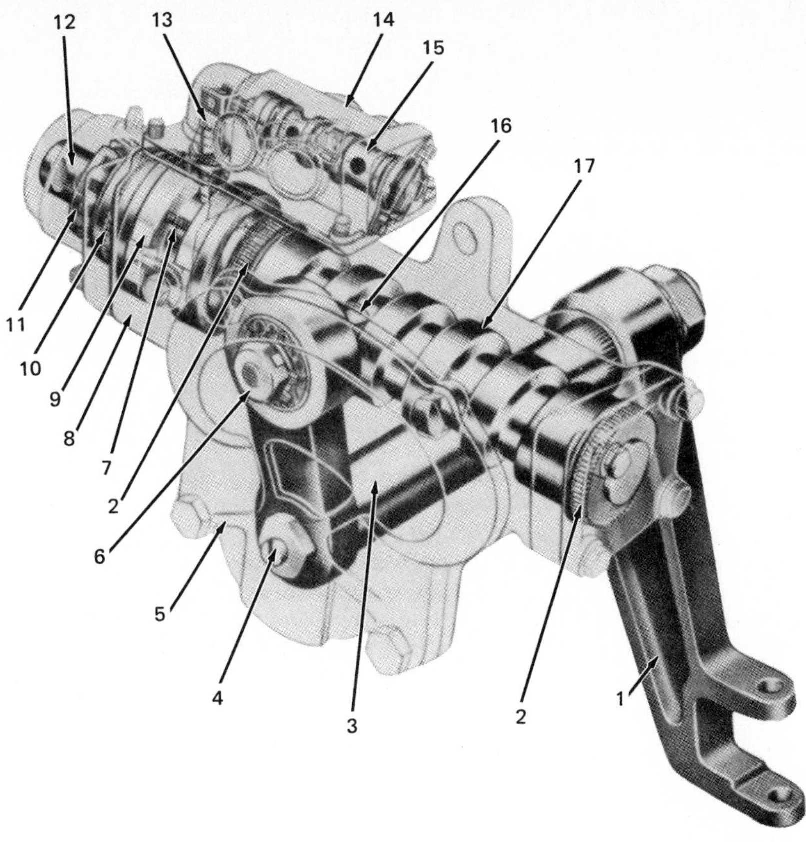

1. Pitman arm
2. Cam bearings
3. Lever shaft
4. Adjusting screw & locknut
5. Steering gear housing
6. Stud bearing unit
7. Centering spring
8. Actuator housing
9. Actuator
10. Thrust bearing & washers
11. Adjusting nut
12. Shaft
13. Actuator lever
14. Steering valve assembly
15. Steering valve spool
16. Stud
17. Cam

Fig. 7-51 Phantom view of a semi-integral steering gear and valve. (*Terex Division of General Motors*)

ing system then flows through an orifice into the return line. This causes a slow reduction in the steering system pressure but, in the event of engine failure, it gives the operator adequate time to steer the machine to a safe stop. When the engine is restarted, the transmission oil pressure closes the check valve, allowing the steering system pressure to build up.

NOTE The oil flow within the valve spool during a left- or right-hand turn is the same as that

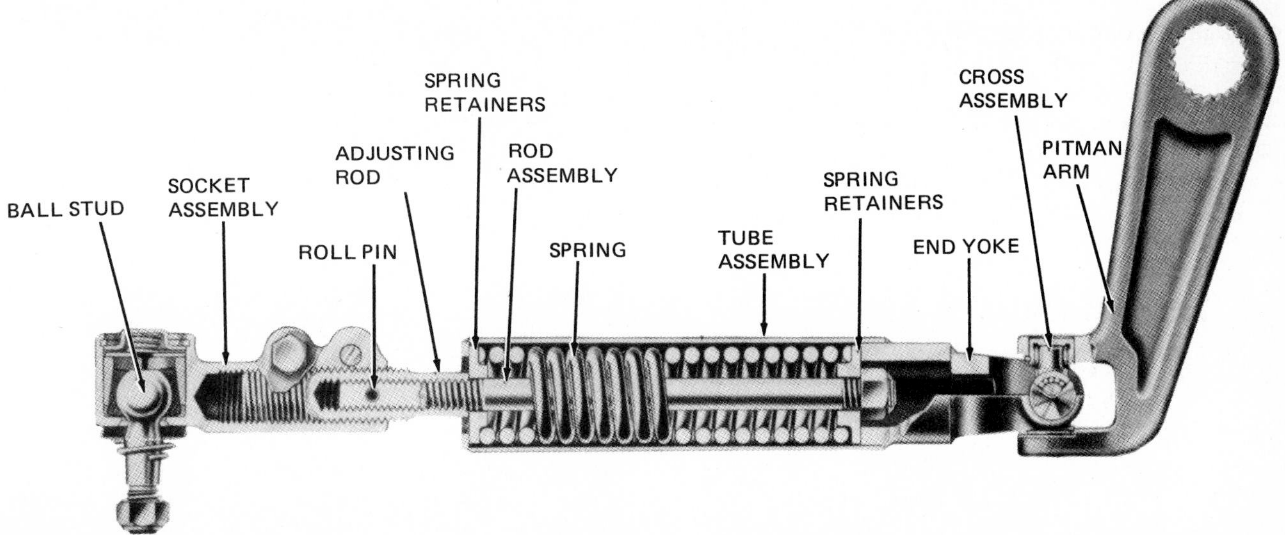

Fig. 7-52 Sectional view of followup link. (*Terex Division of General Motors*)

explained earlier in this unit in the section on semi-integral power steering gear. However, the oil pressure forces one piston rod to extend and the other to retract, and this pushing action pivots the front end of the machine, tractor, or loader, to the left or right or pivots the front wheels to the left or right.

As the steering wheel is turned, the pitman arm semirotates (partly rotates) at a maximum travel of about 1.5 in [3.81 cm] (Fig. 7-52). If the motion is to the left, the force is placed onto the universal joint, cross-end, and spring retainer, compressing the spring as the tube assembly slides off the left-hand spring retainer. When the pitman arm pivots to the right, the yoke and tube assembly is pulled to the right. Again, the spring is compressed but this time the force is applied from the right-hand side. Any shock loads which may occur are absorbed by the spring. When the rotating force of the steering wheel is below 25 lb [111 N] and the energy of the followup link is in the static state, the pitman arm has moved the cam, which in turn moves the actuator, and the springs of the actuator force its lever to pivot, moving the steering valve spool to neutral.

ADJUSTMENTS Two very important adjustments have to be made to ensure that the steering system operates properly: The length of the followup link must be as specified in the service manual, and the valve spool must be centered.

To adjust the followup link to the specified length, first loosen the ball stud clamp nuts and then remove the ball stud from the frame. Next, turn the ball socket clockwise to reduce the overall length, or counterclockwise to increase the length. **NOTE** For this steering system, the length is measured from the center of the ball stud to the center of the universal joint bore in the yoke. Before tightening the clamp nuts, reinstall the ball stud and align the followup link so that the ball stud center line is 90° from the center line of the universal joint.

To adjust or check the valve spool adjustment, remove the cap screws, washers, seal retainer, water seal, spool cover, and retainer ring. Place a straightedge across the housing and valve spool—both surfaces should form a straight line. If the straightedge does not form a straight line, remove the cover over the clevis yoke, loosen the locknut and then, with a screwdriver, turn the valve spool so that the spool face is flush with the valve housing. Lock the adjustment, recheck it, and then reinstall the parts previously removed.

HYDROSTATIC STEERING SYSTEMS

In this type of steering system, the hydraulic components and oil flow control and move the front wheels, or manipulate an articulated tractor or machine. They are full-power steering systems having no mechanical linkage from the steering wheel to the front wheels or front frame. See Fig. 7-53. Hydrostatic steering systems are used almost exclusively on off-highway motortrucks, tractors, and machines, mainly because they can be modified to suit small or large units simply by increasing the oil flow and/or pressure and the size (diameter) of the steering cylinders—which means the steering capacity is nearly unlimited.

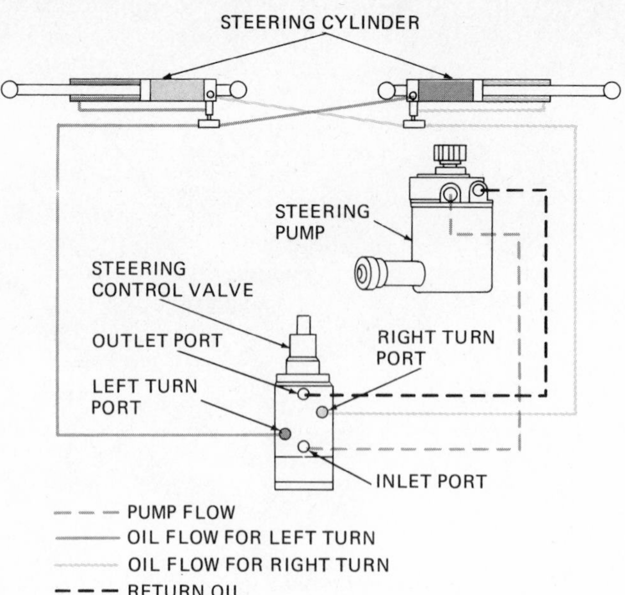

Fig. 7-53 Schematic view of a hydrostatic steering. *(J I Case Agricultural Equipment Division)*

Although hydrostatic steering system designs differ they nevertheless function on the same principle and use similar hydraulic components: a reservoir and filters, a hydraulic pump, a steering control valve, steering cylinders (of either the single- or double-action design), and hydraulic hoses and tubing. The system may be designed with the hydraulic pump, reservoir, filter, and steering relief valve as one unit, or these components may be separately mounted, or the hydraulic system's reservoir may also serve as the reservoir for the steering system. Moreover, on some hydrostatic steering systems, one of the dual hydraulic pumps supplies oil to the steering system.

The purpose of all of the components just mentioned is to supply clean oil to the steering system and to protect the system against high pressure. The purpose of the control section is to provide steering control, and the purpose of the steering cylinders is to convert hydraulic pressure into lineal force.

Although all hydrostatic steering systems serve the same purpose, their components vary in size and design. The metering sections (manual pump) are of the gerotor design, and they too vary in size and design. The steering control valve, if used, may be of the closed center or open center design. Some hydraulic systems use pilot-operated steering control valve(s), and when the oil is supplied from the main pump the system may use a flow divider combination valve (which includes a steering relief and pressure-reducing valve). When the main hydraulic pump is of the variable displacement design, an unloading valve and a metering valve are used, with a combination valve for the steering system. In some instances an accumulator is also used.

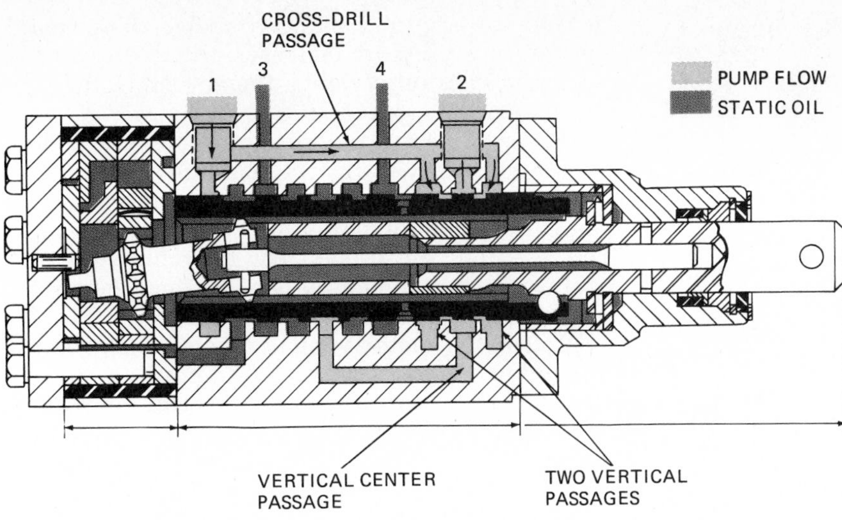

Fig. 7-54 Schematic view of steering control (right-hand turn, engine running). (*J I Case Company Agricultural Equipment Division*)

Steering Control Valve Design One of many steering control valve designs is shown in Fig. 7-54. The valve body has two ports to connect it with the pump inlet port 1, and outlet port 2, and two ports for the left-hand turn outlet port 3; port 4 then becomes a return port. For the right-hand turn, port 4 becomes the outlet port and port 3 becomes the return port. Internally the body is machined and has 10 spool lands. This steering control valve is of the open center design. When the engine is operating, oil flows from the pump, into port 1, around the spool valve, through the cross-drilled passage, downward through the two vertical passages, around the spool, and by the spool lands into the center vertical passage. It then flows upward and out of port 2 and back to the reservoir. Oil also flows from the lower right-hand spool land through a passage to the center of the spool where the spool land blocks the oil flow. When the spool is in neutral, the spool land also blocks the oil flow toward ports 3 and 4, preventing the oil from flowing to and from the steering cylinders.

CONTROL VALVE SECTION Components 17 to 29 make up the control valve section. Its purpose is to direct oil from the power steering pump back to the steering wheel or the steering shaft with the input shaft, to actuate the spool, and to support and seal the output shaft. **NOTE** Shims are used to position the spool correctly to the body.

CONTROL VALVE SECTION Components 17 to 29 comprise the control valve section. Its purpose is to direct oil from the power steering pump back to the reservoir when the steering wheel is held in a fixed position. When the steering wheel is rotated, it directs oil from the steering pump to the metering section, and then from the metering section to the steering cylinders. The oil returning from the steering cylinders passes through the metering section, out through the outlet port, and back to the steering pump.

METERING SECTION This section consists of components 30 to 42. The purpose of the commutator, commutator ring, and manifold is to direct the flow of oil to and from the gerotor and control valve section. The gerotor controls the oil flow to the steering cylinders. When the engine is not operating but the steering wheel is turned, the pump supplies oil to the steering cylinders. The input shaft is linked with the gerotor, commutator, and spool through the torsional bar that is pinned to the input shaft. The other end of the torsional bar is flexibly pinned to the drive link. One end of the drive link is splined to the gerotor, and the other to the spool. Its pin rests in the commutator slot. The output shaft is also linked to the spool through the actuator ball which rests in the groove of the shaft and in the sleeve.

Operation (Engine Operating) When the steering wheel is held in a fixed position, the torsion bar is straight (untwisted) and the spool is therefore in the neutral position. The spring force holds the left- and right-hand check valves on their seats. The oil from and to the steering cylinders' ports is blocked, holding the steering cylinder piston in a fixed position. If, under this condition, the front wheel(s) of the motortruck, tractor, etc., hit an obstruction, thereby placing a side force onto one or both wheels, the pressure within the cylinders rises. The check valve of one oil line, say, for example, in the line leading to port 3, is forced open and redirects the oil within the valve out of port 4. This reduces the pressure but maintains the steering cylinders full of oil.

When the steering wheel is rotated to the left or right, several actions occur simultaneously. Say the steering wheel is turned to the left—this rotates the input shaft to the left, the actuating ball moves the spool to the right, and the torsion bar, in effect, tries to rotate the drive link. As a result, oil from the steering pump flows past the spool lands and into the hollow center of the spool, charges the metering section, and the three charging pockets formed by the gerotor and stator are filled with oil (see Fig. 7-56). **NOTE** The seventh pocket is in neutral—it changes from charging to discharging. The rotor and the commutator, however, resist rotation because the oil pressure in the three charging pockets must increase to overcome the steering cylinder pressure required

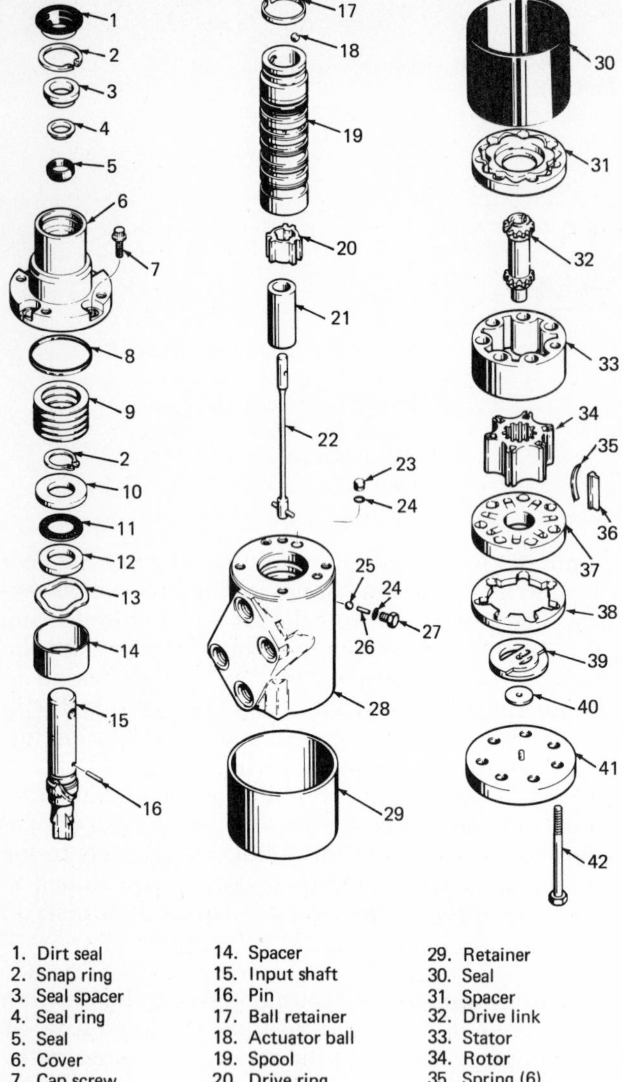

Fig. 7-55 Exploded view of steering control valve components. (*J I Case Company Agricultural Equipment Division*)

to move the front wheels (or the front of the articulated machine). The torsion bar is then further twisted and the actuating ball moves the spool further to the right, increasing the spool land openings from the steering pump to the metering section, and to the steering cylinders. At the same time the gerotor and commutator rotate, directing oil to the valve body, around the spool lands, and out of the left-hand steering ports. Oil returning from the steering cylinder enters the right-hand steering port, flows around the spool, and passes by the spool lands into the horizontal passage, out of the return port, and back to the reservoir. **NOTE** Since the link is splined to the spool, it also rotates the spool. If the required steering force is too high or the steering cylinders have reached the end of their travel, the metering section cannot discharge the oil, and as a result the pressure increases, which unseats the steering system relief valve, thereby protecting the system against high pressure.

If the operator reduces the steering effort, the torsion bar untwists. The spool then moves to the left, reducing the oil flow to and from the metering section. If the operator holds the steering wheel in a fixed position, the torsion bar fully untwists, the spool returns to the neutral position, and the tractor or machine steers in the fixed direction.

To steer the motor vehicle, tractor, etc., from a left-hand turn into a straight-ahead position, the operator has to turn the steering wheel to the right—which moves the spool to the left. The oil flow reverses within the spool body and metering section, and the former low return pressure for a left-hand turn becomes steering pressure while the former steering pressure becomes low return oil pressure.

Operation (Engine Not Operating) When the engine is not operating or the steering pump fails, the motor vehicle, tractor, etc., can be steered when the steering wheel is turned, because the gerotor now becomes a pump and supplies oil for the steering action (see Fig. 7-57). Assume that the motor vehicle has to be steered to the left. As the steering wheel is turned to the left, the action that occurs within the steering control valve and metering section is the same as that when there is an oil flow from the power steering pump. The spool partly rotates and is moved to the right, opening the spool lands to and from the control valve section, metering section, and steering cylinders. The torsion bar is twisted and the twisting motion is transmitted to the gerotor. When the twisting force overcomes the cylinder pressure, the gerotor and commutator rotate. The three charging pockets create a low pressure and draw makeup oil from the steering reservoir, and also use the oil returning from the steering cylinders. The oil discharged from the gerotor passes into the body passage by the open lands. Oil returning from the steering cylinder passes by the spool lands, opens the recirculating valve, and flows to the center of the spool into the three charging pockets. The displaced oil from the steering cylinders helps to charge the gerotor pump. To steer the tractor under this condition, a much greater turning effort is required—not only is more turning force needed, but also more steering wheel rotation.

Emergency System A hydrostatic steering system which uses two emergency steering pumps is shown in Fig. 7-58. This system is designed as a backup in the event the main hydraulic pump fails or loses its volume. Each emergency hydraulic pump is driven by a dc electric motor. The current is supplied from the batteries. The actuation of the electric motor is controlled through a switch which is mounted within easy reach of the operator. In addition to the emergency pumps, a shuttle valve and a pressure relief valve are required in order to make the system operational and to protect the hydraulic pump and motors.

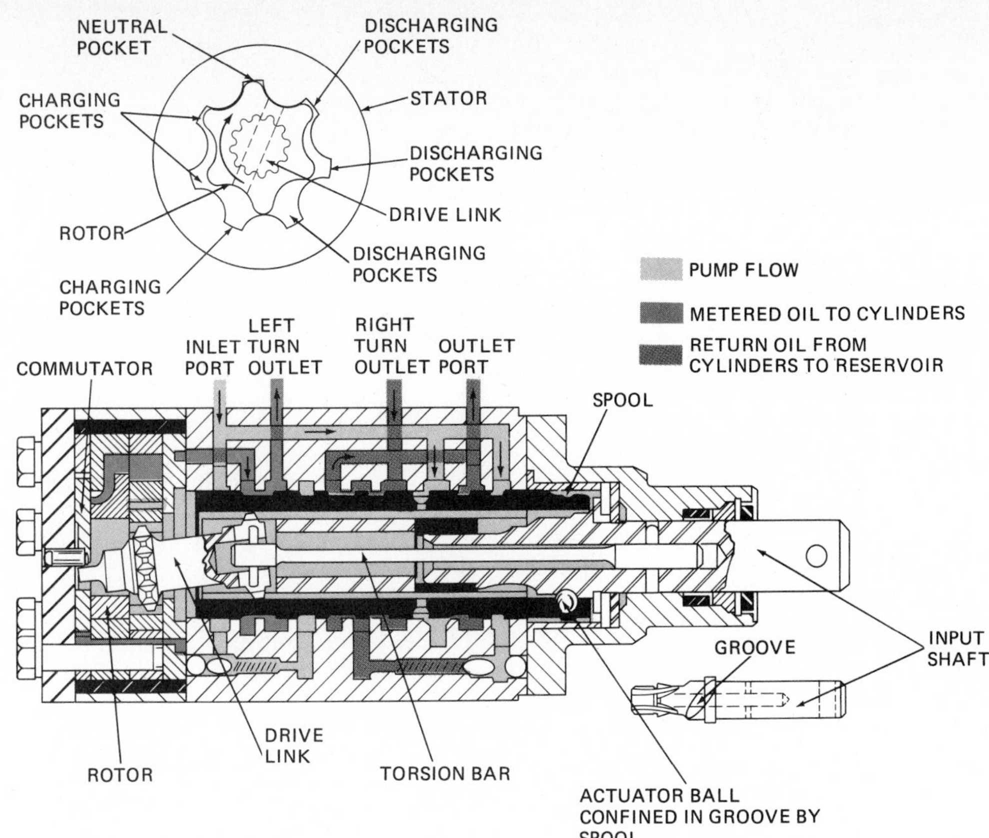

Fig. 7-56 Schematic view of steering control oil flow (left-hand turn) with engine running. Counterclockwise rotation of input shaft moves actuator ball to top of groove and spool out of valve. (*J I Case Company Agricultural Equipment Division*)

OPERATION When the switch is not energized and the engine is operating, oil from the left-hand main pump flows to the flow divider, where about 30 gal [113.55 l] from the 80-gal [302.8-l] hydraulic pump is directed to the shuttle valve. The valve shifts to the left, closes the port to the emergency pumps, and opens the port to the steering control valve. The remainder of the oil is directed to the hoist directional control valve. When the steering wheel is in a fixed position, the spool is in neutral position. Oil is directed from the steering control valve to the flow control valve, to the hoist directional control valve, and from there back to the reservoir.

If for any reason the operator encounters reduced steering response, perhaps because the engine is operating at low idle speed or because of reduced pump efficiency or malfunction of the flow divider valve, the emergency motor switch can be activated. Battery current will then flow to the two electric motors and drive the hydraulic pumps. The two pumps supply about 25 gal/min [94.62 l/min] to the shuttle valve, and as the pressure increases the shuttle valve is forced to the right, closing the port to the flow divider and opening the port to the steering control valve. The oil from the steering control valve flows back to the divider valve, to the hoist directional control valve, and from there back to the reservoir.

Pilot-Operated Hydrostatic Steering System Several different types of pilot-operated hydrostatic steering systems are used. The purpose of these sys-

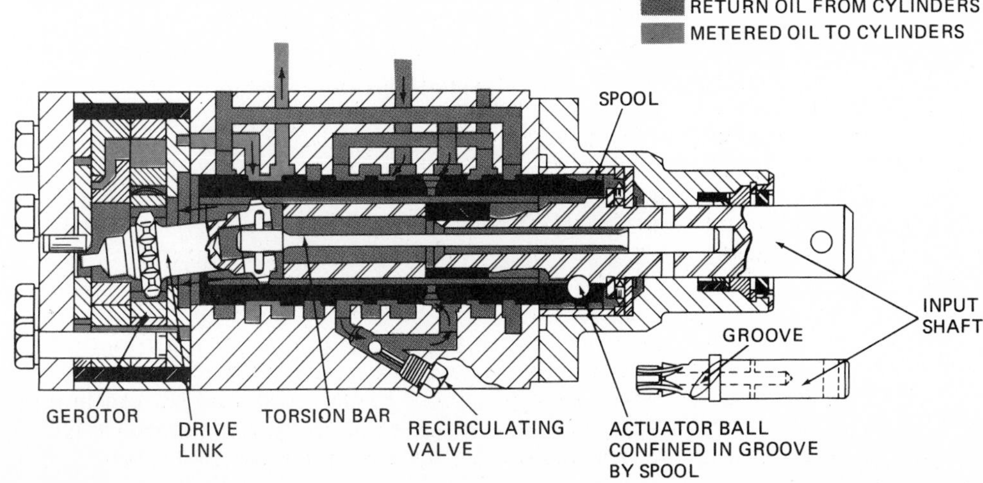

Fig. 7-57 Schematic view of oil flow (left-hand turn) engine not running. Counterclockwise rotation of input shaft moves actuator ball to top of groove and spool out of valve. (*J I Case Company Agricultural Equipment Division*)

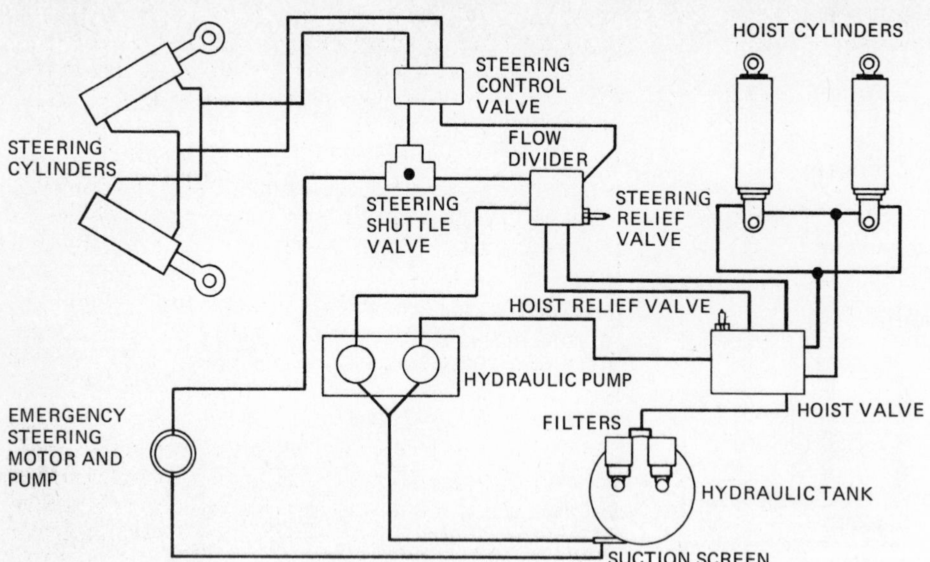

Fig. 7-58 Schematic view of a dump truck hydraulic system. (*Caterpillar Tractor Co.*)

tems is to improve the steering control when the distance from the steering control valve to the steering cylinder is exceptionally long. Despite any differences between the types, the steering system can be divided into two individual sections: the pilot section and the steering section. The pilot section consists of the steering control valve (manual pump and metering unit) and neutralizer valve. The steering section consists of the steering control valve and the steering cylinders. (See Fig. 7-59.) Also, depending on the required steering effort and characteristics of the machine, the power supply, relief valve, reservoirs, etc., could be the same in design as any of the hydrostatic systems previously explained.

The hydrostatic steering system shown in Fig. 7-59 utilizes the right-hand pump of the dual pump. The filter is an in-line filter and the pressure relief valve and flow control valve are part of the closed center directional (steering control) valve. The purpose of the neutralizer valve is to stop the steering action just before the tractor or machine completes its full left- or right-hand turn.

HAND METERING UNIT The steering control valve (hand metering unit) used is slightly different from that previously explained. The steering shaft is supported in a housing that is bolted to the valve body. The steering wheel is splined to one end of the shaft, and the spool to the other. The spool is linked with the sleeve through a multileaf spring, and the left-

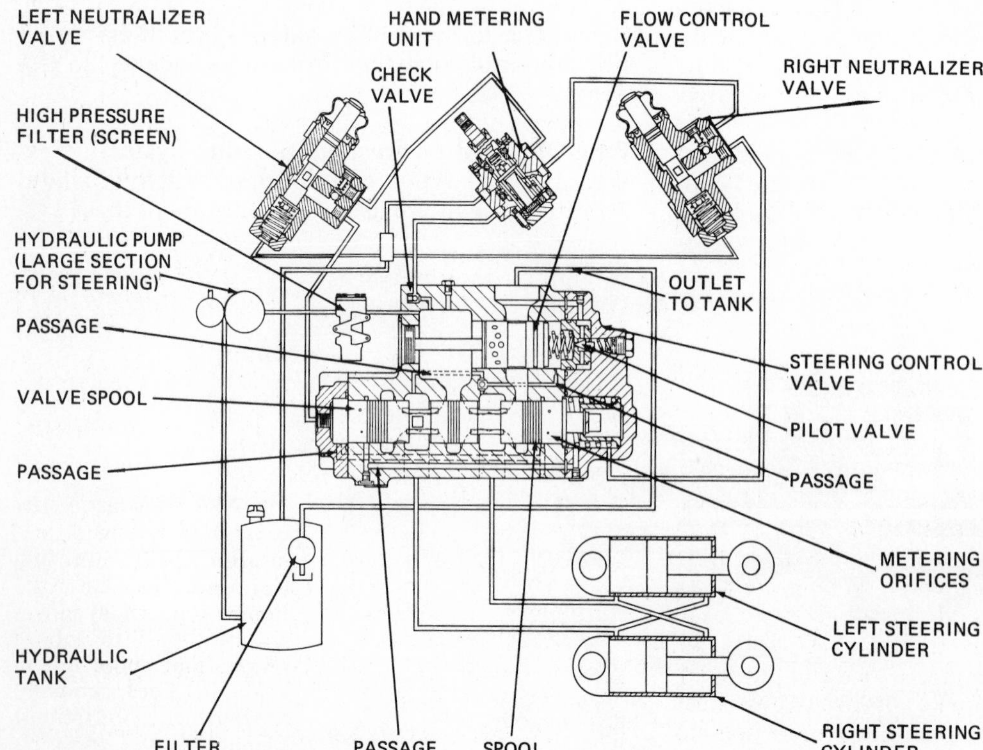

Fig. 7-59 Schematic view of a pilot-operated hydrostatic steering system. (*Caterpillar Tractor Co.*)

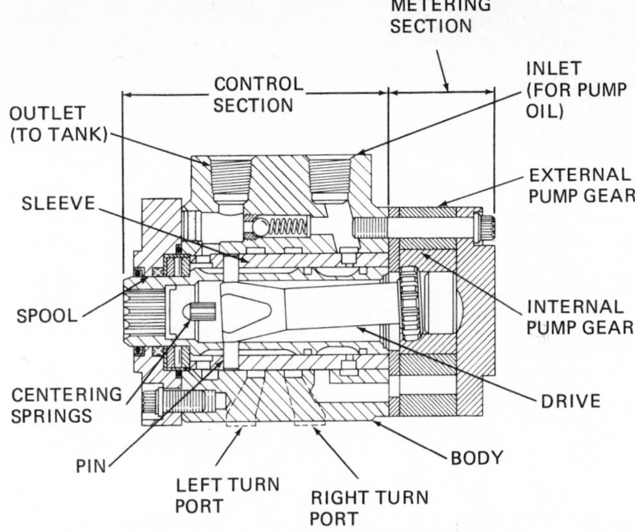

Fig. 7-60 Sectional view of the hand metering unit. (*Caterpillar Tractor Co.*)

hand end of the drive is loosely linked, through a pin, with the spool and sleeve. The other end of the drive is splined to the gerotor. See Fig. 7-60.

STEERING CONTROL VALVE This valve is a three-position closed center pilot-operated spool valve having a flow control valve and relief valve within. Its two lower ports are connected with the steering cylinders; the lower left- and right-hand ports are connected to the left- and right-hand neutralizer valves, the upper right-hand port is connected to the reservoir, and the upper left-hand port serves as the pump inlet port and also supplies oil over the check valve to the steering control valve.

NEUTRALIZER VALVES These two-position spring-opened valves close off the pilot oil flow when the valve spool contacts the striker stud, because this mechanical action forces the valve spool into the closed position.

OPERATION (ENGINE OPERATING AND STEERING WHEEL IN A FIXED POSITION) Oil from the large hydraulic pump flows through the in-line oil filter, into the steering control valve, and from there over the check valve to the hand metering unit. Because both valves are of the closed center design, the oil flow causes a pressure rise which moves the flow control valve. Oil then passes to the outlet port and back to the reservoir, maintaining a fixed pressure within the system. Under this condition, the oil pressure within the steering cylinders and in the left- and right-hand outlet ports is equal and is exerted through the passages onto the pilot valve (see Fig. 7-59). Therefore, if the system pressure exceeds the maximum set pressure because the front wheels resist turning, or an external side force is placed on either front wheel, the pilot valve is forced open. As a result the pressure will then reduce to the set operating pressure, thereby protecting the entire hydraulic system as well as the spindle, axle, frame, etc.

OPERATION (RIGHT-HAND TURN) When the steering wheel is turned to the right, the steering shaft turns the spool, which force is transmitted to the drive pin and to the drive, which turns the gerotor. The steering shaft's rotating force is also transmitted to the leaf springs; however, the sleeves resist rotation and the leaf springs bend before the rotating force moves the sleeve. This creates a difference of a few degrees between the sleeve and the spool and brings the holes in the sleeve into alignment with the grooves in the spool. (See Fig. 7-61.) Pump oil can then flow through the lower holes in the sleeve, into the left-hand grooves in the spool, and to the three charging pockets in the gerotor. The three discharging pockets of the gerotor force the oil into the body, routing it as follows: through the fourth row of holes in the sleeve, into the spool groove, out through the fifth row of holes in the sleeve, out through a port to the neutralizer valve, into the inlet port, around the spool, and out of the outlet port into the left port of the steering control valve. Oil returning from the right-hand port of the steering control valve flows to and through the right-hand neutralizer valve and from there into one port of the hand metering unit. It then passes through the sixth row of holes in the sleeve, into the spool groove, out through the seventh row of holes in the sleeve to the return port, and back to the reservoir. The pilot oil that enters the left-hand port of the steering control valve flows into the left-hand chamber and into a passage, but it is blocked by the valve spool at the right (see Fig. 7-62). The pilot pressure moves the spool to the right because an orifice reduces the oil flow (pressure drop) in passage 17 and in chamber 21. This spool movement now allows pump oil to flow past the spool land and into and then out of the left outlet port to the steering cylinders. The steering oil (under pressure) is directed over an orifice onto the pilot valve, and at the same time seats the resolver valve, closing the passage to the right turn outlet. Oil re-

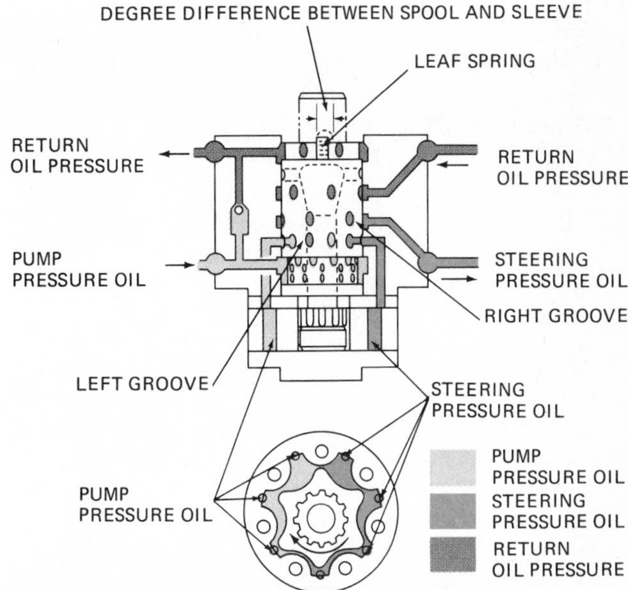

Fig. 7-61 Schematic view of oil flow in a right-hand turn. (*J I Case Company Agricultural Equipment Division*)

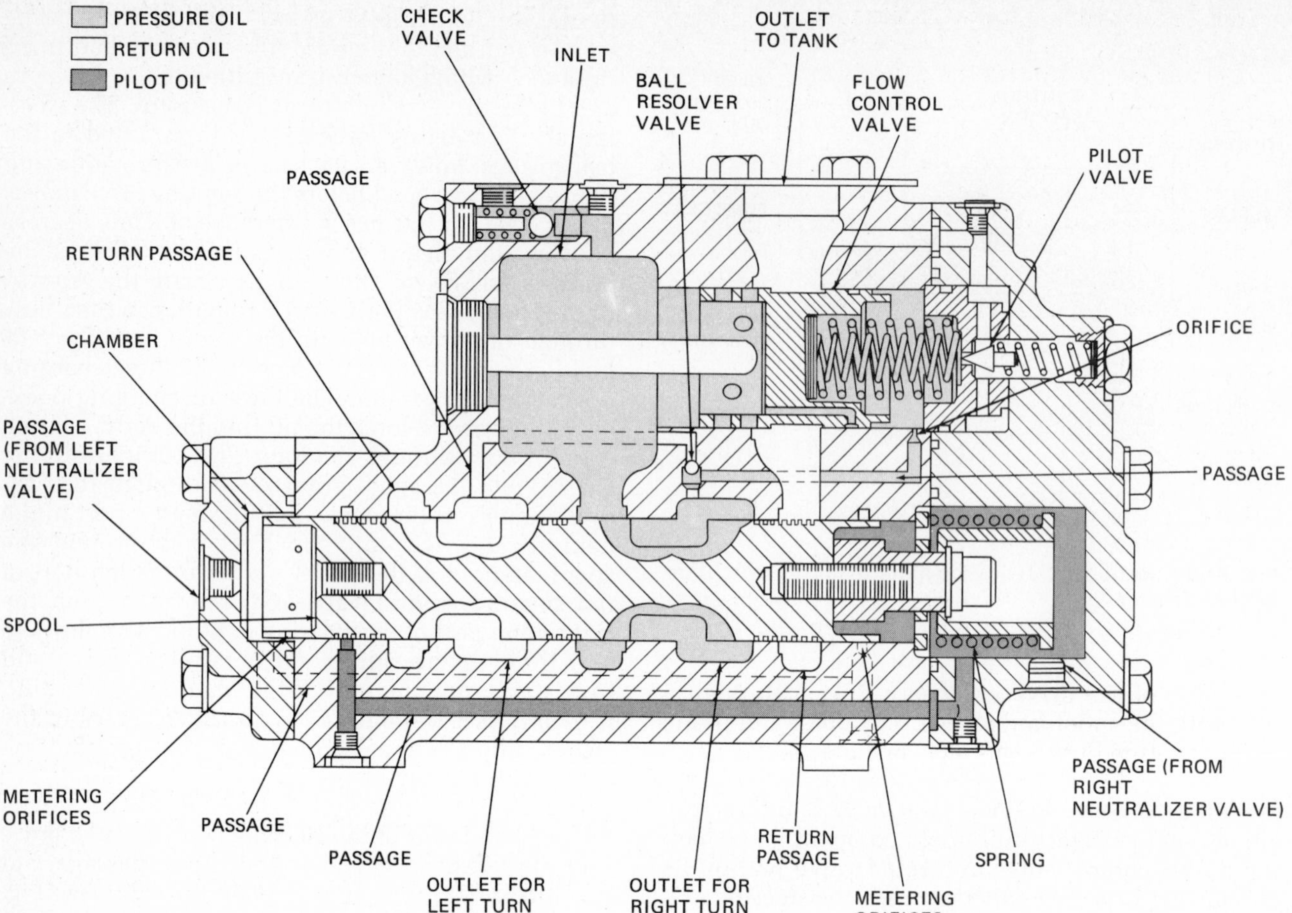

Fig. 7-62 Steering control valve in right-hand turn position. (*Caterpillar Tractor Co.*)

turning from the steering cylinders enters the right port, flows past the spool land into a passage, and flows through the tank outlet.

When the steering wheel rotation is stopped, the pilot oil flow is stopped and the spool spring moves the spool to the left (neutral position). In order to move the spool to the left, the oil pressure in the chamber must be released, and this is done by allowing the oil to flow through the orifice and passage into the spring area. Now the spring can move the spool to neutral, confining the oil to the steering cylinders.

NOTE As the steering wheel is turned quickly, the variation between the spool grooves and sleeve holes is reduced, which causes an increase in pilot oil flow. The gerotor therefore meters more oil, and causes the steering valve to move farther. Therefore more oil flows to and from the steering cylinders. When the steering wheel rotation speed is reduced, less pilot oil will flow to the steering valve because the gerotor meters less oil; then the leaf springs have reduced alignment between the spool grooves and the sleeve holes.

When the steering wheel rotation ceases or when the wheel is held in a fixed position, all motion within the steering control valve stops. The leaf springs then move the sleeve to a position where no holes align with the grooves. This blocks the oil flow from the power steering pump to the metering section.

The oil flow and mechanical action within the steering control valve for a right-hand turn is precisely the reverse. The components which were moved to the left now move to the right. The former pilot pressure now becomes return pressure, and the control valve spool is moved to the left rather than to the right.

If, during a left- or right-hand turn, the front wheels come to the end of a complete turn, the neutralizer spool contacts the striker stud and the spool moves to the right against its spring force. As this action blocks the pilot oil flow from the steering control valve, the pilot oil pressure from the steering valve opens the ball check valve, allowing the oil to flow to the steering control valve and thus causing the spring of the steering valve to center its spool (neutral).

Troubleshooting a Hydrostatic Steering System Although different hydrostatic steering systems may be subject to different problems because of the variations in their steering control valves and additional hydraulic valves, nevertheless there are some basic troubleshooting rules applicable to all systems. For instance, when testing, checking, or inspecting, move the motor vehicle, tractor, etc., onto level ground away from the general work area. Have only one person operate the motor vehicle, etc., during testing. Block the rear wheels and safely position the loader, grader blade, backhoe, etc.

Before beginning physical checks, visuallly inspect the entire steering system (hydraulically as well as mechanically). Check the oil level and color—if it is milky, air has entered the system. Check the hoses, tubings, and fittings for leaks or damage and for kinks or twists. Inspect the oil filter and, if you deem it necessary, analyze the contamination. When testing, use a flowmeter to determine the performance of individual components.

Here are some basic problems common to all systems:

1. Steering wheel turns but there is no steering response. The problem could be excessively low oil level, worn or damaged steering control valve, sticking or damaged control valve spool, damaged sleeve and body, damaged steering cylinder piston seals, excessively worn steering pump, damaged drive coupling, relief valve spring broken, or valve sticking in the open position.
2. Steering wheel is hard to turn, or very slow to respond. The cause could be cold oil, incorrect oil viscosity, steering pump or drive coupling failure, hydraulic lines improperly connected, damaged or worn parts in the steering control valve or steering valve, damaged relief valve, steering control valve incorrectly assembled, damaged steering cylinder, low tire pressure, high mechanical friction, or kingpins worn or broken.
3. Left-hand turn responds faster than right-hand turn, or vice versa. The cause could be a sticky, worn, or damaged steering control valve spool or sleeve, flow control valve out of adjustment, sticking steering valve spool, or broken spring.
4. Machine veers. The cause could be a sticking spool or sleeve (or both), broken leaf springs, steering valve spool sticking, spring broken, or plugged orifices.

TESTING If the steering system fails to operate properly and external checks have not revealed the problem, install a flowmeter (T hookup—see material on hydraulics) and test the efficiency of the supply system and for air entering the system. Check the efficiency of the power steering pump. Check the relief valve setting and efficiency of the steering cylinders.

If these tests do not expose the cause of failure, measure the steering wheel slippage to determine if the steering control valve and steering valve are worn. To do this, install a socket to the steering wheel nut, using a torque wrench as the handle. Start the engine and operate it at the speed recommended in the service manual. Now rotate the torque wrench and note the required torque effort (pound-inches [Newton-meters]) to maintain rotation of the steering wheel. If the torque is below specification, then the steering control valve or the steering valve spool is worn. To determine which is at fault, stop the engine and repeat the procedure. If the rotating torque has gained one-half the previous value, the oil leakage causing the steering wheel to slip is in the steering valve. If the torque remains the same, the oil leakage is caused by a worn or damaged spool or sleeve, or the body of the steering control valve is worn or damaged.

Another method recommended by some manufacturers to determine steering wheel slippage is as follows: Operate the engine at the recommended speed and turn the steering wheel sufficiently to bring the front wheel against either stop. Now place a torque wrench on the steering nut, rotate the wrench and maintain a torque of about 3 lb · ft [43.8 N · m]. The rate of steering wheel slippage should not exceed the given specification, which is about 5 rpm. If the slippage is higher, stop the engine and repeat the procedure. If the slippage rate drops to half the rpm, the problem is in the steering valve. If the steering slippage remains the same (above 5 rpm), the problem is in the steering control valve.

TURNING ANGLE AND STEERING CYLINDER ADJUSTMENT To prevent steering cylinder damage, the turning angle must be properly adjusted. This can be achieved by the following methods: adjusting the ball joint to bring the overall length of the steering cylinders to the specified dimension, adjusting the striker stud, or adjusting the stop studs. In all cases, the piston is prevented from hammering on the cylinder gland (head) when the vehicle makes its maximum left- or right-hand turn.

To check the adjustment, if possible raise the front end and block the machine. Check the toe-in and if necessary adjust it. Start the engine; turn the steering wheel slowly to bring the left- or right-hand spindle against the axle stop. If the spindle does not contact the axle *fixed* stop, loosen the ball joint clamp nut and turn the piston rod. If this is not possible, remove the steering cylinder ball joint from the steering arm and then turn it counterclockwise to increase the overall length of the steering cylinder so that the spindle contacts the stop before the steering cylinder piston bottoms out. Reinstall and torque the ball stud nut to the recommended torque and, if applicable, install the cotter pin. Repeat this procedure with the other steering cylinder.

NOTE Make certain that the hoses and fittings clear all obstructions when the axle is tilted against its stop and the wheels are against the left- or right-hand stop bolt.

Another service manual recommends the following: Jack up the front axle. Then measure and if necessary adjust the toe-in. Next, disconnect the steering cylinder piston rods from the steering spindles and turn the front wheel by hand until the stop bolt is against the axle housing. Lay a straightedge, as shown in Fig. 7-63, against the machined axle flange and measure the distance from the right-hand side of the straightedge to the center of the steering spindle bore. If the measurement is less or more than specified, loosen the jam nut and turn the stop bolt to achieve the proper distance; then lock the adjust-

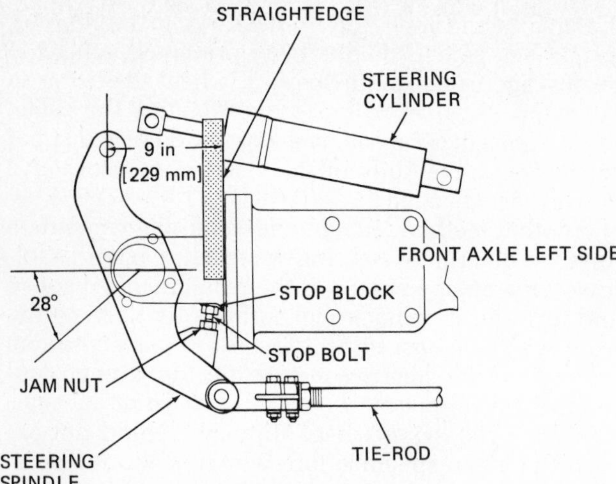

Fig. 7-63 Method used to check and adjust front wheel turning angle. (*J I Case Company Agricultural Equipment Division*)

ment and repeat the procedure at the right-hand front wheel. **NOTE** When the adjustment is made, the front wheels are limited to a turning angle of 28° and the steering cylinder piston will not bottom.

To check the adjustment of the neutralizer valve (axle stop), raise the bucket, release the brakes, and place a piece of putty or similar material of about 0.6 in [15.24 mm] in thickness onto each side of the front frame stop. Then operate the engine at low idle speed. Now, quickly steer the (articulated) machine into left- and right-hand stops. Stop the engine and measure the thickness of the inserted material. If it is between 0.38 and 0.50 in [9.7 and 12.7 mm], the striker stud is adjusted properly. If the thickness is greater, adjust the stud. This is done by loosening the locknut, turning the stud clockwise, and then locking the adjustment. This brings the neutralizer valve into the shutoff position later. If the material thickness is less than 0.38 in [9.7 mm], turn the striker stud counterclockwise, as this will bring the neutralizer valve earlier to the shutoff position.

Self-Steering Axles To reduce trailer drag and increase maneuverability, tire life, load capacity, and fuel economy, self-steering axles are used (Fig. 7-64). They are of the conventional front axle design, with a relatively large positive caster to ensure immediate reaction to side thrust when cornering and to automatically bring the wheels into a turn. To fulfill these functions a torpress chamber is fastened to the axle beam and adjusting rods are bolted to the left- and right-hand sides of the chamber ends. Heavily constructed brackets are clamped to the tracking bar (tie-rod) and, when the vehicle travels in a straight direction, a clearance of less than 0.04 in [1 mm] exists between the adjusting screw and the brackets. An air-actuated mechanical lock is used to lock the track bar, converting the self-steering axle into a fixed axle. The air system components used to charge and maintain a fixed pressure within the torpress chamber and to actuate the backup lock are shown in Fig. 7-65. The pressure-variation valve is a three-position pressure-reducing valve. When in the shutoff position, the reservoir air is blocked, exhausting the air pressure from the chamber. When in the half- or full-charge position, the valve maintains the desired air pressure within the torpress chamber. The two-way valve shown in the illustration is used to actuate the backup lock.

The self-steering axle beams can be fastened to nearly all suspensions since the operation of the axle is independent of the suspension. They may be mounted any place between the trailer and tractor tires, or in front of or behind a tandem or single-drive axle or dead axle, or behind the tandem axle of a semitrailer. See Figs. 7-66 and 7-67 for two examples of placement. **NOTE** Self-steering axles having an air suspension can be lifted up through the action of air cylinders.

WHEEL ALIGNMENT

Wheel alignment is the measuring of the interrelated angles and distances between axles, wheels, and

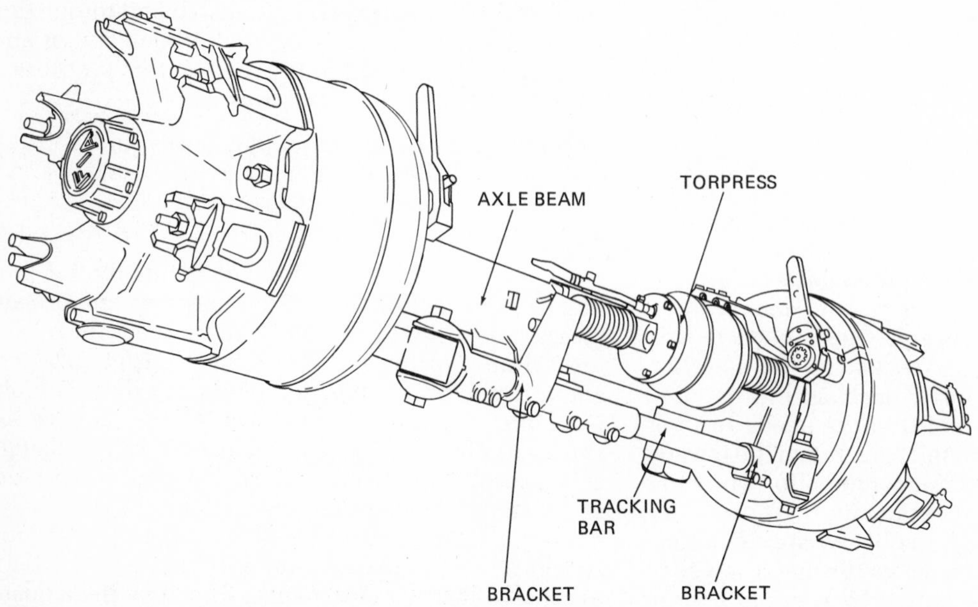

Fig. 7-64 View of a self-steering axle.

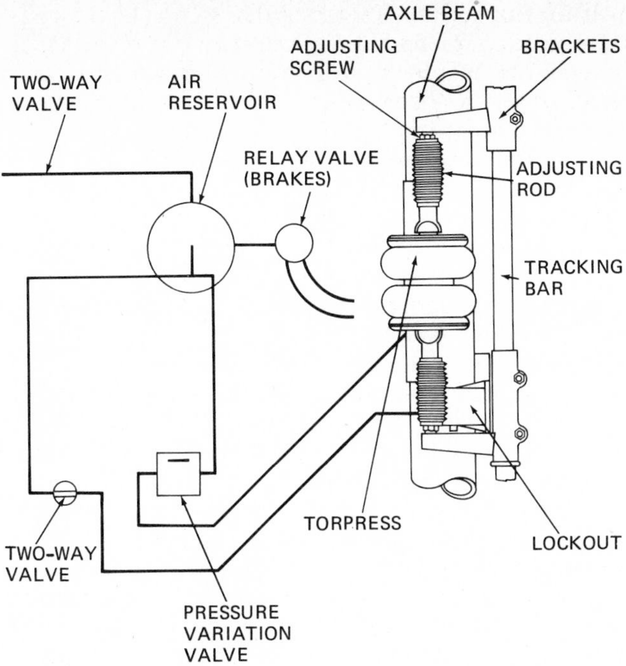

Fig. 7-65 Schematic view of air system and axle components.

Fig. 7-66 Forty-five-foot semitrailer with a center steering axle.

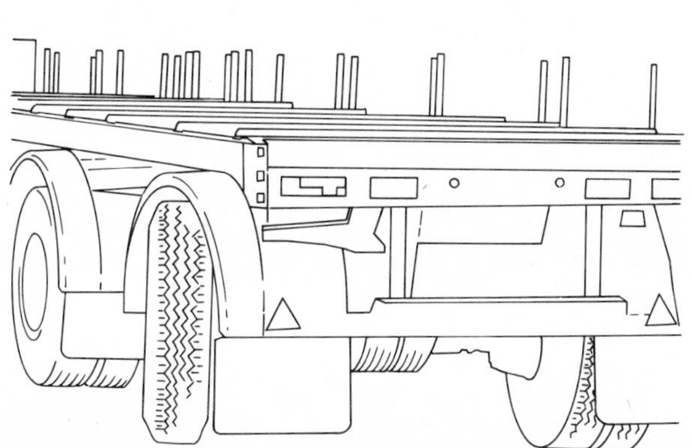

Fig. 7-67 Rear-rear trailer self-steering axle during a left-hand turn.

frames, as well as the adjustments needed to make those angles and distances agree with service manual specifications. The correct relative position of all wheels to the frame and axles assures a true free-rolling movement over the road either in the straight-ahead direction or during a turn.

When neglected, wheel alignment can be a most costly maintenance factor. It increases tire and suspension wear, while it decreases ease of handling, safety, and fuel mileage. Unfortunately, alignment angles and distances change over a period of time even under average or ordinary operating conditions. It is therefore essential that the entire motor vehicle be checked and serviced at regular intervals to reduce overall wear, to prevent perhaps a fatal accident, and to reduce repair costs and vehicle downtime.

Preliminary Checks If a wheel alignment is to be meaningful, numerous preliminary checks must first be made. If you have a scuff gauge (Fig. 7-68) to check toe-in of the front and rear wheels, check first the tire pressure and adjust it as needed to the recommended specification. Next, check the toe-in of the front and rear wheels. To do this, drive the motor vehicle very slowly over the scuff gauge while firmly holding the steering wheel. For an accurate reading use at least a 20-ft [6.1-m] straight approach. As the front or rear tires roll over the scuff gauge platform, each tire comes in contact with a blade. Because of the side drag (scuff action) of the tires, the blades move toward each other if the motor vehicle has toe-in, and apart if it has toe-out. The movement of the blades is transferred over levers and rods to a dial, or electronically transmitted to a dial which indicates the combined slip of both tires in feet per mile [millimeters per kilometer]. A toe-in reading of 0 to 3 ft per mi [0 to 915 mm per 1.61 km] for the front axle indicates the toe needs no adjustment. However, the rear tire should register a toe-in reading of not more than 1 ft per mi [305 mm per 1.61 km]. Any reading beyond this specification means a thorough check of the motor vehicle and a wheel alignment is required.

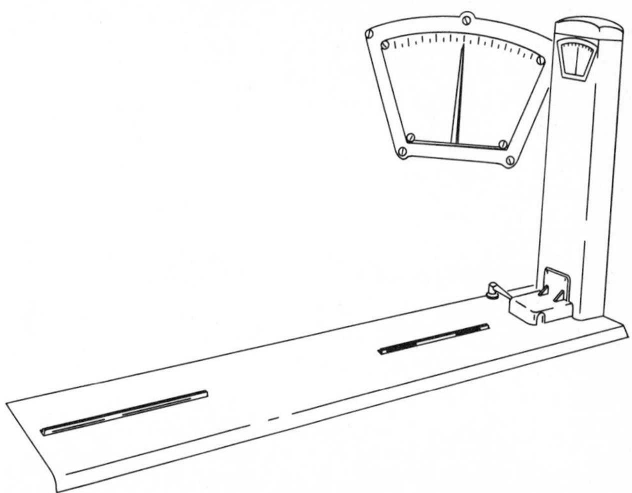

Fig. 7-68 Scuff gauge. (*Bear Manufacturing Co.*)

Following is a checklist outlining other preliminary steps that should be taken (although it is not necessary to do them in the order given here):

1. Check the wear pattern, size, and pressure of the tires.
2. Check for loose wheel mountings.
3. Measure frame and spring heights and if necessary measure frame alignment.
4. Raise the vehicle off the ground, block it securely, and then check for bent rims, high-speed shimmy, and out-of-roundness of the tires. This can be done by spinning the front wheels and driving the rear wheels.
5. Check the wheel bearing adjustment.
6. Check wear of the kingpins, the thrust bearings, or the ball joints.
7. Check the front and rear suspension for damage and wear.
8. Check the condition and mountings of the shock absorbers.
9. Check the tie-rods and drag link for damage or bends and check the ends for wear.
10. Check the adjustment of the steering gear, the tightness of the steering gear and steering column mounting bolts or nuts, and the alignment and tightness of the steering shaft coupling(s).
11. Check the steering gear operation for roughness and stickiness.

Replace the damaged or worn parts and if necessary adjust the wheel bearings, match the tires, balance the wheels, then continue with the wheel alignment.

Suspension and Steering Problems The number of checks can be minimized and time saved if the operator gives a specific complaint or if the tire problem is obvious.

If the tires are scuffed, the problem could be any of the following: incorrect tire pressure, too much toe-in or toe-out, bent rims, tires out-of-round, lack of kingpin lubrication, a damaged thrust bearing, a bent steering knuckle, front wheel bearings adjusted too loosely, or bearings and/or spindle worn. Worn or loose steering linkage parts, kingpins, bushings, or ball joints also lead to tire scuffing.

If the tires are cupped, the cause could be one or more of the following: incorrect tire pressure, wheel assembly (including the brake drum) out of balance, damaged shock absorber(s), weak spring(s), brakes dragging, the wheel bearings adjusted too loosely, bearings or spindle worn, steering linkage parts, kingpins, or ball joint worn or loose, incorrect camber adjustment.

If the complaint is front wheel shimmy, look for any of the following: low or uneven tire pressure, wheel assembly out of balance, front wheel bearings adjusted too loosely, bearings and/or spindle worn, steering gear not adjusted properly (or its mountings are loose), steering linkage damaged or worn, high wheel runout, weak spring(s), damaged shock absorbers, damaged or worn kingpins or thrust bearing, too much toe-out or toe-in, steering knuckle bent, or incorrect or uneven caster.

If the complaint is front and/or rear wheel tramp the cause could be wheel assembly out of balance, uneven tire size, front or rear springs weak or damaged, or shock absorber not operating properly.

If the motor vehicle wanders, the cause could be low or uneven tire pressure, loose steering gear mounting, lack of steering gear lubrication, worn steering gear or gear adjustment too tight or too loose, lack of kingpin lubrication, thrust bearing worn or damaged, too much toe-out or toe-in, broken spring center bolt, worn spring shackles, or bent steering knuckle, spindle, or frame.

If the motor vehicle pulls to one side, check for low or uneven tire pressure, scuffed tires, uneven tire size, weak or broken front and rear spring(s), broken center bolt, worn shackles, excessive or uneven camber or caster, and/or bent frame.

If the motor vehicle pulls to one side when the brakes are being applied, the cause could be low or uneven tire pressure, excessive caster, bent steering knuckle, loose or worn wheel bearings, worn front suspension, weak springs, damaged shock absorber, broken spring or center bolt, contaminated brake linings, excessive flow restriction in a brake line leading to one front wheel.

If the complaint is excessive steering effort, the problem may be low or uneven tire pressure, uneven (front wheel) tire size, worn or damaged kingpins, bushings, or thrust bearing, lack of steering gear and steering linkage lubrication, excessively tight steering gear adjustment, steering bent knuckle or spindle, broken or weak springs, or bent frame.

If the complaint is excessive steering gear movement, the cause could be loosely adjusted steering gear, loose steering gear or steering column mountings, worn or damaged steering linkage parts, worn wheel bearings, kingpins, bushings, or ball joints, or loose wheel bearing adjustment.

Wheel Alignment Checks Numerous types of wheel alignment test equipment are available, ranging from the simple to the very sophisticated, and all measure the difference in angle between the wheel and the true vertical line. As one would expect, the measurement accuracy of the simple devices is $\pm\frac{1}{8}°$ whereas the light beam and electronic test instruments are very precise. However, it is not the test instruments that perform the alignment, it is you, the mechanic. Moreover, the best test instrument is only as effective as you make it.

Simple wheel alignment equipment consists of three test gauges: a turning radius gauge, a toe-in gauge, and a camber/caster gauge (see Fig. 7-69 and 7-70). The purpose of the turning radius gauge is to measure the turning radius of the front wheels. It consists of a sturdy frame to which the turntable (semi- or full-floating) is attached. An adjustable degree scale is attached to the frame, graduated from 0° to 30° right and 0° to 30° left.

The toe-in gauge measures the toe. It consists of an extendable bar, to which two adjustable stands and two adjustable pointers are attached.

The magnetic type caster/camber gauges vary somewhat but all have a magnet to hold the gauge

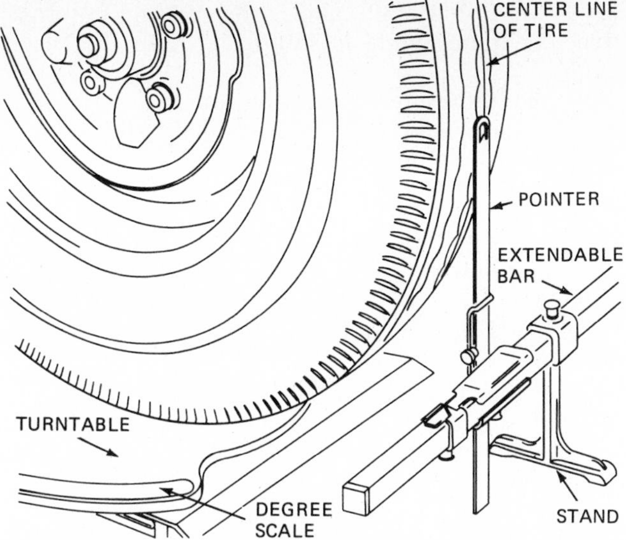

Fig. 7-69 Simple wheel alignment equipment.

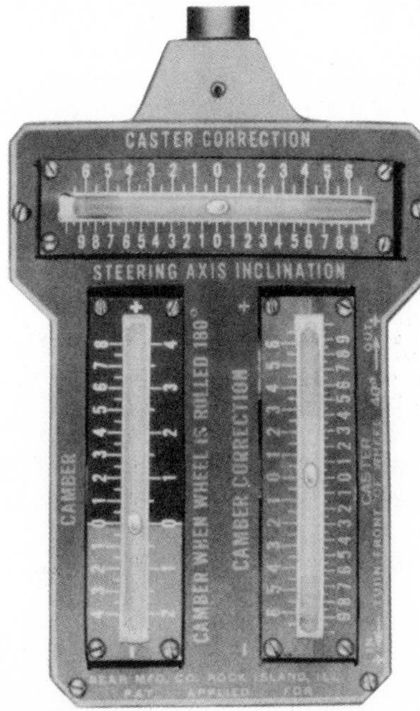

Fig. 7-70 Camber/caster gauge.

to the wheel hub or to a wheel clamp, and have either two or three spirit levels. The one shown in Fig. 7-70 has, in addition, a series of templates (scales) that are calibrated to a certain model of motor vehicle.

SETTING UP THE EQUIPMENT To measure front wheel alignment with the gauges illustrated, just drive the motor vehicle onto a hard level surface. Raise the front end and position one radius gauge (lock pins installed) under each front wheel with the degree scale pointing outward. Turn the steering wheel to point the front wheels into the straight-ahead direction and then lower the tires onto the radius gauges. Make certain that the tires contact the center of the turntable. Remove the two lock pins which hold the turntable in a fixed position and adjust both radius

scales to zero. If the turning gauge is of the full-floating design, apply the brakes. If it is of the semi-floating design, do *not* apply the brakes.

Remove the wheel hub cap or cover. On larger wheels, install the wheel clamps to the wheel (see Fig. 7-71). Clean the gauge and wheel hub surfaces. If necessary, remove nicks and burrs from the latter to assure that the gauge fits true to the hub, and then attach the gauge to the wheel hub or wheel clamp. This is done by placing the center pin onto the spindle center and then the gauge onto the wheel hub.

NOTE On small motor vehicles, first settle the suspension by grasping the front bumper and bouncing the front of the vehicle up and down several times. Now rotate both gauges so that the caster corrective scale bubble is at zero. If applicable, place the specified template onto the four screw stud pins.

MEASURING RUNOUT If you attached the caster/camber gauge to the wheel clamp (Fig. 7-71), the wheel runout must be checked and adjusted to achieve a true camber/caster reading. To do this, first make

Fig. 7-71 Camber/caster gauge attached to wheel clamp. (*FMC Corporation*)

certain that the wheel clamp fingers rest firmly against the rim and that the gauge rests firmly against its seat. Raise the front wheel off the turning radius gauge, note the reading on the camber scale, and, while turning the wheel, further note the point of the highest wheel runout. Mark this point on the tire and position it in the forward or rearward direction. This action brings the true wheel center line into the vertical position, splitting the runout. Next, lower the front end to bring the tires onto the turning radius gauge. **NOTE** If the wheel clamp has a runout adjustment, make the wheel runout with this device. The end result will be the same.

READING THE CAMBER Stabilize the front end and then read the camber from the camber scale by visually aligning the center of the bubble with the left- or right-hand camber graduation. If the bubble has floated toward the plus sign the wheel has positive camber, and if it has floated toward the negative sign it has negative camber.

MEASURING CASTER Whether or not the front wheels have center point steering or are of the inclined kingpin design, the front wheels must be turned from 0° to 20° left, and then from the 20° left position to the 20° right position. This measures the amount the end of the spindle moves downward from the true horizontal.

Whether the motor vehicle has an inclined kingpin or is of the ball joint design, with *no* caster the spindle end, at the end of both the 20° left- and 20° right-hand turns, will have moved downward an equal distance from the true horizontal. However, if the same motor vehicle *has* positive or negative caster, the spindle at the end of the left- and right-hand turns will have moved a different distance down. See Fig. 7-71. When the motor vehicle is of the center point design and has *no* caster, the spindle end during the 40° of rotation travels in the true horizontal line. However, when the same motor vehicle *has* positive or negative caster, the spindle ends behave as shown in Fig. 7-8. It is therefore very important that you start the caster measurement at the correct wheel position; otherwise your reading will be reversed. In addition, when the motor vehicle is designed to carry loads, the service manual may give the caster specification for the loaded or unloaded condition (or both). If you measure the caster angle when the specification given is for the loaded condition you must, if your vehicle is not loaded, measure the frame angle in order to obtain the correct caster angle. In most cases it will be negative because the rear suspension rises more than the front suspension.

Listed below are some relatively simple rules to help you determine the correct caster angle:

1. If the frame angle is negative and the caster reading is positive, both angles must be added.
2. If the frame angle and caster reading are both negative, the frame angle is subtracted from the caster angle.
3. If the frame angle and caster reading are positive, the frame angle is subtracted from the caster angle.
4. If the frame angle is positive and the caster reading is negative, both angles are added. Suppose that the caster angle measurement is 3° positive, and the frame angle is $\frac{1}{2}$° (30′) negative (high at the rear). The correct caster angle would be: $3 + \frac{1}{2} = 3\frac{1}{2}$°, or 3°30′. Comparing this total angle against the specification will determine if an adjustment is necessary.

To check caster, zero both turning radius scales, then turn the steering wheel to make a right-hand turn so that the left-hand front wheel is turned to 20° (pointing toward the center). Center the left-hand wheel caster gauge bubble by turning the adjusting screw. Next, turn the steering wheel to the left so that the left-hand front wheel is at the 20° left-hand turn position. Rotate the gauge to level it and then, by visually aligning the center of the bubble with the left- or right-hand caster graduation, read the degree of caster. If the bubble is toward the positive sign, the caster is positive; if it is toward the negative sign, the caster is negative. **NOTE** Had you started when the front wheel was turned 20° to the left, and then turned it 40° to the right, you would have the same caster reading but with the "opposite" sign (positive or negative).

If the caster (or camber) on one or both wheels is excessively out of specification (which in most cases would involve a negative reading) and yet the wear of the kingpins, bushings, or ball joints is minimal and the wheel bearings are adjusted to specification, you may assume that the spindle, steering knuckle, or axle is bent, or on an independent front wheel suspension that the steering knuckle, spindle, upper or lower control arms are bent. To confirm any one of these, attach the camber/caster gauge to the spindle nut using the attachments supplied with the gauge and perform a caster check. This will now check the steering axle inclination because the gauge is attached to the spindle end. See Fig. 7-72.

When checking the camber angle of the rear wheels to determine if the axle is bent, install the wheel clamps to the rear wheels and attach the caster/camber gauge to it. Check the wheel runout and then from the gauge read the camber angle.

MAGNETIC CASTER/CAMBER GAUGE The magnetic caster/camber gauge shown in Fig. 7-73 has two scales fastened to the knob, and two spirit-leveling devices. The outside (camber) scale, divided into eighths of degrees, indicates 0° to 2° positive and 0° to 2° negative camber. The inner (caster) scale has identical graduations. When turning the knob, the camber/caster scale rotates with the knob, and through a screw and lever the camber/caster spirit leveller is tilted up or down depending on the knob rotation. The inner scale can be rotated independently by turning the bolt head.

When the magnetic gauge is attached to the wheel hub or the wheel clamp, center (by rotating the gauge) the inside spirit level bubble, then turn the knob until the camber/caster spirit level bubble is in

Fig. 7-72 Method of attaching gauge to check steering axis inclination. (*Bear Manufacturing Company*)

the center. Now read from the camber scale the camber degree. Figure 7-73 shows the camber is about $\frac{3}{8}$° negative.

To measure caster, turn the steering wheel to the right so that the left-hand turning radius gauge reads 20°. Rotate the gauge to center the inside bubble, and by turning the knob center the caster/camber spirit level bubble. Now turn the bolt head which turns the caster scale and set it to zero. Next, rotate the front wheels to the left until the left-hand turning radius gauge scale is at 20°. Again rotate the gauge to center the bubble and rotate the knob to center the caster/camber spirit level bubble. **NOTE** The rotation of the knob turns both scales. Now read the caster angle from the inner caster scale.

Camber and Caster Adjustment for I-Beam Axle Most motor vehicles with an independent front wheel suspension use the same method to adjust caster and camber, and *all* I-beam axles use the same method to adjust caster—that is, by placing tapered shims between the spring and axle seat (Fig. 7-74). Where shims are already being used but an increase of caster is necessary, replace the shim with one having a greater taper. Never use two shims, as they will not stay in place. When the shim is positioned with the thicker part toward the rear, the caster will increase toward the positive. When placed with the thicker part toward the front, the caster will increase toward negative.

Assuming you have equal caster on both front wheels and you have to increase positive caster by 2°30′, first apply penetrating oil to the U-bolt threads (spring clips), loosen the nuts about 10 turns, and raise the front frame. This will create a space between the frame and axle spring seat. Now insert a 2°30′ shim (having the same width as the spring) in the space created, so that the thicker end faces toward the rear, the center bolt rests in the slot or shim hole, and the shim is equally spaced from the ends of the axle seat. Next, lower the frame and retorque the nut to the specified torque.

If the inequality of the caster angle exceeds $\frac{1}{2}$° (30′), or the camber angle of one or both sides is incorrect, you will need special equipment to correct the axle twist or bend. This equipment consists of an axle correction attachment, hydraulic jacks of at least 50 tons [45 t], and a heavy-duty pit rack. See Figs. 7-75 to 7-77, which show attachments and jack installation to correct camber and caster.

Camber and Caster Adjustment for Independent Front Wheel Suspensions The method used to adjust caster and camber depends upon the design of the independent front wheel suspension (see the section on independent front wheel suspension in Unit 6). However, some of these designs, as well as the twin I-beam suspension, cannot be adjusted—that is, the angles are fixed, and when the caster and camber are not within specification the worn, damaged, or bent parts must be replaced before the specified caster or camber angle can be achieved.

The most common adjustment is the changing of the mounting points of the upper control arm shaft. This alters the front and rear pivot points of the upper control arm, thereby changing the position of the upper control arm ball joint. In Fig. 7-78, the upper control arm shaft is bolted to the inside of the frame bracket, whereas on others it may be bolted to the outside. Shims positioned between the frame bracket and shaft are used to make the adjustment. For this type of suspension, alignment is done in two steps—first for caster and then for camber angle. To change the caster angle, loosen both shaft mounting nuts by about three turns. The weight of the vehicle will separate the control arm shaft from the bracket when inboard-mounted; otherwise you have to take the weight off the wheels. Now, according to the in-

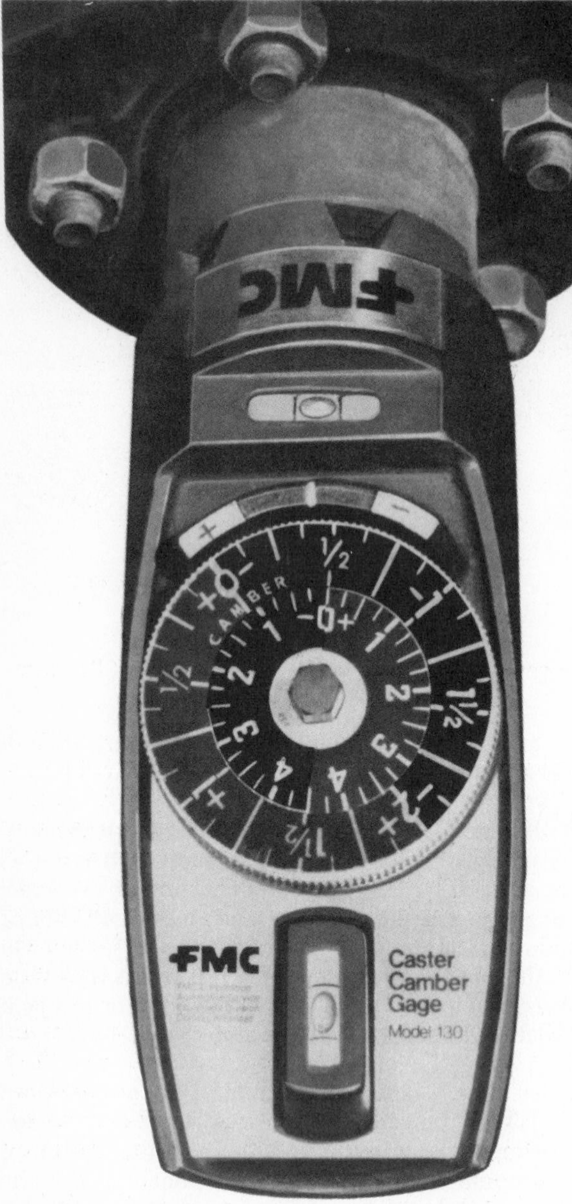

Fig. 7-73 Camber/caster gauge. (*FMC Corporation*)

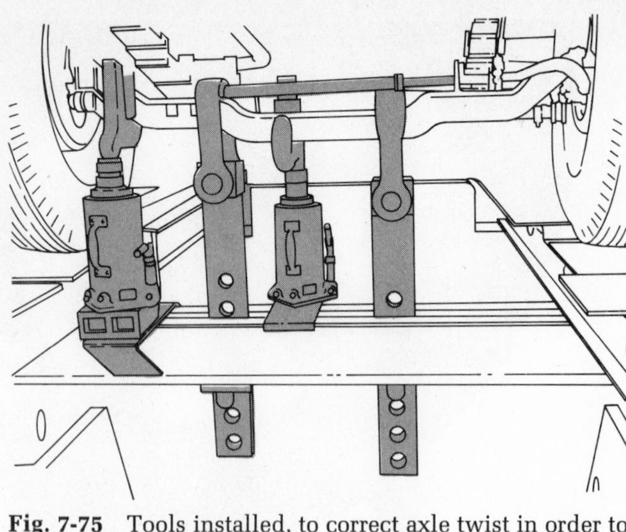

Fig. 7-75 Tools installed, to correct axle twist in order to equalize caster. (*Bear Manufacturing Company*)

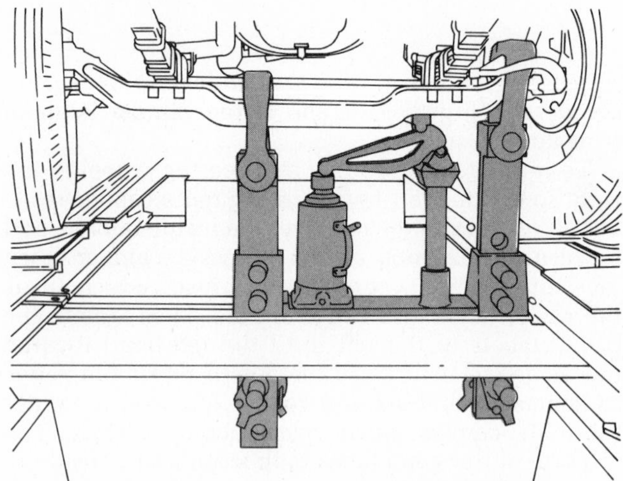

Fig. 7-76 Tools installed to increase left-side camber toward positive. (*Bear Manufacturing Company*)

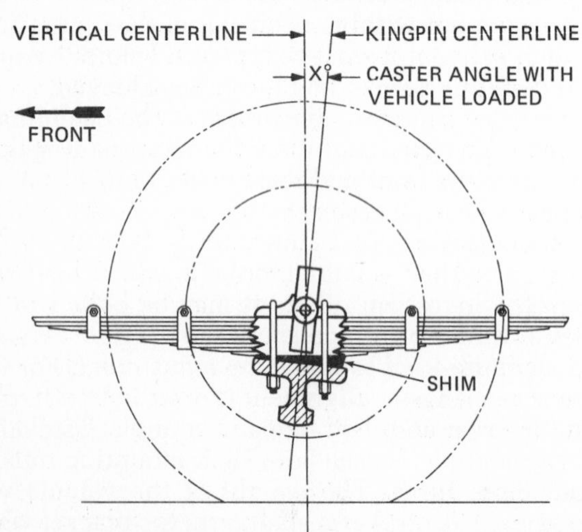

Fig. 7-74 Caster angle adjustment (positive). (*Bear Manufacturing Company*)

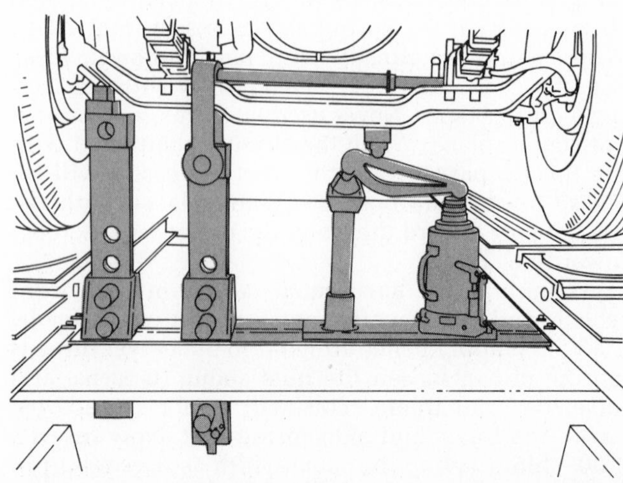

Fig. 7-77 Tools installed to decrease right-side camber. (*Bear Manufacturing Company*)

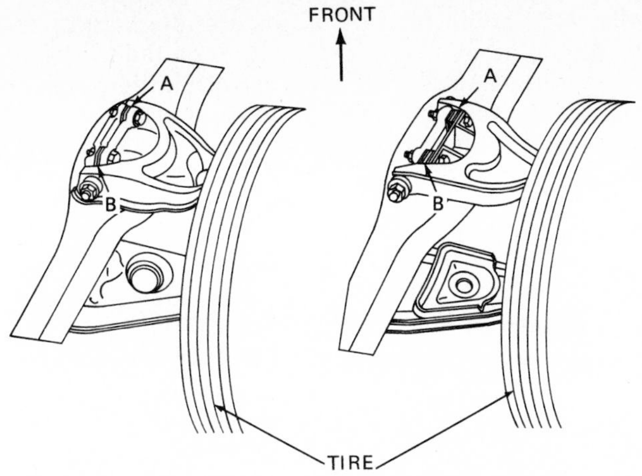

Fig. 7-78 Difference in camber and caster shim location between an inboard and outboard control arm shaft mounting. (*Bear Manufacturing Company*)

tended adjustment, install or remove shims at the points labeled A or B in Fig. 7-78, but first refer to the service manual to obtain the specified shim thickness. For example, one particular service manual states that, when inboard-mounted, a 0.30-in [7.62-mm] shim varies the caster angle by $\frac{1}{4}$°. By adding shims at point A, it will change the caster angle toward negative with practically no change in camber. In other words, if the caster angle were 2° positive or 2° negative, and a 0.30-in [7.62-mm] shim were added, then the caster angle would be $1\frac{3}{4}$° (1°45′) positive caster or $2\frac{1}{4}$° (2°15′) negative caster, respectively. Adding shims at point B, on the other hand, would change caster toward positive and camber toward negative. This means that, if the caster angle were 2° positive or 2° negative, by adding a shim of 0.30 in [7.6 mm] the caster would be $2\frac{1}{4}$° (2°15′) positive or $1\frac{3}{4}$° (1°45′) negative, respectively.

After the caster angle is adjusted and the upper control arm shaft nuts torqued to specification, check the camber angle. If it requires an adjustment, loosen the shaft nuts once more and remove an equal thickness of shim from points A and B to change camber toward positive. On the other hand, by *adding* equal thickness of shims at points A and B, camber will be changed toward the negative.

If the upper control arm shaft is bolted to the outside of the frame bracket, you must raise the front end of the motor vehicle in order to separate the shaft from that bracket. To change camber and caster, reverse the procedure outlined when the shaft is mounted on the inside.

For an independent front wheel suspension where the upper control arm (Fig. 7-79) is attached to the frame bracket through bushings, the camber and caster angles are adjusted by a cam. Basically camber and caster adjustment on this type of suspension is the same as that for the shim adjustment design, except that, instead of shims being added, two cams, one on the outside of each bushing end, are rotated to move the pivot point in or out. To change camber, loosen the nuts from the rear and front cam bolt. Now turn both cam bolts by the same amount. When rotating them in a clockwise direc-

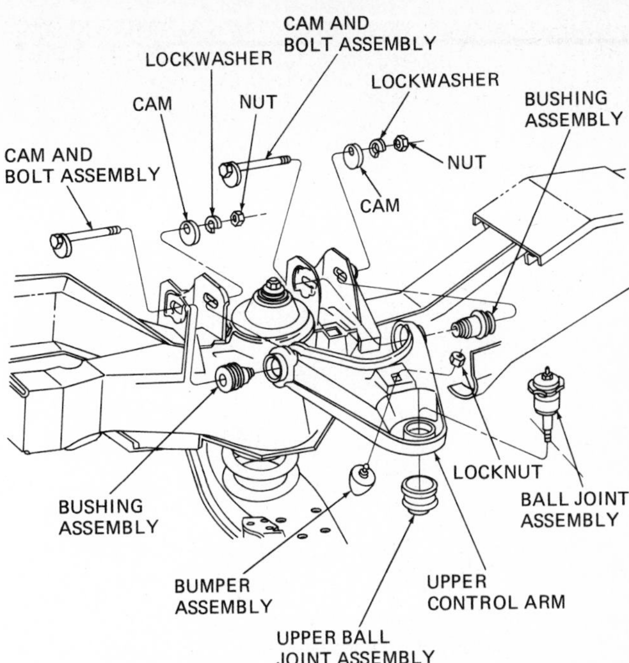

Fig. 7-79 Exploded view of upper control arm (disassembled). (*Chrysler Canada Limited*)

tion the camber is moved toward negative, and when in a counterclockwise rotation it is moved toward positive. Once camber is checked and adjusted, tighten the nuts temporarily and then check the caster angle.

To move caster toward positive, loosen the front cam bolt nut and turn the bolt counterclockwise. To move the caster toward negative, turn the cam bolt clockwise.

When the caster adjustment cannot be made with the front cam bolt, loosen the rear cam nut and then turn the rear cam bolt clockwise to move caster toward positive. Turn it counterclockwise to move caster toward negative. Note, however, that this adjustment will also change camber.

Although there are several other methods used on small trucks to adjust camber and caster, they are based on the two principles previously explained, with one exception, and that is where the caster is adjusted by lengthening or shortening the strud rod. To shorten the strut rod, the inside strut nut is turned counterclockwise and the outer clockwise. This pulls the lower control arm forward and moves caster toward positive. When the strut rod is lengthened, caster is moved toward negative. The camber adjustment on this suspension is made by turning the cams (which are located on both ends of the lower control arm). By rotating the cams clockwise, the lower control arm is moved inward and camber is moved toward positive. When they are rotated counterclockwise, the lower control arm is moved outward and camber is moved toward negative. Another method used is the one shown in Fig. 7-80.

Measuring Toe-In When using the toe-in gauge shown in Fig. 7-69, drive the motor vehicle onto a hard, level surface. Next, scribe a chalk line 1 in [25.4 mm] wide down the center of the entire

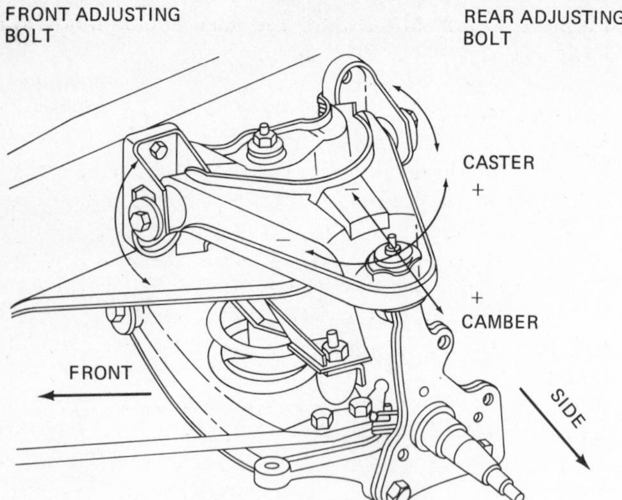

Fig. 7-80 View of alignment adjustment locations and directions. (*Chrysler Canada Limited*)

circumference of each front tire. (Scribing is done by raising the vehicle's front end, positioning a tire scriber against a tire so that its needle is under tension when resting on the center of the tire tread, and then rotating the tires forward 360°.) When the tires have been so scribed, lower the motor vehicle and drive it backward about 20 ft [6.1 m] and then forward. By driving it forward, all existing tolerances in the front suspension and steering linkage are taken up and both are under near driving conditions. This step is necessary because the front wheels will not return to their normal operating position when they have been jacked up.

Next, center the steering wheel. On small units it is possible to settle the steering linkage and the front suspension by (1) bouncing the front end of the motor vehicle up and down, and (2) with your hands positioned against the inside of the wheels spread the front of the wheels apart. Now place the toe-in gauge at the rear of the front tires, extend the bar, adjust the pointer height to the spindle height, adjust the pointers to the scribed lines on the tires, and set the indicator to zero. Next, position the gauge in front of the tires so that the indicator scale is at the left and the right-hand pointer aligns with the scribed line of the right-hand tire. Adjust the left-hand pointer until it lines up with the scribed center line on the left-hand tire. You can now read from the indicator scale the amount of toe-in or toe-out.

A faster method to check toe is by using the equipment shown in Fig. 7-81. The optical light projector is fastened to the magnetic caster/camber gauge or to a special magnetic base, or the camber/caster gauge is attached to wheel clamps to accommodate large wheels. When the two projector units are electrically connected to the motor vehicle batteries, the light from the left-hand unit is projected to the right-hand target screen and vice versa. By focusing the optical lens and adjusting the projector heights using the guide rods, the correct toe reading can be obtained by adding or subtracting the readings from each scale. For example, when the steering gear is centered, the steering wheel spokes are horizontal, and the toe reading of both scales is the same, say a toe-in of 0.0625 in [1.59 mm], then the toe-in is 0.125 in [3.18 mm]. However, if the left-hand target screen reads 0.125-in [3.18-mm] toe-in and the right-hand target screen reads 0.125-in [3.18-mm] toe-out, then the toe-in is zero. Note, however, the left-hand wheel, not the right, is toeing out because it is the left-hand wheel projector that projects to the right-hand scale. The advantage of using this type of toe-in gauge is that the toe adjustment can be observed as the correction is made.

Adjusting Toe-In To adjust toe-in, again check and center the steering gear. This should bring the steering wheel spokes into the horizontal position. If the front wheels point straight ahead, apply penetrating oil to the tie-rod threads and to the clamp bolt threads. Loosen the clamp nuts and count the

Fig. 7-81 Optoe Liner installed. (*FMC Corporation*)

threads per inch on the tie-rod. Say, for example, they have 16 threads per inch and the toe-in measurement was 0.125-in toe-out (not toe-in), and say the correct toe-in according to the service manual should be 0.125 in. You would then have to extend both tie-rods by 0.125 in (which is precisely one complete turn of the tie-rods) since both tie-rods extend by 0.0625 in. After the adjustment has been made, align the tie-rods and the tie-rod clamps, and then tighten the nuts to the specified torque.

If, however, the front wheels point to the left, you will have to remove one tie-rod end. If you remove the one on the left, you should then turn the tie-rod end one complete right-hand turn. This will shorten the tie-rod by 0.0625 in and will move the right-hand wheel to the right. To compensate for the toe-in and to move the left-hand wheel to the right, rotate the left-hand tie-rod end two full turns counterclockwise. The left-hand wheel will move 0.125 in to the right, giving the front wheels the correct toe-in and position.

Toe-Out on Turns The last alignment measurement is toe-out on turns. Unfortunately, many truck service manuals do not include specifications for this and you must therefore go to the dealer or manufacturer for the information if the motor vehicle is hard to handle during a turn or has excessive tire wear.

Assume you are making the toe-out on turn check and that the front wheels are on the turning radius gauge, the locking pins removed, and both scales are zeroed. Turn the steering wheel to the left so that the left-hand turning radius gauge scale reads 20° or as specified, and from the right-hand scale note the degree to which the right-hand wheel has turned. It will always be less than 20° and will vary with the wheel base and wheel spacing. Next, turn the steering wheel to the right so that the right-hand wheel is at 20°, and from the left-hand scale note the degree to which the left-hand wheel is turned. If the toe-out on turn is not within $\frac{1}{2}$° (30′) of the service manual specification, then the steering arm is bent or twisted and must be replaced. **CAUTION** Never attempt to straighten bent steering linkages or suspension components, as this could weaken them so that they might break or bend during operation and cause a serious accident. **NOTE** The turning angle adjustment or check should be the last check made on motor vehicles, tractors, or machines.

Measuring Wheel Alignment with Light Beam Equipment There are several different types of light beam alignment equipment, and all are basically the same in design and operating principle. They may consist of a fixed raised ramp, or a portable raised ramp, or a hydraulically operated raised ramp, or of various types of pit racks. Their purpose is to position the motor vehicle in a horizontal plane and to allow the mechanic to work on the steering system and suspension components from below. The ramp or pit rack beam spacing can be adjusted to accommodate different-sized wheel spacing, and the ramp or rack may be made of sheet steel or of a heavy-duty twin I-beam pit rack design. See Fig. 7-82.

Alignment equipment includes a set of optical light projectors having within their housings the camber, toe-in, and caster scales. The projectors are attached through wheel clamps to the rim flange or they are positioned on side rails to the front left- and right-hand pit rack beams in line with the center of the turning radius gauge (see Fig. 7-83). In the latter case, angle convex mirrors are attached to the rim flange through wheel clamps. The purpose of the optical projectors is to project the vertical position of each front and rear wheel onto a target screen. The purpose of the front and rear convex mirrors is to measure, through the light beam, the wheel position and flash this measurement onto the target screen.

To measure the front and rear wheel alignment using the equipment shown in Fig. 7-82, drive the motor vehicle straight onto the pit rack and then pull or push it onto the center of the turning radius gauge. Remove the radius gauge lock pins. Install the front and rear wheel convex mirrors. Make certain that the wheel clamp finger rests firmly against the rim flange and that the mirrors are in the center of the wheel hubs, and then center the steering gear switch on the optical projectors. Turn the selector knobs of the optical projectors to flash the camber scale onto the screen. Move the optical projectors toward the wheels until the cross hair and the locator spot (having the vertical line) align. See Fig. 7-84. Raise the front wheels off the radius gauge, measure

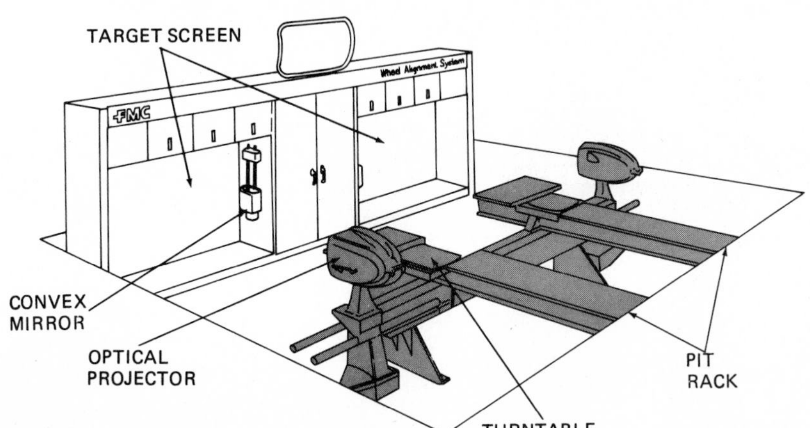

Fig. 7-82 Schematic view of an extra-heavy-duty pit visualiner system. (*FMC Corporation*)

Fig. 7-83 An optical system.

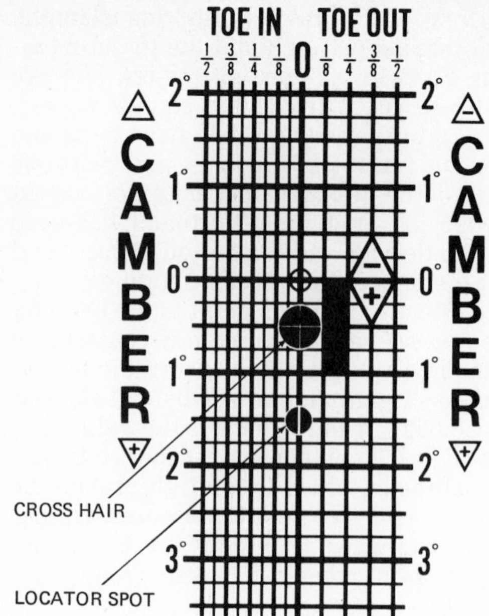

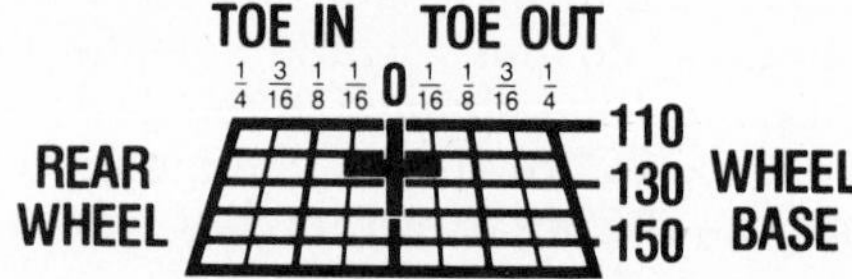

Fig. 7-84 Camber and toe-in screen.

and adjust the wheel runout, then lower the tire back onto the gauge. Stabilize the suspension, center the steering wheel, and again align the crosshair and locator spot. Now you can read the right-hand-wheel camber and toe directly from the right-hand scale, and from the left-hand scale, the left-hand-wheel camber and toe, since four independent light beams are transferred from each projector to the wheel mirrors, back to the projectors, and onto the screen. See Fig. 7-85. Light beam 1 is projected from lamp 1 to one projector mirror, reflects to the front wheel mirror, back to a second projector mirror, and from there onto the screen. Light beam 2 is projected from lamp 2 to one projector mirror, reflects to the front wheel mirror, back to a second projector mirror, and from there onto the projector screen. Light beam 3 projects the camber/caster chart from lamp 3 onto the screen, and light beam 4 projects the rear cross hair from lamp 3 onto the screen. Therefore any changes in the relationship between the wheel mirrors and the optical light projectors will vary the reflection angles of light beams 1, 2, and 4, and project the angle changes onto the screen. However, the chart light beam 3 always remains the same. If the image of the left-hand wheel has $\frac{1}{2}°$ (30′) positive camber and zero toe-in, and the right-hand image, say, shows the same camber but has 0.125-in [3.18-mm] toe-out, then the right-hand wheel is pointing outward and

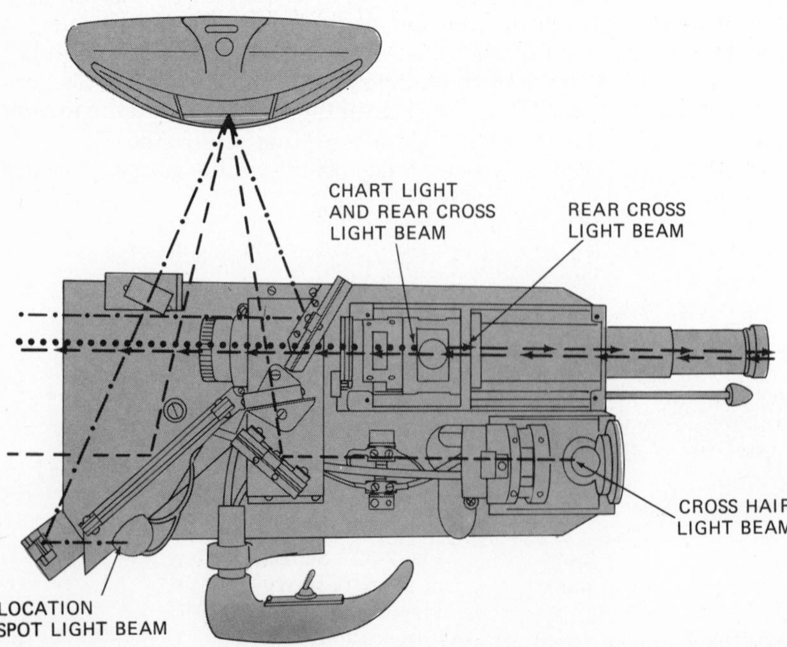

Fig. 7-85 Sectional view of the projector. (*FMC Corporation*)

the right-hand tie-rod must be adjusted to bring the toe to specification.

To check the rear wheel toe and rear axle tracking, read the left- and right-hand scales to determine toe. If both rear crosshairs are at zero, the toe at the rear wheels is correct and the rear wheels precisely track the front wheels. However, if both rear toe scales show toe-out by identical amounts, the rear axle is bent backward.

If one scale shows toe-in or toe-out, only that side of the axle is bent (forward or backward). If one scale shows toe-in and the other shows toe-out by the same amount, say 0.25 in [6.35 mm], then the frame or axle is bent or the suspension is worn or damaged.

To check caster, select and position both caster scales by turning the selector knobs on the projectors. Turn the steering wheel to the right. **NOTE** The specification for this alignment equipment requires a 15° wheel position. Now turn the selector knobs to bring the caster scale crosshairs to the zero line. Next, turn the steering wheel to the left so that the left-hand radius gauge reads 15°. You can then take the caster reading from the left-hand caster scale. Figure 7-86 shows $1\frac{1}{2}$° (1°30′) positive caster. At the same time take from the right-hand caster scale the toe-out on turn reading.

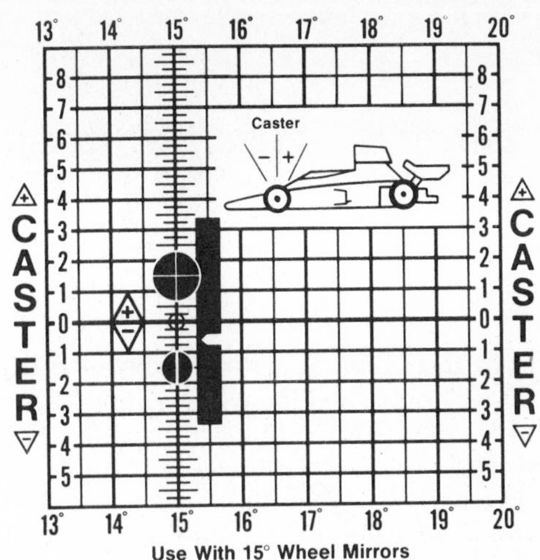

Fig. 7-86 View of caster target screen showing 1½ degree positive caster. (*FMC Corporation*)

Wheel and Axle Alignment Test Equipment By maintaining good tracking and specified front wheel toe-in, tire wear and rolling resistance are reduced, thereby decreasing fuel consumption. To quickly check, with a high degree of accuracy, wheel tracking and front and rear wheel toe-in on motortrucks or truck-tractors (or the entire rig), several different types of wheel and axle alignment test equipment are used, similar in design to the light beam type of wheel alignment equipment just discussed.

The optical projector shown in Fig. 7-87 uses a laser beam projector which is attached to an adjustable wheel clamp. The wheel clamp is secured to the inside of the rim with three thumb screws, and the mounting plate of the projector is adjustable to compensate for wheel runout. Two measuring gauges (one at the front and one at the rear) are

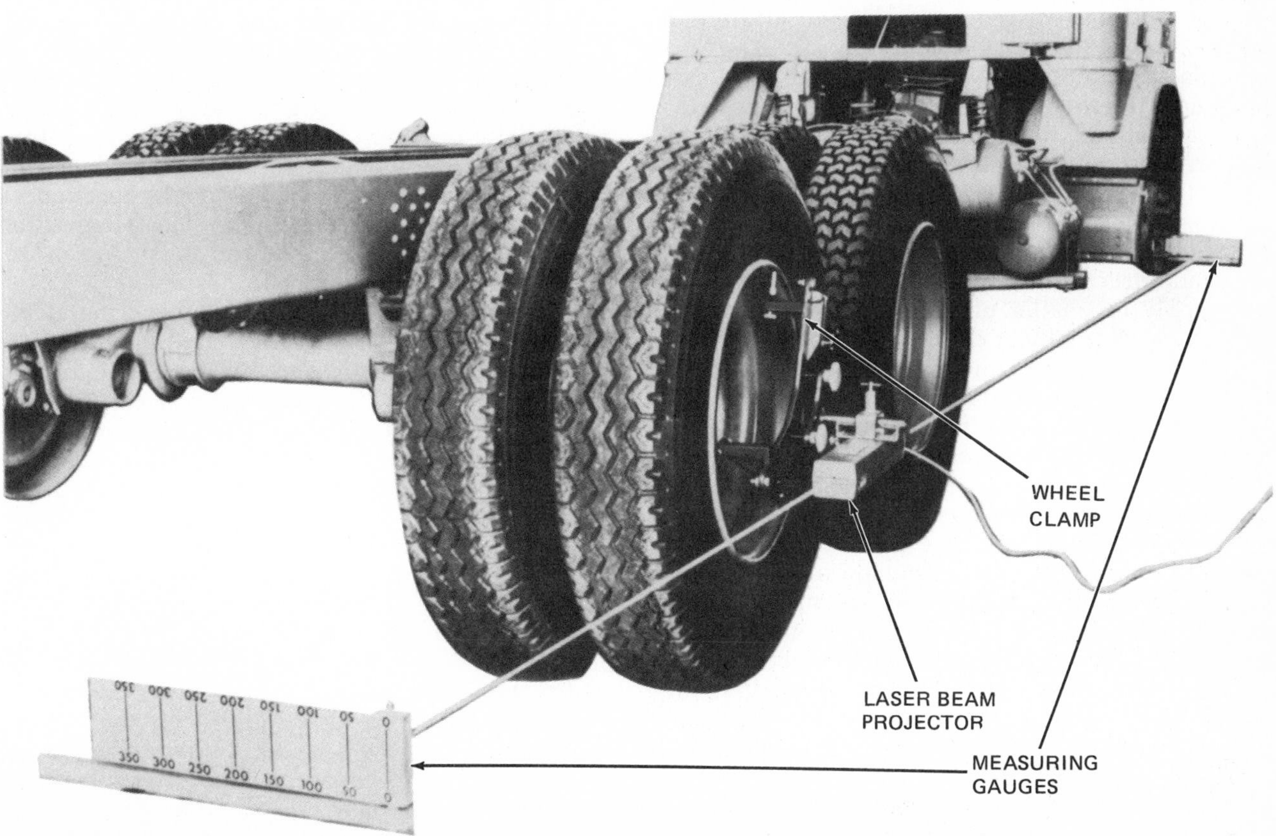

Fig. 7-87 View of laser beam axle and wheel alignment equipment installed.

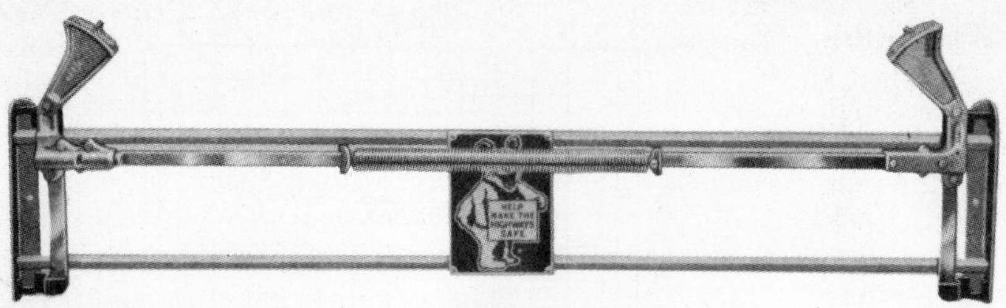

Fig. 7-88 Toe-in alignment gauge. (*Bear Manufacturing Company*)

fastened to the frame at an equal distance from the frame center line. When the wheel runout is adjusted on both left- and right-hand rear drive axle wheels, and the laser beams are projected toward the front measuring gauge, a reading can be recorded from the left- and right-hand sides of the gauges. The laser beam projector is then rotated so that the beam points toward the rear measuring gauge and the readings again recorded. Both readings (from the left- and right-hand sides) can be compared; and if the left front and rear and the right front and rear are equal, the rear drive axle is parallel with the center of the frame. If the readings are not equal, check the front rear drive axle and the steering axle and record the readings. However, remember that the readings of the front axle will differ by the amount of toe-in. When all measurements are recorded, they should then be compared to determine if the axles or frame are out of alignment.

Alignment of Off-Highway Wheel-Type Tractors, Trucks, and Machines Wheel-type tractors, motortrucks, or machines which are steered by pivoting the front wheels (but have a nonadjustable built-in camber and caster) require only two alignment checks, that is, toe-in and tracking.

If (on small units) you suspect that the front axle or spindle is bent or twisted, you could measure the kingpin inclination or the camber to determine the former, or measure the caster to determine if the axle is twisted.

Several methods can be used to check toe, some of which are applicable to both small and large tractors, motortrucks and machines, and others which only apply to smaller units. Prior to checking the toe, several preliminary checks are essential. For instance, you must check the tire pressure, the steering linkage, steering cylinder, kingpins, bushings, and wheel bearings for wear. If applicable also check the mechanical steering gear adjustment and the radius rod pivot pin and bushing for wear, and make sure that the radius rod-to-axle is properly secured.

To check the toe-in using the toe-in alignment gauge shown in Fig. 7-88, raise the front end of the motor vehicle, measure the wheel runout, and mark each tire at its highest runout point; then lower the wheels to the ground. Turn the steering wheel until the front wheels point straight ahead, then drive the motor vehicle at least 12 ft [3.66 m] backward and then forward again to settle the suspension and steering linkage. Make certain the runout marks on both tires are on the top. If applicable, center the steering gear; the steering wheel should then be in the horizontal position. Now compress the alignment gauge and position it between the lower part of the left- and right-hand front wheel rims so that the toe-in scale faces forward and the gauge lugs rest firmly against the rim flanges. Now take the reading from the left and right toe-in scales. Assume the service manual specification is zero toe-in. Under this condition, each scale should read zero also. However, if both scales have the same reading, say 0.25 in [6.35 mm], then there is a toe-in of 0.5 in [12.7 mm]. To correct the toe-in to zero toe, loosen both ball joint clamp nuts, place a pipe wrench at each end of the tie-rod, and turn the tie-rod counterclockwise until both scale gauge readings are zero. Align the ball joints and adjusting clamp and then retighten the adjusting clamp nuts.

If the motortruck, tractor, etc., has a hydrostatic steering system and one scale, say the right-hand one, reads 0.5 in [12.7 mm] and the other reads zero, split the toe-in by moving the front wheels until each scale reads 0.25 in [6.35 mm] and then adjust the tie-rod to bring both scales to zero. Recheck the turning radius and wheel stop.

If, however, the motortruck, etc., has a manual steering gear, loosen both the left- and right-hand ball joint adjusting clamp nuts, remove the right-hand ball joint from the steering arm, and then turn it clockwise the calculated number of turns. Reposition the ball joint, torque the nut to specification, and install the cotter pin. You may now have to turn the tie-rod slightly in either direction to achieve the specified toe, but in any event do not forget to check the center position of the steering wheel. Reposition the tie-rod clamps and the tie-rod as recommended, then torque the nuts to specification.

Follow the same procedure to check toe of the rear wheels. However, if there is too much toe-in or toe-out, the axle housing should be replaced, or bent to correct the toe with special tools. See Fig. 7-89.

Another method, although slow, but which becomes necessary as the tire size increases, or because there is no toe alignment gauge, is as follows: Drive the tractor, motor truck, or machine, onto a hard, level surface and make the usual preliminary checks. Next, raise the front end so that the tires just clear the ground and scribe a center line around the entire circumference of the tire tread using the method explained earlier in this unit. Next, lower the front end, center the steering wheel, and, with a measuring stick or tape, measure (at spindle height) at the front and rear the distance between the two scribe lines. Then compare the measurements. They should be equal when the toe is zero.

If the tires have super ground or rock grip treads, this method will not bring about the desired results.

Fig. 7-89 Method used to increase toe-in. (*Bear Manufacturing Company*)

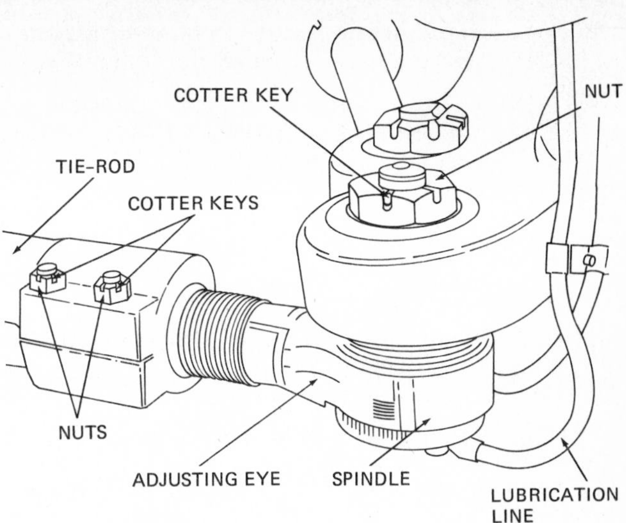

Fig. 7-91 Method of adjusting toe-in. (*WABCO, An American-Standard Company*)

In these cases, you must proceed as follows: Drive the motortruck onto a hard, even surface and center the steering wheel with the wheels in a straight-ahead position. If the motortruck has Hydrair suspension you must, in addition to the preliminary checks, measure and possibly adjust the piston to the recommended height. (See material on Hydrair suspension.)

Next, by using a plumb bob (and an extension to allow the plumb bob line to clear the tire) from the front rim flange and rear rim flange, project the points onto the ground. Mark these points sharply and clearly as shown in Fig. 7-90. Press a thumb tack into one drive lug in the center of each tire. Position the tire as shown in Fig. 7-90. Hold the plumb bob line to the thumb tack and project this point onto the ground. Again mark this point and then rotate the tire 180°, hold the plumb bob to the thumb tack (which is now at the rear), and project *this* point onto the ground. When all the front wheel points are projected, scribe a line which connects the front points, the rear points, and the rim points. Measure at both the front and rear of the tire the distance between the points where the lines cross, and this should give you a measure of the toe. See Fig. 7-90 for more about these steps.

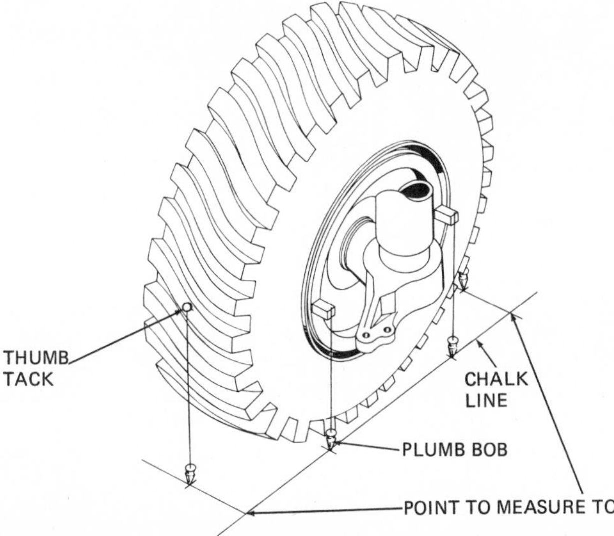

Fig. 7-90 Preliminary steps to measure toe-in. (*WABCO, An American-Standard Company*)

If the toe-in exceeds, or is less than specified, remove the cotter pin from the ball joint stud nut and adjusting clamp nuts. Next, loosen the clamp nuts and loosen and remove the ball stud nut and ball stud from the spindle arm. To make the adjustment, measure the thread pitch. If it has, say, 18 threads per inch it will take one complete revolution to move the ball stud in or out 0.055 in [1.397 mm]. You must, therefore, rotate the ball stud the calculated number of turns in a clockwise direction to shorten the tie-rod, or in a counterclockwise direction to lengthen it in order to arrive at the correct toe.

Reinstall the ball stud and torque the nut to specification, which in this case would be 2000 lb · ft [29,187 N · m]. Install the cotter pin and align the tie-rod so that both ball stud housings are parallel with the spindle arm. In this position, tighten the clamp nuts to specification, and install the cotter pins. See Fig. 7-91.

Review Questions

1. What three factors (other than the steering system) assist in the steering stability and the natural inclination to steer straight ahead?
2. What is the difference between a constant-ratio steering system and a variable steering system?
3. How does a leaf spring suspension of a rear axle assist in steering?
4. Define (*a*) understeer, (*b*) oversteer, and (*c*) slip angle.
5. Assume you are using a spring scale to measure the rotating torque of the steering and it reads 8 lb [3.63 kg]. The diameter of the steering wheel is 20 in [508 mm]. Calculate the rotating torque.

6. Why is the worm diameter of a worm-and-roller steering gear not equal throughout?
7. (*a*) How are the camshaft bearings adjusted on a cam and lever steering gear? (*b*) How is the stud mesh adjusted?
8. When the front wheels are pointing in the straight-ahead position, the steering gear must be precisely in the center. Why is this so important?
9. List the four components essential to any power-assist steering.
10. Explain the difference between linkage power steering and semihydrostatic steering.
11. Outline the differences between hydrostatic steering and semihydrostatic steering.
12. Explain how to check the turning radius of the front wheel.
13. List five reasons why a power-assist steering system could lose steering power or steering speed.
14. What could cause an operator to complain of (*a*) slow steering system recovery? or shimmy? (*b*) the motor vehicle wandering? (*c*) delayed steering action?
15. Explain why the hydrostatic steering system is nearly unlimited in its capacity (force) and application.
16. Why are pilot-operated hydrostatic steering systems used?
17. On a hydrostatic steering system, why is it so important to check, and if necessary to adjust, the turning angle of the front wheels or of the articulated machine?
18. On a self-steering axle, what action causes the tires to follow the turning radius of the motor vehicle or vehicle?
19. Which part(s) or component(s) would first indicate wear if one or more angle (and/or distance) were above or below specification?
20. Explain why a motor vehicle or vehicle would pull to the side of the under-inflated tire (*a*) when the brakes are applied, or (*b*) when the suspension is broken.
21. Why would an out-of-balance wheel assembly cause the tire tread to show a cupped-wear pattern?
22. Why is it important to measure the wheel runout when using a wheel clamp to attach the camber/caster gauge?
23. Assume the frame angle is $2\frac{1}{4}°$ negative and the measured caster angle is $1\frac{1}{2}°$ positive. What is the true caster angle?
24. List two common omissions of procedure which could result in an incorrect toe measurement.
25. What are the advantages of using light beam alignment equipment over a magnetic camber/caster tool and toe-in bar?

Unit 8
Track-Type Undercarriages

Tracks have been used over the last 60 years on tractors both large and small, as well as on medium and large cranes, shovels, log loaders, and other specially designed equipment such as rock drills, rocket launchers, etc. Recently, however, the number of track-type carriers has grown to include small units such as hydraulic excavators, shovels, and cranes. Credit for the steady increase in popularity of track-type tractors and carriers is due to their capability of improving the tractor or machine traction (pulling power), load-carrying capacity, stability, and maneuverability.

As you are aware, the weight of a wheel-type tractor is carried by the tire surface area that is in contact with the road, which also constitutes the tire's traction area. The stability of such tractors depends basically on the wheel base, the wheel spacing, and the tire size, all of which affect the center of gravity, while maneuverability depends upon the design of the steering system.

On track-type tractors and carriers, the increased traction, load-carrying capacity, and stability, are achieved through the design of the undercarriage—that is, they are related to the track frame, track rollers, track chains, and track shoes. The load-carrying capacity and traction depend on the size and design of the track shoes. Both vary with the gross weight and operating condition of the machine.

The average track shoe ground pressure for small and midrange tractors ranges from 3 to 6 psi [20.67 to 41.34 kPa]. In comparison, 3 psi [20.67 kPa] is about the pressure that an average-sized individual exerts when standing on the ground. Track-type tractors, therefore, can be driven on any surface on which a person can walk. The track shoe ground pressure on larger tractors and machines is on the whole higher, that is, from about 10 to 40 psi [68.9 to 275.6 kPa]. These machines are generally not used on soft terrain and are more or less designed for greater load-carrying capacity and/or pulling power.

As a rule, track-type tractors are rated by their pulling power (in pounds or kilograms), but many manufacturers also specify engine power, the total gear and drive reduction, the gross weight, and the track shoe design and size.

In order to reduce wear and excessive strain on the rotating drive components, the tractor drive train, track chain, and track shoes are designed to permit track slippage of about 3 percent when the tractor reaches its maximum drawbar pull.

UNDERCARRIAGE COMPONENTS

Tractor Undercarriages There are two designs of track-type undercarriages—the tractor and the crawler types. Both types and their components are discussed in this unit. The greatest difference between these two designs is in the functions of the undercarriages. The carrier undercarriage on the crawler design is only to support and propel the machine and to provide stable footing, whereas the tractor-type undercarriage is also designed for pulling power and maneuverability. Practically all tractor undercarriages consist of the following components: Two track roller frames with recoil and adjusting mechanisms, the track rollers, the track carrier (support) rollers, track (front) idlers, sprockets, and the track chains with the track shoes. (See Fig. 8-1.)

Track Roller Frames The track roller frames must support the tractor and provide the support surfaces for the front idler, track and carrier rollers, track adjustment and recoil mechanism, stabilizer bar or spring, and track guards. In addition it provides the mountings or pivot points which keep the track roller frames in alignment with the tractor.

Most track roller frames are fabricated from special steel into sections, and then welded into a rigid frame. However, as a rule, small tractors use two-channel iron rails, bolted or welded to a rigid track frame. The top and bottom of the rails are machined parallel to provide precision alignment of the track roller frame with the track and carrier rollers and front idler. The bearing supports are then machined to assure track roller frame alignment with the tractor. Next, the necessary holes are drilled (and in some cases tapped) for the bolt-on components. See Figs. 8-2 and 8-3. Depending on the tractor design, the track roller frames are secured at the rear by a pivot shaft and by the sprocket shaft outboard bearing; or the outside pivot point is attached to an independent shaft that is fastened in front of the sprocket to the tractor frame. See Fig. 8-4. A stabilizer (equalizer) bar or multileaf spring is pivot-fastened to the tractor frame (Fig. 8-5). Each end of the stabilizer bar or spring ends rest in a bracket that is fastened to the track roller frames. The stabilizer bar supports the front end of the tractor, thereby transferring the tractor weight at the front onto the track roller frames. This design allows the individual track roller frames to oscillate a specific distance, counteracting the movement of one track roller frame against the other.

NOTE Some loader tractors do not have oscillating track roller frames; instead, the front of the track roller frame is bolted to the tractor frame. Such a mounting gives the tractor loader greater stability (see Fig. 8-2).

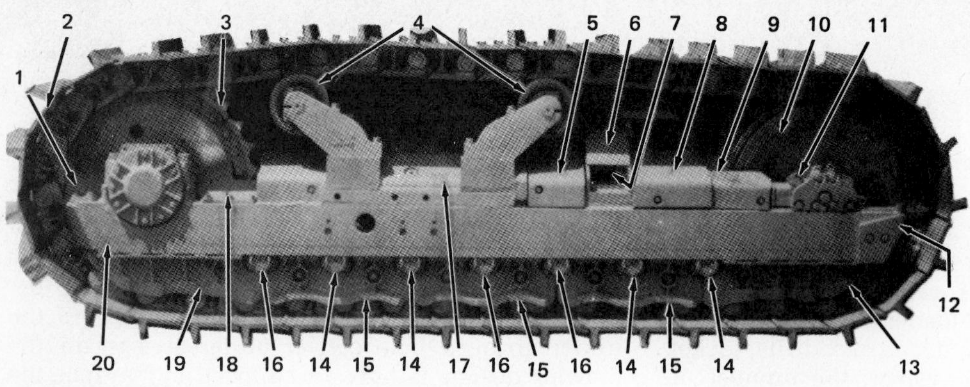

1. Rear sprocket guard
2. Track
3. Sprocket segment
4. Carrier rollers
5. Rear track release guard
6. Equalizing beam bracket
7. Equalizing beam
8. Intermediate track release guard
9. Front track release guard
10. Track idler
11. Idler guard
12. End guard
13. Front roller guard
14. Double flange rollers
15. Intermediate roller guard
16. Single flange rollers
17. Track release housing
18. Front sprocket guard
19. Rear roller guard
20. Track frame

Fig. 8-1 View of right-hand side undercarriage components (medium-sized tractor). (*Fiat-Allis*)

Front Idler and Yoke The purpose of the front idler and yoke is to align the track chain as the chain changes direction and to provide, in conjunction with the recoil and adjusting mechanism, a protecting device and track adjustment. The front idlers are either of a prefabricated welded structure or of a one-piece steel casting. The flanges and thread surfaces are then machined to a specific width, height, diameter, and angle. To provide a good self-alignment feature, the average flange and thread angle surface is tapered about 4° since any belt will run toward the greater diameter. Therefore, the track chain aligns with the front idler when the tractor moves in the straight-ahead or reverse direction, and does not come into contact with the inside or outside idler flanges.

The center of the idler is machined to accommodate the seals and the bearings. The bearings may be of the roller, tapered roller, or bushing design. The seals used may be of the duo-cone, metal cone floating seal, or bellows mechanical seal design.

NOTE Double lip-type seals are used only on small tractors.

The idler shaft is fastened through a bolt or pin to the left- and right-hand idler bracket (block). The guide plates and shims allow a lateral adjustment of the front idler. The assembly supports align and guide the front idler on the track roller frame guide rails (see Figs. 8-6 and 8-7). The idler yoke is either a one-piece steel casting or cast in two halves and then bolted to make a single unit. It is the link be-

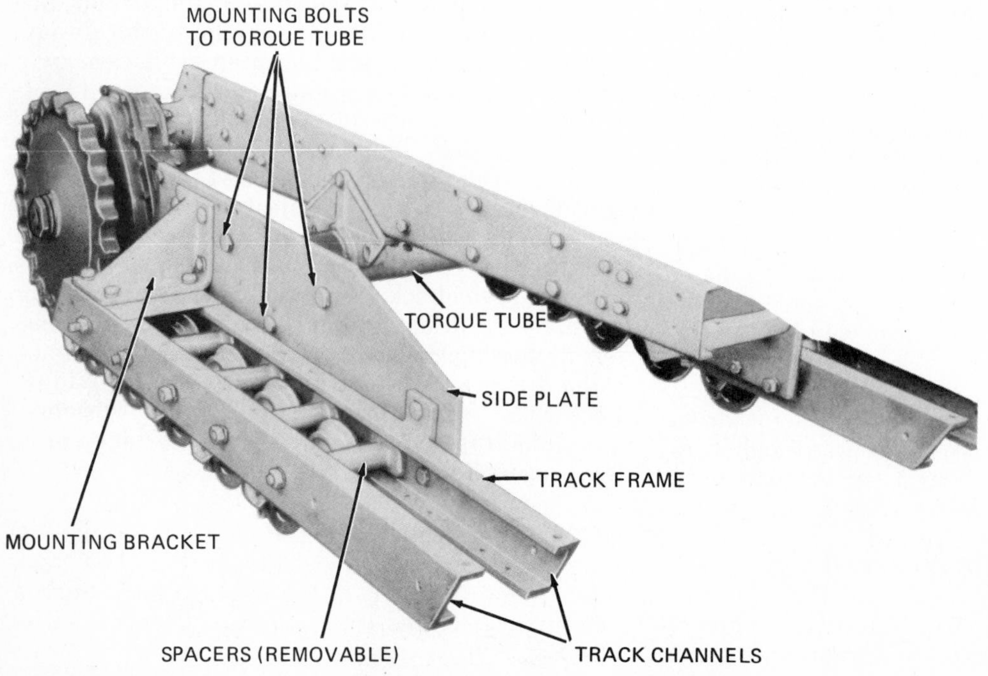

Fig. 8-2 Fixed-mounted track frame. (*J I Case Company Agricultural Equipment Division*)

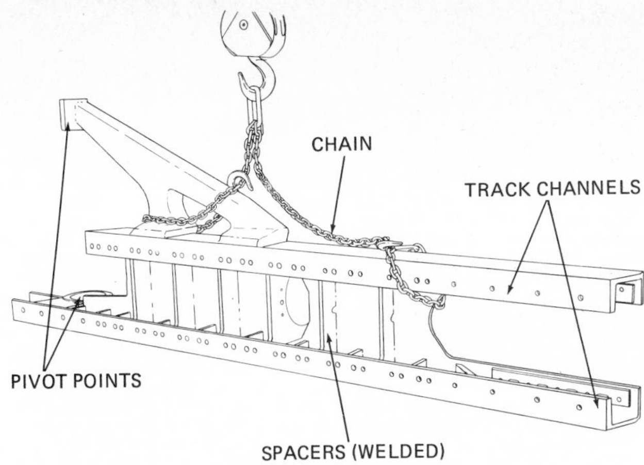

Fig. 8-3 Pivot-mounted track frame. (*Fiat-Allis*)

tween the track-adjusting mechanism and front idler bracket.

Drive Sprockets The purpose of the drive sprockets is to transmit rotary motion to the track chains by pulling the chains in clockwise or counterclockwise rotation onto the sprockets, rolling the tractor on the track links in a forward or reverse direction. **NOTE** Only alternate teeth engage with the track bushings and, since the sprockets are of the hunting tooth design (an uneven number of teeth), a particular sprocket tooth engages with a track bushing on every second sprocket revolution. Only after several track revolutions will the same bushings and teeth again engage. This design retards deterioration of the sprocket teeth and track bushings.

The sprockets are one-piece steel-cast (see Fig. 8-8) and may be splined (tapered or straight splines) to the sprocket or planetary carrier shaft. On the other hand, the sprocket hub may be splined to the sprocket or planetary shaft, in which case either a one-piece sprocket ring is bolted to the sprocket hub or individual sprocket segments are bolted to it.

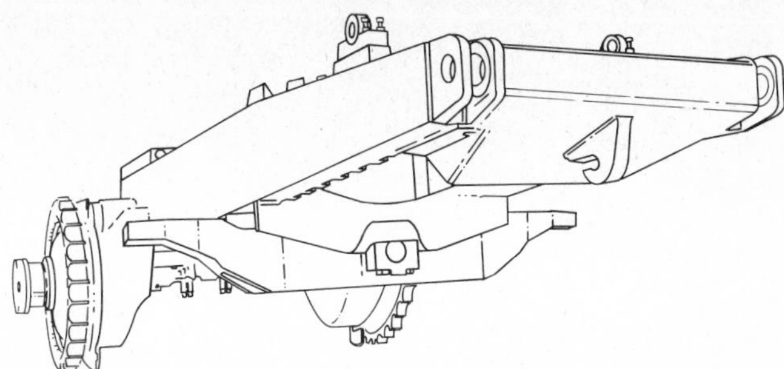

Fig. 8-5 View of tractor frame and equalizer bar.

Track-Adjusting and Recoil Mechanisms These components are bolted to each track frame and coupled to the front idler yoke. Although individual parts, they actually work together as a unit. The purpose of the track adjuster is to adjust the track chain so that a specific tension between the drive sprocket and front idler can be maintained when worn track bushings and pins or worn sprocket teeth reduce the tension. The purpose of the recoil mechanism is to act as the counter force to the track-adjusting mechanism. Moreover, it allows the front idler to move toward the sprocket if a large object should lodge between the sprocket teeth and bushings or between the track chain and front idler. In such an instance, excessive strain is placed on the track pins, bushings, front idler, and drive sprocket shafts. When this occurs, a spring of one type or another compresses, reducing the strain on the components. The same action also takes place when the front idler is accidentally forced rearward. The force is absorbed by the spring (recoil mechanism), thereby protecting the idler and yoke against serious damage. Four types of recoil mechanisms and adjustments are used.

COIL SPRING RECOIL MECHANISM AND MECHANICAL TRACK ADJUSTMENT A coil spring recoil mechanism having a screw track-adjusting mechanism is shown

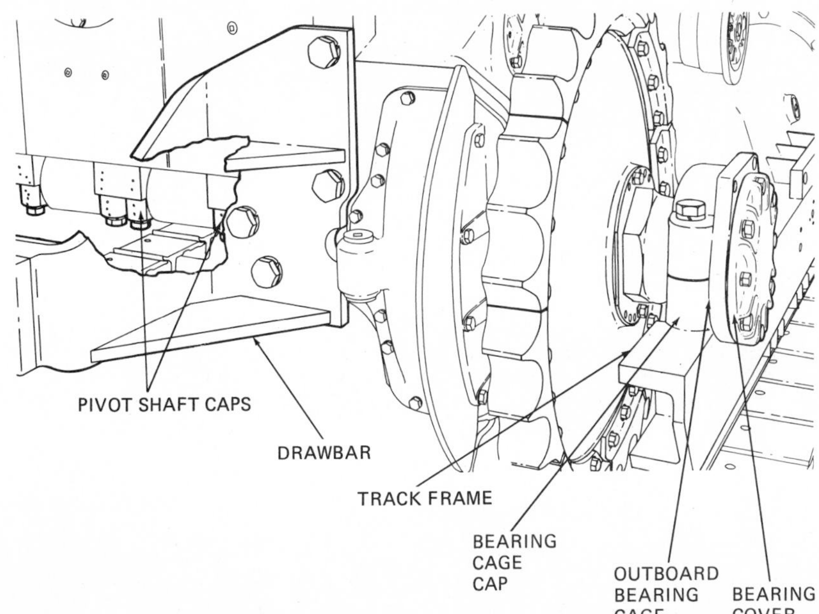

Fig. 8-4 View of a pivot-mounted track frame. (*Fiat-Allis*)

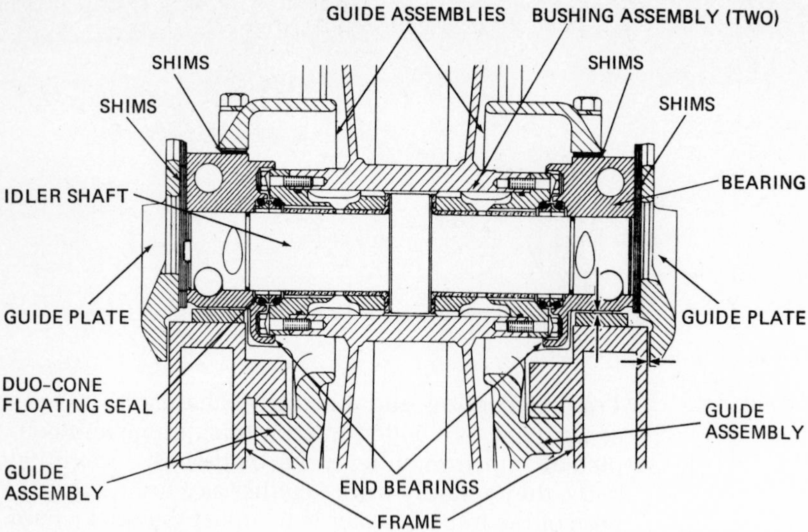

Fig. 8-6 Sectional view of front idler assembly. (*Caterpillar Tractor Co.*)

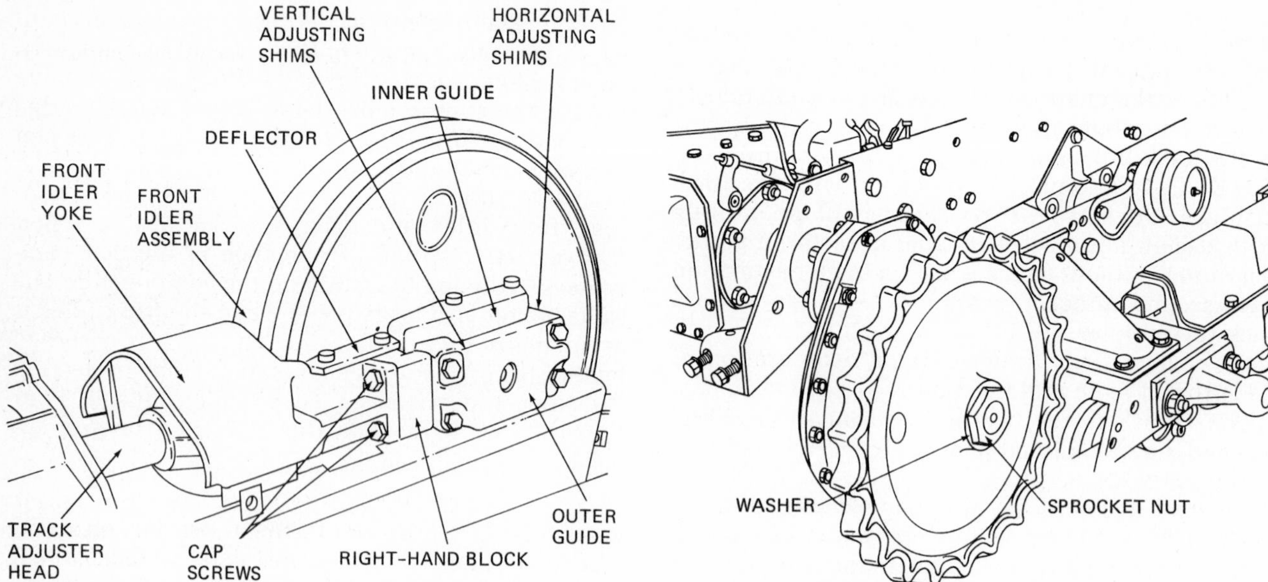

Fig. 8-7 View of right-hand front idler. (*Deere & Company*)

Fig. 8-8 View of a one-piece steel-cast sprocket. (*J I Case Company Agricultural Equipment Division*)

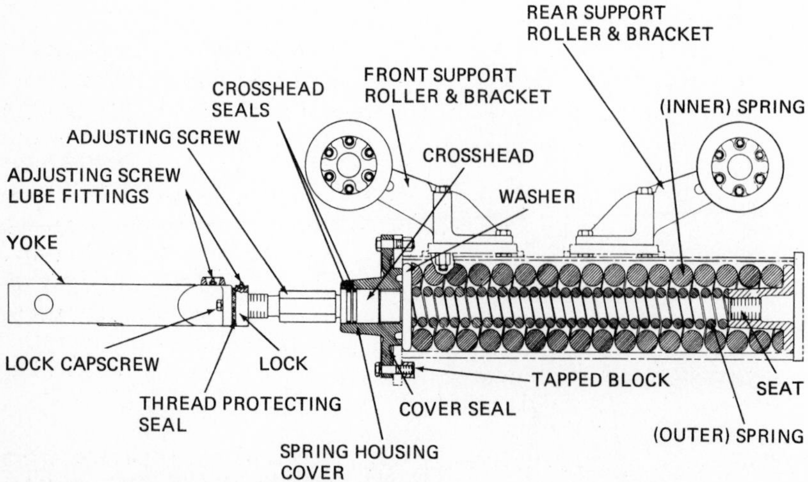

Fig. 8-9 Sectional view of a coil spring recoil mechanism and mechanical track adjustment. (*Fiat-Allis*)

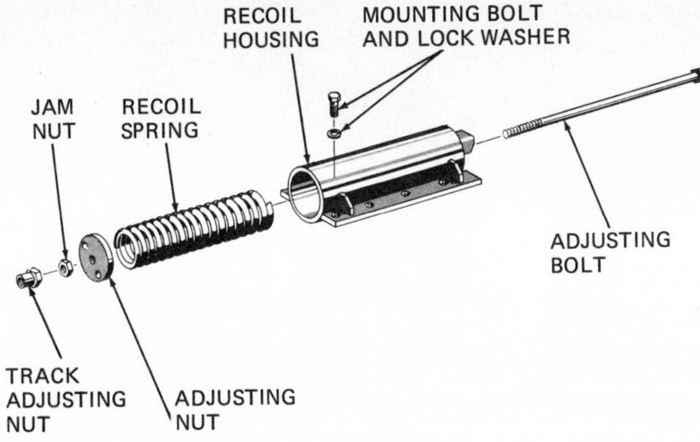

Fig. 8-10 Exploded view of a coil spring recoil mechanism and mechanical track adjustment. (*J I Case Company Agricultural Equipment Division*)

in Fig. 8-9. The two recoil springs are installed under a predetermined force (energy), in the recoil housing which is bolted or welded to each track frame. In this design, the spring housing cover confines the springs and seals the housing. The adjusting screw socket rests in the crosshead. One end is sealed with an O ring to the housing cover, and the other is screwed into the front idler yoke. A seal placed between the yoke and locking device protects the threads. The locking device is fastened to the yoke with two cap screws. In the recoil mechanism illustrated in Fig 8-9, the spring housing is sealed and partly filled with oil, but on some designs the track-adjusting screw socket rests directly on the spring washer.

There are also coil spring recoil mechanisms (Fig. 8-10) which have the coil spring compressed to a predetermined length (energy) through the track-adjusting bolt and a large adjusting nut. A specially designed track-adjusting nut is screwed onto the adjusting bolt and rests in the bore of the front idler yoke.

Operation and adjustment If, for one reason or another, the front idler is forced to the right, the yoke, the adjusting screw, and the crosshead are also forced to the right against the spring washer and the springs are further compressed, thus removing the tension from the track chain. As the force from the front idler is removed, the coil springs expand and the washer comes to rest against the spring housing cover, positioning the front idler to its static position.

To adjust the track tension, remove the two cap screws and then, using a wrench, turn the adjusting screw clockwise to tighten the track chain and counterclockwise to loosen it. After the adjustment is made, turn the lock plate tight against the seal and reinstall the two cap screws.

COIL SPRING RECOIL MECHANISM AND HYDRAULIC TRACK ADJUSTMENT A coil spring recoil mechanism having a hydraulic (grease) track adjustment mechanism is shown in Figs. 8-11 and 8-12. The coil spring is located between the spring adapter that rests against the housing of the pivot shaft and the track-adjuster

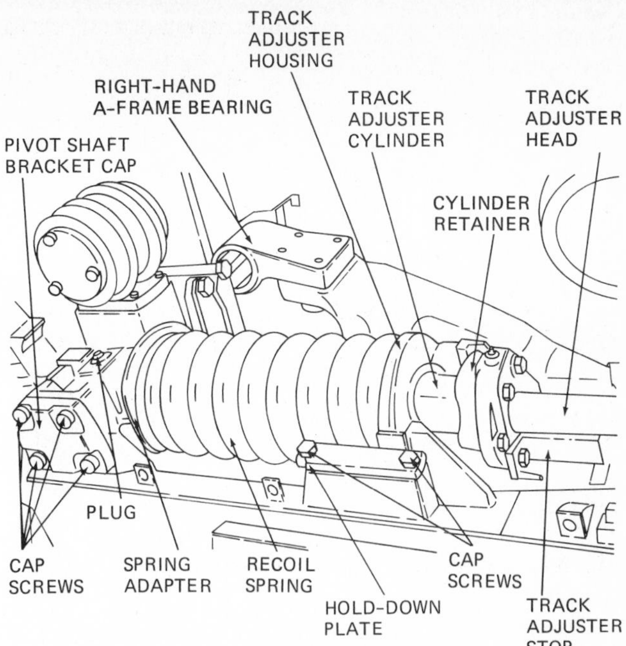

Fig. 8-11 View of a coil spring recoil mechanism and hydraulic track adjuster. (*Deere & Company*)

housing that rests against two track frame rail lugs. The piston spacer and one end of the track-adjusting cylinder is located within the track-adjuster housing. The other end of the cylinder is fastened through a retainer ring to the cylinder retainer. The retainer is bolted to the track-adjuster head, and the other end of the head rests in the bore of the front idler yoke. Inside the track-adjuster cylinder is the track-adjuster piston, which has two fiber wear rings and one cup seal. Depending on the manufacturer, the mechanism may have a conventional grease fitting screwed into a combination ball check valve and a vent fitting that is screwed into the cylinder retainer, or it may be designed as shown in Fig. 8-13 with a special filler valve having two ball check valves and a special relief valve screwed into the retainer. When the filler valve and the relief valve are tightened, their tapered ends rest against the tapered seats, thereby sealing (confining) the grease within the cylinder.

Operation To remove the track tension, turn the relief valve one complete turn counterclockwise. This will allow the grease (which may be under high pressure) to flow into the vertical slot, into the unthreaded area, and out of the vent hole. To tighten the track chain, tighten the relief valve, fasten a grease gun to the filler valve, and then pump grease into the fitting. The grease flows past the first and second check valves to the front of the track piston seal. As the pressure rises, the track-adjuster head, the cylinder retainer, and the track-adjusting cylinder are forced to the right, moving the front idler and tightening the track chain.

STAKED CONE SPRING PLATES AND HYDRAULIC ADJUSTER A recoil mechanism using staked cone spring plates is shown in Fig. 8-13. It consists of 55 cone spring

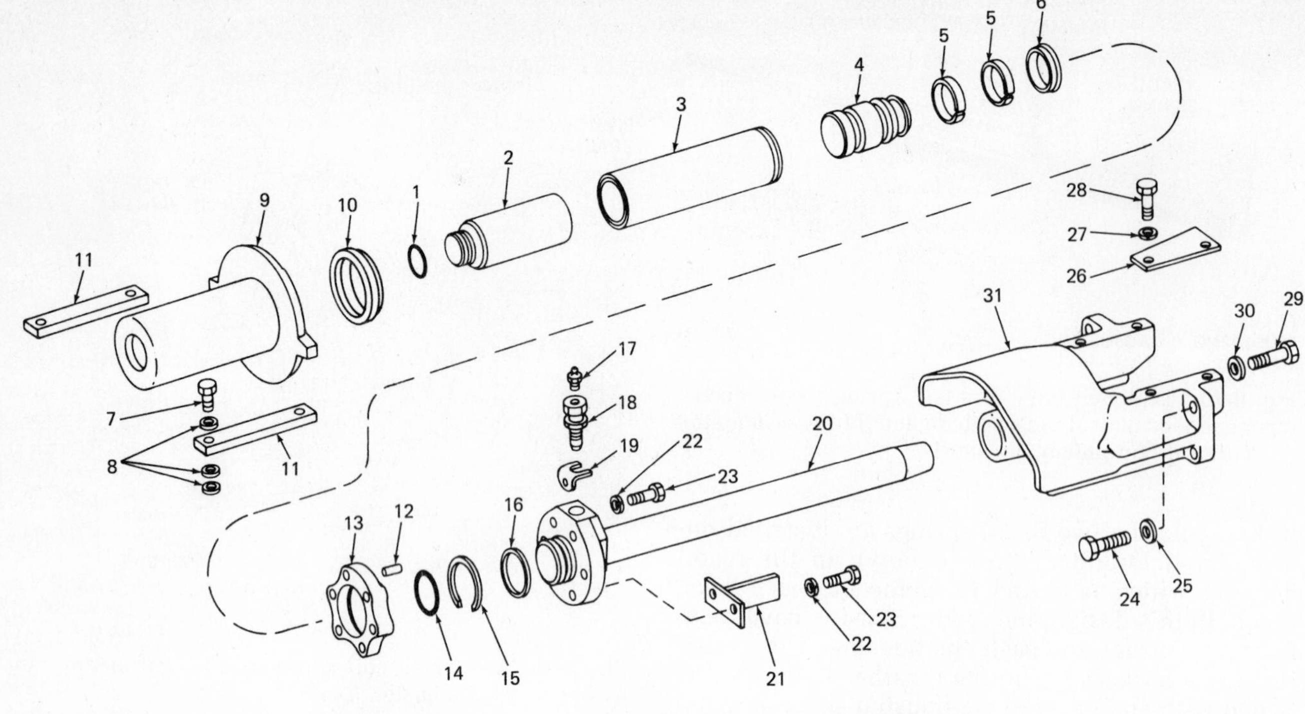

1. O Ring
2. Piston spacer
3. Track adjuster cylinder
4. Track adjuster piston
5. Piston wear ring (two)
6. U-Cap seal
7. Cap screw (four)
8. Special washer
9. Track adjuster housing
10. Wiper seal
11. Holddown plate (two)
12. Spring pin
13. Cylinder retainer
14. O Ring
15. Snap ring
16. Backup ring
17. Straight grease fitting
18. Ball check valve
19. Fitting guard
20. Track adjuster head
21. Track adjuster stop
22. Lock washer (six)
23. Cap screw (six)
24. Cap screw (four)
25. Special washer (four)
26. Deflector (two)
27. Lock washer (four)
28. Cap screw (four)
29. Cap screw
30. Special washer
31. Front Idler yoke

Figure 8-12 Exploded view of hydraulic track adjuster components. *(Deere & Company)*

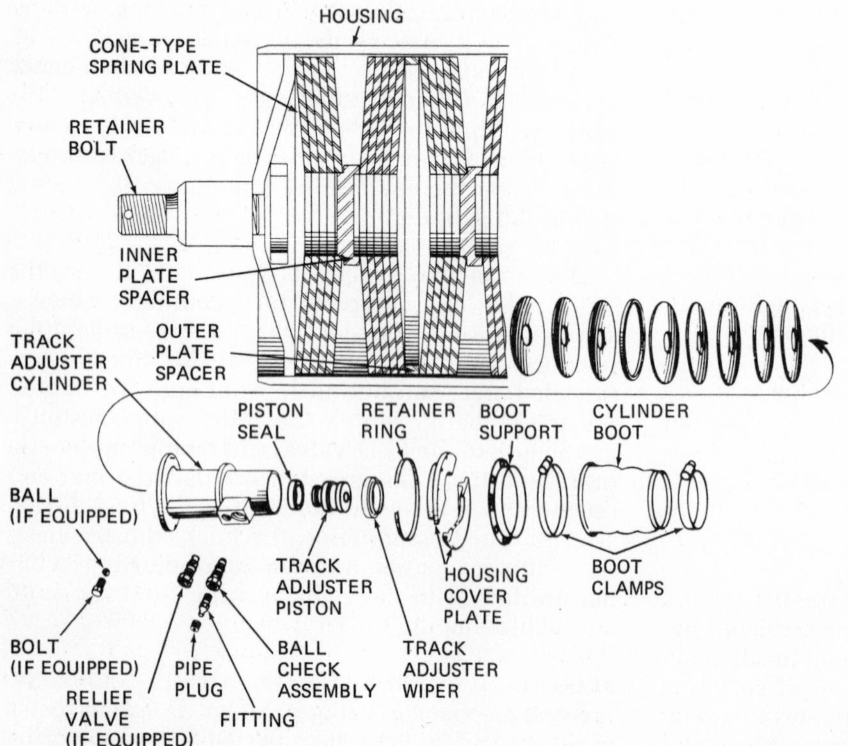

Fig. 8-13 Exploded view of the track spring and hydraulic track adjuster assembly. *(International Harvester Company)*

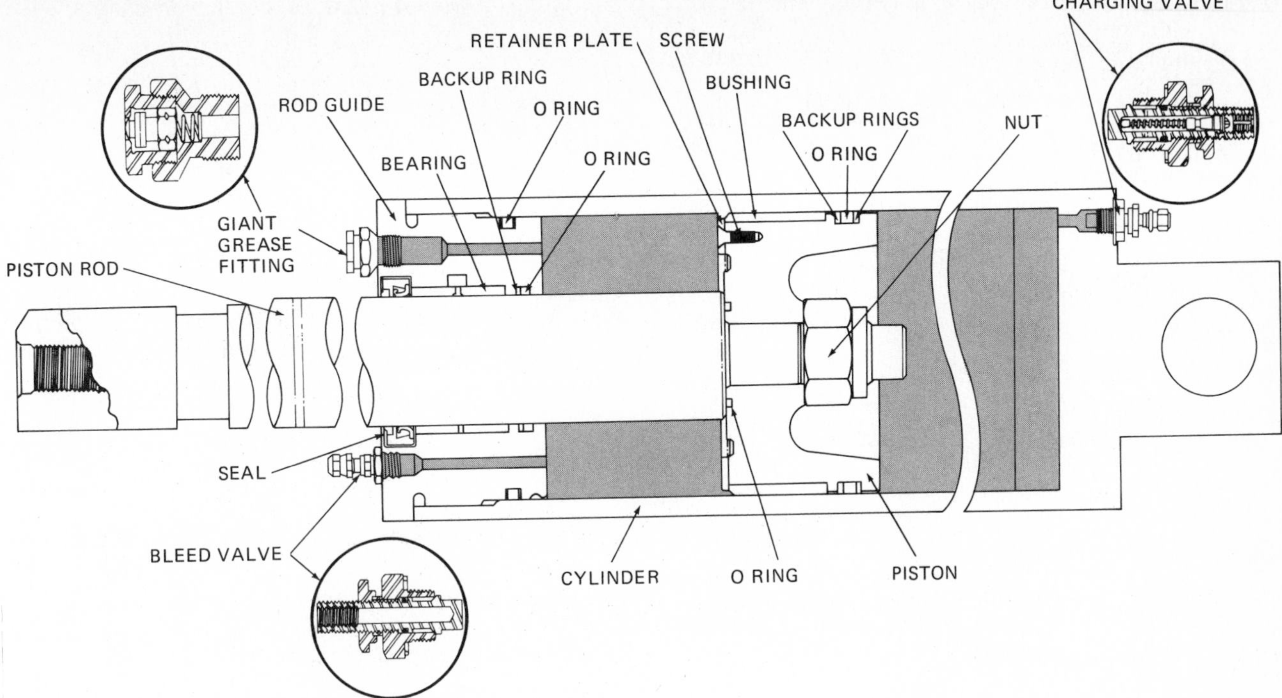

Fig. 8-14 Cutaway view of typical recoil nitrogen recoil cylinder and hydraulic adjuster. (*Terex Division of General Motors Corporation*)

plates, staked in sets of five. The cones are positioned between the inner and outer spacers, with the cone faces opposite each other. They are situated within the track spring housing under a predetermined energy. An hydraulic track-adjuster mechanism, which is similar in design to the one previously described, is bolted to one end of the front idler yoke (not shown). The retainer bolt on the other end is pinned to the track frame.

NITROGEN GAS RECOIL MECHANISM AND ADJUSTER The sectional view of a recoil mechanism (cylinder) which uses nitrogen gas as the recoil spring and grease as the adjuster is shown in Fig. 8-14. One end of the recoil cylinder is pinned to the track frame bracket. The nitrogen-charging valve is screwed to the right-hand side of the cylinder. The cylinder contains the piston with its seals, the backup washers, and the bushing (piston bearing) which divides the cylinder into two parts. The piston rod is supported and sealed by the rod guide which, in turn, is sealed to the cylinder through an O ring. The grease fitting and bleed valve is screwed into the rod guide.

Operation Assume the recoil cylinder is a rebuilt one and the right-hand side is charged with nitrogen to a pressure of 1500 psi [10,335 kPa] (see material on Hydrair suspension for the charging procedure). The piston and piston rod would have been forced to the left and the piston would be resting against the piston rod guide. To retract the piston and rod and bring it to the required installation length, grease is pumped through the grease fitting into the area in front of the piston until the piston rod has retracted to the specified distance. The recoil cylinder is then installed, and fastened to the front idler and track frame bracket.

To tighten the track chain, the bleed valve is *opened* about three-quarters of a turn to allow grease to bleed from the cylinder. As the grease escapes from the cylinder, the gas pressure forces the piston, the piston rod, the front idler yoke, and the front idler to the left, tightening the track chain. **NOTE** When the track is correctly adjusted, the nitrogen gas pressure should be rechecked and if necessary bled, or charged, precisely to the pressure given in the service manual.

To release the track tension, attach a grease gun to the fitting and pump grease into the cylinder. This moves the piston, the piston rod, and the front idler to the right and thereby removes the track tension.

CAUTION Whenever you release the track tension, the grease may be forced out at very high pressure; therefore, *never* inspect at eye level or use your hands to check whether or not grease is bleeding from the check valve. Moreover, do not relieve the track tension by removing either valve, as this could also cause a serious accident.

Track Rollers The purpose of the track rollers is to transfer the tractor or carrier weight evenly onto the track links, to reduce rolling friction, and to guide the track chain.

Two types of track rollers are used—the single flange and the double flange (see Figs. 8-15 and 8-16). The track roller halves are steel-forged, welded, machined to the required internal dimensions, and then heat-treated. **NOTE** The flanges are manufactured to an angle of approximately 4° to assist in guiding the track links onto the track roller

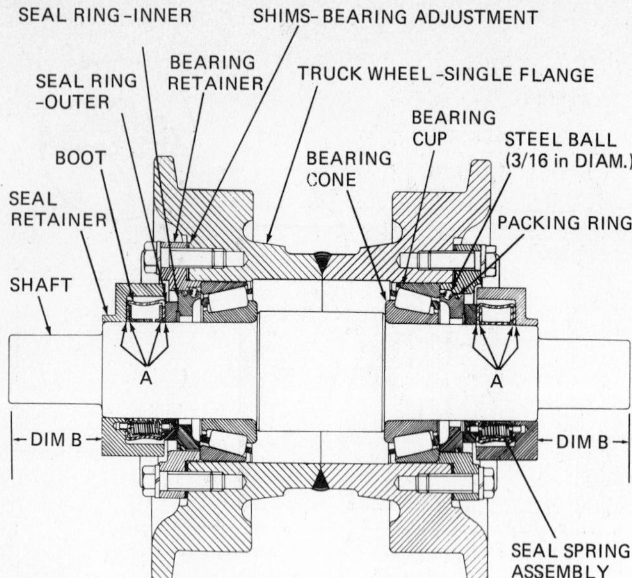

Fig. 8-15 Sectional view of single-flange track roller using tapered roller bearing and mechanical seals. (*Fiat-Allis*)

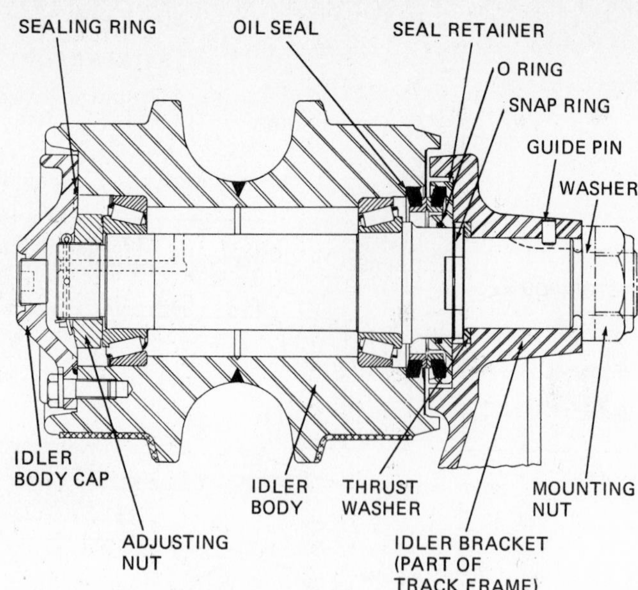

Fig. 8-17 Sectional view of a track carrier roller using tapered roller bearings and metal seal ring assembly. (*International Harvester Company*)

tread surface. Bushings or tapered roller bearings support the track roller housing on the track roller shaft. When tapered roller bearings are used, they provide the roller-body-to-roller-shaft alignment. When bushings are used, the thrust bushings and the shaft retainer cap (end collar) provide the alignment. Otherwise, the alignment is provided by the track roller flange and bushing that is pressed into the bushing housing, the latter being bolted to the sides of the roller body (see Fig. 8-15).

Mechanical seals, duo-cone seals, or metal floating ring seals are used to maintain the oil within the track roller and to keep out foreign matter. Each end of the track roller shaft has a machined flat surface which rests against the frame rail flange. The retainer cap (end collar), located over the shaft, positions and holds the track roller in alignment with the frame rails.

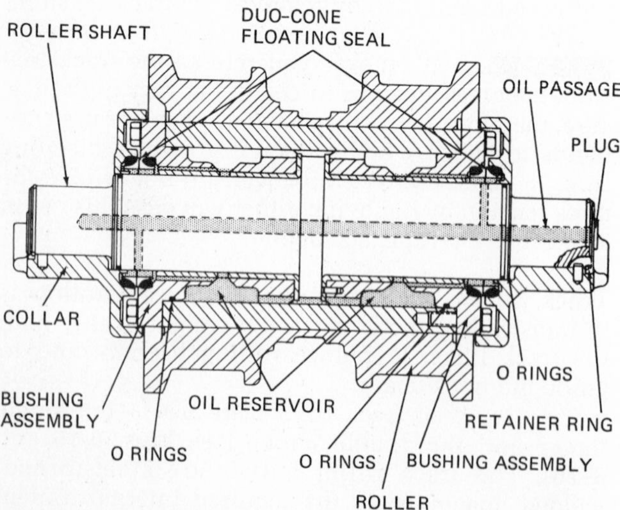

Fig. 8-16 Sectional view of double-flange track roller using bushing and duo-cone floating seal. (*Caterpillar Tractor Co.*)

NOTE Some track rollers use locating dowels to position the track roller shaft and prevent it from rotating should the roller body mounting cap screws become loose.

Most track rollers use oil as a lubricant and for this reason the track roller body must have one or two reservoirs. The track roller shaft must be center-drilled and must have several partly cross-drilled passages to provide lubricant to the seals and/or the bushings and thereby prolong the shaft, bushing, and seal life.

Track Carrier Rollers It is the function of the track carrier rollers to support and guide the track chain. Although they are basically similar in design to the track rollers, most carrier rollers have the flanges in the center and the tread surfaces on the outside. Furthermore, they nearly all use tapered roller bearings to support and align the roller body (see Fig. 8-17). In most cases, only one end of the roller shaft is fastened to the specially designed carrier roller brackets; therefore, only one roller shaft seal is required. The seals may be of the same design as those used with track rollers. The bearing preload may be adjusted through shims or through the nut that is threaded onto the right-hand side of the shaft. When oil is used as the lubricant, the housing is designed with an oil reservoir.

Track Chains The purpose of the track chain is to transform drive sprocket rotation into linear motion and thereby roll the tractor or carrier in a forward or reverse direction. It also serves as the mounting pad for the track shoes. The track chain is a combination of individual left- and right-hand links joined through the track pins and bushings to form a chain. The track chain ends are joined through a master pin (master links and bushing) to become an endless chain. The overall design of all track chains is the

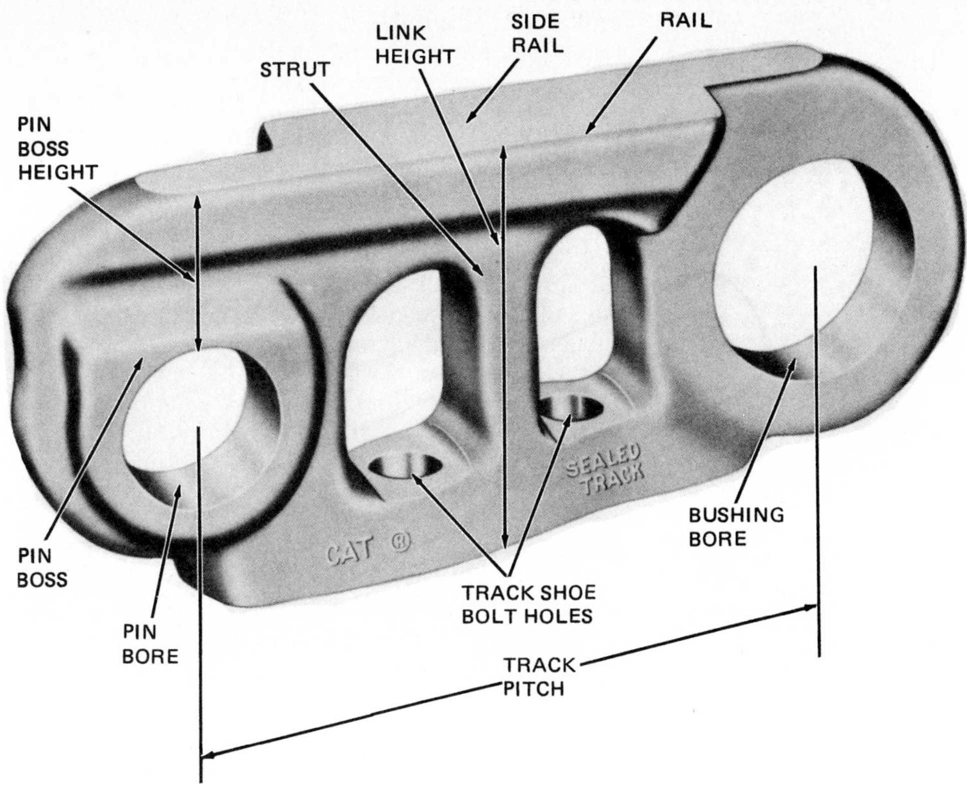

Fig. 8-18 View of a right-hand track link. (*Caterpillar Tractor Co.*)

same notwithstanding the varying sizes of the tractors and carriers and the relatively larger or smaller track pins and bushings, the greater or shorter track pitch, or the lighter or heavier construction of the track links.

Track pitch, which is the distance measured between the center of one track pin and the center of the adjacent pin, is the most important factor in track chain design. Furthermore, the track pitch and sprocket pitch must match to ensure smooth track chain rotation, as well as to reduce wear on the pins and bushings and sprocket teeth. Since wear accelerates when the pitches do not match, you should not use a new track chain with a worn sprocket, or a worn track chain with a new sprocket. Wear rate also accelerates if a new track chain is used with worn track rollers or with worn front idlers, or if new track rollers and front idlers are used with a worn track chain.

The track links are forged with a massive strut and heavy body to increase strength and minimize fatigue, then hardened to increase resistance to wear. See Fig. 8-18. One side of each track link has a bushing bore, and the other a pin bore. Both bores are broached for a precision fit with the pin and bushing. Each link has two holes, one at each side of the strut, to mount the track shoe. The link ends are formed in such a way that, when joined together, they prevent particles from lodging between them. The track pins and bushings are made from special steel and hardened to increase their service life. Track links may vary somewhat in design, shape, composition, and heat-treating method, but the most noticeable difference is the method by which the links are joined to one another.

TYPES OF TRACK CHAINS The oldest track chain design is the *open* type, also called the *flush* type (see Fig. 8-19*a*). In this design, the bushing is flush with the narrow ends of the track links. When the links

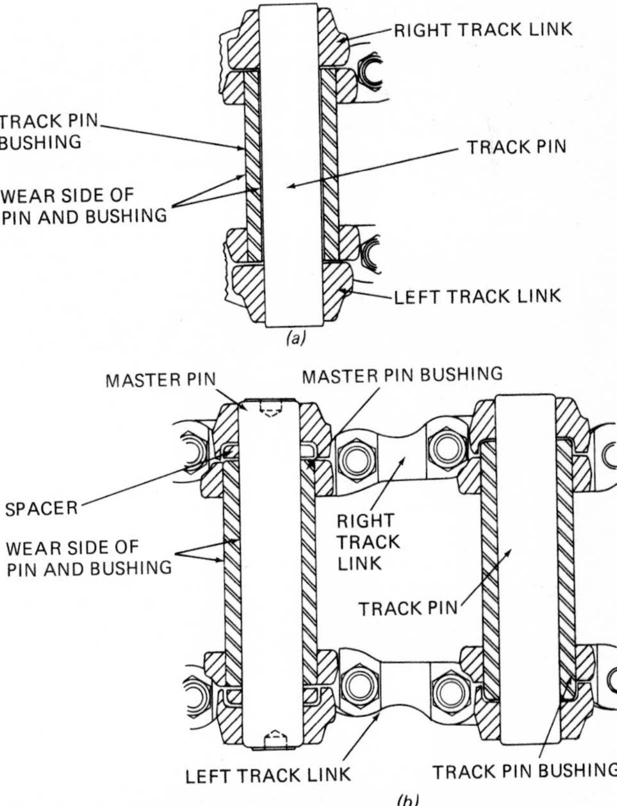

Fig. 8-19 (a) Sectional view of an open track; (b) sectional view of an interlocking-type track. (*Fiat-Allis*)

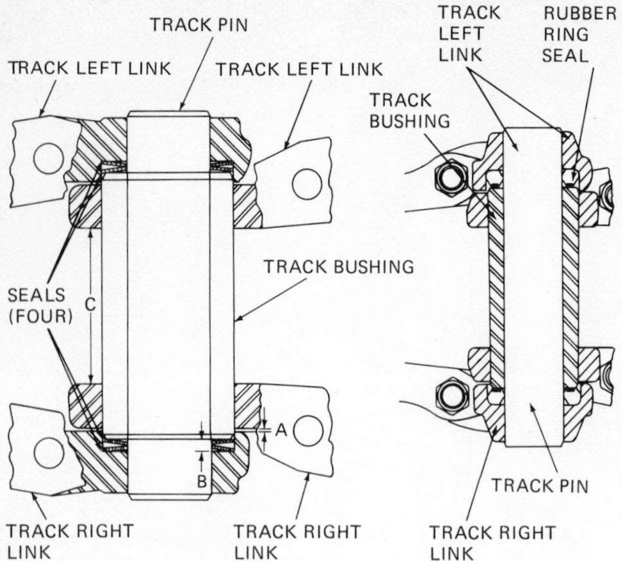

Fig. 8-20 Sectional view of two types of sealed track chains. (*Deere & Company*

are assembled there is a small clearance between the narrower and wider link ends, and the two joining links (with the wide spacing) lie with a very small margin against the inner links. There is no difference between the master links and the standard links, but the master pin is slightly smaller than the standard track pins. Nevertheless, that master pin is tightly fitted into the track link bore and held in position by pins.

The second design is the interlocking type (see Fig. 8-19*b*). Here the bushing extends past the end surfaces of the track links, and the extending ends fit loosely in the counterbore of the wider track link ends. The purpose of this design is to increase the pin and bushing wear area (thus reducing pin and bushing wear), and also to cover the joint areas and so prevent contaminants from lodging between the joints, pins, and bushings. The master link bushing therefore is shorter and is flush with the links. To compensate for this shortness, two ring spacers are used. The master pin is of the same design as the open track master pin.

The third type of track chain design is the interlocking seal type. Several different kinds of seals are used. They come in various shapes, may be of synthetic rubber, or may be cone disk seal washers. In any case, their function is to prevent contaminants from lodging between the track pin and bushing. See Fig. 8-20. **NOTE** The convex side of the outside cone seal washer faces outward, sealing the links, and the convex side of the inside cone seal washer faces inward, sealing the track pin. A track chain of this design uses a master pin, master link bushing, and ring spacers similar to those used by the interlocking type.

In an effort to reduce maintenance costs caused by external track pin and internal bushing wear, manufacturers are continually experimenting to develop different composition materials and/or hardening methods. The Caterpillar Tractor Company, however, has used another approach: It has designed and manufactured a lubricated and sealed track chain (see Fig. 8-21). Basically, it is an interlocking design. However, the track pins are center- and cross-drilled, permitting the oil to be stored and also permitting it to flow to the bushing and seals. One end of the track pin is plugged by a rubber stopper and a polyethelyne plug. Instead of cone seal washers, a thrust ring and rubber-back polyurethane seal assembly is used. The thrust ring rests on the track pin, and the seal assembly surrounds it. The inner side of the crescent seal is forced, through a soft rubber load ring, against the track pin, and the outer side is forced against the face of the track link.

Because of the design of the sealed and lubricated track chain and the size of the individual links, a different method is used to join the link ends (see Fig. 8-67). The master link is comprised of two diagonally shaped left- and right-hand link halves, interlocked through gear teeth. The two halves are held in this position by the ground bolts, which also serve as the track shoe bolts. Unlike the conventional track shoe, this arrangement requires a master track shoe because of the variation of the bolt hole pattern. **NOTE** When a sealed or lubricated track chain is used, equidistance at A and B (Fig. 8-20) is very important to assure an effective seal and to achieve the required distance (clearance) at C.

Track Shoes The purpose of the track shoes is to support the tractor or carrier weight and to provide flotation and/or traction. In addition, they are designed to provide protection to the track chain and thereby reduce wear. This is achieved (1) by slightly curving the front of the shoe downward and the rear of the shoe upward (when the track chain is straight, the adjacent track shoe overlaps at the front and the shoe at the rear underlaps), and (2) by positioning the grouser bar as far forward as possible over the link pin bores.

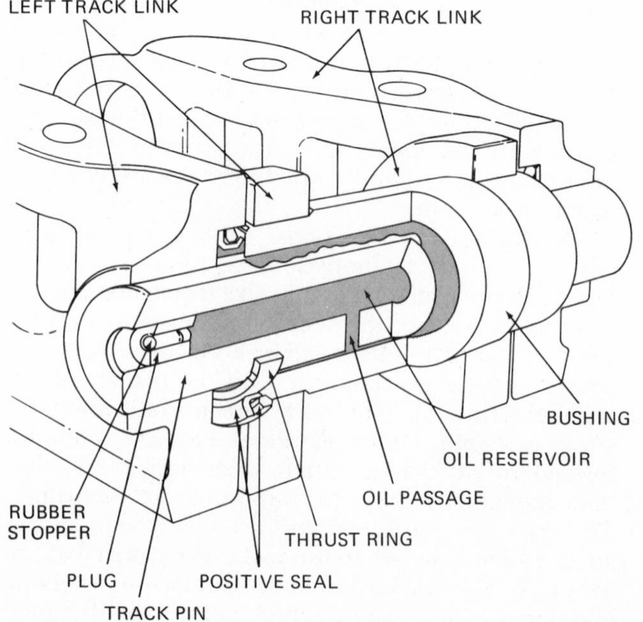

Fig. 8-21 Schematic view of a sealed and lubricated track chain. (*Caterpillar Tractor Co.*)

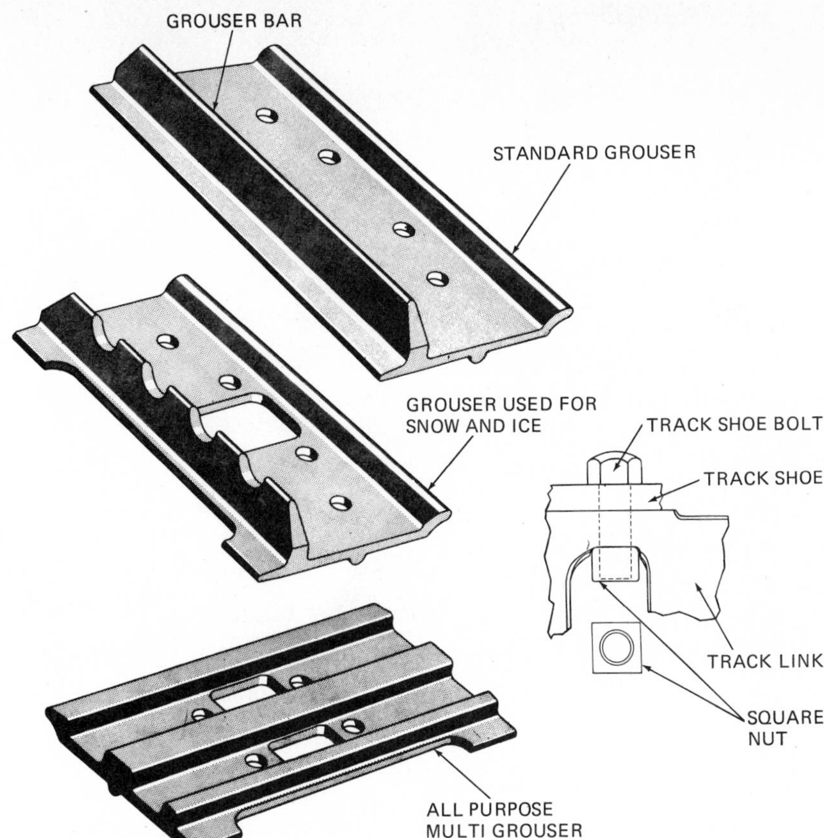

Fig. 8-22 The three most common track shoes. (*J I Case Company Agricultural Equipment Division*)

Track shoes of various widths, lengths, and designs are manufactured to meet particular needs and applications. Dozer tractors and carriers which require good ground penetration may use one of the track shoe designs shown in Fig. 8-22. However, numerous types are available, varying from the standard grouser having a single fairly high grouser bar, with or without the center relief hole, to the special grouser which also has a single grouser bar but which is manufactured to withstand a greater impact and abrasive terrain. To reduce turning resistance of loader tractors and carriers and thereby prolong the undercarriage life, a *double* or *triple grouser* (also called *multigrouser*), with or without the center relief hole, is used. Where the track shoes have two or three grousers, the grouser bar height is only half or less that of the standard grouser bar. For special operating conditions such as ice, snow, mud, dirt, or semiskeleton ice, grousers are also used. When operating on pavement or hard surfaces, flat track shoes of various designs are bolted to the track chain, or rubber pads are bolted to the track shoes.

To hold the track shoe to the track links, specially designed track bolts and nuts are required. The bolt threads are rolled to give greater strength, and the nuts are square. When installed, the nut rests in the provided cutout, making the assembly self-locking.

Track Roller, Idler, and Sprocket Guards The purpose of the track roller guards is to prevent particles from lodging between the track rollers and track chain, and to protect the track rollers from impact. The front idler and sprocket guards protect the sprockets and idlers by preventing large particles from falling onto the track chain. Not only would a continuous impact of rocks and large particles cause damage to those components, but if they entered the track assembly it could cause the track to become excessively tight, accelerating track roller wear and also damaging the sprocket teeth, the final drive, and the front idler. The guards are either of the prefabricated welded design or cast of steel, and are bolted to the track roller frame.

Crawler Carrier Undercarriages Basically two kinds of track-type undercarriages are used on crawler carriers: the tractor type and the crawler carrier type. Tractor undercarriages are commonly used on small and midrange excavators, cranes, shovels, etc., and are nearly identical in design to the tractor undercarriage previously covered. There are three differences, however: The side frames are bolted (at the front and rear) to mounting brackets or cross beams, which, in turn, are bolted to the lower carrier body (car frame, turntable); the drive sprocket shaft is supported by inside and outside bearings, the housings of which are bolted to the frame side rails; and the front idlers and track rollers use bushings exclusively, whereas the carrier rollers may use tapered roller bearings to support the roller body. Seals, such as those used on track-type tractors, seal the idler or roller shafts (see Fig. 8-23 for an example of this). Except that the track chains and track shoes may be larger in design, they are otherwise identical to the tractor-type track chain, and single- or multigrouser track shoes are also used.

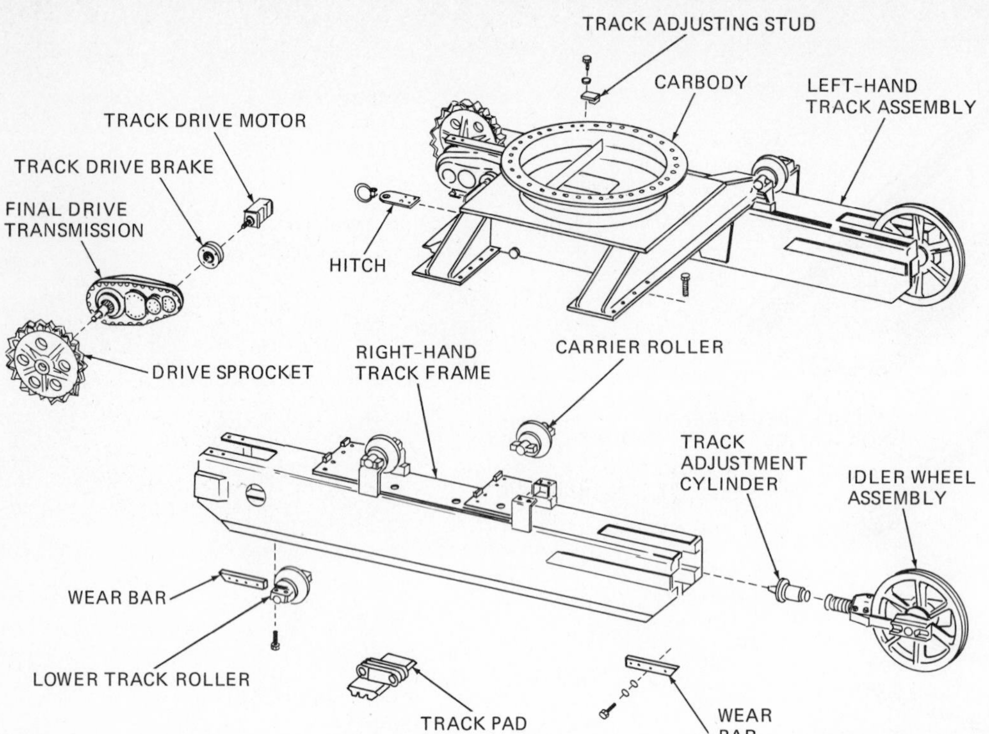

Fig. 8-23 Exploded view of an excavator track frame assembly. (*J I Case Company Agricultural Equipment Division*)

Crawler Carrier Undercarriage Design The overall design of the crawler carrier undercarriage is similar to the tractor undercarriage, although the design of the components differs. This is because the main purpose of the carrier undercarriage is to support the carrier weight and to provide a stable, secure footing to enable the superstructure to perform to capacity.

NOTE Although some component names may be different, their purposes and functions are identical to those of analogous components in tractor undercarriages.

SIDE FRAMES The crawler side frames are either of a prefabricated welded structure or are cast from steel. Because the undercarriages are designed to support the superstructure, there is no need for track roller guards. On large undercarriages the roller shafts are supported in the bores of the side rail, and on smaller machines they are bolted to the side rails. See Fig. 8-24. The two side frames are bolted to I beams or frame brackets, which are bolted to the lower turntable (gear box) frame. Depending upon the drive application, adjusting devices may be attached to the side frames to move the drive tumbler and sprocket, to adjust the drive chain, and to move the front idler tumbler in order to adjust the crawler belt.

BELT ROLLERS AND IDLER TUMBLERS The belt rollers, carrier rollers, and idler tumbler bodies are sup-

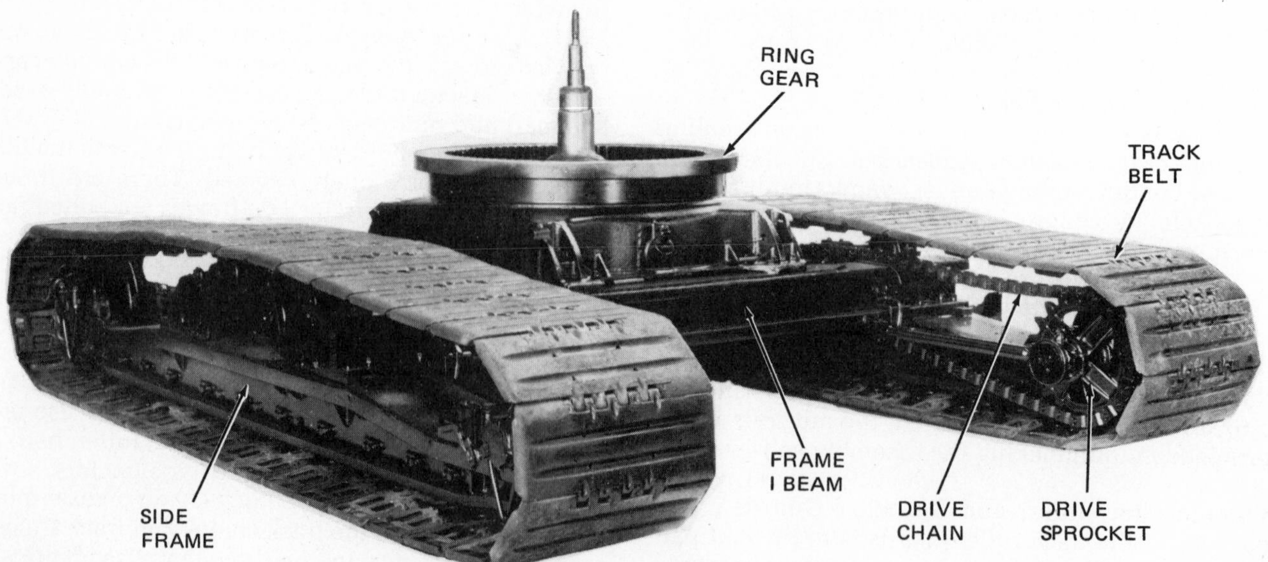

Fig. 8-24 View of track frame assembly. (*Northwest Engineering Company*)

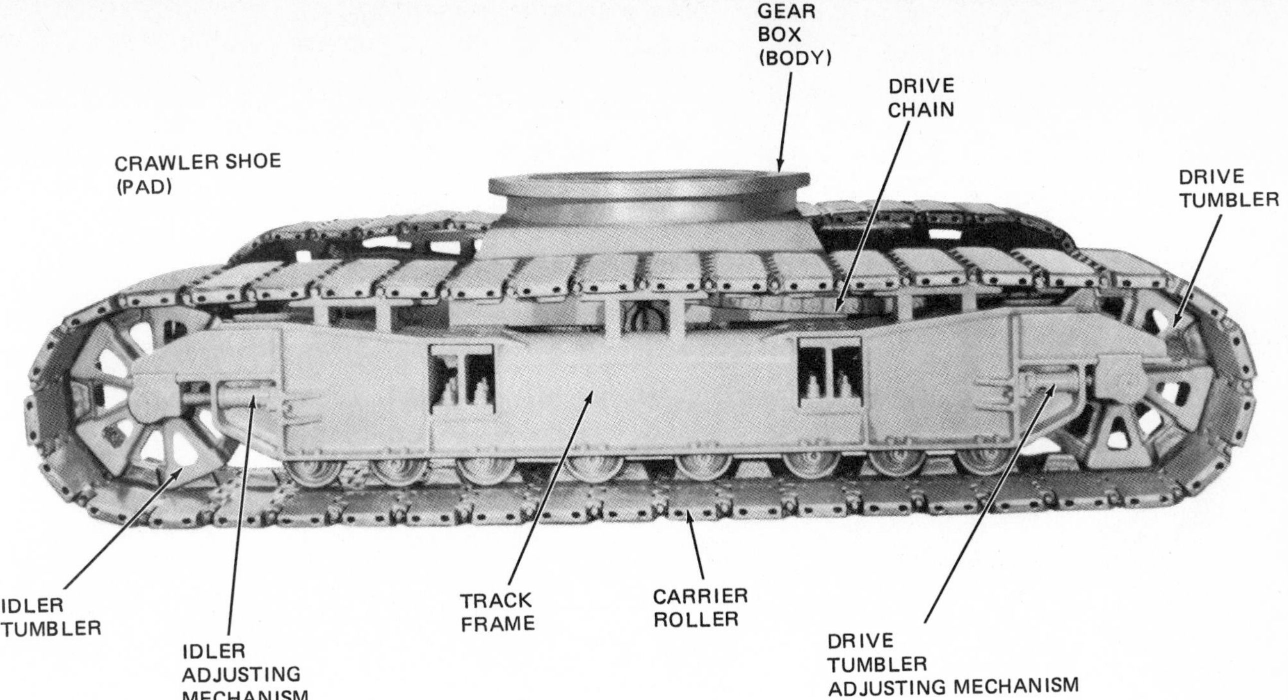

Fig. 8-25 View of left-hand track frame. (*American Hoist and Derrick Company*)

ported on their respective shafts by bushings. As a rule, no seals are used; the thrust washers retain the grease and also prevent contaminants from entering the rollers.

NOTE The weight of the belt rollers varies from 200 to 900 lb [90.8 to 408.6 kg]. Rollers smaller in weight may use lip-type seals. The belt roller shaft is secured in the bore side frame rail through bolts and nuts or through cap screws. The idler tumblers are either cast from steel or are of a prefabricated welded structure. See Fig. 8-25. The shaft ends are supported in bearing blocks, and shims, placed between the idler bearing block and the side frame rails, are used to adjust the belt tension. Otherwise the bearing blocks are fastened to a yoke and a screw adjusting mechanism is used, or each bearing block is attached to a screw belt adjuster mechanism. See Fig. 8-26.

Whatever the type of adjusting mechanism used, it nevertheless serves another purpose, which is to align the idler tumbler with the track frame. The outer circumference of the rollers and tumblers vary in that the larger-sized machines have specially rounded rollers and tumblers to permit treat oscillation and symmetrical distribution of the machine weight when operating on uneven ground (see Fig. 8-27), whereas other idler tumblers have a lower-profile tooth pattern or are designed similarly to the tractor front idler. The belt roller and carrier roller may have the same external appearance (shape) as a (tractor) track-carrier roller.

DRIVE TUMBLER The drive tumbler and drive sprocket (when a chain drive is used), or the gear (when a final drive transmission is used), are splined to the final drive shaft. When a final drive transmission is used, the bearing blocks that support the final drive shaft are bolted to the side frame rails. When the tumblers are driven through roller chains, the bearing blocks are supported and guided on guide rails and shims can be used to move the drive tumbler and sprocket rearward to tighten the roller drive chain; each individual bearing block can be moved by using a screw-type adjusting device. However, both methods also provide the drive-tumbler-to-track-frame alignment.

The drive tumblers are cast from steel but the design of the outer circumference varies. Some have

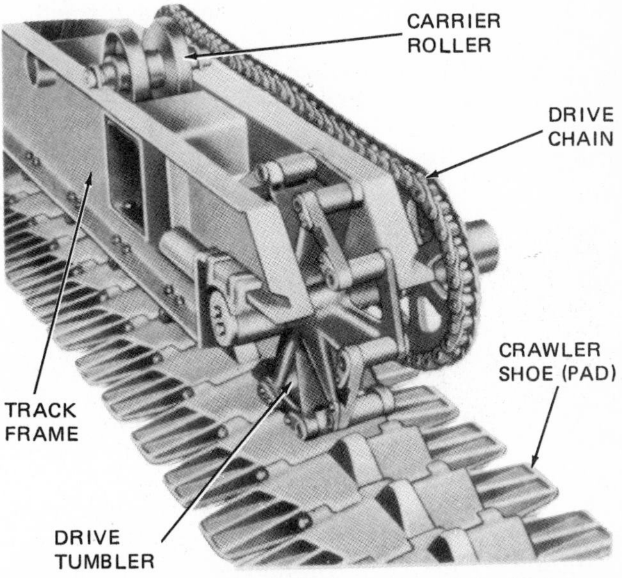

Fig. 8-26 View of left-hand track frame. (*Schield Bantam Division of Koehring Company*)

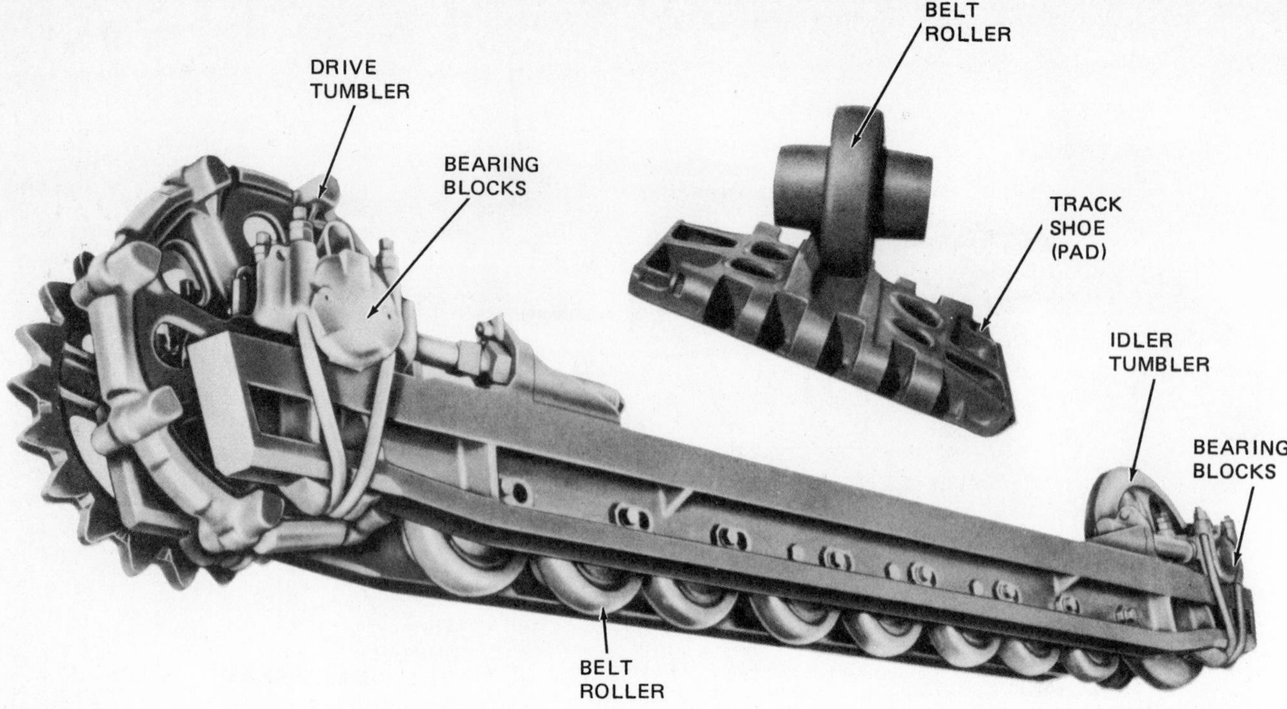

Fig. 8-27 View of right-hand track frame. *(Northwest Engineering Company)*

large drive lugs equally spaced to the belt pitch. Others are designed as shown in Fig. 8-26, where hardened rollers turn on hardened pins which are attached to the drive tumbler in order to provide a rolling friction contact between the tumbler and track shoe lug. This design not only reduces the wear of the drive tumblers, final drive, crawler shoe lugs, pins, and bores, but also reduces the repair costs and downtime.

TRACK BELT AND SHOES The crawler belt (track belt) is composed of individual crawler shoes (treads) or pads cast from steel with reinforced ribs, drive lugs, and link pin eyes. The outsides of the crawler shoes are commonly flat; however, some have traction grooves cast into them. The size of the shoes varies—some are relatively small, 16 in [40.6 cm] in width, whereas others are large, about 58 in [147.32 cm] wide—the size used depends on the weight of the machine and the ground conditions of the terrain where it will operate. The same rule that applies to tractors also applies here, which is that the smallest crawler shoe possible should be used to reduce wear. For example, one manufacturer recommends using a 24-in [60.96-cm] shoe when operating on a solid ground or uneven, rocky terrain, and a 32-in [81.28-cm] shoe for all-purpose construction work. When working in soft, swampy, or marshy terrain, a shoe width of 40 in [101.6 cm] is recommended to achieve a low ground contact pressure. When using the 40-in [101.6-cm] crawler shoe, the ground pressure of the machine is reduced to 3 psi [20.67 kPa].

It is possible to interchange one individual shoe with any of the three sizes or to interchange one entire crawler belt with another that has larger or smaller crawler shoes, without any alteration to the crawler undercarriage because the crawler belt pitch on all three shoe sizes is the same.

The track pins (link pins, shoe pins) which couple the individual crawler shoes to an endless belt may be straight hardened pins, or specially designed pins. They are secured through cotter pins, specially designed keepers, or as shown in Fig. 8-28 through a bolt and nut. No master link or master pins are used because all crawler shoes and pins are equal;

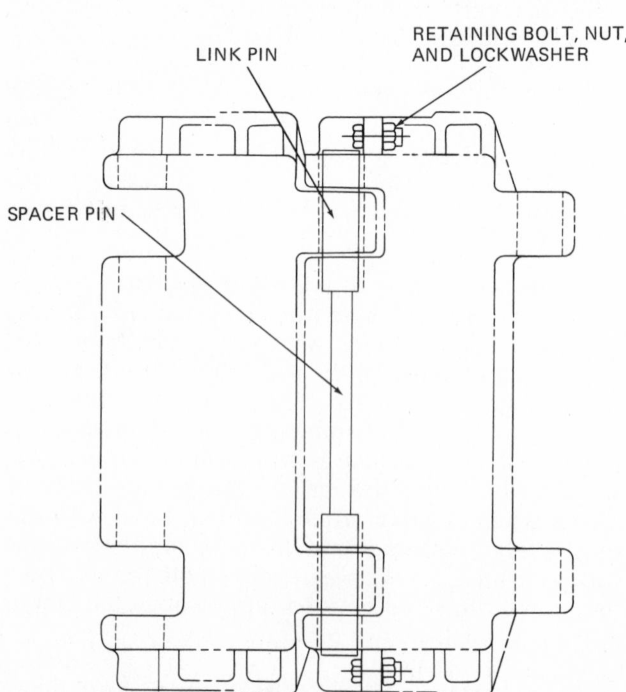

Fig. 8-28 Schematic view of a crawler shoe assembly. *(Harnischfeger Corporation)*

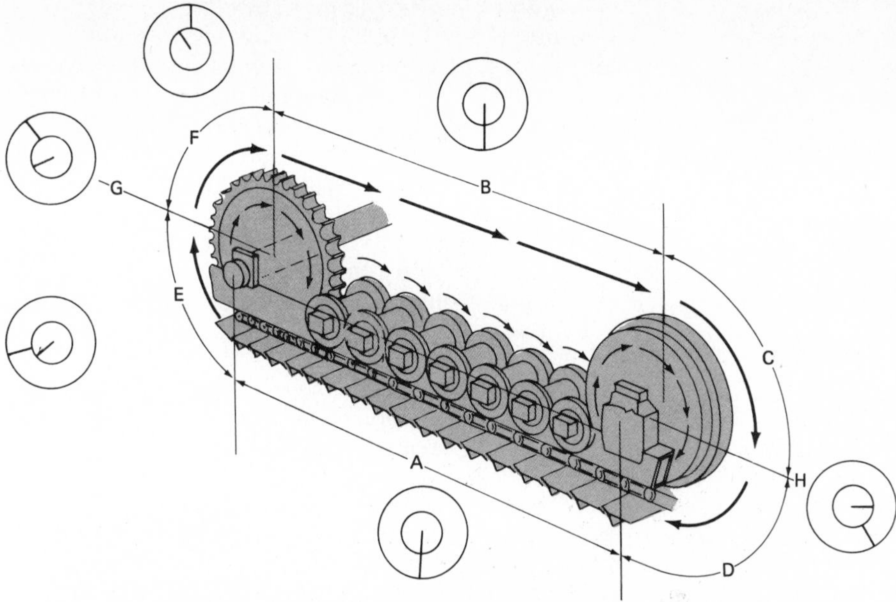

1. At "A" track chain is standing still. No track pin or bushing movement
2. Track then speeds up "E" and at "G". Maximum pin and bushing rotation has occurred
3. From this point on, ("F"), the track further increases and rotation of pins & bushings reverses
4. At "B" the track chain speed is twice the tractor travel speed
5. The track chain speed then reduces ("C"), and again track pins and bushings rotate. At "H" they are in the maximum rotated position
6. At "D" the track chain further reduces in speed, and the track pins and bushings reverse rotation

Fig. 8-29 Track chain action.

therefore, the crawler belt can be split at any crawler shoe.

Track Chain and Belt Action As the tractor moves, the track links or shoes located between the center line of the drive sprocket and the front idler remain stationary. When both drive sprockets or tumblers are driven in a clockwise rotation, the track links or shoes which are in the sprocket or tumbler rotate with the sprocket. One track shoe is lifted off the ground onto the sprocket, while at the top one track link leaves the sprocket. This action pulls the tractor forward. At the same time, one track link or shoe leaves the front idler and one track link or shoe is placed onto the ground. This action repeats until the drive sprocket rotation stops.

If the drive sprocket is rotated in a counterclockwise direction, the entire action reverses. One track link after another at the top is pulled onto the drive sprocket, while below one track link after another leaves the drive sprocket and is placed onto the ground. Simultaneously, in regard to the front idler one track link after another is lifted off the ground onto the idler while at the top one link after another leaves the front idler. As a result the tractor is pulled and rolls in reverse direction onto the stationary track links.

Several mechanical actions occur as the track links come on and off the sprocket and front idler. For instance, assume that the track chain is rotating in a clockwise direction: (1) As the individual track links move from the horizontal to the vertical and then return to the horizontal position, they semirotate at the pivot points of the track bushings and pins. (2) The rotation speed of the track links on the drive sprocket increases to twice that of the moving tractor. (3) At the front idler, the rotation speed of the track links diminishes to zero when the track shoe is laid onto the ground. See Fig. 8-29. In other words, the greatest friction between track bushings and pins occurs while they are on the drive sprocket and front idler. As an example, when the ground speed of the tractor is 1 mph [1.61 km/h], the top track links' speed (between the sprocket and front idler) is precisely 2 mph [3.22 km/h].

When the track frames are pivot-mounted and one track frame, say the right-hand one, rolls over an obstacle, the track frame is forced upward and the equalizer pivots, transferring the force to the left-hand track roller frame. However, the left-hand track is on the ground; therefore the upward motion of the right-hand track frame is restricted.

If the right-hand track frame rolls into a hole, the equalizer bar mounting restricts the downward movement.

If the front idler hits an obstruction, or the track chain is shortened because a rock lodges between a bushing and a sprocket tooth or between the track roller and track links, the recoil mechanism is compressed. When this happens, the strain exerted on the bushings and track pins, the sprocket, the sprocket shaft and bearings, the front idler shaft and bearings, and the yoke is reduced. After the obstruction is overcome or the rock is expelled, the recoil mechanism expands again, returning the track once more to its normal tension.

UNDERCARRIAGE MAINTENANCE

The cost of the tires on highway motortrucks or truck-tractors may amount to 3 percent of the total

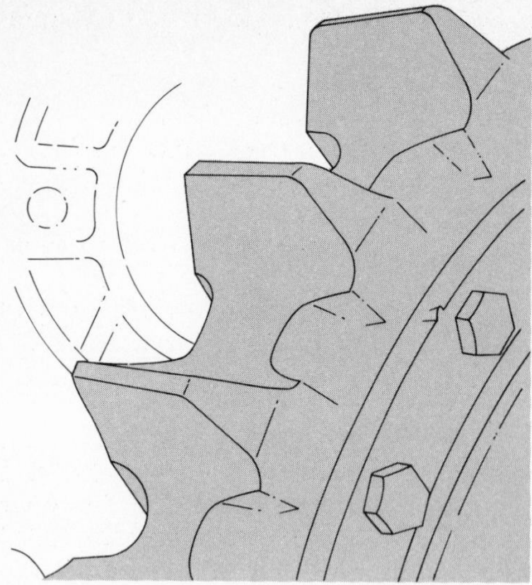

Fig. 8-30 Relief-tooth sprocket segments. (*Terex Division of General Motors Corporation*)

purchase price of the vehicle, whereas the cost of the undercarriage on a track-type tractor amounts to about 28 percent. Costs for tire maintenance, including replacement, may amount to approximately 1.7 percent of the total maintenance costs of the wheel-type vehicle, whereas the maintenance costs of an undercarriage on a track-type tractor may reach 50 percent of the total, or more if the tractor is used regularly under severe operating conditions. For these reasons alone careful selection of undercarriage components and a good maintenance program are mandatory if the operating costs and the downtime are to be kept to a minimum.

UNDERCARRIAGE COMPONENTS AND WEAR The causes of undercarriage wear can be classified into four groups:

1. Undercarriage components not suited to the operating condition
2. Component misalignment due to severe operating conditions
3. Poor maintenance
4. Tractor constantly operated at high speed

Although the service technician has little control over (1), (2), and (4) above, it should be obvious when the undercarriage components do not match the operating conditions or when the tractor attachments are causing an unbalanced weight distribution. It is your responsibility to suggest component replacement in the interest of economy. You should also be aware that, if the tractor operates in ice and snow, or in sticky soil, the drive sprocket should be of the relief-tooth design (see Fig. 8-30), since this type allows the dirt to escape as the bushing enters the root of the tooth. In that case also, track shoes of the open center grouser design should be used (see material on track shoes). Open center shoes prevent ice or mud from building up in the pockets formed between the links, bushings, and track shoes. When operating on ice, an ice shoe should be used to provide good penetration and thereby prevent track spin-out. In this instance you, as the mechanic, could forestall undercarriage wear by removing the track roller guards to allow the ice, snow, or mud to be squeezed out. If, because of the guards such material remains trapped, the friction from the rotating components will increase. In fact, the track rollers could even be prevented from rotating, and this would cause flat spots on the tread surface and result in link surface and pin boss wear.

It is also your responsibility to grease the track roller (using a low-pressure grease gun) when applicable, and on a daily basis if so required. You should check the final drive oil level at least every week. **NOTE** Apply grease to the components only until you feel a resistance, otherwise you could damage the seals.

Manufacturers usually recommend that the tractor operate with the narrowest track shoe possible for the job since unnecessary extra width adds extra load onto other parts of the undercarriage system. The narrower width could increase track slippage, but it reduces the lever force from the track shoes to the track links, and then against the track roller flanges, drive sprockets, and front idler flange (see Fig. 8-31). The probability of the track shoes bending or becoming loose as the shoe ends are forced upward would then be minimized. On the other hand, if the operation demands a maximum drawbar pull, a shoe having the required width and cross section must be used; otherwise the track will spin out, reducing the work capacity and increasing undercarriage wear.

Track slippage and high operating speed (forward or reverse) do by far the most to accelerate wear of track pins, bushings, and sprockets because every rotating part is speeded up, which increases friction. High slippage may be the result of worn grouser shoes, in which case the track shoes must be replaced. It can also occur when the operator tries to push a load greater than the track traction capacity. To overcome this, the operator should shift down to a speed that does not cause abuse to the undercarriage.

To reduce undercarriage wear, the weight of the tractor and attachments must be evenly distributed

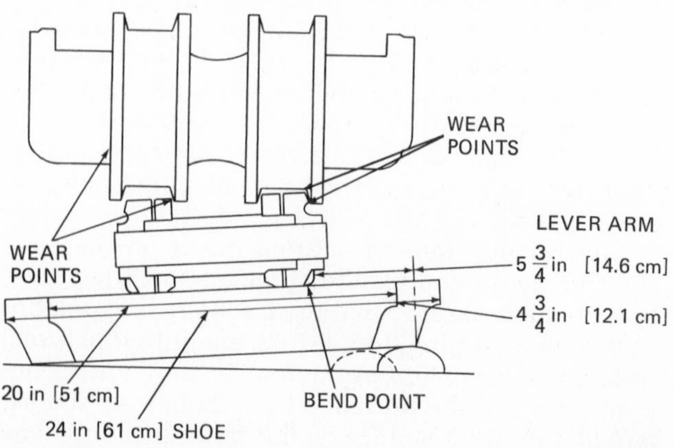

Fig. 8-31 Track shoe selection. (*Terex Division of General Motors Corporation*)

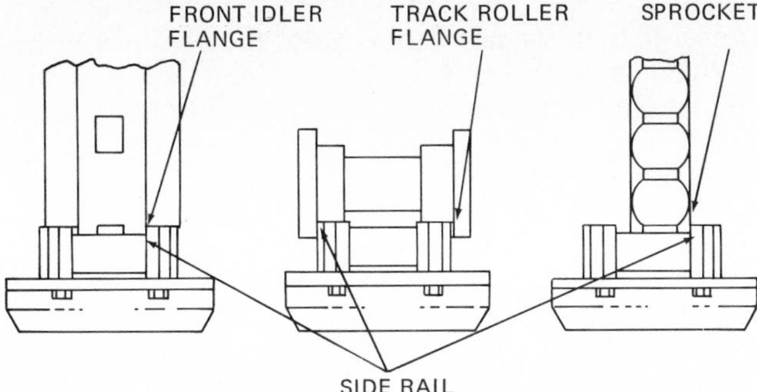

Fig. 8-32 Wear point on downhill side. (*Fiat-Allis*)

onto the track rollers and track chains. If the tractor is heavy at the front because no counterweight or attachment is used to offset the loader or dozer weight, the wear rate of the front idler, the front track frame, and the first two track rollers will increase. If the tractor is heavy at the rear due to the combined use of winch and a heavy ripper, the wear rate of the two rear track rollers will increase. To offset these conditions and to achieve balance, add weight to the front or remove one or more ripper shanks.

UNDERCARRIAGE WEAR DUE TO OPERATING CONDITIONS A cause of undercarriage wear over which you have little control is the kind of operating conditions the tractor may encounter. Examples are as follows:

- *When the tractor has to work in water or excessively wet terrain.* Fine amounts of contamination will be swept into cavities and pockets, especially between pins and bushings and between bushings and sprockets, and will abrade them like emery cloth.
- *When the tractor is used exclusively for push-loading or for ripping.* Excessive wear will occur on the two front or two rear track rollers because of the weight transfer during the operation.
- *When the tractor must work on a side slope.* This forces the entire tractor weight to the downhill side (see Fig. 8-32). Although the track shoes hold the tractor on the slope, most of this weight is placed, through the track links, onto the track roller flanges, front idler flanges, and sprockets. As a result, increased wear will occur at each of these points.
- *When the tractor is used continuously for loading operations.* It may be required to turn excessively, in which case the undercarriage wear will be similar to that found when the tractor must operate on a slope.
- *The ground surface on which the tractor must operate, such as sand, topsoil, shale, clay, rocks, or coal.* Each has a different degree of abrasiveness which affects the life of the undercarriage. Sand and rock formation, for instance, cause a high wear rate, whereas coal, due to its lubricant quality (graphite), reduces the wear and therefore prolongs undercarriage life.

UNDERCARRIAGE WEAR DUE TO POOR MAINTENANCE AND MISALIGNMENT Since maintenance means so much to the life of the undercarriage, its importance cannot be overemphasized. Maintenance should include

1. Keeping the undercarriage clean
2. Maintaining correct track chain tension
3. Regularly lubricating the track rollers, idlers, and final drive
4. Making regular visual checks for loose or missing parts
5. Visual checks to determine misalignment, and where necessary making minor repairs such as replacing or rotating track rollers, replacing track shoes, and turning pins and bushings

It is even more important to keep the undercarriage clean when the tractor is used in geographic locations where the ambient temperature falls below freezing or on terrain that tends to stick to the undercarriage and congeal overnight. Such coagulated buildup and hardened mud or snow prevent the track rollers from rotating and could prevent the recoil mechanism from operating. An additional incentive for keeping the track undercarriage clean is that the track adjustment can then be checked with ease and loose track shoes and oil leaks at the rollers, idlers, and sprockets can be detected early. If any of these conditions are noted, the tractor should be serviced immediately to prevent further undercarriage wear, as procrastination will only result in double or triple repair costs and downtime at a later date.

Improper track tension Track adjustment neglect is another primary cause of excessive undercarriage wear. A *loose* track becomes snakelike and will not stay aligned between the sprocket and front idler. The track links, therefore, rub on both sides of the roller and idler flanges, and on both sides of the sprocket teeth. When the tractor changes direction from forward to reverse, the top of the track whips against the track carrier rollers. The resultant hammering effect may bend the carrier roller shafts and/or the carrier roller bracket and cause a tremendous strain on the sprocket teeth and final drive components. A loose track also increases track pin and bushing wear because the individual track links follow the contour of the ground. Moreover, none of them mate as well with the track rollers, idlers, and sprocket teeth, and on the top the track bends and kinks as the links move over the carrier rollers. Still another problem is that a loose track could allow the sprocket to jump one or more teeth as the tractor direction is changed from forward to reverse. This would cause excessive strain and wear on the pins and bushings, sprocket teeth, and final drive components. Finally, when a track is loose and the tractor is operating on a slope, undercarriage wear is accelerated by about 50 percent because, under this condition, the track may jump on and off the track rollers, or the track links roll on the roller flanges and cause additional track link, roller flange, idler flange, and sprocket teeth wear. On larger tractors the deterioration will be even speedier because of greater misalignment due to the longer track chain.

A track chain which is adjusted *too tightly* is not unusually destructive to the undercarriage. However, if the recoil mechanism is damaged, its full energy is exerted on the front idler and after a short operating period the track pins and bushings will cease to pivot because of the resulting high friction. The operator should notice this malfunction immediately because the tractor begins to lose power. It must be stopped immediately, or the pins and bushings and sprocket teeth will start to disintegrate, and within about 6 h of operation the tractor will break down. Furthermore, during this interval, extreme force is placed on the front idler and final drive components.

If the track chain is only moderately overtight, the friction between the track pins and bushings would increase, resulting in accelerated wear on the pins and bushings, sprocket teeth, final drive components, front idler shaft, and bearings. Unfortunately, under this condition the operator may not notice the loss of power.

Checking for Wear and Loose or Missing Components Motortrucks, truck-tractors, and other wheel-type motor vehicles having steering components which are loose, bent, or out of alignment show a specific tire wear pattern. This is also true for track-type tractors in the sense that a specific wear pattern will occur on the undercarriage components and that wear will accelerate if the cause is not immediately corrected. It is therefore important to check the undercarriage components as often as possible for bent or loose parts. You should also check the wear (and wear pattern) of the sprockets, front idler, track and carrier rollers, and track links, to determine not only the undercarriage's remaining life span, but also if there is misalignment.

If the track shoes are loose or bent, they interfere with each other and cause excessive stress on the track links, rollers, idlers, and sprockets. Track shoes in this condition would also allow segments of terrain to pass by the individual shoes and then be forced into the track links and onto the track rollers. If the track shoes are loose over a long period of time, the holes in the shoes and links will elongate, making tightening of the shoes impossible. For these reasons, the track shoe bolts should be retorqued after about 100 h of operation. Although this may be time-consuming, it is worth the effort in the long run.

Check all pivot points of the equalizer bar and the track roller frame for wear, and make certain that the bearing cap bolts are torqued to specification. Periodically check the torque of the sprocket segment nuts or cap screws. If they become loose and remain so, not only will the sprocket teeth deteriorate more quickly, but the sprocket and sprocket hub holes will elongate. Furthermore, the track pins and bushings will wear because of the increased track pitch.

Check that the track, the sprocket, and the idler guards are in place and are not bent out of shape. Otherwise they will not serve their intended purpose and will contribute to accelerated undercarriage wear. If they are defective, replace them with new ones. If they do not fit properly, they should be removed, straightened, and/or welded before being reinstalled. All manufacturers provide one or more track wear gauges which, when properly used and interpreted, can be used to evaluate the undercarriage condition and the approximate length of future component life.

Checking Track Chain Wear Track pins, bushings, and sprocket teeth, because of their interrelation (track pitch), affect track life more extensively than any of the other components. The extent of the exterior bushing wear can be determined by using an outside caliper (see Fig. 8-33) to measure the distance between the caliper legs, and then comparing this distance with the measurement recommended in the service manual. For example you may find the service manual states that a new bushing should have a diameter of 3.04 in [77.22 mm] and a service limit of 2.87 in [72.90 mm]. To be acceptable for reuse, the bushing to be reused must measure within these tolerances. If the bushing wear limit is less than 2.87 in [72.90 mm], the bushings and pins should be turned.

The internal wear of the bushings and pins (track pitch) must be measured. There are two methods by which this can be done: by using the track wear gauge (Fig. 8-34), or by measuring the distance between a number of pins. In either method, the track should be tightened by placing a track pin in one sprocket tooth and then driving the tractor backward. Next, apply the brakes, or tighten the track by using the track adjuster, or place a hydraulic jack between the track chain and track frame, then extend the jack to raise the track.

To measure track pitch by the first method mentioned above, place the track wear gauge as shown in Fig. 8-34 with one edge of the gauge in line with the right-hand inside pin bore. The opposite edge of the gauge indicates the wear. If the pin and bushing are worn no more than the specified limit, they may be turned, but if worn further they should be rejected.

NOTE Since individual companies produce their own wear gauges, always read the relevant instruction manual carefully to ensure correct evaluation of measurement.

Repeat the procedure by measuring the wear of the master pin and bushing.

NOTE The wear rate at the master pin and bushing is greater when their contact area is less than the contact area of a standard pin and bushing. When

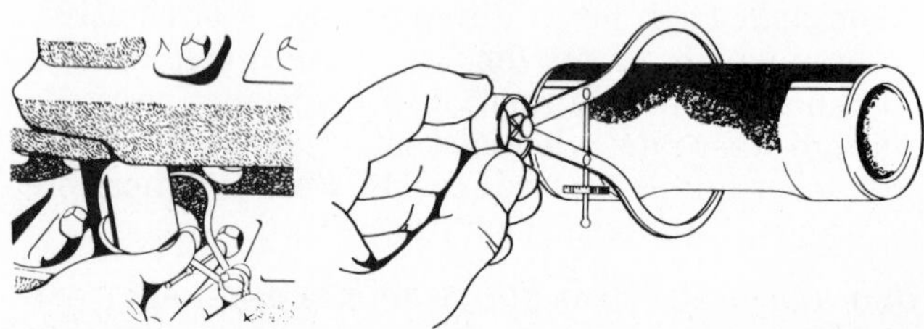

Fig. 8-33 Checking bushing wear with an outside caliper. (*J I Case Company Agricultural Equipment Division*)

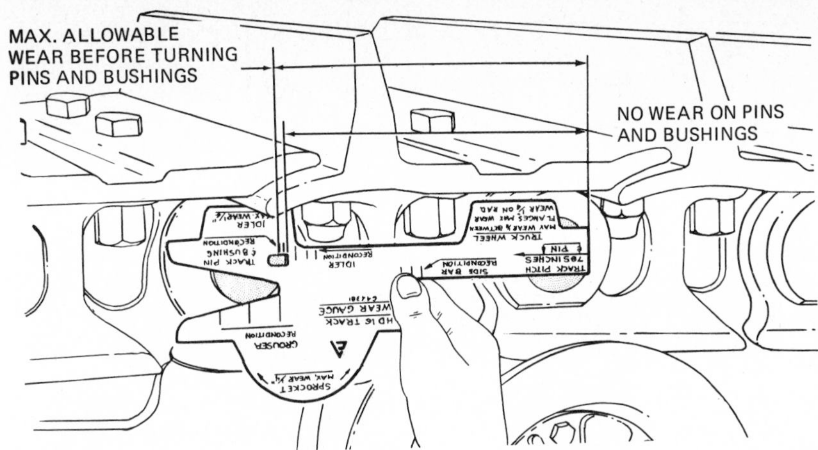

Fig. 8-34 Measuring track pin and bushing wear (track pitch) with special gauge.

that is the case, the wear rate of the two adjacent pins and bushings will also increase. It is therefore recommended that the master pin and bushing be replaced when the wear on them is one-half the maximum allowable amount for the other pins and bushings, in order to reduce the wear on the sprocket and the adjacent pins and bushings.

The second method referred to above is carried out as follows: When the track is tight, measure the distance from one pin boss bore to the fifth pin boss bore or from one side of one pin to the same side of the fifth pin. Divide that distance by the number of link sections, that is, five, as recommended in most service manuals (see Fig. 8-35). To determine the total wear of the pins and bushings, subtract the pitch dimension given in the service manual from the measured value. For example, when the actual track pitch is 10.25 in [260.35 mm], the maximum recommended track pitch service limit is 10.37 in [263.40 mm], and the total distance you have measured over four links is 41.25 in [1047.75 mm], then the total wear is

$$0.25 \times \frac{41.25}{41.00} = 0.25 \text{ in } [6.35 \text{ mm}]$$

The wear at each pin and bushing is 0.25/4 = 0.062 in [1.57 mm]. Thus the pins and bushings are within the wear limit and do not require turning. To determine master pin wear repeat the procedure for the master pin.

Checking Sprocket Wear Next, measure the sprocket tooth wear with the track wear gauge. Place the gauge, as shown in Fig. 8-36, with the rounded portion against the root of the tooth. Read the wear from the gauge. If the sprocket tooth is worn at 1 and 5 it is normal wear caused by the rotation of the bushings as they leave the sprocket when moving forward, while if worn at 2 it is normal wear of the sprocket caused by the rotating bushings as they enter it when traveling in reverse. If worn at 3 and 6, the wear is due to increased track pitch; and if worn at 4, the bushings are sliding from side to side, indicating that the track frame to sprocket is out of alignment. Heavy wear on the inside or outside of the sprocket teeth should then be noticeable. If heavy contact is on the inside of the sprocket teeth, the track frame is *toed out*. In this case heavy contact would show also on the inside two rear track roller flanges, on the outside flange of the rear carrier roller, and on the inside of the inside track links. If the track frame is *toed in*, heavy contact or wear would appear on the opposite side of the sprocket teeth, track and carrier rollers, and track links.

If the track frame at the pivot point is out of alignment due to a bent shaft, a worn bushing, or misadjustment, accelerated wear will occur on the sprocket teeth, the track links, and the track and carrier roller flanges. When the track frame is misaligned toward the outside, a heavy contact would show on the inside of the sprocket teeth, on the inside of the inside track links, on the outside of the two rear track roller flanges, and on the outside flange of the rear carrier rollers. If the track frame is misaligned toward the inside, however, the heavy contact area would appear on the opposite sides of all components just listed. If the track frame pivot point is bent upward (the track frame is leaning inward on the top), heavy contact would show on both sides of the sprocket, on the inside of both track links, on the inside flanges of the two rear track roll-

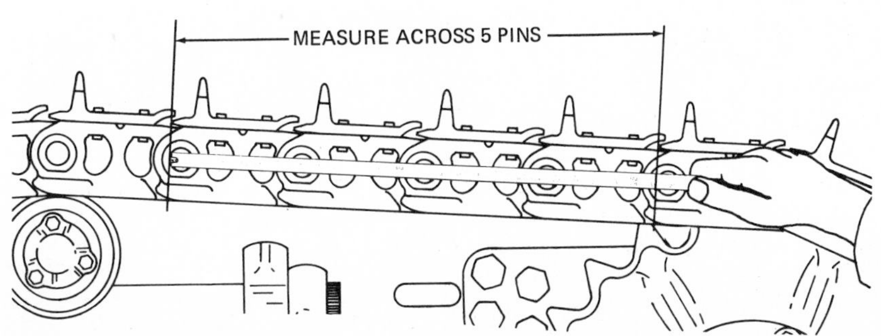

Fig. 8-35 Measuring track pin and bushing wear (track pitch) with straightedge.

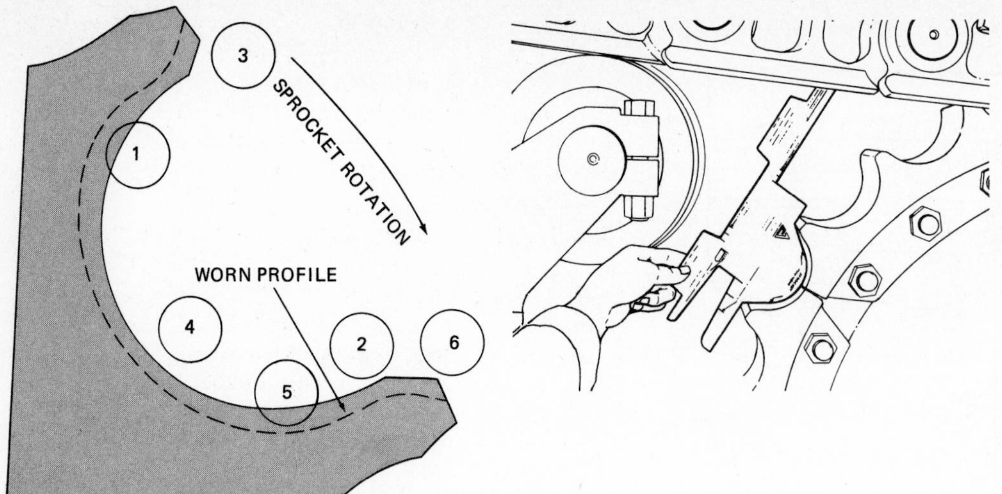

Fig. 8-36 Measuring sprocket wear and determining its cause.

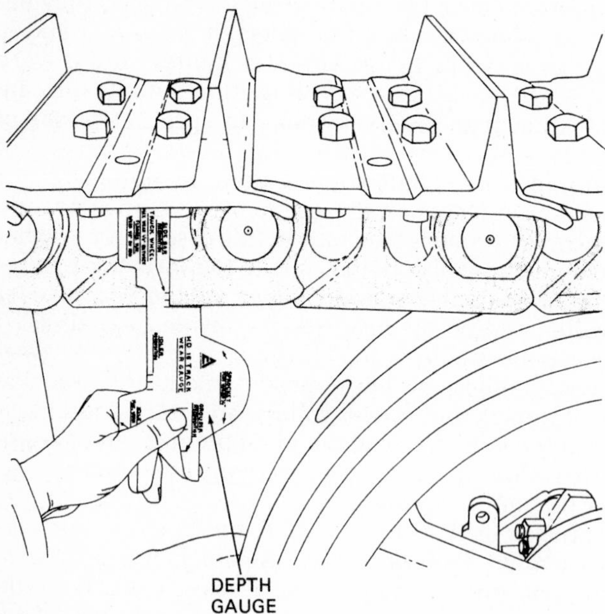

Fig. 8-37 Measuring track link height using a wear gauge.

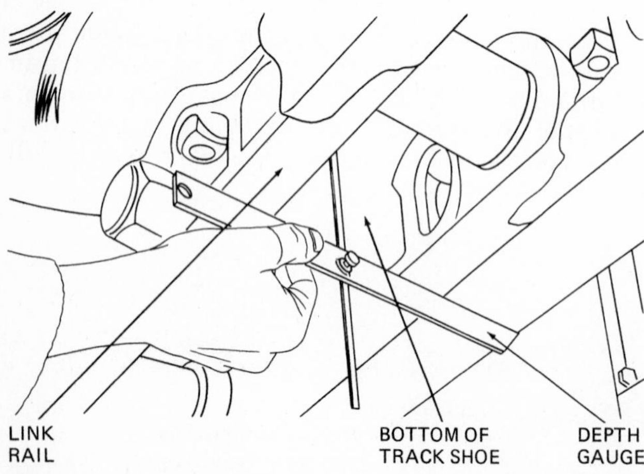

Fig. 8-38 Measuring track link height using a depth gauge.

ers, and on the outside flange of the rear carrier rollers.

Checking Track Link Wear You can measure the track link wear (height) with a wear gauge (see Fig. 8-37), or with a depth gauge (see Fig. 8-38). If the links are worn beyond the recommended maximum wear limit, the pin bosses are too low and could damage the track roller flanges; moreover, the track roller flanges would then wear the track pin bosses. In these circumstances, the track links must be rebuilt or replaced.

If the pin bosses show wear, but the track link is within the wear limit, the track roller thread surfaces are worn beyond an acceptable limit. Some manufacturers recommend measuring the pin boss clearance to detect possible track roller flange damage and pin boss damage. To make this measurement without removing the track guards, measure the track link and the track roller wear, and then subtract the combined wear measurements from the measured clearance of the pin boss when new. For example: Assume that the service manual clearance of the (new) pin boss is 0.50 in [12.7 mm]. Assume that the measured track link wear is 0.15 in [3.81 mm], and the track roller wear is 0.25 in [6.35 mm]. The pin boss clearance in this instance would be $0.50 - (0.15 + 0.25) = 0.10$ in [2.54 mm]. See Fig. 8-39.

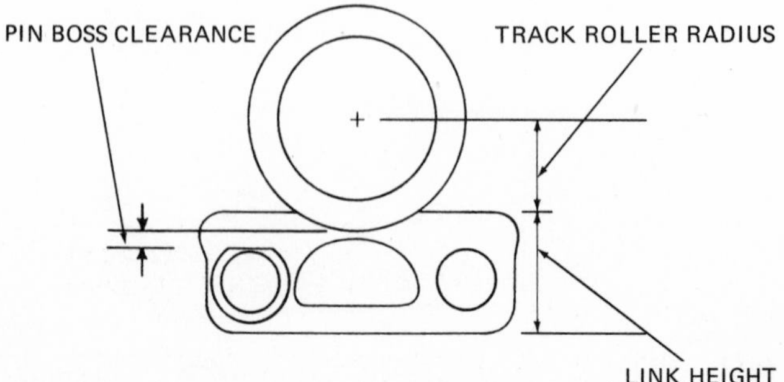

Fig. 8-39 Method of measuring pin boss to roller flange clearance.

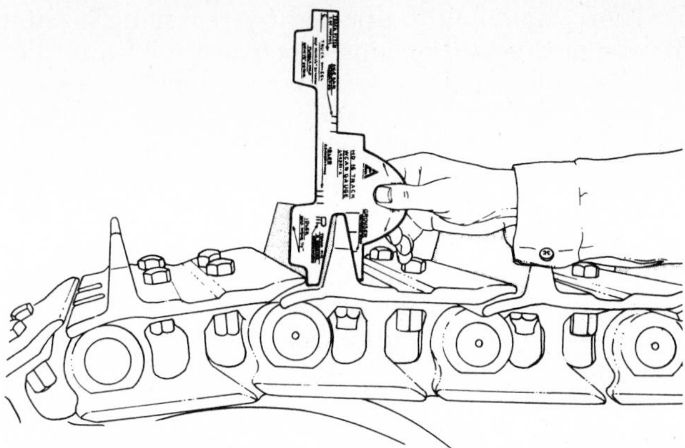

Fig. 8-40 Method of checking grouser wear. (*Fiat-Allis*)

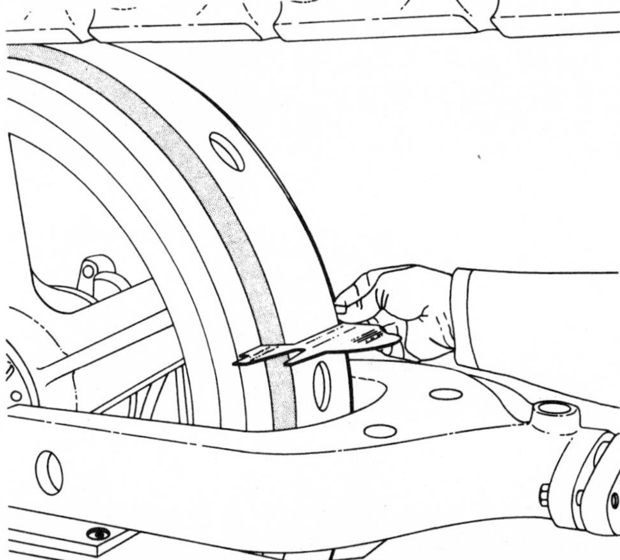

Fig. 8-41 Method of checking idler tread and flange wear. (*Fiat-Allis*)

HEAVY CONTACT ON
IDLER OUTER FLANGE

LIGHT TO NO CONTACT
ON IDLER INNER FLANGE

HEAVY CONTACT ON INNER SIDE
OF OUTER SIDE BARS

LIGHT TO NO CONTACT ON INNER
SIDE OF INNER SIDE BARS

NOTE: MORE CONTACT ON OUTER ROLLER
FLANGE THAN INNER FLANGE (NOT SHOWN)

Fig. 8-42 Wear pattern when front idler is off-center toward outside. (*Fiat-Allis*)

Checking Grouser Wear Next, check the grouser wear by placing the gauge onto one grouser. If the wear is beyond the lowest mark on the gauge, the shoes should be replaced or the grousers rebuilt; otherwise there may be track slippage, and possibly bending of the track shoes. See Fig. 8-40.

Checking Front Idler Wear Next, place the gauge onto the idler flange to check the front idler tread (rim) surface and flange for wear (see Fig. 8-41). If uneven wear is noticeable, or if there is an uneven wear pattern (that is, evidence of heavy and light contact), the front idler is out of either vertical or lateral alignment. If the contact on each of the sides of the idler flanges, and on the insides of both links and the two front track roller flanges is even, the front idler is properly aligned. However, if the outside idler flange contact is heavy, the inside surfaces of the outside track links show heavy contact, and the two front track rollers show heavy contact on the outside flanges, the front idler is laterally offset toward the *outside* (see Fig. 8-42). If the front idler is laterally offset toward the *inside* then the heavy contact appears on the opposite flanges of the front idler and track rollers, and on the opposite side of the track links.

If there is a heavy contact on the inside of the front idler flange, on the outside track links' inner surface, and on the two front outer track roller flanges, the top of the front idler is tilted toward the inside (negative camber) (see Fig. 8-43). But if the heavy contacts are on sides and parts opposite to those just described, it is tilted on the top toward the outside (positive camber).

If the heavy contact is on the outside of the front idler flange, on the inner surface of the outer track links, and on the inner flange of the two front track rollers, the front idler is toed in (see Fig. 8-44). If on

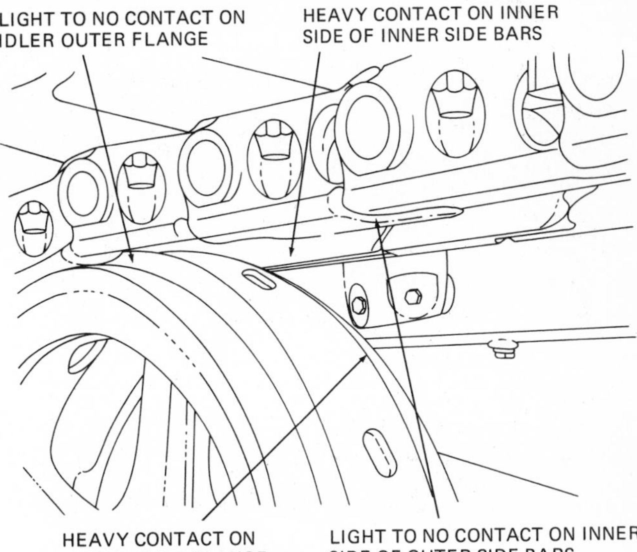

NOTE: MORE CONTACT ON INNER ROLLER
FLANGE THAN OUTER FLANGE
(NOT SHOWN)

Fig. 8-43 Wear pattern when front idler is off-center toward inside. (*Fiat-Allis*)

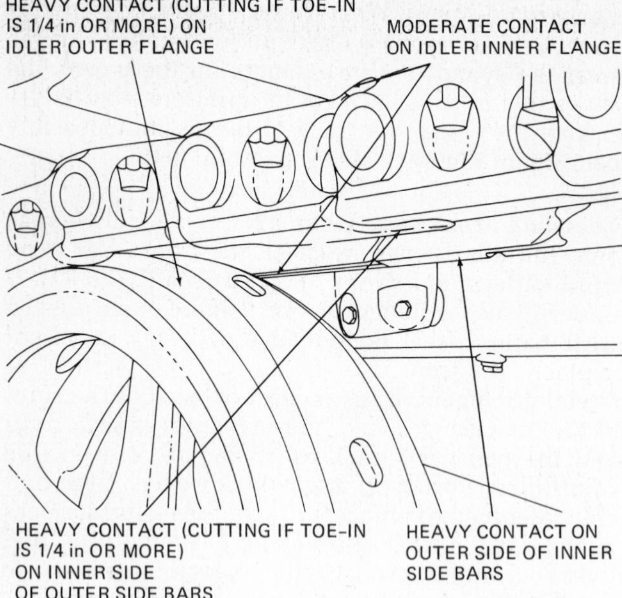

Fig. 8-44 Wear pattern when front idler is toeing in. (*Fiat-Allis*)

the opposite parts and surfaces, though, it is toed out (Fig. 8-45).

Adjusting Front Idler to Compensate for Wear To adjust the front idler in order to correct camber or toe, always refer to the appropriate service manual. However, before making any adjustment check for loose bolts on the idler brackets and bracket guide plates, and check for worn or damaged idler brackets, idler guide plates, and slide bars. If any of these defects are present, correct as necessary; that is, retorque the bolts and/or replace the worn, damaged, or bent part.

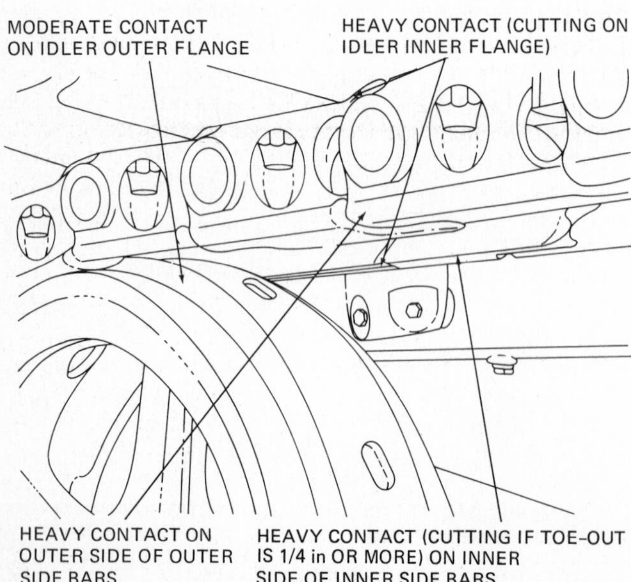

Fig. 8-45 Wear pattern when front idler is toeing out. (*Fiat-Allis*)

Toe is commonly adjusted by removing a shim from one side and placing it between the front idler bracket and guide plate. To correct camber, a shim is removed from between either the top or bottom of the slide bar and frame rail and then reinstalled in the opposite position. To correct the front idler offset in an effort to center the idler position, shims are removed from one side of the front idler bracket guide plate and reinstalled between the idler bracket and guide plate on the opposite side (see Figs. 8-6 and 8-46). **NOTE** If idler wear is excessive, remove the idler from its bracket, turn it 180°, and reinstall it. This will prolong the life not only of the front idler, but of track links and track rollers too.

Checking Track and Carrier Roller Wear Next, with a track wear gauge, check the track and carrier rollers for wear. When proceeding by this method, you must remove the track roller guards and loosen the track tension. Place a 12 × 12-in [30.48 × 30.48-cm] block behind the drive sprocket and drive the tractor onto the block until the sprocket is in the center of the block. Apply the brakes. You can now place the gauge onto each track roller to determine the flange and surface (tread) wear.

If the front track rollers are beginning to wear, the track rollers may be rotated or moved to the rear or the center to prolong roller life. Some manufacturers recommend not only rotating the track rollers, but also interchanging those on the left with those on the right.

A faster method to check track and carrier roller wear, though not quite as accurate, is as follows: Measure the distance from the center of the track

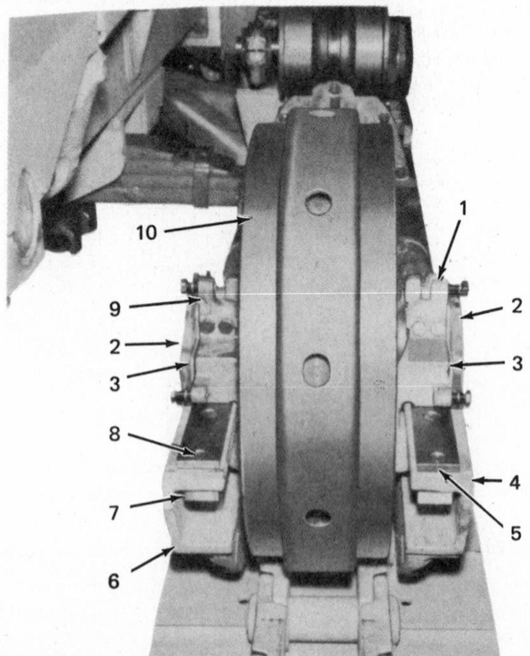

1. Outer idler bracket
2. Guide plate
3. Guide plate shims
4. Truck frame outer channel
5. Slide bar shims
6. Truck frame inner channel
7. Lower slide bar
8. Upper slide bar
9. Inner idler bracket
10. Track idler

Fig. 8-46 Front idler adjustment components. (*Fiat-Allis*)

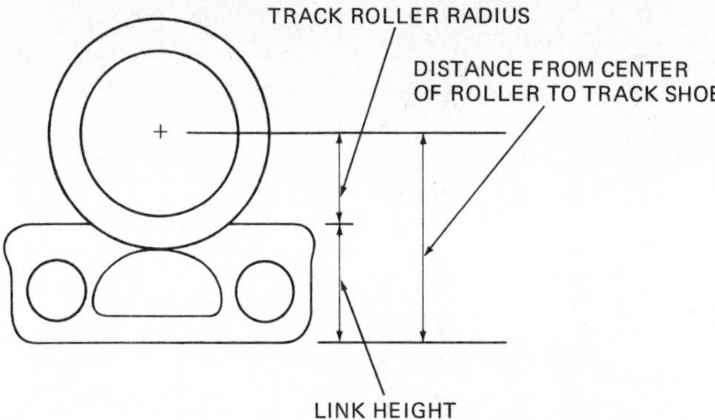

Fig. 8-47 Method of determining roller wear.

roller to the inside surface of the track shoe. Then measure (at the top) the track link height. Subtract the last measurement from the first, and subtract this measurement from the radius diameter of a new track roller. For example, say the distance from the center of the track roller to the track shoe is 9.30 in [236.22 mm], the measured link height is 4.80 in [121.92 mm], and the track roller radius of a new track roller is 4.53 in [115.06 mm]. The calculated wear on the track roller is then 9.30 − 4.80 = 4.50, and 4.53 − 4.50 = 0.03 in [0.76 mm]. See Fig. 8-47.

Checking Track Frame Alignment If you suspect that the track roller frame is out of alignment, bent, twisted, cracked, or broken, that the pivot point is bent, or that the front idler is misaligned, the track frame alignment must be checked. This procedure may vary for the products of different manufacturers (as may the tools used for checking alignment), but the following steps are common to all:

Before doing anything else, steam-clean the undercarriage thoroughly, adjust the track chain, and then drive the tractor straight ahead onto a level cement surface. Do not make any steering corrections during the approach.

To check toe and/or track frame parallelness, measure with a toe-in bar or steel ruler the distance between the ends of the left- and right-hand track roller shafts at the front of the tractor, as well as the distance between the ends of those shafts at the rear. Then compare the measurements. If the measured difference is more than specified in the service manual, the track frame or the pivot shaft is bent. It is usually bent rearward (see Fig. 8-48). In order to determine which is the case (track frame or pivot shaft), the track frame must be checked.

To check for a twisted track frame and a bent (upward) pivot shaft you may use a protractor and measure the frame from side to side, horizontally. To do this, place the protractor on a machine-cleaned transmission or steering clutch housing surface and then center the bubble of the protractor. Clean the track frame flanges in front of the sprocket and in front of the slide bar. Lay a straightedge across the frame rails and place the protractor onto the straightedge, or use the method shown in Fig. 8-49. The bubble position indicates whether the track frame corresponds with the machined surface or not, and if not, it indicates the difference in minutes and/or

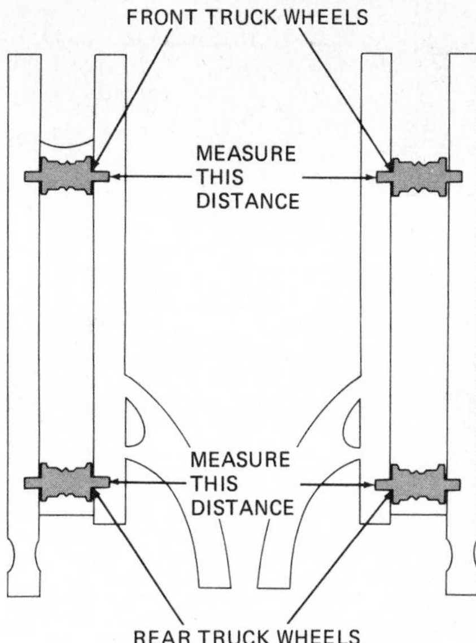

Fig. 8-48 Measuring points to determine bent track frame. (*Fiat-Allis*)

degrees. **NOTE** Do not rotate the protractor 180° when you move it from the machined surface onto the straightedge, as this will give you an incorrect measurement. Repeat these steps at the front of the sprocket. If both degree readings coincide, say they show ½° (30′) negative, the pivot shaft is bent upward. However, if the bubble, when measuring near the rear frame, is in the center, but shows ½° (30′) negative when measuring near the front, the track frame is twisted.

If after analyzing the front idler wear pattern you suspect that the idler is leaning (on the top) toward the inside, first measure the idler center position. To do this, lay a straightedge against the inside surface of the outside top slide bar, or against the track frame flange edge, and measure the distance between the straightedge and the outside surface of the idler flange. Repeat this procedure with the inside top slide bar or frame flange edge. An acceptable distance would be equal to, or at least within, the maximum variation. If this is not the case, release the track tension, remove the outer and inner guide plates, remove one shim from the side to which the idler is to be moved, and install the removed shim

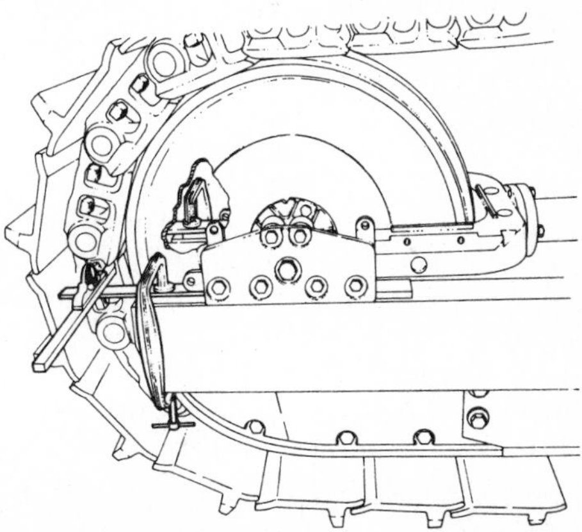

Fig. 8-49 Checking track frame level. (*Fiat-Allis*)

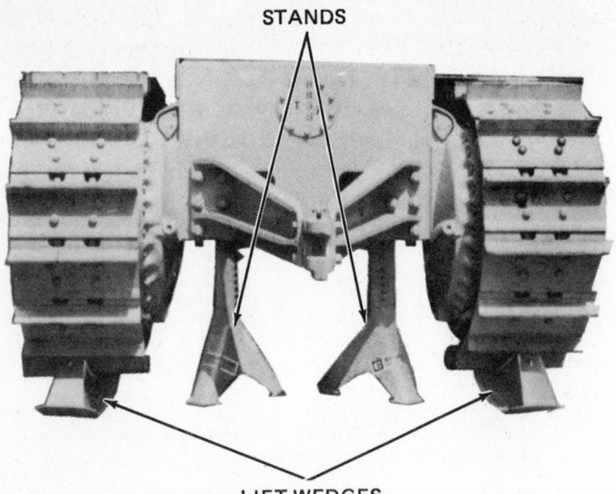

Fig. 8-50 Method of raising and blocking tractor in order to remove track roller. (*Caterpiller Tractor Co.*)

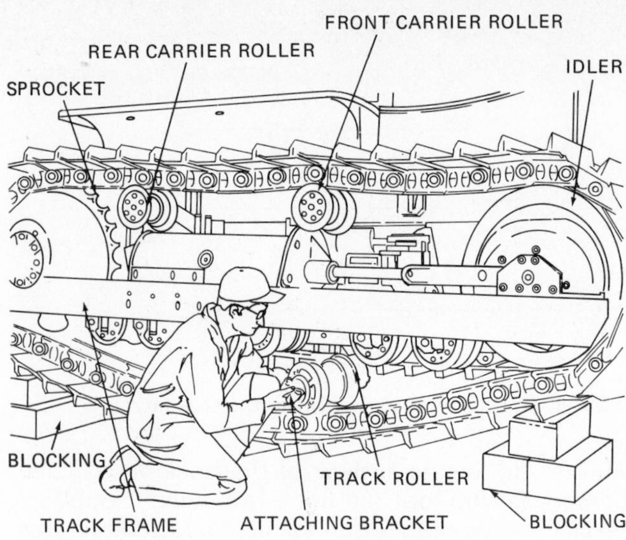

Fig. 8-51 Method or raising tractor off the ground. (*Fiat-Allis*)

to the other side; then reposition the guide plates, retighten the bolts to the specified torque, and check the vertical position of the idler. To adjust the front idler vertical position, split (uncouple) the track and slide the idler from the track frame. Remove one shim from below the outside top slide bar and insert it onto the lower outside slide bar. This will achieve the required outward tilt of the idler on the top. See Fig. 8-46.

UNDERCARRIAGE SERVICE

Replacing Track Rollers To replace a track roller, you must first remove the track roller guards. This, of itself, may be a major undertaking if, for instance, the cap screw heads are worn and therefore no socket will fit the head, or if the cap screws should break, or if the guards are so twisted that no socket can be placed onto the cap screws. Again, there are occasions when the twist tension of the guards is so great that removal of the cap screws is extremely difficult.

Nevertheless, once the guards are removed, steam-clean the undercarriage, if possible, or dislodge the mud or dirt, and then drive the tractor onto level ground, preferably inside a workshop. After removing the track tension, if the tractor is small, use hydraulic jacks to jack up the front and rear ends. Make certain the jacks are correctly positioned and supported so that they cannot sink into the ground or slip off the tractor frame or housing (see Fig. 8-50). If you do not have a hydraulic jack and/or if the tractor is large and heavy, position blocking material as shown in Fig. 8-51, or place a specially designed wedge about 12 in [304.8 mm] in front of the front idler, and drive the tractor forward until the block or wedge is under the first track roller. Then place the same type of block or wedge against the rear track shoe and back the tractor over the second block, far enough to place both blocks or wedges in the center of the idler sprocket. The slack of the track chain should then be at the bottom, in which case apply the parking brakes and block the tractor with blocking material or steel stands. You can now measure the roller, treads, and flanges for wear. You should also check for oil leaks and, with the aid of a crowbar, pry the rollers up to feel the bushing and end play wear.

To remove a track roller, place short pieces of 2 × 4- or 2 × 6-in wood between the track links, and with additional blocking material support the rollers. Next, loosen and remove the cap screws and the shaft brackets, or shaft retainers, and roll the rollers from the wood onto the ground.

To remove a track roller on a large tractor where the roller weight is more than 100 lb [45.4 kg], loosen and remove the shaft brackets, or shaft retainers, and the cap screws from the three rear rollers and then back the tractor onto the rear blocks (you can also carry out this procedure on the front three rollers and then drive the tractor onto the front block). This lowers the track chain and the roller slides from between the frame side rails. It is also good practice to lay pieces of wood between the track links to facilitate removal of the roller. **NOTE** If you have a fork lift, place the forks under the track chain and raise the forks to support the roller. Remove the cap screws and shaft retainers, then lower the track chain and remove the roller. Or you may use a tool similar to that shown in Fig. 8-52. If you notice any worn or damaged threads, use a tap to restore them.

The track roller reinstallation procedure is precisely the reverse of the removal procedure.

CAUTION Take care not to damage the roller flanges or to endanger your fingers as you push/lift the roller into position. Align the shaft retainers, and the roller shaft, then install the cap screws and tighten them to the recommended torque.

Replacing Track Carrier Rollers To replace a track carrier roller, first remove the track tension. On small tractors, raise the track chain with a crowbar

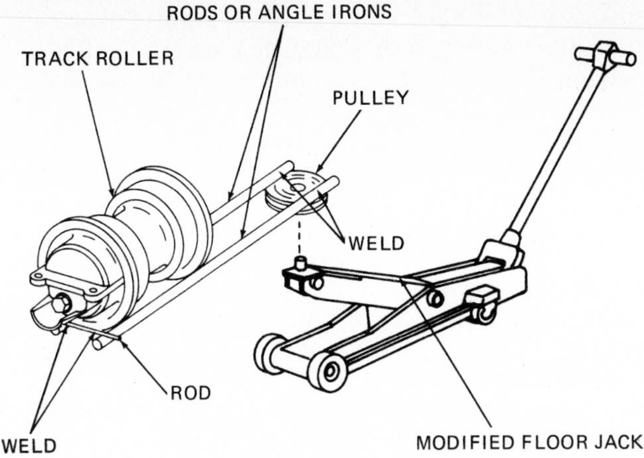

Fig. 8-52 Track roller removal and installation tool. (*Deere & Company*)

or pipe and support the track chain by using two blocks, one on each side of the carrier roller bracket. On large tractors use a hoist and sling, raise the track chain, and then block the track. Next, in order to remove the carrier roller, either remove the cap screws that hold the carrier roller mounting brackets to the side rail, or else remove the two cap screws and place a heavy-gauge sheet metal in the bracket slot; then reinstall the cap screws. Tighten them against the sheet metal as this will spread the bracket and ease removal of the shaft. Then remove the carrier roller.

Reinstall the carrier roller in precisely the reverse order of steps by which it was removed, but make certain, if applicable, that the two dowels in the end collar are properly inserted into the support bracket holes, or that the machine groove in the end of the roller shaft aligns with the support bracket holes.

Inspecting Crawler Belt Rollers To inspect or to replace one or more crawler belt rollers, one must be able to approach the machine from below. Small machines can be raised according to the procedures outlined earlier for tractors. However, for large machines this method is too difficult and time-consuming. Therefore the following method is recommended: Dig a hole about 1 ft [0.305 m] deep, one-third wider than the belt and about one-half the overall length of the side frame, then drive the machine over the hole so that one or two belt rollers are exposed for inspection and the shaft and bushings can be checked for wear.

To check the shaft and bushings, place a suitable bar between the roller and belt shoe and as you lift the roller, measure the clearance between the shaft and bushing, using a ruler or dial indicator. **NOTE** This may be difficult as some rollers weigh nearly 1000 lb [454 kg]. If a replacement is necessary because of the excessive clearance you must release the belt tension in order to gain slack between the crawler belt and rollers. Next, use blocking material to support the rollers so that they remain snugly in place as the roller shaft is removed, remove the retainer or locking device which holds the roller shaft to the side frame rail or, if applicable, drive out the shaft (your service manual will instruct from which side it is to be driven out). Use a suitable lifting device to lower the belt roller from between the side frame rails and then, using sheer muscle power or a hoist and lift, remove the roller from the crawler belt. The reinstallation procedure is precisely the reverse of the removal procedure.

Track Carrier Roller Service

DISASSEMBLY Thoroughly clean the track carrier roller exterior. Next, remove the inner retainer cap screws and screw the pusher cap screws into the threaded holes of the retainer, or use a hydraulic puller arrangement to pull the bearing retainer, seal retainer, and seal from the shaft and body. (See Fig. 8-53 for a sectional view of these parts.) Remove the

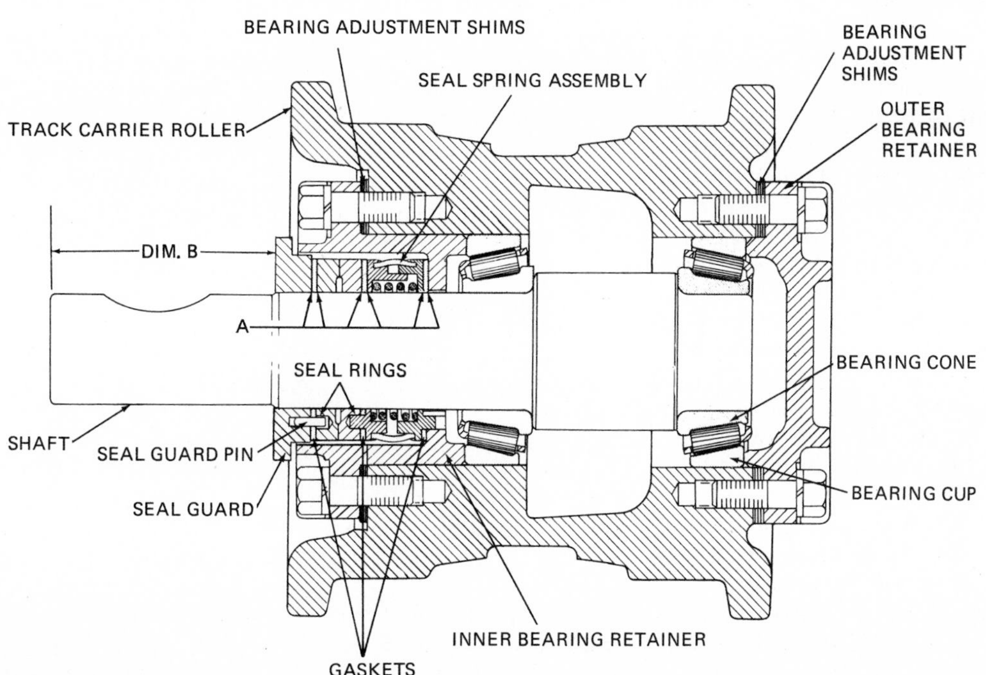

Fig. 8-53 Sectional view of a track carrier roller. (*Fiat-Allis*)

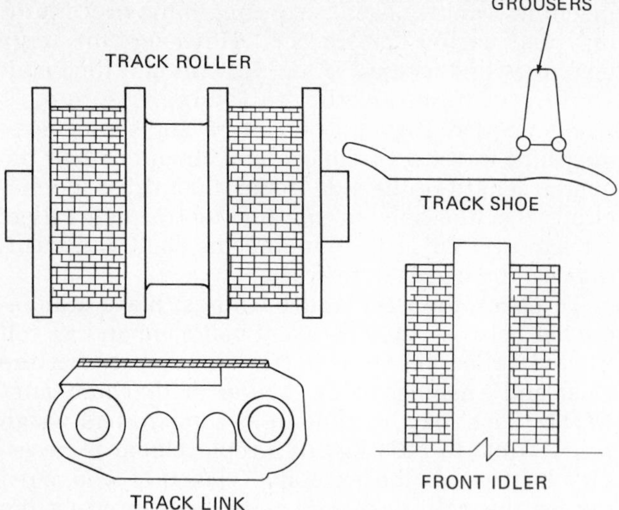

Fig. 8-54 Rebuilding the roller body schematically illustrated. (*Terex Division of General Motors Corporation*)

seal assembly from the seal retainer and remove the seal ring from the inner bearing retainer. When employing the puller screw method, use a soft-face hammer and tap on the retainer to ease removal. Next, remove the outer bearing retainer cap screws, the retainer, and shims.

NOTE Attach the shims to the inner and outer retainers to speed up the reassembly later. Install a three-jaw puller over the outer roller flange and the puller screw against the shaft to remove the inner bearing cup and shaft. Use a hammer puller or a soft iron punch to remove the outer bearing cup. Place the shaft with the bearing cone on a notched adapter plate and the plate onto the press bed, then press the bearing from the shaft. Repeat this procedure with the other bearing cone.

INSPECTION If the roller body flange tread surfaces are worn, the bearing cups are loose in their bores, or the weld is cracked, the roller body must be replaced or rebuilt. [Rebuilding means restoring the tread and flange surfaces through welding and then later regrinding them to the correct dimension (see Fig. 8-54). The bores are sleeved and then machined to the specified bore diameters.] Check the shaft for warpage and cracks, and for wear at the seat of the bearing cones. If the shaft shows any of these defects, and depending on the extent of the defect, the shaft must be rebuilt or even possibly may need to be replaced. The bearing cups and cones should be cleaned thoroughly and inspected (see material on antifriction bearings).

The mechanical seal shown in Fig. 8-53 is no longer commonly used. It has been replaced by the metal floating ring seal, which seals more effectively. However, when inspecting a mechanical seal, check the sealing surfaces for nicks, scratches, and burrs. When checking the seal spring assembly, if you find the bellow cracked, the spring weak, or the guide dowels damaged, the seal assembly must be replaced.

REASSEMBLY Clean all parts thoroughly, especially the roller body. Next, install the seal assembly following the procedure recommended in the service manual.

Press the bearings onto the shaft (you may heat them to facilitate installation) until they are seated firmly against the shaft shoulder, then lubricate them. Insert the shaft into the roller body. Place the same number of shims as removed onto the inner and outer retainers. Install the retainers one at a time, to the body. Tighten the inner bearing retainer cap screws to the specified torque and then torque the outer cap screws. While doing so, rotate the shaft to ensure that the bearings are not overly preloaded and then check the preload by checking the rotating torque of the shaft (Fig. 8-55). If the rotating torque is too low, remove the outer bearing retainer, remove a shim, replace the retainer, and recheck the rotating torque. Then again remove the outer retainer. Stand the roller on its shaft. Attach a high-volume grease gun to the grease fitting and pump grease into the roller until lubricant is forced from between the upper tapered roller bearings. Then reinstall the retainer.

Track Roller Service The procedure for servicing a track roller having roller bearings or tapered roller bearings parallels that previously outlined for the track carrier roller. However, when bushings replace bearings, and/or when metal floating ring seals with rubber toric seal rings are used, the servicing procedure differs slightly.

DISASSEMBLY To service the track roller shown in Fig. 8-56, first remove the shaft plug. Remove the left- and right-hand retainer (lock) rings and, with two prybars, pry the collar straight from the shaft ends. Lift the metal floating ring seal and the toric seal rings from the collar and bushing assembly. Discard the toric seals, tape the two seal halves together, and store them safe from possible damage.

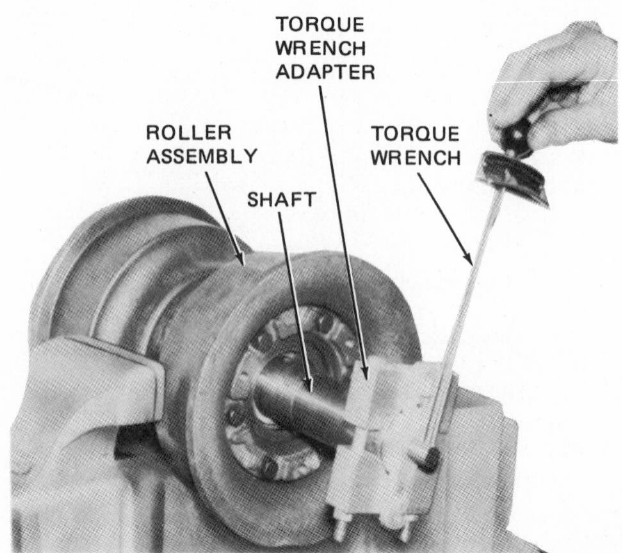

Fig. 8-55 Method of checking bearing preload. (*Fiat-Allis*)

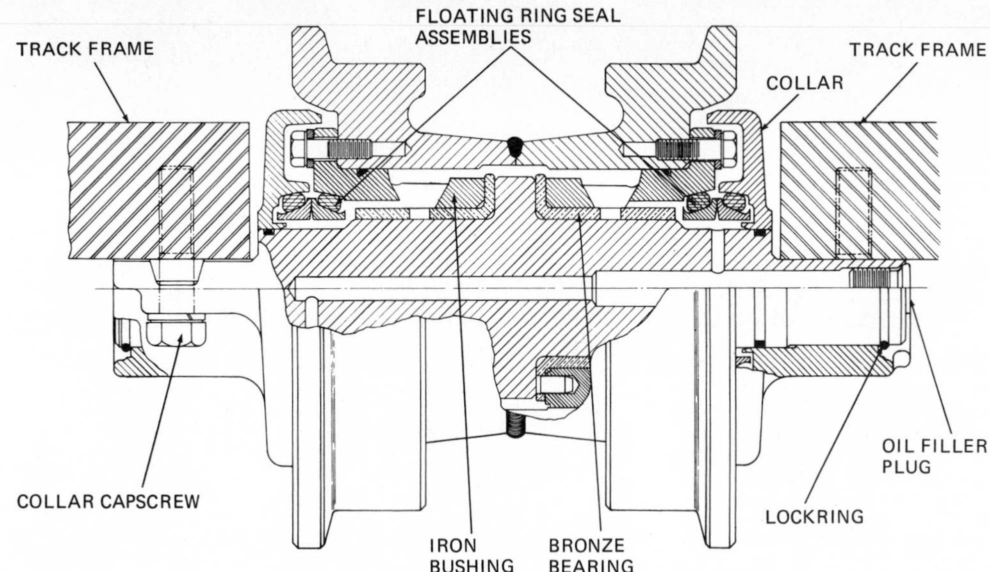

Fig. 8-56 Sectional view of a track roller. (*J I Case Company Agricultural Equipment Division*)

Next, remove the cap screws which secure the bushing assembly (iron bushing) to the roller body. Then place the roller assembly onto the press bed so that the roller is supported by its flange. Next, press on the shaft to force the bushing assembly from the roller body. Repeat this procedure for the other side.

INSPECTION Clean the shaft, the two bushing assemblies, and the two rollers. Inspect and measure the shaft for wear and to determine if it is bent. If bent or worn beyond specification, it must be replaced or rebuilt. If the bushing assembly is externally damaged or the bearing (bushing) has turned in the bore, the entire track roller assembly must be replaced.

BEARING REPLACEMENT If only the bearings are to be replaced, position one bushing assembly, face down, onto the press bed so that the bushing supports the assembly, and place an adapter onto the bearing; then press out the bearing. Repeat this procedure with the other bushing. With a hacksaw, saw off the locating pins and with a file smooth the bushing surface. Clean the bushing, align the bearing holes with the bushing holes, then press the bearing into the bushing so that the bearing flange rests firmly against the bushing. Now on each side of the bearing flange drill two holes opposite one another, through the bearing flange and into the bushing. (Both should be 0.30 in [7.62 mm] in diameter and about 0.88 in [22.35 mm] deep.) Do not drill into the oil grooves, as this will reduce lubrication. Install two pins into the holes to secure the bearing to the bushing housing, and if necessary use a file to smooth the surface. Check for nicks and burrs at the seal counterbore surface, and remove any that are present with a scraper or emery cloth. Again clean all components and dry them with compressed air.

REASSEMBLY Install the O-ring seal to each bushing assembly (without twisting or rolling them). Using the specified lubricant or an antiseize compound, lubricate the inner bore of the track roller and the outer surface of the bushing assembly. Position the roller onto the press bed. Align the bushing assembly by using the special assembly tool (Fig. 8-57) if available, or by inserting three guide pins into the bushing holes and into the holes of the roller body. When aligned, press the bushing assembly into the roller body until it rests firmly against the roller body shoulder. Install and tighten the cap screws to the specified torque. Turn the track roller over 180°, lubricate the bearing and shaft, and then insert the shaft into the roller body. In a like manner, press the other bearing assembly into the roller body. Install and torque the cap screws to the specified torque. When the shaft is installed, measure its end play, which should be within specification. If it is not, the shaft must be replaced.

Next, clean the metal floating ring seals using the recommended cleaning fluid if available, or alcohol, and examine the sealing surfaces. If the surfaces are scratched, or show an uneven or undefined wear pattern, or if the wear pattern has passed the center of the sealing surfaces, the set of seals must be replaced. If they are reusable, install the new toric seals, but make sure the sealing rings are not twisted and that they rest firmly in the relief of the seal ring. With your fingers, install the assembly by pressing on the outside of the toric seal ring to force it into the bushing assembly counterbore (Fig. 8-58).

Fig. 8-57 Preparing to press bushing assembly into track roller.

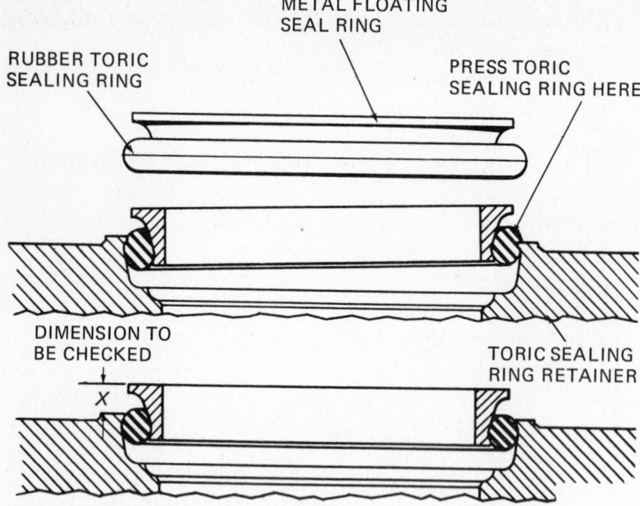

Fig. 8-58 Correct procedure to install metal floating seal ring and toric sealing rings. (*Caterpillar Tractor Co.*)

Repeat these steps to position the other half of the floating ring seal into the counterbore of the collar. Before placing the collar onto the roller, again clean both sealing surfaces with a lint-free cloth and alcohol to remove any minute particles or fingerprints. Then discharge one drop of oil onto the cloth and lubricate both sealing surfaces. You may now place the collar onto the shaft and position the lock ring. Repeat these steps precisely to install the other floating ring seal. Pay particular attention to cleaning instructions since minute dirt particles or fingerprints on the sealing surface will cause an oil leak, which could result in many thousands of dollars in downtime and repair costs. **NOTE** Do not use any kind of lubricant on toric seal rings.

LUBRICATION The final step before installing the track roller is to lubricate the track roller. To do this, screw the special nozzle into the shaft end. Position the roller shaft horizontally, that is, with the flat side or the pin groove in the shaft facing upward so that the shaft holes align with the reservoir holes. Now pump oil into the roller until air-free oil flows out from around the threads of the nozzle. Next, remove the nozzle and install the plug to the specified torque.

Front Idler and Yoke Service Because of the similarity in design between a front idler and a track roller or carrier roller, the service procedures and inspections are almost identical. Front idlers use the same type of bearings to support the idler on the idler shaft as do track rollers or carrier rollers, although most front idlers use floating metal ring seals. Small tractors and carriers use roller bearings, whereas larger tractors and machines use tapered roller bearings or bushings. The variance in procedure when servicing the front idler may be narrowed down to the method by which you connect the idler shaft to the yoke, adjust the idler to achieve alignment between the track roller frame and front idler (see material on front idler design and adjustment earlier in this unit), and install the floating ring seal. Therefore, rather than reoutlining all procedures here, only the installation of a different type of metal floating ring seal will be covered.

RING SEAL INSTALLATION The serviceability checks and cleaning procedure for the metal floating ring seal shown in Fig. 8-16 are the same as those for a duo-cone floating ring seal. (However, the procedure is slightly different for the seal shown in Fig. 8-59.) After the two seal halves are cleaned, place a plastic retainer band around them to hold them together as a unit. **NOTE** This band disintegrates after a few hours of operation and allows the halves to float free. Next, install a rubber ring at each side. Some rubber rings are of a standard design, whereas others have projecting lips or taps. When the latter is the case, the seal, with the taps, must be placed into the idler or roller counterbore. Before installing the seal into the seal retainer, idler, or roller, make certain the counterbores are free of nicks, burrs, and oil. Then using your fingers only, force the rubber ring into the counterbore so that the edge rests in the corner of the bore. Next, place the assembly onto the front idler counterbore and install the other rubber ring in the counterbore.

INSPECTION AND REASSEMBLY While removing the idler from the roller frame and during the disassembly, examine the yoke for damage and/or wear, and check for twist. Check the inside and outside bearings (also known as "idler caps," "blocks," or "brackets"), the inner and outer guide plates, and

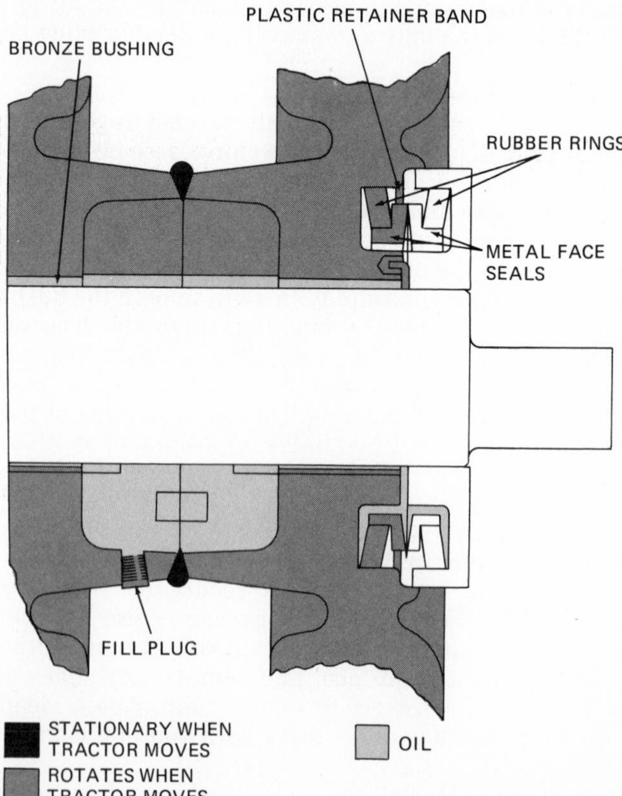

Fig. 8-59 Sectional view of an idler roller having metal face seal. (*J I Case Company Agricultural Equipment Division*)

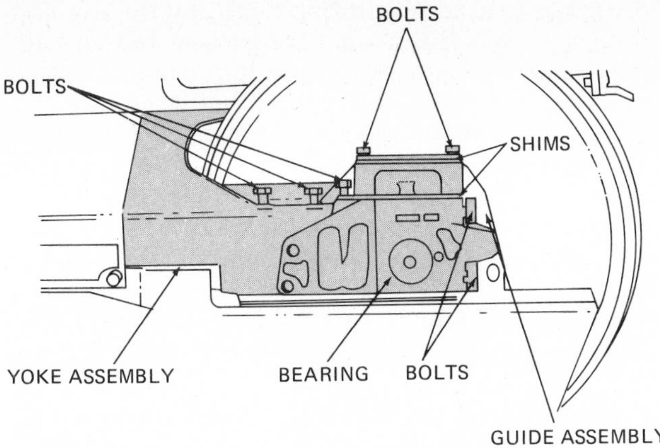

Fig. 8-60 Side view of right-hand front idler in the low position with guide removed. (*Caterpillar Tractor Co.*)

the upper and lower slide bar (wear plates) for wear. Replace all worn or damaged parts and then reassemble the yoke to the idler shaft. Position the front idler to the roller frame, and install the same number of shims between the guide plates and bracket, and between the slide rails and frame, as were previously used, and then check the front idler alignment.

NOTE On most Caterpillar tractors, the bearings that support the ends of the idler shaft on the wear plate can be placed in either the high or low position. This is possible because the idler shaft hole in the bearing is not in the center. Therefore, when reassembling the idler shaft, you must take into consideration the intended tractor application. For instance, when the tractor is to be used for drawbar pull, it is recommended that the idler shaft be positioned above the horizontal center line of the bearing, and, when a loader or dozer is attached, the idler shaft should be positioned below the center line (see Fig. 8-60).

Servicing Track Recoil and Track-Adjusting Mechanisms As a rule, these two mechanisms usually operate trouble-free and are therefore often overlooked during routine maintenance. The low failure rate may be attributed to the fact that most adjusting mechanisms are hydraulic, and the coil spring(s) is (are) fully enclosed so that no mud and dirt can build up in the recoil spring housing.

Recoil mechanism failure is identifiable by the track becoming suddenly too loose, or fiddle-string-tight, in which case the mechanism must be removed for service. Removal can be dangerous in that some springs positioned within the spring housing are energized to many tons and if improperly removed could cause injury to the mechanic. On the other hand, if the recoil spring is broken, or if the tractor uses a nitrogen recoil cylinder, the removal procedure is not so hazardous. The service procedure for a nitrogen recoil cylinder is similar to that for a hydraulic cylinder, except that in the former case after the grease is bled from the cylinder, the nitrogen must also be bled prior to servicing.

When servicing a coil spring recoil mechanism where the full power of the coil spring(s) rests on the end cap housing or against the spring stop, first read the service manual before taking any action and then meticulously follow each step outlined so as to avoid injury to yourself or others.

REMOVAL AND REPLACEMENT OF A RECOIL MECHANISM The procedure to replace the recoil mechanism shown in Fig. 8-61 is as follows: Split the track, support the front of the tractor, and remove the equalizer bar and the track carrier roller bracket. In some cases you may have to remove the front idler. When all this is done, remove the track-adjusting screw from the spring housing cover, apply grease or oil to the bolt threads and to the outside spacer surface, install the two spacers, and thread the special bolt into the right-hand spring seat. Tighten the bolt until the assembly turns in the housing or until the bolt head has moved about 0.25 in [6.53 mm] inward, and then loosen and remove the nuts, lockwashers, and bolts that hold the cover to the spring housing. Pull the spring out and place it and the cover onto the press bed. Adjust the press bed height, extend the piston rod so that you have a release stroke of about 8 in [20.3 cm], and then place the rod end against

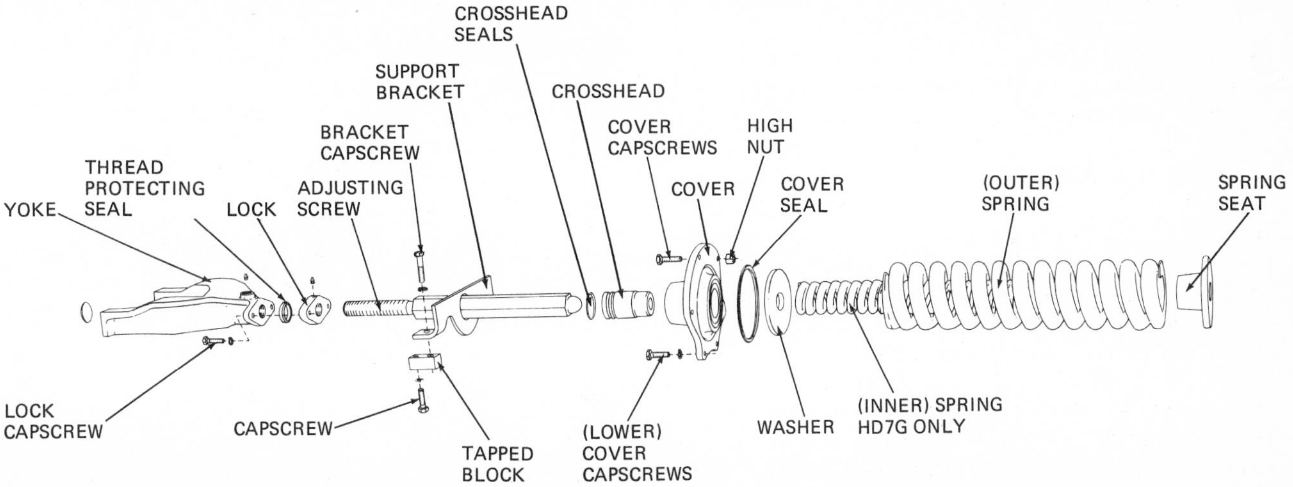

Fig. 8-61 Exploded view of the track recoil and track-adjusting mechanisms. (*Fiat-Allis*)

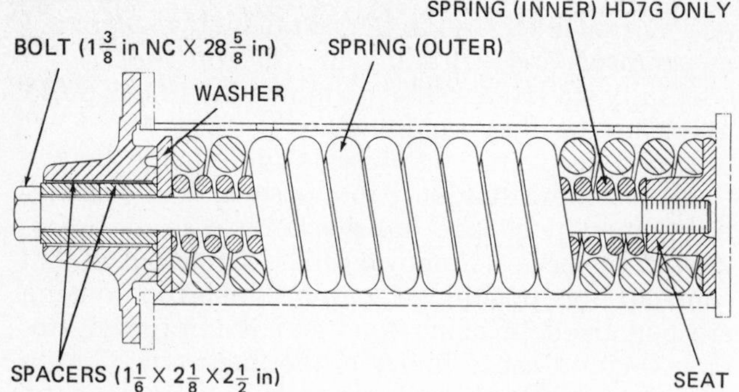

Fig. 8-62 View of recoil spring compressed. (*Fiat-Allis*)

the spring seat and slightly compress the spring. Now, simultaneously turn the bolt counterclockwise and release the hydraulic force until the force from the spring is fully removed.

Next, clean the interior of the housing, the cover, the bore, and the springs, or if necessary, replace the springs. Reverse the procedure when compressing the springs to the specified overall length. Reinstall the springs into the spring housing in precisely the reverse order of removal. Figure 8-62 shows a compressed recoil spring.

If, for some reason, the bolt cannot be threaded into the spring seat, but the springs are not broken, proceed as follows: Place a hydraulic jack against the cover; fully extend the jack piston and secure the jack to the roller frame. Remove the cover nuts, washers, and bolts, and then slowly release the hydraulic force to allow the springs to emerge from the spring housing.

SERVICING A TRACK-ADJUSTING MECHANISM Service for a mechanical track-adjusting mechanism consists basically of cleaning and restoring the adjusting screw threads and the threaded bore in the yoke or the adjusting nut. The service procedure for a hydraulic adjusting mechanism is comparable to that for a small hydraulic cylinder.

Track Chain Service This service may be classified into four groups:

- Track shoe replacement
- Track chain replacement
- Turning pins and bushings or replacing them
- Track link replacement

TRACK SHOE REPLACEMENT Although track shoe replacement in the shop is relatively simple, it can be an arduous task in the field because of the time-consuming cleaning procedure required prior to placing a socket wrench onto the track shoe cap screws, or the necessity of cutting the screw head with a cutting torch if the bolt heads are rounded off. In any event, when in the shop, begin with steam cleaning and use an impact wrench to loosen and remove the cap screws. When in the field use a six-point socket and a torque multiplier wrench to loosen the cap screws. If any of the cap screws or nuts show wear, replace them. After the shoes are removed, use a wire brush to clean the link surfaces and the aligning grooves in the links, and then place the rebuilt, straightened, or new track shoe into position. Align the bolt holes, install the bolts and nuts, and tighten the track bolts to the specified torque. **NOTE** If the track nuts have beveled corners, the nuts must face toward the link holes, and, if the track shoes have equally spaced track-shoe bolt patterns, the grouser bar must be positioned toward the track bushing.

REMOVING A TRACK CHAIN There are several methods by which track may be replaced. The one to be used will depend on the size of the track and the conditions under which the mechanic must make the change. In the field, for instance, drive the tractor, when possible, onto a level, hard surface where there is room to work and to fully roll out the tracks. Position one of the two track master pins of one track chain half-way up the sprocket, and then place a block at the sprocket end, under the grouser bar. Start the engine. Hold or place both steering levers in the neutral position to prevent the tractor from moving, shift the transmission into reverse, or, if applicable, disengage the clutch and then shift the transmission into reverse. Next, slowly engage the engine clutch or increase the engine speed, and at the same time release the brake on the side (left or right) on which you have placed the block. As the sprocket begins to slightly rotate, promptly apply the brakes and stop the engine. This action removes some tension from the master pin and bushing. If applicable, remove the master pin lock, and then, with a drive tool made from soft steel and a sledge hammer, drive the master pin out (see Fig. 8-63). The service manual will indicate to which side the pin must be driven. **CAUTION** When undertaking this task, the mechanic must wear a face shield and gloves as protection against flying steel chips.

If the sprocket and track vibrates heavily but the pin does not move, place a hydraulic jack between the master link and tractor frame to force the track chain against the sprocket.

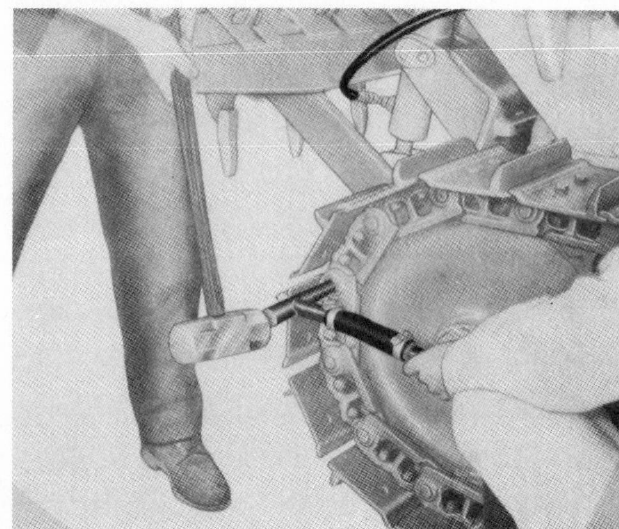

Fig. 8-63 Removing master pin. (*J I Case Company Agricultural Equipment Division*)

When the tracks are to be removed in the shop, use hydraulic jacks to raise the front and rear end of the tractor just enough to allow the track shoes to clear the ground, and in this position block the tractor. Start the engine, shift the transmission into gear, and, by manipulating the steering lever and/or brakes, position both tracks until one of the master pins is half-way up the sprockets.

Once the master pin is removed, there are two methods to lay the track onto the ground:

- *Method one.* If a hoist is available, attach the free end of the track chain to it and then lift the track from the top of the sprocket; pull it over the carrier roller and over the front idler, and lay it flat on the ground.
- *Method two.* Insert a crowbar into the master link bushing and hold the bar in front of you as you face toward the front of the tractor. A second mechanic then holds both steering levers in neutral position—or applies the brake hydraulically and then starts the engine. Engage the transmission in low speed forward, and slowly release the brakes to turn the sprocket forward. Meanwhile, hold the bar firmly in your hands, but be aware that as the track chain becomes free from the sprocket teeth it may pull you forward. When the track is free from the sprocket, carry the end of the chain over the carrier roller, then over the front idler, and let it slowly roll onto the ground.

CAUTION As the track starts to roll onto the ground the weight on your crowbar will continually increase.

NOTE During removal keep your hands and feet clear of the track and do not allow others to come near.

INSTALLING A TRACK CHAIN There are several methods for installing a new or rebuilt track, and the one you will employ will depend upon your circumstances. When in the field roll the new track out on the ground in front of the old track, and then, using a pin or bar, link the new track with the old track links (Fig. 8-64). Then space the tracks to match the distance between the sprockets. Again, *be careful*—keep your fingers and your feet clear. Then roll or drive the tractor onto the new track so that the sprocket is above the third track pin.

Another method is to raise and block the tractor at the front and rear, and then pry the track from below the track rollers until clear. Next, roll up the track, secure it, and then move it out of the way. Roll the new track parallel with the track roller frame, so that the bushing end of the track chain points to the front. Next, roll the track out (using a crowbar), and ease it under the track rollers until the third last track pin is below the center of the sprocket. Lower the tractor, but check that the track roller flanges do not come to rest on the track chain links.

Yet a third method is to use a crane, tractor, or other mobile equipment to skid the track from below the track rollers. In a like manner, pull the new track into position. When the track is in position, lift the last three track links onto the sprocket, and with a block hold the links against the sprocket. If a hoist is available, attach the other track end to it and pull the track over the front idler and carrier roller, and onto the sprocket. You may have to use a crowbar to engage the proper bushing with a sprocket tooth to ensure that both track ends meet. When there is no hoist available, you can install the track in one of two other ways: (1) If the track chain can be carried without mechanical help, first use a crowbar and engage it with the front end of the track link. Two able-bodied individuals can then lift the track and carry it over the front idler and carrier roller, and onto the sprocket. (2) If the track is extremely heavy, engage the crowbar into the rear chain link to pick up the last link, lay the bushing onto one sprocket tooth, and hold it there. Now have a second person hold both steering levers in the neutral position, then start the engine, engage the transmission in forward low gear, and slowly release the brakes and the steering lever to rotate the sprocket forward. As you walk forward, carry and guide the track over the carrier rollers and front idler. Apply the brakes just before the sprocket starts to roll the tractor forward, and then lift the last three links onto the front idler and with a block hold it in this position.

To join the track ends when the track links are of the open design, use a prybar and align the bushing and pin bores. Insert the master pin, and with the same tools used to remove the master pin drive it into position. **NOTE** Check your service manual to determine which end of the master pin should be inserted, and whether it should be inserted from the inside or outside.

For an interlocking or sealed track, use the following method to join the two ends: Move the last lower track link slightly outward and away from the sprocket, then clean the counterbores. Install the two-coned disk seal washers, and spacer, as specified in the service manual, and use the service tool supplied by the manufacturer to hold the seal assembly in place. Otherwise, cut two pieces off a flat bar, 0.75 in [19 mm] in width and about 1.0 in [25.4 mm] longer than the pin bore diameter, and two other pieces of the same width but about twice this length. Drill in each bar a 0.375-in [9.525-mm] hole

Fig. 8-64 Method of installing the track chain. (*International Harvester Company*)

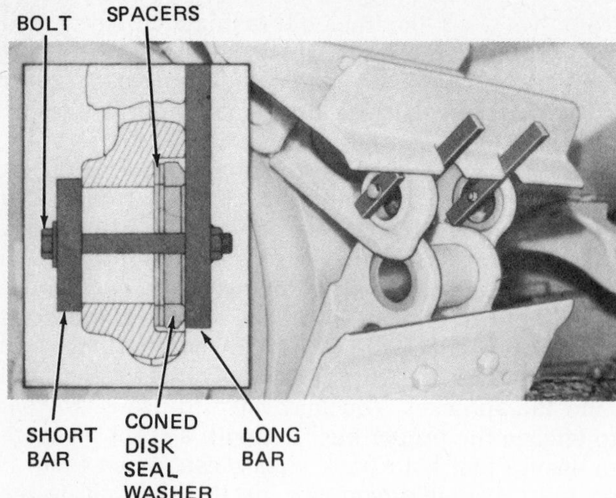

Fig. 8-65 Seal-holding tools (installed). (*Caterpillar Tractor Co.*)

and braise a 0.375-in [9.525-mm] nut to the longer bars. Then install them as shown in Fig. 8-65. Next, using a hammer, tap the links toward the sprocket until the bushing end of the link holds the spacers and seals in place. Remove the holding tools, align the pin and bushing holes, and then install the master pin.

REPLACING TRACKS ON LARGE TRACTORS Drive the tractor onto a level, hard surface with room enough to operate a hoist and to allow the tracks to be rolled out. Position one of the master pins between the carrier rollers, and then remove the track tension. Make certain that the hydraulic pressure is fully released and the front idler does not hang up. You may have to move the tractor back and forth to retract the front idler, or do so by using the track pin method. Place a large block in front of the idler against the track shoe grouser bar, and drive the tractor forward against the block to bring the track chain slack to the top.

Install the track master pin press and press out the master pin according to installation instructions supplied with the tool. (One of several kinds of master pin presses is shown in Fig. 8-66.) Once the master pin is removed, remove the track master pin press, the two spacers and the four-coned seal washers, and then the block from the front of the idler.

CAUTION As you remove the block, the chain may roll forward. If it does not, drive the tractor slowly forward to roll the track off the front idler, then drive it slowly backward to rotate the track off the sprocket. Now position the new track in front of the old and join them together. If space will not allow this, drive the tractor onto a plank having a thickness which brings it to the combined height of the track chain and track shoes and a width corresponding to the track link spacing or wider. Then roll up the old chain, move it aside, and lay the new track chain tightly against the front of the plank. Now drive the tractor onto the new tracks.

If the job must be done within the shop, also position the tractor so that there is room to use a hoist and to roll the track from the track frame. Use lifting wedges to raise the front and the rear of the tractor, block it, and then drive the lifting wedge out from under the track.

Next, start the engine, engage the transmission, and by manipulating the steering lever and brake, position the master link at the sprocket so that a wedge block can be placed under the track shoe grouser bar next to the master link (see Fig. 8-67). Then place the transmission in reverse so that the drive sprocket removes the track tension from the master link. Now apply the brake and stop the engine. With a track press, remove the master pin, or when a two-piece master link is used remove the track shoe (ground) bolts and the master shoe. When this is done again start the engine, engage the transmission, and drive the sprocket in a forward direction to move the wedge out. This will disengage the lower track chain end from the sprocket teeth and drive the top track chain end from the top of the sprocket teeth, causing the track chain to roll from the carrier rollers and the front idler to roll onto the ground. Skid the old track from below the track rollers and position the new track so that the pin end

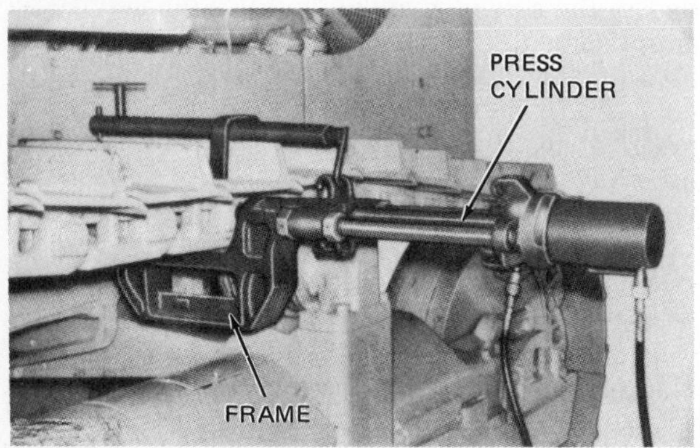

Fig. 8-66 View of removing master pin. (*Caterpillar Tractor Co.*)

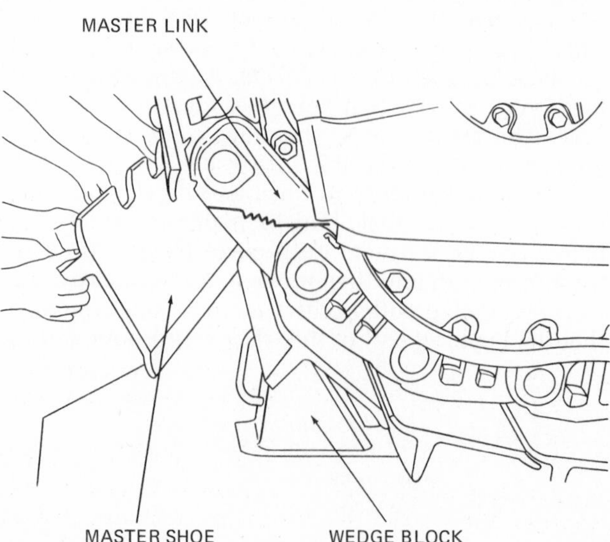

Fig. 8-67 Splitting a track chain having a two-piece master link. (*Caterpillar Tractor Co.*)

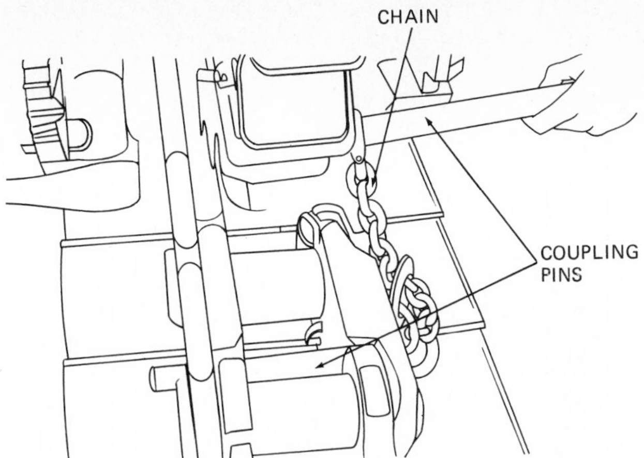

Fig. 8-68 Method used to lift chain end onto sprocket. (*Caterpillar Tractor Co.*)

of the track chain faces to the rear and the third track pin is under the center of the sprocket.

To lift the track end onto the sprocket, attach a chain to the first link and a bar to the other end of the chain, and place the bar into one sprocket tooth root. Now drive the sprocket in a forward direction, to pull the track onto the sprocket (see Fig. 8-68). When the track end has passed the top sprocket center, apply the brakes and remove the chain and bars. In order to guide the track over the carrier rollers and onto the front idler roller, the spaces between the sprocket and carrier roller, and between the two carrier rollers and the carrier roller and front idler, must be filled. Use either the guide tools supplied by the manufacturer or blocking material. When the spaces are filled, slowly release the brakes and drive the sprocket forward. This pulls the track onto the sprocket and pushes the top end over the carrier rollers and over and onto the front idler.

CAUTION Make certain the master link or the two master link halves do not hang up as the track is pushed forward. As the two track ends come close together at the front idler, apply the brakes and with a chain, couple the ends together.

Remove the guide tools or the blocking material and then slowly release the brakes and drive the sprocket in a forward direction. This rotates the entire track clockwise. As the master link ends are lifted off the floor, apply the brakes and place a track wedge below the grouser bar as shown in Fig. 8-69. With the wedge in position, shift the transmission into reverse and slowly release the brake. This action drives the sprocket counterclockwise, pulls the lower track link bushings onto the sprocket teeth, and allows the master links to meet the lower master links, or the top track bushing end to meet the link pin end. As this occurs, apply the brakes and stop the engine.

Remove the chain and clean the pin bores and the counterbores of the seals, or clean the master link serration, the link bore, and threaded bores. Install the seals and spacer, and couple the track ends together as outlined previously. When a serration master link is used, lubricate the threaded bores and the

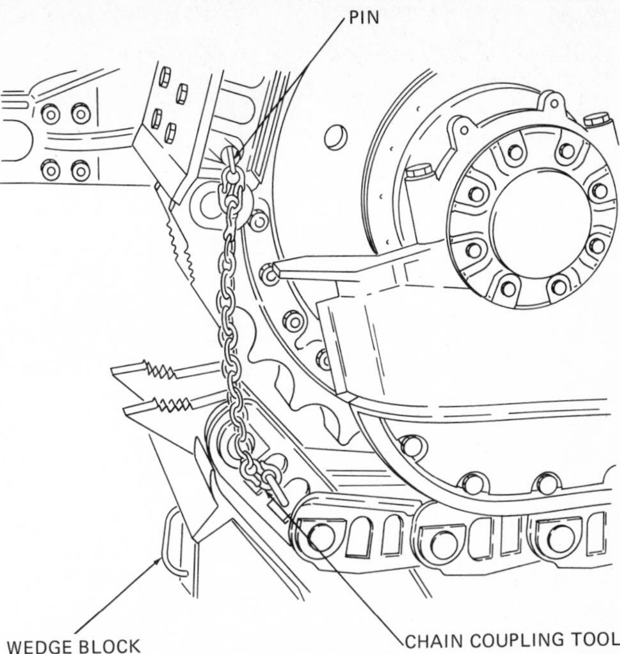

Fig. 8-69 Master link in position to start master link reconnection. (*Caterpillar Tractor Co.*)

track shoe bolts, align the bolt holes (using a hammer), and, with your fingers, start to thread in the bolts to check the alignment. If the alignment is satisfactory, remove the bolts, position the master shoe, and then install and tighten the track ground shoe bolts. Start the engine and drive the sprocket forward so that the track shoe bolts can be torqued to specification. Use the lifting wedges to raise the tractor. Remove the stands, lower the tractor onto the track chain, and then adjust the track tension.

ADJUSTING TRACK TENSION Although much has been said about track tension because of its overall importance, one question still remains: When is the track chain properly adjusted? To decide this, you would normally measure the track sag and adjust it to the specification given in the service manual (see Fig. 8-70). However, during this process, mistakes can be made which result in too loose or too tight a track. A common error is neglecting to position the track pin over the carrier roller, in which case the sag (distance) increases. The normal inclination then is to tighten the track chain in order to come within the specified sag, but this results in the track chain becoming too tight. Another mistake is to measure the track sag immediately after driving the tractor or carrier in reverse. Driving in reverse tightens the track at the top and places the slack on the bottom. Thus, to achieve the specified sag you would probably remove some track tension, which would mean that the track, when in operation, would be too loose. On the other hand, you may have the track properly adjusted before the tractor or machine has been put to work, but it may become too tight as the vehicle is operating.

Following are some simple, basic rules which, if put into practice, will assure correct measurements so that you will obtain the specified track sag:

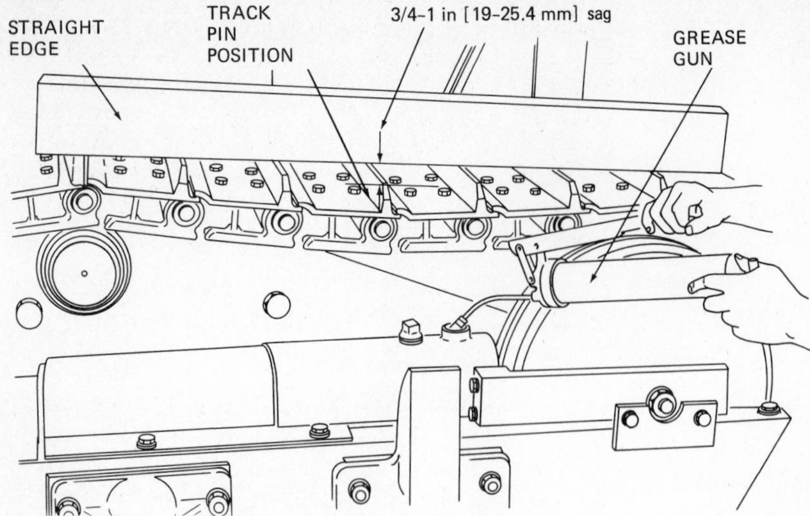

Fig. 8-70 Measuring and adjusting track tension (sag). (*J I Case Company Agricultural Equipment Division*)

1. Regardless of the measuring method used, the tracks must be adjusted at the working site.
2. Before starting measurements and adjustments, the tractor must be driven in a forward direction and a track pin must be in the center of the carrier roller.
3. There must be no master pin between the carrier roller and the front idler (or drive sprocket) during the measuring and adjusting.

A recommended procedure which is fast and accurate is as follows:

1. Drive the tractor a short distance in a forward direction, then stop the engine.
2. Tighten the track chain, but stop doing so as soon as the packed buildup starts to squeeze from between the track bushing and sprocket teeth (or you should stop as the track chain is almost straight between the carrier roller and front idler).
3. Measure from the front idler yoke to any fixed point on the track roller frame.
4. Reduce the track tension by bleeding grease from the adjusting cylinder, or by pumping grease into the cylinder for a nitrogen recoil mechanism, or by using the track adjusting screw.
5. Force the front idler rearward by placing a track pin (or any large pin) between one sprocket tooth and the track link, and then drive the tractor in a reverse direction until the track pin is on top (see Fig. 8-71). Next, drive the tractor forward to remove the inserted pin.
6. Now tighten the track until the front idler has moved forward 0.5 in [12.7 mm] less than the distance measured when the track chain was tightly adjusted. For example, say the measured distance with a tight track chain is 10 in [25.4 cm], then the new distance forward of the front idler yoke should be 9.5 in [24.13 cm]. This adjustment may not quite equal the track sag recommended in the service manual, but it will provide a track tension which will reduce wear on the undercarriage.

Turning Track Pins and Bushings This entails removing the track chain from the tractor, pressing out the pins and bushings, rotating them 180°, and reinserting them. Turning the pins and bushings should be done before they reach the maximum service limit since it can extend the track chain life by approximately the mileage already achieved by the tractor up to this point in its use. See Fig. 8-72, which shows worn and turned pin bushings.

When performing this service, use the specially designed track pin and bushing presses which have adapter tools for whatever specific track chain might be involved. Briefly, the servicing steps include:

1. Cleaning the track
2. Removing the track shoes (on some tracks you need only to remove the bolts and nuts from the links on one side of the track chain)
3. Simultaneously pressing out one pin and one bushing from one side of the track link, and then pressing out the bushing from each of the other links
4. Cleaning all pins and bushings in solvent, once they have been removed
5. Inspecting the links, pins, bushings, seals, and spacers for wear
6. Reassembling and pressing the pins and bushings into the links (to the specified spacing dimension)
7. Reinstalling the track shoes

Track Link Replacement When, for one reason or another, one or more track links break on the job, the broken section(s) or link(s) can be replaced in

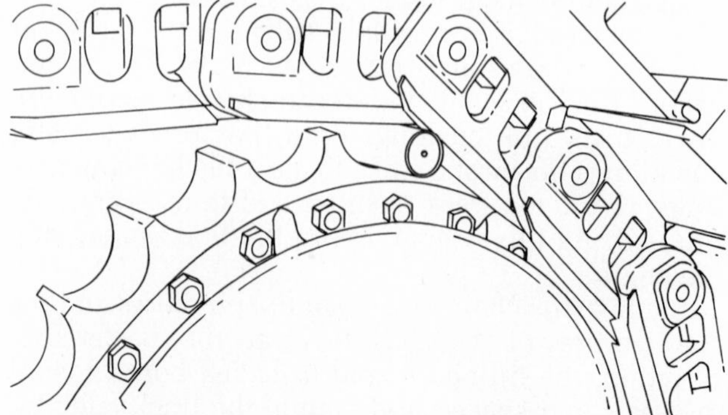

Fig. 8-71 Method used to pull front idler toward drive sprocket. (*Caterpillar Tractor Co.*)

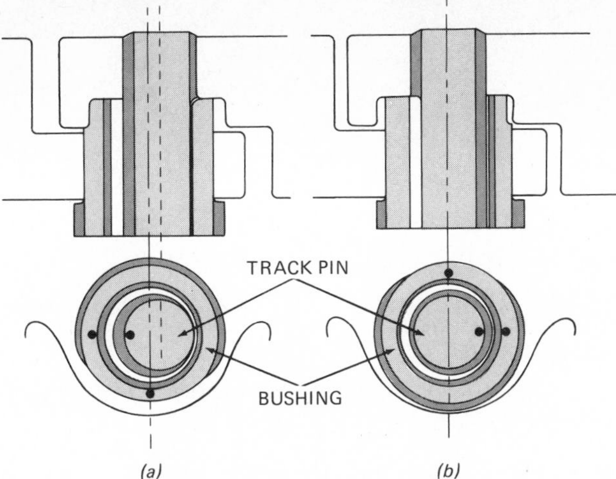

Fig. 8-72 (a) Worn and (b) turned pin bushings. (*Terex Division of General Motors Corporation*)

the field if you have a cutting torch and a portable track pin press. To begin with, you should, if possible, drive the tractor forward to bring the broken link or section to the top. Next, release the track tension and remove the track shoes from the damaged track links. Also remove the track shoes on each side of the last damaged link. Span a chain and cinch across the damaged section to hold the track together while the repair is being made. However, if the track is broken, it must be removed in order to be repaired. This task may be simple or extremely arduous because of the slope or condition of the ground on which the tractor is situated or because of the location of the track chain after the breakage.

Next, clean the bushings and links which are to be replaced so that you can cut the bushings and pins as close as possible to the inside surfaces of the links. (See Fig. 8-73). Secure the pins and bushings by welding them together. Install the pin press and force the pin and bushing ends from the damaged links; then clean the seal counterbores. Now, join the two ends by pressing a master pin bushing into

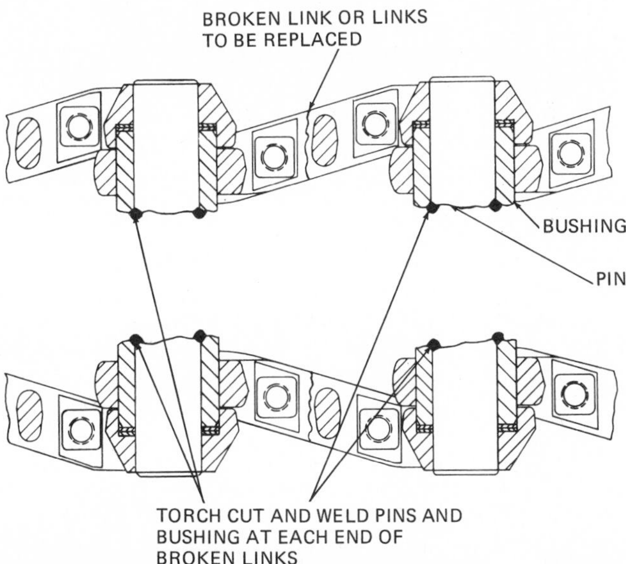

Fig. 8-73 Method of removing damaged links. (*International Harvester Company*)

the new left- and right-hand links, and a master pin bushing into the links attached to the track. Install the coned seal washers and spacer into the link counterbores, align the holes (using a smaller pin), and press a standard track pin into the links. If the track was removed, reinstall it and then couple the two ends as previously outlined. Reinstall the track shoes and adjust the track tension.

Crawler Belt Service Since crawler belts are made up of crawler shoes pinned together, it is easy to service and replace them without special tools.

REPLACING A CRAWLER SHOE If one or more crawler shoes are damaged, or the link pins or drive lugs are broken or damaged, propel the machine onto level ground. Clean the crawler shoes, and position the damaged shoe onto the drive tumbler. Release the belt tension, and chain the two shoes which are adjacent to the damaged shoe tumbler. Remove the link pin locks and drive out the two link pins. By muscle power or by hoist and a sling, lift the damaged shoe off the tumbler and insert a new one in its place. Align one set of the link holes, insert the link pins, then position and lock the pins. Repeat this procedure to join the crawler belt. Finally, remove the chain and adjust the belt tension.

REPLACING A CRAWLER BELT To replace the crawler belt, you may have to dig a hole of appropriate dimensions (i.e., three crawler shoe widths) and then propel the machine (front tumbler) over it. See Fig. 8-74. Next, remove the belt tension and the crawler shoe link pin retaining bolts, nuts, and washers from the shoe (one-third up on the idler tumbler), and then remove the left- and right-hand link pins and spacer. **CAUTION** Stand clear when removing the link pins. For small machines, use crowbars to force the belt to roll off the drive tumbler onto the ground. For large machines, attach a sling to the front portion of the crawler belt, and position a tractor behind the rear of it at a distance of about $1\frac{1}{2}$ times the overall length of the side frame. Attach a wire rope to the sling and pull on the crawler belt.

CAUTION Make certain that no one is near the side frame or in the vicinity of the wire rope, in case the belt, when pulled, starts to roll freely from the carrier rollers and drive tumbler, due to its own weight.

Fig. 8-74 Step 1 when removing crawler belt. (*Harnischfeger Corporation*)

Fig. 8-75 Final step in crawler belt installation. (*Harnischfeger Corporation*)

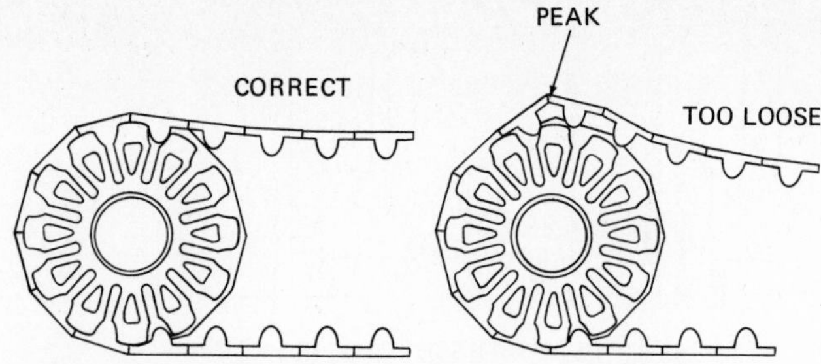

Fig. 8-76 Correct crawler belt tension, and belt too loose. (*Harnischfeger Corporation*)

Next, split the crawler belt in two, close to the drive tumbler. Remove the half of the belt which does not support the machine. (See the section on inspecting and replacing crawler belt rollers.) When both (the new and old) halves are connected, propel the machine, or use a tractor to pull it onto the new section of the crawler belt. Next, replace the second worn crawler belt half with a new (or rebuilt half) and join the two new halves together.

When this is accomplished, propel or pull the machine so that the drive tumbler is near one belt end. Attach a sling to the other belt end shoe and a wire rope to the sling. Run the wire rope over the carrier rollers and over the idler tumbler, to the tractor. Now, pull the wire rope onto the winch drum (or drive the tractor to pull on the crawler belt), and at the same time propel the machine slowly in a forward direction until the top end of the crawler belt is three-quarters over the idler tumbler (see Fig. 8-75). Disconnect the sling and, with a suitable lifting device, or with jacks, raise the lower belt shoes and lay them against the tumbler. Align the link holes, install the link pins and spacers, and then adjust the crawler belt tension.

CHECKING CRAWLER BELT TENSION A common method to check belt tension is to propel the machine in a forward direction and observe the action of each individual crawler shoe as it leaves the drive tumbler. When the crawler belt is correctly adjusted, it will have a gentle slope (sag) toward the side frame. If it is too loose, the shoe that leaves the drive tumbler will push upward instead of straight forward. (see Fig. 8-76). If the belt is too tight, the top line of the belt shoes will be nearly straight, with very little or no sag.

If an adjustment is necessary, check first the wear patterns on the drive tumbler and on the belt shoe lugs. If the wear patterns are even, the idler tumbler must be moved evenly forward. If one side shows a heavy wear pattern, the opposite side must be moved farther forward than the worn side, to compensate for the excessive wear. See Fig. 8-77.

Drive Sprocket Service Drive sprocket service may be divided into four topics:

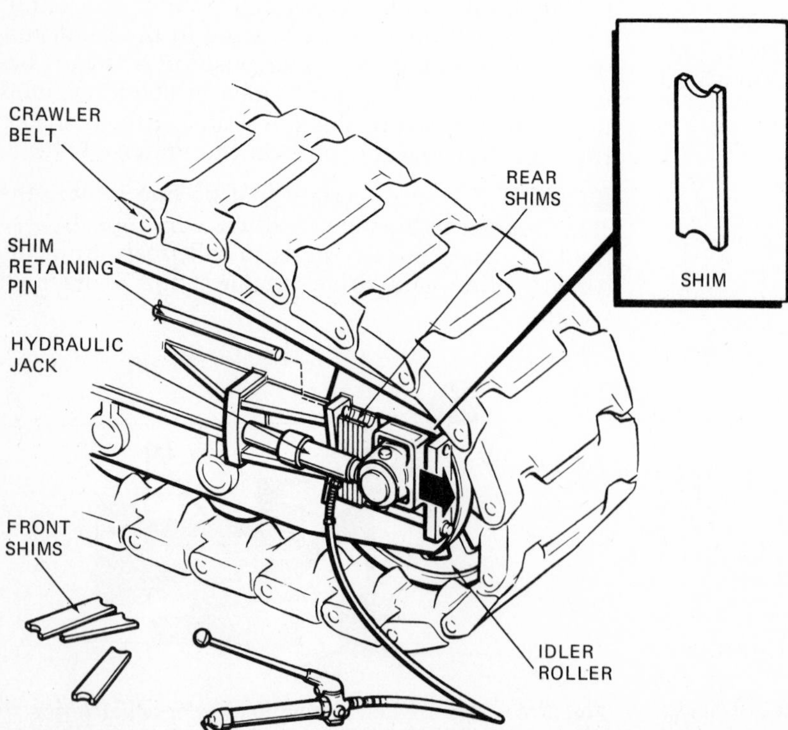

Fig. 8-77 Method used to adjust crawler belt tension. (*Harnischfeger Corporation*)

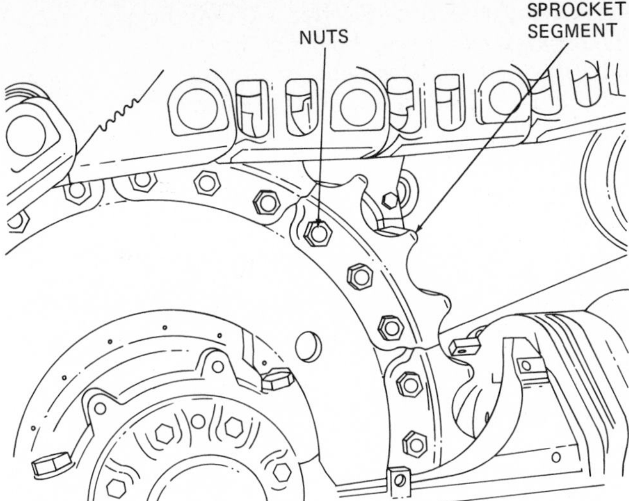

Fig. 8-78 Position of drive sprocket for the replacement of sprocket segments. (*Caterpillar Tractor Co.*)

- Replacing the one-piece drive sprocket, or switching it to the opposite final drive
- Replacing or switching the one-piece sprocket ring
- Replacing the individual sprocket segments, or alternating one set from one side to the other sprocket hub
- Rebuilding (rewelding) the drive sprocket teeth

To replace the drive sprocket or the sprocket ring, the track must be split, and, depending on the undercarriage or final drive designs, the side frame must be removed and part of the final drive must be disassembled. When sprocket segments are used (bolted to the sprocket hub), they can be replaced or switched with ease since the individual segments can be replaced without splitting the track. However, to replace the sprocket hub the track must be split and the final drive must be partly disassembled.

REPLACING SPROCKET SEGMENTS To replace individual sprocket segments, remove the final drive guard and steam-clean the sprocket. Drive the machine in a forward or reverse direction until one sprocket segment is free from the track chain, and then loosen and remove the nuts, the segments, and the bolts. Clean the hub surfaces and bolt threads and lubricate them with the recommended antiseize compound. If you are switching sprocket segments, also clean the segment mating surfaces. Next, position the bolts in the sprocket hub and the segments on the bolts, and then install and tighten the nuts to the specified torque. Start the engine and drive the tractor forward to position the next sprocket segment. Repeat these steps until all segments are replaced or switched; then reinstall the sprocket guard. See Fig. 8-78 for the position of the drive sprocket during this procedure.

REPLACING A ONE-PIECE OR A RING DRIVE SPROCKET When a one-piece or ring drive sprocket is used, and the side frame is either rigidly fastened to the tractor frame or pivot-fastened to an individual shaft in front of the drive sprocket, replacing the drive sprocket is a relatively simple and quick procedure. Assume that the track is split, and a one-piece sprocket is used. Begin by removing the lock from the sprocket nut, and with a socket and torque multiplier loosen and remove the nut. If the sprocket is splined onto a straight splined final drive shaft, use a lead hammer to drive the sprocket off the shaft. If the sprocket is splined to a tapered shaft, use a puller arrangement to pull the sprocket off.

NOTE You may have to rotate the sprocket slightly in order to clear the side frame outside rail.

After the sprocket is removed, check the splines on the final drive shaft for wear. If they are damaged, the shaft must be replaced. If an oil leak is visible, disassemble the final drive to replace the damaged oil seal or worn bearings. When no damage is visible, clean and lubricate the splines, place the sprocket onto them, and drive it or press it into position. Install the sheet metal washer and then the nut. Hold the sprocket by applying the brakes or by wedging a block between a sprocket tooth and the side frame, and then, with a socket torque multiplier and torque wrench, tighten the nut to the specified torque. Next, lock the nut by bending the washer against one flat of the nut. **NOTE** See material on final drive in Unit 9 for instructions on how to replace a one-piece sprocket or sprocket hub that is fastened to the sprocket shaft or hub.

To replace a one-piece sprocket from a track-type carrier, the basic procedure is as follows: After the track is split, raise and block the front and rear in order to take the weight of the machine off the side frame rails. Disconnect the inner and outer pillar block (bearing housing) from the side frame rails (see Fig. 8-79) and the mounting bolt from the front frame rails, and then roll the side frame forward on the

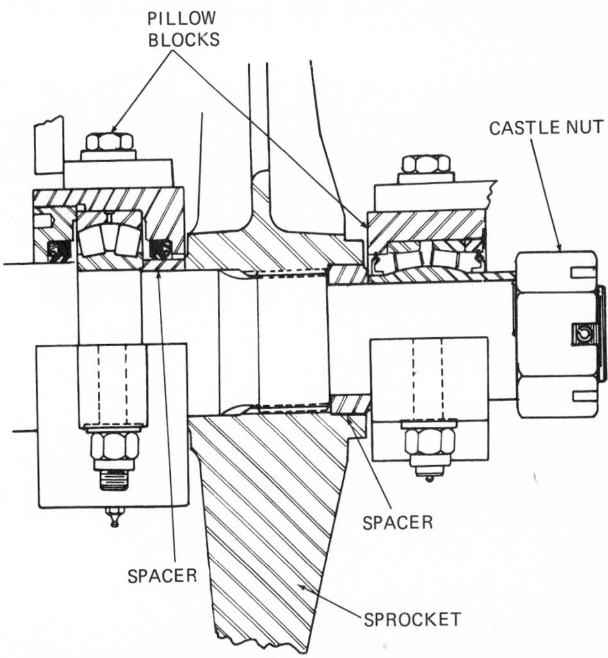

Fig. 8-79 Sectional view of drive sprocket mounting. (*J I Case Company Agricultural Equipment Division*)

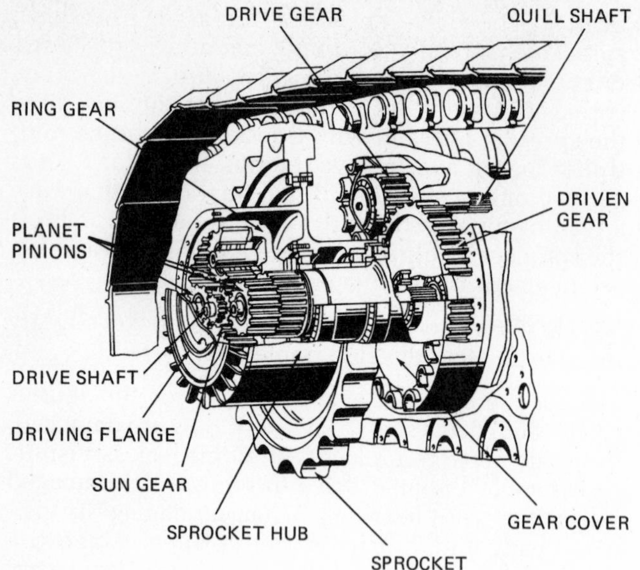

Fig. 8-80 Cutaway view of final drive components. (*Terex Division of General Motors Corporation*)

track chain. On some track-type carriers removal of the final drive transmission is recommended (see material on final drive track-type steering in Unit 9). After the side frame or transmission is removed, remove the lock from the castle nut and the nut from the transmission output shaft, and then, with a puller, remove the outer pillar block and the sprocket. Reassemble in precisely the reverse order of procedure.

REPLACING A ONE-PIECE SPROCKET RING Common methods of attaching the ring sprocket are (1) to bolt it to the outside of the sprocket hub, or (2), when a planetary final drive is used (see Fig. 8-80), either bolting it to the sprocket hub or positioning the ring between the sprocket hub and planetary housing. In order to replace the sprocket ring on the latter final drive design, it is necessary to remove the planetary housing (including the planetary gears). See material on servicing final drives in Unit 9.

Track Roller Frame Service When the roller frame is broken, the pivot bearings are worn, the pivot shaft or dead axle is bent, or the roller frame is out of alignment, all of which cause accelerated wear to the rotating components, the roller frame must be removed and serviced. Because of the variety of track roller frame designs, there are numerous ways in which they can be removed and reinstalled. Following are two very common procedures to remove, check, test, and install a track roller frame—one where the frame is pivot-attached and the other where it is fixed-mounted.

PIVOT-ATTACHED FRAME When the roller frame is pivot-attached to the final drive outboard bearing, or is attached to an independent shaft and a diagonal brace is used to stabilize the roller frame, the removal and reinstallation procedure is as follows:

1. Remove the sprocket, front idler, and recoil guards.
2. Steam-clean the undercarriage.
3. Drive the tractor onto a level, hard surface.
4. Raise the front and rear of the tractor to the recommended height (about 10 in [25.4 cm]) and block the tractor securely.
5. Block the hydraulic equipment to stabilize the tractor.
6. Split the tracks.
7. Attach a sling or chain to the carrier rollers and then hook it to a crane or hoist.
8. Remove the stabilizer bar, which, in some cases, means removing the front idler, the oil, and the transmission guards.
9. With a crane or hoist, take the weight from the roller frame.
10. Mark the pivot shaft bearing caps to ensure that they will be reinstalled in the same position.
11. Remove the diagonal brace pivot shaft cap screws and cap(s).
12. Remove the outboard pivot shaft bearing cap screws and caps.
13. For the track roller frame shown in Fig. 8-81,

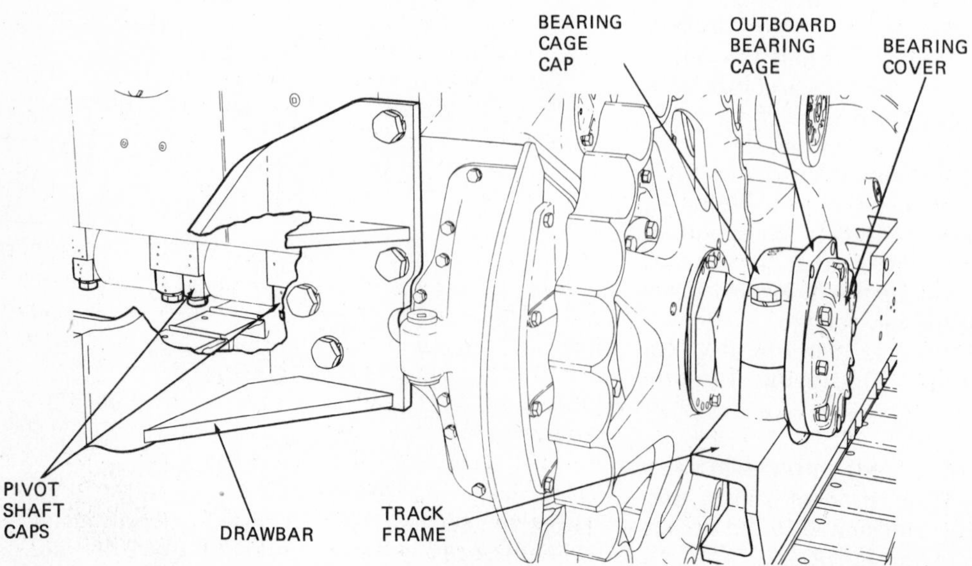

Fig. 8-81 View of track uncoupled for track frame removal. (*Fiat-Allis*)

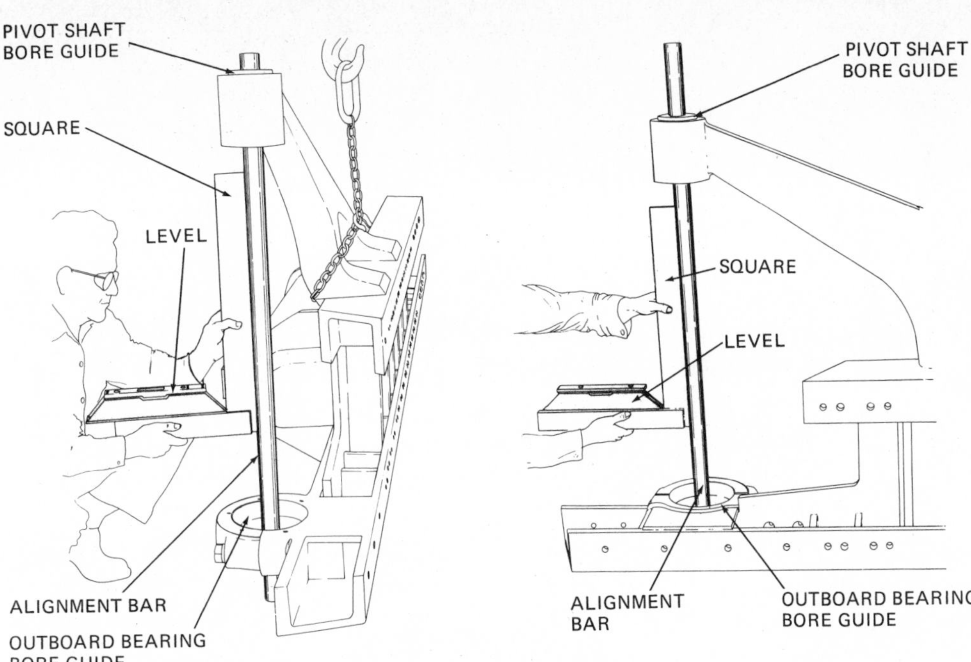

Fig. 8-82 Leveling track frame prior to alignment checks. (*Fiat-Allis*)

you must in addition remove the bearing cover, and then wire the shims to the cover. Remove the cotter pin and loosen the bearing retainer nut about five turns (located under cover—nut not shown in the illustration); then with a three-jaw puller, pull the bearing cage out against the nut. This prevents damaging the bearing cage and shims during removal and installation.

14. Lower the track roller frame to clear the diagonal brace from the steering clutch and bevel gear housing.

15. Swing the frame from the tractor. **NOTE** You may have to force the rear of the frame down in order to swing it free from the tractor.

16. Remove the carrier roller mounting brackets, recoil mechanism, front idler, track roller guards, and track rollers—in other words, strip the frame of all components and cap screws.

17. Clean the frame using a power wire brush or sand blaster.

18. Position the track roller frame on a level, hard surface, install the outboard bearing cap, and install into the pivot bores the aligning plugs and the aligning bar. If the diagonal brace bearings (bushings) are worn, replace them before checking the alignment. But when the alignment shaft will not align with the second bore in the diagonal brace or outboard bearing bore because of a bent frame end and/or diagonal brace, correct this misalignment first.

19. With a square and level, measure and level the roller frame to the horizontal and vertical positions by using wedges (see Fig. 8-82).

20. Then with a square and bevel, measure the roller frame for twist and, by using a long straightedge and level, measure the inside and outside frame rails for bend (toe-in or toe-out). **NOTE** Some manufacturers recommend screwing two cap screws—one at each end—into the track roller mounting holes and laying the straightedge onto the bolt head (see Fig. 8-83).

21. Screw about four cap screws (equally spaced) into each side rail of the track roller mounting holes; then measure the frame rails for parallelness. All measurements must fall within the maximum allowable bend or twist limits; otherwise the track frame must be straightened. **NOTE** If the track frame is straight but the measurement prior to removal indicates that the frame is misaligned then the pivot shaft or dead axle is bent (see material on final drives in Unit 9). Track frame straightening is a specialized job and should not be undertaken by a mechanic unskilled in the relevant procedures.

After the frame is straightened and undercoated, you should

1. Measure the wear of the diagonal brace pivot shaft pin, and bushing. If they fall within the wear limit, only the lip-type seals need be replaced. If the bushings are worn, use a portable ram and adapter to replace them. See Fig. 8-84.

2. If the outboard bearing bore is damaged or out-of-round, replace the bearing cap.

3. Restore all threaded bores by running a tap into the holes, and then clean the holes using compressed air. **CAUTION** Wear goggles.

4. Reinstall the removed components to the roller frame in precisely the reverse order of removal.

Some manufacturers provide a shim adjustment to align the track roller frame to the sprocket when the roller frame is pivot-fastened to the outboard bearing, whereas others do not since the components are meticulously machined to provide precision alignment. When shims are used, they are removed from between the outboard bearing cage and bearing cover to move the roller frame out, and are added to move the roller frame in. **NOTE** When shims are used between the bearing cap and track roller frame to compensate for outboard bearing wear, make

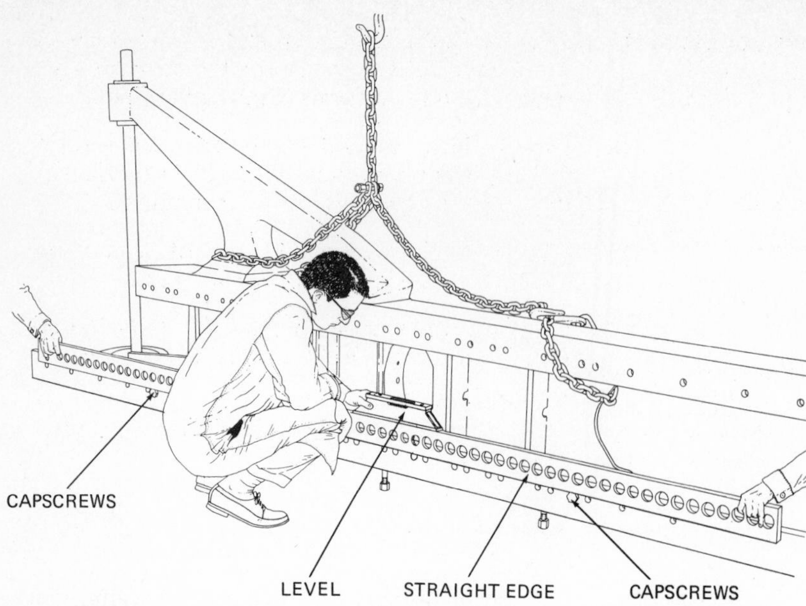

Fig. 8-83 Method of checking track frame toe-in/toe-out. (*Fiat-Allis*)

certain you follow the procedure recommended in the service manual to prevent bearing cap breakage or an improperly secured roller frame. The track roller frame is properly aligned when the drive sprocket is in the center of the rear track roller.

FIXED FRAME The procedure for removing and installing a fixed-mounted track roller frame is faster than that for a pivot-mounted roller frame because the track roller frame is independently mounted (and not attached to the final drive) and a misalignment is nearly impossible. Before removing a fixed track roller frame, first make certain (by measuring and checking the roller frame alignment) whether or not the roller frame or mounting brackets, I beam, or torque tube has caused track frame misalignment.

To remove a fixed-mounting track roller frame, you must raise and support the tractor, support and block the hydraulic equipment to stabilize the tractor or machine, split the tracks or crawler belts, and then remove the front idler or front tumbler. Securely attach a sling and crane, or hoist to the track roller frame and raise it so that the weight is removed from the tractor or crawler frame. Next, loosen all mounting cap screws or nuts which secure the roller frame to the tractor. If the sprocket shaft (transmission output shaft) pillar blocks are fastened to the frame side rails, loosen and remove their mounting bolts or cap screws first, and then remove the remaining cap screws or bolts. Swing the roller frame forward and lower it onto the track chain or belt; then move it to your work area. The reinstallation procedure is precisely the reverse of removal. **CAUTION** Always recheck the toe and the roller frame alignment before reinstalling the tracks or crawler belts.

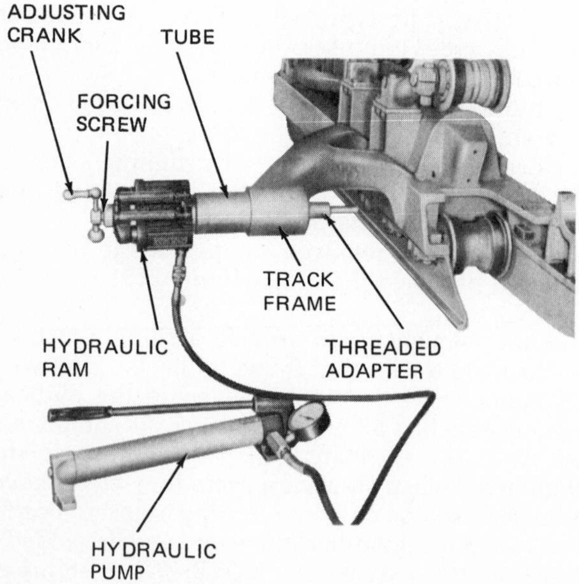

Fig. 8-84 Method of removing pivot shaft bushing. (*Fiat-Allis*)

Review Questions

1. In your opinion, what factors have contributed to the steady production increase of track-type tractors and carriers?
2. List the seven basic components of a track-type undercarriage.
3. What is the main difference between a drive tumbler and a drive sprocket?
4. When the tractor or carrier is driven in a forward or reverse direction, at which point do the track pins and bushings rotate to the greatest degree?
5. List the four main groups into which tractor or carrier undercarrier wear are classified.
6. When the tractor is used continuously for loading operations, which parts or components are subject to excessive wear?
7. Explain why track chain wear will be accelerated if the chain is (*a*) too loose, or (*b*) too tight.

8. What defective undercarriage components would contribute to a wear pattern on the left-hand outside sprocket teeth? the right-hand front idler flange? the right-hand inside track rail?
9. Briefly outline two methods for checking the track pitch.
10. Explain how to measure the wear of (*a*) pins and bushings, (*b*) the rails, (*c*) the master pin, and (*d*) track shoes.
11. Using a training track-type tractor: (*a*) measure its frame alignment. (*b*) List the safety steps and procedures you followed when measuring the frame alignment.
12. Outline the preliminary steps to replace the front track rollers of the tractor on which you have just made a frame alignment check.
13. Explain how to (*a*) disassemble a track roller, (*b*) check the components for their serviceability, and (*c*) reassemble the mechanism.
14. List the indications which would suggest that a recoil mechanism requires service.
15. How would you decide that it is the correct time (neither too early nor too late) to turn the track pins and bushings.
16. List the major differences between a track chain (track) and a crawler belt.

Unit 9 **Final Drives and Steering Mechanisms**

The chief purpose of a final drive or final drive transmission is to reduce the output speed of the transmission in order to gain torque through the use of various types of gears and gear arrangements. In addition, the final drive lowers the output shaft and thereby brings the drive sprocket closer to the ground.

The principal purpose of the steering mechanism is to control the action of the individual track or crawler belts. Although the final drive and the steering mechanism are actually two independent devices, one is required in conjunction with the other in order to drive the tractor and to control the tractor steering (see Fig. 9-1). Some of the design variations are (1) the number of reduction gear sets and the type of gears used, (2) the manner in which the gears are supported, (3) the way in which the drive sprocket is connected to the final drive, (4) the type of steering clutch used, (5) the method by which the clutches and brakes are activated, (6) the method used to lubricate the final drive, and (7) the size of the individual components.

Final Drive Designs For tractors, three types of final drives have been designed to increase output torque and to reduce speed. They are the single-reduction, the double-reduction, and the double-reduction planetary final drives. These designs vary to some extent among different models and manufacturers; however, all final drives use straight cut gears, with the single exception of those for specially designed tractors or carriers which use herring bone gears.

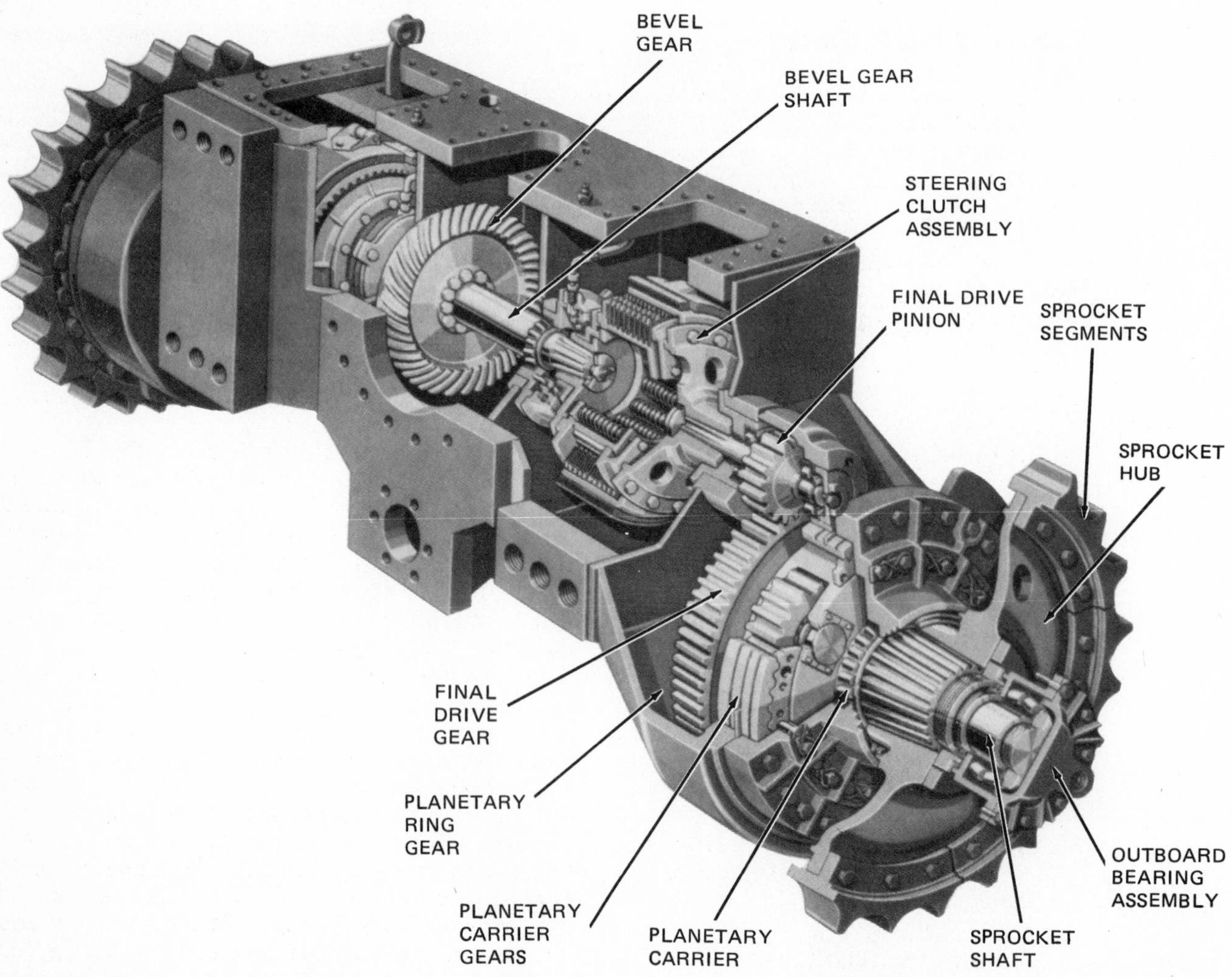

Fig. 9-1 Cutaway view of a (large) final drive and steering clutch assembly. (*Fiat–Allis*)

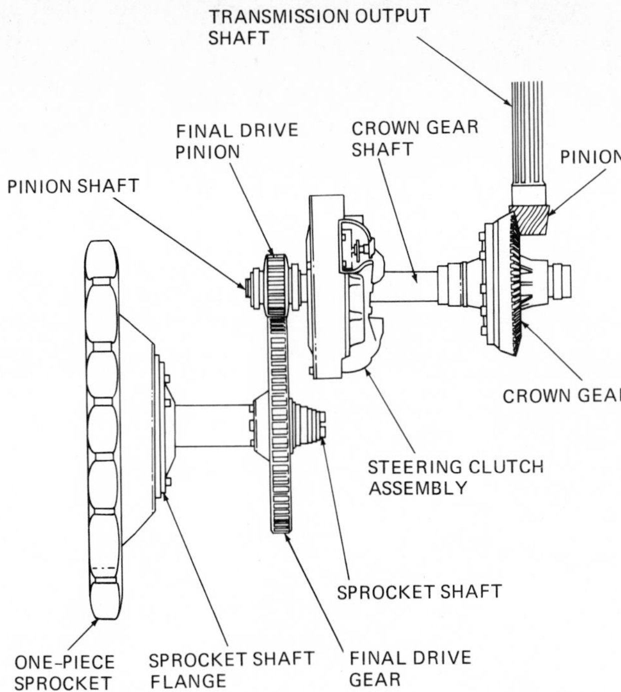

Fig. 9-2 Drive line components of a single-reduction final drive and steering clutch. (*Deere & Company*)

Single- and Double-Reduction Final Drives A single-reduction final drive has one gear set, comprised of the pinion gear and the sprocket shaft gear (bull gear or final drive gear) (see Fig. 9-2). Small tractors usually have a one-piece-cast final drive housing, which is bolted to the steering clutch housing. The pinion gear, which is either splined or part of the pinion shaft, is supported in the inner and outer final drive housing by roller bearings, ball bearings, or tapered roller bearings. The final drive gear is splined to the sprocket shaft, which in turn is supported by ball bearings or tapered roller bearings. **NOTE** All pinion or sprocket shafts are sealed with lip-type, mechanical, or metal floating ring seals.

Gear and bearing lubrication is done through the splash method—that is, as the final drive gear rotates, it picks up the oil and throws it against the pinion gear and inner walls of the housing and bearings. On some designs the lubricant is directed through channels to the bearings.

A double-reduction final drive (see Fig. 9-3) has two sets of reduction gears, which are located either in a one-piece or two-piece housing. The inner housing of a two-piece final drive housing is part of the steering clutch housing, while the outer final drive housing or cover is bolted to it. The top pinion is supported by tapered roller bearings, and shims are used to adjust the bearing preload. The brake drum hub is splined to the right-hand side of the top pinion and secured to it by the hub retainer cap screw. A double-lip-type seal is used between the bearing cage and brake drum hub to prevent oil from flowing to the steering clutch housing. The correct oil level is maintained within the housing by allowing the oil, in excess of the oil level, to flow back into the bevel gear housing. The intermediate pinion, to which the intermediate gear is splined, is supported by tapered roller bearings, and shims are used to adjust the bearing preload. The sprocket shaft gear is splined to the sprocket shaft, which is also supported by tapered roller bearings, and again, shims are used for the bearing preload adjustment. The sprocket hub is splined to the left-hand side of the shaft and affixed to it by the sprocket nut. One seal is positioned between the intermediate bearing cage and the sprocket hub, and another is positioned within the sprocket nut and against the outboard bearing cage to seal the final drive housing. The bearing cages and bearing bores position the shafts to cause the top pinion to mesh with the intermediate gear, and the intermediate pinion to mesh with the sprocket gear.

Although most double-reduction final drive bearings are pressure-lubricated, the one illustrated in Fig. 9-3 relies on splash lubricating for the lower gears and bearings, with only the inside top pinion bearing being pressure-lubricated.

Planetary Final Drive There are several reasons for using a planetary gear set as the last reduction unit: (1) It reduces the overall size (diameter and width) of the final drive, (2) it can transmit a greater torque than a single set of gears having the same reduction, and (3) it reduces the spreading force of the gear and therefore has less bearing wear and gear failure.

Overall, double-reduction planetary final drive designs are much the same, the two primary differences that occur being the method by which the power from the final drive gear (bull gear) is transmitted to the sun gear, and the method used to connect the sprocket hub to the planetary carrier.

One of several planetary final drives is shown in Fig. 9-4. In this illustration, the pinion (final drive or quill) shaft is supported in the final drive housing and final drive housing cover by tapered roller bearings. The brake hub is splined to the right-hand side of the shaft. Shims are used to adjust the bearing preload.

In other designs, the shaft is supported by roller bearings and the pinion is splined to the shaft. The final drive (bull) gear is splined to the sun pinion (drive) shaft, to which the sun gear of the planetary gear set is splined. The shaft is supported on the right-hand side by a roller bearing and on the left-hand side by the sun gear (which is in mesh with the three planetary gears).

In yet other designs, the shaft is supported on the right-hand side by two roller bearings, and on the left-hand side by the sun gear. The planetary (internal) ring gear is a one-piece casting that is splined to the final drive housing (gear cover). The sprocket hub to which the planetary carrier housing and sprocket is bolted is supported on the final drive housing cover by tapered roller bearings. A metal floating ring seal is used to seal the rotating sprocket hub with the housing cover. The planetary carrier housing has three planetary gear sets which are supported on their respective shafts by roller bearings, and the housing is bolted to the sprocket hub. On

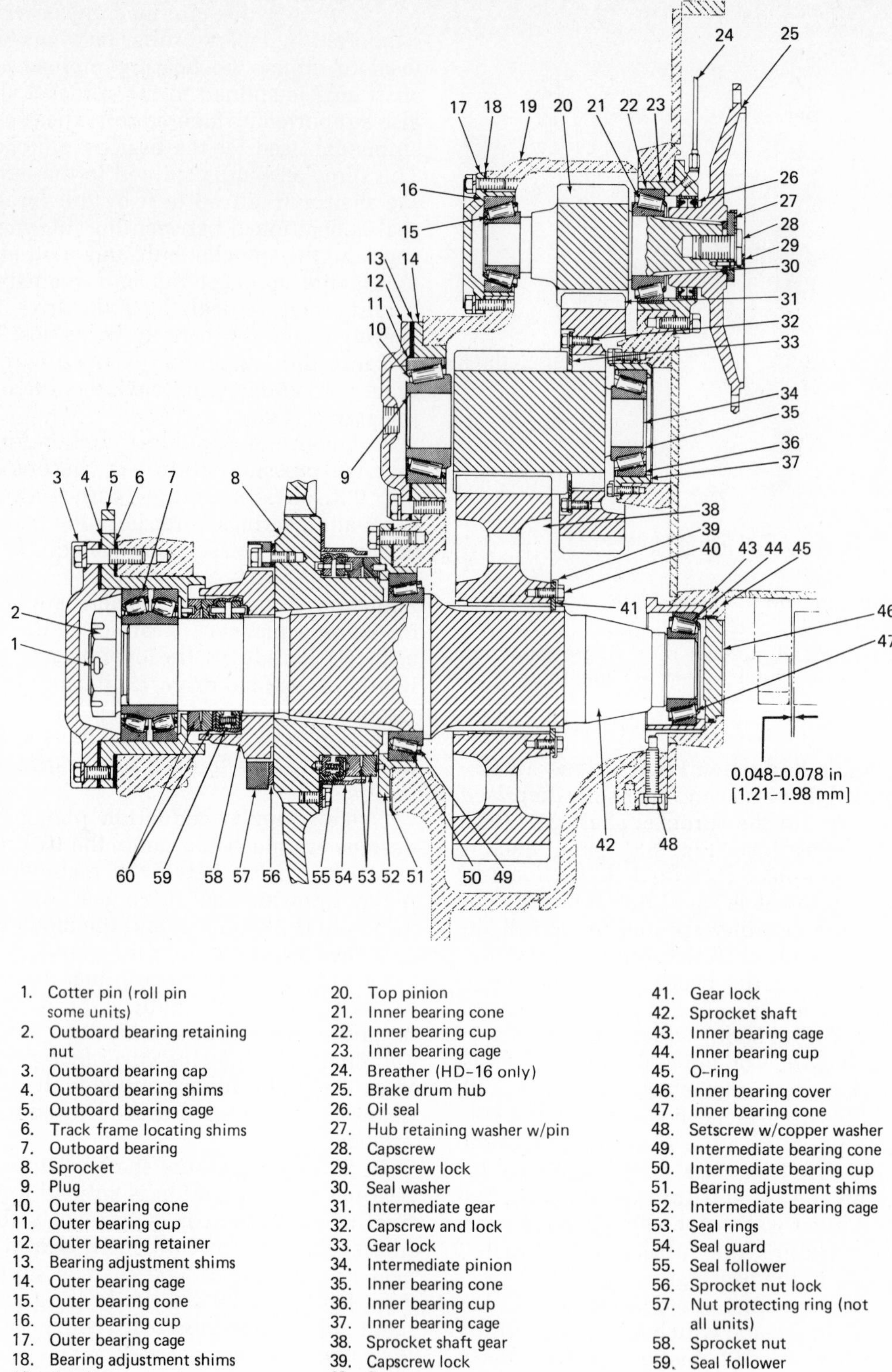

Fig. 9-3 Sectional view of a double-reduction final drive. *(Fiat–Allis)*

some designs the carrier gears are supported by roller bearings.

The planetary final drive shown in Fig. 9-5 is slightly different in design than the one shown in Fig. 9-4. Here the final drive pinion is supported by roller bearings in the inner final drive housing and final drive case. The final drive pinion flange is splined to the left-hand side and is secured to the shaft by a nut. A duo-cone seal is used to seal the final drive with the steering clutch housing. The sprocket shaft is press-fit into the bevel gear housing and then bolted to the inner housing. The final drive gear assembly is bolted to the final drive hub, which in turn meshes with the final drive pinion. That gear assembly consists of the hub with the sun gear, and the final drive gear (bolted to the

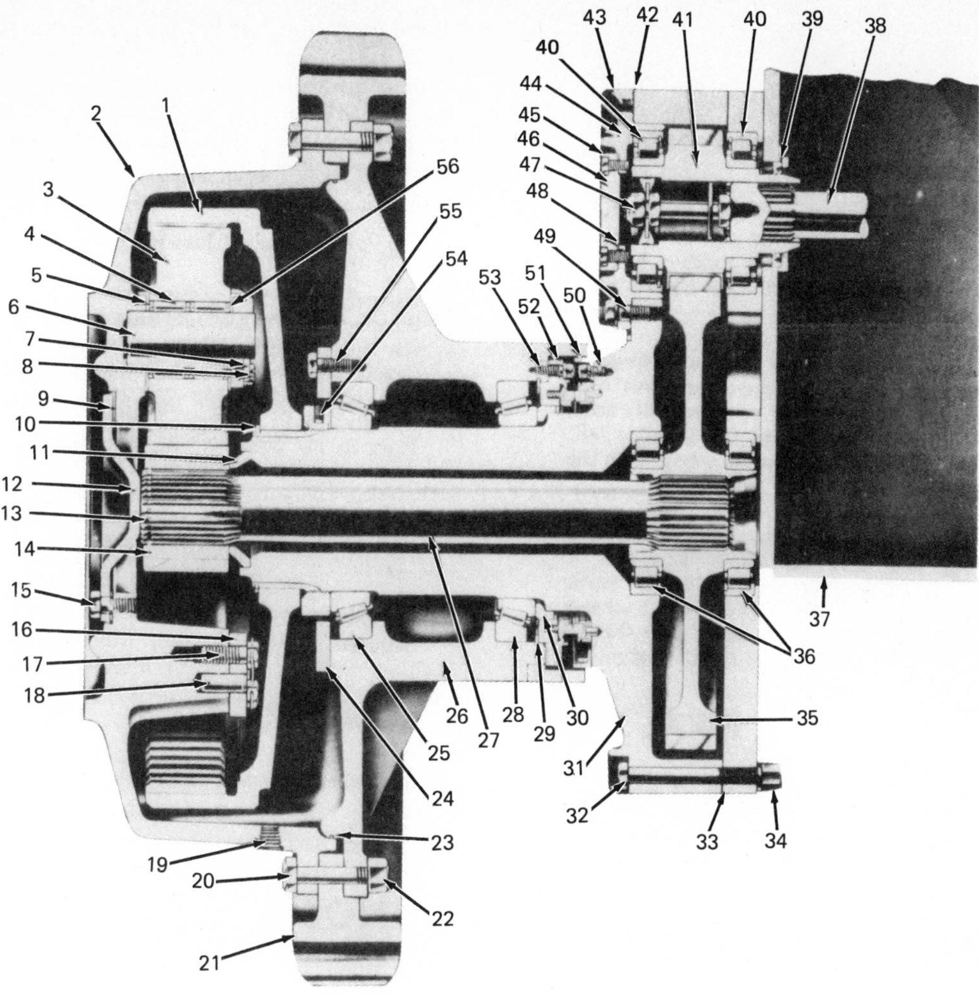

1. Internal ring gear
2. Planetary housing
3. Planetary pinion
4. Roller bearings
5. Thrust washer
6. Pinion pin
7. Pin retainer
8. Retainer bolt
9. Cover gasket
10. Snap ring
11. Thrust collar
12. Thrust collar
13. Snap ring
14. Sun pinion
15. Lock bolt
16. Retainer ring
17. Bolt
18. Dowel pin
19. Drain plug
20. Bolt
21. Sprocket
22. Nut
23. O ring
24. Bearing retainer
25. Roller bearing
26. Sprocket hub
27. Drive shaft
28. Roller bearing
29. Snap ring
30. Spacer
31. Gear cover
32. Bolt
33. Gasket
34. Nut & lockwasher
35. Driven (bull) gear
36. Driven gear bearings
37. Drive case
38. Quill shaft
39. Oil seal
40. Drive gear bearings
41. Drive gear
42. Gasket
43. Set screws
44. Bearing retainer
45. Lock bolt
46. Cover plate
47. Quill shaft retainer
48. Gasket
49. Nut, lockwasher & stud
50. Bolt & lockwasher
51. Ring
52. Seal
53. Retaining bolt
54. Locknut assembly
55. Bolt
56. Thrust washer

Fig. 9-4 Sectional view of a planetary final drive. (*Terex Division of General Motors Corporation*)

hub). The left-hand side of the hub is supported on the sprocket shaft by the final drive hub support (roller) bearing and the right-hand side is supported by the carrier housing. The carrier housing has three planetary gears which are supported on their respective shafts by rollers. The carrier is supported on the left by the carrier support bearing positioned between the carrier housing and final drive case, and on the right by tapered roller bearings positioned between the sprocket shaft and carrier housing and between the carrier housing and the support (outboard bearing) cage. The cage is supported on the final drive shaft by a tapered roller bearing, and the bearing preload is adjusted by the support retainer nut. The sprocket hub is splined onto the tapered splines of the carrier housing, and further secured

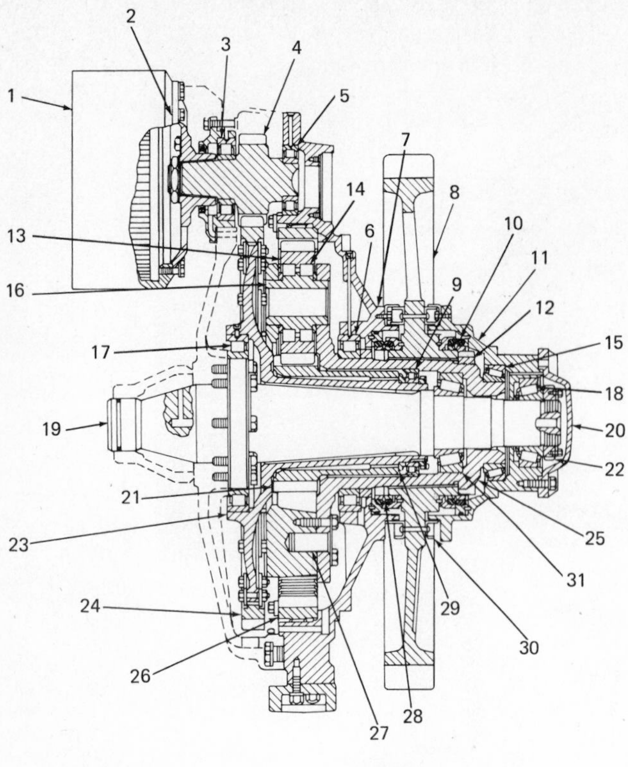

1. Brake drum
2. Final drive pinion flange
3. Final drive pinion inner bearing
4. Final drive pinion
5. Final drive pinion outer bearing
6. Carrier support bearing
7. Final drive case
8. Sprocket
9. Final drive gear hub support bearing
10. Duo-Cone seal
11. Support
12. Sprocket retaining nut
13. Planet gear
14. Planet gear rollers
15. Support bearing
16. Planet roller hub
17. Final drive gear hub support bearing
18. Support bearing
19. Sprocket shaft
20. Support cap
21. Sun gear
22. Support retaining nut
23. Final drive gear hub
24. Final drive gear
25. Carrier
26. Ring gear
27. Dowels (six)
28. Duo-Cone seal
29. Spacer
30. Dust guard
31. Carrier support bearing

Fig. 9-5 Sectional view of a planetary final drive. (*Caterpillar Tractor Co.*)

by the sprocket nut. Two duo-cone seals, one between the sprocket hub and final drive case and one between the sprocket hub and support, seal the rotating sprocket hub against the final drive. To prevent or reduce dirt or dust from contacting the duo-cone seals, each is protected by a dust seal.

The final drive is splash-lubricated through the final drive gear and carrier housing, and the bearings are pressure-lubricated through a gear pump (see Fig. 9-6). The pump is bolted to the final drive case and meshes through a tang with the final drive pinion. Steel tubing connects the pickup strainer, located in the lower half of the final drive, with the gear pump. A line connects the gear pump with a junction which has a ball check valve capable of closing through its own ball weight. A second line connects the check valve (over a fitting and a passage) with the oil filter. From the filter, oil is directed to a fitting where it then is divided, and flows (1) to the final drive pinion and bearings, and (2) through passages to the left-hand end of the sprocket shaft, into the center of the shaft, and to the right-hand side of the sprocket shaft, lubricating the three tapered roller bearings. **NOTE** When the tractor is driven in reverse, the ball check valve seats, preventing a reverse oil flow from the filters to the pump. If the oil filter becomes plugged, the bypass valve within the filter housing opens to provide bearing lubrication.

Steering Clutch and Brake Designs A steering clutch is a coupling between the bevel gear and the final drive. It is used in conjunction with the brakes to steer and stop the tractor. Steering clutch and brake component parts are located within the steering clutch housing. With the exception of tractors produced by one particular firm, most use brake bands which are applied mechanically or are hydraulically assisted and spring-released, and use multiplate steering clutches which are spring-applied and hydraulically released. Some older tractor models use conventional engine clutch pressure plate assemblies which are mechanically linked with the steering levers and brake mechanism to release the clutch and apply the brakes. Steering clutches which have multiplate friction disks are much the same in design. Their components are shown in Fig. 9-7. Any differences that exist lie in the size of the components and the method by which the brakes are applied and released.

The bevel gear shaft is supported in the bevel shaft bearing cage by tapered roller bearings, the cage being bolted to the steering clutch housing. The steering clutch hub is splined to the left-hand end of the shaft and secured to it with a washer and cap

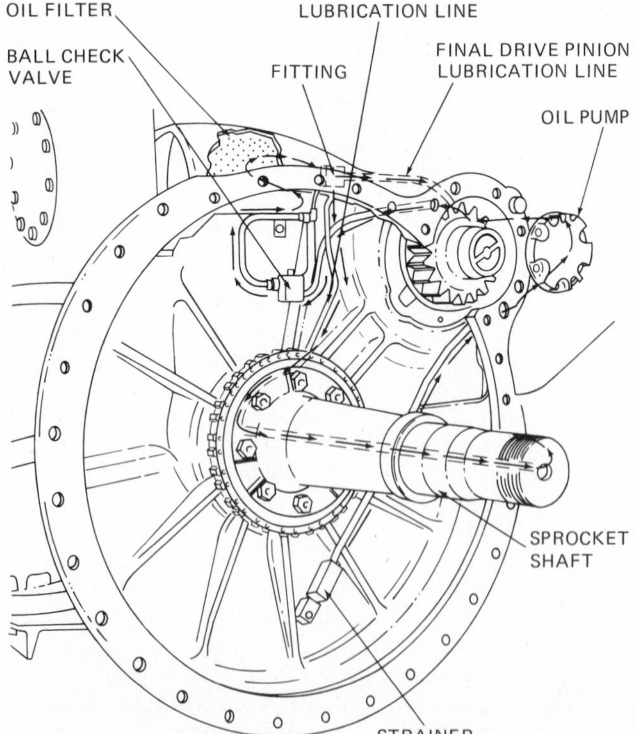

Fig. 9-6 A pressure lubrication system. (*Caterpillar Tractor Co.*)

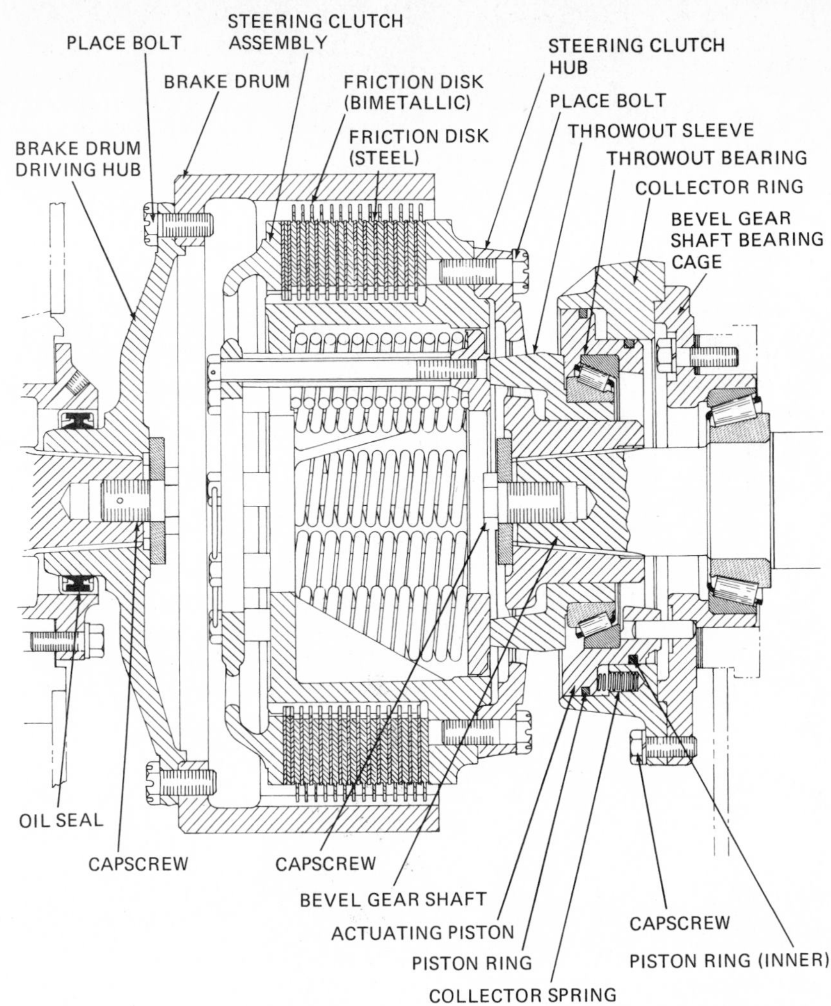

Fig. 9-7 Sectional view of a steering clutch. (*Fiat–Allis*)

screw. Shims are used to adjust the preload of the bevel gear shaft bearings. The steering clutch hub is bolted to the steering clutch driving hub. The clutch hub has external splines to which steel friction disks are loosely splined. Between each two steel friction disks lies one bimetallic friction disk, loosely splined to the internal splines of the brake drum. The friction disks are held firmly together (between the steering clutch assembly and steering clutch hub) by the energy of the coil springs. Throwout plate cap screws hold the coil springs compressed between the steering clutch hub and the throwout plate. **NOTE** The cap screws pass through the holes in the steering clutch assembly, through the center of the coil springs, and then are threaded into the throw-out plate. The cap screws are secured by wire to prevent them from coming loose. The brake drum is bolted to the brake drum driving hub, which is splined to the pinion shaft.

The clutch release mechanism consists of the throwout sleeve, the tapered roller bearing, the actuating piston, and the collector ring. The throwout sleeve rests on the steering clutch hub and its finger passes through the steering clutch hub and rests against the throwout plate. A tapered roller bearing positioned between the actuating piston and throwout sleeve allows the actuating piston to remain stationary when the steering clutch is disengaged. The collector ring (cylinder) is bolted to the steering clutch housing by the same cap screws that secure the bevel gear shaft bearing cage. Within the collector ring is the actuating piston and the coil springs which maintain the piston to the left.

The brake band is located around the brake drum, one end resting in a fixed bracket and the other (live) end, if mechanically actuated, connected through pins and levers to the brake pedal. If the brake application is hydraulically assisted, the linkages are connected to the brake booster.

Another steering clutch design is shown in Fig. 9-8. The difference between this clutch and the one shown in Fig. 9-7 is that here the actuating piston is within the steering clutch drive hub, and it acts directly onto the throwout plate. A guide is used to support the piston, and both turn when the piston is hydraulically moved to the right.

STEERING CLUTCH OPERATION—MECHANICAL ACTION When the steering clutch is engaged, that is, when there is no oil pressure on the steering clutch piston, the power from the transmission output shaft is transmitted to the bevel gear pinion and onto the bevel gear. Here the power is divided to the left and right toward the bevel gear shafts. The power from the bevel gear shafts is transmitted to the steering clutch driving hub, to the steering clutch hub, over the friction disks, to the brake drum, and to brake drum driving hub. From there it is transmitted to the

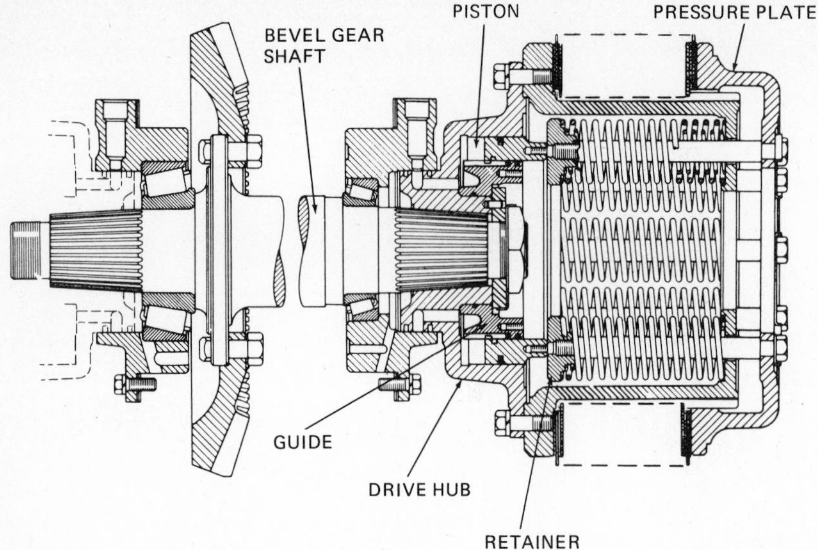

Fig. 9-8 Sectional view of a steering clutch. (*Caterpillar Tractor Co.*)

pinion, the intermediate gear and pinion, the sprocket shaft gear, and the sprocket shaft, driving the sprocket hub and causing the tractor to move in a straight-ahead direction.

When oil from the steering control valve is directed into one piston area, the piston is forced outward, directly or indirectly moving the throwout sleeve or the retainer, thereby further compressing the coil springs, and moving the cap screws and the steering clutch assembly or pressure plate. Consequently, the force from the friction disks is fully or partially released, depending on the hydraulic pressure. Accordingly, the power to the brake drum is now fully or partially interrupted, the track idles, or is only partially powered because of the slippage between the steel and bimetallic friction disks, and the tractor makes a slow turn or does not turn at all, depending on the operating terrain and the tractor's immediate task.

When the brake is applied under these circumstances, the brake band holds the drum in a fixed position, or allows the drum to partially rotate, again depending upon the force exerted onto the brake band and the rotating force of the track. The track is held stationary or allowed to partly rotate, thereby controlling the tractor's turn.

STEERING CLUTCH OPERATION—HYDRAULIC ACTION Hydraulic systems that actuate and release the steering clutches have much in common apart from design variations of the pressure control, flow control, and directional control valves and the oil flow variations involved when a hydrostatic, powershift, or standard transmission is used.

A schematic illustration of a hydraulic steering control circuit is shown in Fig. 9-9. The steering control valve is mounted on top of the bevel gear housing (or steering clutch housing), and the steer-

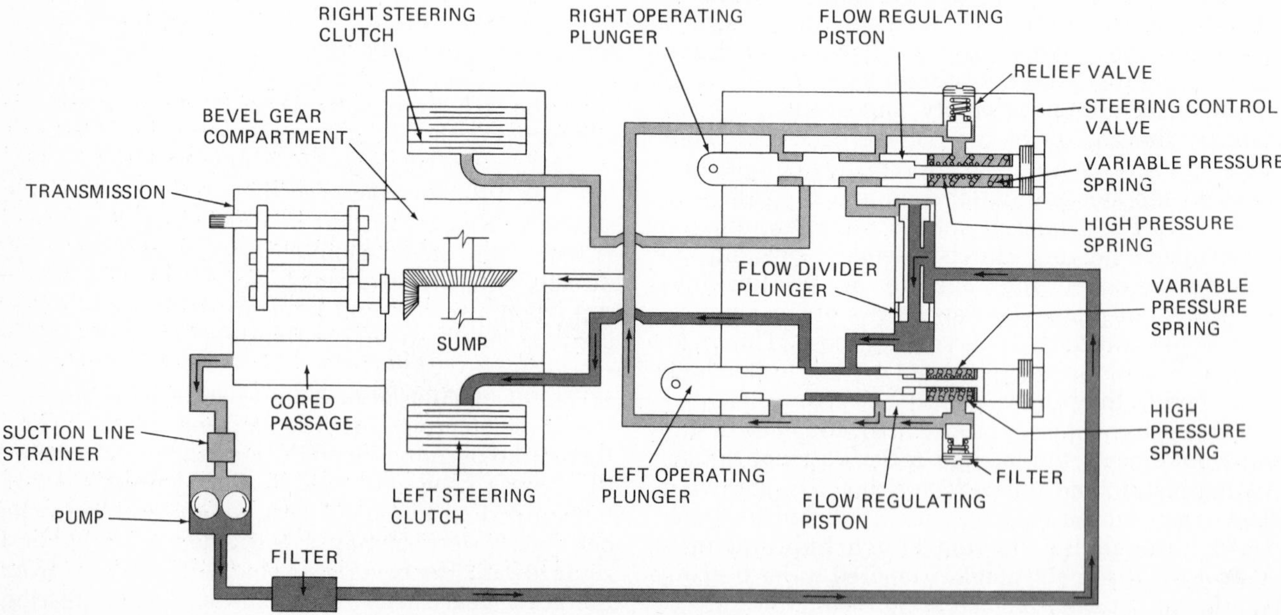

Fig. 9-9 Schematic view of hydraulic steering control components and oil flow when left-hand steering clutch is disengaged (powershift transmission). (*Fiat–Allis*)

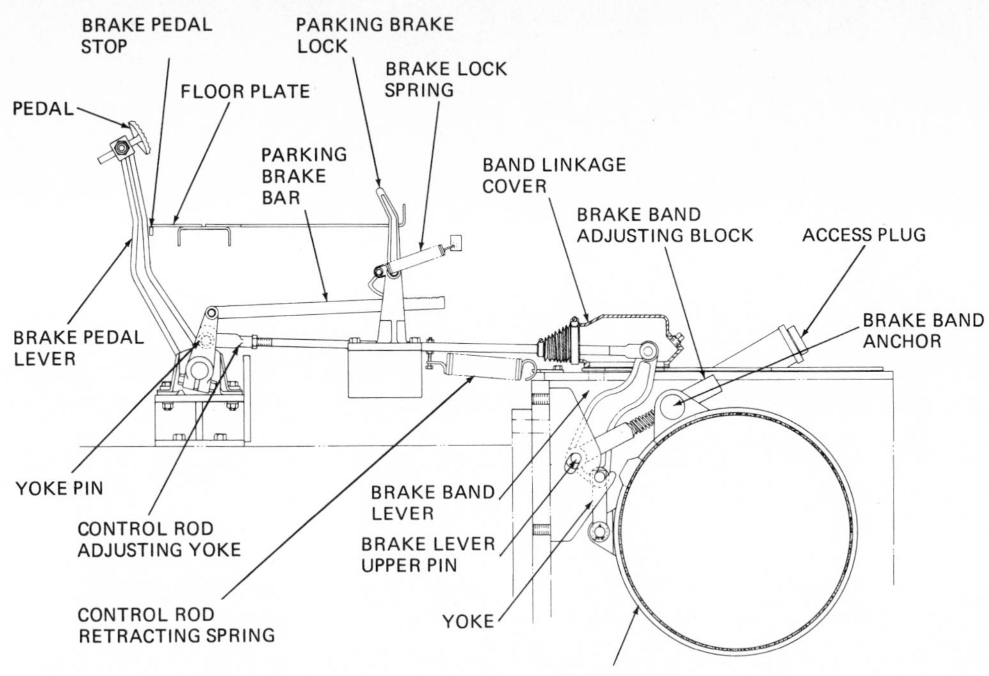

Fig. 9-10 Brake and brake control linkage components. (*Fiat–Allis*)

ing valve spools are linked through linkages and levers with the steering control levers. The valve spool plungers are of the open center design, and each steering clutch is protected by the flow regulator piston and the high-pressure spring.

When the engine is operating and both steering valve plungers are in the neutral position, oil from the steering pump is directed through the filter to the steering control valve, where it flows around and through the center of the flow divider plunger, and from there to the left- and right-hand steering plungers. The oil flows around both plungers, by both spool lands, out of the steering control valve, into the return line, and back to the bevel gear housing sump.

When the left-hand steering plunger is pulled fully to the left through the action of the steering lever and linkages, the plunger land fully opens the port leading to the left-hand steering clutch piston. This causes the high-pressure and variable-pressure springs to force the flow regulator piston to the left, closing or reducing the return oil flow into the return line. This increases the line pressure and the pressure on the steering clutch and the flow regulator piston. The flow divider plunger then shifts upward, reducing the oil flow to the right-hand steering plunger. These actions, combined, assure a smooth but quick pressure buildup to engage the left-hand clutch. When the set pressure, about 500 psi [3445 kPa], is reached, the increased force on the flow regulator piston moves it to the right against both spring forces and opens the port leading to the return line, thereby maintaining the specified pressure.

The purpose of the relief valve is to prevent a hydraulic lock on the flow regulator piston, and at the same time prevent a reverse oil flow onto the piston.

NOTE This valve opens at very low pressure.

If the left-hand steering plunger is moved only partly to the left, the action outlined above takes place. However, the steering valve plunger only partly opens the port to the steering clutch piston, and the variable-pressure spring controls only the movement of the flow regulator piston. In this circumstance a reduced flow, at reduced pressure, is directed into the steering clutch piston cavity and the friction disks are only partly separated, thereby reducing the power to the left-hand track. When the left-hand steering lever is moved to the neutral position, the steering valve plunger and the flow regulator piston are moved to the right. The flow regulator piston then directs the oil into the return line, and the steering valve plunger allows the oil from behind the steering clutch piston to flow past its plunger land into the common return line.

BRAKE BAND APPLICATION (MECHANICAL) When the operator forces the brake pedal lever down over the lever and control rods, the transmitted motion multiplies, causing the brake band lever to pivot and pull the brake band adjusting pin and the lever end of the brake band against the brake drum. If the tractor is moving in a forward direction, the brake band, due to its self-energizing action, wraps more tightly against the drum. If the tractor is moving in reverse, there is no self-energizing action and the brake application is reduced.

To park the tractor, the operator places the transmission in neutral and forces both brake pedal levers downward. Then, by pulling the parking lever rearward, the parking brake bar is locked, holding the pedal shaft lever in a fixed position and maintaining the brake application. See Fig. 9-10, where the brake system is illustrated.

BRAKE BAND APPLICATION (HYDRAULIC-ASSIST) A hydraulic steering linkage and brake booster system is

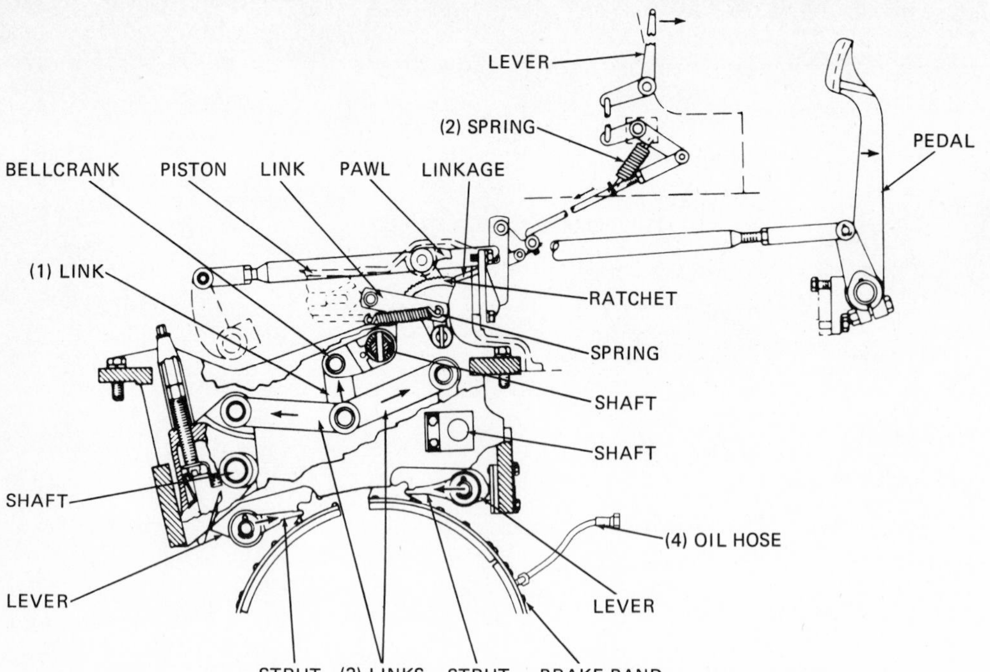

Fig. 9-11 Steering linkage components. (*Caterpillar Tractor Co.*)

shown in Figs. 9-11 and 9-12. The assembly is attached to and located within the booster control housing cover. The cover is bolted to the top of the steering clutch housing. When the hydraulic brake booster is in the release position and the engine is operating, oil is directed over a check valve, located within the housing cover, into the cavity (2). Oil, over a separate line (4), is directed to the brake band to cool the brake drum and band.

When the brake pedal is forced down over lever and linkage, the shaft (9) rotates, pivoting the lever (8) to the right and moving the plunger and valve to the right also. In this position, the valve closes the passage in the piston, and at the same time passages (5), (6), and (7) open. This allows oil from cavity (2) to flow into cavity (11), and as the oil pressure increases it moves the piston, thereby pivoting the bell crank. As the bell crank pivots, it pulls the link (1) up, forcing the toggle links (3) outward. The levers on each end pivot on their respective shafts, and force the struts that rest (in the lugs) on the brake band ends toward each other. This squeezes the brake band against the brake drum. **NOTE** Regardless of the direction of tractor travel, with an hydraulic booster the brake bank is always self-energized.

To lock the brake in the applied position, the parking brake lever is moved downward over rods, linkages, and levers. The pawl is then moved against the ratchet, holding the link in a fixed position. Since the link is connected to the bell crank, the brake application holds firm.

To release the brake, the operator must depress the brake pedal and pull the parking lever upward. This engages the pawl and the link is free to move. The spring (2) and the springs within the hydraulic booster, in effect, try to pull the lever links to the neutral position. The two springs (10) force the valve (3), the plunger (1), and the lever (8) to the left, thus opening passage (4) and allowing the oil from behind the piston to flow into the steering clutch housing. At the same time passages (5), (6), and (7) are

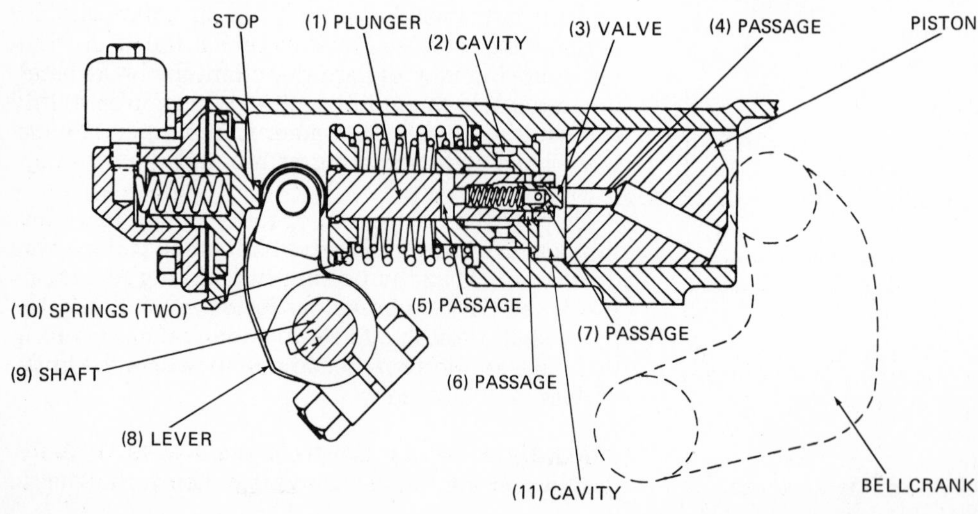

Fig. 9-12 Sectional view of hydraulic booster components. (*Caterpillar Tractor Co.*)

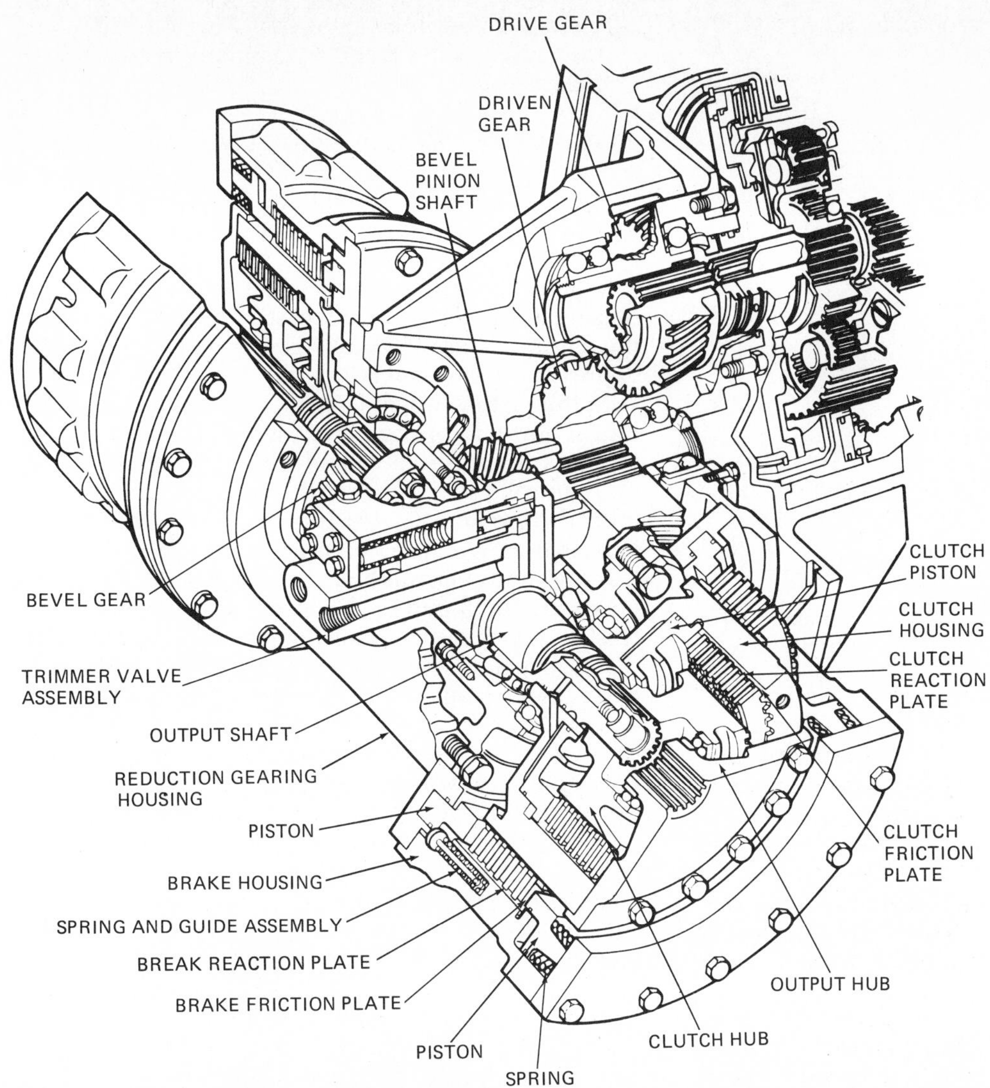

Fig. 9-13 Cutaway view of a steering clutch and reduction gear. (*Terex Division of General Motors Corporation*)

blocked and oil from the pump is trapped in cavity (2). This allows the bell crank to follow the retracted piston and causes the link to move downward, the toggle links to pull toward each other, each lever to pivot, and the struts to pull outward, removing the force from the brake band.

Hydraulically Applied Steering Clutch Figure 9-13 illustrates a steering clutch that is hydraulically applied, and that has hydraulically applied service brakes plus spring-applied brakes that automatically go into action when the steering or transmission system loses its oil pressure. (Note the reduction gear between the transmission and bevel gear pinion.) The smaller helical (drive) gear of the reduction gear is splined to the transmission output shaft, and the larger helical (driven) gear is splined to the bevel gear pinion shaft. The output shafts are splined to the bevel gear, and the clutch hub is splined to the other ends of the shafts. A roller bearing located on the output hub (bolted to the clutch housing) supports the outer side of the clutch hub. The quill shaft (not shown) that drives the final drive pinion gear fits into the splines of the output hub. Roller bearings in the bearing race (bolted to the bevel gear housing) support the internally and externally splined clutch housing. Reaction plates (steel friction disks), positioned between the bimetallic friction disks, are splined to the inside splines of the clutch housing. The friction disks are splined to the clutch hub. The clutch piston is located within the inner end of the clutch housing, and the steel and bimetallic friction disks are positioned between the clutch piston and output hub.

The brake housing (which surrounds the clutch housing) is bolted to the brake anchor. The clutch housing has internal splines to which the steel friction plates (disks) are splined. Bimetallic friction disks are located between the steel plates which are externally splined to the clutch housing. The brake anchor is bolted to the bevel gear housing which contains the hydraulically actuated brake piston. **NOTE** The spring and guide assembly holds the inner piston in the released position. Coil springs between the outside piston and anchor plate press the friction disks against the inner piston and hold the clutch housing stationary whenever the hydraulic pressure from the cavity of the outside piston is released.

Hydraulic Steering Control and Brake System This system consists of the components shown in

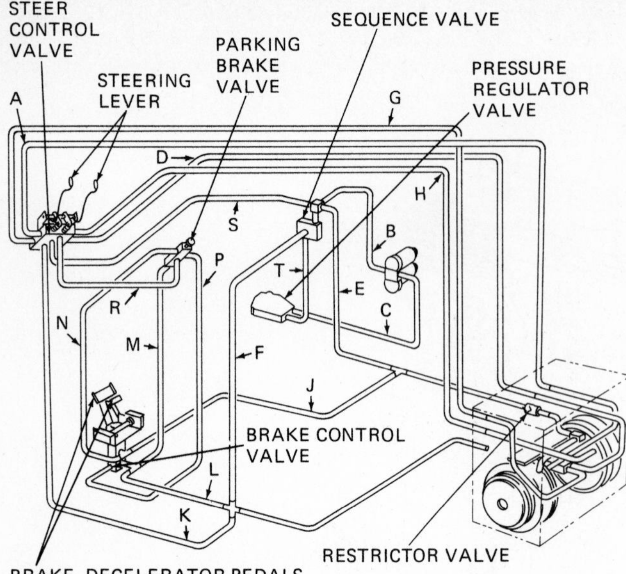

Fig. 9-14 Schematic view of hydraulic brake system. (*Terex Division of General Motors Corporation*)

Fig. 9-14 (all letters in the following descriptions refer to this illustration). When the engine is not operating, there is no oil pressure within the lines, and the pressure from behind the outside and inside brake pistons and the steering clutch pistons is therefore released. As a result the brake coil springs force the brake friction disks firmly together, holding the clutch hub, the quill shaft, the final drive, and the tracks stationary. This action separates the steering clutch friction plates and releases the steering clutch.

When the engine is operating, the parking brake pedal is in the released position, and the steering levers are in neutral, oil from the powershift transmission's hydraulic system flows to the pressure relief valve. From there it flows through line C to the filters, and over line B to the junction where it divides into three streams:

- *Stream No. 1.* Oil flows into line E over a restricted fitting, into the left- and right-hand steering clutches, and to the left- and right-hand outside brake pistons. This causes the piston to retract and the springs to compress, thereby releasing both brakes. From line E, oil flow is T'd off (flows in two directions) into line J leading to the brake valve, then over line N to the parking brake valve, and from there over line R into the steering control valve where the oil flow is blocked. Lines H and A connect the steering control valve with the steering brake pistons.
- *Stream No. 2.* Oil flows over line S into the steering control valve, around the valve spool, and out of lines D and G to the sequence valve. From the sequence valve, it flows to the left- and right-hand steering clutch piston cavities thereby applying the steering clutches.
- *Stream No. 3.* Oil flows into the sequence valve. Since the pressure-regulating valve is connected with the sequence valve through line F, when system pressure is reached, the oil from the sequence valve flows over line F to join the common return lines L and K, maintaining the system pressure.

BRAKE ACTION When both parking brake pedals are released, oil from the transmission flows into port D, around the spool, through orifice A, into the center of the spool, and out of port C into the common return line. See Fig. 9-15.

When one or both brake pedals are depressed, the decelerator pedal is also forced down, decelerating the engine before the brake is engaged. Brake pedal depression forces the regulating spring down, along with the piston cup and spool. This action closes the return port and opens port D, allowing oil to flow to the parking brake valve and from there to the steering control valve. From the steering control valve, oil is directed over either line A or H (or both) to the inside brake piston, compressing the disks and thereby applying the brakes. At the same time, the brake pressure moves the steering valve spool, releasing the pressure from the steering clutch(s) (on the side where the brake is applied). The amount of brake pressure applied depends on the force exerted on the brake valve regulating spring. The brake control valve acts like an air treadle valve and balances when the oil pressure equals the spring force.

When the brake pedal force is removed, the oil

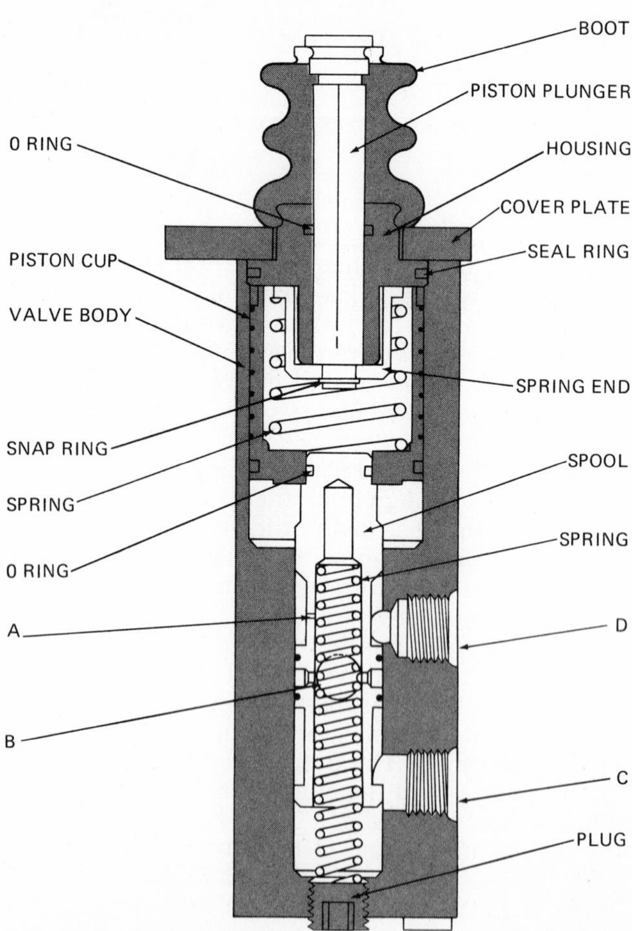

Fig. 9-15 Sectional view of brake control valve. (*Terex Division of General Motors Corporation*)

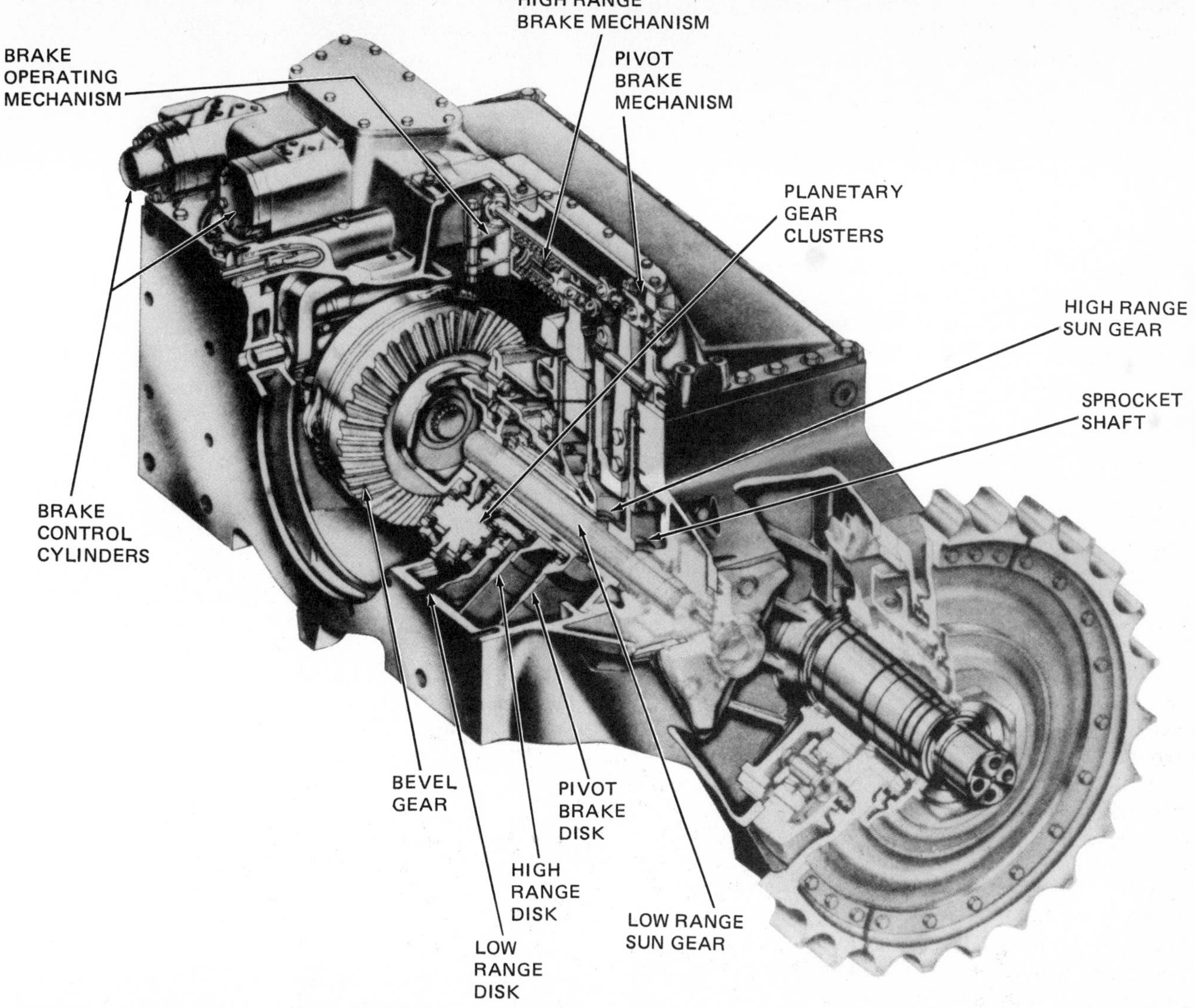

Fig. 9-16 Cutaway view of planetary power drive. (*International Harvester Company*)

pressure forces the valve upward, closing the oil pressure inlet port and opening the return port. Brake pressure is then released over the steering valve, line R, parking brake valve, line M, and line L to the reservoir. As the brake pressure is released, the steering valve spool directs oil to the steering clutch and both tracks are again driven at equal speed.

PIVOT TURN To make a right-hand pivot turn, the operator pulls the right-hand steering lever back to its maximum. This action moves the right-hand steering control valve spool and allows oil to flow through line H into the cavity of the inside brake piston, thereby applying the right-hand brake. Simultaneously, the spool blocks the oil flow to the right-hand steering clutch but opens the return port, thus allowing oil from the steering clutch to flow over line D, through the steering valve, and into line K, where it returns to the sump.

GRADUAL TURN To make a gradual right-hand turn, the right-hand steering lever is only partially pulled back. This action only partially moves the steering valve spool, but blocks the oil supply to the steering clutch and brake and opens the return port, allowing oil from the right-hand steering clutch to flow to the sump. **NOTE** If the brake is not applied but the steering clutch is disengaged, the track idles.

The steering action and oil flow for a pivot left- or gradual left-hand turn are the same as for right-hand turns. However, in left-hand turns, the left-hand steering clutch is disengaged and the left-hand brake is applied.

When both steering levers are pulled completely back, the power to both tracks is interrupted and both brakes are applied. If under this circumstance the parking brake is activated, the parking brake valve spool blocks return line R, thus maintaining brake action.

Planetary Power Drive (Steering) A quite different method (shown in Fig. 9-16) is used to transmit the power from the bevel gear to the final drive pinion. Furthermore, the gear and brake arrangement in the planetary power drive not only transmits the power, but provides steering capability by maintaining full power to both tracks during steering. In addition its hydraulic system and brake arrangement provide the tractor with the capacity to make pivot turns.

NOTE When making a pivot turn, the track being held by the pivot brake is without power.

DESIGN The planetary power drive consists of two identical sections bolted to the left- and right-hand sides of the bevel gear and positioned in the rear main frame housing. The bevel gear carrier center, the carrier cover, and the bevel gear carrier ends are bolted to each side of the bevel gear. Tapered roller bearings (not shown in Fig. 9-16) on the outside of the carrier ends support the assembly to the main housing. Bearings are positioned in the adjustable bevel gear carrier cage to provide bearing preload adjustment and bevel-gear-to-pinion adjustment. Three cluster gears are roller-bearing-supported on shafts within the carrier ends and carrier cover. Each gear set includes three straight cut gears of different sizes. Inside the carrier ends are three roller-bearing-supported shafts. The outside shaft is the low-range sun gear; the middle shaft (located within the low-range sun-gear shaft) is the high-range sun gear, within which the sprocket drive shaft is located.

The low-range sun gear is in mesh with the low-range gears of the three cluster gears (the second smallest gears on the cluster), and the low-range disk is splined to the right-hand side of the low-range sun gear.

The high-range sun gear is located over the sprocket drive pinion shaft, and the sun gear is in mesh with the three (larger) high-range cluster gears. The high-range disk is splined to the right-hand side of the high-range sun gear. The sprocket drive shaft is positioned within the high-range sun gear, to which the sprocket drive pinion gear is splined. The drive pinion gear is in mesh with the smallest of the three cluster gears. The pivot brake disk is splined to the center of the sprocket drive shaft, and the final drive pinion is splined to the outside of this shaft. Each side has a multipurpose disk brake assembly which is positioned above and partly between the low-range, high-range, and pivot brake disks. See Fig. 9-17.

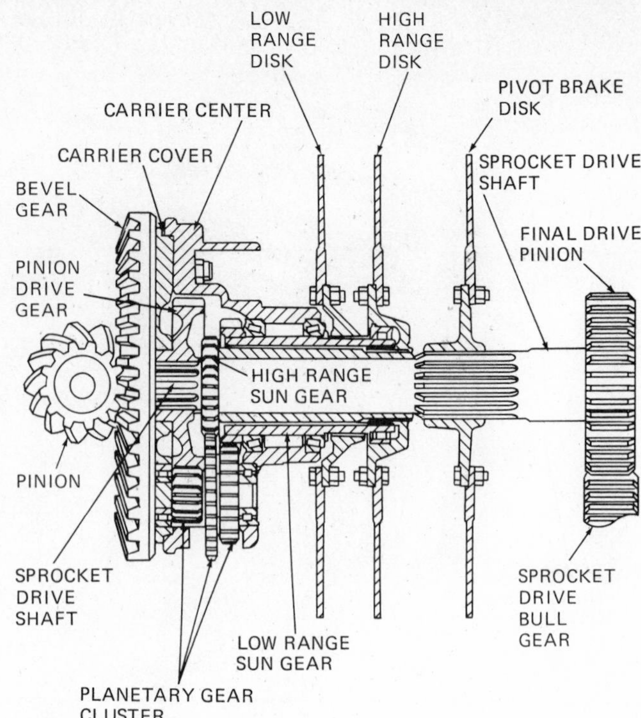

Fig. 9-17 Sectional view of planetary drive showing the right-hand side drive and steering components. (*International Harvester Company*)

HYDRAULIC SYSTEM The hydraulic system components, hydraulic line connections, and disk brake assemblies are shown in Fig. 9-18. When the engine is operating with the main transmission in neutral and the steering hand control levers in high range, the oil flows as follows: As soon as the pump rotates and creates low pressure, oil from the reservoir flows through the filter into the piston pump. From the pump, it is directed through the high-pressure filter to the combination unloading and pressure relief valve, and from there to the accumulator and then to the steering control valves. **NOTE** The bypass valve within the filters opens when there is a pressure differential of more than 44 psi [303 kPa].

Within the control valve are seven valves: two high-range release sequence valves, two low-range sequence valves, one pressure-reducing valve, and two pivot brake valves. Therefore, to control one track, one high-range, one low-range, and one pivot brake valve are used. A steering lever pivots a cam to actuate the valves. The pressure-reducing valve reduces the pressure to both low-range sequence valves to 900 to 1000 psi [6205 to 6894 kPa]. Both pivot brake valves, in addition to their function as directional valves, are independent reducing valves. Maximum brake pressure is 750 psi [5171 kPa].

HIGH-RANGE OPERATION When both steering control levers are placed in high range, none of the valves are moved. Therefore the high-range release and sequence valves block the oil flow to the left- and right-hand high-range brake pistons, causing the high-range brake pressure springs to hold the high-range disks stationary. Since the low-range sequence valves block the oil flow, no pressure is exerted on the low-range brake pistons, and the pivot brake valves block the oil flow to the pivot valve brake pistons.

The system pressure increases quickly to the unloading pressure, 1250 psi [8618 kPa], and the unloading valve directs the pump output oil back to the reservoir. If the system pressure drops, say due to internal leakage or to the activation of the disk brakes, and falls below 1150 psi [7928 kPa], the unloading valve reacts and directs the piston pump output oil to the system and accumulator until the system pressure again reaches 1250 psi [8618 kPa]. The unloading valve again reacts, whereupon oil is then pumped back to the reservoir.

When the transmission is now shifted into forward-first or forward-second gear, or into reverse-

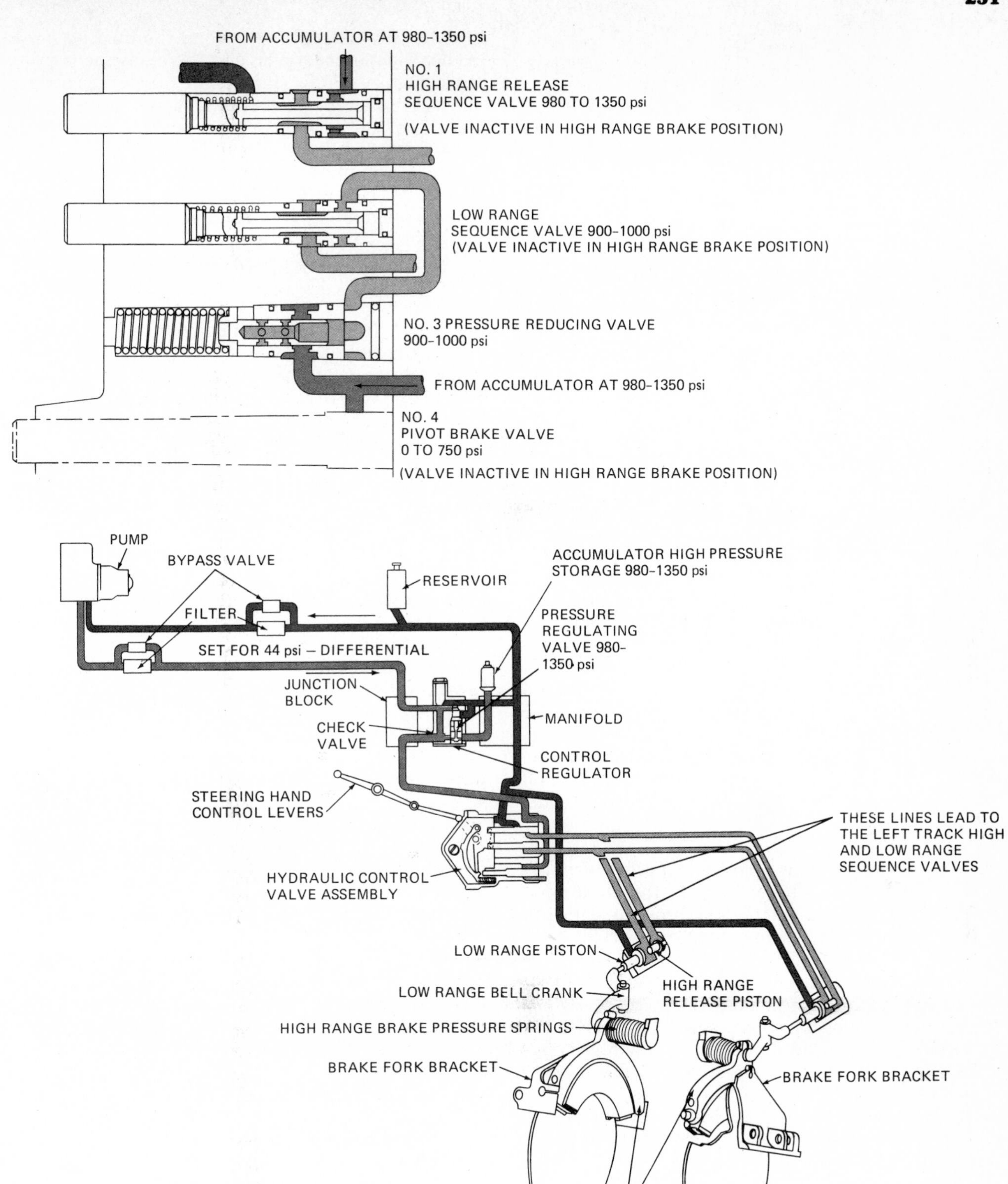

Fig. 9-18 Schematic view of planetary drive showing hydraulic system and components (high range). (*International Harvester Company*)

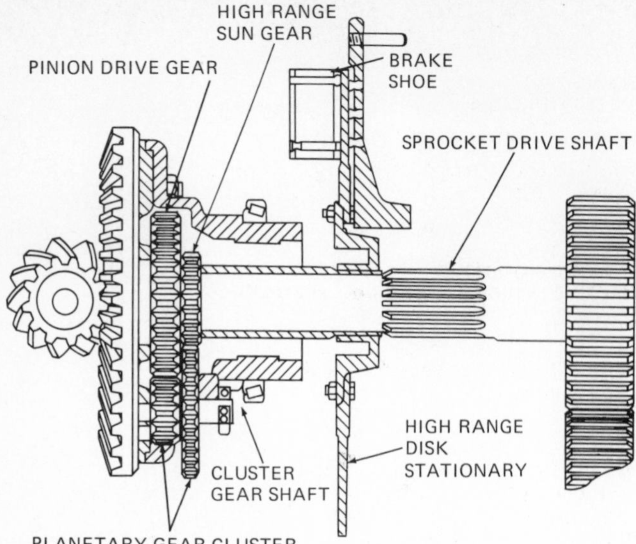

Fig. 9-19 Sectional view of planetary drive, in high range. (*International Harvester Company*)

first or reverse-second gear, the engine power is transmitted over the transmission to the bevel gear pinion, rotating the bevel gear, carrier centers, carrier covers, and carrier ends, and with them the planetary cluster gears rotate as a unit. However, the high-range sun gears are held by the left- and right-hand high-range disk brakes, causing both left- and right-hand sets of cluster gears to rotate on their shafts around the high-range sun gears. Consequently, the pinion cluster gears drive the pinion drive gears, the sprocket drive shafts, and the final drive pinions, and the tracks are then driven at equal speed. See Fig. 9-19.

HIGH-RANGE PIVOT TURN To make a pivot turn, say by stopping the right-hand track, the right-hand steering lever (right-hand track) is brought to the full pivot position. This action moves the right-hand brake pivot valve and the right-hand high-range release sequence valve, and the latter directs oil to the right-hand high-range brake piston. The brake piston is forced out by the oil pressure, thereby pivoting the bell crank. The crank compresses the high-range brake pressure springs, which releases the high-range brake, and the disk is then free to rotate.

At the same time, the pivot brake valve directs oil to and moves the pivot brake piston. Through linkages the right-hand pivot brake is actuated, thus holding the pivot brake disk, the sprocket drive shaft, the final drive pinion, and therefore the right-hand track. See Fig. 9-20. However, because of the pivot brake valve design, only a maximum oil pressure of 750 psi [5171 kPa] can be exerted on the pivot brake piston. With full engine power on the left-hand track, the tractor makes a pivot turn to the right. **NOTE** Under this condition, the sprocket drive shaft and gear do not rotate, but are held stationary.

If the right-hand steering lever is eased away from the full pivot position, the pivot pressure is reduced from its maximum of 750 psi [5171 kPa]. This allows the pivot disk to rotate and the track to move in the direction of travel, and increases the turning radius because the right-hand cluster gears are forced to rotate on their shafts, thereby causing the high- and low-range sun gears and disks to rotate freely. **NOTE** If the left-hand steering lever is also placed in the pivot position, the tractor comes to a stop because now the left-hand high-range release sequence valve releases the high-range brake disk, and the left-hand pivot brake valve directs oil to the left-hand pivot brake piston, thus applying the pivot brake. See Fig. 9-21.

LOW-RANGE OPERATION When both steering control levers are placed in the low-range position, the high-range release sequence valves move, directing high system pressure to both high-range brake release pistons. The bell cranks pivot, compress the high-range brake pressure springs, and release the high-range disks. At the same time, the low-range sequence valves move, allowing the oil at system pressure to enter the reducing valve. This valve reduces the system pressure to about 900 to 1000 psi [6205 to 6894 kPa] and then directs the oil to the low-range sequence valves. Oil flows through both low-range sequence valves and out to both low-range brake pistons. The pistons' movement pivots both bell cranks and forces the brake shoes against the low-range disks, holding the disks. See Fig. 9-22. With both low-range brake disks held stationary, the low-range sun gears are also held stationary. As a result, both sets of cluster gears are forced around the stationary low-range sun gears, driving both left- and right-hand drive pinion gears and the sprocket drive shafts, and thereby propelling the tracks at reduced but equal speed. See Fig. 9-23.

To make a right-hand turn, the operator must differentiate between a sharp turn or a power turn. If a power turn is necessary, the operator shifts the left-hand track into high range by placing the left-hand

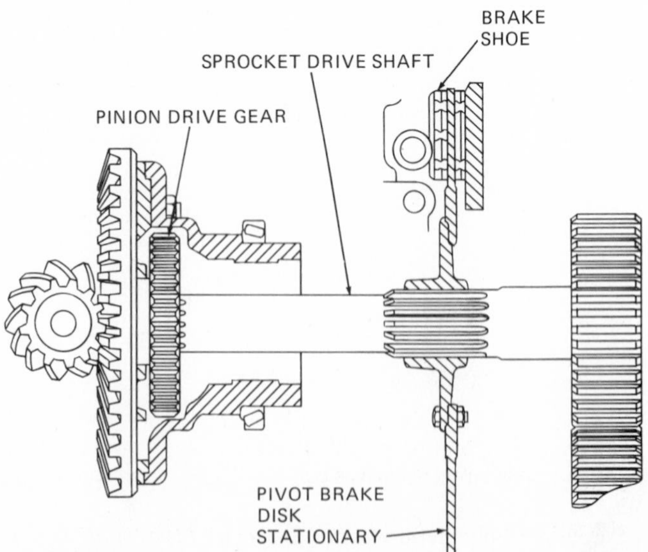

Fig. 9-20 Sectional view of planetary drive with the right-hand side in the pivot brake position. (*International Harvester Company*)

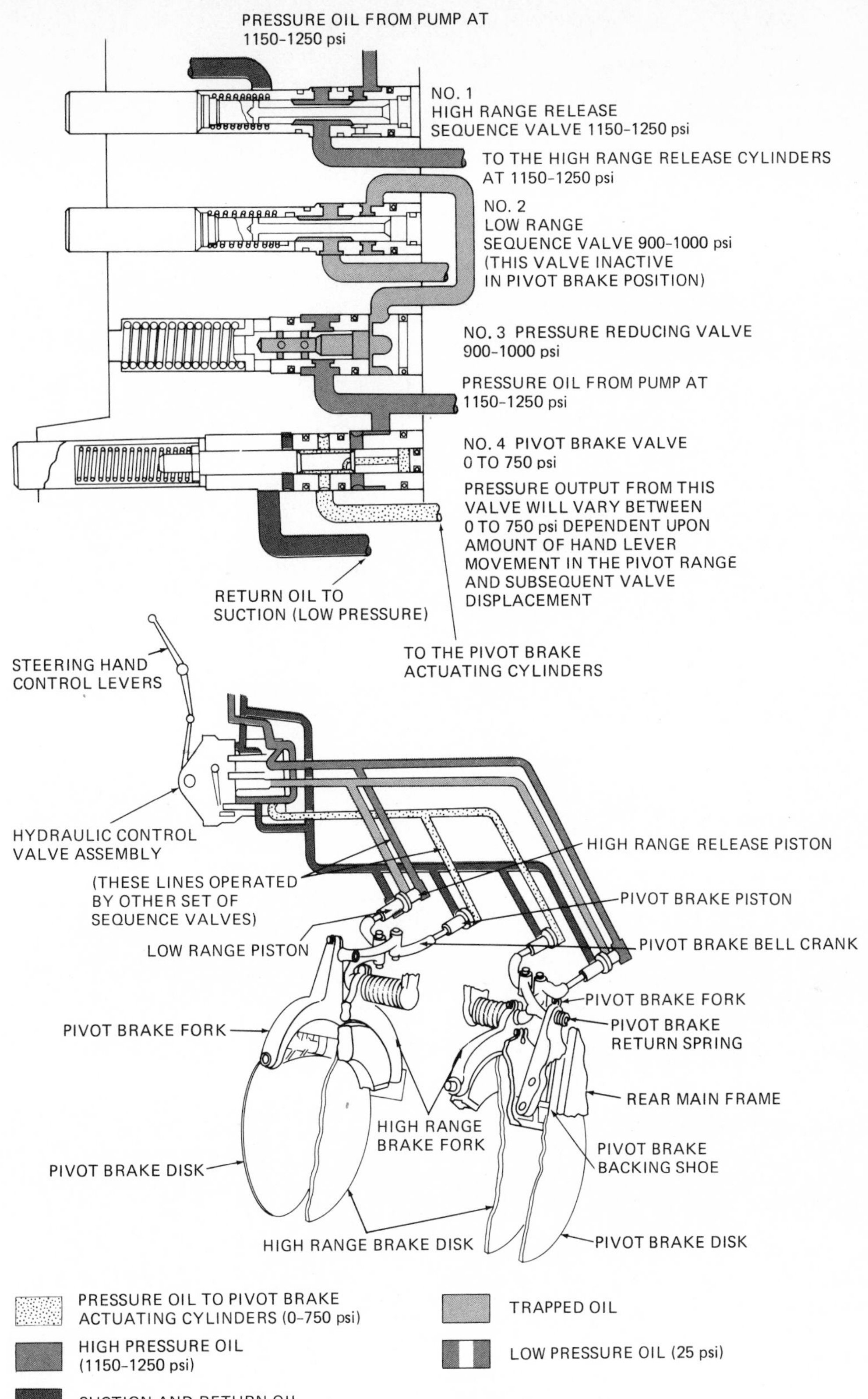

Fig. 9-21 Schematic view of planetary drive showing valve position and oil flow when both left- and right-hand pivot brakes are applied. *(International Harvester Company)*

steering lever into the high-range position. To make a sharp turn to the right, the right-hand steering lever is placed into the pivot position, and (depending on the lever position) maximum or reduced brake pressure is exerted onto the pivot brake piston. Under this circumstance, the high-range release sequence valve and the low-range sequence valve are shifted and system pressure is directed to the high-range release cylinder, forcing the piston to move the bell crank, which in turn disengages the high-

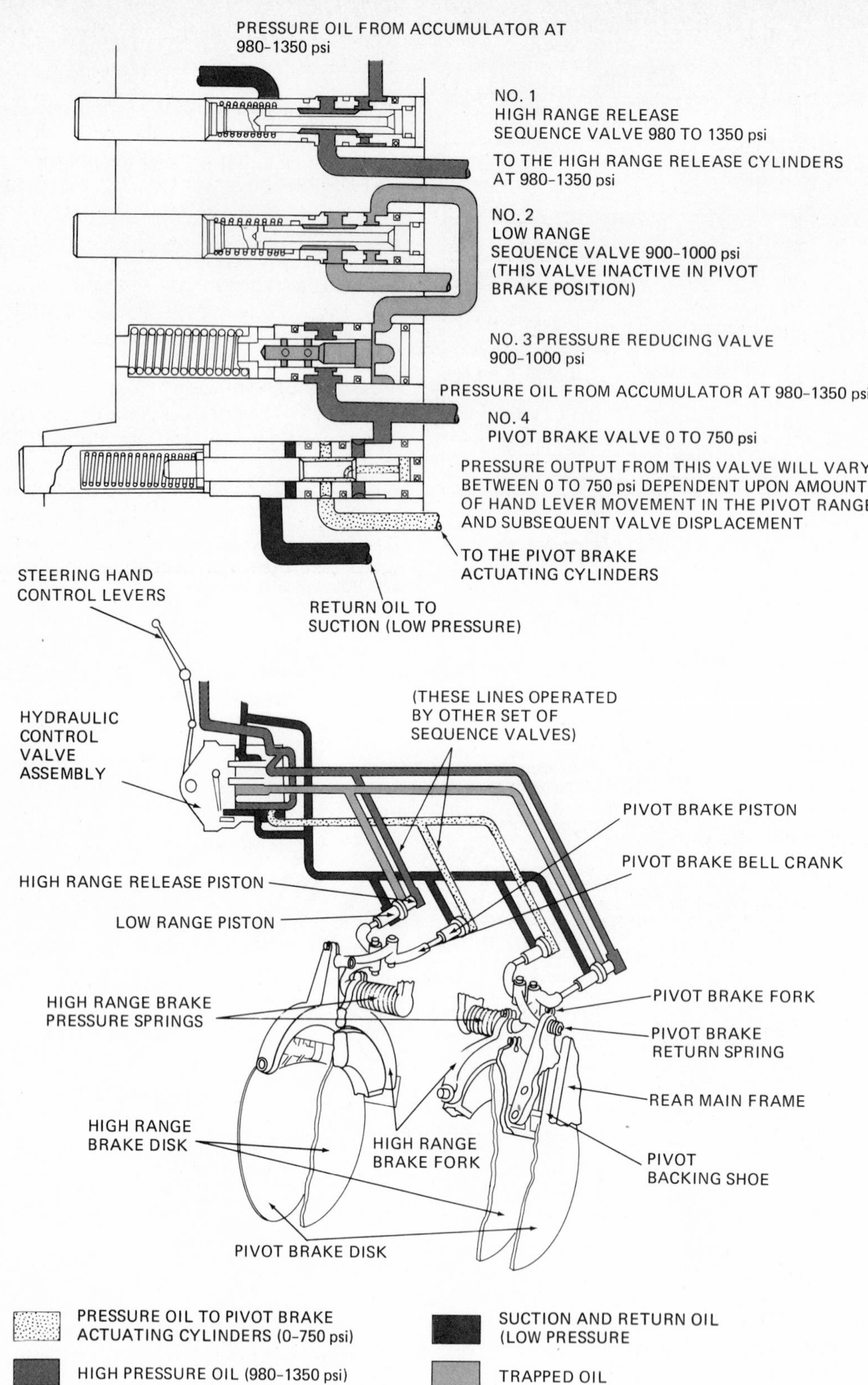

Fig. 9-22 Schematic view of planetary drive showing valve position and oil flow when both left- and right-hand planetary drives are in low-speed range. (*International Harvester Company*)

range disk brake. Oil pressure from the low-range brake system is simultaneously released. Consequently the track can idle or can be held by the pivot brake, depending upon the steering lever position.

Track and Crawler Carrier Drives and Steering Mechanisms Track and crawler carriers (excavators, shovels, cranes, etc.) which are propelled through hydraulic or electric motors are equipped

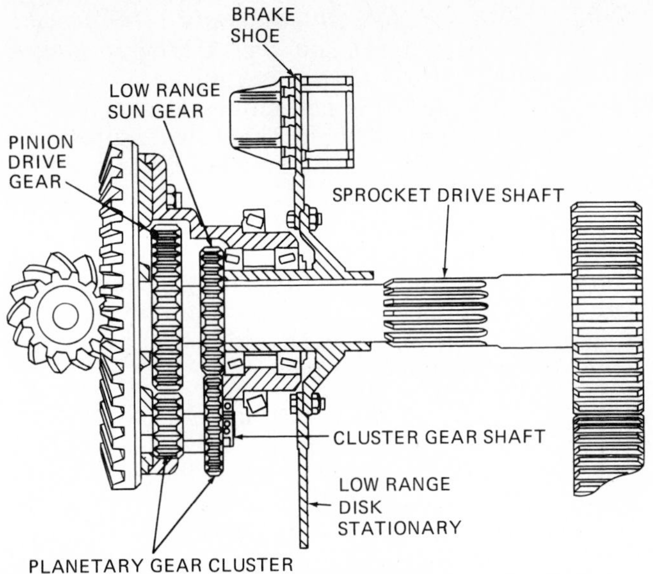

Fig. 9-23 Sectional view of planetary drive, in low-speed range. (*International Harvester Company*)

with a final drive transmission rather than a final drive.

FINAL DRIVE TRANSMISSION DESIGN These transmissions are usually double- or triple-reduction units bolted to the track roller or crawler frame (see Fig. 9-24). The final drive transmission illustrated is used on a hydraulically propelled excavator. The left-hand side of the output shaft is supported in the gear case and gear case cover by ball bearings, and the right-hand side is supported by two sets of barrel bearings located in pillar blocks bolted to the side rails of the roller frame. The drive sprocket is splined between the inside and outside bearings, and the output gear is splined to the output shaft, within the gear case. The intermediate shafts are supported on roller bearings and ball bearings. **NOTE** The intermediate pinion gear is usually *machined* to the shaft but the intermediate output gear is *splined* to the shaft. The right-hand side of the input shaft is splined to the input gear and is supported in the gear case by roller bearings. The brake assembly is

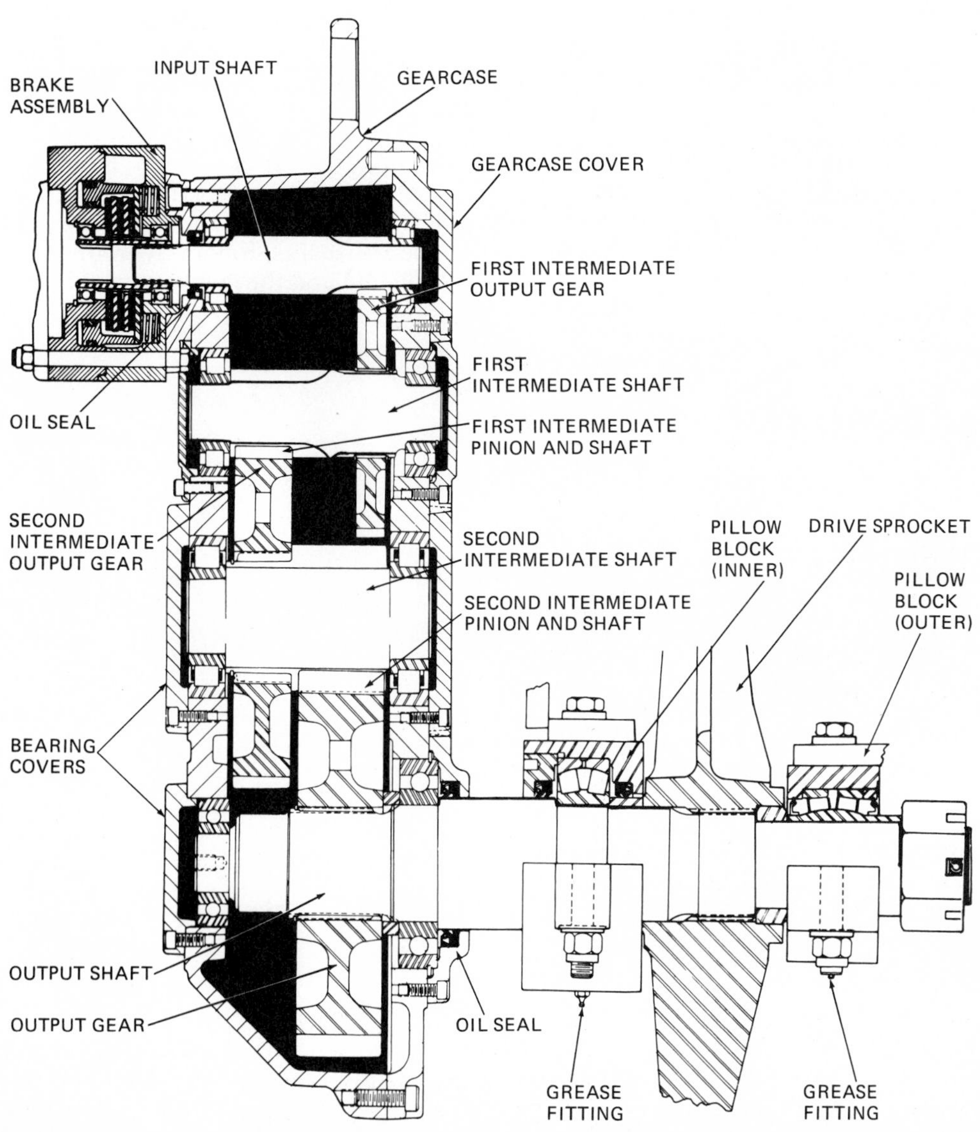

Fig. 9-24 Sectional view of an excavator final drive transmission. (*J I Case Company Agricultural Equipment Division*)

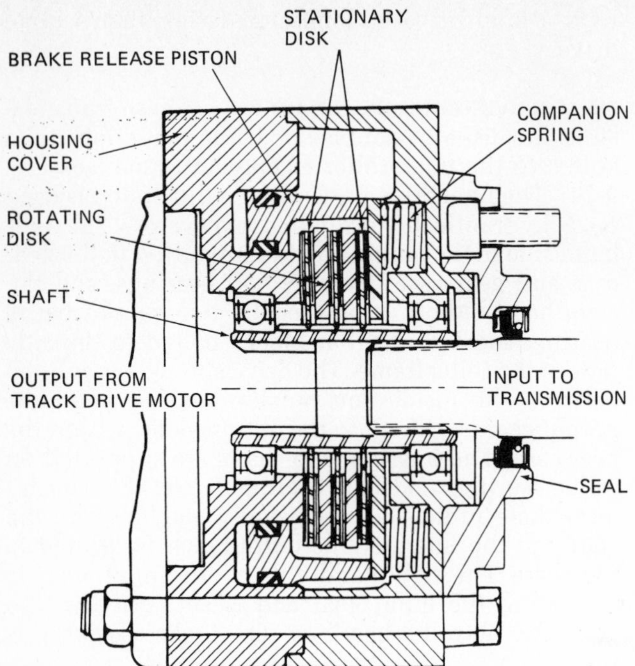

Fig. 9-25 Sectional view of a brake assembly.

bolted to the gear case. Brakes of the multidisk brake design, very similar to a steering clutch, are used (see Fig. 9-25).

The brake used on the excavator, however, has three steel and three bimetallic friction disks. The bimetallic friction disks are splined to the external splines of the shaft, and the steel friction disks pass through the cutout of the piston and are held to the housing by their two lugs. The shaft is supported on roller bearings in the inside and outside brake housing cover. The right-hand shaft's internal splines mesh with the external splines of the input shaft, and the left-hand internal splines fit over the hydraulic motor output shaft. The activating piston is located within the outside housing cover cylinder, and sealed to the cylinder bore by an O ring and backup washer. The compression springs, located within the right-hand side of the housing cover, force the activating piston into its cylinder bore and force the friction disks firmly, one after another, against the housing cover shoulder, thereby holding the output shaft and the track.

OPERATION When the brakes are released, by sending oil from a directional control valve into the brake piston cavities, the piston moves to the right against the spring force, separating the disks. (See material on hydrostatic drives in Unit 12.) If now both directional control valves direct oil to the hydraulic motors to drive them in a clockwise rotation, oil returning from the motors is redirected back to the directional valves and then to the reservoir. See Fig. 9-26. The motor rotation is transmitted to the splined brake shaft, which relays the power to the input shaft. The input shaft then drives the first intermediate gear and pinion, which in turn drives the second intermediate gear and pinion, thereby driving the output gear, output shaft, and drive sprocket.

If both directional valve spools are shifted into the opposite direction, the oil flow to the hydraulic motor reverses and both tracks are driven in the opposite direction. In either case, both tracks are propelled at equal speed—that is, if both hydraulic motors are equally efficient and the components of each

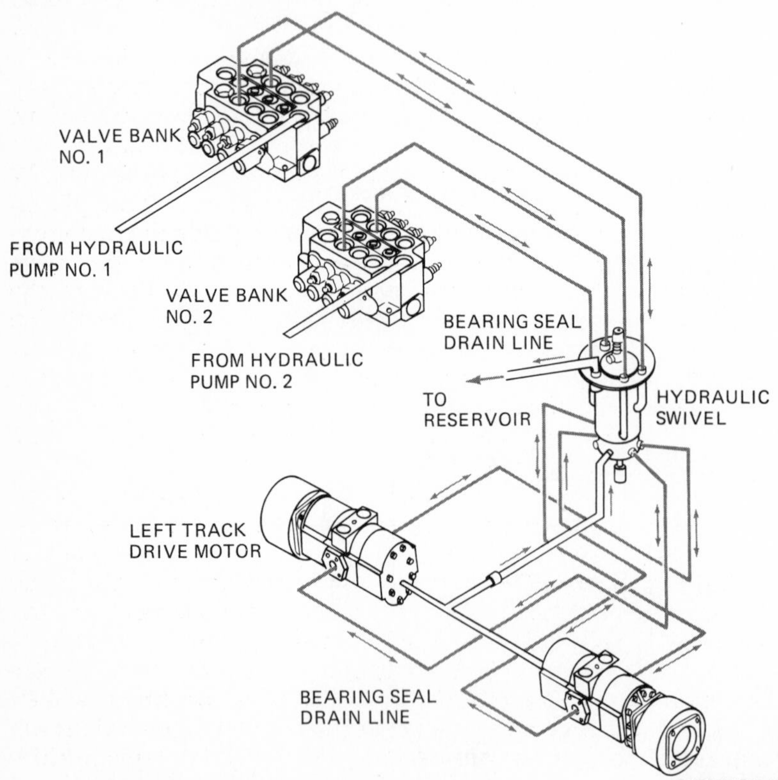

Fig. 9-26 Schematic view of track drive motor circuits.

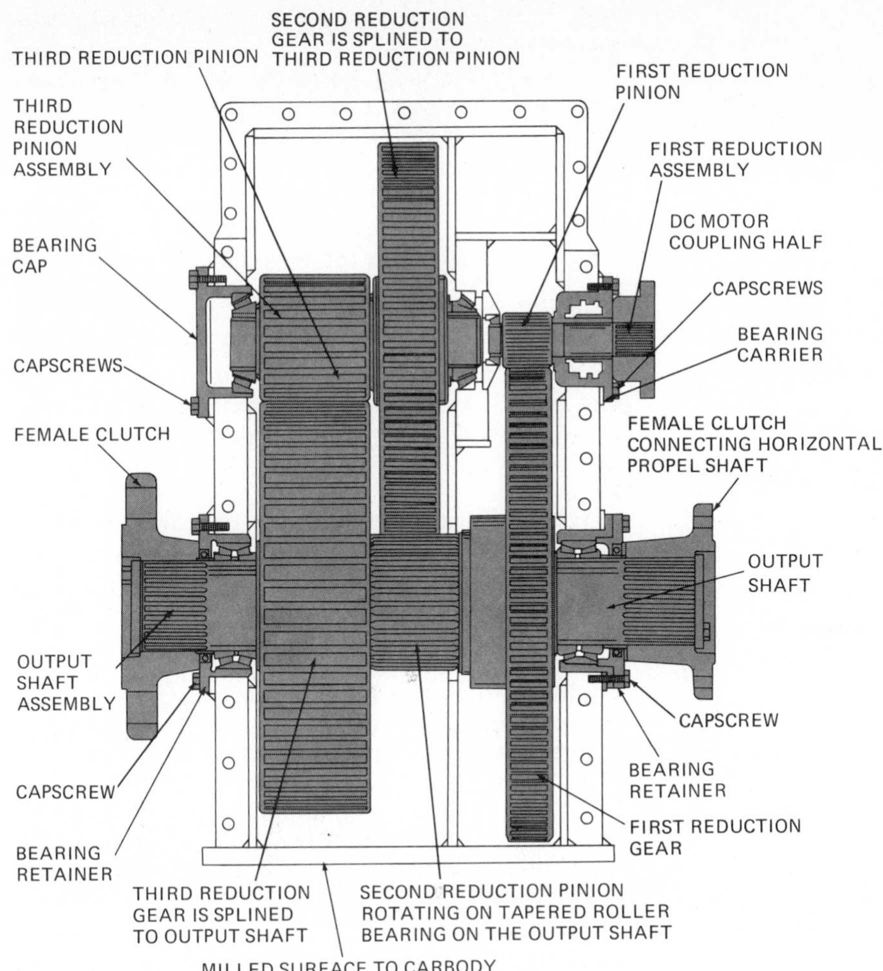

Fig. 9-27 Sectional view of a propel transmission's major components. (*Harnischfeger Corporation*)

transmission and undercarriage are not damaged. Maximum speed range is between 1.5 and 2.5 mph [2.41 and 4.02 km/h].

There are several methods by which a hydraulically propelled excavator can be steered, each depending upon the design of the hydraulic system: A power left- or right-hand turn can be achieved (1) by positioning one directional control valve in the maximum oil flow position, thereby directing maximum flow to one hydraulic motor, and through manipulating the other directional control valve so that it reduces the oil flow to the other hydraulic motor; (2) by stopping the oil flow to one hydraulic motor and driving the other with either the maximum or reduced oil supply; or (3) by driving one motor in the forward and the other motor in the reverse direction.

NOTE It is not the purpose of the brakes to control steering, but to hold the track or crawler belt stationary during digging or loading operations.

Electrical Propel System One of several methods to propel and steer a crawler carrier electrically is shown in Figs. 9-27 to 9-29. The assembly consists of a dc reversible propel motor, propel transmission, horizontal propel shaft, final drives, clutches, and brakes. The dc motor is connected to the triple-reduction propel transmission through a coupling. The female section of the propel jaw clutch is fastened to the left-hand side of the transmission's output shaft and to the horizontal propel shaft, which is coupled through a jaw clutch to the right-hand side of the transmission. **NOTE** Both propel clutches are located within the propel brake area.

The final drive assembly consists of the final-reduction drive pinion shaft and the final drive shaft (to which the gear and the drive tumbler are splined). Propel brake wheels (brake drums) of a V-type design are splined to the final drive pinion shafts. The wheels are slotted to guide the male propel jaw clutch members which ride on the brake wheel hubs. The male jaws protrude through the slots and can be engaged or disengaged with the female jaw members through a lever and yoke arrangement activated by a double-acting air cylinder. The pivot shafts of the propel steer linkage levers link with one another through an interlocking pipe. See Fig. 9-29.

When the propel jaws are engaged with the female members, the power from the propel transmission output shaft and horizontal propel shaft is transmitted over the jaw clutches, onto the brake wheel hubs, and to the final drive shafts. When the jaws are disengaged from the female jaw members, the power is interrupted.

The propel brake consists of the brake wheel, lower and upper brake arms to which the linings are bolted, a single-acting air cylinder (air-applied, spring-released), and the levers to apply and release the brake.

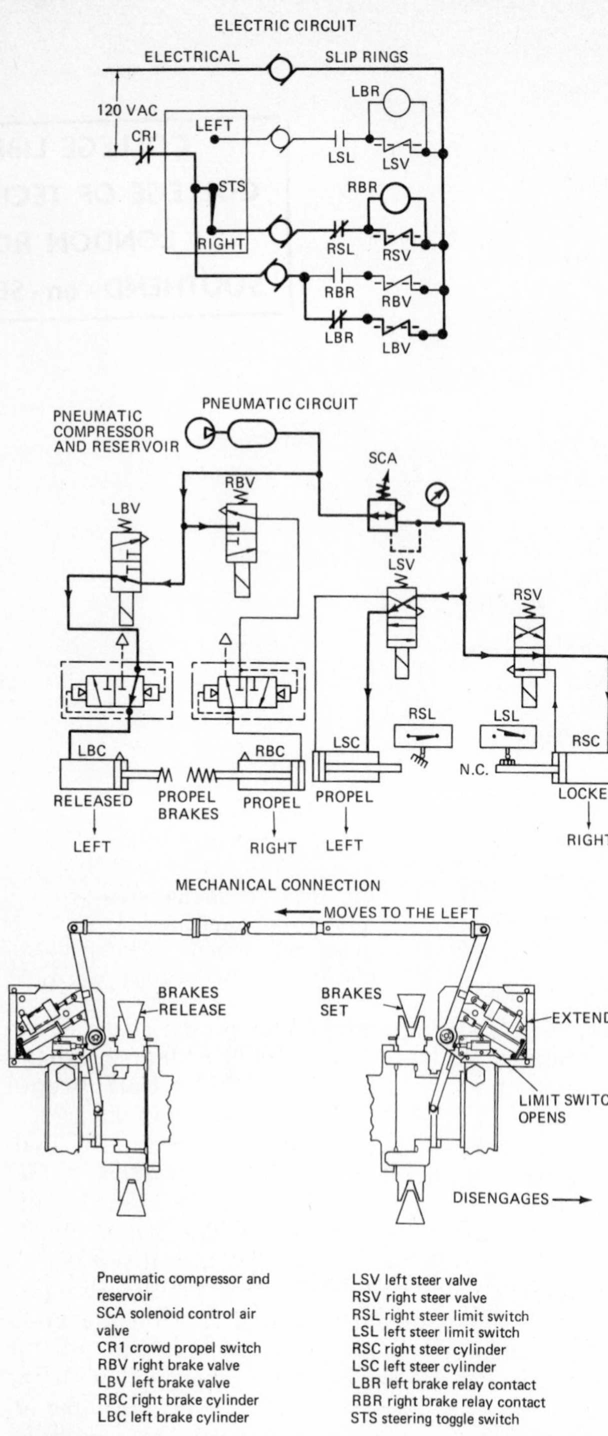

Pneumatic compressor and reservoir	LSV left steer valve
SCA solenoid control air valve	RSV right steer valve
CR1 crowd propel switch	RSL right steer limit switch
RBV right brake valve	LSL left steer limit switch
LBV left brake valve	RSC right steer cylinder
RBC right brake cylinder	LSC left steer cylinder
LBC left brake cylinder	LBR left brake relay contact
	RBR right brake relay contact
	STS steering toggle switch

Fig. 9-28 Schematic view of electrical, air, and mechanical components when in right-hand turn. (*Harnischfeger Corporation*)

STEERING Steering is controlled through toggle switches in the operator cab. However, current to the toggle switch is interrupted until the crowd propel switch is placed in the propel position. When any of the toggle switches are placed in a steer position, three systems—electrical, air, and mechanical—interrelate to achieve the various steering modes.

When the operator places the crowd propel switch in the propel position, it energizes the left- and right-hand brake valves; the valve spool shifts and allows air to flow over the quick release valve into the left- and right-hand brake cylinders. This action moves the piston rod out, compressing the spring, and the lever action releases the brakes. Because both left- and right-hand steering switches are open (deenergized), the left- and right-hand steering valves remain in a position which allows the air to pass into the rod ends of the steering cylinders and hold both jaw clutches engaged. When the dc propel motor is energized, it rotates (clockwise or counterclockwise) so that the motor rotation (power) is transmitted to the triple-reduction propel transmission, and from the transmission output shaft and horizontal propel shaft to the female jaw members. The male jaw members then drive the brake hubs, which transmit their rotation to the final drive pinions and from there to the final drive gears and tumblers.

When one of the steering toggle switches is placed in the right-hand steering position, first the brake valve and then the right-hand steering valve energize and shift, directing air to the air chambers and thereby applying the right-hand brake and disengaging the right-hand jaw clutch. As a result, the machine pivots on its stationary carrier belt and makes a right-hand turn. When the steering toggle switch is moved from the right- into the left-hand steering position, the right-hand brake is released and the right-hand jaw clutch is engaged. At the same time, the left-hand brake is applied and the left-hand jaw clutch is engaged through the actions of the brake valves, the steering valves, and the air chambers. See Fig. 9-28.

Mechanically Propelled Carriers and Their Swing Systems Crawler carriers which mechanically (i.e., through gears and chains) propel the carrier also use some of the propel components to swing the superstructure. One such machine is shown in Fig. 9-30. The power from the engine is transmitted from the engine clutch over a multiroller chain drive to the drive shaft, and from there over a gear set to the horizontal swing shaft. A swing clutch drum is fastened to each end of the horizontal swing shaft, and the bevel gear pinion is attached to the swing clutch hub. The bevel gear pinions mesh with the bevel gear fastened to the vertical reverse shaft. The reverse shaft gear (splined to the reverse shaft) is in mesh with the vertical swing shaft drive gear, and the latter is in mesh with the vertical propel shaft drive gear. The two latter gears are cast with jaws and are supported on their respective shafts by bushings. The shafts are bushing-supported in the upper housing. The swing pinion gear, which is in mesh with the internal ring gear, is fastened to the bottom end of the vertical swing shaft. The swing brake drum is fastened to the top of the shaft. Pivot-fastened above the vertical propel shaft drive gear and vertical swing shaft drive gear are the jaw clutches which, though keyed to their shafts, can slide up and down on their shafts.

SWING OPERATION Because of the intermechanical action of the propel and swing components, it is impossible to propel the machine and simultane-

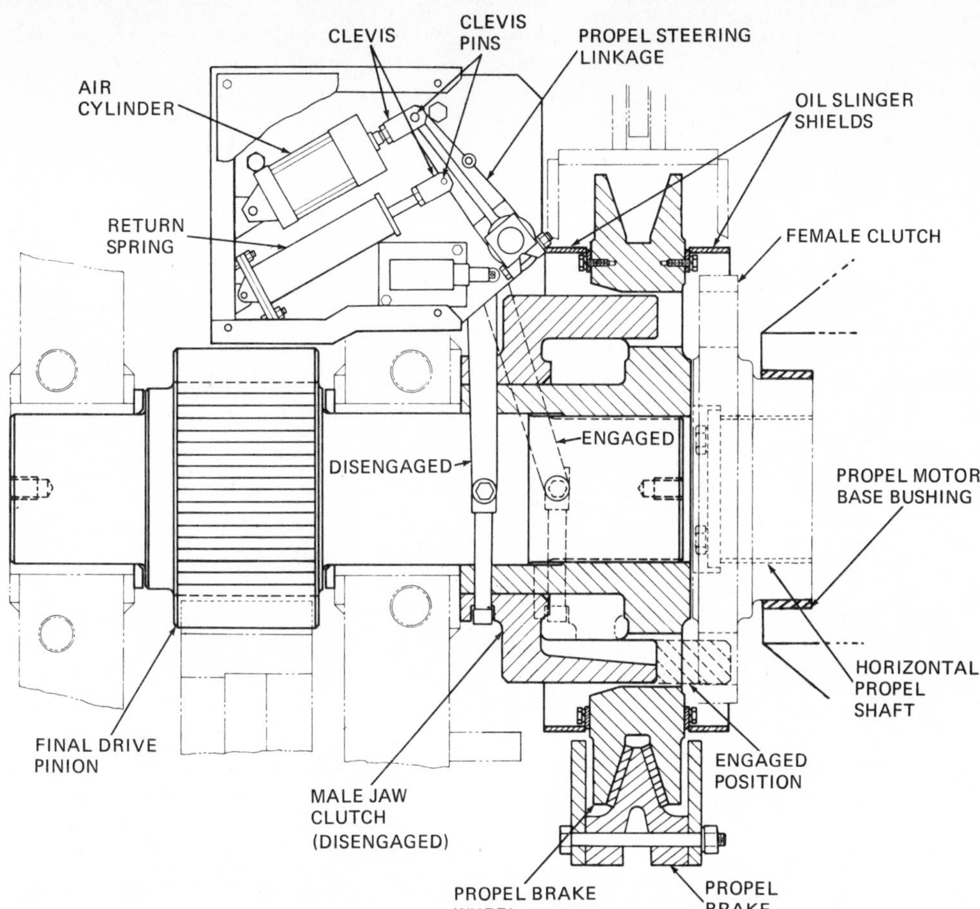

Fig 9-29 Sectional view of left-hand propel steering and brake components. (*Harnischfeger Corporation*)

ously swing the superstructure: To swing the superstructure the propelling drive gear travel lug must be *engaged*, while to propel the machine the swing brake must be applied, which means the propelling lug must be *disengaged*. When the engine is operating, and the master clutch is engaged, the horizontal swing shaft with clutch drums rotate as a unit. However, no power is transmitted because neither swing clutch is engaged; therefore the bevel gear pinions are not driven.

In order to make a left-hand swing, the operator manipulates the air directional control valve, and air from the valve is directed over a swivel joint into the center-drilled passage of the horizontal swing shaft, and from there over an air line to the two air brake chambers located inside the left-hand swing brake drum. The air pressure extends both air cylinder pushrods which, through levers, cause the internal band clutch to apply, thereby locking the clutch drum to the clutch hub. At the same time air is directed to engage the swing jaw clutch, locking the swing drive gear to the vertical swing shaft. By manipulating the brake valve (releasing the swing brakes) and controlling the air pressure to the swing clutch air cylinders, the superstructure rotates to the left because the left-hand bevel gear pinion drives the bevel gear and the vertical reverse shaft in a clockwise rotation. The power from the vertical gear is transmitted to the swing gear, which drives the vertical swing shaft and its pinion. The pinion rotates within the internal ring gear, maneuvering the superstructure in a left-hand-turn direction. When the operator reduces the air pressure to the left-hand swing clutch air cylinders and at the same time directs air to the right-hand swing clutch air cylinders, the swing action comes to a smooth stop.

Another way in which the operator can stop rotation (swing) is to reduce the air pressure to the left-hand swing clutch air cylinders and at the same time direct air to the swing brake air cylinders. Doing this stops the drive to the bevel gear, and the brake band clamps around the brake drum, holding the vertical shaft and bringing the superstructure to a stop. When air is directed to the right-hand swing clutch air cylinders, the brake drum and clutch hub engage and the right-hand bevel gear pinion is locked to the horizontal swing shaft. Now the right-hand bevel gear pinion drives the bevel gear and the vertical reverse shaft in the opposite direction (counterclockwise), causing the superstructure to rotate in the right-hand direction.

PROPELLING AND STEERING To propel the machine forward or backward

1. Apply the swing brakes.
2. Engage both jaw clutches with the horizontal propelling shaft by placing the air shaft lever in neutral. This releases the air pressure, and the spring force engages both jaw clutches.
3. Shift the swing to travel—that is, disengage the swing jaws and engage the propel jaw clutch.
4. Release the travel brakes.

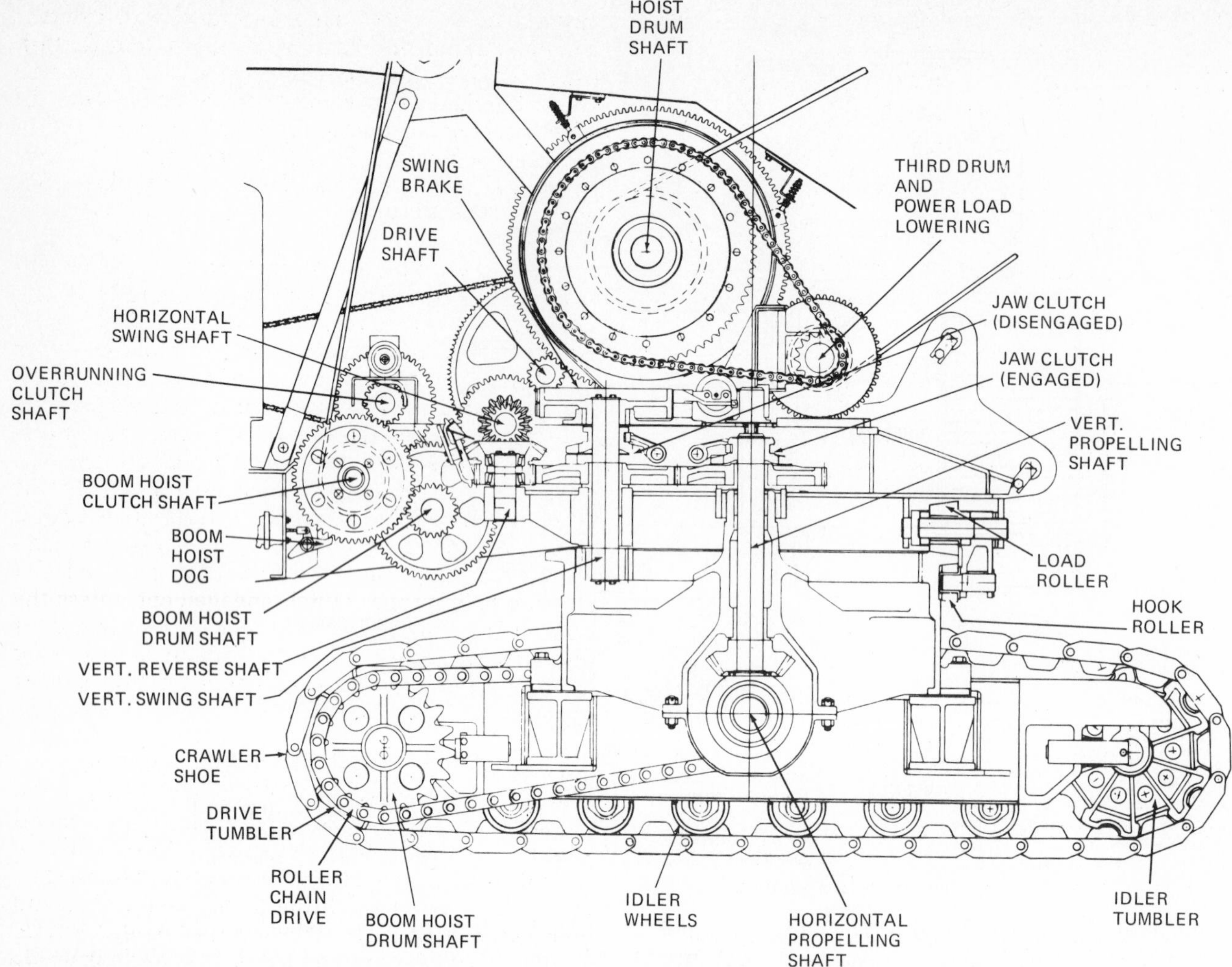

Fig. 9-30 Sectional view of crane hoist, swing, and drive components. (*Harnischfeger Corporation*)

Then select forward (or reverse) by directing air to the left- or right-hand swing clutch. This drives the bevel gear and the vertical reverse shaft clockwise or counterclockwise, respectively. Power is then transmitted to the vertical reverse shaft gear and to the swing drive gear (which idles on the vertical swing shaft), and drives the vertical propelling shaft drive gear. Since the jaw clutch is engaged, the gear drives the vertical propelling shaft and its pinion. The pinion drives the bevel gear on the horizontal propelling shaft as well as the drive chains. The drive chains transmit the motion to the left- and right-hand chain sprockets, driving the tumblers, and one crawler shoe after another reaches the ground, pulling the machine in the desired direction.

To steer the machine into a left- or right-hand turn, the air valve is placed in the desired (left- or right-hand) steering position. (See Fig. 9-31). This directs air to the steer air rotor chamber and the brake air rotor chamber. Both pushrods are forced out, causing the left- or right-hand jaw clutch to disengage and the propel brake (not shown in Fig. 9-31) to apply. With the driving power removed from the chain sprocket and the brake applied, the crawler belt is stopped and the machine pivots on this now stationary belt.

If the air valve is placed in the neutral position, the air exhausts from both rotary chambers, thus releasing the propel brakes, and the spring force engages the propel jaw clutch. As a result the machine travels in a straight line in the desired direction. **NOTE** Long-distance travel in the idler tumbler (reverse) direction is not recommended since it increases track belt wear.

Final Drive and Steering Clutch Troubleshooting and Testing Steering clutch and/or brake trouble or final drive failure, although not common, can arise due to inadequate or procrastinated maintenance. For example, brake adjustment and lubrication checks may not be made early enough, or may be made after steering difficulties have arisen, or maintenance may not be undertaken until noise indicates bearing or gear failure.

Final drive and steering clutch failure may be classified in two groups: mechanical failure and hydraulic system failure.

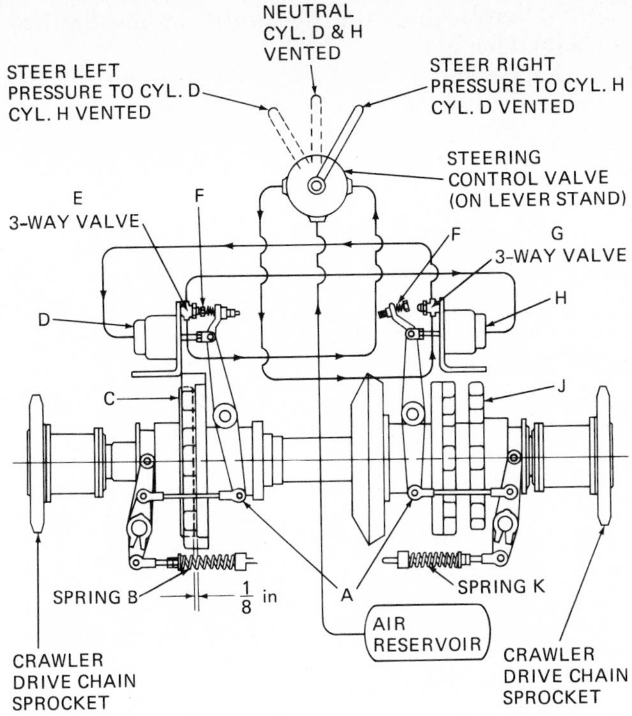

Fig. 9-31 Schematic view of drive and steering components when in a right-hand turn. (*American Hoist & Derrick Company*)

MECHANICAL FAILURE OR MALFUNCTION Mechanical failure within the final drives or steering clutches can arise from bearing or gear failure caused by

- Improper bearing installation and/or preload
- Inadequate lubrication or not using the recommended lubricant
- Welding on the tractor or machine and inadvertently directing current over a bearing set or gear teeth, due to improper welding clamp position
- Loose tracks causing a hammering effect or sharp impact on the gears, shaft, and bearings
- Excessively misaligned track frame
- Operating conditions where the track direction is constantly being reversed under power, without stopping the machine before the directional change is made

Bearing and gear failure may be recognized by excessive noise or change of noise pattern, evidence of oil leakage, and/or overheating of the steering clutch or final drive. If the faulty bearing(s) and/or gear(s) are not replaced at this time, the gears, shafts, and the remaining bearings will continue to deteriorate and cause misalignment, and a major repair job will eventually become necessary.

Mechanical malfunction which will adversely affect tractor steering can arise from bearing failure on the bevel gear shafts and/or final drive pinion shafts. Either will cause misalignment of the steering clutch and could cause insufficient clutch release. Tractor steering will also be adversely affected by damaged or overheated steering friction disk(s), brake drums, or hubs, by grooved steering clutch hub or drum splines, or by worn or bent internal and external friction disk teeth. Worn, bent, or twisted friction disks may hang up, allowing power to be transmitted to the final drive when in release position. Still other problems can arise from broken parts within the steering clutch or final drive such as shafts, drive splines, broken teeth, and damaged or broken linkages.

HYDRAULIC SYSTEM FAILURE Hydraulic system failure can stem from any one of the hydraulic system components—for example, the reservoir if it has insufficient oil, or a plugged vent or strainer which reduces the oil flow to the steering pump. A damaged or worn pump could cause delayed steering and delayed brake action or overheating of the steering clutch and brakes. A plugged return filter, or a misadjusted or damaged pressure relief valve or steering valve spool, may cause inadequate clutch release and/or brake application. **NOTE** A damaged actuating piston or seal will not cause delayed steering or improper clutch engagement unless the oil leak is equal to half the steering pump output. If the latter were so, the operator would note a delay in steering clutch disengagement at low engine speed.

HYDRAULIC SYSTEM TESTING If the operator complains that the tractor or machine will not steer to either the left or right, the problem may be in the oil supply, the filters, or the pressure release valve, or the steering linkage may be completely misadjusted. In any case, the oil level should be checked first, and then the steering valve linkage adjustment. Next, install a flowmeter (when possible) and pressure gauges to the respective test plugs. See material on hydraulics for flowmeter testing.

Operate the tractor or machine until the steering oil temperature is about 180°F [82°C]. At the recommended speed, test the supply system, the steering pump, and then the relevant pressures at the points recommended in the service manual. Check the pressure responses on release and engagement of the steering clutch and brakes to determine steering valve condition and (if applicable) the necessity for internal adjustment.

If the operator complains of power loss on both tracks, the track adjustment may be too tight, the engine may not be producing full power, or the transmission may be slipping. If the complaint is power loss on one track, the tractor or machine would also wander to the side which had lost power. In that instance, the problem may be a mechanical failure within the steering clutch, a misadjusted steering spool, or a damaged spool or valve body allowing oil to flow to the steering clutch and thereby partly disengaging the clutch.

If the tractor or machine continues to turn after the steering control lever is released back to neutral, the problem may be a mechanical failure within the steering clutch (on the side to which the tractor or machine wanders). A broken steering valve spool return spring, or a bent or damaged spool, would

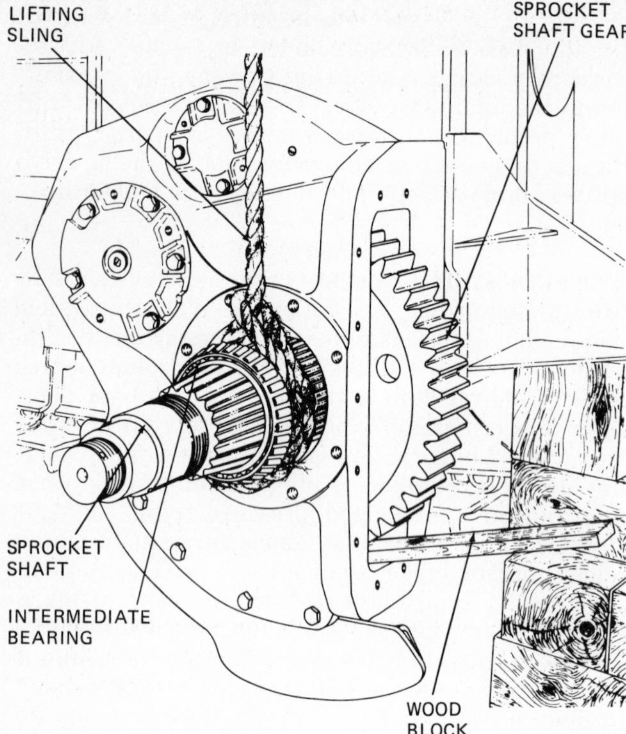

Fig. 9-32 Proper method of removing sprocket shaft. (*Fiat–Allis*)

produce the same effect, as would an internal valve spool misadjustment.

If the tractor or machine will not turn in one or both directions, drive it forward in low gear and at half engine speed; apply the left- and then the right-hand brake. If in both cases the engine rpm falls off, the brakes are working properly and the steering clutches are not slipping. The steering trouble is not within the machine; it is caused by the unfavorable operating conditions. However, if the engine rpm remains at half speed when either the left- or right-hand brake is applied, the problem may be worn brake linings, misadjusted brakes, incorrect oil pressure to the brake booster, misadjusted directional valve, or mechanical linkages damaged or broken.

To determine if there is hydraulic failure within the system, install a flowmeter and pressure gauges at the specific test plugs, then test the system as specified in the service manual.

Final Drive and Steering Clutch Service To attempt to include in one textbook precise service procedures for all the various kinds of final drives and steering clutches would be impractical, particularly since individual service manuals have been written dealing with each particular type. However, the following "dos and don'ts" cannot be overemphasized. Make certain that you

1. Make all necessary tests and checks to determine which components caused the final drive or steering clutch failure.
2. Learn the reason for the component failure.
3. Correct the cause of failure promptly.
4. Safely support and block the tractor or machine and, if applicable, the hydraulic or mechanical working attachments.
5. Follow the removal steps recommended in the service manual and do not use any shortcuts or unsafe practical procedures when lifting or removing components to gain access to the final drive or steering clutch.
6. Use a fiber or synthetic rope (as they will not slip or damage the components or parts) when lifting a gear assembly cover from or onto a shaft or housing (see Fig. 9-32).
7. Properly attach the press arms, rods, etc., and make sure the adapter, spacer, etc., is fully screwed onto the shaft or correctly positioned when removing or installing press-fitted parts or components (see Fig. 9-33).
8. Use pullers to remove bearings and do not drive them off, or into, position with a punch and hammer. Otherwise, use a bearing heater or one of the methods outlined in the material on friction bearings.
9. Properly seat each bearing and seal, and make sure that the bearings have the specified preload and that the adjustment is locked.
10. Replace any bearing, gear, seal, clutch, disk, or shaft, if you have reason to question its effectiveness. Replacement is always far less expensive than a second repair attempt.
11. Do not exceed or go below specifications of cap screws, nuts, torque or rotating torque, shaft clearance, or dimensions of shafts, bores, hubs, or covers, or the wear limit of the brake bands or friction disks.
12. Properly place the clutch housing and safely position the hydraulic compression tool and adapter when removing the coil spring force from the steering clutch assembly.
13. Double-check every step of the reassembly to

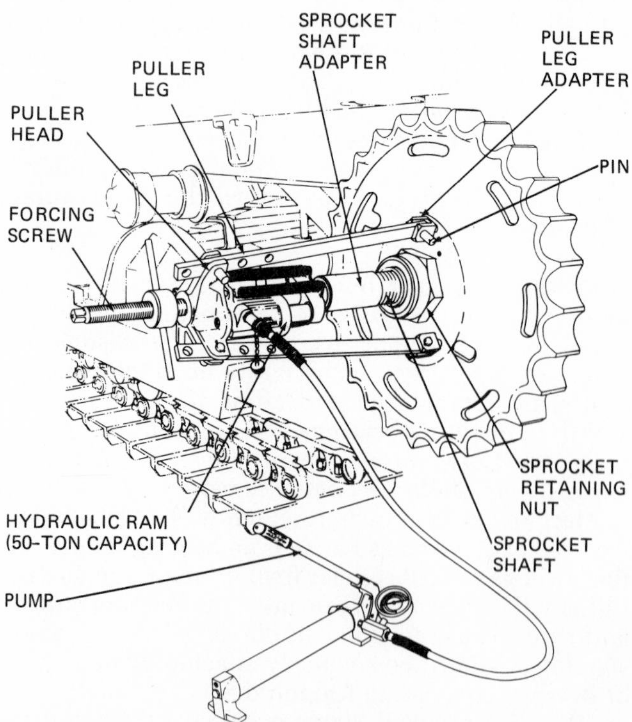

Fig. 9-33 Removing the sprocket. (*Fiat–Allis*)

ensure that each part is positioned and inserted as specified in the service manual.

14. See that all adjustments conform with the service manual specifications.

15. Recheck the oil levels after the tractor or machine's hydraulic system is tested and adjusted.

Review Questions

1. On a track-type tractor, what is the function of (*a*) the final drive? (*b*) the steering mechanism?
2. What are the main advantages of a double-reduction planetary final drive over a double-reduction final drive?
3. Which type of seal is commonly used in track rollers and final drives to prevent an oil leak?
4. Explain why the steering clutches are engaged through spring force, but disengaged mechanically or hydraulically.
5. What are the two functions of the steering clutch brake mechanism?
6. List the main advantages of a track-type tractor having a planetary power drive (steering) over one having steering clutches.
7. List the drive and steering combinations of the planetary power drive tractor described in the text.
8. Why is a final drive transmission necessary on the track of a track-type tractor, excavator, etc., which is powered through a hydraulic or electric motor?
9. Fully outline the three methods used to steer a hydraulic drive track machine.
10. Trace, in sequence, the transmission of the power flow of a mechanically driven track machine as it rotates the drive tumbler.
11. Final drive failure is usually caused through oil leaks which bring about bearing, gear, and shaft failure. List eight factors contributing to bearing failure.
12. Steering problems within the steering assembly could originate from hydraulic or mechanical malfunctions. List eight mechanical malfunctions which would affect steering.

Unit 10
Mechanical Clutches

A clutch is a device which allows an engagement and disengagement between drive and driven members, or between two shafts which lie in the same plane, or which allows a shaft and a wheel, hub, gear, etc., to rotate freely or as a unit. Without one or more clutches, a motortruck, tractor, or other motor vehicle could not function. Clutches are most commonly associated with engine operation. However, clutches are used by on- and off-highway equipment in many other ways also.

Clutches may be divided into four major groups:

- Clutches which rely on friction to connect the drive and driven members
- Clutches which connect the members mechanically
- Clutches which rely on fluid to make the connection
- Clutches where magnetism achieves the engagement

Each group can be subdivided further, and each clutch is named to identify its design, purpose, application, or, in some cases, the method used to accomplish engagement or disengagement.

FRICTION CLUTCHES

Friction clutches are used where a smooth engagement or disengagement to the driven member or shaft is required, without a time loss and/or interruption in transmission of the power. They may be subdivided or classified by types

1. Single disk
2. Double disk
3. Multidisk
4. External band
5. Internal band
6. Internal shoe
7. Cone
8. Internal expanding tube

The first three are used as engine, power takeoff, powershift transmission, steering, and winch clutches, and are also used in positive traction differentials. The remaining five are used on winches or as propel or swing clutches.

Disk Engine Clutches An engine clutch links the engine and transmission and is therefore the first component of the power train. The power train consists of the clutch, the transmission, the drive line, and the components that divide the power equally to the wheels or sprockets.

Although many types of disk engine clutches are manufactured, they are all basically very similar since they depend on friction to achieve clutch engagement. And being similar, they all have the capacity to (1) disconnect the power train from the engine so that the engine can be started, (2) allow the motor vehicle or machine to stop without stopping or stalling the engine, (3) connect with the power train to set the motor vehicle in motion, (4) enable the motor vehicle to start moving without grab or chatter, (5) reduce or dampen torsion vibration, (6) provide quick shifting of gears with ease, and (7) transmit the engine torque without slippage.

As you can see, an engine clutch is a multipurpose component. Moreover, it must be matched to the engine torque and to the gear train ratios in order to have a long service life. For instance, a clutch designed for an engine having a torque of 40 lb · ft [54.2 N · m] and operating at 2000 rpm could not be used on an engine having a torque of 100 lb · ft [135.5 N · m] because it would burn up. Conversely, a clutch designed to transmit 1500 lb · ft [2032.5 N · m] torque would grab and chatter on an engine having 100 lb · ft [135.5 N · m] torque, and may fly apart at 2000 rpm. Furthermore, the cost would be prohibitive for this application.

Single-Disk Clutch A typical single-disk clutch using a direct-acting multispring pressure plate is shown in Fig. 10-1. **NOTE** "Direct-acting" means that the force of the pressure springs acts directly on the pressure plate.

An engine clutch consists primarily of four parts: clutch disk, pressure plate assembly, release mechanism, and the reaction member (flywheel).

FLYWHEEL The cast-iron flywheel is bolted to the engine crankshaft and provides one friction surface for the clutch disk facing. The clutch shaft (transmission input shaft) is supported through the pilot bearing or bushing, snugly fitted into the flywheel center bore. Cast iron is used because it provides a good friction surface, good heat dissipation, and some lubrication due to the graphite in its composition. The flywheel's diameter and shape (flat or having the friction surface recessed) depends upon the type of clutch used and the engine design. In addition, the flywheel is an engine balancer, in that it smoothes out the power impulses. It also provides the mounting surface for the ring gear.

CLUTCH DISK The friction disk hub is splined to the clutch shaft, to which the flat steel disk is riveted, and the clutch facing is riveted to the disk. The disk hub splines are broached, and fit with close toler-

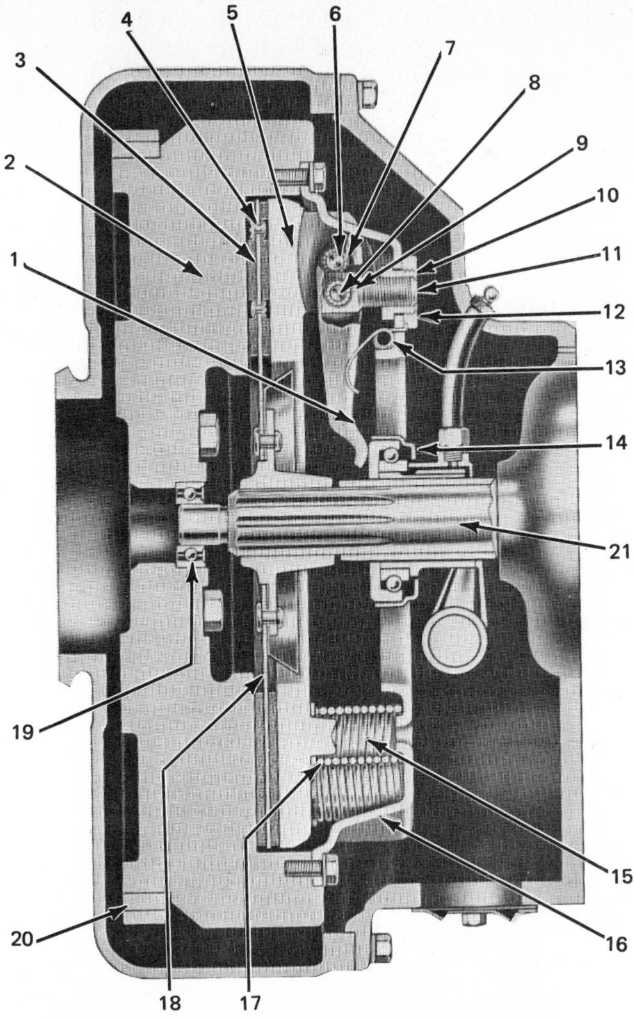

1. Release lever
2. Engine flywheel
3. Facing
4. Facing rivet
5. Pressure plate
6. Pressure plate pin
7. Needle bearing (pressure plate pin)
8. Eyebolt pin
9. Needle bearing (eyebolt)
10. Adjusting nut
11. Eyebolt assembly
12. Locknut
13. Retractor spring
14. Release bearing
15. Pressure spring
16. Clutch flywheel (ring cover)
17. Insulating washer
18. Driven disk assembly
19. Pilot bearing
20. Ring gear
21. Transmission input shaft clutch shaft

Fig. 10-1 Sectional view of a single-disk multicoil spring pressure plate. (*Lipe-Rollway Corporation*)

ance on the clutch shaft, allowing the hub to slide lengthwise, but there is very little side clearance (backlash) between the splines on the hub and on the clutch shaft. This assures a smooth transmission of power without jar or shock, thus reducing the wear on both components.

Some engines require a flexible clutch hub in order to reduce torsional vibration from the engine to the transmission. This hub is usually equipped with coil springs positioned in the slot provided in the hub flange. Two specially formed friction rings enclose or hold the springs in position. See Fig. 10-2. The three parts are then riveted together with special stop pins so that the clutch hub can move independently (clockwise or counterclockwise) from the

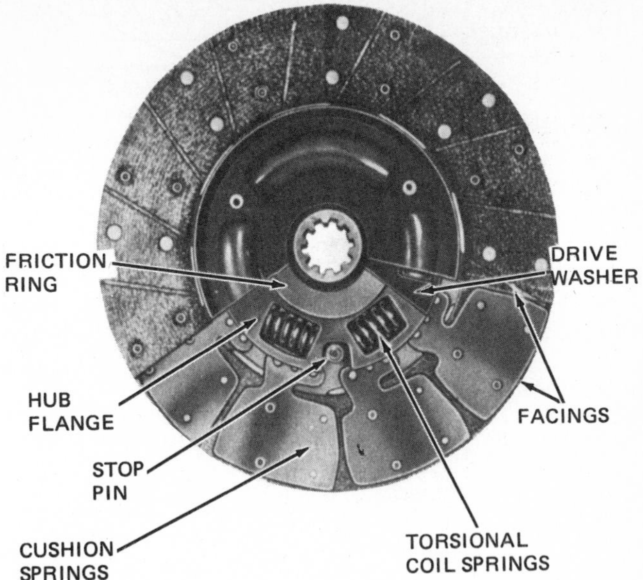

Fig. 10-2 Cutaway view of a clutch disk.

friction rings. The movement is dampened by compressing the torsional coil springs, and consequently the crankshaft rotates at a more uniform rate, thereby limiting some torsional vibration to the transmission. To limit the hub-to-friction ring variation to about 15° without transmitting the torque over the springs, the clutch hub, after rotating 15° more or less than the friction ring, comes to rest against the stop pins; or the two spring supports that guide the spring (and thereby reduce wear between the hub slots, friction ring opening, and spring ends) limit the compression of the springs (see Fig. 10-3). Another way in which torsional vibration can be reduced is by bonding the clutch hub to the steel disk with rubber.

Single-disk clutches with a flexible center commonly have a damping device between the two facings to achieve a smooth engagement without chatter. Several methods are used to provide this cushion or flexing between the facings: The disk may have slots or cutouts, or individual sections may be riveted to the hub so that the remaining disks can be formed into a curved or waved pattern to which the clutch facing is then riveted. When the clutch starts to engage, the waves or curves of the disk begin to flatten out, becoming completely flat when the clutch is wholly engaged. This flattening ensures a

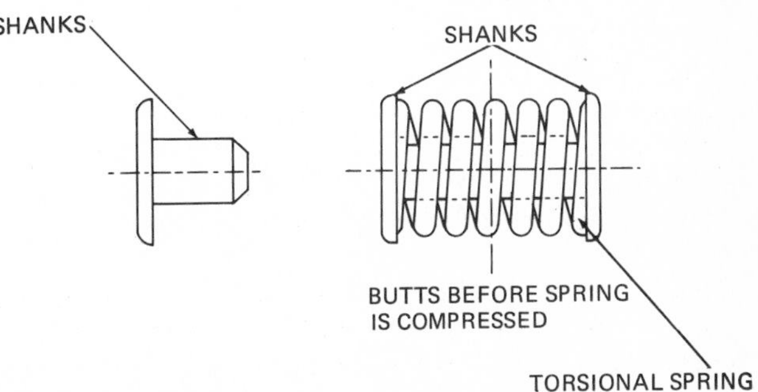

Fig. 10-3 View of a torsional spring having spring supports.

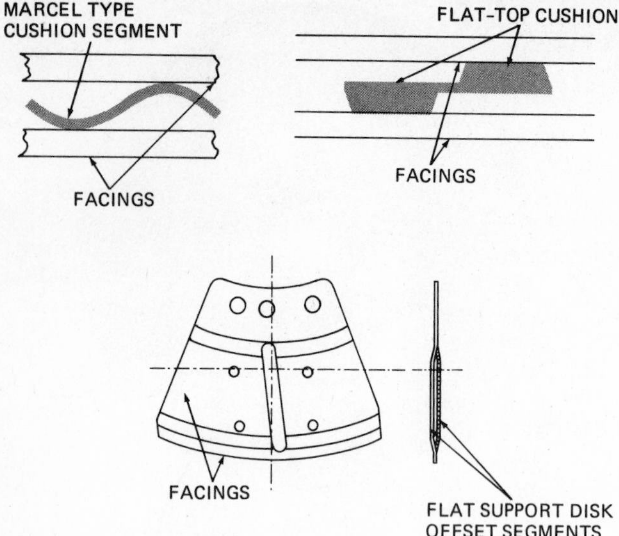

Fig. 10-4 Three methods used to achieve smooth engagement.

smooth engagement. See Fig. 10-4, which illustrates three methods of achieving smooth engagement.

Clutch facings Although the material from which the clutch facings are made varies, it must permit slippage when the clutch is being engaged to ensure a smooth, chatter-free transmission of power, but it must not allow slip after the engagement is made. During the engagement interval, a great amount of heat is developed which, if not quickly dissipated, will burn the facings, weaken the pressure springs, and harden or heat-spot the pressure plate. Any material from which the clutch facing is made, therefore, must be able to withstand this heat and hold the maximum engine torque while it is being generated. Furthermore, the facing area must be precisely calculated with regard to the pressure to be applied.

Clutch facings are usually made from woven or molded asbestos fibers with additives similar to those used for brake blocks and brake linings. The material is cured at a high temperature, pressed to size, and ground to dimension, and the holes are drilled and countersunk. When the engine torque is high or motor vehicle operation causes a high clutch temperature, facing material having a higher coefficient of friction is required, such as ceramic, sinter bronze, or bimetallic. Although these types of lining materials withstand a greater heat and have a longer wear life, they may cause greater flywheel and pressure plate wear. See Fig. 10-5, where different types of disk clutch facings are shown.

PRESSURE PLATE ASSEMBLY The main parts of a pressure plate assembly are the pressure plate cover, pressure plate, pressure springs, release levers, and eye-bolt assemblies. The pressure plate cover, which is bolted to the flywheel, may be press-formed from plates of steel, or may be cast steel. The pressure springs are precompressed between the pressure plate and cover, and the spring ends rest in the lugs or in counterbores of the pressure plate and cover. Some pressure plates use heat-insulating washers, located between the spring and pressure plate, to prevent the transfer of heat from pressure plate to springs, and thereby prevent weakening of the springs. The cast-iron pressure plate is cast with reinforcing ribs, spring lugs, and pin lugs. The release levers are attached to the pin lugs. To enable the torque to be transmitted from the pressure plate cover to the pressure plate, all pressure plates have some type of drive lugs which fit into slots or recesses in the pressure plate cover. See Fig. 10-6.

The release levers are steel-cast or press-formed and attach to the fulcrum point (the eye bolt). The eye bolt is screwed into a flange nut, which is locked by the locknut. This arrangement provides the clutch release lever adjustment. The outer ends of the release levers are pinned to the pressure plate. On some clutch pressure plate assemblies, the release lever pins are supported by needle bearings.

CLUTCH RELEASE MECHANISM A clutch release mechanism consists of the clutch release bearing assembly, the clutch yoke, cross shaft and levers, and linkages and rods that connect the clutch pedal to the cross shaft or yoke.

Basically two mechanical release mechanisms are used—one in which the clutch pedal is linked (over levers, linkages, and rods) with the release fork, and the other where the link between the clutch pedal

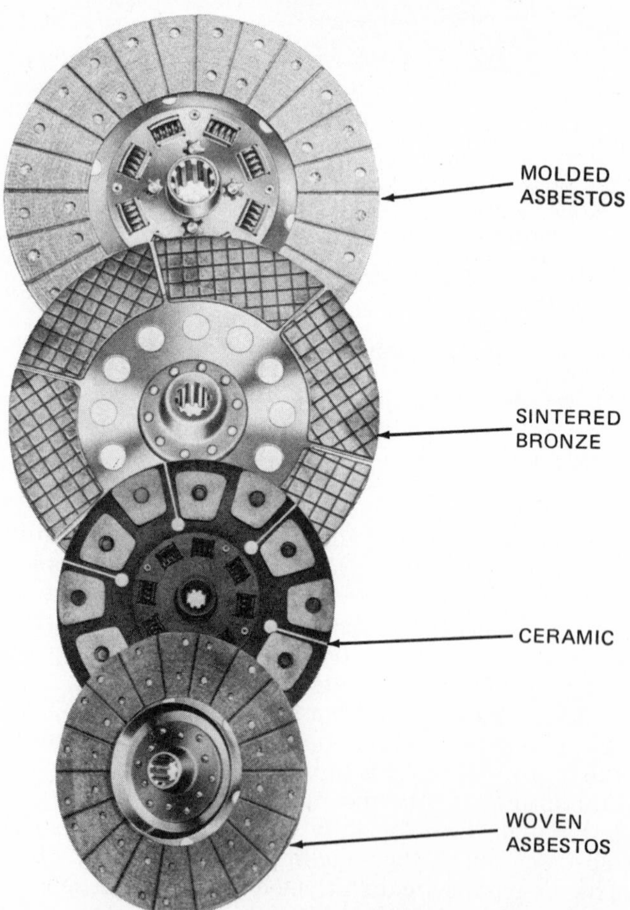

Fig. 10-5 Four types of clutch disk facings.

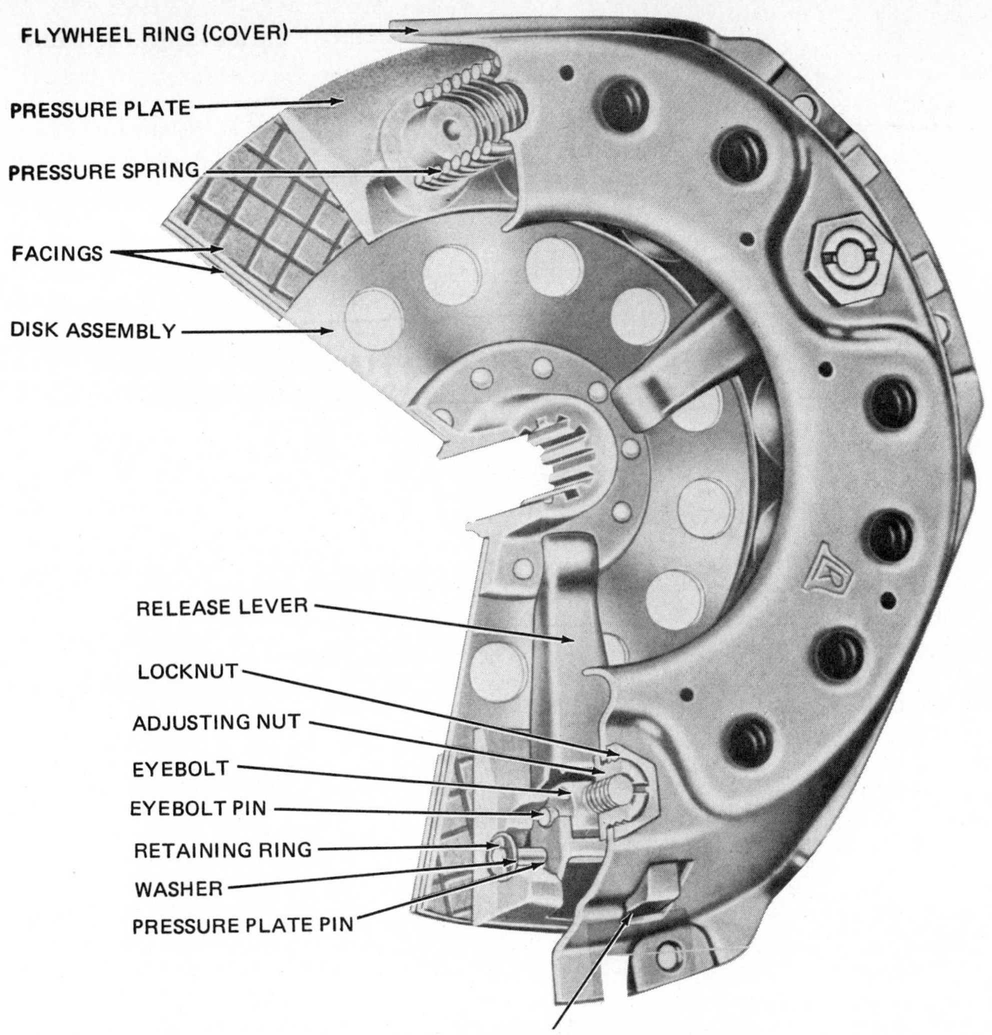

Fig. 10-6 Cutaway view of a clutch disk and pressure plate. (*Lipe-Rollway Corporation*)

and release fork is made through a specially designed clutch control cable. One of the cable designs for the latter is shown in Fig. 10-7. Connected to each end of the movable center blade is an adjustable yoke, and each yoke in turn connects with a pin to the actuating clutch release levers on the cross shaft and clutch pedal shaft. The center blade rides between two sets of ball bearings (positioned in guides), held to the center blade by two races. The assembly is enclosed by a flexible outer shell.

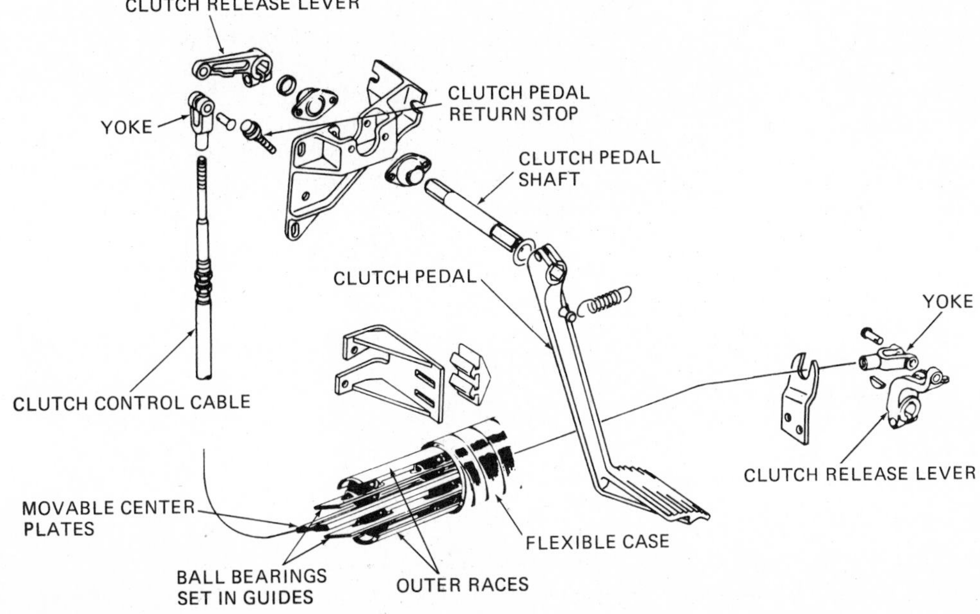

Fig. 10-7 View of a cable clutch control linkage. (*International Harvester Company*)

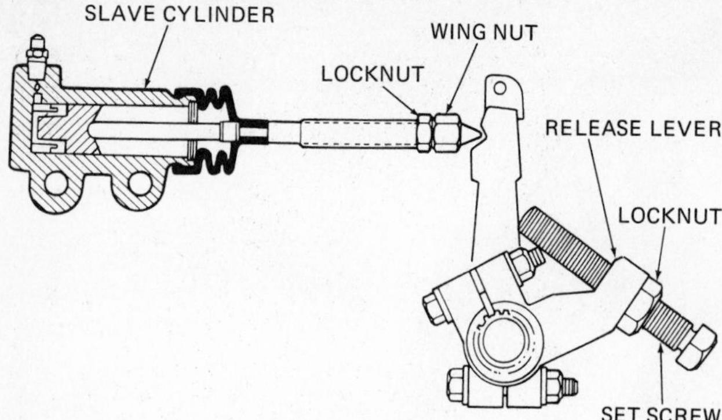

Fig. 10-8 View of a hydraulic clutch control. (*Ford Motor Co.*)

Either type of mechanism provides a means of adjusting the clutch pedal free travel, and both have clutch pedal stops and springs to return the mechanism to the release position.

If the clutch is released through hydraulic action, the clutch release mechanism consists of a clutch master cylinder linked with the clutch pedal, and a clutch slave cylinder linked through an adjustable yoke with the clutch release lever, the latter being fastened to the cross shaft (see Fig. 10-8). If the clutch is released through air action, a clutch treadle valve is used in place of the clutch master cylinder and a diaphragm or rotary air chamber is used instead of the slave cylinder.

The clutch release bearing assembly (Fig. 10-9) consists of a thrust bearing and a release sleeve or throwout bearing sleeve. The thrust release bearing, commonly of the seal type, is fitted snugly to the release sleeve (bushing support sleeve). The release sleeve is slide-fitted over the clutch shaft or the clutch shaft bearing retainer. On larger clutches, the release sleeve is supported on bushings to reduce friction and wear.

Fig. 10-9 Sectional view of a clutch release sleeve and bearing assembly. (*GMC Truck and Coach Division*)

OPERATION When the clutch is released, there is a small clearance between the clutch release levers and the release bearing. If the engine is operating, the entire assembly, with the exception of the release bearing and release sleeve assembly, rotate as a unit at engine speed. The engine torque is directly transmitted from the flywheel to the clutch cover, over the drive lugs, to the pressure plate, to the clutch disk, and to the clutch hub, or over the coil springs and torque stop, and then to the clutch hub.

When the operator depresses the clutch pedal, the motion is transmitted over linkages and levers to the release fork (semirotating the fork). The first 1 in [25.4 mm] of clutch pedal travel brings the release bearing into contact with the release levers. Any further movement of the release bearing (toward the flywheel) pivots the release levers on their eyebolt pins, and consequently the outer ends of the levers are forced in the opposite direction and lift the pressure plate against the force of the pressure springs away from the right-hand clutch facing. As soon as this occurs, the clutch disk starts to slip and then loses contact with the flywheel and pressure plate friction surfaces. The clutch disk and clutch shaft are then driven by the transmission.

If the operator now places the transmission in neutral, the clutch shaft and disk slow down until they come to a stop. If the operator shifts the transmission into gear again, the clutch shaft and clutch disk are driven once more by the transmission. Now when the operator releases the clutch pedal, the release sleeve and the release bearing assembly are pulled away from the flywheel, and the release levers follow the bearing because of the force of the pressure springs. As a result, the outside lever ends, and pressure plate, are moved toward the flywheel and the clutch facings are gripped between the pressure plate and flywheel surfaces, completing the engagement. See Fig. 10-10.

Diaphragm Clutch (Pressure Plate) A diaphragm pressure plate assembly having a bent finger diaphragm spring and a single clutch disk is shown in Fig. 10-11. The main difference between it and the coil spring pressure plate is that a one-piece conical (diaphragm) spring is used which has a solid outer ring and individual tapered fingers. The tapered fingers also serve as release levers. The release mechanism consists of a clutch fork that is fastened through a ball socket to the clutch housing.

NOTE Two types of conical springs are used. One is only slightly coned and the other has bent fingers, although both are identical in operation.

The pressure plate cover is bolted to the flywheel, and the diaphragm spring is attached to the inside by means of special rivets and steel rings. The diaphragm spring rests against the upper and the lower ring. The steel rings make up the spring fulcrum. The solid outer ring of the diaphragm spring rests against the cast nose of the pressure plate. The pres-

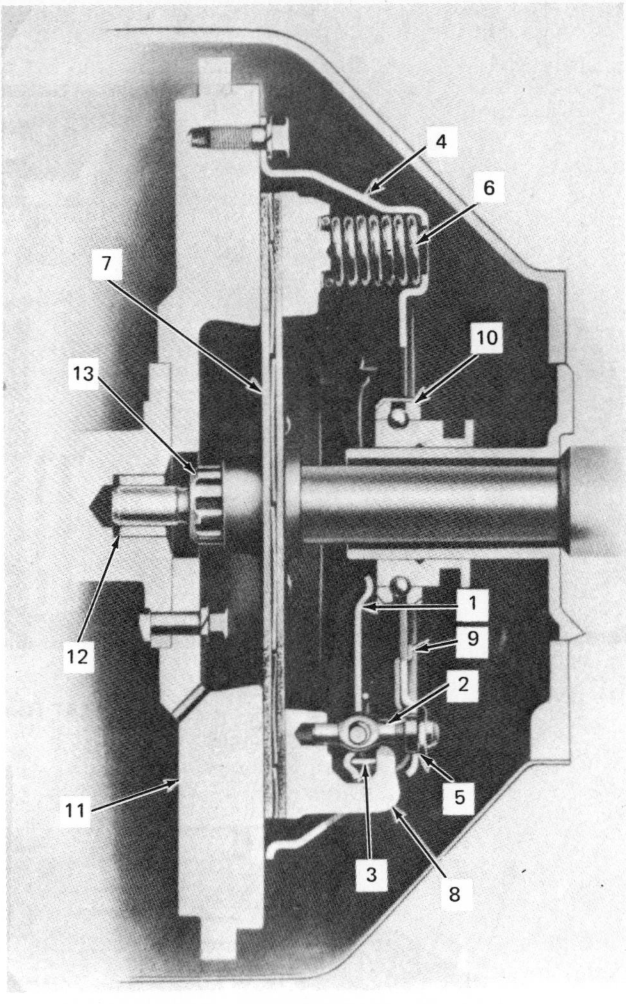

1. Release lever
2. Eyebolt
3. Strut
4. Cover
5. Adjustment nut
6. Coil spring
7. Drive disk
8. Pressure plate
9. Antirattle spring
10. Throwout bearing
11. Flywheel
12. Pilot bushing
13. Clutch shaft

Fig. 10-10 Sectional view of a medium-sized coil spring clutch assembly. (*GMC Truck and Coach Division*)

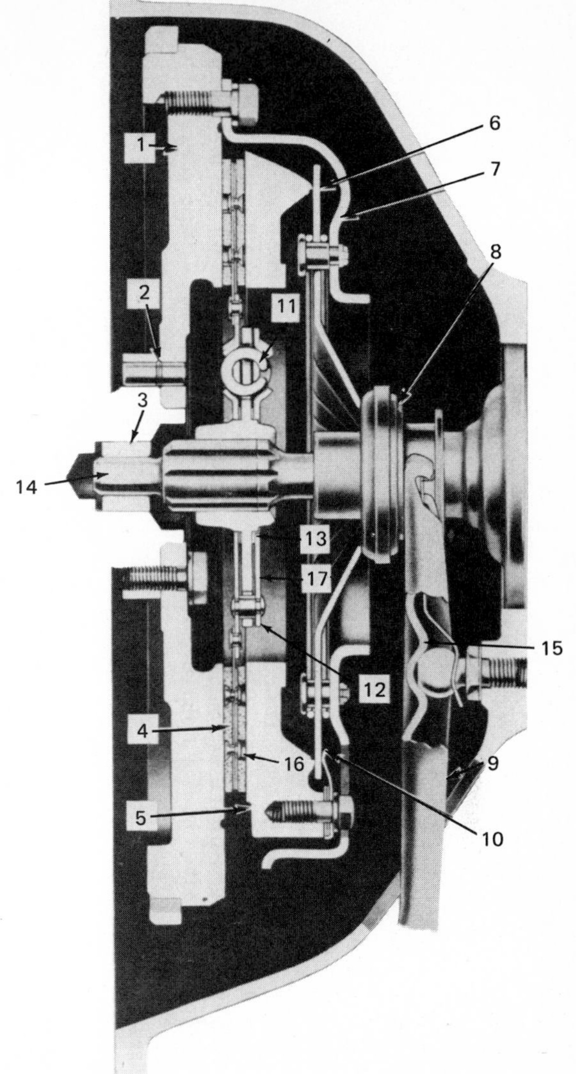

1. Flywheel
2. Dowel pins
3. Pilot bushing
4. Clutch disk facings
5. Pressure plate
6. Diaphragm spring
7. Pressure plate covers
8. Throwout bearing
9. Clutch fork
10. Retraction spring
11. Torsional spring
12. Stop pin
13. Disk hub
14. Clutch shaft
15. Ball socket
16. Special rivets
17. Rings

Fig. 10-11 Sectional view of a diaphragm clutch assembly. (*GMC Truck and Coach Division*)

sure plate is held to the diaphragm spring by three retraction springs. Cap screws, screwed into the pressure plate, hold the three springs in place.

OPERATION When the clutch is in release position, the energy of the conical spring forces the pressure plate toward the flywheel, and the clutch facings are grabbed between the pressure plate and flywheel friction surfaces. When the operator depresses the clutch pedal, the motion pulls the fork to the right and it pivots on the ball socket and moves the throwout bearing against the diaphragm finger end, forcing the fingers toward the flywheel. This pivots the diaphragm spring on the two steel rings and moves the outer (solid) end away from the pressure plate. Since the retraction springs lie on the outer diaphragm surface, the pressure plate is moved away from the clutch facing.

The clutch disk starts to slip until it becomes free, whereupon the clutch disk and clutch shaft are then driven by the transmission. When the operator releases the clutch pedal, the energy of the diaphragm spring moves the throwout bearing away from the flywheel. Consequently, the outer circumference of the diaphragm spring moves toward the flywheel and forces the pressure plate toward the flywheel, and the clutch facings are grabbed between the flywheel and pressure plate friction surface.

Angle Link Clutch (Pressure Plate) A single-disk multispring indirect-acting clutch pressure plate (angle link) is shown in Fig. 10-12. The clutch, due to its lever arrangement, multiplies the pressure

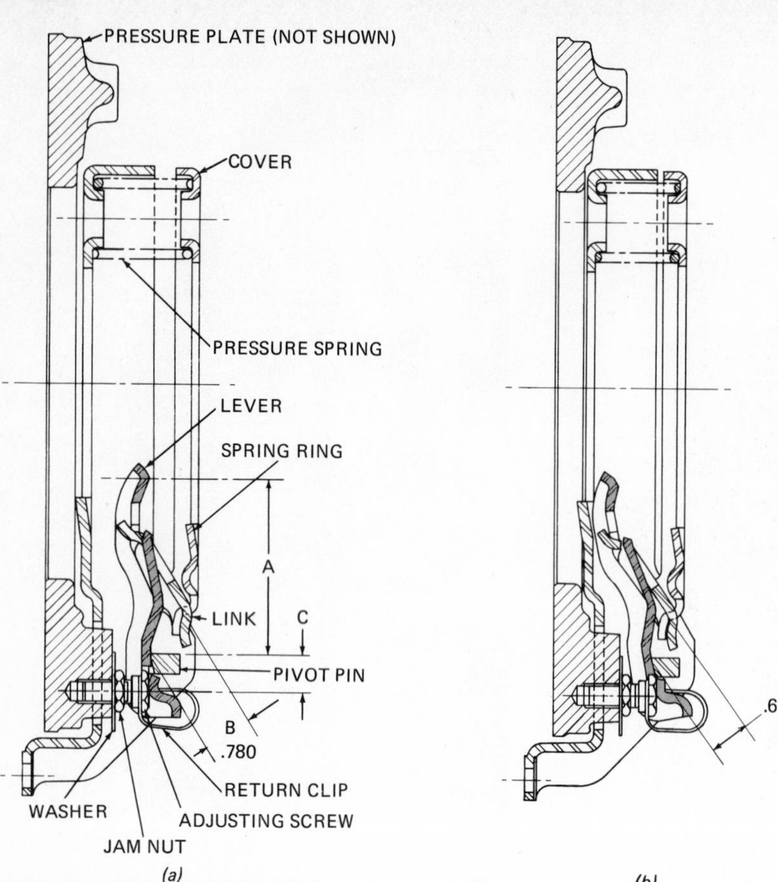

Fig. 10-12 Sectional view of an angle link clutch in the (*a*) engaged position and (*b*) in the released position. Lever advantage (ratio of A to B, ratio of B to C) increases at the same rate as the spring load loss occurs. (*Dana Corporation, Spicer Transmission Division*)

spring force and maintains the same coil spring energy when the clutch facings and friction surfaces wear. **NOTE** The pressure springs do not contact the pressure plate; therefore, a longer spring service life can be expected. The cast-iron pressure plate, with its drive lugs, fits into the slots of the bracket (pressure plate cover) and is held to the bracket by three adjusting bolts and three return clips. The six coil pressure springs are located between the bracket and spring ring and are held in position by the protruding shoulders on the spring ring and bracket. The spring ring is held to the bracket by compressing the springs to a predetermined energy through three links. The three links are hooked into the spring ring and the inside ends of the links are hooked to the lever.

OPERATION When the clutch is in the release position, the pressure springs have forced the spring ring to the right. The outside ends of the links move to the right and pull the levers to the right by pivoting them on their pins. This forces the outside ends of the levers against the adjusting bolts, and the pressure plate toward the flywheel. When the operator depresses the clutch pedal, the throwout bearing moves against the release levers, pivoting the levers on their pins *toward* the flywheel and the outside ends *away from* the flywheel. Since the return clips connect the levers with the adjusting bolts, the pressure plate is moved away from the clutch facings. During the clutch release, the links slide in the release lever slots; therefore, the pressure springs are not compressed further and the clutch pedal force remains virtually the same during the entire engagement cycle (see Fig. 10-12). When the clutch pedal is released, the release levers are forced (through the links) to follow the retracting throwout bearing. Consequently, the levers pivot on their pins, the outside ends force the pressure plate over the adjusting bolts toward the flywheel, and the facings are grabbed between the pressure plate and flywheel friction surface, completing the engagement.

Pull Clutches Two types of pull clutches will be discussed—one of the multispring design and the other of the angle spring design. Both clutch assemblies are designed for heavy-duty service and may utilize either a single or double clutch disk.

Double-Disk Coil Spring Pull Clutch This type of clutch and its release mechanism are illustrated in Figs. 10-13 and 10-14. The two clutch disks are splined to the clutch shaft (also note the hub position). The inside disk rests against the flywheel friction surface and against the cast-iron intermediate plate, and the second disk rests against the intermediate plate and pressure plate. The intermediate plate is loosely fastened to the fly-wheel by four intermediate plate drive pins which are locked to the flywheel by set screws. The flywheel ring (clutch cover) is bolted to the engine flywheel, and the pressure plate drive lugs extend into the mating slots of the flywheel ring. The release levers are attached to the ring through eyebolts screwed into the adjusting

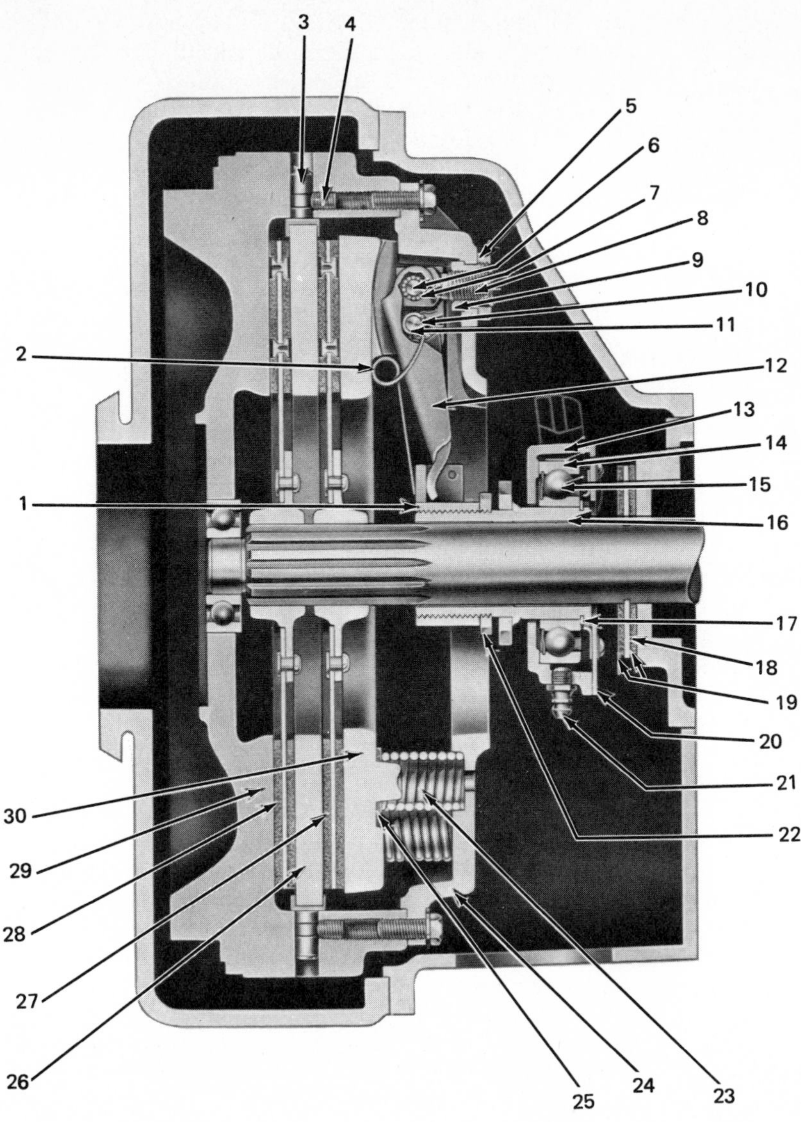

1. Release lever spider
2. Retractor spring (lever spider)
3. Intermediate plate drive pin
4. Socket head (Allen) set screws
5. Locknut
6. Eyebolt pin
7. Needle bearing (eyebolt)
8. Eyebolt
9. Adjusting nut
10. Needle bearing (pressure plate)
11. Pressure plate pin
12. Release lever
13. Release bearing housing
14. Bearing retaining spring
15. Release bearing
16. Sleeve & bushing assembly
17. Snap ring
18. Steel disk (clutch brake)
19. Friction disks (clutch brake)
20. Bearing housing cover
21. Lubrication fitting
22. Sleeve locknut
23. Pressure spring
24. Flywheel ring (cover)
25. Insulating washer
26. Intermediate plate
27. Driven disk assembly (pressure plate side)
28. Driven disk assembly (flywheel side)
29. Engine flywheel
30. Pressure plate

Fig. 10-13 Sectional view of a double-disk coil spring pull clutch assembly. (*Lipe-Rollway Corporation*)

nuts which are locked by locknuts. The outer ends of the release levers are attached with pins to the pressure plate. **NOTE** The eyebolt pins are supported on needle bearings.

Each release lever has a retraction spring to hold the release lever spider against the release levers. (See Fig. 10-13.) The release lever spider is screwed to the left-hand side of the bushing support sleeve, and the sleeve locknut is screwed to the spider. The release bearing assembly fits onto the right-hand side of the sleeve, and a snap ring is used to hold the bearing assembly to the sleeve. **NOTE** A clutch brake is used when the transmission is nonsynchronized to aid in making initial shifts into low, forward, or reverse, or to upshift the transmission without gear clash. The clutch brake consists of the

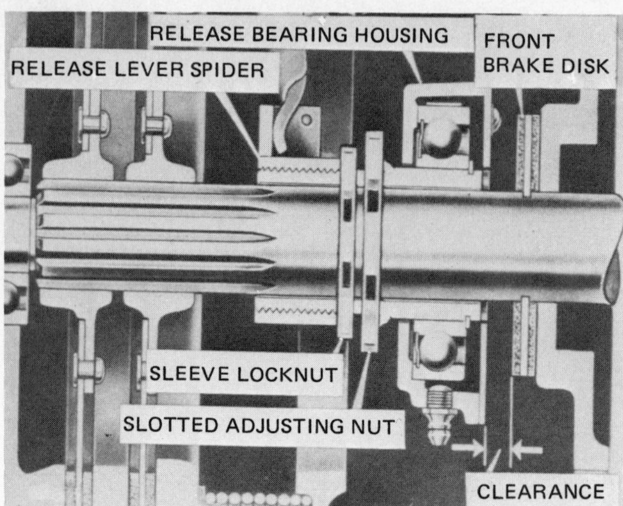

Fig. 10-14 Sectional view of clutch release mechanism. (*International Harvester Company*)

steel disk splined to the clutch shaft, and two friction disks. The right-hand friction disk rests against the friction surface of the clutch shaft bearing retainer cover. When the clutch is properly adjusted, a specific distance exists between the bearing housing cover and the first friction disk of the clutch brake, and there is a small clearance of about 0.125 in [3.17 mm] between the release yoke and the bearing carrier wear pads.

OPERATION When the engine is operating, the entire clutch assembly rotates as a unit with the exception of the release bearing housing. As the clutch pedal is being depressed, the first 1 in [25.4 mm] of movement takes up the free play; then the release bearing, the sleeve, and the bushing assembly are pulled toward the transmission. This also pulls the release levers toward the transmission and causes the pressure plate to be pulled away from the first clutch disk facing, thereby releasing the force from the intermediate plate and the forward clutch disk. Both clutch disks slide on the clutch shaft toward the transmission, and the intermediate plate slides on the drive pins toward the transmission also, releasing the clutch. The clutch shaft and the two clutch disks are now driven by the transmission. If the engine is not operating or the transmission is shifted into neutral, an additional movement of the clutch pedal brings the bearing housing cover into contact with the friction disks and squeezes the three disks against the friction surface of the clutch shaft bearing retainer cover, stopping the clutch shaft. When the clutch pedal is gradually released, the bearing assembly and the release levers move toward the flywheel, also forcing the pressure plate toward the flywheel. This sequence forces the right-hand clutch disk against the intermediate plate, and the intermediate plate then forces the left-hand clutch disk against the flywheel, completing the clutch engagement.

ADJUSTMENT If the free travel and the clutch brake distance between the brake disk and bearing housing are less than specified, the following steps must be taken to adjust them. First, check all linkages and pins for wear and if necessary replace them. Next, depress the clutch pedal, hold it down, and then loosen the release sleeve locknut. Release the clutch pedal but keep a light tension on it to hold the release lever spider snugly against the release lever. Turn the slotted adjusting nut clockwise to increase to service manual specification the distance between the bearing housing cover and friction disk. When the adjustment has been made, depress the pedal and turn the sleeve locknut tightly against the release sleeve spider. Depress the clutch pedal several times and measure the distance between the brake disk and bearing housing cover. (See Fig. 10-14.) If the clutch brake is properly adjusted, it will engage when the clutch pedal is about 1 in [25.4 mm] from the floorboard. After finishing with these procedures, check the clutch free travel and if necessary adjust it by lengthening or shortening the rod or yoke to increase or decrease the travel distance.

Angle Spring Clutch (Disk Type, Pull Type) Angle spring clutches (Fig. 10-15) are indirect-acting. Due to their location and the changing position of the pressure springs, they provide a constant pressure plate force throughout the wear life of the clutch facing(s). The flywheel ring is cast with drive lugs, spring seats, and reinforced ribs. It is bolted to the flywheel, and the adjusting ring is screwed to its internal threaded bore. The adjusting ring is locked through the adjusting ring lock. In some cases, an automatic adjusting device, instead of the manual

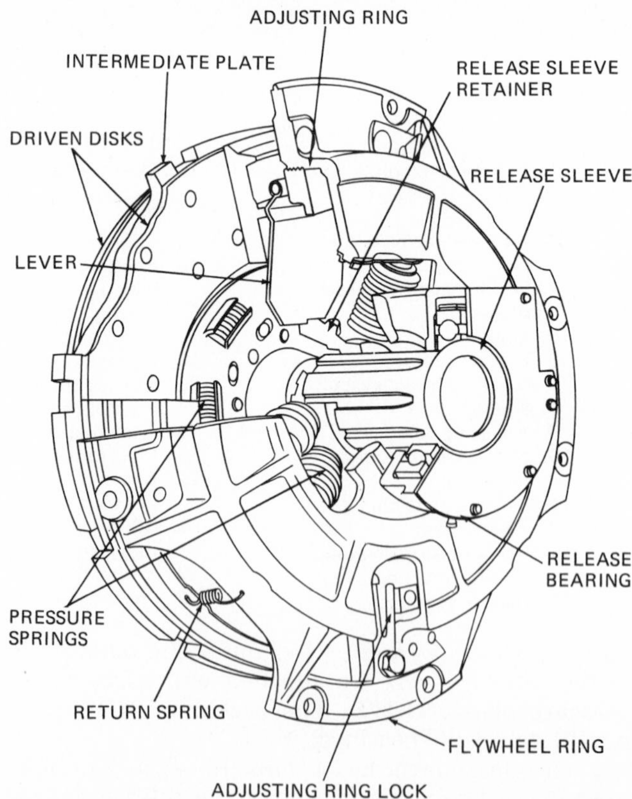

Fig. 10-15 Cutaway view of an angle spring clutch assembly. (*International Harvester Company*)

lock, is bolted to the flywheel ring. Six release levers are attached to the adjusting ring. The pivot point on the pressure plate provides the fulcrum. The pressure plate is held to the flywheel ring with four return springs, and the drive lugs of the pressure plate fit between the drive lugs on the flywheel ring. The raised contour of the release levers rests against the raised contour of the pressure plate, and the inner ends of the release levers rest in the release sleeve retainer groove. Located between the release sleeve retainer and the flywheel ring are the pressure springs. Their ends rest on pivots to ease the spring angle changes as the clutch is disengaged or as the clutch facing and friction surface deteriorate. The spring pivots rest on lugs cast on the release sleeve retainer and flywheel ring. The release bearing is positioned onto the right-hand side of the release sleeve and rests against the shoulder of the sleeve. The release sleeve retainer is positioned onto the left-hand side and is held to the release sleeve by two release sleeve ring halves. A snap ring secures the release sleeve ring to the release sleeve retainer. **NOTE** The intermediate plate may be cast with drive lugs that fit into the grooves of the flywheel, or drive pins may be used to drive the intermediate plate.

When two clutch disks are used, the clutch disk hubs are not identical. When installing the clutch disks, therefore, it is very important to make sure they are positioned to the flywheel as shown in Figs. 10-13 and 10-14. For instance, if the left-hand clutch disk were installed backward, the clutch would slip because the clutch disk would not be parallel with the friction surfaces. After a short operating period the two clutch hubs would bottom against each other and the clutch would lose almost half its holding torque.

CLUTCH BRAKE When the transmission is of a nonsynchronizing design, a clutch brake is used. But for angle spring clutches, the clutch brake may be torque-limiting, which is a slightly different design than those commonly used. See Fig. 10-16. The assembly is enclosed, two brake facings are bonded to the outside, and two brake facings are positioned inside between the friction disk hub and belleville springs. The hub is splined to the clutch shaft. The torque-limiting feature is provided by the internal bellevilles which are positioned between the friction disk and drive hub. The hub will slip after approximately 30 lb · ft [40.65 N · m] torque has been exerted. A driver cannot use a torque-limiting clutch brake to slow down a vehicle because of this slip.

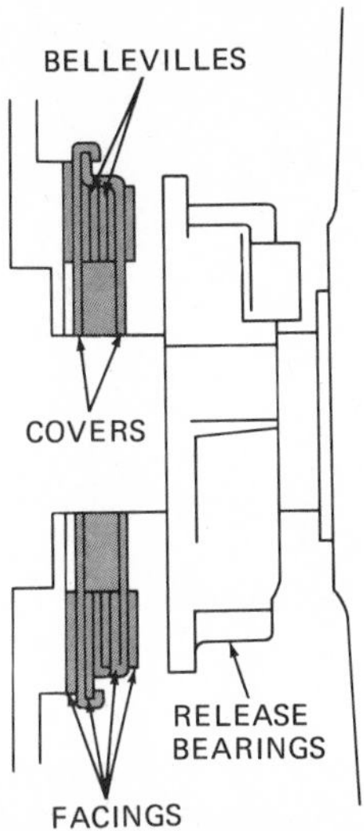

Fig. 10-16 Sectional view of a torque-limiting clutch brake. (*Dana Corporation, Spicer Transmission Division*)

ANGLE SPRING CLUTCH OPERATION When the engine is operating, the entire clutch assembly rotates, with the exception of the release bearing housing. As the clutch pedal is depressed and the free travel is taken up, the release fork contacts the wear plates located on the bearing housing. The release bearing assembly, release sleeve, and release sleeve retainer are then pulled toward the transmission, but only slightly compress the pressure spring. With the movement of the release sleeve retainer, the inner ends of the release levers are moved to the right, removing the force from the pressure plate. The return springs pull the pressure plate away from the first clutch disk, allowing the intermediate plate and the second clutch disk to move slightly toward the transmission. This disengages the clutch disks from the friction surfaces of the flywheel intermediate plate and pressure plate. See Fig. 10-17.

When the clutch pedal is gradually released, the clutch release bearing assembly, the release sleeve retainer, and the release levers are forced toward the flywheel (through the pressure springs), causing the release levers to force the pressure plate also toward the flywheel. This reduces the gap between the clutch facings and friction surfaces, and the clutch disks increase or decrease in speed to match the rotating speed of the flywheel until the clutch is fully engaged, whereupon the entire assembly rotates as a unit.

ADJUSTMENT If the clutch is not designed for automatic adjustment (Fig. 10-15), it must be manually (internally) adjusted. To check the clutch adjustment, remove the clutch housing cover and measure the clearance. This can be done by holding the specified-size wire rod between the release fork and bearing housing wear plate, and by holding a rod of specified thickness between the clutch brake friction disk and the release bearing housing cover. **NOTE** If the clutch does not have a clutch brake, hold a rod of specified thickness between the release bearing and flywheel ring.

If the clutch brake clearance is not within specification, turn the flywheel until the adjusting ring lock is removable and then remove the lock, release the clutch, and hold it released. Now, with a large screwdriver turn the adjusting ring counterclockwise to increase the space between the clutch brake friction disk and the release bearing housing cover, or clockwise to reduce the distance. You may reinstall the cap screw, for use as the fulcrum, to ease the turning of the adjusting ring. **NOTE** Each

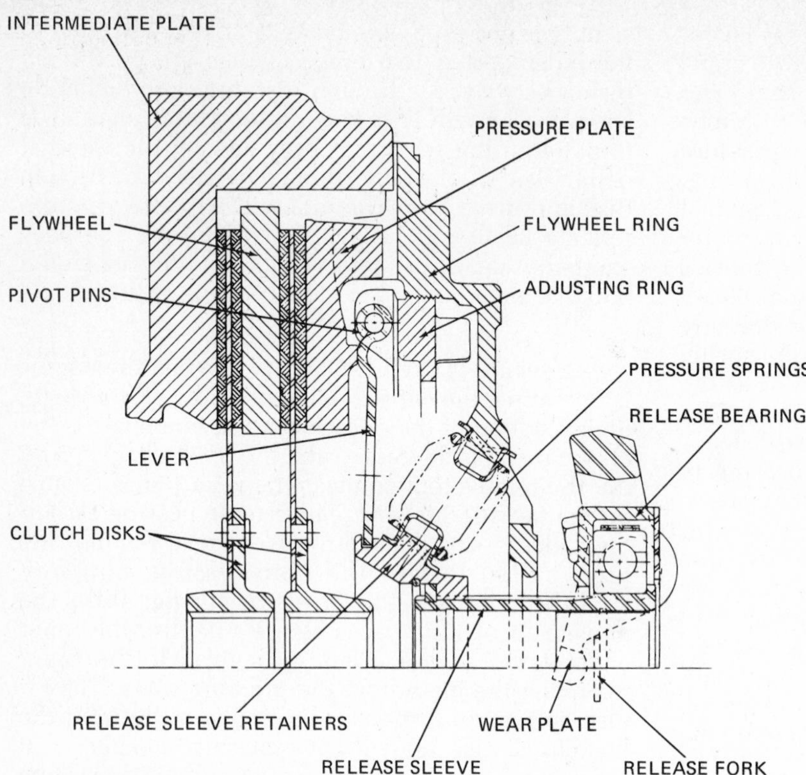

Fig. 10-17 Sectional view of an angle spring clutch at the start of release. (*Dana Corporation, Spicer Transmission Division*)

notch on the adjusting ring moves the release bearing about 0.02 in [0.5 mm].

Once the adjustment is made, reengage the clutch and again measure the distance. When properly adjusted, reinstall the adjusting ring lock and then check the pedal free travel, that is, the clearance between the clutch fork and wear plate. To increase or decrease the clearance, adjust the external linkage in order to get 0.125-in [3.17-mm] or 0.5-in [12.7-mm] clearance between the release fork and bearing housing wear plate. This will give you a pedal free travel of about 1.5 in [38 mm].

SELF-ADJUSTER The self-adjuster (Fig. 10-18), when used, is bolted to the flywheel ring so that the worm ring rests in one notch of the adjusting ring, and the actuator arm ball socket rests in the groove of the release sleeve retainer. Assuming the clutch is properly adjusted and is now being disengaged, the release sleeve retainer moves toward the transmission. This action pivots the actuator arm upward, forcing the worm ring to the right against its spring force, and the adjuster ring moves in the direction of the compressed spring. Upon clutch engagement, the actuator arm pivots downward and the adjuster spring forces the worm ring and adjuster ring to return to their original positions. However, if, due to clutch facing wear, the release sleeve retainer travel extends, thereby necessitating an adjustment, the actuator lever cam locks in the cam on the worm ring, and, as soon as the clutch disengages, the adjusting lever rotates the worm ring, which turns the

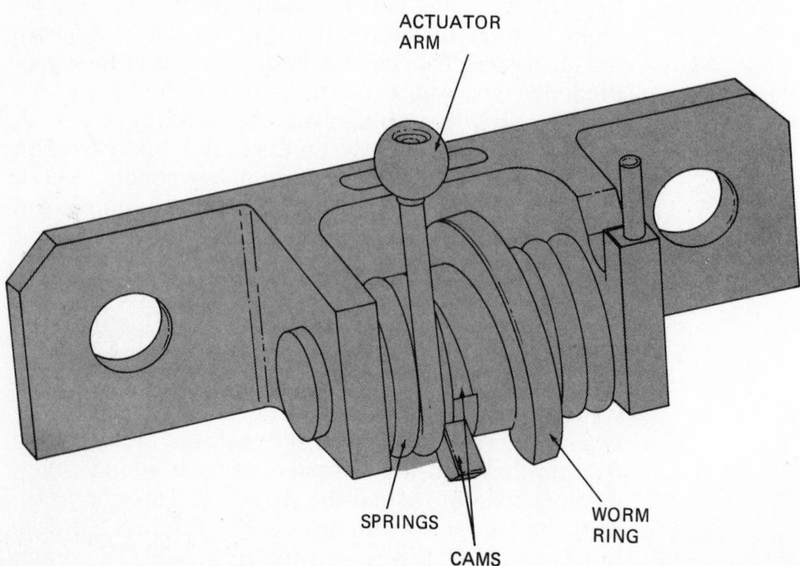

Fig. 10-18 The self-adjuster mechanism. (*Dana Corporation, Spicer Transmission Division*)

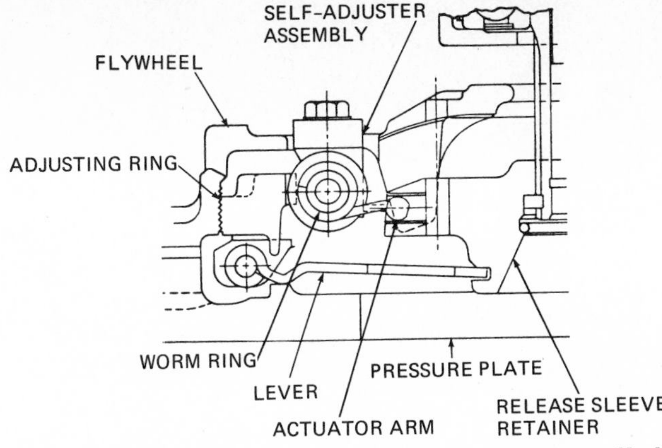

Fig. 10-19 Schematic view of self-adjuster installed. (*Mack Canada Inc.*)

adjusting ring in a clockwise direction to adjust the clutch. See Figs. 10-18 and 10-19.

Multidisk Push-Type Wet Clutch The multidisk direct-acting engine clutch shown in Fig. 10-20 is of the wet design—that is, it uses oil to lubricate and cool the clutch. In addition, it has a wet clutch brake and uses an air-control system to disengage the clutch and to engage the clutch brake. This clutch is much the same as a standard coil spring clutch, with the following exceptions: (1) where the center hub to which the four friction disks are splined is splined to the main drive pinion (clutch shaft); (2) where the clutch facings are bonded to steel disks and are of special fibrous materials, designed for operating in oil; (3) where the three steel disks and the pressure plates are splined to the clutch drive ring, which is bolted to the flywheel (**NOTE** The flywheel provides the friction surface for the first friction disk.); (4) where the special, hardened, self-locking adjusting screws are screwed into the ends of the release levers (although the major clutch adjustment is made through the eyebolts, the adjusting screws are used to make fine clutch adjustment); and (5) where the release collar assembly slides on the drive pinion cover.

LUBRICATION The lubrication and cooling of the clutch components are achieved through a simple device known as a *collector ring and pitot tube*. The

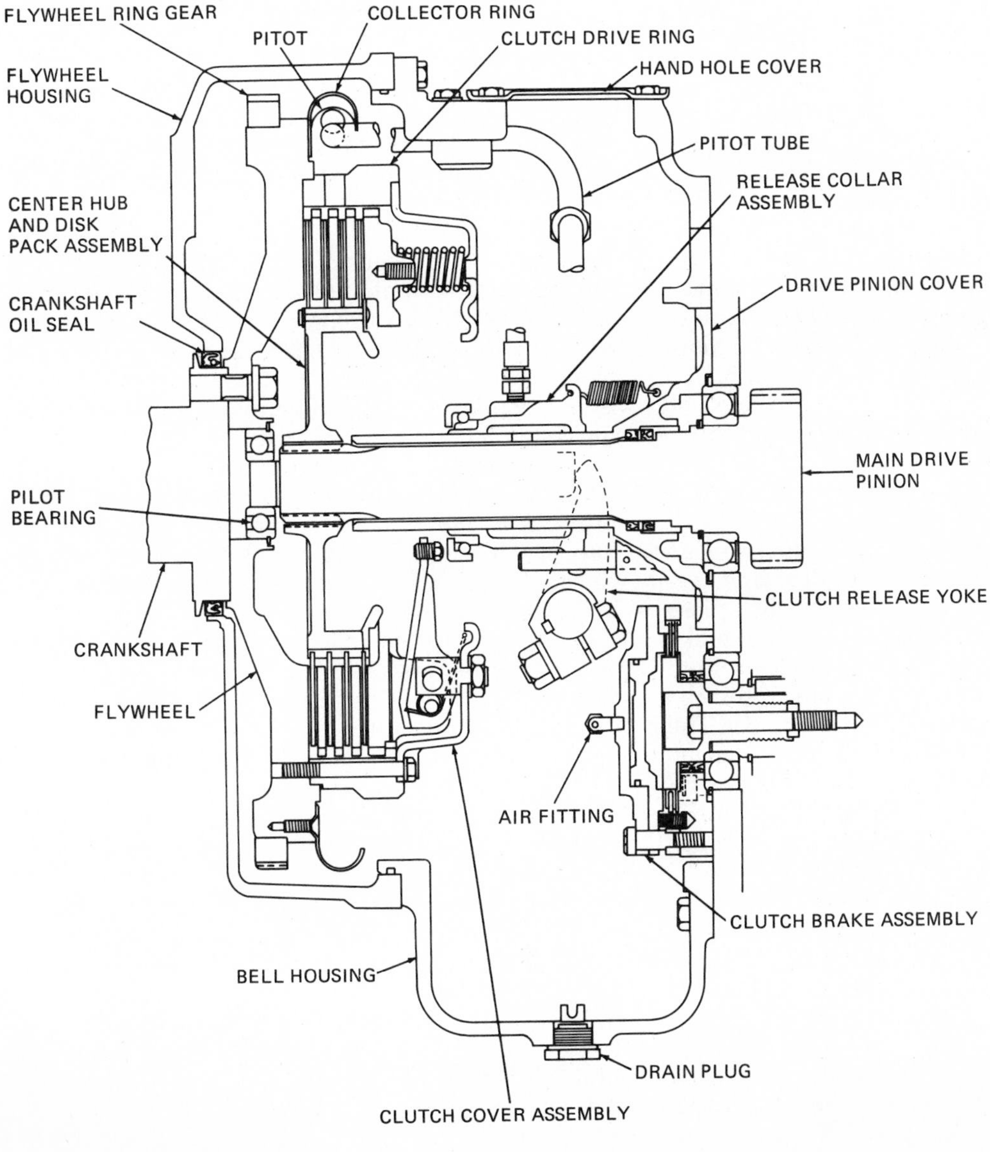

Fig. 10-20 Sectional view of Dynamax clutch. (*Mack Canada Inc.*)

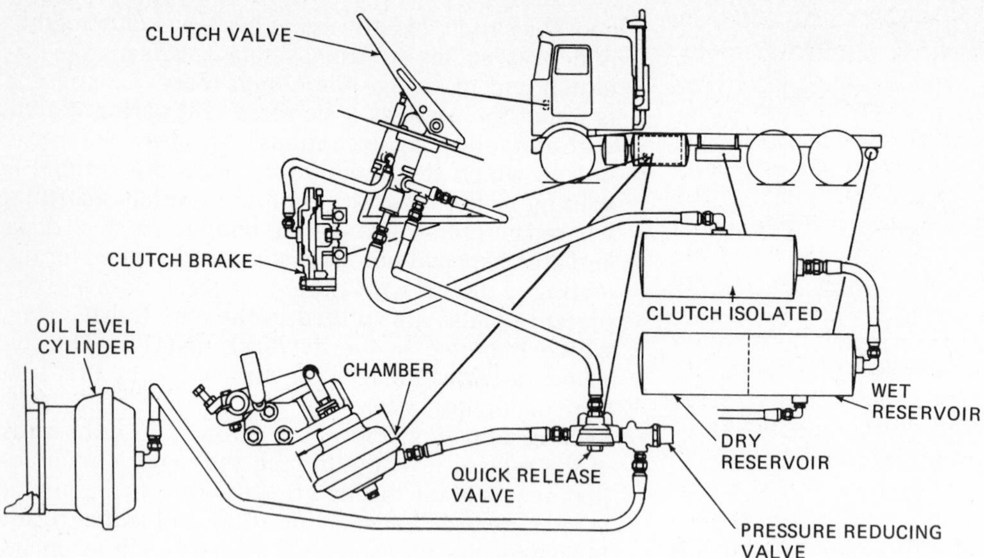

Fig. 10-21 Schematic view of a typical air control system. (*Mack Canada Inc.*)

collector ring is screwed to the flywheel and its lower portion is always submerged in oil. The opening of the pitot tube is located in the top curved portion of the collector ring, and the tube is connected through a flexible hose to the clutch release collar. When the engine is operating, the oil in the collector ring is swirled around with the rotating flywheel and forced into the opening of the pitot tube, through the tube and flexible hose, and into the clutch release collar. From there it flows along the main pinion shaft to the center of the clutch, where centrifugal force throws the oil from the shaft and onto the friction disks.

CLUTCH BRAKE The clutch brake used with the multidisk push-type wet clutch serves the same purpose as any other type of clutch brake. However, it is more crucial than others because, when the clutch is disengaged, there is a viscous drag caused by the oil on the friction disk and steel disk, so that the main drive pinion rotates with the flywheel. In order to stop the main drive pinion, the lower countershaft must be held stationary.

The brake, in this case, is of the multidisk design and the brake facings are composed of the same type of material as the clutch facings. The friction disks are splined to the disk retainer and the clutch brake piston is located within the clutch brake cover. Both components are bolted to the bearing cover, but the piston flange can slide on the cap screw shanks. The steel disks are splined to the clutch brake sleeve, which is screwed into the lower countershaft and further secured with a bolt. Note the air line fitting in Fig. 10-20 that is screwed into the clutch brake cover.

CLUTCH AND BRAKE CONTROL SYSTEM This system consists of the components shown in Fig. 10-21, as well as the oil temperature warning light circuit, the clutch air reservoir low-pressure warning light circuit, and the oil pressure gauge, none of which are shown. As you can see from the illustration, air is used to disengage the clutch and to apply the clutch brake, and a combination air chamber/oil reservoir (oil level cylinder) is bolted to the lower part of the bell housing. The clutch control valve used is of a design similar to an air treadle valve, and the clutch brake control valve is fastened to the bracket of the clutch control valve so that the plunger is located underneath the clutch control pedal. The clutch brake control valve is used to apply the brake after the clutch is disengaged. Through it, the operator can sense when the clutch brake is being applied.

When the engine is operating and the clutch reservoir is at system pressure, the same air pressure is present in the inlet valve of the clutch control valve. When the clutch control valve is being depressed, the exhaust valve closes and the inlet valve opens, allowing air to flow to the clutch brake valve, where it is stopped. At the same time air flows over a quick release valve to the clutch release air chamber, and from the quick release valve over a pressure-reducing valve to the oil level cylinder. The purpose of the pressure-reducing valve is to reduce the system air pressure to about 20 psi [137.8 kPa]. The air pressure in the clutch chamber moves the pushrod outward, pivoting the clutch release lever, the clutch release shaft, and the clutch release yoke. This moves the release collar assembly toward the flywheel, pivoting the release levers, and the release levers lift the pressure plate away from the friction disk, removing the force from the clutch disk and disengaging the clutch. At the same time, the oil level cylinder diaphragm is moved to the left, forcing the oil from the reservoir into the bell housing sump, and the collector ring picks up more oil, increasing both the lubrication to the clutch components and the cooling capacity.

If the clutch control valve pedal is further depressed (to the detent position), the brake control valve directs air to the clutch brake, and the piston forces the brake friction and steel disk against the bearing cover, stopping the rotation of the lower countershaft, and thereby stopping the main drive pinion (clutch shaft). **NOTE** If the vehicle is moving, the transmission must be shifted into neutral before the clutch brake is engaged; otherwise the clutch brake acts as a service brake to stop the motor vehicle.

When the clutch control valve pedal is released, first the inlet valve of the clutch brake control valve closes and then the exhaust valve opens, releasing the air pressure from the clutch brake piston; the return springs release the clutch brake. The exhaust valve of the clutch control valve then opens and the air pressure escapes from the clutch release air chamber and the oil level cylinder. This pivots the clutch release lever, clutch release shaft, and clutch release yoke, and allows the release collar assembly to be forced (through the release levers) toward the transmission, and the pressure plate to be forced toward the engine, engaging the clutch. As the oil level cylinder diaphragm moves to the right through its spring force, the oil from the sump is drawn back into the reservoir, reducing the oil level in the sump.

ADJUSTMENT On this type of clutch, the only adjustment necessary is to the clutch brake control valve. Clutch free travel is not adjustable, but the free travel of the clutch chamber pushrod should be checked periodically in order to determine the wear rate of the clutch assembly. When the free travel of the pushrod is less than 0.0675 in [1.7 mm], the clutch should be serviced. Note, however, that when the clutch is serviced, the free play must be adjusted to 0.5625 in [14.3 mm]. This is done by turning the clevis on the pushrod of the air chamber.

To adjust the clutch brake control valve, loosen the adjusting screw locknut and retract the adjusting screw. Next, place a 0.05-in [1.3-mm] feeler gauge between the pedal roller and actuating piston and fully depress the clutch pedal. Hold it in this position while screwing the head of the adjusting screw against the clutch control pedal. Then lock the adjustment with the locknut and recheck the adjustment. See Fig. 10-22.

Overcenter Clutches The method of engaging and disengaging an overcenter clutch is completely different from the methods previously outlined for other kinds of clutches. The basic principle of this clutch is that the pressure plate is forced indirectly over levers and links against the clutch disk. When the clutch is enaged, the levers and links come over the center of the fulcrum (pivot point) and lock the engagement.

An overcenter clutch can be used as an engine or power takeoff (PTO) clutch. In either case, the operating principle does not change, only the size of the components and the number of clutch disks.

Overcenter Engine Clutch One of several types of overcenter clutches is shown in Fig. 10-23. It is an oil-type multidisk clutch having a multidisk clutch brake and is designed for use on a track-type tractor. The oil that is used to lubricate and cool the clutch components is provided from the steering control valve. It enters port A (see Fig. 10-23), and flows into the housing and into the center- and cross-drilled passages of the clutch shaft to cool and lubricate the

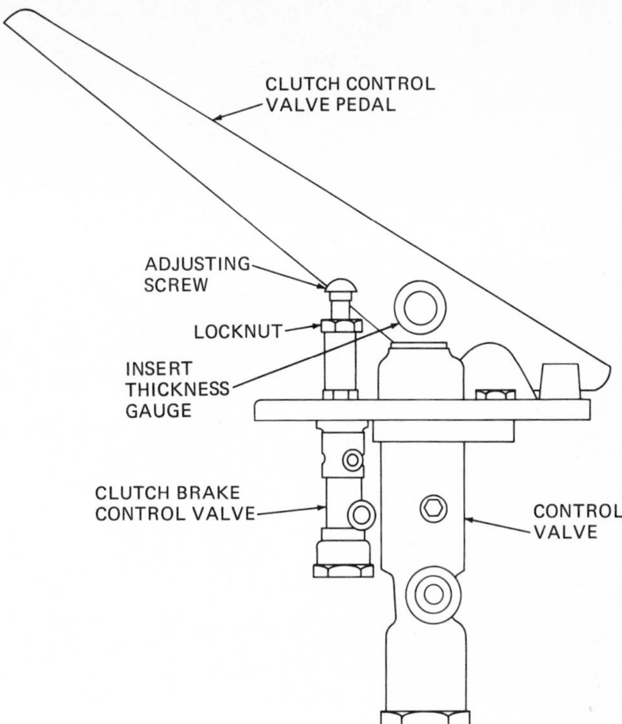

Fig. 10-22 The clutch and brake control valves. (*Mack Canada Inc.*)

clutch components. Two seals, one on each side of the clutch shaft's vertical passage, seal the shaft to the housing so that the lubricating oil is directed into the cross- and center-drilled passages.

The clutch shaft is supported at the left by the pilot bearing which is fitted snugly into the flywheel, and at the right by a roller bearing located in the housing. The accessory drive sleeve is supported on the clutch shaft, on the left by a bushing and on the right by a needle bearing. The sleeve is splined to the back plate and is held to it with two snap rings, and the accessory drive gear is bolted to the right-hand side of the sleeve. The center (clutch hub) is splined to the left-hand side of the clutch shaft and held to it through a snap ring. The back plate and driving ring are bolted to the flywheel. Four bimetallic friction plates are splined to the center (clutch) hub, and the three steel friction plates and the pressure plate are splined to the driving ring. The clutch adjusting ring is threaded into the back plate and locked to it with a locking device. Positioned inside the adjusting ring is the adjusting ring (wear) plate.

The pressure plate is cast with pin lugs, to which the cam shafts are pinned. The cam shafts are connected through yoke pins to the connecting links, and the connecting links are pinned to the throwout bearing sleeve. The bimetallic friction plates are splined to the clutch brake hub, which is splined to the clutch shaft. Snap rings secure the hub to the shaft. The steel friction plates and the brake pressure plate are splined to the rear cover. The clutch brake apply plate is threaded to the throwout bearing carrier and secured to it with a set screw.

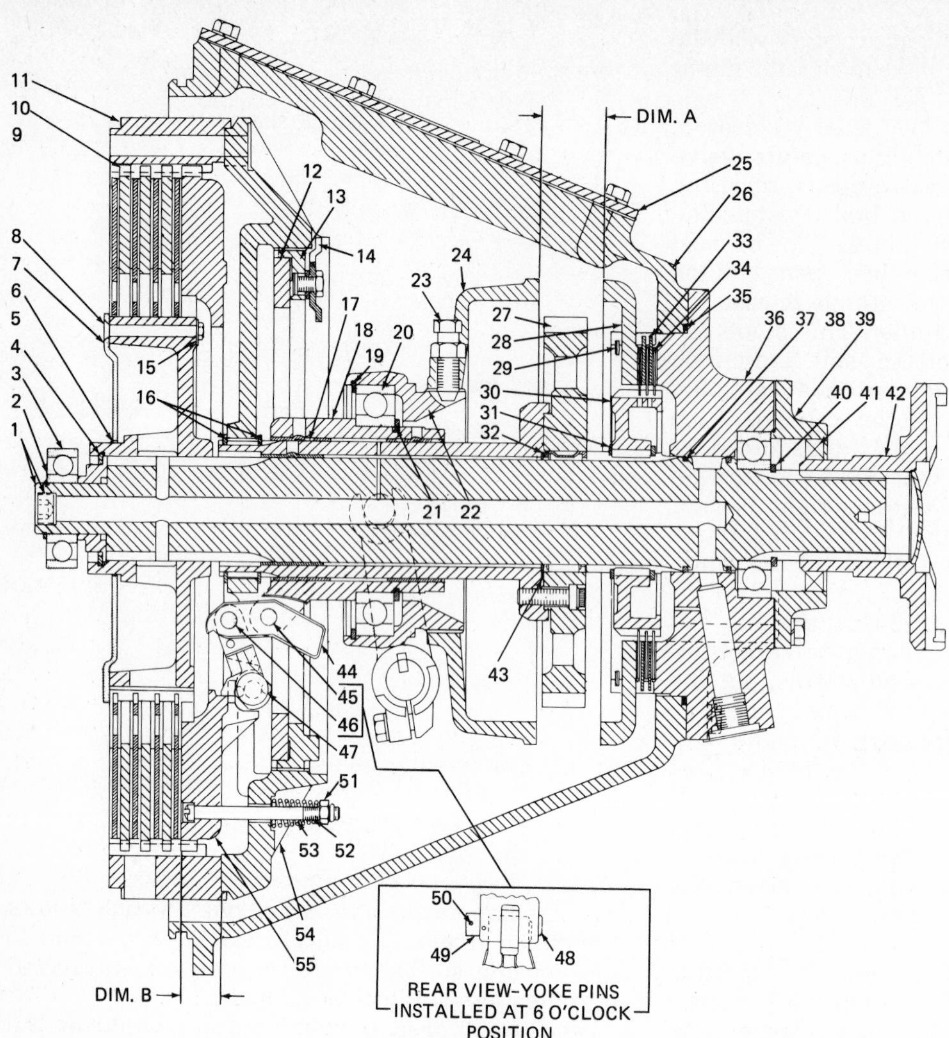

1. Clutch shaft w/drilled plug
2. Snap ring
3. Pilot bearing
4. Spacer
5. Snap ring
6. Center (clutch hub)
7. Cover
8. Rivet
9. Clutch friction disk—bimetallic
10. Clutch friction disk—steel
11. Driving ring
12. Adjusting ring plate
13. Clutch adjusting ring
14. Adjusting ring lock
15. Washer
16. Snap ring
17. Accessory drive gear sleeve
18. Throwout bearing sleeve
19. Snap ring
20. Throwout bearing
21. Snap ring
22. Throwout bearing carrier
23. Setscrew
24. Clutch brake apply plate
25. Access cover
26. Housing
27. Accessory drive gear
28. Brake pressure plate
29. Retaining ring
30. Clutch brake hub
31. Snap ring
32. Bearing
33. Brake friction plate steel
34. Brake friction plate—bimetallic
35. O-Ring
36. Rear cover
37. Shaft sealing rings
38. Rear bearing
39. Rear bearing retainer
40. Snap ring
41. Rear oil seal
42. Drive shaft front yoke
43. Thrust washer
44. Connecting link
45. Yoke pin
46. Yoke pin
47. Camshaft
48. Head end of yoke pin
49. Collar
50. Roll pin
51. Lock nut
52. Capscrew
53. Return spring
54. Back plate
55. Pressure plate

Fig. 10-23 Sectional view of an overcenter engine clutch and clutch brake. (*Fiat–Allis*)

OPERATION When the engine is operating and the clutch is engaged, all components rotate at engine speed except the throwout bearing carrier and clutch brake plate, which do not rotate. The engine power is transmitted from the flywheel to the driving ring, friction plates, clutch hub, clutch shaft, and the drive shaft front yoke. At the same time, engine power is transmitted from the flywheel to the back plate, and to the accessory drive gear sleeve, rotating the accessory drive gear, which drives the hydraulic pump (not shown in Fig. 10-23).

When the operator pulls the hand lever to the right, the motion is transmitted to the shifting yoke shaft, pivoting the yoke. The yoke then pulls the throwout bearing sleeve, the connecting links, throwout bearing carrier, and clutch brake apply plate, to the right. This pivots the camshaft, and the camshaft lobes move away from the adjusting ring plate, allowing the pressure plate to be moved to the right through the return spring. This sequence of actions removes the force from the steel and bimetallic friction plates, disengaging the clutch, and the

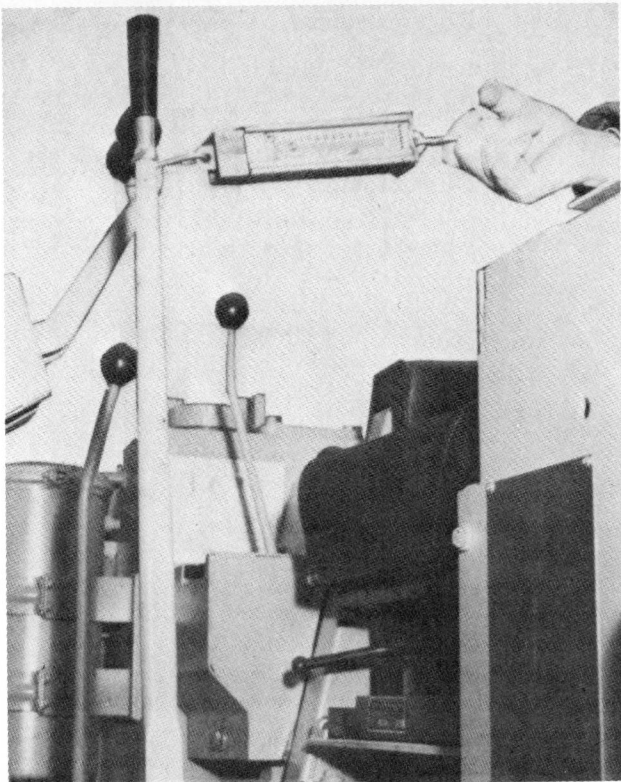

Fig. 10-24 Checking pull required to engage engine clutch. (*Fiat–Allis*)

engine power to the clutch shaft is interrupted. Note, however, that the hydraulic pump is still being driven, and due to the viscous residue on the steel and bimetallic friction plates the clutch shaft may rotate slightly.

If the operator wishes to shift the transmission into a gear, the clutch lever is pulled further to the right, and as the clutch brake apply plate contacts the brake pressure plate the steel and bimetallic friction plates are squeezed between the brake pressure plate and the friction surface on the rear cover, applying the clutch brake, stopping the clutch shaft.

When the operator moves the clutch lever to the left (to engage the clutch), the motion is transmitted to the throwout bearing sleeve, carrier, clutch brake apply plate, and the connecting links, releasing the clutch brake, and the connecting links pivot the camshaft. The camshaft lobes come against the adjusting ring plate, forcing the pressure plate toward the flywheel. The steel and bimetallic friction plates are thus squeezed between the pressure plate and flywheel friction surface, engaging the clutch.

ADJUSTMENT To maintain 100 percent clutch and shift efficiency, the clutch and brake adjustment must be periodically checked. To check the clutch, first stop the engine. Remove the access cover. Turn the flywheel until the adjusting ring lock is under the cover opening. To determine the pull required to engage the clutch attach a spring scale to the engine clutch hand lever (at the center of the hand grip) and pull on it while observing the scale reading (see Fig. 10-24). If the pull is less than specified, unlock the adjusting ring lock and, with a large screwdriver, turn the adjusting ring (clockwise) one notch, then recheck the adjustment. When the adjustment has been made, lock the adjusting ring, engage the clutch, and then measure the distance between the clutch brake apply plate and clutch brake pressure plate. If the distance is not within specification, loosen the locknut, turn the set screw out of the lock groove, and turn the clutch brake apply plate either counterclockwise to decrease the distance or clockwise to increase it. When the adjustment is correct, tighten the set screw, lock it, and install the access cover.

TROUBLESHOOTING OVERCENTER CLUTCHES Overcenter clutches are relatively trouble-free and have a long service life as long as the correct clutch adjustments are maintained and the clutch is moved to the engaged position whenever the tractor transmission is in neutral. If the latter action is not taken, the camshafts, connecting links, yoke pins, and throwout bearing sleeve will be subject to excessive wear, which may result in clutch slippage and/or cause hard clutch engagement. However, clutch slippage can also originate from excessively worn steel or bimetallic friction plates, or hung-up plates caused by worn teeth or grooves in the clutch hub or driving ring. If the gears clash when shifting the transmission, it may be because the clutch brake is misadjusted, the clutch brake steel or bimetallic friction plates are worn or damaged, or the plates hung up.

Power Takeoff Clutches An overcenter clutch (single- or multidisk) is commonly used as a power takeoff clutch to disengage and engage the engine power to accessory machinery such as rock crushers, winches, converter belts, cement mixers, farm implements, etc. The PTO clutch may be mounted directly to the flywheel housing, to the front of the cylinder block, or to the rear of the tractor transmission.

Single-Disk Overcenter PTO Clutch A single-disk overcenter clutch is shown in Fig. 10-25. Although it is basically similar to the multidisk overcenter engine clutch previously discussed, it has the following dissimilarities:

- The outer clutch pressure plate is fastened through a taper and key to the clutch drive shaft.
- The right-hand side of the clutch drive shaft is supported in the clutch housing by two sets of tapered roller bearings.
- The drive shaft retainer bearing is used to adjust the bearing preload.
- The clutch facings consist of a single ring with external gear teeth or of three independent segments with teeth which are splined to the driving ring.
- The facing material is of an asbestos compound.
- The inner pressure plate is connected through the clutch release levers and links to the clutch release sleeve.

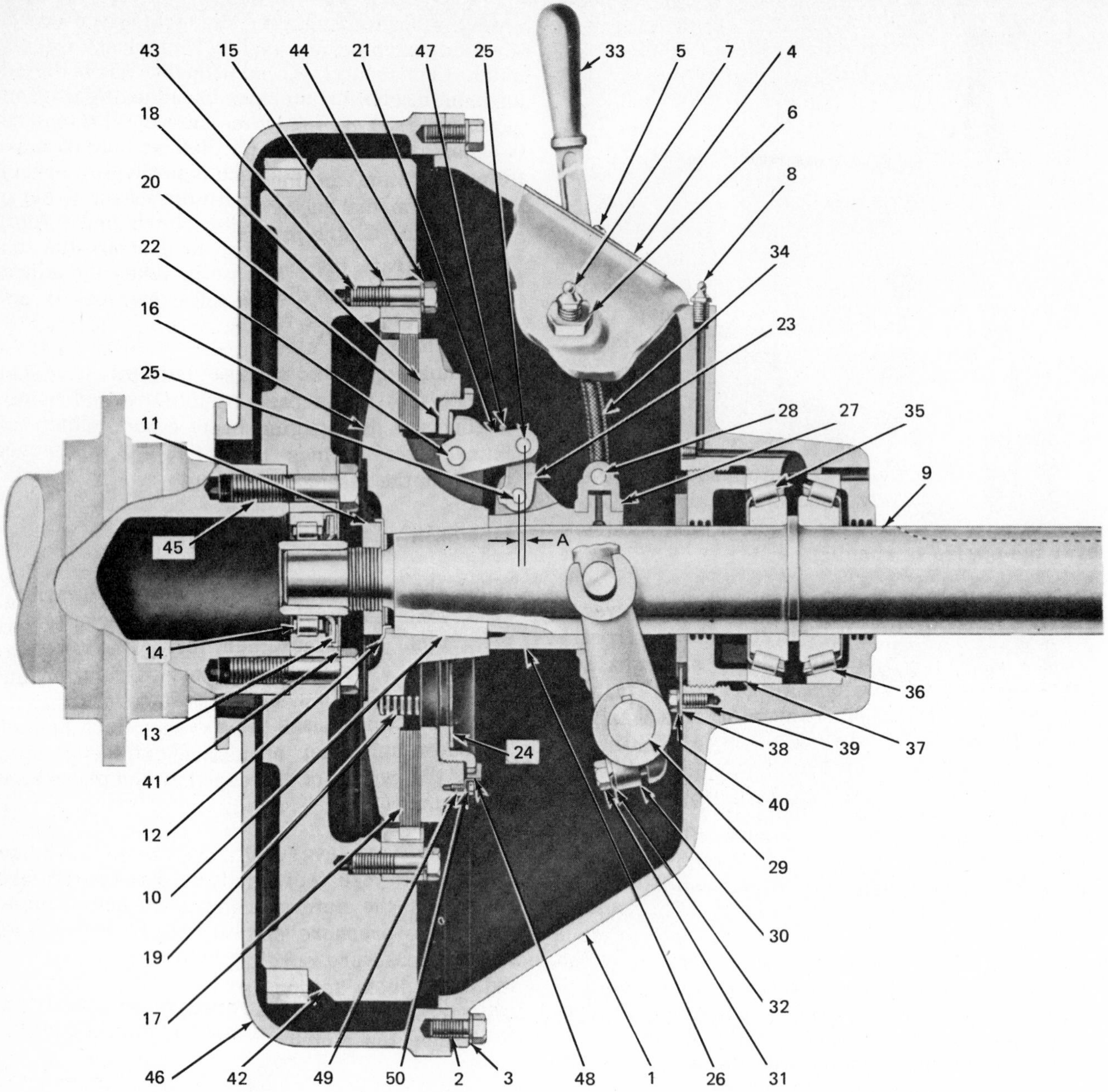

1. Housing—clutch
2. Bolt—clutch housing
3. Lock washer
4. Cover—inspection hole
5. Screw—cover
6. Nut—flexible tube to clutch housing
7. Fitting—grease
8. Fitting—grease
9. Shaft—clutch drive
10. Key—drive shaft
11. Nut—drive shaft
12. Lock washer—drive shaft
13. Seal—pilot bearing oil
14. Bearing—clutch drive shaft pilot (roller)
15. Ring—clutch driving
16. Plate—clutch pressure (outer)
17. Clutch facing (one piece)
18. Plate—clutch pressure (inner)
19. Spring—pressure plate separator
20. Ring—clutch adjusting
21. Lever—clutch release
22. Pin—release lever to pressure plate
23. Link—release lever
24. Plate—adjusting ring wear
25. Pin—release lever to link and sleeve
26. Sleeve—clutch release
27. Collar—clutch release sleeve
28. Bolt—release sleeve collar
29. Shaft—clutch release
30. Yoke—clutch release
31. Bolt—yoke to shaft
32. Lock washer
33. Lever—clutch hand
34. Flexible tube assy
35. Bearing assy.—roller (inner)
36. Bearing assy.—roller (outer)
37. Retainer—drive shaft bearing
38. Lock plate—bearing retainer
39. Bolt—retainer lock plate
40. Lock washer
41. Retainer—pilot bearing
42. Flywheel assy
43. Bolt—clutch driving ring
44. Lock washer
45. Bolt—flywheel
46. Housing—flywheel
47. Spring—clutch release
48. Lock—clutch adjusting ring spring
49. Screw—adjusting ring spring lock
50. Lock washer

Fig. 10-25 Sectional view of power takeoff overcenter clutch. (*GMC Detroit Diesel Allison Division*)

- The yoke end fits in the lugs of the clutch release collar.
- The clutch adjusting ring is threaded into the inner pressure plate and locked to it with the clutch ring adjusting lock.
- The clutch release yoke is keyed to the clutch release shaft.
- The clutch release sleeve slides on the clutch drive shaft.
- The clutch release bearing is a two-piece clutch release collar bolted together over the flange on the clutch release sleeve.
- The pressure plate separator springs are placed between the inner and outer pressure plate.

OPERATION When the clutch is engaged and the engine is operating, the entire assembly rotates, with the exception of the clutch release collar. When the clutch hand lever is pulled to the right, the motion pulls the clutch release collar, the clutch release levers, and the three links to the right. This action moves the clutch release levers down, causing the nose on the clutch release levers to move away from the adjusting ring wear plate, and also causing the pressure plate separator springs to force the inner pressure plate away from the clutch facing. This allows the facing to move away from the outer pressure plate, disengaging the clutch, while the clutch drive shaft, the outer pressure plate, and the clutch release collar remain stationary.

When the clutch hand lever is moved toward the flywheel, the motion forces the clutch release collar, the clutch release sleeve, and the three release lever links to the left. The links pivot on their pins and move the right-hand ends of the release levers outward, forcing both the release lever nose against the adjusting ring wear plate and the inner pressure plate toward the flywheel, and the clutch facing is grabbed between the two pressure plate surfaces. The engine power is transmitted from the clutch driving ring to the clutch facing and to the outer and inner pressure plates, driving the clutch shaft at engine speed. When the clutch is fully engaged, the clutch release sleeve has moved the link–to–release-sleeve-pin link pins past the center line of the link–to–release-lever-pin link pins, thus locking the clutch in engagement (see Fig. 10-25, distance *A*).

NOTE When the clutch is of the double-facing design, the clutch driving ring is wider and a one-piece intermediate plate is splined to that ring.

ADJUSTMENT To compensate for clutch facing and pressure plate surface wear, the clutch can be adjusted to maintain 100 percent engagement. This clutch is adjusted somewhat differently from the multidisk clutch shown in Fig. 10-23.

To check the clutch adjustment, disengage the clutch and attach a spring scale to the center of the hand grip of the clutch hand lever. Pull on the scale to engage the clutch and note the reading (which registers in pounds or kilograms). **NOTE** The pull required varies according to the hand lever length and the diameter of the clutch facing; therefore, check the service manual before making any adjustment. For example, say the hand lever is 25 in [63.5 cm] and a 14.5-in [36.83-cm] diameter clutch facing is used. The pull would be specified as 75 lb [34.05 kg]. If the measured pull is less, say only 50 lb [22.7 kg], the clutch requires an adjustment. To make this adjustment, disengage the clutch, remove the inspection plate cover, and turn the flywheel to bring the clutch-adjusting ring lock below the inspection cover opening. Release the adjusting ring lock and, with a large screwdriver or prybar, turn the adjusting ring one notch, counterclockwise. Recheck the adjustment. You may have to repeat the procedure several times to achieve the required pull. If a new clutch is installed and the required pull is higher than specified, then you must turn the adjusting ring clockwise to achieve the required pull. When the clutch is correctly adjusted, lock the adjusting ring and reinstall the inspection plate cover.

Multidisk Hydraulically Activated PTO Clutch A clutch of this design is shown in Fig. 10-26. Note the hydraulic pump which is driven by a gear splined to the clutch input shaft. The clutch input shaft is supported by two ball bearings in the PTO and hydraulic pump drive housing. The right-hand end of the clutch drive shaft is splined into the engine flywheel, and the left-hand end is splined to the clutch input shaft. The steel friction disks are splined to the external splines on the clutch input shaft. Sintered clutch plates and the output shaft are splined to the piston carrier. The clutch piston is located inside the piston carrier, which is externally machined to a coned brake friction surface. The brake piston is located in the bore of the PTO and hydraulic pump drive housing. This piston is cast with a brake shoe to which the brake lining is bonded.

OPERATION When the clutch is disengaged—that is, when the oil pressure is removed from behind the clutch piston—the piston return spring moves the clutch piston to the left, allowing the steel and clutch friction disks to separate, and the input and output shafts to disconnect from each other. At the same time, the oil pressure from the right-hand brake piston area is removed and the brake piston return spring moves the brake piston to the right, forcing the brake lining against the piston carrier friction surface.

If the engine is operating, the rotation from the flywheel is transmitted over the clutch drive shaft to the clutch input shaft, and over the drive gear and idler gear to the hydraulic-pump-driven gear, pump drive shaft, and pump input shaft, but the piston carrier and output shaft are held stationary by the brake. When oil is directed into port A (Fig. 10-26), it divides into two streams—one that flows through the center passage of the brake piston into area A, and the other that flows into the PTO housing passage. From there it flows into the piston passage and into area B. As the oil pressure increases, the brake piston is forced to the left, releasing the brake from the piston carrier, and the clutch piston moves to

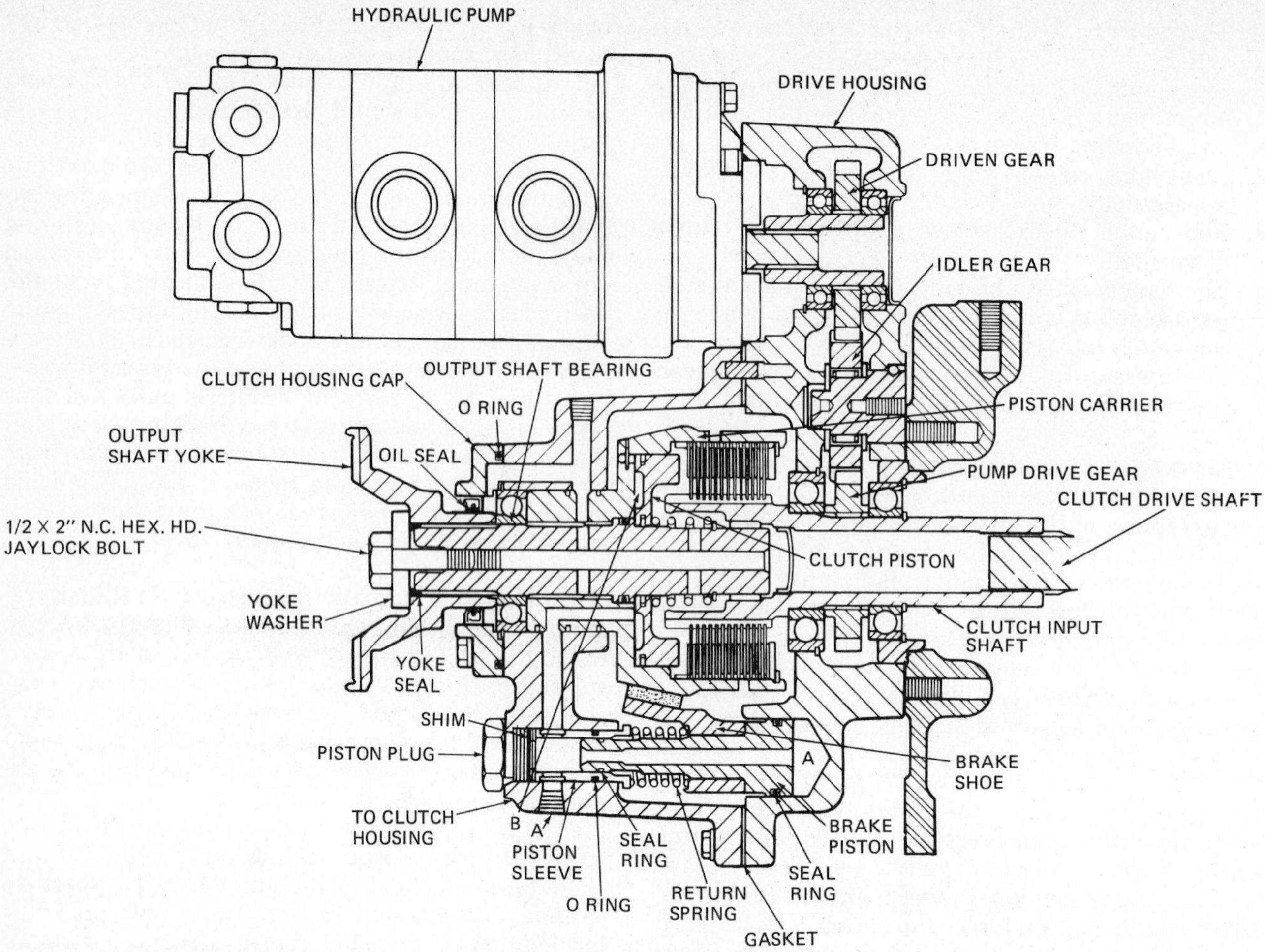

Fig. 10-26 Sectional view of a multidisk PTO clutch. (*J I Case Company Agricultural Equipment Division*)

the right, forcing the steel and clutch disks to the right. The input shaft engages with the piston carrier, and drives the output shaft at engine speed.

Shoe and Band Clutches The different types of shoe and band clutches are too numerous to be covered completely, but a few will be discussed.

An internal shoe clutch is very similar in design to a shoe brake. Furthermore, it may be of the servo or nonservo (double-anchor) design and may be air-, brake-fluid-, or oil-activated.

Air-Activated External Band Clutch A self-energizing external half-band clutch is shown in Fig. 10-27. The dead ends of the clutch bands are pinned to the clutch spider, and the live ends are connected by levers to the rotary air chambers. The two air chambers are connected by a T fitting to the air application line. The lining material is commonly woven asbestos, riveted to the brake band. Since both ends of the brake bands are alike, they can be interchanged to increase their service life, thereby compensating for the heavier wear at the dead end.

OPERATION In the disengaged position, the air pressure is removed from the rotary air chambers and the coil spring within the chambers moves the

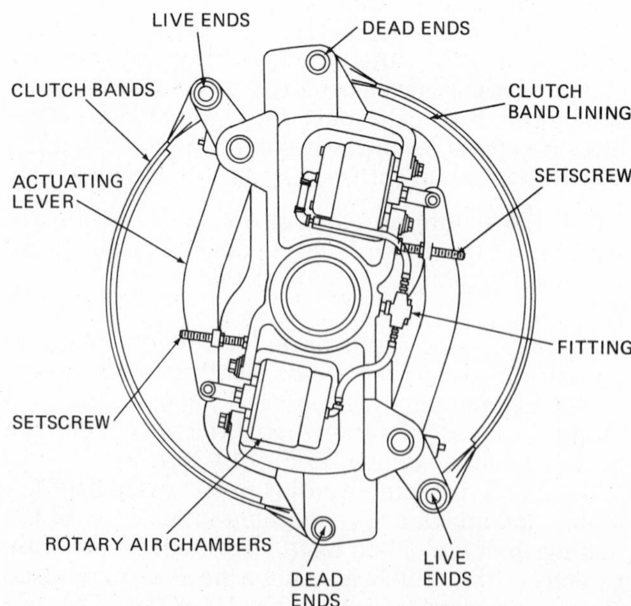

Fig. 10-27 Schematic view of an external half-band clutch. (*American Hoist & Derrick Company*)

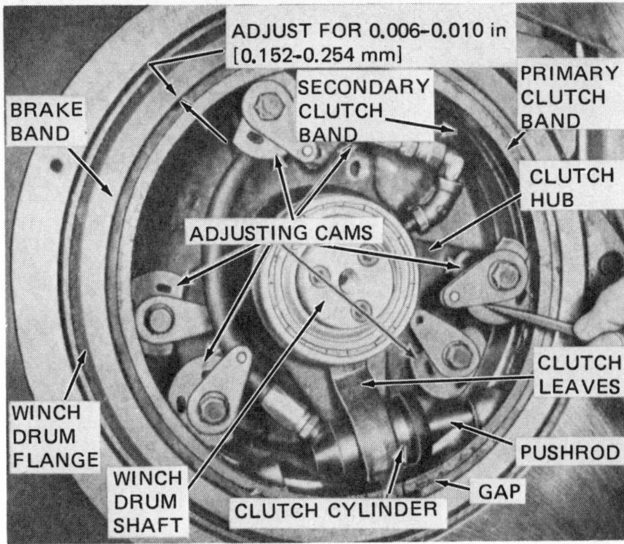

Fig. 10-28 View of winch clutch and brake. (*J I Case Company Agricultural Equipment Division*)

pushrod inward. This pivots the actuating levers, and the lever ends push the clutch bands in the direction of the dead anchors, away from the clutch drum.

When air from the clutch valve is directed to the T fitting, it flows into the rotary air chambers, forcing the pushrods outward. This pivots the actuating levers on their pins and pulls the clutch bands in a clockwise direction onto the clutch drum, and the clutch band facing then contacts the clutch drum friction surface, transmitting the rotation to the clutch drum. Clutch application can be controlled through the clutch air valve (treadle valve); therefore, a smooth clutch engagement and disengagement can be achieved and clutch slippage can be controlled.

Clutch adjustment to compensate for lining wear is made through the set screws.

Hydraulically Activated Internal Band Clutch A clutch of this design is shown in Fig. 10-28. It is used on a winch. The winch drum flange extends to form a combination clutch and brake drum. The clutch friction surface is the internal surface of the drum, and the brake friction surface is the external surface. The clutch hub (on which the clutch release lever pivots) is splined to the drum shaft. The clutch lever is attached to the clutch cylinder, and the end of the clutch lever rests between the gap of the primary and secondary brake bands. The cylinder is connected with fittings and hoses to the winch drum shaft, and the clutch pushrod rests in the socket of the primary clutch band. The heel end of the secondary clutch band rests against the lever arm that is attached with a pin to the clutch hub (not shown in the illustration). The clutch linings are bonded to the clutch bands.

OPERATION When the hydraulic pressure is removed from the clutch cylinder, the inherent retraction tension of both clutch bands moves them away from the clutch drum friction surface until they come to rest against the adjusting cams. When the engine is operating, the drum shaft, clutch hub, and clutch band rotate clockwise, but the winch drum is held stationary by the brake band. As fluid under pressure enters the gland (not visible in Fig. 10-28 since it is behind the bearing), it flows into the clutch shaft passage, through the fittings and hose, and into the clutch cylinder, forcing the piston and pushrod outward and the toe end of the primary band against the drum. The heel of the primary band and the toe of the secondary band are forced (by means of the clutch lever) against the clutch drum friction surface. As the band facings come into contact with the drum friction surface, the applied force of the primary clutch band is multiplied through self-energizing action, and the increased force is transmitted onto the clutch lever, increasing the spreading force onto the secondary clutch band. Rotation is transmitted from the clutch band to the clutch friction surface, causing the winch drum to rotate. The amount of slippage between the brake bands and clutch drum depends on the hydraulic pressure that is applied to the clutch cylinder. **NOTE** Because of the direction of drum rotation, the brake force is released; but it automatically applies when the drum rotation stops.

ADJUSTMENT To ensure good clutch action, an even clearance between both clutch bands and friction surfaces is necessary. Clearance varies among various clutch designs and in this case 0.010 in [0.25 mm] is recommended. Adjustment is made as follows: Remove the end cap and the hydraulic line from the hydraulic tube and master cylinder, then remove the clutch cover. Loosen the adjusting cap screw of the primary band; then turn the adjusting cams until the flat side of that band faces toward the clutch band. Remove the clutch slave cylinder pushrod and the primary clutch band. Next, loosen the secondary cam cap screws slightly, and place a 0.010-in [0.25-mm] feeler gauge at or near the cam between the clutch band facing and drum. Turn the cam, using a screwdriver, to force the lining against the feeler gauge. When adjusted, turn the cap screws to the specified torque. Repeat the procedure with the remaining two cams. When this is done, reinstall the primary clutch band and the pushrod, and adjust the former. Next, adjust the clutch rod so that no slack exists between the clutch lever and clutch hub while maintaining the required clutch lining clearance. Reattach the removed components and bleed the hydraulic system.

Internal and External Tube Clutches Clutches of this type are similar in design to the external expanding tube brake (see material on brakes). The clutch-actuating member is an oval reinforced rubber tube bonded to either the internal or external surface of the drive or driven member. In the case illustrated (Fig. 10-29), it is bonded to the clutch hub, which in turn is splined to the drive shaft and held to the shaft with a snap ring. It is so positioned that the air passage in the hub leading from the air

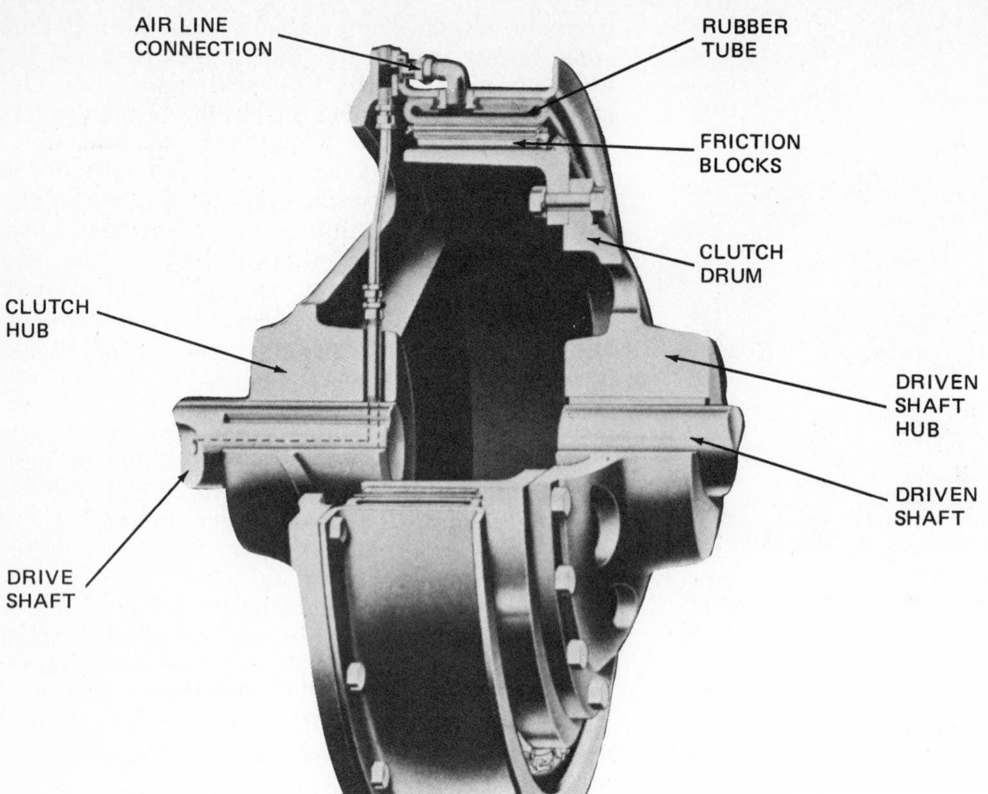

Fig. 10-29 Cutaway of an internal expanding tube clutch. (*Eaton Corporation*)

tube to the center bore aligns with the air passage in the drive shaft. Clutch shoe pads are bonded to the outer circle of the tube to which the clutch shoes are pinned. The driven member (clutch drum) is positioned inside the air clutch and is attached to the driven shaft hub.

OPERATION When the air pressure is exhausted from the air tube, the inherent energy of the rubber returns the tube to its original shape. Consequently, the clutch shoe linings are pulled away from the clutch drum surface and no power is transmitted to the clutch drum. To engage the clutch, the operator depresses the air clutch treadle valve, and air flows from it over an air line to the air swivel joint attached to the clutch drive shaft (not shown in Fig. 10-29). Air flows through the center-drilled passage of the shaft into the clutch hub passage and into the tube. The air pressure decreases the inner circumference of the tube, forcing the brake shoe linings against the drum friction surface and transmitting rotation to the clutch drum. Depending upon the applied air pressure, either the clutch hub and clutch drum rotate at the same speed, or there is a slippage and the clutch drum rotates at a reduced speed. To reduce the time of clutch engagement and disengagement, a quick-release valve or relay valve is inserted into the application circuit.

DISADVANTAGES The tube clutch cannot be adjusted, and therefore with increased shoe lining wear the engagement time increases, since more air is needed to force the shoe lining against the clutch drum. Another drawback to this type of clutch may be excessive heat. If the clutch heat deteriorates the bond, the brake shoes or the air tube could come loose and cause clutch failure.

Another type of tube clutch is shown in Fig. 10-30.

MECHANICAL CLUTCHES

These clutches may be divided into the following three groups (each group being variously designed): jaw clutches, spline or collar clutches, and one-way (or overrunning) clutches.

Jaw and Collar Clutches Jaw clutches (Fig. 10-31) and collar clutches (Fig. 10-32) are used on all types of manual transmissions and for crawler carriers, to engage and disengage the front axle drive from the main transmission, to engage and disengage an interaxle differential carrier, or to lock the differential so as to achieve a positive traction differential. In other words, they can normally be used wherever two shafts need be connected. They are relatively trouble-free and have a long service life since the wear rate is minimal.

To accomplish an engagement when using a jaw or collar clutch either both shafts must rotate at nearly the same speed, or both shafts (drive and driven) must be held stationary. To disengage the clutch, the torque must first be removed from the shafts.

Jaw and collar clutches have many similarities. For instance, when engaged they cannot slip, although a misalignment between the male and female (drive or driven) members may cause a disengagement. Both types of clutches use one sliding member

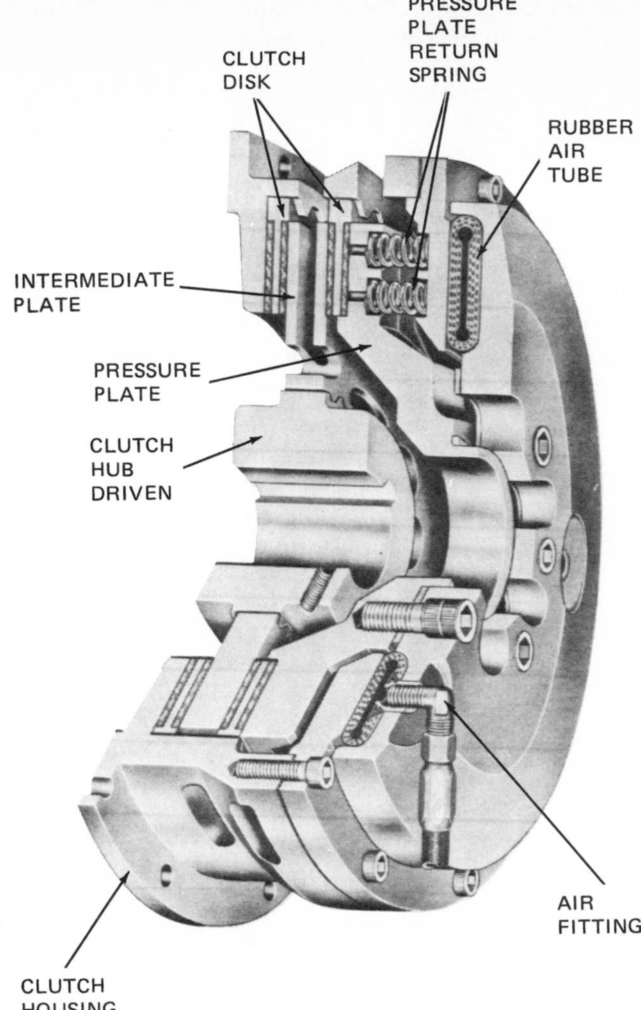

Fig. 10-30 Cutaway view of a Witchita air clutch.

that is splined loosely to the drive or driven shaft, and one or two clutch members that are either fastened to the driven or drive shaft or are supported through bearings on the driven shaft. (See material on transmissions in Unit 11.) The sliding member

Fig. 10-32 View of sliding collar clutch. (*Mack Canada Inc.*)

commonly has a circular groove in which the shift fork rests. The main differences between the jaw and collar clutches are that their male and female clutch members are unalike in shape, and that the clutch members of a jaw clutch are located on the side whereas, on the collar clutch, the male collar clutch members are around the outer circumference and the female collar clutch members are on the inner circumference. The jaw clutch members (male or female) are relatively larger than the collar clutch members.

Jaw Clutches The jaw clutch shown in Fig. 10-31 is used in a transmission to select high- and low-range gears. The sliding-jaw male members are loosely splined to the transmission output shaft and bolted to each side of the shift fork. Two gears (one on each side of the male jaw clutch) are supported on the output shaft and are free to rotate on it, but are governed by the gear ratio between them and the counter shaft gears.

OPERATION To engage the left-hand male jaw clutch with the left-hand female jaw clutch, the engine clutch is disengaged and the shift rail and fork are moved from the neutral position to the left. The engagement is assisted and maintained through the design of both jaw clutches (male and female), but

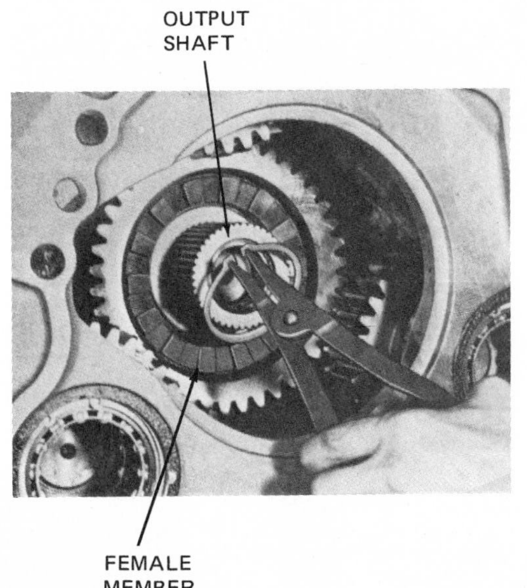

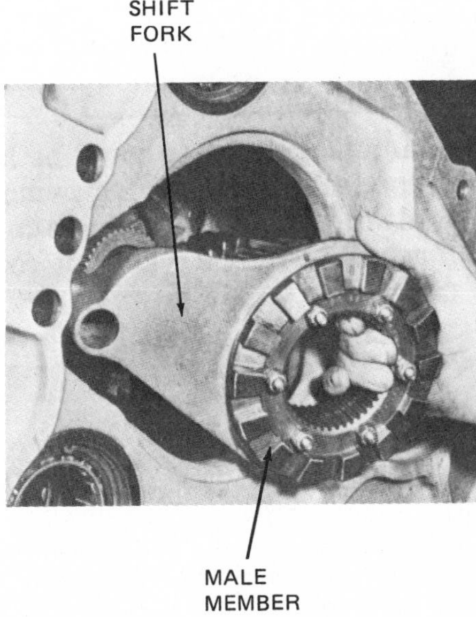

Fig. 10-31 View of a jaw clutch. (*Mack Canada Inc.*)

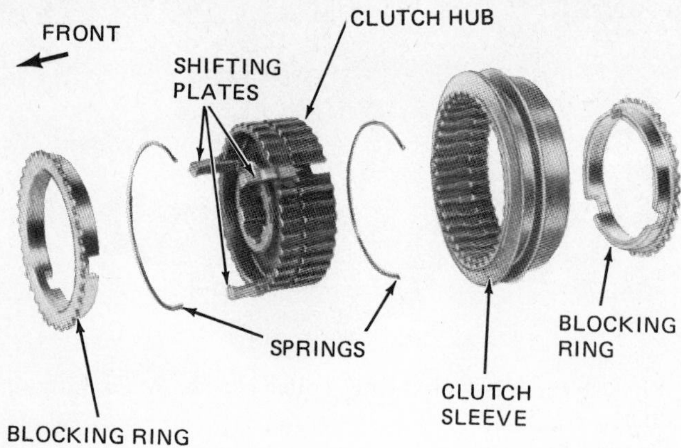

Fig. 10-33 Exploded view of a cone synchronizer. (*International Harvester Company*)

the shift rail detent and ball hold the shift rail in position, thus holding the male jaw clutch engaged.

Collar Clutches One of several types of collar clutches is shown in Fig. 10-32. (Also see material on differential lock.) Its male clutch member is similar to a straight cut gear, and the female clutch member is similar to an internal gear. To make engagement easier, the toothlike clutch member ends are slightly tapered.

Collar clutches which have an additional clutch to synchronize the drive and driven shaft are shown in Figs. 10-33 and 10-34. One is called a *cone synchronizer* and the other a *pin synchronizer*. Each performs the same function—that is, to equalize the speed of both shafts so that the sleeve can engage the output shaft with the gear.

CONE SYNCHRONIZER The clutch hub has external and internal splines. It is splined and secured to the output shaft by two snap rings. The clutch sleeve, which is internally splined, has a small internal groove and a large external groove in which the shift fork rests. When the sleeve is centered over the clutch hub and the two insert springs are positioned under the three shifting plates (inserts), the small nose on the inserts rests in the internal groove of the sleeve, holding the inserts to the hub. Both hub ends are machined to allow space for the blocking rings. The bronze blocking rings have external teeth, their hubs have external coned friction surfaces, and each one has three cutouts in which the shifting plates rest. The coned surfaces, in addition, have numerous small radial (lubrication) grooves (see Fig. 10-33).

When assembled, a very small clearance exists between the hub, blocking ring, and the joining gear; therefore no contact is made between the coned friction surfaces. The blocking ring teeth are aligned with the internal sleeve teeth, but the blocking ring can move only one-half a tooth length to the left or right.

Operation When the transmission is in first gear and the synchronizer in neutral, all synchronizer components rotate with the output shaft, and the left- and right-hand gears are driven at different speeds by the countershaft gears (see Fig. 10-35). To shift the transmission into left drive, the engine clutch must be disengaged and then the gear shift lever should be moved. This forces the shift rail, shift fork, and the sleeve to the left. As the sleeve is moved to the left, the three inserts are also forced to the left because the insert nose rests in the internal groove of the sleeve. This forces the left-hand blocking ring coned friction surface against the coned surface of the clutch shaft gear. Their contact causes the speed of the gear to equalize (synchronize) with the output shaft speed. As speed equalization nears, the sleeve slides over the external teeth on the blocking ring and over the external teeth on the drive gear; then the collar clutch is engaged, locking the output shaft to the gear (see Fig. 10-36).

To disengage the left gear from the output shaft and to shift into right gear, the engine clutch must be disengaged as the shift fork is moved to the right. This pulls the sleeve to the right, disengaging it from the left gear.

Now the inserts lock into the internal groove of the sleeve. As the sleeve moves to the right, the right-hand blocking ring is forced (by means of the inserts) against the coned friction surface on the

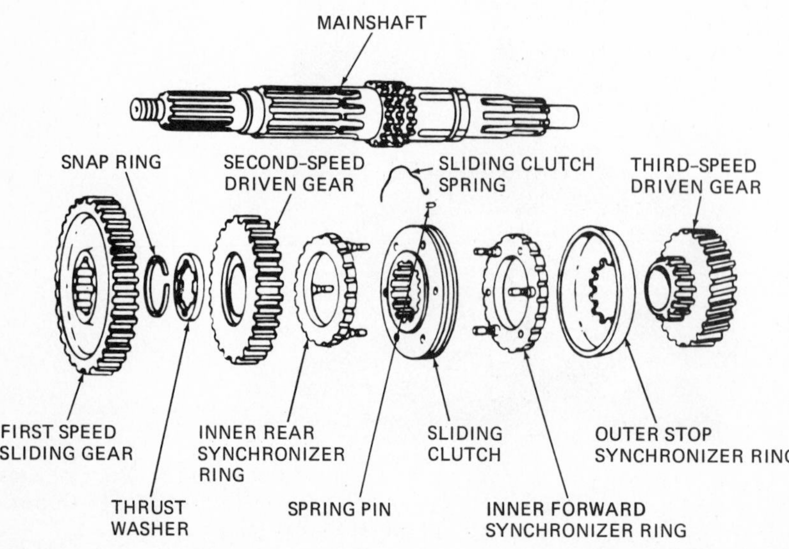

Fig. 10-34 Exploded view of a pin synchronizer. (*International Harvester Company*)

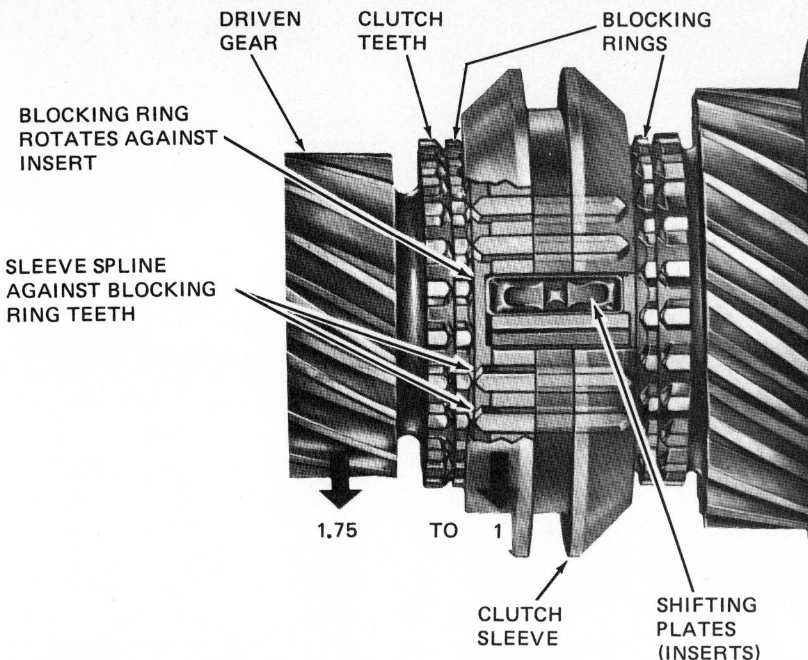

Fig. 10-35 View of cone synchronizer when in neutral. (*International Harvester Company*)

right gear. When the output shaft and gear speeds are equal, the sleeve slides over the external teeth on the blocking ring, then over the teeth on the gear, completing the engagement. **NOTE** Troubleshooting and service is covered in the material on standard transmissions (Unit 11).

PIN SYNCHRONIZER The clutch drive gear, which has internal and external splines, is splined to the output shaft and secured to it with two snap rings or is part of the main shaft. The sliding clutch gear is loosely splined to the clutch drive gear. In some cases the sliding clutch gear is loosely splined to the mainshaft. (See Fig. 10-34). The sliding clutch gear is machined with a flange, and it has six holes with slightly tapered ends. The shift fork is positioned on the flange. The aluminum alloy (or bronze) synchronizer blocking rings have coned friction surfaces which also have several radial grooves. Three pins are fastened to each blocking ring, and each pin is machined with two different diameters. The outer rings or the gears are machined with an internal coned friction surface, and the bores have internal teeth. Each outer ring is splined to the adjoining gears' male collar clutch members and the smaller-diameter ends of the blocking ring pins rest in the holes of the sliding clutch gear.

Operation When the transmission is in gear, the truck is operating, and the synchronizer (Fig. 10-34) is in neutral, the output shaft (the clutch drive gear),

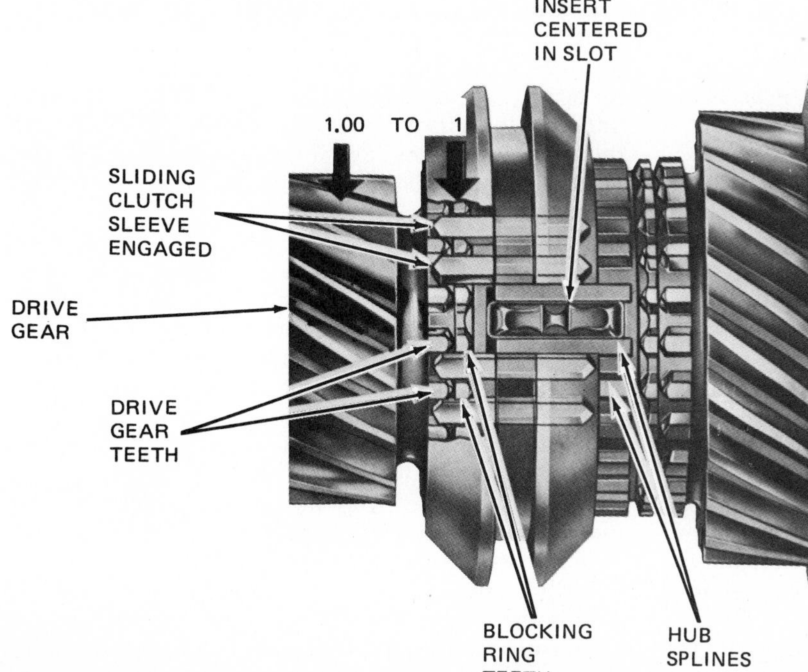

Fig. 10-36 Cone synchronizer in the engaged position. (*International Harvester Company*)

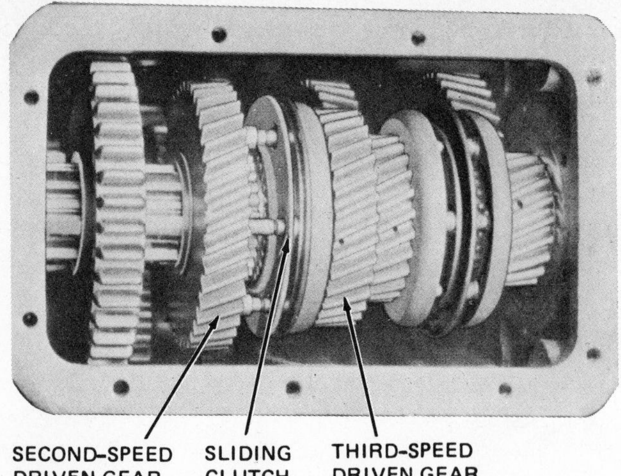

Fig. 10-37 Pin synchronizer position with transmission in third speed. (*International Harvester Company*)

the sliding clutch gear, and the blocking ring rotate as a unit. The left- and right-hand gears, as well as the outer rings, are driven at different speeds by the countershaft gears. To shift into the right-hand gear, the engine clutch must be disengaged and then the shift lever moved. This moves the shift rail, shift fork, and the sliding clutch gear to the right (see Fig. 10-37). The three holes in the sliding clutch gear come against the left-hand side of the larger-diameter ends of the three pins on the blocking ring, and force the blocking ring to the right. The two coned friction surfaces of the blocking and outer rings come into contact, resulting in equalization of speed between the third-speed driven gear and the output shaft. At this point, the sliding clutch gear holes slide over the pins, and the internal teeth of the sliding clutch gear slide over the external teeth of the gear, completing the clutch engagement.

To disengage the gear from the output shaft, the operator disengages the engine clutch and at the same time moves the shift lever to neutral. This moves the shift fork and the sliding clutch gear to the left, disengaging the sliding clutch gear teeth from the gear teeth.

One-Way (Overrunning) Clutches This third type of mechanical clutch, as the name indicates, transmits power in only one direction of rotation; when the drive rotates in the opposite direction, it automatically disengages. It is used in powershift transmissions, winches, cranking motor drives, etc. Basically, all types of one-way clutches depend on the same principle, that is, wedging the clutch members between the inner and outer races. There are three major types of one-way clutches: where the locking elements are steel balls, where they are steel rollers, and where they are sprags (cam-profiled shaped elements). All one-way clutches have an inner and outer race, with the inner race commonly fastened to the drive shaft and the outer to the driven shaft.

Sprag Clutch On a sprag clutch, the sprags are equally spaced between the inner and outer races.

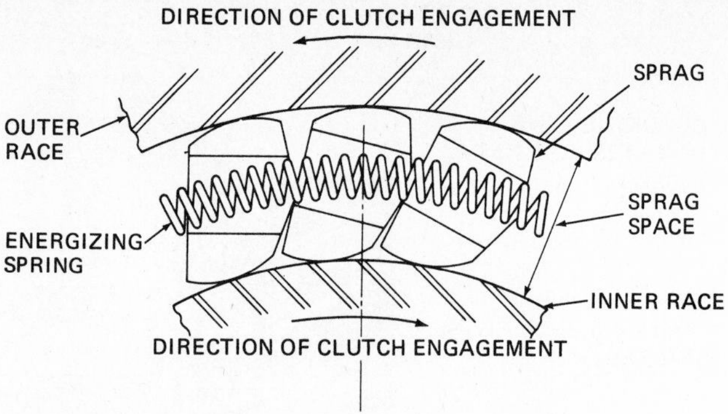

Fig. 10-38 Diagram of sprag one-way clutch.

The shape of the individual sprags determines their angle; nevertheless, they can be installed in the direction shown in Fig. 10-38, or turned 180°.

Some sprag clutches have an energizing spring to hold the individual sprags against the inner and outer race surfaces. On others, the sprags are spaced through an outer cage and an energizing spring is used.

OPERATION When the inner race is rotating in a clockwise direction, its friction surface moves the inner ends of the sprags ever so slightly in the same (clockwise) rotation. This action tilts the sprags, wedges them between the inner and outer race surfaces, and therefore forces the outer race to rotate in the same direction and at the same speed. If for some reason the outer race rotates (clockwise) faster than the inner race, the outer ends of the individual sprags move in a clockwise direction, tilting the sprags in this direction. The wedging action is then removed and no power is transmitted from the outer race to the inner race, or vice versa. If the inner race is rotated in a counterclockwise direction the inner ends of the sprags follow the direction of rotation, also removing the wedging action, and no power is transmitted to the outer race.

If the outer race is rotated counterclockwise, the outer ends of the sprags move in the same direction and are therefore wedged between the inner and outer race surfaces, driving the inner race. **NOTE** If the one-way drive is to be reversed, the sprags should be turned 180°.

Ball and Roller One-Way Clutches On these clutches, either the inner or outer race has several ramplike cutouts in which the clutch elements (rollers or balls) lie (see Fig. 10-39). A spring (which can be of different designs) is positioned in front of the roller or ball. Its purpose is to hold the elements against the ramp and race surfaces.

OPERATION When the inner race is rotated in a clockwise direction, the friction between the inner race surface and balls or rollers moves them ever so slightly in the same direction. This wedges the balls or rollers between the ramps and surface of the inner race, causing the outer race to be driven at the same speed as the inner. If the outer race is rotated faster

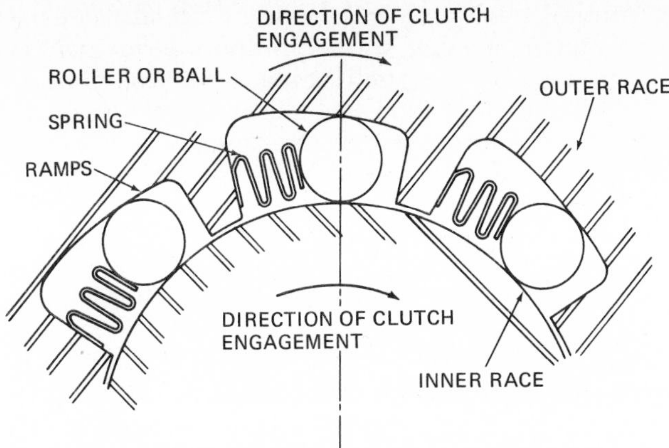

Fig. 10-39 Diagram of a ball or roller one-way clutch.

than the inner, the distance between the ramp and the surface of the inner race increases, removing the wedging action of the clutch element, and no power is transmitted from the inner race to the outer, or vice versa.

If the outer race is rotated in a clockwise direction, the friction surface of the ramp moves the balls or rollers to a slight degree in the same direction. This wedges the elements between the ramp and inner race surface, causing the inner race to be driven at the same speed as the outer race. **NOTE** A torque of about 5 lb · in [0.56 N · m] is required to engage a one-way clutch.

FLUID COUPLINGS AND MAGNETIC CLUTCHES

Fluid Couplings Fluid couplings are no longer used as engine clutches on modern off- and on-highway trucks, tractors, or machines. However, they are used to drive large converter belts, water or oil pumps, etc., where a friction clutch could not transmit the required torque. Generally speaking, fluid couplings are used today where the engine torque required is greater than 1500 lb · ft [2032.5 N · m]. See material on torque converters in Unit 12.

Magnetic Clutches Magnetic clutches are used on on- and off-highway trucks and tractors as cooling fan and air conditioning compressor hub clutches. They are also used as winch clutches and on equipment where the required engine torque is greater than 1500 lb · ft [2032.5 N · m].

Air-Conditioning Compressor Magnetic Clutch Figure 10-40 schematically illustrates an air-conditioning compressor magnetic clutch. The coil housing, which is held in place by a snap ring, is attached to the compressor shell hub. Within the coil housing is the coil, one end of which is connected to a ground and the other of which is connected over a switch or thermostatic switch circuit breaker to the positive side of the battery. A double-row angle thrust ball (clutch pulley) bearing is pressed to the

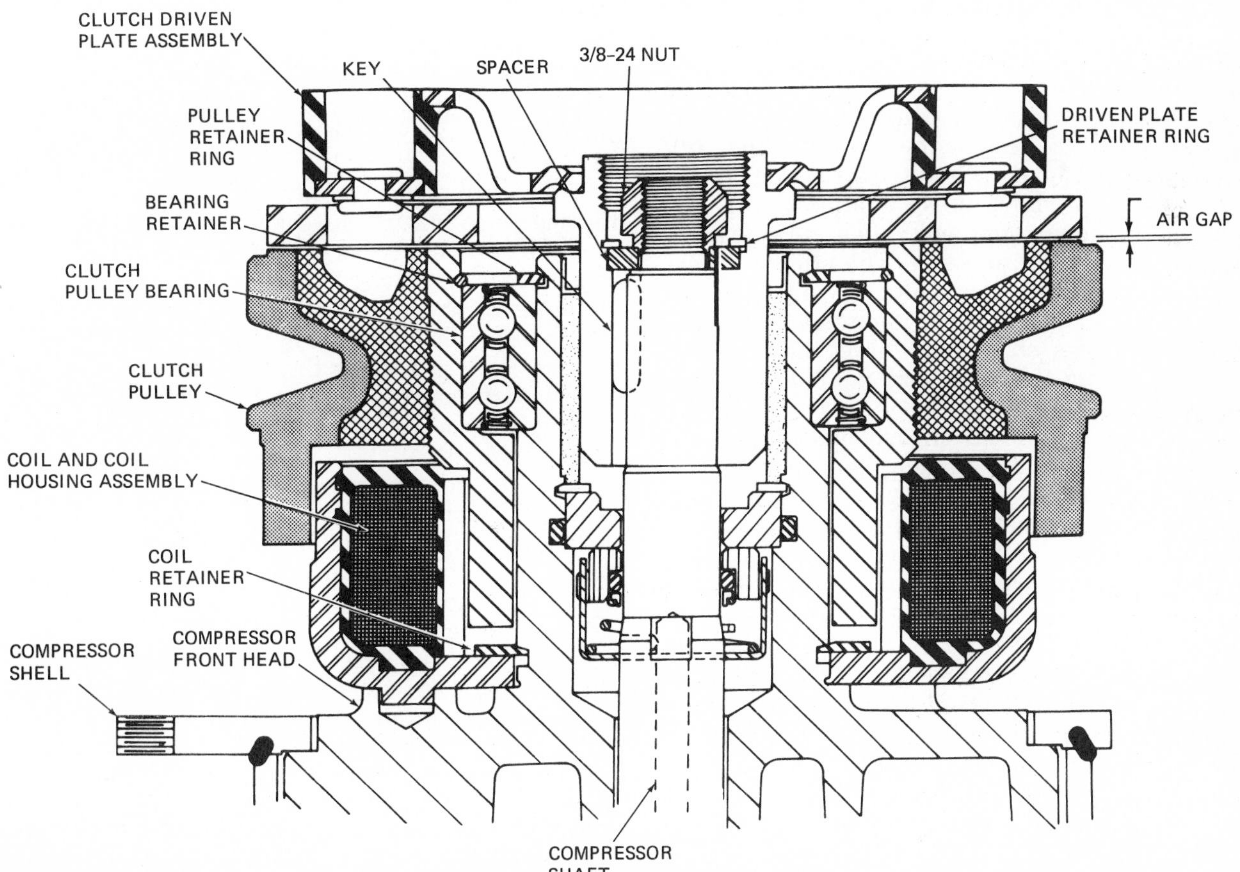

Fig. 10-40 Sectional view of a magnetic clutch and pulley assembly. (*Mack Canada Inc.*)

shell's outer hub, and the clutch pulley is pressed onto the outer bearing race. The clutch pulley and clutch pulley bearing are secured (through the bearing retainer ring) to the compressor shell hub. Inside the clutch pulley is the rotor. Positioned onto the compressor shaft and resting against the inner bore of the compressor shell hub is the seal assembly and seal seat. Both are held in position through the seal retainer. Inside the compressor shell's inner hub bore is the absorbant sleeve, within which is the clutch drive plate assembly. The latter is keyed to the compressor shaft and secured to it through a spacer, drive-plate retainer ring, and the $\frac{3}{8}$-24 nut. The right-hand side of the clutch drive-plate assembly is protected with a dust cover. The armature is attached to the drive plate assembly with special rivets and can move laterally on those rivets. When the clutch is properly assembled, there should be an air gap clearance of 0.022 to 0.057 in [0.55 to 1.44 mm] between the clutch armature and clutch pulley.

On other types of magnetic clutches, the coil is located within the clutch pulley and its ends are electrically connected to slip rings. A brush is positioned onto each slip ring. One brush is grounded, the other is connected over a switch and fused to the ignition switch. The brush holders are fastened to the compressor shell. (See material on magnetorque clutches.)

OPERATION When the engine is operating and the coil is de-energized, only the clutch pulley rotates on the clutch bearing, and the compressor shaft remains stationary. When the electric circuit is closed, current flows through the coil, and the magnetic lines of force flow from the coil to the rotor, to the armature, and then back to the rotor and the coil, completing the magnetic circuit. This action creates an electromagnet which pulls the armature against the rotor because the rotor and clutch pulley cannot move on the compressor shaft. The armature now solidly connects with the rotor, driving the compressor shaft. When the electric circuit is opened, the magnetic lines of force collapse, the armature moves away from the rotor, and the clutch pulley rotates freely.

To ensure good clutch engagement and disengagement, it is essential to have the correct (specified) air gap between the armature and rotor, and also to make sure that the armature is not bent, warped, or cracked, and that it can move on its special rivets; if the armature is damaged in any way, the clutch will slip. Clutch slippage can also be caused by low battery voltage, high circuit resistance, a shorted coil, or a damaged rotor surface. If the clutch does not engage, the problem may be an open circuit, an open coil, or a damaged switch.

Magnetorque Clutch Another type of magnetic clutch called the *magnetorque* is shown in Fig. 10-41. These clutches are used on crawler cranes, and provide the operator with a superstructure swing control. Each of these magnetorque clutches consists of an outer member splined to the intermediate reduction shaft, the shaft being supported through roller bearings on the bevel pinions. Two sets of barrel-type roller bearings, pressed into each side of the frame, support the assembly. The inner member, to which the field coil and slip rings are attached, is splined to each bevel pinion. The brush holder assembly is fastened to the nonrotating frame. Note that, in design, it is very similar to an alternator.

OPERATION Whenever the engine is operating, the alternator produces an alternating current which is rectified to direct current and controlled through the control system (diodes, resistors, voltage regulator, and capacitators). It is then directed to the manual control swing controller. The swing controller's positive leads are connected to one brush, and the negative leads to the other brush. When the engine operates and the engine clutch is engaged, the brakes must be applied, so that the sprocket can drive the swing shaft. If the operator now moves the swing lever to swing the superstructure to the left (Fig. 10-42), the swing controller moves, closing one set of points. Direct current is then directed over one brush, the slip ring, and into the field coil of the left magnetorque. The current returns to the slip ring, the other brush, the swing controller, and back to the control system. This creates magnetic lines of force and the unit becomes a rotating magnet; the inner member is magnetically clutched to the outer member and therefore forced to rotate along with it. The inner member now drives the bevel pinion, which in turn drives the intermediate swing shaft, and the intermediate swing shaft drives the swing shaft assembly. The swing pinion rotates within the internal ring gear, rotating the superstructure. See Fig. 10-43.

If the current flow is low, the magnetic lines of force are also low, thus weakening the magnetic energy. The inner member, therefore, can slip and consequently turns slower than the outer member. If the swing lever is pulled farther back, the swing controller responds by directing higher current through the field coil, increasing the magnetic lines of force, the magnetic energy, and the swing speed, but retaining a speed differential between the inner and outer members.

When the swing lever is pushed in the opposite direction in order to change to a right-hand swing or to stop the swing action, the field coil circuit to the left-hand magnetorque unit opens and the electric circuit to the right-hand magnetorque unit closes. The inner member of the right-hand magnetorque then, in effect, tries to drive the pinion, which in turn drives the intermediate swing shaft. The intermediate shaft drives the swing shaft assembly, and the swing pinion rotates within the internal ring gear and tries to force the superstructure in the opposite direction. This brings the superstructure to a smooth stop, unless the lever remains in the right-hand swing position, in which case the pinion then rotates the superstructure for a right-hand swing.

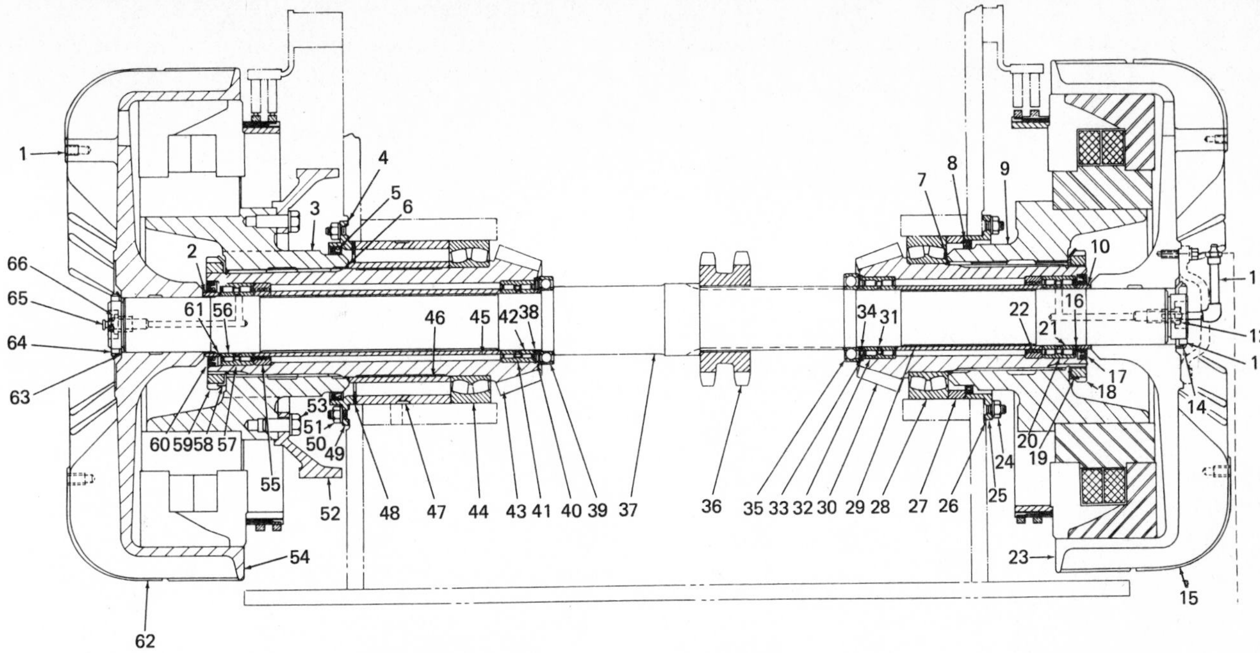

1. Capscrew
2. Spacer
3. Field member assembly
4. Gasket
5. Oil seal
6. O-ring
7. O-ring
8. Oil seal
9. Field member assembly
10. Spacer
11. Grease fitting
12. Plug
13. Bearing lock nut
14. Bearing lockwasher
15. Shroud
16. O-ring
17. Oil seal
18. Bearing lock nut
19. Bearing lockwasher
20. Bearing (outer ring)
21. Bearing (inner ring)
22. Grease retainer
23. Clutch rim
24. Lockwasher and nut
25. Bearing retainer
26. Shims
27. Spacer
28. Bearing
29. Spacer
30. Bevel pinion
31. Bearing (inner ring)
32. Bearing (outer ring)
33. Snap ring
34. Spacer
35. Bearing
36. Sprocket
37. Shaft
38. Spacer
39. Bearing
40. Snap ring
41. Bearing (outer ring)
42. Bearing (inner ring)
43. Bevel pinion
44. Bearing
45. Spacer
46. Spacer
47. Spacer
48. Shims
49. Bearing retainer
50. Lockwasher
51. Nut
52. Brake drum
53. Capscrew
54. Clutch rim
55. Grease retainer
56. Bearing (inner ring)
57. Bearing (outer ring)
58. Bearing lockwasher
59. Bearing lock nut
60. Oil seal
61. O-ring
62. Shroud
63. Bearing lockwasher
64. Bearing lock nut
65. Grease fitting
66. Plug

Fig. 10-41 Sectional view of swing clutch shaft assembly with magnetorque units.

CLUTCH TROUBLESHOOTING

Although the service life of any clutch depends on many variables, three common causes of clutch deterioration are hard or improper use by the driver or operator, constant overload on the motor vehicle, and improper maintenance (particularly in regard to adjustment and/or lubrication).

Clutch Problems Due to Improper Use If two drivers operate identical vehicles over the same haul route, or operate identical tractors on the same terrain, one may soon have much more clutch deterioration than the other. As a rule, the operator whose vehicle is constantly in for repair may be guilty of any of the following: (1) repeatedly starting the motor vehicle in one of the higher gears instead of the low gear, (2) shifting into a higher gear before the engine has reached the shift rpm, (3) starting to engage the clutch at a very high engine speed, and/or (4) keeping a foot continuously resting on the clutch pedal. In each of these instances, the clutch, during

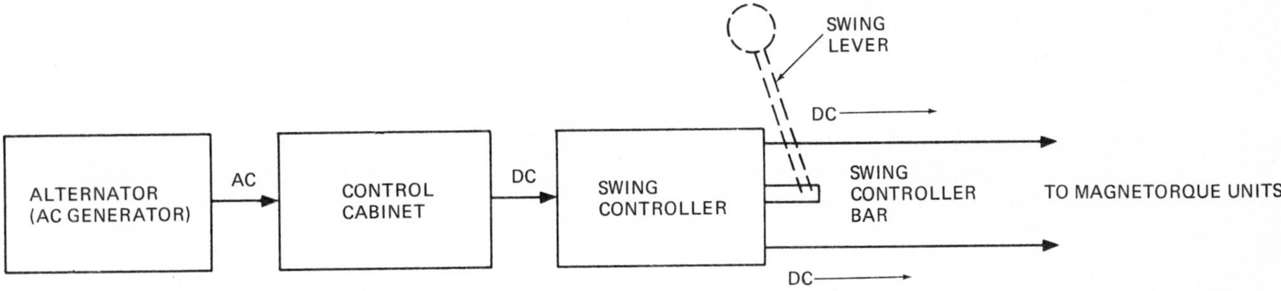

Fig. 10-42 Simplified block diagram of magnetorque system. (*Harnischfeger Corporation*)

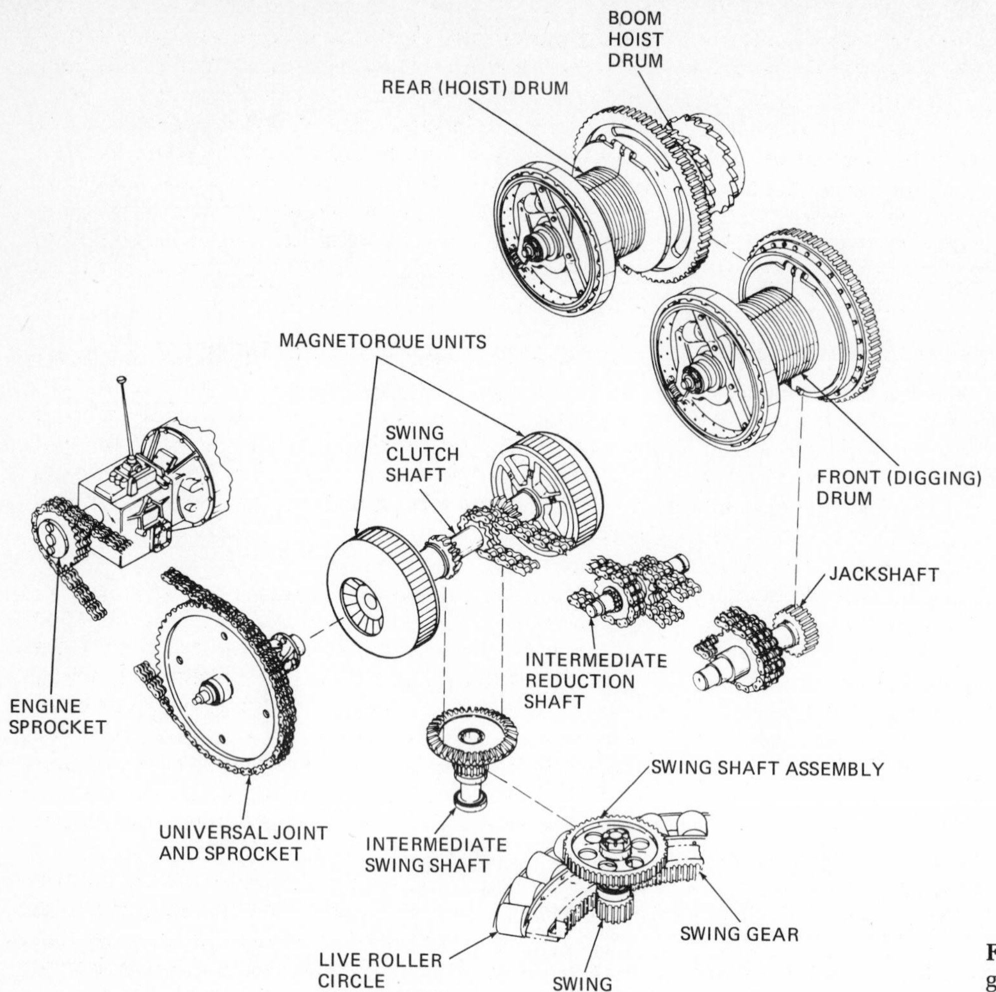

Fig. 10-43 Diagram of gear train. (*Harnischfeger Corporation*)

engagement, will create more heat than it can dissipate. As a result, the clutch temperature may reach a point where the metal flows on the friction surface of the flywheel, intermediate plate, and pressure plate, causing high spots, hard spots, and heat checks. This excessive heat can also warp or even crack the pressure plate and intermediate plate, weaken the friction disk, and reduce the energy of the pressure springs. Under such conditions, the bonding material of the clutch facing will burn and be drawn to the outside of the facing, causing loss of friction and further heat generation until the facing rapidly disintegrates.

Clutch Problems Due to Overload An overloaded vehicle, regardless of the competence of the driver, will always cause increased clutch wear since clutches are matched to the motor vehicle's kinetic capacity. When overloaded, a higher engine speed must be used to start the vehicle rolling, and therefore a greater rise in clutch temperature is experienced. Where this condition exists constantly, clutch life is obviously reduced.

Normally, the driver selects low gear and depresses the throttle only enough to raise the engine rpm without causing the engine to stall, maintaining this rpm until the clutch becomes fully engaged. Only then is the rpm increased. Under this condition, the engine may run at 900 to 1000 rpm, which shortens the clutch slip period to engage the clutch so that the heat developed during the engagement can readily be dissipated by the clutch. When the driver operates the engine during clutch engagement at say, 2000 rpm, however, the time required to engage the clutch increases, as does the temperature because of the higher rotating speed of the clutch disk. For example, say a truck-tractor is equipped with a 14.5-in [36.83-cm] double-disk clutch and the engine is operating at 1000 engine rpm during clutch engagement. The outer edge of the clutch disk would have a speed of about 3794.1 feet per minute (ft/min) [1156.5 meters per minute (m/min)]:

$$\frac{14.5 \times 3.14 \times 1000}{12} = 3794 \text{ ft/min } [1156.5 \text{ m/min}]$$

When engaged at 2000 rpm, the speed at the outer edge of the friction disk would double, that is, it would be about 7588.2 ft/min [2312.9 m/min]. However, the temperature would perhaps triple.

Clutch Failure or Reduced Life Due to Lack of Maintenance A clutch with little or no pedal free travel will cause excessive wear on the clutch release bearing, and this problem, if not remedied, will soon cause the clutch release lever to wear. Moreover, the clutch may slip. If the clutch is internally misadjusted, this may also reduce the applied force and cause slippage. If the clutch linkage is worn, the engine or the transmission mounts loose or broken, the clutch housing cracked, the brake adjustment too tight (brake drag), or the universal joint worn, clutch chatter may result. Clutch chatter is caused through excessive play or delayed motion between clutch components, so that power from the engine to the transmission is transferred with a hammering effect. This will wear down the clutch hub and the clutch drive shaft until it finally causes delayed engagement or disengagement when the clutch disk hub hangs up on its spline.

Inadequate lubrication of the clutch linkages and/or release bearing may cause an increase in the disengagement and engagement cycle, and extend clutch slippage, whereupon greater heat develops. Too much grease pumped into the release bearing may hydraulically lock the bearing, preventing it from rotating, thereby causing excessive release lever wear. None of these problems will occur if a good preventive maintenance program is followed.

Complaints Indicating Clutch Trouble As previously stated, clutch trouble is the result of many variables. It could originate within the clutch itself or from the power train components. The five most common complaints associated with the clutch are that it slips or fails to transmit power, it disengages poorly, thus causing poor shifting, it is noisy (chatters), it grabs (does not transmit the power smoothly), and/or it vibrates. After one or more complaints have been registered, you should first check the clutch adjustment and if applicable the brake adjustment. Check the clutch linkage for wear, the disengagement and engagement, and at the same time the brake action. If necessary, lubricate the linkage and release bearing and again check disengagement and engagement. Check for loose mounting bolts and/or broken mounting brackets.

CLUTCH SLIPS If the clutch slips even though the clutch linkages are not worn, do not lack lubrication, and do not bind, the cause may be worn or glazed clutch facings or cracked, heat-checked, or warped pressure plate, intermediate plate, or flywheel friction surface. Slippage can also be caused by weak pressure springs, or oil or grease on the friction surfaces. Binding of the pressure plate drive lugs or intermediate plate drive pins will hold the intermediate plate or pressure plate partly disengaged and therefore could also cause slippage.

If the clutch fails to transmit power, the cause may be that the clutch drive disk has broken loose from the disk, the clutch drive shaft is broken, or the clutch hub or clutch drive shaft splines are worn.

CLUTCH DISENGAGES POORLY If the clutch release is unsatisfactory but the clutch adjustment is correct and the clutch linkages are not worn or binding, the cause may be loose or broken engine or transmission mounting(s), loose or worn clutch facings, worn or rusted clutch hub or clutch drive shaft splines, or a damaged or worn release bearing. If the pedal is hard to depress, the cause may be a bent or cracked pressure plate or intermediate plate, or damaged or worn release sleeve collar, release bearing carrier, or friction or steel disk teeth. A grooved release fork and/or grooved wear pads on the release bearing housing or driving ring, or lack of lubrication between clutch drive shaft (or clutch drive shaft bearing cover) and release sleeve collar or carrier also leave the pedal hard to depress.

If the clutch cannot be released at all, the cause may be a bent or cracked pressure plate and/or intermediate plate, twisted or bent clutch shaft, burred or worn clutch hub or clutch drive shaft splines, bent clutch disk or friction disk, facing broken loose from the disk, or excessive misalignment between engine and transmission.

NOISY CLUTCH If the clutch is noisy (chatters) during engagement, the malfunction may be within the clutch due to worn or damaged release fork, wear pads, or clutch release linkages, or grooved, worn, or burred clutch drive shaft, clutch drive shaft bearing cover, or release sleeve. On the other hand, the release levers may be unevenly adjusted or not parallel, or the pilot bearing may be worn. The chatter also could come from any loose or broken accessory mounting brackets, including a loose or broken radiator shroud, loose or broken transmission mounting brackets, loose or cracked bell housing or clutch housing, misalignment between the engine and transmission, worn or damaged universal joints, weak or broken rear springs, loose rear axle mountings, worn or broken spring shackles, or a dragging brake.

If the clutch makes a noisy squealing sound when disengaged or during disengagement, the problem may be a worn or damaged pilot bearing or release bearing. However, if a rubbing or grinding noise occurs during engagement or disengagement, the cause may be a worn or damaged release bearing. If, during engagement and disengagement, a thumping noise is audible, the crankshaft may have too much end play or the engine or transmission mountings may be loose or broken.

If there is a rattling noise while the clutch is being engaged, look for loose clutch cover mounting bolts, too much backlash in the power train, some broken clutch disk hub springs, a broken or loose hub and/or friction ring, or a misfiring engine. If the rattling noise occurs when the clutch is being engaged or disengaged, the problem may be a worn clutch hub or clutch drive shaft splines, or a worn or damaged pilot or release bearing. In addition, the intermediate plate or the pressure plate, drive lugs, or clutch cover may have too much clearance. The return spring may be broken or missing, or there may be excessive backlash in the power train caused by a misfiring engine.

CLUTCH GRABS If the clutch grabs or does not transmit the power smoothly during engagement, the problem may be within the clutch, due to a burred, damaged, or worn clutch drive shaft, clutch drive shaft bearing cover, and/or release sleeve; the clutch pressure plate may be bent or worn, the clutch disk, hub, and clutch drive shaft splines may be twisted, the clutch drive shaft may be twisted, or the pressure plate or intermediate plate may be bent or twisted. Clutch grab can also originate from misalignment between engine and transmission, too much backlash in the drive train, worn or loose clutch linkages, or a binding clutch pedal.

VIBRATION If vibration is noticeable when the clutch is engaged, the cause could be unbalanced power train components, misadjusted drive line angle, misalignment of drive line components, worn universal joints, loose or broken engine or transmission mounts, or out-of-balance clutch and/or flywheel. If the vibration occurs only while the clutch is being engaged and disengaged, the cause may be a bent clutch drive shaft, worn clutch drive shaft splines, or misalignment of power train components.

Misalignment of power train components could occur from a loose flywheel, dirt or burrs between flywheel and crankshaft mounting surface, a damaged or broken pilot bearing, cracked or broken flywheel housing, loose or broken engine or transmission mount, worn or damaged clutch drive shaft bearing, and/or bent frame rails.

Clutch Service Because there are so many varieties of engine and PTO clutches, it is not possible to outline a service procedure applicable to them all. Furthermore, it would be impractical to detail each one, particularly since service manuals are produced for this purpose. Nevertheless, there are numerous generalities applicable to replacing any clutch assembly, and these will be covered.

REMOVING THE CLUTCH The first step should be to determine whether the clutch trouble is within the clutch assembly or whether it originates from other parts of the motor vehicle. If you are sure it is within the assembly, refer to the applicable service manual for the procedures by which to remove the clutch, and follow them precisely.

Park the motor vehicle or machine where there is plenty of room in which to work and where a hoist or crane can be utilized to lift the heavier components from it. Next, if applicable, block the hydraulic equipment in such a fashion that you have easy access for the removal of the transmission and clutch. Apply the parking brake or block the wheels or tracks. Remove the battery ground cable and attach a sign "PERSON WORKING ON MACHINE" to the dashboard.

Disconnect the drive line, tape the bearing to the universal cross, and secure the end to the frame. Remove the clutch linkage and, if necessary, the hydraulic lines, in order that the transmission can be removed. Support the transmission's weight, align and position the floor jack, and clean the floor area so that the jack can be rolled rearward without interference; otherwise attach a sling and hoist to the transmission. Remove two mounting cap screws or bolts, and install two guide bolts to guide and maintain the transmission alignment during the removal (that is, until the clutch drive shaft is clear from the clutch disk hub splines). By omitting this step you could damage or distort the clutch disk.

When the transmission is removed, mark the position of the clutch to the flywheel, remove two cap screws, and replace them with two long guide bolts. On larger clutches, the pressure plate force must be removed from the clutch disk facing; otherwise it would be very dangerous to remove the clutch cover from the flywheel. On coil spring clutches, insert hold-down cap screws in the holes of the clutch cover and screw them into the threaded holes of the pressure plate (see Fig. 10-44). Tighten them evenly to compress the pressure spring and thereby remove the pressure plate force from the clutch facing. On pull clutches you may first install a clutch disk aligning tool to prevent damage to the clutch release levers and release sleeve retainer. Then disengage the clutch. Place a piece of wood 0.75 in [19 mm] thick on each side between the release bearing housing and clutch cover (flywheel ring), and then reengage the clutch (see Fig. 10-45). This will hold the pressure plate away from the clutch disk. Next, remove two clutch cover (flywheel ring) cap screws and install two guide bolts. On larger clutches, attach a sling and hoist to the clutch to lift it from the flywheel. This will compensate for your loss of strength while working in an awkward position. Remove the cap screws, the clutch cover with pressure plate, the first clutch disk, the intermediate plate,

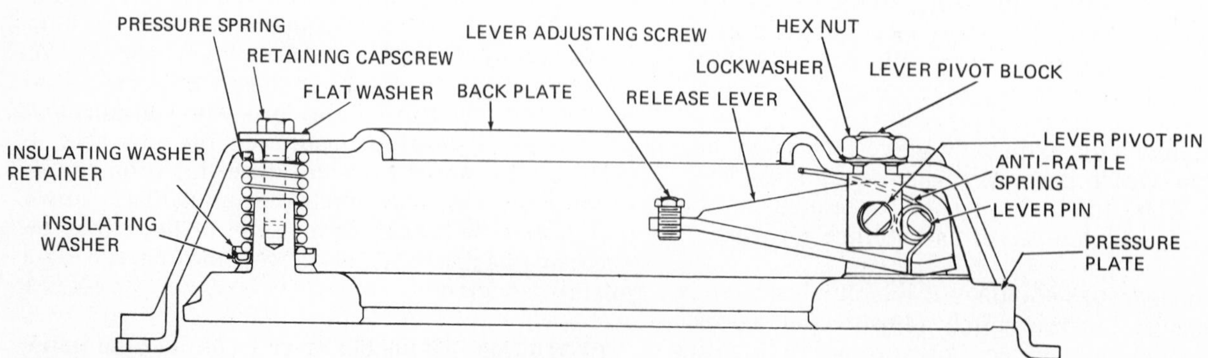

Fig. 10-44 Sectional view of a multicoil spring clutch with retaining cap screw installed. (*International Harvester Company*)

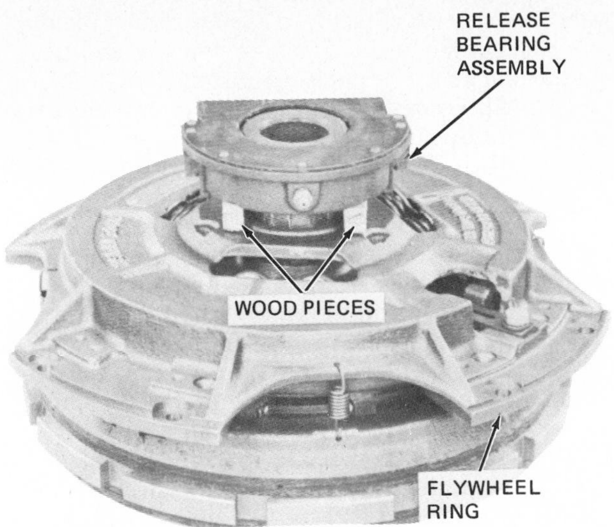

Fig. 10-45 View of angle spring clutch with the pieces of wood in place.

and the second clutch disk, and then disassemble the clutch.

INSPECTION, CHECKS, AND MEASUREMENTS Inspect and measure the clutch components and compare your measurements with the service manual specifications.

Check for wear and damage Check the clutch cover (flywheel ring) for distortion and cracks, the flanges for straightness, the pins and cap screw holes for wear, and the threaded holes for damage. Check the pressure plate slots for wear and, if applicable, check the adjusting ring for cracks. Check the pin holes for wear, and the clutch cover and adjusting ring threads for damage and wear. Inspect the eyebolt assembly for damage or worn ends and check the bores. As a general rule, the eyebolt assembly should be replaced.

Inspect the flywheel, the pressure plate, and the intermediate plate for heat checks, cracks, and

Fig. 10-46 A damaged flywheel that must be replaced. *(Lipe-Rollway Corporation)*

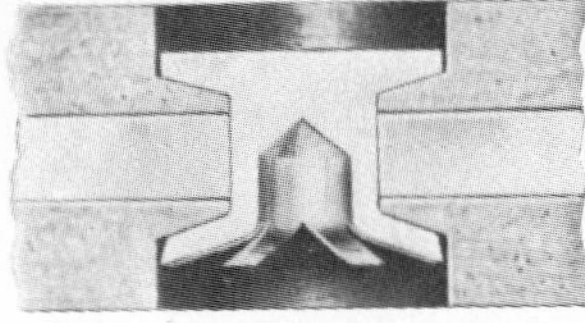

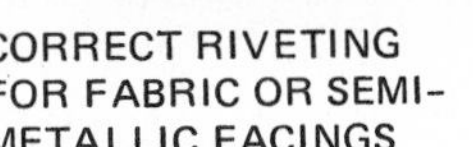

Fig. 10-47 Correct clutch disk riveting. *(Lipe-Rollway Corporation)*

scored friction surfaces (see Fig. 10-46). Measure them for straightness. Check the intermediate plate drive lugs or slots for wear. If the pressure and intermediate plate friction surfaces can be restored through grinding, make certain that no more than the recommended amount of material is removed; otherwise you will lose some clutch heat dissipation capability.

Inspect the clutch disk for worn or damaged splines; check for distorted, loose, cracked, or broken disks. If the clutch disk has a flexible center, check the torsional springs and the slots for wear. When replacing the clutch facing, use a suitable riveting machine to remove and install the rivets, and use the proper riveting technique (Fig. 10-47). See also material on brake lining replacement.

Check the clutch release bearing assembly for wear or damaged bushings, and check the wear plates or lugs and the bearing support housing cover for wear. **NOTE** Release bearings are normally replaced.

Inspect the clutch release linkages and yoke holes for worn or damaged bores. Check the pivot points for wear, and the rod levers and linkages for damage, bends, or cracks.

Inspect the flywheel friction surface for wear, taper, and heat checks. Check the intermediate drive pins for wear, and measure the alignment with a square and feeler gauge (see Fig. 10-48). Check the threaded bores for worn or damaged threads, and at this time check the ring gear for worn, damaged, or broken teeth.

If the clutch housing or flywheel must be replaced, the components must be aligned and redowelled. If the old clutch chattered or vibrated, the flywheel and clutch housing must be checked for alignment.

Measure runout To check the flywheel housing bore runout, attach a dial indicator holder (or place a magnetic base) onto the crankshaft or flywheel. Attach a dial gauge to it so that the pointer rests squarely on the inner surface of the bore (Fig. 10-49). Zero the dial and then turn the crankshaft one complete revolution. Record readings at 90° intervals. The reading at any point must not exceed an average concentricity (runout) tolerance of 0.005 in [0.12 mm]. Next, check the flywheel housing face runout. To do so, relocate the dial gauge so that the pointer rests against the flywheel housing flange (see Fig. 10-49). Force the crankshaft forward to remove end play; then zero the dial. Turn the crankshaft one

Fig. 10-48 Aligning drive pins in flywheel using mechanist square and feeler gauge. (*Lipe-Rollway Corporation*)

complete revolution and record readings at 90° intervals. **NOTE** Make sure the crankshaft is placed forward when taking the readings. The average allowable maximum face runout is about 0.010 in [0.25 mm].

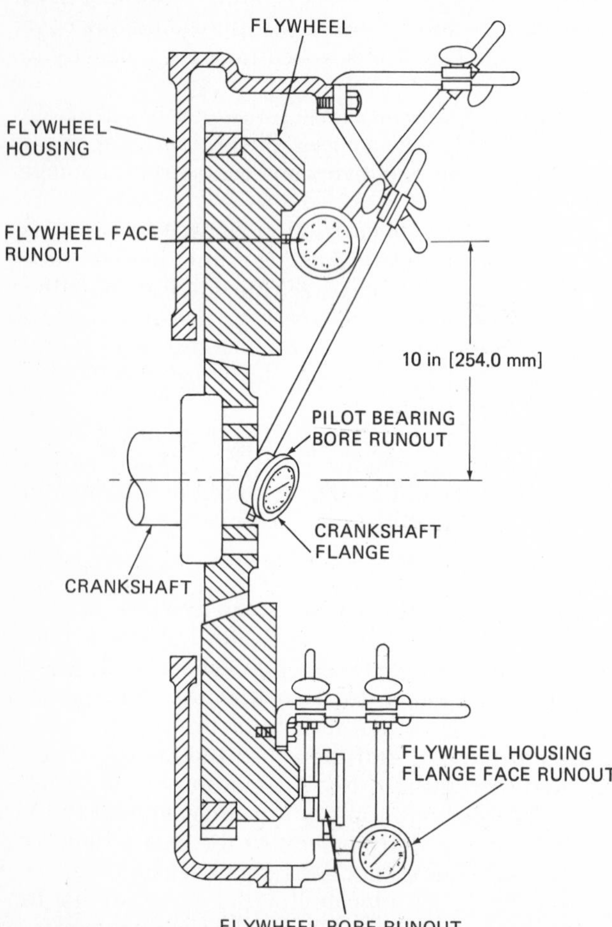

Fig. 10-49 Measuring flywheel–to–flywheel-housing alignment.

To check the flywheel face runout, attach the dial indicator holder to the flywheel housing and position the dial gauge squarely against the flywheel face (Fig. 10-49). Force the crankshaft forward and zero the dial, following the measuring procedure previously outlined. The average maximum runout should not exceed 0.0005 in [0.012 mm] for each 1 in [25.4 mm] of radius. For example, when the pointer of the dial is 10 in [254 mm] from the center of the crankshaft, safe engine and clutch operation dictates that the maximum runout should not exceed 0.005 in [0.127 mm].

To check the pilot bearing bore runout, relocate the dial gauge so that the pointer rests squarely against the pilot bearing bore (see Fig. 10-49). Runout should not exceed 0.005 in [0.127 mm]. If it does, however, the flywheel and/or flywheel housing must be repositioned and redowelled.

CLUTCH INSTALLATION Correctly position the lubricated pilot bearing into the flywheel bore. Install the first clutch disk, but, if it is not centrally positioned on the hub make certain that the shorter clutch hub side faces in the direction outlined in the service manual, or as marked on the clutch disk. Next, install the intermediate plate and measure the clearance between the drive pin and slots if not previously measured. Next, install the second disk and, with a sling and hoist, lift the clutch against the flywheel and install three guide bolts to hold the assembly to the flywheel. Insert the aligning tool, a pilot shaft, or a clutch shaft, into the first and second clutch hubs and then into the pilot bearing bore (see Fig. 10-50). Install and tighten the clutch cover (flywheel ring) cap screws progressively and evenly to the specified torque. Make certain the scribed marks on the flywheel and pressure plate are aligned. Remove the retaining cap screws so that the pressure

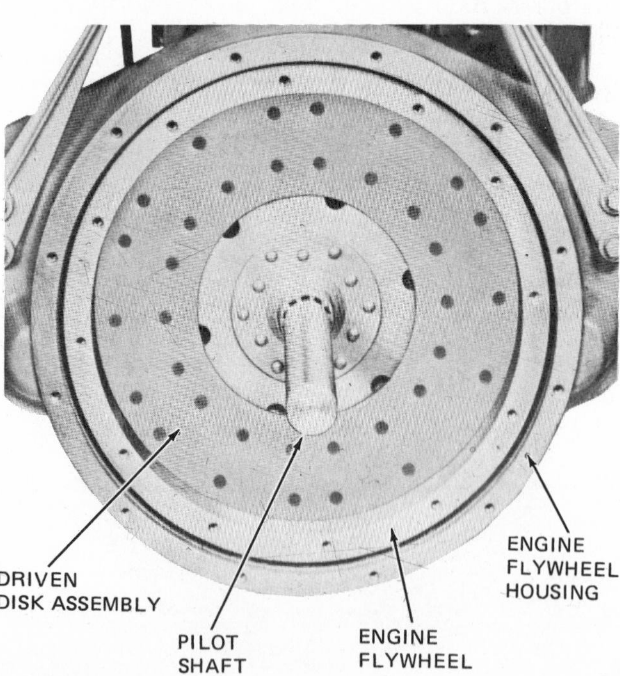

Fig. 10-50 Use of pilot shaft when installing clutch. (*International Harvester Company*)

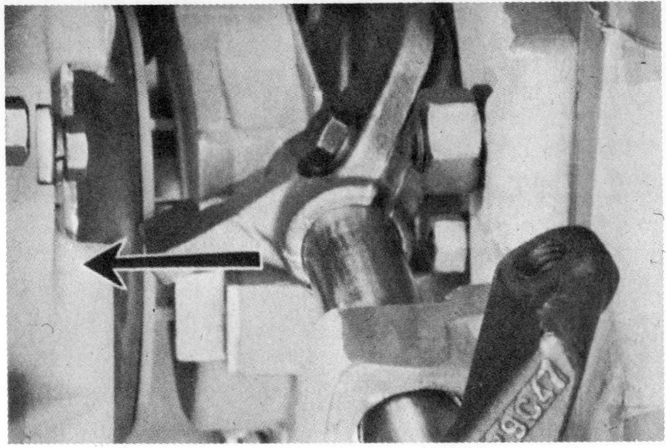

Fig. 10-51 Guiding yoke finger over release bearing assembly. (*International Harvester Company*)

plate forces the friction disks and intermediate plate against the flywheel. If necessary, readjust the release lever height to the specification given in the service manual. **NOTE** If the clutch is of a pull-type design, the wood pieces should fall free during the tightening of the cover cap screws; otherwise, remove them.

Remove the aligning tool. Lubricate the clutch drive shaft lightly with the recommended grease to prevent rusting, fretting, and corrosion, and to ease the transmission installation. Install two alignment bolts, place the transmission in gear, raise the transmission into position, align it with the flywheel housing, and then push the transmission toward the flywheel and guide the clutch drive shaft into the bore of the release bearing assembly. All the while, check and constantly adjust the squareness and alignment between transmission and flywheel housing as you push the transmission (that is, the clutch drive shaft) into the clutch hub splines and pilot bearing bore.

NOTE You may have to turn the transmission output shaft in order to engage the clutch drive shaft splines with the clutch hub splines.

If the clutch is a pull type, you must at the same time engage the yoke with the release bearing housing, as well as keep an eye on the assembly during the installation (see Fig. 10-51). **CAUTION** Do not exert force or use bolts to draw the transmission against the flywheel housing, as this will distort the clutch disks. If the clutch drive shaft will not enter the clutch hub or pilot bearing freely, check squareness and alignment. You may have to remove the transmission again in order to check the clutch-disk–to–pilot-bearing alignment. After the transmission is installed, make the necessary clutch adjustment and grease the release bearing.

Review Questions

1. (*a*) What is the purpose of a clutch? (*b*) List the different types of clutches.
2. List seven capabilities an engine clutch must have.
3. Outline the differences between the various kinds of (*a*) flywheels, (*b*) clutch disks, (*c*) pressure plates, and (*d*) release mechanisms. (*e*) State the main purposes of the mechanisms listed in (*a*) through (*d*).
4. Describe the methods used to increase the torque transmission of a clutch assembly.
5. (*a*) Explain why some clutch assemblies use a clutch brake. (*b*) Which component is affected when the clutch brake is engaged?
6. Regardless of which type of pressure plate is used, the clutch must be correctly adjusted in order to function properly and prevent decreased service life. Outline the methods used to adjust the clutch pedal free play and the clutch brake for (*a*) an angle spring clutch and (*b*) multispring clutch.
7. When is it advantageous to use (*a*) a wet-type clutch or (*b*) a multidisk wet-type clutch in preference to a single- or double-disk dry-type clutch?
8. List the factors which could cause both incorrect clutch engagement and disengagement. What factors would contribute to undue clutch noise?
9. Explain the mechanical action of the overcenter clutch (Fig. 10-23) when the operator moves the clutch lever to achieve clutch engagement.
10. (*a*) In which applications will you find band or shoe-type clutches? (*b*) Why do these applications use these types of clutches?
11. (*a*) List the three groups into which mechanical clutches may be divided. (*b*) Describe how each group achieves clutching (engagement and disengagement).
12. What is the underlying principle of magnetic clutch engagement?
13. List two factors, other than maintenance, which will prolong the service life of any friction clutch.
14. List the preventive maintenance checks and/or adjustments which will prolong the service life of a friction clutch.
15. List the general procedural steps and safety precautions to be taken when removing an engine clutch.
16. List the checks which must be made and/or measurements which must be taken before installing the clutch assembly of the (*a*) flywheel and (*b*) bell or clutch housing.
17. List the usual steps required to install a double-disk clutch which uses an angle spring pressure plate.

Unit 11
Standard Transmissions

A transmission is a device that is used to transmit power from the engine or motor to the output shaft and to increase the engine or motor torque. Power can be transmitted and the torque multiplied by any one of four basic methods: by belts and pulleys (sheaves), by chain(s) and sprockets, by a set of gears, or by using fluid (torque converter).

The latter two methods are the most commonly used; however, all four methods apply the same principle—that is, the lever principle: For the same force, a longer lever will result in a greater movement or torque. In a transmission, the "levers" are usually the diameters of gears or pulleys. The principle is applied by making the diameter of the driven pulley greater than that of the drive pulley, or by giving the driven sprocket or gear more teeth than the drive sprocket or gear. The torque converter, which is a special transmission with the lever built in, is covered in the next unit.

The difference between the drive- and driven-pulley diameters, or between the number of teeth on the drive or driven sprocket or gear, provides the reduction ratio (increasing torque).

The Need for Transmissions You may have wondered why manufacturers prefer to build a transmission to increase torque, rather than building an engine having a higher torque to operate the motor vehicle, machine, etc. One reason is that an engine at low speed has low torque, and a specific rpm is required to develop its maximum torque. But this rpm would be too high to start engagement with a transmission. Therefore the engine speed must be lowered, which means the engine torque is also lowered. Thus a reduction unit (transmission) is used to increase the motor vehicle torque and allow the engine to accelerate to higher speeds. When the engine reaches maximum torque speed and the transmission has additional reduction gears, the driver can select a higher speed ratio thereby increasing the output shaft's speed; however, this reduces the torque. For example if the engine develops a torque of 50 lb · ft [67.8 N · m] at 1000 rpm, and a total reduction of 6:1 is built into the truck-tractor or machine, then the torque at each axle shaft is (50 × 6)/2 = 150 lb · ft [203.3 N · m]. However, when the total reduction is 150:1, then the torque to each axle shaft (assuming it has a single drive axle) would be (50 × 150)/2 = 3750 lb · ft [5081.3 N · m]. If it has a tandem drive axle, the torque to each wheel would be 937.5 lb · ft [1270.3 N · m]. Assume that, at maximum engine torque speed, the motor vehicles ground speed is 2 mph [3.22 km/h]. If the transmission were shifted into another gear and the total gear reduction were 75:1, then the ground speed would be doubled to 4 mph [6.4 km/h], and the torque to each wheel would be reduced to half of the previous value, that is, to 468.8 lb · ft [635.2 N · m].

The highest reduction at present is on a specially designed 12 × 8 motortruck, where the reduction ratio is 341:1 and the engine has a torque of 1250 lb · ft [1693.8 N · m]. Therefore, the maximum torque at each driving wheel is 26,640.6 lb · ft [36,098.0 N · m] (1250 × 341 = 426,250 lb · ft of torque altogether, and 426,250 ÷ 16 = 26,640.6 lb · ft at each driving wheel).

Transmissions of various designs and ratios are built to match a particular engine torque, and to provide the motortruck, truck-tractor, or machine with the speed ranges required to allow it to perform according to its intended usage.

MECHANICAL (STANDARD) TRANSMISSIONS

We shall use the term "mechanical transmission" to mean a device which uses gears to transfer the engine power, and which is able to change the torque and speed ratio, and/or reverse the direction of travel of the motor vehicle or machine.

Commonly the transmission is the second unit of the power train, and is therefore attached to the flywheel housing. However, on off-highway machines or tractors, more than one transmission may be used, in which case their locations are governed by the intended use of each particular transmission.

Types of Transmissions Mechanical transmissions can be divided into two major groups: special-purpose transmissions and speed range transmissions. The special-purpose transmissions are identifiable by name; for example: swing transmissions—used to rotate a superstructure; propel transmissions—used to transmit the power to the tracks; crowd transmissions—used to pivot the dipper handle; transfer cases—used to transfer the power from the transmission to the front and rear drive axles; forward-reverse (shuttle) transmissions—used to change the direction of tractor travel; PTO transmissions—used to transmit the engine power to an accessory machine; and the machine deck of a crane, shovel, or excavator—the purpose of which is to transmit the engine power to the individual winches, swing transmissions, and propel transmissions.

The second group, that is, the speed range transmissions, are designed with from two to twenty speed ranges. These transmissions are subdivided into groups according to the number of forward speed ranges they permit and the method used to engage the forward gears with the output shaft. The

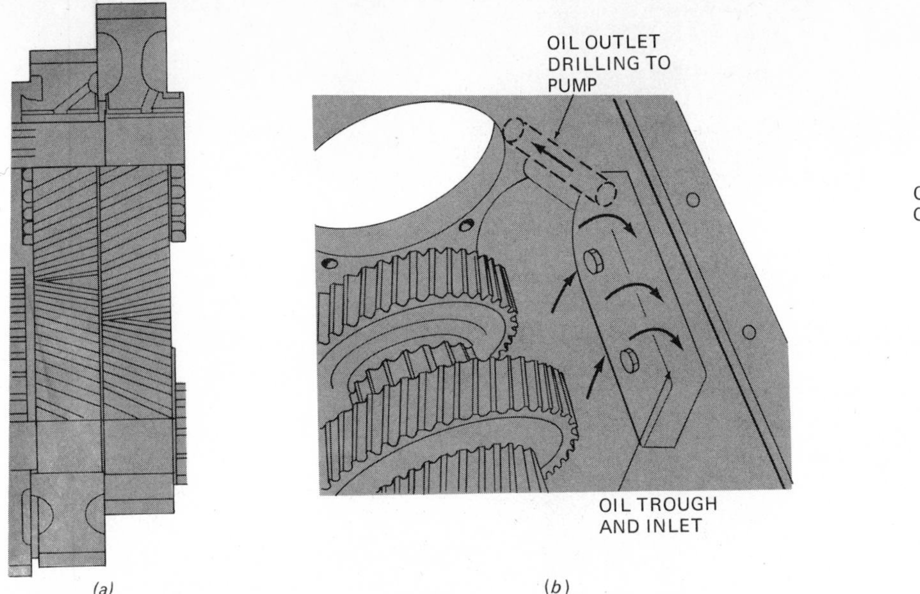

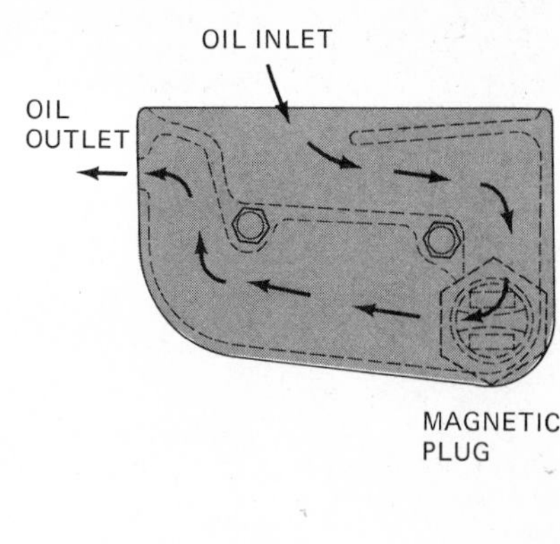

Fig. 11-1 (*a*) Oil passages in transmission gears. (*b*) Channels cast onto transmission walls direct lubricating oil. (*c*) Cleaning the transmission oil.

forward speed transmission groups are three-, four-, five-, six-, nine-, ten-, eleven-, thirteen-, fourteen-, fifteen-, sixteen and twenty-speed types; the methods used to engage the gears are (1) sliding-gear transmission, (2) collar shift transmission, and (3) synchronized transmission.

The collar and synchronized transmissions are further divided into: single countershaft, twin countershaft, and triple countershaft.

Since this text has previously introduced you to swing, propel, crowd, and PTO transmissions, to a machine deck of a crane and shovel, and to electrically and hydraulically driven propel transmissions, the remainder of this unit will be restricted to the other major types of transmissions.

Transmission Lubrication Of the several different methods of lubricating bearings, bushings, clutches, and shafts, the most common is splash lubrication. When the engine is operating, whether the transmission is in neutral or in gear, the countershaft gears (on a constant-mesh transmission), or the oil slinger (on a sliding-gear transmission), throw(s) [splash(es)] the oil onto the areas to be lubricated. In some cases, deflector shields are used to direct the splash in a specific direction and to ensure that unsplashed bearings receive lubrication.

In another lubrication method, channels cast on the inside walls of the transmission direct the oil to predetermined areas. To provide positive lubrication to the special steel bushings or needle bearings which support the driven gears on the main shaft, the gears or gear hubs have one or more diagonal passages leading to the bearing or bushing (see Fig. 11-1*a*). When the engine is operating and the transmission is in neutral or in gear, the rotation of the main shaft and countershaft gears forces the oil inward, thereby lubricating the bearing or bushing. If the gear has one passage or more leading from the root of the gear tooth to the bearing, oil is forced through this passage each time this tooth meshes with the countershaft gear tooth; or if the gear has one or more passages leading from the side to the bearing surface, oil is forced through this passage into the bearing whenever the transmission is operating (see Fig. 11-1*b*).

A third lubrication method is through a vane pump (see material on triple countershaft transmissions later in this unit).

To rid the oil of metallic particles, one or more magnetic plugs are used. Some transmissions additionally include an oil filter bolted to the PTO opening of the transmission (see Fig. 11-1*c*) to remove nonmetallic particles. In this case, the oil is splashed into the filter housing by the fourth/third-speed driven gears and drained through the filter before it reenters the transmission through the center opening.

Transfer Cases These transmissions are of the constant-mesh design and use either straight-cut or helical gears. They are among the simplest transmissions and may be of either the single-reduction or the two-speed design. Each design has a collar clutch to engage or disengage the drive to or from the front-to-rear drive axle.

The transfer case shown in Fig. 11-2 is used on an articulated wheel-type loader. The transfer case housing is bolted to the transmission housing; the transmission output drive gear is splined to the transmission output shaft, and the output shaft is supported by roller bearings in the transfer case housing. Its idler gear is supported by tapered roller bearings on the idler shaft which is fastened to the housing. The front output shaft (supported by ball bearings) has the output drive gear and the output flange splined to it. The parking brake shoe assembly is attached to the backing plate, and the brake drum is bolted to the output flange. The rear output shaft

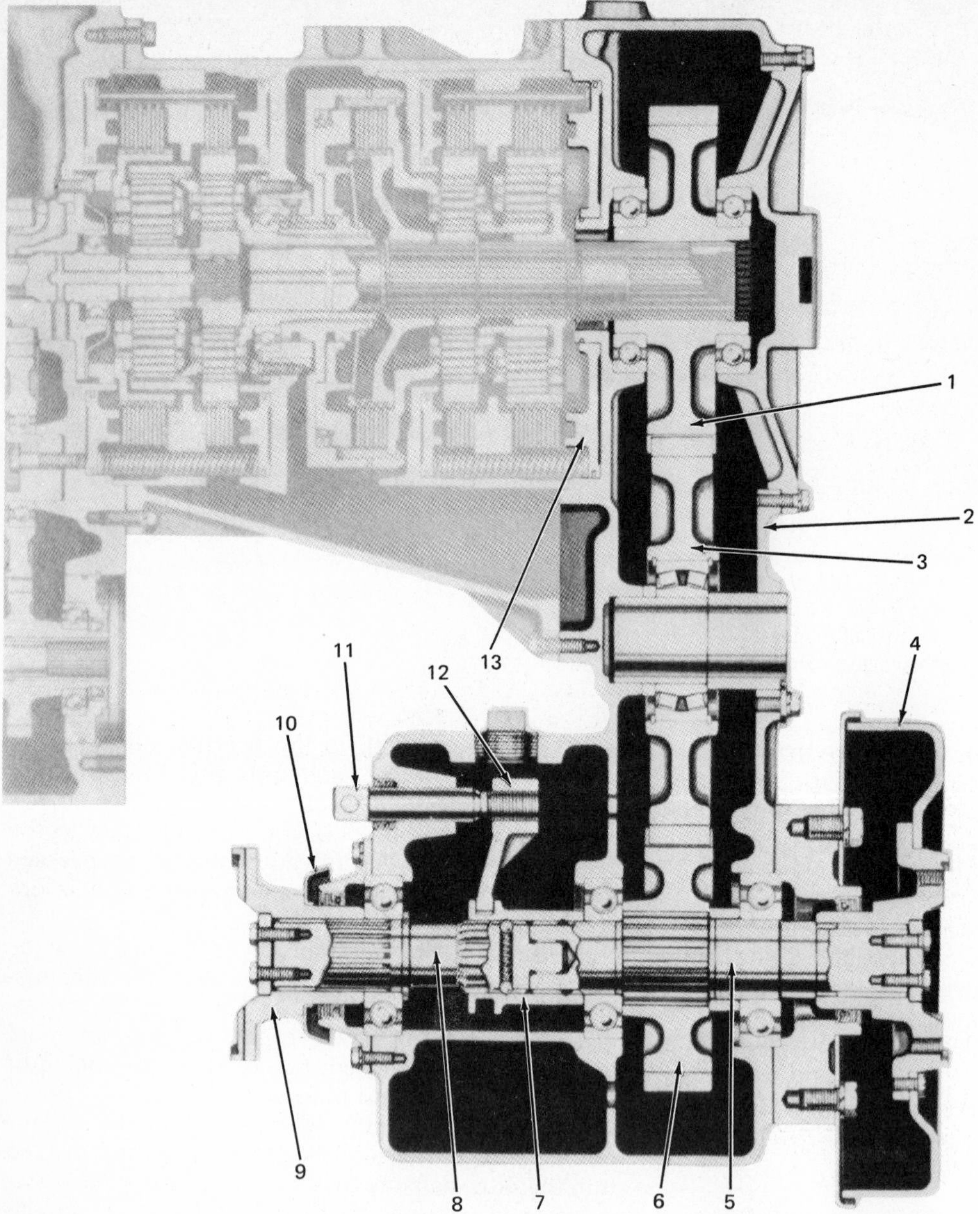

1. Output drive gear
2. Housing
3. Idler gear
4. Brake drum
5. Front output shaft
6. Output driven gear
7. Disconnect clutch
8. Rear output shaft
9. Output flange
10. Dust shield
11. Shift fork shaft
12. Shift fork
13. Low range piston

Fig. 11-2 Sectional view of a transfer case using straight-cut gears. (*Terex Division of General Motors Corporation*)

is supported on the left-hand side by a roller bearing, and on the right-hand side by a bushing that is pressed into the bore of the front output shaft. The left-hand end of the front output shaft and the right-hand end of the rear output shaft are splined. Consequently, when the disconnect clutch is positioned (engaged) as shown in Fig. 11-2, the rear output shaft and front output shaft are clutched (splined) together.

When the transmission is in gear, its output shaft drives the output drive gear, which drives the idler gear. The idler gear drives the output shaft driven gear, which in turn drives the rear and front output shaft. **NOTE** When one idler gear is placed between the drive and a driven gear, the direction of rotation of the drive and driven gears is the same—that is, when the drive gear rotates clockwise, the idler gear rotates counterclockwise, and the driven gear rotates clockwise. See Fig. 11-3.

To disengage the transmission of power to the rear output shaft, either the torque to the transfer gear must (for a split second) be reduced, or the loader transmission must be placed into neutral. The shift fork shaft, the shift fork, and the disengage clutch can then be pulled (as a unit) to the right, causing the internal splines of the clutch to disengage from the external splines of the rear output shaft. All engine torque is then transferred onto the front output shaft and from there onto the front drive axle.

Two-Speed Transfer Case The two-speed transfer case shown in Fig. 11-4 is used on a large 6 × 6

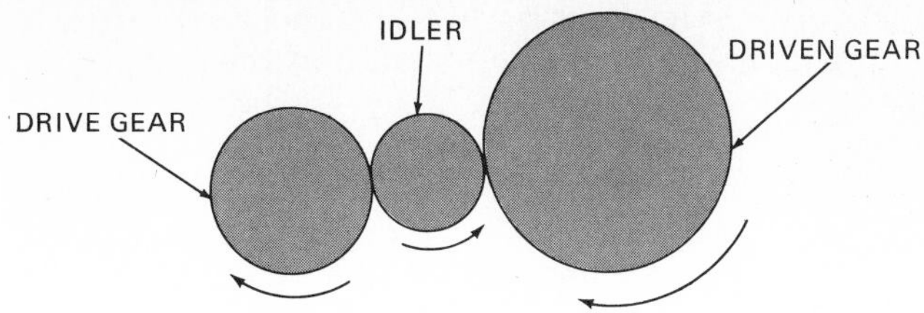

Fig. 11-3 Use of an idler gear so that the drive and driven gears rotate in the same direction.

motortruck. Since it is of the constant-mesh transmission design, it uses helical gears to increase the torque transfer and to reduce gear noise. A jaw clutch is used to engage and disengage the positive drive to the front axle, and a collar clutch is used to engage the high and low ranges. A planetary gear positioned between the rear drive shaft and the front drive shaft serves as a center differential and automatically compensates front-wheel–to–rear-wheel speed differential. See Fig. 11-5. All shafts are supported by tapered roller bearings, but the right-hand end of the front drive shaft is supported by a bushing which is pressed into the bore of the rear drive shaft.

The main shaft and the low-range gear form one piece. The high-range gear is keyed to the shaft which has the drive yoke splined to its left-hand side. Attached to the right-hand side is a small gerotor pump whose inner rotor member is keyed to the shaft. The countershaft has two individual splines—one on which the collar clutch is posi-

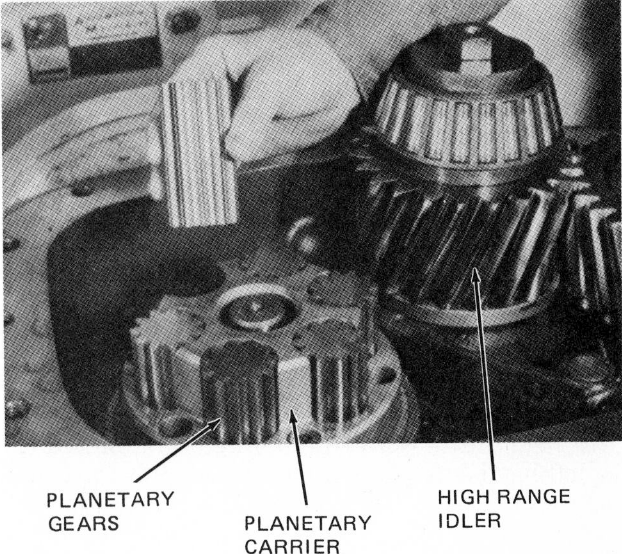

Fig. 11-5 View of the planetary carrier and gears. (*Mack Canada Inc.*)

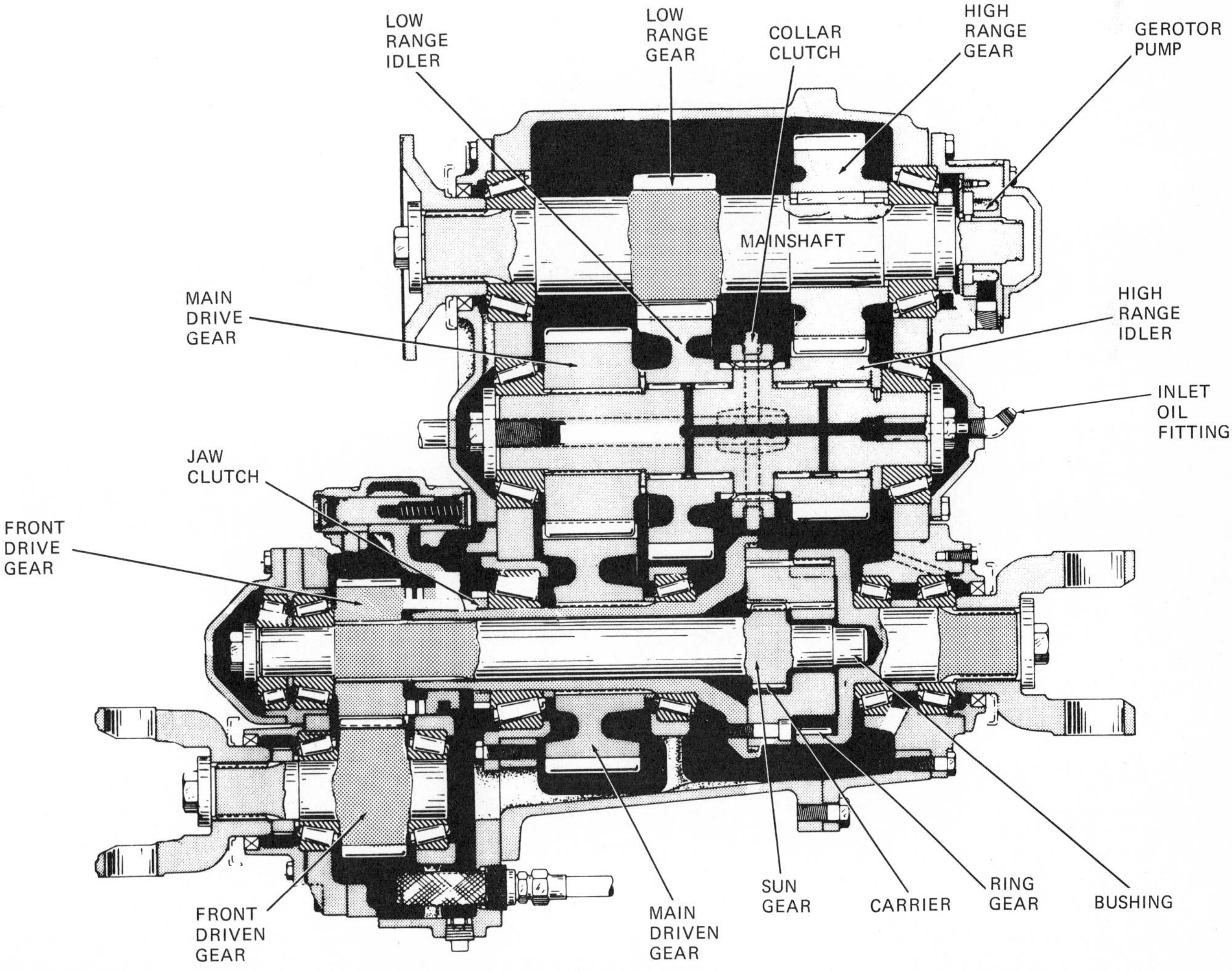

Fig. 11-4 Sectional view of a two-speed transfer case using helical gears. (*Mack Canada Inc.*)

tioned, and the other which splines the main drive gear to it. Both high- and low-range idler gears are supported on the countershaft by cage needle bearings. The main drive shaft also has two individual splines—one to which the main driven gear is splined, and the other to which the male jaw clutch member is loosely splined. The planetary carrier housing is splined and secured with bolts to the flange of the main drive shaft. Individual planetary gears are positioned in the six bores of the planetary carrier housing. The rear drive shaft is cast with the planetary ring gear, and the gear drive yoke is splined to the right-hand side of the shaft. The front drive shaft and the planetary sun gear form one piece. The sun gear meshes with the six planetary gears, and they mesh with the ring gear. Splined to the left-hand side of the front drive shaft is the front drive gear. The front driving shaft and gear are one piece, and the front drive yoke is splined to it. The oil line fitting, with screen, is threaded into the transmission housing and is connected with an oil line to the pump inlet. The pump outlet is connected with the oil filter (not shown) and from the oil filter it is connected to the inlet fitting, which is attached to the countershaft.

OPERATION When the main transmission is in gear and the engine is operating, the (transfer) main shaft rotates at the same speed as the main transmission's output shaft. When the high- and low-range collar clutch is in neutral, only the high- and low-range driven gears rotate on the stationary countershaft.

As the main shaft rotates, the inner rotor of the gerotor pump rotates, creating a low pressure, and the atmospheric pressure forces the oil into the pump inlet. The outlet oil is pumped through the filter and is then directed to the countershaft, where it flows through the center- and cross-drilled passages to lubricate the needle bearings of the high- and low-range driven gears. **NOTE** The other bearings are lubricated through splash lubrication.

When the high/low-shift rail moves to the left, the shift fork and the female clutch collar move to the left and engage with the male collar on the low-range gear. Conversely, when the shift rail moves to the right, it engages with the high-range gear. In each case the rotation from the main shaft is transmitted to the countershaft and main gear. However, when engaged with the high-range gear, the countershaft rotates faster than when engaged with the low-range gear. The main drive gear transmits the rotation to the main driven gear, which transmits it to the main drive shaft, rotating the planetary carrier housing, and the carrier gears transmit the power to the ring gear and sun gear. The ring gear drives the rear drive shaft, and the sun gear (which is part of the front drive shaft) drives the front drive gear, which in turn drives the front driven shaft.

If extreme traction conditions exist, the driver shifts the front jaw clutch to direct air from the air brake reservoir into the piston area, and forces the shift rail, shift fork, and male clutch jaw to the left. The male clutch jaw then meshes with the female jaw on the front drive gear. This action locks the planetary carrier housing to the planetary sun gear, and both the front driving shaft and the rear drive shaft rotate at equal speed.

Sliding-Gear Transmission These types of transmissions are no longer used on today's on-highway motortrucks or tractors, which now have either collar shift or synchronized transmissions. Sliding-gear transmissions are used only on off-highway tractors or machines. A four-speed sliding-gear transmission, using a sliding reverse idler, and having a high/low-range transmission attached to it, is shown in Fig. 11-6. Note, however, that the range transmission uses a collar clutch.

The outer (range) shaft and sliding-gear shaft are supported by ball bearings and roller bearings. The countershaft, however, is supported by tapered roller bearings because the pinion forms part of it and the shaft must therefore absorb side thrust. The inner (PTO) shaft passes through the hollow range shaft and onto the PTO transmission. High and low drive gears are splined to the range shaft, and the high and low driven gears are supported on the sliding-gear shaft by needle bearings. The clutch collar is positioned between the two gears and is loosely splined to the sliding-gear shaft. The one-piece first and second gear, and the one-piece third- and fourth-speed drive gear, are loosely splined to the sliding-gear shaft. The first-, second-, third-, and fourth-speed driven gears are splined to the countershaft, also called the *pinion shaft*. The idler shaft is solidly fixed to the transmission housing, and the reverse idler gear is supported by needle bearings on the (idler) shaft. The location of the reverse idler shaft as shown in Fig. 11-6 is inexact, in that, when actually installed, the idler gears are so located that, when the gears are shifted into reverse, they mesh with the first-speed driven gear on the countershaft and with the second-speed sliding gear.

OPERATION When the shift levers are in neutral, none of the four-speed transmission gears are in mesh and the sliding collar clutch of the range transmission is not engaged with any gear. When the engine is operating, the power is transmitted to the PTO and range shafts and the high- and low-range drive gears drive the high- and low-range driven gears. Because the clutch collar is not engaged, no power is transmitted to the sliding-gear shaft.

If the operator shifts into either high or low range, say for instance into low range, he or she depresses the clutch pedal to disengage the engine clutch. After a few seconds, the range shaft stops but the power of the PTO shaft is not interrupted. The operator then moves the shift lever which moves the shift rail, shift fork, and collar, and the female collar engages with the male collar on the low gear. Power is then transmitted through the collar onto the sliding-gear shaft, but no power is transmitted to the countershaft of the main transmission because no sliding gear is in mesh with the countershaft gears.

If the operator now elects to shift into first gear, again he or she has to disengage the engine clutch, wait a few seconds, and then move the shift lever.

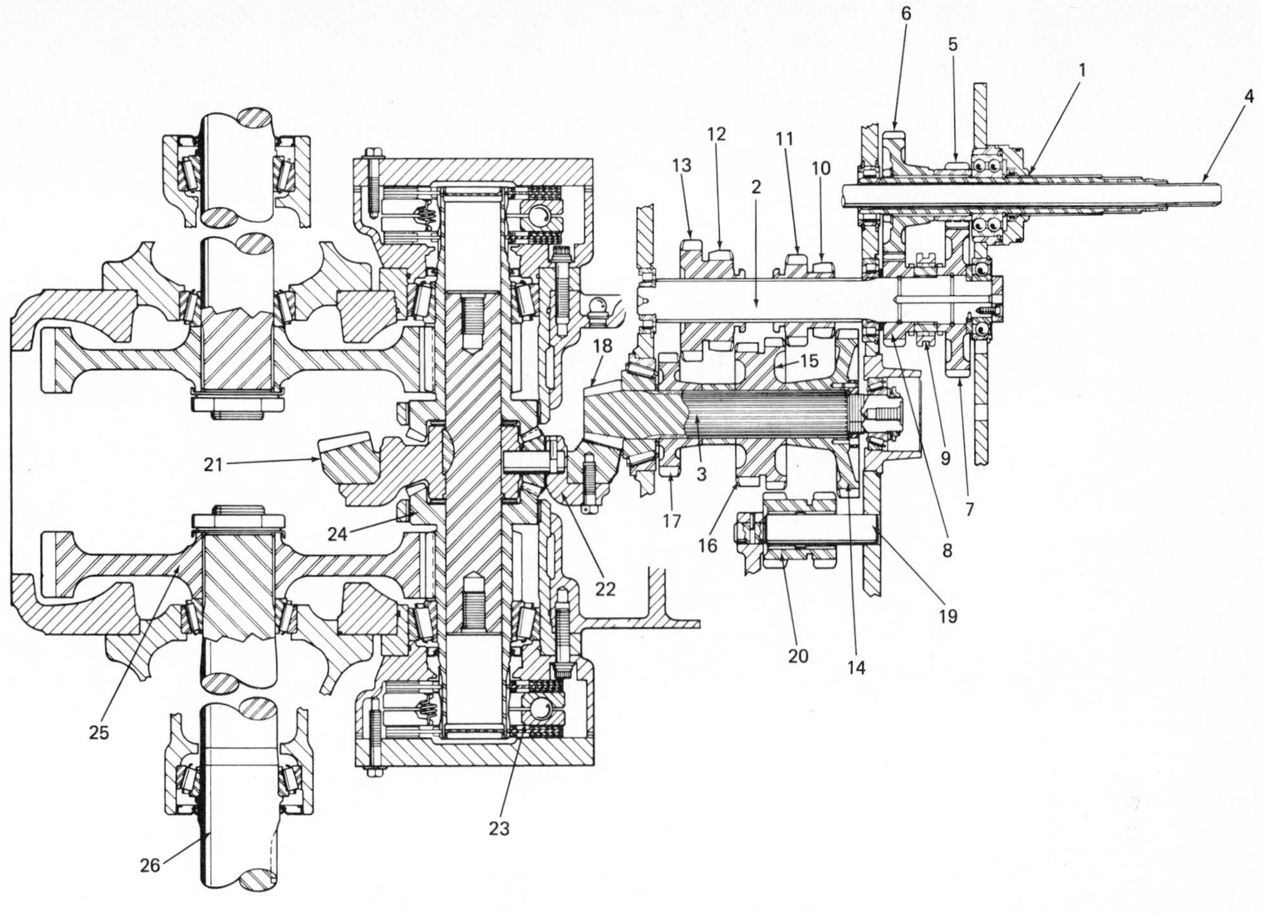

1. Range shaft
2. Sliding gear shaft
3. Connector shaft
4. PTO shaft
5. Low range drive gear
6. High range drive gear
7. Low range driven gear
8. High range driven gear
9. Collar clutch
10. First speed drive gear
11. Second speed drive gear
12. Third speed drive gear
13. Fourth speed drive gear
14. First speed driven gear
15. Second speed driven gear
16. Third speed driven gear
17. Fourth speed driven gear
18. Pinion gear
19. Reverse idler shaft
20. Reverse idler gears
21. Crown gear
22. Differential housing
23. Differential disk brake
24. Side gear and drive pinion
25. Bull gear
26. Drive axle

Fig. 11-6 Sectional view of a tractor power train. (*J I Case Company Agricultural Equipment Division*)

This moves the shift rail and shift fork and the first-speed drive gear to the right, and the drive gear meshes with the driven gear. When the clutch is engaged, the power is transmitted from the range shaft to the low-range drive gear, to the low-range driven gear, over the clutch collar, onto the sliding-gear shaft, to the first-speed drive gear, to the first-speed driven gear, and onto the countershaft and pinion, which drives the crown gear.

When the operator elects to change the tractor direction from forward to reverse, he or she disengages the engine clutch, applies the brakes, and moves the shift lever to neutral. This action pulls the first-speed sliding gear out of mesh with the first-speed driven gear. The operator then moves the shift lever to select reverse. This moves the right-hand gear of the reverse sliding gear into mesh with the first-speed gear on the countershaft, and at the same time moves the left-hand gear of the reverse sliding gear into mesh with the second-speed sliding gear. When the clutch is now engaged, the power from the low-range gear is transmitted to the low-range driven gear, to the collar, onto the sliding gear shaft, to the second-speed sliding drive gear, and onto the left- and right-hand gears of the reverse idler, whereupon the right-hand gear of the reverse idler drives the first-speed gear on the countershaft.

NOTE To identify which set of gears is first speed, which is second, which is third, etc., look at the diameter of the gear set—the smallest drive gear and the largest driven gear always form the lowest speed range of the transmission; and the largest drive gear and the smallest driven gear always form the highest speed range of a sliding-gear transmission. However, if the collar or synchronized shift transmissions have overdrive, this would not be so.

Mechanical Forward-Reverse (Shuttle) Transmission One of the forward-reverse constant-mesh transmissions using a cone synchronizer shift clutch is shown in Fig. 11-7. **NOTE** A range transmission is bolted to it. To show the reverse idler support more clearly, the meshing position of the left-hand countershaft gear with the output shaft gear had to be omitted from the illustration. The input shaft and

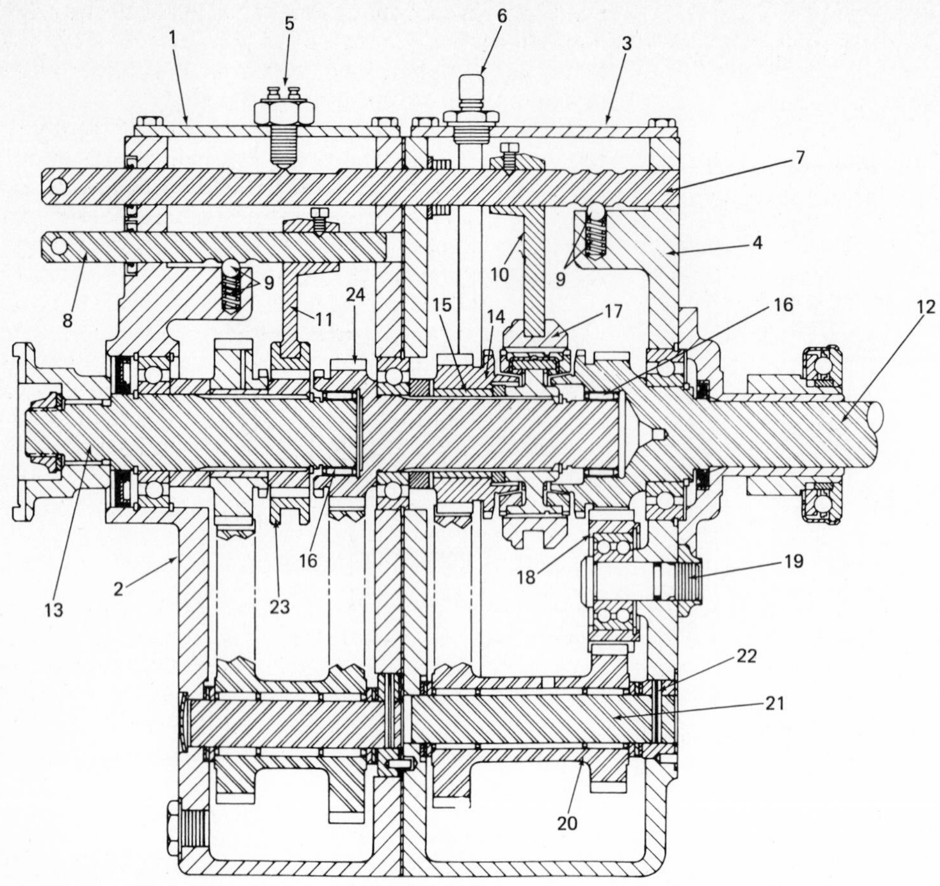

1. Range housing cover
2. Range housing
3. Shuttle housing cover
4. Shuttle housing
5. Neutral start switch
6. Breather
7. Shuttle shift rail
8. Range shift rail
9. Detent balls and springs
10. Shuttle shift fork
11. Range shift fork
12. Input shaft and gear
13. Output shaft
14. Output gear
15. Bushing
16. Needle bearings
17. Cone type synchronizer
18. Idler gear
19. Idler shaft
20. Countershaft
21. Connector shaft
22. Thrust bearing
23. Collar clutch
24. Low range drive gear

Fig. 11-7 Sectional view of a shuttle and range transmission. (*J I Case Company Agricultural Equipment Division*)

the input shaft gear form one piece; and the output shaft and the range transmission input shaft gear form one piece. The input shaft is supported by ball bearings in the forward-reverse gear housing, and the right-hand side of the output shaft is supported by needle bearings, located in the bore of the input shaft. The output gear of the forward-reverse transmission is supported on a specially designed bushing that is splined to the output shaft. The cone synchronizer hub is splined to the output shaft and secured to it with two snap rings. The idler shaft is bolted to the transmission housing, and the idler gear is supported on the shaft with a double-row ball bearing. The countershaft is press-fitted into the bores of the housing, and the gear set is supported by two needle bearings. End thrust is absorbed by needle thrust bearings.

OPERATION When both forward and reverse transmissions and the range transmission are in neutral, the shift rail of the forward-reverse transmission has raised the neutral starting switch plunger and it has closed the switch contact. The detent ball, as well as the range transmission shift rail detent ball, rests in the neutral detents of the shift rails. If the ignition switch is now activated, it closes the solenoid circuit to the cranking motor, thereby cranking the engine. However, if the starting switch is misadjusted, or the forward-reverse transmission is in gear, the solenoid circuit of the cranking motor is open and therefore no cranking is possible.

When the engine is operating and the forward-reverse synchronizer is in neutral, the input shaft gear drives the reverse idler, the idler drives the countershaft gears, and the left-hand countershaft gear drives the output shaft gear, but no power is transmitted to the high/low-range transmission.

If the operator shifts into forward, the forward-reverse shift rail moves to the right and the detent ball locks into the forward detent on the shift rail. At the same time the synchronizer sleeve engages with the clutch collar teeth on the input gear. The power is now transmitted from the input shaft clutch collar, to the synchronizer sleeve, to the synchronizer hub, and to the output shaft, whereupon all gears in the range transmission rotate but no power is transmitted to the speed range transmission. If the high/low-range transmission is placed into high range, the power from the forward-reverse output shaft is transmitted from the clutch collar teeth to

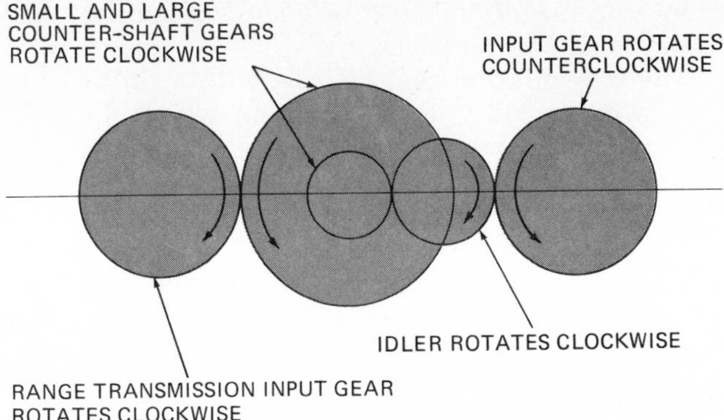

Fig. 11-8 Power flow when shuttle transmission is in reverse.

the range transmission high-range gear and output shaft, driving the input shaft of the main transmission through a drive line.

If the operator selects low range, the range shift rail fork and clutch collar move to the left, the ball detent locks into the low-range detent in the shift rail, and the clutch collar teeth engage with the teeth on the range transmission drive (input) gear. Power is now transmitted from the forward-reverse output shaft and range transmission input gear to the countershaft gears, from the left-hand countershaft gear to the output shaft gear, and over the clutch collar to the range transmission output shaft.

If the operator wishes to change the tractor's direction of travel, she or he disengages the engine clutch and moves the shift lever to the right, which moves the forward-reverse shift rail, shift fork, and synchronizer sleeve to the left. The detent ball locks into the reverse shift rail detent, and the synchronizer sleeve engages with the clutch collar teeth on the input shaft gear. Power is now transmitted from the input shaft gear to the idler, then to the countershaft gears, and the left-hand countershaft gear then drives the output shaft gear. From there the power is transmitted to the clutch collar teeth and to the synchronizer sleeve, and from there to the synchronizer hub, to the output shaft, and to the range input shaft gear. See Fig. 11-8.

Four-Speed Tractor Transmission The four-speed transmission shown in Fig. 11-9 is used on a backhoe in conjunction with the forward-reverse and high/low-range transmission previously covered. The transmission is bolted to the transaxle assembly

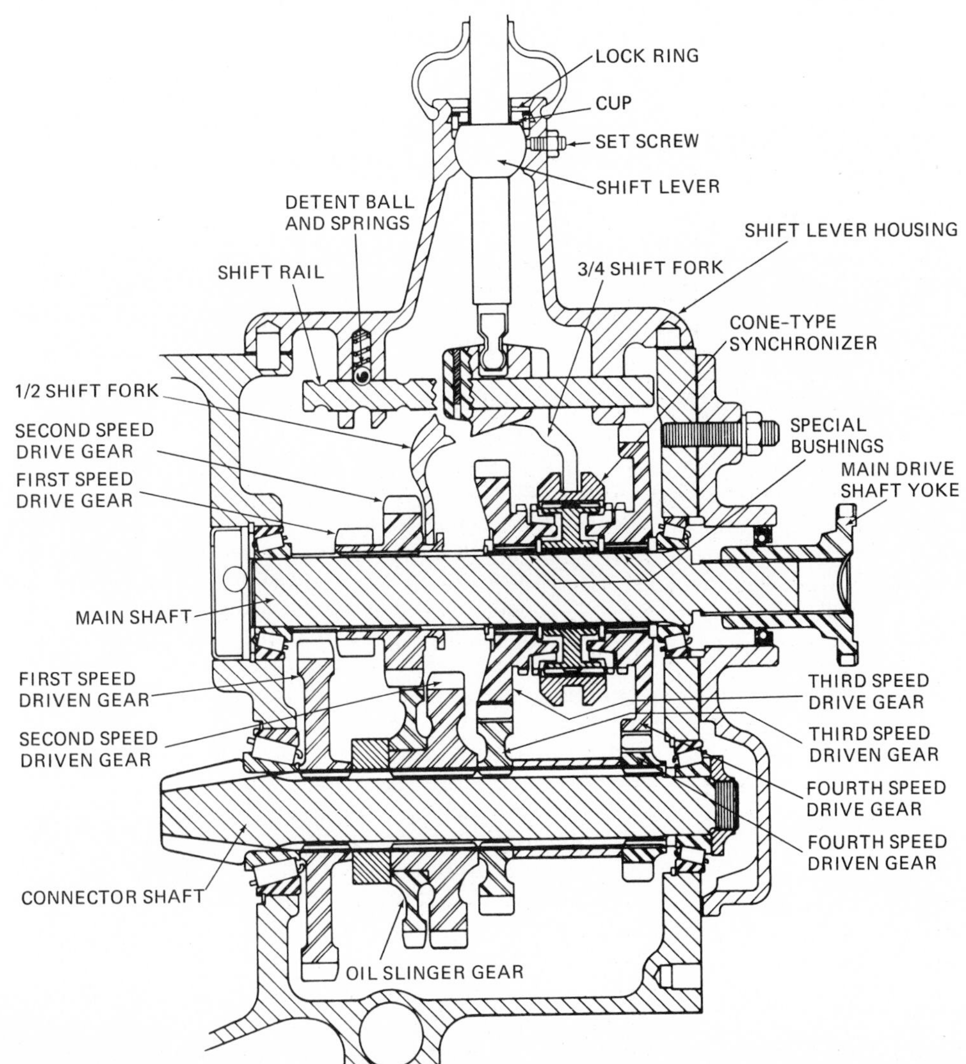

Fig. 11-9 Sectional view of a four-speed tractor transmission. (*J I Case Company Agricultural Equipment Division*)

so that the countershaft pinion meshes with the crown bevel gear. A transaxle assembly is one in which the crown gear and differential are located. Both the countershaft and main shaft are supported by tapered roller bearings, and selective spacers are used to adjust the preload.

This transmission is of a combination synchronized and sliding-gear design. The third- and fourth-speed drive gears are in constant mesh with the third- and fourth-driven gears on the countershaft. The first-speed and second-speed drive gears are engaged by sliding them into mesh with the first- and second-speed driven gears. A cone synchronizer clutch is used to engage third and fourth speeds. The main shaft drive yoke is connected with the range transmission through a drive line. Splined to the countershaft and spaced by spacers (from left to right) are the first-speed driven gear, the second-speed driven gear, and the fourth-speed driven gear. The oil slinger is positioned on the hub of the second-speed driven gear. The third- and fourth-speed drive gears are supported on specially designed steel bushings which are splined to the main shaft, and the synchronizer hub is located between the bushings. All three parts are secured to the shaft with snap rings. The first- and second-speed sliding clutch gear is loosely splined to the left-hand side of the main shaft.

The third- and fourth-speed shift fork rests in the sleeve groove, and the shift rail is supported in the bores of the transmission cover. The first- and second-speed shift fork rests in the side groove on the second-speed drive gear. Its shift rail is also supported in the transmission cover. Each shift rail has three detents and, when the transmission is in neutral, the detent balls rest in the center rail detent, holding the shift rails in the neutral position. A shift interlock plug is positioned between the two shift rails (see Fig. 11-10). Its purpose is to prevent, under normal circumstances, both shift rails from moving at the same time. If one shift rail is moved from its neutral position, the interlock plug is forced to the left or right and the plug end is forced into the groove on the second shift rail, locking the shift rail to the transmission cover.

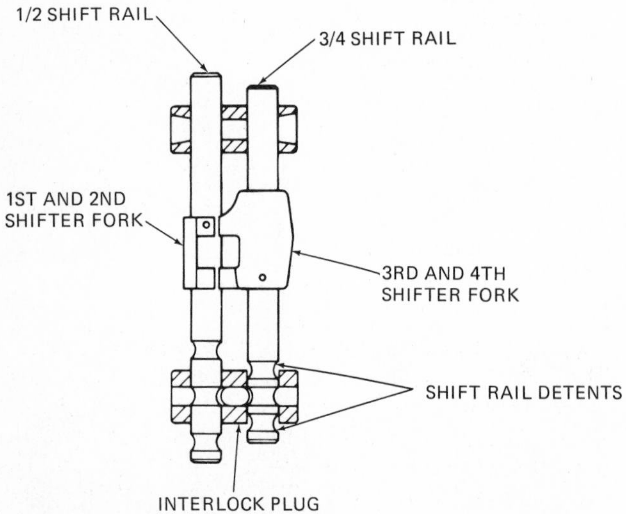

Fig. 11-10 Schematic view of a shift mechanism.

The transmission cover is cast with a shift tower that is machined with a socket, in which the ball socket of the hand shift rests. A shift lever seat and snap ring are used to hold the ball socket to the housing socket. A vertical groove machined into the ball socket provides a rest for the retainer screw, thereby preventing the shift lever from rotating. When in neutral, the lower shift lever ball socket rests between the cutouts of the two shift forks. Operation (shifting and power flow) is similar to the sliding-gear transmission previously covered.

Four- and Five-Speed Motortruck and Truck-Tractor Transmissions These transmissions are used on motortrucks and truck-tractors which have an engine torque ranging between 250 and 800 lb · ft [338.7 and 1084.0 N · m]. The differences between a transmission built to transmit a torque of 250 lb · ft [338.7 N · m] and one built to transmit 800 lb · ft [1084.0 N · m] are several. The strength of the transmission housing or case varies, as do the types of bearings used to support the clutch shaft, main shaft, countershaft, and idler shaft. There is also a difference in the diameter of the shafts and the width of the gears.

NOTE You should also be aware that where constant-mesh transmissions use helical gears, the gears are cut in the same direction; therefore the side thrust on the countershaft is rearward when the transmission is in forward gear, and forward when it is in reverse.

FOUR-SPEED TRANSMISSIONS The newer four-speed transmissions are of the constant-mesh design and use either a cone or pin synchronizer clutch. Reverse speed is accomplished by sliding the sliding reverse idler gear into mesh with the countershaft gear and with the first-speed gear. See Fig. 11-11.

When all gears are of the helical design, including the reverse gear, reverse speed is achieved by sliding the sliding reverse gear (on the mainshaft) into mesh with the reverse idler gear, which is always the drive gear on the countershaft.

When the four-speed transmission uses a sliding clutch gear (having a collar clutch) to clutch the first- and second-speed driven gears to the main shaft, reverse speed is accomplished by placing the transmission in neutral and then shifting the sliding reverse gear into mesh with the countershaft gear and the sliding clutch gear. See Fig. 11-12.

On yet another four-speed transmission design, the second-, third-, and fourth-speed driven and countershaft gears are in constant mesh, a cone synchronizer clutch is used to engage third speed with the main shaft and fourth speed with the clutch shaft gear, and a half-cone synchronizer is used to engage the second-speed drive gear with the main shaft. **NOTE** The first-speed sliding gear is used to shift the second-speed synchronizer sleeve in order to engage the synchronizer sleeve with the second-speed male collar clutch. See Fig. 11-13.

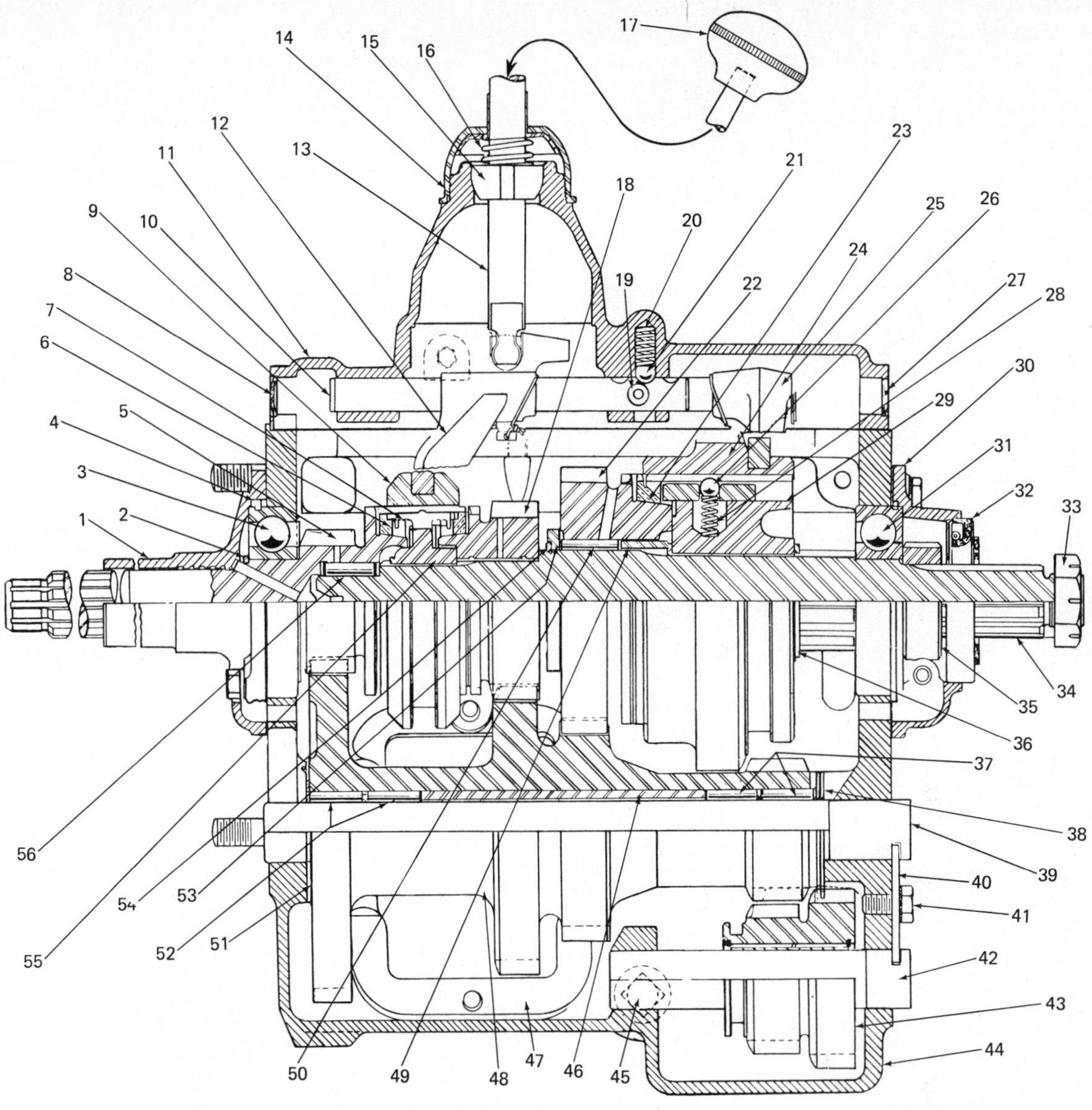

1. Main drive gear bearing retainer
2. Snap ring
3. Main drive gear bearing
4. Snap ring
5. Main drive gear
6. Synchronizer blocking ring
7. Shifting plate
8. Expansion plug
9. Sleeve (3rd & direct)
10. Shift rail
11. Transmission cover
12. Shift fork (3rd & direct)
13. Control lever
14. Control housing cap
15. Fulcrum ball
16. Control lever spring
17. Control lever ball
18. Mainshaft 3rd speed gear
19. Interlock plunger
20. Poppet spring
21. Poppet ball
22. Mainshaft 2nd speed gear
23. Synchronizer blocking ring
24. Mainshaft 1st & 2nd speed gear
25. Shift fork, 1st & 2nd speed
26. Poppet ball
27. Expansion plug
28. Poppet spring
29. Clutch hub, 1st & 2nd speed
30. Mainshaft rear bearing retainer
31. Mainshaft rear bearing
32. Rear bearing retainer seal
33. Mainshaft flange nut
34. Mainshaft
35. Speedometer drive gear
36. Snap ring
37. Countershaft roller bearing
38. Countershaft rear thrust washer
39. Countershaft
40. Lock plate
41. Lock plate capscrew
42. Reverse idler shaft
43. Reverse idler gear
44. Case
45. Drain plug
46. Countershaft bearing spacer
47. P.T.O. opening
48. Countershaft gear cluster
49. 2nd speed gear bearing spacer
50. 2nd speed gear roller bearing
51. Countershaft front thrust washer
52. Countershaft roller bearing
53. 2nd speed gear thrust washer
54. Snap ring
55. Clutch hub, 3rd & direct
56. Mainshaft pilot bearing

Fig. 11-11 Sectional view of a four-speed transmission using a sliding reverse idler gear. (*International Harvester Company*)

When the first-speed sliding gear is shifted into first gear, it moves into mesh with the countershaft first-speed gear. Reverse speed is accomplished by placing the transmission in neutral and sliding the reverse idler right-hand gear into mesh with the countershaft gear, and the left-hand gear of the reverse idler into mesh with the first-speed driven gear.

FIVE-SPEED TRANSMISSIONS All five-speed transmissions are basically similar in design in that the second-, third-, and fourth-speed drive and driven gears, the main drive (clutch shaft) gear, and the countershaft driven gear are in constant mesh. The countershaft drive gear, PTO gear, fourth-speed, third-speed, and second-speed drive gears are keyed to the countershaft. The reverse, the second-speed,

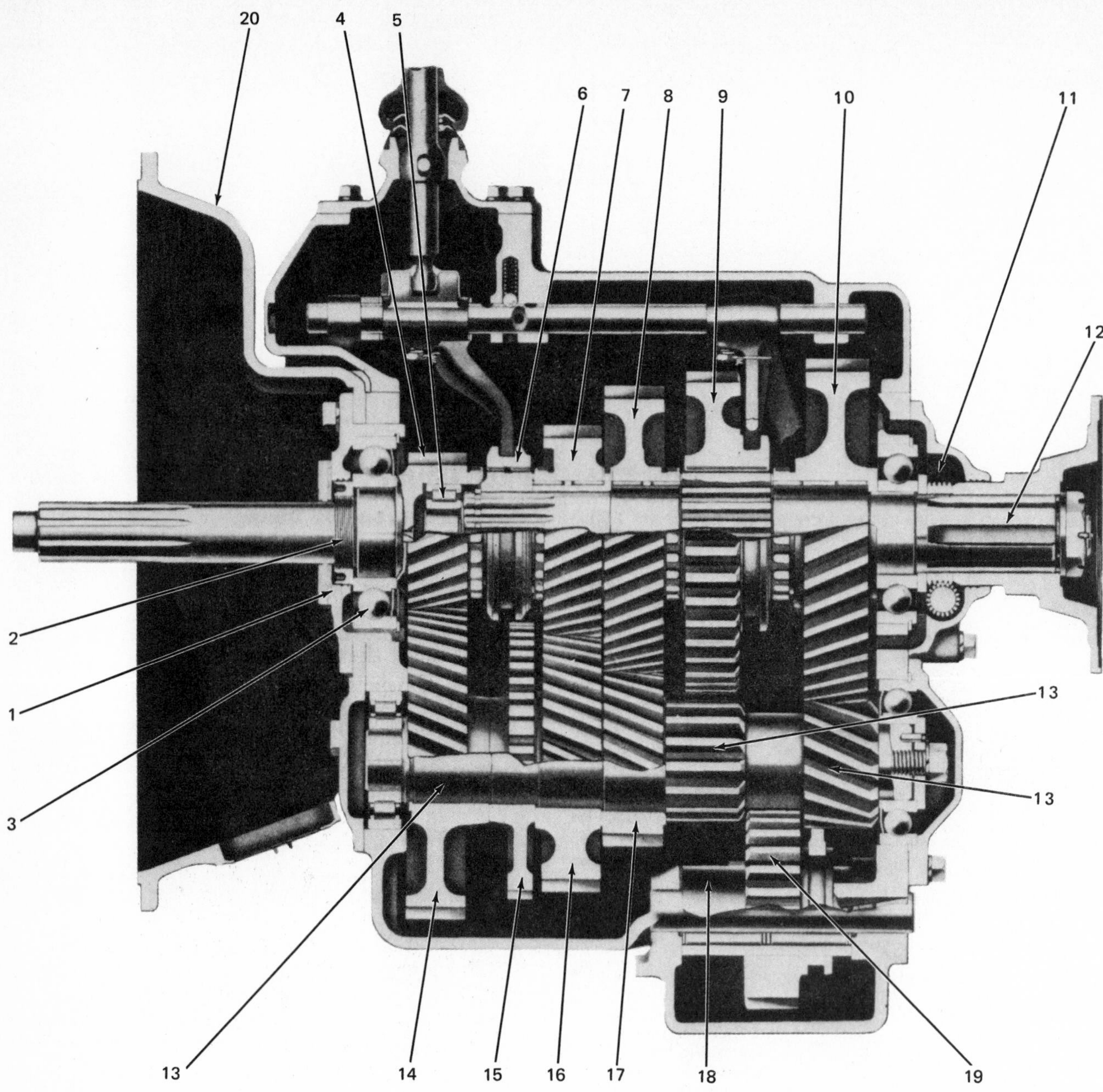

1. Bearing cap
2. Seal
3. Ball bearing
4. Main drive gear
5. Pilot bearing
6. 4/3 speed synchronizer
7. Third-speed driven gear
8. Second-speed driven gear
9. Clutch gear
10. First-speed driven gear
11. Speedometer gear
12. Mainshaft
13. Connecter shaft with first speed and reverse
14. Connecter shaft driven gear
15. PTO drive gear
16. Third speed drive gear
17. Second speed drive gear
18. Reverse idler shaft
19. Reverse idler gear
20. Clutch housing

Fig. 11-12 Sectional view of a four-speed transmission using a sliding reverse idler. (*Dana Corporation, Spicer Transmission Division*)

and the first-speed drive gears are commonly part of the countershaft. The second-, third-, and fourth-speed driven gears are supported on specially designed steel bushings that are splined or locked to the main shaft; otherwise the main shaft (at the point where the gears are located) is specially machined to provide support and lubrication. The reverse idler (nonsliding design) is supported on the idler shaft by cage needle bearings or needle bearings.

The first-speed drive gear shown in Fig. 11-14 is a sliding clutch gear as well as the reverse idler gear. To shift into first speed, the first-speed driven gear is moved to the right, on the main shaft, whereupon it fully engages with the first-speed drive gear on the countershaft. To shift into reverse, the reverse idler is moved on the idler shaft to the right, whereupon the right-hand gear of the reverse idler engages with the reverse idler drive gear on the countershaft and with the first-speed clutch gear. As mentioned, usually two cone or pin synchronizers are used—one to

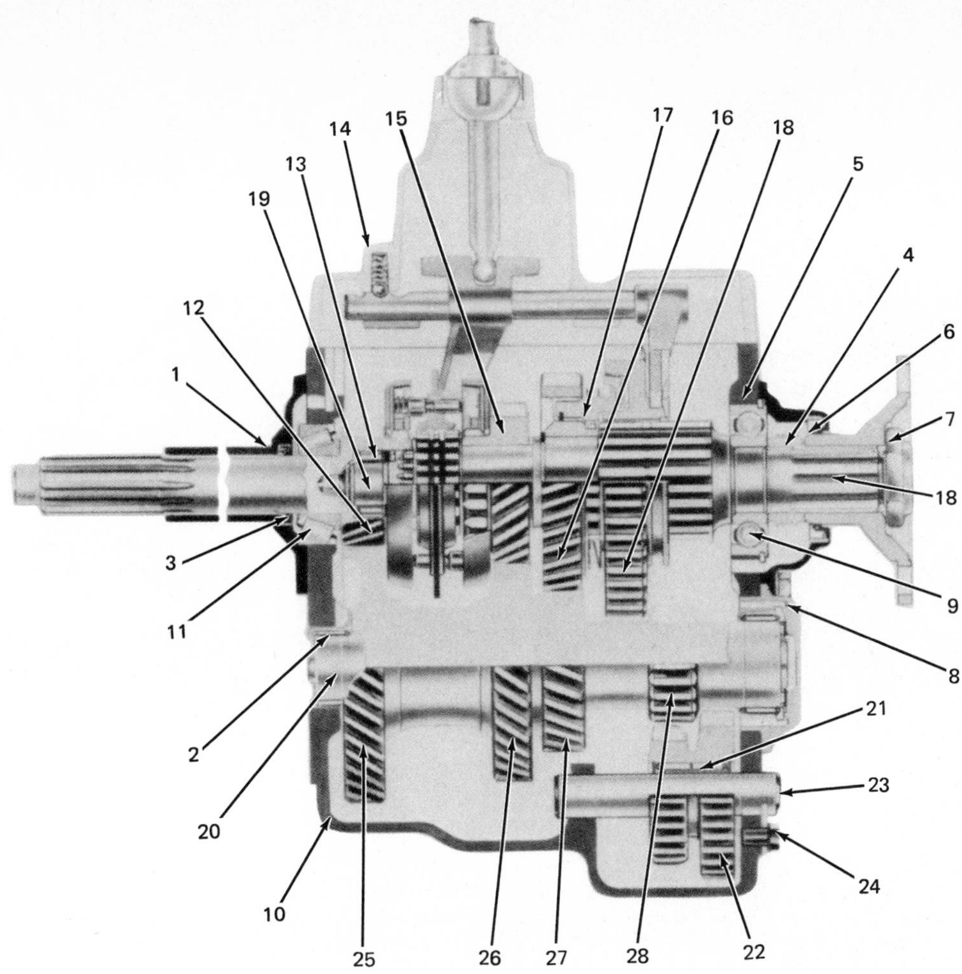

1. Main drive gear retainer
2. Bearing (roller, countershaft front)
3. Main drive gear seal
4. Speedometer drive gear
5. Mainshaft rear bearing retainer
6. Mainshaft rear seal
7. Companion flange nut
8. Countershaft rear bearing retainer
9. Mainshaft rear bearing
10. Transmission case
11. Main drive gear bearing
12. Main drive gear
13. Mainshaft pilot bearing
14. Third and fourth-speed synchronizer
15. Third-speed gear
16. Second-speed gear
17. Second-speed synchronizer
18. First-speed gear
19. Mainshaft
20. Countershaft
21. Roller reverse idler
22. Reverse idler gear
23. Reverse idler gear shaft
24. Reverse idler gear shaft lock plate
25. Countershaft driven gear
26. Third-speed drive gear
27. Second-speed drive gear
28. First-speed drive gear

Fig. 11-13 Sectional view of a four-speed transmission using first-speed driven gear to achieve reverse. (*International Harvester Company*)

clutch the fourth-speed driven gear and the clutch shaft drive gear to the main shaft and the other to clutch the third- and second-speed driven gears to the main shaft. However, the fifth-speed transmission shown in Fig. 11-15 uses a collar clutch to clutch the fourth-speed driven gear and the drive shaft gear to the main shaft.

Figure 11-16 shows a transmission in which the reverse idler is not of the sliding design; the left-hand gear of the reverse idler is in constant mesh with the reverse idler drive gear on the countershaft. To shift into reverse, the sliding first/reverse clutch gear is moved on the main shaft to the right, until it fully engages with the right-hand reverse idler gear. To shift into first gear, the sliding first/reverse clutch gear is moved on the main shaft to the left, until it is fully in mesh with the first drive gear on the countershaft. **NOTE** To shift any one of these five-speed transmissions into first, forward, or reverse speed, the engine clutch must be disengaged and the countershaft must not rotate.

The designs of the shifter housing, shift tower, shift rail (bar), shift fork, shift rail poppet balls, and shift rail interlocks are similar to those on the four-speed tractor transmissions. However, the transmission, having a first/reverse clutch gear, uses a first/reverse shift block having a spring-loaded interlock plunger. The shift block is fastened to the first/reverse shift rail (see Fig. 11-17). To shift this transmission into reverse, the shift lever is pushed to the right. This moves the shift lever lower ball socket against the spring-loaded shift rail interlock plunger, and allows the ball socket to engage in the cutout in the first/reverse-speed shift block. When the shift lever is pushed forward or pulled backward, the first/reverse-speed sliding clutch gear engages with the adjacent gear. When the transmission is placed in neutral and the operator removes her or

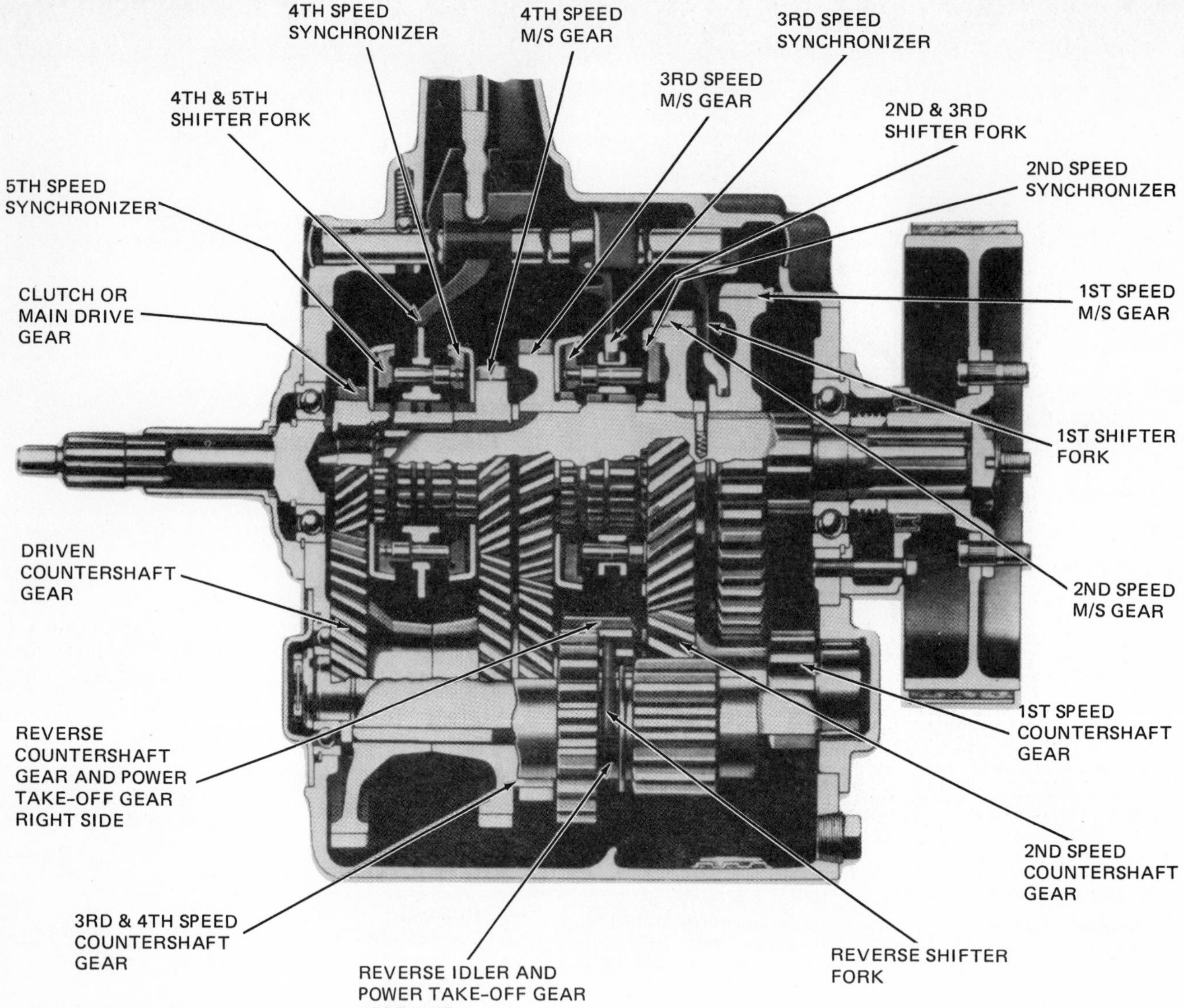

Fig. 11-14 Sectional view of a five-speed transmission having sliding first-speed clutch gear and a reverse idler. (*GMC Truck and Coach Division*)

his hands from the shift lever, the shift rail interlock plunger spring forces the lower ball socket out of the cutout on the first/reverse-speed shift block, and between the cutouts of the fourth/fifth-speed shift fork and the third/second-speed shift fork. The power flow through the different speed ranges parallels that of the four-speed transmission.

Auxiliary Transmissions These are additional transmissions used to increase the speed range; that is, to increase gear reduction (torque) to the wheels. However, their popularity has gradually lessened since the introduction of the modern double and triple countershaft transmissions.

Auxiliary transmissions are individual two-, three-, or four-speed constant-mesh transmissions designed very similarly to a main transmission except that they have no reverse gear. (Reverse is shifted in the main transmission.) The auxiliary transmission is connected to the main transmission through a drive line. Those which use collar clutches are designed to transmit a higher torque than those which use pin synchronizer clutches.

A four-speed auxiliary transmission designed to transmit a maximum torque of about 700 lb · ft [948.5 N · m] is shown in Fig. 11-18. The first-speed, second-speed, and overdrive gears are supported on the main shaft by needle bearings, or by specially designed bushings. The countershaft driven gear and the second- and third-speed drive gears are keyed to the countershaft, and the first-speed drive gear is part of the countershaft. Depending on the torque limitation of the transmission, the countershaft is supported on roller, ball, or tapered-roller bearings. The left-hand end of the main shaft is supported by a cage roller bearing positioned inside the bore of the drive gear.

Upon examining the drive and driven gears on the countershaft, you will notice that the countershaft driven gear has a smaller diameter than the third-speed drive gear; therefore the fourth speed is overdrive. The ratio of this specific transmission in

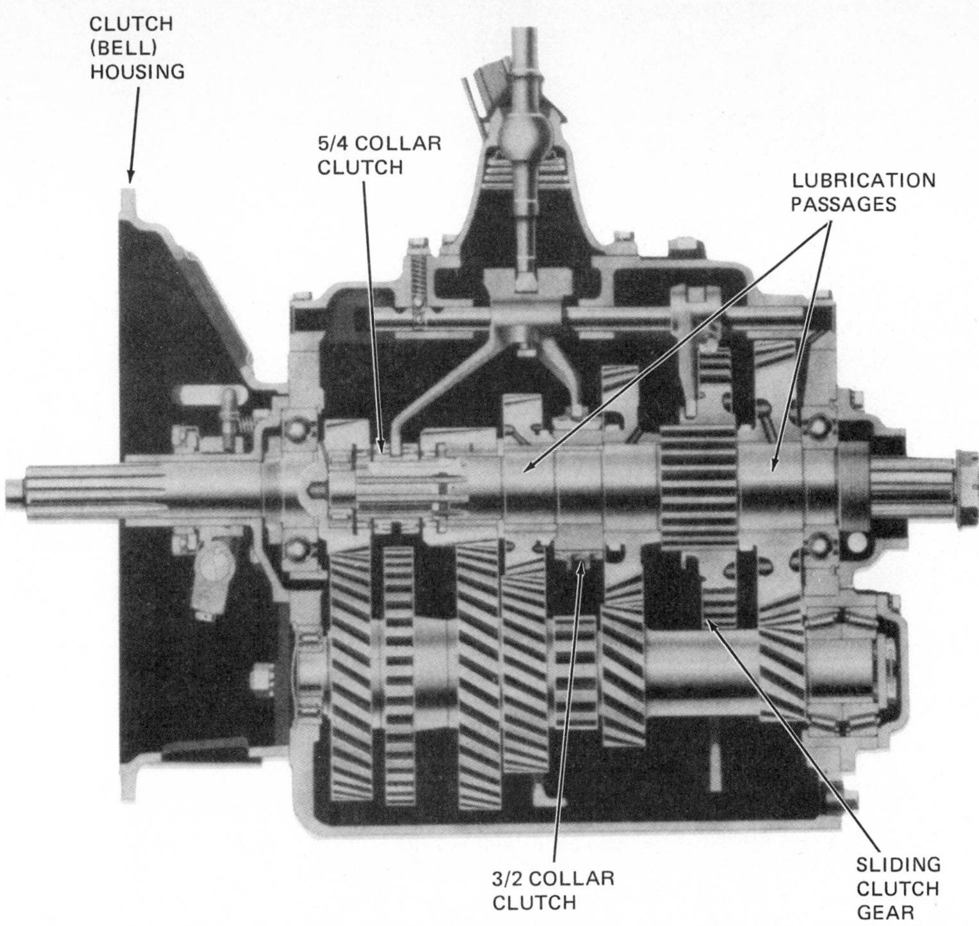

Fig. 11-15 Sectional view of a speed transmission using collar clutch to shift fifth/fourth and third/second speeds and a clutch gear shift in first gear and reverse gear. (*International Harvester Company*)

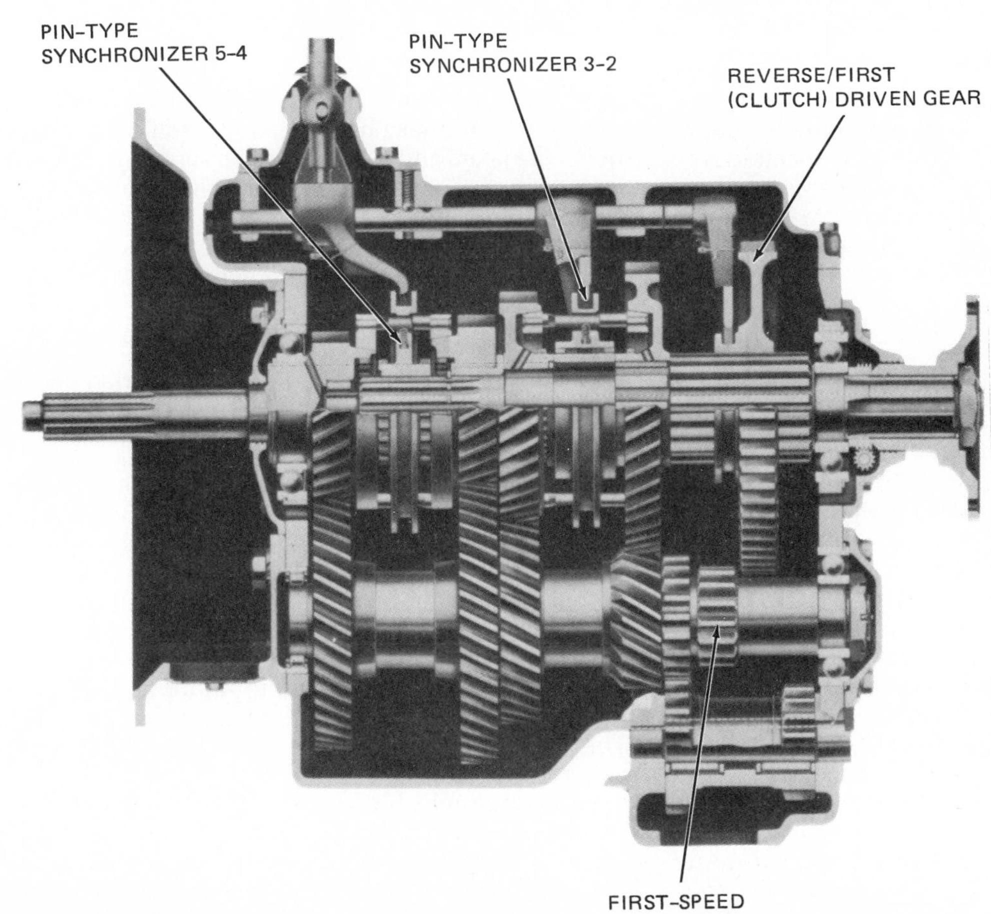

Fig. 11-16 Sectional view of a five-speed transmission using pin synchronizer to shift fifth/fourth and third/second speeds and a clutch gear to shift first and reverse speeds. (*Dana Corporation, Spicer Transmission Division*)

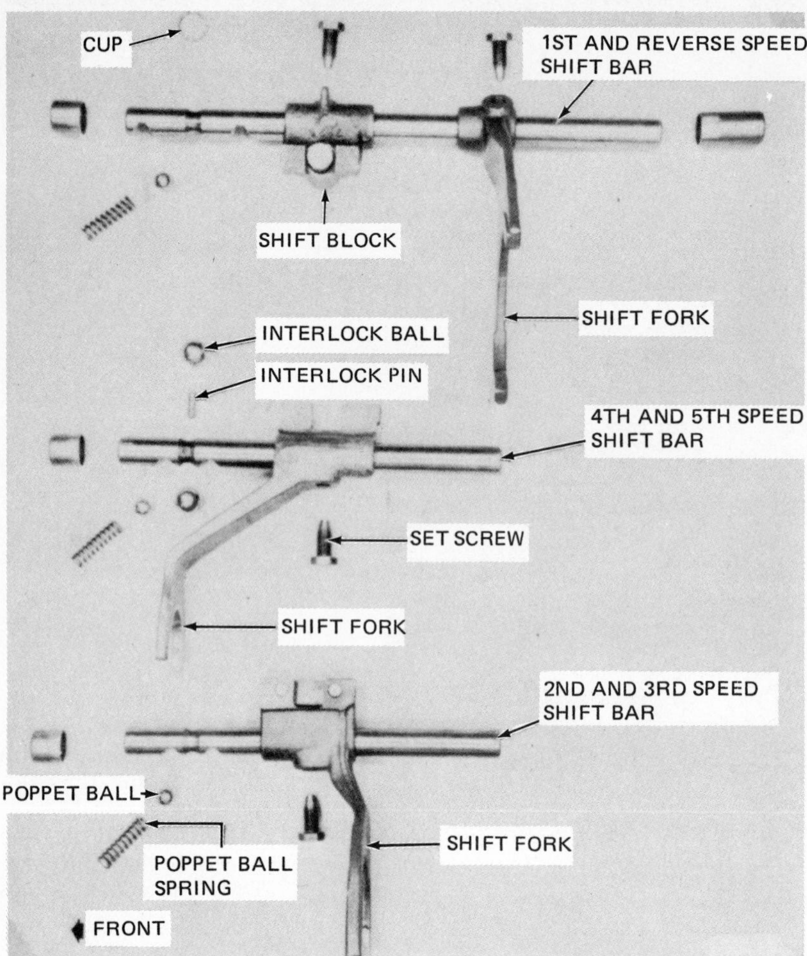

Fig. 11-17 Shift bar housing parts in their relative positions. (*International Harvester Company*)

first gear—that is, when the first-speed driven gear is clutched to the main shaft through the collar clutch—is 2.14:1.00. When the second-speed driven gear is clutched to the main shaft, the second speed has a reduction of 1.24:1.00. When the main shaft is clutched to the clutch shaft drive gear, the third speed is direct, 1.00:1.00. When the overdrive gear is clutched to the main shaft, the fourth speed is an overdrive: 0.86:1.00.

Compound Transmissions When the four-speed auxiliary transmission shown in Fig. 11-18 or a two-, three-, or another four-speed auxiliary transmission is bolted directly to a four- or five-speed main transmission, the assembly is called a *compound transmission*, and a numbering system is used to identify each of the forward speeds in both the main and rear unit (auxiliary transmission): 3 × 4, 4 × 3, 4 × 4, 5 × 4, etc. The first digit indicates the number of forward speeds in the main transmission and the second the number of forward speeds in the rear unit. A 4 × 4 compound transmission of the overdrive design is shown in Fig. 11-19. **NOTE** These types of transmissions may be interchanged with twin countershaft transmissions.

REAR-UNIT DESIGN The driven gear and second/third-speed drive gears are keyed to the countershaft, and the first-speed drive gear is part of the shaft. The countershaft is supported by roller bearings in the auxiliary housing, and a self-locking nut holds the gears and bearings to the shaft. The splines on which the male first/second collar clutch (gear) slides form part of the main shaft but the direct and overdrive male collar clutch (gear) slides on a splined sleeve fastened to the main shaft. The first-speed, second-speed, and direct driven gears are supported by needle bearings on the main shaft.

NOTE The gears provide the outer bearing races, and the gear sleeves (which are positioned on the main shaft) are the inner races.

The rear-unit drive gear is splined to the rear-unit main shaft. The rear-unit main shaft is supported on the left by a cage roller bearing, positioned in the bore of the main transmission's main shaft, and supported on the right-hand side through a ball bearing. The rear unit very closely resembles the main transmission. The main difference between the main and auxiliary transmissions is in the shifter housing and the shift lever control (stick control) to the rear units. The shift lever assembly (to shift the rear unit) is bolted to the housing of the main transmission, and is linked through shift rods with the two rear shifter housing cross-shaft levers. See Fig. 11-20A. The inner shift fingers are fastened to the ends of the cross shafts, and their ball sockets rest in the cutouts of the shift forks.

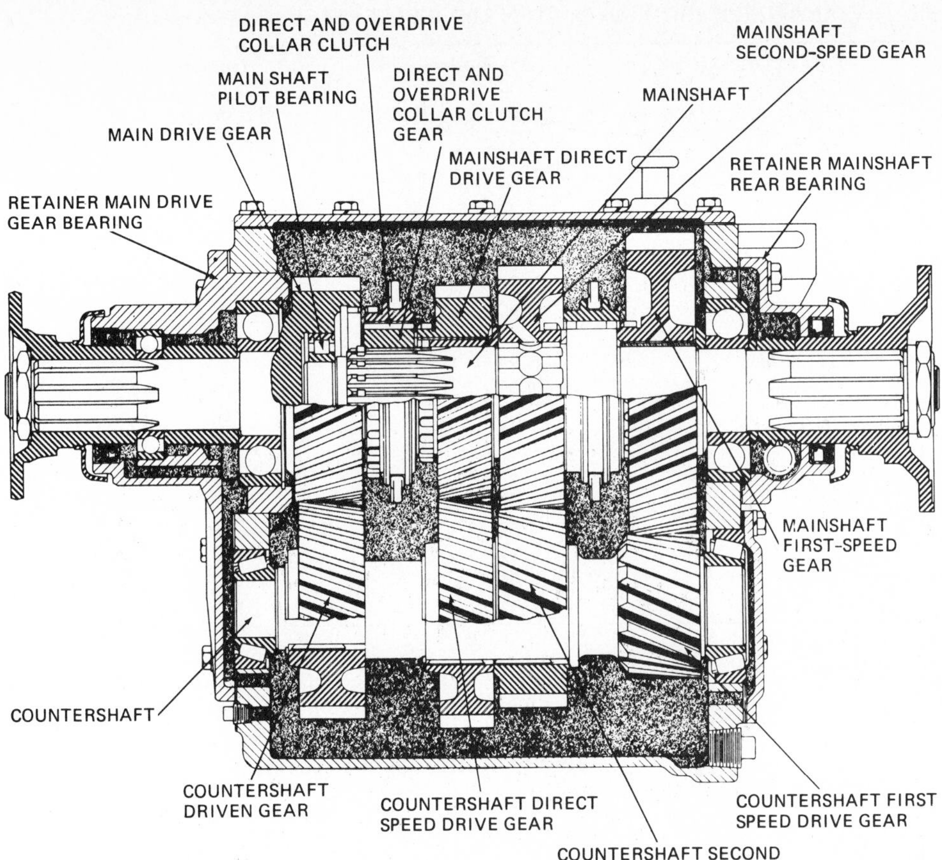

Fig. 11-18 Sectional view of a four-speed (overdrive) auxiliary transmission. (*International Harvester Company*)

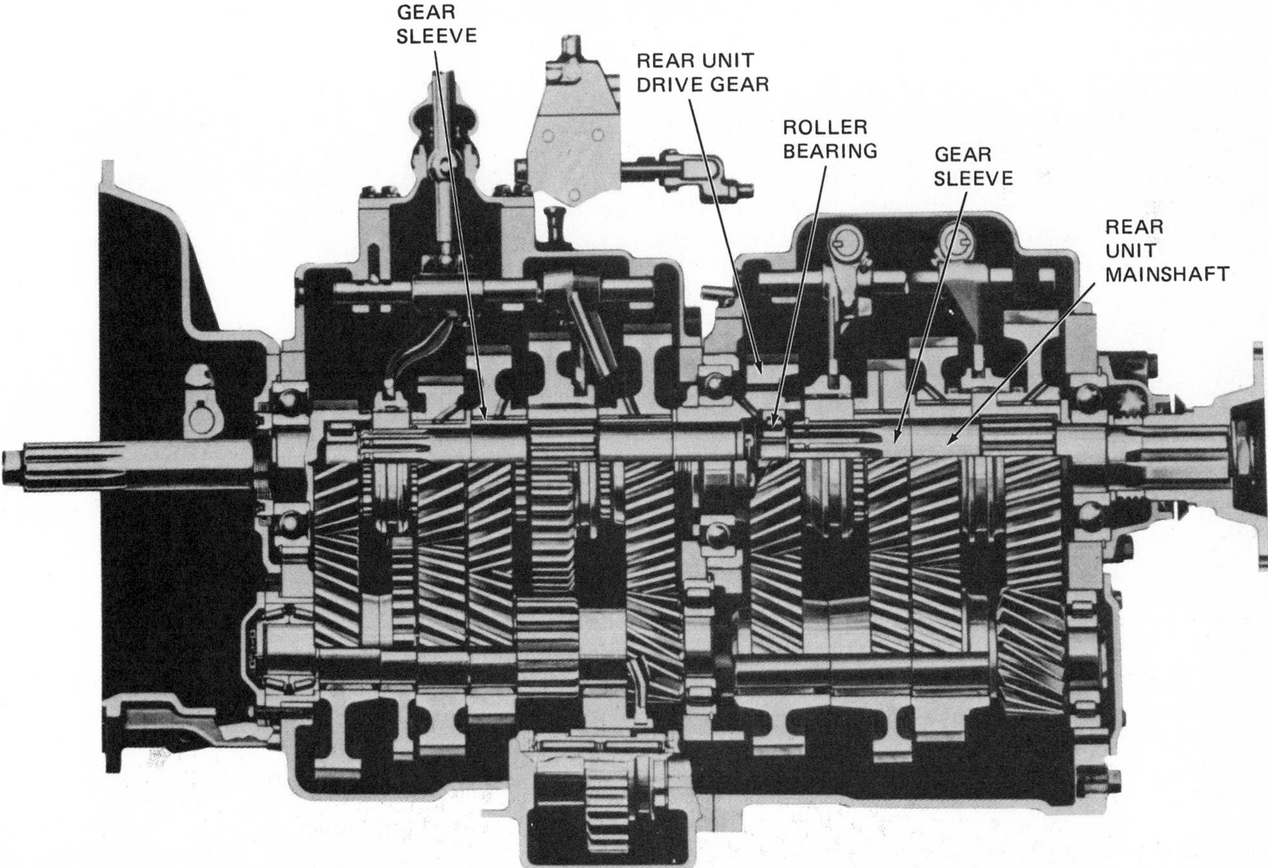

Fig. 11-19 Sectional view of a 16-speed (4 × 4) compound transmission. (*Dana Corporation, Spicer Transmission Division*)

Table 11-1 EXAMPLES OF GEAR RATIOS AND STEPS FROM SPEED TO SPEED FOR SEVERAL TRANSMISSIONS

	Transmission 1		Transmission 2		Transmission 3		Transmission 4	
Gear	Ratio	Step, %	Ratio	Step, %	Ratio	Step, %	Ratio	Step, %
1	8.53		8.53		12.35		12.35	
2	5.52	54	4.87	75	10.41	19	10.41	19
3	3.57	55	3.00	62	7.53	38	7.05	48
4	2.27	57	1.90	58	6.34	19	5.94	19
5	1.51	50	1.33	43	4.67	36	4.17	42
6	1.00	51	1.00	33	3.93	19	3.50	19
7					3.29	19	2.75	27
8					2.76	19	2.31	19
9					2.36	17	1.97	17
10					1.98	19	1.66	19
11					1.66	19	1.39	19
12					1.39	19	1.17	19
13					1.19	17	1.00	17
14					1.00	19	0.84	19
Rev.	8.53		8.53		12.35		12.35	
					10.41		10.41	
					8.86		8.86	
					7.47		7.47	

CALCULATION OF COMPOUND GEAR REDUCTION Although gear reduction calculations can hardly be considered a probable daily encounter, they should at least be within the capacity of a good mechanic to carry out, should the need for them arise. Let us assume you need to calculate the total gear reduction on a tractor loader having a forward/reverse, high/low-range, and four-speed main transmission. To calculate the total reduction, the following formula is used:

$$\frac{\text{Driven gear} \times \text{driven gear}}{\text{Drive gear} \times \text{drive gear}} = \text{total reduction}$$

That means you must multiply together the number of teeth on the driven gears, and divide this number by the product of the number of teeth on the drive gears. This operation is illustrated in Fig. 11-20B. For each calculation, whole-number ratios have been chosen, although in actual fact each set of transmission gears has an uneven number of teeth. In this simplified compound gear train, the forward/reverse transmission is in reverse, the high/low-range transmission is in low, and the main transmission is also in low. The numbers that apply to the *drive* gears are circled.

NOTE All three- or more-speed transmissions and all range and splitter transmissions are built with one or more different gear ratios to accommodate the special applications. For instance, the ratio step from speed to speed on some transmissions is maintained as evenly as possible, whereas others have a gathered (uneven) ratio. Four examples of gear ratios and steps are shown in Table 11-1.

TWIN- AND TRIPLE-COUNTERSHAFT TRANSMISSIONS

With the ever increasing demand for higher engine torque, single-countershaft transmissions had to be

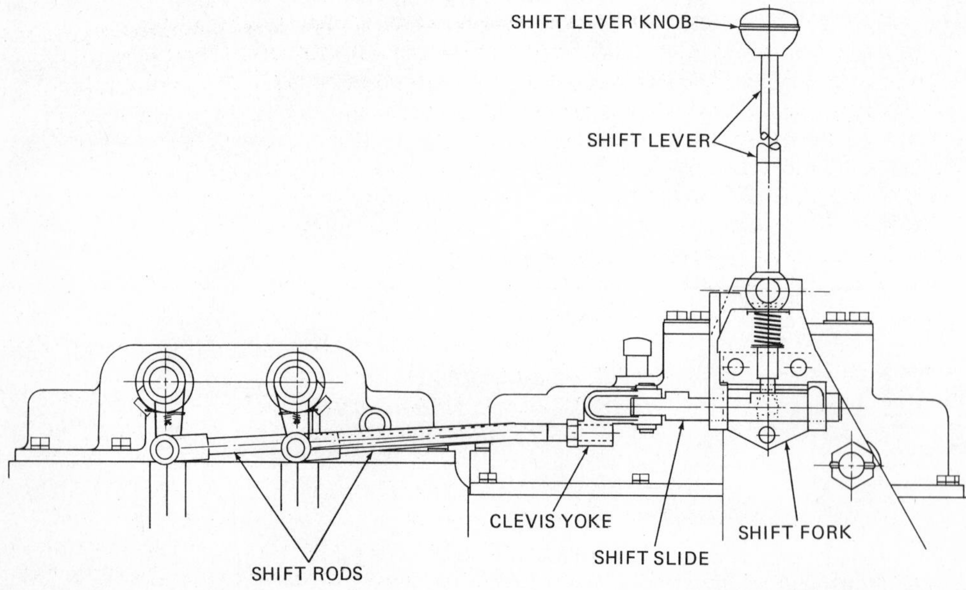

Fig. 11-20A Schematic view of the stick control rear units. *(Dana Corporation, Spicer Transmission Division)*

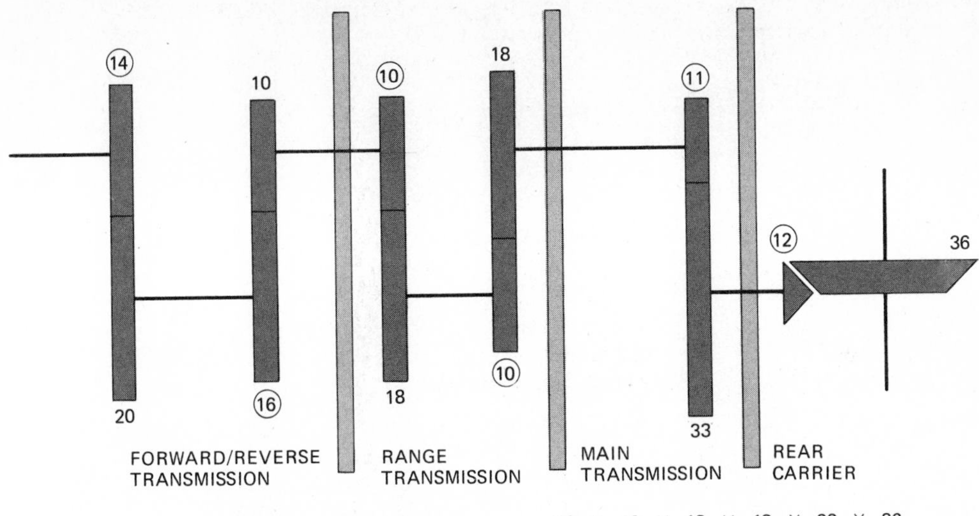

$$\text{GEAR RATIO} = \frac{\text{DRIVEN GEAR} \times \text{DRIVEN GEAR}}{\text{DRIVE GEAR} \times \text{DRIVE GEAR}} = \frac{20 \times 10 \times 18 \times 18 \times 33 \times 36}{⑭ \times ⑯ \times ⑩ \times ⑩ \times ⑪ \times ⑫}$$

$$= \frac{26.03}{1} = 26.03{:}\ 1$$

Fig. 11-20B The calculation of the overall gear reduction for a compound gear train.

built larger and stronger. These transmissions consequently reduced payload and were difficult to install. And as the engine torque on a single-countershaft transmission climbed to 1250 lb · ft [1694.75 N · m], the spreading force between the drive and driven gears increased to such an extent that the gears, bearings, shafts, and transmission housings could no longer stand up to the high torque. To resolve these problems, twin- and triple-countershaft transmissions were designed. These allow the engine torque to be equally divided between two or three countershafts and then again placed onto the main shafts. Consequently, it is not only possible to increase the transmission torque capacity, but also to reduce the transmission's overall weight and size. See Fig. 11-21.

All transmissions so designed are of the constant-mesh type, and use collar clutches to shift the main transmission, with jaw clutches and/or pin or cone synchronizers to shift the range transmission. All designs, regardless of the speed ranges, use straight-cut (spur) gears, and use splash lubrication to lubricate the bearings, clutches, and gears. However, the triple-countershaft transmission, in addition, uses a positive vane pump to lubricate the bearings, shafts, and clutches. Attached to the drain plugs are magnetic plugs; in addition some have magnetic disks

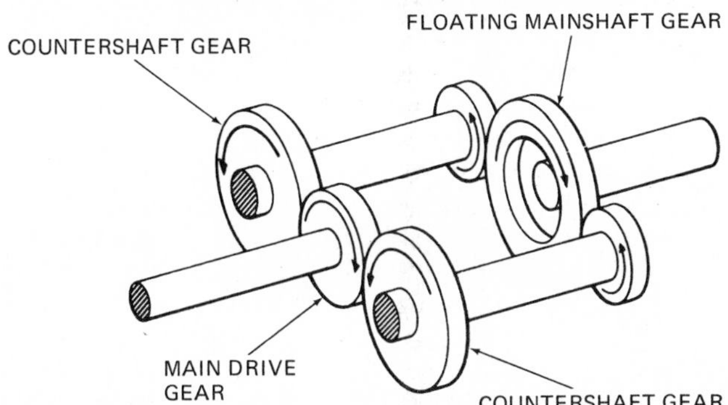

Fig. 11-21 Schematic view of transmitting power in a twin-countershaft transmission. (*Eaton Corporation*)

to attract and hold metallic particle deposits that may be in the oil. The transmission main housing has two PTO openings—one on the side, to which a light-duty (six-bolt) PTO transmission can be bolted, and one on the bottom of the housing, to which a heavy-duty (eight-bolt) PTO can be bolted. When either PTO is installed, the PTO driven gear is in constant mesh with the PTO drive gear on the countershaft.

Five-Speed Twin-Countershaft Transmissions Two companies build twin-countershaft transmissions which are very similar to each other (see Figs. 11-22 and 11-23). The basis of these is a five-speed forward and one-speed reverse transmission. Commonly, the reverse- and first-speed gears are part of the countershaft, and the other gears are keyed to the shaft. The arrangement of gears and the design of countershafts vary not only between both manufacturers, but also among models. The gears are keyed to the countershaft in the following order (Figs. 11-22 and 11-23, from left to right): countershaft driven gear, PTO, fourth-, third, and second-speed drive gears. The only difference between the left- and right-hand countershafts is in the number of teeth of the PTO gears. On the transmission shown in Fig. 11-23, only the countershaft reverse drive gear is part of the countershaft, and the PTO gear is splined to the fourth-speed driven gear. The countershafts on both transmissions are supported at the front by ball bearings and at the rear by tapered roller or roller bearings. Also, both manufacturers support the left- and right-hand reverse idler gears with cage needle bearings, and the clutch shaft (input shaft, or drive gear shaft) with a roller bearing.

On both transmissions, the main-drive gear is keyed to the clutch drive shaft, but the support of the main shaft differs between the two companies. The Fuller transmission's (Fig. 11-22) main shaft is merely guided or held in position by the front and rear quills which are pressed into the bore of the main shaft. The mesh of the drive and driven gears

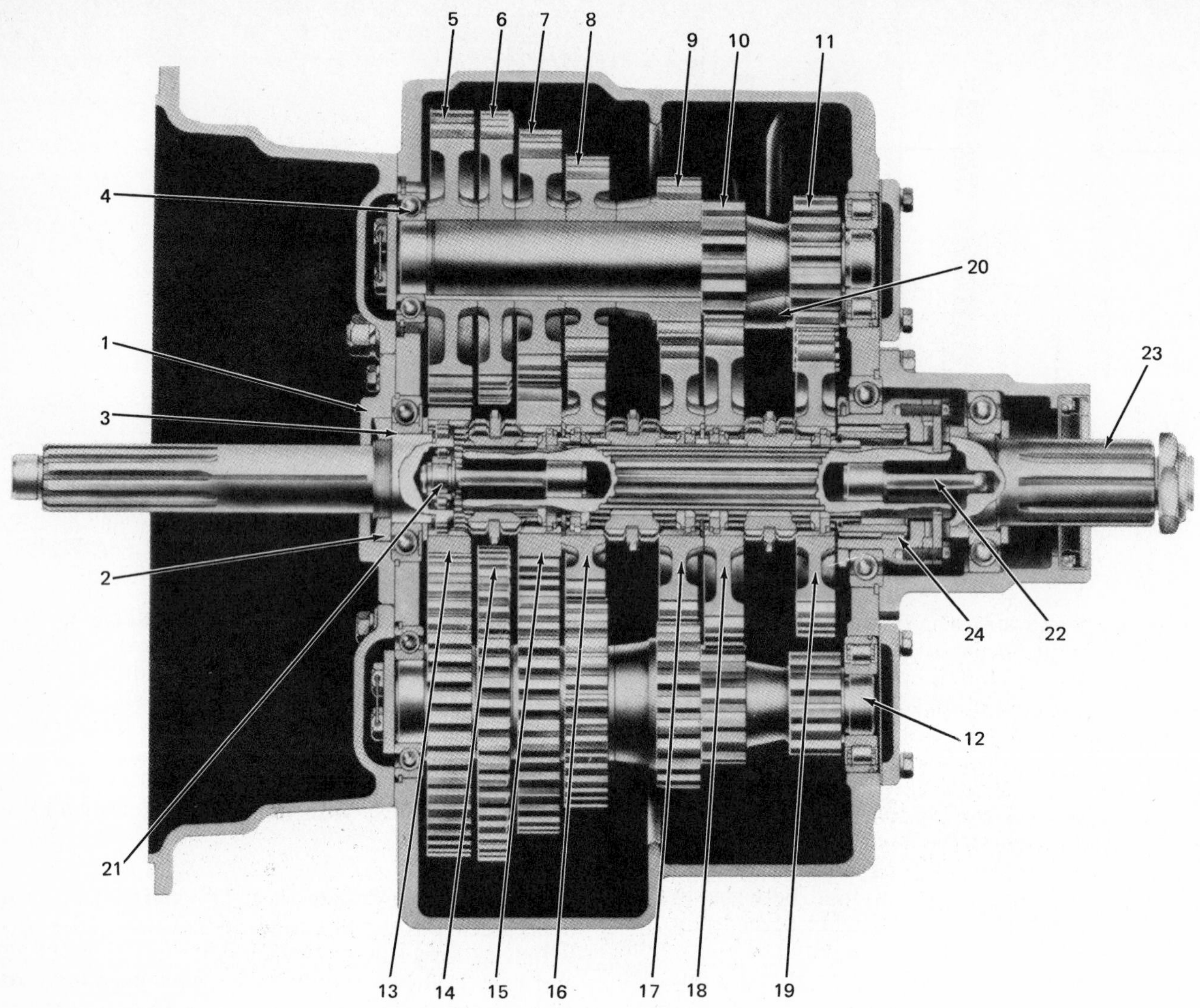

1. Drive gear bearing cover
2. Drive gear nut
3. Drive gear bearing
4. Countershaft ball bearing
5. Countershaft driven gear
6. Countershaft PTO gear
7. Countershaft fourth speed drive gear
8. Countershaft third speed drive gear
9. Countershaft second speed drive gear
10. Countershaft first speed drive gear
11. Countershaft reverse speed drive gear
12. Countershaft
13. Main drive gear
14. PTO drive gear (left)
15. Fourth speed driven gear
16. Third speed driven gear
17. Second speed driven gear
18. First speed driven gear
19. Reverse speed driven gear
20. Reverse idler gears
21. Front quill
22. Rear quill
23. Tail shaft
24. Coupling gear

Fig. 11-22 Sectional view of a five-speed twin-countershaft transmission. (*Eaton Corporation*)

actually floats the main shaft between the front and rear quills, allowing the gears to find the best tooth contact during operation. The front quill is supported by a cage roller bearing positioned in the bore of the drive gear, and the rear-quill ball socket rests in the bore of the tail shaft. The tail shaft coupling gear couples together the main and tail shafts. The latter is supported at the right by a roller bearing located in the bearing cover, and by a roller bearing located in the rear bore of the transmission housing.

The main shaft of the Spicer transmission (Fig. 11-23) is supported at the right by a ball bearing positioned in the bore of the transmission housing, and at the left by a cage needle bearing positioned inside the drive gear bore.

The driven gears are loosely held to the main shaft through externally splined (gear) spacers, the teeth of which mesh with the internal teeth of the driven gears. Gear washers, one on each side, are keyed to the main shaft and snap rings hold them to the main shaft, thereby positioning the driven gears on the shaft. See Fig. 11-24.

The Fuller transmission uses three collar clutches—one for reverse/first speed, one for second/third speed, and one for fourth (direct)/fifth speed; the Spicer transmission uses one additional half-collar clutch to clutch the fourth-speed driven gear to the main shaft. **NOTE** The male and female collar (gear) clutches have conical teeth to improve their engagement. There are three shift rails in the shift

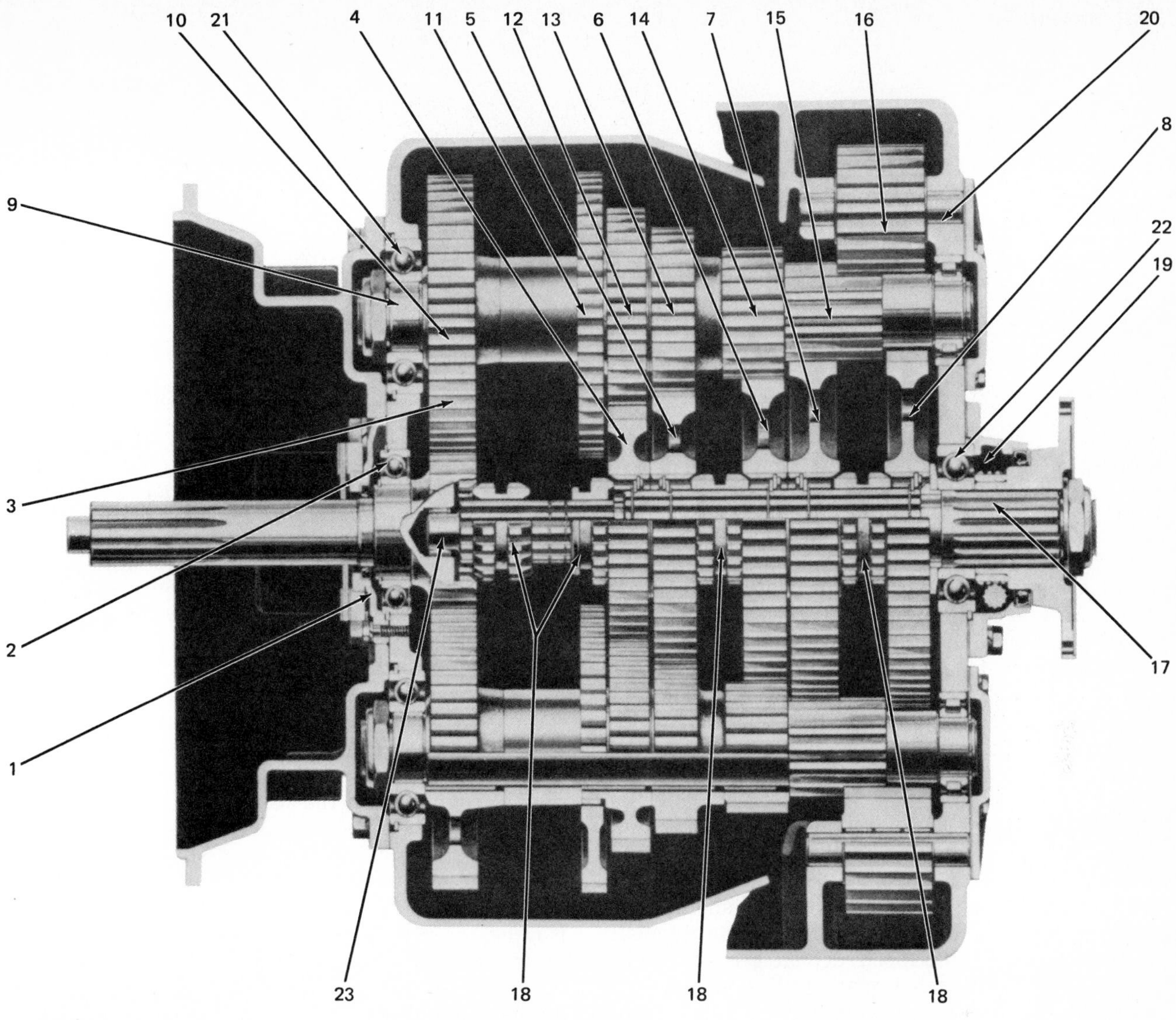

1. Main drive gear ball bearing
2. Main drive gear ball bearing
3. Main drive gear
4. Fourth speed driven gear
5. Third speed driven gear
6. Second speed driven gear
7. First speed driven gear
8. Reverse speed driven gear
9. Countershaft
10. Countershaft driven gear
11. Countershaft PTO gear
12. Countershaft fourth speed drive gear
13. Countershaft third speed drive gear
14. Countershaft second speed drive gear
15. Countershaft first/reverse speed drive gear
16. Reverse idler
17. Main shaft
18. Collar clutch
19. Speedometer gear
20. Countershaft roller bearing
21. Countershaft ball bearing
22. Mainshaft ball bearing
23. Mainshaft needle bearing

Fig. 11-23 Sectional view of a five-speed twin-countershaft transmission. (*Dana Corporation, Spicer Transmission Division*)

cover (housing) of both transmissions; however, the Spicer transmission has one additional shift fork fastened to the fourth and fifth shift rails. A shifter block is attached to the first/reverse shift rails of both transmissions. On a Fuller transmission the shift lever ball socket is held to the shift lever housing through a tension spring, the latter being held to the transmission by the spring washer.

OPERATION When the transmission is in neutral, neither collar clutch is engaged with a driven gear; therefore, when the clutch shaft is rotated, the main drive gear drives the driven gear on the countershafts, and the right- and left-hand countershaft assemblies rotate in a counterclockwise direction (see Fig. 11-25). As a result all gears, including the reverse idler, rotate.

To shift the transmission into any one of the five forward gears, the engine clutch must be disengaged and the shift lever moved (to the left or right) to select the speed. This movement places the shift lever's lower ball socket into the selected cutout of the shift fork. The shift lever is then moved either forward or backward, to shift the transmission into the desired gear (see Fig. 11-26). The movement of the shift rail, in turn, moves the shift fork and the male

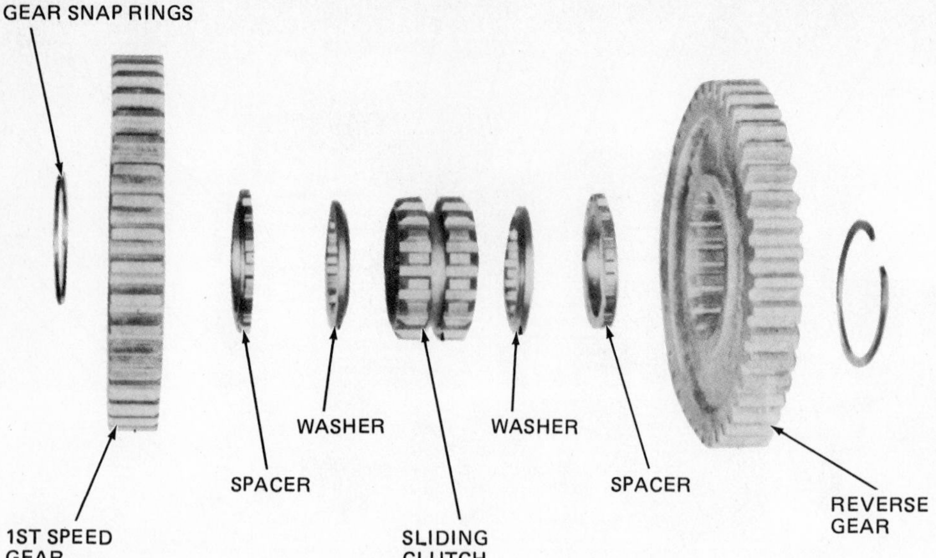

Fig. 11-24 Method used to support driven gear on the main shaft of transmission shown in Fig. 11-21. (*Eaton Corporation*)

collar clutch. The latter slides on the main shaft and clutches the selected gear to the main shaft. Say it is the fourth speed that is clutched and that the engine is operating. The torque from the engine clutch is then directed to the clutch shaft and main drive gear. The drive gear transmits the torque to the left- and right-hand driven gears on the countershaft, rotating it, and the fourth-speed drive gears (on the countershaft) drive the fourth-speed driven gear (on the main shaft). The torque is transmitted from the fourth-speed driven gear over the collar clutch onto the main shaft. (On the Fuller transmission the torque is transmitted from the main shaft to the tail shaft coupling gear, and then to the tail shaft.)

As the torque is transmitted from the countershaft gears onto the fourth-speed driven gear, the left-hand countershaft drive gear applies an upward force onto the driven gear, and the right-hand countershaft drive gear applies a downward force onto the driven gear. On a Fuller transmission, this removes all force from the main shaft.

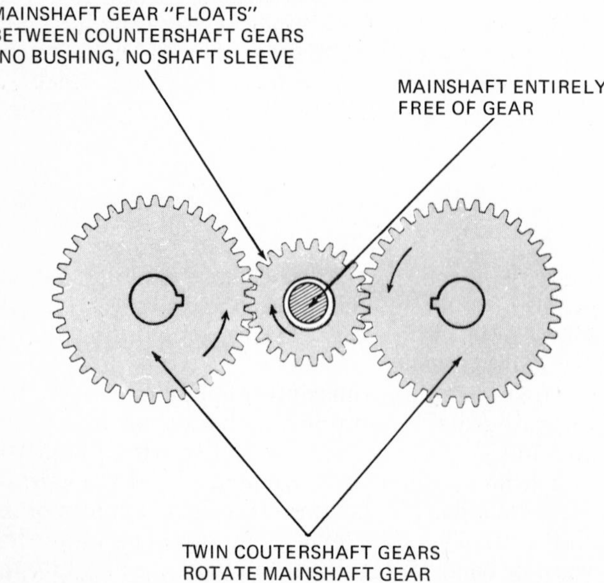

Fig. 11-25 View of countershaft rotation in a five-speed twin-countershaft transmission. (*Eaton Corporation*)

To select reverse (gear) speed, the shift lever is moved to the right, whereupon the lower ball socket forces the blocking plunger inward and the ball socket then engages in the cutout of the interlock block (see Fig. 11-26). The shift lever is then pushed forward, causing the collar clutch to engage with the reverse-speed driven gear, which clutches the driven gear to the main shaft. The torque from the countershaft reverse-speed drive gears is transmitted to the reverse idlers. From the idlers, the torque is transmitted onto the reverse-speed driven gear, over the collar clutch, and onto the main shaft.

If for some reason the five-speed transmission must be converted into an overdrive transmission, it must be entirely disassembled and the following must be done: The countershaft driven gears must be interchanged with the fourth-speed drive gears on the countershaft, and the drive shaft gear must be interchanged with the fourth-speed driven gear on the main shaft.

Six- to Fifteen-Speed Twin-Countershaft Transmissions Several different designs enable gear ratios to be added to the basic five-speed twin-countershaft transmissions, making them versatile enough to be used for medium- and heavy-duty on- and off-highway applications. For example, to increase the speed range on Fuller twin-countershaft transmissions from five speed to six, seven, nine, ten, thirteen, and fifteen speeds, an auxiliary transmission is bolted to the standard transmission or the gears in the five-speed transmission are rearranged and an auxiliary transmission is bolted to it. Similarly, Spicer five-speed twin-countershaft transmissions are modified to produce six-, seven-, ten-, eleven-, and fourteen-speed transmissions.

RT906 and T955 Six-Speed Transmissions (Fuller) The Fuller company manufactures two six-speed transmissions—one (T955) where a five-speed main transmission is used, to which a range transmission is bolted, and the other (RT906) (see Fig. 11-27) where the five-speed transmission is reduced to three speed and one reverse, and a two-speed aux-

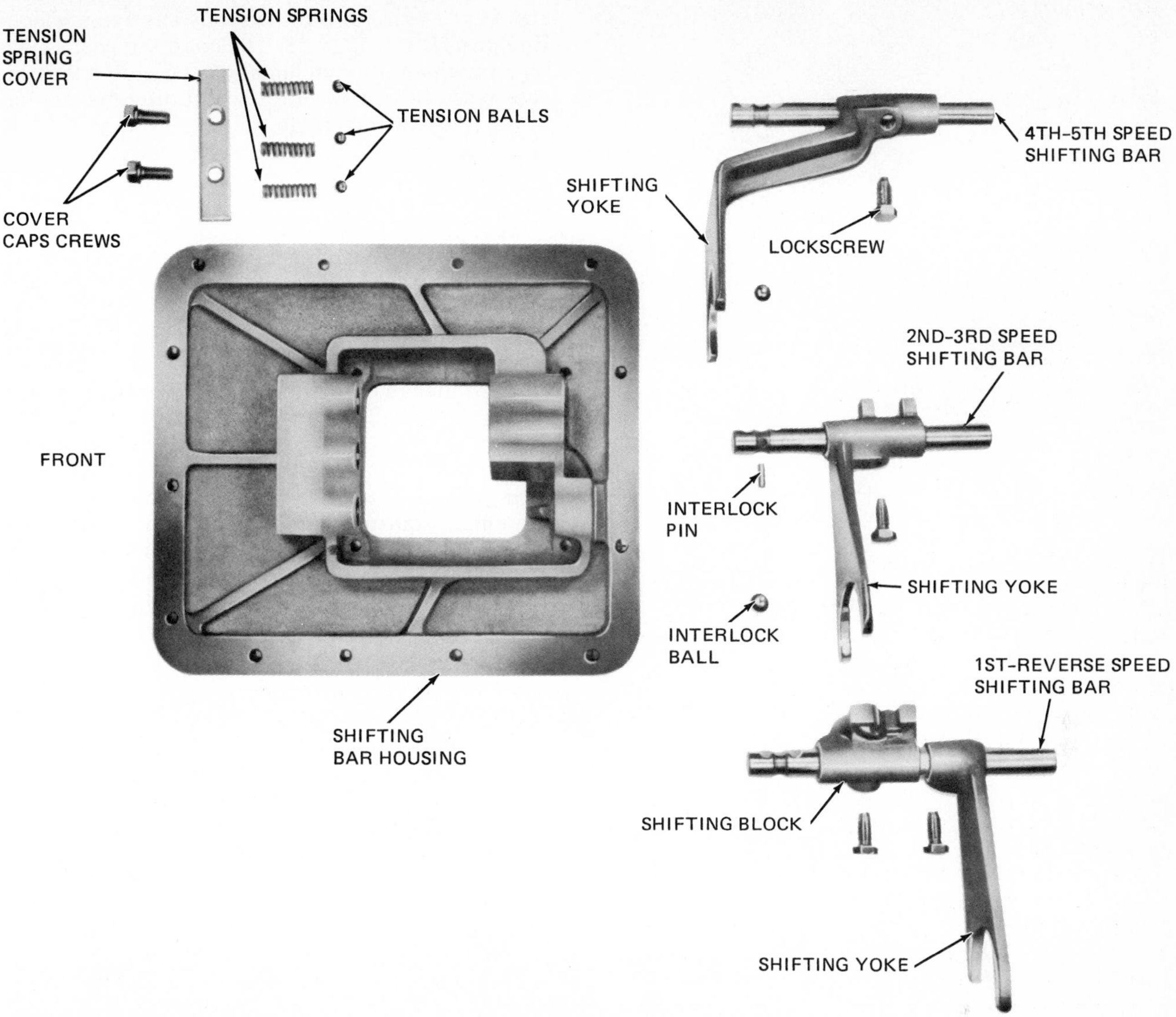

TENSION SPRINGS
TENSION SPRING COVER
TENSION BALLS
COVER CAPS CREWS
4TH-5TH SPEED SHIFTING BAR
SHIFTING YOKE
LOCKSCREW
2ND-3RD SPEED SHIFTING BAR
FRONT
INTERLOCK PIN
SHIFTING YOKE
INTERLOCK BALL
1ST-REVERSE SPEED SHIFTING BAR
SHIFTING BAR HOUSING
SHIFTING BLOCK
SHIFTING YOKE

Fig. 11-26 Exploded view of the shift mechanism. (*Eaton Corporation*)

iliary transmission is bolted to the main transmission. We will discuss the RT906 first.

In the RT906 transmission, the driven countershaft gear and the PTO third-, second-, first-, and reverse-speed gears are keyed to the countershaft. The second-, first-, and reverse-speed driven gears are attached through the spacer and washers to the main shaft. This assembly provides the main transmission with three speeds forward. Third speed is achieved by clutching the clutch shaft gear to the

CLUTCH HOUSING
FRONT SECTION
CASE
AUXILIARY SECTION

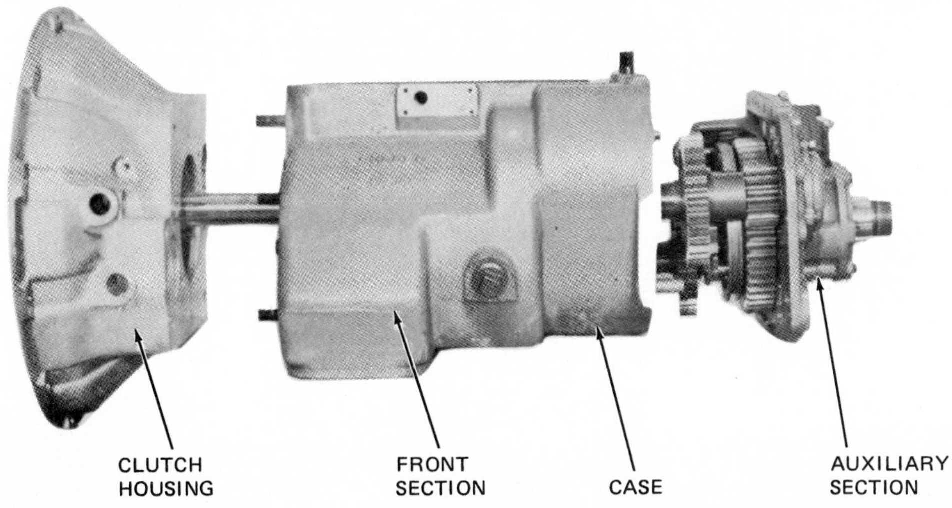

Fig. 11-27 View of the three major components of an RT906 transmission. (*Eaton Corporation*)

Fig. 11-28 Installing coupling gear in bore spline of auxiliary gear and on splines of main shaft (RT906 transmission). (*Eaton Corporation*)

main shaft. Second, first, and reverse are achieved by clutching the respective driven gears to the main shaft.

To transmit the torque from the main shaft to the auxiliary transmission, the auxiliary gear is supported by a ball bearing in the rear main housing and is connected to the main shaft through a coupling gear. See Fig. 11-28. The coupling gear is machined with an internal female collar clutch that engages with the pin synchronizer sliding male collar clutch. The sliding male collar clutch is loosely splined to the right-hand side of the auxiliary main shaft (output or tail shaft). A coupling gear is used to spline the auxiliary gear to the main shaft. The splined washer, two washers, and two snap rings (similar to those used on the main transmission) attach the low-speed driven gear to the auxiliary main (tail) shaft (Fig. 11-29).

The main (tail) shaft is supported by two sets of tapered roller bearings, one located in the rear plate and the other in the tail shaft rear cover. The auxiliary countershaft and low-speed drive gear is a single unit to which the auxiliary shaft driven gear is keyed. The countershafts are supported by roller bearings—one located in the rear cover and the other in the main transmission housing.

The shift housing has only two shift bars (rails) to which shift yokes (forks) are fastened (see Fig. 11-30). Positioned between the two shift rails and extending past the raised housing (cover) is the actuating plunger. When the shifter housing is installed and the main transmission is in neutral, the actuating plunger's tapered cone ends are forced

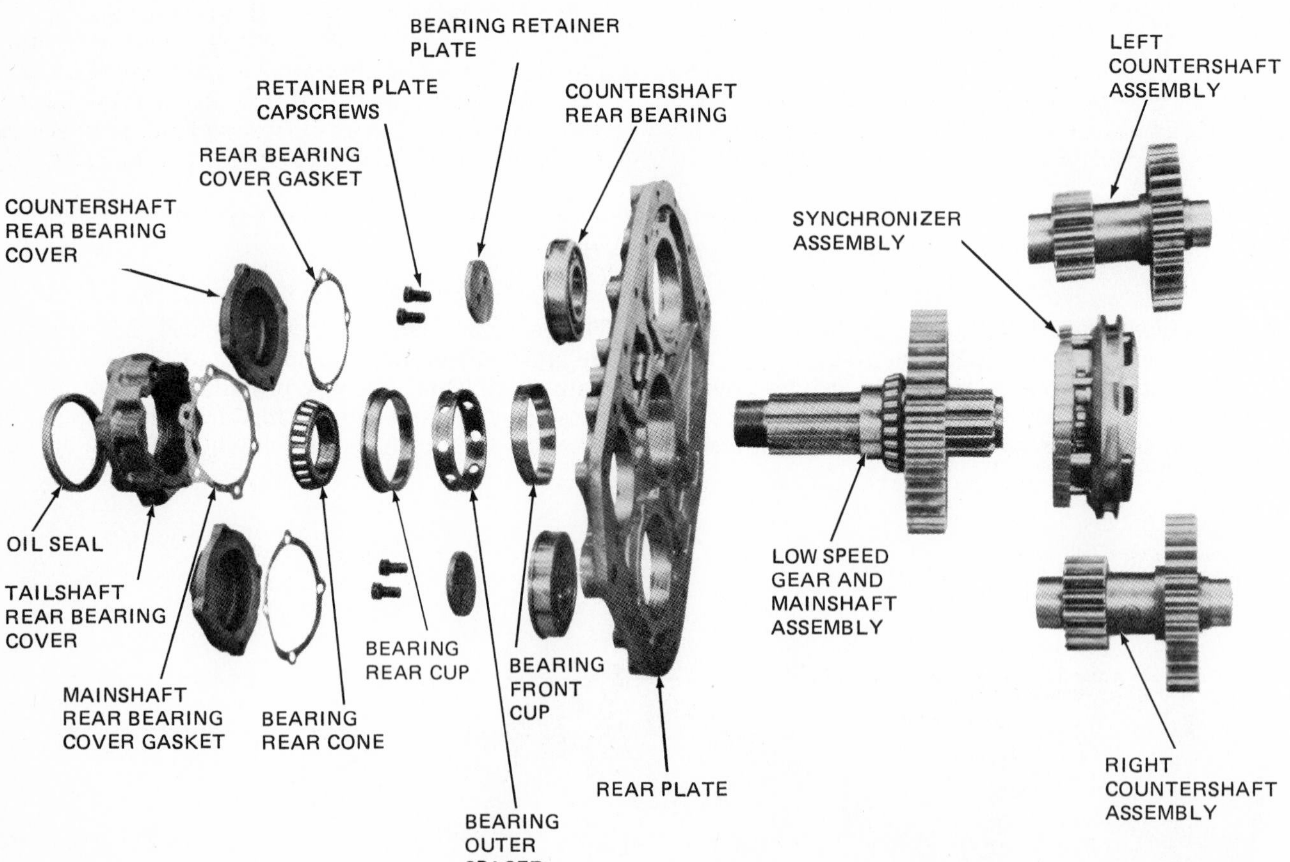

Fig. 11-29 Exploded view of the auxiliary section of an RT906 transmission. (*Eaton Corporation*)

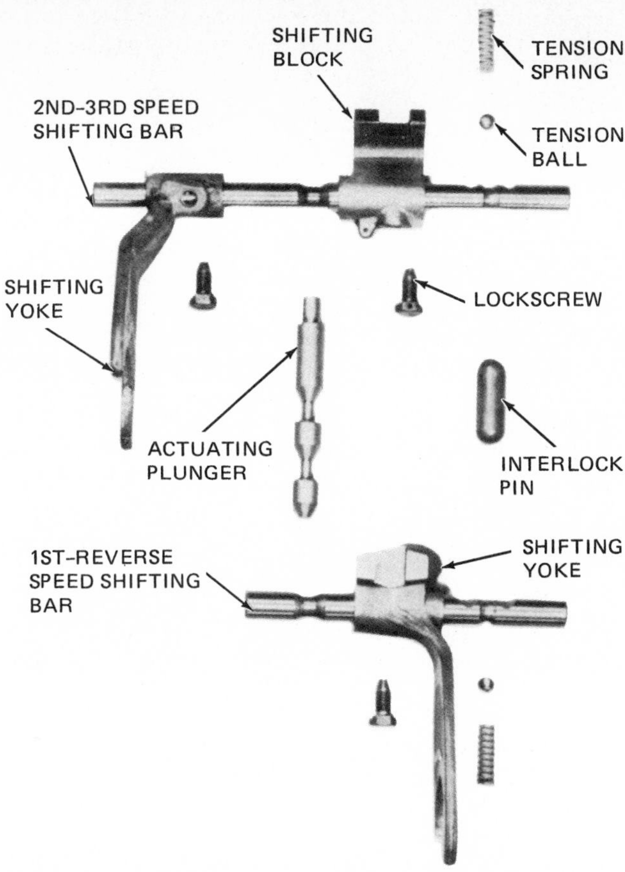

Fig. 11-30 Exploded view of shift bar housing assembly for an RT906 transmission. (*Eaton Corporation*)

into the grooves on the shift rails through the actuating pin spring force. This action moves the pin end out of the groove in the air valve spool.

The range transmission is shifted through a double-action air cylinder bolted to the rear cover. The air supply comes from the air brake reservoirs. The shifting bar is fastened on one end to the air piston, and the range shift fork is fastened to the other end. **NOTE** The range transmission has no neutral.

The shift bars have two detents, low and high (direct), and, depending on the bar position, the spring-loaded detent ball rests in either low or high position.

AIR CONTROL SYSTEM The air control system for the RT906 transmission consists of the components shown in Fig. 11-31. The range control valve is used to direct air to the air valve. The air valve is used to direct air onto the left- or right-hand side of the air cylinder piston. The air regulator reduces the reservoir pressure to around 60 psi [413.4 kPa] and the air filter cleans the air before it enters the control system. The air valve is a two-position spool valve, activated by air pressure; and the control valve is an on and off valve. When the air system is under pressure, the transmission in neutral, and the range valve is in high range, air flows from the reservoir through the air filter onto the air regulator. Here the air pressure is reduced, and then air flows to the control valve where it is blocked. At the same time, air flows from the air valve onto the left-hand side of the spool valve; then the valve spool shifts to the right and directs air onto the left-hand side of the range piston.

OPERATION To start the RT906 rig rolling, the operator pushes the control valve down (see Fig. 11-32). This directs air to the air valve (right-hand side), causing the valve spool to direct air onto the right-hand side of the air cylinder piston, moving the piston, piston shift bar, shift fork, and auxiliary sliding synchronizer clutch to the right, and engaging the sliding clutch with the female collar on the low-range driven gear. The operator then selects and

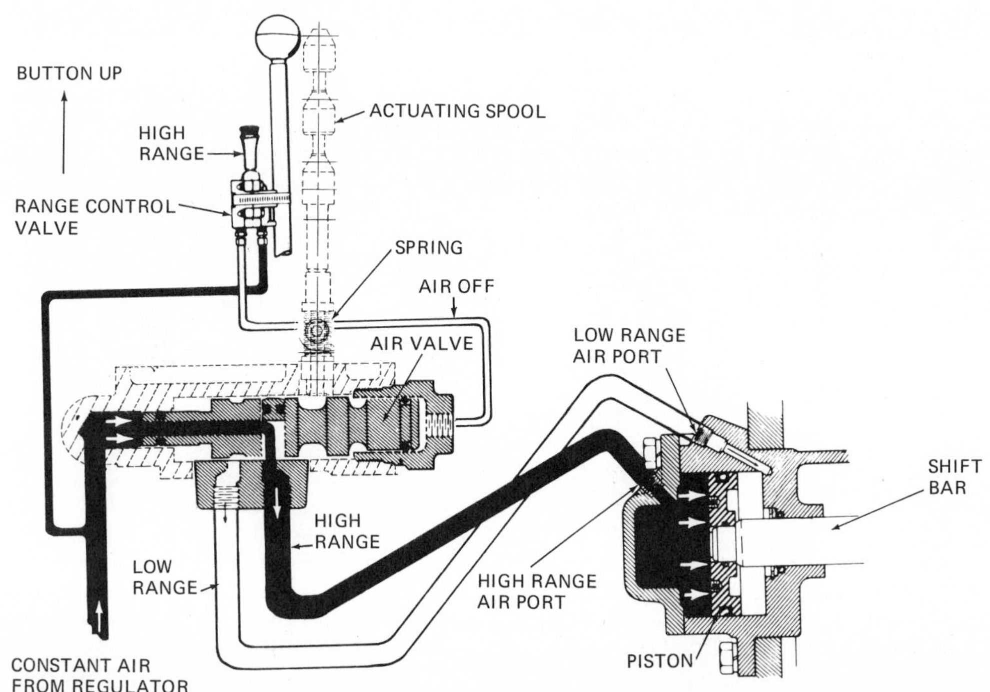

Fig. 11-31 Schematic view of the air control system in high range (RT906 transmission). (*Eaton Corporation*)

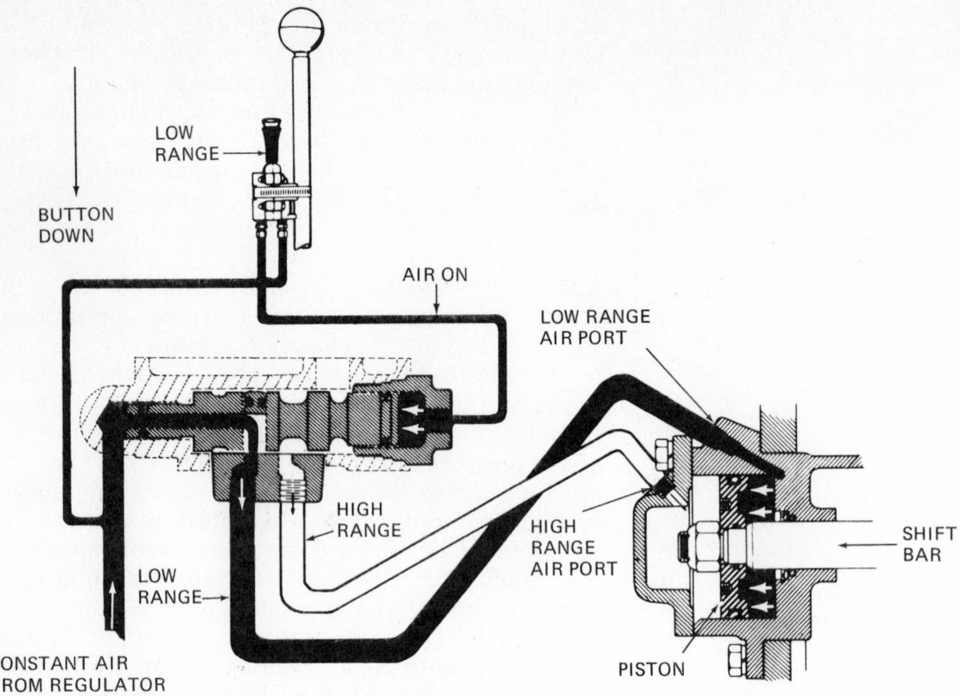

Fig. 11-32 Schematic view of the air control system in low range (RT906 transmission). (*Eaton Corporation*)

shifts into first speed gear in the main transmission. The torque now is transmitted from the clutch shaft main gear to the countershaft driven gears, and from the first-speed drive gear (on the countershaft), to the first-speed driven gear (on the main shaft), and over the collar clutch to the main shaft and auxiliary drive gear. From there it is transmitted to the left- and right-hand countershaft driven gears and low-speed drive gears, over the synchronizer clutch, and onto the tail shaft.

The operator then progressively shifts from first to second and then to third speed. When the engine speed approaches shift speed, she or he preselects high range by pulling the range control valve button up (see Fig. 11-31). This blocks the air flow to the air valve and air then exhausts from the right-hand side of the valve spool. As the operator shifts from third to first speed (in main transmission) and the shift rail passes through neutral, the actuating plunger and actuating pin are moved inward and the air pressure on the left-hand side of the air valve shifts the valve spool to the left. The air valve now directs air to the right-hand side of the piston. Consequently the piston, shift bar, shift fork, and synchronizer sliding male collar clutch slide to the left, clutching the tail shaft to the auxiliary drive gear. The torque from the main shaft is then directly transmitted to the tail shaft, nullifying the range transmission. The operator can now shift progressively from first to second and from second to third speed in the main transmission, which gives the operator fourth, fifth, and sixth speed.

Downshift When the main transmission is in first speed high range (fourth speed) and a downshift must be made, the operator pushes the range valve down (see Fig. 11-32). As he or she shifts from first to third speed in the main transmission, the range transmission shifts to low-range speed. The operator can now downshift in the main transmission from third to second speed, and then to first speed if so required.

T955 and T955 ALL Transmissions (Fuller) The T955 is a six-speed transmission and the T955 ALL is a seven-speed twin-countershaft transmission which uses a five-speed main transmission to which a two-speed auxiliary transmission is bolted. The auxiliary transmission is similar to that used on the RT906 six-speed transmission, except that the auxiliary transmission gears on the T955 are positioned in a separate housing. On the RT906 series, the gears can be located in the main transmission housing since there are fewer gears in the main transmission.

Other differences are in the identification of the main transmission gears, which are referred to (from left to right in Fig. 11-33) as fifth, fourth, third, second, and reverse, and that the first-speed gear is located in the tail shaft in the range transmission. The torque from the main shaft on the T955 is also transmitted over an auxiliary drive gear onto the auxiliary countershaft driven gear; however, the auxiliary drive gear is splined directly onto the main shaft. The auxiliary countershaft and driven gear and low reverse drive gear form one piece. Instead of a cone synchronizer, a collar clutch is used to shift into first speed and low reverse (see Fig. 11-34), and the shifting is done manually rather than by air-assist.

OPERATION To start the rig rolling (in first speed forward), the engine clutch is disengaged. Next, the shift lever is moved to the left to engage its lower ball socket with the reverse/second-speed shift block that is fastened to the reverse/second-speed shift bar. The lever is then pulled backward to engage the second-speed collar clutch with the second-speed driven gear. When in the second-speed position, the shift lever is pushed again to the left. This engages the

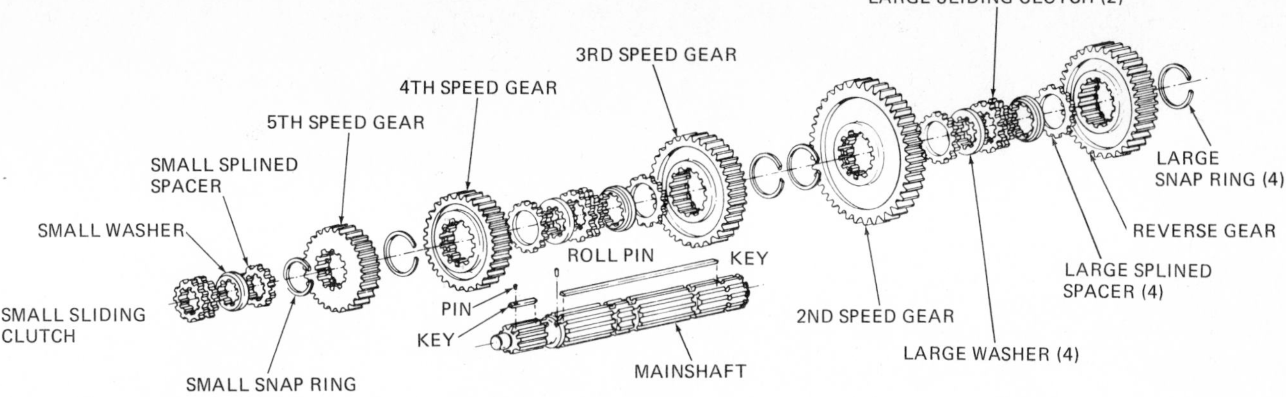

Fig. 11-33 Exploded view of the T955, or T955 ALL mainshift components. (*Eaton Corporation*)

lower shift lever ball socket in the first/low reverse shift block that is fastened to the first/low reverse shift bar. The lever is then pushed forward, which engages the male collar clutch (range transmission) with the female collar clutch on the low-speed driven gear. See Fig. 11-35. When the engine clutch is now engaged, the torque is transmitted from the clutch shaft drive gear onto the countershaft driven gears, and from the countershaft second-speed drive gears, onto the second-speed driven gear, and then over the collar clutch onto the main shaft and auxiliary drive gear. From the auxiliary drive gear, it is transmitted onto the auxiliary countershaft driven

Fig. 11-34 View of the auxiliary unit (T955). (*Eaton Corporation*)

gears, and from the low-speed drive gears onto the first-speed driven gear, over the collar clutch, and onto the output (tail) shaft, rotating the propeller shaft, and starting the rig moving.

To shift into second speed, the shift lever is pulled rearward. This disengages the first-speed driven gear from the output shaft and the male collar clutch engages with the auxiliary drive gear. Now the power from the countershaft second-speed drive gears in the main transmission is transmitted to the second-speed driven gear, over the collar clutch, onto the main shaft, auxiliary drive gear, and collar clutch, and finally onto the output shaft.

To shift into reverse, the shift lever is pulled to the left. This engages the lower ball socket with the second/reverse-speed shift block. The lever is then pushed forward to engage the second/reverse-speed male collar clutch with the reverse driven gear on the main shaft. The torque now is transmitted from the countershaft reverse driven gears, onto the reverse idlers, from there onto the reverse driven gear, over the second/reverse-speed collar clutch and onto the main shaft, auxiliary drive gear, and collar clutch, and finally onto the tail shaft.

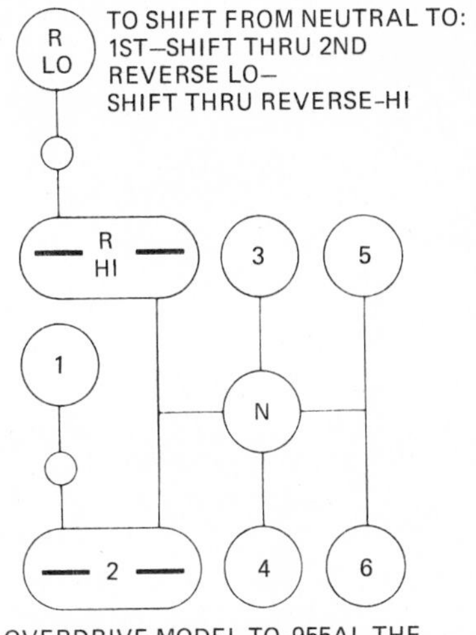

Fig. 11-35 Schematic view of T955 series shift pattern. (*Eaton Corporation*)

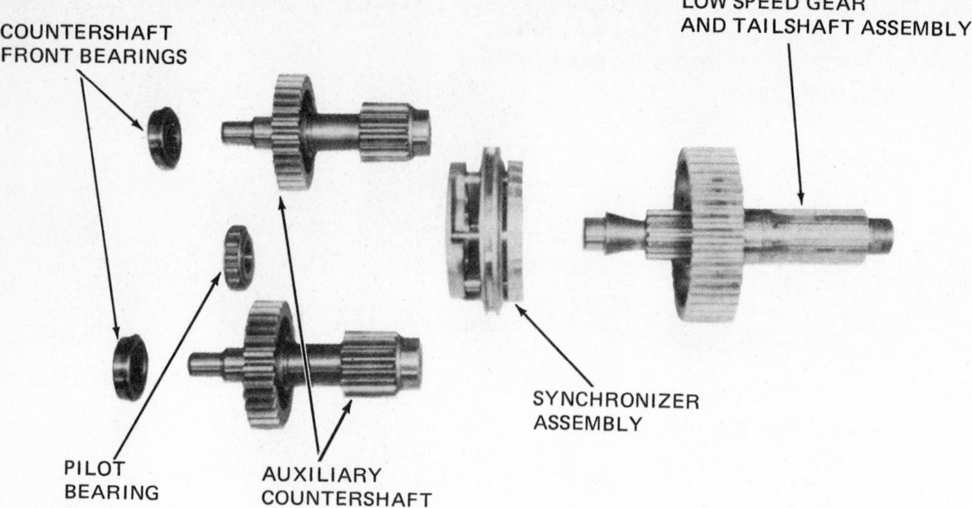

Fig. 11-36 Exploded view of the auxiliary section (RT610 transmission). *(Eaton Corporation)*

If a higher reverse ratio (low reverse) is required, the engine clutch is disengaged and the shift lever moved to the extreme left. This engages the lower ball socket in the cutout of the first/low reverse speed shift block. The shift lever is then moved forward to engage the male with the female collar clutch on the first-speed driven gear. The torque now is transmitted from the reverse driven gear in the main transmission, over the collar clutch onto the main shaft, to the auxiliary drive gear, to the auxiliary countershaft driven gears, and from the countershaft first-speed drive gears onto the first-speed driven gear and over the collar clutch onto the tail shaft.

To make a T955 ALL seven-speed forward transmission out of a T955 six-speed transmission, the two-speed auxiliary transmission is replaced with a three-speed auxiliary transmission. (See also material on thirteen- and fifteen-speed transmissions below.)

RT610 Ten-Speed Transmission (Fuller) The ten-speed Fuller transmission consists of a standard five-speed main transmission and a two-speed auxiliary transmission. The drive from the transmission main shaft to the auxiliary countershaft is also over an auxiliary drive gear assembly. However, it is splined directly onto the mainshaft. The auxiliary transmission is very similar to the RT906 six-speed transmission previously covered, although the countershaft, as well as the output shaft, are slightly longer. (See Fig. 11-36.) It is otherwise identical in design, with the air system components and the operation the same on both transmissions.

OPERATION Since the main transmission has five speeds forward and the auxiliary transmission has high and low range, the ten forward speeds are obtained by shifting the auxiliary transmission to low range and using, progressively, the five speeds in the main transmission, then shifting the range transmission into high range and once again using the five speeds in the main transmission.

RT613 Thirteen-Speed Transmission (Fuller) This transmission uses a standard five-speed twin countershaft main transmission and a three-speed auxiliary transmission. It has thirteen forward and three reverse speeds. The five-speed ratios in the main transmission are selected and shifted by one lever, and the range transmission selection (low, intermediate, and direct range) is made through a three-position air selector valve.

The main transmission is almost identical to the RT906, except that the main transmission main shaft on the RT613 is longer and extends into the auxiliary transmission. The main shaft is supported at the right through the combined effort of the rear bearing retainer, the spring-loaded center ring, and the rear ball bearing. See Fig. 11-37. The auxiliary drive clutch gear is loosely splined to the main shaft. The intermediate shift fork rests in the groove of the auxiliary drive gear/clutch gear assembly. The shift bar is connected to one side of the assembly, and the other side of the shift bar is connected to the low-speed air cylinder piston. The intermediate drive gear is splined to the drive gear and bolted to the rear end of the main shaft (Fig. 11-37). The auxiliary countershaft low-speed and intermediate gear is one piece to which the countershaft driven gear is keyed. The countershafts are supported at the rear by ball bearings, and at the front by roller bearings. Two sets of tapered roller bearings support the tail shaft—one located in the rear bearing housing and the other in the auxiliary rear housing, to which the low-speed gear is attached through a splined spacer, step washer, and washer. **NOTE** The low and intermediate drive gears have internal female collar clutches and coned friction surfaces. A pin synchronizer is used to achieve low and direct range. It has a sliding male collar clutch loosely splined to the tail shaft. The shift fork which rests in the groove of the sliding male collar clutch is attached to the shift bar; the other end of the shift bar is fastened to the low/direct double-acting air cylinder piston. When the male collar clutch engages with the low gear

1. Auxiliary housing
2. Left countershaft assembly
3. Right countershaft assembly
4. Extended main shaft
5. (a) Auxiliary drive gear
   (b) Auxiliary clutch gear
6. Intermediate shift fork
7. Main transmission housing
8. Rear ball bearing
9. Bearing retainer
10. Intermediate gear

Fig. 11-37 View of the auxiliary housing and components (RT613 transmission). (*Eaton Corporation*)

female collar clutch, the low-range driven gear is clutched to the tail shaft, and when the male collar clutch engages with the female collar clutch in the intermediate drive gear, the tail shaft is clutched to the main shaft. See Fig. 11-38.

AIR SYSTEM The air system (Fig. 11-39) consists of the air filter, air regulator (not shown), slave air valve, intermediate shift cylinder, auxiliary shift cylinder (low and direct), air control valve, and necessary air hoses. When the system is under pressure,

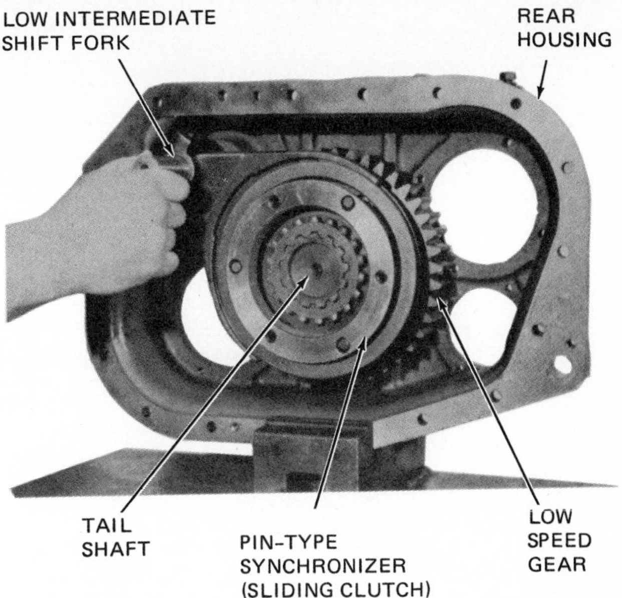

Fig. 11-38 View of rear housing (RT613 transmission). (*Eaton Corporation*)

this pressure is exerted on the control valve, the slave air valve, and the intermediate shift cylinder piston's left-hand side, shifting the piston to the right. The slave air valve is a two-position valve and its piston is air-actuated. The auxiliary and intermediate air cylinders are double acting.

OPERATION—LOW RANGE The air control valve is a three-position semirotating valve. When it is in the low position (with the main transmission in neutral), air is directed from the control valve to the slave air valve, and through the slave valve piston action air is directed onto the right-hand side of the auxiliary air piston. The piston, shift bar, shift fork, and synchronizer sliding male collar clutch move to the left, and the male collar clutch engages with the low-speed female collar clutch, clutching the low-speed gear to the tail shaft. Because no air pressure from the control valve is exerted on the intermediate shift cylinder, the insert valve and piston remain in the same position. See Fig. 11-39. The torque from one of the three forward speeds, or the one reverse speed, is transmitted from the clutch gear, onto the countershaft driven gears and low-range drive gears, and from there onto the low-range driven gear, over the synchronizer sliding clutch, and onto the tail shaft.

OPERATION—INTERMEDIATE RANGE When the control valve is placed in the intermediate range, the slave valve and auxiliary shift cylinder remain in the same position. The control valve directs air to the intermediate shift cylinder. This shifts the insert valve, which then closes a port and prevents the air from flowing onto the right-hand side of the intermediate piston. Air exhausts from the right-hand side of the piston; the intermediate piston, shift rail, shift fork, and male collar clutch are moved to the left. This disengages the clutch gear from the countershaft driven gears, and that gear then engages

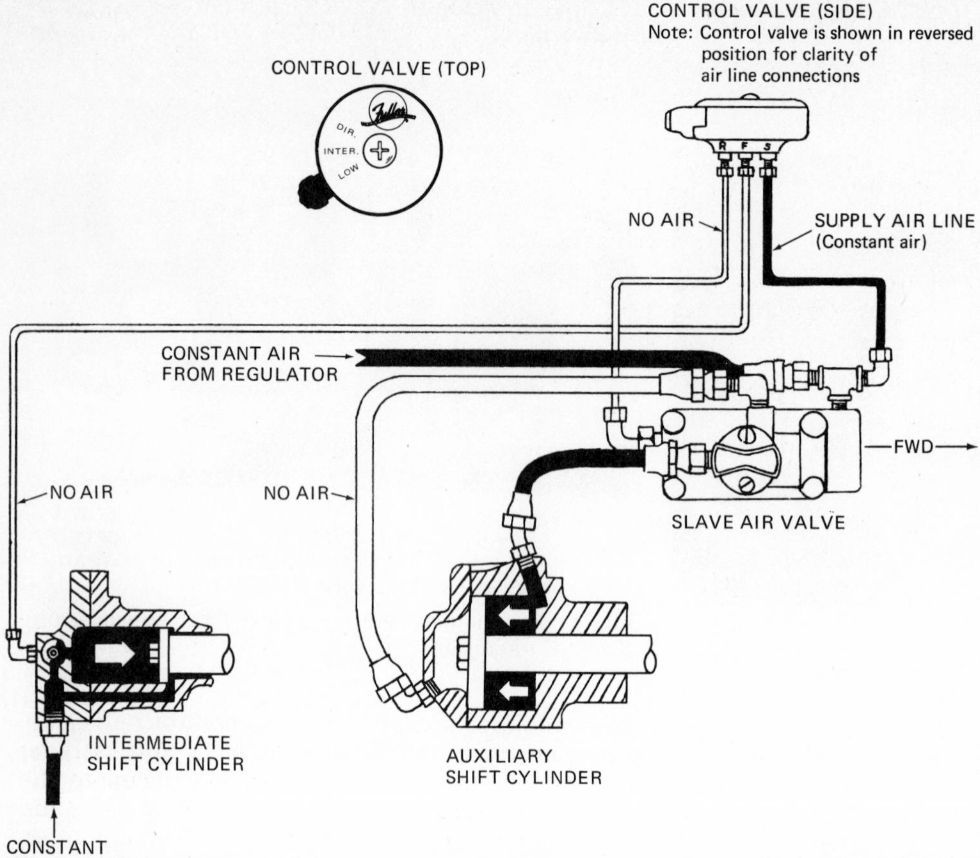

Fig. 11-39 Schematic view of the air system when the control valve is in the low position (low range) (RT613 transmission). (*Eaton Corporation*)

with the intermediate gear. Torque from one of the five forward gears or from the reverse gear is transmitted over a collar clutch onto the main shaft, from the drive gear/clutch gear to the intermediate drive gear and onto the intermediate countershaft gears, and from the countershaft low-range drive gears, onto the low-range driven gear, and over the synchronizer sliding male collar clutch onto the tail shaft. See Fig. 11-40.

OPERATION—DIRECT RANGE When the engine speed approaches shift speed, the operator semirotates the control valve into the direct position, which directs air to the left-hand side of the slave air valve piston. As the main transmission is shifted from fifth to first speed, the shift rail passes through neutral and the slave valve piston is moved by the air pressure. Now it directs air onto the left-hand side of the auxiliary piston and at the same time exhausts the air from the right-hand side. The auxiliary piston, shift rail, shift fork, and synchronizer sliding male collar clutch move to the right, and the latter disengages from the low-range gear and engages with the intermediate gear female clutch collar. The range transmission is then in direct drive, therefore the transmission is in the ninth speed (see Fig. 11-41). Torque from one of the five forward speeds or from the reverse speed is transmitted over the collar clutch, onto the main shaft, over the drive/clutch gear, to the intermediate gear, and over the synchronizer sliding male collar clutch onto the tail shaft.

RT9513 and RT12513 Thirteen-Speed Transmissions (Fuller) The RT9513 and RT12513 have a slightly different range transmission (Fig. 11-42) in that the splitter gear is attached to the tail shaft through a splined spacer, step washer, plain washer, and snap rings. The splitter shift fork rests in the groove of the male splitter sliding collar clutch, which is splined loosely to the left-hand end of the tail shaft. The shift bar is fastened to the splitter shift cylinder piston. **NOTE** The splitter shift cylinder of the RT9513 and RT12513 transmissions is the same as the intermediate shift cylinder on the RT613. The short auxiliary main shaft is supported through a bushing and bearing on the tail shaft quill, which is press-fitted into the tail shaft. Also, the low-range gear is attached (through a splined spacer and coupler) to the auxiliary main shaft. The pin synchronizer sliding male collar clutch is loosely splined to the auxiliary main shaft. The rotation from the main shaft to the auxiliary countershaft driven gears is achieved through an auxiliary drive gear that is splined to the main shaft. See Fig. 11-43. The auxiliary drive gear and the low-range drive gears have female collar clutches and coned friction surfaces.

The air system consists of an air filter, air regulator, air valve, splitter and range shift cylinder, and two air control valves. One of these valves, the splitter control valve, is two position semirotating, and the other, the range control valve, is two position push/pull.

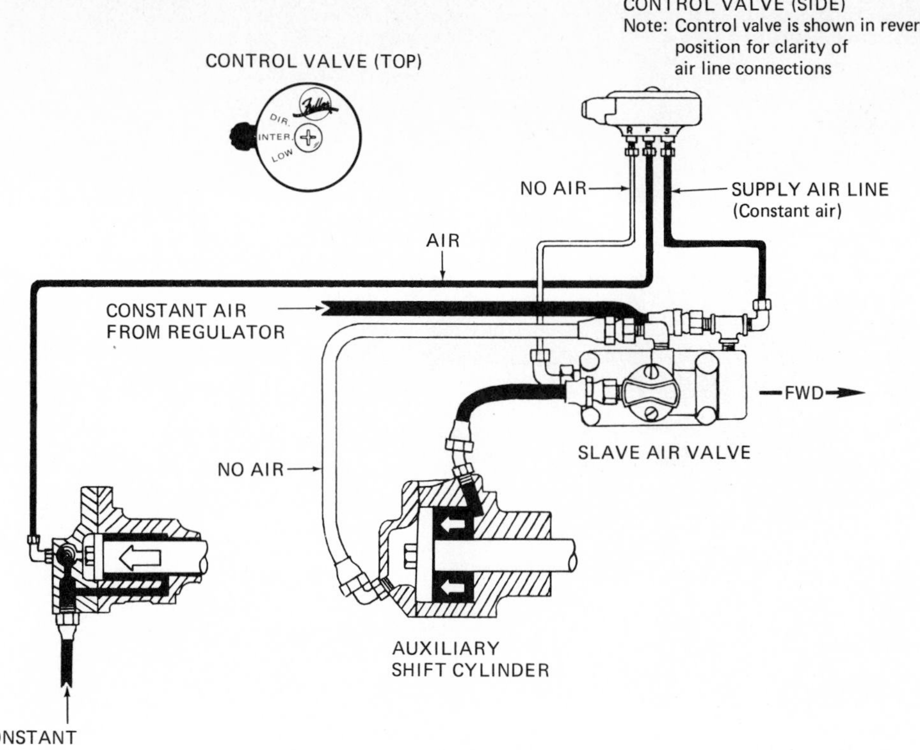

Fig. 11-40 Schematic view of the air system when the control valve is in the intermediate position (intermediate range) (RT613 transmission). (*Eaton Corporation*)

OPERATION This gear arrangement in the auxiliary transmission provides thirteen speeds forward and two reverse. When the air system is under pressure and the range and splitter control valves are rotated to the low position (see Fig. 11-44), air from them is directed over the air valve to the range air cylinder, and onto the right-hand side of the piston. This shifts the synchronizer sliding male collar clutch to the right, and it engages with the low-range driven gear. The range/splitter control valves block the air flow to the splitter air cylinder, thereby causing the insert valve to shift so that air is directed onto the

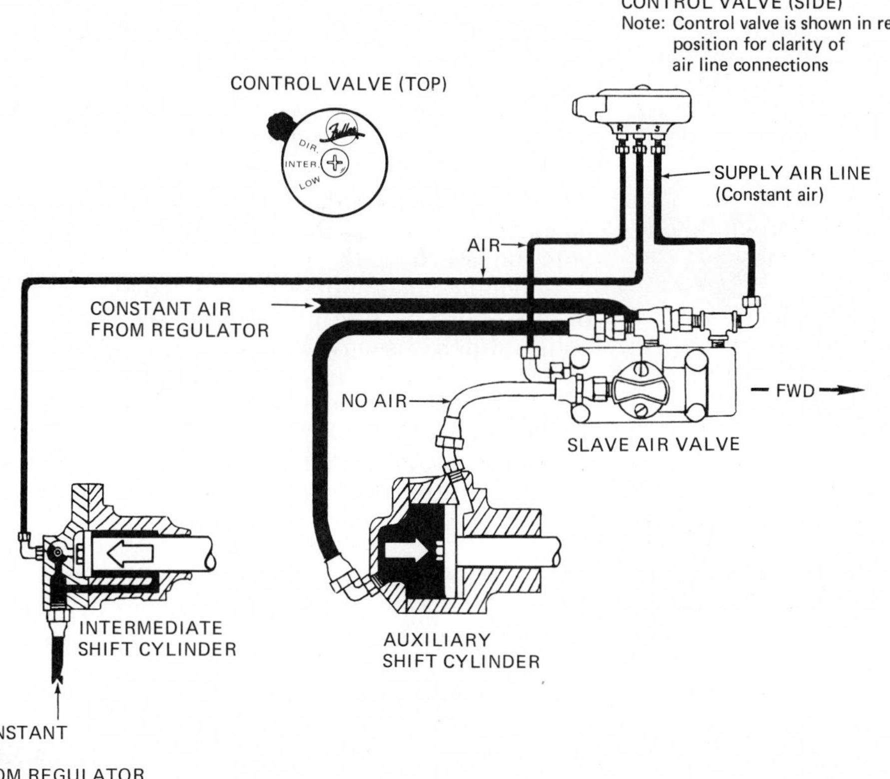

Fig. 11-41 Schematic view of the air system when the control valve is in the direct position (direct range) (RT613 transmission). (*Eaton Corporation*)

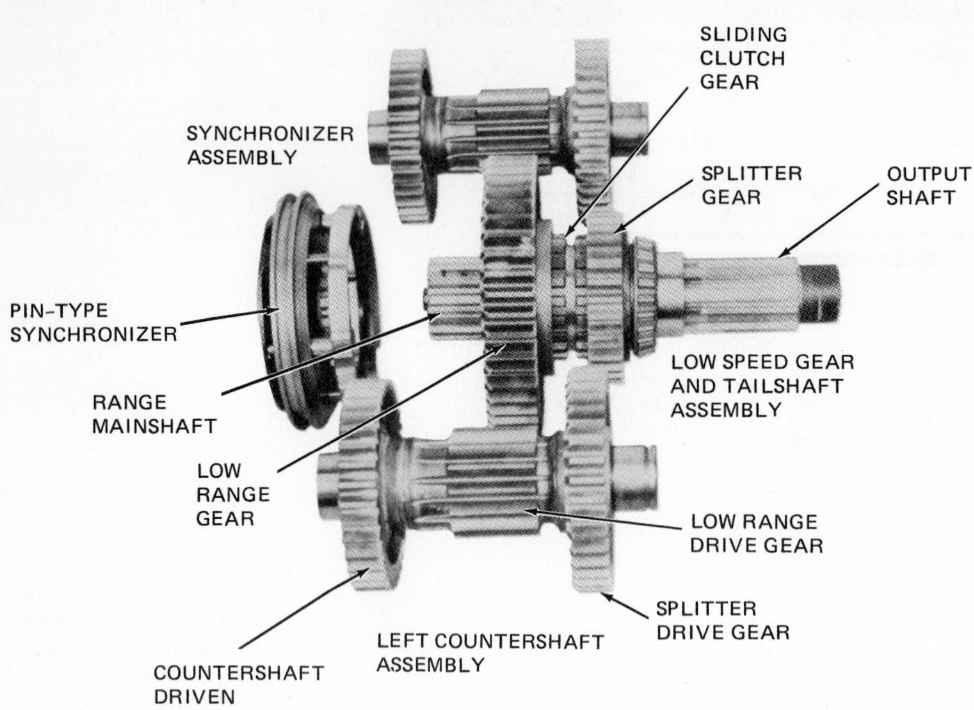

Fig. 11-42 View of the auxiliary gear train for RT9513 and RT12513 transmissions. (*Eaton Corporation*)

left-hand side of the splitter piston. The male collar clutch then engages with the auxiliary main shaft, clutching it to the tail shaft. The torque from the main transmission's main shaft is transmitted to the auxiliary drive gear, to the auxiliary countershaft driven gears, and to the low-range drive gears. From there it is transmitted onto the low-range driven gear, over the synchronizer collar clutch, onto the auxiliary mainshaft, and over the splitter collar clutch onto the tail shaft.

ROLLER BEARING
AUXILIARY
COUNTERSHAFT
MAIN
SHAFT
RIGHT MAIN
TRANSMISSION
COUNTERSHAFT
LEFT MAIN
TRANSMISSION
COUNTERSHAFT
AUXILIARY
DRIVE
GEAR
ROLLER BEARING
AUXILIARY
COUNTERSHAFT

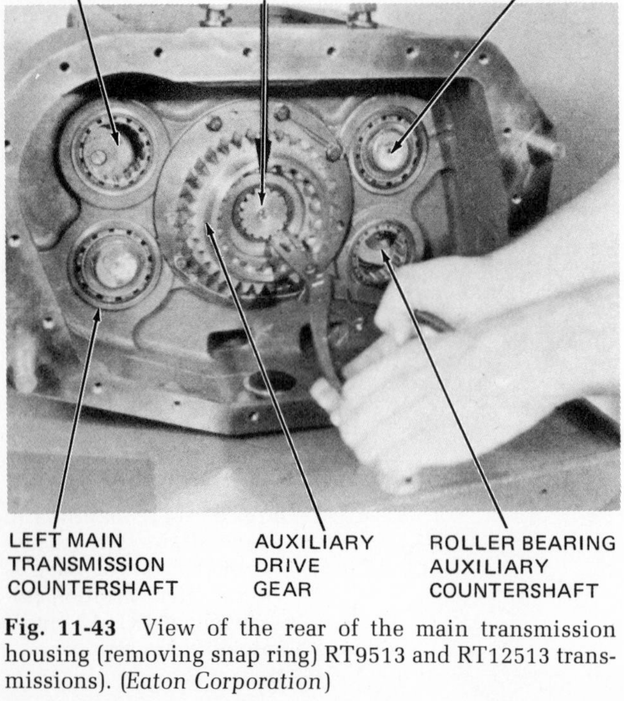

Fig. 11-43 View of the rear of the main transmission housing (removing snap ring) RT9513 and RT12513 transmissions). (*Eaton Corporation*)

To shift into direct range, the range/splitter control valves are rotated to direct position (see Fig. 11-45). This directs air to the left-hand side of the range cylinder, causing the synchronizer sliding male collar clutch to disengage from the low-range driven gear and engage with the auxiliary drive gear female clutch, thereby clutching the auxiliary main shaft to the main shaft. With the range/splitter selector in high range, the sliding male collar clutch remains engaged with the auxiliary main shaft and disengages from the splitter gear. As a result, the auxiliary transmission is in direct drive. The torque is then directed from the auxiliary drive gear over the synchronizer sliding collar clutch, onto the auxiliary main shaft, and over the sliding male collar clutch onto the tail shaft.

When the range/splitter selector valve is placed in the low position (see Fig. 11-46), the sliding male collar clutch disengages from the auxiliary main shaft and engages with the female collar clutch on the splitter gear. Now torque is transmitted over the auxiliary drive gear, to the auxiliary countershaft driven gears and splitter drive gears, and from there onto the splitter gear and over the collar clutch onto the tail shaft.

RT915 Fifteen-Speed Transmission (Fuller) The main and auxiliary transmissions and air control valves of the RT915 are nearly identical to those of the RT9513 except for the gear ratio in the auxiliary transmissions (see Fig. 11-47). Also, the RT915 technically has only 12 usable gear ratios; some ratios of the deep reduction overlap. Deep reduction means a very high reduction ratio.

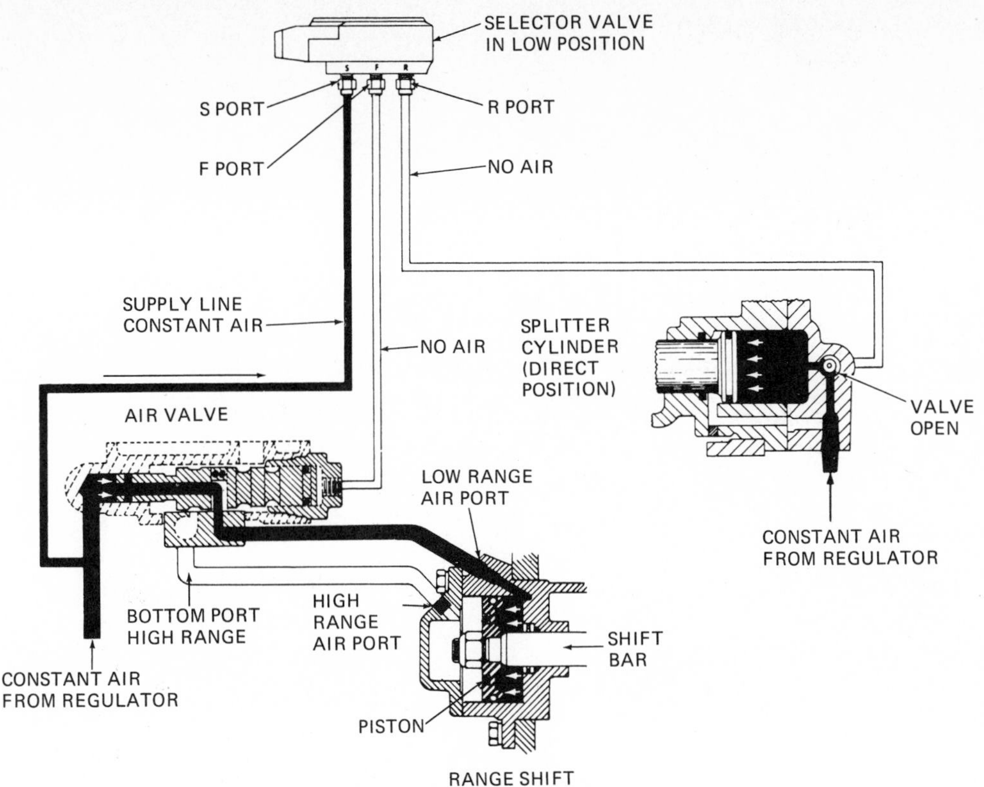

Fig. 11-44 Schematic view of the air control system (low range) (RT9513 and RT12513 transmissions). (*Eaton Corporation*)

Six-Speed Transmission (Spicer) To increase the number of gear ratios on a Spicer twin countershaft transmission from five to six speeds forward, one additional gear is placed on the countershafts between the PTO gear and countershaft driven gear, and another one is positioned on the main shaft between the direct shift collar clutch and the fourth-speed shift collar clutch. See Fig. 11-48. It is then necessary to change the direct drive shift rail in order to shift the collar clutch into fifth speed.

Seven- and Eleven-Speed Transmissions (Spicer) To increase this six-speed transmission to a "6 + 1" (seven speed), or to eleven speeds forward, a high/low-range transmission is bolted to the rear of the main transmission housing, and a jaw clutch is used

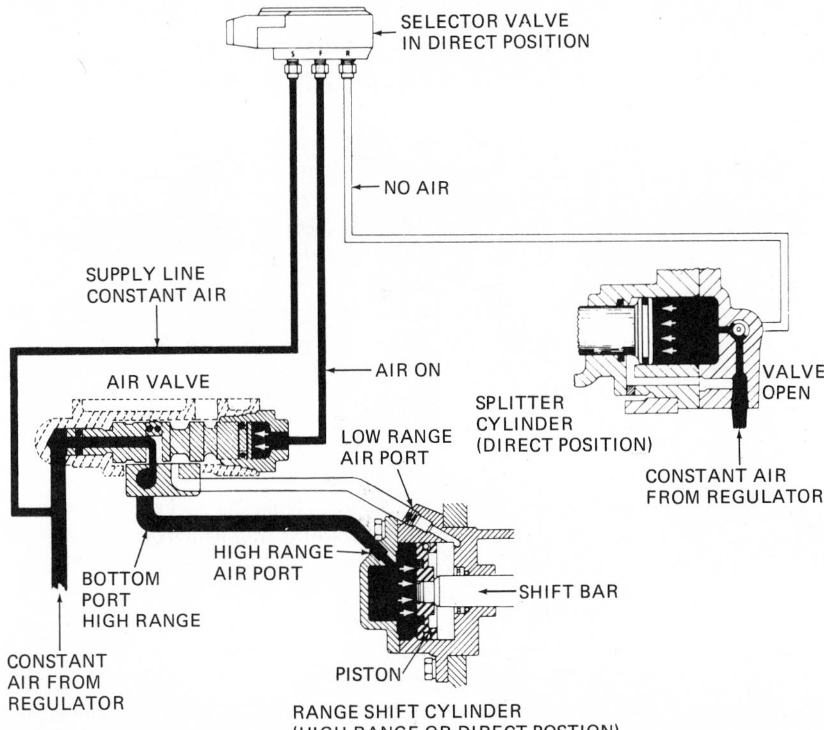

Fig. 11-45 Schematic view of the air control system in direct range (RT9513 and RT12513 transmissions). (*Eaton Corporation*)

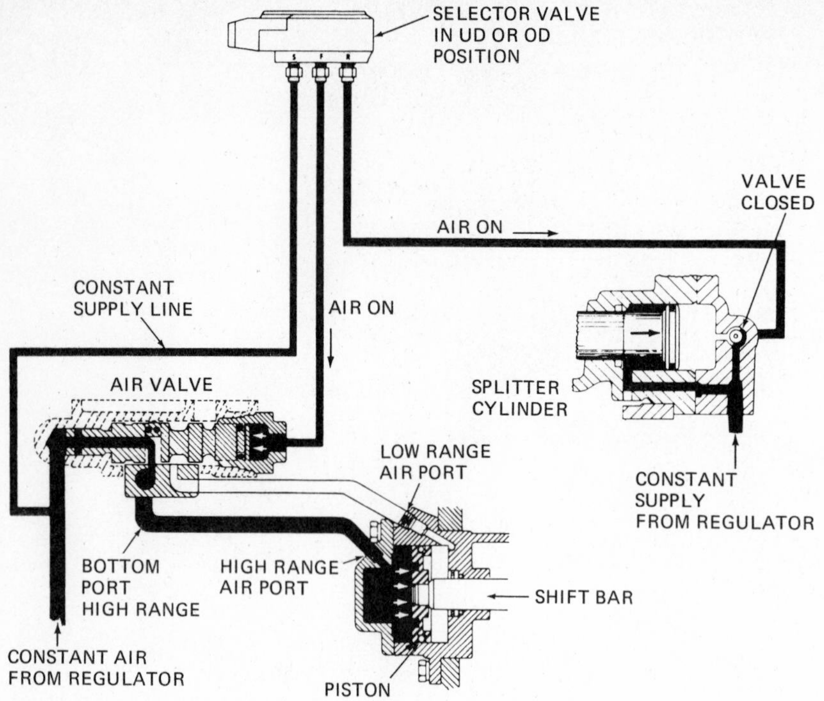

Fig. 11-46 Schematic view of the air control system in splitter range (RT9513 and RT12513 transmissions). *(Eaton Corporation)*

to engage the high- or low-range driven gears to the output shaft. However, note that the range transmission has no neutral position. See Fig. 11-49.

The range transmission, countershaft, and right-hand (low-range) drive gear form one piece, and the left-hand gear is keyed to the countershaft. The countershafts are supported in the rear case (cover) by tapered roller bearings, and the preload is adjusted through shims. The low-range and range transmission drive gears are cast with female jaw clutches. The range drive gear is splined to the main shaft and the low-range driven gear is supported on the output shaft. The output shaft is supported on the right by a ball bearing positioned in the housing,

Fig. 11-47 View of the RT915 auxiliary countershaft. *(Eaton Corporation)*

and on the left by the main shaft and a roller bearing. The roller bearing is positioned in the center bore of the output shaft. The male jaw clutch is splined to the left-hand side of the output shaft (see Fig. 11-49).

On a 6 + 1 (seven-speed) transmission, the shift cover and rail are so designed that, when the transmission is in reverse or first gear, the high and low range can be shifted to give the transmission one additional low gear and one reverse gear, but the range transmission shifter is blocked out in all other gears.

On the eleven-speed transmission, the shift cover and rails are so designed that, when the transmission is in reverse or in first, second, third, fourth, or fifth speed forward, high and low range can be shifted. This gives the transmission eleven speeds forward and two reverse speeds.

To make this shifting possible, a double-acting air cylinder is attached to the rear housing, and the piston is fastened to the piston rod, to which the jaw clutch is attached. An air shift valve (high and low) is fastened to the shift lever, and an air filter and pressure regulator are placed between the truck air reservoir and air distributor block, the latter being bolted to the air cylinder.

Ten-Speed Transmission (Spicer) To convert a six-speed to a ten-speed transmission, the front section of the six-speed transmission must be changed. See Figs. 11-50 and 11-51. The clutch shaft is extended, and the splitter jaw clutch gear is splined to it. The jaw clutch collar clutch slides on the splitter jaw clutch gear. The high splitter drive gear is partially supported on the clutch shaft and partially in the transmission housing using two sets of ball bear-

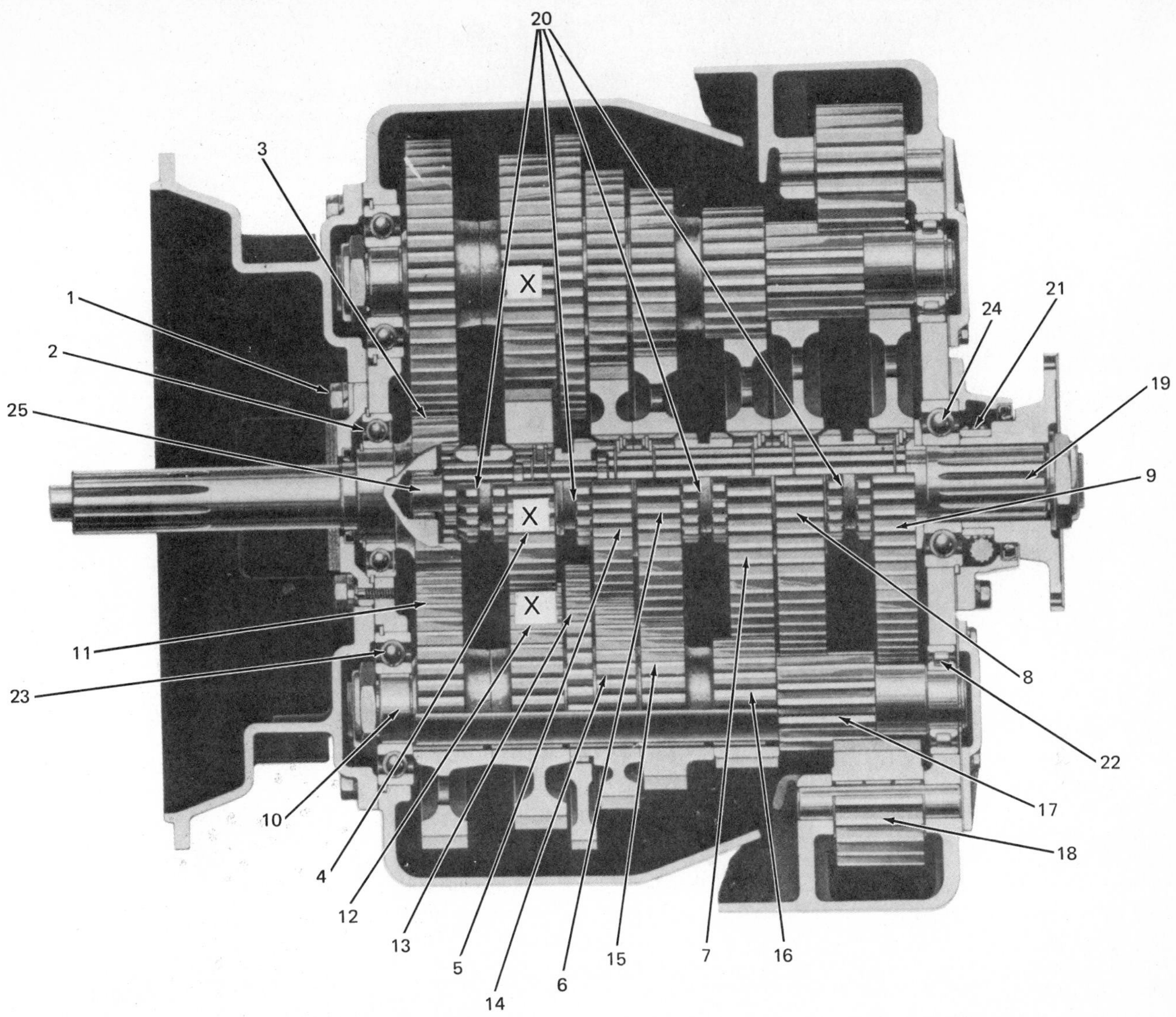

1. Main drive gear bearing cover
2. Main drive gear ball bearing
3. Main drive gear
4. Fifth-speed driven gear
5. Fourth-speed driven gear
6. Third-speed driven gear
7. Second-speed driven gear
8. First-speed driven gear
9. Reverse-speed driven gear
10. Countershaft
11. Countershaft driven gear
12. Countershaft fifth-speed drive gear
13. Countershaft PTO gear
14. Countershaft fourth-speed drive gear
15. Countershaft third-speed drive gear
16. Countershaft second-speed drive gear
17. Countershaft first/reverse-speed drive gear
18. Reverse idler
19. Main shaft
20. Collar clutches
21. Speedometer gear
22. Countershaft roller bearings
23. Countershaft ball bearings
24. Main shaft ball bearing
25. Main shaft needle bearing

Fig. 11-48 Sectional view of a six-speed twin countershaft transmission (Note: The gears marked with an X are added). (*Dana Corporation, Spicer Transmission Division*)

ings. The low splitter drive gear is supported at the left on the main shaft through an external spline thrust washer, a collar, and snap rings. An air cylinder is attached to the shaft housing and the air piston is connected, through the piston rod, to the splitter (high- and low-range) shift fork. This arrangement gives the transmission ten speeds forward and two reverse speeds.

OPERATION When the air selector valve is placed into the low position, the air piston, piston rod, shift fork, and male jaw clutch are pulled to the right. The male jaw clutch then engages with the female jaw clutch on the low splitter gear. The operator then shifts into first gear. The torque from the engine is now transmitted from the clutch drive shaft over to the low splitter clutch gear, male jaw clutch, low splitter drive gear, and from there onto the countershaft low splitter driven gear and first-speed countershaft drive gears. From that point, it is transmitted to the low-speed driven gear (on the main shaft), and over the collar clutch onto the mainshaft.

To shift into second speed, the engine clutch is disengaged, and at the same time the air splitter valve is placed into high. This disengages the male jaw clutch from the low splitter drive gear, and

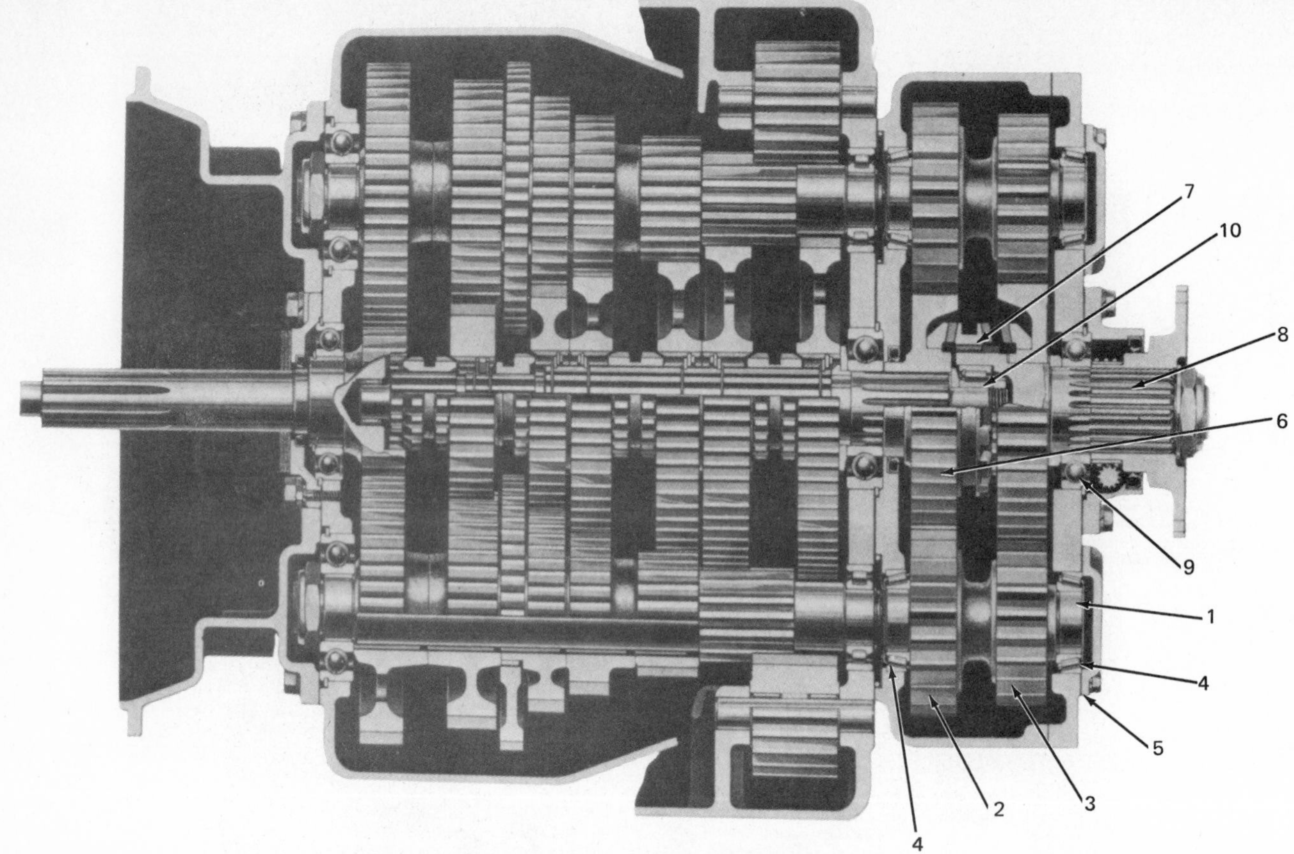

1. Range transmission countershaft
2. Countershaft driven gear
3. Low range drive gear
4. Tapered roller bearings
5. Shims
6. Range transmission drive gear
7. Jaw clutch
8. Output shaft
9. Output shaft ball bearing
10. Output shaft roller bearing

Fig. 11-49 Sectional view of a "6+1" twin countershaft transmission. (*Dana Corporation, Spicer Transmission Division*)

engages it with the high splitter drive gear, clutching the high splitter gear to the clutch shaft. Torque is now transmitted from the high splitter drive gear to the countershaft driven gears, and from the first-speed countershaft drive gear to the first-speed driven gear on the main shaft.

To shift into third speed, the operator first places the air valve into the low position, and when the engine speed reaches the shift rpm then shifts the main transmission into second speed. As the shift rail moves through neutral and onto the second speed, air is directed to the splitter air cylinder, and then the piston, piston rod, shift fork, and male jaw clutch move to the right. The male jaw clutch engages with the female jaw clutch on the low splitter gear, and the transmission is now in third speed.

Fourteen-Speed Transmission (Spicer) To convert a ten-speed into a fourteen-speed transmission, a range transmission similar to that used on the eleven-speed transmission is bolted to the main transmission housing, and a special four-piston air selector valve is fastened to the shift lever. The latter is connected with air lines to the splitter and range air cylinders (Fig. 11-52).

Maxitorque Triple-Countershaft Five-, Six-, Ten-, and Twelve-Speed Transmissions These are manufactured by Mack Truck Inc. for use on their trucks only. The basic triple-countershaft transmission is also a five-forward/one-reverse-speed transmission designed for on-highway truck and tractor operation, and is particularly suitable for long-distance hauls. All gears, except for the sliding reverse driven gear, are in constant mesh with one another. This five-speed transmission is splash-lubricated.

As the name indicates, the triple-countershaft transmission has three countershafts. They are equally spaced around the main shaft, with the lower one positioned below it. See Fig. 11-53. Each of the rear countershafts is splined to the front countershaft. The ends of the rear countershafts are supported by ball bearings, and the center by a roller bearing.

NOTE On the five-speed transmission, there is no upper left-hand rear countershaft.

Five-Speed Transmission (Maxitorque) The reverse-speed drive gear is machined to each of the two rear countershafts and an oil slinger is splined to the lower rear countershaft. The first-speed drive

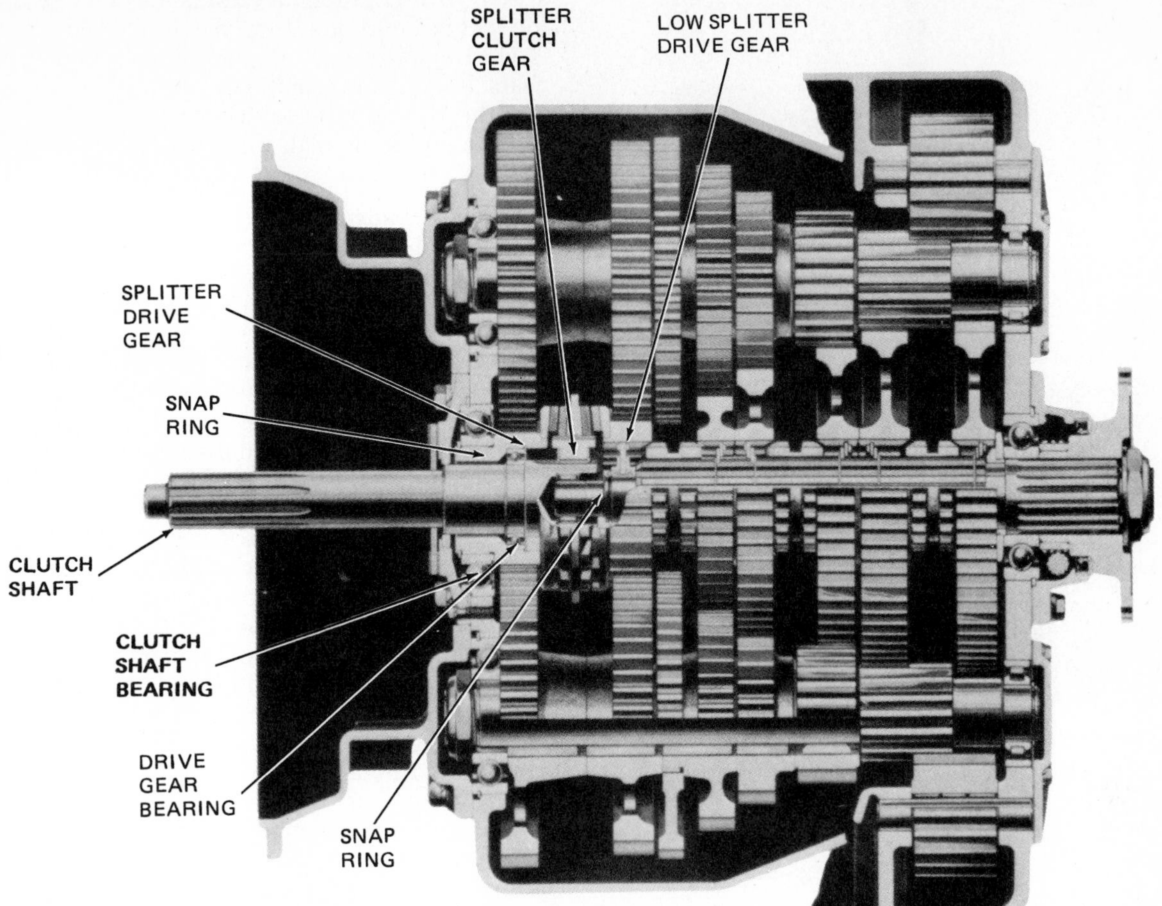

Fig. 11-50 Sectional view of a ten-speed twin countershaft transmission. (*Dana Corporation, Spicer Transmission Division*)

gear is machined to each of the front countershafts, and to these, the second-, third-, and fourth-speed, countershaft drive gears are keyed. The clutch drive shaft (main driving pinion assembly) is a one-piece unit supported by a ball bearing located in the main housing. It supports the left-hand side of the main shaft through a roller bearing, located in the bore of the clutch shaft. The right-hand side of the main shaft is supported by a ball bearing. The sliding reverse gear is loosely splined to the rear portion of the main shaft, and the reverse-speed shift fork rests in the machined groove of the gear. All other driven gears on the main shaft have female collar clutches. The driven gears are positioned to the main shaft through selected spacers and snap rings, and float between the three countershaft drive gears.

The short fifth/fourth-speed male collar clutch is loosely splined to the main shaft and positioned between the clutch shaft drive gear and the fourth-speed driven gear; and the fifth/fourth-speed shift fork rests in the center groove. The long third/second-speed male collar clutch is loosely splined to the larger portion of the main shaft, and the male collar clutch is positioned between the third- and second-speed driven gears. The third/second-speed shift fork rests in the groove machined on the right-hand side of the clutch collar. The short, one-sided, male collar first-speed clutch is loosely splined to the third/second-speed male collar clutch, and its shift fork rests in the machined groove of the clutch collar. The two reverse idlers are supported by roller bearings and are in constant mesh with the countershaft reverse-speed drive gears.

The three shift rails (first/reverse, second/third,

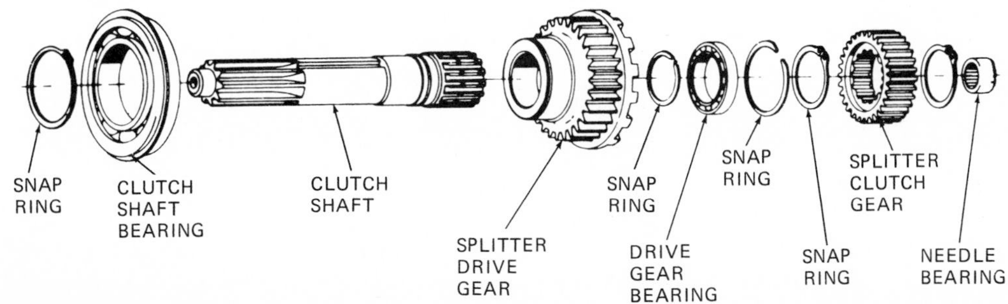

Fig. 11-51 Exploded view of clutch shaft assembly (ten-speed twin gearshaft transmission).

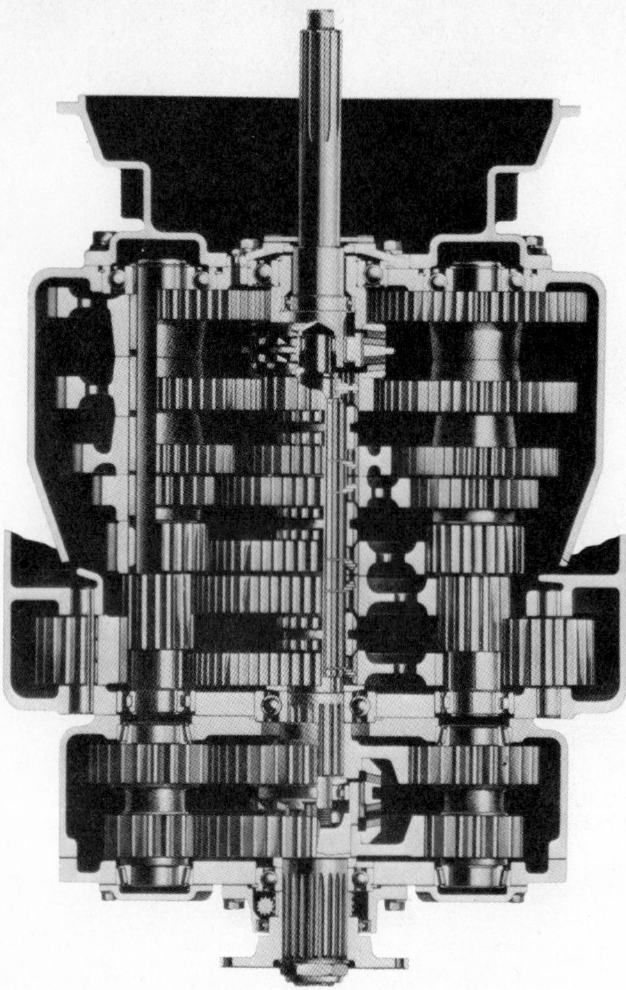

Fig. 11-52 Sectional view of a fourteen-speed transmission. (*Dana Corporation, Spicer Transmission Division*)

and fourth/fifth speeds) are supported in the bores of the transmission housing, and the shift lever or shift control lever lower ball socket rests in the cutout of the second/third-speed shift block and fourth/fifth-speed shift fork. See Fig. 11-54.

OPERATION Shifting into any one of the five forward gears closely resembles the shifting of any five-

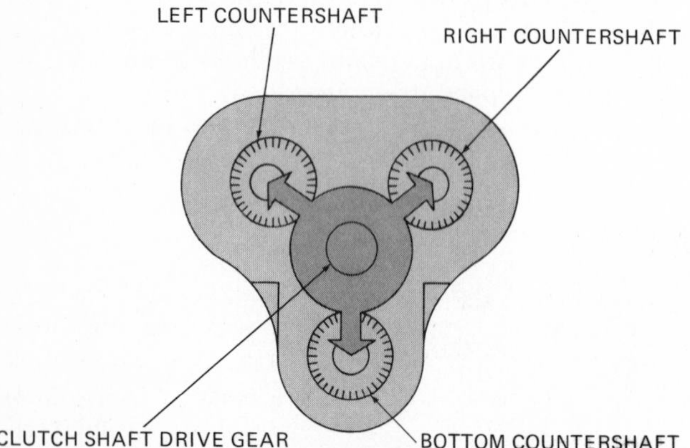

Fig. 11-53 Schematic showing position of countershafts on a triple-countershaft transmission. (*Mack Canada Inc.*)

speed twin-countershaft transmission, except that the incoming torque from the clutch shaft drive gear is split equally onto the three countershaft driven gears. Furthermore, achieving reverse differs only in that the sliding reverse driven gear is moved to the right to engage it with the reverse idler gears.

Six-Speed Transmission (Maxitorque) To convert a five-speed to a six-speed triple-countershaft transmission requires several changes. The rear countershafts are no longer splined to the front countershafts—instead, they are independently supported. Refer to Fig. 11-55. The left-hand sides of the front countershafts are supported by ball bearings, and the right-hand sides by roller bearings. The left-hand sides of the rear countershafts are supported on the front countershafts by roller bearings, and on the right-hand side by ball bearings. The reverse-speed drive gear and low- and direct-range drive gears are keyed to each rear countershaft. The main shaft is now comprised of a two-piece unit—the main shaft and the output shaft. Although these shafts support each other, the output shaft is also supported at the right by a ball bearing positioned in the transmission housing and by a roller bearing located in the rear bearing cover. On its right-hand side, the main shaft is supported by a roller bearing located in the bore of the output shaft, and on its left it is supported by a ball bearing positioned in the bore of the clutch shaft. The sliding reverse driven gear is loosely splined to the right-hand side of the output shaft, and the low-range driven gear is supported through a thrust washer and positioned, through snap rings, to the output shaft. The low/direct range male collar clutch is loosely splined to the left-hand side of the output shaft, and the direct drive gear is splined to the right-hand side of the main shaft.

Since low range for the second, third, fourth, and fifth speeds is impractical to use because the ratio is almost identical to the ratio in high range (direct), the transmission has only six usable forward speeds and five reverse speeds.

LUBRICATING PUMP In addition, this transmission has an eccentric shuttle pump (vane pump), located in the clutch shaft, with which it pressure-lubricates the collar clutches and gears located on the main and output shafts. The pump has one moving part—a double-ended reciprocating vane positioned in the clutch shaft bore. The eccentric ring is positioned inside the clutch shaft bearing cover.

When the engine is operating, the rotation is transmitted over the clutch shaft to the countershaft and main shaft gears. Consequently, oil from the gears is thrown into the reservoir (see Fig. 11-56), where ferrous metallic particles, if present, are removed by the magnet. The oil then flows to the pump inlet through a passage in the transmission housing and clutch drive shaft bearing cover. When the clutch drive shaft rotates, the vane pump reciprocates due to the eccentric (chamber) ring. This causes the vane ends to seal against the ring, and as each end in turn traps the oil in the eccentric chamber the valve port leading to the center of the shaft

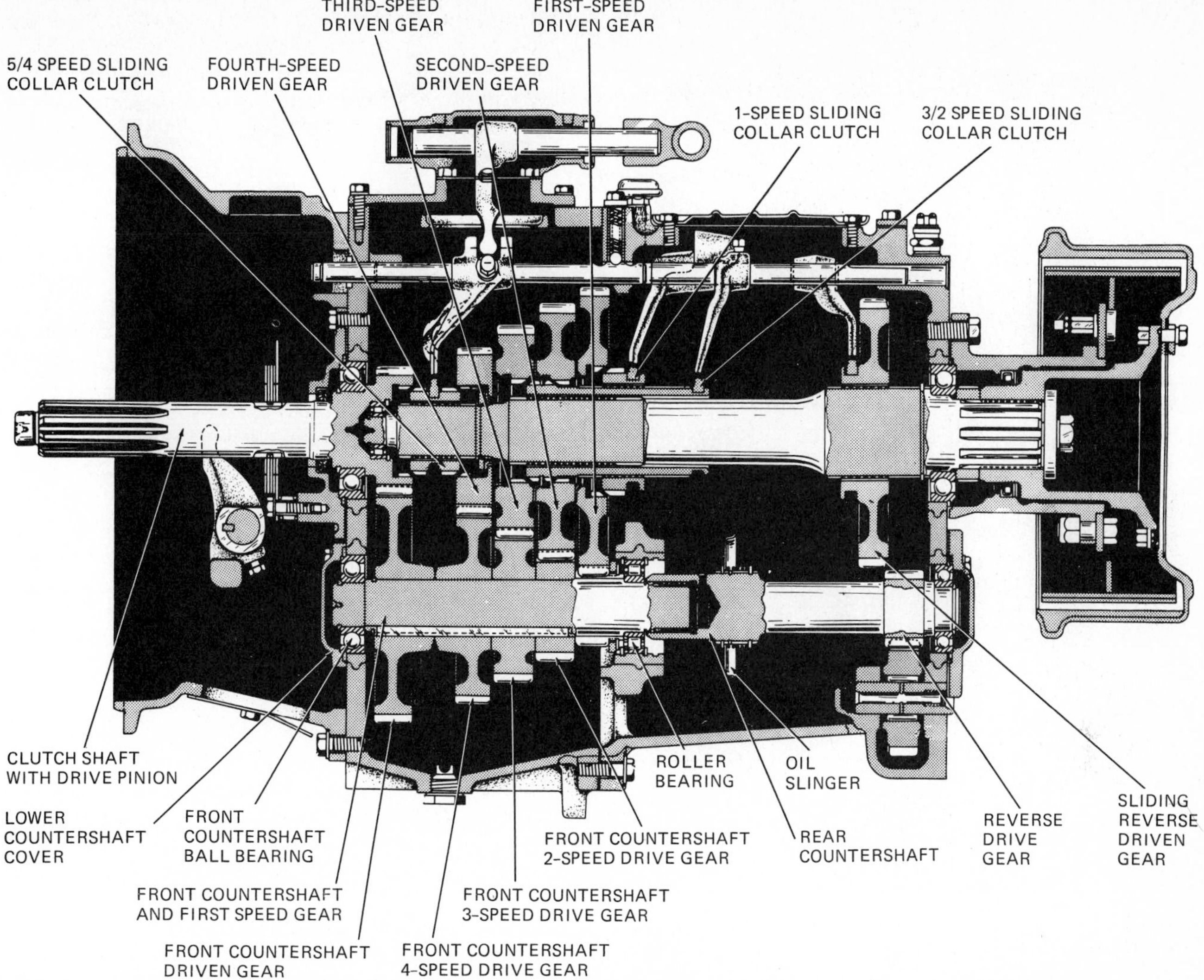

Fig. 11-54 Sectional view of a five-speed triple-countershaft transmission. (*Mack Canada Inc.*)

closes. The oil is carried around the vane end, opening the valve port, and it is then forced into the center of the clutch drive shaft and into the main and output shafts. **NOTE** A bronze nipple is used to bridge the gap between the clutch drive shaft and main shaft, but there is enough clearance to allow oil to pass by and lubricate the ball bearing on the main shaft.

Ten-Speed Transmission (Maxitorque) The ten-speed forward and five-speed reverse transmission shown in Fig. 11-57 is nearly identical to the six-speed Maxitorque transmission but for some minor exceptions: the low-range drive and driven gears have a ratio different from the six-speed transmission, the compound gear sets become a splitter section instead of a collar clutch, a jaw clutch is used, and the reverse and the splitter sections are shifted by air.

The air control system (Fig. 11-58) is similar to a Fuller or Spicer air shift transmission, consisting also of an air filter, two air regulators (pressure-reducing valves), a four-position semirotating air control valve, a quick release valve, and the necessary hoses to connect the components. The air control valve has two levers—one for selecting reverse and the other for selecting low and direct. When the air system is under pressure and the reverse air selector lever is in neutral, air (at reservoir pressure) is directed over port 4, onto the right-hand side of the reverse cylinder piston, retaining the reverse shift rail in neutral. If the air selector range lever is placed in the LOW position, the air is directed over the pressure-reducing valve, into port 1 and to the left-hand side of the splitter air cylinder piston, moving the piston, shift rail, shift fork, and male jaw clutch to the right. The male jaw clutch engages with the low-range gear female jaw clutch, clutching the low-range gear to the output shaft.

OPERATION To start the rig rolling, the operator shifts into first gear, whereupon the torque is transmitted from the main shaft, over the splitter low-range countershaft gears, onto the low-range drive gears, and over the jaw clutch onto the output shaft. As the engine shift speed is reached, the engine clutch is disengaged, and at the same time the range air selector lever is turned to DIRECT. This exhausts

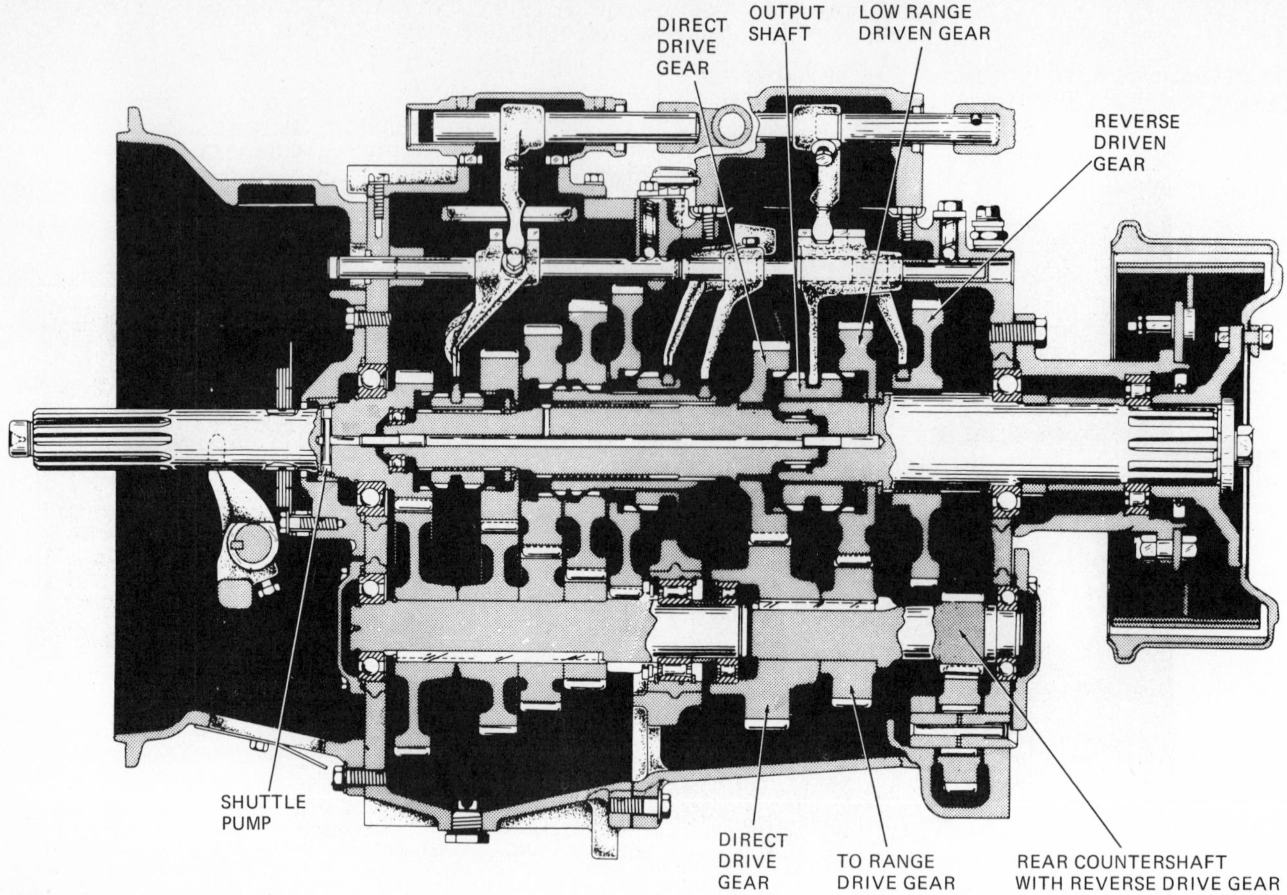

Fig. 11-55 Sectional view of a six-speed triple-countershaft transmission. (*Mack Canada Inc.*)

air from the left-hand side of the piston and directs it over the pressure regulator, into port 2, and to the splitter air cylinder piston, and consequently the piston, shift rail, shift fork, and male jaw clutch move to the left, and the jaw clutch disengages from the low-range gear and engages with the direct drive gear, clutching the output shaft to the main shaft. When the engine speed again reaches shift speed, the operator disengages the engine clutch and at the same time shifts the main transmission into second speed and turns the range air selector lever to LOW. This shifts the splitter into low range.

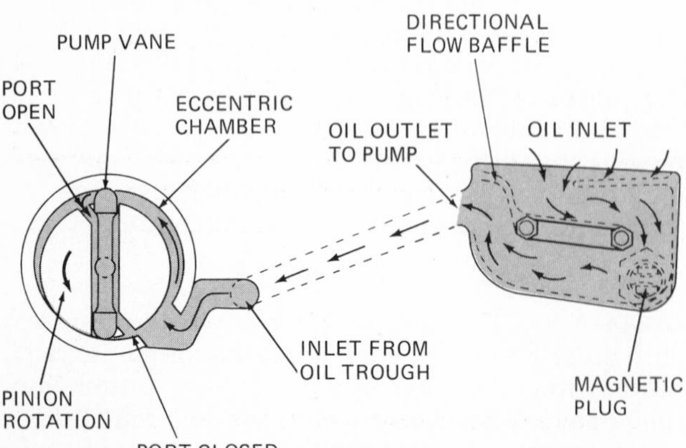

Fig. 11-56 Schematic showing oil flow from oil cleaner to oil pump in a six-speed triple-countershaft transmission. (*Mack Canada Inc.*)

To shift into reverse, the reverse selector lever is placed into reverse and the range selector switch into neutral. Air is then directed over the quick-release valve into port 3 and onto the reverse air piston, whereupon air promptly exhausts from the left-hand side of the piston through the air control valve. The piston, shift rail, shift fork, and sliding reverse gear are moved to the right, and the sliding reverse gear meshes with the reverse idlers. Now the operator can select any of the five gears in the main transmission to achieve five reverse speeds. **NOTE** When the transmission is in reverse, the shift rail closes the backup switch, warning the driver that it is in reverse.

Twelve-Speed Transmission (Maxitorque) The twelve-speed forward, five-speed reverse transmission is a ten-speed transmission to which a compound gear set is bolted (see Fig. 11-59). This would appear to give the transmission actually fifteen speeds forward and ten reverse, but due to a positive interlock low range in the front compound gear set can only be shifted when the main transmission is in first gear, not in any other. This gives the transmission two additional low-speed ratios—one 18.56:1.00 and the other 14.44:1.00.

OPERATION To achieve the low-low-speed ratio of 18.56 (first speed), the shift lever of the front compound gear set is pushed forward. This moves the

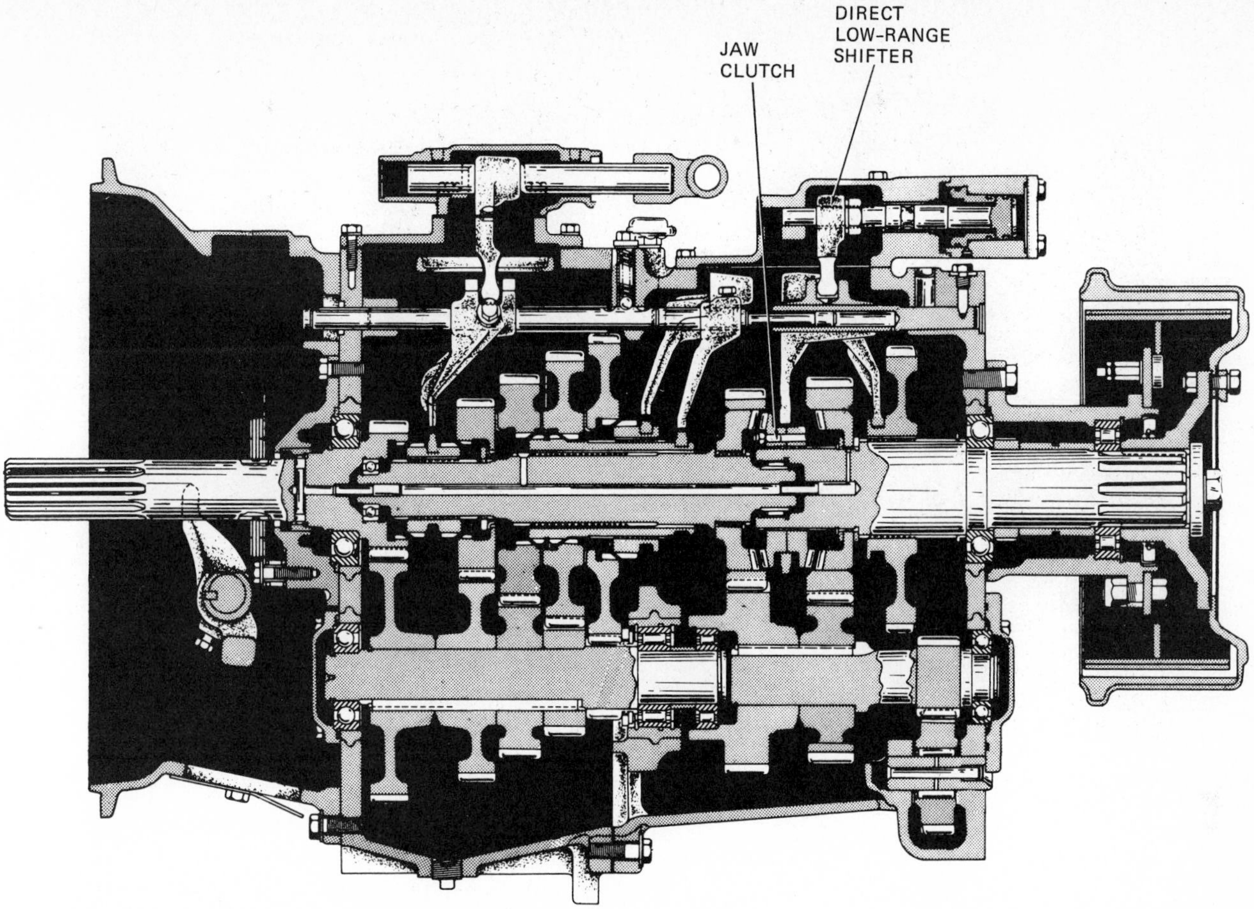

DIRECT LOW-RANGE SHIFTER

JAW CLUTCH

Fig. 11-57 Sectional view of a ten-speed triple-countershaft transmission. (*Mack Canada Inc.*)

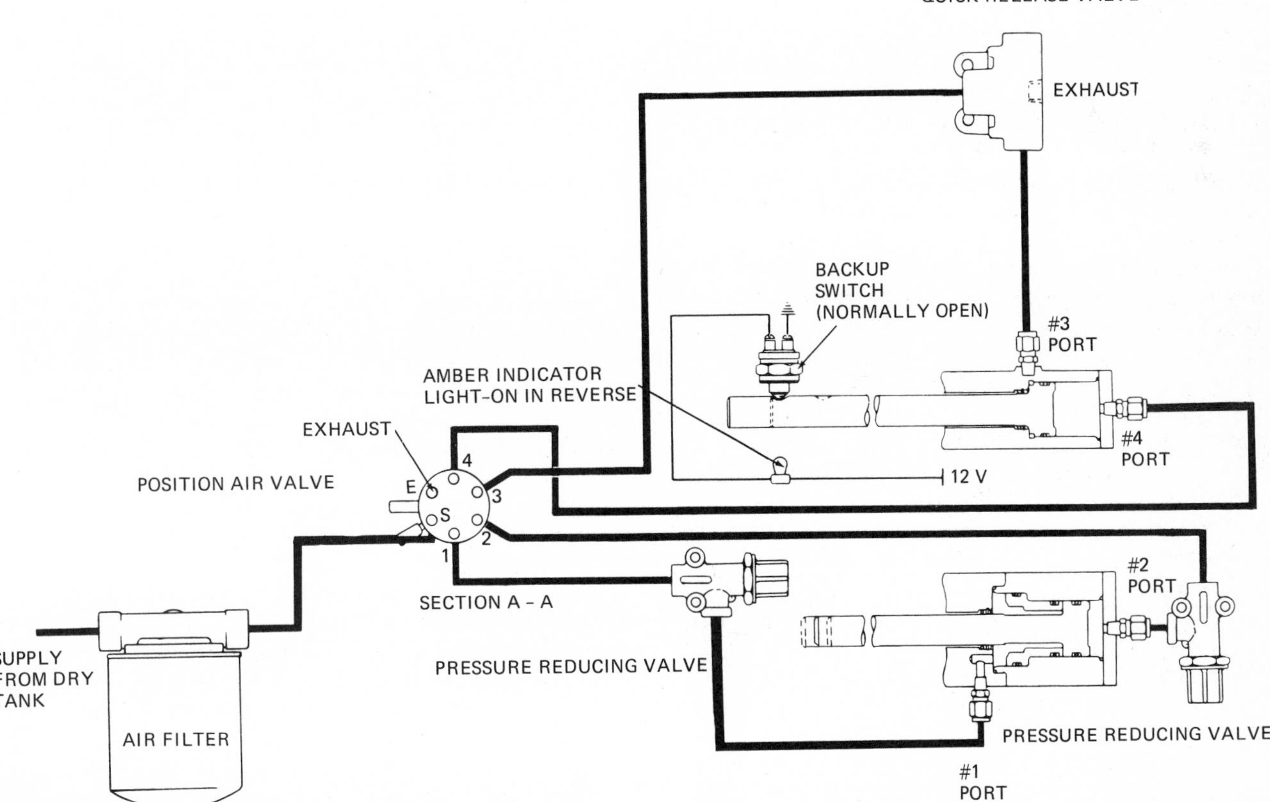

Fig. 11-58 Schematic view of the air control system (ten-speed triple-countershaft transmission). (*Mack Canada Inc.*)

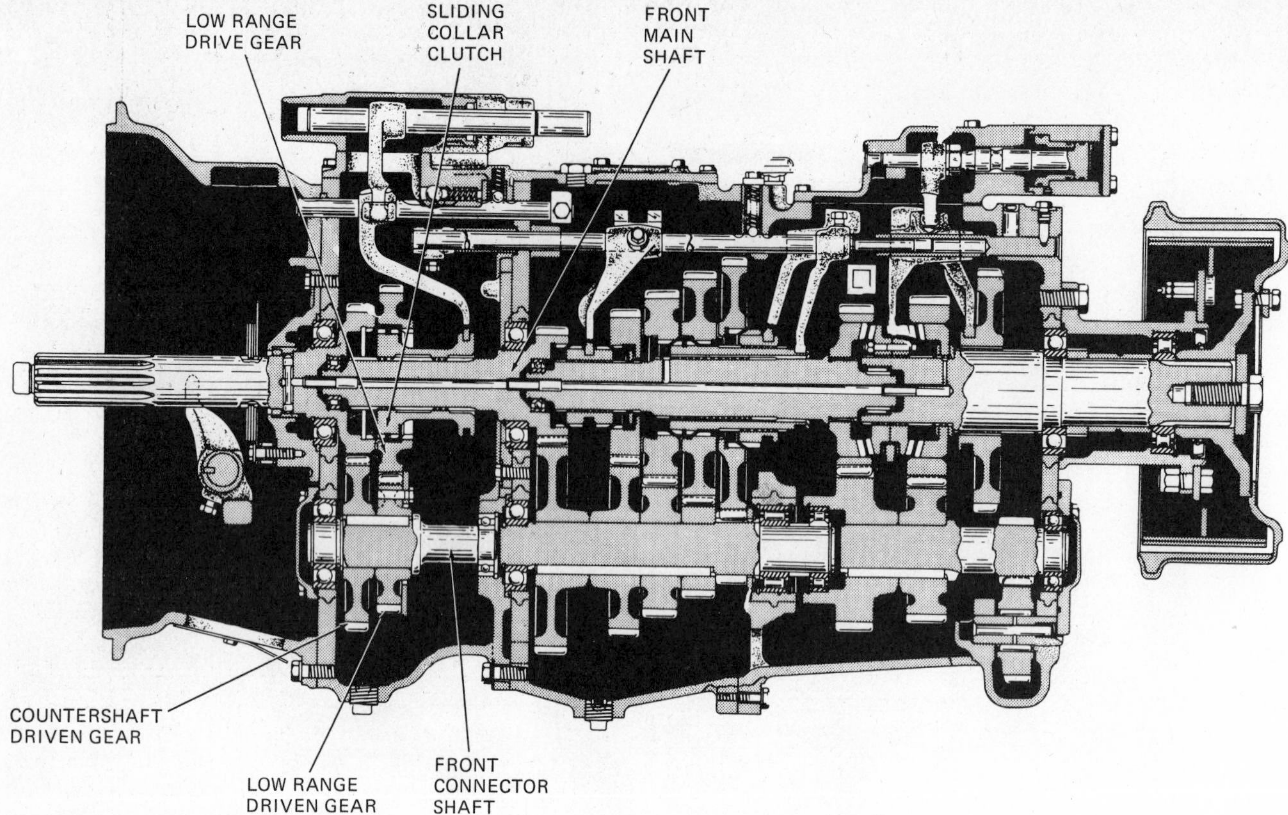

Fig. 11-59 Sectional view of a twelve-speed triple-countershaft transmission. (*Mack Canada Inc.*)

shift rail, shift fork, and male collar clutch to the right, and engages it with the low-range driven gear, clutching that gear to the front main shaft. At the same time, the range air selector lever is positioned in low range, causing the low-range driven gear in the splitter section to clutch to the output shaft. The torque is now directed from the clutch shaft drive gear, onto the front-section countershaft driven gears, and to the low-range drive gears. From there it is directed onto the low-range driven gear, over the collar clutch, onto the front main shaft and drive gear, onto the main transmission countershaft driven gears, and to the first-speed countershaft drive gears. From the drive gears, it is transmitted onto the first-speed driven gear and over the collar clutch onto the main shaft and splitter main drive gear. It is then transmitted onto the splitter countershaft driven gears and splitter low-range drive gears, onto the splitter low-range driven gear, and over the jaw clutch onto the main shaft.

To shift into second speed (low range, 14.44:1.00), the range air selector is shifted into direct. This clutches the jaw clutch to the splitter main drive gear, placing the splitter transmission in direct drive.

To achieve third speed, the splitter is shifted into low range, and at the same time the front compound gear set is manually shifted into direct, that is, the male collar clutch engages with the clutch drive shaft gear, nullifying the front compound gear set. From this point on, to achieve the remaining nine forward speeds, the transmission is shifted as outlined for the ten-speed transmission previously covered.

TRANSMISSION TROUBLESHOOTING

The most effective way in which to extend transmission life at minimum cost is through good maintenance, which includes checking the oil level, the condition of the oil, and the condition of air and oil filters.

Checking and Changing Transmission Oil and Filters Inadequate filters allow water, acid, and dirt to combine with the oil, thereby reducing its lubricating effectiveness and allowing corrosive oxides (which act like lapping compound) to form. Eventually, surface fatigue and small edge holes (pitting) on gears and bearing contact surfaces will occur. Unless the oil is changed and the transmission flushed, destructive pitting will cause total surface damage, or develop into flakeout areas (spalling), and result in gear tooth breakage and bearing failure. An oil filter in bad condition will not remove the fine metal particles which originate from normal wear or from clashing of gears, and these fine particles will accelerate wear on bearings, bushings, gears, shafts, and clutches, as well as cause the bearings to skid rather than roll. If the air filter is plugged, the transmission cannot breath and the seals and/or gaskets will start to leak, reducing the lubricant level. Reduced lubrication leads to increased oil temperature, and eventually to lubrication breakdown. A damaged air filter, of course, will allow dirt and other contaminants from outside to enter the transmission.

When changing the transmission oil, flush the transmission thoroughly with diesel fuel and at this time clean all magnetic plugs and change the filter. Then fill the transmission with the oil recommended by the manufacturer, but take care not to overfill it, as this causes excessive heat and oil leakage. If the oil level is low and you do not know what type of oil is in the transmission, it is safer to drain out the oil, flush the transmission and refill it with the kind recommended. Adding new oil to the oil already present may result in a mixture that would, when heated and agitated, become unstable and break down, which again would reduce lubrication.

There is no special yardstick by which you may be sure when to change the oil—some change it yearly, some change it in summer and once again at the beginning of winter, while some change it after every 25,000 mi [40,250 km]. Others take oil samples to determine whether the oil should be changed. For off-highway equipment, the oil is commonly changed after 1000 h of service. In any event, it is essential to change oil often enough to prolong the service life of the transmission components.

Other Preventive Maintenance Checks Other preventive maintenance steps which should be given high priority include checking for loose transmission or clutch housing cap screws or nuts, and for broken engine transmission mounts, as they cause misalignment. Check for a loose output flange nut and for splines on the flange and output shaft. Check for a worn output shaft bearing since this also causes misalignment as well as a hammering effect on the transmission with every gear shift. Check for oil leaks at the seals and gaskets, the welch plugs, and the drain plugs, and check for external seal damage. Service as necessary to stop any oil leaks.

If shifting is achieved over linkages, check them for binding and wear as well as adjustment, since any of these defects could prevent the collar clutch or jaw clutch from engaging fully with the driven gear. The clutch might then slip out, damaging or chipping the clutch teeth. Check the air control system for leaks and promptly repair them, especially when they are within the air cylinders. **NOTE** Change or clean the air filter at the same time you change the transmission oil, as this will reduce corrosion and wear on the air valves and air cylinders.

At least once a year check the air pressure regulator setting and if necessary adjust it to the recommended pressure. If the setting is too high, it could cause damage to the jaw clutch or collar clutch, and if too low it could prevent the clutch from engaging fully. Check the engine clutch and clutch brake adjustment (see material on various clutches and their adjustment in Unit 10.)

Another effective method of preventing transmission failure is to train vehicle operators adequately—teach them how to shift into first and reverse without gear clashing. Show them the correct shift pattern, the correct sequence of preselecting the shift rpm spread between various gear ratios, and when and how to downshift. Suggest to them that they report to the service manager or their supervisor any irregularities (minor or major) that may have occurred during the last trip or last work shift.

Transmission Problems Although a good preventive maintenance program will extend the service life of any transmission, nevertheless the transmission can eventually create noise, develop oil leaks, or walk out of a gear. Shifting may become difficult or the gears may stick. Any of these can arise after normal wear of bushings, gears, clutches, shafts, and seals.

TRANSMISSION NOISE All transmissions are somewhat noisy; by noise we therefore mean additional noises such as hissing, thumping, metallic rattle, growling, squealing, or whining. Any of these may originate from within the transmission, or may originate elsewhere and be amplified by the transmission. It is therefore advisable to accompany the operator as he or she drives the vehicle or machine so that you can personally assess the situation as the gear ratio is changed in regard to the engine rpm. You should also assess the engine while it is operating with the transmission in gear.

If the additional noise occurs when the transmission is in neutral, the cause could be from any loose accessory or accessory driven component. On the other hand, it may be that the air intake system is leaking, the engine is misfiring or has a defective vibration damper, or that the crankshaft, flywheel, or clutch assembly is out of balance. The noise could also arise from a loose flywheel or clutch assembly, or misalignment between engine and transmission.

If the noise occurs when the vehicle is in motion and becomes more audible with increase in travel speed, it may be originating from any of the causes listed above, or, in addition, may come from worn or damaged universal joints, damaged drive-line centering bearing, worn, damaged, or out-of-balance drive line, damaged or worn gears or bearings in the rear or front carrier, worn or damaged drive axle bearings, or weak or broken rear springs or shackles. It could also occur if the parking or service brake is adjusted too tight, the wheels are out of balance, or the tires and wheels are incorrectly mounted.

If a metallic rattle occurs when the transmission is in neutral but no other abnormal noise is audible, the engine may be transmitting its torsional vibration to the transmission, it may be misfiring, or the idling rpm may be too low. A metallic rattle can also be caused through worn or damaged countershaft(s) or main shaft bearing(s), or from pitted, spalled, or scuffed gears, or through a bent main or countershaft.

If a growling or humming sound can be heard, the problem may be damaged, chipped, or spalled gears.

If the transmission makes a hissing or thumping sound, it indicates worn or damaged bearings. If it is more of a squealing sound which increases with acceleration, it indicates that one or more driven gears on the main shaft have started to seize, or that the thrust washer or snap rings are worn and are allowing the gears on the main shaft to rub against one another. The latter possibility can be quickly checked by shifting the transmission through its speed ranges. **NOTE** The noise will disappear when the defective gear is clutched to the main shaft.

If the transmission has a whining sound when operating, it indicates that the drive and driven gears are not meshing properly. Poor gear meshing can result from worn or damaged countershaft bearings, in which case the sound should disappear when the transmission is in direct drive.

WALKING OUT OF GEAR (SLIP-OUT) Slip out is the demeshing of the clutch or gear. The male collar clutch or sliding gear walks out of engagement if there is a malfunction within the transmission and maximum torque is placed onto the gear train, or when the torque is reversed (that is, when the vehicle drives the power train). On the other hand, a gear or clutch can be pulled out of engagement when the vehicle hits a bump. However, this may not be the fault of the transmission; rather, it may be caused when the whip of the shift lever moves the shift rail. It is more likely to happen when the shift lever is loose in its socket or if it is heavy or long. **NOTE** Some large, single-countershaft transmissions have a specially machined relief, called a *hopping guard,* machined onto the main shaft and in the male collar clutch or sliding gear. When the collar clutch or gear is engaged, it locks into the hopping guard, preventing disengagement under load. See Fig. 11-60.

Walking out of gear can be due to misalignment (see Fig. 11-61). When the clutch shaft gear and collar clutch are misaligned due to bearing failure, direct drive can walk out. When the output shaft bearing is worn, the first-, second-, and reverse-speed gears can walk out. When excessive end play exists on the clutch shaft, main shaft, or countershaft, due to worn bearings, retainers, or thrust washers, it

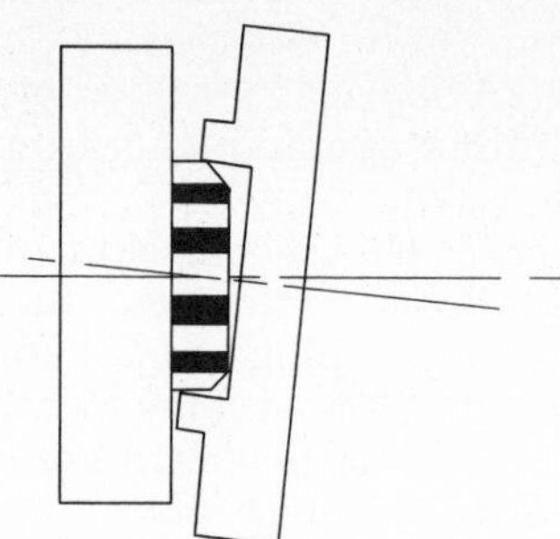

Fig. 11-61 Misadjustment that causes slipout.

causes the gear(s) to move away from the male collar clutch or drive gear, reducing the tooth contact. When the clutch collar (male or female) teeth are shortened or worn to a taper, after normal usage or continuous gear clashing, this also reduces the tooth contact and/or causes misalignment (see Fig. 11-62). When the internal or external splines on the shaft or collar clutch are worn, misalignment may occur between the drive and driven gears, or between female and male collar clutch teeth. When the shift rail or shift fork is bent, the collar clutch or gear can only partly engage. When the shift rail detents are worn or the detent spring is weak, the rail cannot hold engagement. A loose or sloppy shift lever will whip after any small bump, pulling the rail and the clutch or gear out of engagement. Binding shift linkages or linkages which are out of adjustment can also cause only partial engagement of the collar clutch or gear. A damaged air cylinder or low air pressure may prevent the piston from moving its full distance, which results in reduced engagement.

DIFFICULT SHIFTING AND STICKING IN GEAR Although not common, this trouble is caused more often when the shifting is accomplished over linkages, in which case any additional friction at the linkage or support points would require an increased effort to shift on the part of the operator. However, difficult shifting or a sticking gear or clutch could also result from worn (galled) splines (Fig. 11-63), collar clutches, or

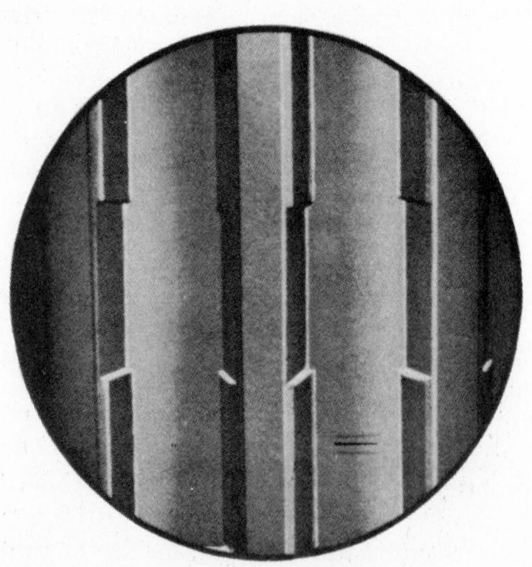

Fig. 11-60 View of mechanical relief called a *hopping guard.* (*Dana Corporation, Spicer Transmission Division*)

Fig. 11-62 View of worn collar clutch teeth due to shifting with mating parts out of synchronization.

Fig. 11-63 View of damaged splines. (*Dana Corporation, Spicer Transmission Division*)

gears, which cause increased friction too. A bent shift rail, a shift rail which interferes with the interlock plug, or a split shift rail detent ball can make shifting difficult. Many of these defects cause the gears or clutches to clash since the operator must overcome the higher friction, caused by the defective parts. In addition the shift time extends, causing loss of synchronized speed between the drive or driven gear or clutch. Hard shifting or sticking in gear can also be caused by badly burred-over clutch teeth.

Transmission Service It would be an impractical duplication of available service manuals to attempt to outline individual service procedures for the myriads of transmissions used in on- and off-highway equipment. Therefore, only the salient general procedures which help prevent repeat transmission failures will be covered.

REMOVING A TRANSMISSION Before attempting to remove a transmission for service, first road-test or shop-test it to determine if transmission *needs* to be removed. Many transmission problems, such as shifting trouble, replacing the output shaft bearing(s) and seal, and (on some transmissions) replacing PTO gears, do not require removal.

When it is necessary to remove the transmission, drain the oil, examine the magnetic plug, and take a sample of the last few drops of oil leaving the transmission. Evaluating the sludge on the drain plug and the drained transmission oil will often reveal the cause or causes of the trouble, in which case you can pay special attention to these points during the disassembly. Refill the transmission with diesel fuel so that it acts as a cleaning agent while you drive the vehicle to your work area. Having a clean assembly will help you to make a thorough inspection during its disassembly.

Next, position the vehicle so that you can use lifting devices to lift out components or the entire transmission. Block, if applicable, the hydraulic equipment and wheels or tracks. Remove the battery ground cable and place a "Machine being serviced" or similar sign, on the dashboard. If you are removing the transmission for the first time, read the service manual before you begin, and follow precisely the recommended steps. In this way, many unnecessary steps can be saved, particularly when removing a transmission from a backhoe, tractor loader, or other off-highway equipment. Steam-clean the surrounding work area before placing the machine in position, drain the diesel fuel, and then remove and steam-clean the transmission itself. When possible, mount the transmission to a holding fixture, as this enhances safety and speeds up disassembly.

When removing the output flange nut, use a torque multiplier rather than an impact wrench, as the wrench could brinell the bearings. When removing bearings, use the recommended pullers and do not drive them from a bore or shaft. Driving may not only damage the bearings but may also harm the shaft or bore. This is especially true for press-fit gears. If these parts must be removed, support them firmly and use the recommended puller or press arrangement to prevent damaging the reusable parts. Unless a complete disassembly is mandatory, remove only those parts necessary to gain access to the faulty components. On twin-countershaft transmissions use the recommended disassembly tools to hold the countershaft in the required position in order to lift out the main shaft assembly. Use rope slings to lift heavy assemblies from the transmission case, as such slings will not slip and will not nick or burr shafts or gears. **NOTE** If the main shaft driven gears are supported by needle bearings, count each bearing set to make certain that none is stuck to a gear or to the inside of the transmission housing. When shims are used to achieve bearing preload, bearing spacing, or gear spacing, tie the shims to the shaft, cover, etc., to facilitate reassembly. During the disassembly, examine every part that you lift, press, or pull from the transmission or shaft so as to determine the cause of the trouble. Pay special attention to parts which are completely defective, since they will indicate the cause of transmission failure.

Number each shift rail, shift fork, and shift block before removal to prevent possible mixup with others which are nearly identical. (When placed on a different shift rail, or when a different shaft is used, the clutch will only partially engage.) And as a final precaution, place a shop towel over the detent ball hole before removing the shift rail. This might well prevent an accident since the spring-loaded detent ball could fly out with considerable force.

INSPECTION Most transmission trouble starts with bearing or bushing failure, which need not have occurred had bearings and bushings been properly installed. Improper installation can damage the races, bearing shields (Fig. 11-64), or the ball separator, preventing the balls, rollers, and needles from rotating freely. If the bearing is driven on the shaft, or into the bore, misalignment between the inner and outer race or false (caused by the hammering effect) brinelling may result.

Other causes of bearing failure which could be prevented through a good maintenance program are insufficient lubricant, abrasives in the lubricant, and/or contaminating moisture (an acid by-product of the lubricant), all of which reduce lubrication, create excessive heat, and double the wear rate. Vibration is another cause of bearing failure because it results in brinelling and fretting. The cap screws, therefore, should be kept tight, the engine and the universal in good operating condition, and the wheels and drive lines in balance.

The final source of bearing failure worth mention-

Fig. 11-64 Bearing shield damaged due to improper removal or installation. (*Dana Corporation, Spicer Transmission Division*)

ing, but over which you have no control, is shock loading on the transmission due to overloading or placing excessive radial thrust on it.

Abrasives and contaminants in the lubricant attack the gears and shafts, and form specific destructive patterns on them. To identify *destructive* patterns, though, you must first know what normal patterns a new gear has. Figure 11-65 shows these latter: hob marks, shaving marks, and lipping patterns, which are tool marks produced during the machining of the gear. Note the direction in which they lie.

A gear which is highly polished or has a slightly greyish color on the teeth surfaces shows that it has operated in good alignment and with good lubrication. If there is any other pattern on those surfaces, the gear may need to be replaced. Irregular surface profile and/or some pitting indicate gear fatigue. Fatigue is a weakening of the metal surface caused by lengthy, continuous use or strain. If the gear was

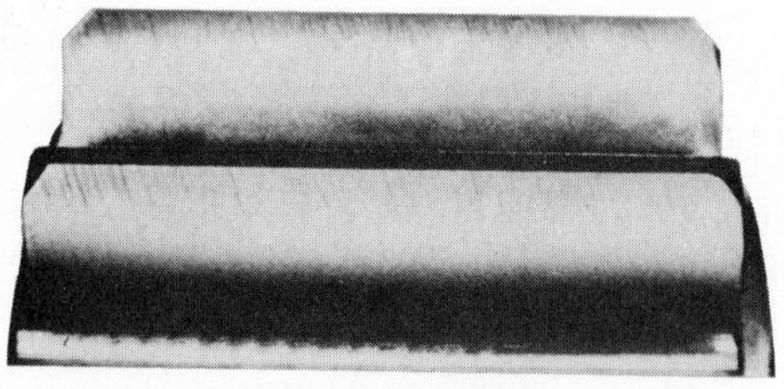

Fig. 11-65 Pattern marks on a new gear. (*Caterpillar Tractor Co.*)

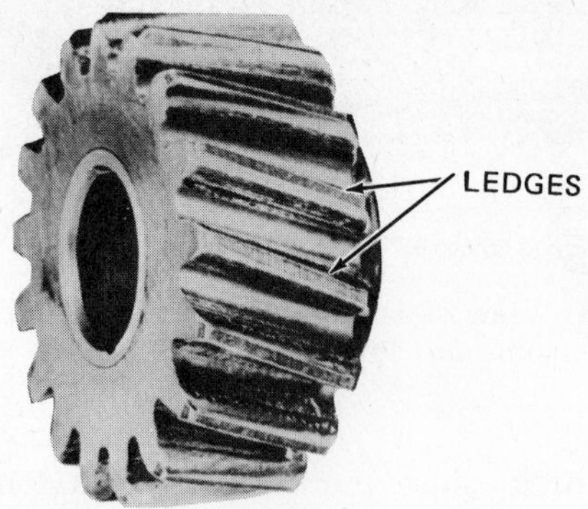

Fig. 11-66 Plastic yielding pattern from improperly hardened gear. (*Caterpillar Tractor Co.*)

improperly hardened, the surface metal may have flowed to the gear tip, which is called *plastic yielding* (see Fig. 11-66). This is not to be confused with *lipping*, in which metal lips form on the tips of the teeth (see Fig. 11-67).

The most common gear surface condition you will encounter is *pitting* (Fig. 11-68), which is caused from abrasive wear, or from corrosion, and which attacks the gear surface, thereby reducing the contact surface area. If the holes are few and small, like pin holes, it is termed *initial pitting*. If the hole sizes increase, and the holes increase in number, it is called *severe pitting;* and when flakes or chips have broken from the surface, it is called *spalling* (see Fig. 11-69).

NOTE A gear that shows a limited amount of initial pitting can be reused because it usually takes longer to reach the severe pitting stage than it did to reach initial pitting.

If the gear surfaces show light scratches or small patches of seizing, it is called *scoring* (see Fig. 11-70). Scoring is caused from high points on the gear surface or on the mating gears. It does not ruin the surface; however, if it is caused by lack of lubrication and the lubrication remains inadequate, the surface flakes out and totally destroys the gear surface as well as the mating gear. This stage is called *welding*.

If the gear teeth surfaces show longitudinal cracks, and if in addition the surfaces are chipped out, *fatigue fracture* has occurred as a result of fatigue or impact. The tooth or part of a tooth will break when insufficient strength remains to carry the load. See Fig. 11-71.

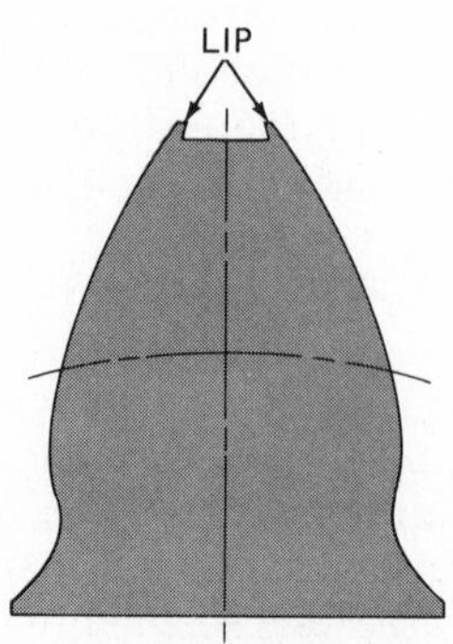

Fig. 11-67 Lipping pattern on tip of gear teeth. (*Caterpillar Tractor Co.*)

Fig. 11-68 Destructive pitting on gear surface. (*Caterpillar Tractor Co.*)

Fig. 11-69 Spalled gear. (*Caterpillar Tractor Co.*)

Fig. 11-70 Scored gear. (*Caterpillar Tractor Co.*)

Fig. 11-71 Fatigue fractured gear. (*Caterpillar Tractor Co.*)

Chipped teeth edges should be ground to remove the high spots and/or any partly broken pieces from the gear teeth. Chipped areas on the gear face should *not* be ground, however, as this will reduce the contact surface area.

Shafts should be checked for straightness (using V blocks and a dial indicator); if the out-of-roundness (see Fig. 11-72) is more than specified, it could cause gear seizure. Check the splines for wear and remove small nicks and burrs with a hand grinder. Check the bearing surfaces and the bearing for fit. If the bearing is loose by 0.001 in [0.025 mm] or more, it could rotate in the bore or on the shaft.

REASSEMBLY AND INSTALLING Before reassembling the transmission, clean all parts thoroughly and lay them out in the order to be reassembled, but keep the bearings in their packings until they are to be installed. If new gears are being installed, make certain the drilled passages are free of obstructions; otherwise the gears will not receive sufficient lubrication. Reassemble the transmission as recommended in the service manual, without taking shortcuts, as you may then miss a clearance check or an adjustment.

CAUTION Pull, press, or push parts into position and do not drive them in or on.

When reassembling a twin- or triple-countershaft transmission, follow the outlined timing procedure, and double-check the timing after the countershafts are in position. If the timing is off, the transmission will seize. Check clearances as recommended and make sure they are within specification before proceeding with the next reassembly step. Rotate semi-assembled components to make certain they are free and, before placing the shift cover into position, shift the transmission through its speed ranges with a large screwdriver, one at a time, check the gear or clutch engagement, and then rotate the clutch drive shaft. When in the speed ranges, the gear should rotate smoothly without hesitation. After the shift cover is installed, repeat the procedure.

NOTE Torque and secure each cap screw, bolt, and nut as specified, and, where required, wire-lock the

Fig. 11-72 Measuring mainshaft for out-of-roundness. (*International Harvester Company*)

set screws, cap screws, and nuts, then check that the wire does not interfere with any component parts.

If you have to mount a PTO to the transmission, engage and bolt it loosely (without the gaskets) to the transmission base. Then, with a feeler gauge, measure the space between the PTO flange and transmission face. Select a gasket of the same thickness as the feeler gauge, as well as one having the recommended gear backlash dimension thickness. Remove the PTO, place the gasket and PTO into position, tighten the cap screws to the recommended torque, and recheck the PTO gear backlash.

Before reinstalling the transmission, remove the clutch assembly to check for wear and if necessary to replace or service the worn parts. At this time also measure the clutch housing alignment and check the drive-line angle. (See material on drive lines in Unit 13.)

Review Questions

1. (*a*) Define transmission, and (*b*) identify the three most common power transmitters.
2. Transmissions are used to increase the engine or motor torque and reduce speed; or to increase speed and reduce torque. Outline other functions of the transmission.
3. (*a*) Name the two mechanical transmission groups, and (*b*) identify the transmission in each group.
4. Describe the methods used to lubricate the bearings, shafts, and gears of a transmission.
5. What two common methods are used to support the (*a*) countershaft? (*b*) the reverse-idle shaft?
6. What is the main difference between a sliding-gear transmission and a constant-mesh transmission?
7. How would you decide whether a transmission is of an overdrive or direct-drive design?
8. How many gears has the countershaft when the transmission is of (*a*) the sliding first/reverse-speed gear design? (*b*) a four-speed forward, no reverse-speed design? (*c*) a five-speed forward, one-speed reverse with a sliding reverse idler design? (*d*) a ten-speed forward, one-speed reverse with a sliding reverse idler design?
9. Which devices are used (*a*) to maintain the shift rail in position? (*b*) to prevent two gears from being engaged simultaneously?
10. Which type of clutches are used to engage a transmission's (*a*) speed range? (*b*) range speed?
11. List the main differences between a compound transmission and an auxiliary transmission.
12. Explain why it is necessary for manufacturers to build twin-end triple-countershaft transmissions.
13. Trace the power flow of a five-speed twin-countershaft transmission when it is in (*a*) reverse-speed gear and (*b*) third-speed gear.
14. List the methods used to increase the number of forward gears of a five-speed twin-countershaft transmission to: six, seven, ten, thirteen, fourteen, and fifteen.
15. Outline the main differences between a six-speed twin-countershaft transmission and a six-speed triple-countershaft transmission.
16. List the preventive maintenance checks which will prolong the service life of a transmission.
17. List the problems which could create noise when the transmission is in (*a*) neutral, (*b*) direct drive, (*c*) any forward gear other than direct, and (*d*) reverse.
18. List the problems which could cause the gear to "walk out" (*a*) when under forward torque or (*b*) when under reverse torque (load pushing the motor vehicle).
19. List the problems which could cause difficult or sticky shifting.
20. List the safety and removal steps which are basic to all types of transmissions.
21. Describe the appearance of the gear teeth surfaces when (*a*) there are abrasives in the oil, (*b*) one or more teeth have a high point, and (*c*) the transmission oil level is too low.
22. Outline the procedure to achieve the specified PTO backlash between the driven gear and drive gear.

Unit 12 Fluid Couplings, Torque Converters, and Powershift Transmissions

Fluid couplings and torque converters are mechanical "hydrodynamic drive" devices which transmit torque solely through dynamic fluid action, in a designated recirculating path, within a closed housing or shell. However, there is one great difference between them. The fluid coupling is designed to transmit torque without increasing it. The torque ratio from the power source to the output shaft of the fluid coupling is equal to the speed ratio, and therefore the output torque is equal to the input torque.

A torque converter, due to its (floating fulcrum) oil flow angle, has the ability to change the torque ratio (multiplying the engine torque). Although the torque ratio depends on many factors, generally speaking, it follows the speed ratio; that is, the higher the speed differential between the drive and driven member, the higher is the torque ratio.

FLUID COUPLINGS

A fluid coupling (Fig. 12-1) has two elements—one is fastened to the power source, the other to the output shaft. Each element (or member) of the fluid coupling or torque converter has a single row of flow-directing blades (vanes). The member fastened to the power source is the *impeller* (also known as the *drive member, pump,* or *drive torus*), and the member fastened to the output shaft is the *turbine* (also known as the *driven member,* or *driven torus*) (see Fig 12-2). The drive and driven tori are convex shaped, steel or aluminum alloy castings having directional blades. Both members are enclosed in a housing or shell. The internal design of the impeller and turbine are comparable, but their outsides differ because the impeller is usually bolted to the flywheel and is supported on the output shaft through a bearing or bushing. The turbine is splined to the output shaft.

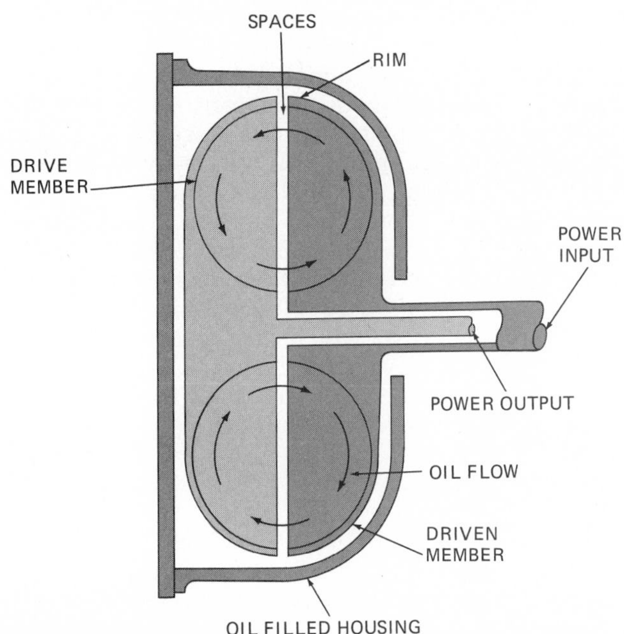

Fig. 12-1 Schematic view of a fluid coupling. (*Clark Equipment*)

Fig. 12-2 Schematic view of the drive and driven members.

When the fluid coupling is assembled, only a narrow space exists between the two members to increase the oil flow from member to member. The oil is either confined within the fluid coupling housing, or is directed into the center of the coupling through a passage in the output shaft. In the latter circumstance, a pressure and directional control valve is used to control the maximum oil pressure and the oil flow from the reservoir to the coupling, or viceversa.

Operation of a Fluid Coupling The variable speed coupling shown in Fig. 12-3 consists of two

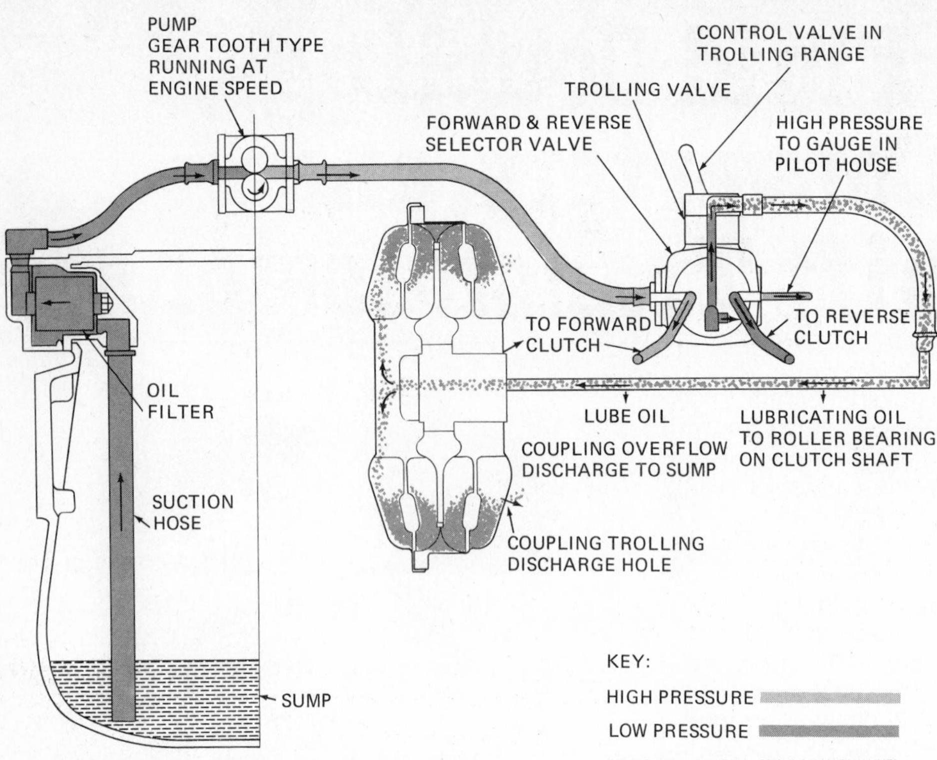

Fig. 12-3 Schematic diagram of a two-speed fluid coupling.

couplings in one coupling housing. When the engine is not operating, the lower halves of both fluid coupling members remain full of oil; and when the engine is started, both impellers rotate at engine speed. At this time the sprocket drive assembly transmits the rotation to the hydraulic pump, and oil flows from the pump into the directional valve, through the center of the output shaft, and into the coupling, increasing the oil volume and pressure. Air escapes past the support sleeve and bearing into the transmission, and when it is removed a small amount of oil follows in its path. This provides a constant flow of oil through the fluid coupling, maintaining the oil temperature below the maximum of 250°F [121°C]. Some fluid couplings have, in addition, discharge holes to control the internal pressure.

While all this is taking place, the (drive member) impeller carries the oil around in pockets formed by the vanes and torus. Because of the shape of the torus and the centrifugal force, the oil is forced to flow into the pockets of the turbine. The flow pattern now established is called *vortex flow*. Because the oil velocity at engine startup is low, and the oil flow angle onto the turbine vanes (driven members) is small, the torque exerted on the turbine is low and the turbine remains stationary. However, when the transmission is in neutral, the turbine may start to rotate. As the engine speed increases, more oil is circulated (pumped) from member to member (vortex flow). The oil velocity increases and, because of the greater speed differential, the oil flow angle increases. This places a greater impact on the turbine vanes, resulting in a higher torque transmission to the turbines. If the output shaft resistance is higher than the oil velocity impact on the turbine vanes, the shaft remains stationary, and the engine must be speeded up to maximum to increase the oil velocity. At this maximum speed differential, the oil flow angle and the velocity at which the oil is forced onto the turbine vanes is the greatest; therefore the maximum impact (torque) is transmitted to the turbine. When the turbine starts to rotate, it rotates in the same direction as the impeller, and simultaneously the vortex flow decreases and changes to rotary flow. See Fig. 12-4.

To reduce the oil turbulence and to increase the vortex flow, a split guide ring is positioned in each member.

As the turbine speed gradually increases to that of the impeller, the vortex flow gradually decreases and the rotary flow gradually increases. At the maximum rotary flow the oil molecules form a solid mass and start to clutch both members together. If both speeds were absolutely equal, the assembly—that is, the two members and the oil within—would rotate as a unit. However, in actual fact a fluid coupling at this stage slips about $\frac{1}{2}$ to 3 percent, depending on the design of the coupling and the type of oil used.

Some on- and off-highway machines or industrial applications use fluid couplings similar to the one shown in Fig. 12-3, which can be converted into variable speed drives simply by reducing the oil pressure within the coupling, thus increasing the slippage and reducing the output shaft speed.

TORQUE CONVERTERS

Externally, a torque converter appears to be similar to a fluid coupling because the impeller and turbine are fastened to the same components. However, internally torque converters are quite different.

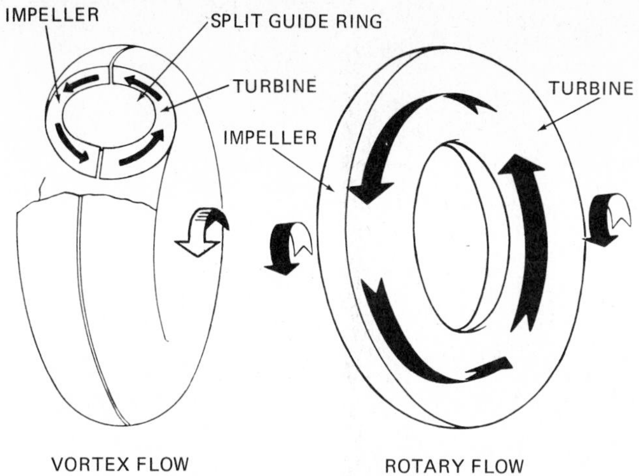

Fig. 12-4 Schematic view of the oil flow within a fluid coupling. (*General Motors Corporation*)

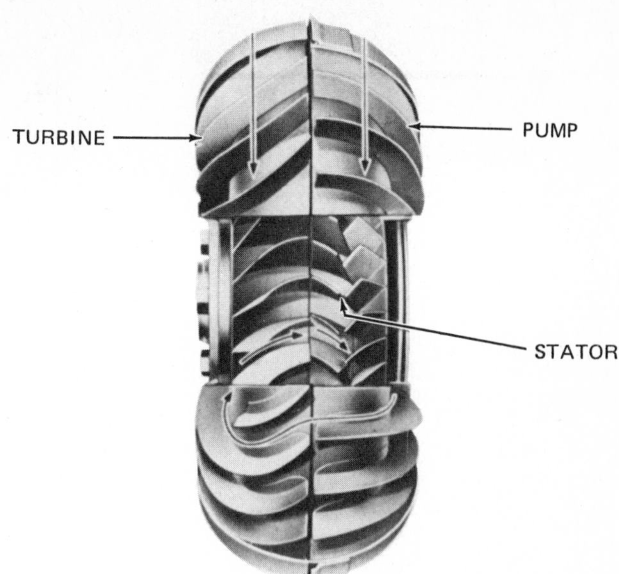

Fig. 12-5 Schematic view of a torque converter.

Conventional Torque Converters A conventional torque converter consists of three members (see Fig. 12-5). The additional member, known as the *reactor* (also called the *stator*), is centered between the impeller and turbine and is either splined or positioned on a one-way clutch to the converter ground sleeve. The ground sleeve is a stationary shaft to which the stator or one-way clutch is fastened. Additional directional vanes are fastened or cast to the impeller and turbine. The impeller vanes are positioned and designed so that the vanes are curved slightly toward the direction of rotation, and the areas between the vanes at the center (where the oil enters) are larger than at the trailing edge (where oil leaves the impeller). The impeller vane angles vary between 5° and 15° depending on the torque converter torque ratio. The vanes in the turbine are curved in the opposite direction from the vanes in the impeller, and the areas at the outer rim (where the oil enters the turbine) are larger than at the center. The turbine vanes curve about 45° to 50° away from the direction of rotation. The vanes on the reactor (stator) are curved about 90° toward the direction of rotation to allow the oil from the turbine to be directed without turbulence into the reactor vanes, and from the reactor, to the impeller. To reduce turbulence and increase vortex flow, half-guide rings are used, and on most torque convertors the vanes on the turbine, impeller, and reactor are aerodynamically designed. They are round at the end where the oil enters, and tapered off to a very fine edge at the oil exit.

PHASES VERSUS STAGES The torque converter just described (and shown in Fig. 12-6) is of a single-phase, single-stage design. "Phase" is the functional arrangement of the working members, and when a functional change is produced through an additional device such as a one-way or other clutch, the number of phases changes. "Stages" indicates the number of turbines within the torque converter. If the torque converter had the reactor attached to a one-way clutch, it would be a two-phase, single-stage torque converter (see Fig. 12-10).

DESIGN The torque converter shown in Fig. 12-6 is splined to the flywheel through the external gear teeth on the rotating housing. It is supported in the center and in the flywheel by the input hub and bushing, the latter being bolted to the rotating housing. The assembly is bolted to the engine block through the converter housing. The impeller is bolted to the rotating housing and the right-hand side is supported by a ball bearing positioned on the converter ground sleeve. The accessory drive gear is bolted to the impeller, and the ground sleeve is bolted to the output hub to which the reactor (stator) is splined. The output shaft is supported by roller bearings—one in the output hub and the other in the rotating housing. The turbine is splined to the output shaft and positioned to it through the spacer and bearing retainer.

When properly assembled, there is a designated space between the turbine and the impeller, and between the impeller, turbine, and reactor. Note the lubrication passages in the left-hand side of the output shaft.

The torque converter/transmission hydraulic pump is bolted to the top right of the converter housing, and the steering brake/hydraulic pump is splined to the steering pump drive gear.

OPERATION When the engine is not operating, oil is trapped in the lower halves (below the output shaft) of the torque converter. As the engine starts, however, the following happens (see Figs. 12-7 and 12-8): The hydraulic pump directs oil to the filter and from there to the torque converter (filling it), while the torque converter safety valve prevents excessive inlet pressure. The oil leaving the converter is directed to the transmission sump. Oil is then directed to the transmission. The oil enters the torque converter through a passage in the ground sleeve. From there it flows between the reactor and impeller. As the oil pressure increases, the air escapes through the space between the impeller and turbine. The oil

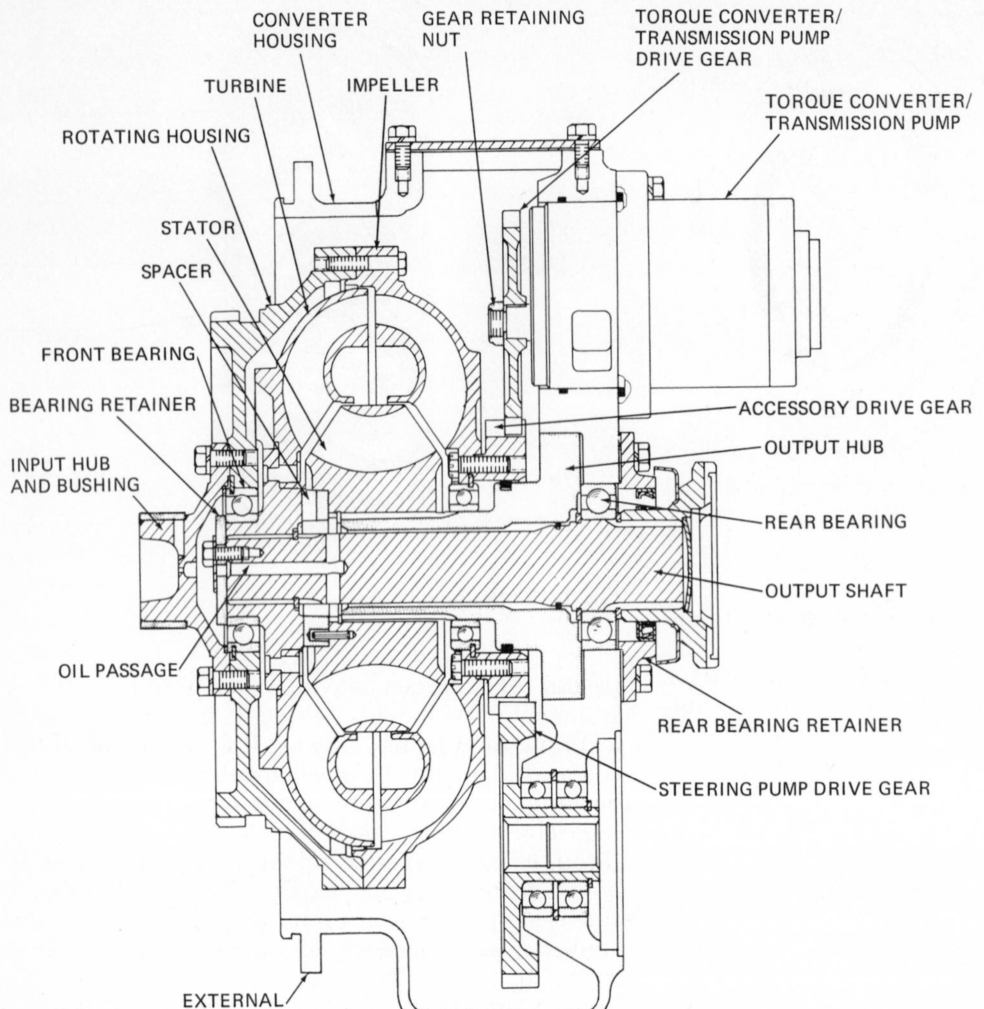

Fig. 12-6 Single-phase, single-stage torque converter. (*International Harvester Company*)

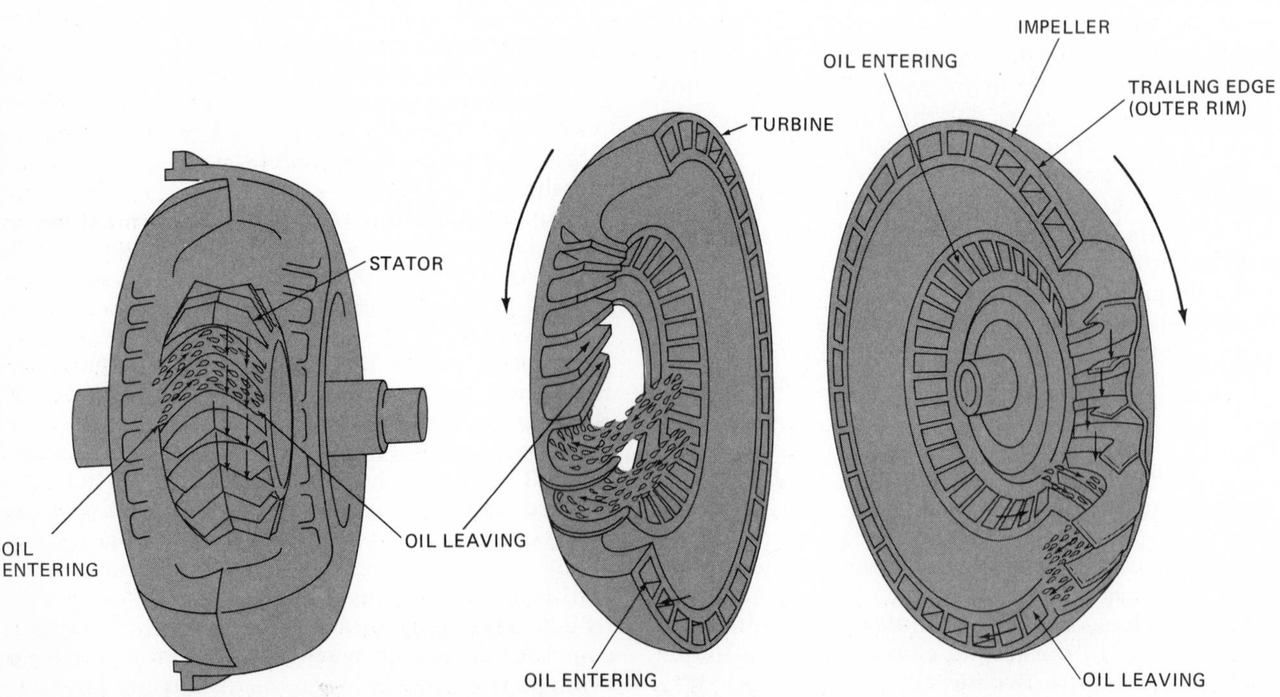

Fig. 12-7 Schematic view of the oil flow within the three torque converter components. (*International Harvester Company*)

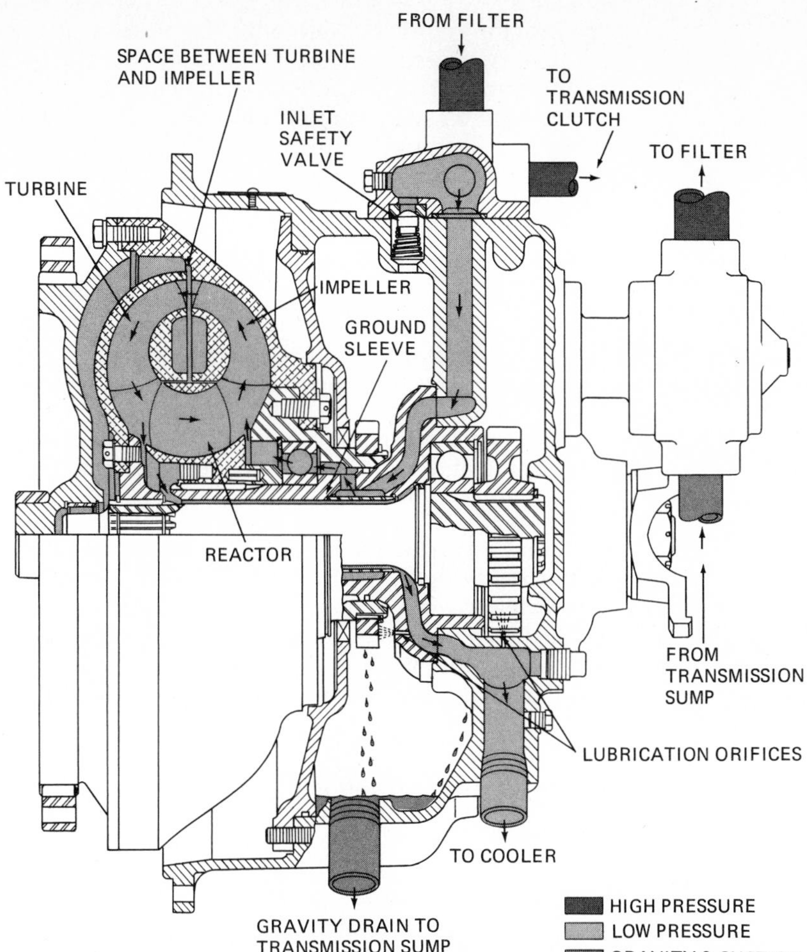

Fig. 12-8 Schematic view of the oil flow within a torque converter. (*Clark Equipment of Canada*)

that leaves the torque converter passes between the reactor and turbine, is directed to the ground sleeve, and returns over the oil cooler back to the transmission sump. The oil that lubricates the output shaft, the gears, and the bearings, as well as the oil that passes by the converter elements, is collected in the base of the converter housing, from which a scavenging pump (not shown) draws the oil out and pumps it back into the transmission sump, or gravity drains it to the transmission sump.

Oil is carried by the rotating impeller around in the pockets formed between the vanes and torus, and it is forced out into the pockets of the turbine through the pumping action (centrifugal force) of the impeller. **NOTE** The oil is thrown into the pockets of the turbine in the direction of the impeller rotation. At low engine speed and with the turbine stationary (motor vehicle not moving), the angle at which the oil is thrust onto the turbine vanes is small, but it increases with increased impeller speed. The oil enters the individual turbine pockets and, due to the decreasing pocket area and the curved contour of the vanes, its velocity increases. The oil that leaves the turbine pockets hits the stationary reactor vanes (fulcrum), and an additional fluid force (torque) is exerted upon the turbine. A comparable action which you may have experienced when washing your car occurs as you lay the end of the garden hose on the ground—the hose end starts to whip. At low water velocity it will not whip much, but with increasing velocity it will bounce about more. A similar reaction occurs within the turbine, but the precalculated oil flow, and the entering and leaving angles from all three members create a force greater than that on the end of a water hose. As the oil strikes the reactor vanes, it is redirected to the impeller. This causes a reduction in oil velocity and the oil, at reduced velocity, enters the impeller pocket and hits the impeller vanes from behind, helping the engine to rotate. (See Fig. 12-9.)

When the output shaft resists motion, the engine speed—that is, the impeller speed—must be increased in order to increase the oil velocity. The impeller speed not only increases the oil velocity, however, but also the oil impact angle onto the turbine. If the output shaft remains stationary, the engine speed will drop to (converter) stall speed. Stall speed is the maximum engine-torque speed for a specific torque converter and is about 150 rpm below droop speed when a diesel engine is used. Droop speed is the reduced speed from high idle after a load is placed on the engine. It may be as high as 2000 rpm below maximum speed (5000 rpm) on a gasoline engine.

At converter stall, the torque converter is at its maximum torque ratio. This could be between 2.1:1 and 3.8:1 on a single-phase, single-stage torque converter. At this point, the oil temperature rises very quickly above safety temperature because of the very high oil velocity and its great impact on the turbine

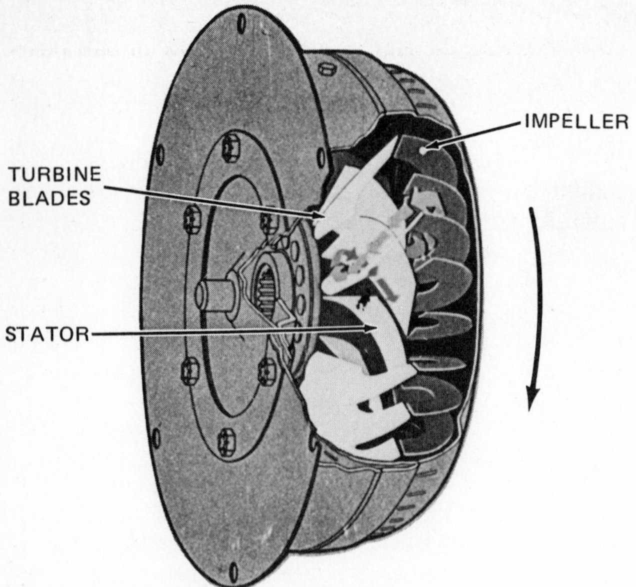

Fig. 12-9 Oil flow within the torque converter at stall speed. (*Clark Equipment of Canada*)

and reactor. Consequently, when the temperature exceeds 250°F [121°C] the rotating parts are deprived of lubrication and may cause the oil to break down, or the tolerance may reduce and then totally destroy the torque converter and perhaps the transmission.

When the turbine starts to rotate, the vortex flow and the impact angle gradually decrease because the turbine now rotates in the same direction as the impeller. Torque (oil velocity) onto the turbine is reduced, whereupon the torque converter gradually reduces its torque ratio. When the turbine rpm reaches about 80 percent of the impeller rpm, the torque converter becomes something of a fluid coupling, although very inefficient because of the fixed reactor. The temperature again starts to rise because the reactor vanes interfere with the oil flow and direction. As a result, the oil is directed onto the front of the impeller vanes, retarding the engine.

For this reason, where a fluid coupling phase is required (highway application), the reactor is mounted on a one-way clutch. When the torque converter begins to act as a fluid coupling in the "coupling phase," that is, when the oil is directed onto the back of the reactor vanes, the one-way clutch disengages from the ground sleeve and allows the reactor to rotate with the impeller and turbine.

When the engine rpm is reduced (retarded) and the turbine rpm remains high, the turbine then acts as the impeller and the oil flow reverses somewhat, causing a very high turbulence, and consequently the engine and torque converter act as a small retarder.

Torque Converter Variation There are several different methods by which the efficiency of a torque converter can be increased. The simplest is to replace the fixed-blade reactor with a variable-blade (variable pitch) reactor. See Fig. 12-10. The individual reactor blades are pivot-mounted in the reactor housing, and one end of each blade is linked through a belt crank to the air or hydraulic piston. From turbine stall speed up to about 65 percent of the impeller speed, the vanes are positioned at their greatest redirectional angle. From this point on, the operator can and should direct air to the reactor air piston.

When torque conversion is automatic, the engine speed is sensed by the governor, which then directs oil to the shift valve, causing the shift valve to direct oil to the hydraulic piston. In either case, the end result is the same—the air or hydraulic pressure forces the piston to move, which in turn moves the bell crank and causes the reactor vanes to decrease their angle, extending the torque multiplication range.

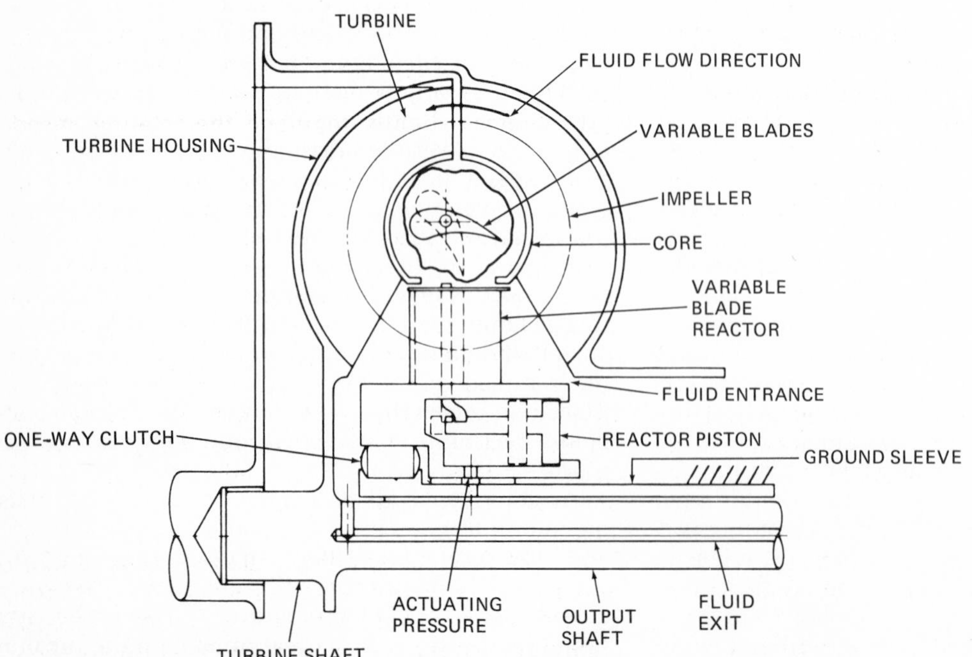

Fig. 12-10 Schematic view of a two-phase, single-stage torque converter having a variable-blade reactor. (*General Motors Corporation*)

Three-Phase, Single-Stage Torque Converter Another way to increase the torque converter efficiency is to use two reactors instead of one. Performance will then be comparable to a variable-blade reactor. In addition, a lockup clutch may be used. See Fig. 12-11.

Basically, all torque converters are very similar to the one shown in Fig. 12-6. However, the torque converter shown in Fig. 12-11 has two reactors and a lockup clutch. When using two reactors, the total reactor vane angle can be increased to about 170° providing a greater reaction, up to about 85 percent of turbine speed.

DESIGN AND OPERATION The lockup clutch plate is riveted to the turbine hub, and the friction material is bonded to each side of the outer circle of the clutch plate. The lockup clutch piston is positioned inside the bore of the flywheel. The lockup piston reaction plate is keyed to the flywheel and held by the impeller bolted to the flywheel. To reduce vibration and to compensate for minor misalignment between the torque converter and engine, a flex plate connects the flywheel to the crankshaft and, additionally, the flywheel is supported in the center bore of the crankshaft.

The center oil passage in the turbine shaft leads into the lockup piston area. Clutch lockup can be achieved in two ways—by manually directing oil to the lockup clutch, or by a governor that senses engine speed and then actuates a lockup clutch shift valve, which in turn directs oil to the lockup piston. See material on powershift transmissions later in this unit.

Operation of this torque converter (Fig. 12-11) is the same as the single-phase single-stage torque converter previously covered, with a single exception—at about 65 percent of turbine speed, the oil from the turbine starts hitting the first reactor vane from behind and causes the reactor to unlock from the ground sleeve; it then starts to rotate with the turbine and impeller. This removes about half of the total redirectional angle because the second reactor is now the only redirectional member, with a very flat angle. Torque multiplication is extended to about 85 percent of the turbine speed. At this point, the second reactor unlocks and the torque converter becomes a fluid coupling (see Fig. 12-12). If the torque converter has a lockup clutch, the operator or governor at this time directs oil to the lockup clutch piston. The piston is forced to the right, clutching the turbine to the flywheel, and the entire assembly rotates at engine speed.

Two-Phase, Two-Stage Torque Converter The two-phase, two-stage torque converter shown in Fig. 12-13 uses another method to increase its efficiency, and could have a torque ratio as high as 6.1:1.00.

DESIGN The torque converter in Fig. 12-13 is a remote-mounted unit. It is connected (through a drive line and coupling) to the torque converter input shaft.

The impeller is bolted to the torque converter drive cover, which is bolted to the input shaft. It is supported on the right by a double row of ball bearings positioned on the ground sleeve, and at the left by a roller bearing positioned on the hub of the first turbine support assembly. The reactor is splined to the ground sleeve. The first turbine is locked to the first turbine support assembly, which is splined to the first turbine shaft. **NOTE** The support assembly also has vanes. The second turbine is splined to the second-turbine drive gear shaft. The left-hand side of the second-turbine drive gear shaft, and the first-turbine drive gear shaft, are supported (through two sets of ball bearings) by the output shaft and torque converter drive cover.

The first-turbine drive gear is splined to the first-turbine drive gear shaft. The first-turbine drive gear is in mesh with the first-turbine driven gear, the latter being part of the one-way clutch. The free wheel cam of the one-way clutch is bolted to the second-turbine driven gear, and the free wheel rollers are positioned between the cam and hub on the first-turbine driven gear.

OPERATION The oil flow within the two-phase, two-stage torque converter follows the same route as the flow within the converters previously outlined. Note, however, that the oil from the lower part of the torque converter housing returns to the transmission through a pipe.

When the engine is operating, the transmission is in gear, and a high torque is required (say, to move the tractor), the speed difference between the impeller and turbines is high (high vortex flow). Under this condition, the impeller directs oil to the first turbine, then to the second turbine, then to the reactor, and back to the impeller. The applied torque on the first turbine is transmitted to the first-turbine driven gear, causing the one-way clutch to lock up, clutching the first-turbine driven gear to the second-turbine driven gear. As a result, the first turbine transmits the torque over the one-way clutch to the second-turbine driven gear shift.

When both turbine speeds are at about 65 percent of the impeller speed, the oil from the impeller hits the first turbine from behind, removing the torque and therefore slightly reducing the rotating speed compared with the speed of the second turbine. This unlocks the one-way clutch and now only the second turbine transmits the torque over the overdrive gear set (second-turbine drive and driven gears) to the transmission. At about 85 percent of the impeller speed the governor responds and through its action oil is directed to the lockup clutch piston. The piston is forced to the right, clutching the turbine to the flywheel. Now the entire assembly rotates at engine speed. As soon as the speed differential between the impeller and turbine increases, the vortex flow hits the first turbine in the front, and consequently the one-way clutch locks up again.

Planetary Gear Set and Drive Combination Before moving on to the next type of torque converter, it is essential to understand the different types of planetary drive combinations in relation to their

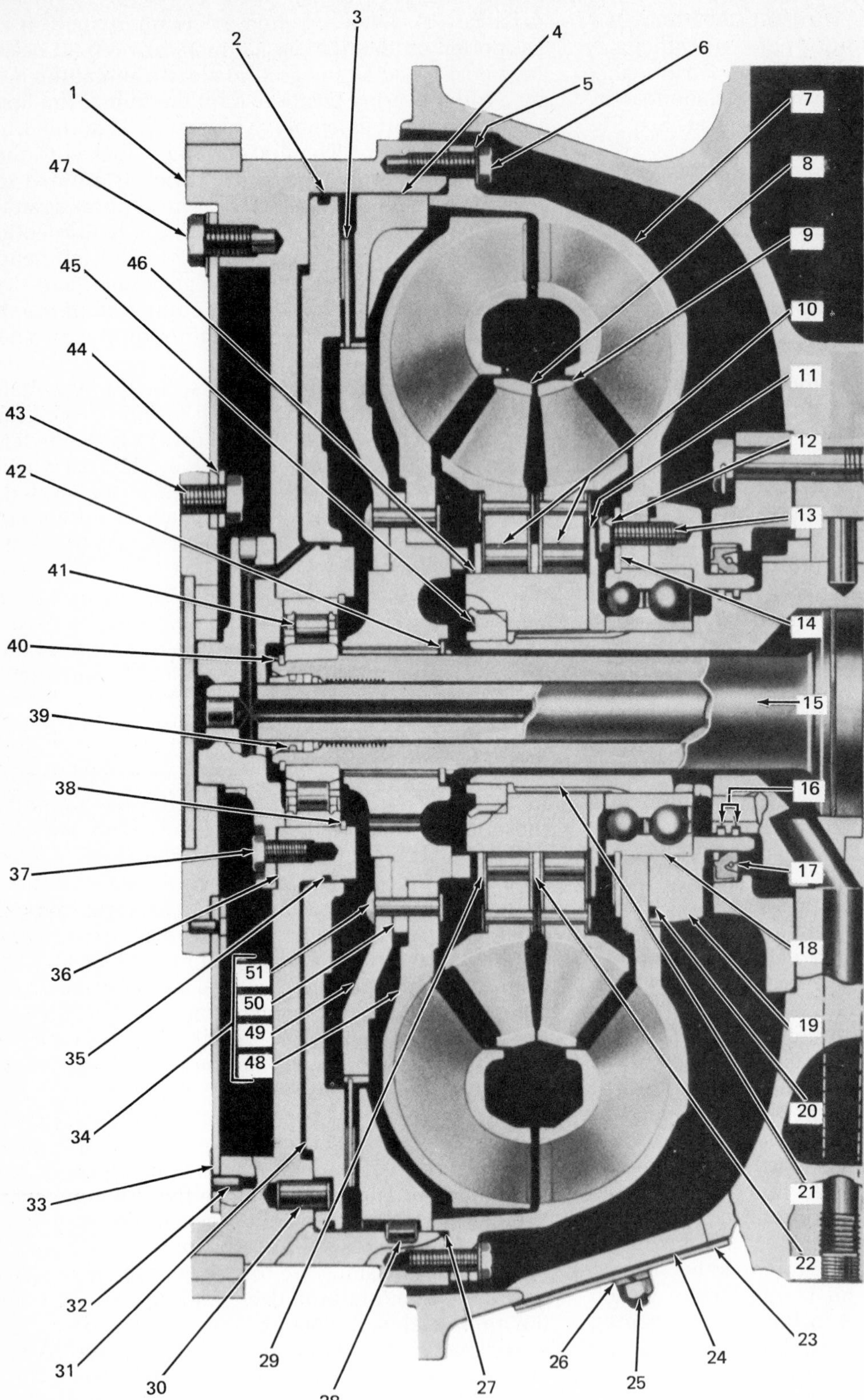

1. Flywheel
2. Seal ring—lockup clutch piston (outer)
3. Plate—clutch friction
4. Plate—lockup clutch reaction
5. Washer—converter pump-to-flywheel bolt
6. Bolt—converter pump to flywheel
7. Pump—converter
8. Stator assembly—first
9. Stator assembly—second
10. Roller—freewheel
11. Spacer—freewheel roller race
12. Strip—converter pump-to-hub bolt locking
13. Bolt—converter pump to hub
14. Plates—converter pump hub bearing retaining
15. Shaft—transmission main
16. Seal ring—converter ground sleeve
17. Oil seal—ground sleeve retainer
18. Bearing—converter pump hub
19. Hub—converter pump
20. Seal ring—converter pump to hub
21. Sleeve—converter ground

Fig. 12-11 Sectional view of a three-phase, single-stage torque converter. (*General Motors Corporation*)

Table 12-1 POSSIBLE PLANETARY DRIVE COMBINATIONS

Drive	Held	Driven	Direction	Gear Ratio
1 Sun	Ring	Carrier	Same as drive	$\frac{30+120}{60}=\frac{150}{60}=2.5{:}1.00$
2 Ring	Sun	Carrier	Same as drive	$\frac{30+120}{120}=\frac{180}{120}=1.5{:}1.00$
3 Carrier	Ring	Sun	Same as drive	$\frac{60}{30+120}=\frac{60}{120}=0.5{:}1.00$
4 Carrier	Sun	Ring	Same as drive	$\frac{120}{30+120}=\frac{120}{150}=0.8{:}1.00$
5 Sun	Carrier	Ring	Reverse	$\frac{120}{60}=2{:}1$
6 Ring	Carrier	Sun	Reverse	$\frac{60}{120}=0.5{:}1$

consequences (reduction, overdrive, or direct drive). Although the planetary gear set covered so far (planetary wheel hubs) had only one purpose—to increase the gear reduction (torque)—planetary gear sets can nevertheless perform many functions.

A standard planetary gear set consists of the components shown in Fig. 12-14. Its gear ratio depends upon the number of teeth which each member has, and whether the member is the drive or driven member, or is held stationary. Moreover, the gear set function can change from overdrive, to reduction, or to reverse drive depending on whether the member is the drive or driven member, or is held stationary.

At this time, it is important to point out that every reaction of the planetary gear set depends on the action of the planetary carrier, that is (1) when the carrier is held (stationary) a direction change is always made, (2) when the planetary carrier is the driven member a reduction ratio is always achieved, (3) when the planetary carrier is the drive member an overdrive ratio is always achieved, and (4) when the drive is exerted on two members and both members rotate at equal speed, the third member does not rotate and direct drive is achieved.

GEAR RATIO CALCULATION Assume the members of the planetary gear set shown in Fig. 12-14 have the following number of gear teeth: sun gear 60; carrier gears 30; ring gear 120. To calculate the gear ratio, the following formulas are used:

For overdrive:

$$\text{Gear ratio} = \frac{\text{driven gear} + \text{affected teeth (ring gear)}}{\text{drive teeth}}$$

For reduction:

$$\text{Gear ratio} = \frac{\text{driven teeth}}{\text{drive teeth} + \text{affected teeth (ring gear)}}$$

The possible drive combinations and their gear ratios are given in Table 12-1.

NOTE When the sun gear is the drive member, a higher reduction is achieved than when the ring gear is the drive member. When the sun gear is held stationary, a lower overdrive ratio is achieved than when the ring gear is held stationary. In reverse, the carrier gears are reverse idlers and have no effect on the gear ratio.

Ratio calculation for other drive combinations To help visualize the various planetary drive combinations and to arrive at the gear ratio (see Fig. 12-15), draw a straight line on a piece of paper. Next, measure the distance between the center of the sun gear and the center of a carrier gear and transfer, in proportion, the measurement onto the straight line. Next, measure the distance from the center of a carrier gear to the root of one tooth on the ring gear, and also transfer that distance proportionally onto the straight line (Fig. 12-15). Now, using any drive combination listed below, move the drive member, sun gear, ring gear or carrier any distance (say, 0.39 in [10 mm]), and draw a line from this point to the member that is held stationary, and extend the line straight out. You will notice the reaction of the driven third member and you can then measure the distance which it has moved in comparison to the

22. Washer—thrust (bronze)
23. Cover—housing
24. Gasket—handhole cover
25. Stud—handhole cover
26. Nut—handhole cover
27. Seal ring—converter pump to flywheel
28. Key—reaction plate locking
29. Washer—thrust (bronze)
30. Dowel pin—flywheel
31. Piston—lockup clutch
32. Dowel pin—flexible drive disk-to-hub and flywheel
33. Disk—flexible flywheel
34. Turbine assembly
35. Shaft—transmission main
36. Gasket—bearing retainer cover
37. Bolt—bearing retainer cover
38. Snap ring—flywheel pilot bearing retaining
39. Seal ring—input pump drive shaft
40. Snap ring—flywheel pilot bearing-to-main shaft
41. Roller bearing—main shaft pilot
42. Snap ring—turbine assembly to main shaft
43. Bolt—flexible disk to hub
44. Plate—flexible flywheel disk
45. Nut—freewheel roller race lock
46. Race—freewheel roller
47. Bolt—flexible disk to flywheel
48. Turbine—converter
49. Plate—clutch drive
50. Hub—turbine
51. Rivet—clutch drive plate

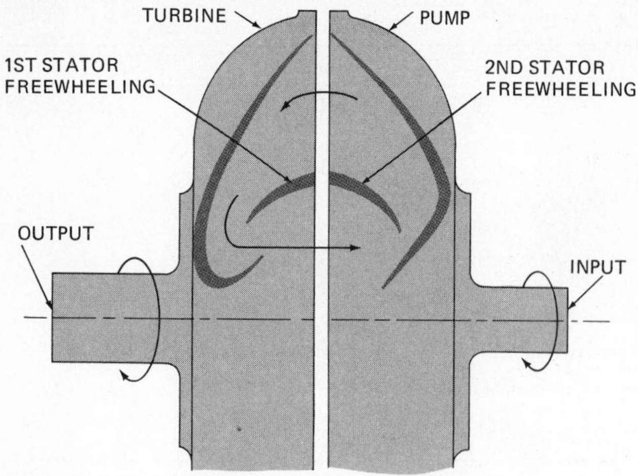

Fig. 12-12 Schematic view of oil flow when the torque converter is in the third phase (coupling phase). (*GMC Truck and Coach Division*)

drive member. This gives you the planetary gear ratio.

Drive combinations Refer to Fig. 12-15. 1(*a*) When you drive the sun gear in a clockwise rotation and then also start to drive the ring gear in a clockwise rotation, the 2.5:1 gear reduction decreases with increased ring gear speed. When both rotate at the same speed, the carrier also rotates at the same speed, resulting in direct drive. 2(*a*) The reaction is the same as outlined above when the ring gear and the sun gear are both the drive members.

1(*b*) When you drive the sun gear in one direction and then drive the ring gear in the opposite direction, the gear reduction increases from 2.5:1 with increased ring gear speed, and at a certain speed the planetary gear set becomes neutral. In other words, the carrier does not rotate. If you drive the ring gear even faster, the carrier rotation reverses from that of the sun gear. 2(*b*) The reaction is the same as 1(*b*) when the ring gear and the sun gear are both the drive members.

1(*c*) When you drive the carrier in a clockwise direction and at the same time start to drive the ring gear in a clockwise rotation, the overdrive ratio of 0.4:1.00 gradually decreases with increased ring gear rotating speed, and then becomes direct drive. 2(*c*) The reaction is the same as 1(*d*) when you drive the carrier and the sun gear.

1(*d*) When you drive the carrier in one direction and then drive the ring gear in the opposite direction, the overdrive ratio of 0.4:1 gradually increases. 2(*d*) The reaction is the same as 2(*b*) when you drive the carrier and the sun gear.

FOUR-MEMBER PLANETARY GEAR SET The planetary gear sets used with some powershift transmissions have inner and outer planetary gears. The inner planetary gears are in mesh with the sun gear and the outer planetary gears, and the outer planetary gears are in mesh with the ring gear.

The purpose of this design is to achieve reverse by holding the ring gear, since designing a transmission in which the carrier is held to achieve reverse is extremely difficult.

When the ring gear is held stationary and either the sun or the carrier is the drive member, the other one (the driven member) is always driven in the opposite direction (see Fig. 12-16). However, if the sun gear is the drive member, the carrier is driven at a speed less than that of the sun gear, and when the carrier is the drive member the sun gear is driven at higher speed than that of the carrier.

Torque Divider The Caterpillar Tractor Company manufactures a special torque converter for use on their track-type tractors. See Fig. 12-17. It is referred to as a *torque divider* because it has a planetary gear set within the torque converter housing. As a result the engine torque is transmitted along two different torque paths onto the output shaft. Along one path it travels over the planetary gear set, and along the other over the torque converter—but in each case to the output shaft.

DESIGN The impeller is bolted to the rotating housing, which is splined to the engine flywheel, and the assembly is enclosed by the torque converter housing that is bolted to the engine crankcase. The torque divider housing, in conjunction with the rear support housing (carrier) supports (through a tapered roller bearing) the rotating housing at the left. At the right, the torque divider housing is supported by a ball bearing positioned on the planetary carrier hub. The planetary ring gear is splined to the flange assembly and held to it by a snap ring. The turbine is also splined to the flange assembly, and both the flange assembly and turbine are supported at the left by a roller bearing and at the right by the ball bearing in the rotating housing. The sun gear is splined to the engine flywheel and held to it by retainers that are bolted to the flywheel. See Fig. 12-18. The output shaft is supported by two roller bearings—one in the center flywheel bore and the other in the rear support housing. The planetary carrier is splined to the output shaft. The reactor is pinned and bolted to the rear support housing. The hydraulic pump drive gear, which is bolted to the impeller, meshes with the driven gear on the hydraulic pump. **NOTE** The purpose of the hydraulic pump is to remove the oil used to lubricate the bearings, gears, and shaft from the torque divider housing and to remove the oil that passes by the torque converter members during operation.

OPERATION When the engine is started, several actions occur almost simultaneously. The hydraulic scavenging pump, driven by the rotating impeller, removes the oil from the divider housing and pumps it to the transmission sump. The transmission pump supplies oil to the torque converter, transmission, and torque converter inlet relief valve. Oil enters the converter at the inlet port, flows through the passages in the rear support housing, into the converter, and between the reactor and turbine. Oil that leaves the converter passes between the impeller and reactor into the passages in the rear support housing,

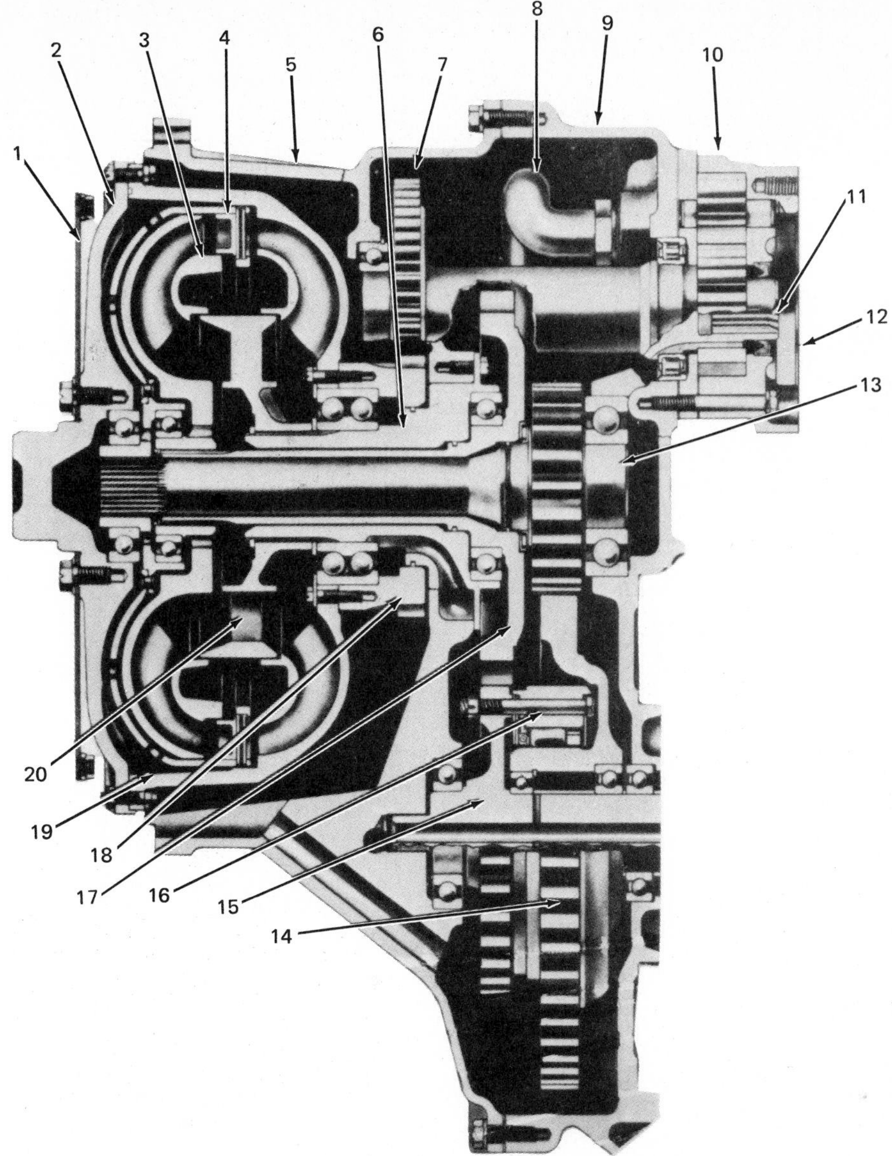

1. Flex disk drive
2. Torque converter drive cover
3. Second turbine
4. First turbine
5. Torque converter housing
6. Torque converter ground sleeve
7. Accessory driven gear
8. Oil suction tube
9. Transmission housing
10. Oil pump assembly
11. Accessory drive splines
12. Accessory mounting pad
13. First turbine drive gear
14. First–turbine driven gear
15. Second–turbine driven gear gear
16. Freewheel clutch
17. Second–turbine drive gear
18. Accessory drive gear
19. Torque converter pump
20. Torque converter stator

Fig. 12-13 Sectional view of a two-phase, two-stage torque converter. (*General Motors Corporation*)

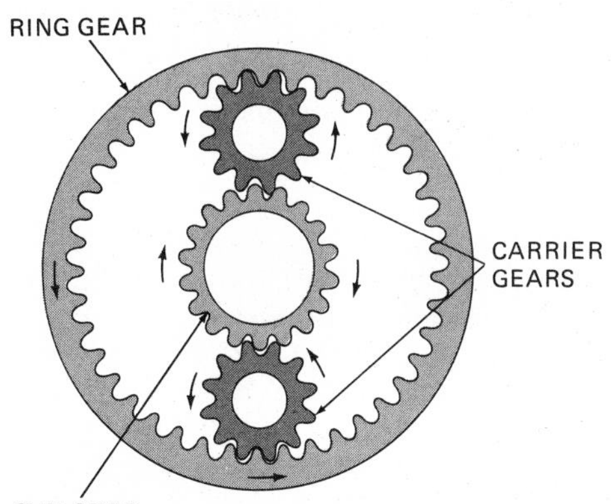

Fig. 12-14 Schematic view of a standard planetary gear set. (*Ford Motor Company*)

out of the outlet port, over an outlet relief valve, through the oil cooler, and back to the main transmission sump. **NOTE** The outlet relief valve controls the converter pressure, whereas the converter inlet relief valve protects the converter against excessive pressure.

Assume the engine is operating and the transmission is in gear, but the torque divider output shaft is not rotating. Under this condition, the sun gear and the rotating housing (including the impeller) rotate at engine speed. Because the output shaft is stationary, the planetary carrier is also stationary; the sun gear drives the planetary carrier gears, forcing the ring gear and turbine to rotate in a direction opposite to that of the sun gear. However, at the same time the fluid velocity from the impeller to the

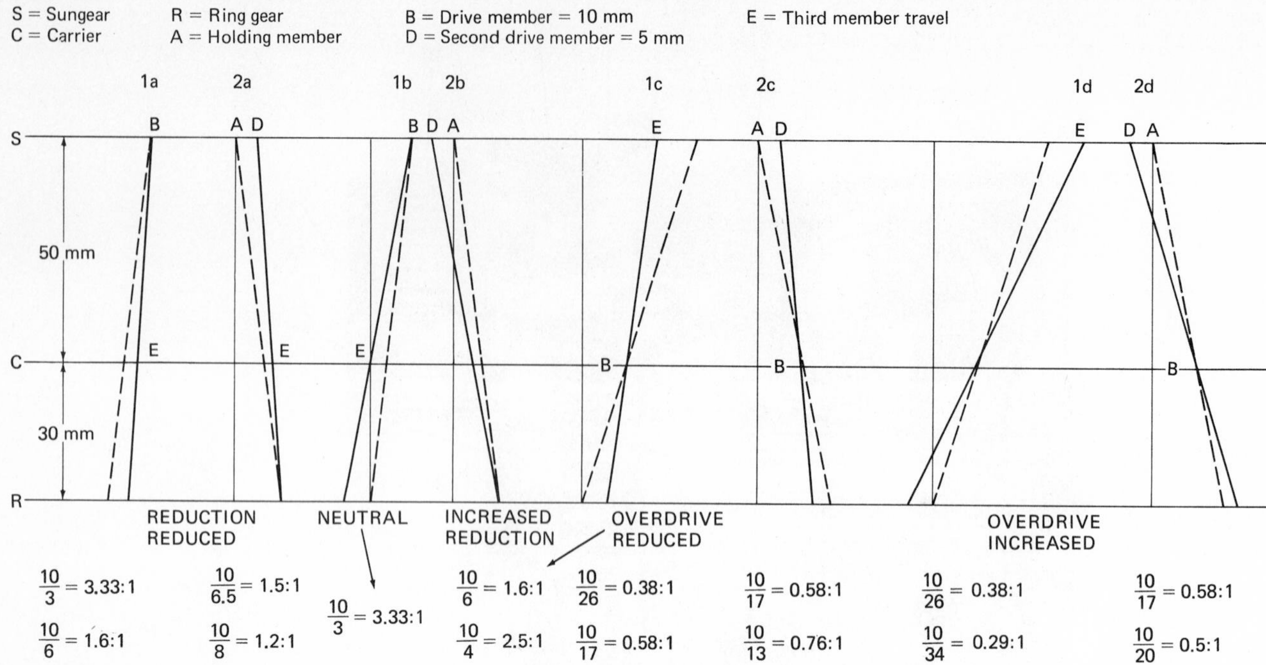

Fig. 12-15 Ratio calculations and other drive combinations.

turbine, and from the turbine to the reactor, causes the turbine alternately to become stationary, and then to rotate in the same direction as the impeller. The engine torque is transmitted to the sun gear and over the impeller to the torque converter turbine and ring gear. As a result, the sun gear and ring gear rotate in the same direction; however, the sun gear rotates at engine speed, and the ring gear at this point may rotate very slowly or not at all.

In a planetary drive combination, when the ring gear is held stationary and the sun gear is the drive, maximum gear reduction is achieved from the planetary gear set, and the carrier gears rotate within the ring gear, driving the carrier and the output shaft. if the impeller (engine) speed increases to its maximum, the turbine then has maximum torque

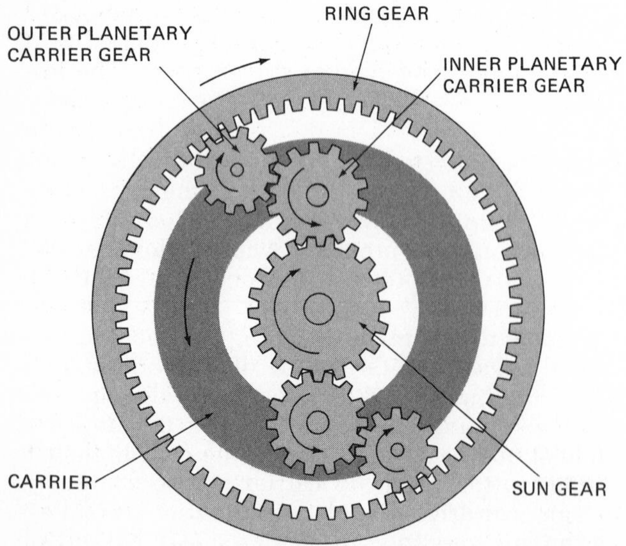

Fig. 12-16 Schematic view of a four-member planetary gear set.

and starts to rotate, slowly at first, but gradually increasing in speed. As the carrier (output shaft) speed increases, the planetary gear ratio decreases, and when the turbine speed reaches about 70 percent of the impeller speed, the carrier rotates nearly at the speed of the turbine; at this point the transmission should be shifted into higher gear. See material on powershift transmission using compound planetary gear sets.

POWERSHIFT TRANSMISSIONS

The purpose of a powershift transmission is the same as that of a standard transmission. However, a powershift transmission has the ability to shift from one forward speed to another (up- or downshift), or from one reverse speed to another (up- or downshift), without loss of torque to the output shaft. This transfer of torque without loss or hesitation during the up- or downshift is made possible through the interaction of hydraulic and multiplate clutches, which is why they are called "powershift" transmissions.

NOTE About 99 percent of all powershift transmissions operate in conjunction with a torque converter.

Powershift transmissions may be divided into three groups: transmissions that automatically shift up and down, transmissions that are semiautomatic (that is, some of the speed ranges are shifted automatically and some are manually shifted), and transmissions that must be manually shifted (that is, the directional valve is manually moved to direct oil to the clutch being engaged).

Each group may be further subdivided into transmissions that use planetary gear sets exclusively,

sage leads into the reverse clutch piston areas. At the right, sealed through seal rings, are two cross-drilled passages (not shown) leading into the cover and then to the directional control valve.

The clutch drum is fastened to the turbine shaft, and the forward and reverse clutch pistons are located inside the left- and right-hand cylinder bores. The clutch pistons are held against the center wall of the clutch drum through the clutch release springs, the latter being held in place through the retainer. The clutch friction disk plates are splined to the inner diameter of the clutch drum, and the steel clutch drive plates are splined to the forward and reverse drive clutch hub.

OPERATION When the engine is operating, oil from the main hydraulic pump flows onto the main relief valve, from which excess oil flows to the converter relief valve and from there excess oil flows to the lubrication relief valve. This provides three different pressures. The main clutch pressure is directed to the lockup clutch and forward/reverse directional valve. The torque converter oil (pressure) is directed to the torque converter, from the converter through the filter and oil cooler (heat exchanger) back to the lubrication relief valve, and then to the transmission sump. The lubrication relief valve maintains lubrication pressure. The lubrication oil is directed into the area around the center tube in the turbine shaft, from the shaft through passages to the tapered roller bearings, and onto the spring and clutch plate areas.

When the operator moves the directional control valve to forward, oil is directed into the top passages of the turbine shaft and into the forward clutch piston area. This forces the piston to the left, clutching the clutch drum to the forward drive clutch hub. The power from the turbine shaft is directed over the clutch drum, clutch friction and drive plates, and clutch hub, to the forward drive gear, to the driven gear, and onto the output shaft. When the engine speed reaches shift speed, the governor directs oil to the lockup clutch directional valve. The valve shifts, whereupon oil is directed through the center passage to the lockup piston. The clutch then engages, and the turbine shaft rotates at engine speed.

To shift into reverse, the spool valve is shifted to reverse, thereby blocking the oil flow to the forward clutch piston and directing it into the reverse clutch piston. As the pressure in the reverse clutch piston builds up, the pressure in the forward clutch piston is reduced through both the directional valve and the small passage in the clutch piston. See Fig. 12-20.

Torque Divider Transmission The torque divider transmission shown in Fig. 12-21 is a fully automatic, three-speed forward transmission. It is manufactured by the Caterpillar Tractor Company for use on their dump trucks and tractor-scrapers, and is used in conjunction with a three-speed-forward, one-speed reverse range transmission.

DESIGN This transmission consists of a single-phase, single-stage torque converter, a planetary gear set, two clutches, and a one-way clutch. The output flange is splined to the flywheel through its outer teeth and is also supported at the center by the flywheel. The planetary carrier is fastened to the input flange.

Within the input flange is clutch piston 1, which has two dump valves. Between the piston and the input flange friction surfaces, clutch friction plate 1 is positioned. The plate is splined to the outer teeth of the planetary ring gear (clutch ring gear 1). The output shaft is supported at the left and right by ball bearings, and the planetary ring gear is splined to the right-hand side of the output shaft. The impeller is supported on the output shaft at the right by a tapered roller bearing, and at the left by a roller bearing. The left-hand side of the impeller has splines to which clutch gear 2 is splined. The sun gear is splined to the left-hand side of the clutch gear, and clutch friction disks 2 are splined to the left-hand side. Clutch pressure plate 2 is bolted to the torque divider housing. The one-way clutch cam is bolted to the turbine, and the turbine is supported by a ball bearing. The one-way clutch outer race is splined to the output shaft. The reactor (stator) is bolted to the torque divider housing.

HYDRAULIC SYSTEM The hydraulic system consists of the components shown in Fig. 12-22. The purpose of the pressure relief valve is to maintain a maximum pressure of about 360 psi [2480 kPa], while the reducing valve must reduce the pressure to about 250 psi [1722.5 kPa]. The purpose of the torque

---

33. Bushing—valve adapter body
34. Adapter—input pump drive
35. Gear—input pump drive
36. Shaft—input pump drive
37. Cover—input pump
38. Shaft—input pump idler gear
39. Gear—input pump idler
40. Body—input pump
41. Plug—main shaft oil hole
42. Seal ring—main shaft (rear)
43. Lock nut—roller bearing retaining
44. Roller bearing—main shaft (rear)
45. Roller bearing—reverse drive gear
46. Spacer—reverse drive gear bearing
47. Roller bearing—reverse drive gear
48. Cover—transmission end
49. Gasket—transmission end cover
50. Gear—reverse drive
51. Key—clutch drum to shaft retaining
52. Hub—reverse drive clutch
53. Spring—clutch release (inner)
54. Plate—clutch friction
55. Spring—clutch release (outer)
56. Dowel—key locating (converter shaft)
57. Seal ring—clutch piston (inner)
58. Plate—clutch drive
59. Retainer—clutch release spring
60. Snap ring—release spring retainer
61. Hub—forward drive clutch
62. Roller bearing—forward drive gear
63. Gear—forward drive
64. Stud—support
65. Spacer—forward drive gear bearing
66. Roller bearing—forward drive gear
67. Seal ring—main shaft (front)

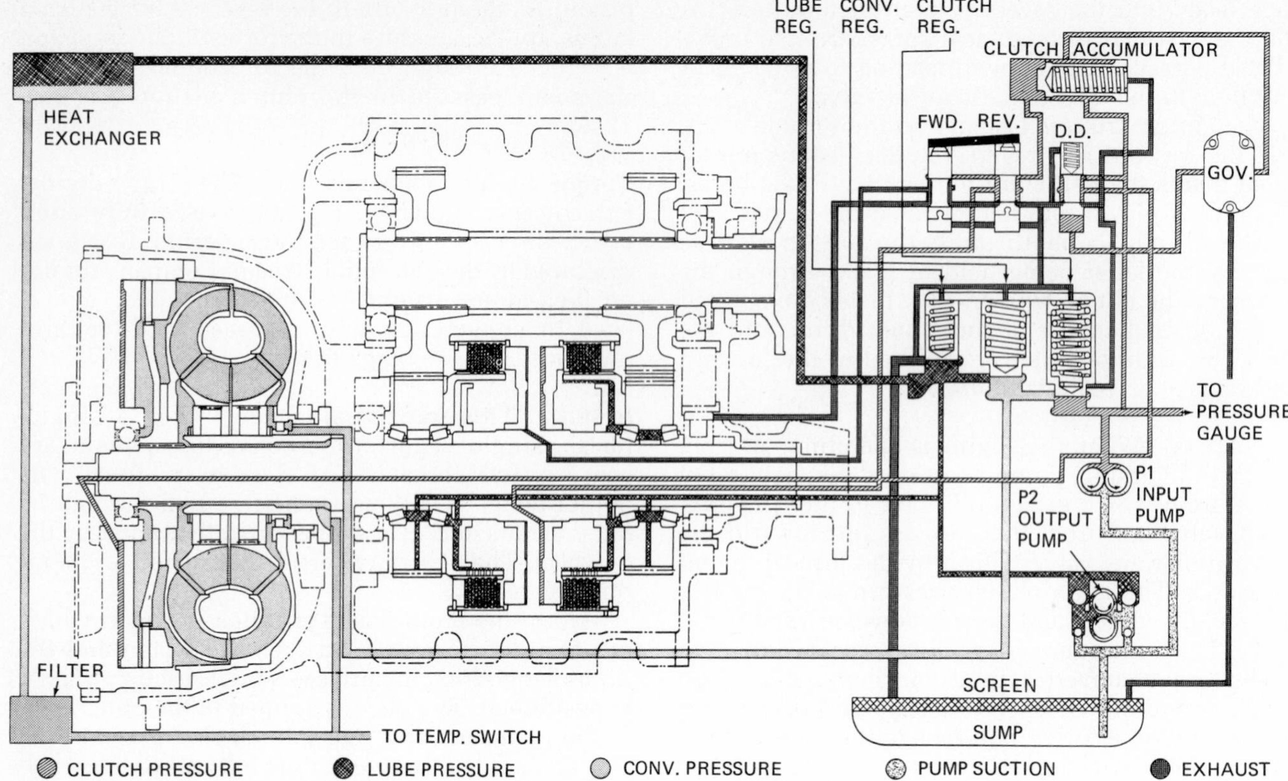

Fig. 12-20 Transmission oil flow diagram for reverse gear direct drive (lockup). (*General Motors Corporation*)

converter charging valve, in conjunction with the torque converter speed valve, is to control the converter pressure. The torque converter hold valve (when used) holds the transmission at converter speed. The throttle-pressure-reducing valve reduces the pressure to about 60 psi [413.4 kPa], and the differential valve reduces this pressure to about 40 psi [275.6 kPa]. It is the purpose of both valves to produce two throttle pressures that act against the mechanical force of the governor and thereby control (at a specific speed) the up- and downshift. The two shift valve accumulators maintain a nearly constant pressure when the shift valves are moved to the left or right during upshift or downshift. The shift valves block or direct oil to clutch piston 1 or 2. The flow divider valve directs a flow of 9 gal/min [34.06 l/min] to clutch 1, and only a flow of about 4 gal/min [15.14 l/min] to clutch 2. This, in conjunction with the torque converter charging valve and accumulator, assures a smooth up- and downshift. The accumulator charging valve is used to direct oil to the accumulator when clutch 1 is being engaged, and to direct the accumulator oil to clutch 2 when shifted from direct to overdrive. The governor is driven by the output shaft, and its lever force is directed onto both shift valves. Its purpose, in conjunction with the throttle pressure, is to upshift or downshift the transmission at a specific output shaft speed.

TORQUE CONVERTER SPEED When the engine is operating and the range transmission is in neutral, first-, second-, third-, or reverse-speed gear, both clutches in the torque divider transmission are disengaged. The oil from the main hydraulic pump flows through the filters, and from there it flows into three different circuits. It flows to the main pressure relief valve, which limits the maximum system pressure to the range transmission pressure control valves, and to the pressure-reducing valve. As the main pressure rises to the set pressure, the pressure relief valve opens and directs oil to the torque converter and to the torque converter charging valve.

The oil returning from the torque converter flows into the charging valve, around the valve spool, and from this valve to the oil cooler. From the cooler it flows to the lubrication valve, where it is then directed to the range transmission and torque divider transmission lubrication circuits. The main controlled oil pressure flows to and through the pressure-reducing valve and from there to the flow divider valve, and to the torque converter speed valve onto the torque converter hold valve. The flow divider valve directs oil to clutch shift valves 1 and 2, where it is then blocked. The spring of the torque converter speed valve then moves the valve spool to the right, whereupon the oil is directed to the right-hand end of the torque converter charging valve, increasing its spring force. Torque converter pressure increases because the return flow is restricted. When the torque converter inlet pressure is reached, the torque converter charging valve spool is forced to the right, allowing more oil to return to the oil cooler, thereby maintaining a pressure of about 100 psi [689.0 kPa].

The oil under pressure that enters at the torque converter hold valve flows past the valve spool, and onto the throttle-pressure-reducing valve, where the pressure is reduced to 60 psi [413.4 kPa]. the oil is

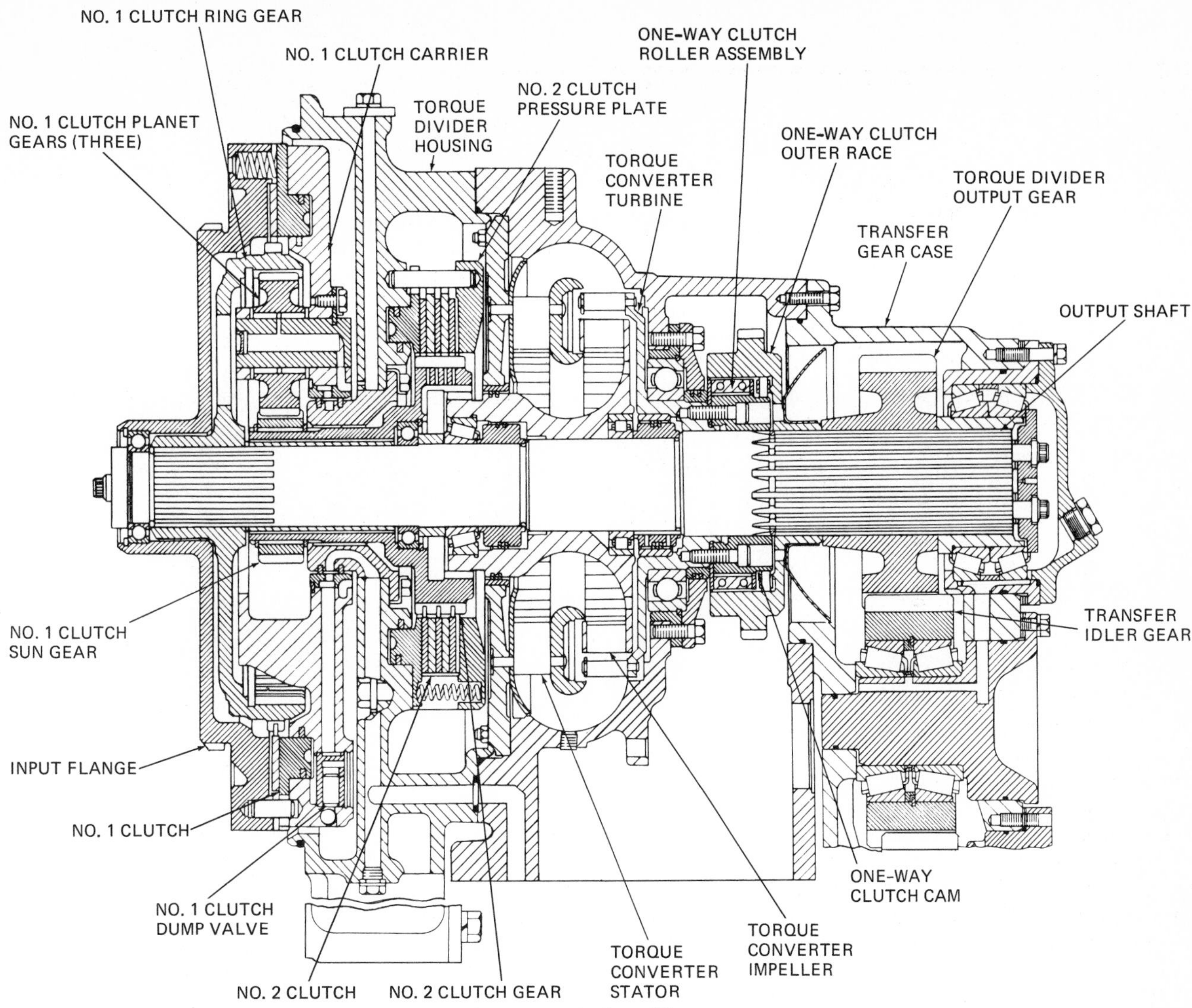

Fig. 12-21 Sectional view of the torque divider transmission. (*Caterpillar Tractor Co.*)

then directed to the differential valve, from there to clutch shift valve accumulator 2, and onto the right-hand side of shift valve 2. The differential valve reduces the pressure to about 40 psi [275.6 kPa], and directs the oil to shift valve accumulator 1 and over a check valve onto the right-hand side of shift valve 1. The throttle pressures hold the shift valves to the left.

TORQUE CONVERTER DRIVE OPERATION Under the hydraulic circumstances just outlined, both clutches are disengaged, the torque converter pressure is about 100 psi [689 kPa], and the output shaft is not rotating. Therefore the planetary ring gear is also stationary. The rotation (torque) from the engine is transmitted to the output flange and planetary carrier, and the carrier gears drive the sun gear, clutch gear 2, and the impeller because the ring gear is held stationary. **NOTE** The planetary gear set is in overdrive ratio. This action locks the turbine through the one-way cam, rollers, and one-way clutch outer race to the output shaft. As the output shaft and planetary ring gear start to rotate, the sun gear and impeller speed reduce, and with increased ring gear speed the planetary gear set gradually becomes direct drive. See Figs. 12-22 and 12-23.

Direct drive At about this point, the output shaft speed has caused the mechanical governor to create enough force to overcome the throttle pressure force and move shift valve 1 to the right. Oil at a volume of 9 gal/min [34.06 l/min] is then directed into three passages: to clutch 1, over the one-way check valve to the torque converter speed valve, and to the accumulator charging valve.

The oil flowing into clutch 1 moves the piston to the right, clutching the planetary ring gear (output shaft) and the carrier (engine flywheel) together. This causes the output shaft to be driven at engine speed. During the time the clutch is filled, the pressure rises and forces the torque converter speed valve to the left. Oil pressure is then removed from the right-hand side of the torque converter charging valve, whereupon only the spring force controls the torque converter pressure, dropping it to about 30

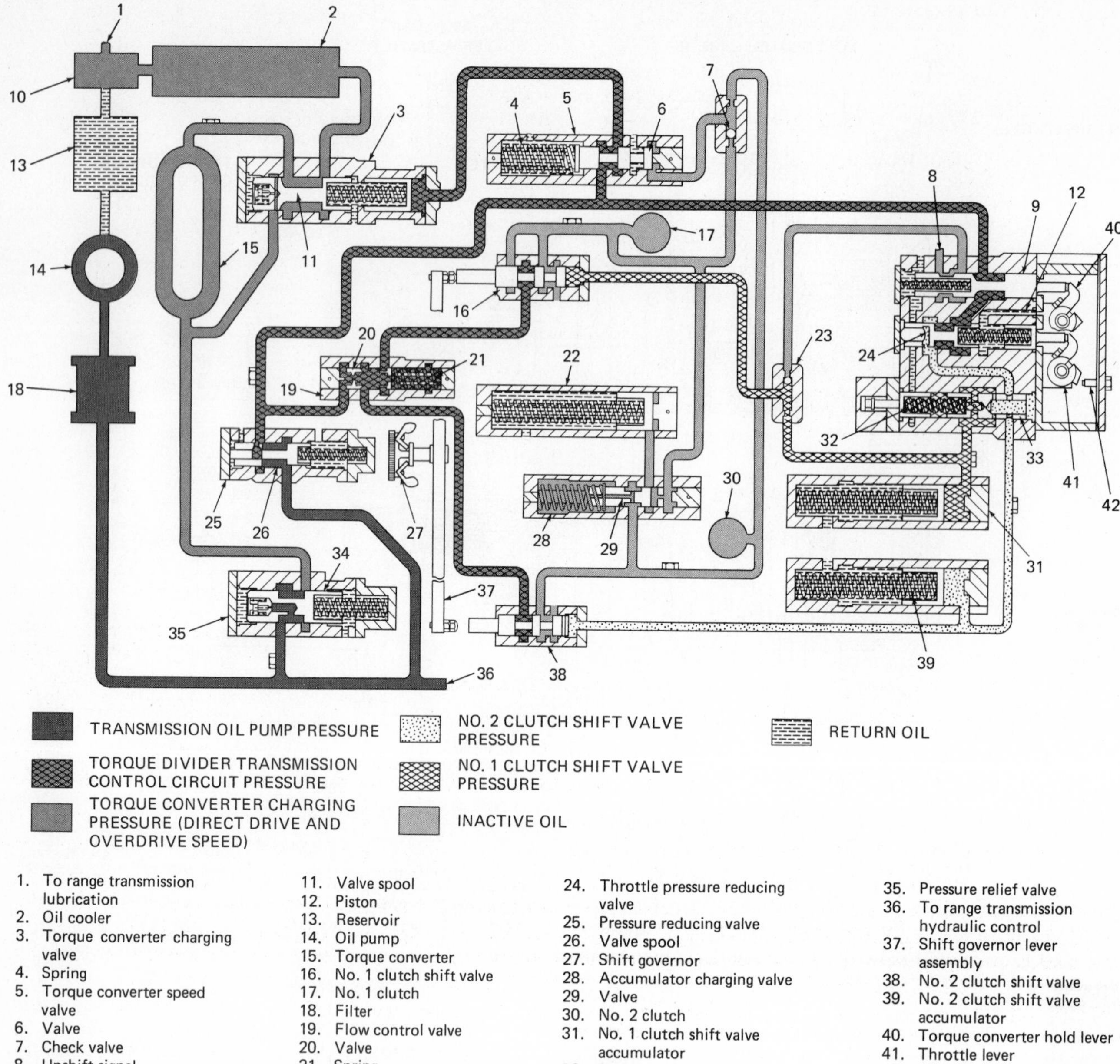

1. To range transmission lubrication
2. Oil cooler
3. Torque converter charging valve
4. Spring
5. Torque converter speed valve
6. Valve
7. Check valve
8. Upshift signal
9. Torque converter hold valve
10. Lubrication valve
11. Valve spool
12. Piston
13. Reservoir
14. Oil pump
15. Torque converter
16. No. 1 clutch shift valve
17. No. 1 clutch
18. Filter
19. Flow control valve
20. Valve
21. Spring
22. No. 2 clutch accumulator
23. Check valve
24. Throttle pressure reducing valve
25. Pressure reducing valve
26. Valve spool
27. Shift governor
28. Accumulator charging valve
29. Valve
30. No. 2 clutch
31. No. 1 clutch shift valve accumulator
32. Piston
33. Differential valve
34. Valve
35. Pressure relief valve
36. To range transmission hydraulic control
37. Shift governor lever assembly
38. No. 2 clutch shift valve
39. No. 2 clutch shift valve accumulator
40. Torque converter hold lever
41. Throttle lever
42. Stop screw

Fig. 12-22 Schematic view of torque divider transmission hydraulic controls (torque converter speed). (*Caterpillar Tractor Co.*)

psi [206.7 kPa]. This combined action assures a speed change without a torque loss. See Fig. 12-24.

Hold action If operating circumstances compel the operator to maintain the transmission in torque converter drive, she or he moves the torque converter hold valve to the hold position. This moves the valve spool, and oil under a pressure of about 250 psi [1722.5 kPa] is then directed over the check valve, onto shift valve 1. Because of the high oil pressure, the mechanical force of the governor is overcome, and the valve shifts to the left, blocking the oil flow to clutch 1. With the pressure removed, clutch dump valves 1 shift outward and allow the oil from the clutch piston to drain into the transmission, disengaging clutch 1. Consequently, the pressure from the torque converter speed valve is removed and causes the torque converter charging valve to restrict the return flow, and the torque converter is again charged with a higher pressure.

Overdrive When the transmission is in direct drive and the governor force is increased due to increased output shaft speed, the governor moves shift valves 1 and 2 to the right. Shift valve 1 now blocks the oil flow to the clutch and to the torque converter speed valve and torque converter charging valve. This action reduces the oil pressure in clutch 1 through the action of the dump valve in clutch carrier 1.

Shift valve 2 now directs oil to clutch 2, and onto the torque converter speed valve. Because the accumulator charging valve has lost its application

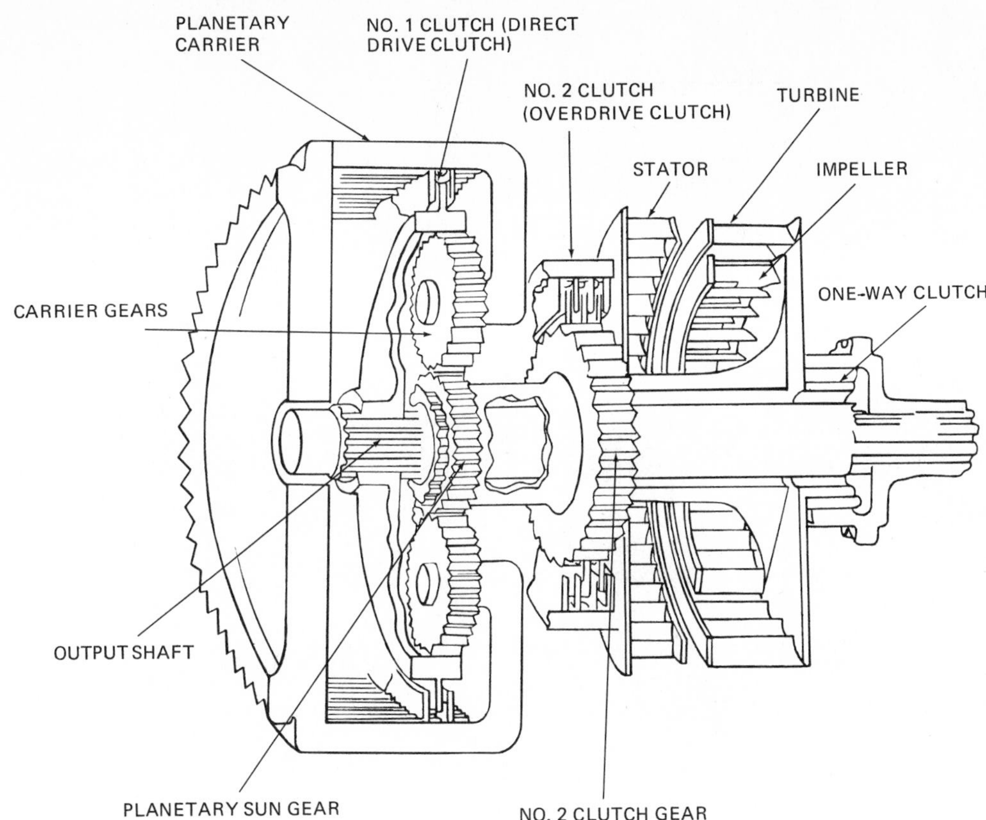

Fig. 12-23 Schematic view of the torque divider transmission. (*Caterpillar Tractor Co.*)

pressure, it moves to the right, allowing the accumulator oil to help fill clutch 2.

NOTE The pressure on the torque convertor speed valve is maintained. See Fig. 12-25.

The oil pressure in piston 2 forces the piston to the left, clutching the clutch gear to the torque divider housing, and holding the sun gear, as well as the impeller, stationary. This places the planetary gear set into an overdrive ratio because the sun gear is held stationary and the carrier gears drive the ring gear (output shaft) at higher speed than the carrier.

Downshift If the output shaft speed decreases, the governor force also decreases, and at a certain speed the combined force of throttle pressures 1 and 2 are higher than the force of the governor. Under this circumstance shift valves 1 and 2 are moved to the left. Clutch shift valve 2 blocks the oil flow to clutch 2, and at the same time it opens a return port, allowing the oil from clutch 2 to flow out, disengaging the clutch. Clutch shift valve 1 now directs oil to clutch piston 1, engaging it, and the transmission is now in direct drive. If the output shaft decreases further, throttle pressure 1 moves shift valve 1 to the left, causing the transmission to shift to torque converter drive.

If the range transmission is upshifted, a signal pressure is directed to the torque converter hold valve, and flows around that valve to the check valve and onto the right-hand side of shift valve 1. These actions assure that, when the range transmission is upshifted, the torque divider transmission will shift into torque converter speed. However, when the range transmission is downshifted, the torque divider transmission is allowed to select its own range, depending upon the governor force and throttle pressure.

Planetary Powershift Transmissions All planetary powershift transmissions are nearly equivalent in design and operation. Any differences which exist among the numerous types lies mainly in (1) the hydraulic system, (2) the number of forward and reverse speeds, and (3) the torque capacity.

Their basic principle is to utilize more than one single planetary gear set and to fasten a member of the first planetary gear set to a member of a second set, and perhaps a member of the secondary planetary gear set to a member of the third set. See Fig. 12-26. Such a system is called a *compound planetary gear set.* The multiplate clutches used to hold one member of a planetary gear set (to achieve the individual speed ranges) are hydraulically applied and spring released.

Three-Speed Forward and Three-Speed Reverse Powershift Transmission A three-speed forward and three-speed reverse transmission is schematically illustrated in Figs. 12-27 to 12-30. The sun gears of the reverse and forward planetary gear sets are splined to the turbine shaft (or transmission input shaft). The reverse carrier can be clutched to the transmission housing. The reverse planetary ring gear is fastened to the forward planetary carrier, and fastened to the latter is the clutch drum of the intermediate range. The high-range planetary carrier is fastened to the intermediate clutch drum, and the low-range sun gear is fastened to the high-range planetary carrier.

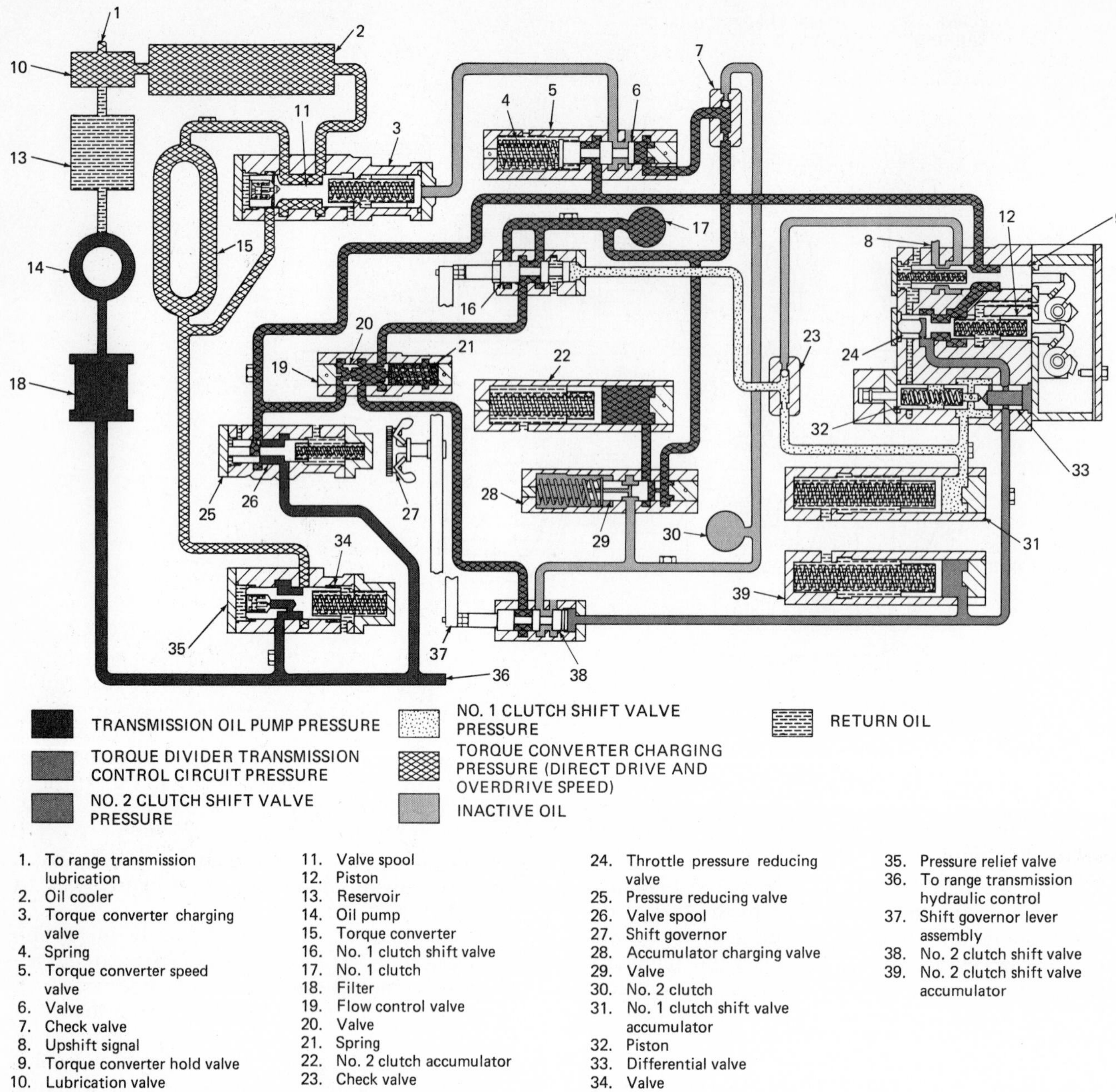

Fig. 12-24 Schematic view of torque divider transmission hydraulic controls (direct drive speed). (*Caterpillar Tractor Co.*)

The ring gears of the forward high and low ranges can be clutched to the transmission case, and the intermediate clutch drum can be clutched to the intermediate clutch hub. Fastened to the output shaft are the low-range planetary carrier, the high-range sun gear, and the intermediate-range clutch hub. To achieve a transfer torque from the turbine to the transmission output shaft, two clutches must be engaged—one range clutch (low, intermediate, or high), and either the forward or reverse clutch.

OPERATION For low forward operation, the forward and low-range clutches are engaged through hydraulic action. This holds the forward and low-range ring gears stationary. The rotation (torque) from the turbine shaft rotates all gears; however, the torque is transmitted into the transmission from the forward sun gear only. The sun gear drives the carrier gears, causing the carrier, the intermediate clutch drum, the high-range carrier, and the low-range sun gear to rotate in the same direction as the forward sun gear. The low-range sun gear drives the carrier gears, causing the carrier and the output shaft to rotate in the same direction as the forward sun gear. **NOTE** Two planetary gear sets are used to achieve first speed (low range 5.27:1.00). See Fig. 12-27.

When shifting into intermediate range (second speed), the intermediate clutch is engaged, and it clutches the forward carrier to the output shaft. Now only one planetary gear set is used to achieve second (speed) range at a ratio of 1.9:1.00. See Fig. 12-28.

When shifted into high range, the high-range ring gear is clutched to the transmission case, holding the righ gear stationary and converting the high-range planetary gear set into overdrive ratio. The rotation (torque) from the turbine shaft is transmitted

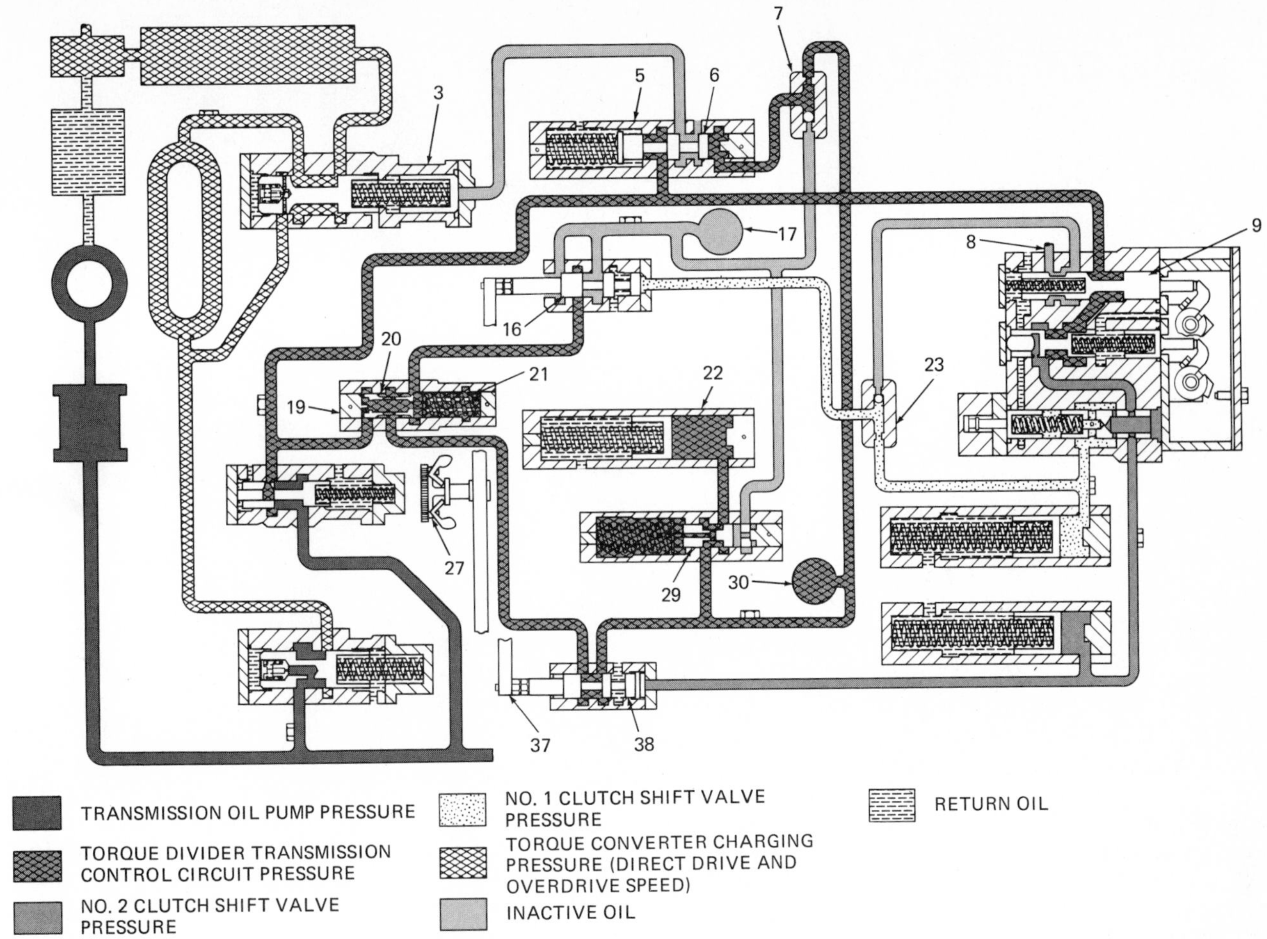

TRANSMISSION OIL PUMP PRESSURE	NO. 1 CLUTCH SHIFT VALVE PRESSURE
TORQUE DIVIDER TRANSMISSION CONTROL CIRCUIT PRESSURE	TORQUE CONVERTER CHARGING PRESSURE (DIRECT DRIVE AND OVERDRIVE SPEED)
NO. 2 CLUTCH SHIFT VALVE PRESSURE	INACTIVE OIL
RETURN OIL	

3. Torque converter charging valve
5. Torque converter speed valve
6. Valve
7. Check valve
8. Upshift signal
9. Torque converter hold valve
16. No. 1 clutch shift valve
17. No. 1 clutch
19. Flow control valve
20. Valve
21. Spring
22. No. 2 clutch accumulator
23. Check valve
27. Shift governor
29. Valve
30. No. 2 clutch
37. Shift governor lever assembly
38. No. 2 clutch shift valve

Fig. 12-25 Schematic view of torque divider transmission hydraulic controls (overdrive speed). (*Caterpillar Tractor Co.*)

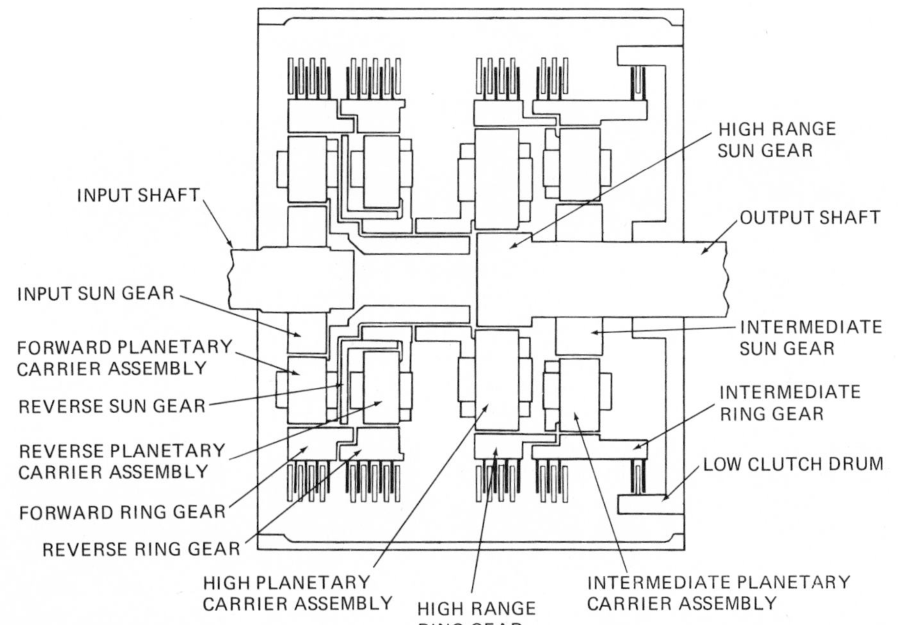

Fig. 12-26 Schematic view of transmission gearing.

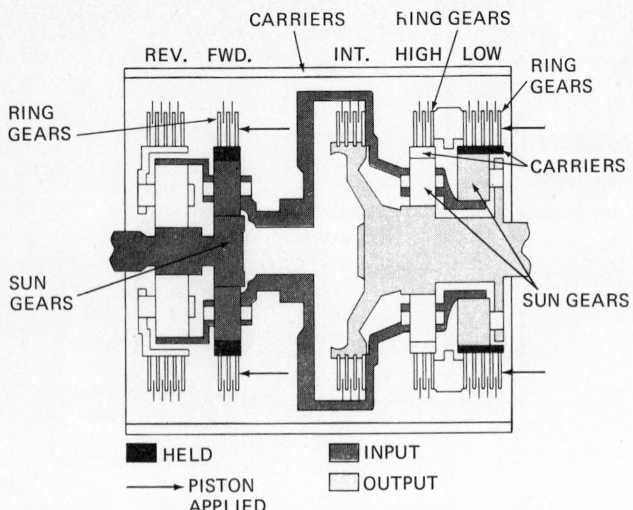

Fig. 12-27 Schematic view of a compound planetary gear set in low range forward.

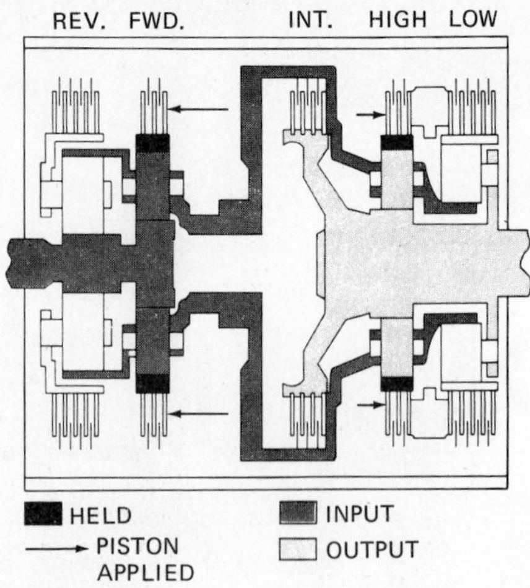

Fig. 12-29 Schematic view of a compound planetary gear set in high range forward.

to the forward sun gear, the forward carrier intermediate clutch drum, the high-range carrier, and the low-range sun gear. The high-range carrier gear drives the high-range sun and output shafts at a ratio of 0.65:1.00. See Fig. 12-29.

To achieve the three reverse ranges, the reverse clutch is engaged, and this holds the reverse carrier to the transmission housing. Now one of the three range clutches is engaged—say, for instance, low range. The rotation of the turbine shaft and reverse sun gear drive the planetary gears, which drive the reverse ring gear, the forward carrier, the intermediate clutch drum, the high-range carrier, and the low-range sun gear in reverse rotation to the turbine shaft.

The transmission just described is used on a front-end wheel loader. When it is used on a track-type loader or dozer, no transfer case is used.

DESIGN The turbine shaft is supported by two ball bearings, and the transmission main shaft is supported by a roller bearing on the turbine shaft and at the right by two sets of ball bearings. Splined to it, from left to right (Fig. 12-30) are the intermediate-range clutch hub, high-range sun gear, low-range carrier, and the output drive gear. The low- and high-range clutch pistons are positioned in the bore of the high/low range anchor that is fastened to the transmission housing, and the steel clutch plates are fastened through pins to the high/low anchor. The clutch friction plates are splined to the outside splines on the high- and low-range ring gears. The intermediate-range drum is splined to the forward carrier, and both are supported by a ball bearing. The clutch piston is positioned in the bore of the intermediate-range drum. The steel clutch plates are splined to the drum, and the clutch friction plates are splined to the intermediate-range clutch hub. The reverse sun gear and turbine shaft form a single unit to which the forward sun gear is splined. The reverse anchor is fastened to the transmission housing, and the forward and reverse steel clutch plates are pinned to it. The clutch pistons for both clutches are located in the bore of the transmission housing. The clutch friction plates of the reverse clutch are splined to the reverse planetary carrier hub, and those of the forward clutch are splined to the forward planetary ring gear.

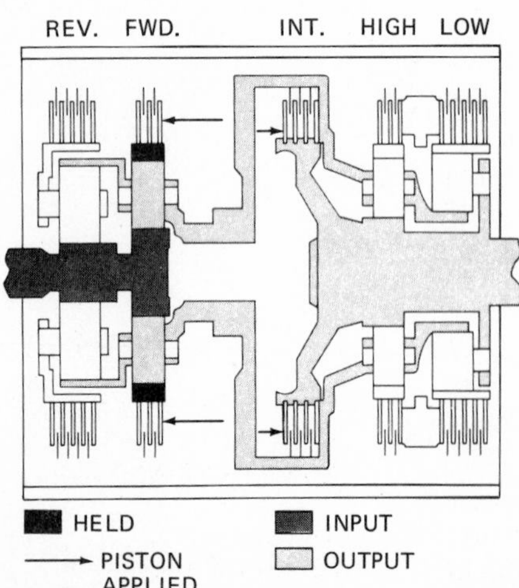

Fig. 12-28 Schematic view of a compound planetary gear set in intermediate range forward.

HYDRAULIC SYSTEM Of the hydraulic system components schematically illustrated in Fig. 12-31, you will see one component with which you may not be familiar, the clutch cutoff valve.

The purpose of this valve is to disengage the directional clutch when the service brake is applied.

If both selector valves are in neutral when the engine is operating, the oil from the hydraulic pump flows through the oil filter, to the main pressure regulator, and to the range selector valve, where it is stopped. Oil also flows through the forward/reverse selector valve, through the cutoff valve, and again to the forward/reverse selector valve, where it is also stopped. The pressure then rises, and the main pressure regulator valve directs the excess oil to the converter relief valve. The converter valve maintains the specific converter "in" pressure, and the excess oil is dumped back into the transmission sump. The oil from the oil cooler is directed into the center passages of the turbine shaft and main transmission

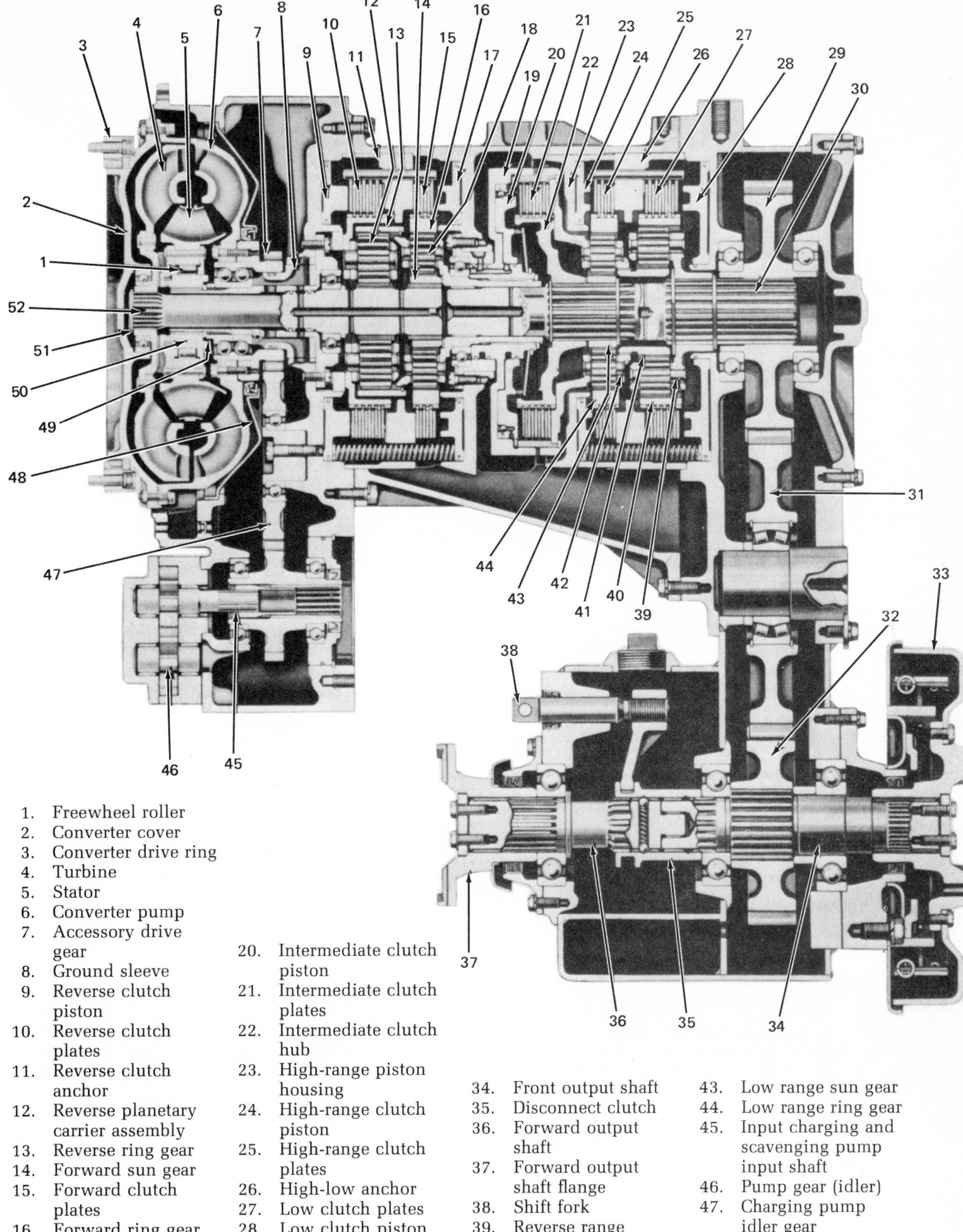

1. Freewheel roller
2. Converter cover
3. Converter drive ring
4. Turbine
5. Stator
6. Converter pump
7. Accessory drive gear
8. Ground sleeve
9. Reverse clutch piston
10. Reverse clutch plates
11. Reverse clutch anchor
12. Reverse planetary carrier assembly
13. Reverse ring gear
14. Forward sun gear
15. Forward clutch plates
16. Forward ring gear
17. Forward clutch piston
18. Forward planetary carrier assembly
19. Intermediate-range drum
20. Intermediate clutch piston
21. Intermediate clutch plates
22. Intermediate clutch hub
23. High-range piston housing
24. High-range clutch piston
25. High-range clutch plates
26. High-low anchor
27. Low clutch plates
28. Low clutch piston
29. Output drive gear
30. Transmission main shaft
31. Output idler gear
32. Output driven gear
33. Parking brake
34. Front output shaft
35. Disconnect clutch
36. Forward output shaft
37. Forward output shaft flange
38. Shift fork
39. Reverse range planet pinion
40. Reverse range ring gear
41. Low range carrier
42. Reverse range sun gear
43. Low range sun gear
44. Low range ring gear
45. Input charging and scavenging pump input shaft
46. Pump gear (idler)
47. Charging pump idler gear
48. Turbine housing
49. Ground sleeve
50. Freewheel roller race
51. Snap ring
52. Input shaft

Fig. 12-30 Sectional view of a powershift transmission. (*Terex Division of General Motors Corporation*)

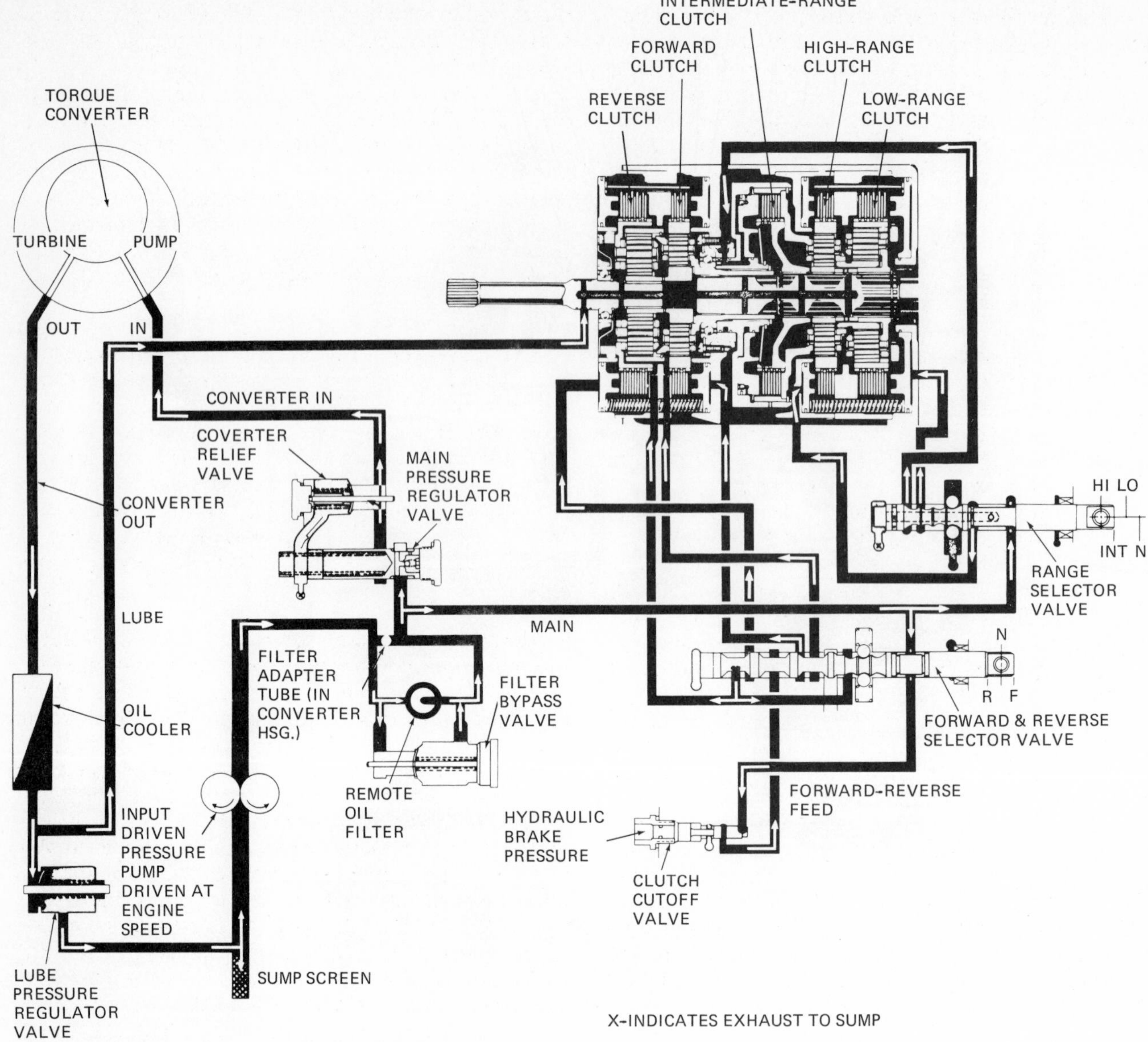

Fig. 12-31 Schematic view of the transmission hydraulic system. (*Terex Division of General Motors Corporation*)

shaft, providing lubrication to the shafts, gears, bearings, and clutches, and then it drops into the sump. If the lubrication oil pressure exceeds the set pressure, the excess oil is directed to the sump.

When the operator selects and moves the range selector valve to the low position, oil is directed into the low-range piston area, engaging the low-range clutch. He or she then selects and moves the forward/reverse selector to the forward or reverse position, engaging one of the clutches. If the operator applies the service brake (air or hydraulic), the clutch cutoff piston is moved to the right, and the oil flow to the forward or reverse clutch is blocked. At the same time the return port is opened and the oil pressure is removed in the clutch being engaged, interrupting the torque to the range gears.

Five-Speed Planetary Transmission The five-speed forward, one-speed reverse transmission shown in Fig. 12-32 is a fully automatic transmission. However, due to its hydraulic control, it can be held to four-speed forward automatic upshift and downshift, or to three- or two-speed, or it can be held in first gear.

In forward low, it has a ratio of 3.19:1.00; in first 1.89:1.00; in second 1.55:1.00; in third 1.24:1.00; and in fourth (direct) 1.00:1.00. However, when in the one-, two-, three-, and four-speed ranges, the transmission also shifts into lockup when the pitot governor (velocity governor) sends a signal to the lockup shift valve. The transmission has four planetary gear sets and six clutches.

DESIGN The output shaft is supported by two sets of ball bearings, and splined to it is the low-range planetary carrier, the rear governor, and the speedometer drive gear. The low clutch anchor, which includes the first clutch piston, is fastened to the transmission housing, and the steel clutch plates are splined to the anchor. The low-range clutch piston is located in the rear cover assembly. The low-range ring gear is fastened to the reverse planetary carrier assembly that is splined to the front planetary ring gear. The low-range sun gear is splined to the main transmission shaft, and the reverse planetary carrier is supported on the shaft through a roller bearing.

The clutch friction plates are splined to the low-range and reverse planetary ring gears. The steel clutch plates are splined to the low and reverse clutch anchors. The center planetary ring gear is splined to the reverse sun gear which, in turn, is splined to the main transmission shaft, and the center carrier is splined to the front planetary ring gear. The center planetary sun gear and the shaft form one piece that is supported on the main transmission shaft by two sets of roller bearings. Splined to the center planetary sun gear shaft is the front planetary sun gear, and splined to its left-hand side is the fourth clutch drum.

The front planetary carrier is supported on the center sun gear shaft by a roller bearing, and splined to the carrier hub are the friction clutch plates. The steel clutch plates are splined to the forward clutch anchor. The forward planetary clutch piston and the fourth clutch piston are positioned in the bores of the center support housing. The latter is fastened to the transmission housing and is supported through roller bearings on the center sun gear shaft. The steel clutch plates are internally splined to the fourth clutch drum, and the friction clutch plates are splined to the forward clutch hub. Located within the fourth clutch hub is the fourth clutch piston. The friction clutch plates of the third clutch are externally splined to the fourth clutch drum, and the steel clutch plates are splined to the third clutch anchor.

The forward clutch drum is splined to the turbine shaft (within which is the clutch piston), and the steel clutch plates are splined to it. The friction clutch plates are splined to the forward clutch hub, which in turn is splined to the transmission main shaft. The large gear of the hydraulic pump is fastened through a pin to the impeller hub, and the small gear is supported on the gear shaft. Fastened to the front clutch drum is the pitot collector ring. The pitot is fastened to the forward support, within which are the main pressure regulator, the lockup shift valve, and the converter bypass valve. (The last three items listed are not shown in Fig. 12-32.)

HYDRAULIC SYSTEM The schematic diagram of the hydraulic system (Fig. 12-33) may at first be quite confusing, but actually it is simple when you relate the new names for the components to functions you already understand.

The oil flow with which you are familiar originates from the gear pump (driven by the impeller) and flows to the main regulator. From there it is distributed into 10 individual hydraulic circuits: to the converter bypass valve and torque converter, and then to shift valves 4–5, 3–4, 2–3, and 1–2, the trimmer regulator valve, the lockup valve, and relay valve 2–3. From relay valve 2–3 oil flows to relay valve 1–2, and from there to shift valve 1–2. Oil also flows over the selector valve to the rear governor and to the modulator valve. A reduced pressure from the main pressure regulator is directed to the selector valve, and this pressure is used to engage the forward clutch.

When the set main pressure is reached, the excess oil is directed to the torque converter and the converter bypass valve. Excess oil passes by the converter bypass valve onto the lubrication valve. The return oil from the torque converter, flows through the oil cooler, onto the converter bypass valve, and then into the lubrication circuit. The lubrication pressure regulator controls the maximum lubrication pressure.

Rear governor The rear governor senses output shaft speed, whereupon it moves the valve spool either to the left or right. When the valve spool is moved to the right, the output shaft speed is low, resulting in low governor pressure which is derived from the main pressure. When it is moved to the left, the output shaft speed is high, resulting in a higher governor pressure. The regulated governor pressure is directed onto one side of the four shift signal valves.

Modulator pressure regulator The modulator pressure regulator is actually a throttle pressure regulator. It is linked over the mechanical actuator with the throttle. When the throttle is depressed toward maximum fuel, the valve spool is moved to the left against its spring force, reducing the main line pressure; the reduced pressure is exerted onto the right-hand side, resulting in a modulated pressure. When the throttle allows the valve spool to move to the right, the modulator pressure increases because, in addition to the spring force, the modulator pressure moves the valve to the right, creating a larger valve spool opening. The (regulated) modulator pressure is directed to shift signal valves 4–5, 3–4, and 2–3, the trimmer regulator valve, and the lockup valve. The combined governor and modulator pressure act against the calibrated spring force of the shift valve. At a given governor pressure, and an increased modulator pressure (throttle pressure), a signal valve will upshift, and with a reduced modulator pressure, a downshift occurs if the governor pressure cannot hold the shift valve open.

Trimmer regulator valve and trimmer valve The trimmer regulator is a remote-control pressure regulator that responds to the various modulator pressures, thereby reducing the main pressure. The regulated (modulator) pressure is directed onto the bottom of the low clutch, first clutch, second clutch, and third clutch trimmer valves. The trimmer valves act as accumulators, thereby preventing harsh clutch engagement. They are connected in parallel with the clutch application line. When the trimmer regulator pressure is low, because of a high modulator pressure (low idle) there is less oil below the trimmer plug. When the clutch is engaged, more oil can flow into the trimmer valve and out of the exhaust port, resulting in a low initial clutch application pressure. With a low modulator pressure (increased fuel), the trimmer regulator pressure is higher; therefore there is more oil below the trimmer plug. As a result, less

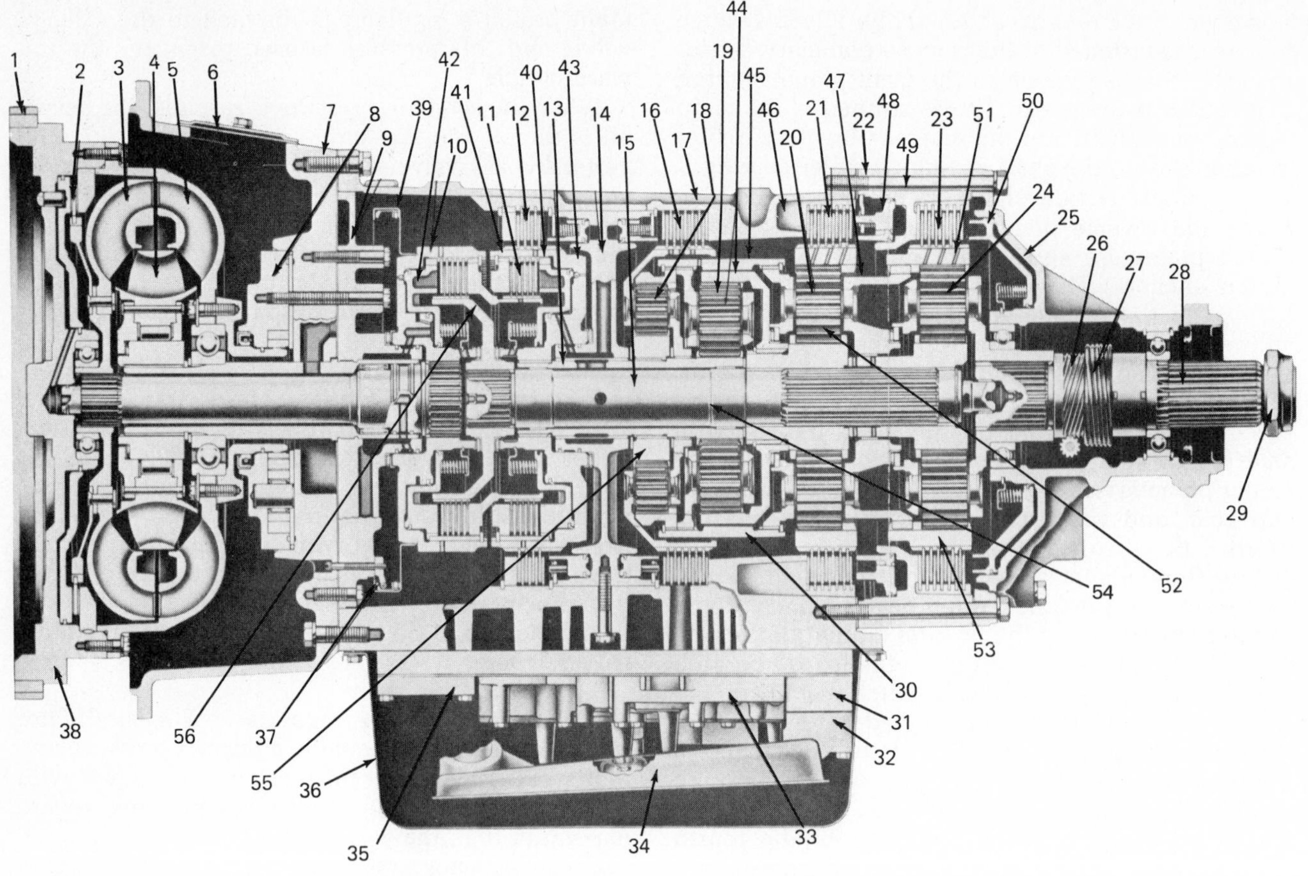

1. Starter ring gear
2. Lockup clutch
3. Torque converter turbine
4. **Torque converter stator**
5. Torque converter pump
6. Accessory cover
7. Torque converter housing
8. Trans. input pump
9. Forward support & valve assembly
10. Forward clutch drum
11. Fourth clutch assembly
12. Third clutch
13. Sun gear and shaft assembly
14. Center support housing assembly
15. Main shaft assembly
16. Second clutch
17. Transmission housing
18. Front planetary carrier
19. Center planetary carrier
20. Rear planetary carrier
21. First clutch
22. Adapter housing assembly
23. Low clutch
24. Low carrier
25. Rear cover assembly
26. Governor drive gear
27. Speedometer drive gear
28. Output shaft
29. Output flange retaining nut
30. Gear unit connecting drum
31. Low shift valve assembly
32. Low trimmer valve assembly
33. Control valve assembly
34. Oil filter
35. Cover plate
36. Oil pan
37. Pitot tube
38. Flywheel
39. Pitot collector ring
40. Fourth clutch piston
41. Third clutch anchor
42. Fwd. clutch piston
43. Fourth clutch drum
44. Center planetary ring gear
45. Front planetary ring gear
46. Reverse anchor
47. Reverse planetary carrier
48. First clutch piston
49. Low clutch anchor
50. Low clutch piston
51. Low range ring gear
52. Low range sun gear
53. Reverse sun gear
54. Center planetary sun gear
55. Front planetary sun gear
56. Fwd. clutch hub

Fig. 12-32 Sectional view of a five-speed automatic transmission. (*General Motors Corporation*)

oil can flow into the trimmer valve and out of the exhaust port, causing a quick clutch application pressure rise.

Hold regulator valve The hold regulator valve's purpose is to prevent the transmission from shifting higher than selected, by directing a reduced main line pressure to the shift signal valves. When shifted in D4 (fourth speed), the hold pressure is directed to shift signal valve 4–5; when in D3 (third speed), it is directed to shift signal valves 4–5 and 3–4; and when in D2 (second speed), it is directed to shift signal valves 4–5, 3–4, and 2–3.

Priority valve The purpose of this valve is to maintain sufficient clutch pressure during an upshift or downshift.

Front governor (lockup circuit) The front governor pressure originates at the pitot when the forward clutch drum is driven by the turbine shaft. The oil in the collector ring is then forced into the pitot orifice, and the resultant oil pressure is directed onto the top of the lockup valve. The pitot pressure increases with increased turbine speed, and, when the combined pitot and modulator (throttle) pressure overcome the spring force, the main line pressure is then directed to the lockup clutch.

Relay valves Relay valves 1–2, 2–3, 3–4, and 4–5 are remote-control directional valves that direct main line oil to the respective clutchs and are activated through the shift signal valves. **NOTE** Each clutch has its own circuit—a shift valve, trimmer valve, and a relay valve—except the forward clutch,

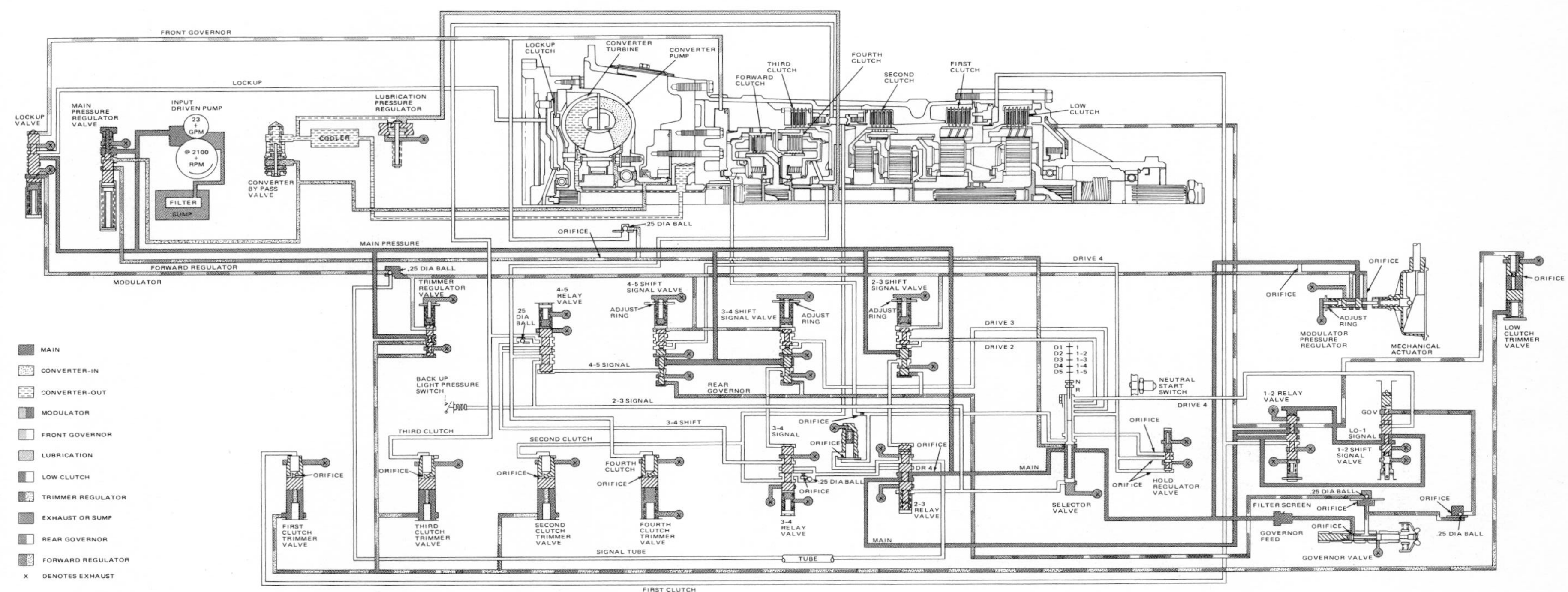

Fig. 12-33 Schematic view of the five-speed automatic transmission hydraulic system. (*General Motors Corporation*)

which is directly connected from the selector valve to the forward clutches.

Selector valve The selector valve is a seven-position spool valve. It receives two different pressures from the main pressure regulator valve—main line and forward clutch pressure; due to its porting, it can direct oil to seven different circuits—relay valve 2–3, the hold regulator valve, shift signal valves 1–2, 2–3, 3–4, and 4–5, and the priority valve.

When the selector valve is placed in position D1, oil is directed to relay valve 2–3, from there to relay valve 1–2, then to shift signal valve 1–2, and from there onto the top of relay valve 1–2, causing the low clutch to be engaged. At the same time, the hold regulator valve pressure directs oil to shift signal valve 5–4, and then to the selector valve, and the latter directs the oil on to shift signal valves 3–4, 2–3, and 1–2, preventing an upshift to second speed.

When the selector valve is placed in position 1–2, the hold regulator valve removes the pressure from shift signal valve 1–2, and an upshift to second speed occurs as soon as the governor pressure shifts signal valve 1–2. The oil pressure from the top of the relay valve is removed. The relay valve now directs oil to the first clutch and at the same time drains oil from the low clutch.

When the selector valve is placed in position 1–3, the hold regulator valve removes the oil pressure from shift signal valve 2–3, and as soon as the governor pressure increases, due to the increased output shaft speed, shift signal valve 2–3 is forced upward and directs oil to relay valve 2–3. The 2–3 relay valve responds, and as it directs oil to the second clutch it also blocks the oil flow to signal valve 1–2 and relay valve 1–2, so that signal valve 1–2 is moved downward by the rear governor pressure. Consequently the pressure from the top of relay valve 1–2 is removed and that valve responds and disengages the low clutch.

When the selector valve is placed in position 1–4, the hold regulator valve removes the oil pressure from shift signal valve 3–4. The transmission upshifts to fourth speed as soon as the governor pressure overcomes the shift signal valve spring force 3–4.

When the selector valve is placed in position D1–5, the low clutch engages through relay valve 1–2; oil is then directed from the selector valve, over the priority valve, and to relay valve 2–3, and the hold regulator pressure is removed from all shift signal valves. When the governor pressure and modulator pressure, or the governor pressure alone, is sufficient to shift signal valve 1–2, it directs oil to relay valve 1–2. When the governor pressure increases and shifts shift valve 2–3, the latter directs all to relief valve 2–3, whereupon the second clutch is engaged. A further increase in governor speed causes a 3–4 upshift and 4–5 upshift. Whenever an upshift occurs, the relay valve, which directs oil to and engages a clutch, also disengages, in sequence, the next lower speed clutch.

When the rear governor pressure drops (and the transmission is in fifth speed), its pressure on shift signal valve 4–5 is less than its spring force. Consequently the shift signal valve moves down, exhausting the pressure which is exerted on relay valve 4–5. The relay valve moves upward, exhausting the oil from the fourth clutch, and at the same time it directs oil to the third clutch. This sequence recurs at shift valve 3–4, and then at relay valve 3–4 when the governor pressure is further reduced. It then recurs at shift signal valve 2–3 and at relay valve 2–3 when the governor pressure again drops, and also on shift signal valve 1–2 and on relay valve 1–2. **NOTE** A lockup could occur with the transmission in any of the five speeds, when the pitot pressure is higher than the combined force of the modulator pressure and the valve spring force. In this case, the lockup valve is moved downward, and main line oil pressure is directed to the lockup piston. If the pitot governor pressure is less than the combined modulator pressure and spring force, the lockup valve spool is moved upward, disengaging the lockup clutch.

NEUTRAL OPERATION When the selector valve is in neutral, oil is directed over relay valve 2–3, through shift signal valve 1–2, and onto the top of relay valve 1–2. This causes the relay valve to shift and to direct main line pressure to the low clutch, holding the low-range planetary ring gear, rear planetary carrier, and front planetary ring gear. Rotation, therefore, is not transmitted beyond the clutch hub, preventing unnecessary gear rotation. At the same time, the oil flow to the forward clutch is plugged by the selector valve. See Fig. 12-34.

FIRST-GEAR OPERATION In first gear, the forward and low clutches are engaged, and the low clutch has clutched the rear planetary ring gear to the transmission housing. The forward clutch locks the forward clutch drum (which is splined to the turbine shaft) to the clutch hub (which is splined to the transmission shaft), and consequently they rotate as a unit. Engine torque is transmitted through the torque converter to the turbine and mainshafts. The low sun gear drives the low planetary carrier gears, causing the low carrier and the transmission output shaft to rotate in the same direction as the sun gear, but at a reduction of 3.19:1. See Fig. 12-35.

SECOND-GEAR OPERATION In second gear, the forward clutch remains engaged and the first clutch is engaged. Through this engagement, the first clutch planetary ring gear is clutched to the transmission housing. Since the rear planetary sun gear and low planetary sun gear are splined to the main shaft, they drive both planetary carrier gears. With the rear planetary ring gear held stationary, the rear planetary carrier and low planetary ring gear rotate in a clockwise direction because both are splined together. Now two members—the low planetary ring gear and the low planetary sun gear—are driven members, but rotate at different speeds. This causes the low planetary carrier to be driven at a higher speed than that of the rear planetary carrier, but at a speed reduction of 1.89:1. See Fig. 12-36.

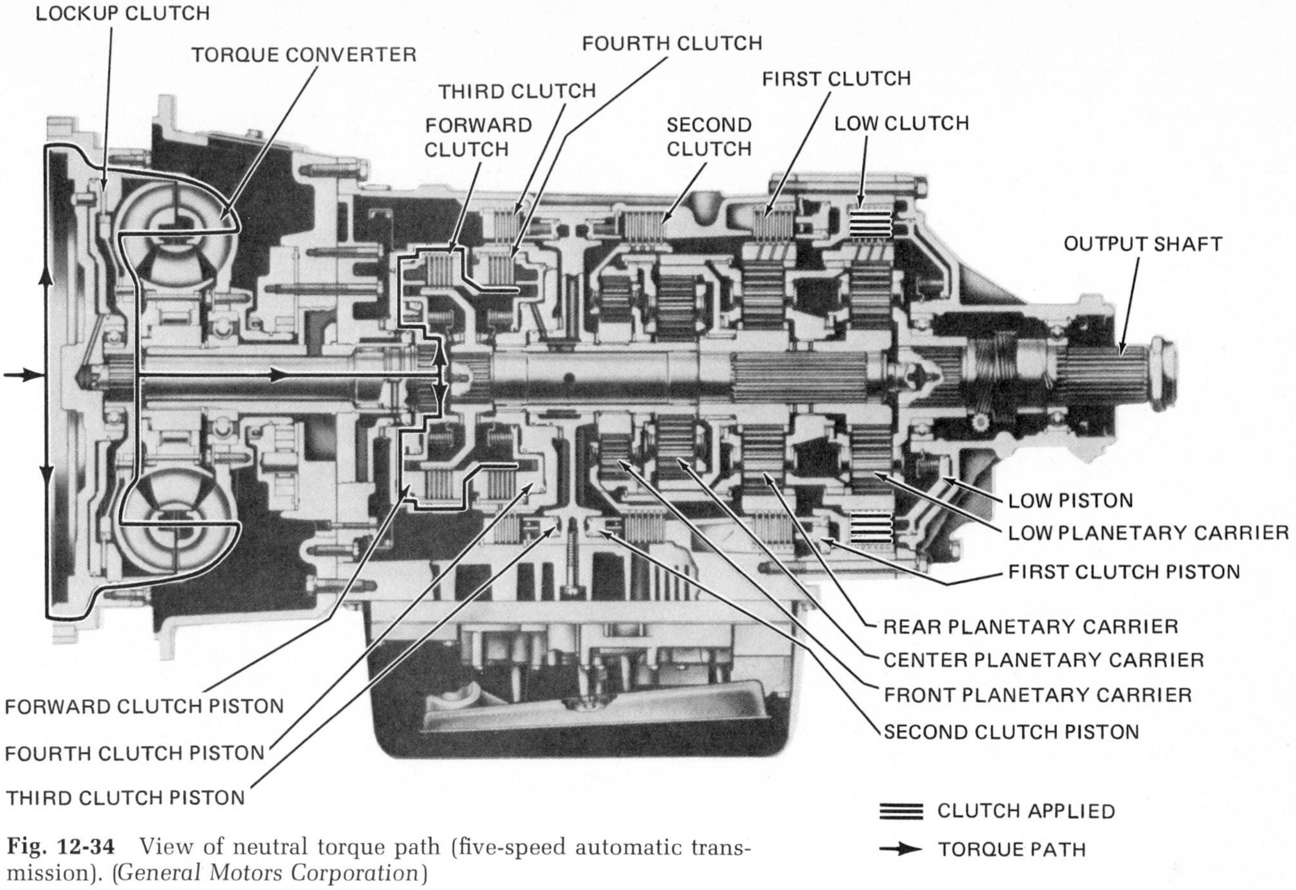

Fig. 12-34 View of neutral torque path (five-speed automatic transmission). (*General Motors Corporation*)

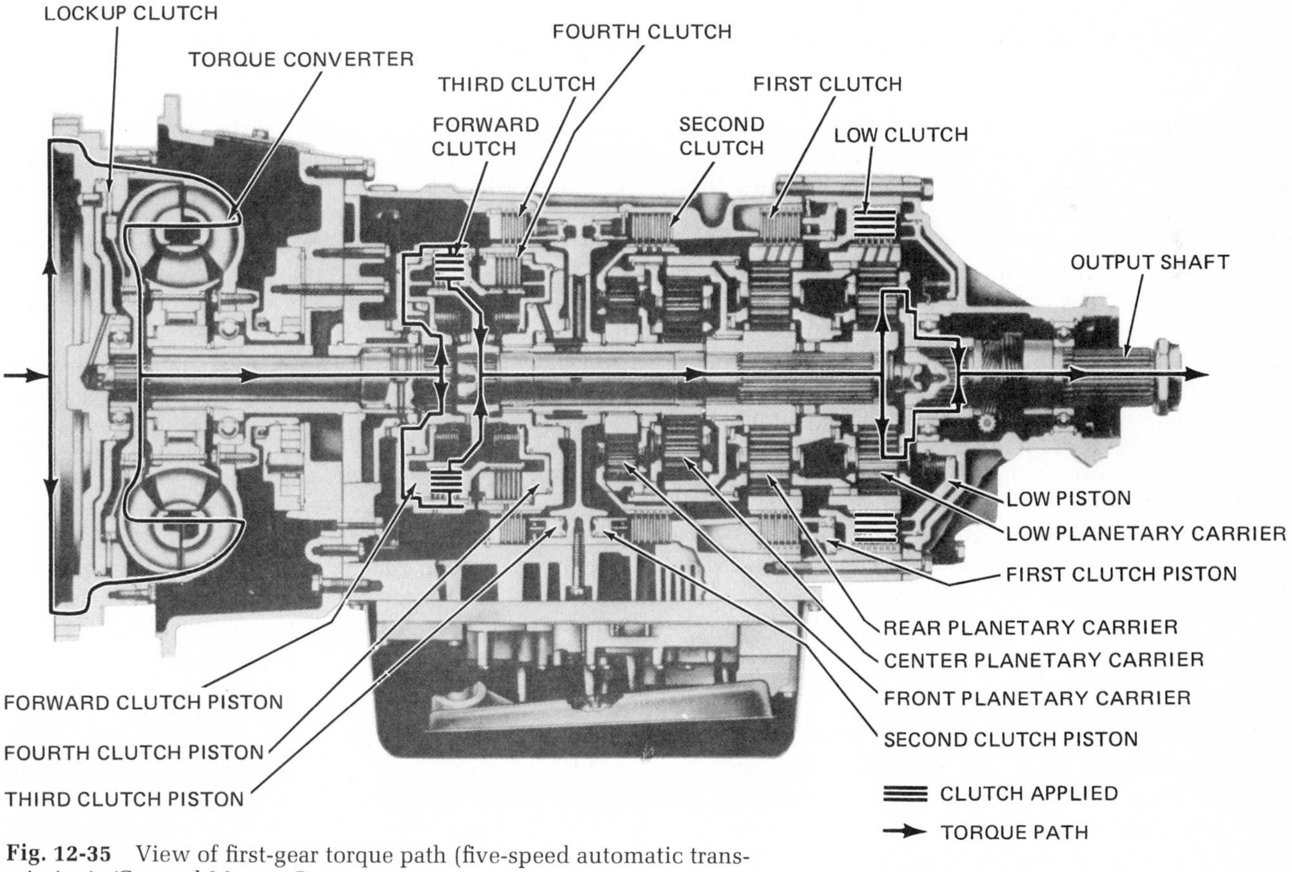

Fig. 12-35 View of first-gear torque path (five-speed automatic transmission). (*General Motors Corporation*)

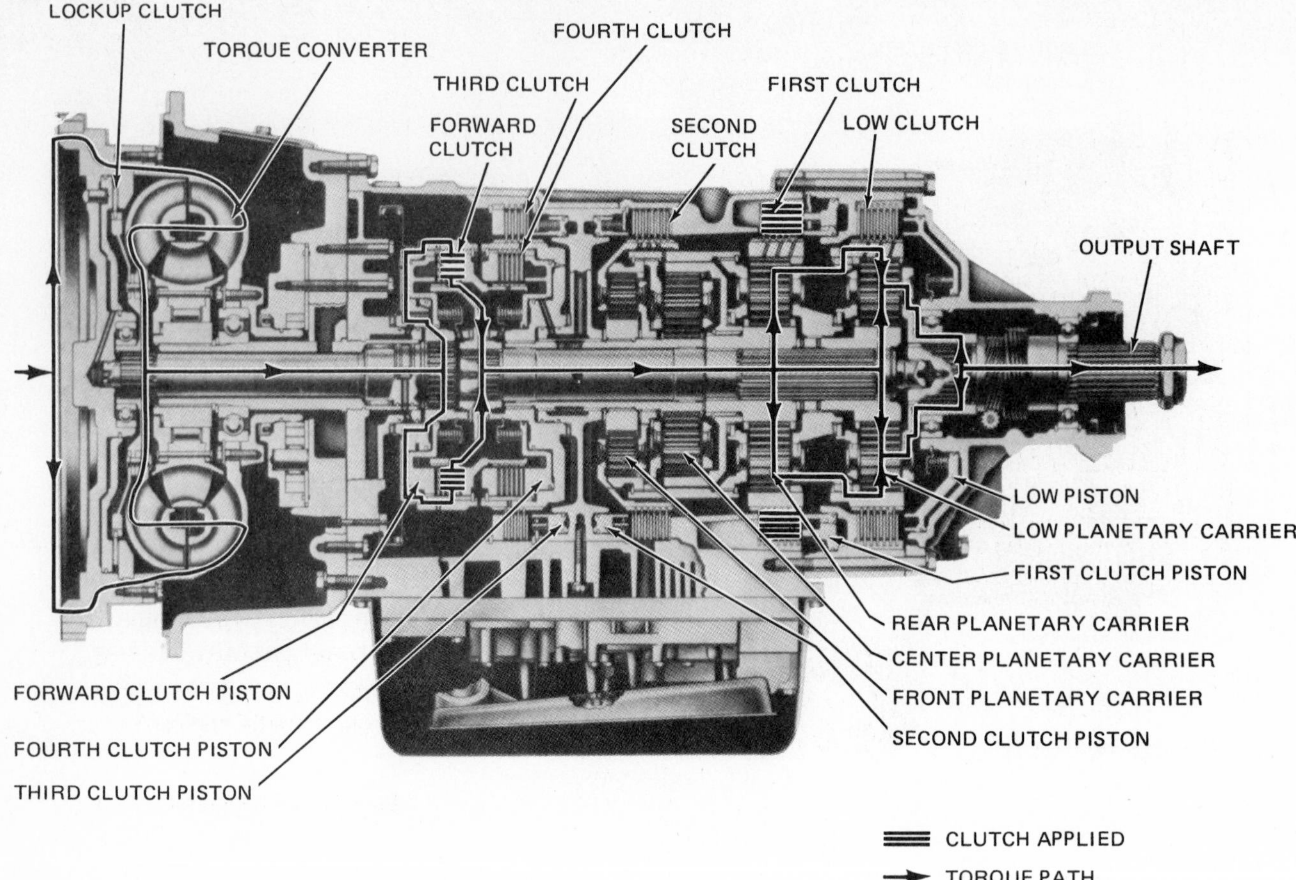

Fig. 12-36 View of second-gear torque path (five-speed automatic transmission). (*General Motors Corporation*)

THIRD-GEAR OPERATION In third gear, the forward clutch remains engaged and the second clutch is engaged, thereby holding the front planetary carrier stationary. The main shaft rotation (torque) is transmitted to the rear sun gear and front planetary carrier center ring gear because they are splined together. The ring gear, therefore, drives the front planetary carrier, and as a result the carrier gears (through the sun gear) drive the center sun gear shaft, since the front planetary sun gear is splined to the sun gear shaft. Consequently the center sun gear drives the front carrier gears, which drive the front planetary ring gear along with the rear planetary ring gear. **NOTE** The rotation speed of all three components is the same. The low planetary ring gear now drives the low planetary carrier gears, and the low planetary sun gear (driven by the main shaft) also drives the low planetary carrier gears. As a result, the low planetary carrier and output shaft are driven at a speed reduction of 1.55:1. See Fig. 12-37.

FOURTH-GEAR OPERATION In fourth gear, the forward clutch remains engaged and the third clutch is engaged. The third clutch, via the fourth clutch drum, clutches the center sun gear shaft to the transmission housing. The rear planetary sun gear is splined to the main shaft and to the center ring gear, and rotates at turbine speed.

With the center planetary sun gear held stationary, the center planetary ring gear drives the center planetary carrier gears, thereby driving the center planetary carrier. Because this carrier and the rear planetary ring gears are splined together, the low planetary ring gear drives the low planetary carrier gears. The low-planetary sun gear is driven by the transmission main shaft, which also drives the low planetary carrier gears. Consequently, there is a further change in ratio from that produced in the center planetary gear set, to a reduction of 1.24:1.00. See Fig. 12-38.

FIFTH-GEAR OPERATION In fifth gear, the forward clutch remains engaged and the fourth clutch is engaged. The fourth clutch clutches the center planetary sun gear and the rear and low planetary sun gears (over the fourth clutch) to the forward clutch drum. **NOTE** The forward clutch drum is splined to the center sungear shaft, and the forward clutch hub is splined to the turbine shaft. The center sun gear and the center ring gear are then driven at the same speed, and as a result the center planetary carrier also rotates at that speed. Consequently the rear planetary carrier and the low planetary ring gear also rotate at the same speed. With both the low planetary ring gear and the low planetary sun gear driven at turbine speed, the low planetary sun gear set is in direct drive. See Fig. 12-39.

REVERSE-GEAR OPERATION In reverse gear, the fourth and the low clutches are engaged. The low

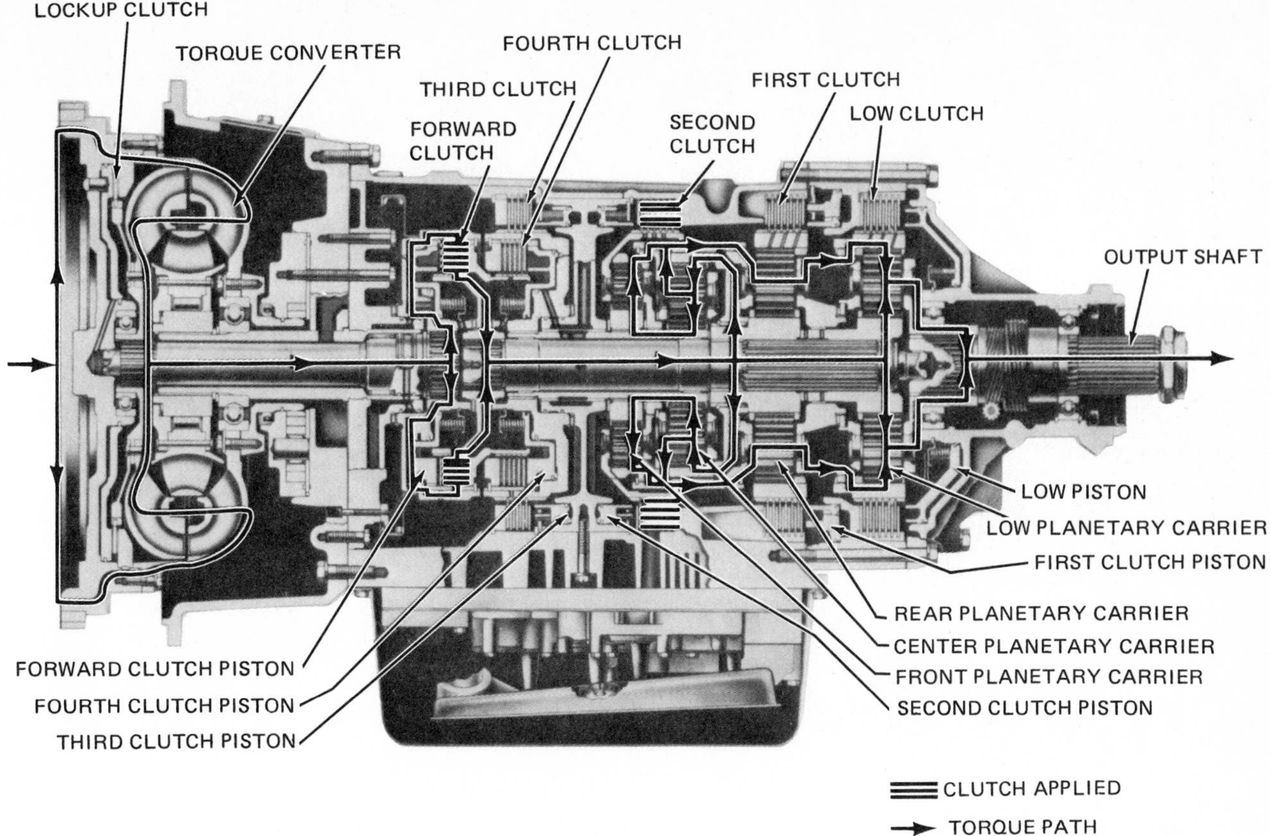

Fig. 12-37 View of third-gear torque path (five-speed automatic transmission). (*General Motors Corporation*)

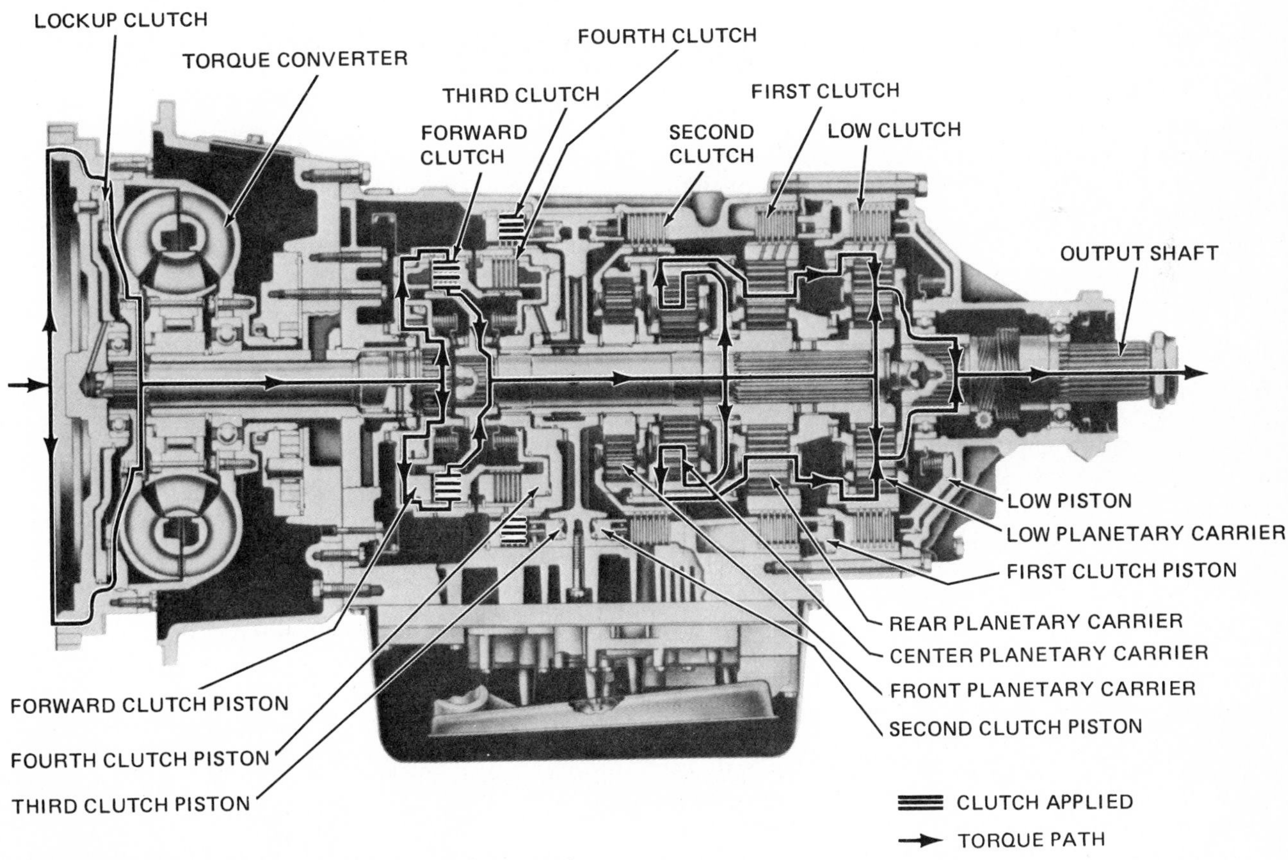

Fig. 12-38 View of four-gear torque path (five-speed automatic transmission). (*General Motors Corporation*)

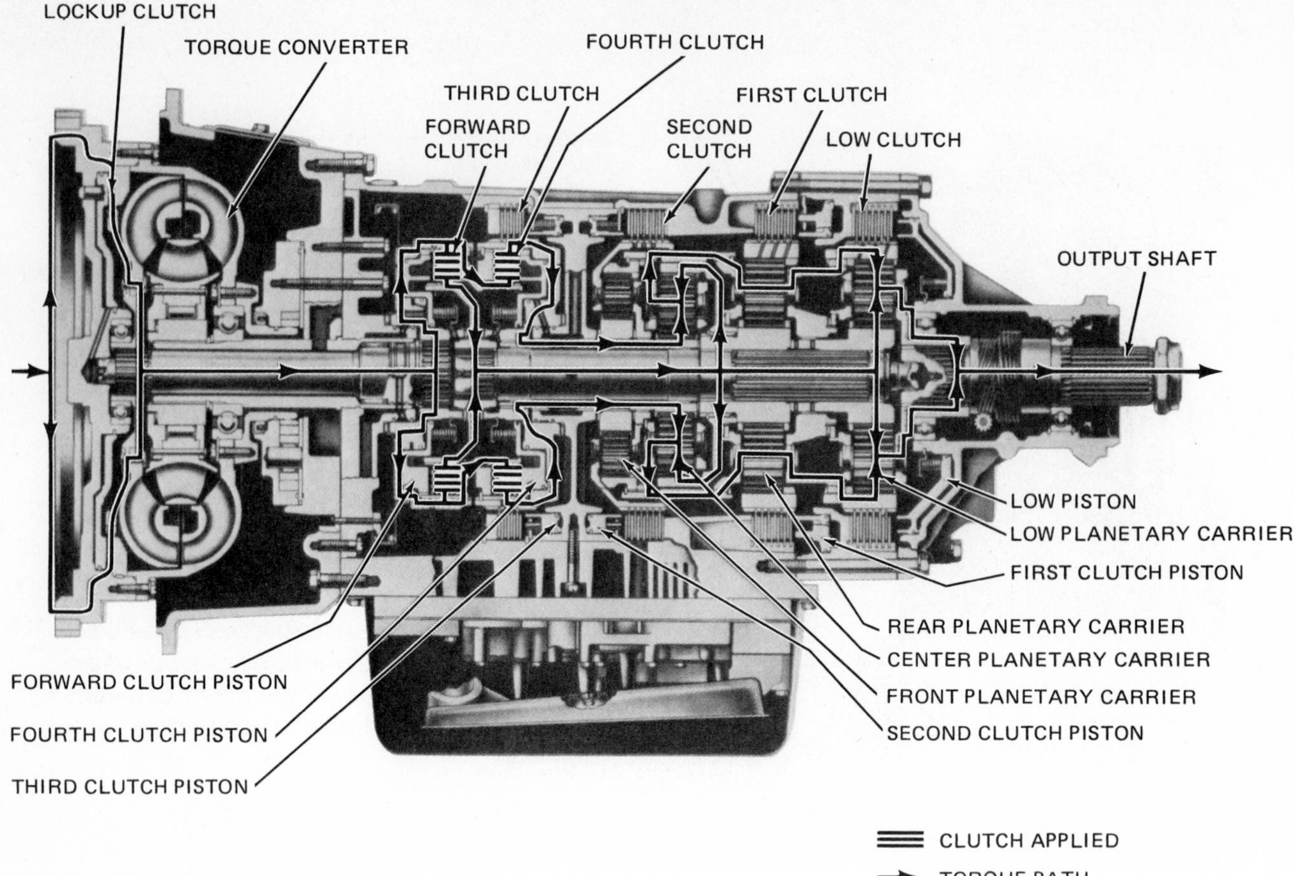

Fig. 12-39 View of fifth-gear torque path (five-speed automatic transmission). (*General Motors Corporation*)

clutch locks its ring gear to the transmission housing, and the fourth clutch clutches the fourth clutch drum to the forward clutch drum.

Rotation (torque) from the turbine shaft is transmitted over the forward clutch drum, and from the fourth clutch drum onto the transmission main shaft.

NOTE The low planetary ring gear, rear planetary carrier, and center planetary carrier are splined together, thereby holding the center planetary carrier stationary.

Since the center planetary sun gear rotates at turbine speed, it drives the center planetary gears, forcing the center planetary ring gear and rear planetary sun gear to rotate in a direction opposite to that of the center sun gear. The reverse rotation is transmitted through the rear planetary sun gear onto the transmission main shaft and low planetary sun gear. The low planetary sun gear drives the carrier gears, which, in turn, drive the carrier and output shaft in a direction opposite that of the turbine shaft. See Fig. 12-40.

Multicountershaft Powershift Transmissions A counter shaft powershift transmission transmits the rotation (torque) to the output shaft over several gear sets and shafts. The number of forward and reverse ratios for which the transmission is designed determines the number of shafts and clutches necessary to achieve the different ratios and directions.

Two-Speed Forward and Two-Speed Reverse Countershaft Transmission To convert the forward/reverse transmission previously covered (see Fig. 12-19) to a two-speed forward and two-speed reverse transmission, one shaft having two clutch packs is added, and, in order to drive the hydraulic pump, a drive gear is splined to the impeller. A clutch pack consists of a set of friction and reaction plates confined within the clutch drum. The transmission shown in Fig. 12-41 is one used on a small fork lift. Its hydraulic system consists of the components shown in Fig. 12-42, all of which should be familiar to you.

NEUTRAL OPERATION When the engine is operating, the transmission in neutral, and the service brake released, oil from the pump flows through the filter, to the main pressure regulator, through the inching valve to the forward/reverse selector valve, to the high/low selector valve, and through an orifice into the torque converter. Excess oil from the main regulator valve flows into the torque converter and acts on the torque converter regulator. Oil from the torque converter flows to the cooler and from there to the forward/reverse clutch packs to cool the clutches. It then returns to the transmission sump.

NOTE The torque converter regulator controls the "in" pressure; that is, the pressure is controlled at the inlet of the converter.

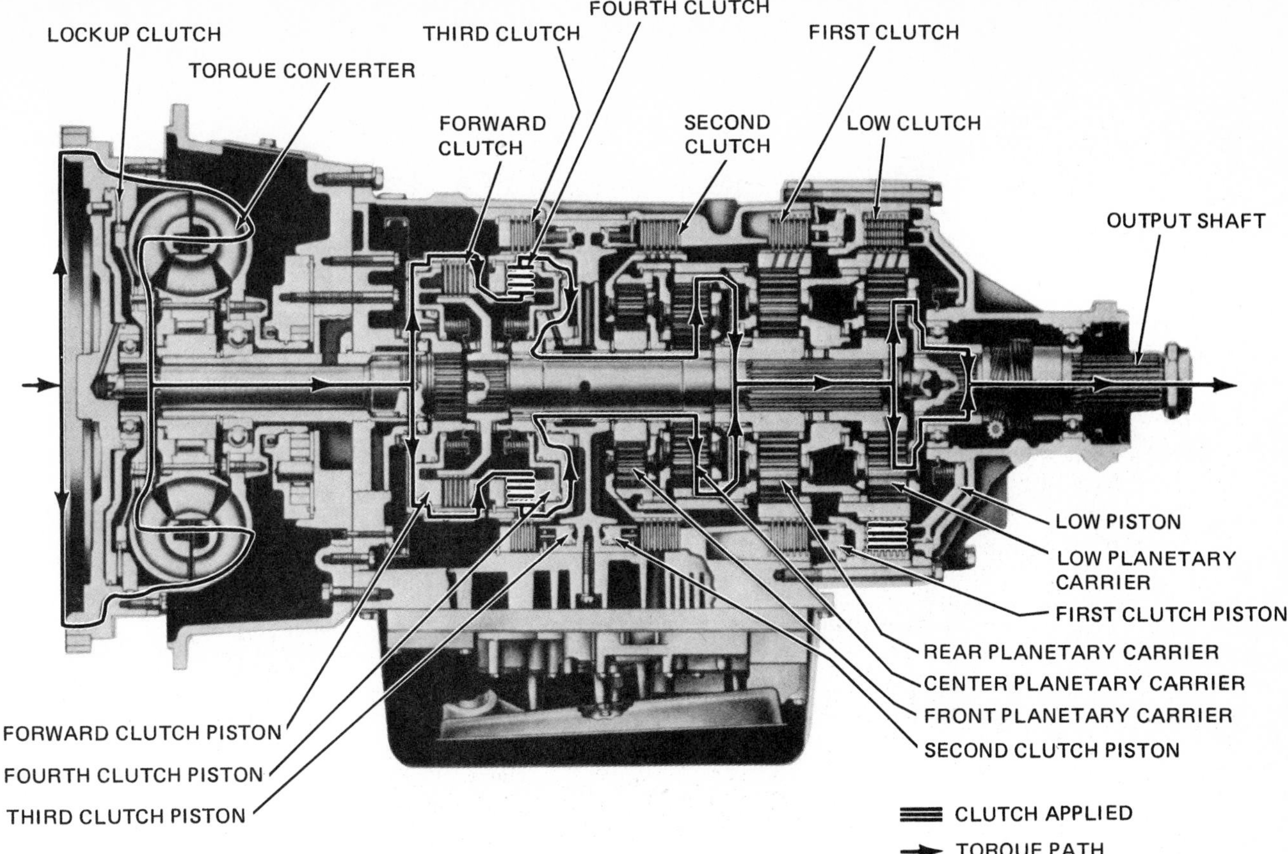

Fig. 12-40 View of reverse-gear torque path (five-speed automatic transmission). (*General Motors Corporation*)

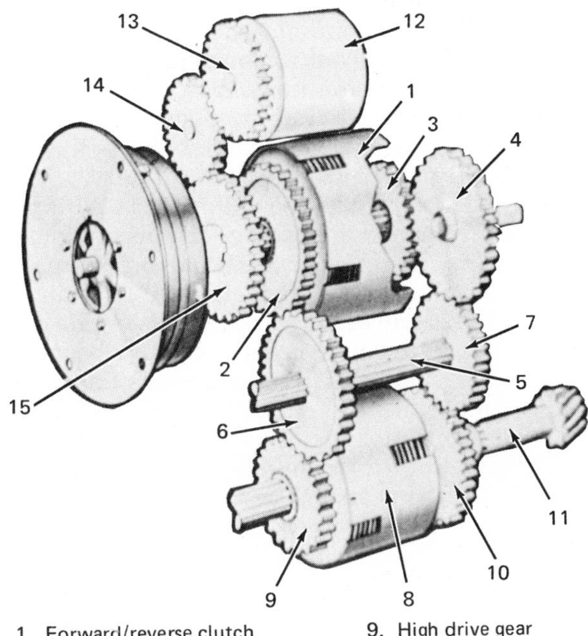

1. Forward/reverse clutch pack
2. Forward drive gear
3. Reverse drive gear
4. Reverse idler
5. Idler shaft
6. High idler gear
7. Low idler gear
8. High/low clutch pack
9. High drive gear
10. Low driven gear
11. Output shaft with pinion
12. Pump
13. Pump gear
14. Idler gear
15. Converter pump drive gear

Fig. 12-41 Schematic view of a two-speed forward and two-speed reverse powershift transmission. (*Clark Equipment of Canada*)

LOW/FORWARD OPERATION To shift the transmission into forward and low gear, the operator moves the forward/reverse selector valve spool to FORWARD position, and the high/low selector valve to LOW position. Oil is now directed into the forward and low clutch-pack piston areas, thereby clutching the clutch hubs and gears to the clutch drums. Rotation from the turbine shaft is then transmitted to the forward/reverse clutch shaft, over the clutch pack, to the forward clutch gear, to the idler gear, to the low clutch gear, and over the clutch pack to the output shaft.

HIGH/FORWARD OPERATION In high gear, oil is directed to the high clutch pack, and the rotation is then transmitted from an idler driven gear onto the idler shaft and driven gear, which, in turn, drives the high clutch drive gear; rotation is then transmitted over the clutch pack to the output shaft. **NOTE** When the high clutch pack is being engaged (and during engagement), the applied oil is also directed through the orifice into the low clutch pack. Correspondingly, when the low clutch pack is engaged, the oil is directed through the orifice into the high clutch pack. The resultant lubrication reduces clutch wear and effects a smooth clutch engagement.

REVERSE OPERATION When the operator moves the forward/reverse selector valve to reverse, the reverse clutch pack engages and the rotation from the forward/reverse shaft is then transmitted over the clutch pack to the reverse clutch drive gear, onto the

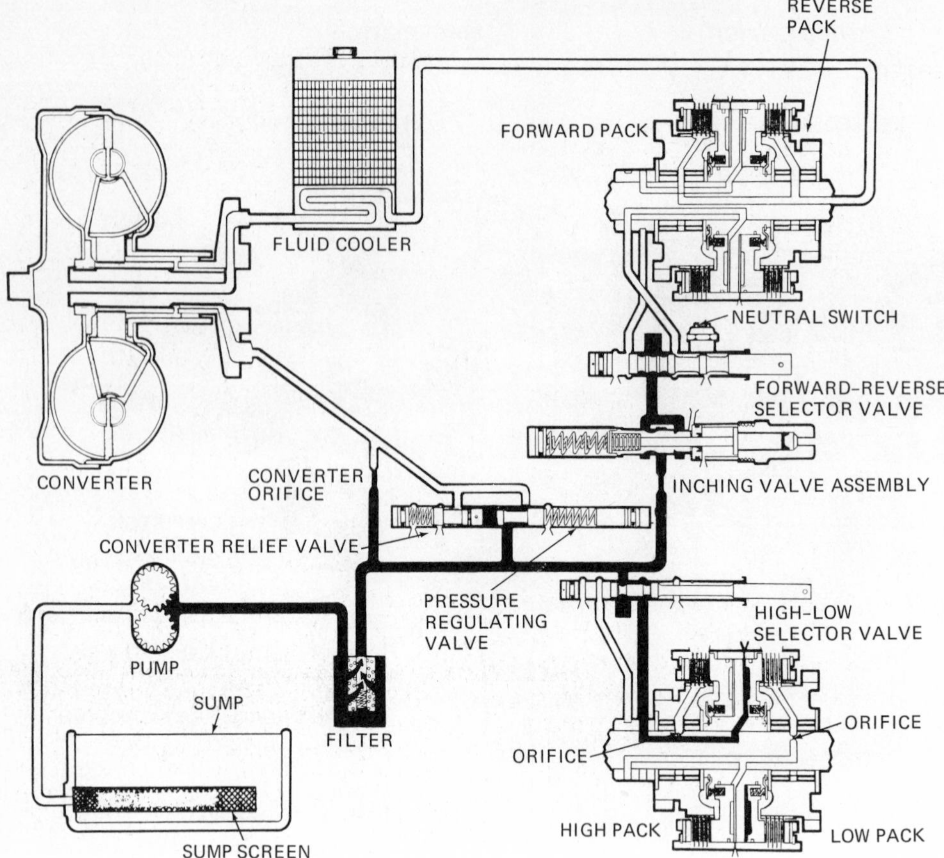

Fig. 12-42 Hydraulic circuit in neutral-low (two-speed forward, two-speed reverse powershift transmission). (*Clark Equipment of Canada*)

reverse idler gear. From the reverse idler gear, torque is transmitted onto the driven gear on the idler shaft, whereupon (depending on whether the operator choses the high or low selector valve position) it is either directed onto the high clutch drive gear, or over the driven gear to the low clutch pack drive gear.

INCHING OPERATION To slow the travelling speed, or to come to a gradual or a quick stop, the hydraulic service brake is applied. The applied brake pressure is directed upon the inching valve, forcing the inching piston and valve spool to the left. This reduces the oil flow to the forward/reverse selector valve, and at the same time opens the return passage, reducing the applied oil pressure of the clutch being engaged. Depending on the brake application pressure, the inching piston and valve spool are only partially moved, or else the oil flow to the clutch is blocked, and the return passage fully opens and effects a partial or full engagement of the applied clutch.

Five-Speed Forward, One-Speed Reverse Countershaft Transmission To change the two-speed forward, two-speed reverse transmission just discussed to a five-speed forward, one-speed reverse transmission, a range clutch shaft having two clutch packs is added.

DESIGN The forward clutch shaft, reverse clutch shaft, compound shaft, and the range clutch shaft are supported in the transmission housing by roller bearings, and the output shaft is supported by two sets of tapered roller bearings. The clutch shafts have three passages (bores). The upper and lower passages are connected at the right (through the bearing cap) to the two-position closed center solenoid-actuated spool valves. At the center these passages are connected to the piston housing and dump valves. The center passages are also connected internally to the lubrication supply line which extends from the lubrication regulator valve. See Fig. 12-43.

Each clutch shaft has two clutch packs which are separated by the piston housing. The piston housing has two dump valves, and, when pressure is applied to the inlet port of one dump valve, it directs oil into one piston area and at the same time opens the drain port and allows the oil to drain from the other clutch piston area. The clutch pistons are positioned into the left- and right-hand sides of the piston housing bore. The steel clutch plates are splined to the clutch hubs, which in turn are splined to the clutch shaft. The clutch drive gears are welded to the drive gear ring (clutch drum), and the friction plates are splined to its internal bore. The assembly is supported on the clutch shaft by roller bearings, and a thrust bearing (not shown in Fig. 12-43) is placed between the clutch shaft shoulder and the drive gear ring (clutch drum hub) to reduce friction.

To transmit rotation from the forward shaft to the output shaft, the shafts are so positioned that the second and fifth clutch drive gears, as well as the third and sixth clutch drive gears, are in mesh. The forward clutch shaft and the reverse clutch shaft drive gears are splined to their shafts and are in mesh with one another. The first, second, and third compound driven gears are splined to the compound shaft. The first compound shaft driven gear is in

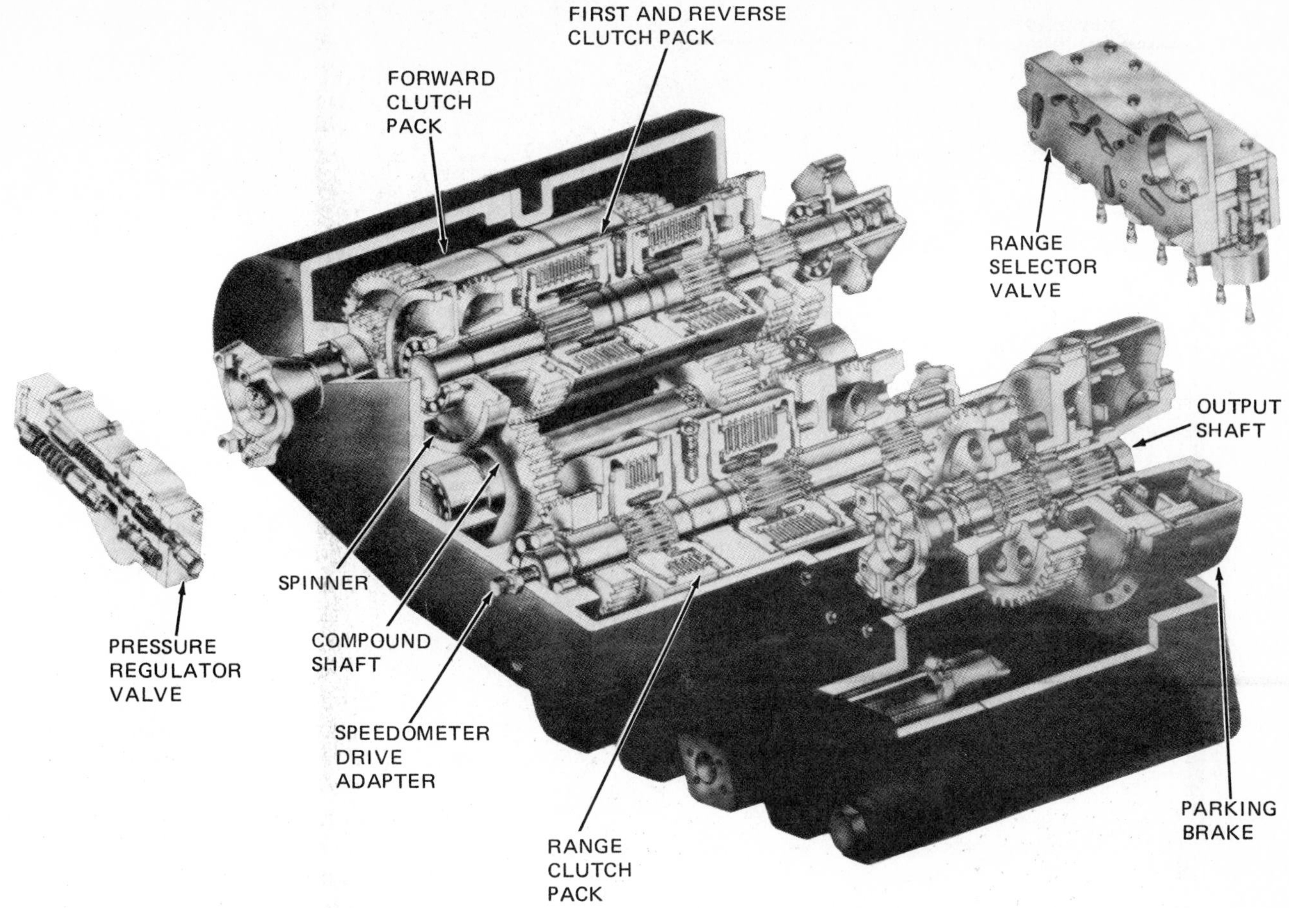

Fig. 12-43 Cutaway view of five-speed powershift transmission. (*International Harvester Company*)

mesh with the compound shaft drive gear and the low-range clutch drive gear. The second compound shaft driven gear is in mesh with the high-range clutch drive gear. The third compound shaft driven gear is in mesh with a clutch drive gear. The range shaft drive gear is in mesh with the output shaft driven gear, the latter being splined to the output shaft. See Fig. 12-44.

HYDRAULIC SYSTEM The hydraulic system consists of the components shown in Figs. 12-45, 12-46, and 12-47, and includes a valve not previously covered, that is, the flow-sensing valve. It is used to reduce lockup shift shock by sensing the pitot pressure. If the pressure drops due to a shift (low engine speed), it moves to the right, causing the lockup valve to move and disengage the lockup clutch. If the pitot pressure increases due to increased engine speed, a lockup will occur because the pitot pressure moves the lockup valve, whereupon main oil line pressure is directed to the lockup clutch. **NOTE** The range selector valves are solenoid-operated through a rotating switch (range selector control).

OPERATION When the engine is operating, both hydraulic pumps are driven, causing the scavenging pump to draw oil from the the torque converter and pump it into the reservoir (transmission sump). The transmission charging pump directs oil over the filter to to the main pressure regulator and lockup shift

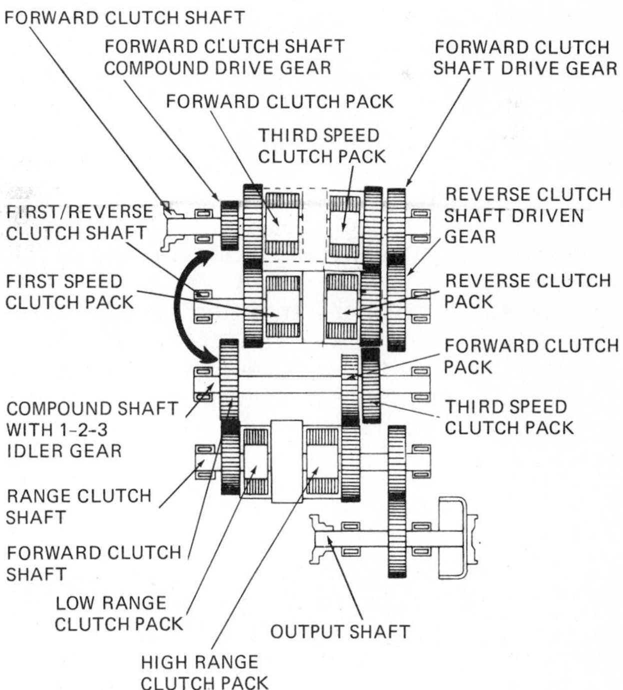

Fig. 12-44 Schematic view of the power train (five-speed powershift transmission)

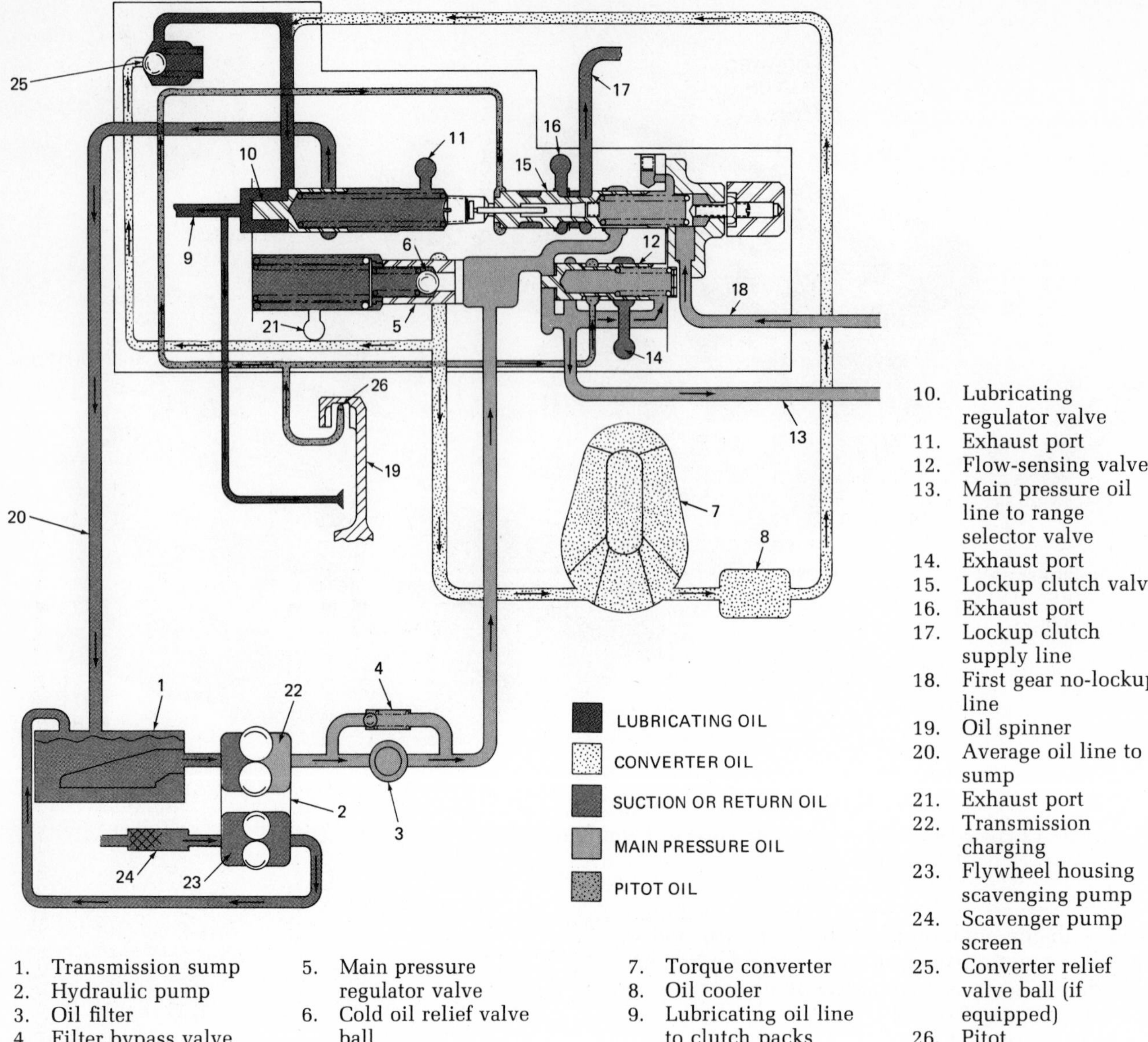

Fig. 12-45 Hydraulic system with five-speed transmission in first gear and pressure regulator valve in lockout. (*International Harvester Company*)

valve, where it is then blocked. Oil also flows to the flow-sensing valve, from there to the transmission range selector valve, and from the range selector valve to the accumulator. With the range selector spools in neutral, the oil flow to the clutches is blocked. the main pressure regulator valve controls the main line pressure, and the excess oil is directed into the torque converter. From the torque converter, excess oil flows to and through the oil cooler to the lubrication regulator. The oil directed to the torque converter relief valve controls the converter pressure, and excess torque converter oil is directed to the lubrication regulator valve. This valve directs oil to the oil spinner (collector ring) and to the range transmission selector valve. Through passages in the transmission housing and in the clutch shafts, oil is directed to the bearings, into the clutch pack, and to the accumulator.

First gear When the operator semirotates the range selector switch to first gear, the electric circuit to solenoids 5 and 8 closes. As a result, the two solenoids shift the two valve spools, and oil is directed into the bearing cap ends, into the top passage of the first and reverse clutch shafts, and into the top passage of the range clutch shaft. The oil pressure exerted on the dump valves forces them open, allowing the oil to enter clutch piston areas 5 and 8. As the dump valves allow oil to flow into the clutch piston areas, they simultaneously open the clutch pack piston areas into the return oil passage. The applied oil pressure engages the clutches, locking the gears to the shaft. During the engagement, a pressure drop would normally occur, but this is prevented by the accumulator, thereby assuring a smooth shift. When clutch 5 is engaged, the same applied oil pressure is directed to the lockup valve, forcing it to the right

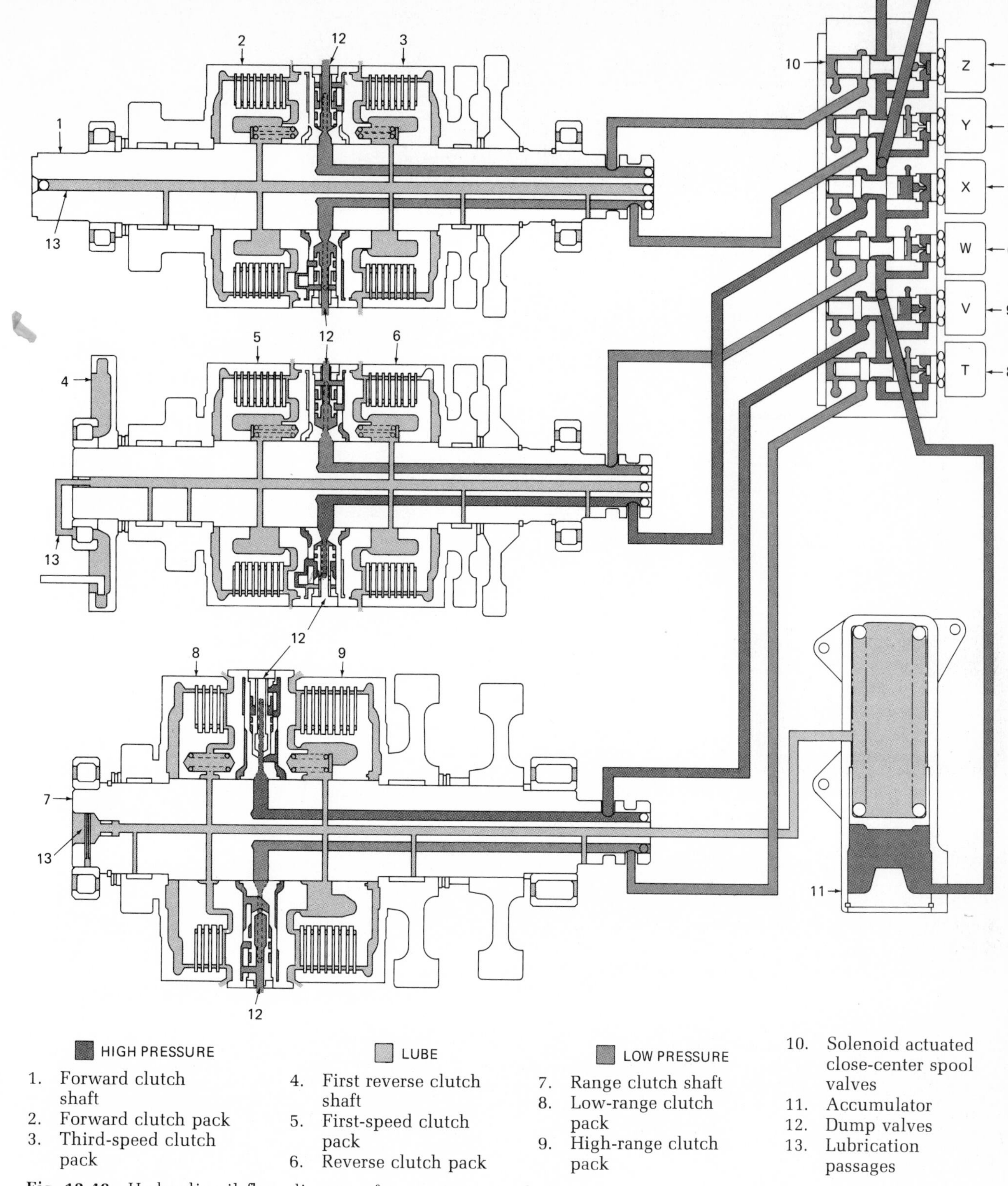

Fig. 12-46 Hydraulic oil flow diagram of transmission in first gear (five-speed powershift transmission). (*International Harvester Company*)

and blocking the oil flow of the pitot pressure, thereby preventing a lockup in first gear. See Fig. 12-46.

Rotation from the turbine shaft is transmitted over the drive line to the forward clutch shaft and forward clutch shaft drive gear. Because the forward clutch shaft drive gear and the reverse clutch shaft drive gear are splined to their shafts and are in mesh, the reverse clutch shaft is forced to rotate. With clutch 5 engaged, the rotation therefore is transmitted over the clutch pack to the compound shaft and to driven gears 1, 2, and 3. Driven gear 2 drives clutch gear 8,

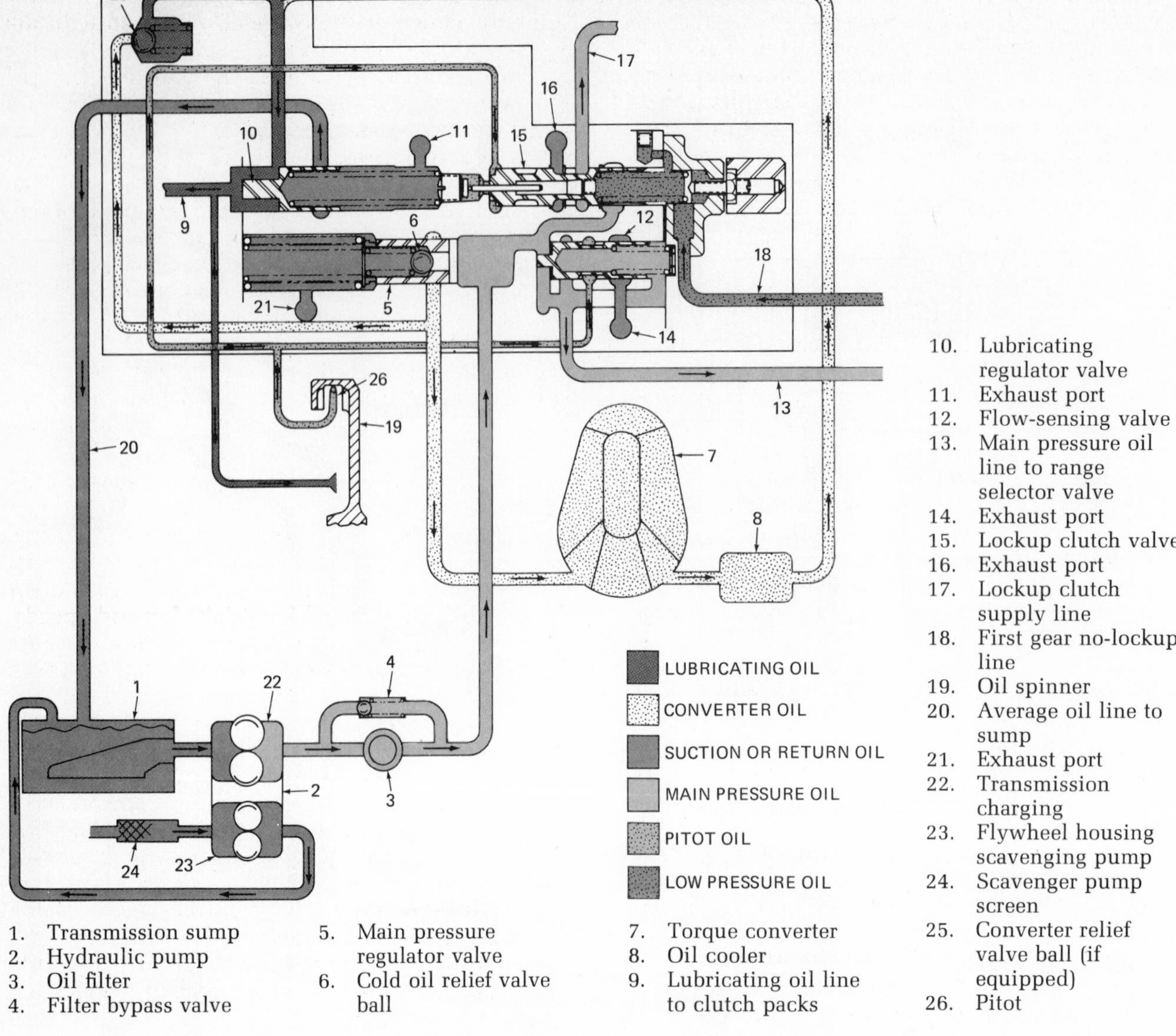

Fig. 12-47 Hydraulic system with the pressure regulator valve in second through fifth and reverse gears—lockup. (*International Harvester Company*)

and the torque is transmitted over the clutch pack to the range shaft and range shaft drive gear, and then to the output shaft gear and shaft.

Second gear When the operator shifts to second speed, solenoid 5 deenergizes, solenoid 2 energizes, and solenoid 8 remains energized. This results in the disengagement of clutch 5 and the engagement of clutch 2. See Fig. 12-44.

The rotation from the forward shaft is transmitted over clutch pack 2 to the drive gear and compound shaft driven gear. From here on, torque transmission is the same as in first gear.

Third gear When the operator shifts to third speed, solenoid 2 deenergizes and solenoid 3 energizes and solenoid 8 remains energized. This action disengages clutch 2 and engages clutch 3, and clutches the drive gear to the forward clutch shaft. The forward clutch shaft drive gear transmits the rotation to clutch pack drive gear 6 (which now acts as an idler). From here rotation is transmitted onto the compound shaft third driven gear, after which the transmission of torque is the same as in first and second gear.

Fourth gear When the operator shifts to fourth speed, solenoids 3 and 8 deenergize and solenoids 2 and 9 are energized, and consequently clutch packs 3 and 8 disengage and clutch packs 2 and 9 engage. Rotation is transmitted from the forward clutch shaft, over the drive gear, onto the compound shaft, to driven gear 1, from there onto clutch pack drive gear 9, over the clutch pack, onto the range clutch shaft and drive gear, and to the output shaft driven gear and output shaft.

Fifth gear When the transmission is shifted into fifth speed, solenoid 2 deenergizes, solenoid 3 energizes and solenoid 9 remains energized. This action disengages clutch 2 and engages clutch drive gear 3 to the forward clutch shaft. Rotation is transmitted to the clutch pack drive gear 6 (now an idler) and to compound shaft driven gear 3, thereby rotating the shaft. Compound driven gear 1 transmits the rotation to clutch pack drive gear 9, over the clutch pack, onto the range clutch shaft and drive gear, and from the range shaft drive gear to the output shaft driven gear and shaft.

Reverse gear When the selector control valve is switched to reverse, solenoids 6 and 9 are energized and consequently clutch packs 6 and 9 engage. Rotation from the forward clutch shaft is transmitted to the reverse clutch shaft drive gear, and because clutch 6 is engaged the rotation is transmitted to the compound shaft third driven gear. The second driven gear drives clutch drive gear 9, causing the range clutch shaft and drive gear to rotate. The drive gear, in turn, drives the output shaft driven gear and shaft in a direction opposite that of the forward clutch shaft.

Eight-Speed Forward, Four-Speed Reverse Countershaft Transmission To convert the five-speed transmission to an eight-speed forward, four-speed reverse transmission, one clutch shaft (reverse) having a single clutch pack is added. See Fig. 12-48.

DESIGN The input and reverse clutch shafts are supported by ball bearings, and the idler, first/third, and second/fourth speed clutch shafts are supported by a combination of roller and double tapered roller bearings. The input shaft, however, is further supported by two sets of tapered roller bearings.

The clutch packs, although not equal in diameter, are identical in design. The clutch hubs 1–2 and 3–4 (to which the clutch friction plates are splined) are splined to the clutch drum support sleeves (which are bolted to the transmission housing). The clutch drum is supported on the support sleeve by a ball and roller bearing, and the steel clutch plates are splined to the drum. The clutch drum drive gears (with the exception of drive gears 1 and 2) are welded to the clutch drum. The larger drive gears 1 and 2 are splined to smaller gears, and the latter are welded to the clutch drum. See Fig. 12-49. Each clutch drum has a one-way check (ball bleed) valve to assist in the release of the clutches. **NOTE** The shaft arrangement shown in Fig. 12-48 is for clarification only. The actual arrangement is shown in Fig. 12-50. The input clutch shaft (forward, high, and low) is located at the top left. Splined to the shaft is the reverse drive gear, and supported by roller bearings is the clutch support sleeve assembly to which the forward/high clutch gear and clutch hub are splined. The reverse clutch shaft is located at the top right. The reverse driven gear, which is splined to the reverse clutch shaft, is in mesh with the forward driven gear. The reverse clutch drive gear is in mesh with the right-hand idler driven gear, and the latter is splined to the idler shaft. The forward/low clutch drive gear is also in mesh with the right-hand idler driven gear.

The idler shaft is centered between the forward high/low clutch shaft, the reverse clutch shaft, and clutch shafts 1–3 and 2–4. Splined to the idler shaft are three driven gears. Driven gear 1 is in mesh with the first and second clutch pack drive gears. The second driven gear is in mesh with the forward/high clutch pack drive gear, and the third driven gear is in mesh with the reverse, forward/low, and the third and fourth clutch-pack drive gears. The output shaft is centrally positioned beneath clutch shafts 1–3 and 2–4, and two driven gears are splined to it. Driven gear 1 is in mesh with the drive gear splined to clutch shaft 2–4, and the second driven gear is in mesh with the drive gear splined to clutch shaft 1–3.

HYDRAULIC SYSTEM This system consists of the components shown in Fig. 12-51 and a hydraulic shift control (Fig. 12-52). The hydraulic shift control is a nine-position valve which, through its porting, can hydraulically shift the valve spools in the hydraulic shift cover to achieve eight forward speeds, four reverse speeds, and torque converter lockup. The hydraulic shift control cover is bolted to the top of the transmission housing. It has the following components within (Fig. 12-52)—from right to left, the torque converter inlet relief valve (safety valve), clutch pressure regulator valve, shutoff valve, forward/reverse shift valve, range spool forward high/low shift valve, and shift valves 1, 2, and 3. The valves are connected to one another through internal passages which lead to ports, and the ports are connected through steel tubing to the clutch piston areas. Hydraulic lines connect the hydraulic shift control valve with the main line pressure and with the individual valve spools and lockup clutch.

OPERATION When the engine is operating and the shift control is in neutral, the hydraulic pump is driven by the impeller drive gear and oil is directed over the oil filter to the hydraulic shift control cover, and to the hydraulic shift control. With the hydraulic shift control valve in neutral, the oil pressure from the shutoff valve is removed and the spring force then moves the valve downward and blocks the oil flow to the forward/reverse valve spool. Consequently, the main pressure relief valve opens and directs oil over the torque converter inlet relief valve to the torque converter. From the torque converter, oil is directed over the torque converter outlet relief valve to the oil cooler, and from there back into the hydraulic shift control cover. From there the oil is directed through various internal passages and steel tubings to the bearings to provide lubrication.

NOTE An hydraulic line connects the transmission with the torque converter to allow oil to drain (through gravity) back to the transmission.

First gear When the shift lever is placed into first speed, oil is directed to the shutoff valve, forcing the valve spool upward and allowing main line

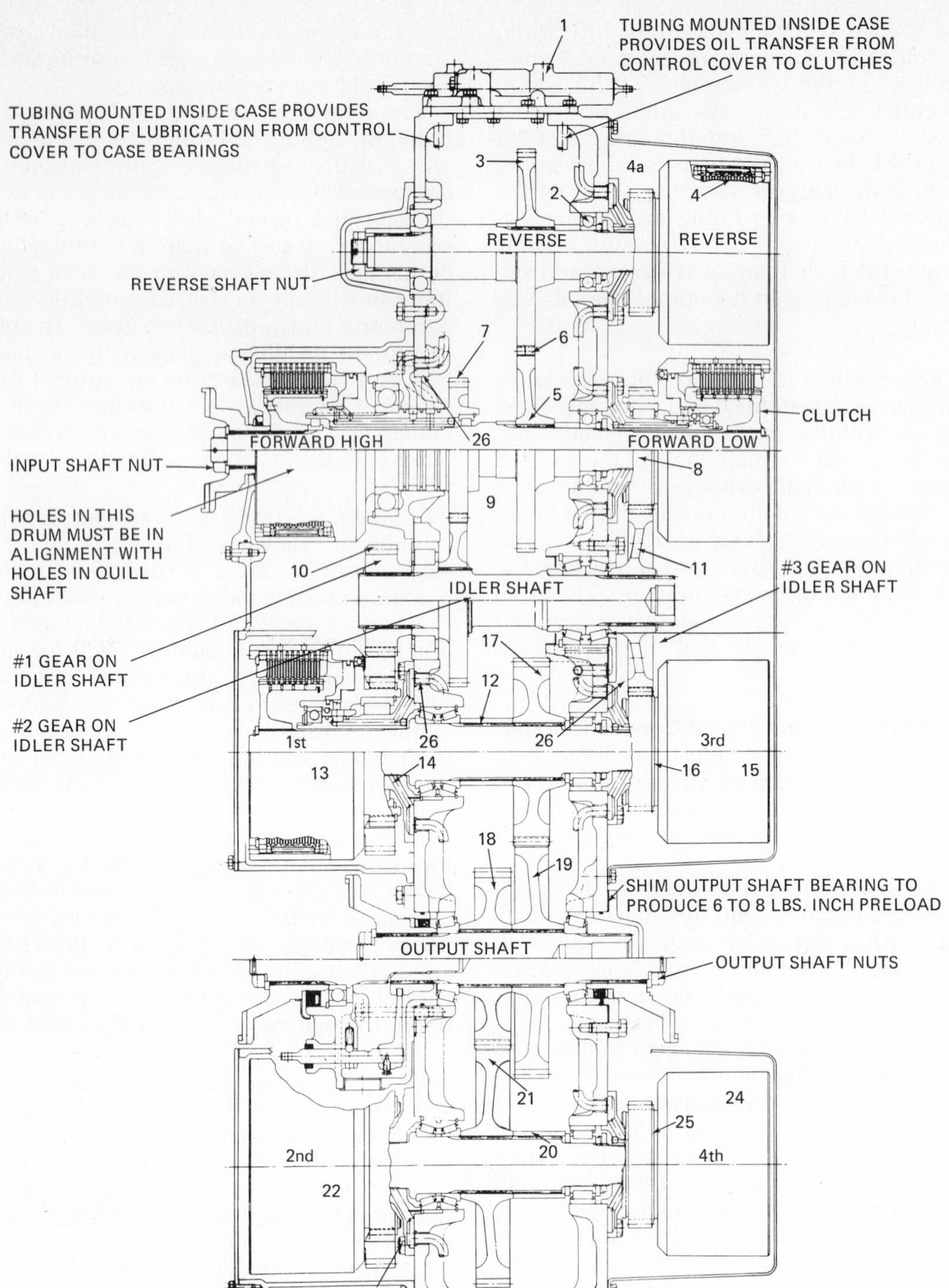

1. Shift cover
2. Reverse clutch shaft
3. Reverse drive gear
4. Reverse clutch
4-a. Reverse clutch drive gear
5. Forward clutch shaft (input shaft)
6. Forward clutch shaft driven gear
7. Forward drive high drive gear
8. Forward drive low drive gear
9. Idler shaft driven gear
10. Idler shaft drive gear (first speed)
11. Idler shaft reverse idle driven gear
12. First/third speed clutch shaft
13. First speed clutch
14. First speed clutch drive gear
15. Third speed clutch
16. Third speed clutch drive gear
17. First/third speed clutch shaft drive gear
18. Output shaft drive gear
19. Output shaft driven gear
20. Second/fourth clutch shaft
21. Second/fourth clutch shaft driven gear
22. Second speed clutch
23. Second speed clutch driven gear
24. Fourth speed clutch
25. Fourth speed clutch drive gear
26. Bearing cover

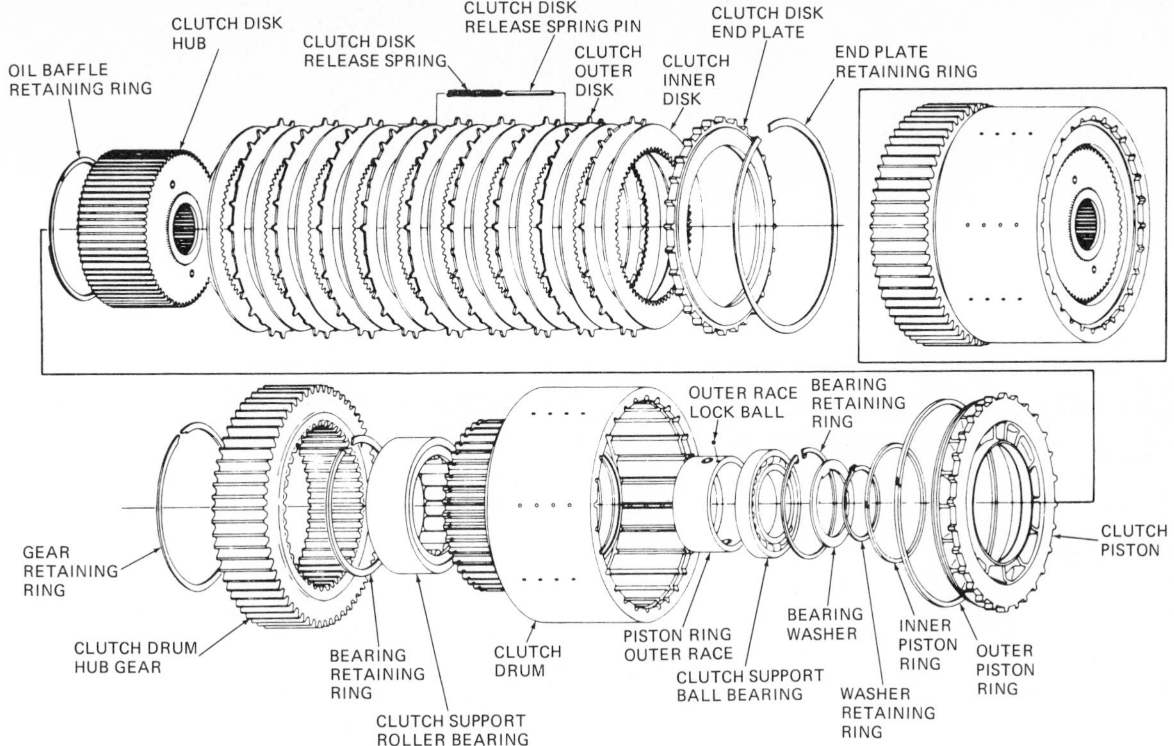

Fig. 12-49 First- and second-gear clutch components. (*Clark Equipment of Canada*)

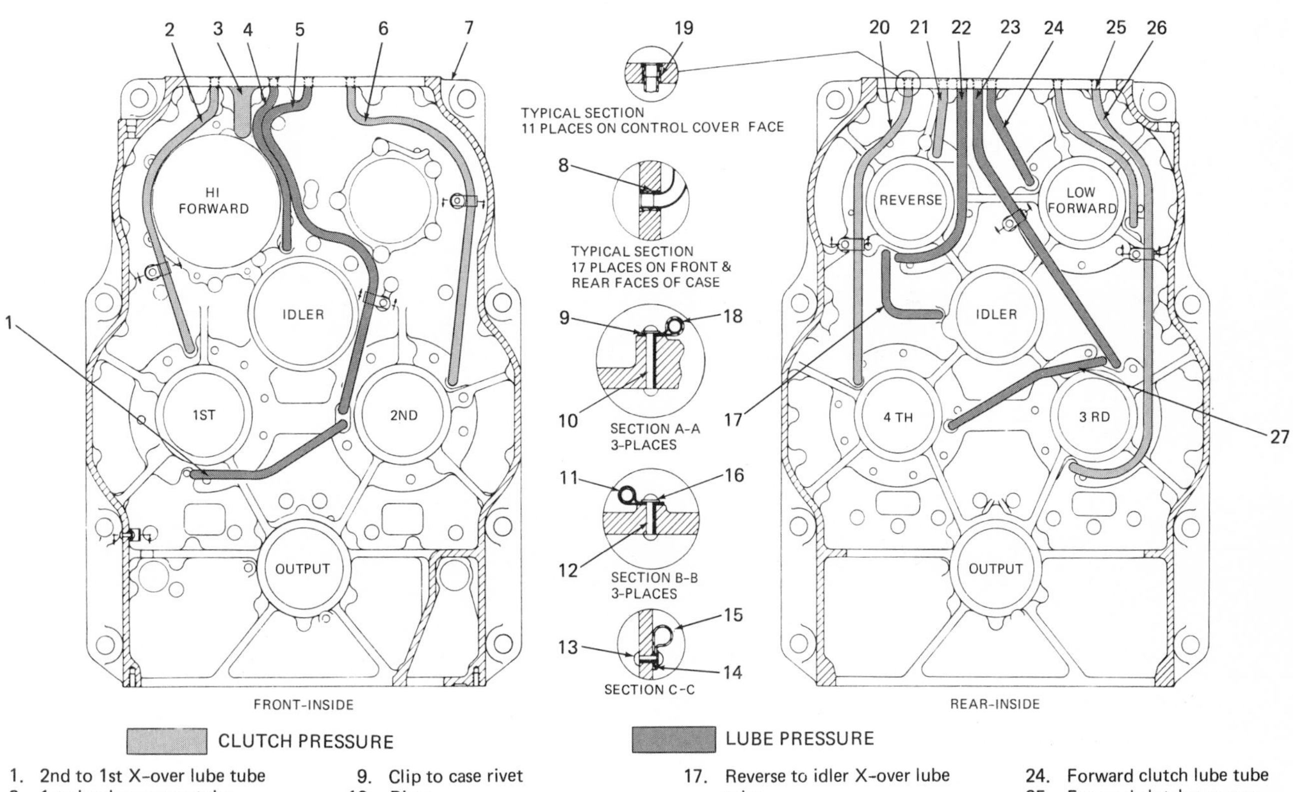

1. 2nd to 1st X-over lube tube
2. 1st clutch pressure tube
3. High forward pressure port
4. Idler shaft lube tube
5. 2nd clutch lube tube
6. 2nd clutch pressure tube
7. Transmission case
8. Tube sleeve
9. Clip to case rivet
10. Rivet
11. Tube clip
12. Clip to case rivet
13. Clip to case rivet
14. Clip to case washer
15. Tube clip
16. Clip to case washer
17. Reverse to idler X-over lube tube
18. Tube clip
19. Tube sleeve
20. 4th clutch pressure tube
21. Reverse clutch pressure tube
22. Reverse clutch lube tube
23. 3rd clutch lube tube
24. Forward clutch lube tube
25. Forward clutch pressure tube
26. 3rd clutch pressure tube
27. 3rd to 4th X-over lube tube

Fig. 12-50 View of the left- and right-hand sides of the transmission case showing the internal tubing and shaft locations (eight-speed countershaft powershift transmission). (*Clark Equipment of Canada*)

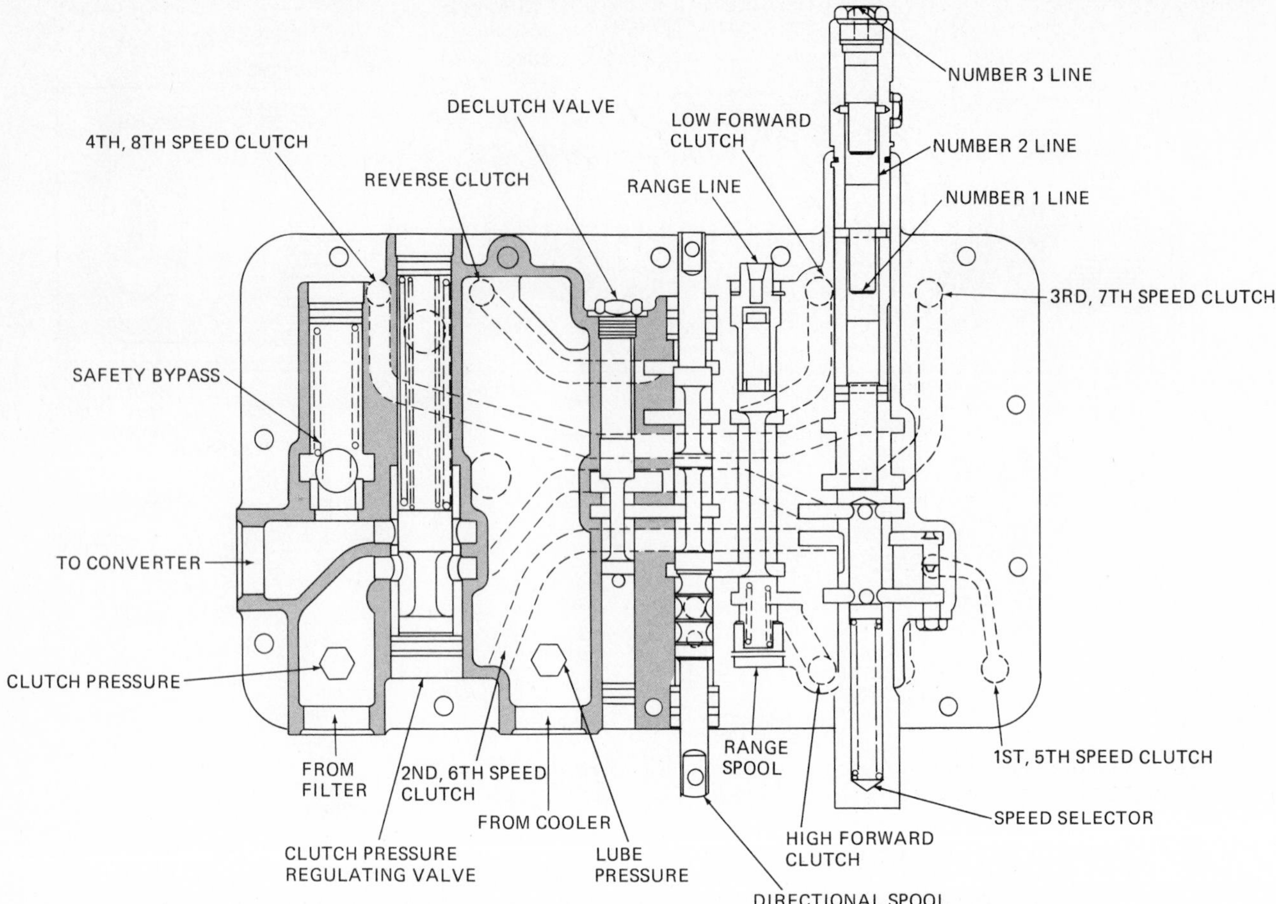

Fig. 12-51 Sectional view of the eight-speed hydraulic shift transmission cover. (*Clark Equipment of Canada*)

oil pressure to flow onto the forward/reverse, forward high/low, and 1, 2, and 3 shift valves. As a result of the oil pressure exerted on shift valve 1, it shifts downward and now directs oil into clutch piston area 1, clutching both the forward/low drive gear to the input shaft and the first clutch drive gear to clutch shaft 1–3.

Rotation (torque) is transmitted from the input shaft over the forward low clutch pack, to the drive gear, and onto the third driven gear on the idler shaft, which in turn drives clutch drive gear 1 and clutch shaft 1–3, whereupon clutch shaft drive gear 1–3 drives output shaft gear 2 and its shaft.

Second gear When the transmission is shifted into second speed, the forward/low clutch remains engaged; however, the pressure is removed from line 1 and oil is directed over line 2 into port 2. This shifts speed valve 2, which then directs oil into clutch piston area 2 and causes the drive gear to clutch to clutch shaft 2–4. The torque transfer to the idler shaft remains the same, but now drive gear 1 on the idler shaft transfers the rotation to the second clutch drive gear and subsequently onto clutch shaft 2–4.

Third gear When shifting into third speed, the forward/low clutch remains engaged, the oil pressure in line 2 is removed, and oil is directed over line 3 into port 3; this shifts the third-speed valve and allows oil into clutch piston area 3. Torque from the idler shaft is now transmitted over the third clutch drive gear, to clutch shaft 1–3 and its driven gear, and onto the second driven gear on the output shaft.

Fourth gear When the shift lever is placed into fourth speed, no oil is directed into lines 1, 2, or 3. This allows the spring force to move speed valve 1 upward, so that it now directs oil into fourth-gear clutch piston area. See Fig. 12-53.

Fifth through eighth gears When shifting into fifth speed, oil from the hydraulic shift control is directed to the forward high/low shift valve and into port 1. The high/low shift valve then moves upward and directs oil to the forward/high clutch piston area and, at the same time, one port opens to reduce the pressure in the forward low-clutch piston area. The drive gear then clutches to the forward high/low clutch shaft, and clutch drive gear 1 clutches to clutch shaft 1–3.

The shift into sixth, seventh, and eighth speeds, and the transfer of torque to the output shaft, is mechanically the same as it is in the first four speeds, except that now the torque to the idler shaft is transmitted from the forward high-clutch drive gear to driven gear 2 on the idler shaft.

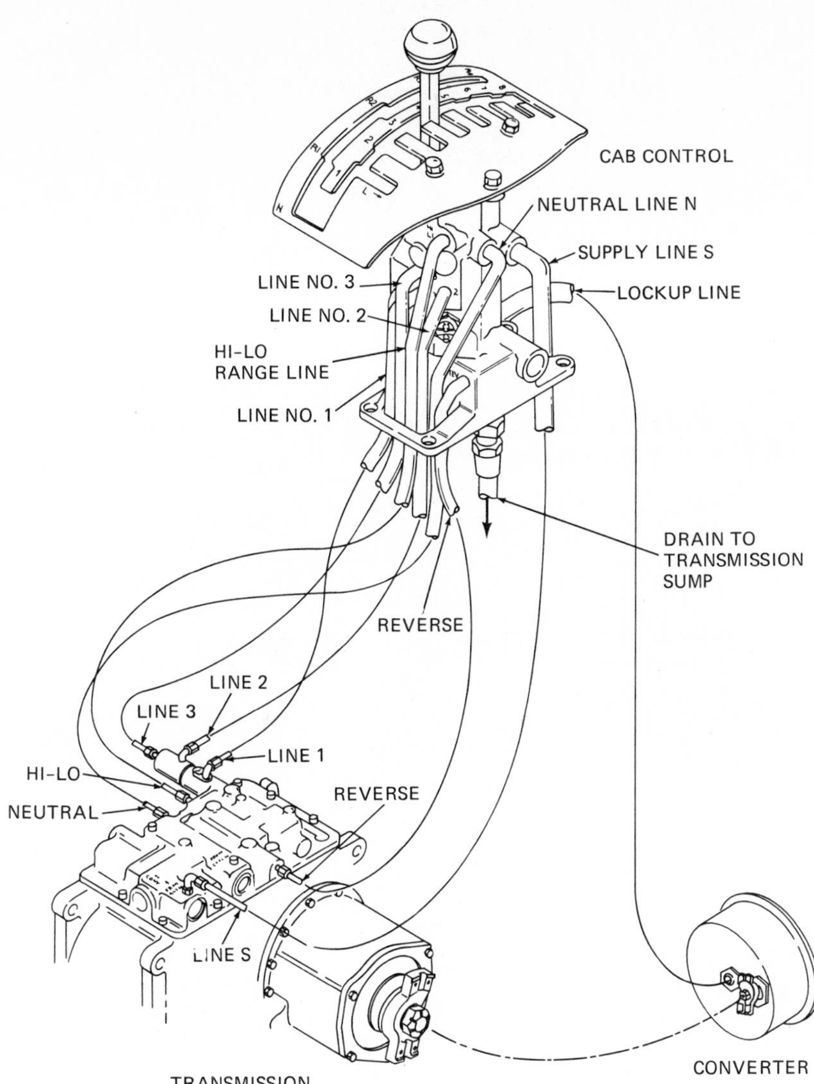

Fig. 12-52 Schematic view of the hydraulic shift control eight-speed forward, four-speed reverse transmission with lockup. (*Clark Equipment of Canada*)

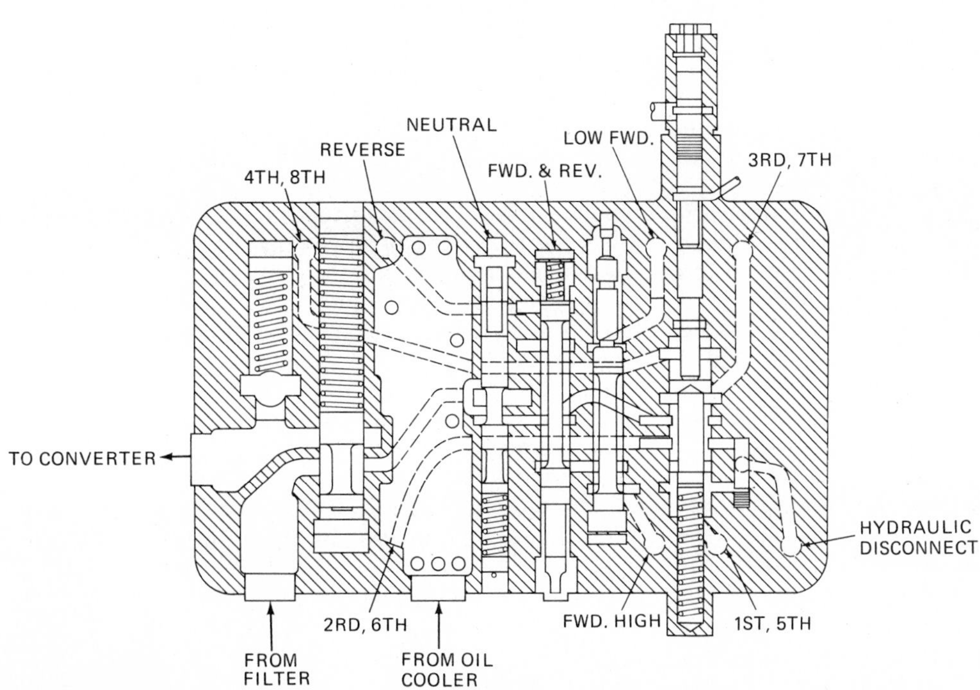

Fig. 12-53 Control valve position when in fourth gear (eight-speed countershaft, powershift transmission). (*Clark Equipment of Canada*)

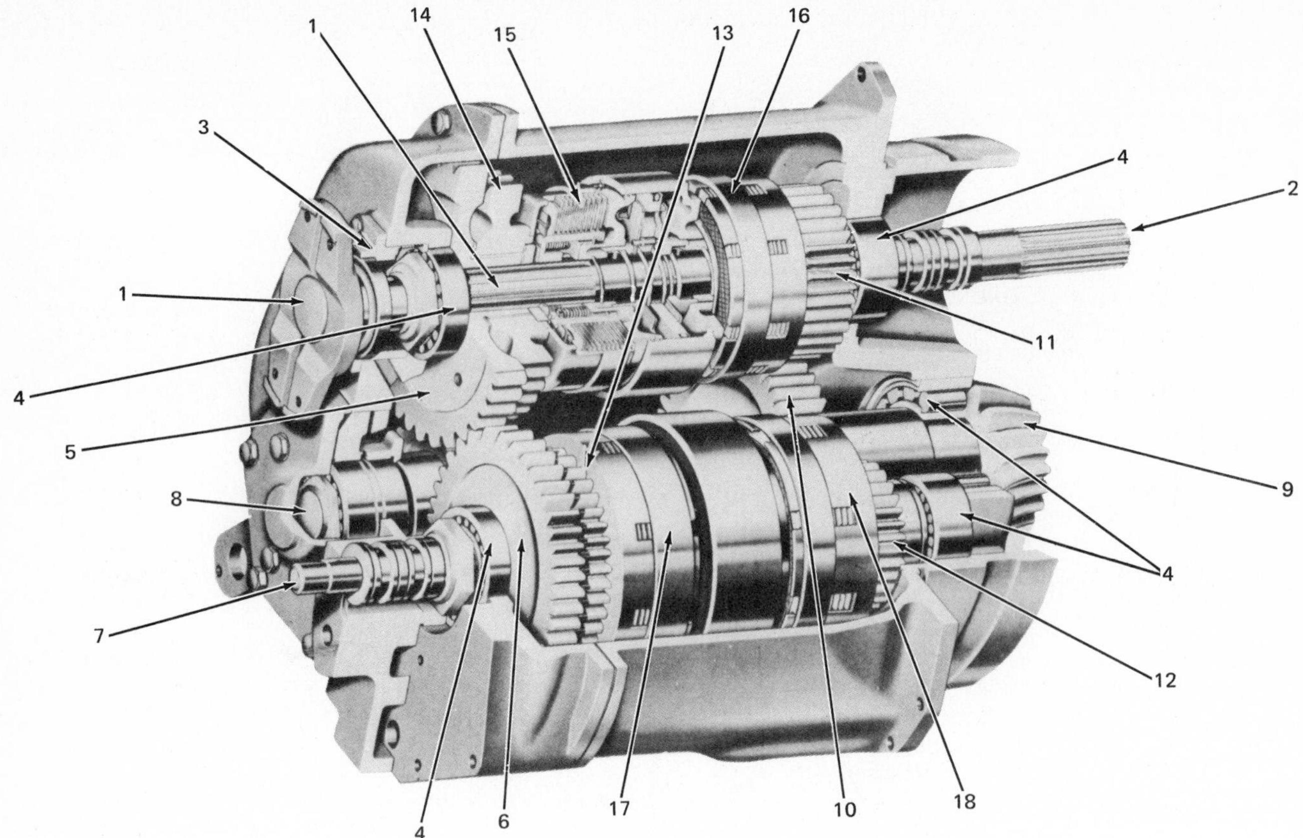

1. Input shaft (reverse shaft)
2. Input shaft to PTO drive
3. Bearing cap
4. Roller bearing
5. Input shaft drive gear
6. Forward driven gear
7. Forward shaft
8. Countershaft
9. Pinion
10. Speed driven gear
11. First speed reverse drive gear
12. First speed forward drive gear
13. Second speed reverse drive gear
14. Second speed forward drive gear
15. Reverse second speed clutch pack
16. Reverse first speed clutch pack
17. Forward second speed clutch pack
18. Forward first speed clutch pack

Fig. 12-54 Cutaway view of the two-speed forward, two-speed reverse powershift transmission. (*International Harvester Company*)

Reverse gears When the shift lever is placed in the first reverse-speed position, oil from the hydraulic shift control is directed into port 1, and consequently clutch 1 engages. At the same time oil is directed to the forward/reverse shift valve, forcing it upward, thereby directing the oil into the reverse clutch piston area. The drive gear then clutches to the reverse clutch shaft.

Rotation is transmitted from the input (forward high/low-clutch) shaft drive gear, to the reverse clutch shaft driven gear, over the reverse clutch pack, and onto the drive gear. It is then transmitted to the third driven gear on the idler shaft, causing the idler shaft to rotate opposite to the input shaft.

Torque transfer from the idler shaft is the same in all four reverse-speed ranges as in forward first, second, third, or fourth speeds.

Two-Speed Forward, Two-Speed Reverse Countershaft Transmission This type, as well as the five-speed forward, one-speed reverse transmission, has the clutch shafts and countershafts positioned in a triangle, whereas on the two-speed forward and two-speed reverse transmission (Fig. 12-41) the two shafts are parallel. The transmission illustrated in Fig. 12-54 is the kind used on a track-type tractor having a two-speed planetary drive.

DESIGN The two clutch shafts (forward and reverse) are supported by roller bearings, and the bevel pinion (counter-) shaft is supported by ball bearings. The first-speed driven gear is splined to the bevel pinion shaft (toward the pinion), and the second-speed driven gear is splined to the other end of the shaft. The first-speed driven gear is in mesh with the first-speed reverse clutch drive gear, and with the first-speed forward clutch drive gear. The second-speed driven gear is in mesh with the second-speed reverse and the second-speed forward clutch drive gears. The input shaft forward drive gear (which is in mesh with the forward driven gear) is splined to the reverse clutch shaft, and the forward driven gear is splined to the forward clutch shaft.

The clutch shafts are center-drilled, and a tube is positioned in the bore to separate and direct the clutch-applied oil flow to the left- and right-hand clutch piston areas. The separator plate is splined to the clutch shaft. This plate has six large and six small oil transfer holes, and four guide pin holes, in which guide pins are located, to hold the steel disk

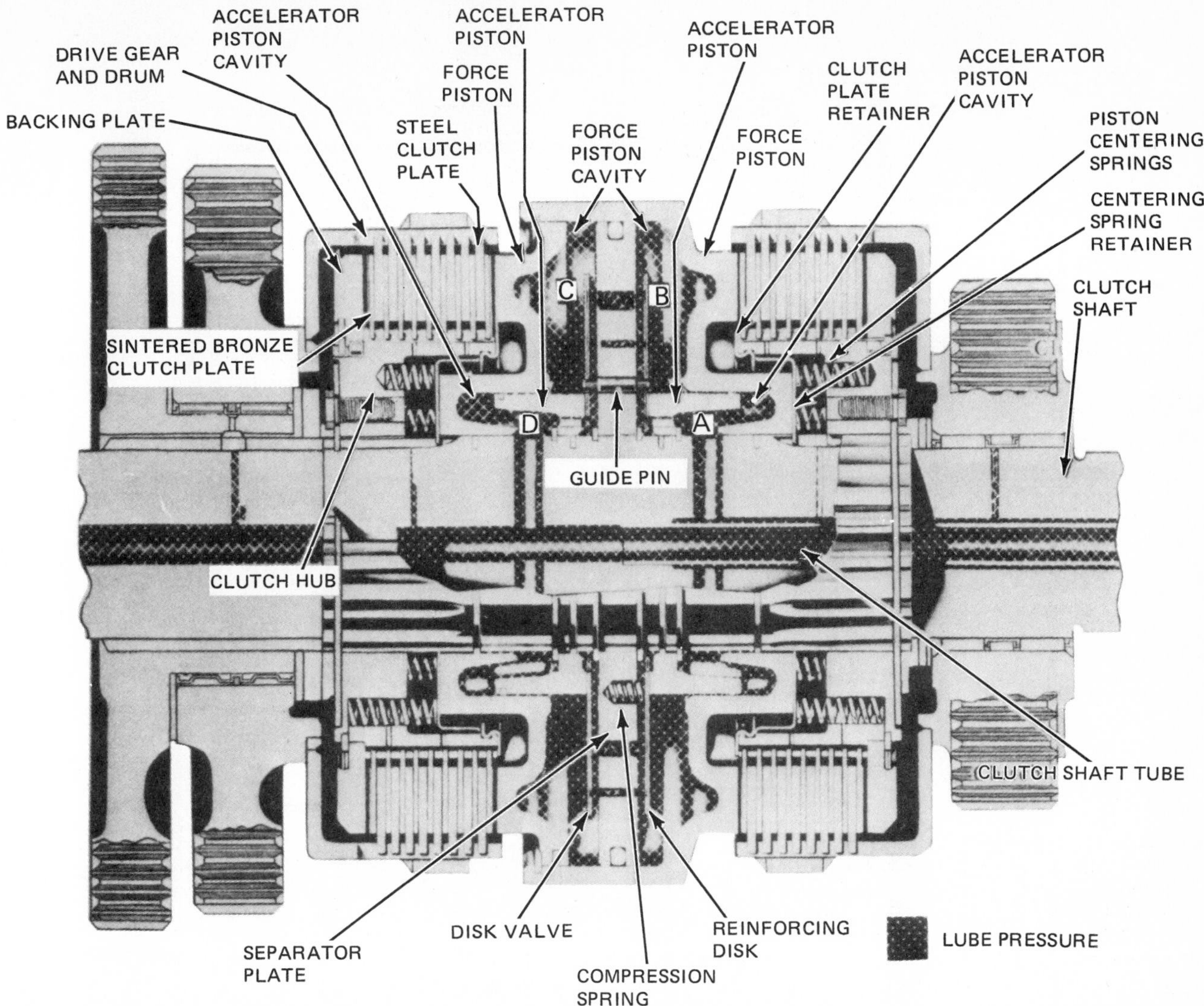

Fig. 12-55 Sectional view of the clutch shaft assembly when clutches are disengaged (two-speed forward, two-speed reverse powershift transmission). (*International Harvester Company*)

valve and reinforcing disk over the oil transfer holes. In addition, there are six countersunk holes on each side of the separator in which the compression springs are located. The force piston is fastened, through a snap ring, to the force piston housing, which is positioned over the separator plate. The accelerator pistons are positioned within the force piston and force piston housing. The (inside) ends of the accelerator pistons rest against the reinforcing disk. **NOTE** Piston travel is limited through snap rings.

The friction clutch plates are splined to the clutch hubs, which in turn are splined to the clutch shaft, and when assembled the piston centering springs push the force piston into the center position. The clutch drive gears are welded to the clutch drums, and the steel clutch plate lugs are positioned in the slots of the clutch drums. The assemblies are supported by roller bearings on the clutch shaft. See Fig. 12-55.

HYDRAULIC SYSTEM The hydraulic system that controls the oil flow to the torque converter, as well as to the direction and speed ranges, is schematically illustrated in Fig. 12-56. Components with which you may not be familiar are the signal pump, signal brake cylinder, pilot control valve, and shuttle valve. The signal pump is a small gear pump which is driven by the final drive. In conjunction with the signal brake and shuttle valve, it allows a shift from forward to reverse or vice versa only when the tractor is coming to a halt (track no longer moving). The main purpose of the pilot control valve is to direct signal oil pressure to the range selector valve spools and the lockout valve spool. The pilot control valve is a five-position valve—neutral, reverse high, reverse low, forward high, and forward low. The selector valve has a forward range, reverse range, and lockout spool. All three are remote-controlled and of the closed center valve spool design.

NEUTRAL OPERATION When the engine is operating and the shift lever is in neutral, the spool centering springs center the forward range, reverse range, and lockout spool, and close the two lower check valves in the shuttle valve. The oil pressure and mechanical

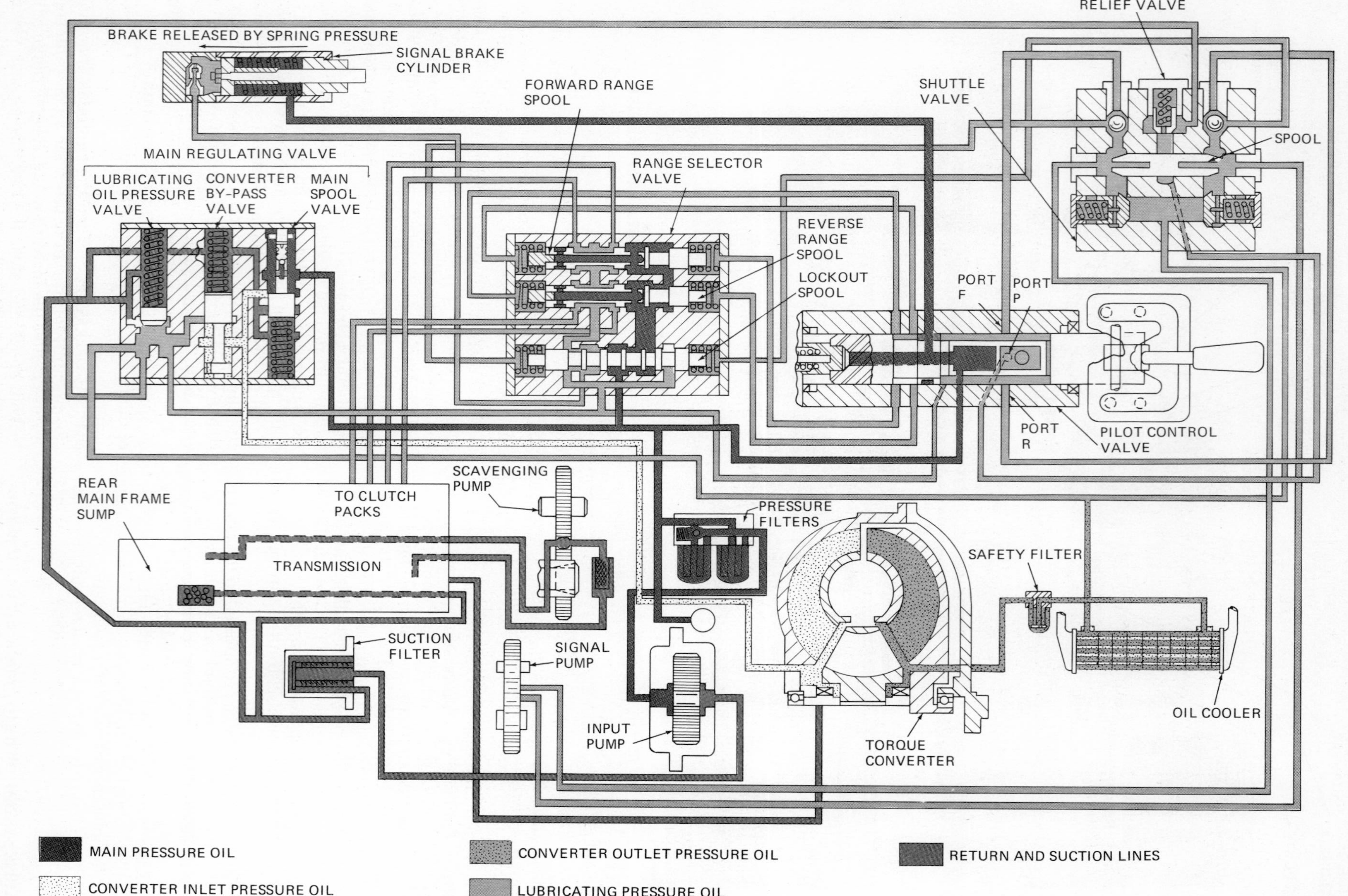

Fig. 12-56 Schematic view of the hydraulic system with transmission in neutral (engine operating). (*International Harvester Company*)

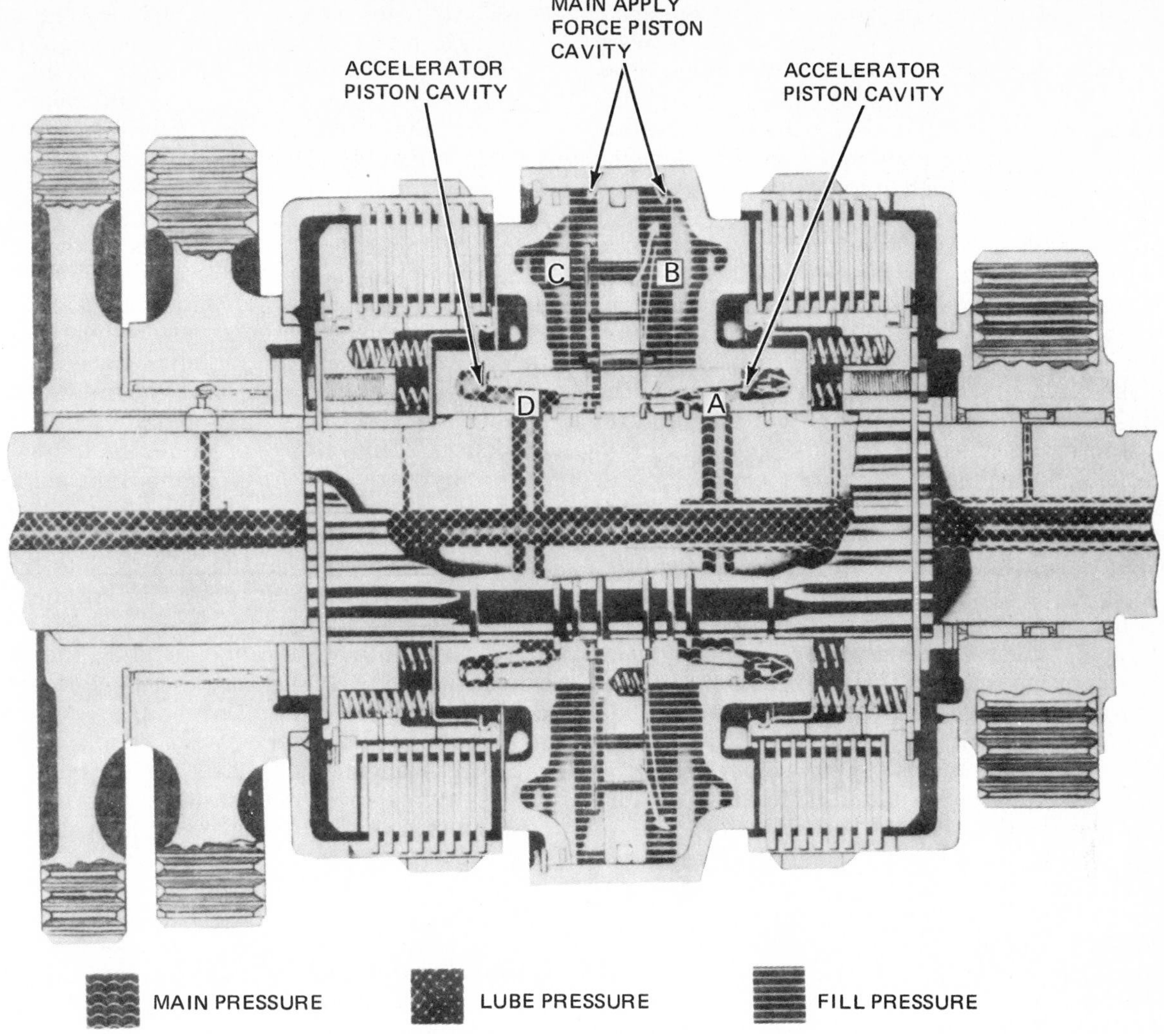

Fig. 12-57 Sectional view of flow of oil through clutch during the engagement (two-speed forward, two-speed reverse powershift transmission). (*International Harvester Company*)

energy of the signal brake spring release the brake. The oil from the input pump flows through the filter, onto the main spool (pressure relief) valve, over the pilot control valve, and onto the right-hand side of the signal brake cylinder, then passes through the lockout spool onto the forward and reverse range valve spools where the oil is then blocked. See Fig. 12-56. Excess oil is directed to the torque converter bypass valve, and *its* excess oil is directed to the lubrication pressure relief valve. Oil from the lubrication valve is directed to the range selector valve, and subsequently to the four transmission clutch packs. It is also directed over the pilot control valve to the shuttle valve, onto the two lower check valves, and from there to the signal pump.

Oil from the torque converter bypass valve flows into the torque converter, from there through the oil cooler, and then into the lubrication circuit. The scavenging pump pumps the oil from the torque converter into the transmission sump.

FORWARD HIGH- AND LOW-RANGE OPERATION When the operator rotates the shift lever to the left, the pilot valve spool directs main line oil over line 1 and onto the left-hand side of the forward range spool (low range). The spool subsequently shifts to the right and thereby directs the main line oil over the bearing end cap, into the outer area of the center tube, into the cross-drilled passage A, and then into the accelerator piston cavity. The higher oil pressure forces the accelerator piston to the left, causing it to force the reinforcing disk and valve disk against the separator plate. This compresses the compression springs and closes the six valve ports.

At the same time, the increased oil pressure forces the forcing piston to the right, preengaging the clutch. This increases the volume in force piston cavity B, and reduces it in cavity C; as a result, the pressure in cavity C increases, thereby forcing the ends of the disk valve and the reinforcing disk away from the separator plate. Oil can then flow into cavity B until the pressure in both cavities is equal, whereupon the disk valve reseats. During this time, oil from the accelerator piston cavity flows through the orifice into force piston cavity B. The combined action of the accelerator piston and force piston effects a smooth clutch engagement. **NOTE** At the time of engagement and during engagement of the clutch, the needle bearings of the drive gear are lubricated by main line pressure. See Fig. 12-57.

With the forward low-range clutch pack engaged, the low-range drive gear is clutched to the forward clutch shaft. The rotation is transmitted from the reverse clutch shaft drive gear to the forward clutch shaft driven gear and shaft. From there the rotation is transmitted over the low-range clutch pack to the clutch drive gear and then onto the low-range driven gear on the countershaft.

As the tractor is driven forward, the signal pump pumps oil over line 2 onto the right-hand side of the shuttle spool. The spool moves to the left, as does the left-hand lower check valve. This forces the oil to flow past the ball check valve 1, into line 3, onto the right-hand side of the lockout spool, over the shuttle valve, into line 4, through the pilot control valve into line 5, over the ball check valve 2, into line 6, and onto the left-hand side of the lockout spool. The spool is now held in neutral (balance) through hydraulic pressure. See Fig. 12-58.

When the operator moves the shift lever forward, the pilot valve spool moves to the left into high range, but ports P and F remain as in first gear. The valve spool, however, now directs oil into line 7 and at the same time removes the oil pressure from line 1. The forward range spool then shifts to the left, and oil is thereby directed onto the forward high clutch pack, over the bearing cap center tube, and into the high range accelerator cavity. Oil pressure in the low-range accelerator piston cavity and in force piston cavity B is removed through the repositioning of the forward range valve spool. The mechanical action and oil flow within the low-range clutch pack is a repetition of that within the high-range clutch pack and, as a result, while the high-range clutch is being engaged, the low-range clutch disengages, effecting a smoother transfer of torque from low to high range.

A downshift from high to low has the same hydraulic and mechanical result as an upshift. The engagement of the high-range clutch clutches the drive gear to the forward clutch shaft. Rotation now is transmitted from the reverse shaft drive gear to the forward shaft driven gear and shaft, over the high-range clutch pack to the drive gear, and from there onto the high-range driven gear and the bevel pinion shaft.

REVERSE LOW- AND HIGH-RANGE OPERATION When the operator semirotates the shift lever to the right and at the same time pulls it back, the pilot control valve spool is semirotated clockwise and moves to the right. This positions port P with port R. Consequently main line oil is directed over line 8 onto the right-hand side of the reverse range spool, shifting it to the left. However, the signal pressure in line 6 is removed by the pilot control valve, leaving only lubrication pressure at the left-hand side of the lockout spool. Since the tractor has not yet come to a halt, the signal pressure is still exerted on the right-hand side of the lockout spool. The spool is therefore shifted to the left, blocking the oil flow to the reverse range spool and directing oil over line 10 into the left-hand side of the signal brake cylinder, thereby applying the brake. See Fig. 12-59.

When the tractor comes to a stop, the signal pump no longer rotates. Consequently the signal pressure is removed from the right-hand side of the lockout spool, causing the spool to come into balance (neutral). See Fig. 12-60. It now allows oil to flow to the reverse range spool and from there to the reverse low-range clutch pack. The reverse low-range drive gear then clutches to the reverse clutch shaft. Rotation from the reverse clutch shaft is transmitted over the reverse low-range clutch pack to the drive gear, and then onto the low-range driven gear on the (bevel pinion) countershaft. As soon as the tractor travel reverses, the signal pump rotation reverses. As a result, line 11 is now pressurized and the shuttle valve is forced to the right; signal oil is then directed past ball check 2, into line 6, and onto the left-hand side of the lockout valve. At the same time, signal pressure oil is also directed over the shuttle valve into line 4, into port P, out of port R, into line 12, over ball check valve 1, into line 3, and onto the right-hand side of the lockout spool, holding the spool in balance (neutral).

To shift into high-range reverse, the operator moves the shift lever forward, which causes the pilot control valve to direct oil over line 9 onto the left-hand side of the reverse range spool, and the oil pressure from the right-hand side is released. The reverse range spool then shifts to the right and directs main line oil to the reverse clutch shaft bearing cap and into the center tube passage, to engage the high-range reverse clutch. Rotation is now transmitted from the reverse clutch shaft, over the high-range reverse clutch pack, to the drive gear, and then to the high-range driven gear on the bevel pinion shaft.

HYDROSTATIC DRIVES

Hydrostatic drives convert engine power first to fluid power and then to mechanical power (torque), which drives the wheels or the tracks of a tractor, or rotates a superstructure, etc. They only transmit engine torque and do not multiply it, as do the hydrodynamic units (torque converters). Almost all hydrostatic drives have infinite speed ranges in both directions and some, in addition, have a two-speed range.

The principles which apply to mechanical transmissions also apply to hydrostatic drives; that is, torque is reduced as motor speed increases. Maximum engine torque is transmitted and is present at the motor output shaft when maximum pressure is applied to the hydraulic system, which is usually when the output shaft of the hydraulic motor is standing still.

NOTE Torque is reduced in proportion to the increase in motor output shaft speed.

Hydrostatic drives have several advantages over mechanical transmissions—their power loss is less than that of a mechanical drive; they can be installed almost anywhere and in any position; they are smaller in size and weigh less than other mechanical drives; they have infinite speed ranges; they transfer

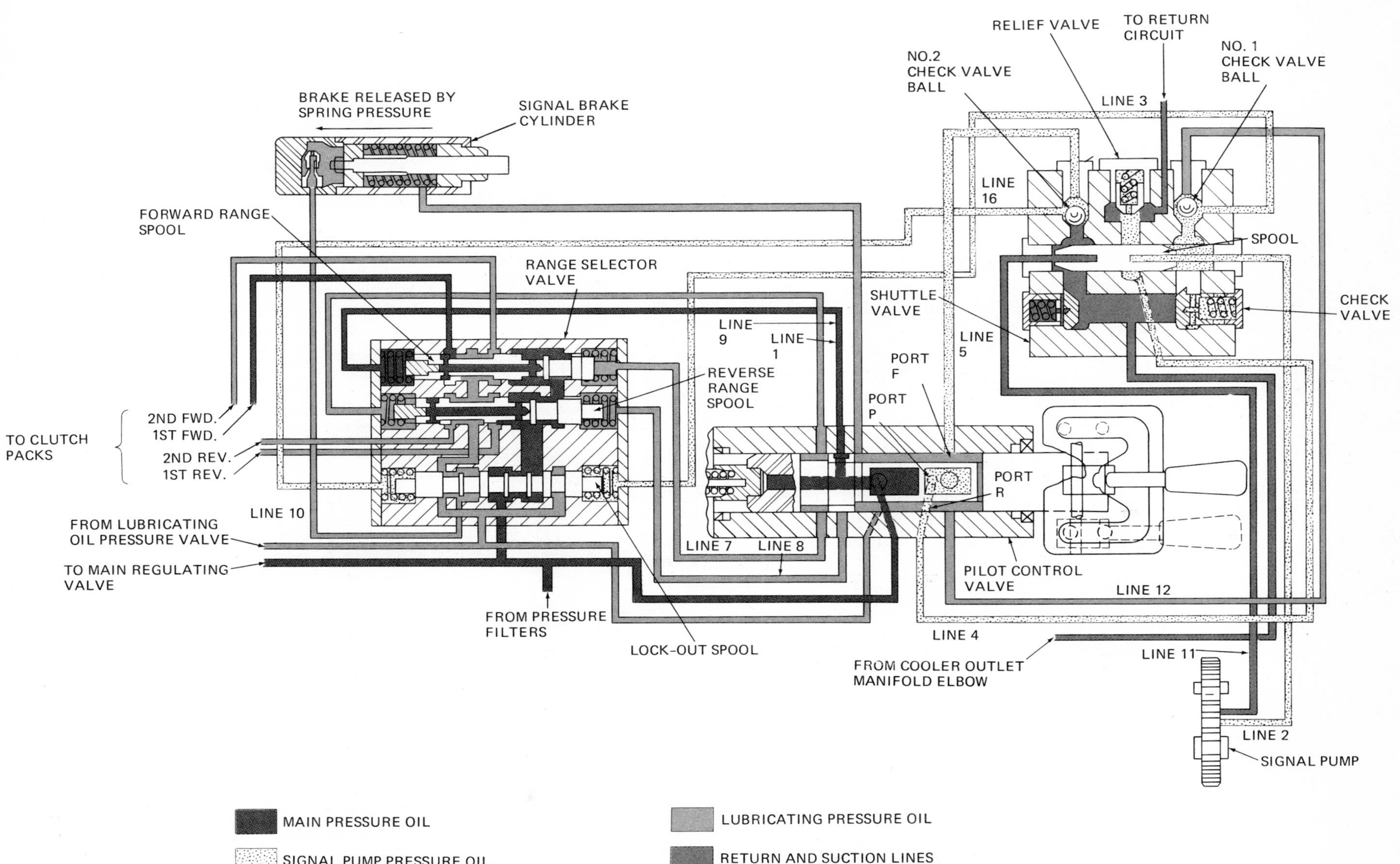

Fig. 12-58 Schematic view of hydraulic oil flow diagram (tractor in first speed forward) (two-speed forward, two-speed reverse powershift transmission). (*International Harvester Company*)

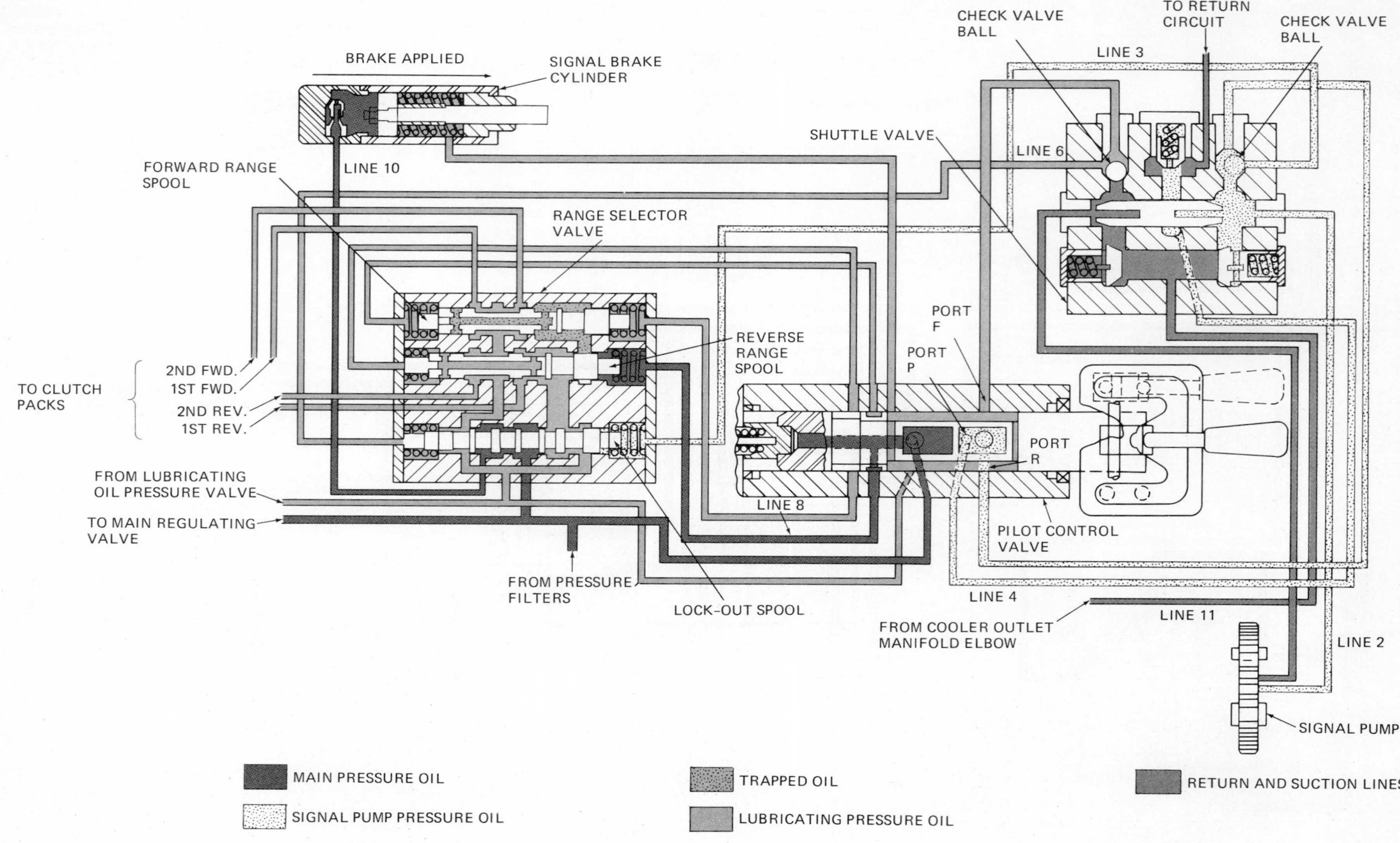

Fig. 12-59 Schematic view of hydraulic flow (tractor in first speed reverse, yet still moving forward) (two-speed forward, two-speed reverse powershift transmission). (*International Harvester Company*)

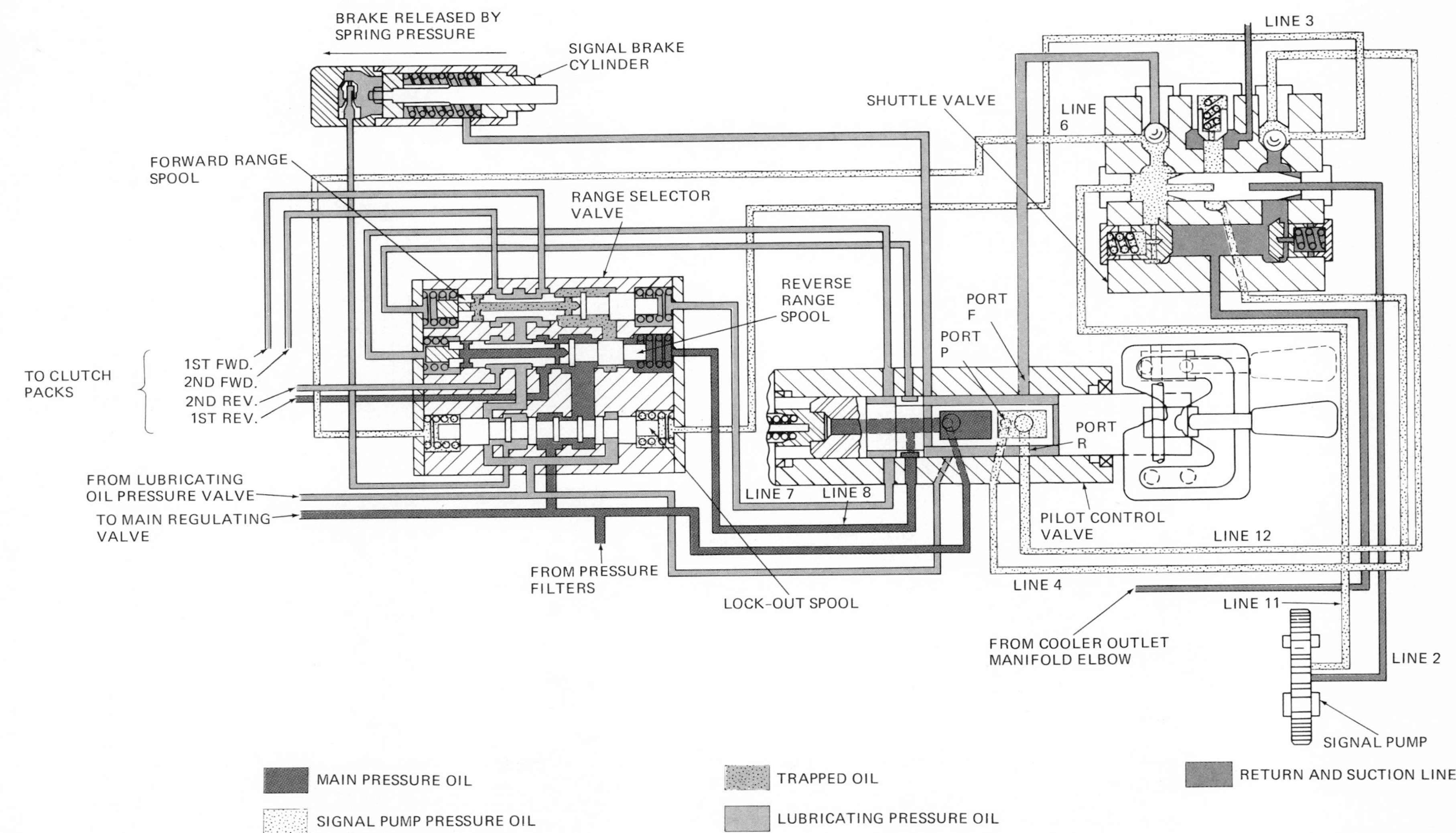

Fig. 12-60 Schematic view of hydraulic oil flow, tractor in first speed reverse (two-speed forward, two-speed reverse powershift transmission). (*International Harvester Company*)

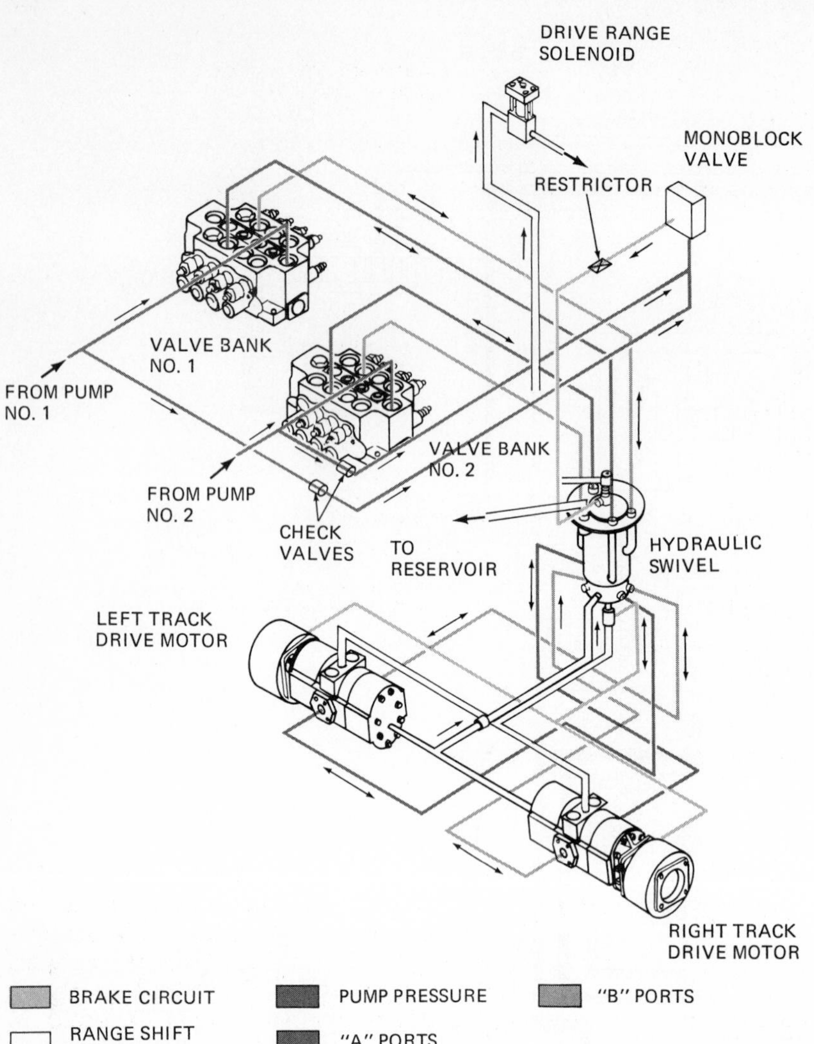

Fig. 12-61 Schematic view of a hydrostatic system. *(J I Case Company Agricultural Equipment Division)*

engine torque and speed smoothly and without hesitation; they do not require a clutch (the system itself is the clutch); and they can change direction more quickly and smoothly than other mechanical drives and can use this feature as a dynamic brake.

All hydrostatic drives are relatively the same in design. The power source (engine or motor) provides the rotation to the hydraulic pump. The hydraulic pump provides the flow rate, and the flow rate provides the motor speeds. The pressure of the oil transmits the power to the motor, and the motor transforms the oil pressure into torque. Directional change of the oil flow provides directional change of the motor output shaft, and the valves provide control and safety for the system.

Differences among the various systems occur in: (1) the type and size of the hydraulic pump and motor, (2) the flow rate, (3) the system's operating pressure, (4) the type of system (closed hydraulic loop system or an open system), (5) the type or number of speed ranges (infinite-speed and/or a two-speed system), and (6) whether or not a mechanical transmission is additionally used.

Open Hydrostatic System A typical open hydrostatic drive system is shown in Fig. 12-61. "Open" means that the oil returning from the motor is directed back to the reservoir. This system is an electrically controlled, two-speed track drive, used on an excavator. It operates at a maximum pressure of 3000 psi [20,670 kPa], and each hydraulic pump provides a flow rate of 47 gal/min [177.89 l/min] when operating at 2000 rpm and at 2000 psi [13,780 kPa]. Both directional control valves are of the open center design. The track drive motors are tandem external gear motors (see Fig. 12-62). The rear motor section includes the two oil ports which are connected through passages over the speed selector (hydraulically actuated poppet) valves to the front motor section oil ports. The two check valves direct bleed oil to the drive-range solenoid valve, instead of directing oil from the lower to the upper poppet valve, or vice versa. This prevents the poppet valve from closing. The drive-range solenoid valve is connected externally over the selector switch and override button to the ignition switch. See Fig. 12-63.

LOW-RANGE OPERATION When the engine is operating, both hydraulic pumps are driven; pump 1 supplies oil to valve bank 1, and pump 2 supplies oil to valve bank 2. At the same time, oil flows to the monoblock valve. See Fig. 12-61.

When both directional valve spools that control the oil flow to the motors are in neutral, the oil re-

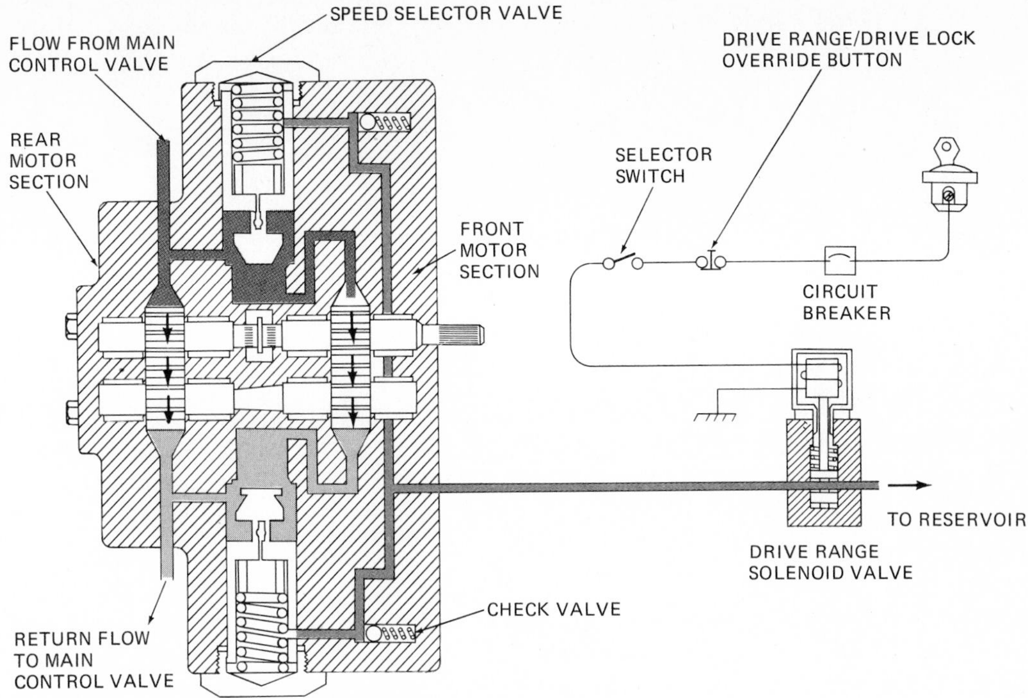

Fig. 12-62 Schematic view of one track drive motor in low range (open hydrostatic system). (*J I Case Company Agricultural Equipment Division*)

turns to the reservoir. When the drive brake switch is deenergized, the monoblock valve blocks the oil flow to the digging brakes and the spring force applies the brakes.

If the operator places the drive brake switch in the BRAKE OFF position, the solenoid energizes and opens the port to the digging brake cylinders. However, the oil pressure is low because the pump oil is directed back to the reservoir; therefore the digging brake remains applied.

If the operator moves only directional valve spool 2 to the forward drive direction, oil is directed over the hydraulic swivel and into the top port of the right-hand track drive motor; in effect the oil tries to rotate the motor gear. This causes a pressure rise in the motor application line and the line leading to the monoblock, and from there onto the brake cylinders. At this point, two separate hydraulic actions occur—the brakes start to release, and the top poppet valve lifts off its seat, whereupon oil is directed to the front motor section. When the outlet oil pressure of the front motor section is exerted against the lower poppet, oil is then directed into the common return line. From there it flows over the swivel to the directional valve in valve bank 2, on to the oil cooler, and then to the reservoir.

Under the above circumstances, both the rear and front motors are driven. This drives the reduction

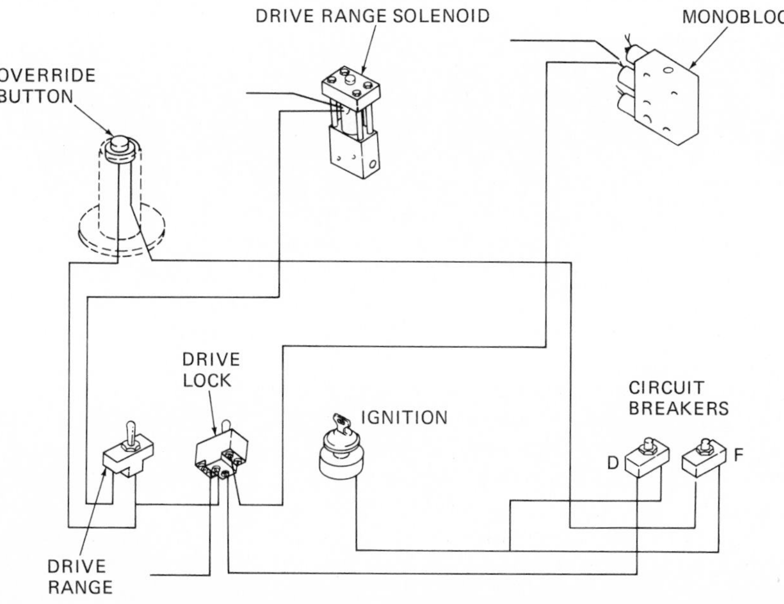

Fig. 12-63 Schematic view of drive lock and drive-range circuits (open hydrostatic system). (*J I Case Company Agricultural Equipment Division*)

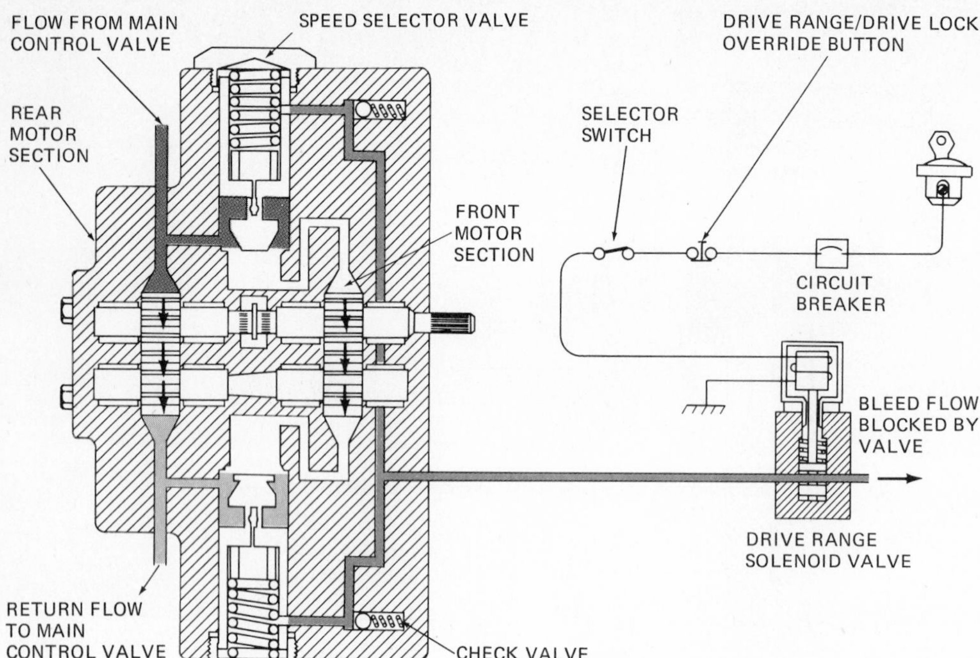

Fig. 12-64 Schematic view of one track drive motor in high range (open hydrostatic system). (*J I Case Company Agricultural Equipment Division*)

transmission, which then drives the right-hand track, thereby turning the excavator on the left-hand track.

NOTE The left-hand track can rotate in either direction because the brake is released.

When the directional valve spool of valve bank 1 is moved in the same direction as valve bank valve spool 2, the left-hand track is also driven and the excavator moves at slow speed in a forward direction. The speed is slow because the oil 47 gal/min [177.89 l/min] is directed to the rear and front motor sections.

If for one reason or another, one or both tracks resist rotation, the pressure in one or both supply systems increases. Under such circumstance, the track would start to rotate and the main pressure relief valve in one or both valve banks would be forced open to protect the individual systems against excessive pressure.

If the valve spool of valve bank 1 is moved in a direction opposite to that of valve bank valve spool 2, the oil flow to the left-hand track drive motor is reversed. As a result, the left-hand track is driven in a direction opposite to that of the right-hand track, causing the excavator to make a tight left-hand turn.

HIGH-RANGE OPERATION To increase the travel speed, the drive range switch is flipped to HIGH. This energizes the drive-range solenoid, which blocks the bleed off line. Consequently the pressure on the spring areas of the poppet valve increases sufficiently to close the valve and to block the oil flow to and from the front motor section. All the pump oil is now supplied to the rear motor, increasing the motor rotation and therefore the travel speed.

NOTE The hydraulic system and the electric circuit are not designed to switch one track drive motor into low and the other into high range. See Fig. 12-64.

Closed Loop Hydrostatic Drive The components of a closed loop hydrostatic drive are shown in Fig. 12-65. It is referred to as "closed loop" because the hydraulic pump and the hydraulic motor are directly connected, or are connected through hydraulic lines. The hydraulic motor is a fixed-displacement swash plate piston motor, and the hydraulic pump is a hydraulically controlled reversible variable-displacement swash plate pump. To protect the hydraulic motor, the hydraulic pump, and the lines against excessive pressure, one hydraulic pressure relief valve is placed in parallel to the motor supply lines. Since this is a closed system, a separate charging system must be used. The charging system consists of the reservoir, the charging pump, the charging relief valve, two charging check valves, a shuttle valve, a charge pressure relief valve, and an oil cooler. To control the tilt angle of the swash plate, a closed center, four-way, three-position directional valve is used which may be actuated manually, by air, or hydraulically.

NEUTRAL OPERATION When the control handle is released, the directional valve is forced into neutral through the force of its springs. When the piston pump is driven, the charging pump is also driven and oil is forced over both charge check valves to the inlet ports of the piston pump. Oil also flows to the directional valve, and there it is blocked. When the directional valve is in neutral, the servo control cylinder ports are open to the sump; because the charging pressure is exerted onto the pump pistons, the swash plate is forced to the neutral position. The third charging circuit extends to and around the high-pressure relief valves and oil is directed through passages onto each end of the shuttle valve, thereby centering it and blocking the oil flow to the charge pressure relief valve. If the charge pressure exceeds specification, the charge pressure relief valve is forced open and the charge pressure returns

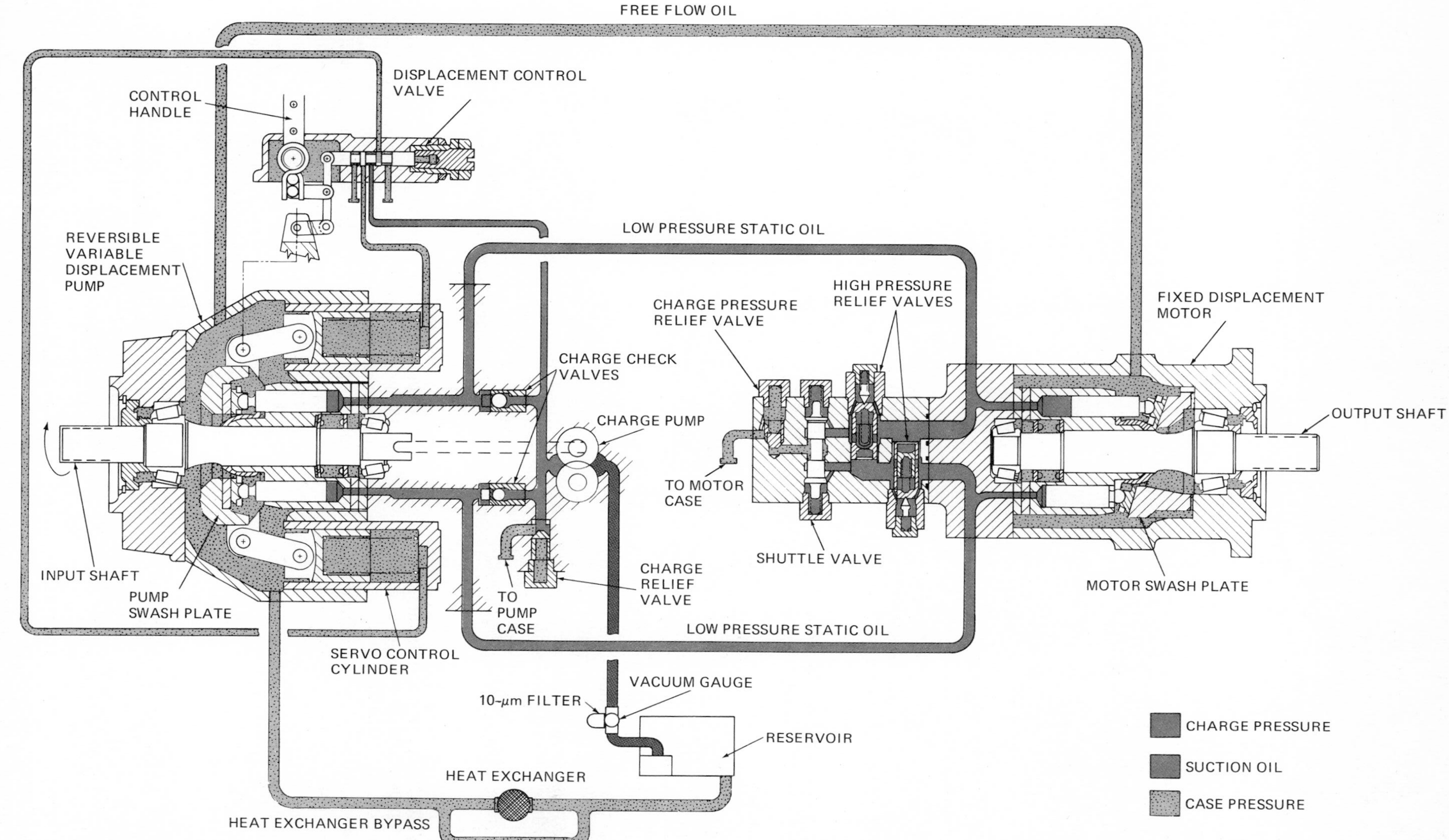

Fig. 12-65 Schematic view of a typical fixed motor-variable pump closed loop hydrostatic transmission (neutral). (*Sundstrand Corporation*)

to normal. **NOTE** The excess charging oil is directed from the charge pressure relief valve into both the pump housing (case) and the motor housing. Oil from both housings is directed over the oil cooler to the reservoir.

FORWARD OPERATION When the operator moves the control handle to the FORWARD position, the directinal valve spool moves to the right and charge pressure is directed to the lower servo control cylinder. Oil pressure forces the piston to the left, pivoting the swash plate. The angle to which the swash plate is forced depends upon the amount of oil that is directed into the servo control cylinder. Four pump piston cylinders are charged, and four pump pistons pump oil to four motor pistons, forcing the output shaft to rotate in a clockwise direction, whereupon four pistons discharge the oil into the charging system. High main circuit pressure is not exerted against the shuttle valve, and the valve spool is forced downward, allowing the charging oil to flow to the charge pressure relief valve. Since the discharge pressure is relatively high, the charge pressure relief valve is forced open, maintaining the low charge pressure. See Fig. 12-66.

REVERSE OPERATION To change the rotation of the hydraulic motor from forward to reverse, the operator moves the directional spool to the right. Oil is then directed to the top servo cylinder, and opens the lower servo cylinder port to the oil sump, causing the swash plate to move through neutral and then to the left. During this time, the transmission of power is reduced to nil, after which it gradually increases. Oil is now pumped into the lower main circuit, driving the output shaft in a counterclockwise direction. **NOTE** At maximum pump speed and maximum swash plate angle, the pump supplies the maximum flow rate to the main circuit. With reduced pump speed and/or reduced swash plate angle, the flow rate decreases. See Fig. 12-67.

POWERSHIFT TRANSMISSION TROUBLESHOOTING

Overly simplified, transmission malfunctions may be divided into two groups: hydraulic system adjustment or failure, and mechanical failure. Mechanical failure can usually be identified through additional noises originating from worn bearings, shafts, or splines that cause misalignment of gears, clutch drum, or clutch hub. Such problem areas can usually be isolated by shifting the transmission through the various ranges because each speed range (in either forward or reverse) functions around a particular set of gears.

When a tractor transmission is overly noisy, it is usually because the bearings of the forward and/or reverse planetary gear are worn or damaged. Hydraulic problems are more difficult to locate, and you therefore must use a flowmeter and test gauges.

Maintenance To maintain the powershift transmission in good operating condition and to minimize transmission trouble, good maintenance is essential. Good maintenance requires checking the entire hydraulic system. Check the tubings, hoses, and fittings for damage and leaks; make certain they are not twisted or bent, not rubbing on metal parts, and *are* well secured. When an air oil cooler is used, check the oil cooler core for contamination. Inspect the transmission air breather; if it is plugged it may cause the transmission seal to leak. Check for loose or broken mounting brackets and/or loose mounting cap screws or nuts. Inspect and test the control valve adjustment. Check the linkage rods for bends which would cause either improper positioning of the valve spool, resulting in a delay in upshift or downshift, or improper clutch engagement.

When checking and correcting the oil level, closely follow the manufacturer's recommendations. The level must be no lower or higher than recommended if the transmission is to be guarded against high oil temperature. Moreover, when checking and adjusting the oil level, make certain that no dirt enters the transmission and that you use only the oil recommended. Furthermore, use clean filling devices to prevent contaminants from mixing into the oil.

Briefly, one procedure to check the transmission oil level is as follows:

1. Start the engine and bring the oil temperature to at least 160°F [71°C].
2. Shift the transmission through all ranges in order to fill all piston cavities and passages.
3. Operate the engine at low idle.
4. Place the transmission in neutral and then check the oil level. It should be at the full-level mark.

Good maintenance also requires changing the transmission oil, filter, and air breather at the recommended intervals. Furthermore, the drained oil should be checked for contaminant content. Note, however, that oil which has been used for some period of time may contain a small amount of powdered clutch friction material, some minute steel particles, or a small amount of water. This is normal and not unduly harmful. On the other hand, if coolant has infiltrated from the oil cooler, the oil lubrication quality will quickly deteriorate; therefore the leak must be repaired immediately. if there are large metal particles in the oil sump, the oil pan should be removed, if possible, to locate their source, or the transmission should be serviced.

It is more expedient in the long run to check the torque converter and the transmission pressure after an oil change, and then to perform a torque converter stall test to determine if the converter and transmission are in good hydraulic and mechanical condition. To make a stall test and/or to locate the trouble within the transmission, you must first have a thorough knowledge of the transmission and of the hydraulic system, and you must know the test specifications.

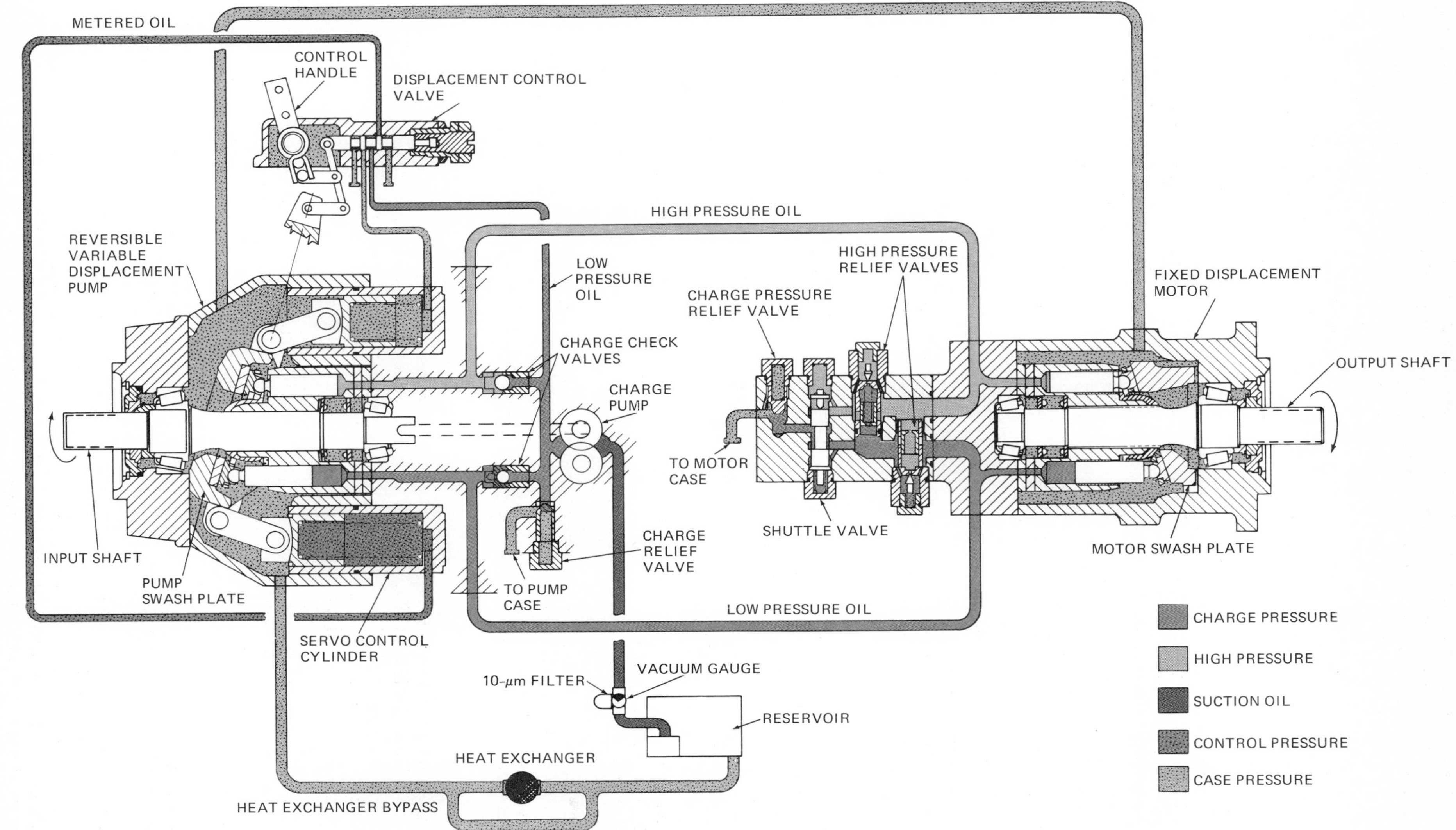

Fig. 12-66 Schematic view of a typical fixed motor, variable pump, closed loop hydrostatic transmission (forward). (*Sundstrand Corporation*)

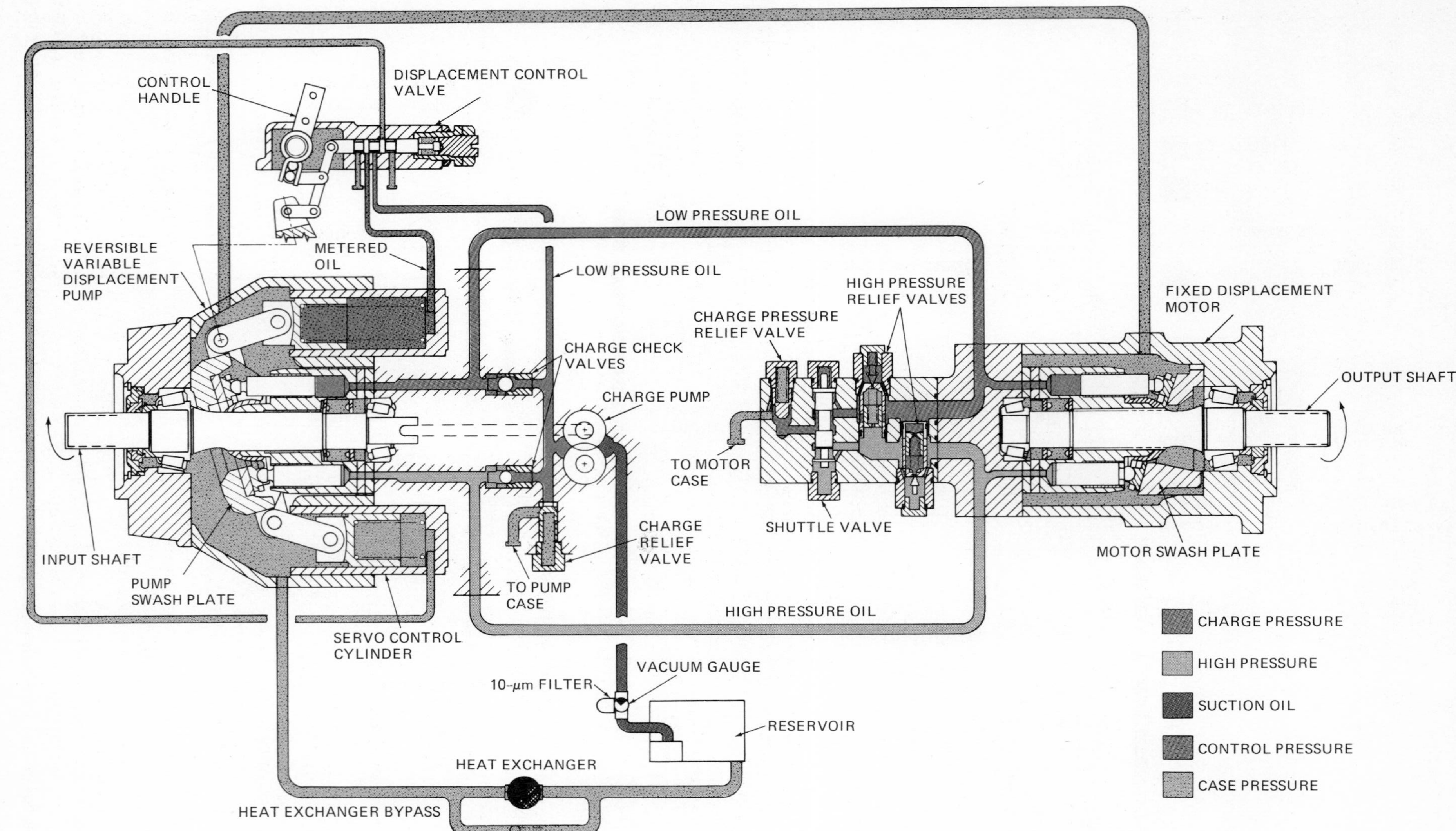

Fig. 12-67 Schematic view of a typical fixed motor, variable pump, closed loop hydrostatic transmission (reverse). (*Sundstrand Corporation*)

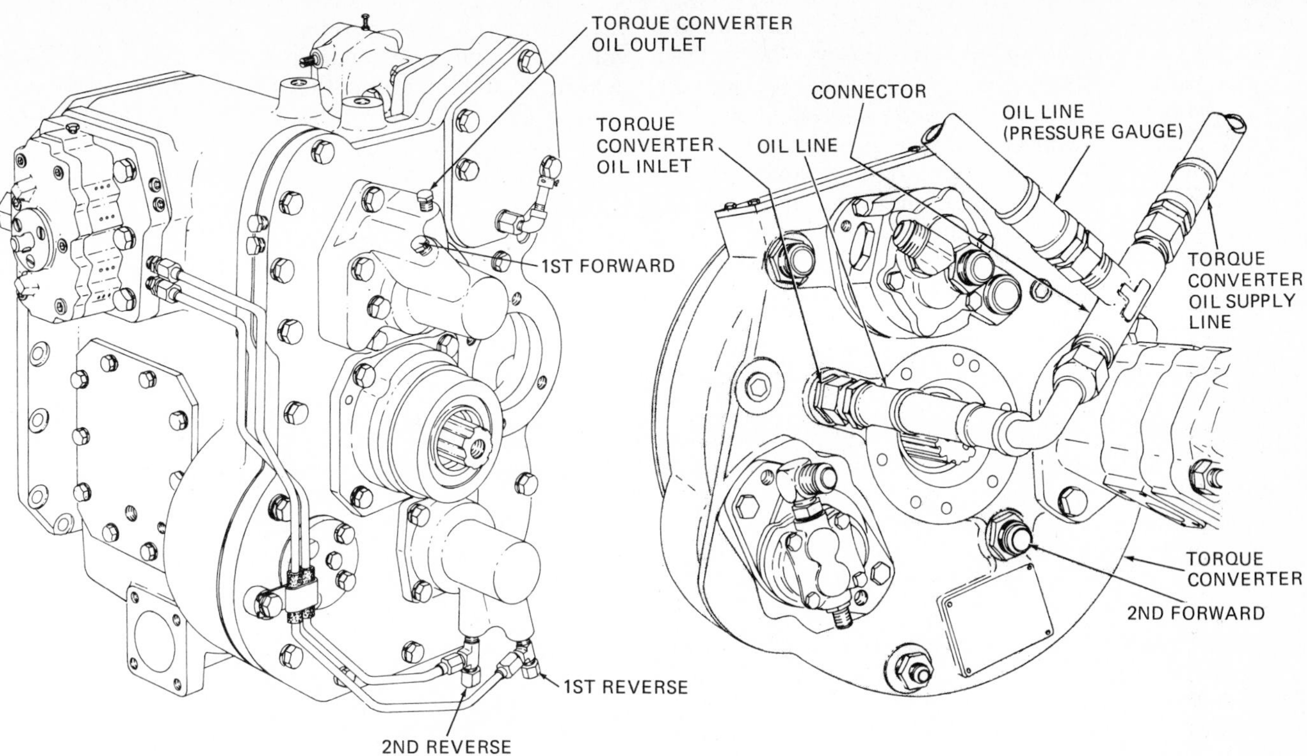

Fig. 12-68 View of transmission and torque converter test plug locations. (*International Harvester Company*)

Pressure Testing Powershift Transmission Install the pressure gauges having the recommended pressure ratings into the recommended test plugs. See Fig. 12-68. You may (for some transmissions) require as many as 10 gauges in order to check all pressures simultaneously: the hydraulic pump pressure gauge, range and directional clutch pressure gauges, governor pressure gauge, throttle pressure gauge, converter "in" and "out" pressure gauges, oil cooler "in" and "out" pressure gauges, and the lubrication pressure gauge.

When the engine is checked and the gauges are connected, start the engine and operate it at about 1500 rpm to bring the oil to 180°F [82°C]. To do this, block the wheels, apply the brakes, and shift the transmission into high range. During warmup, note and record the oil pressure gauge readings. When the oil is at 180°F [82°C], accelerate the engine to the recommended rpm (with the transmission in neutral) and record the main line pressure reading. If the pressure is lower than specified, make the necessary adjustment to raise it to the recommended setting. Now repeat the test and record the torque converter "in" and "out" pressures, and the oil cooler "in" and "out" pressures. If all those are low, the cause could be one or more of the following: (1) misadjusted main relief valve, (2) badly worn main hydraulic pump (low flow rate), (3) inlet filter plugged, (4) the inlet line restricted, (5) the torque converter inlet regulator not adjusted properly, and for (6) the torque converter damaged due to worn bearings or contamination.

To check the flow rate, the inlet restriction, or for air in the hydraulic system of the transmission, install a flowmeter and test the system. To check the mechanical condition (leakage) of the torque converter, you may check the converter drain flow by disconnecting the drain line and measuring the flow rate. If it exceeds specification, the torque converter must be serviced.

If the torque converter pressure is too high and the oil cooler pressure "out" is low, it is an indication that the oil cooler is plugged, that the outlet relief valve is adjusted improperly, or that the connecting tube or hose to the oil cooler is restricted. However, if all pressures are higher than specified, the main relief valve may be misadjusted or stuck in the closed position.

Following is an example of test pressures:

	psi	kPa
Main	300	2067
Torque converter "in"	80	551.2
Torque converter "out"	60	413.4
Oil cooler "in"	40	275.6
Oil cooler "out"	20	137.8
Lubrication	15	103.35
Torque converter leakage 4.75 gal/min [18 l/min]		

The next step in the pressure test is to engage the range clutch and then the directional clutch; check their applied pressures and if necessary make any required adjustments. When the pressure rise is slow or the pressure of the individual clutch packs is less than specified (indicating high leakage), install a flowmeter to determine which component or clutch pack is causing the excessive leakage. **NOTE** The circuit leakage (gal/min [l/min]) can vary, even between transmissions produced by the same manufacturer, because some transmissions use the clutch apply pressure oil to lubricate the bearings and/or the adjacent clutch. Low pressure can occur as the result of worn or damaged piston seals or any valve to which main line pressure is directed. Next, check the throttle or the modulator pressure, and last, if applicable, the lockup clutch pressure.

To make a lockup clutch test, install a pressure gauge in the test plugs, operate the engine at high idle or at the recommended rpm, and note the pressure gauge reading. The lockup pressure reading should be the same as main line pressure. Now, gradually decrease the engine rpm until the gauge drops to zero, at which point note the engine rpm. It should be as specified in the service manual. **NOTE** If during the testing, the pressure fluctuates more than specified, that is, more than 5 psi [34.5 kPa], it indicates that either there is air in the hydraulic system or the valve which is being tested is sticking.

Torque Converter Stall Test After the pressure checks have been made, you may wish to perform a torque converter stall test if there is any doubt about the combined performance of the engine and transmission. **CAUTION** Do not perform a converter stall test when the transmission is in first forward or first reverse gear, as the high torque developed during the test could damage the transmission drive line or rear carrier.

Position the motor vehicle or tractor on level ground, and at a spot with good amount of space since the vehicle might start to move during the test. Apply the service and parking brake, block the wheels or tracks, and lower the hydraulic equipment to the ground. Warn any workers nearby that you are about to conduct a torque converter stall test.

After the transmission and engine oil have reached operating temperature, place the transmission in the highest gear; then accelerate the engine to full throttle and note the engine rpm and the torque converter temperature. As the temperature approaches about 250°F [121°C], reduce the engine rpm to about half-throttle, and at the same time place the transmission in neutral. This will reduce the torque converter oil temperature as well as the engine temperature. Under no circumstances shut off the engine after a stall test. To do so would not only damage the engine, but would also allow the oil in the torque converter to boil, thereby necessitating a major repair job.

If the engine rpm is within stall test specification, you know that the engine and torque converter are in good operating condition and the transmission clutch does not slip. If the engine rpm is lower than specified, the engine does not develop maximum torque. However, if it is higher than specified, shift into the next low range and repeat the test. If the engine develops the same rpm as when in the higher gear, you can assume that the forward clutch is slipping, or that the torque converter is not developing the torque multiplication for which it was designed. Assuming the torque converter pressures are correct, the torque converter slippage may originate from the following: damaged or worn bearings or bushings which would increase the clearance between the torque converter members; damaged turbine, impeller, or reactor vanes; or if applicable, slipping of the reactor one-way clutch. Under any of these conditions, the vertex flow within the torque converter would be reduced, and consequently the torque multiplication. On the other hand, should the engine rpm remain high, you may assume that the forward clutch pack is slipping, in which case you should place the transmission in high reverse and then repeat the converter stall test to verify forward clutch slippage.

Operator Complaints If the operator complains that the engine and/or transmission temperature is too high during operation, she or he may be operating the machine in a gear which is too high for the load or road incline, or the ambient temperature in which the vehicle is operated may be above 100°F [38°C].

When the operator complains of rough shifting, or the upshift or downshift occurs late or too early, the malfunction may be in the governor, the shift valve, or the accumulator. However, the problem may be a damaged clutch drum, a damaged clutch hub, or damaged clutch plate splines, causing the plates to hang up so that they do not engage or release the clutch quickly enough. Again, the problem may be a plugged passage within the application circuit. When the operator complains that the transmission does not shift into lockup, the cause could be a worn or damaged lockup clutch.

Review Questions

1. What are the three major differences between a fluid coupling and a torque converter?
2. Which part of a fluid coupling or torque converter reduces the oil turbulence and at the same time increases vortex flow?
3. (*a*) Why are stators mounted on a one-way clutch? (*b*) Why do torque converters have two stators with each mounted on a one-way clutch?
4. (*a*) Describe the oil flow within a torque converter when the engine operates at torque speed and the transmission output shaft is not rotating. (b) What terminology is used to define the condition described above?
5. List the methods used (other than the stator variation) to increase the efficiency and/or the ratio of a torque converter.
6. (*a*) Name the four components of a standard planetary gear set. (*b*) Which component governs the drive combination? (*c*) Which two planetary actions achieve direct drive?
7. What advantage does a torque divider have over a torque converter?

8. List the three advantages of a powershift transmission over a standard transmission.

9. Why are the range and the speed directional valves on all powershift transmissions of the closed center design?

10. Through which valve is the torque divider transmission (*a*) held in torque converter speed? (*b*) converter charging pressure varied (converter speed to direct or overdrive speed or vice versa)? (*c*) shifted into direct drive? (*d*) shifted into overdrive? (*e*) What two forces shift the transmission into direct drive and overdrive, or from overdrive to direct drive, or from direct drive to converter drive?

11. Explain the power flow of the transmission in Fig. 12-28 when it is (*a*) in second speed forward, and (*b*) in first speed reverse.

12. (*a*)Identify the three types of governors which sense road speed; (*b*) identify the one which senses engine speed.

13. (*a*) Explain why most modern powershift transmissions utilize a lockup clutch. (*b*) Which member of the torque converter is locked (through the clutch) to the engine flywheel?

14. Outline the methods and/or components which manufacturers use to achieve a smooth and sequenced upshift or downshift.

15. Trace the oil flow and describe the mechanical action when the transmission of Fig. 12-43 is shifted (*a*) into fourth speed, and (*b*) into reverse.

16. Outline the differences between the five-speed forward, one-speed reverse transmission (Fig. 12-43) and the eight-speed forward, two-speed reverse transmission (Fig. 12-48).

17. Outline the power flow of a track-type tractor two-speed forward, two-speed reverse transmission when it is (*a*) in second speed forward, and (*b*) in first-speed reverse.

18. State the purpose of each of the following: (*a*) signal pump, (*b*) pilot control valve, and (*c*) shuttle valve.

19 (*a*) List the primary advantage of any type of hydrostatic drive over all other types of transmissions. (*b*) List five other advantages of the hydrostatic drive over nearly all types of transmissions.

20. Outline the two basic methods of reversing the direction of the output on a hydrostatic drive.

21. Explain why hydrostatic drives require some type of transmission.

22. (*a*) Define "closed loop hydrostatic drive." (*b*) Name its essential components.

23. List the maintenance checks necessary to prolong the service life of a powershift transmission.

24. List the problems which could be assumed to be present if, when testing the transmission hydraulically, (*a*) all test point pressures measure out below specification, (*b*) the torque converter inlet pressure is too high, (*c*) the torque converter inlet pressure is too low, (*d*) the main clutch pressure is too low, and/or (*e*) one clutch pack pressure is too low.

Unit 13
Drive Lines

It is the function of a drive line to transmit torque at a uniform speed from the transmission to the rear carrier and/or the front carrier, or from one carrier to another. A drive line consists of two or more universal joints, one slip yoke (joint), one or more connecting (propeller) shafts, the transmission and carrier flanges or yokes, and sometimes a center bearing. See Fig. 13-1.

Universal Joints The purpose of the universal joint is to link together the ends of two components which do not operate on the same plane. The universal joint consists of a forged cross and four bearing cups. Most bearing cups have internal needle bearings, and use seals (of various designs) to keep out dirt. Washers rest between the individual cups and the cross-shaft shoulders, thereby limiting universal joint side play when installed. The cross shaft has lubricant passages which lead from the grease nipple to the bearings. See Fig. 13-2.

A special universal joint is shown in Fig. 13-3. It has a lubrication control system built into each needle bearing guide, and includes a triple lip seal and a waffle design thrust washer. The large passages and the area below the needle bearing guide form the grease reservoir. A fine-mesh filter screen prevents contaminants from entering the needle bearings. The orifice controls the flow of lubricant to the bearings at a pressure of about 500 psi [3445 kPa] during rotation and also prevents a reverse flow of heated lubricant from the bearings back to the reservoir. The triple lip seal maintains lubrication and prevents contaminants from entering the needle bearing. The waffle thrust washer allows the old lubricant to flow, with ease, from the bearings as new lubricant is pumped in.

Several different methods are employed to hold the bearing cups to the bores of the yokes (see Fig. 13-4). Since the size of the cross and the bearing cups are precisely calculated by the manufacturer to prolong service life, they should never be exchanged with universal joints of a different size.

However, all universal joints of this type have one drawback—they operate at an angle (small or large) and therefore do not transfer uniform rotating speed since the turning radius of the driven yoke changes constantly during the 360° rotation. This results in continual velocity changes (fluctuating speeds) of the propeller shaft (see Fig. 13-5). The propeller shaft speed rises above and below the drive yoke speed twice in every revolution. **NOTE** The propeller shaft velocity changes with increased propeller shaft angle, but not with increased rotating speed. When the universal joint operates at an angle of, say, 10° and the propeller shaft cross is as shown in Fig. 13-5, the lever is shortened. This reduces the rotating speed by about 75 rpm below that of the drive yoke. As the cross shaft rotates 180°, the rotation increases in speed until it reaches 75 rpm more than the rpm of the drive yoke because the lever arm lengthens. When the cross rotates an additional 270°, the rotation decreases in speed by 75 rpm less than the rpm of the drive yoke because the lever arm shortens. When rotated 360°, the cross rotation speed is again 75 rpm above drive yoke speed. The speed variation increases with increased angle variation.

To compensate for the inconsistent propeller shaft velocity, the propeller shaft yoke ends are phased to allow the other universal joint to reduce the twisting action of the propeller shaft. It is therefore important to make certain, when replacing a drive-line yoke, or when separating a slip joint, that the yoke phase remains precisely the same; otherwise vibration and excessive universal joint wear will occur.

Slip Yoke (Joint) The purpose of the slip yoke is to lengthen and shorten the drive line. When the carrier is fixed-mounted (as in a track- or wheel-type tractor), a slip joint is not necessary. But when the carrier is mounted to an axle housing and is attached to the frame through a suspension, a slip joint is needed because of the constant change (during operation) of the drive-line length—from the transmission flange to the carrier flange on a two-joint assem-

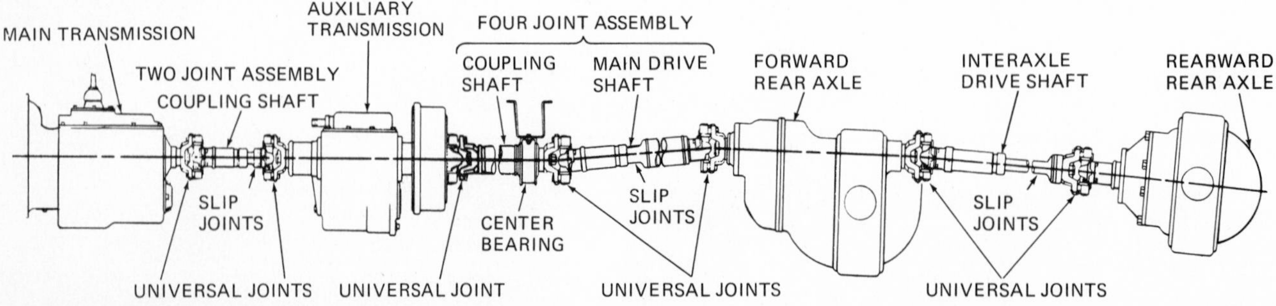

Fig. 13-1 A typical propeller shaft arrangement for a tandem rear axle. (*Ford Motor Company*)

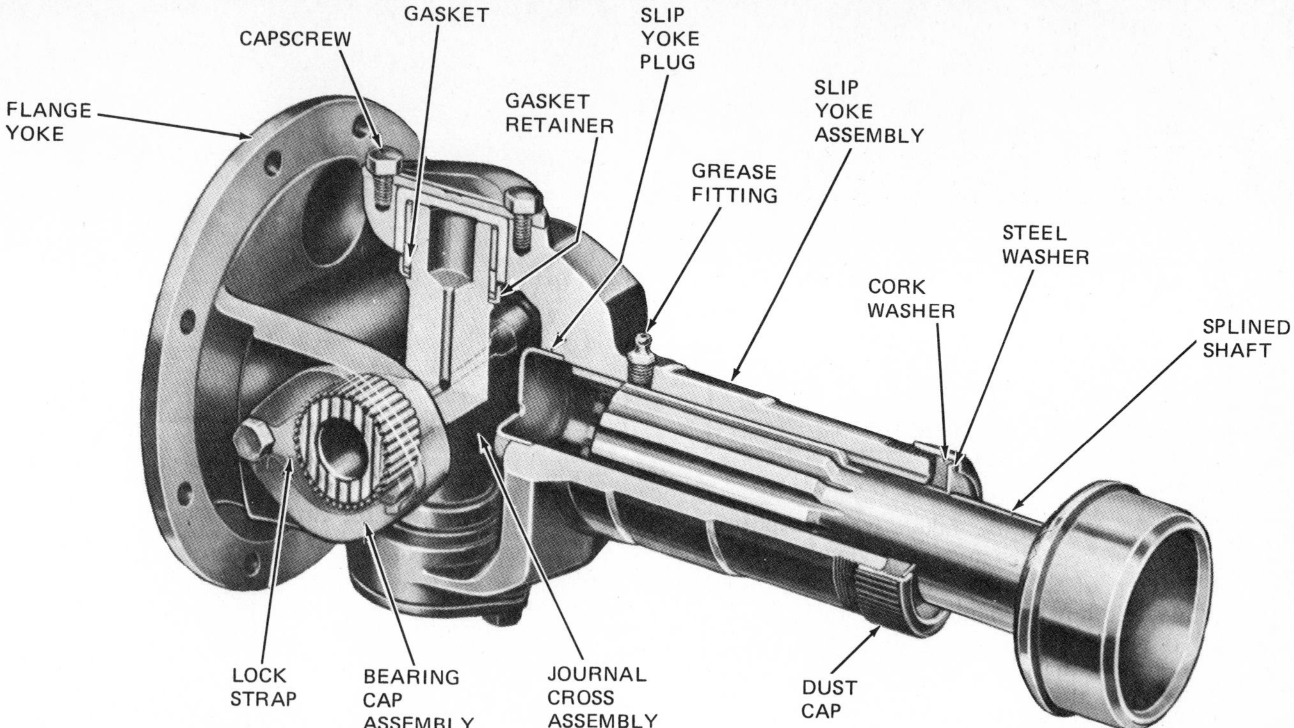

Fig. 13-2 Cutaway view of a flange (bearing cap) joint-type universal joint attached to a slip yoke. (*Mack Canada Inc.*)

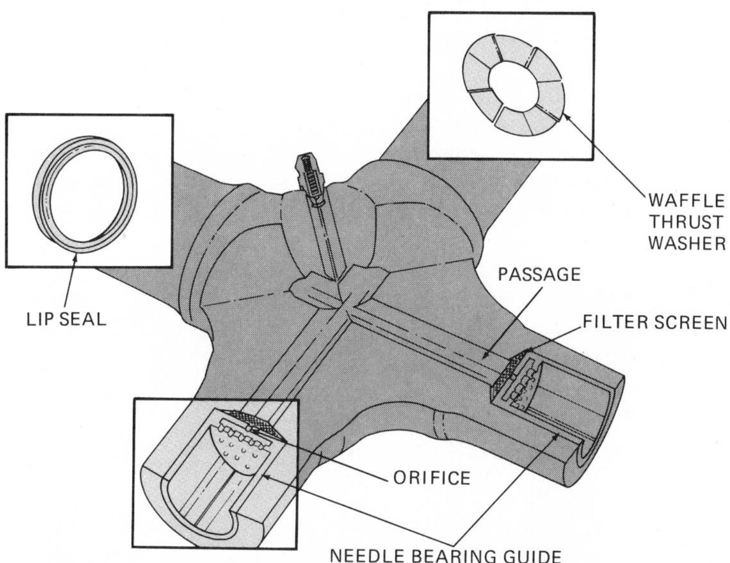

Fig. 13-3 Cutaway view of a special universal joint.

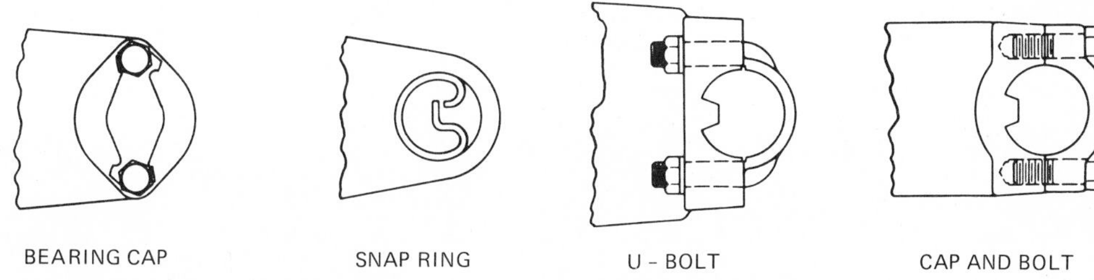

Fig. 13-4 With alternate yoke construction, different methods are used to hold bearing cups.

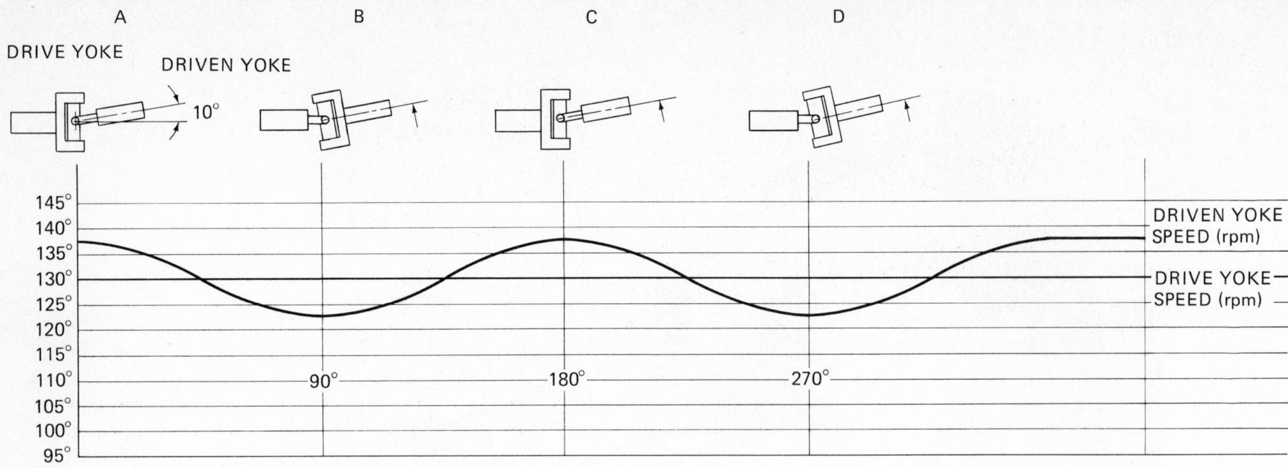

Fig. 13-5 Graph of a standard (Cardan) universal joint during one 360° rotation.

bly, or from the last center (steady) bearing of a three-, four-, or five-joint assembly to the carrier flange. The change of length occurs as a result of the loaded and unloaded condition of the suspension during rebound, and jounce, acceleration and braking, or due to road conditions.

SLIP YOKE DESIGN The yoke of a conventional universal joint is extended to a strong steel tube (see Fig. 13-6). The tube has internal splines which are in mesh with the shaft splines. The left-hand side has a seal and washer which are held to the yoke tube through the dust cap. The splined shaft on which the slip yoke slides is welded to the propeller shaft tube.

NOTE Some splines are coated with polymer nylon (to increase slippage), thereby reducing thrust and shock load under high torque conditions to the transmission bearings, carrier bearings, and shafts.

A recent slip yoke (joint) design known as a roll yoke, is shown in Fig. 13-7. The splined shaft, as well as the ball joint steel tube, have four grooves. Seven steel balls are positioned in each groove and are held in the middle of the splined shaft by coil springs. This design not only has lower sliding friction, but requires less maintenance (lubrication) and has less tendency to seizure under high torque; therefore, less stress is placed on the power train components.

Propeller Shafts Propeller shafts are steel tubes whose diameters and wall thicknesses vary according to shaft length. Either forged yokes are welded to each end of the propeller shaft, or one end may have a splined shaft welded to it. The shafts are designed to be as short in length and as large in diameter as possible, considering the intended application, in order to transmit the drive and braking

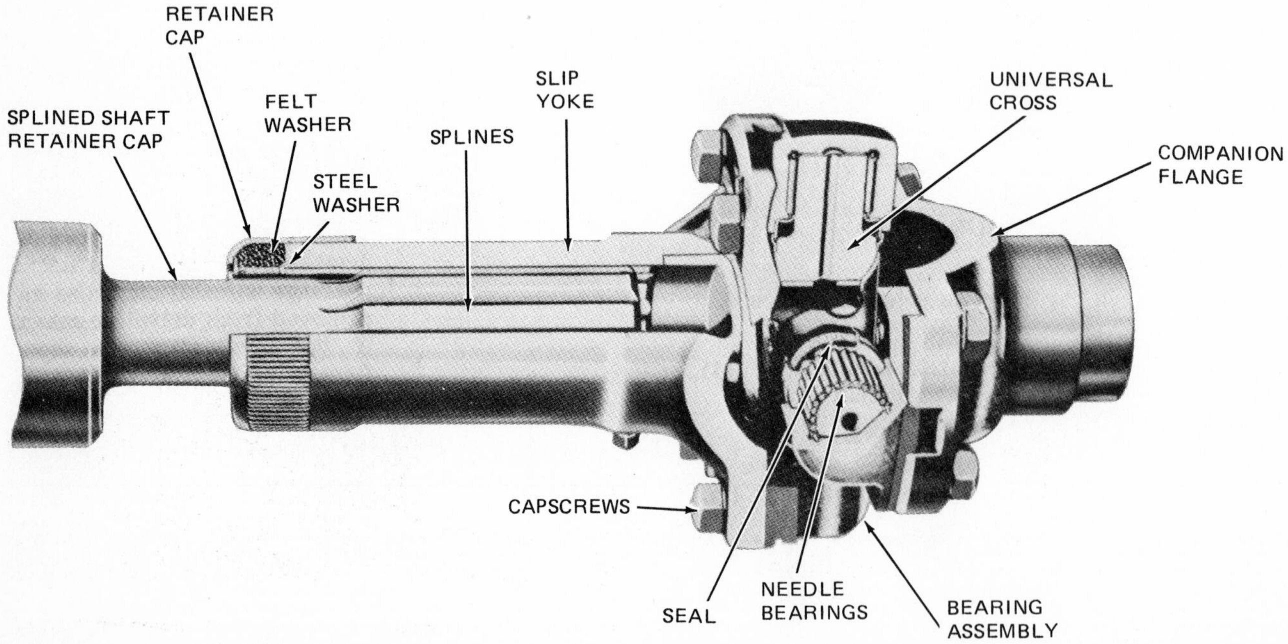

Fig. 13-6 Cutaway view of universal and slip joint assembly. (*Terex Division of General Motors Corporation*)

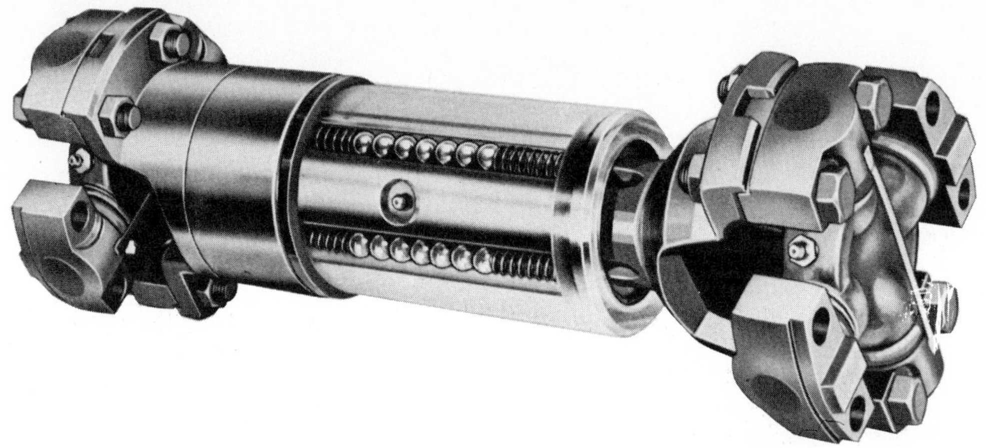

Fig. 13-7 Cutaway view of a roll joint (roll yoke). (*Rockwell International, Automotive Operations, Troy, Michigan*)

torque to the carrier without bending or vibrating. They are also designed to be flexible enough to take up minute speed differences. Propeller shafts having a length of more than 60 in [152.4 cm] could bend and vibrate. For this reason three, four, or five propeller shafts having the same number of universal joints are used. However, the increased number of shafts require one or more center bearings (steady bearings) to secure the shaft end and to maintain alignment.

The center bearing consists of a sealed or nonsealed ball bearing that is mounted in a synthetic rubber support to insulate the shaft from the frame. It is enclosed by a dust seal and a steel mounting bracket which is bolted to the frame crossmember. See Fig. 13-8.

Track- and wheel-type tractors use two universal joints, back to back, to make up a constant velocity joint, because an alignment at such short distance (between the torque converter and transmission) is not always possible. This type (Fig. 13-9) is called a wing universal joint because the bearing flanges are fastened through cap screws to the yoke, and lock wire or lock plates are used to secure the cap screws.

Drive-Line Troubleshooting To extend the life of the drive line, and specifically the lives of the universal joints and slip yokes (joints), two factors are significant—lubrication and alignment. Although you are limited in what you can do with regard to lubrication when the universal joints are sealed, you should nevertheless check them regularly for excessive end play and wear. If worn, they should be replaced; otherwise the universal or slip yoke will cause vibration which could damage the transmission bearings and carrier bearings. Lubricate the universal joints and slip yokes at regular intervals (about every 30,000 mi [48,300 km]) with the recommended grease and in such a way that all old grease is purged out and new grease is visible at every bearing seal. To grease the slip joint, remove the dust cap. Then pump grease into the joint until new grease comes out of the dust cap end. Next,

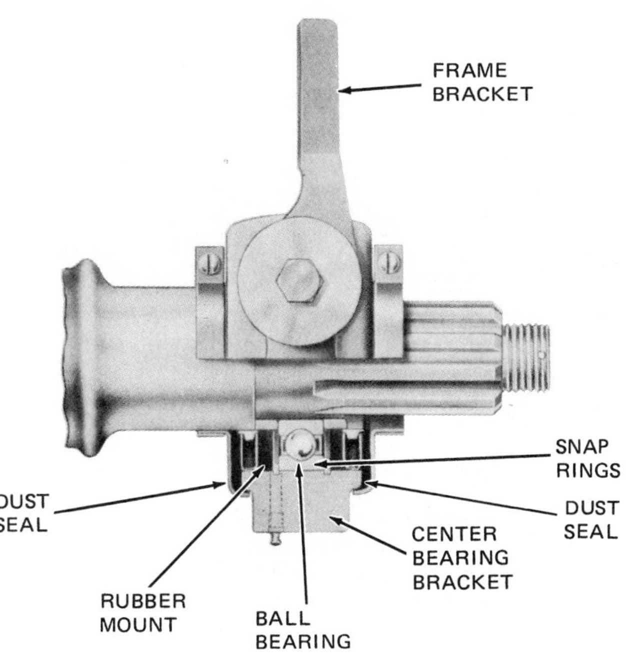

Fig. 13-8 Cutaway view of a center bearing. (*Mack Canada Inc.*)

1. Torque divider output flange
2. Universal joint bearing caps
3. Transmission input flange
4. Capscrews

Fig. 13-9 View of a wing universal joint installed. (*Caterpillar Tractor Co.*)

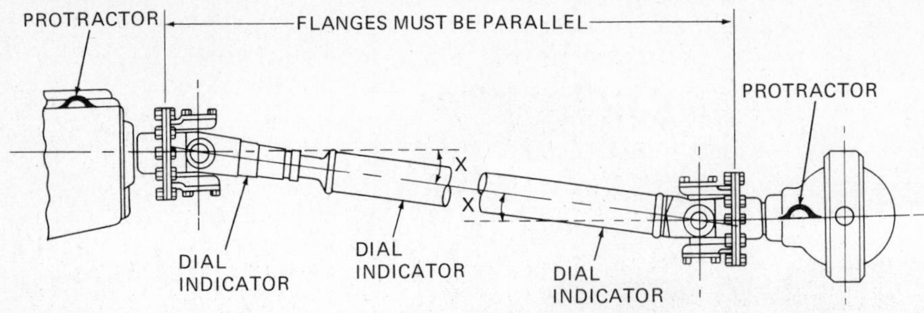

Fig. 13-10 Schematic view of a two-joint assembly.

clean the joint, position the seal and washer, and then replace and firmly tighten the dust cap.

Alignment should be checked and measured when vibration or noise is reported. However, before commencing alignment procedures, make certain that the vibration does not originate elsewhere by testing and checking the entire drive-line suspension. Personally drive the motor vehicle to pinpoint the origin of the noise and/or the cause of vibration. It may come from the carrier or transmission, or from loose transmission mountings. It may be that the emergency brakes were inadvertently applied. You may discover that the brake drum is out of balance, the suspension is damaged or worn, the torque arms or radius rods are worn or bent, the wheel assembly is out of balance, or the tires are worn.

When noise and/or vibration occurs regardless of road speed, the cause could be damaged or worn universal or slip yokes (joints), loose flange nuts, bent or distorted flanges or yokes which cause high propeller shaft runout, and/or high bearing friction. The slip yoke (joint) or universal joint bearing may be seized, the propeller shaft could be bent or damaged, or road dirt (tar) may be sticking to the shaft. It is also possible that the balance weight could have broken off the propeller shaft tube. Any of the above could cause an unbalanced condition.

Angular Alignment Checks and Adjustment Prior to checking the propeller shaft alignment, check the entire power train and suspension as outlined above; make any necessary repairs and then again test drive the motor vehicle. If the vibration and/or noise still persists, check the alignment. The first step is to read the service manual to determine if the alignment checks are to be made under loaded or unloaded conditions. Next, drive the motor vehicle onto a level surface, that is, level from front to rear and from side to side. Do not jack up the axles to achieve he level. Next, check and, if necessary, inflate the tires to the operating pressure and record from the service manual the alignment and the maximum propeller shaft runout specifications.

Two-Joint Assembly Alignment To check alignment of a two-joint assembly (Fig. 13-10), first check runout of the propeller shaft at the transmission end, at the center, and at the carrier end. Thoroughly clean the exterior of the shaft tube at these points with emery cloth. Attach a dial indicator so that you can measure the shaft runout at each point. If the runout at the transmission or carrier ends is above specification, indications are that the universal joint or slip joint is worn, the flanges or yoke bores are distorted, or the flange nut is loose. If the runout at both ends is within specification but the runout at the center of the propeller shaft is higher than specified, it indicates that the propeller shaft tube is bent.

If the runout is within specification, remove the front and rear universal joint in order to remove the propeller shaft; or when the bearing cups are held by lock plates, remove one lock plate from each joint. Next, clean and inspect the transmission flange and carrier flange for looseness and distortion. If they have nicks and burrs which cannot be removed, or if they are twisted or bent, they must be replaced. Next, attach a dial indicator and measure the flange runout.

NOTE One wheel must be jacked up in order to rotate the carrier flange. The runout should not exceed 0.005 in [0.127 mm]; if it does, it should be replaced or straightened.

With a protractor, measure the angle of the crankshaft. [This is done by placing the protractor on a horizontal, clean surface (cylinder head, cylinder block, or transmission). Center the spirit bubble and read from the scale the degree the engine is tilted downward.] Record your reading.

Next, repeat the same procedure on the carrier and record the measurement. If measurements of both the engine and carrier angles are within specification, which is, say, 20° 30′ on the transmission and −2° 15′ on the carrier, the drive-line angles are within specification. If the transmission flange angle is greater than specified, lower the transmission or raise the front end of the engine. If the angle must be increased, raise the transmission or lower the front end of the engine by means of shims, washers, or plates, or by adjusting the mounting bolts. If the carrier angle is too great or too small, tilt the axle housing by installing a greater or smaller wedge between the spring and housing spring saddle.

Measuring the Offset Alignment (Parallelness of the Flanges) To check the parallelness of the flanges, clamp a straightedge to the bottom of the frame rail between the transmission and carrier, and by using a large square, square the straightedge with the frame. Next, plumb the center of the rear axle spindle and the rear edge of the straightedge onto the ground, then measure the distance (Y) (see Fig. 13-11) at each side between the points plumbed on the ground. They should be within 0.062 in [1.5 mm] of each other. If they are not, check for worn shackles, broken center bolts, damaged or worn torque or radius arms, loose spring clamps, or a bent frame.

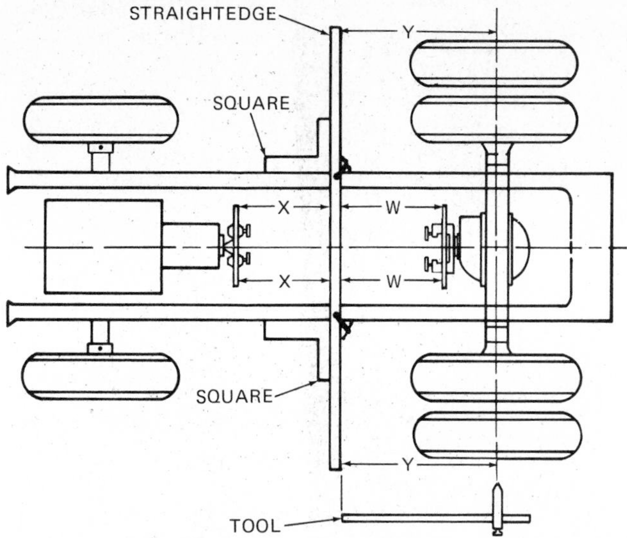

Fig. 13-11 Schematic view of checking the horizontal alignment of yokes. (*Rockwell International, Automotive Operations, Troy, Michigan*)

Next, clamp a square bar (about 36 in [91.44 cm] length) to the flanges, or insert a round steel rod through the yoke bores and secure them so that the ends are an equal distance from the center of the transmission and pinion shaft. Then measure the distances on both sides of W and X (Fig. 13-11). The two measurements should not vary by more than 0.062 in [1.5 mm]. If they are within the 0.062-in [1.5-mm] limit, the flanges are parallel. If not, the transmission and/or suspension must be moved to achieve parallelness. However, first check the suspension for wear or for broken or bent components, and check the frame to determine if it is bent or twisted.

If the vibration still persists after all these tests and adjustments have been made, you can assume the propeller shaft is out of dynamic balance.

Balancing the Propeller Shaft To check the dynamic balance of the propeller shaft, lift the rear axle so that the tires just clear the ground, and then support the axle. With a piece of chalk, mark the front and rear end of the propeller shaft tube. Attach and position a wheel balancer pickup to the propeller shaft, once at the transmission, and then at the carrier end as close as possible to the universal joint. Start the engine, shift the transmission into high gear, and measure the balance condition of the propeller shaft. If the unbalanced point and weight is determined, clamp the required weight to the tube, using a radiator hose clamp as shown in Fig. 13-12, and recheck the balance condition of the propeller shaft.

If you do not have wheel-balancing equipment, you can check and dynamically balance the propeller shaft by the following method: With a hose clamp, clamp a weight (near the spline shaft) to the propeller shaft tube. Use a 1-ounce (oz) [0.028-kg] weight for a large propeller shaft, or a ½-oz [0.014-kg] weight for a small propeller shaft. With the tires off the ground, start the engine, place the transmission in high gear and note the vibration of the propeller shaft. If the vibration has increased the added weight is in the wrong position, or too much weight was added. Stop the engine and reposition or reduce the weight. These steps have to be repeated (by the trial and error method), that is, by repositioning the weight around the shaft until the least vibration is apparent. When the dynamic balance is achieved, weld the weight to the tube, but keep the weld to a minimum; otherwise it could cause an unbalanced condition.

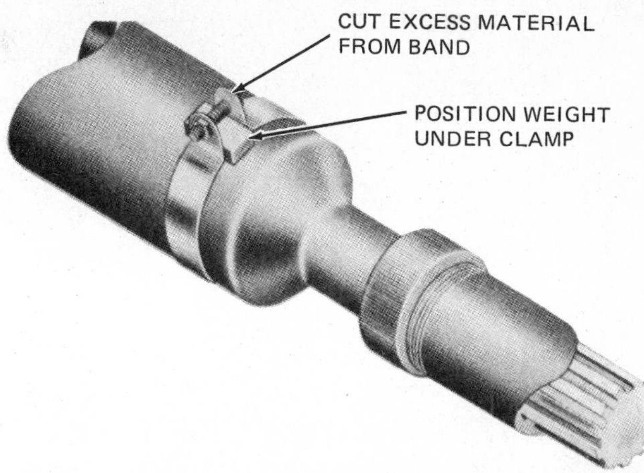

Fig. 13-12 Positioning weight for shaft balancing. (*Mack Canada Inc.*)

You may be able to reduce propeller shaft vibration by disassembling the drive line and rotating one end of the shaft 180° from its phase position. Then reinstall the drive line and test-drive the vehicle. If the vibration has not disappeared, return the propeller shaft to its original phase position and make a dynamic balance of the propeller shaft.

Multipropeller Shaft Angle Checks Checking the drive-line angle of a multipropeller shaft (Fig. 13-13) requires the same preparation as when checking the angles of a two-joint assembly. First, clean the exterior of the propeller shaft; then measure the runout of the drive lines. Next, measure the angles of the transmission (1), the front-rear carrier (3), and the rear-rear carrier (5). Then measure the propeller shaft angles. **NOTE** Turn the drive line so that the yoke bores of the propeller shaft are horizontal before measuring the drive-line angles. This takes the end play out of the universal joint, assuring a correct measurement.

Assume for the moment that the angles you have measured are as follows—the engine or transmission angle (1) is 4°30′ down; the main propeller shaft angle (2) is 7°00′ down; the front carrier (3) is 4°00′ up; the interaxle propeller shaft (4) is 7° down; and the carrier (5) is 4°15′ up. To calculate the working angle of the main propeller shaft (a) at the transmission, subtract the transmission angle from the main propeller shaft angle: 7°00′ − 4°30′ = 2°30′. To calculate the working angle at the front-rear carrier (b), subtract from the main propeller shaft angle the front-rear carrier angle: 7°00′ − 4°00′ = 3°00′. To calculate the interaxle propeller shaft angle at the front-rear carrier (c), subtract the carrier angle from the inter-

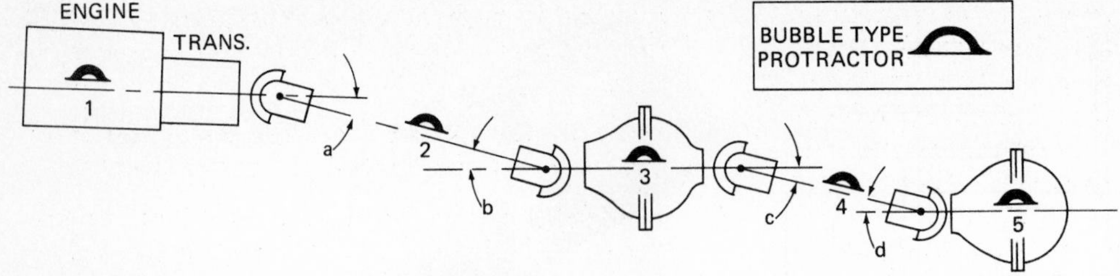

Fig. 13-13 Schematic view of a multipropeller shaft assembly. (*Dana Corporation, Spicer Transmission Division*)

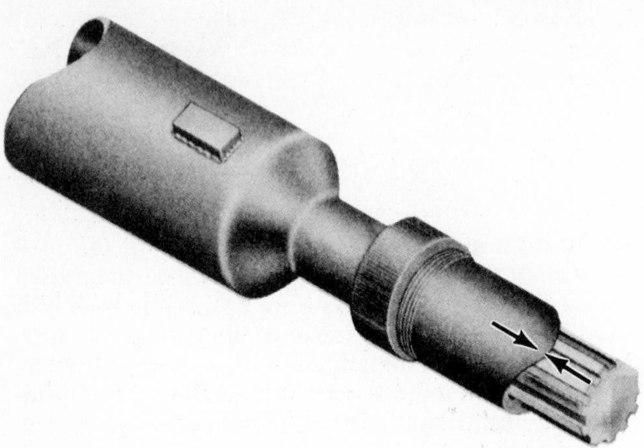

Fig. 13-14 Phase angle marking. (*Mack Canada Inc.*)

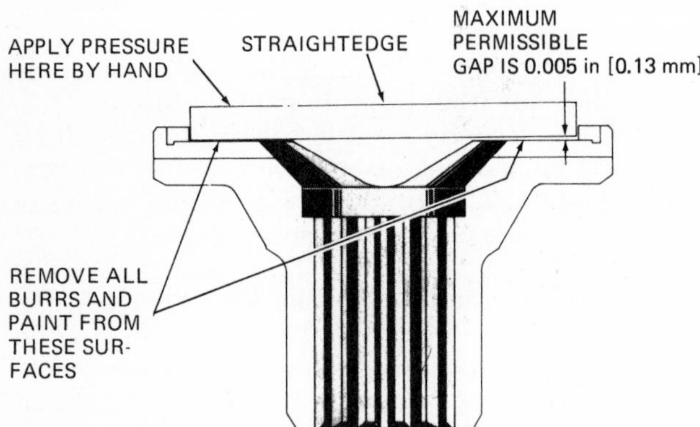

Fig. 13-15 Checking parallelism of flange. (*Terex Division of General Motors Corporation*)

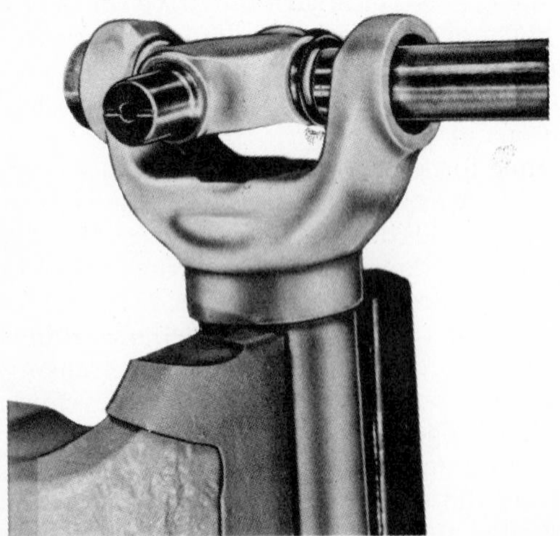

Fig. 13-16 Removing bearing from yoke. (*Terex Division of General Motors Corporation*)

axle shaft angle: 7°00′ − 4°00′ = 3°00′. To calculate the working angle at the rear-rear carrier (d), subtract the rear-rear carrier angle from the interaxle shaft angle: 7°00′ − 4°15′ = 2°45′.

After completing the measurements, compare them with those given in the service manual. If the flange angles of the front-rear and rear-rear carriers have to be changed, again refer to the service manual with regard to the type of suspension and the steps and methods to be used to tilt the front and rear axle in order to achieve the desired flange angles.

Servicing the Drive Line As a general rule, it is easy enough to replace worn drive-line parts without specially designed tools or resorting to specialty shop service. On the other hand, if the propeller shaft tube is damaged or bent, or the yoke bores or flanges are distorted, the entire assembly must be replaced, or perhaps sent to a specialty shop for repair and assembly balancing.

As mentioned, the service is not complex; nevertheless there are several checks, measurements, and precautions to be taken to prevent failure or repeat failure. The most basic measurements and precautionary steps are the following:

1. Remove the battery ground cable.
2. Hang a warning sign on the steering wheel: "MACHINE BEING SERVICED."
3. Check the phase angle markings and, if none are present, scribe the shaft and joints (see Fig. 13-14).
4. When removing long or heavy propeller shafts, support them with rope so they will not fall to the ground and become damaged.
5. If the universal joints have to be partially disassembled in order to remove the drive line, always carefully follow the procedure recommended in the service manual. With masking tape, attach the removed bearing cups to the cross journals. Check the components for damage and wear as you remove them.
6. Check the transmission flange and carrier flange for nicks and burrs, and check for loose nuts. Measure, using a dial indicator, the flange runout.
7. Using a round bar having the same diameter as the bearing cups, measure the alignment of the yoke bores, or use a straightedge and feeler gauge to check the parallelness of the flanges (see Fig. 13-15). When disassembling the universal joints, use a soft punch; otherwise you could damage the yoke bores or distort the flanges or the snap ring grooves. See Fig. 13-16.

8. Inspect the splines for wear and the cross bearing surfaces (trunion journals) for damage. If the journals show any wear, pitting, spalling, or discoloration, they must be replaced. Otherwise remove the needle bearings, clean all parts of the universal joint in solvent, and dry them with compressed air. When reassembling the universal joint, use the recommended grease and the recommended procedure. (Do not use a steel hammer and punch.) If the center bearing rubber is deteriorated or the dust shields are distorted, the assembly must be replaced

NOTE Refer to the service manual to determine the preferred method of holding the dust shield to the shafts.

9. During reinstallation of the drive line, make certain all cap screws or U clamp nuts are torqued to specification and that the phase angle is as specified.

Review Questions

1. What is the purpose of a drive line?
2. Name the essential components of a drive line.
3. When operating a Cardan universal joint at an angle, why is the rotation of the output shaft not uniform?
4. *(a)* What is the function of a slip joint? *(b)* Why, in some cases, are one or more center bearings used?
5. What are the two foremost factors which contribute to reduced drive-line service life?
6. List the problems that could cause vehicle vibration which *(a)* have to do with the drive line, and *(b)* do not have to do with the drive line.
7. Why is it essential to position the motor vehicle on a level surface and to check the inflation pressure of the tires before performing a drive-line adjustment check?
8. If, when measuring the propeller shaft runout, you find the carrier end to be above specification, what component or components might be defective?
9. Describe two methods to check the dynamic balance of a drive line.
10. Calculate the working angle of the propeller shaft when the engine angle is 2°30′ down, the propeller shaft angle is 6° down, and the carrier is 5° up.

Unit 14 Front-and Rear-Drive Units (Carriers)

The purpose of a carrier is to transmit torque to the drive axle. In doing so it (1) multiplies the torque, (2) divides the torque equally onto both drive axles, (3) allows one drive axle to increase and the other to decrease by the same number of revolutions per minute, (4) because of its design, changes the drive angle (torque) by 90°.

Of the different types of carriers for the multitude of on- and off-highway motortrucks, truck-tractors, machines, etc., all except the bevel gear drives used on track-type machines (and winches) perform three of the four functions listed above. The bevel gear drives do not allow the drive axles to rotate at different speeds.

To transmit and multiply the torque coming from the transmission or drive line, and to change the drive torque angle by 90°, carriers of the bevel gear drive sets consisting of the drive pinion and ring gear (also known as the *crown gear*) are used. The gear ratio, which is the torque multiplying factor, varies according to the intended application.

There are four types of gear sets: bevel gear, spiral bevel gear, hypoid bevel gear, and amboid bevel gear sets. (See Fig. 14-1.) On a bevel gear set, both the ring gear and the drive pinion have straight teeth, and when assembled the drive pinion and ring gear center lines are on the same plane. The teeth of the spiral bevel gear set are slightly curved, and the center lines of both gears are also on the same plane. The teeth of a hypoid bevel gear set are curved more than those of a spiral bevel gear set, and the center line of the pinion is lower than the center line of the hypoid ring gear. The teeth of an amboid bevel gear set curve in a direction opposite to that of a hypoid gear set because its drive pinion center line is higher than the center line of the amboid ring gear.

The reason for these different types of bevel gear sets is that *tooth contact area* will be different for gears having teeth of each design. For instance, a bevel gear set and a straight gear set can have a tooth contact area of about 1.33 teeth through which the torque is transmitted; a spiral gear set and a helical

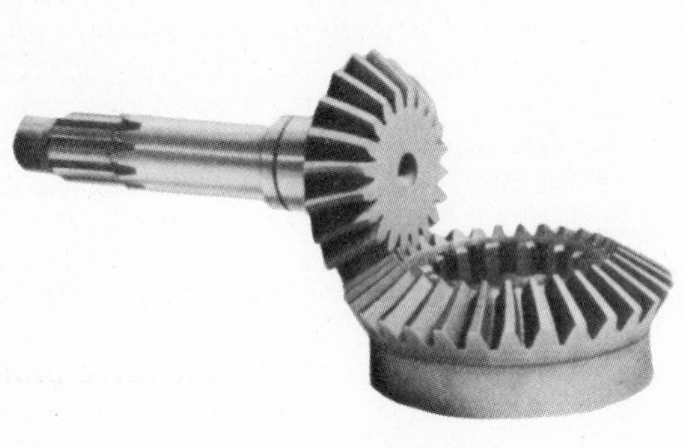

(a) Bevel gear set

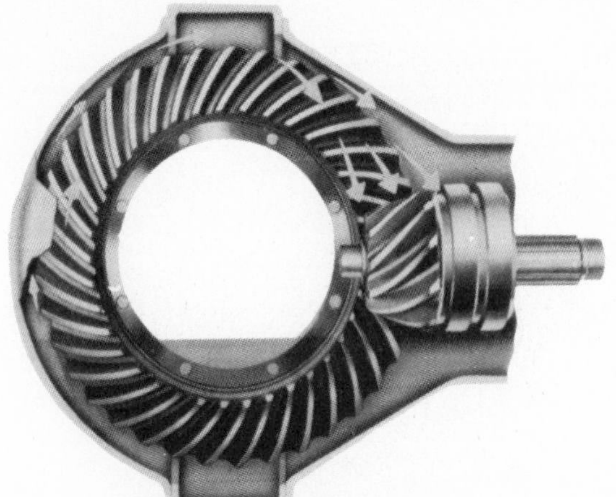

(b) Spiral bevel gear set
NOTE The lube oil is channelled and directed to the pinion bearings and gear mesh point

(c) Hypoid gear set

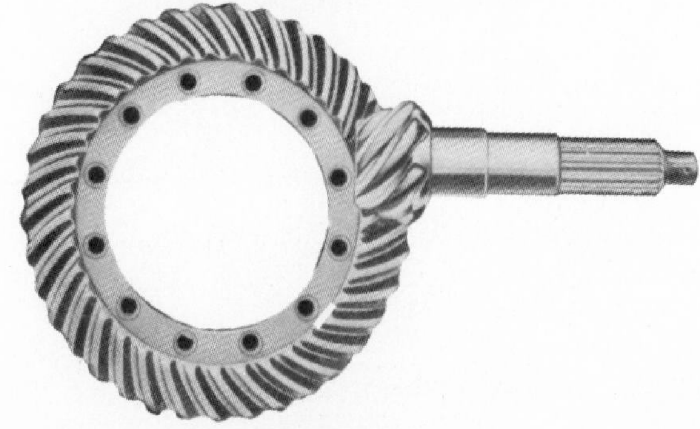

(d) Amboid gear set

Fig. 14-1 Four types of gear sets.

Fig. 14-2 Cutaway view of a powershift transmission and bevel gear. (*Fiat-Allis*)

gear set can have a tooth contact area of about 1.66 teeth; and a hypoid or amboid gear set and a herringbone gear set can have a tooth contact area of about 2.24 teeth. The tooth contact figure varies according to gear and ring gear diameter, increasing with an increase in gear diameter and decreasing with a decrease in gear diameter. **NOTE** Amboid gear sets are used in front and rear carriers to decrease the drive-line angle and minimize the drive-line spline movement, thereby reducing the shock load to the pinion.

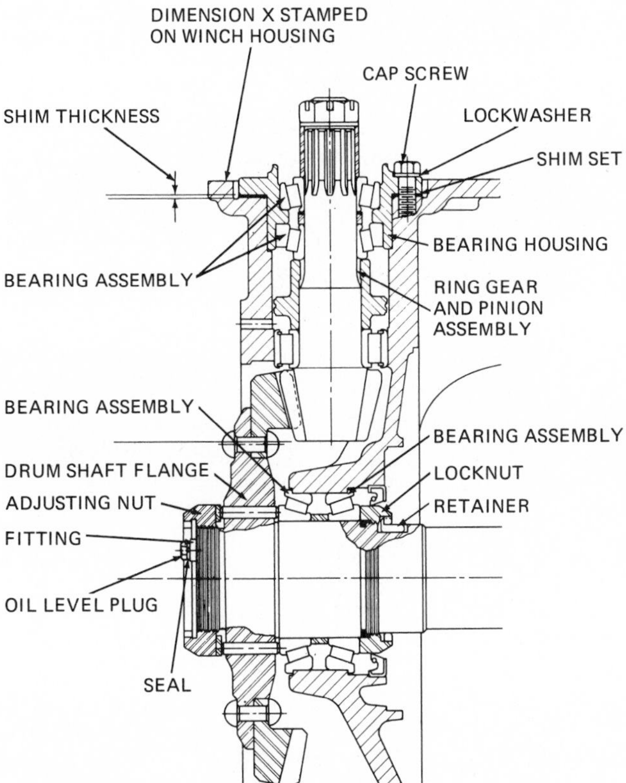

Fig. 14-3 Sectional view of a bevel gear installation (for a winch). (*Gearmatic Co.*)

Drives for Track-Type Machines and Winches Track-type machines or winches can use a bevel gear set or a spiral bevel gear set since their structure permits using a larger diameter ring gear to provide adequate tooth contact. (Note also that production cost of a bevel or spiral-bevel gear set is considerably lower than a hypoid or amboid gear set.) A typical spiral bevel gear drive used on a track-type machine is illustrated in Fig. 14-2 and one used on a winch is shown in Fig. 14-3. On a track-type machine, the pinion may be part of the transmission output shaft or may be splined or keyed to the shaft, and the spiral bevel gear is bolted to the bevel gear shaft. (See material on steering clutches and transmissions earlier in this book.)

In most track-type applications, the drive pinion is fixed (cannot be moved), but to achieve the correct tooth contact the bevel gear shaft can be moved by removing shims (located between the bearing cage and bevel gear housing) from one side and transferring them to the other. See Fig. 14-4.

The winch drive pinion is supported by two sets of tapered roller bearings positioned within the bearing housing (the latter being bolted to the winch housing), and the spiral bevel gear is riveted to the winch drum shaft flange. The shaft is supported at the pinion end by tapered roller bearings and at the other end by a ball bearing, the bearing being located in the bores of the clutch cover and gear cover. The drum shaft, with bearings, can be moved to the left or right by the two adjusting nuts. The drive pinion can be moved in and out by adding or removing shims positioned between the bearing housing flange and the winch housing.

OPERATION When the transmission is in gear and the engine is operating, clockwise rotation (torque)

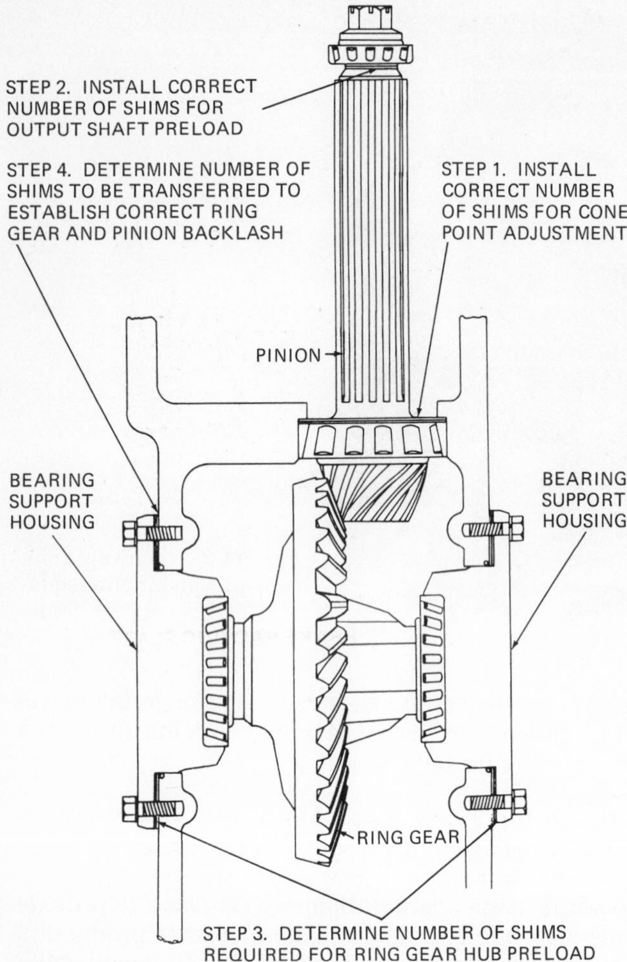

Fig. 14-4 Schematic view of a track-type bevel gear drive and method of adjustment. *(Deere & Company)*

is transmitted to the drive pinion, which in turn drives the ring gear and the bevel gear shaft (or the winch drum shaft), at less rpm than that of the drive pinion, but at greater torque. When both steering clutches are then engaged, both final drive pinions are driven, each at half the torque of the ring gear. For example: Assume the torque at the pinion is 1000 lb·ft [1355 N·m] and the gear set ratio is 3.5:1. The torque at each final drive pinion would be (1000 × 3.5)/2 = 1750 lb·ft [(1355 × 3.5)/2 = 2371.25 N·m]. If, however, one steering clutch is disengaged, all torque is then placed on the other final drive pinion. The torque on this final drive pinion would be 1000 × 3.5 = 3500.0 lb·ft [1355 × 3.5 = 4742.5 N·m].

DRIVE AXLES AND CARRIERS

The carriers used on motortrucks, truck-tractors, loaders, scrapers, etc., are bolted to the rear or front drive axle housing. The carrier is either front- or top-mounted, which means it is vertically or horizontally positioned onto the axle housing. The carriers are classified by a numbering and/or a lettering system which is stamped on the carrier housing, or by an identification tag. The numbering and lettering system identifies the carrier design (type), load capacity, and the drive axle on which it can be used. Carriers may be typed as follows:

1. *Single reduction.* The carrier has only one reduction (the pinion and the ring gear).
2. *Double reduction.* The carrier has a second reduction gear set in addition to the drive pinion and ring gear.
3. *Planetary double reduction.* The carrier has a planetary gear set as the second reduction gear.
4. *Two speed.* These carriers also have a planetary gear set which can be placed in reduction or in direct drive (two speed through the action of a shift mechanism).
5. *Double reduction, two speed.* The carrier has two additional reduction gear sets as well as the drive pinion and ring gear. Either one of the second reduction gear sets can be engaged through a jaw clutch to give the carrier constant double reduction, but at different ratios (two speeds).

The axle housing is usually a one-piece unit (*banjo housing,* so called because of its similarity in appearance to the musical instrument), or it may be a split type. The latter is used on off-highway machines and may comprise two or three pieces bolted to a unit. The one-piece or split axle housing may be made from stamped steel welded or bolted to form a unit, or it may be of cast steel. On a full floating axle, the forged, heat-treated spindle is welded to the ends of the axle housing. On a steering axle housing, the yoke is either bolted or welded to the ends of the housing. If the live axle is of the semifloating design, the inner bore of the axle housing ends are machined to accommodate the drive axle bearings.

A full floating axle means that the axle shafts are relieved of all loads or stress. Its sole purpose is to transmit torque from the carrier side gear to the wheel hubs, or to transmit braking torque to the side gears. The inner end of the axle shaft is loosely splined into the side gear, and the outside end (the flange) is bolted to the wheel hub.

On a semifloating axle, 50 percent of the load and thrust is carried by the outside ends of the axle housing, and 50 percent is carried by the axle shaft. Here, also, the inner end of the axle shaft is loosely splined to the side gears; however, the outside axle shaft end is supported by roller, ball, or tapered roller bearings positioned in the axle housing bores. See Fig. 14-5, which illustrates both full floating and semifloating axles.

Single-Reduction Carriers The single-reduction carriers used on motortrucks or truck-tractors differ from the bevel gear drives used on track-type machines or winches in that (1) the carrier components are attached or fastened to the carrier housing, (2) a differential (Fig. 14-6) consisting of two side gears, two or four side pinion gears, and the spider is used, and (3) the axle shaft ends are loosely splined to the side gears. The gear ratio used on single reduction units can vary from 3.4:1 to 6.67:1.

The purpose of the differential is to act as a torque

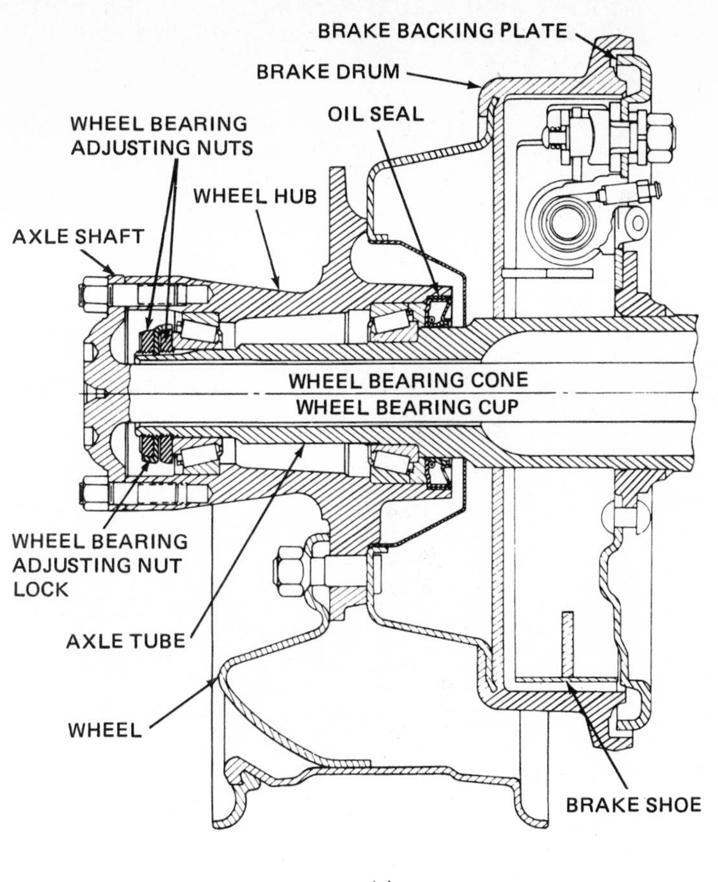

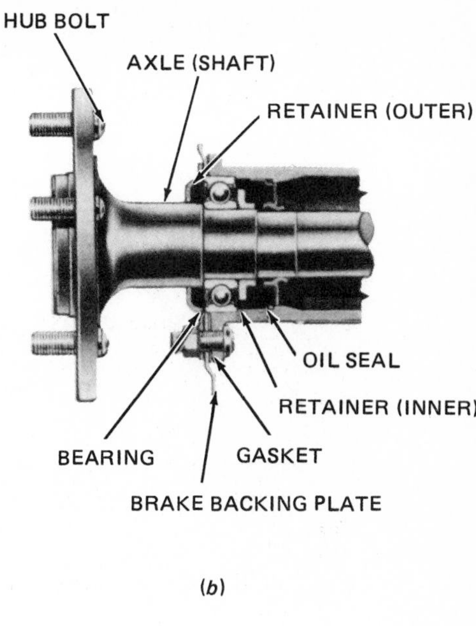

Fig. 14-5 (*a*) Schematic view of full floating axle. (*b*) Schematic view of a semifloating axle.

divider and at all times to transfer equal torque from the differential case, over the spider and the side pinion gears, and onto the side gears, allowing a 2:1 speed variation between the two axle shafts insofar as the rotating speed of the differential case (ring gear) is concerned. The axle shaft speed variation could occur from uneven tire size, from road contour variations (dips or bumps), and when the vehicle makes a turn.

DESIGN The drive pinion is supported by two sets of tapered roller bearings which are held to the pinion bearing cage through the companion flange and a slotted nut. The bearing preload is adjusted through shims or by exchanging the spacer (varying the thickness of the spacer). The drive pinion is sealed through a combined felt and lip-type seal positioned in the seal retainer. The seal assembly is protected through a shield which is pressed onto the companion flange. A roller bearing or a double-row ball bearing is used as the pinion end bearing (pinion pilot bearing) to absorb the side thrust which is placed on the pinion during operation. This reduces tooth contact distortion under high torque.

The differential case (housing) consists of two halves bolted to form a unit, the cap screws being lock-wired. The case is supported by two tapered roller bearings. The bearing cones are press-fitted to the ends of the case, and the bearing cups are positioned in the half-bores (pedestals) of the carrier housing and the bearing caps. Adjusting nuts, one on each side, are used to adjust the position of the differential cage and the differential case bearing preload. The adjustment is locked through the adjusting locks and cotter pins, and the bearing cap cap screws are lock-wired. The ring gear is bolted or riveted to the left-hand half of the differential case in order to rotate it in a forward direction. When the carrier is used on a front axle the ring gear is positioned on the left-hand side.

Inside the differential case, and supported on the spider, are the spider pinion gears. The ends of the spider are supported in the bores of the differential case. Coned pinion thrust washers are placed between the pinion gear and differential case to reduce friction and wear. The side gears are supported in the machined bores of the differential case, and thrust washers are also positioned between the gears and the differential case to reduce friction and wear. The spider pinion gears and side gears are of the bevel gear design. When assembled into the differential case, they possess the necessary backlash and end play between the meshed teeth, washers, gear ends, and housing case. See Fig. 14-7.

OPERATION: STRAIGHT AHEAD, GOOD TRACTION When the motor vehicle transmission is in forward gear, the clockwise rotation (torque) of the drive pinion is transmitted to the ring gear and differential case, rotating the assembly in a forward direction. The differential case transmits the torque onto the spider and from there to the side pinion gears. If the motor

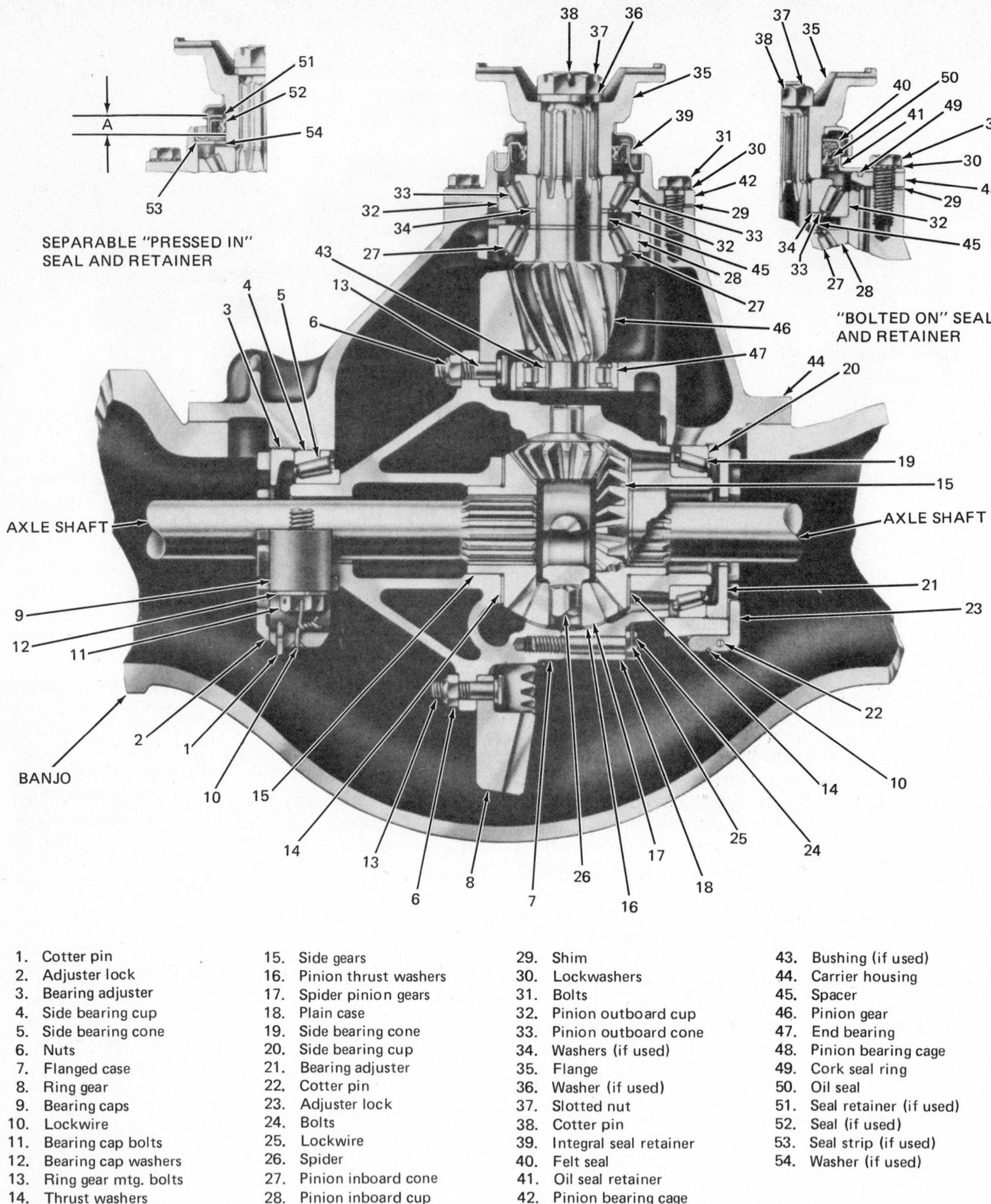

1. Cotter pin
2. Adjuster lock
3. Bearing adjuster
4. Side bearing cup
5. Side bearing cone
6. Nuts
7. Flanged case
8. Ring gear
9. Bearing caps
10. Lockwire
11. Bearing cap bolts
12. Bearing cap washers
13. Ring gear mtg. bolts
14. Thrust washers
15. Side gears
16. Pinion thrust washers
17. Spider pinion gears
18. Plain case
19. Side bearing cone
20. Side bearing cup
21. Bearing adjuster
22. Cotter pin
23. Adjuster lock
24. Bolts
25. Lockwire
26. Spider
27. Pinion inboard cone
28. Pinion inboard cup
29. Shim
30. Lockwashers
31. Bolts
32. Pinion outboard cup
33. Pinion outboard cone
34. Washers (if used)
35. Flange
36. Washer (if used)
37. Slotted nut
38. Cotter pin
39. Integral seal retainer
40. Felt seal
41. Oil seal retainer
42. Pinion bearing cage
43. Bushing (if used)
44. Carrier housing
45. Spacer
46. Pinion gear
47. End bearing
48. Pinion bearing cage
49. Cork seal ring
50. Oil seal
51. Seal retainer (if used)
52. Seal (if used)
53. Seal strip (if used)
54. Washer (if used)

Fig. 14-6 Cutaway view of a typical differential. (*Terex Division of General Motors Corporation*)

vehicle travels in a straight-forward direction, the ground surface is level, the tires have equal rolling radius and equal tire traction, then both axle shafts are forced to rotate with the differential case. The axle shafts rotate with the differential case because the side pinion gears, which are levers having equal lever arms, transfer equal force to the side gears. See Fig. 14-7. **NOTE** The spider pinion gears and side gears do not rotate, but during torque transmission the drive pinion tends to climb up the ring gear, causing the axle housing to rotate and lift the companion flange upward.

The torque placed on the axle housing is absorbed and transferred over the suspension onto the frame.

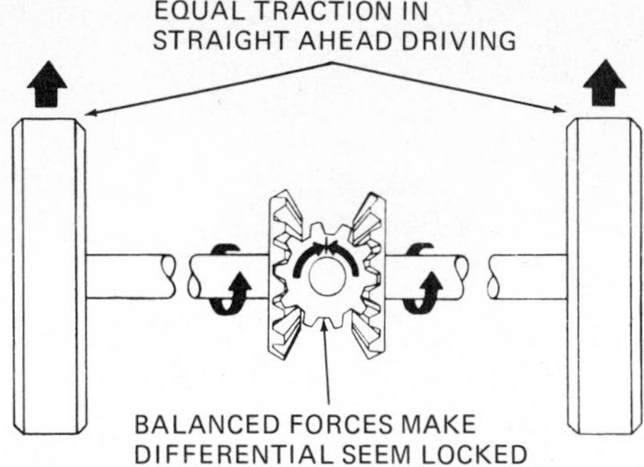

Fig. 14-7 Schematic view of differential when active. (*GMC Truck and Coach Division*)

During deceleration or braking, or when the motor vehicle is driven in reverse, the torque placed on the axle housing is reversed, causing the pinion to climb down the ring gear. This forces the axle housing to rotate in a forward direction and the companion flange to move downward.

OPERATION: TURNS If, however, the motor vehicle is in a turn, say a right-hand turn, and the tires have equal traction and rolling radius, then the outside left-hand tires have a greater turning radius than the inside right-hand tires. The outside tires now have to travel a greater distance, which increases the axle shaft rpm; the inside tires travel a shorter distance, consequently reducing the axle shaft rpm. Say for example, that the speed of the outside tires has increased 10 rpm more than the speed of the differential case because of the increased travel distance of the tire. The outside tire or tires cause the left-hand side gear to rotate in a forward direction 10 rpm more than the differential case and it now, in turn, rotates the spider pinion gears (see Fig. 14-8). The spider pinion gears transfer the rotation to the right-hand side gear. Because the spider pinion gears are idler gears, the speed of the right-hand side gear is reduced by 10 rpm in comparison to the differential case, or by 20 rpm in comparison to the left-hand side gear. **NOTE** The relation of 2:1 remains constant regardless of the number of spider pinion gear and side gear teeth, since the spider pinion gears are idlers.

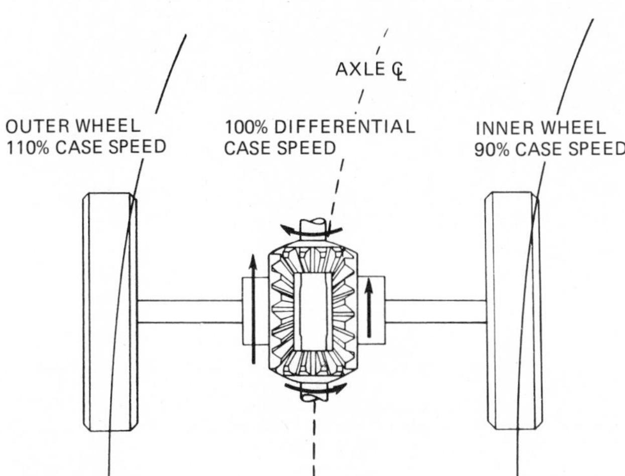

Fig. 14-8 Schematic view of differential action during a right-hand turn. (*GMC Truck and Coach Division*)

OPERATION: LOSS OF TRACTION If one side of the motor vehicle loses tire traction, say for instance that the right-hand side tires are on ice, and only a torque of 10 lb·ft [13.55 N·m] is required to rotate the right-hand wheel then the left-hand side would also have only 10 lb·ft [13.55 N·m]. This torque, however, may be insufficient to drive the motor vehicle in either a forward or reverse direction. The left-hand tires would therefore remain stationary, and the right-hand tires would rotate forward at twice the rpm of the differential case. Because the left-hand side gear is stationary and the differential case rotates (say at 1000 rpm), the spider pinion gears would be forced to rotate on the left-hand side gear, driving the right-hand side gear in a forward drive direction at a speed of 2000 rpm. If the right-hand tires' traction were to increase, the torque on both axle shafts would also increase, and if the torque increased sufficiently to propel the vehicle forward, the rpm of the right-hand tires would instantly decrease by the same number of revolutions per minute by which the left-hand tire rotation increased.

Remember that the torque to each axle shaft is no greater than the torque to the axle shaft having the smallest torque. For this reason, different types of mechanical devices are designed to limit or reduce tire slippage and to transfer all or a portion of the unused torque from the tires that have lost traction to the tires that have retained it (see material on control traction differential). **NOTE** The common single-reduction ratios vary between 3.4:1 to 6.67:1.

Lubrication of the carrier bearings is achieved through the rotation of the differential case, which picks up the oil and directs it through a wiper blade to the differential bearing. The oil is then directed to the pinion bearing cage through an oil collector ring and flows through a passage onto the pinion bearings. See Fig. 14-1*b*.

Two-Speed and Planetary Double-Reduction Carriers These carriers are both very similar in design in that they use a planetary gear set as the second reduction gear set. The major difference between them is that the planetary sun gear on the two-speed carrier can be moved into two positions, whereas on the planetary double-reduction carrier the sun gear is held in one position.

Planetary Double-Reduction Carrier First the planetary double-reduction carrier is discussed.

DESIGN The planetary double-reduction carrier (Fig. 14-9) is much like the single-reduction carrier described in the last section, except in the double-reduction carrier

1. The ring gear and the planetary ring gear are one piece.
2. The carrier gear pins, on which the carrier gears are loosely positioned, are fastened to the differential case.

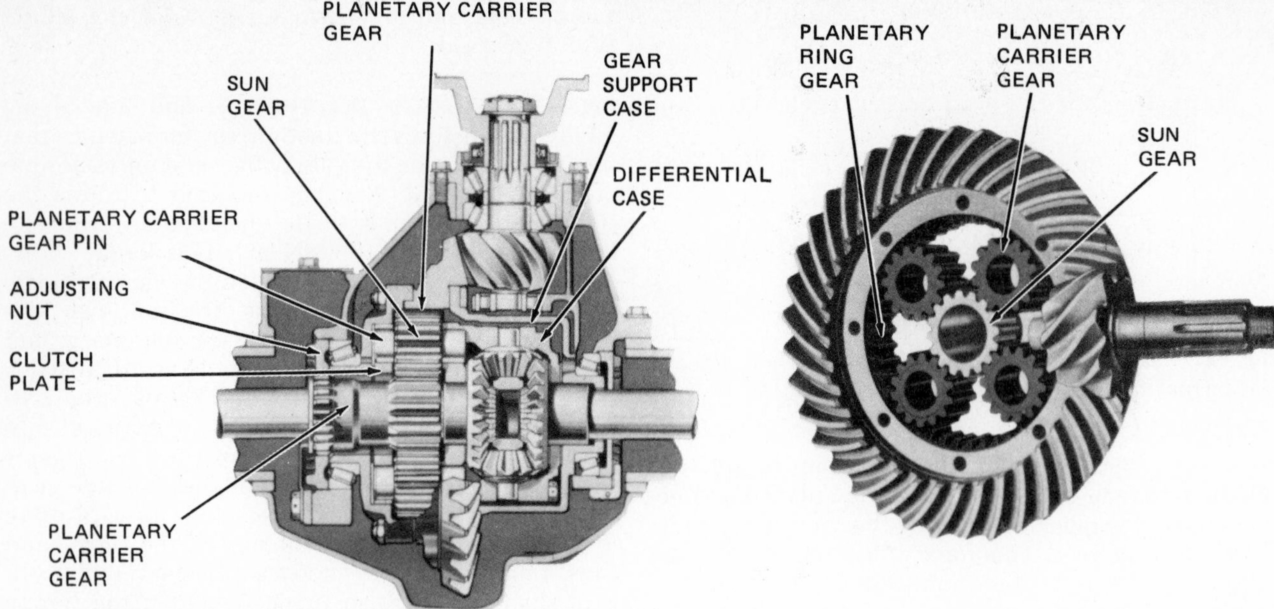

Fig. 14-9 Sectional view of a planetary double-reduction carrier. (*International Harvester Company*)

3. The clutch plate, which supports the carrier gear pins, has internal splines and is bolted to the differential case.
4. The differential case is positioned inside the right-hand half of the gear support case, which in turn is positioned in the counterbore of the ring gear. The left- and right-hand gear support cases are bolted to the ring gear. Each end of the gear support case is supported in the carrier housing by tapered roller bearings.
5. The left-hand adjusting nut has internal splines.
6. The sun gear fits loosely over the left-hand axle shaft. At the left-hand side, it is in mesh with the internal splines of the adjusting nut, and at the right-hand side it is in mesh with the planetary carrier gears.

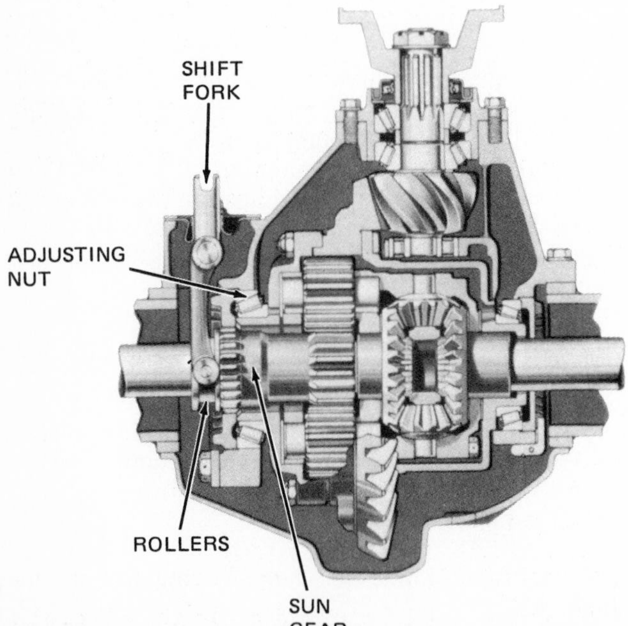

Fig. 14-10 Sectional view of a two-speed carrier. (*International Harvester Company*

OPERATION Rotation (torque) from the drive pinion is transmitted to the ring gear, rotating it and the planetary ring gear in a forward direction. Because the sun gear is held stationary, the planetary ring gear drives the carrier gears around it. This forces the planetary carrier, which is part of the differential case, to rotate in the same direction but at fewer revolutions per minute than the ring gear. The ratio of a double-reduction carrier is usually between 7.59:1 to 8.86:1.

Two-Speed Carrier Differences between a two-speed carrier and a planetary double-reduction carrier are that in the former

1. The sun gear has a groove on the left-hand side in which the shift fork rollers rest.
2. A shift fork, pivot-fastened to the carrier housing, is used (see Fig. 14-10).
3. A seal is required to seal the shift fork.
4. An air shift system, an electric-over-air-shift system, or an electric system is used to shift the sun gear.

AIR SHIFT SYSTEM This system consists of the components shown in Fig. 14-11. The purpose of the semirotating two-speed shift valve is to select a direct ratio or a reduction ratio. The purpose of the air solenoid valve is to direct air to the shift valve when the ignition key is in the ON position. The quick-release valve assures quick air release, and the axle shift unit moves the shift fork. The purpose of the speedometer adapter is to compensate for the speed differential on the speedometer when the two-speed axle is in direct drive.

When the ignition key is in the ON position, the air solenoid valve is deenergized, thereby allowing

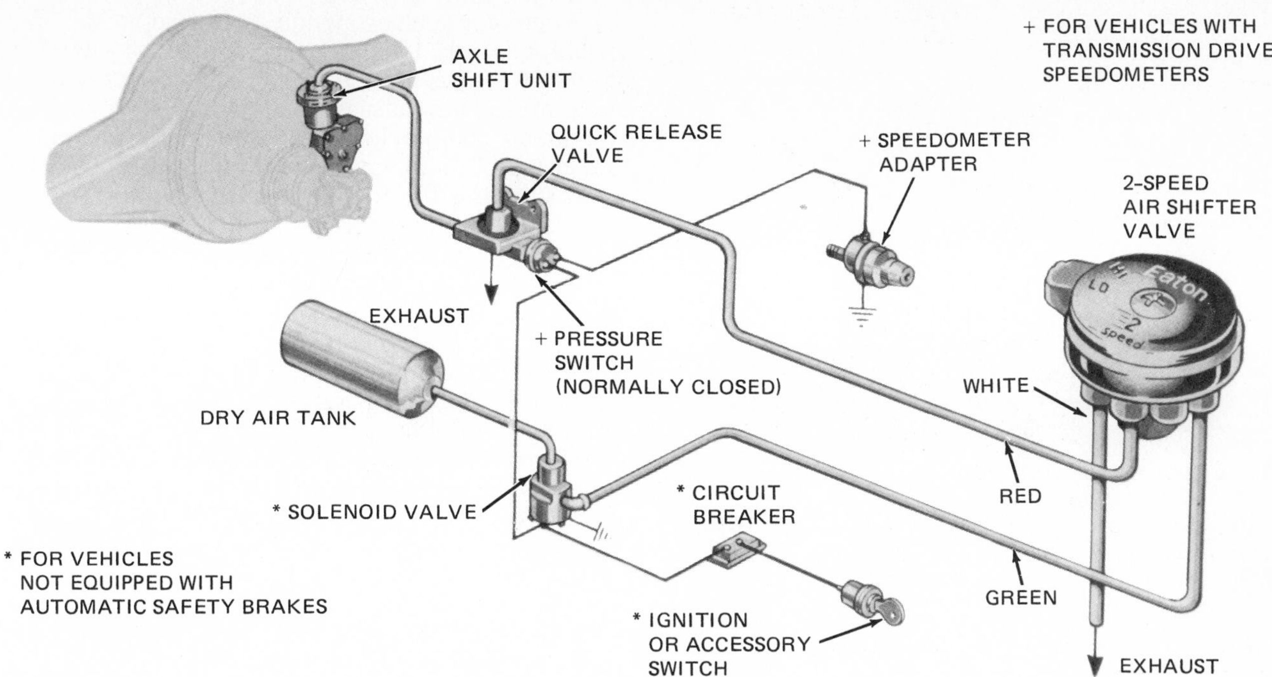

Fig. 14-11 Schematic view of a single-axle air shift system. (*Eaton Corporation*)

air to pass to the two-speed shifter valve. When the two-speed shifter valve is in the low position, the air is blocked to the axle shift unit and the axle shift unit spring force moves the shift fork. This moves the sun gear to the left and locks it into the splines of the adjusting nut. The power flow in this shift condition is exactly the same as that of the planetary double-reduction carrier.

When the engine reaches shift point speed, the operator momentarily disengages the engine clutch or removes his or her foot from the throttle as he or she simultaneously moves the shift knob of the axle shifter valve to the high position. Air is now directed over the quick-release valve onto the piston of the axle shift unit and moves the piston, whereupon the push rod pivots the actuating lever which moves the shift fork and the sun gear. The sun gear slides out of mesh with the adjusting nut splines, and meshes with the splines in the clutch plate. In doing so, two members (the sun gear and the carrier) of the planetary gear sets are locked together, converting the planetary gear set into direct drive, thereby nullifying the planetary gear ratio and making the carrier into a single-reduction unit. A motor vehicle using a two-speed carrier then has one additional speed ratio for each transmission speed ratio. In other words, if the motor vehicle had a five-speed transmission, it would now have a ten-speed unit.

ELECTRIC SHIFT SYSTEM An electric shift consists of the reversible motor, a push/pull control switch, and speedometer adapter (see Fig. 14-12). When the control switch knob is pushed down, current flows over the control switch to terminal D, and through the right-hand motor winding to ground. This rotates the motor and the drive screw in a clockwise direction, thereby causing the drive nuts and the spring winding lever to travel upward and wind the torsion

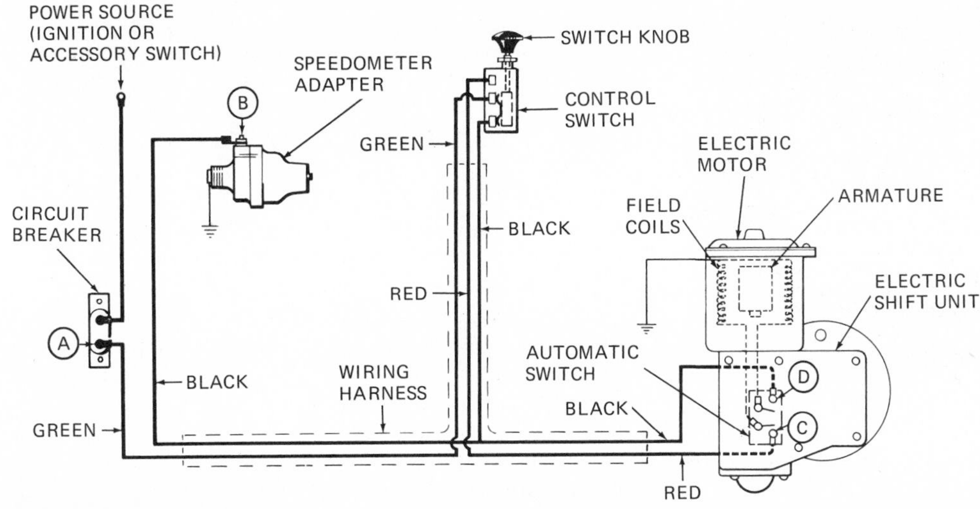

Fig. 14-12 Schematic view of the electric shift system. (*Mack Canada Inc.*)

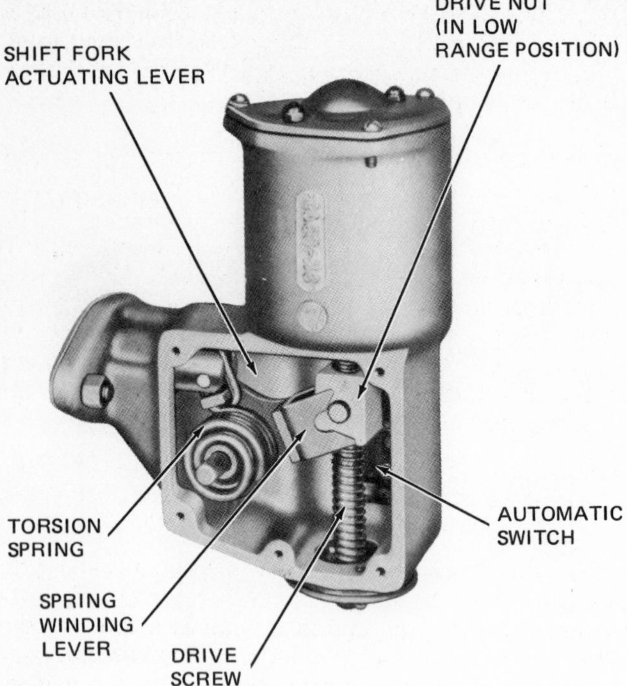

Fig. 14-13 View of the electric shift unit. (*Mack Canada Inc.*)

spring for a shift to low range. The torsion spring moves the shift fork actuating lever, which in turn moves the shift fork and the sun gear so that the latter meshes with the adjusting nut. When the drive nut has traveled a fixed distance, its contact bumper opens a contact set, which in turn opens the motor circuit, stopping the motor. **NOTE** The nut is held by a ball detent spring which prevents it from moving on the drive screw. See Fig. 14-13. (The ball detent is not illustrated.)

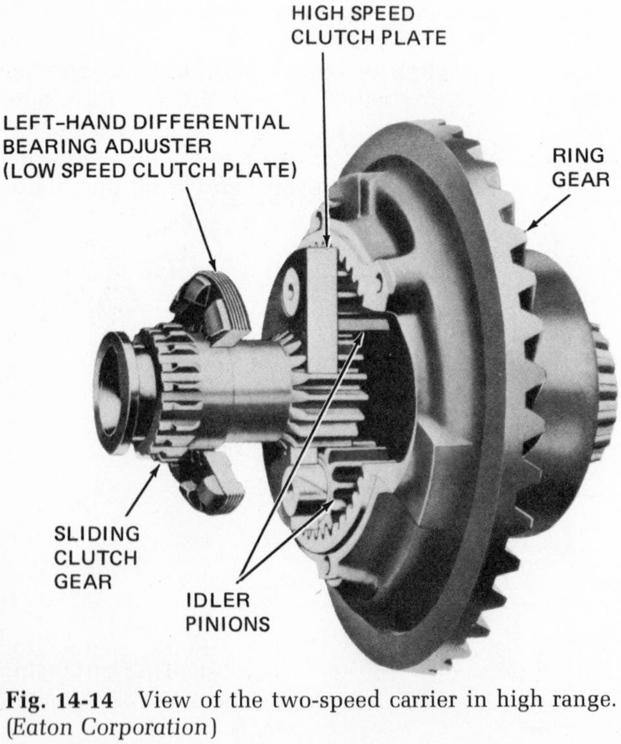

HIGH SPEED
CLUTCH PLATE
LEFT-HAND DIFFERENTIAL
BEARING ADJUSTER
(LOW SPEED CLUTCH PLATE)
RING
GEAR
SLIDING
CLUTCH
GEAR
IDLER
PINIONS

Fig. 14-14 View of the two-speed carrier in high range. (*Eaton Corporation*)

When the control switch is moved to the high position, current flows over the control switch to terminal C, and through the left-hand motor winding to ground. This causes the motor and drive screw to rotate in a counterclockwise direction, which moves the drive nut and spring winding lever downward, thus winding the torsion spring counterclockwise for a shift into high range (see Fig. 14-14).

Double-Reduction Carrier A double-reduction carrier is used to increase the torque to the drive axles. The gear ratio of this unit can vary from 4.41:1 to 9.76:1, depending on the intended application of the motor vehicle. Moreover, it may be of the front-mounted or top-mounted design. Commonly the first drive reduction set (pinion and ring gear) is comprised of spiral bevel gears, and the second set is of the helical gear design. Both gear sets and the drive pinion are supported by tapered roller bearings.

DESIGN There are the following differences between single-reduction and double-reduction carriers. On the double reduction carrier:

1. The bevel gear is on the left-hand side of the drive pinion to permit the differential case to be driven in a forward direction.
2. The helical drive gear forms part of the bevel gear shaft and has the bevel gear keyed to it.
3. The bearing preload and ring gear adjustment is achieved through shims placed between the bearing cage and the carrier housing.
4. The helical driven gear is bolted to the left-hand half of the differential case and the two halves of the differential case are bolted together.
5. The spider pinion gears have bushings. See Fig. 14-15.

Double-Reduction, Two-Speed Carrier This type of carrier serves primarily the same purpose as do those of the double-reduction design but it has two

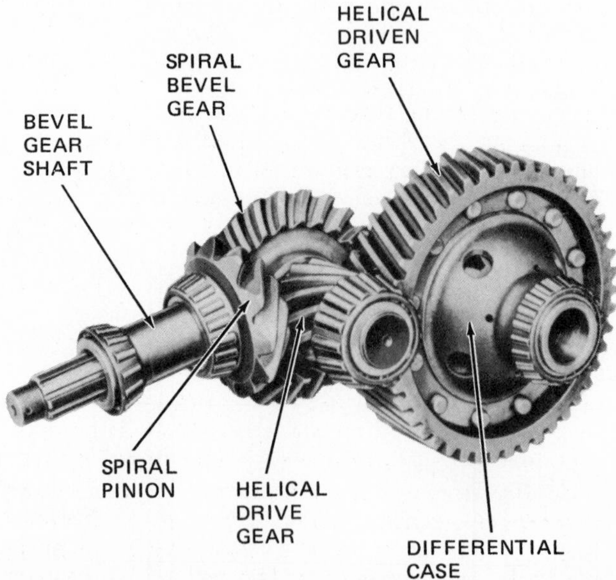

Fig. 14-15 View of a double-reduction carrier. (*International Harvester Company*)

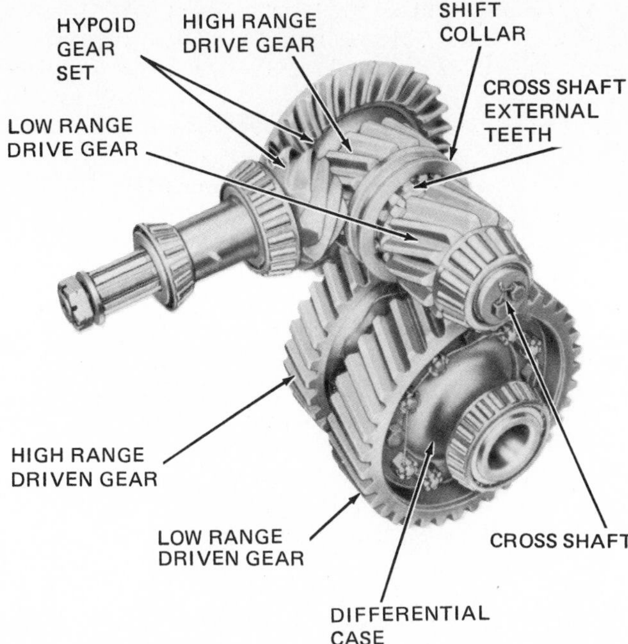

Fig. 14-16 View of a double-reduction, two-speed carrier gear train. (*International Harvester Company*)

secondary reduction gear sets, either one of which can be selected to give the motor vehicle one additional speed ratio for each transmission speed ratio. The first reduction gear set (pinion and ring gear) is of the spiral or hypoid gear design. It is available with gear ratios of 2.91:1 to 3.81:1. The high- and low-speed gear sets are of the helical gear design, with available low-speed ratios of 2.99:1 to 5.36:1 and high-speed ratios of 1.47:1 to 3.29:1. This could give the carriers an overall ratio in low of 5.90:1 to 9.17:1, and an overall ratio in high of 4.38:1 to 7.10:1.

The varying available ratios lend such versatility to the double-reduction, two-speed carrier that it can be used on many single-axle units. See Fig. 14-16.

DESIGN (TOP-MOUNTED UNIT) In the center of the cross shaft (Fig. 14-17) are external gear teeth over which the shift collar is positioned. Three spring-loaded detent pins are positioned in the bore of the cross shaft, thereby holding the shift collar engaged. The low- and high-range helical drive gears (which are free to rotate on the cross shaft) have external (side) clutch teeth (see Fig. 14-17). The hypoid bevel gear is pressed and keyed to the left-hand side of the cross shaft. The bearing cones, which are pressed onto the cross shaft, are held in position by the plate that is bolted to the shaft ends. The shift fork rests in the groove of the shift collar, and the shift shaft is connected, over a bell crank, to the electric shift unit (which is similar in design to the shift unit used on a plain two-speed carrier). The shift fork travel is adjusted through the set screw. **NOTE** The high/low reduction shift clutch has no neutral—the clutch is engaged with either the low-range drive gear or the high-range drive gear. The differential case consists of two halves. The high-reduction drive gear is bolted to the left-hand half, and the low-reduction drive gear is bolted to the right. The differential case bearings as well as the drive-gear–to–driven-gear alignment are adjusted through the adjusting nut (ring) (not shown in Fig. 14-17).

OPERATION Assume that the operator has shifted the second reduction gear set to low range. This moves the clutch collar over the external clutch teeth on the low-range drive gear, thereby clutching the low-range drive gear to the cross shaft. The clockwise rotation (torque) from the drive pinion is transmitted to the ring gear, reversing the rotation of the cross shaft and low-range drive gear. The low-range drive gear then drives the low-range driven gear and the differential case in a forward direction.

NOTE The high-range driven gear drives the high-range drive gear, which freely rotates on the cross shaft.

To shift from low into high range after the engine reaches shift speed, the operator momentarily disengages the engine clutch or moves a foot off the throttle. At the same time he or she moves the control switch to high. The motor is energized, the drive screw turns, and the nut and the torsion spring lever are moved to the high-range position. The torsion spring then moves the shift rail, which pivots the bell crank and moves the shift shaft, shift fork, and clutch collar to the left. This engages the clutch collar with the external teeth on the high-range drive gear and clutches the gear to the cross shaft. See Fig. 14-18.

The rotation (torque) is now transmitted from the high-range drive gear to the high-range driven gear and to the differential case, and the low-range driven gear drives the low-range drive gear, which rotates freely on the cross shaft.

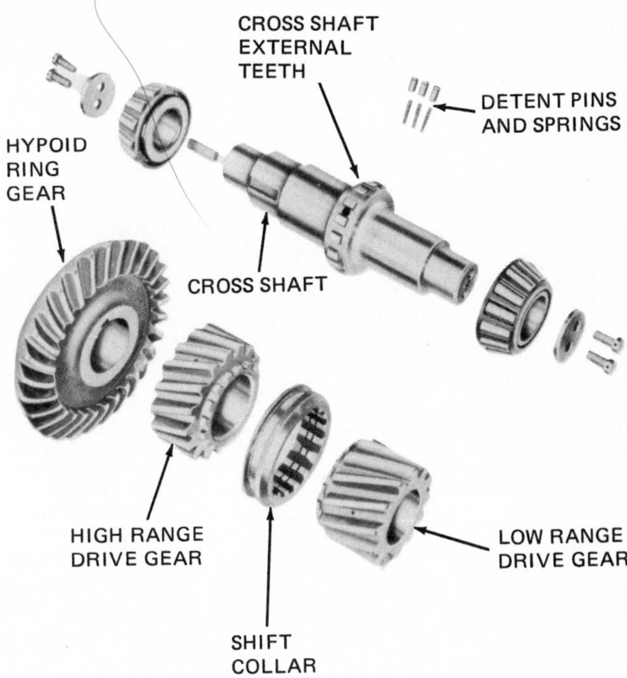

Fig. 14-17 View of the cross shaft (double-reduction, two-speed carrier gear train). (*International Harvester Company*)

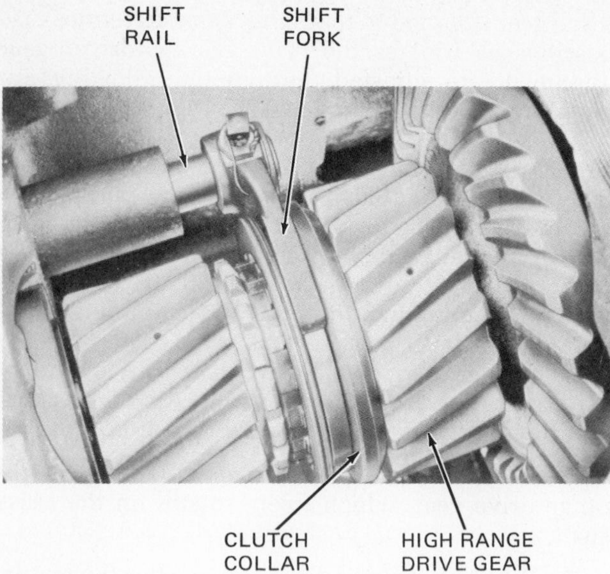

Fig. 14-18 View of clutch engaged with high-range drive gear. (*International Harvester Comnpany*)

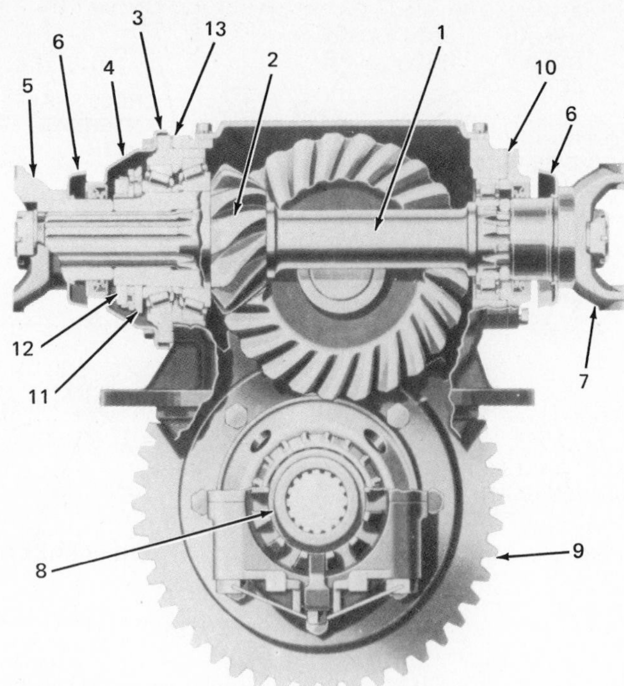

1. Through shaft
2. Pinion
3. Drive pinion bearing cage
4. Drive pinion bearing cage cover
5. Input yoke
6. Slinger
7. Output yoke
8. Cross shaft
9. Driven gear
10. Through–shaft rear bearing cover
11. Adjusting nut
12. Locknut
13. Shim pack

Fig. 14-19 Sectional view of a double-reduction, thru-drive, front-rear carrier. (*International Harvester Company*)

TANDEM DRIVE AXLE CARRIERS

The carrier used in the rear-rear axle of a tandem drive axle could be single reduction, two speed, planetary double reduction, or double reduction top- or front-mounted. **NOTE** Double-reduction, two-speed carriers are not designed for tandem drive axles. Front-rear carriers are slightly different in design since they must transmit the rotation from the front-rear carrier to the rear-rear carrier.

Two basic front-rear axle carrier types are manufactured—one for off-highway motortrucks and truck-tractors (see Fig. 14-19) and the other for on-highway motortrucks and truck-tractors (see Fig. 14-20). The carrier shown in Fig. 14-19 is of the thru-drive design. A thru-drive is where the rotation from the drive line is placed onto the thru-shaft and from the thru-shaft onto the rear-rear axle pinion. The pinion is keyed to the thru-shaft and the shaft is supported on each end by a tapered roller bearing (or as shown in the illustration). The bearing preload is achieved through the adjusting nut, and drive pinion adjustment is achieved through shims placed between the bearing cage and carrier housing. A drive line connects the thru-shaft flange or yoke with the rear-rear axle drive pinion flange or yoke. Therefore when the thru-shaft is driven, the rear-rear axle drive pinion is driven at the same rpm. This type of thru-drive has one advantage and some disadvantages. Its advantage is that there is no torque loss when the front-rear or rear-rear axle tires lose traction—full torque is placed on the carrier which has the tires with the most traction. The drawbacks are the following: (1) During the periods that the rolling radiuses on the front-rear and rear-rear axles are not equal, wear on the traction tires is increased. (2) Because the two carrier drive pinions always rotate at the same rpm, the motor vehicle does not steer and handle as easily as motor vehicles having an interaxle differential. (3) When one axle is lifted or falls due to road surface conditions, the tires on that axle slide over the surface in order to keep up with the axle on the level surface. In other words, the front-rear axle and the rear-rear axle shafts rarely turn at the same speed.

Interaxle Differentials On-highway motortrucks and truck-tractors also use thru-drive front-rear axle carriers. However most on-highway motortrucks and truck-tractors use a power divider (interaxle differential) which is bolted to the front carrier. The purpose of the power divider is to provide an interaxle differential, that is, to divide the torque equally between the front-rear and rear-rear axle carriers, thus allowing either drive pinion to increase or decrease in rpm. The interaxle differential is designed and operates as a conventional differential, thereby minimizing tire wear, maximizing handling (steering stability), and reducing rolling resistance.

DESIGN The front-rear axle carrier of a single-reduction, tandem-drive, interaxle differential is shown in Fig. 14-20. The pinion is supported by two sets of tapered roller bearings positioned in the bearing cage, as well as through the pilot bearing positioned in the carrier housing. The helical drive gear is splined to the pinion shaft, and the bearing preload is adjusted by changing the spacer thickness.

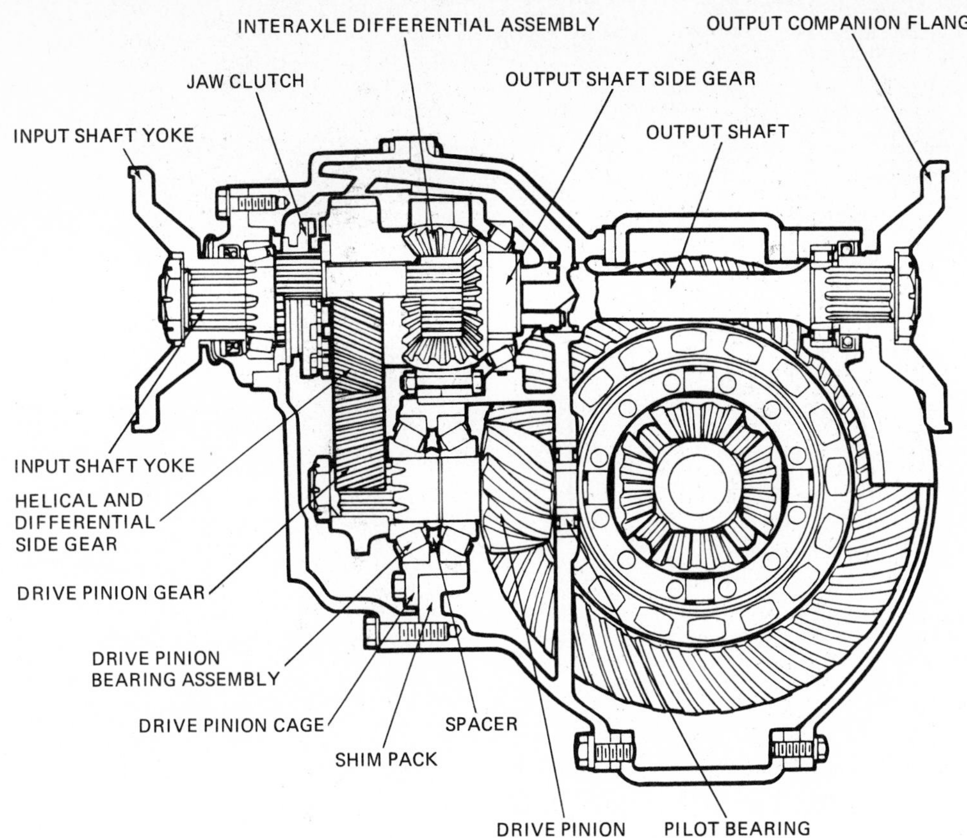

Fig. 14-20 Sectional view of a single-reduction, front-rear carrier with interaxle differential. (*International Harvester Company*)

The bearings, driven gear, and drive pinion are held to the pinion bearing cage by the pinion nut. The bearing cage is bolted to the carrier housing, and shims (located between the cage and housing) are used to move the pinion in or out. The input shaft is splined in the center and at both ends. The companion flange is splined to the left-hand side of the input shaft. The sliding (jaw) clutch is loosely splined to the center splines. The shift fork rests in the groove of the clutch, which is of the jaw-clutch design. The side gear and the helical drive gear form a single unit supported on the shaft by bushings.

NOTE The helical drive gear has the other half of the jaw clutch machined to it.

The interaxle differential assembly is splined to the input shaft's right-hand side splines. It consists of two equal interaxle differential halves, one spider, and four spider pinion gears. The input shaft is supported on the left by a tapered roller bearing, on the right by a tapered roller bearing located on the output shaft side gear, and by a bushing on the output shaft. The bearing preload is adjusted by placing shims between the bearing cover and carrier housing. A sheet metal shield fastened to the companion flange protects the (combined) felt- and lip-type seal. The output shaft is splined on both ends. The output shaft companion flange is splined to its right-hand side and is secured through a nut. The right-hand side gear is splined to the output shaft's left-hand side and is supported by a tapered roller bearing. The right-hand input shaft end is additionally supported on the output shaft through a bushing. **NOTE** The ring gear is positioned on the left-hand side of the pinion in order to drive the ring gear in a forward direction.

LUBRICATION Some carriers have a positive lubrication system to provide pressurized lubrication to the input shaft components. The gear pump is bolted to the left-hand side of the carrier housing, and its driven gear is in mesh with the input shaft splines. The inlet and outlet ports of the pump are internally connected through ports leading to the sump and oil filter. When the input shaft is rotated, the gear pump supplies oil over the oil filter to the metering orifice and through the differential case window into the differential (not shown in Fig. 14-20). Oil is forced through distributing channels to other vital parts which need lubrication (see Fig. 14-21).

OPERATION Assume that the tires of the front-rear axle and the tires of the rear-rear axle have the same rolling radius, that the vehicle is traveling on a flat surface, and that the interaxle differential clutch is disengaged. Clockwise rotation (torque) is transmitted onto the input shaft and the differential case, because under this condition equal torque is required to drive the front-rear and the rear-rear drive pinions. The spider pinion gear teeth are in mesh with, and apply equal force to the side gears, and consequently both side gears are forced to rotate with the interaxle differential case. Now the right-hand side gear drives the output shaft and the rear-rear axle pinion, and the left-hand side gear drives the helical driven gear and the front-rear axle drive pinion. Suppose the torque input is 1000 lb·ft [1355 N·m] and the carrier gear ratio is 3.5:1; then each

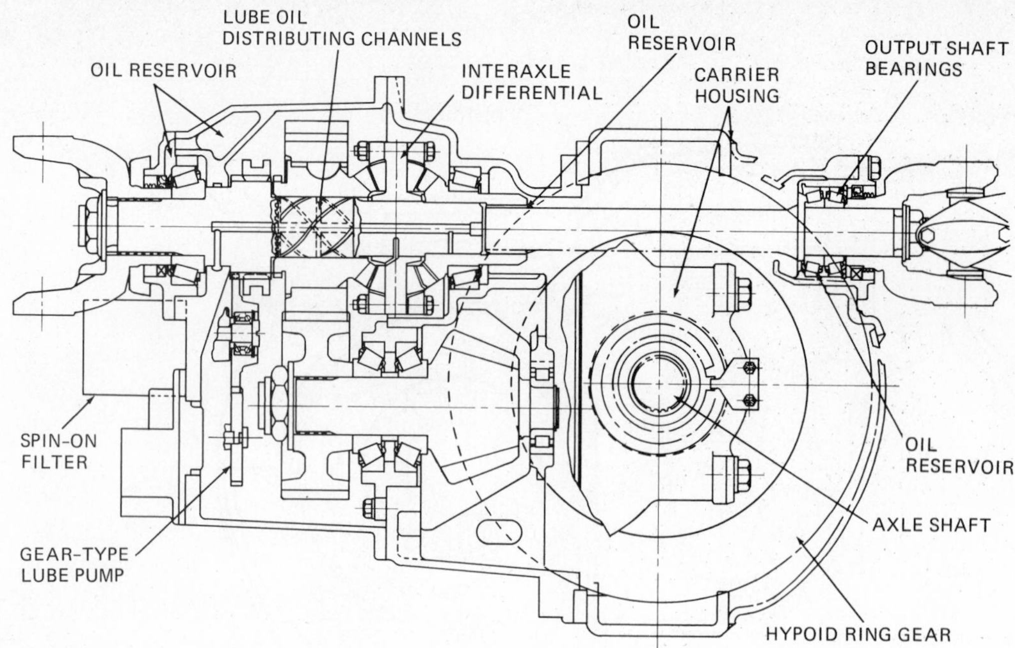

Fig. 14-21 Schematic view of the pressurized lubrication system. *(Ford Motor Company)*

carrier has an input torque of 500 lb·ft [677.5 N·m], and each axle shaft would have a torque of 815 lb·ft [1185.62 N·m]: (500 × 3.5)/2 = 815 lb·ft [(677.5 × 3.5)/2 = 1185.62 N·m] (see Fig. 14-22).

If the tires on both sides of one axle (say the front-rear) have a greater rolling radius, or they climb momentarily over a surface bump, the following action takes place within the interaxle differential. The front-rear carrier drive pinion is forced to rotate faster than the rear-rear drive pinion because of the increased tire rotation. The increased rotation is transmitted to the left-hand side gear, over the spider pinion gears, to the right-hand side gear, output shaft, and rear-rear axle drive pinion, causing the rear-rear drive pinion to reduce rpm. This prevents tire skidding and tire wear, and improves steering and handling. **NOTE** If only the tires on say, the left-hand side have a greater rolling radius or only the tires on the left-hand side climb over a bump, then the carrier differential compensates for the speed variation. If, however, the tires of one axle shaft (one set of tires) were to lose some traction, not only would *they* lose torque, but so would the remaining three axle shafts. When the tires of one axle shaft are off the ground (say the left-hand rear-rear axle tires), the motor vehicle tends to come to a stop because all torque is wasted by the axle shaft whose tires are off the ground. To overcome this condition, the operator momentarily disengages the engine clutch or reduces engine rpm and at the same time directs air onto the lockout piston. The piston moves the piston rod, the shift fork, and the jaw clutch. The jaw clutch engages with the helical drive gear (which is part of the left-hand side gear). This clutches the left-hand side gear to the input shaft and differential case, thereby preventing interaxle differential action. This converts the front-rear carrier to a thru-drive. As a result all torque is directed to the front-rear axle drive pinion.

Mack Interaxle Power Dividers The power divider used on Mack front-rear axle carriers (see Fig. 14-23) is a torque proportional differential. It serves the same purpose as an interaxle differential, but, unlike the conventional type, it can vary the distribution of torque. If one or both sets of tires of one axle lose traction, it is designed to automatically redirect up to 75 percent of the total available transmission output torque to the carrier (axles) with better tire traction. This also protects the axle shaft from becoming twisted or broken.

DESIGN The interaxle power divider is bolted to the top-mounted double-reduction carrier housing. The power divider lockout housing is bolted to the interaxle power divider housing. The driving cage is supported in the lockout housing by a double row of ball bearings. Inserted into the two staggered rows of the slotted bores in the cage ring are 24 short radial (driving) plungers (wedges), which are free to slide a short distance inward and outward. The companion flange is splined to the splined end of the driving cage.

When a power divider lockout is used, the internally splined sliding clutch is loosely splined to the driving cage splines, and the shift fork rests in the clutch groove. The shift fork is fastened to the shift rod (which is part of the air actuator). The male half of the clutch is machined at the right-hand end, and the female half is machined to the left-hand end of the outer cam. The inner cam is splined to the through shaft. Each row of cams has six lobes offset from one another. The through shaft passes through the hollow bevel pinion and is supported by a pilot bearing positioned in the outer cam. The universal joint flange is splined to the right-hand side of the shaft. The hollow bevel pinion is supported in the divider housing by two sets of tapered roller bearings, and the outer cam is splined to it.

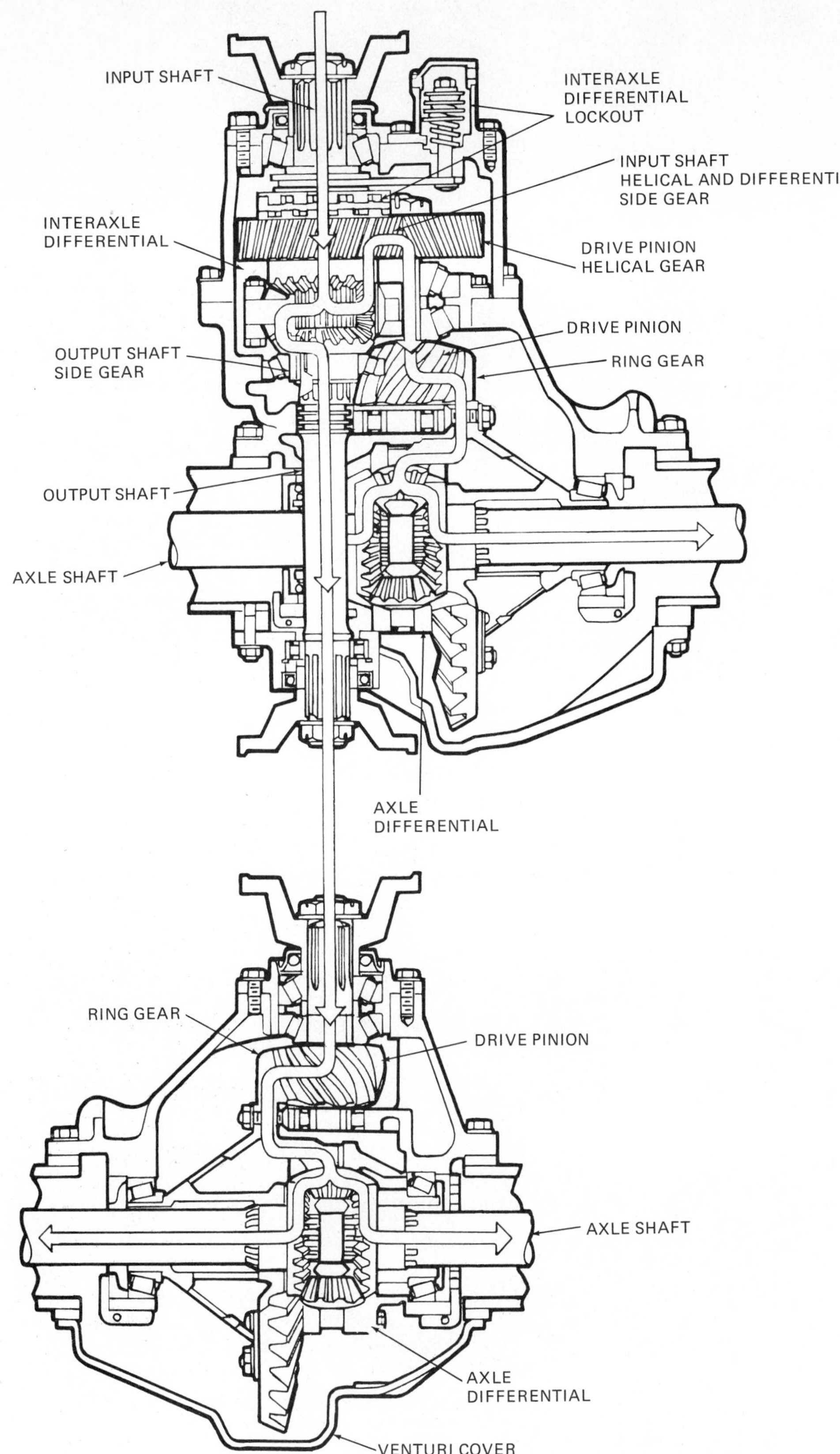

Fig. 14-22 Power flow with equal torque on both drive pinions. (*Ford Motor Company*)

The assembly is held to the divider housing through the bevel pinion nut, which is also used to adjust the bearing preload. When the power divider is assembled, the inner end of the radial plunger rests against the inner cam surface, and the outer ends rest against the outer cam surface. The bevel pinion adjustment is achieved by removing or adding shims between the divider housing and carrier housing.

OPERATION When the motor vehicle is driven in either direction and the tire traction on the front-rear and rear-rear axles is equal, the torque to drive the inner and outer cams is then also equal. This causes

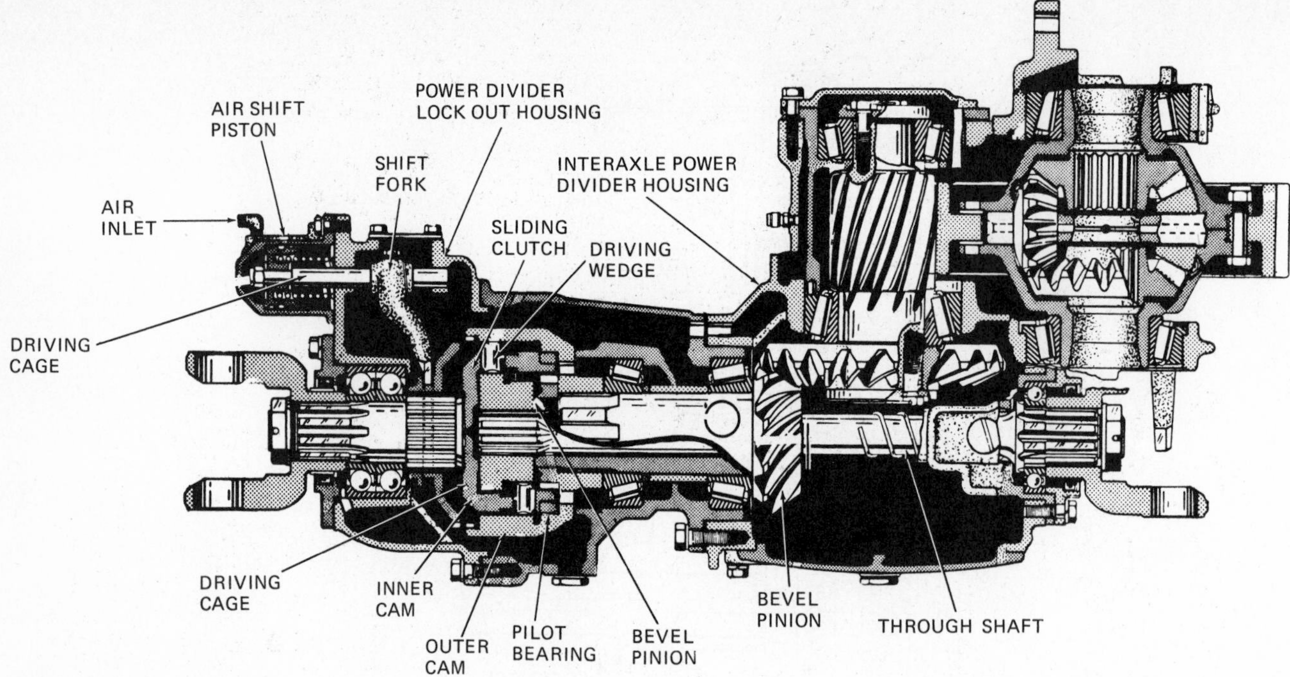

Fig. 14-23 Sectional view of the front-rear-axle carrier with interaxle power divider. (*Mack Canada Inc.*)

the blunt radial plungers to wedge against the contour of the inner and outer cams, thereby locking the assembly so that it rotates as a unit. Because the plungers (levers) have equal lever arms, equal force is applied to the inner and outer cams, and both bevel pinions are driven at equal rpm. See Fig. 14-24.

If, due to road conditions, either bevel pinion, and consequently the inner or outer cam, is forced to rotate faster than the driving cage, either the inner or the outer cam overruns the driving cage. This forces 12 plungers to slide down and 12 plungers to slide up the inner cam, constantly changing the plunger lever arm on the cams. The cam that overruns the speed of the driving cage by a certain number of rpm forces the other cam (through the plunger) to reduce its speed by a like amount.

With a conventional interaxle differential, when one of the driving tires loses traction, say by 80 percent, torque loss of 80 percent to all tires would occur. Such is not the case on a Mack interaxle power drive because of the torque bias of 3:1 and the designed angle of the plungers and cams. The remaining 20 percent of torque from the slipping tire is multiplied in a 3:1 ratio by the cams and plungers and directed to the tires (axle shafts) having traction. However, under no circumstance can torque greater than 75 percent of the total be placed on one axle because the power divider protects every axle against such an excessive amount.

Bus Coach Carrier As a rule, coaches use single-reduction units. However, due to the location of the engine at the rear of the coach and its position square to the coach frame, the drive from the transmission to the carrier is at an angle. See Fig. 14-25.

The essential difference between a single-reduction carrier and the one illustrated in Fig. 14-25 is that the drive pinion in the latter is angled about 38° from the center line of the carrier to the center line

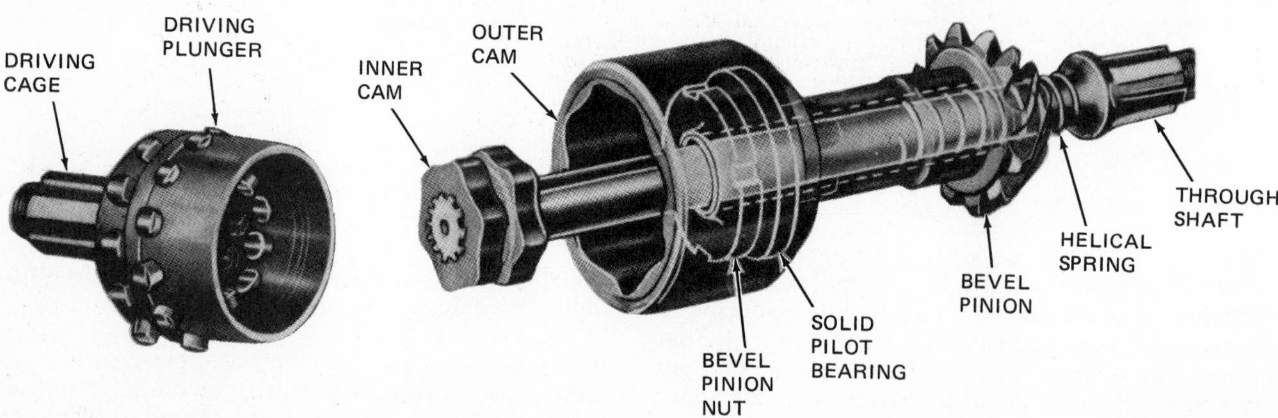

Fig. 14-24 Exploded view of the interaxle power divider.

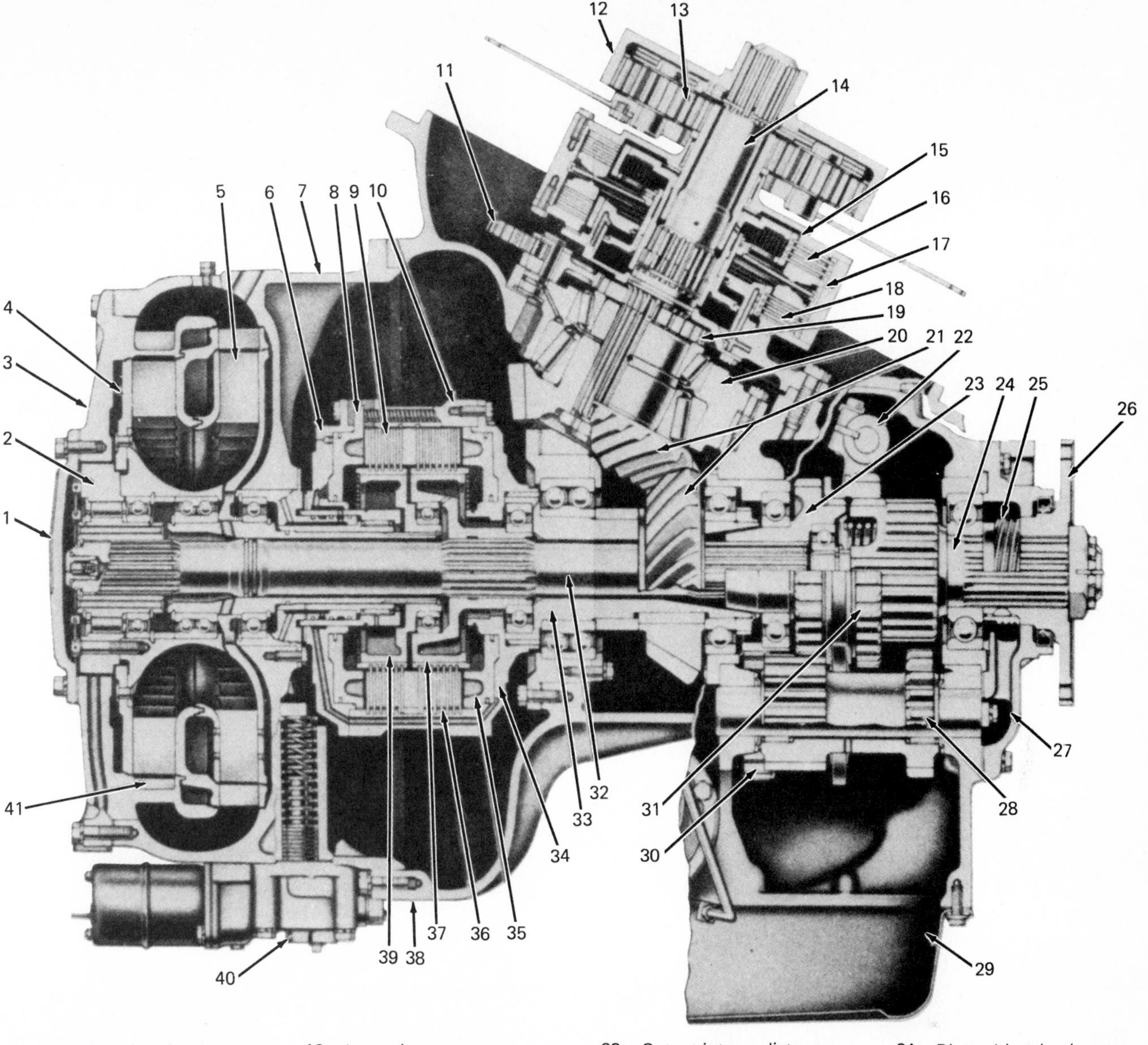

1. Converter housing cover cap
2. Over-running clutch assembly
3. Converter housing cover
4. Torque converter turbine
5. Torque converter pump
6. Hydraulic drive clutch cover
7. Converter housing
8. Hydraulic drive clutch piston
9. Hydraulic drive clutch
10. Direct and hydraulic clutch drum
11. Oil pump idler gear
12. Input ring gear
13. Input carrier assembly
14. Input shaft assembly
15. Sun gear assembly
16. Splitter direct drive clutch
17. Splitter clutch drum
18. Splitter overdrive clutch
19. Oil pump drive gear
20. Bevel pinion gear bearing retainer
21. Matched bevel gears
22. Shifter fork
23. Output intermediate gear
24. Output shaft
25. Speedometer, governor drive gear
26. Output flange
27. Output end cover assembly
28. Reverse idler gear
29. Oil pan
30. Reverse shifter gear assembly
31. Output shifter gear
32. Drive shaft assembly
33. Bevel gear sleeve
34. Direct drive clutch cover
35. Direct drive clutch piston
36. Direct drive clutch
37. Direct drive clutch hub
38. Transmission main housing assembly
39. Hydraulic drive clutch hub
40. Control valve
41. Stator vanes

Fig. 14-25 Sectional view of a V-drive automatic transmission. (*Allison Division of General Motors*)

of the drive pinion and the drive pinion and bevel gear are therefore of a special design.

Torque-Selector Front-Rear Axle Carrier The torque selector is actually a range transmission which is bolted to the case cover. The interaxle differential components are positioned within the case cover. The purpose of the torque selector is to give the motor vehicle one additional gear ratio for each transmission ratio. If the motor vehicle has a five-speed transmission and uses two-speed carriers, it would give the motor vehicle ten ratios. If in addition a torque selector is used, it would give the motor vehicle twenty ratios.

For example, first-gear ratio would be achieved by placing the transmission in low gear, the two-speed carrier in low speed, and the torque selector in underdrive. Second speed would be achieved by shifting the carrier into direct drive, and third speed would be achieved by shifting the torque selector into direct drive. Fourth speed would be achieved by shifting the transmission into second, the carrier

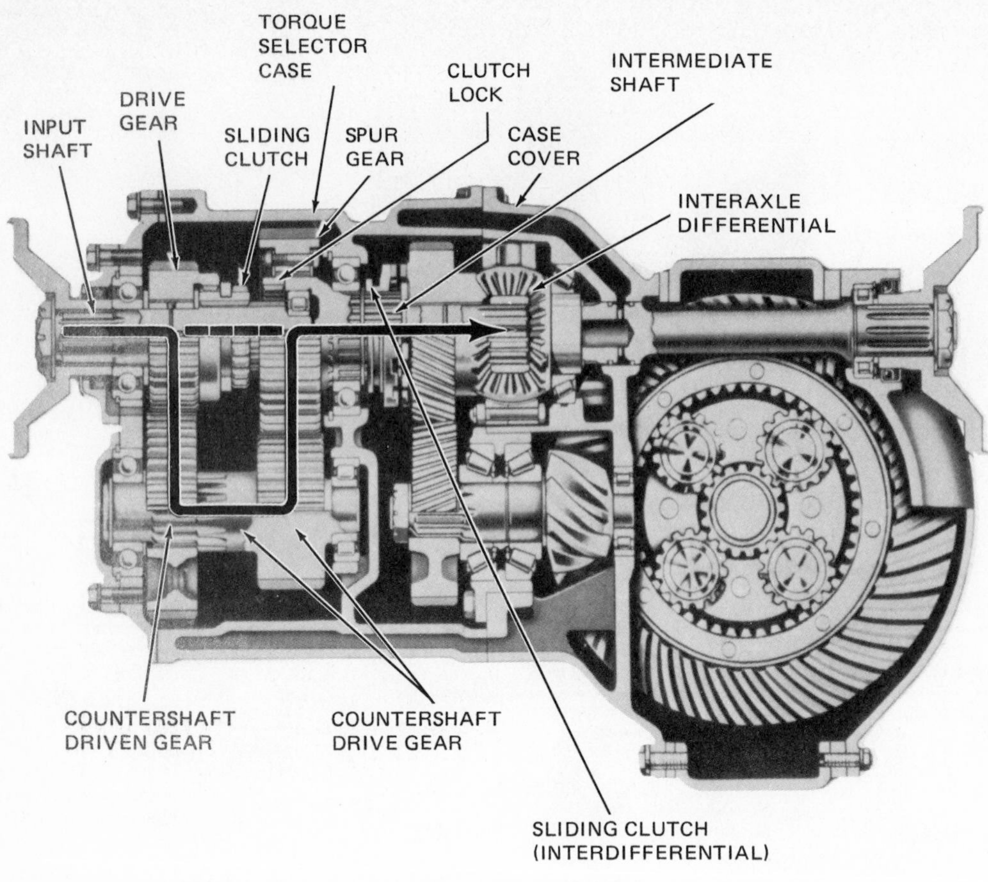

Fig. 14-26 Sectional view of a tandem front-rear axle carrier equipped with a torque selector unit. (*Eaton Corporation*)

into low speed, and the torque selector into underdrive.

DESIGN The countershaft drive gear forms part of the shaft, and the countershaft driven gear is splined to the countershaft. The countershaft is supported on the right by a roller bearing and on the left by a ball bearing. The ends of the input shaft are splined, and it is supported at the left by a ball bearing and at the right by a roller bearing. The drive gear is supported on the input shaft by bushings, and the male jaw clutch member is machined to its right-hand side. The female jaw clutch member is loosely splined to the input shaft, and the shift fork of the air-operated torque selector shift unit rests in the groove of the sliding clutch. Splined to the left-hand input shaft is the companion flange. The clutch lock (internal gear teeth) is machined to the spur gear, which is splined to the intermediate shaft. The intermediate shaft rests on the inner race of the roller bearing, and the spur driven gear is splined to its left-hand side. See Fig. 14-26.

OPERATION When the operator shifts the torque selector into underdrive, the sliding clutch moves to the left and engages with the spur drive gear. This clutches the drive gear to the input shaft. Rotation (torque) is transmitted from the input shaft to the drive gear, then to the countershaft driven gear, countershaft, and countershaft drive gear, onto the driven gear, and to the intermediate shaft.

If the operator selects direct drive, the sliding clutch engages with the clutch lock (driven gear), clutching the input shaft to the intermediate shaft. Torque is now transmitted directly from the input shaft, over the clutch, and to the intermediate shaft.

Tractor Carriers Because of the transmission and final drive design, the carriers of some tractors, loaders, etc., are located inside the final drive or transaxle housing. See Fig. 14-27. In this case, a four-speed transmission is bolted to the final drive housing.

The tractor carrier differs from a single-reduction carrier in the following ways

1. The drive pinion is part of the transmission output shaft.
2. Only the spider pinion gears are inside the differential center wheel.
3. The cross shaft is pressed into the bore of the differential center wheel (ring gear) and locked to it with a pin.
4. The side gears have the final drive gear machined to them and are supported on the cross shaft through bushings. The three friction clutch disks are splined to the outside ends.
5. The cross shaft assembly is supported on each side by tapered roller bearings.
6. The bearing preload as well as the ring gear adjustment is achieved through shims placed between the brake housing and final drive housing.
7. Each end of each axle shaft is supported by a tapered roller bearing, and the driven gear is splined

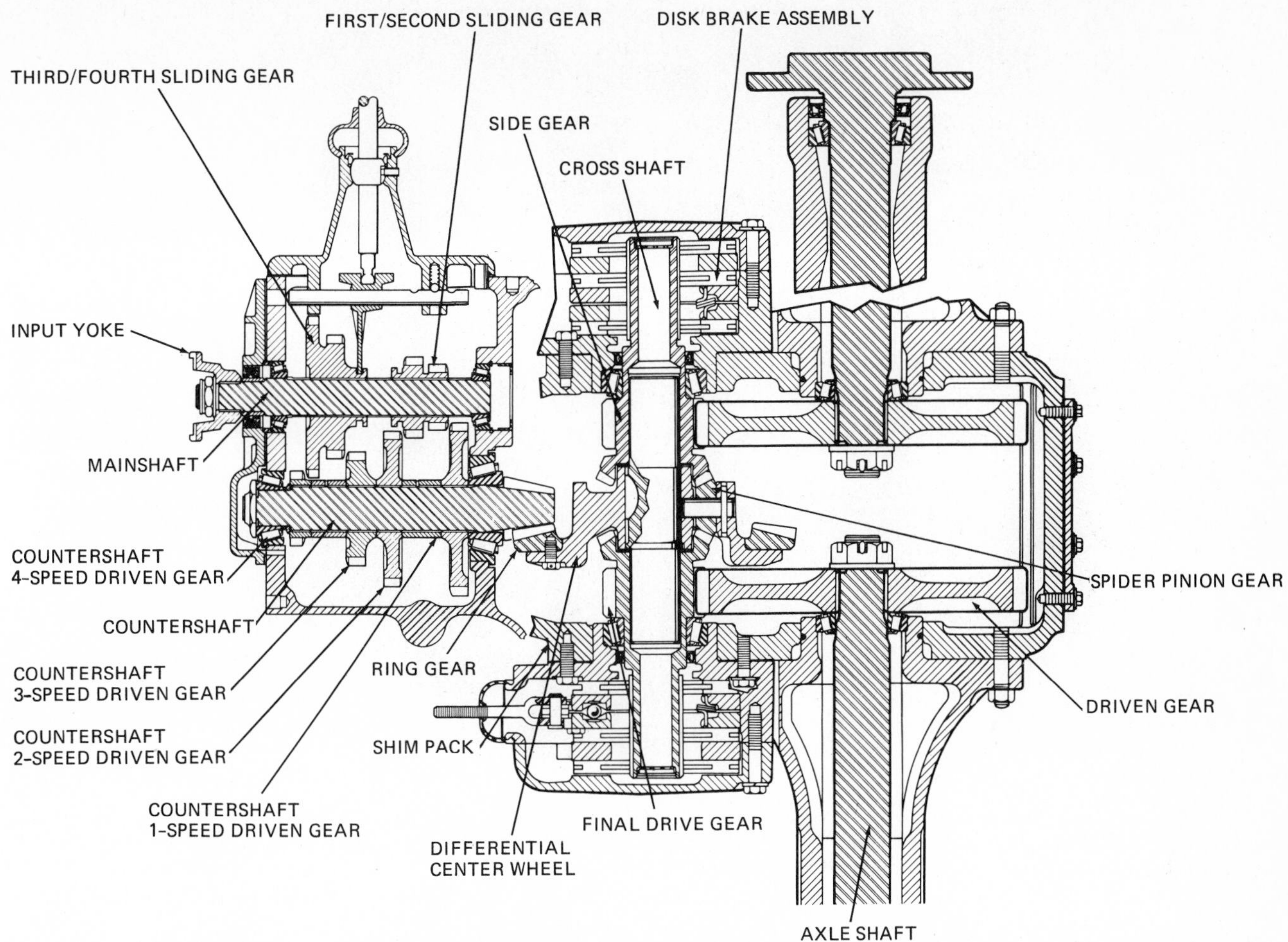

Fig. 14-27 Sectional view of a tractor transmission, carrier, and final drive. (*J I Case Company Agricultural Equipment Division*)

to the inside ends of the axle shaft. The bearing preload is adjusted through the axle shaft nut.

Although the normal drive action of this carrier is the same as that of any other, the rotation is transmitted from the side gears' final drive gears to the driven gears and axle shafts. Moreover, it has two inherent features not found in other types of carriers: (1) The brakes can be used as a traction equalizer when one tire loses traction. In this case (Fig. 14-27), the disk brake is applied, thereupon reducing or stopping the side gear rotation (which simulates tire traction), increasing the torque to the tire that is not slipping. (2) The brake can also be used to assist in steering. For example, to make a sharp left-hand turn, the operator turns the steering wheel so as to position the front tire into a left-hand turn. At the same time she or he applies the left-hand brake. This stops the left-hand drive wheel and also the left-hand side gear. Now all torque from the differential center wheel is directed to the right-hand side, pivoting the tractor on the left-hand tire.

Traction Equalizers There are many mechanical devices intended specifically to prevent or reduce tire slippage. Some are simple in design, while others are somewhat intricate.

Differential Locks The simplest traction equalizer is the differential lock type, one of which is shown in Fig. 14-28. Its clutch collar has internal splines and can slide on the splines of the final drive shaft. The planetary sun gear is splined to the left-hand side of the final drive shaft. The left-hand end of the differential hub quill is machined with external splines. Shoes which rest in the groove of the clutch collar fit into the bores of the yoke. The yoke is keyed to the shaft, and the shaft is connected over a lock arm to the lock pedal. A torsion spring is used to force the yoke into the disengaged position—that is, to force it to the left-hand side.

OPERATION When the terrain on which the tractor is operated is such that one of the tires loses traction, the operator stops the tractor and depresses the differential lock pedal. This moves the clutch collar to the right, over the splined end of the differential hub quill; as a result the final drive shaft clutches to the differential hub quill. (The side pinion gear therefore cannot rotate.) However, both final drive shafts rotate with the differential hub, but the torque from the differential hub (case) is directed to the final drive shaft of the tire with the most traction.

To disengage the differential lock, the operator momentarily moves a foot off the throttle or disen-

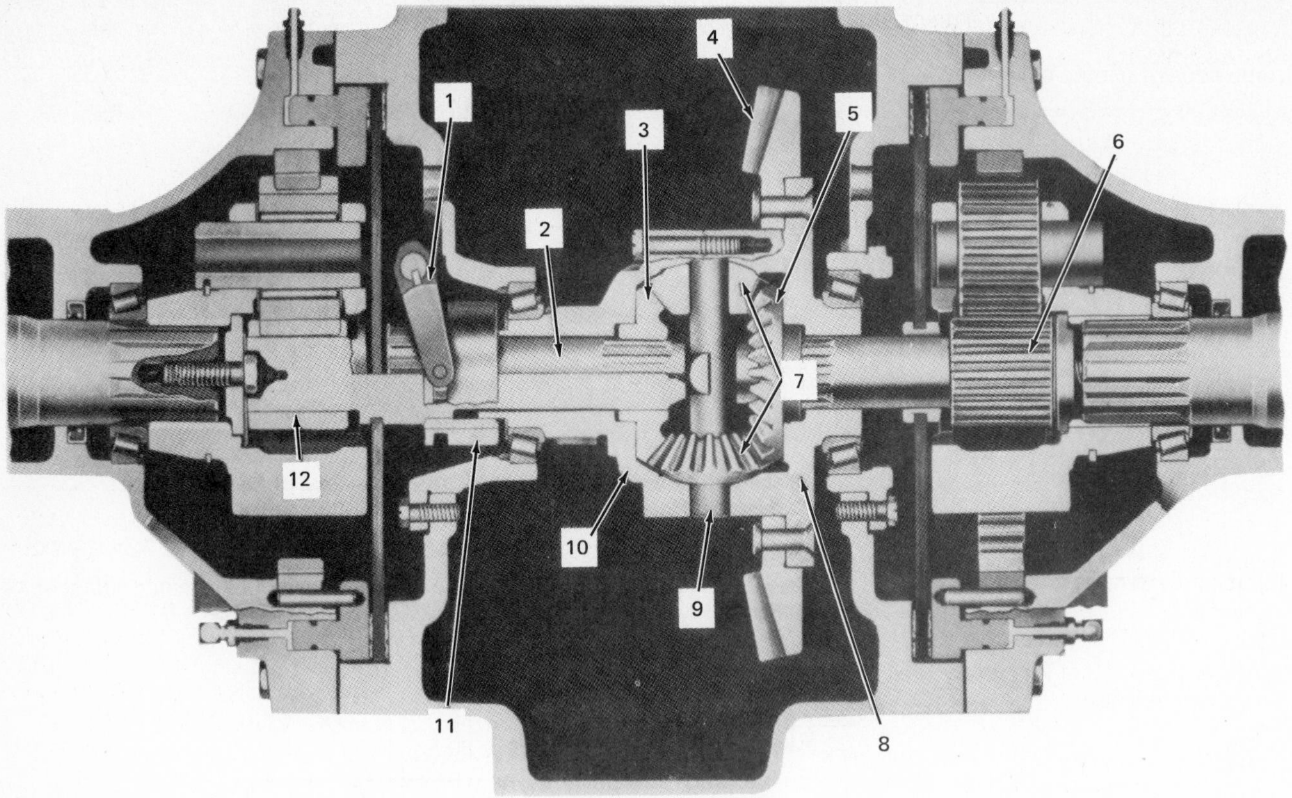

1. Differential lock lever
2. Final drive shaft
3. Left bevel gear
4. Ring gear
5. Right bevel gear
6. Sun pinion
7. Bevel pinion
8. Differential hub
9. Bevel pinion shaft
10. Differential hub quill
11. Differential lock collar
12. Sun pinion

Fig. 14-28 Sectional view of a bevel gear drive with differential lock and final drive. (*Deere & Company*)

gages the engine clutch. This removes the torque from the final drive shaft, and the torsion spring force moves the yoke to the left, thereby disengaging the clutch collar from the splines of the differential hub quill.

Mack Power Divider Differential The Mack power divider differential (Fig. 14-29) is a true differential and the oldest traction equalizer in use. It is designed in basically the same way, and serves the same purpose, as the interaxle power divider. Un-

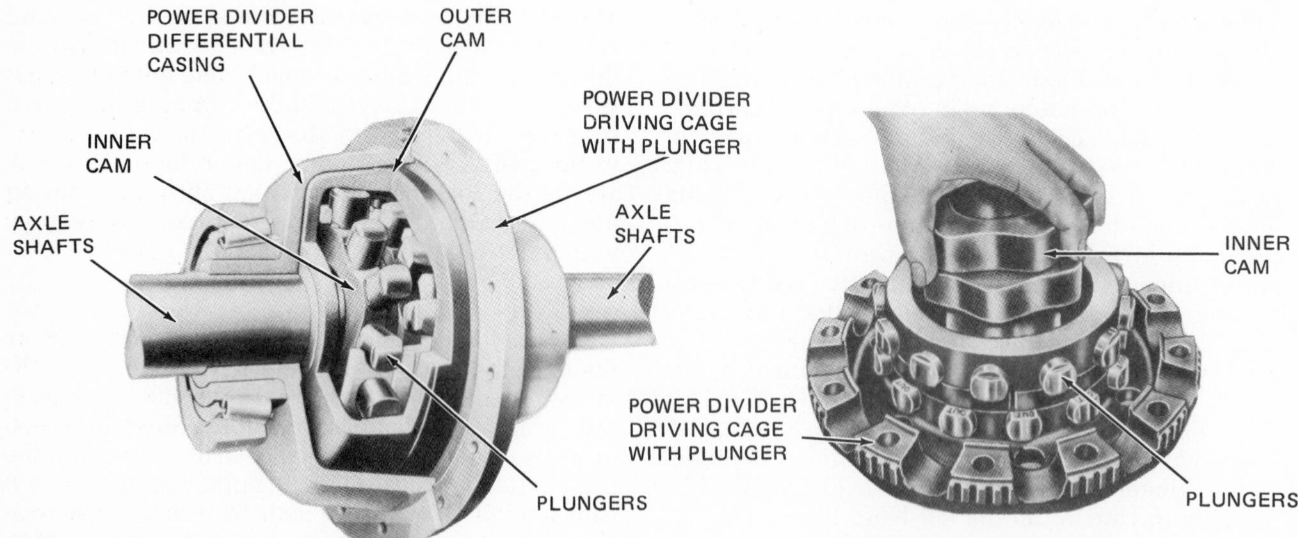

Fig. 14-29 Schematic view of the Mack power divider differential. (*Mack Canada Inc.*)

derstandably, it is located within and forms part of the differential case.

DIFFERENTIAL CASE DESIGN The differential case consists of two halves—the power divider differential casing and the driving cage. The second reduction driven gear (bull gear) is externally splined to the driving cage splines, and the differential casing, the bull gear, and the driven cage are bolted as a unit. This assembly is supported in the carrier housing by tapered roller bearings. The bearing preload and bull gear alignment are achieved through the differential adjusting nuts. Inside the differential case assembly are the outer and inner cams, which are supported by bushings in the bores of the casing and driving cage. The axle shaft ends are splined to the outer and inner cams. **NOTE** Since the operating principle of this design is exactly the same as that of the interaxle power divider, an explanation of it will not be given here. See the previous discussion above for details of how it works. The differential case can also transfer and multiply torque (this time in a 3:1 ratio) from the axle shaft of the tire which is slipping to the axle shaft having more traction.

Torque Proportional Differential Another kind of power divider is shown in Fig. 14-30. This type relies on the lever principle, as does the Mack power divider differential. It uses spider pinion gears and side gears with teeth differently contoured from the conventional bevel gear design, and in addition the side pinion gears have an odd number of teeth.

OPERATION When road conditions permit equal tire traction and the tractor or tractor-loader operates on level ground, the spider pinion gears are so positioned that the lever arms L2 and L3 (and L1 and L4) are equal in length and form an angle of 90° to the tooth contact lines A and B. This exerts an equal force from the spider pinion teeth to the side gear teeth, negating gear rotation and equalizing the torque onto each side gear.

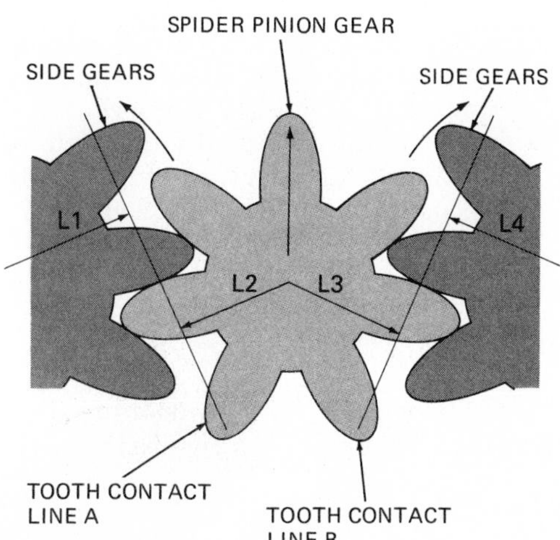

Fig. 14-30 View of the torque proportional differential gear when equal tire traction exists. (*J I Case Company Agricultural Equipment Division*)

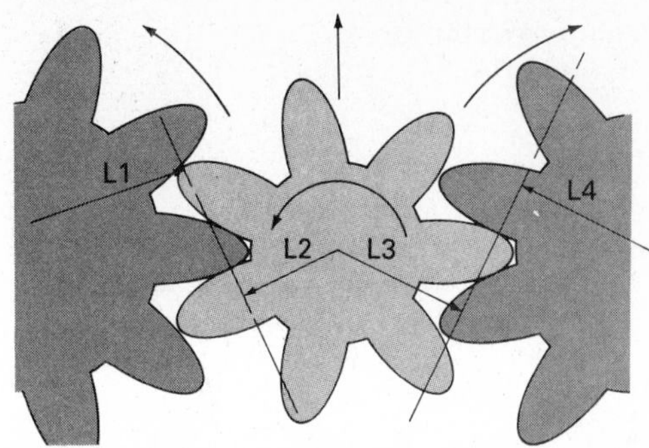

Fig. 14-31 View of the torque proportional differential gear when low right traction exists. (*J I Case Company Agricultural Equipment Division*)

When the tractor makes a turn, the differential reacts like a conventional differential. However, when the left- or right-hand tire loses traction, the lever arm lengths constantly change. The gear position which transfers a maximum torque of 27 percent is shown in Fig. 14-31. Note, however, that this maximum torque position exists only for a split second. At this point the right-hand tooth of the spider pinion gear is fully engaged with the right-hand tooth of the right-hand side gear, and the tooth of the left-hand spider pinion gear is only partly engaged with the left-hand side gear. This tooth position increases the torque of the lever L3 arm 27 percent more than that of the lever arm L2. If the torque on the right-hand side gear were only 100 lb·ft [135.5 N·m], then due to the additional lever arm leverage of 27 percent, more torque—that is, 127 lb·ft [172.08 N·m]—would be transferred from the spider pinion tooth onto the left-hand side gear. The increased leverage is small, but nevertheless enough to prevent tractor wheel spinout.

As stated, this position remains only for a split second because the right- and left-hand side gears are rotating due to the slipping tire. The right-hand side gear therefore takes a low torque transfer position, and a loss of 27 percent (from the 100 lb·ft [135.5 N·m]) will occur. In other words, it will have a lower torque of 73 lb·ft [98.91 N·m]. In this position, the right-hand side gear and pinion would have the shorter lever arm, and the left-hand side gear and pinion would have the longer lever arm. From this, you can see that the torque proportional differential cannot constantly multiply and transfer the maximum torque. The increase and decrease in torque is noticeable as jerkiness in the tractor's movement.

Traction Equalizer Differentials Basically there are two types of this kind of differential—one which relies on multiclutch friction and the other on friction between gears. They are both designed to prevent torque loss.

Multiclutch Friction Traction Equalizer The traction equalizer differential shown in Fig. 14-32 is relatively simple. It has conventional spider pinions and side gears and two sets of multiplate clutches. The clutches are continuously engaged, but will slip above (although not below) the torque value.

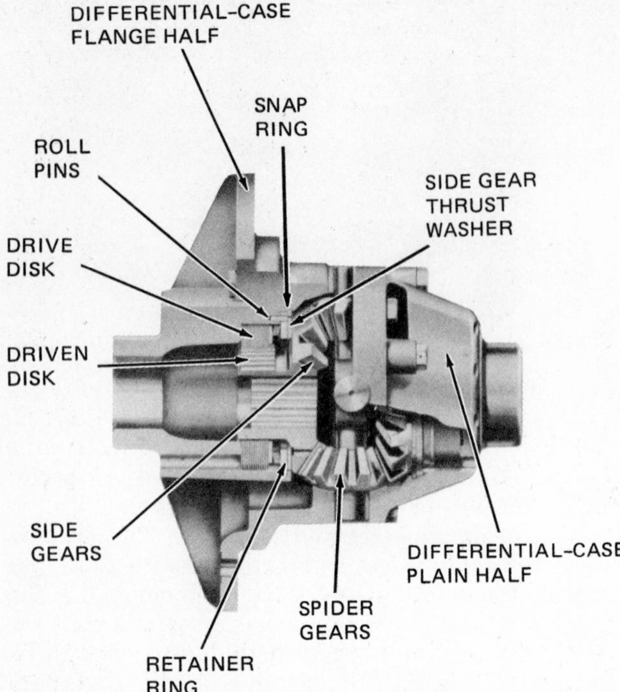

Fig. 14-32 Cutaway view of a self-contained traction equalizer. *(International Harvester Company)*

DESIGN To accommodate the traction equalizer (the multiclutches), the differential case flange half and the differential case plain half are internally machined with grooves in which the lugs of the drive disk rest. The left- and right-hand side gears are machined with external splines on which the driven disks are positioned. To achieve the predetermined friction, four cone clutch springs are positioned between the first (thicker) drive disk and the retainer ring (shown in Fig. 14-32). The retainer ring is splined to the differential case.

OPERATION When the motor vehicle is driven with equal torque (equal tire traction) on the axle shafts, the clutches prevent the side gears from rotating. When the motor vehicle makes a turn and the torque on the inner and outer axle shafts exceeds the clutch friction (for one type of clutch the friction is equal to 300 lb·ft [406.5 N·m]), the clutch starts to slip, allowing the inside side gear speed to decrease in proportion to the increase in speed of the outside gear. If the torque on one axle shaft drops below the torque value, neither side gear can rotate because the clutch with lower torque remains engaged. This enables the vehicle to maintain an appreciable amount of torque on the axle shaft of the tires having traction.

A disadvantage with this type of traction equalizer differential is that the clutch disk wears, and the spring becomes weaker. Either of these conditions reduces clutch friction and therefore reduces torque transmission. Another drawback is that the static friction coefficient of the lubricant could be higher than the sliding coefficient of the clutch if a limited-slip-differential oil were not used. That situation could cause slippage and/or jerky clutch action.

Controlled Traction Equalizer Another type of traction equalizer differential is shown in Fig. 14-33. It is termed a "controlled traction equalizer" because a collar clutch is used to engage the multiclutch.

DESIGN The differential support case forms part of the differential case. Splined to its inner left-hand bore are the drive friction disks. The left-hand half of the differential case and ring gear are bolted to the support case, as is the right-hand half of the differential case. The assembly is supported in the carrier housing by tapered roller bearings. The friction plate driver has external and internal splines, and the driven friction disks are splined to the external splines. The clutch collar also has internal and external splines. The internal splines are in mesh with the splines on the axle shaft, and the external splines can engage with the internal splines of the friction plate drive. The clutch disks, through the compression spring, are forced against one another, and against the side of the support case. The fork end of the pivot-mounted shift fork rests in the groove of the sliding clutch collar, and the other end connects to an air cylinder.

OPERATION For normal on-highway operation, the sliding clutch collar is moved to the left so that it is no longer splined to the friction plate driver. The controlled traction differential is now a conventional differential.

When tire traction difficulties are encountered, the operator directs air to the air actuator, causing the sliding clutch collar to engage with the friction plate driven splines. This clutches the axle shaft and the left-hand side gear to the differential support plate, whereupon the left-hand side gear cannot rotate independently, the differential locks up, and the torque is then proportionately divided. For instance, assume that one side of the vehicle is lifted up, or that one side is on ice. Very little torque would be required to rotate the tires in either position. Under this condition, the torque would be directed in two directions: (1) Very little torque would be directed from the differential support case to the multiclutch, over the sliding clutch collar, and to the left-hand axle shaft, and (2) nearly all torque would be directed from the differential case to the spider, the spider pinions, and side gears, to the right-hand axle shaft. If, however, the torque of either axle shaft exceeds the designed torque value of the multiclutch, the clutch slips and only this torque value is exerted onto the axle shafts. **NOTE** The torque value of this differential, when new, is 4000 lb·ft [5420 N·m]. This torque value protects the axle shafts from becoming twisted or broken.

Planetary Differential The limited slip differential shown in Fig. 14-34 relies on two basic principles—planetary drive and gear ratio.

DESIGN Special helical gears supported in the center bores of each differential half are used as side gears. Six specially curved helical gears replace the conventional differential spider pinion gears. Three

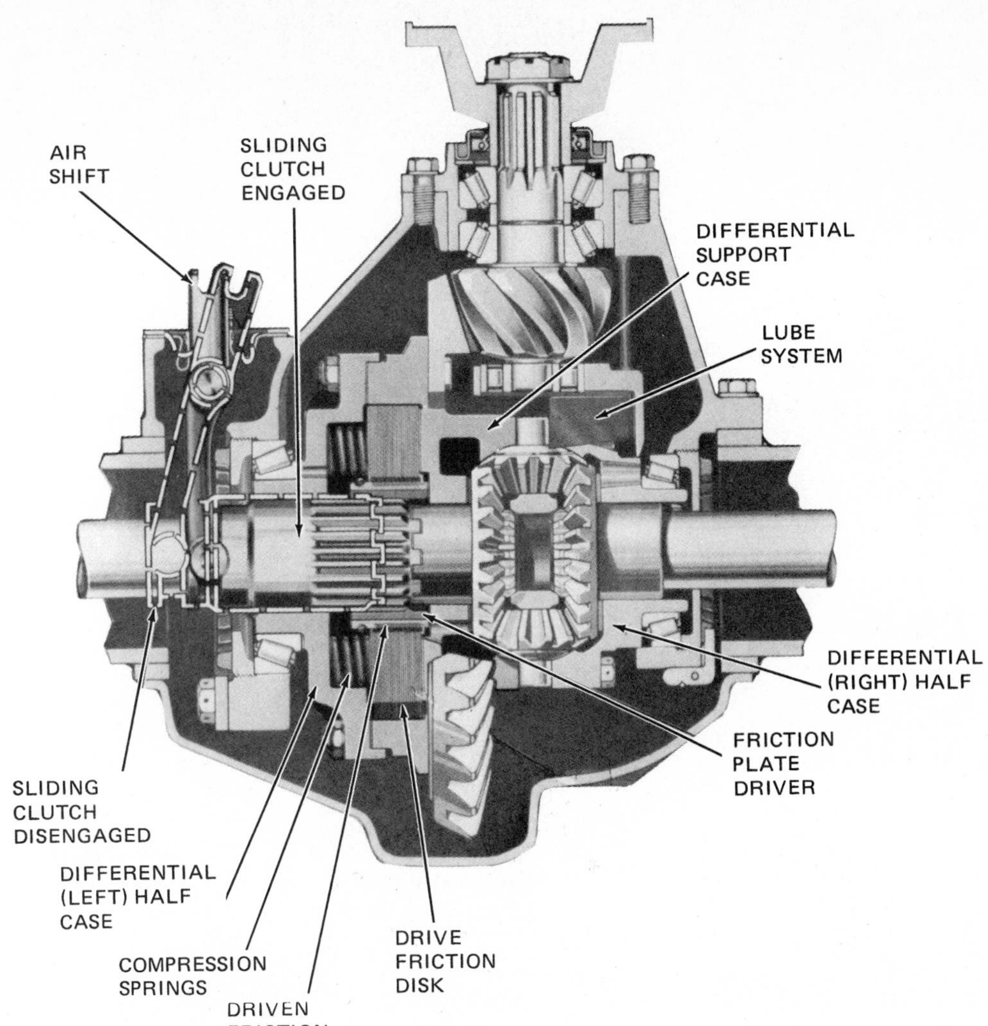

Fig. 14-33 Sectional view of a single-reduction carrier with controlled traction equalizer. (*Eaton Corporation*)

helical pinion gears are supported in the bore of the right-hand half of the differential flange and partly in the bore of the left-hand half, while three are supported in the bores of the left-hand half and partly in the bore of the right-hand half. When assembled, the three supported in the right-hand differential half are in mesh with the right-hand helical side gear, and the three which are supported in the left-hand plain differential half are in mesh with the left-hand helical side gear. In addition, each of the three helical pinion gears in the left- and right-hand halves of the differential case are in mesh.

OPERATION When the motor vehicle is driven straight ahead, the tires have equal traction and equal rolling radius. Rotation (torque) is transmitted from the ring gear to the differential case, to the helical pinion gears, and onto the helical side gears, driving both axle shafts at the same rpm as the ring gear. When the vehicle is in a turn, say a left-hand turn, the right-hand helical side gear drives the three right-hand helical pinion gears. Since each is in mesh with one left-hand helical pinion gear, those gears too are driven and subsequently drive the left-hand helical side gear, but at reduced rpm. The rpm of the left-hand helical side gear is reduced by the increased rpm of the right-hand helical side gear.

If the tire(s) on one side lose traction, torque is then placed onto the other axle shaft. This is due to the helical gear design and the overdrive ratio between the side gear and pinion gears (about 1:2.4). The tires without traction do not have sufficient torque to drive the helical pinion gears, therefore the other side gear having traction also does not have traction, and the planetary differential becomes a nonslip differential.

Nonspin Differential The nonspin differential transmits 100 percent torque to the tires having traction with full differential action.

DESIGN The nonspin differential is a mechanical device without friction clutches: it can be exchanged with a conventional differential or vice versa. There are three different types of nonspin differential designs—the standard, the silent, and the silent overrunning. A nonspin differential is shown in Fig. 14-35, which distinguishes the components used in the most recent designs, the silent and silent overrunning types.

An important difference between the silent and the silent overrunning nonspin differential is that, when in a turn, the latter remains disengaged whereas with the former the outside driven clutch

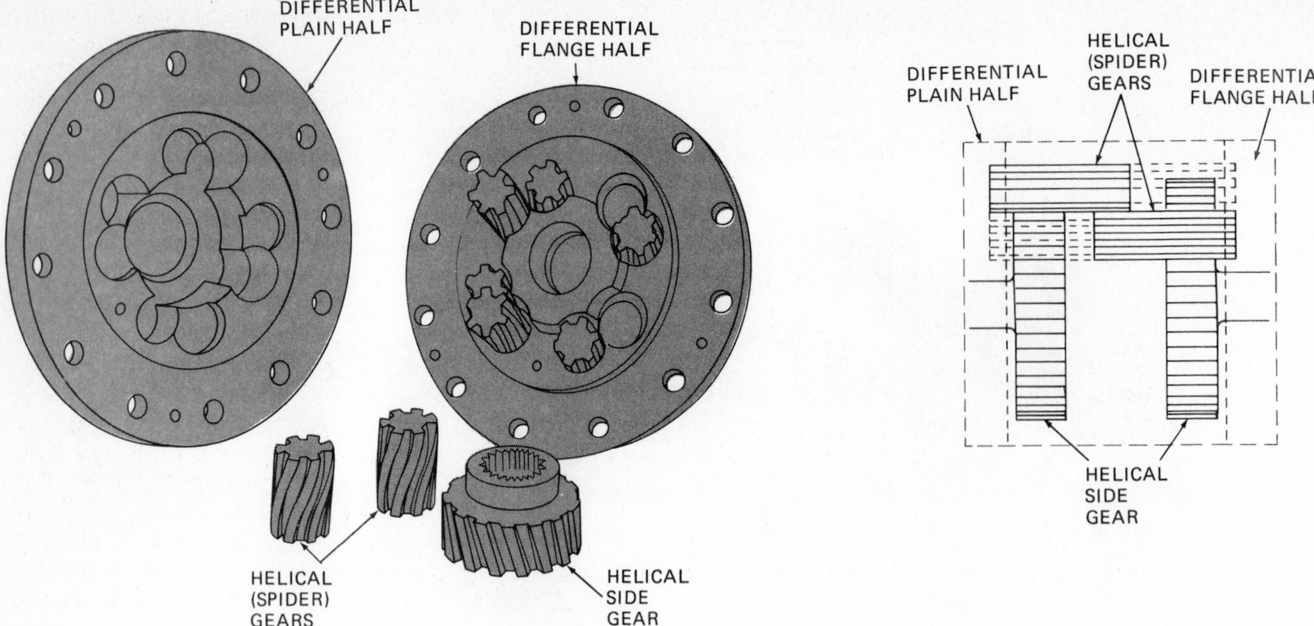

Fig. 14-34 Exploded view of a planetary differential.

returns to full engagement after the clutch jaws have passed by the spider jaws. A slight clicking sound is audible during reengagement. The spider has a slightly inwardly tapered jaw clutch on each side. Its journals are secured in the differential case bores. Inside the center bore of the spider is the center cam, which has clutches of a lug design and a cutout in which the holdout ring lugs rest during normal operation. The holdout rings are positioned in each driven clutch and held in place through the friction spring. On the outer circle side face of the driven clutches are jaw clutches, which are engaged with the spider jaw clutches. On the inner circle side face are lug clutches which are engaged with the lugs on the center cam. The spring retainer and side gears are loosely splined to each driven clutch, and the springs (located between them) force the driven clutches to the spider and center cam.

OPERATION When the motor vehicle is driven straight ahead on a level surface, and the tires have equal rolling radius, the driven clutch jaws are fully engaged with the spider jaw clutch, their inner lugs rest in the center cam, and the holdout rings rest in the center cam cutouts (seats) (see Fig. 14-36). Rotation (torque) is transmitted from the differential case to the spider, and from the spider to the driven clutches and side gears, placing equal torque onto the axle shafts.

On a conventional differential during a turn, the outside tires turn faster than the ring gear speed, while the inside tires turn slower than that speed.

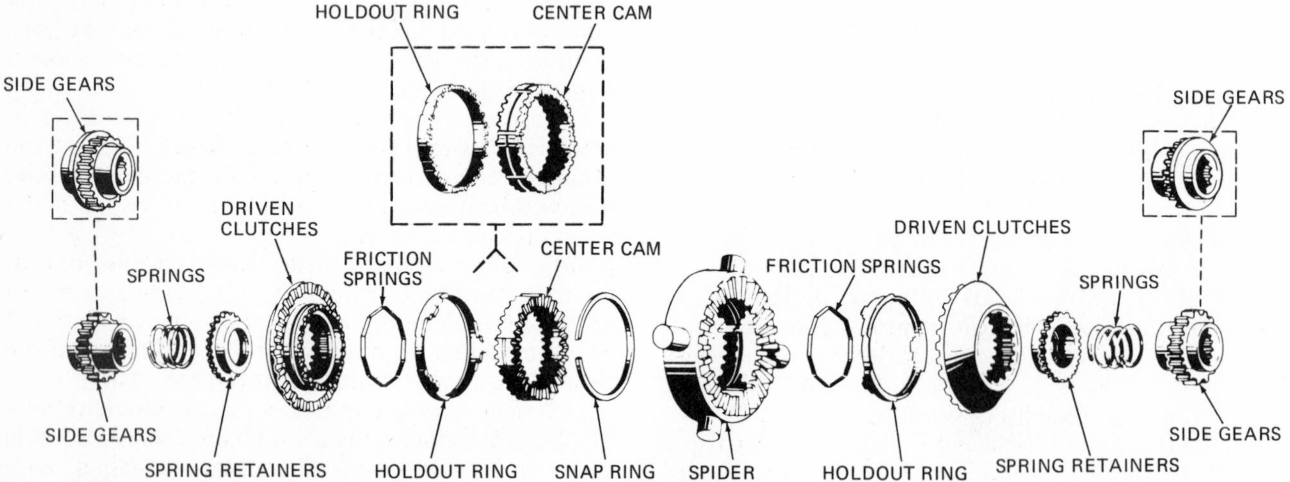

Fig. 14-35 Exploded view of a silent nonspin differential. The silent overrunning nonspin differential of this design will be the same except in the use of different side gears, holdout ring, and center cam, shown in the boxed illustration. (*Terex Division of General Motors Corporation*)

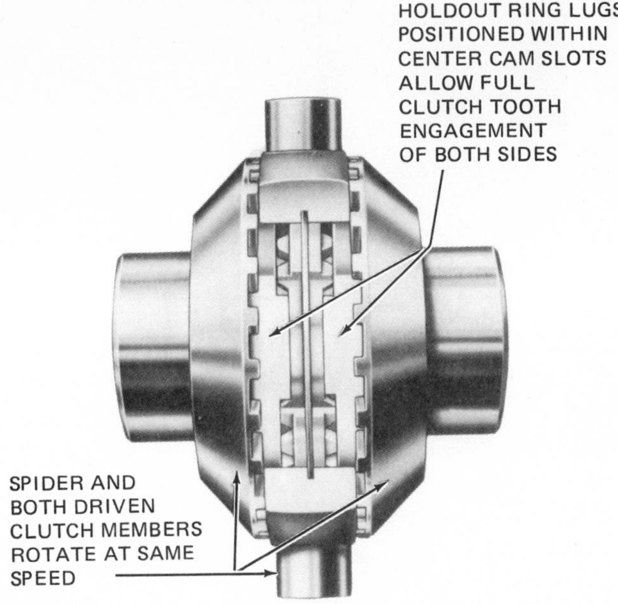

Fig. 14-36 View of the nonspin differential in the locked position. (*Terex Division of General Motors Corporation*)

Such is not the case with any of the three nonspin differentials. During a turn they allow either the left- or the right-hand tire(s) to turn faster than the ring gear speed, but do not permit either one to turn slower than that speed. If the motor vehicle is making a turn, say to the right, the left-hand tires have to cover a greater distance than the right-hand (in this case inside) tires. This forces the left-hand driven clutch and holdout ring to ride up the center cam (see Fig. 14-37). Consequently the left-hand driven clutch jaw separates from the spider and disengages the inner lugs from the center cam, thereby assuring positive engagement of the right-hand driven clutch.

Rotation (torque) now is directed from the differential case to the spider, and over the jaw clutch to the right-hand driven clutch and side gear, driving it with torque equivalent to that of the spider. The left-hand jaw clutch remains disengaged until the driven clutch reaches the same, or almost the same, speed as that of the spider. When the left-hand driven clutch slows down to the speed of the spider, the holdout ring is carried with it (through the friction of the friction spring), causing the holdout lugs to reengage with the center cam cutouts (seats). The left-hand driven clutch then reengages with the spider, producing a positive drive to both axle shafts.

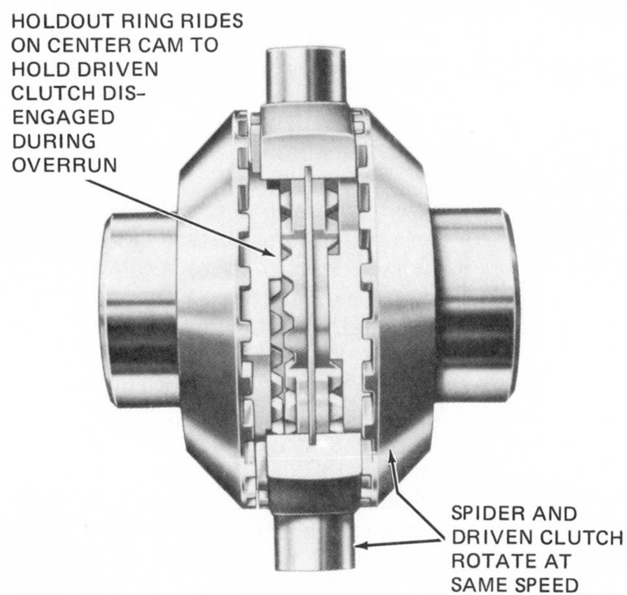

Fig. 14-37 View of the nonspin differential in the overrunning position. (*Terex Division of General Motors Corporation*)

The nonspin differentials can be used as interaxle differentials (see Fig. 14-38). In that case, the spider is splined to the input shaft, the right-hand driven clutch to the output shaft, and the left-hand driven clutch to the helical driven gear, which assembly is supported by bushings on the input shaft. An interaxle nonspin differential operates in the same way as a silent nonspin differential—that is, it reengages after the drive clutch jaws pass by the jaws on the spider.

CARRIER SERVICE

Sources of Carrier Noise One of the first symptoms of carrier trouble is increased carrier operating temperature, which, if ignored, will eventually lead to noise. Increased carrier temperature can be attributed to overload conditions, low oil level, worn or damaged oil pump, plugged oil filter, using oil other than that recommended for the carrier, using oil after it has deteriorated, and misalignment [that is, to a bent axle housing or to twisted axle shaft(s)].

If the carrier is excessively noisy in drive, and the problem is not one of the foregoing conditions, check for a worn or damaged differential bearing case or drive pinion bearings. If the bearings are inadequately adjusted, they will increase end play or backlash, which, in turn, will alter the tooth contact and cause noise. A loose companion flange nut would have the same effect. Other causes of carrier noise are too high bevel gear runout, loose ring gear, damaged wheel hub bearings, dragging brakes, and/or damaged or unbalanced drive line.

If excessive noise occurs only when driving in reverse or when coasting, the backlash between the drive pinion and bevel gear may be too small, or the pinion bearings may be adjusted too loosely, thereby reducing the backlash.

If the carrier noise is constant, check for one or more of the following: bent axle shaft(s), bent or twisted axle housing, slightly damaged or flat spot on carrier bearings or wheel hub bearings, and/or a damaged or unbalanced drive line.

If the noise occurs only during a turn, the problem is within the differential. Check the spider, the side gears, or the spider pinion gears for damage or wear. Check for excessive backlash due to worn or damaged thrust washers or housing. Excessive backlash could damage or wear down the axle shaft splines, which would also result in noise.

If the motor vehicle has an interaxle differential,

A. Forward rear axle shaft
B. Input shaft
C. Interaxle differential (nonspin)
D. Drive pinion gear
E. Ring gear
F. Helical gears
G. Differential carrier
H. Output shaft
I. Axle housing

Fig. 14-38 Sectional view of a front-rear axle carrier with an interaxle differential nonspin.

carrier noise could result from this differential being damaged. Such damage or wear could occur from unmatched tires which would cause the differential gears to rotate constantly during vehicle operation. If the interaxle differential or the two-speed carrier fails to shift when electrically actuated, check the electric circuit for an open, a short, or a ground; check the operation of the shift motor or solenoid with a voltmeter, or use an ohmmeter to check the resistance of the coil or motor winding. If it is actuated by air, check the air pressure, the actuating valve operation, and the control valve operation.

Before removing the carriage for service, make every attempt to determine the origin of the noise so that there is no doubt whether or not the carrier is at fault. Drain some oil from the carrier to evaluate its overall condition and whether it is contaminated. Check the drive line and universal joints for wear and damage and for loose drive pinion nut(s). It may be more expedient in the long run to jack up the rear of the vehicle and check the wheel bearing adjustment, while at the same time checking the tires for excessive runout. Also check the suspension for loose and/or damaged components, either of which could cause drive-line misalignment.

If all of the above checks prove satisfactory, test-drive the motor vehicle to further assist you in assessing the noise origin. Only when you are positive the trouble is within the carrier should you remove it for service.

Removal and Inspection Assuming that the above procedure has proven the need for an overhaul, park the vehicle where there is adequate room to remove the carrier. Block the tires, and if applicable, secure the hydraulic equipment; then remove the ground cable from the battery. The removal procedure now depends on whether the carrier is top-mounted or front-mounted, and whether it is used on a motor-truck, a truck-tractor, or in a tractor, loader, or machine. Follow the appropriate service manual instructions exactly. Do not disregard any safety rules in order to take short cuts.

After removing the axle shafts (see Fig. 14-39), check them for twists and fatigue (cracks). Such defects would appear on the outer surface of the shaft. If the shafts are twisted, they must be replaced. The usual cause of twisted axle shafts is torque or stress in excess of the strength of the metal, sometimes from severe operating conditions, sometimes from abusively operating the motor vehicle or equipment, and sometimes from a combination of both.

If the axle shaft shows fatigue near the flange or is broken off at or near the flange end, the cause is probably misalignment between the wheel hub and differential side gear as a result of misadjusted, worn, or damaged wheel bearings, or a bent or sprung axle housing. If the axle shaft itself is twisted or shows fatigue, or the tires show abnormal inside wear, the axle housing may be bent in either of two directions (see Fig. 14-40). When it is bent from the

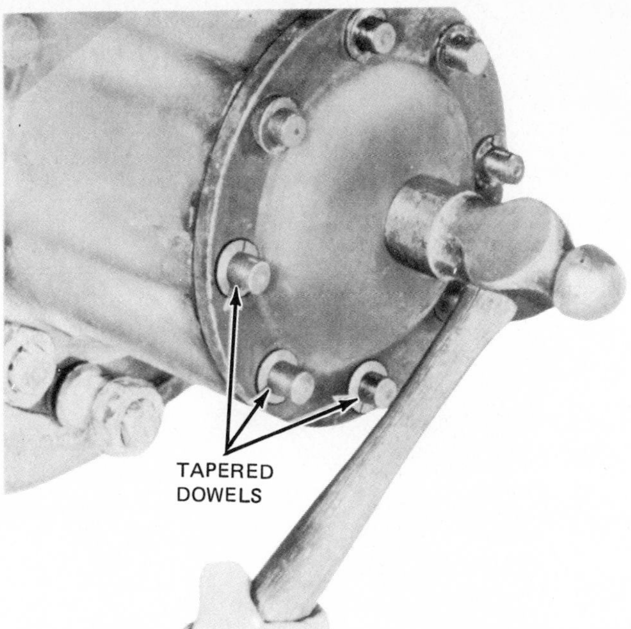

Fig. 14-39 Method of loosening dowels in axle shaft flange. (*International Harvester Company*)

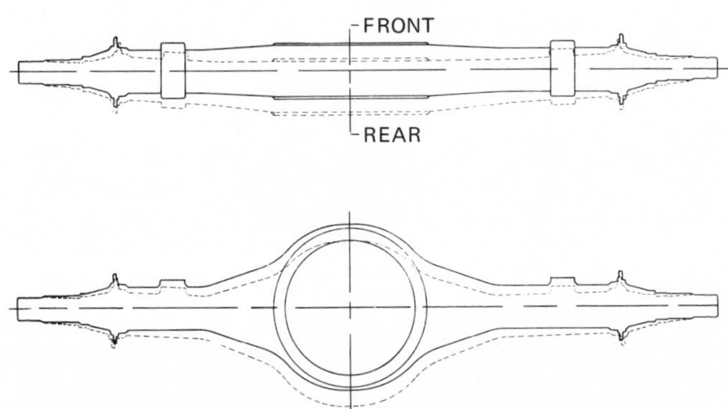

Fig. 14-40 Schematic view of axle housings. (Dotted lines indicate distortion (due to bend). (*International Harvester Company*)

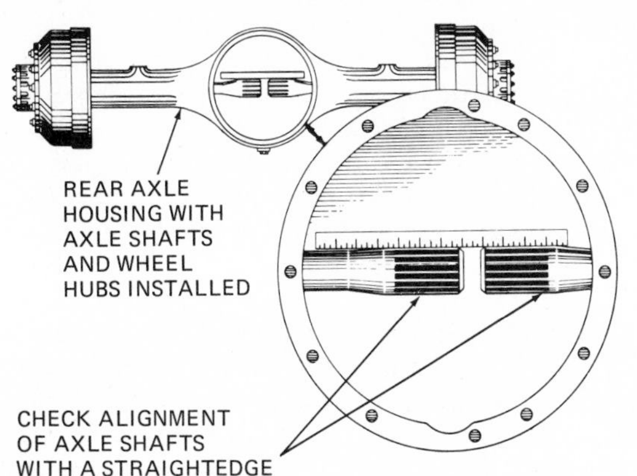

Fig. 14-41 Method used to check axle housing alignment. (*International Harvester Company*)

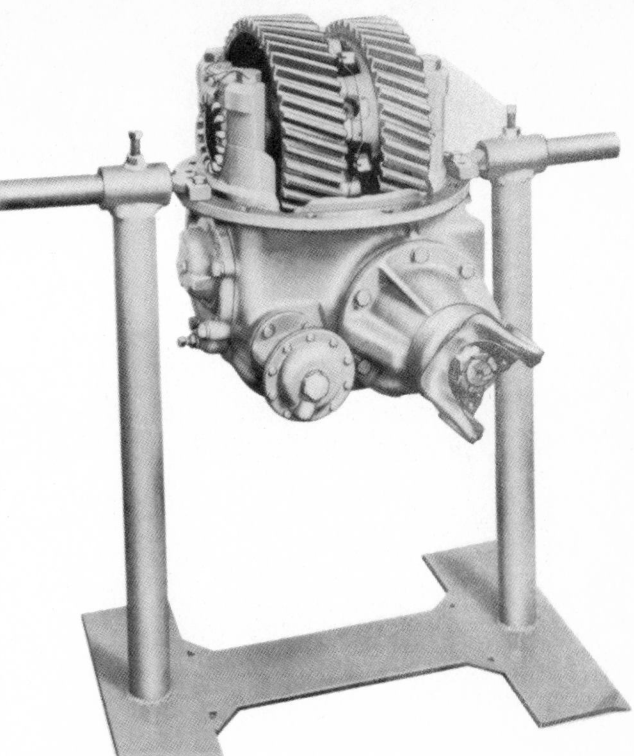

Fig. 14-42 Carrier mounted to a service stand. (*International Harvester Company*)

center downwards (shown by the dotted line), it is due to excessive overload; when bent rearward, it is commonly the result of impact.

To check the alignment of the axle housing, reinstall the wheel hubs and axle shafts and then check the alignment as shown in Fig. 14-41. Next, hold a straightedge to the axle shaft, 90° from the first position shown in the illustration. If the axle housing is bent in either direction, it should be straightened, but this must be done in a shop which has the appropriate tools, equipment, and experience. Otherwise the failure may occur again.

Disassembly All types of motortrucks or truck-tractor carriers are disassembled in much the same manner; the hints given below will speed up this service.

1. Always make certain the carrier housing and gears are clean before starting the disassembly.
2. Mount the carrier to a service stand (see Fig. 14-42).
3. Center-punch (for identification) parts which may be inadvertently interchanged.
4. Loosen the pinion nut first with a companion flange holding tool similar to the one shown in Fig. 14-43 and a torque multiplier and socket. Do not use an impact wrench, as this could damage the pinion bearings.
5. Cut and remove all lock wires, then loosen all cap screws and nuts.
6. After removing components, examine each part thoroughly for damage, wear, twist, or bends and check the threaded bores for damage. Do not forget

Fig. 14-43 Method of removing pinion nut. (*International Harvester Company*)

to check the bearing bores or the machined surfaces for wear or damage.

7. Lay out components on a clean surface, consecutively as removed. If shims are used, wire them to the bearing caps.

8. When lifting heavy parts from the carrier, have an assistant help, or use a rope sling and hoist.

9. Use a press or puller arrangement to remove press-fitted parts. Do not use a punch and hammer, as this could injure you and/or damage the components.

10. If the ring gear is riveted to the differential case or the differential halves are riveted together, use a drill 0.0312 in [0.78 mm] smaller than the rivet body to remove the rivet head. Do not use a cold chisel and hammer, as this could elongate the rivet holes and thereby cause a loose fastener. Press out the rivet so as not to damage the holes (see Fig. 14-44). It is common practice to replace all bearings and seals and the ring gear cap screws.

During the disassembly, or when the carrier is disassembled, scrutinize each component to determine the cause of failure.

Failure Analysis Insufficient or incorrect oil is the primary cause of carrier failure. In either case, the

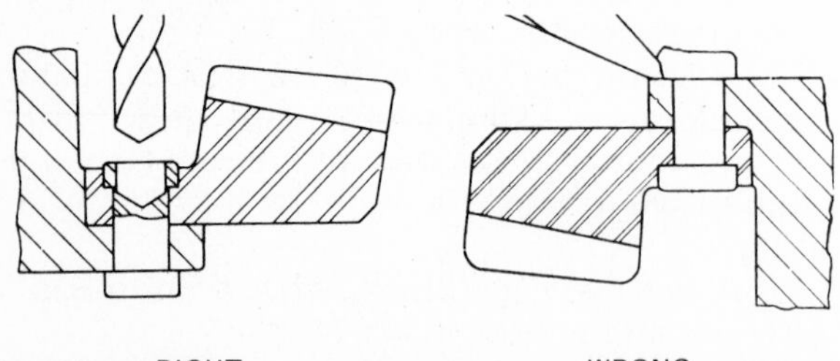

Fig. 14-44 Correct and incorrect method of removing gear rivets.

Fig. 14-45 View of scored and scuffed gear teeth. (*International Harvester Company*)

gear teeth will wear and scuff, due to insufficient lubricating film between the tooth surfaces (see Fig. 14-45). Excessive torque input can also cause the same damage, as even the best lubricant, having a high film strength, can be forced from between the teeth. Although not quite visible in Fig. 14-45, the metal has reached the plastic stage and has been drawn across the teeth surfaces.

If only the coast side of the ring gear and drive pinion are scored or scuffed, the pinion bearings are worn, damaged, or have inadequate preload. This will cause the backlash to decrease and the tooth contact to change. Consequently the contact area is localized, which increases the pressure and thereby reduces the oil film at this point. Carrier failure can also result from fast downhill driving and using the engine clutch to reduce the speed.

FRACTURED GEAR TEETH Fracture on either the toes or heels of the ring gear teeth is caused by improper tooth contact (gear adjustment). Improper adjustment concentrates and reduces the contact area on the teeth, and the input torque cannot be carried by the reduced area. See Fig. 14-46.

PITTED GEAR TEETH Pitted gear teeth, as shown in Fig. 14-47, are either the result of the gear set being adjusted improperly (contact area on the drive face of the ring gear teeth) or the carrier being exposed to extremely severe service. Note that the pitted area in the illustration is near the root and toward the heel of the teeth. Extremely severe operating con-

Fig. 14-46 View of fractured gear teeth. (*International Harvester Company*)

ditions place excessive force on the pinion teeth. The pinion and ring gear will deflect and the tooth pattern (toward the heel and root) will change, with the end result that the contact area will have insufficient lubrication. The high loading force breaks down the lubrication film and then the tooth surfaces become pitted. If the ring gear teeth surfaces do not show pitting, it is because each pinion tooth makes contact with the ring gear teeth several times (the number of times being determined by the gear ratio) before the same pinion tooth contacts the same ring gear tooth. When the pinion is damaged, you should also replace the ring gear because correct tooth contact cannot be achieved between a new and a worn gear, and the carrier will therefore be noisy.

If the planetary gear set or the double-reduction gear set teeth are pitted or show case crushing, these conditions can also be the result of deflection caused by excessive force (loading) on the gear teeth. In this case the tooth contact area on one end of the teeth is reduced, therefore the force placed on the smaller contact areas results in reduced lubrication and a metal-to-metal contact, so that eventually the tooth contact surface breaks down.

FATIGUE FRACTURE Fatigue fracture is the ultimate failure of the gear set after it has developed pitting, scuffing, or case crushing, since any of these conditions reduces the tooth contact surface area and this smaller area must therefore carry all the force. When, momentarily, excessive stress now occurs, such as when the clutch is quickly released or it is necessary to pull out of a difficult spot, one or more gear teeth may fatigue, and eventually total carrier failure (fatigue fracture) will result.

If one or more gear tooth sections are broken off, it is due to shock loading or operating conditions which exceed the designed tooth capacity. However, fatigue fracture on the side gears, as shown in Fig. 14-48, is the result of misalignment between the side

Fig. 14-47 View of pitted bevel pinion teeth. (*International Harvester Company*)

gears and wheel hubs. In this case, the misalignment prevents equal distribution of the stress onto the side gear spline, and places it onto one side. **NOTE** This failure may be the end result of a condition which started much earlier and is, therefore, categorized as *progressive fatigue*.

OVERHEATING An overheated carrier causes bearing failure and tooth surface discoloration, and will, depending upon the length of operation, eventually lead to pitting, scoring, scuffing, etc. As mentioned previously, it is brought about by excessive over-

Fig. 14-48 View of side gear fracture—misalignment. (*International Harvester Company*)

load, low oil level, and/or contaminated or incorrect oil, any one of which will reduce the oil film between the rolling elements and races, and between the gear teeth, thereby causing a metal-to-metal contact. First the bearing will fail, in some cases the pinion and pilot bearings will fuse to the pinion, and the bearing will rotate in the bearing bore.

EXCESSIVE WEAR When the spider pinion gears are seized, or the spider is worn to the extent shown in Fig. 14-49, the machine has seen too much active use from the time of the initial scoring to the end result of metal-to-metal contact of the spider-to-pinion bores. The conditions under which the machine has operated may be one or more of the following: (1) insufficient lubricant, (2) continuous wheel spinning for various reasons (including different tire rolling radiuses), and (3) excessive force on the side gears.

If the bearing bores are scored or worn, it is usually because of bearing failure or seizure, or due to overload conditions.

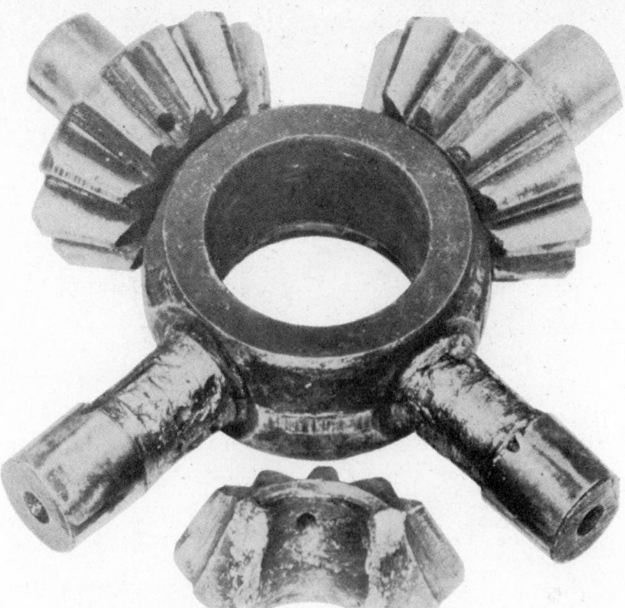

Fig. 14-49 View of scored and seized spider and spider pinion gears. (*International Harvester Company*)

Reassembly Carrier reassembly is not simply the reverse of disassembly, because several measurements and adjustments have to be made during reassembly.

As you are now fully aware, two main factors prevent deterioration of a carrier's operating life and repeat carrier failure: bearing adjustment and proper tooth contact. Other factors which enhance service life are cleanliness during the reassembly, proper installation of press-fitted parts (bearings and gears), proper torque, proper locking of cap screws and nuts, and correct wheel bearing adjustment.

After all parts are thoroughly cleaned, the first step of the reassembly is to record from the service manual the recommended torque specification, the bearing preloads, the pinion depth setting, the maximum ring gear runout, and the ring gear-to-pinion backlash.

Table 14-1 gives an example of these specifications.

Table 14-1 CARRIER TORQUE SPECIFICATIONS

Nuts and screws

Component	Diameter, in	Threads per in	Torque lb · ft	Torque N · m
Pinion shaft nut	1	20	300—400	406.5—542
Differential bearing cap cap screw	3/4	10	230—300	311.6—406.2
Carrier housing cap screws	7/16	20	53— 67	71.8— 90.7
Pinion bearing cage cap screws	7/16	14	53— 67	71.8— 90.7
Cross-shaft bearing cap screws	1/2	20	81—104	109.7—140.9
Cage and cover cross-shaft bearing cap screws	1/2	20	81—104	109.7—140.9
Cross-shaft bearing locknuts	9/16	12	94—120	127.3—162.6
Differential nut	7/16	14	53— 67	71.8— 90.7
Differential adjusting nut lock cap screws	5/16	18	16— 20	21.6— 27.1
Inspection cover cap screws	3/8	16	27— 35	36.5— 47.4
Shift unit mounting cap screws	3/8	16	27— 35	36.5— 47.4

Bearing preload and bearing specifications

Component	Specification
Drive pinion torque	5 to 15 lb · in [0.564 to 1.69 N · m]
Cross-shaft torque	5 to 15 lb · in [0.564 to 1.69 N · m]
Differential bearing	After zero end play tighten adjusting nut $1\frac{1}{2}$ to 2 notches
Pinion-to-ring-gear backlash	0.020 to 0.026 in [0.51 to 0.66 mm]
Pinion depth	3.125 in [79.37 mm]
Ring gear runout	Maximum 0.005 in [0.127 mm]
Shift fork clearance	0.010 in [0.254 mm] minimum
Shift fork adjustment	0.005-in [0.127 mm] clearance when engaged

Table 14-2 PINION BEARING PRELOAD SPECIFICATIONS

Pinion shaft thread size	Specified nut torque		Equivalent press force, tons
	lb · ft	N · m	
1¾ in × 18	300— 400	406.5— 542.0	6
1¼ in × 18	700— 900	948.5—1219.5	11
1½ in × 12	800—1100	1084.0—1490.5	14
1½ in × 18	800—1100	1084.0—1490.5	14
1¾ in × 12	800—1100	1084.0—1490.5	14
2 in × 16	800—1100	1084.0—1490.5	14
2⅛ in × 12	1100—1400	1440.5—1897.0	16

PINION PRELOAD After installing the drive pinion to the pinion bearing cage (using a spacer of the thickness specified, or the one previously used) and after lubricating the bearings with the recommended oil, place the assembly onto the press bed as shown in Fig. 14-50. Next, press the front pinion bearing squarely and firmly against the spacer while rotating the pinion case. These steps are necessary to assure normal bearing contact and to assure that the spacer selected is not too thin (as this would cause too much bearing preload).

Depending on the circumstances, either use the press, as shown in Fig. 14-50, to apply the required force onto the front bearing, or install the companion flange and tighten the pinion nut to the recommended torque in order to measure the rolling torque of the pinion or pinion bearing cage. When you use the press and the assembly (positioned as shown in Fig. 14-50), select from Table 14-2 the recommended force (6 ton [6 t]), which, as you can see, is equal to the pinion nut torque 300 to 400 lb · ft [406.5 to 542.0 N · m]. Apply the force while rotating the cage.

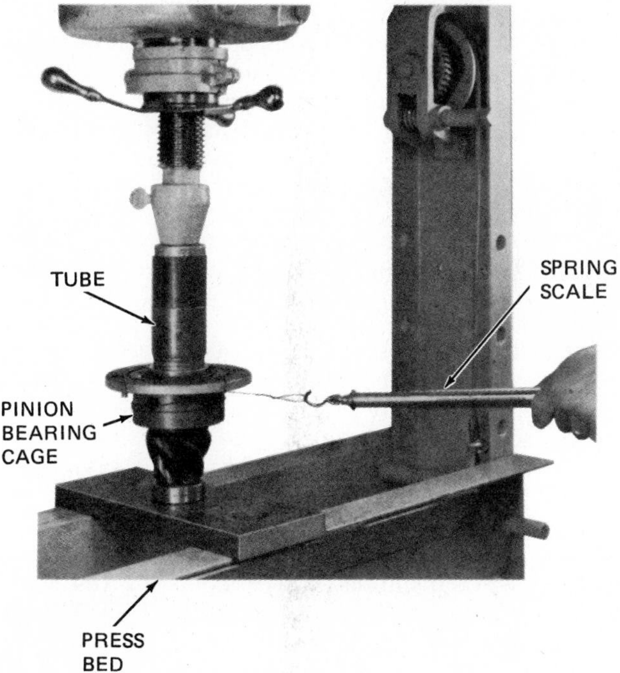

Fig. 14-50 Measuring pinion bearing preload. *(International Harvester Company)*

Next, wrap a string several times around the bearing cage and attach a spring scale to the end of the string. With a 6-ton [6-t] force applied, slowly pull on the spring scale in order to rotate the bearing cage. When the bearing cage rotates freely, note from the spring scale the number of pounds [kilograms] required to maintain rotation. If the pinion bearing cage does not rotate freely, or if it is jerky or sticks, the assembly must be disassembled to determine the cause of the stickiness or jerkiness. **CAUTION** Some service manuals specify pull in pounds or kilograms, whereas others specify the torque.

Assume the spring scale reading is 5 lb [2.27 kg] while the cage is freely rotating, and the service manual specification given is, say between 5 and 10 lb [2.27 and 4.54 kg]. Then the pinion bearing preload is adjusted within specification.

NOTE When new bearings are used, adjust them to the maximum recommended preload.

Suppose the service manual specification is given in torque, and is 5 lb · in [0.564 N · m]. To calculate the (rotation) torque, the radius of the pinion cage must be taken into calculation. If the cage diameter is 6 in [152.4 mm], the radius is 3 in [76.2 mm] and a pull of 5 lb [2.27 kg] on the spring scale would produce a torque of 5 × 3 = 15 lb · in [1.69 N · m]. The bearing preload is then too high. If this method of measuring the pinion bearing preload cannot be applied, install the companion flange and tighten the pinion nut to the recommended torque. Then clamp the pinion cage in a vise having protected jaws, and by using a pound-inch torque wrench and socket measure the rotating torque of the drive pinion.

If the bearing preload is too high, install a spacer of greater thickness than the one being used; this will separate the two bearing cones and thereby reduce the preload. If the preload is too low, install a thinner spacer than the one being used; this will increase the preload.

PINION DEPTH SETTING To achieve the correct tooth pattern, the pinion must be positioned so that the cone point intersects with the center line of, or passes, the ring gear, depending on the gear set design. See Fig. 14-51. There are two methods for establishing this point. One, which is fast and nearly foolproof, is to use one of the various types of pinion depth setting gauges. The other is the trial and error

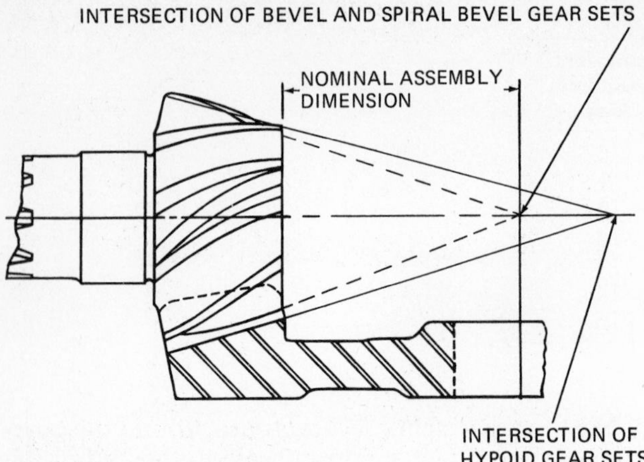

Fig. 14-51 (*a*) Intersection of bevel and spiral bevel gear sets. (*b*) Intersection of hypoid gear sets.

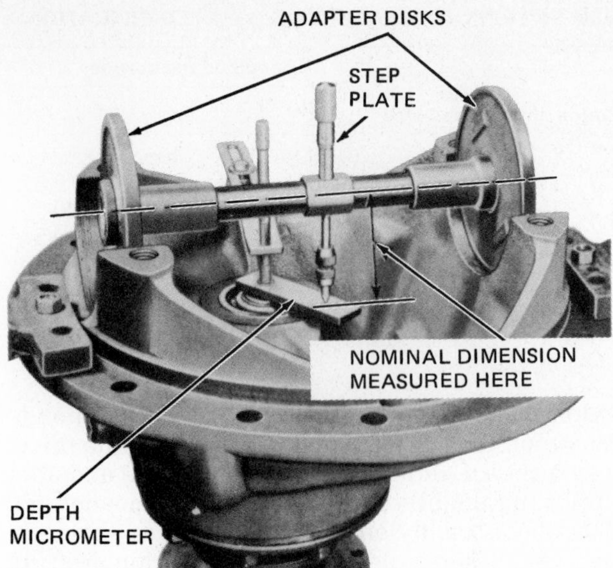

Fig. 14-53 View of a pinion gauge setting tool in position. (*International Harvester Company*)

way of using the printed pattern (tooth contact pattern) on the ring gear to correctly position the pinion. Regardless of the method you are about to use, first install the pinion bearing cage to the carrier housing, placing shims of the same thickness as those used between the bearing cage and carrier housing, and tighten the cap screws to the recommended torque.

If you use a pinion setting gauge, you must understand the figures etched on the pinion (see Fig. 14-52). One number indicates the gear set number. The second + or − number indicates the tolerance of the gear set (in comparison to the master gear set). The third number indicates the pinion depth. A fourth number may be used to indicate the backlash. Make certain all surfaces are clean and the depth micrometer is not out of adjustment, and then place the gauge measuring tool into position, using a C clamp; clamp the step plate or gauge block on top of the pinion. The gauge block is needed to transfer (designate) the pinion height under the spindle of the micrometer. See Fig. 14-53.

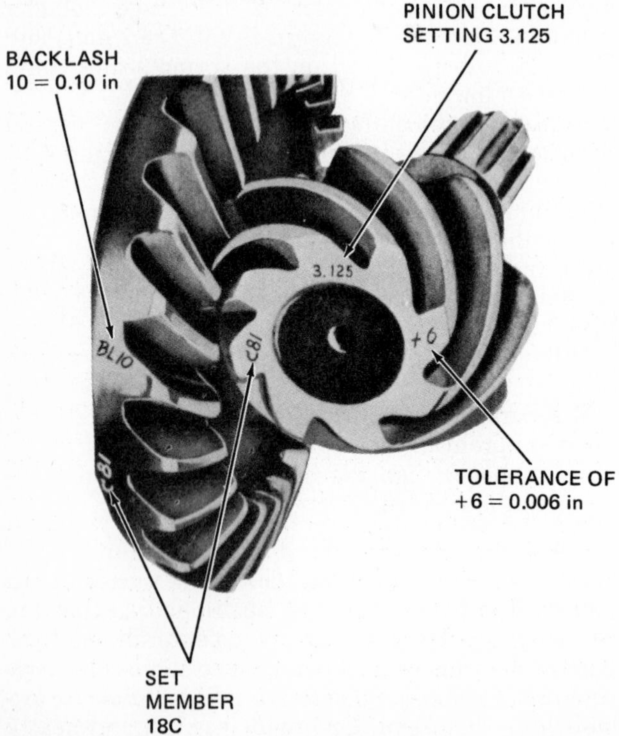

Fig. 14-52 Gear set markings. (*International Harvester Company*)

Assume the pinion depth is 3.125 in [79.38 mm], the step plate thickness and the adapter disk shaft radius are each 0.5 in [12.7 mm], and the etched pinion number is +6 (0.006 in) [0.15 mm]. When the gauge tool is properly positioned, turn the micrometer spindle until the spindle end rests lightly against the step plate or gauge block. Now read the measurement from the depth micrometer.

CAUTION Some gauges are designed to measure the distance from the center line of the adapter disk shaft to the step plate or gauge block, whereas others require that you add the radius of the shaft to the measurement. Assume the micrometer reading is 2.11 in [53.6 mm]. The actual distance to the pinion from the center line of the ring gear would be 3.116 in [79.15 mm]:

2.110 in + 0.5 in (step plate thickness) + 0.5 in (radius of shaft) + 0.006 in (the pinion edge number +6) = 3.116 in [79.15 mm].

This means that the pinion must be moved out by 0.009 in [0.23 mm]; therefore install a 0.009-in [0.23-mm] shim stock between the pinion bearing cage and the carrier housing to bring the pinion depth to 3.125 in [79.38 mm] (see Fig. 14-54). If the gear set were marked −6 (−0.006 [0.15]) and the micrometer reading were the same as above (that is, 2.11 in [53.6 mm]), 0.021 in [0.53 mm] of shim stock must be installed (2.11 − 0.006 = 2.104 + 0.5 + 0.5 = 3.104 + 0.021 = 3.125 [79.38]). **NOTE** On some carriers the pinion depth variation is achieved by varying the shims or spacer thickness between the bearing cone and pinion or between the bearing cone and transmission housing.

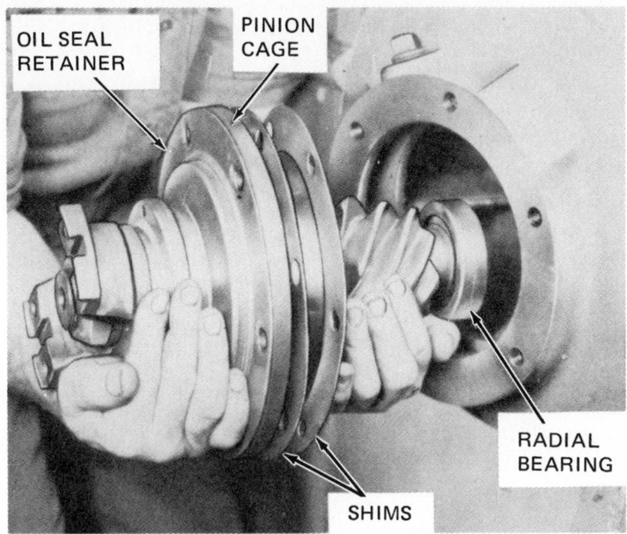

Fig. 14-54 Removing the pinion in order to install required shim. (*International Harvester Company*)

A simpler but equally accurate pinion depth setting gauge is shown in Fig. 14-55. It consists of a tube (cross-bore arbor) which is nearly equal in diameter to the bearing bore. The pinion depth is determined by placing a standard shim or gauge block between the arbor and the end of the pinion and then, with a feeler gauge, measuring the remaining space.

RING GEAR RUNOUT After the drive pinion depth is adjusted, install the differential assembly or cross-shaft assembly. When it has been placed into the carrier housing, and the differential bearing caps, the bearing cups, and the adjusting nuts are positioned, tighten the adjusting nuts evenly and snugly against the bearing cups so that you can feel an end play between the ring gear and pinion, but no end play of the differential assembly. Then install a dial indicator, as shown in Fig. 14-56, onto the back face of the ring gear. Zero the dial, and with prybars try to move the assembly to the left and right while observing the indicator dial. Adjust the bearing nut opposite the ring gear until there is no end play. Now turn each adjusting nut one notch to add bearing preload. Refer to the appropriate service manual for this specification. With chalk, mark the adjusting nut-to-carrier housing position. Again zero the dial and then check the runout by rotating the assembly while observing the dial needle movement. You may, with the chalk, indicate the high runout point. If the ring gear runout exceeds specification (0.005 in) [0.127 mm], the ring gear is not seated properly onto the differential case flange or housing flange, or the differential case flange is damaged or has a high spot, or there may be dirt lodged between the flange and the ring gear. In any event, the ring gear must be removed and the cause of runout determined.

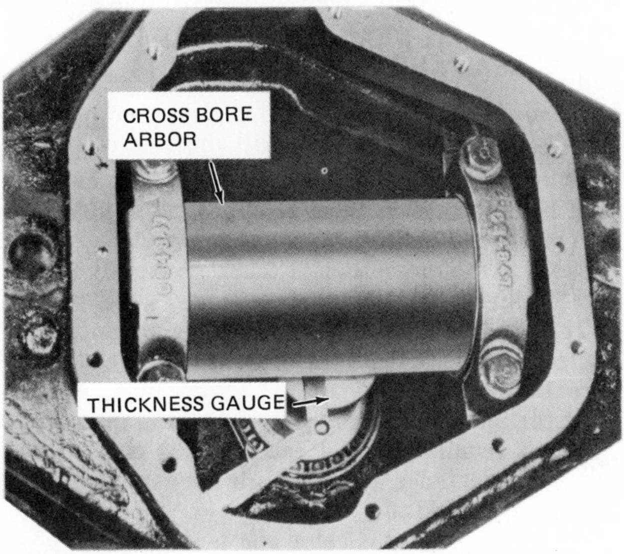

Fig. 14-55 Method of determining shim pack thickness for pinion depth setting. (*Chrysler Corporation*)

Fig. 14-56 Measuring differential bearing preload. (*International Harvester Company*)

RING GEAR BACKLASH When the differential assembly is installed and the bearing preload adjusted, adjust the ring gear backlash. To do this, install a dial indicator as shown in Fig. 14-57. Make certain the spindle is square to the tooth surface; otherwise the backlash reading may not be correct because the spindle end may slip on the tooth surface and an angle larger or smaller than 90° will vary the spindle travel. When positioned, zero the dial indicator and gently rock the ring gear back and forth (without moving the pinion) while observing the needle movement. If the backlash is too high, loosen the four differential cap cap screws, loosen the adjusting nut opposite the ring gear one or two notches, and tighten the (ring gear side) adjusting nut by the same number of notches. Retorque the differential cap cap screws and recheck the backlash. When installing the cross shaft, insert on each side the same number of shims previously used. Tighten the bearing cover

Fig. 14-57 Measuring ring gear backlash. (*International Harvester Company*)

cap screws in a cross pattern to the recommended torque, and while tightening them continuously turn the ring gear to assure that the shaft turns freely and a backlash between the ring gear and pinion is maintained.

CROSS-SHAFT BEARING PRELOAD To measure the cross-shaft bearing preload, use the method shown in Fig. 14-58. **CAUTION** When referring to the service manual, note if it is pound or kilogram pull. If the bearing preload is less than specified, remove a shim from the opposite side of the ring gear to increase the torque. If the rotating torque is too high, install a shim between the carrier housing and bearing cover on the ring gear side. The thickness of the shims to be removed or installed depends on the distance necessary to increase or decrease the rotating torque.

Fig. 14-58 Method used to measure rotating torque. (*International Harvester Company*)

The next check is the ring gear runout and the backlash adjustment. The backlash adjustment is done by removing a shim from one side and adding a shim between the housing and bearing cover on the other side.

GEAR TOOTH CONTACT To correctly interpret the service manual, you need to understand the geometric terms used to describe certain points and areas of the gear teeth. For example, the gear tooth surface (left and right) is called the *profile*. No matter on which side of the differential case the ring gear is positioned, the convex side is the drive side and the concave side is the coast side (these are the reverse on an amboid gear set). A gear tooth is longitudinally divided in two by the *pitch line*. **NOTE** Although the pitch line is the mating line of the gear teeth, it is not in the middle of the tooth.

The upper part of a tooth is known as the *addendum* or *face*, and the lower part as the *dedendum* or *flank*; the top of the tooth is called the *tip* or *tip land*; the lower curved profile is the *root* or *root fillet*. In addition, the gear tooth is divided vertically into three parts—the narrow front part called the *toe*, the large end called the *heel*, and the portion between called the *center*. The space between the root and the tip is known as the *clearance*, and the space between two pitch lines is the *backlash*. See Fig. 14-59, where this terminology is illustrated.

To ensure that the adjustment of the pinion and backlash provide the correct tooth pattern, with a brush apply oily white or red lead lightly to the ring gear teeth. To obtain an effective and true tooth print on the ring gear teeth, use a pry bar to increase the rotation resistance of the ring gear; then gently rotate the pinion in a drive (clockwise) direction until the ring gear has made one full revolution. Next, rotate the pinion in the coast drive (counterclockwise) direction until the ring gear has made one full revolution. Pinion teeth contact with the ring gear teeth will now have printed a pattern on the ring gear and pinion teeth.

Closely examine the printed pattern on the drive and coast sides of the ring gear. If the pinion and backlash are correctly adjusted, both sides (drive and coast) of the ring gear teeth will show an elongated rain drop pattern starting near the toe and stopping about one-quarter of the tooth length from the end of the heel. The center line of the tooth pattern should be the pitch line. See Fig. 14-60. Under operating conditions, the torque causes some deflection of the carrier housing and gears, and the tooth pattern spreads out, moving more toward the heel than the toe.

TOOTH CONTACT PATTERNS AND ADJUSTMENTS If the pinion depth is measured and adjusted with a pinion depth setting gauge, in most cases the tooth pattern will be correct. If, however, the tooth pattern is not satisfactory, increase or decrease the ring gear backlash by moving the ring gear within the limit of backlash specification.

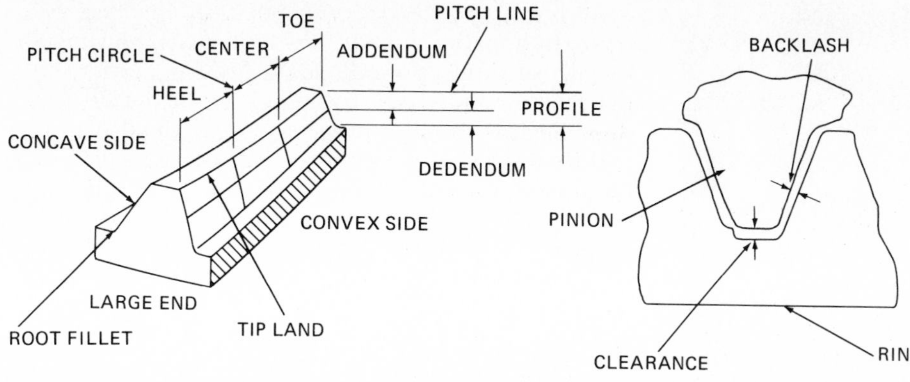

Fig. 14-59 Gear tooth terminology.

If the original gear set is being reinstalled, you may have to move the pinion inward by about 0.002 in [0.05 mm] to compensate for wear on the gear teeth; otherwise the backlash would exceed maximum specification. However, when making this adjustment, avoid overlapping at the worn tooth section. See Fig. 14-61.

If the pinion depth was not set with a depth setting gauge, you may have one of the patterns shown in Fig. 14-62. It may then take hours of work to achieve the correct pattern, and while continuously removing and reinstalling the pinion bearing cage and differential assembly you may even damage the bearings.

The most common pattern is too much toe on the drive and coast sides. In this circumstance, you may increase the backlash to its maximum by moving the ring gear away from the pinion. However, when the drive side shows too much toe and the coast side too much heel, you have to move the pinion (inward) toward the ring gear center line and at the same time move the ring gear away from the pinion to achieve the required backlash.

If the pattern shows too much toe and it is toward the face of the teeth on the drive side, usually the heel and face pattern will show on the coast side (see Fig. 14-62*b*). The pinion must then be moved inward and the ring gear moved away from it in order to attain a good tooth pattern with the specified backlash.

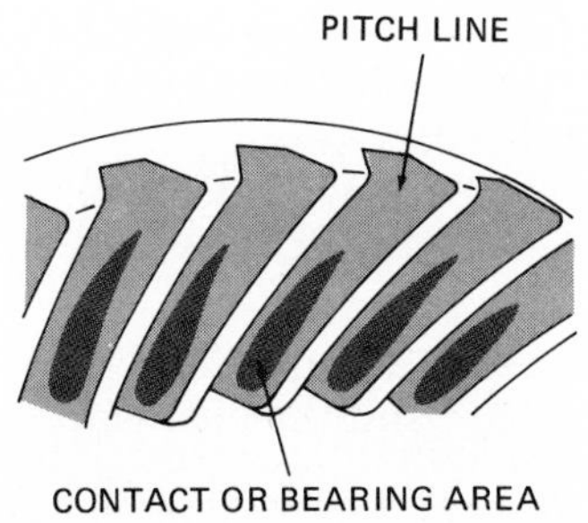

Fig. 14-60 Correct tooth pattern.

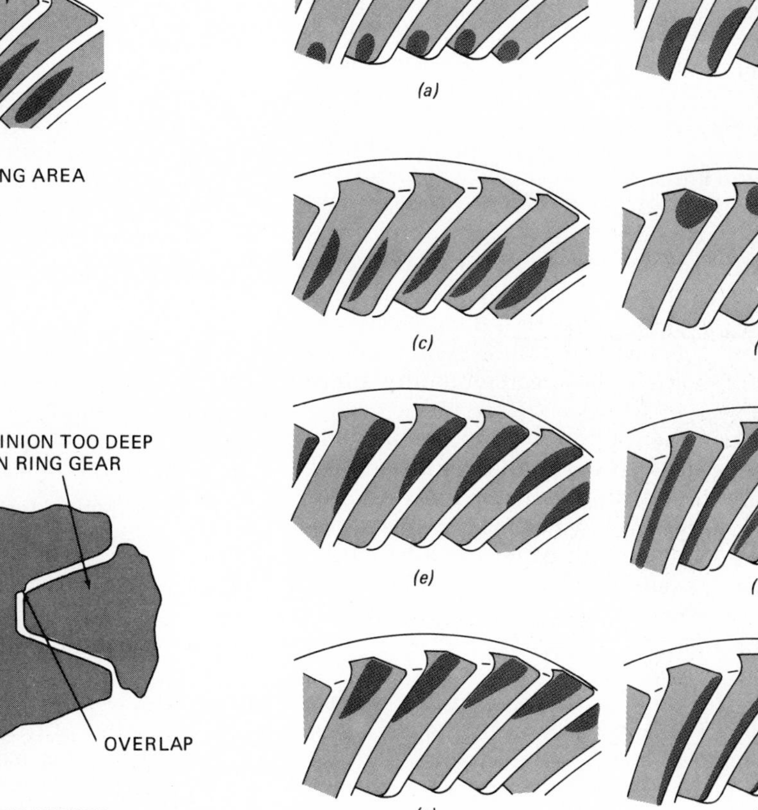

Fig. 14-61 Results of correct and incorrect pinion depth. (*International Harvester Company*)

Fig. 14-62 View of various tooth patterns for left- or right-hand or hypoid ring gears.

Fig. 14-63 Floor jack support carrier. (*International Harvester Company*)

If the pattern shows too much toe and it is toward the flank on the drive side of the teeth (Fig. 14-62*c*), the pattern on the coast side will be on the heel and toward the flank. The pinion must be moved outward and, if necessary, the ring gear moved toward it to attain the required backlash.

If the pattern shows too much heel on the drive side (Fig. 14-62*d*) and too much toe on the coast side, the pinion must be moved outward and the ring gear moved toward it in order to achieve the specified tooth pattern and backlash.

If the pattern is on both the drive and coast sides on the face of the teeth, the pinion must be moved inward and the ring gear moved away from it in order to attain the specified tooth pattern and backlash (Fig. 14-62*h*).

If the pattern is on the flank on both sides of the teeth, the pinion must be moved outward and the ring gear moved toward it to attain the specified tooth pattern and backlash (Fig. 14-62*e*).

If the pattern is on the heel and face on the drive side of the teeth (Fig. 14-62*f*) and on the coast side it is on the toe and face, the pinion must be moved outward and, if necessary, the ring gear must be moved toward it to attain the specified tooth pattern and backlash.

If the pattern on the drive side is on the heel and flank (Fig. 14-62g) and on the coast side it is on the toe and flank, the pinion must be moved inward, and if necessary, the ring gear must be moved away from it to attain the specified tooth pattern and backlash.

When the tooth pattern is correct, recheck the torque of all cap screws, lock-wire them as required, and then install the pinion seal.

Installation Clean the carrier mounting surface and axle housing surface. Check for damaged studs, and if any are damaged replace them; check for damaged threaded bores and if necessary restore them using heli-coils. Place a new carrier gasket onto the axle housing and, with a sling and hoist, lift the carrier from the work stand onto the floor jack (Fig. 14-63). Roll the carrier into position and bolt it to the axle housing. Install new axle seals, and install the wheel hubs and axle shaft. Fill the carrier with the recommended oil to the bottom of the fill level hole. Secure the filler plug, reconnect the drive line, and then operate the motor vehicle at 30 mph [48.3 km/h] for about 5 min to ensure that lubricant reaches all parts of the assembly. Recheck the oil level and if necessary add oil. Lower the motor vehicle onto the ground and, finally, test-drive it.

Review Questions

1. Name the five main components of a carrier.
2. Which main component (*a*) divides the torque equally to both axle shafts, and (*b*) multiplies the engine torque?
3. Name the four types of gear sets used in front and/or rear carriers.
4. What are the two major differences between a track-type and a wheel-type carrier?
5. Explain why the side gears and the spider pinion gears do not need to be supported on any type of antifriction bearing.
6. Explain the power flow from the drive pinion to the axle shafts (*a*) when a two-speed carrier is in reduction and the motor vehicle is traveling in a straight-forward direction, and (*b*) when the motor vehicle makes a left-hand turn. (*c*) Explain why under condition (*b*) the outside rear wheel rotates faster by a ratio of 1:2 as compared to the speed of rotation of the inside rear wheel.
7. What is the main purpose of the torsion spring in the electric shift mechanism?
8. What is the main difference between a double-reduction carrier and a two-speed, double-reduction carrier?
9. (*a*) List the purposes of an interaxle differential; (*b*) explain why interaxle differentials have a lockout clutch.
10. Explain the power flow of the interaxle differential when the lockout clutch is disengaged and the rear-rear axle wheels are forced to rotate faster than the front-rear axle wheels.
11. On a Mack interaxle power divider, explain the basic principle which is used to (*a*) divide the torque equally between the front-rear axle and the rear-rear axle drive pinions, and (*b*) transfer (in a jerky motion) up to 75 percent of the total available torque to the drive pinion having the higher resistance to rotation.
12. For what purpose is a torque selector used on the front-rear axle carrier?
13. List the disadvantages of a differential lock over any other type of traction equalizer.
14. Outline the overall operating principle of the

Mack power divider differential and a torque proportional differential.

15. Explain the disadvantages of the traction equalizer differential shown in Fig. 14-32 when compared to the one shown in Fig. 14-33.

16. List the advantages of a nonspin differential over other differential (other than the planetary type).

17. (*a*) Explain the mechanical action of a nonspin differential when the motor vehicle is making a left-hand turn. (*b*) Why do the left-hand tires rotate at the same speed as the ring gear when the vehicle is making a left-hand turn?

18. The first indication of carrier trouble is increased temperature; the second is undue noise. Explain why the carrier could create excessive noise (*a*) in drive operation, (*b*) when the motor vehicle is in reverse, or is coasting and (*c*) during a turn.

19. What could cause an axle shaft to (*a*) twist? (*b*) fatigue?

20. When disassembling a carrier, why is it a recommended practice to (*a*) mark matched parts, (*b*) not to use an impact wrench, (*c*) to use two mechanics, or a hoist and sling, to lift heavy component parts from the carrier housing, and (*d*) first drill the rivets and then press them out.

21. List the problems which could be assumed when you find, upon examining the carrier gear, that (*a*) the gear teeth surfaces are fractured, (*b*) the gear teeth surfaces show pitting, and (*c*) the gear teeth are fatigue-fractured.

22. Outline the methods to adjust (*a*) the drive pinion bearing preload, (*b*) the drive pinion depth, and (*c*) the differential case or housing bearing preload. (*d*) Explain how to measure the rolling torque of the drive pinion.

23. When using a pinion depth setting gauge to measure and adjust the pinion depth, and the gear set tolerance indicates −5, (*a*) what does the −5 tolerance indicate? (*b*) how does this vary from the pinion depth specification given in the service manual?

24. When measuring the ring gear backlash, why must the spindle of the dial indicator be 90° to the gear tooth surface?

25. Explain why you must move the drive pinion inward and the ring gear away from the pinion when the tooth pattern shows too much toe on the drive side and too much heel on the coast side.

26. List two causes for tooth pattern disparity at quarterly intervals of the ring gear.

Unit 15
Winches and Wire Ropes

A winch is a transmission that converts mechanical, hydraulic, or electric energy into rotary motion to rotate a drum. A wire rope is attached to the drum so that as the latter rotates, the wire rope winds onto or off the drum. It is used to perform work such as pulling an object on or off the ground, raising a load, boom, or blade, closing a grapple or bucket, etc. A winch can only perform work by winding the wire rope onto the drum, as no power can be transmitted when the wire rope is wound off the drum. The wire rope can be wound off the drum by controlling the drum brake and thereby the drum rotating speed. It can also be wound off the drum by using a reverse gear set or a planetary gear set within the winch, or by using a reverse motor. Under the latter three circumstances, the drum reverse speed is controlled by the motor, the engine speed, or the gear ratio of the winch, or through a directional control valve (hydraulically) or by varying the current flow. See Fig. 15-1 for a view of a winch attached to a track-type tractor.

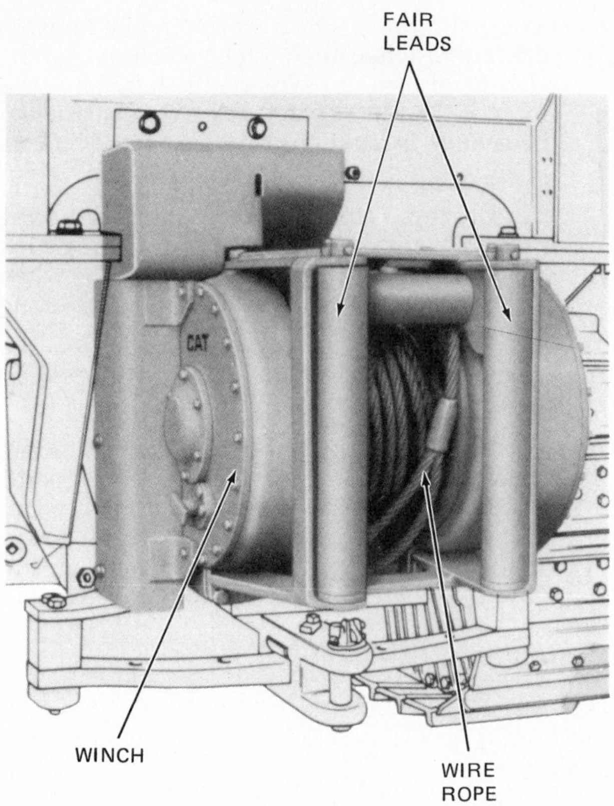

Fig. 15-1 View of a winch mounted to a track-type tractor.

WINCHES

As you are well aware, winches are used on track- and wheel-type tractors, log skidders, cranes, and shovels, or wherever work can be accomplished by reducing the wire length. They may be classified by (1) their pull-in power (line pull) which ranges from about 2000 to 200,000 lb [8896 to 889,644 newtons (N)] on on- and off-highway equipment, (2) their drive method (mechanical, hydraulic, or electric), and (3) their design in regard to line speed, drum capacity, type of application, reverse powerout, automatic brakes, clutch type and clutch actuation, or the method used to transmit power.

As an example of classification, besides the model number and make, a winch might be described as follows: mechanical drive; main line pull on bare drum 100,000 lb [444,822 N]; maximum line speed at rated engine rpm 40 feet per minute (ft/min) [12.2 meters/minute (m/min)]; drum diameter 14 in [35.56 cm]; length 26 in [66.04 cm]; maximum drum capacity 300 ft [91.5 m]; wire rope 1⅛ in [2.86 cm]; multidisk clutch; power reverse; and automatic brakes.

NOTE The maximum line pull is rated at the bare drum; that is, the winch can pull the maximum designed load (kilograms or pounds) until the second layer of wire rope starts to wind onto the drum. The lever arm then increases by the diameter of the wire rope, which reduces the torque and increases, in proportion, the line speed. For example, if in Fig. 15-2 the winch drum shaft torque were 60,000 lb·ft [81,300.0 N·m] and the drum diameter were 12 in [30.5 cm], the line pull then would be (60,000 × 12)/6 = 120,000 lb [533,787 N] pull. If the drum rotated at a speed of 10 rpm, the line speed would be $(10 \times D \times \pi)/12 = (10 \times 12 \times 3.14)/12 = 31.4$ ft/min [9.57 m/min]. After the first layer of wire rope, the drum radius has increased by the diameter of the rope. Say the rope is 1½ in [38.1 mm]; then the

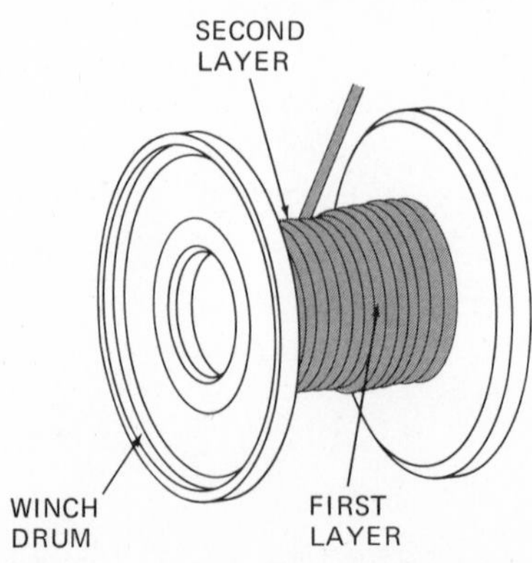

Fig. 15-2 View of a winch drum with a second layer on the winch drum.

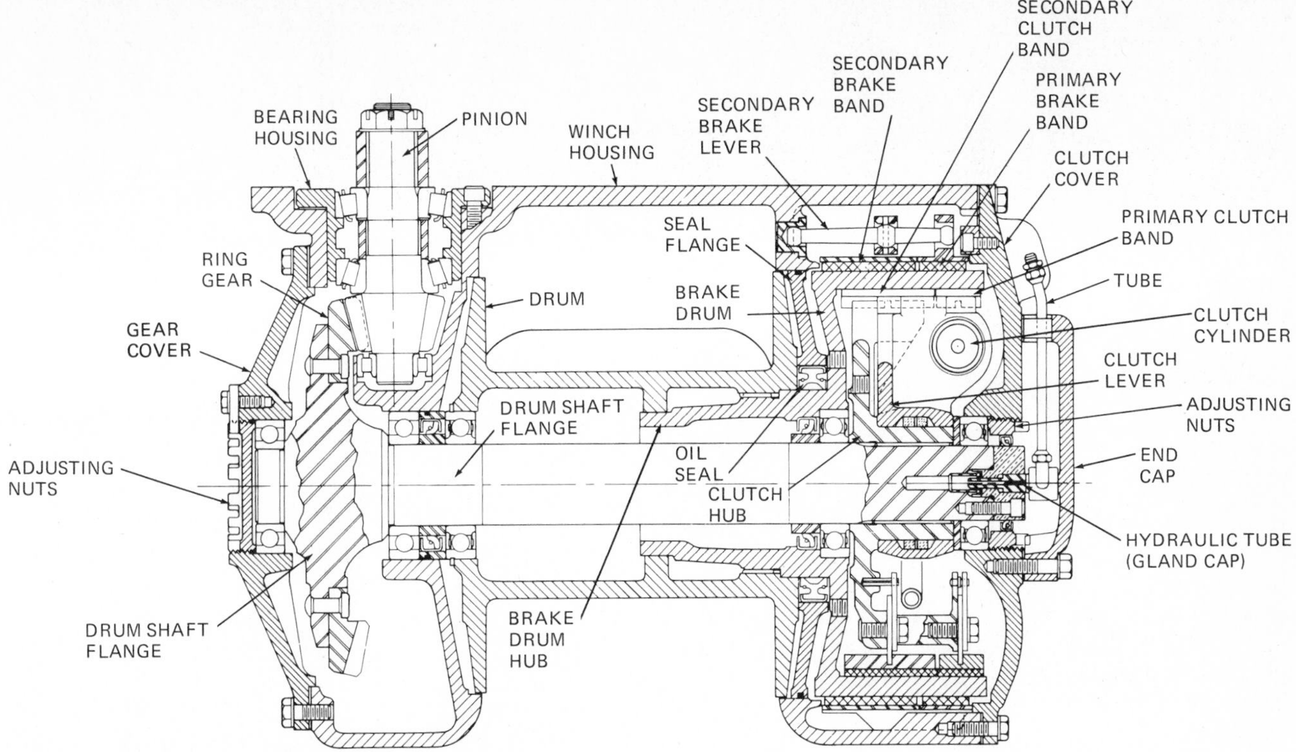

Fig. 15-3 Sectional view of hydraulically controlled mechanically driven winch. (*Gearmatic Co.*)

drum diameter increases to 13.5 in [342.9 mm], which reduces the pulling power to (60,000 × 12)/6.75 = 106,666 lb [48,382 kg] pull and the line speed would increase to (10 × 13.5 × 3.14)/12 = 35.32 ft/min [10.77 m/min].

Track- and Wheel-Type Tractor Winches These types of winches are by far the most commonly used. They are manufactured in an array of sizes, types, and power sources. One of the smaller mechanically driven winches is shown in Fig. 15-3. It is hydraulically controlled, has a maximum line pull of 11,800 lb [52,489 N], and a line speed of 117 ft/min [35.68 m/min]. It is designed to automatically apply the drum brakes after the winch-in operation has stopped. The brake and clutch bands each have self-energizing features. That means the force from the primary brake band or clutch band is transmitted to the secondary band, increasing the brake or clutch force onto the drum. The winch is attached to the transmission case through an adapter housing which contains one or two sets of reduction gears. The power to drive the pinion shaft comes from the tractor's PTO shaft, which can be engaged and disengaged through a separate PTO clutch. The reduction gear set is the link between the PTO shaft and the pinion (not shown in Fig. 15-3). It is used to reduce the PTO shaft speed and to increase torque. **NOTE** Fairleads are used to allow the winch to pull the wire rope onto the drum from any direction; they are bolted to the winch housing.

DESIGN The pinion is supported by tapered roller bearings in the bearing housing and by a roller bearing in the winch housing. A bearing spacer is used to adjust the pinion preload, and shims are used for adjusting the pinion depth. The crown gear is riveted to the winch shaft flange, and the shaft is supported with roller bearings in the gear cover and clutch cover. The adjusting nut and the bearing cap screws are used to adjust the crown gear position by moving the clutch shaft to the left or right. The left-hand side of the winch drum is supported on the winch shaft by a roller bearing. The brake drum hub, which is supported by a roller bearing on the drum shaft, is splined to the right-hand side of the winch drum. The primary brake band (outside) and the secondary brake band (inside) surround the drum. The hydraulic brake cylinder components and brake spring are located in the winch housing, which is linked, through the pushrod and actuating mechanism, with the two brake bands. The clutch hub is splined to the right-hand side of the winch shaft, to which the clutch lever, adjusting device, and actuating mechanisms are attached. The connection between the stationary hydraulic line and the clutch cylinder is achieved through a gland cap that is bolted to the drum shaft, the hydraulic line adapter, and an hydraulic line.

OPERATION When the control handle is in the neutral position, there is no hydraulic pressure on the clutch slave cylinder or brake cylinder (see Fig. 15-4). The brake spring forces the lever block to apply the primary brake band, which in turn applies the secondary brake band. If under this condition the PTO clutch is engaged, the PTO shaft drives the reduction gear set, which drives the pinion and the

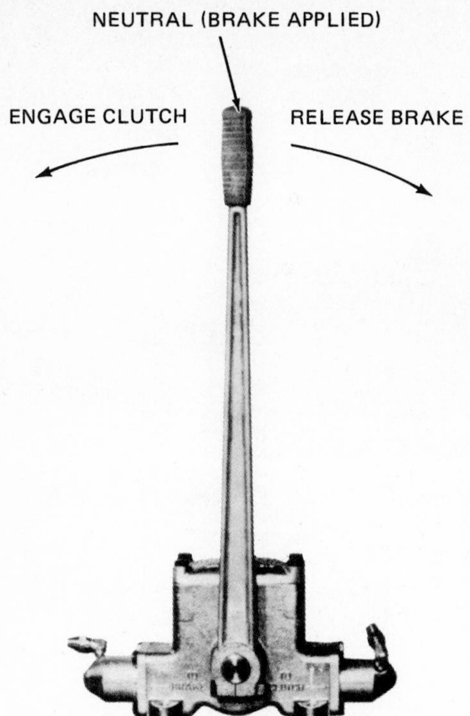

Fig. 15-4 View of the master control (double-acting master cylinder).

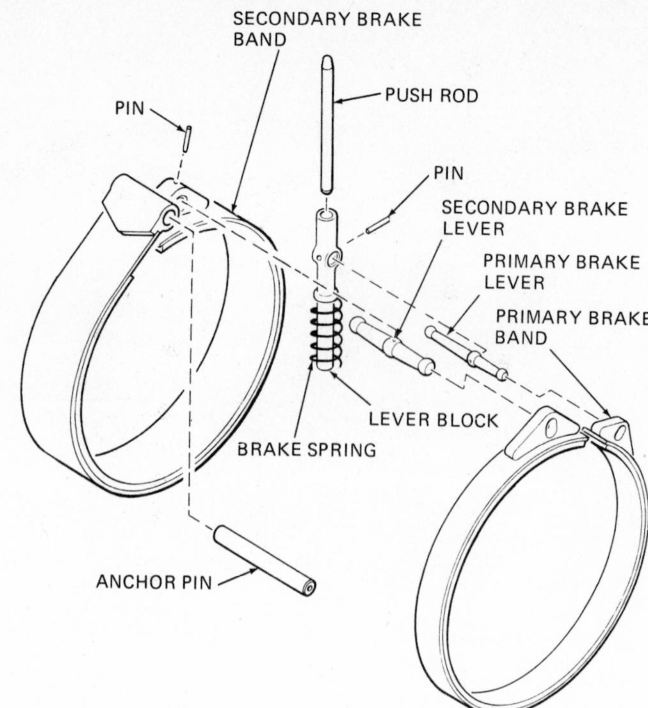

Fig. 15-5 Exploded view of the brake components. (*Gearmatic Co.*)

crown gear, causing the drum shaft to rotate. No power is transmitted because the clutch is disengaged, and the winch drum is held stationary through the primary and secondary brake bands. When the operator moves the control handle fully forward, it locks in this position and the double-ended master cylinder displaces fluid to the brake cylinder. As the pressure builds up, it overcomes the brake spring, forcing the pushrod and lever block downward, releasing the brake bands. (See Fig. 15-5, where the components involved in these operations are illustrated).

The drum will free-spool (rotate freely) but with enough resistance to prevent more wire rope from unspooling from the drum. In other words, when the brake is working properly and the winch is in good mechanical condition, the operator must pull on the wire rope to rotate the drum to wind the wire rope off. **NOTE** If the control handle is moved forward only partly, the brake bands are only partly released.

When the operator positions the handle to the neutral position, as previously outlined, the primary and secondary brake bands are applied. **NOTE** With increased line pull during a pulling operation, the brake band, due to the brake lever, is pulled with higher force against the drum, which results in a higher braking force.

To pull in the wire rope, the operator pulls the control handle rearward. The master cylinder then displaces fluid into the clutch slave cylinder, which partly rotates the clutch lever on the clutch hub. The pushrod then forces the primary clutch band against the internal friction surface of the brake drum, forcing the secondary band against the friction surface. This connects the clutch hub (splined to the drum shaft) with the brake drum (splined to the winch drum). Because of the brake drum rotation (pull-in) and brake band arrangement, the brake band partly rotates, moving the brake levers, which releases the brakes. By increasing or decreasing the pull on the control handle, the hydraulic clutch pressure is varied, giving the operator effective pull-in control.

TROUBLESHOOTING Most winch malfunctions are the result of inadequate maintenance such as insufficient lubrication, which will cause bearings to fail and gears to wear, or improper adjustment, which will cause the clutch or brakes to slip, glazing the friction lining and damaging the drum surface.

Should the clutch slip on the winch as shown in Fig. 15-3, first check the hydraulic fluid level of the master cylinder; then pull the handle rearward, and note if it feels spongy. If it does, there is air in the system, so the pressure developed is insufficient to overcome the spring force. If the handle continues to move rearward there is a fluid leak in the system. Fluid leaks occur from loose fittings, damaged hydraulic lines, or damaged master or clutch slave cylinders. If the control handle travel is excessive, the clutch is out of adjustment.

If none of the above defects is found in a malfunctioning winch, inspect the clutch bands. They may be worn, may have become soaked with brake fluid, or may be glazed from excessive slippage, or water may have leaked into the brake and clutch compartment. Check the drum shaft bearings for wear or damage, which would cause the clutch and brake bands to misalign and result in reduced band contact.

When the brakes will not hold a load (with the

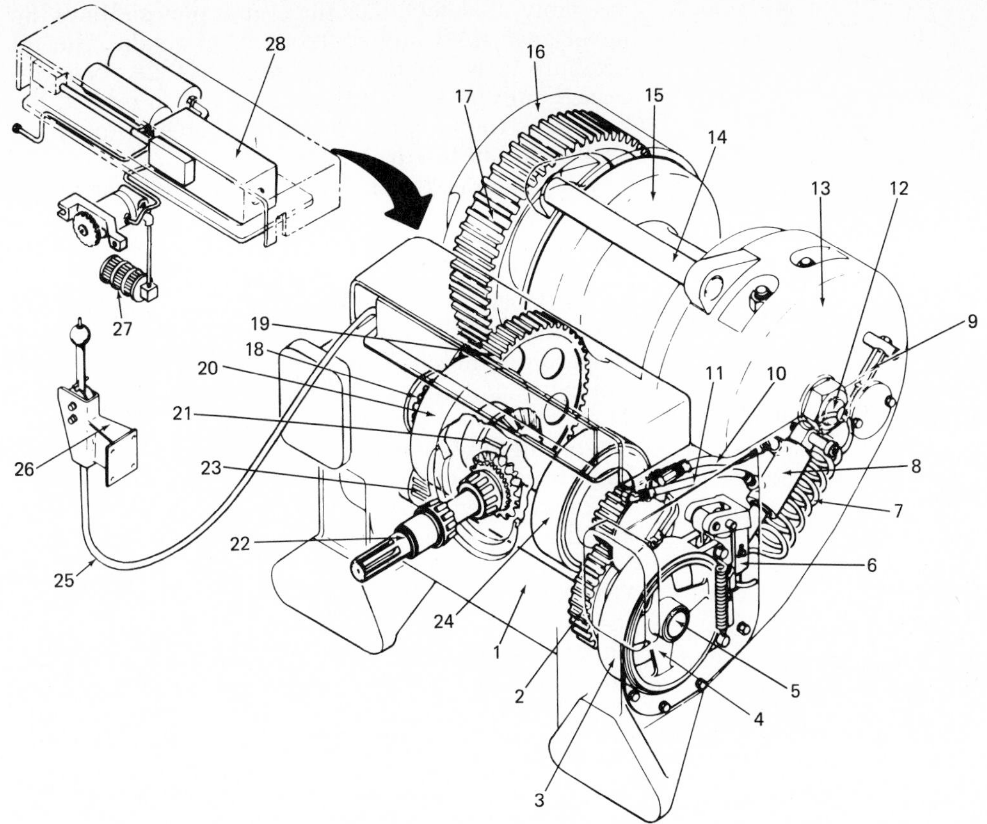

1. Winch case
2. Brake shaft gear
3. Brake band
4. Brake drum
5. Brake shaft
6. Brake arm
7. Brake apply spring
8. Brake release cylinder
9. Brake spring adjustment
10. Brake pressure hose
11. Brake return hose
12. Drum shaft
13. Brake side case cover
14. Cable guard
15. Cable drum
16. Gear side case cover
17. Bull gear
18. Bull pinion
19. Idler shaft gear
21. Bevel gear
22. Bevel pinion
23. Brake shaft pinion
24. Forward clutch
25. Control cable
26. Control stand
27. Suction strainer
28. Control valve

Fig. 15-6 Schematic view of a hydraulically controlled mechanically driven winch. (*Pacific Car and Foundry Co.*)

control handle in the neutral position), check the master cylinder. You may find that the piston hangs up, preventing hydraulic pressure from releasing from the brake cylinder. Check the brake bands for wear, glazing, or brake fluid penetration. Check the brake spring (which may be broken) and the connecting links (which may be damaged or broken), or the brake cylinder piston (which may be hanging up).

If the brake will not release when the control handle is moved forward, and the handle remains firm, the brake cylinder piston may have seized. This would also occur if the connecting links between the cylinder and primary brake bands were damaged or broken. If the control handle resistance gradually decreases when moved into the forward position, it is an indication of fluid leaks at the fittings, or leakage passing by the master or brake cylinder cup.

When the power transmitted to the winch drum is inadequate or nonexistent, it gives the sensation, when the clutch is actuated, that it is slipping. If this occurs, it may be that the PTO clutch is slipping, the crown gear rivets are sheared off from the drum shaft, or the reduction gears or the PTO shaft is broken.

Single-Drum Tractor Winch The schematic drawing of a single-drum tractor winch having a line pull of 150,000 lb [667,223 N] and a maximum line speed of 40 ft/min [12.2 m/min] is shown in Fig. 15-6. It is mechanically driven and hydraulically controlled by a single lever located in the cab, within easy reach of the operator. The control lever is linked through a flexible cable with the four-position open center control valve, located within the winch housing. The drum has a capacity of 400 ft [122 m] of 1-in [25.4-mm] wire rope. The winch is bolted to the rear face of the tractor's main frame, and the PTO shaft is connected through a coupling to the pinion. **NOTE** Whenever the engine is operating, the pinion and winch crown gear shaft and crown gear rotate.

DESIGN The pinion is supported by tapered roller bearings in the carrier housing, which is bolted to the winch housing. Shims are used to adjust the pinion depth to achieve the correct tooth pattern. The bevel gear shaft is supported on both ends by tapered roller bearings which are shim-adjusted for preload and to allow the shaft to be moved for the crown-gear–to–pinion adjustment. Two roller bear-

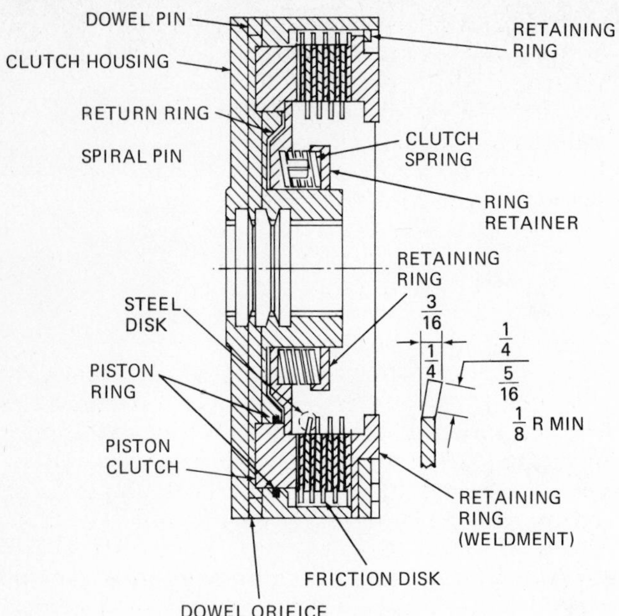

Fig. 15-7 Sectional view of the clutch assembly (without pinion (single-drum tractor winch). (*Pacific Car and Foundry Co.*)

ings near the forward and reverse clutch drum are used to support the middle of the shaft. The clutch pinions, to which the clutch's steel disks are splined, are supported (on the ends of the bevel gear shaft) by roller bearings. The right-hand pinion is in mesh with the brake shaft gear, and the left-hand pinion is in mesh with the large idler shaft gear. The clutch housings are splined to the bevel gear shaft, and the friction plates are splined to the internal teeth of the hubs. See Fig. 15-7. The brake shaft is supported by roller bearings in the winch housing, and the brake shaft gear, the brake shaft pinion gear, and the brake drum are splined to it. Shims are used behind the bearing cover to adjust the alignment between the brake shaft drive and driven gears. The brake cylinder and the actuating mechanism are attached to the brake band and winch housing. The idler shaft gear and bull pinion gear are splined to the idler shaft, which is supported by roller bearings in the winch housing. The bull pinion is in mesh with the drum bull gear, and the idler shaft gear is in mesh with the reverse clutch pinion gear and the brake shaft pinion gear. The cable drum shaft is secured to the winch housing with two nuts; therefore it is stationary. The drum is supported on the drum shaft by two sets of spherical roller bearings, and the drum bull gear is bolted to it. Lip-type seals and O rings are used throughout to prevent oil loss and contamination.

NEUTRAL OPERATION When the operating lever is in the neutral position and the engine is operating, the hydraulic pump draws oil through the filter from the winch housing (which is the reservoir) and forces it through the pressure filter into the directional valve, where it returns back to the reservoir. The oil pressure from the reverse and forward clutch drum cylinder releases and the clutch spring (within each assembly) that separates the clutch plates allows the bevel gear shaft and clutch hub to rotate. The oil pressure from the brake cylinder has also been released and has caused the piston rod to retract, the brake arm to pivot, and the spring force to apply the brake band to the drum.

When, under this condition, a pulling operation takes place, the winch drum cannot rotate because the brake shaft is held stationary by the brake band.

PAY-OUT OPERATION To pull the wire rope off the winch drum, the operating lever must be pushed forward one notch. This moves the directional control valve, and oil is directed into the brake cylinder. The piston rod then extends, pivoting the brake arm, extending the brake spring, and releasing the brake band from the brake drum. With the brake released, the brake, idler, and drum shaft are allowed to rotate, and the wire rope can be pulled off the winch drum.

POWER-OUT OPERATION To power-out the wire rope, the operating lever is pushed two notches forward. This moves the directional control valve, and oil is directed to the brake cylinder; it is also directed into the left-hand end of the bevel gear shaft, through the center- and cross-drilled passages, and into the clutch cylinder. The brake band then releases and the reverse clutch engages. The engagement of the clutch locks the reverse clutch pinion to the clutch hub. The power is now transmitted from the pinion onto the bevel gear shaft, from the reverse pinion gear onto the idler gear, and from the idler bull gear to the bull gear on the winch drum, thereby driving the drum in the reverse direction (power-out direction).

WINCHING-IN OPERATION When the operating lever is pulled fully back, the directional control valve directs oil to the brake cylinder and forward clutch cylinder, releasing the brake and locking the forward clutch pinion to the clutch hub. The pinion rotation is transmitted onto the bevel gear shaft and through the forward clutch pinion gear onto the brake shaft gear, rotating the brake shaft. This causes the brake shaft pinion gear to rotate the idler shaft gear and the idler bull gear. The drum bull gear and the drum are then forced to rotate in the pull-in direction, winding the wire rope onto the drum.

TROUBLESHOOTING AND TESTING Winch problems can generally be divided into four groups: no power or reduced power, no power-out or reduced power-out, brake will not hold or will not release, and the wire rope winds on or off the drum with the directional valve in neutral.

As mentioned previously, the most common cause of winch failure is poor maintenance. When the brake will not hold, first check the brake adjustment. Next, determine if the brake band is contaminated, the lining or drum surfaces glazed, or the lining and/or the drum worn. Also check the working condition of the brake cylinder and actuating mechanism. Either one may be damaged, therefore preventing the brake band from being applied or released. Check the brake shaft bearings. If they are damaged or worn, they cause misalignment, which would affect the brake friction efficiency.

If none of these defects are present, go on to check the directional control valve adjustment. If incorrectly adjusted, the operator should also have complained of reduced power or malfunction in the power-out or pay-out.

If the brake will not release, or the winch has a reduced pull-in power, install a flowmeter into the system and test the hydraulic system to determine its efficiency and the condition of the filters, hydraulic pump, control valve, brake cylinder, and clutches. Check the pressure at the clutch and brake cylinder. When the system pressure is low due to restricted filters, damaged or improperly adjusted control valve, or damaged relief valve, the brakes will not fully release.

NOTE The hydraulic pump has to be badly worn before the pressure is affected. (See your service manual for the procedure to check the system pressure.)

Next, make the following checks:

- The valve spool adjustment
- The brake band adjustment
- The adjustment of the brake and application spring—either one may be adjusted too tight

Improper or inadequate brake release may be the result of defective bearings or gears on the brake idler or drum shafts. However, if these were defective, the winch would be noisy during operation and would lack pull-in power.

If the pull-in is inadequate although the hydraulic system has checked out satisfactorily, the problem may be bearing and/or gear failure, particularly the roller bearings on the clutch pinion. However, it may be that the brake band adjustment is too tight. In each case, the effect would be apparent because of reduced engine rpm when maximum line pull is exerted, or because of increased winch oil temperature. Reduced power could also be the result of mechanical malfunction in the clutch release, which would adversely affect the release of the pinion, and, again, it could occur if there were some defect in the PTO drive.

Power-out or pay-out is also affected by each of the above.

If the wire rope winds on or off the winch drum with the control in neutral, it may be due to a combination of the brake not holding the brake shaft and one or both clutches being mechanically defective, the hydraulic piston hanging up, or the pinion roller bearings being damaged, causing power to be transmitted from the clutch hub to the pinion.

Superstructure Winches The winches used to operate a shovel, crane, etc., are basically the same in regard to design and operation as track-type winches. The most apparent differences are the following

1. The power source used to drive the winch; that is, whether the power source is the engine, an electric motor, or a hydraulic motor
2. The method of controlling the clutch band and brake band actuation
3. The type of clutch band and brake band and method of engagement and release
4. The types of fail-safe devices
5. The line pull, drum capacity, and line speed
6. The winch power-out

DESIGN One of two winches used on a nontelescoping crane is shown in Fig. 15-8. The drum shaft is supported by two sets of tapered roller bearings fastened to the winch frame. The lagging (front or rear drum) is bolted to the clutch drum, and the assembly is bolted to the spool, which is supported on the drum shaft by two sets of tapered roller bearings. The third drum assembly (one-piece-cast) is also supported on the drum shaft by two sets of tapered roller bearings. The clutch assembly of the boom hoist and third clutch is of the internal band design and is splined to the drum shaft (see Fig. 15-9). The drum shaft gear is welded to the drum shaft, to which the planetary ring gear of the boom hoist drum is welded. The sun gear of the planetary gear set is bolted to the spool and therefore turns with the drum shaft. The planetary carrier is cast with a brake surface and is supported on a bushing that is fastened to the exterior of the spool. The external brake bands on the third and boom hoist drums are spring-applied and hydraulically released, whereas the brake band of the planetary carrier is hydraulically applied and spring-released.

NEUTRAL OPERATION When the engine is operating and the engine clutch is engaged, the sprocket shaft and sprocket rotate. **NOTE** Some units use a torque converter instead of a mechanical clutch.

The power from the sprocket shaft is transmitted over a chain reduction drive onto the swing clutch shaft, and from there through a reduction chain drive to the intermediate reduction shaft. From this shaft, the power is transmitted through a chain drive onto the jack shaft. The drive gear is splined to the jack shaft and is in mesh with the drum shaft gear (see Unit 2, "Off-Highway Equipment"). When the winch directional control valve is in neutral, the planetary brake band is released, the brakes apply on the boom hoist and third drum, and both clutches release; therefore no power is transmitted to either drum. The planetary ring gear rotates and drives the carrier gears, but it only rotates the carrier in the same direction as the ring gear (although slower), because the sun gear that is bolted to the spool is held stationary by the front or rear drum brake band.

When the hydraulic system pressure reaches the set pressure, the fail-safe hydraulic cylinder compresses the fail-safe spring, releasing the brake from the boom hoist drum. When the operator now depresses the brake pedal, the brakes are applied through the second hydraulic brake cylinder, and when the brake pedal is released the spring force releases the brakes.

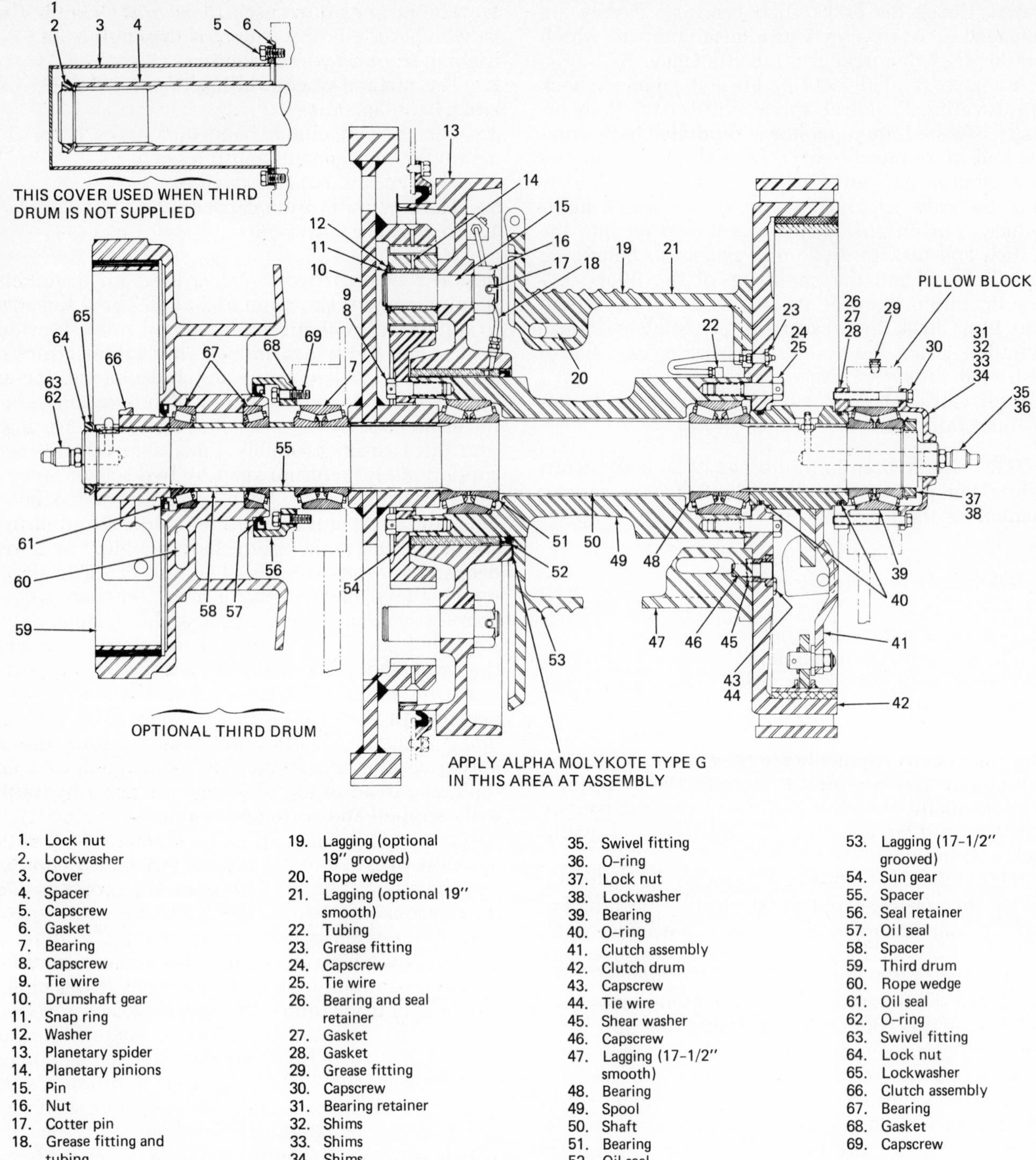

Fig. 15-8 Sectional view of the front drum shaft assembly for winch used on nontelescoping cranes. (*Harnischfeger Corporation*)

RAISING THE LOAD To raise the load, the operator directs oil to the main clutch cylinder, whereupon the clutch band friction connects the clutch drum with the clutch assembly and causes the boom hoist drum to rotate. **NOTE** The drum speed depends on the engine speed and clutch band friction. Because the planetary sun gear and ring gear rotate at the same speed and the carrier gears are therefore stationary (do not rotate), the ring gear, the carrier, and the sun gear rotate as a unit.

To stop the drum rotation and thereby hold the load, the operator gradually reduces the clutch pressure and at the same time depresses the brake pedal, applying the brake. Under this condition, should the hydraulic pressure drop due to the malfunction or hydraulic failure of components, the pressure is removed from the fail-safe piston, and as soon as the pressure is less than spring force the fail-safe spring applies the brake.

LOWERING THE LOAD The operator has two options by which to lower the load: (1) When the load is light, she or he simply releases the clutch and then gradually releases the brake pedal force to reduce

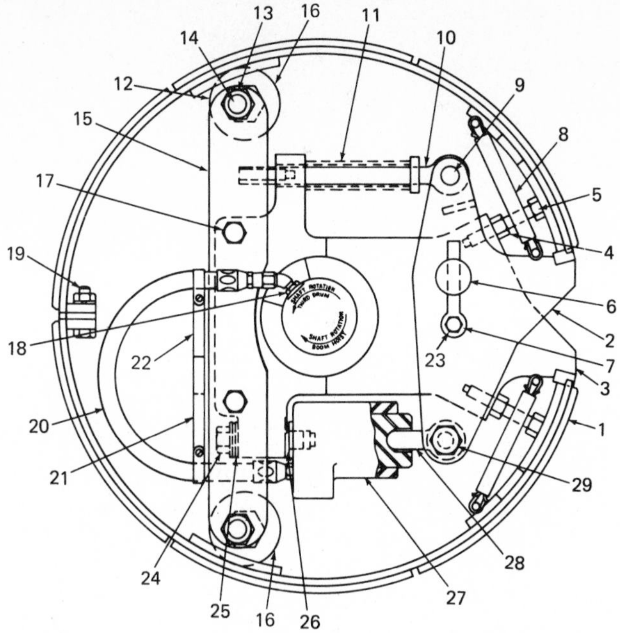

1. Clutch band
2. Spider
3. Lever
4. Nut
5. Adjusting bolt
6. Pin
7. Rod end
8. Spring
9. Pin
10. Eye bolt
11. Spring
12. Roller
13. Nut
14. Adjusting bolt
15. Bracket
16. Washer
17. Capscrew
18. Connector
19. Bolt
20. Hydraulic hose
21. Hose strap
22. Clamp
23. Capscrew
24. Capscrew
25. Washer
26. Washer
27. Cylinder
28. Eye bolt
29. Capscrew

Fig. 15-9 Schematic view of the boom hoist and third drum clutches for winch used on nontelescoping cranes. (*Harnischfeger Corporation*)

the brake cylinder pressure. This reduces the brake force, and now the load forces the drum to rotate. By controlling the brake pressure, the operator controls the lowering of the load.

(2) The lowering of a heavy load by this method would cause excessive heat, however, which could lead to an uncontrolled lowering. The operator therefore has a second option—power-lowering the load. To do this, he or she applies the planetary brake band hydraulically and at the same time releases the drum brake. This holds the planetary carrier stationary. The ring gear now drives the carrier gears which drive the sun gear, the spool, and the clutch drum in a direction opposite to that of the ring gear, unwinding the wire rope from the drum and thereby lowering the load. The lowering speed is controlled by the engine speed and gear reduction.

THIRD DRUM OPERATION The mechanics of winding the wire rope off or onto the third drum are the same as those for the main drum.

If the third drum is used as the boom hoist drum, it then also has a planetary gear set. However, in this case the ring gear is attached to the boom hoist drum assembly, the sun gear is splined to the drum shaft, and the carrier is supported on a bushing that is press-fitted onto the sun gear hub.

Two-Speed Hydraulic Winch A two-speed power-in and power-out hydraulic winch used on a telescoping crane is shown in Fig. 15-10. This winch has two externally mounted, hydraulic gear motors to which the motor valve is bolted.

DESIGN The sprag clutch (sleeve) hub is supported on roller bearings in the winch housing and serves as a coupling between the winch motor shaft and the drum shaft. The brake disk is bolted to the external sprag clutch hub. Two spring-applied, hydraulically-released, caliber brake assemblies are positioned over the brake disk and bolted to the winch housing. The winch drum is supported by roller bearings in the winch housing and sealed with lip-type seals against oil loss and contaminants. The final drive, located in the right-hand housing, consists of two planetary gear sets—outer and inner. They are used to reduce drum speed and to increase torque. Both ring gears are bolted to the housing and are therefore stationary. The outer planetary sun gear

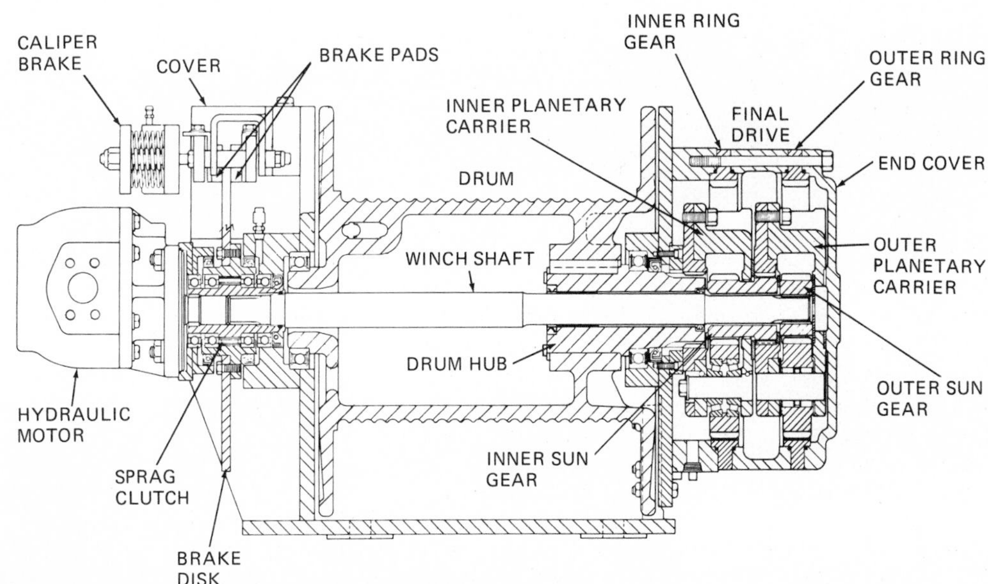

Fig. 15-10 Sectional view of a two-speed hydraulic winch. (*Harnischfeger Corporation*)

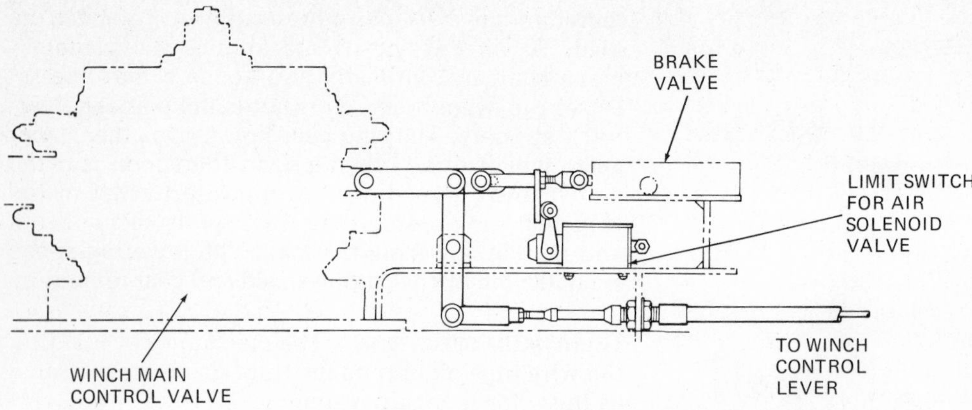

Fig. 15-11 Schematic view of a main winch control and brake valve installation (two-speed hydraulic winch).

is splined to the drum shaft. The inner sun gear is supported on the drum shaft through a bushing and is in mesh with the inner carrier gears and splined to the outer carrier (housing). The carrier of the inner planetary is splined to the drum hub that is press-fitted into the drum. The hydraulic circuit includes a four-position open-center directional control valve, to which the two-position brake control valve is mechanically linked (see Figs. 15-11 and 15-12), and a motor valve (two-position spool valve) is bolted to the hydraulic motors. A two-position solenoid control valve is used to control the motor valve actuation to achieve either high or low speed. A pressure relief valve is used to protect the system from becoming overpressurized.

NEUTRAL AND HOLD OPERATION When the winch directional control valve is placed in the neutral or raised position, the control valve at the same time moves the brake valve, which removes the oil pressure from the brake cylinder. The spring pressure then forces the brake pads against the brake disk, which in effect holds the drum, prevents the spool from rotating, and therefore holds the load stationary.

RAISING THE LOAD When the winch control valve is moved to the RAISE position (to raise the load), oil is directed into one motor valve port. This valve directs oil to both hydraulic motors because the two-speed solenoid valve is automatically in the low-

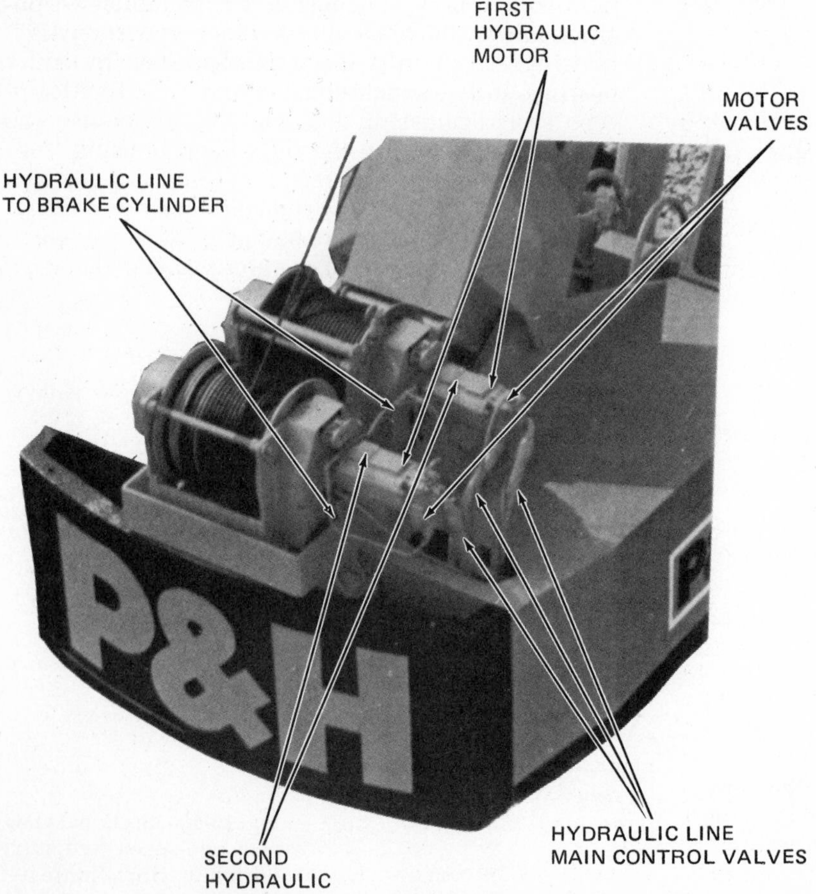

Fig. 15-12 View of the main and auxiliary winch (two-speed hydraulic winch). (*Harnischfeger Corporation*)

speed position and therefore has removed the pressure from the motor valve. Oil from the hydraulic motors returns into the motor valve, flows back to the directional control valve, and then flows back to the reservoir. Because the brake is applied and the motor shaft is turning, the sprag clutch releases. Both hydraulic motors are forced to rotate and drive the drum shaft with its outer sun gear. The outer sun gear forces the carrier gears to rotate within the ring gear, causing the carrier and the inner sun gear to rotate. The inner sun gear drives the inner planetary carrier gears, forcing them to rotate within the planetary ring gear. Consequently the carrier also rotates in the same direction as the hydraulic motors, the drum shaft, and the inner and outer carriers. Because the inner carrier is splined to the winch drum, the drum rotates in the same direction as the hydraulic motors.

When the operator energizes the control switch to achieve high-speed operation, the two-speed control valve is energized. As it shifts, it directs oil to the motor valve; the motor valve then shifts and directs all hydraulic pump oil into one hydraulic motor, resulting in a higher drum speed but lower torque. As soon as the operator de-energizes the control switch, the two-speed solenoid control valve is de-energized (which removes the pressure from the motor valve) and the spring force of the motor valve shifts the motor valve spool so that pump oil is again directed into both hydraulic motors.

LOWERING THE LOAD If the operator shifts the winch control valve to the load lowering position, the brake valve shifts simultaneously and oil is directed into the other motor valve port. As the system pressure increases, it overcomes the brake spring force and releases the brake. Now, because of the hydraulic motor rotation, the sprag clutch locks up and the hydraulic motor output shaft brake disk and the drum shaft rotate as a unit. As a result, the final drive and drum rotation reverse and the load is lowered under hydraulic power control. The operator can also energize the control switch for high-speed operation to lower the load.

When the operator moves the winch control valve into the neutral position, the brake valve shifts simultaneously and oil flow to the motor valve ceases. This removes the oil pressure from the hydraulic motors and the pressure from the brake cylinders. The brake spring forces the brake pads against the brake disk, holding it stationary. The sprag clutch then locks up, holding the drum shaft stationary also.

When the operator moves the winch control valve into the fourth position (which is also a lowering position), oil from the hydraulic pumps is directed back to the reservoir and the oil from the hydraulic motors (which under these conditions are now driven by the drum over the final drive) recirculates from the motors to the motor valve, to the winch directional control valve, and then back to the motor valve and hydraulic motor inlet. As a consequence of recirculating the oil within the circuit, the load can be lowered under controlled free fall.

Hydraulic Tractor Winch Another hydraulic winch is shown in Fig. 15-13. Although it is more prevalent on wheel- and track-type tractors, it can also be used on cranes, shovels, etc. This winch has a maximum line pull of 22,000 lb [97,860.0 N] and a line speed of 60 ft/min [18.3 m/min] on a bare drum in the forward direction, and a line speed of 320 ft/min [97.6 m/min] in reverse. Note, however, that these data are based on an oil flow of 65 gal/min [246.0 l/min] at a pressure of 1900 psi [13,091 kPa].

Some further differences between this winch and the one previously illustrated are the following

1. It has only one gear hydraulic motor which is located in the right-hand (primary) housing, and the sun gear of the primary planetary gear set is splined to the hydraulic motor shaft.
2. The two planetary gear sets are not in the same housing, the secondary planetary set being in the final drive housing. The two planetary gear sets are linked through the sun gear shaft, which is splined on one end to the primary planetary carrier and on the other to the sun gear of the final planetary drive.
3. This winch uses a spring-applied, hydraulically released multidisk brake rather than a single-disk brake. The brake plates are splined to the primary planetary ring gear and the reaction plates are splined to the internal teeth of the primary housing.
4. Rather than one sprag clutch, this winch uses three—one for each primary planetary carrier gear.

NOTE When the winch is driven in the wind-in direction, the sprag clutches allow the carrier gears to rotate on their shafts, and when driven in the spool-out direction the sprag clutches lock up, driving the carrier.

The hydraulic system (Fig. 15-14) consists of the reservoir, the hydraulic pump, a three-position open center directional valve, and filters. **NOTE** Some installations require a heat exchanger, in which case a thermostat is placed in the reservoir to sense the oil temperature and a thermostatic valve is placed in the inlet cooling line to control the cooling flow through the heat exchanger. Apart from the differences outlined, the two winches illustrated are alike in design. The winch drum in each case is supported by roller bearings in the winch housing, and the final drive planetary ring gear comprises part of the final drive housing.

NEUTRAL OPERATION When the engine or any other power source drives the hydraulic pump and the directional control valve is in neutral, oil from the hydraulic pump flows through the open center directional control valve, the heat exchanger, and the filters, and back to the reservoir. At the same time, oil flows from the T fitting preceding the filter, in and out of the primary housing, and back to the reservoir. The purpose of this oil flow is to cool and lubricate the primary housing components.

NOTE When the winch directional control valve is in neutral, or in the pull-in position, the primary

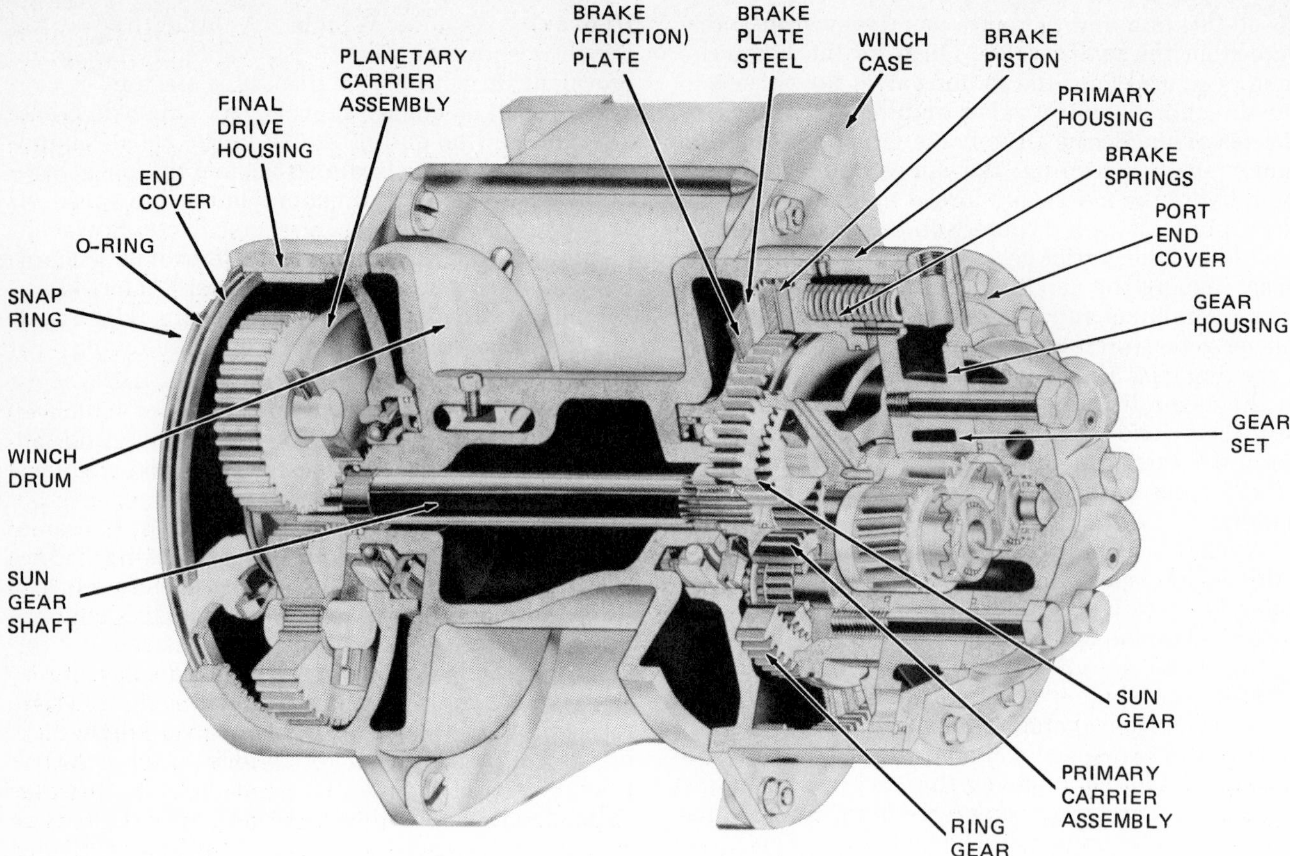

Fig. 15-13 Cutaway view of a hydraulic winch. (*Gearmatic Co.*)

ring gear is held by the brake spring force because the oil pressure is released from the brake cylinder piston. When a pulling operation begins under this condition, the winch drum is held through the combined action of the brake (ring gear) and the carrier gear sprag clutches (Fig. 15-15), because in this case the pull on the wire rope, in effect, tries to rotate the drum in the reverse direction. This causes the primary carrier gears to lock up, and with the ring gear held stationary the drum cannot rotate.

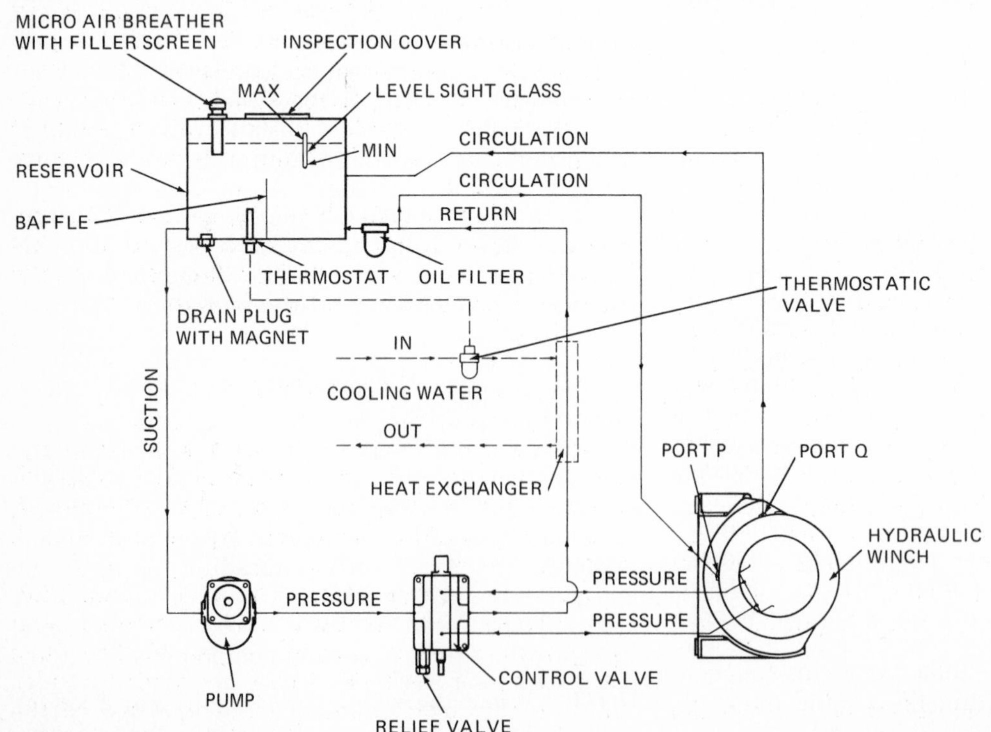

Fig. 15-14 Schematic view of the hydraulic system. (*Gearmatic Co.*)

Fig. 15-15 View of the sprags within a carrier gear. (*Gearmatic Co.*)

PULL-IN When the directional control valve is moved toward the pull-in position, oil flows into the winch motor port P.

NOTE The flow rate is determined by the engine speed and the position of the control valve.

The hydraulic motor is forced to rotate, and the return oil from the motor flows out of port Q, back to the directional control valve, and then to the reservoir. The rotation of the motor shaft causes the primary sun gear to rotate because they are splined together, and this drives the primary carrier gears. Due to the direction of rotation, the sprag clutches allow the carrier gears to rotate within the stationary ring gear, which causes the carrier to rotate in the same direction as the sun gear. The carrier, in turn, now drives the sun gear shaft and the final drive sun gear, which then drives the final drive carrier gears, causing them to rotate within the stationary ring gear. As a result, the final drive carrier and drum rotate in the same direction as the hydraulic motor shaft.

If the system pressure exceeds the set pressure due to increased line pull (above rating), the pressure relief valve unseats and maintains maximum pressure.

POWER-OUT When the operator moves the directional control valve into the power-out direction, oil is directed into motor port Q, then out of port P and back to the directional control valve. At the same time, oil is directed through internal passages to the brake cylinder, releasing the brake and allowing the primary ring gear to rotate. The reverse rotation of the hydraulic motor locks up the sprag clutches of the primary carrier gears and prevents the gears from rotating. This causes the sun gear, the carrier, and the ring gear to be driven as a unit, nullifies the primary reduction, and drives the shaft and the final drive sun gear at the same speed as the hydraulic motor shaft. A lower torque and higher drum speed is then achieved.

Troubleshooting Hydraulic Winches In a broad sense, hydraulic winch problems may be categorized into five groups: no power, low power, no power-out, reduced line speed, and drum not holding load or reduced line pull.

If no power is transmitted to the drum when the winch control is actuated, the (electric or air) control circuit may be defective. To check the electric control circuit, use a voltmeter and check for continuity and the voltage drop of each component connection. Use an ohmmeter to check the solenoid coil for an open, short, or ground. If an air-actuating circuit is used, check (using a pressure gauge) the individual actuating circuits to determine if the pressure at the pressure control valve and directional control valve are as specified, but first check the reservoir level. Visually check the pump and motor drive couplings to determine if the power is transmitted from one shaft to the other. If each of the above checks out satisfactorily, install a flowmeter into the hydraulic circuit and test the circuit resistance; check for the presence of air and the efficiency of the hydraulic pump, the directional control valves, and the hydraulic motor.

If the hydraulic circuit checks out satisfactorily but the winch drum does not rotate, the problem must be within the winch due to broken drive component(s) or the sprag clutches not releasing fully.

If the complaint is low power, check the relief valve setting. To do this, first hook the wire rope end and the tractor to a solid object. Make certain that neither the tractor nor the object can move and that the wire rope is in good condition. Next, gradually increase the engine rpm to the rated speed; move the control lever to the full pull-in position, and note the oil pressure as well as the engine rpm. If the engine rpm drops more than specified, the problem of lower power is not caused by the winch, but by the engine. *Do not adjust* the pressure relief valve under this condition—first check and service the engine. Repeat the test and adjust the relief valve to the specified setting. **NOTE** This stall-pull method is only recommended for small winches.

If the complaint is reduced line speed, the problem either lies in the hydraulic circuit or is due to mechanical failure of bearings or gears, which increases friction.

If the drum will not hold the load or it has reduced line pull, the brakes or clutch is (are) not working properly or the sprag clutches(es) is (are) damaged, thereby preventing a lockup.

WIRE ROPES

Wire ropes are constructed with a central core, around which the wire strands are helically twisted. Each strand is composed of a single wire center, around which individual wires are helically twisted. See Fig. 15-16.

Wire ropes are manufactured with a varying number of strands (the standard number being six) and a varying number of wires in each strand. The grade of steel and/or the type of core are other variables and are contingent upon the intended use of the rope, such as whether it will be subject to excessive

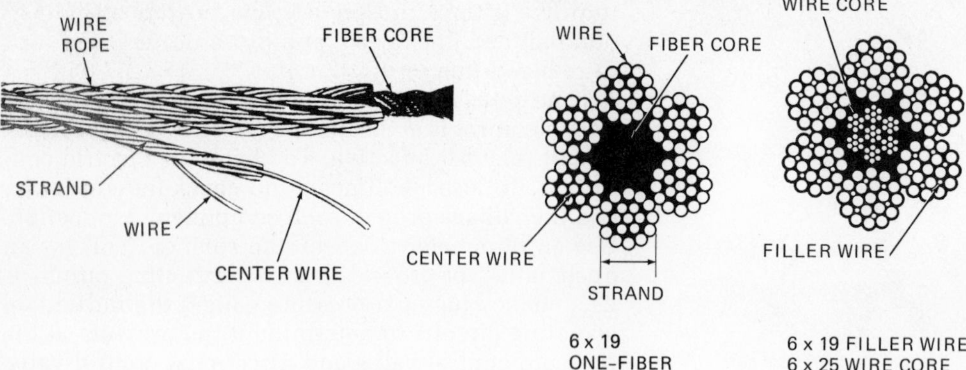

Fig. 15-16 Wire rope. (*Wire Rope Industries Ltd.*)

tension, wear, bending, crushing, and corrosive conditions.

The quality of steel used may range from stainless to improved plow steel, and some wire ropes have the individual wires coated with zinc to reduce corrosion.

The core of the smaller wire ropes may be composed of cotton, jute, or sisal, the latter being the most common. However, when severe crushing or flattening of the rope could occur through use, the core (strand) is of steel. Specialty ropes may use cores of nylon, plastic, paper, etc., and the wire rope used for a mine hoist may have an electric conductor embedded in the fiber.

The diameter of wire ropes varies from 3/16 to 2¾ in (5 to 70 mm). The wires used to form the strand are always equal in diameter but may vary in number from 8 to 49. The wires used to form the core may vary in diameter from those in the strand. The most common number of strands used is six.

Wire Rope Terminology The term "left" or "right" refers to the direction in which the strand rotates around the wire core. The term "regular" or "lang" (lay) refers to the relation of the strands and the wire rotation. The strands of a "right regular (lay)" wire rope twist helically to the right (as a screw thread), and the wire that forms the strands twists helically to the left. In a "left regular (lay)" wire rope, they twist in the opposite direction; that is, the strands twist to the left and the wires of the strands twist to the right. In a "lang (lay)" wire rope, the strands twist around the core in the same direction that the wires twist around their centers. The term "lay" refers to placing or constructing the wire rope in a regular order. It refers to the distance measured along a wire rope between one complete revolution of each strand around its core. **NOTE** A wire rope of a regular lay is commonly shorter in its lay (distance) than that of a lang lay wire rope having the same diameter. See Fig. 15-17, where all three types just discussed are illustrated.

Rope Winding All wire ropes used on winches are right regular or lang lay. Left regular or lang lay wire ropes are manufactured only for special applications.

To assure long wire rope life, to prevent the wire rope from climbing over the next wrap and then piling up, and to obtain a good "drum on" and "unwinding," the wire rope used must be of the correct regular or lang lay, and must be started from the correct drum flange side and correct direction. If started incorrectly on the drum, the wire rope that remains on it will spread apart as soon as the load is slacked off, and may overlap or criss-cross on the drum when wound again onto it, resulting in deformation of the wire rope and early rope deterioration. When the correct wire rope is properly started on the drum, at the correct drum starting point, during the wind-on it will twist slightly in the direction of strand twist and roll against the next drum wrap. Then when the load is slacked off, the wire rope will untwist in the opposite direction, thereby maintaining an even layer.

Depending on the drum power-in rotation, the wire rope is either overwound or underwound onto the drum. When the drum rotates in the counterclockwise (power-in) direction, a right lay wire rope is overwound; that is, the live wire (which is the end that is fastened to the drum) is drawn over the top of the drum, and its end must be attached at or near the left-hand drum flange. When the drum rotates in the clockwise (power-in) direction, a right lay wire rope is underwound; that is, the live wire rope is drawn under the bottom of the drum and its end must be attached at or near the right-hand drum flange.

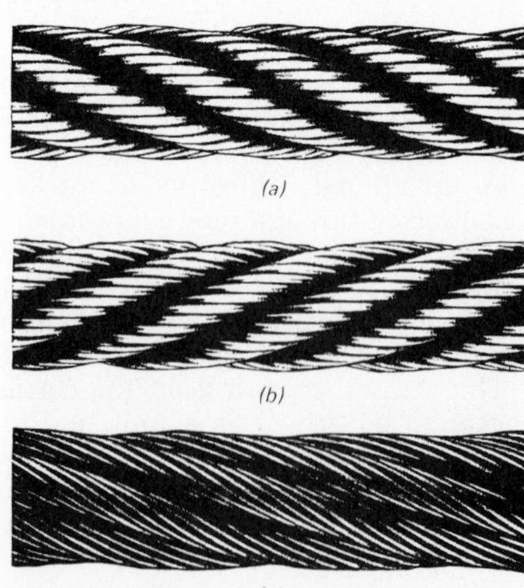

Fig. 15-17 (*a*) Right regular lay rope. (*b*) Left regular lay rope. (*c*) Right lang lay rope. (*Wire Rope Industries Ltd.*)

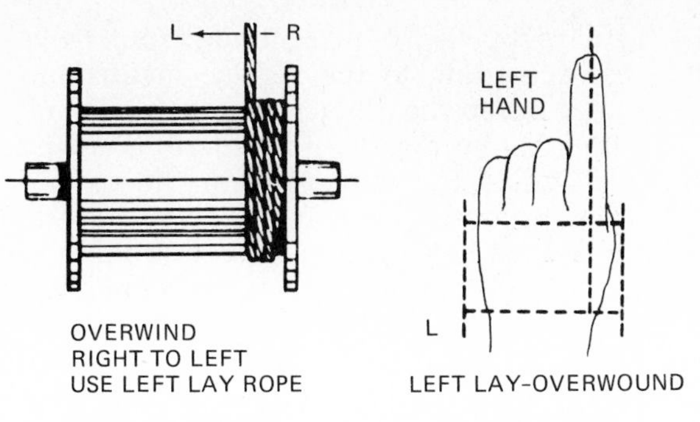

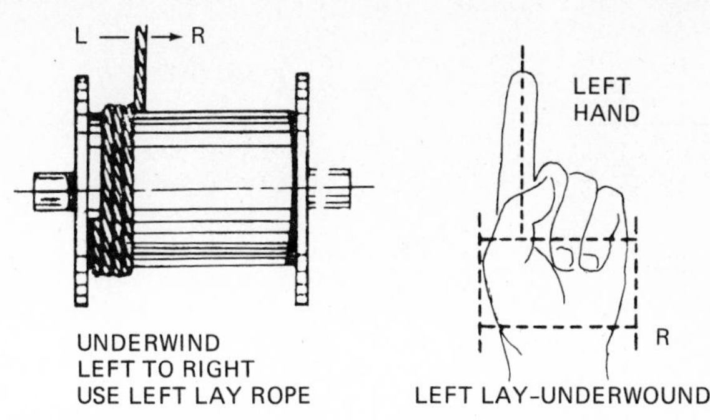

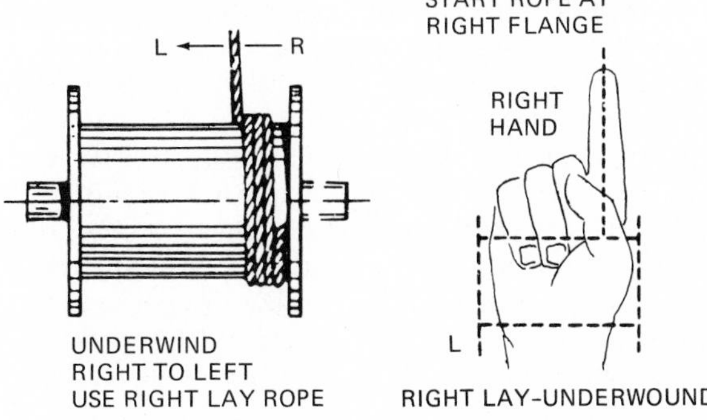

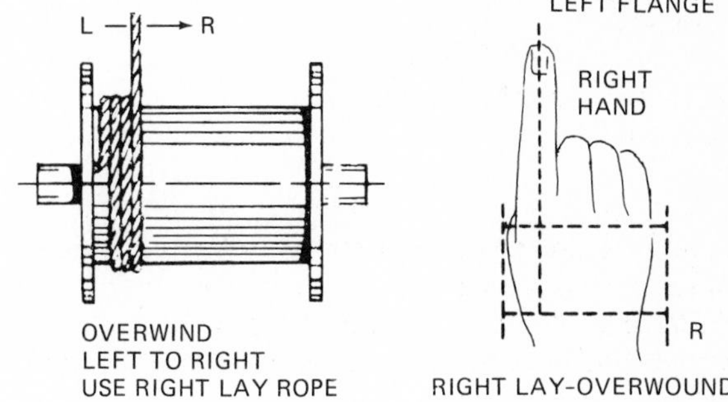

Fig. 15-18 Correct spooling of wire rope onto drum. (*Wire Rope Industries Ltd.*)

The simplest method to remember how to attach a wire rope to a drum is to use your right hand with the palm up representing right-hand drum rotation, and the palm down representing left-hand drum rotation, as shown in Fig. 15-18.

Installing a Wire Rope on a Drum After the old wire is removed from the drum, clean the drum surface thoroughly, especially a drum in which rope grooves are cast. Next, check the drum and flanges for wear, undercut, and cracks and check the drum shaft and bearings for wear. If any one of these conditions exists, the winch must be serviced to prevent any hazard and to increase rope service life.

A new wire rope is usually shipped in a specific length rolled up in a coil, or coiled onto a reel. In either case, it is most important to prevent a kink from forming during the uncoiling process. Once a kink has occurred, no stress can remove it and the wire rope is then unsafe for use. Therefore if a wire rope is supplied coiled up, first position the coil on a clean floor in front of the winch and slowly roll it, like a wheel, on the ground. If the wire rope is wound onto a reel, position the reel in front of the winch, place a pipe through the reel center, and support it with blocks or stands so that the reel can be rotated on the pipe. Next, pull the wire rope from the reel and either pull it onto the drum, or over the specific idler sheave and then onto the drum, depending on the machine. Follow the service manual's instructions and draw the wire rope either over or under the drum through the drum hole, then secure the end with the wedge to the drum. See Fig. 15-19.

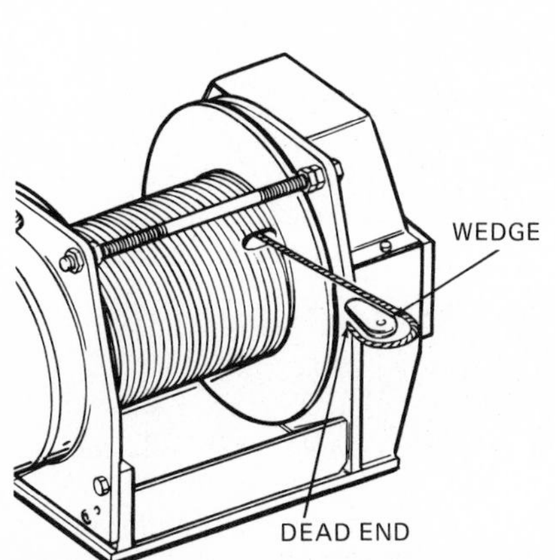

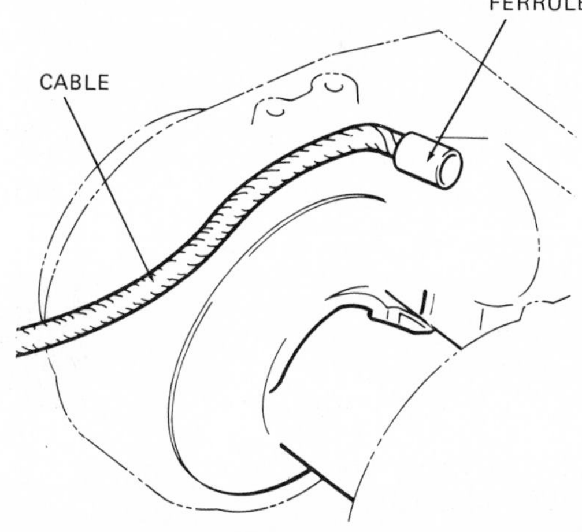

Fig. 15-19 Schematic illustration of two methods used to secure the wire rope dead end to the winch drum.

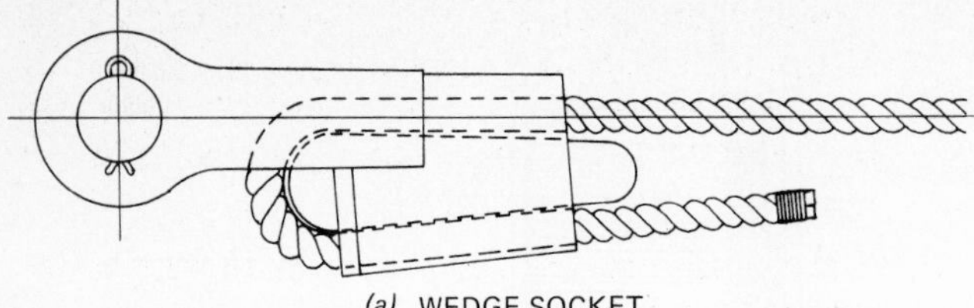

(a) WEDGE SOCKET

(b) HAND SPLICED EYE

(c) STEEL SLEEVE CLEVIS END

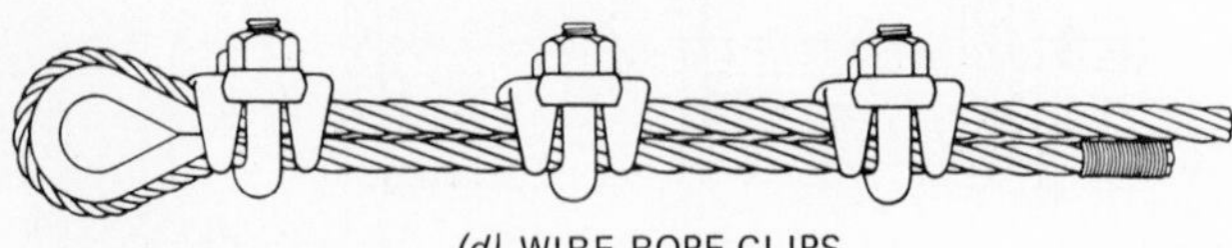

(d) WIRE ROPE CLIPS

Fig. 15-20 Wire rope connections. (*Wire Rope Industries Ltd.*)

NOTE Make certain when using the wedge method that the rope end length is at least 1½ times the length of the wedge to assure secure wedge action.

Now, by controlling the engine speed, and/or clutch engagement, or directional control valve position, slowly wind the wire rope onto the winch drum. **NOTE** For wire ropes with diameter greater than ½ in [12.7 mm], you may need a bronze or lead hammer to tap the rope against the next wrap and to hold tension on the reel so that the drum layers will be even. Under no circumstance use a steel hammer or any other steel device, as it will damage the rope. **CAUTION** To prevent injury while replacing a wire rope, make certain your working gloves are of good quality.

After the wire rope is wound onto the drum, reeve the machine according to the service manual instructions, and fasten the other wire rope dead end to the required connector. See Fig. 15-20. (Reeving is the threading of the wire rope in the recommended order, around the sheaves.) If you have to use wire rope clips to form an eye, you must have (1) good quality clips, (2) the correct number of clips, (3) the clips correctly installed, (4) the clips spaced apart evenly (about six times the diameter of the rope), (5) the nuts torqued down correctly, (6) a thimble in the eye loop, and (7) the clips must be retorqued when the rope is under tension.

Causes of Wire Rope Failure Although wire ropes are extremely durable, they are nevertheless susceptible to damage and eventually wear out. The greatest detriment of wire rope life and cause of early failure is lack of lubrication. During the manufacture of the wire rope, the core, wires, and strands are properly lubricated. This lubrication must be maintained because, as the wire rope is wound on and off the drum as it passes over or under several sheaves, causing the core, wires, and strands to move against each other as well as against the sheave and drum surface. Without sufficient lubrication, the friction increases and accelerates wire deterioration. See Fig. 15-21.

The second most common cause of wire rope wear is incorrect rope selection. For instance, a wire rope which has large wires and is of the lang lay design has a greater bearing surface, a greater resistance to abrasion, and is more flexible than a regular lay wire rope. A wire rope with small wires should never be used in its stead. Do not use rope with a fiber core to lift a heavy load, and do not use it where layer upon layer is wound onto the drum, as the fiber core rope would be crushed. Selecting a wire rope having a greater diameter than the sheaves causes increased friction and may cause rope crushing. Then again, selecting a rope having a smaller diameter than recommended will place a constant overload condition on the rope. It will then stretch, lessening the rope diameter, and the wires will break.

Another cause of reduced wire rope service life or

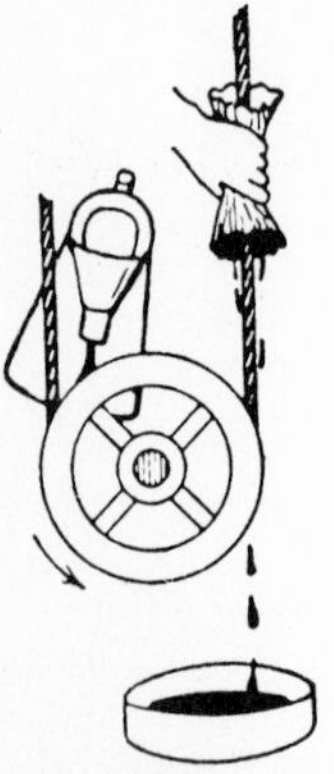

VERTICAL ROPES AT BOTTOM SHEAVE

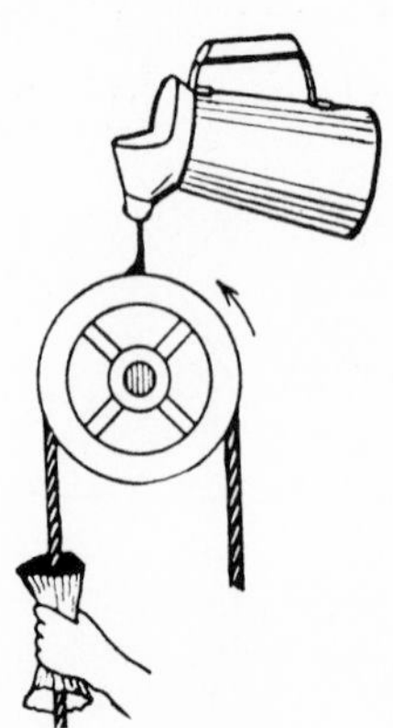

VERTICAL ROPES AT TOP SHEAVE

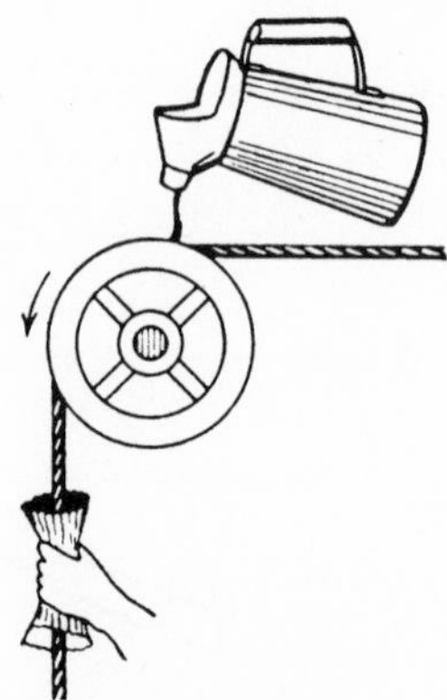

CHANGING DIRECTION AT SHEAVE

Fig. 15-21 Methods recommended to lubricate a wire rope. (*Wire Rope Industries Ltd.*)

rope trouble is brake or clutch failure, which may cause the rope to kink or to crush due to improper winding onto the drum. Brake or clutch failure can also cause rope to jump off the sheave(s) and become wedged and crushed between the sheave and mounting. In addition, damaged sheave(s) or worn or damaged sheave bearings can cause misalignment or prevent the sheaves from rotating. In either case, the rope-to-sheave friction increases, accelerating wire wear.

It is difficult to state specifically when to replace a wire rope without all the facts regarding it. In any case, it should be a matter of safety first, cost second, and determination of the conditions under which the wire rope will be used third. Where a high safety factor must be maintained, a wire rope must be replaced when it is kinked, when the diameter of the wire rope is reduced beyond the specified diameter, when the number of broken wires exceeds the specification, or when the wire is stretched beyond specifications. These rules do not necessarily apply to shovels, cranes, tractors, etc., however; on this equipment, when the wires start to break or become corroded, or when the wire rope diameter has decreased, the rope should be replaced. If a wire rope on a tractor winch snaps in two, both ends respond like a whip, which could kill the operator or others working nearby. Such an occurrence could also cause great damage to the machine and surrounding area. Wire rope replacement, not to mention down time, is costly, but the value of a human life is immeasurable.

Review Questions

1. (*a*) What is the purpose of a winch? (*b*) What power sources can be used to drive a winch?
2. Why cannot other devices be used in place of a winch?
3. Outline the mechanical actions which automatically apply the brakes when the rotation of the winch drum stops.
4. On a mechanically driven winch: (*a*) What two methods are used to pay out the wire rope? (*b*) Elaborate on each method.
5. List the primary variances existing between tractor winches and winches used on cranes, shovels, etc.
6. Explain the hydraulic and mechanical action of the winch shown in Fig. 15-9, when the directional valve is (*a*) in the neutral position, (*b*) moved to raise the load, and (*c*) moved to lower the load.
7. What could prevent the winch brake from holding the drum stationary?
8. List four problems that could reduce line speed and/or reduce power-in on a mechanically driven winch.
9. Describe the methods used to increase or decrease the winch drum speed on (*a*) a mechanical winch, and (*b*) a hydraulic winch.
10. Explain the hydraulic and mechanical action of the hydraulic winch shown in the Fig. 15-10 when the directional control valve is in (*a*) neutral, (*b*) raised position, low speed, and (*c*) high speed.
11. Explain why the planetary carrier gears of the hydraulic tractor winch shown in Fig. 15-13 are positioned on sprag clutches.
12. On a hydraulic winch, which components or valves control (*a*) the maximum winch pull-in power, and (*b*) the line speed.
13. List the problems which could cause a hydraulic winch to have the following problems: (*a*) reduced power, (*b*) reduced line speed, or (*c*) the winch brake not to hold the winch drum.
14. List the parts which make up a wire rope.
15. Define the terms (*a*) left regular lay, and (*b*) right lang lay.
16. When unrolling a wire rope, why is it essential to follow one of the procedures described in the text?
17. If a right lay rope is used, how is it determined (*a*) which way to place it onto the winch drum and (*b*) to which side of the drum end is attached?
18. List the methods used to attach the dead end of a wire rope to the winch drum.
19. Define the term "reeving."
20. List the problems which could accelerate wire rope wear rate.

Unit 16 Air Conditioning and Transport Refrigeration

Air conditioning or refrigeration may be defined as the process of removing heat from a confined space faster than it can reenter, thus lowering and maintaining the temperature below that of the surrounding space.

Both transport refrigeration and air conditioning have been used since as early as 1938, although air conditioning in mobile equipment came into use only in the early 1960s. The three systems, that is, transport refrigeration, on-highway air conditioning, and air conditioning of mobile equipment (off-highway equipment) operate on the same principle.

Transport refrigeration is concerned with the transportation of food products within specially designed motortruck and trailer bodies so as to retard the growth of bacteria and thus prevent or delay the spoilage of those products.

Air conditioning for on-highway motortrucks and mobile (off-highway) equipment is concerned with cooling and dehumidifying the air within the operator's compartment. In most cases, the air conditioning system operates in conjunction with the heating system. Consequently, the driver or operator remains more alert and becomes less fatigued, which increases safety and/or work capacity.

The refrigeration or air conditioning system has five major components: compressor, condenser, receiver-driver, thermostatic expansion valve, and evaporator. In addition, the system requires controls and air distribution ducts. See Fig. 16-1.

To understand how these systems remove heat from a confined space and transfer and dissipate it into the atmosphere, some fundamentals will be reviewed. This review will assist you to more readily analyze system failure and perform the required maintenance and service.

Heat and Cold Generally, the effect of temperature is evaluated by comparing the temperature of a substance or space with your own body temperature. When any amount of heat is added to the substance or space, or removed, you will say it is hotter or colder.

Matter exists in three forms: solid, liquid, and gas. The form can be changed by reducing or increasing the temperature. The speed with which these changes take place depends on the amount of attraction between the molecules. In a solid state, the molecules move very slowly. When enough heat is added to the solid, it becomes fluid, and the molecular motion is increased. When more heat is added, the molecular action increases even further, until

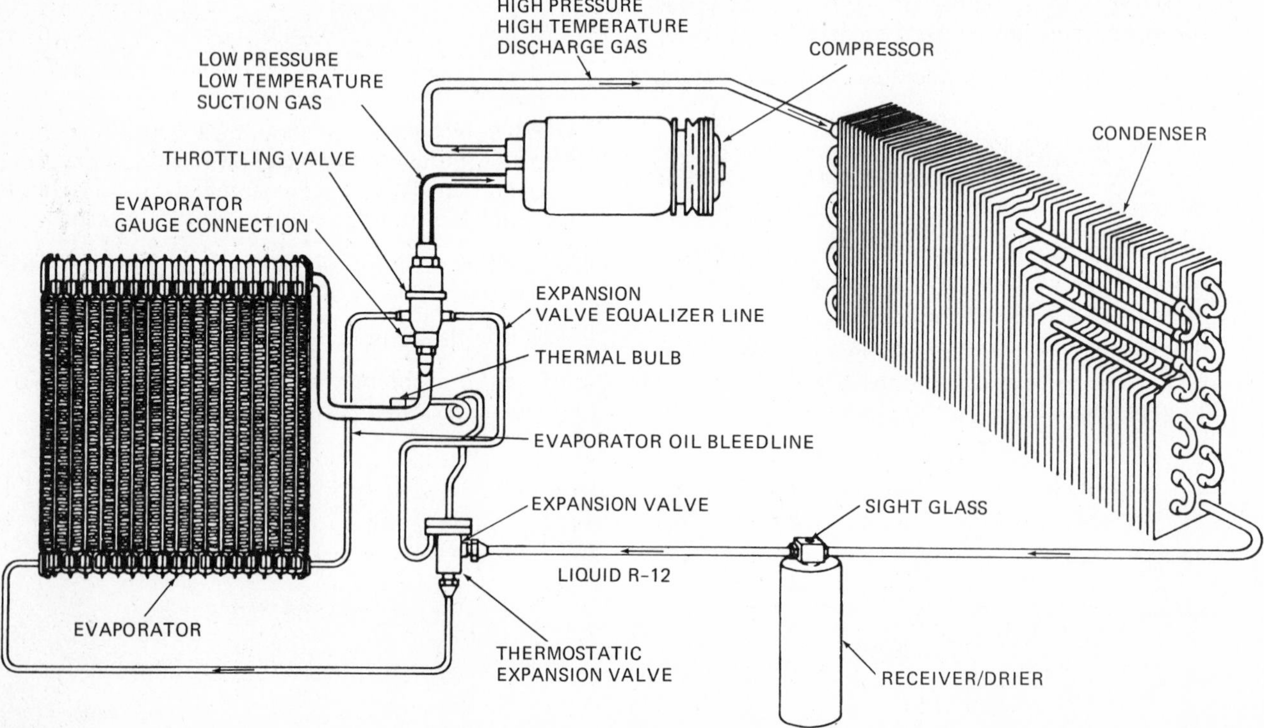

Fig. 16-1 Exploded view of an air conditioning system. (*GMC Truck and Coach Division*)

there is little attraction between molecules. The fluid then becomes a gas.

Heat is a form of energy generated by the transformation of another form of energy. **NOTE** When one form of energy disappears, another form takes its place and heat is generated. Heat remains present within an object or space until its temperature reaches −459°F [−273°C], otherwise known as "absolute zero." At absolute zero a body is wholly deprived of heat.

TEMPERATURE AND PRESSURE A thermometer is used to measure the intensity of heat (sensible heat) in a substance. However, it does not indicate the *amount* of heat contained in the particular substance. For example, compare two air tanks, one large and one small. Both may show the same pressure gauge readings and yet the larger one may contain three times as much air as the smaller one. Similarly, two objects at the same temperature may contain different amounts of heat.

Temperature is usually measured on two scales. On the Fahrenheit scale, the freezing point of water is 32°F and the boiling point of water is 212°F. On the Celsius scale, the freezing point of water is 0°C and the boiling point is 100°C. **NOTE** The two temperature scales are defined at a standard barometric pressure of 29.9 in of mercury (in Hg) [101.32 kPa].

When the pressure acting on liquid is reduced, the liquid will boil at a lower temperature. For instance, when a truck climbs to a height of 10,000 ft [3048.0 m] above sea level, the atmospheric pressure is less than at sea level (standard), and the radiator water at this pressure will boil at 201°F [94°C]. Conversely, when pressure is applied to the liquid, for example, by using a pressure radiator cap, the boiling point of the coolant will rise.

THE MEASURE OF HEAT QUANTITY To measure a quantity of heat in an object or space, the British thermal unit (Btu) is used. 1 Btu is the amount of heat required to raise the temperature of 1 lb of water 1°F at a barometric pressure of 29.9 in Hg. See Fig. 16-2. In the metric system, the quantity of heat in a body or space is measured in joules (J). To raise the temperature of one kilogram of water one degree Celsius at a barometric pressure of 29.9 inches of mercury, 3.343 kilojoules (kJ) are required. **NOTE** This is very important to remember when measuring heat movement in a refrigeration or air conditioning system.

NATURE'S LAW OF BALANCE Whenever fluids at two different pressures are merged, the pressures will always tend to equalize; and, when there is a difference in the heights of two fluids and their containers are somehow connected, the liquids will tend also to seek a common level. When there is a temperature differential in an object, heat will move to the cooler part or space until the temperature equalizes throughout. For example, when you drain hot oil from an engine, at first the oil is hotter than the surrounding air; but it gives off heat to its surroundings and in a short time becomes the same temperature as the surrounding air.

EVAPORATION AND CONDENSATION The changing of state of a substance from liquid to vapor is known as *evaporation*, and the change from the vapor state to the liquid state is known as *condensation*.

NOTE A substance absorbs heat when it evaporates, and gives off heat when it condenses.

LATENT HEAT OF FUSION AND LATENT HEAT OF EVAPORATION Suppose you have an ice block in a container. The temperature of the ice is 32°F [0°C]. When you now apply heat to the container, some of the ice will change from the solid to the liquid state (water). However, the temperature of the ice and of the water remains at 32°F [0°C]. (See Fig. 16-3.) It requires 144 Btu [151.92 kJ] to change 1 lb [0.453 kg] of ice at 32°F [0°C] into 1 lb [0.453 kg] of water at 32°F [0°C]. The heat added to make the change of state is known as *latent heat of fusion* (hidden heat of fusion).

Water boils at 212°F [100°C] at a barometric pressure of 29.9 in Hg [101.32 kPa]. When you have heated 1 lb [0.453 kg] of water to the boiling point and added an additional 970 Btu [1023.35 kJ] of heat, the water will change into 1 lb [0.453 kg] of steam at 212°F [100°C] without changing the temperature of the water. The 970 Btu [1023.35 kJ] is known as the *latent heat of evaporation* of water. As the change of state (water from a liquid at 212°F [100°C] to vapor at 212°F [100°C]) occurs, vapor carries away the 970 Btu [1023.35 kJ] along with it, as this amount of heat was needed to change the water from a liquid to a vapor. When the process is reversed, the latent heat is removed. Thus, 1 lb

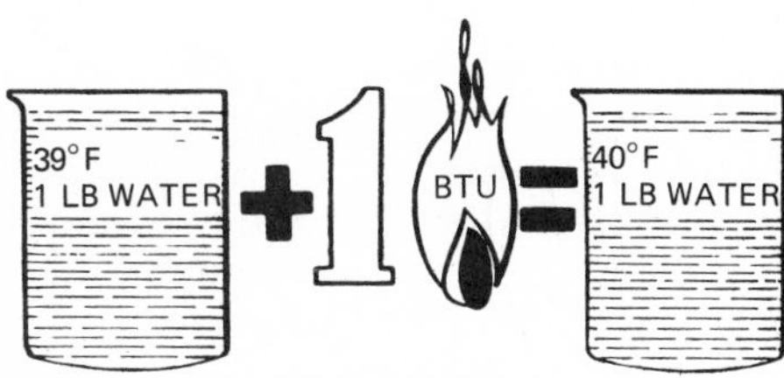

Fig. 16-2 Quantity of heat (Btu).

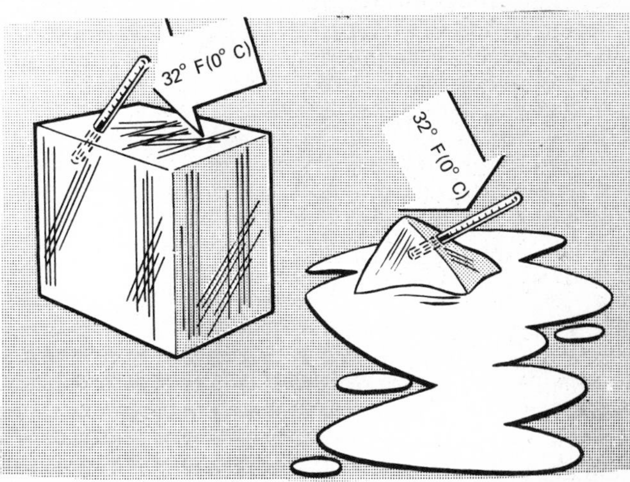

Fig. 16-3 Latent heat of fusion.

[0.453 kg] of steam at 212°F [100°C] will give off 970 Btu [1023.35 kJ] as it condenses into water, without a change in the temperature of the water. This is known as the *latent heat of condensation.* You may note that the water boiled at the same temperature as the steam condensed. This is also true with any other liquid. See Fig. 16-4.

CONDUCTION Conduction is essentially the movement of heat from one part of an object to another part of the same object through the object. A simple demonstration of heat transfer by conduction would be to place a spoon into boiling water. The spoon handle will soon have the same temperature as the boiling water, that is, 212°F [100°C]. Or you can compare heat transfer by conduction with the flow of current (electrons).

NOTE Good electric conductors, such as copper and aluminum, are good heat conductors, while electric insulators retard heat flow.

CONVECTION Convection is the transfer of heat through, or by means of, a liquid, vapor, or gas. Air flow (air current) is the most common means of conveying (by convection) the heat from the hotter to the colder substance or space.

RADIATION Radiation is the transfer of heat by heat rays, which travel in a straight line through space, that does not require some substance to transfer the heat. The best example of heat rays are the sun's rays, which travel in a straight line through space, and heat only the objects that absorb them. Another example of heat rays would be the effect of standing in front of a campfire. The fire's heat rays warm the side of the body facing the fire, while the side not facing it remains cool.

HEAT ABSORPTION You may have felt, on a hot summer day, the tops of two cars—one painted white, the other painted black. You will have noticed that the white car top was cooler than the black one. This is because the lighter color reflects or throws back radiated heat, whereas the darker color absorbs almost all the heat radiated onto it.

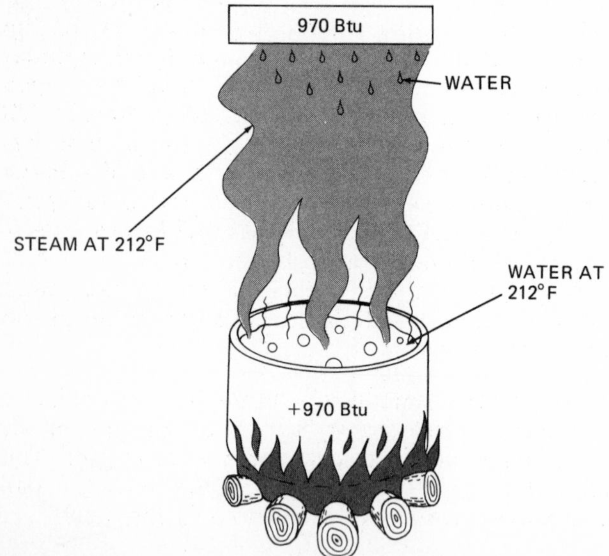

Fig. 16-4 Top, latent heat of condensation. Bottom, latent heat of evaporation.

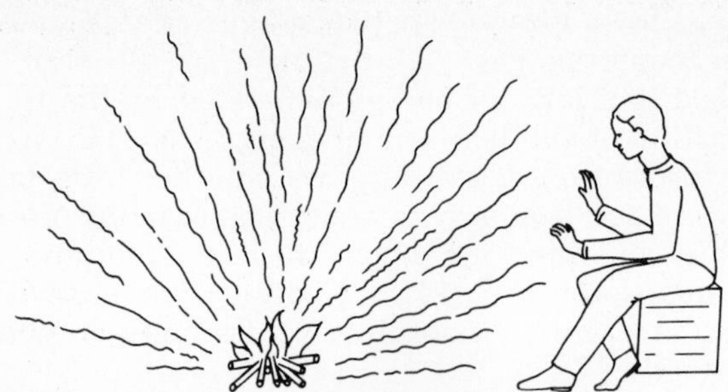

Fig. 16-5 Transfer of heat by heat rays.

Refrigerants The purpose of a refrigerant is to absorb heat as it changes from a liquid to a gas and expel the heat as it changes from a gas to a liquid. Many different types of refrigerant fluids are available for use in air-conditioning and refrigeration systems. One of these, refrigerant 12, is the most widely used because of its desirable characteristics. It is clean, dry, nontoxic, noncorrosive, nonflammable, nonexplosive, and odorless under ordinary usage. Of more importance, refrigerant 12 has a low boiling point of −21.75°F [−29.8°C] at zero pressure (0 psi [0 kPa]) and has a good latent heat of vaporization. In other words, if 1 lb [0.453 kg] of refrigerant 12 is boiled off in the evaporator, it will absorb a very large quantity of heat; therefore less refrigerant is required to be used in the system. This not only reduces the overall size and weight of the refrigeration or air conditioning unit, but is also a savings in engine horsepower.

NOTE When you observe the temperature-pressure relation chart (Fig. 16-6) for refrigerant 12, you will notice the close relationship between the pressure and temperature (21.1 to 84.3 psi [145.3 kPa to 580.8 kPa]) and the temperature of the refrigerant (20 to 80°F [−6.6°C to 26.6°C]). In addition, the low boiling point of refrigerant 12 allows the refrigeration or air-conditioning system to operate at a low temperature and at a pressure range within the evaporator that allows good heat transfer and flow. **NOTE** It is easier to operate in a pressure range than in a vacuum range.

Notwithstanding all the advantages of refrigerant 12, it nevertheless requires certain handling precautions in order to prevent injury to the handler or to others nearby. The most important, even mandatory, precautions or warnings are the following

1. Always wear safety goggles when working with liquid refrigerant, as it could cause blindness if it is splashed into your eyes.
2. Never touch liquid refrigerant, as even a drop on your skin will cause severe and painful frostbite.
3. Do not steam-clean any refrigeration or air conditioning system components when the system is under pressure (charged) because the heat from

°F	°C	Pressure, Psi	Pressure, kPa
−40	−40.0	11.0	75.8
−35	−37.2	8.3	57.2
−30	−34.4	5.5	37.9
−25	−31.6	2.3	15.8
−20	−28.8	0.6	4.1
−15	−26.1	2.4	16.5
−10	−23.3	4.5	31.0
− 5	−20.5	6.8	46.8
0	−17.8	9.2	63.3
5	−15	11.8	81.3
10	−12.2	14.7	101.2
15	− 9.44	17.7	121.9
20	−6.67	21.1	145.3
25	− 3.89	24.6	169.4
30	− 1.11	28.5	196.3
32	0.0	30.1	207.3
35	1.67	32.6	224.6
40	4.44	37.0	254.9
45	7.22	41.7	287.3
50	10.0	46.7	321.7
55	12.8	52.0	358.2
60	15.6	57.7	397.5
65	18.3	63.7	438.8
70	21.1	70.1	482.9
75	23.9	76.9	529.8
80	26.7	84.1	579.4
85	29.4	91.7	631.8
90	32.2	99.6	686.2
95	35.0	108.1	744.8
100	37.8	116.9	805.4
105	40.6	126.2	869.5
110	43.3	136.0	937.0
115	46.1	146.5	1009.3
120	48.9	157.1	1082.4
125	51.7	167.5	1154.0
130	54.4	179.0	1233.3
140	60.0	204.5	1409.0
150	65.6	232.0	1598.4

Fig. 16-6 Pressure–temperature relationships of refrigerant 12.

steam cleaning will raise the refrigerant temperature and pressure to a point where the system could explode.

4. Do not discharge refrigerant from the air conditioning or refrigeration system in an area without sufficient ventilation because refrigerant vapor lacks the oxygen you require to breath.

5. Do not expose a liquid or vapor refrigerant to an open flame, as it then forms into a phosgene gas which, when inhaled, is extremely harmful.

AIR CONDITIONING SYSTEMS

As mentioned, five basic components make up an air conditioning or refrigeration system. Each component may vary to some extent in design or size, but it performs a particular function within the system no matter what its design or size. Furthermore, components are always installed in the same relative position to each other. **NOTE** The refrigeration or air conditioning systems are closed hydraulic systems—there is no starting or ending point of the cycle.

Compressors The purpose of the compressor is to draw the low-pressure, low-temperature gas from the evaporator, to compress it, and to pump it under higher pressure and higher temperature to the receiver-drier. **NOTE** The pressure increase is caused by a restriction created through the expansion valve orifice. Two basic types of compressors are used: a fixed-displacement double-acting axial piston compressor, or a reciprocating piston compressor of the dual-piston or the V four-piston design.

DOUBLE-ACTING AXIAL COMPRESSOR The fixed-displacement double-acting axial piston compressor is shown in Fig. 16-7. It has three double-end pistons 120° apart from one another within the cylinder assembly. Each piston is positioned over the swash plate and is connected to it through two drive balls and ball seats (shoe disks). Each end of the piston has piston rings and an oil scraper and two drilled oil return passages. The central main shaft is supported in the cylinder assembly by needle bearings, and the swash plate is keyed to it. Thrust bearings on both sides of the swash plate reduce the side thrust and friction. Fastened to the right-hand side of the central main shaft is the electromagnetic clutch, and to its left-hand side the gerotor pump (lubrication pump). Positioned onto each end of the cylinder assembly are the front and rear reed plates, onto which are fastened the front and rear discharge valve plate. The compressor shell is formed with an oil reservoir, and the reservoir is connected to the oil pickup, which is connected to the pump. Passages within the compressor connect the left- and right-hand discharge areas, and the left- and right-hand suction areas, with the rear compressor head, to which the suction and the discharge fittings (service valves) are fastened.

Operation When the magnetic clutch is engaged (see material on clutches in Unit 10), the central main shaft, swash plate, and gerotor pump rotate as a unit. This moves all three pistons to the left, creating a low pressure within the right-hand cylinders and opening the front reed valves. At the same time, the pressure in the left-hand cylinder areas increases, causing the discharge valves to open and forcing the vapor into the discharge line. **NOTE** The second piston, which is 120° from the first, has completed one-third of its suction and discharge stroke, and the third piston has completed two-thirds. See Figs. 16-7 and 16-8. This provides a nearly pulsation-free pumping action.

During the main shaft rotation, the gerotor pump supplies oil to the bearings as well as to the piston and piston rings.

RECIPROCATING PISTON COMPRESSOR Basically, a piston compressor is very similar in design to an air compressor and is also commonly water-cooled. The main difference (Fig. 16-9) is in the valves, called *reed valves,* which are made from spring steel.

Operation When the magnetic clutch is engaged, the crankshaft rotates, causing the piston to

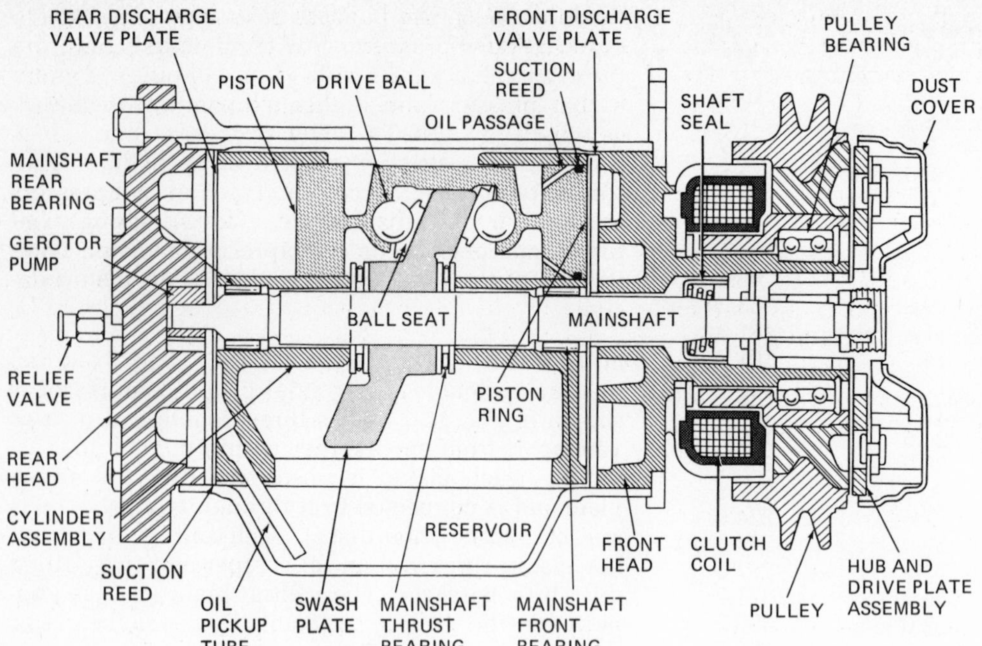

Fig. 16-7 Sectional view of a double-acting axial-piston compressor. (*J I Case Company Agricultural Equipment Division*)

move up and down. When the piston is on the intake stroke (suction stroke), the inlet reed valve opens through the force of the high refrigerant pressure. When the piston is at the bottom of the stroke, the pressure inside the cylinder and the pressure inside the inlet line are equal. As the piston moves upward, the pressure within the cylinder increases and the discharge reed valve is forced open. Refrigerant vapor at a higher pressure and temperature is forced into the charge line. This cycle repeats itself as long as there is a current flow to the clutch coil. When the current flow is stopped, the magnetic clutch disengages.

During the time the compressor operates, some lubrication to the bearings, wrist pins, piston, and piston rings is provided through splash lubrication, and some by the refrigerant that has passed by the piston ring. The mixture of oil and refrigerant is forced to and through the wrist pin and down to the connecting rod bearings. Some compressor oil passes by the piston rings and mixes with the refrigerant throughout the circuit. **NOTE** It is necessary, when replacing the compressor, that you measure the oil level before removing the compres-

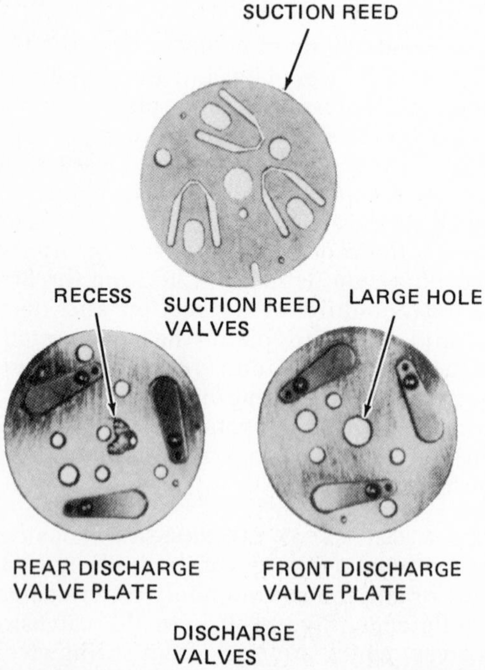

SUCTION REED

RECESS

SUCTION REED VALVES

LARGE HOLE

REAR DISCHARGE VALVE PLATE

FRONT DISCHARGE VALVE PLATE

DISCHARGE VALVES

Fig. 16-8 View of suction reed valves and discharge valves. (*J I Case Company Agricultural Equipment Division*)

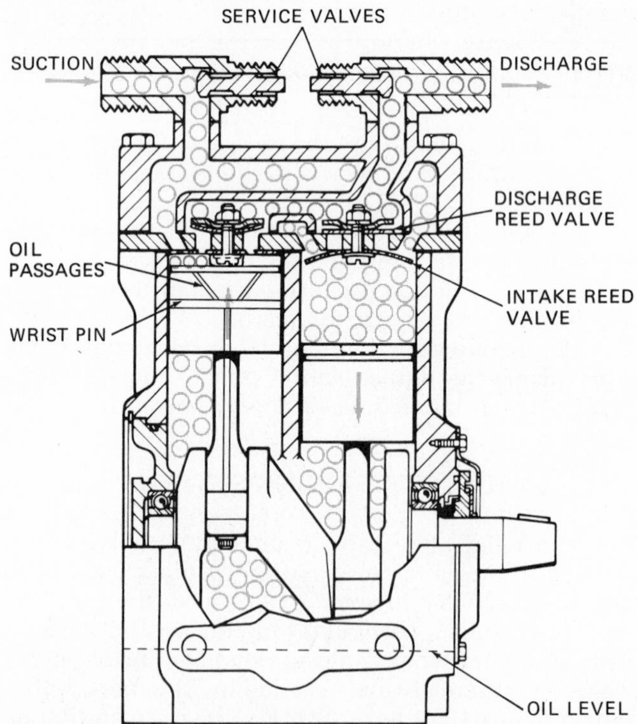

Fig. 16-9 Schematic view of a reciprocating piston compressor. (*J I Case Company Agricultural Equipment Division*)

sor and only fill the new or serviced compressor to the same oil level. Otherwise, too much oil could mix with the refrigerant, which would cause abnormal operating pressure and reduce the performance of the entire system.

Condenser and Evaporator The condenser and evaporator are basically similar in design to a radiator. A copper tube is formed into the shape of the condenser or evaporator, and copper fins are fastened to the tube and support structure. One end of the condenser copper tube is connected to the compressor, and the other to the receiver-drier. One end of the evaporator tube is connected to the receiver-drier, and the other is connected to the suction side of the compressor.

The overall shape, size, and design of both the evaporator and condenser vary, depending on where they are located and on the cooling capacity (Btu [kJ]) of the air conditioning or refrigeration system. The condenser for an air conditioning system could be located in front of the engine radiator or on top of the tractor, motortruck, or truck-tractor cab. The evaporator is commonly part of the cab heating system and is therefore located within the heater system in the driver or operator compartment.

These units serve different functions. The purpose of the condenser is to receive the high-pressure and high-temperature refrigerant gas and convert it into liquid refrigerant. The condenser transfers the latent heat from the inside of the copper tube to the outside air. The cooling capacity can be increased by either of the following methods: (1) On the on-highway motortruck and truck-tractor, the engine fan draws air over the condenser coil and, as well, air is forced, through the movement of the motor vehicle, over the condenser coil and fins. (2) On the off-highway motortruck or tractor, air, forced through electrically driven fans or a squirrel cage blower (Fig. 16-10), removes heat from the coil and fins.

The purpose of the evaporator is to absorb heat from the refrigerated space as it takes in low-pressure gas from the receiver. The heat travels from the evaporator fins to the coil and is absorbed by the refrigerant as it passes through the coil and then onto the suction side of the compressor.

Receiver-Drier This unit has a dual purpose: to store additional refrigerant to compensate for the minute refrigerant loss which occurs over a period of time, and to confine water in minute quantities. Water droplets form during system startup, which, if not confined, will flow into the circuit and possibly freeze up the expansion valve, thereby stopping the flow of the refrigerant into the evaporator.

The receiver-drier (Fig. 16-11) is a tube sealed at both ends. The inlet and the outlet fittings are fastened to the top end. The pickup tube is fastened to the inside of the outlet fitting and reaches downward toward the drier cover. A side glass is positioned in the top end cover to visually indicate the amount of refrigerant in the receiver. The drier dessicant and filter screens are located in the lower part of the tube. **NOTE** The dessicant has the same absorption quality as that of an air drier.

Thermostatic Expansion Valve The purpose of this valve (see Fig. 16-12) is to meter and control the flow of liquid refrigerant into the evaporator. Reducing the flow lowers refrigerant pressure and consequently the temperature; increasing the flow raises the pressure, and therefore the temperature. The valve comprises the body with its inlet port and screen. The thermal sensing valve and diaphragm are fastened to the top of the body, and the inner diaphragm circle rests against the piston. One end of the pin (see Fig. 16-12), located in the bore of the body, rests against the piston, and the other rests against the spring seat, which also serves as the valve seat. The valve, which has a passage (orifice), is screwed into the top part of the body. The super-

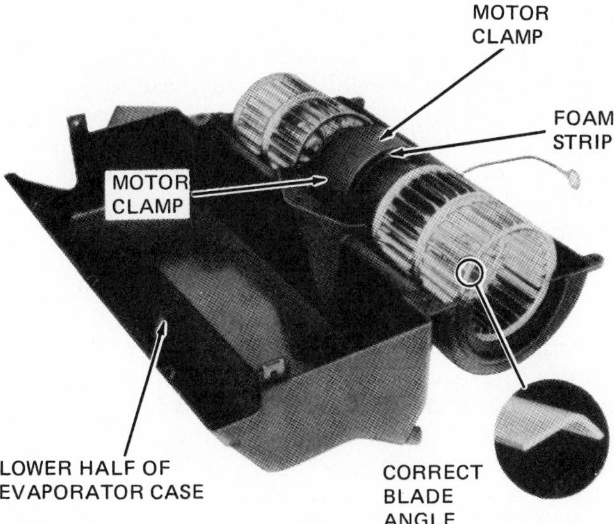

Fig. 6-10 View of exposed squirrel cage blower. (*GMC Truck and Coach Division*)

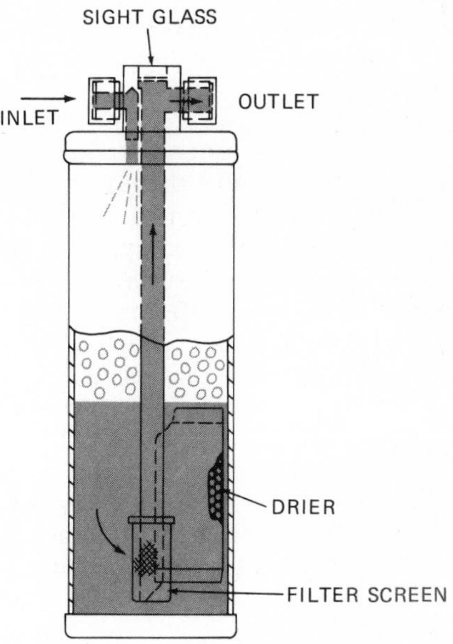

Fig. 16-11 Schematic view of a receiver-drier. (*J I Case Company Agricultural Equipment Division*)

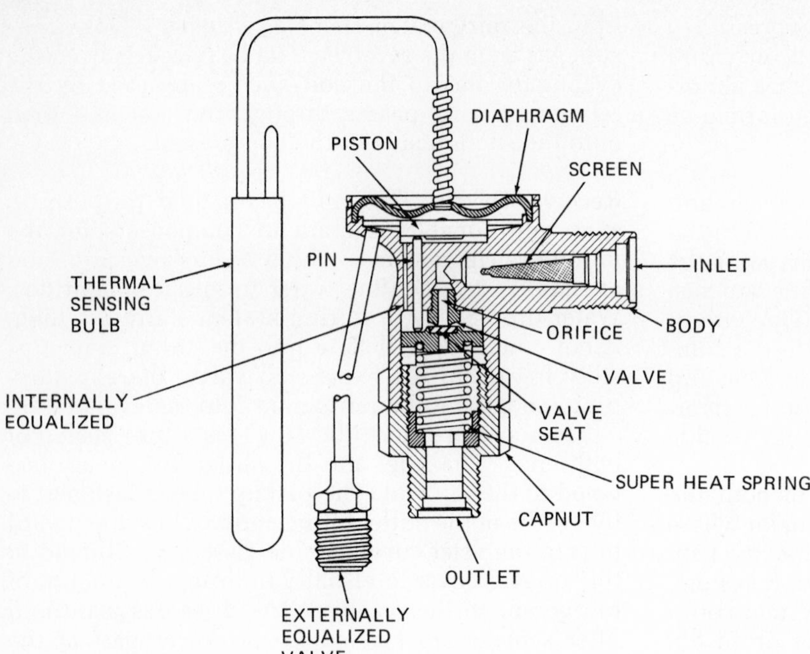

Fig. 16-12 Thermostatic expansion valve. (*J I Case Company Agricultural Equipment Division*)

heat spring is located between the body, cap nut, and spring seat. **NOTE** The thermal sensing bulb must be firmly fastened to the outlet tube of the evaporator in order to sense the outlet temperature of the refrigerant.

OPERATION When the compressor is not pumping, the entire system is under charging pressure, but refrigerant is not flowing. The force of the superheat spring forces the valve against the valve seat. This is because the temperature of the fluid within the thermal sensing bulb (refrigerant or carbon dioxide) is the same as the surrounding air and it therefore condenses, removing the force from the diaphragm. Note, however, that the orifice remains open.

When the compressor is pumping, the fluid refrigerant flows through the orifice, out of the outlet port, and into the evaporator, warming the outlet tube and the sensing valve bulb. This causes the fluid within the bulb to expand and exert a force against the diaphragm. The diaphragm moves the pin and the pin moves the valve seat against the force of the superheat spring away from the valve and orifice, allowing more refrigerant to flow through the evaporator and thereby decreasing the temperature of the evaporator outlet tube and sensing valve bulb. The fluid within the sensing valve bulb senses the lower temperature, and it contracts, reducing the force on the diaphragm, and consequently the refrigerant flow is reduced. To make the expansion valve more sensitive, the refrigerant pressure is directed below the diaphragm, either internally through a passage or through a tube connected from the outlet tube of the evaporator to the expansion valve (see Fig. 16-12). A higher (pressure) expansion of the fluid in the thermal sensing bulb is therefore needed to move the valve seat away from the orifice.

Blower In order to control and properly regulate the confined-space temperature, one or more electrically driven fans or squirrel cage blowers are used. Their purpose is to move the cool air surrounding the evaporator core into the enclosed space of the operator or driver compartment or into the truck trailer body.

Control System The simplest but not the most efficient way to control the temperature within the cab-operator space is to manually actuate the A/C magnetic clutch switch Y-Z (see Fig. 16-13). This engages the clutch and starts the compressor rotating.

When controlling the speed of the blower motor with the blower motor on/off switch (No. 2) W-X placed at the ON position, current flows to the blower switch 1 and subsequently to the resistor assembly, onto the blower motor, through the motor windings, and then to ground. In the example shown in Fig. 16-13, the resistor assembly reduces the voltage to 3.94 V and the current to 4 A, causing the blower motor to rotate at a very low speed. If the operator moves the switch to second speed, it connects terminals 2 and 5 to one another. This circuit connection removes some resistance from the resistor assembly, causing the voltage to increase to 8 V and the amperage to rise to 6.2 A, thereby increasing the motor speed. If the switch is moved to third speed, it connects terminals 2, 4, and 5 to each other and more resistance is then removed from the resistor assembly. Consequently the blower motor rotates faster because now a voltage of 8.9 V is forcing 13 A to flow through the motor windings to ground. In fourth speed, all resistance is bypassed in the resistor assembly because the blower switch connects terminals 1, 2, and 4 with each other; a current of 23 A flows, with maximum battery voltage, say 12.8 V, into wire 260, terminal 1, and wire 261, then into the motor windings.

TEMPERATURE CONTROL THERMOSTAT (THERMOSTATIC SWITCH) To maintain a more even temperature within the operator or driver compartment, and to

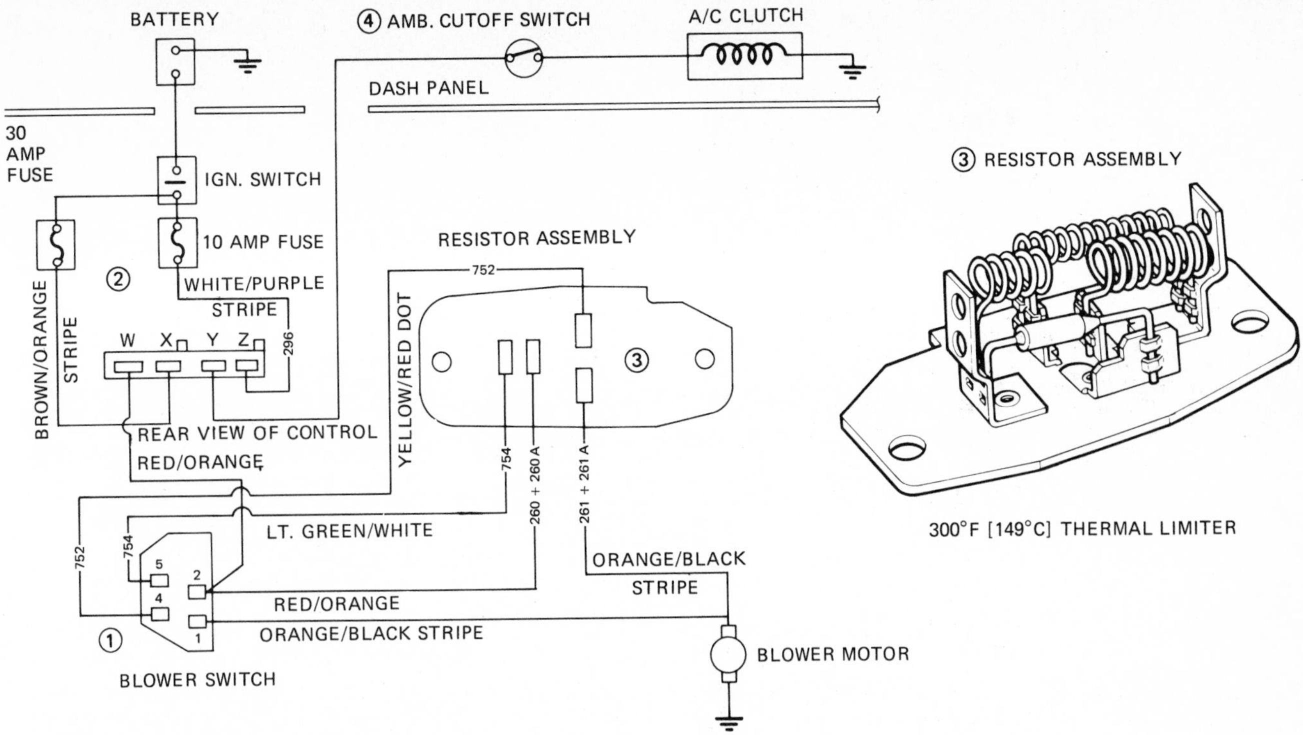

Fig. 16-13 Schematic illustration of an air conditioner electric circuit: (1) Four-position blower switch: (2) W-X blower switch ON/OFF, Y-Z compressor switch ON/OFF; (3) blower resistor assembly.

provide safety features for the system, several components can be added (see Fig. 16-14). These are (1) a thermostatic switch, (2) a low-pressure switch, (3) a high-pressure switch, and (4) a relay.

The purpose of the thermostatic switch is to control the temperature within the cab so as to keep it at the level desired by the driver or operator. The switch senses the cab temperature, and, when it drops below the selected setting, the electric circuit to the magnetic clutch opens, thereby stopping the air conditioning cycle. When the cab temperature rises above the setting of the thermostatic switch, the electric circuit to the compressor clutch closes, starting the air conditioning cycle.

Two kinds of temperature-sensing elements are used to sense and relay the temperature changes to the contact set, opening or closing the electric circuit to the magnetic clutch—the bimetallic and the bulb types. When using the bulb sensing element (see Fig. 16-14), the bulb is fastened to the evaporator coil and the thermostatic switch is positioned within reach of the operator. Figure 16-15 schematically illustrates the switch of this element. An arm is pivot-fastened to the bottom of the switch housing, and the top of the arm is connected to the crossbar of the differential adjusting device. The point of the bellows assembly rests on the right-hand side of the arm, and the temperature range adjusting point rests against the other side. The armature arm is pivot-fastened (near the top) to the switch housing. The top end can slide within the crossbar slot, and its movement to the left can be limited through the differential adjusting screw and limiting bar. The purpose of the differential adjusting device is to change the cutout and cutin temperature. The purpose of the permanent magnet is to prevent the points from opening and closing too slowly. The magnet holds the points closed until the bellows pressure is sufficient to overcome the magnetic force, whereupon the points quickly separate. The purpose of the resistor is to prevent the points from arcing as the contacts separate.

When the differential adjusting screw moves the armature arm to the right, the cutout temperature is raised because the points are separated earlier, and when it moves the armature arm to the left, the cutout temperature is lowered because the points separate later. **NOTE** The adjustment of the range-adjusting screw determines the cutin temperature.

The bimetallic thermostatic switch is very similar in design (see Fig. 16-16). The sensing element is positioned on an arm. When the temperature is, say, 70°F [21.1°C], the sensing element is straight. When the air temperature within the operator cab or driver compartment lowers, the element warps to the left because the brass or steel contracts more than the invar (forcing the arm to the left), thereby opening the contact points. When the air temperature increases, the element gradually straightens up, then warps to the right, allowing the points of the contact sets to close, thus engaging the electric circuits to the magnetic plugs and starting the air conditioning cycle.

HIGH- AND LOW-PRESSURE SWITCHES The high- and low-pressure switches are safety switches, designed to protect the system. The high-pressure switch is positioned within the compressor discharge line and

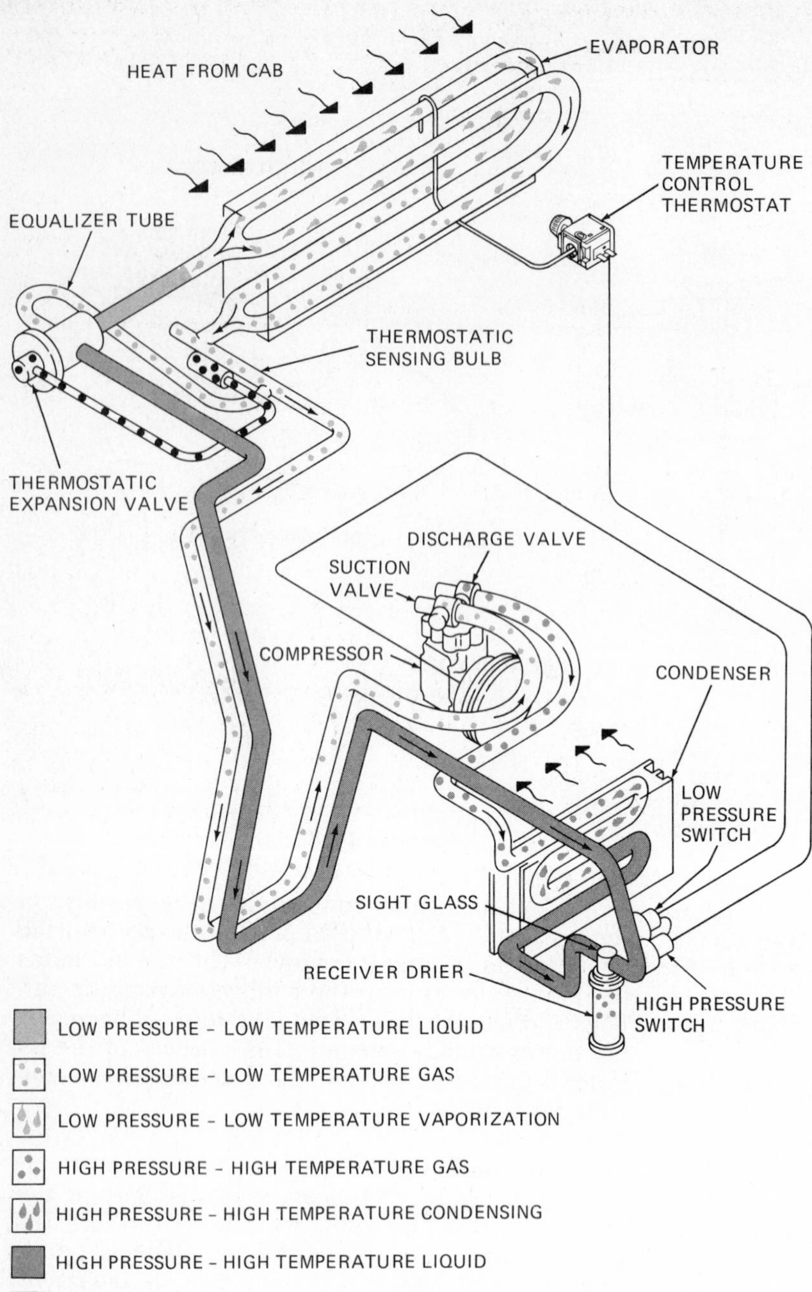

Fig. 16-14 Schematic illustration of a tractor air conditioner system. (*J I Case Company Agricultural Equipment Division*)

opens the electric circuit of the magnetic clutch when the discharge pressure exceeds a preset safety pressure, which is about 350 psi [2411.5 kPa]. The low-pressure switch is positioned within the compressor suction line; it opens the electric circuit of the magnetic clutch when the suction pressure falls below 25 psi [172.2 kPa]. **NOTE** The high- and low-pressure switches are wired in series with the temperature control switch.

RELAY The purpose of the relay is to use a low current flow to close the point-set, over which the higher clutch current then flows.

Air Conditioning Cycle Assume the engine is operating, the air temperature within the operator cab or driver compartment is 80°F [26.7°C], the temperature range is set to 30°F [−1.11°C], and the cutoff temperature is adjusted to 20°F [−6.67°C] (that is, a differential of 10°F [5.56°C]). The operating temperature range of the evaporator would be between 30 and 20°F [−1.11 and −6.67°C]. This setting would maintain a 70°F [21.1°C] temperature within the operator cab. Under these operating conditions, (see Fig. 16-17) the points of the temperature control switch are closed, the magnetic clutch is engaged, and the fluid in the thermostatic sensing bulb has expanded and forced the valve seat in the expansion valve away from the orifice, allowing more refrigerant liquid to flow into the evaporator. Superheat refrigerant vapor at a pressure of 70.3 psi [484.3 kPa] and a temperature of 70°F [21.1°C] enters the compressor, and enters the condenser at a pressure of 271.0 psi [1867.1 kPa] and 196°F [91.1°C]. Super-

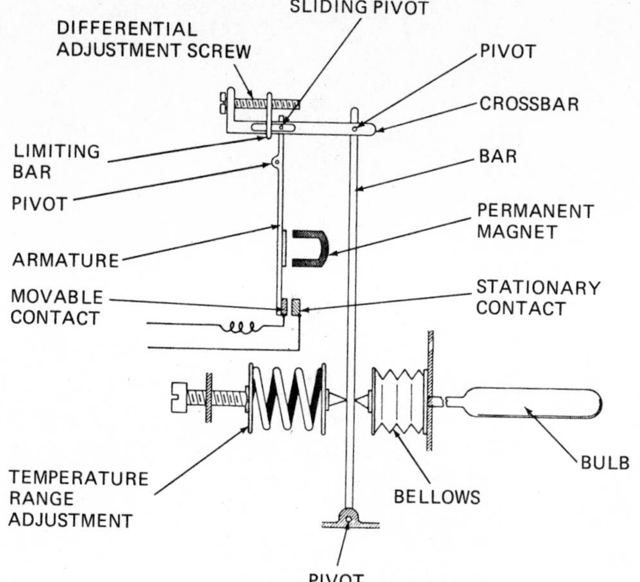

Fig. 16-15 Simplified view of a bellows thermostatic control.

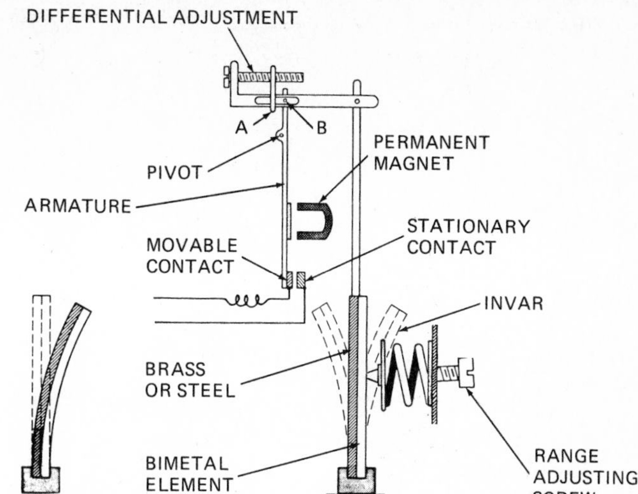

Fig. 16-16 Simplified view of a bimetal thermostatic control.

heat is the heat added to the refrigerant after complete evaporation of the liquid. As heat is removed by the condenser, the temperature and the pressure gradually drop until they reach 100°F [37.7°C] and 117.4 psi [808.1 kPa]. The temperature and pressure in the line to the expansion valve and at the orifice in the expansion valve gradually decrease to, say, 90°F [32.2°C] and 93.0 psi [640.7 kPa]. The orifice and the valve position restrict the refrigerant flow; therefore the compressor creates a low pressure within the line to the evaporator and expansion valve. The pressure of the refrigerant drops to, say, 21.1 psi [145.3 kPa], and the liquid becomes a mixture of liquid and vapor. This reduces the temperature of the refrigerant to, say, 20°F [−6.67°C]. The pressure and temperature of the refrigerant mixture within the evaporator remains the same to near the end of the coil, after which the refrigerant becomes saturated vapor and, from this point on, the pressure and temperature increase because the vapor becomes superheat. As the refrigerant flows to the compressor, the pressure and temperature rise to say, 70.3 psi [484.4 kPa] and 70.1°F [21.1°C].

As the air temperature within the operator cab gradually decreases, it also causes a decrease in the outlet temperature of the evaporator. The fluid in the thermostatic sensing bulb cools and therefore reduces in volume. This closes the valve and the refrigerant can only then flow through the orifice.

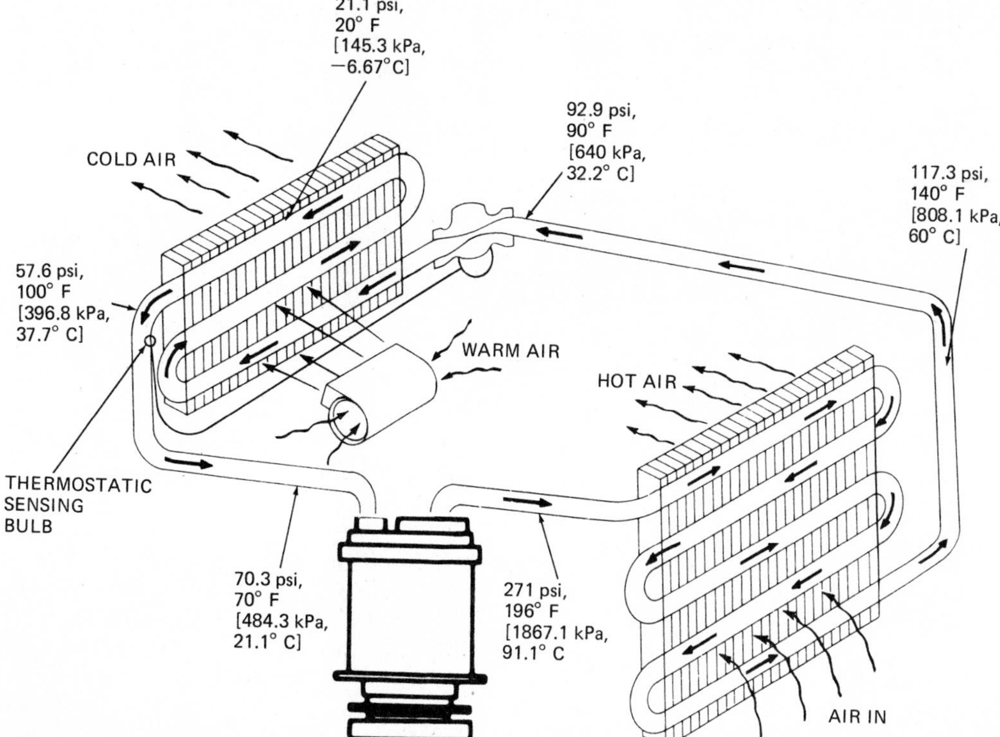

Fig. 16-17 Approximate temperatures and pressures during cooling.

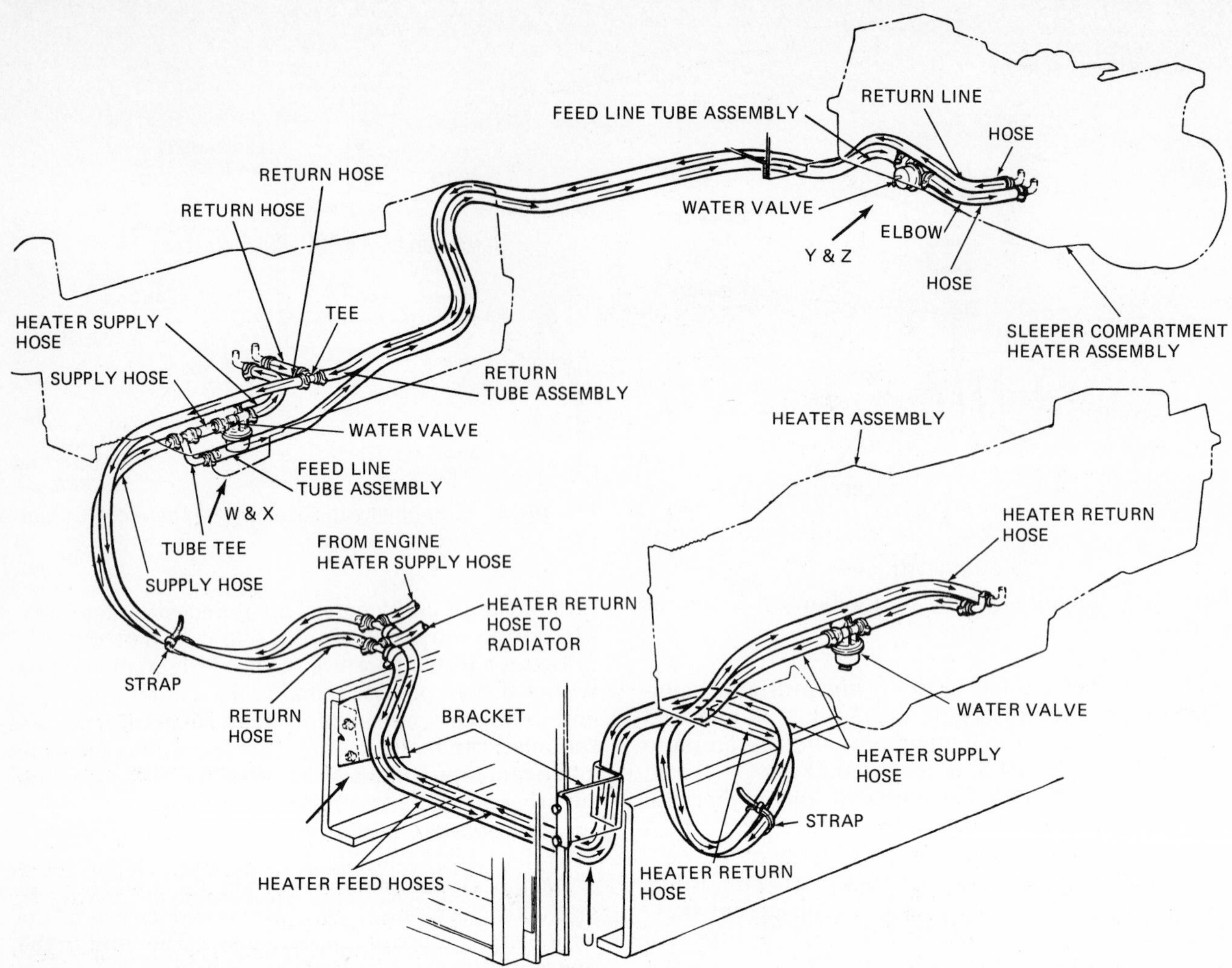

Fig. 16-18 Schematic illustration of a heater system piping. (*Ford Motor Company*)

During the air conditioning cycle, the sensing bulb of the temperature control thermostat responds to the temperature of the evaporator coil. When the fluid in the thermostatic sensing valve retracts sufficiently, that is, to cutout temperature, 20°F [−6.67°C], the temperature range spring forces the points to separate and the compressor clutch to disengage. When the evaporator coil has increased to the cutin setting, the temperature control points close and the air conditioning cycle starts again.

Heating and Air Conditioning Systems To increase the operator comfort (temperature and humidity of the driver compartment), the heater and air conditioning systems must be controlled. In other words, the air must be directed within the environment so that the temperatures in all operating areas are equal, there are no drafts when the system is operating, and the air is sufficiently rich with oxygen.

To achieve these goals, the heater and the air conditioning systems must be combined. Air control doors must be located within the heater and air conditioning distributing systems, and the air distributor tubes and pipes and the air outlet ducts must be positioned where they are most efficient. The valves, actuators (motors), or cable controls must have the ability to select the air flow mode.

One of many different heater and air conditioning installations is shown in Fig. 16-18. The location of the heater hose piping and water valve is schematically illustrated in Fig. 16-19. From these illustrations, you will notice that in the truck-tractor or motortruck cab one heater core (radiator) is positioned below the driver, one core below the passenger seat, and one in the sleeper compartment. **NOTE** The purpose of the water valve is to allow the engine coolant to flow into the heater core or to be blocked off. The valve is opened by creating a low pressure (vacuum) within the vacuum motor, and is closed through spring force as soon as the low pressure increases to atmospheric pressure. The vacuum motors are just like miniature clamp-type brake chambers.

Heating and Air Conditioning Operation The control panels for the heater and air conditioning systems are placed within easy reach of the driver and passenger (see Fig. 16-20). The left-hand driver control panel has two levers to control the heater and air conditioning modes. The operation switches to control the blower motors are on each side of the

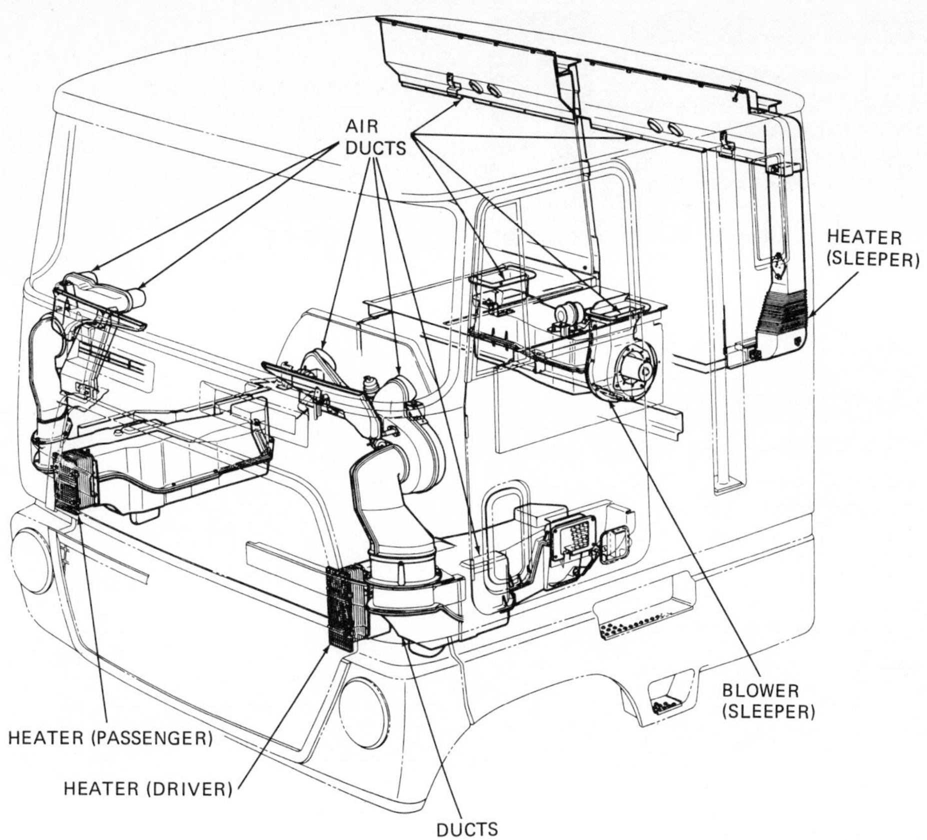

Fig. 16-19 Heater core and air duct locations in a truck-tractor driver compartment.

control panel. The purpose of the temperature control lever (at the top) is to position, manually or automatically, the blend-air modulator valve, which in turn controls the vacuum to the servo control mechanism. The purpose of the servo mechanism is to control the blend-air doors.

When the control lever is in the RECIRC (recirculating mode) position, both heater blend doors, both fresh air doors, both floor outlet doors, and the water valve are closed and the recirculating air doors are open.

The function control lever is located below the temperature control lever. Its position determines the mode of the heater/air conditioning system's operation, that is, the opening and closing of the three water valves, the engagement and disengagement of the compressor clutch, and the opening and closing of the air distributor doors. Located on the left- and right-hand sides of the left-hand control panel are the two four-position blower switch levers. The left-hand one controls the driver side blower and the right-hand one controls the passenger side blower.

The right-hand (passenger) heater control panel has two control levers. The horizontal lever controls the blend door positioned on the passenger side heater, and the right-hand lever controls the blower motor. **NOTE** When the right-hand blower lever of the driver control panel is positioned to RH, the right-hand heater control lever controls the blower motor speed.

The temperature for the sleeper compartment is controlled through a rotary modulator valve within the compartment, which actuates the sleeper blend doors and a three-position blower. This arrangement makes it possible to have heat in the sleeper compartment and at the same time air conditioning for the front driver compartment.

Before detailing the different heat and air conditioning modes, you should first be familiar with the components and connections that make this system functional (see Fig. 16-21). A vacuum generator (pump), driven through an electric motor, is used to create a low pressure vacuum of about 28 in Hg [71.12 cm Hg], and to maintain a nearly constant low pressure a vacuum reservoir is connected, in parallel, to the vacuum distributing manifold. **NOTE** The vacuum pump motor ON/OFF position is controlled through a pressure switch located on the reservoir. The male switch vacuum valve connector is fastened to the left- and right-hand heater control panels. Its purpose is to distribute the selected mode, that is, to remove or allow atmospheric pressure to be present at the various vacuum motors.

When the engine is operating, both left- and right-hand function control levers are in the OFF position and the vacuum reservoir pressure is 28 in Hg [71.12 cm Hg]. The pressure switch opens, causing the vacuum pump motor to stop operating; however, low pressure exists at connection 9 on the mode switch vacuum valve connector, and atmospheric pressure is reduced from the recirculating door motor, and its spring force closes the doors.

When only the temperature lever is moved from "COOL" to any warm position, for instance, moved halfway (see Fig. 16-22), some air is drawn over the blend-air motor modulator valve from the left- and right-hand blend door servo vacuum motors. This places the blend door to about the half-way position.

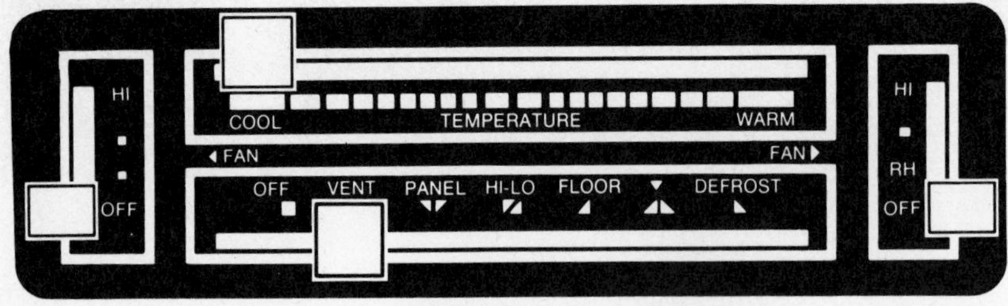

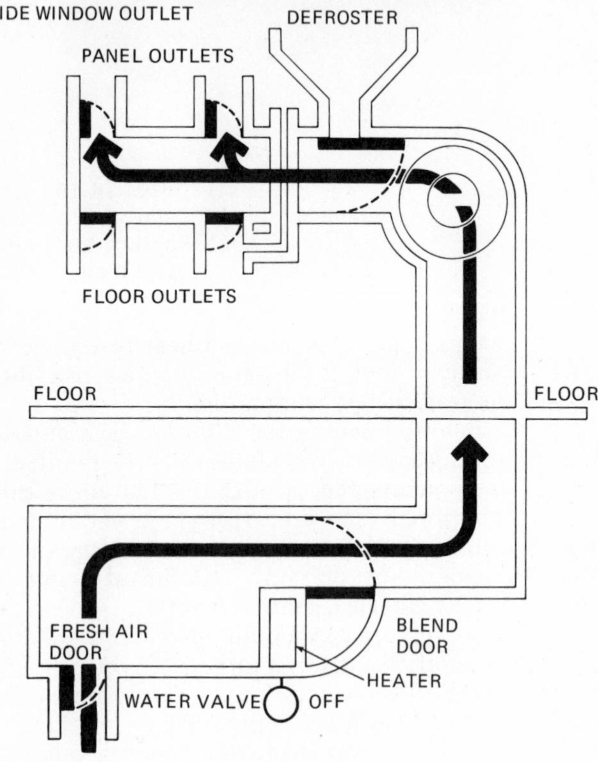

Fig. 16-20 Heater/air conditioner system in the vent mode. (*Ford Motor Company*)

However, the water valves remain closed, so no coolant can flow through the heater core.

VENT MODE If the function control lever is moved to the VENT position, the water valves still remain closed, and atmospheric pressure is removed from both fresh-air door motors, from both blend door motors, and from the panel outlet door motors, closing the doors. At the same time, atmospheric pressure is allowed to flow to the recirculating motor and the spring forces both recirculating doors open. **NOTE** Using this mode, the driver can select any desired blower speed to increase venting, or rely on ram air, that is, air forced into the system by the movement of the motor vehicle.

HEAT MODE When the function control lever is moved to the HIGH/LOW position, two additional vacuum connections are made. As a result: (1) The three water valves are open, allowing coolant to flow through the heater core, and (2) the floor doors are half-open and the compressor clutch electric circuit is closed, engaging the clutch. See Fig. 16-23.

When the function control lever is placed in the HEAT position, two vacuum connections are varied: (1) atmospheric pressure is allowed to flow to the panel outlet vacuum motors, and consequently the spring force closes the doors; (2) the electric circuit to the compressor clutch is opened, disengaging the clutch, and a second vacuum line connection is made to the floor outlet motors, opening the doors fully. The driver can now control the air temperature by varying the speed of either or both blower motors or varying the position of the heater blend doors by moving the temperature lever to the left or the right.

If the function control lever is moved to the HEAT/

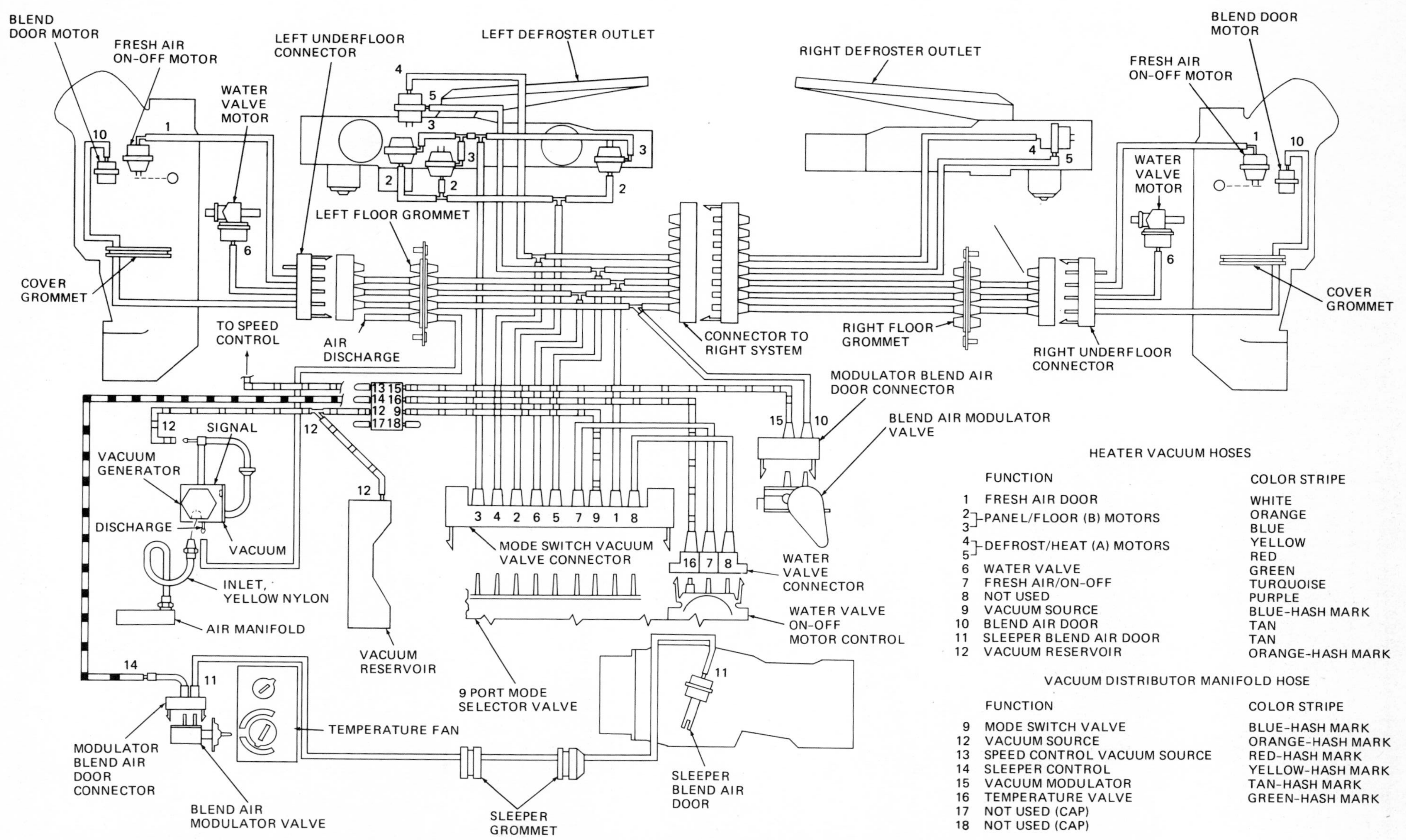

HEATER VACUUM HOSES

	FUNCTION	COLOR STRIPE
1	FRESH AIR DOOR	WHITE
2	PANEL/FLOOR (B) MOTORS	ORANGE
3		BLUE
4	DEFROST/HEAT (A) MOTORS	YELLOW
5		RED
6	WATER VALVE	GREEN
7	FRESH AIR/ON-OFF	TURQUOISE
8	NOT USED	PURPLE
9	VACUUM SOURCE	BLUE-HASH MARK
10	BLEND AIR DOOR	TAN
11	SLEEPER BLEND AIR DOOR	TAN
12	VACUUM RESERVOIR	ORANGE-HASH MARK

VACUUM DISTRIBUTOR MANIFOLD HOSE

	FUNCTION	COLOR STRIPE
9	MODE SWITCH VALVE	BLUE-HASH MARK
12	VACUUM SOURCE	ORANGE-HASH MARK
13	SPEED CONTROL VACUUM SOURCE	RED-HASH MARK
14	SLEEPER CONTROL	YELLOW-HASH MARK
15	VACUUM MODULATOR	TAN-HASH MARK
16	TEMPERATURE VALVE	GREEN-HASH MARK
17	NOT USED (CAP)	
18	NOT USED (CAP)	

Fig. 16-21 Schematic illustration of the heater/air conditioner control components and vacuum hose piping. (*Ford Motor Company*)

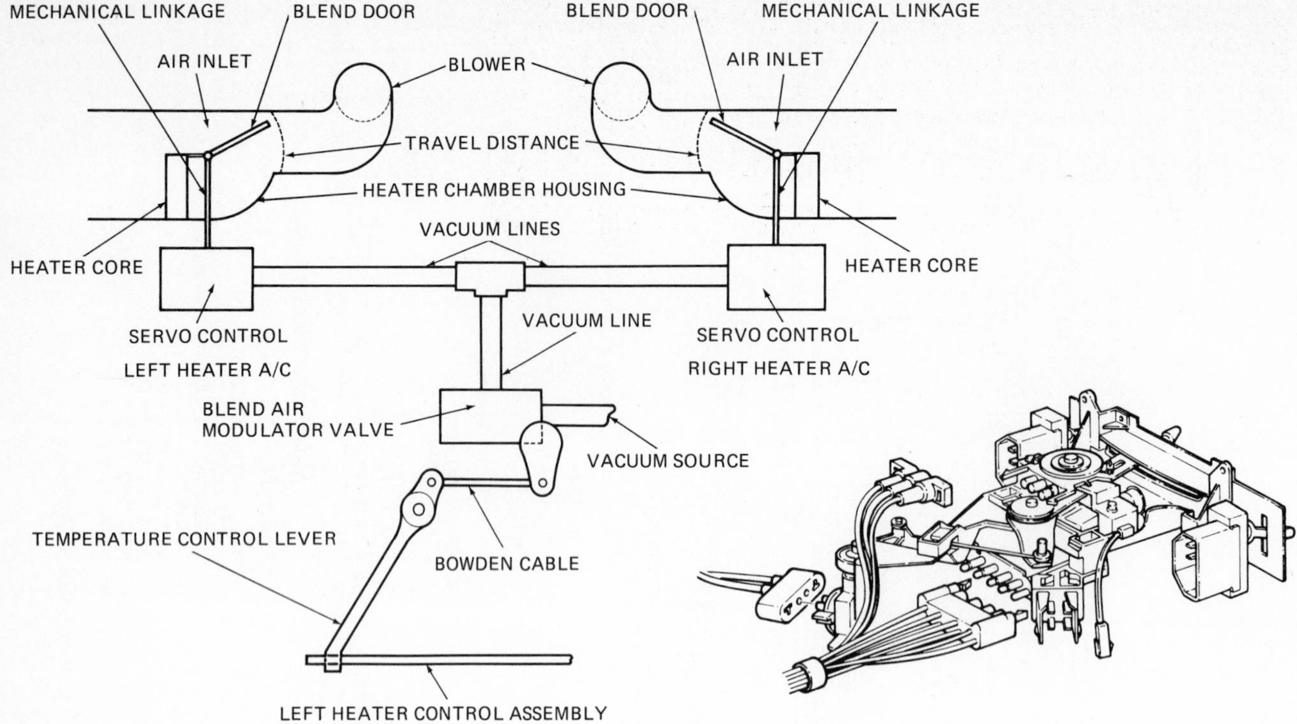

Fig. 16-22 Schematic illustration of the temperature controls. (*Ford Motor Company*)

DEFROST position, one additional vacuum connection is made which opens both defrost doors to the half-way position. However, when the lever is placed in the DEFROST position, only, a second vacuum connection is made to the defrost vacuum motor, which causes the defrost doors to fully open. **NOTE** The driver again has the option of controlling the air temperature and defrosting through the heater control lever or through the speed selection of the blower motor.

AIR CONDITIONING MODE When the function control lever is placed in the AIR CONDITIONING (A/C) position, and the temperature control lever is in any other "fresh air" range position, two vacuum connections occur which cause the floor doors to fully close and the panel outlet doors to open (Fig. 16-24). Again, the driver has the option of selecting both blower speeds or the heater blend doors to control the air temperature within the compartment.

If it becomes necessary to utilize the air conditioning system at maximum capacity, the driver moves the temperature control lever to the OFF position. This places the water valves in the OFF position, closes the heater blend doors, and blocks the air flow through the heater core.

The heater–air-conditioning system in the sleeper compartment can be manually controlled when the left-hand control (driver) panel is in any mode except OFF or VENT.

When the heater–air-conditioning system is of the automatic temperature control design, the temperature control lever is mechanically linked to an arm which is connected to a temperature control thermostat. The thermostat, in turn, controls the vacuum and/or atmospheric pressure to the heater blend motor air doors.

Air-Conditioning–Heating System Service Now we will consider the various problems that can arise in connection with the air-conditioning–heating system, along with the servicing procedures required to correct them.

CHECKS AND TESTS It is unlikely that the heater and the air conditioning system will cause downtime. Furthermore, if the system ceases to function properly it is usually due to some minor failure such as (1) misadjusted controls, (2) bent air doors or controls sticking, or (3) loose or damaged vacuum connections.

Insufficient heat If the operator complains of insufficient heat and/or poor defrosting, first check the engine coolant temperature. If the engine coolant thermostat is damaged, the radiator shutter is not operating properly, or the radiator cap is damaged, you cannot expect much heat from the heater core. The same is also true when the coolant level in the engine is low. This condition will cause aeration or no coolant flow through the heater core.

Next, check the heater hose connections and make sure the hoses are not crossed over, pinched, flattened, or deteriorated, any one of which would cause coolant flow restriction.

Do not forget to check the heater core, for, if the coolant fins are bent or the core is plugged, the air flow through the core will be reduced.

With a voltmeter check the voltage of the switches and resistor assembly while in the various speed

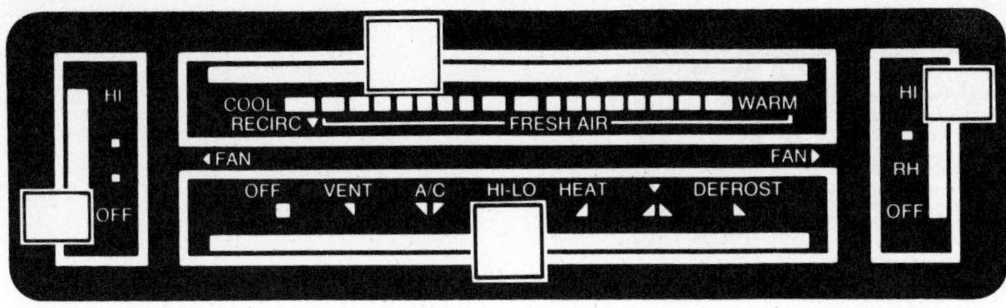

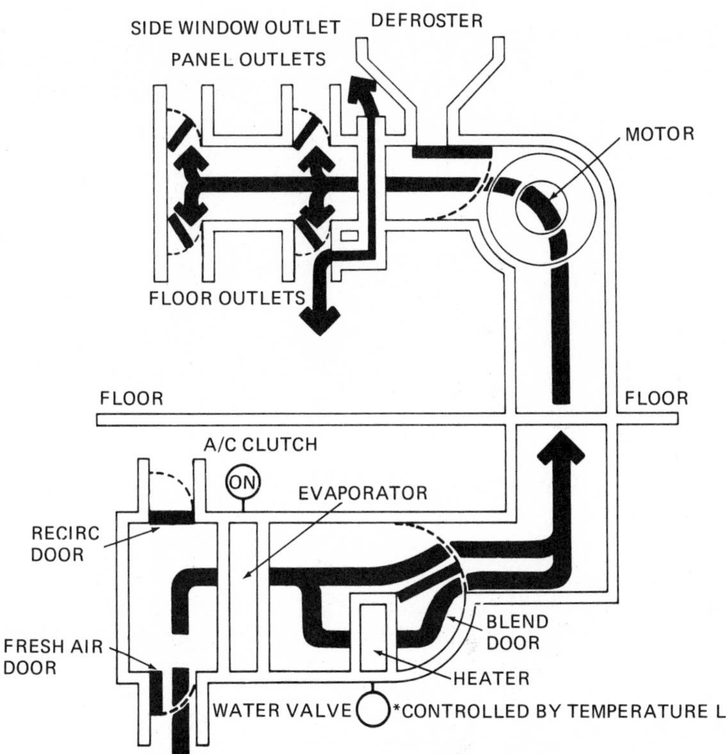

Fig. 16-23 Schematic view of the heater/air conditioner in the high/low mode. (*Ford Motor Company*)

ranges, and compare those readings with the specifications in the service manual. High resistance causes a voltage drop which, in turn, reduces the ampere flow to the blower motor windings. Check the operation of the heater valves by using a vacuum gauge (water valve motors). If the gauge indicates there is not full low pressure at the valves, then they will only partly open, thereby restricting the coolant flow through the heater core.

Next, check the mechanical action of the temperature and function control levers. If the heater system is controlled by vacuum and atmospheric pressure, use a vacuum gauge to check the low pressure (vacuum) on each vacuum motor. Next, make sure that all air doors can be moved, unrestricted, in any position and can be fully closed or opened.

Insufficient cooling If the driver or operator complains that the air conditioning system has no cooling effect, or insufficient cooling, start the engine and operate the system at the maximum efficiency. Look at the sight glass to determine the level of refrigerant within the system. If there is more than one air bubble visible and it is moving very slowly, the refrigerant level is only slightly low. If several air bubbles are present and they are moving fast, the level is low. If you can see foam, the refrigerant level is very low, and, if the sight glass is oily, nearly all refrigerant is depleted. If no air bubbles are visible, it commonly indicates the system is overcharged; however, it could also indicate a complete loss of refrigerant. To check this out, cycle the system (start and stop the compressor clutch), and, if no bubbles occur during the off/on cycle, there is no refrigerant in the system.

Check the heater–air-conditioning controls, especially the air blend doors. If they do not fully close, they allow the heater to inject warm air into the system. Next, check the compressor and the radiator fan drive belts for loose compressor mountings, and the operation of the compressor clutch. Use an ohmmeter to check the resistance of the magnetic clutch coil, and compare the ohmmeter reading with the service manual specification. At this time, visually inspect the compressor clutch for damage and wear. Use a socket and wrench to rotate the com-

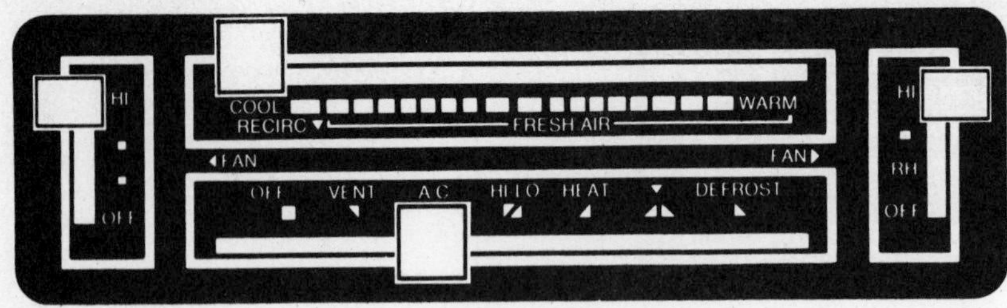

HEATER-AIR CONDITIONER
A/C MAX MODE

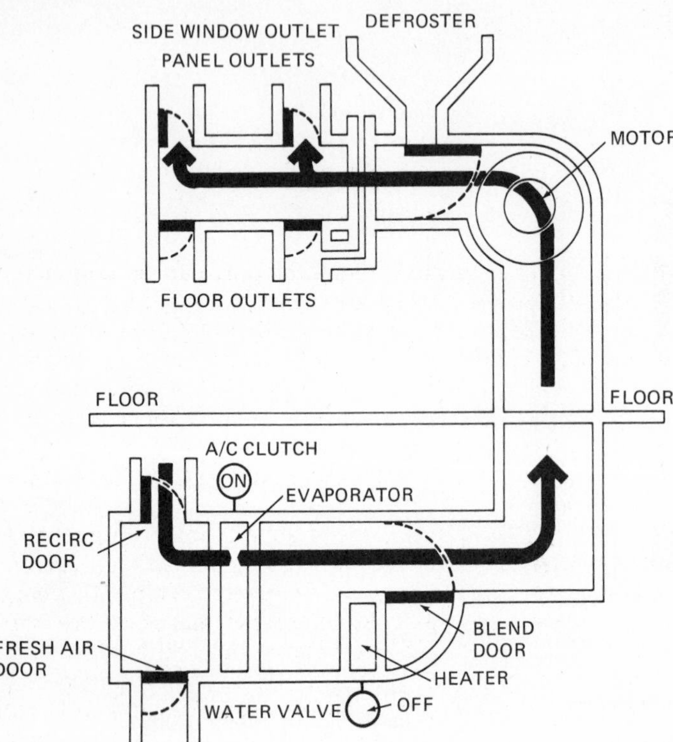

Fig. 16-24 Schematic illustration of the heater/air conditioner in the air conditioning mode. (*Ford Motor Company*)

pressor shaft—it should move freely. Next, use a voltmeter and check the voltage available at the fuse box switches, that is, at the high- and low-pressure switches, the relay, the temperature control thermostat, and the blower motors. Compare the voltmeter readings with the specifications in the service manual.

Air leaks To check for air leaks and to determine the condition of the vacuum pump, install a vacuum gauge into the reservoir. Operate the electric vacuum pump motor and reduce the pressure in the system to its minimum (see service manual for specifications); then stop the engine. Only a slight pressure rise should occur; otherwise the system has excessive leaks.

Place the temperature control lever and the function control lever in their various modes and then check each vacuum line and vacuum motor for air leaks. **NOTE** Do not forget to check the air intake ducts for restrictions, as these would reduce the intake air flow.

Duct temperature check After all checks have been made and the malfunction corrected, start the engine. Set the air conditioning system at the maximum cooling position. Insert a thermostat into an air duct and operate the compressor for 10 min. At the end of this time, the duct temperature should be about average, which is at least 46°F [7.78°C]. See service manual test specifications. If the temperature exceeds service manual specification, the air conditioning system must be tested.

NOTE If the duct temperature is at (or below) the service manual specification during the test but it increases when the motor vehicle is put into operation, the temperature increase could be due to engine overheating, an ambient temperature and humidity higher than normal, excessive stopping and starting of the vehicle, doors and/or windows not closing properly, the cab interior or exterior painted dark in color, or effects of the vehicle traveling on an asphalt road surface during long periods on a hot day.

ADDING REFRIGERANT When adding refrigerant, charging the system, or testing the operation of the air conditioning system, you must use an air conditioning test set, which consists of a vacuum pump,

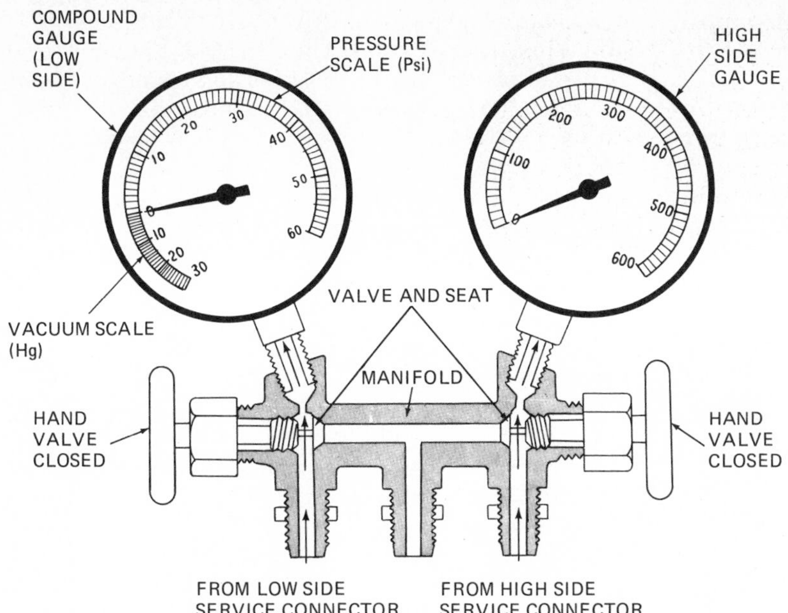

Fig. 16-25 Sectional view of a manifold gauge set. (*J I Case Company Agricultural Equipment Division*)

a charging hose set, a gauge and manifold set (Fig. 16-25), a thermometer, a leak detector, either an electronic or propane torch, and a supply of refrigerant.

The purpose of the vacuum pump is to remove the atmospheric pressure and moisture from the system. The purpose of the charging hose set and gauge manifold is to connect the gauges and the valves to the system in order to (1) remove air and moisture from it, (2) purge it of air, (3) bleed excessive refrigerant from it, (4) fill (charge) it with refrigerant, and (5) discharge the system. The left-hand (low-pressure-side) gauge can register low pressure (vacuum) and pressure, that is, pressure above and below atmospheric pressure. The right-hand (high-pressure side) gauge can only register pressure. **NOTE** The vacuum scale is calibrated in inches of mercury (inHg). The manifold has three inlet connections. The left-hand inlet port is connected to the low-pressure side, and the right-hand inlet port to the high-pressure side. The center port can be connected to the refrigerant supply or to the vacuum pump. When the left- and the right-hand valves are seated toward the center seat, the ports to the gauges are open and the passage to the center port closed off. When either valve is partly or fully opened, the center port is connected to the system and gauges. The purpose of either leak detector device is to locate the refrigerant leak.

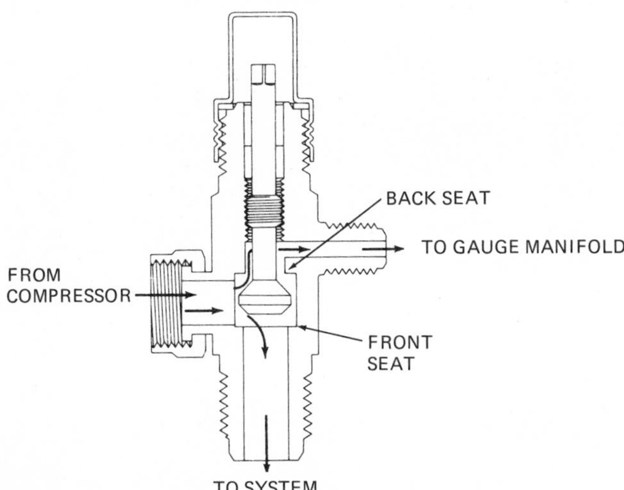

Fig. 16-26 Sectional view of a service valve in the halfway position. (*J I Case Company Agricultural Equipment Division*)

If the sight glass indicates low refrigerant fluid within the system, first clean the service valves, remove the service valve caps and, using the charging hoses, connect the manifold gauge to the service valves. **NOTE** You cannot make a mistake because the connecting fittings are of different sizes. Turn both hand valves clockwise until seated and connect the refrigerant supply to the manifold center port, but leave the hose fittings loose at the manifold. Next, operate, for about 10 min, the engine with the air conditioning set for maximum cooling in order to stabilize the system.

Before charging the system (adding refrigerant), the air in the manifold and charging hoses must be removed. To remove the air, turn the high-pressure-side hand valve slightly counterclockwise and leave it open for about 3 s, then close it and tighten the hose fittings. Repeat this procedure with the low-pressure side.

The next step is to remove the caps from the service valves and rotate both service valve stems clockwise, two full turns, from the back set position (see Fig. 16-26). With the engine operating at the recommended rpm and the air conditioning control set at the maximum cooling capacity, the left- and right-hand pressure gauges should show the pressures within the system. Next, turn the low-pressure-side hand valve counterclockwise to allow refrigerant to flow from the supply source into the low-pressure side of the system. Observe the low-pressure gauge reading—it should not exceed 40 psi [275.6 kPa] so that the added refrigerant will enter the system in vapor form. At the same time, check the sight glass and allow refrigerant to enter the system until the sight glass is free of air bubbles; then close the manifold low-pressure-side hand valve. **NOTE** Refer to the appropriate service manual for the vehicle being serviced, as some manufacturers recommend adding to the system a certain amount of refrigerant, by weight (pounds or kilograms), after the sight glass is free of air bubbles. Next, check the operating pressure of the system. If it corresponds with the performance check, stop the engine and turn both service valve stems counterclockwise until both valves seat firmly against the back seat. Close off the refrigerant supply valve.

CHECKING FOR REFRIGERANT LEAKS Air conditioning or refrigeration systems having even a minute refrigerant leak will very quickly lose their cooling capacity. If the leak is substantial, it will be apparent when you inspect the system, as the leak area will have collected oil and dust.

To verify a minute leak, one of two popular leak detector devices may be used: the electronic detector, or the open flame (propane) torch detector. When using the latter, the area where you are performing the test must be well ventilated.

Testing with a propane torch After the system is stabilized, stop the engine and start the propane torch, adjusting the flame so that you have a good blue flame. Place the flame near each fitting on or near the suspected leak area. If a refrigerant leak exists, the blue will change to yellow or a vivid purplish color. The color variation depends on the extent of the leak. The greater the leak, the more yellow the flame. Next, start the engine, operate the air conditioning, and check the high-pressure side of the system. If the system checks out satisfactorily (has no leaks) but it loses refrigerant, you can assume the evaporator has a leak.

Electronic testing Two basic types of electronic leak detectors are used: One looks like a gun and reveals a leak through an audible signal. Its probe element senses the escaping gas. This leak detector operates on a principle called *dielectric differential.* (2) The second type is the *halogen sensor,* which detects the halogen element inherent in the refrigerant. This test instrument consists of a neon lamp, powered by two D size batteries and a sensor. When the switch is placed in the ON position, the lamp lights, and if the sensor detects a leak it interrupts the current flow to the light.

PERFORMANCE CHECKS (PRESSURE) While the manifold gauge is connected to the system, close both high- and low-pressure-system manifold hand valves, and rotate both service valves clockwise about 1½ turns to open the valve to the mid-position. Next, operate the engine at the recommended rpm, set the air conditioning control for the maximum cooling, and set the blower at maximum speed. The low-pressure gauge should read between 7 and 30 psi [48.2 and 206.7 kPa] and the high-pressure gauge should read between 150 and 270 psi [1033.5 and 1860.3 kPa], depending upon the ambient temperature. Next, record the ambient temperature at a point about 12 to 24 in [31 to 61 cm] from the vehicle radiator and then place the thermometer into the recommended air duct, but make certain that the sensing element does not touch the side wall. Record the thermometer temperature after it has stabilized. Record the high- and low-pressure gauge readings and compare the test results with the service manual operating test chart. See Fig. 16-27 for an example of such a test chart.

If the pressure gauges show a reading which is above or below specification, you can assume there is trouble within the system.

If the low-pressure gauge reading is less than 7 psi [48.2 kPa] or indicates a vacuum, and the high-pressure gauge reading is 100 to 110 psi [689 to 757.9 kPa] the system is low in charge. If, however, the high-pressure reading is around 150 to 180 psi [1033.5 to 1240.2 kPa], probably the expansion valve is not operating correctly, or the high-pressure system side is restricted. To determine where the problem lies, feel the top of the extension valve. If it is as warm as the line to the valve, it is not working properly. If it is cooler, there is a restriction in the high-pressure side, possibly because of a kinked line or a restricted drier desiccant. The valve should be warmer than the line when it is functioning correctly.

High relative humidity

Ambient temperature		Average compressor refrigerant pressure				Passenger inboard outlet air temperature	
		Head		Suction			
°F	°C	psi	kPa	psi	kPa	°F	°C
70*	21	113—143	780— 990	13—17	89—116	46—50	8 —10
80*	26	114—174	990—1190	13—17	89—116	47—51	8.5—10.5
90	32	175—205	1200—1400	14—18	96—124	48—54	9 —12
100	37	208—238	1430—1630	17—21	116—144	51—59	10.5—15
110	43	283—268	1630—1830	20—24	137—164	56—64	13.5—17.8

*System may cycle at these ambient temperatures. Test readings listed are those that will occur just prior to compressor cycling off.

Fig. 16-27 Test chart example for high relative humidity. (*International Harvester Company*)

If the low-pressure gauge reading is high, say above 30 psi [206.7 kPa] and the high-pressure gauge is slightly above the recommended pressure (relevant to the ambient temperature), you may assume that there is air in the system. If so, check the sight glass for air bubbles and feel the suction line. If the suction line is warmer than normal, this indicates air in the system. If the low-pressure gauge reading is above 35 psi [241.15 kPa] and the high pressure is around 150 psi [1033.5 kPa], you can assume that the compressor is not operating properly, possibly due to a malfunction within the compressor or the clutch, or that a drive belt is slipping.

If both the high- and low-pressure gauge readings are high, say around 300 and 40 psi [2067 and 275.6 kPa], it is probably because the condenser is not removing the heat as fast as it should. This may be due to a loose engine fan belt, the radiator shutter system malfunctioning, or the condenser cooling fins being plugged.

Occasionally, the high- and low-pressure gauge readings may be within the recommended pressure range (low 7 to 30 psi [48.2 to 206.7 kPa], high 185 to 275 psi [1274.6 and 1894.7 kPa]) but the operator will complain that, while the system operates satisfactorily in the morning and late evening, it does not function adequately during midday. In this case the drier is probably saturated with moisture which is released during midday when the ambient temperature is high. Such a condition restricts the orifice in the expansion valve through freezing.

BLEEDING AND PURGING THE SYSTEM Whenever a hose, tube, or system component is to be removed, the system must be bled off (discharged). To bleed it, first connect the gauge manifold to the system and place the discharge hose end in a container or wrap it in a shop towel. Operate the engine at the recommended rpm, with the air conditioning system at the maximum cooling setting in order to stabilize the system. Stop the engine. Open both service valves to the midway position and partly open first the low-pressure and then the high-pressure manifold hand valves. **NOTE** If you open a hand valve too far, it will purge the system too fast and consequently excessive compressor oil will be drawn from the system. Close both hand valves when both pressure gauges read zero, and then remove the components which are to be replaced or serviced. Cap all openings to prevent contaminants from entering the system. **CAUTION** Do not discharge an air conditioning or refrigeration system near an open flame, as this could cause phosgene gas to form.

After the components are replaced, the air and moisture which has entered the system during the servicing must be removed. To do this, connect the gauge manifold to the system. Connect the vacuum pump to the center port. Place both manifold hand

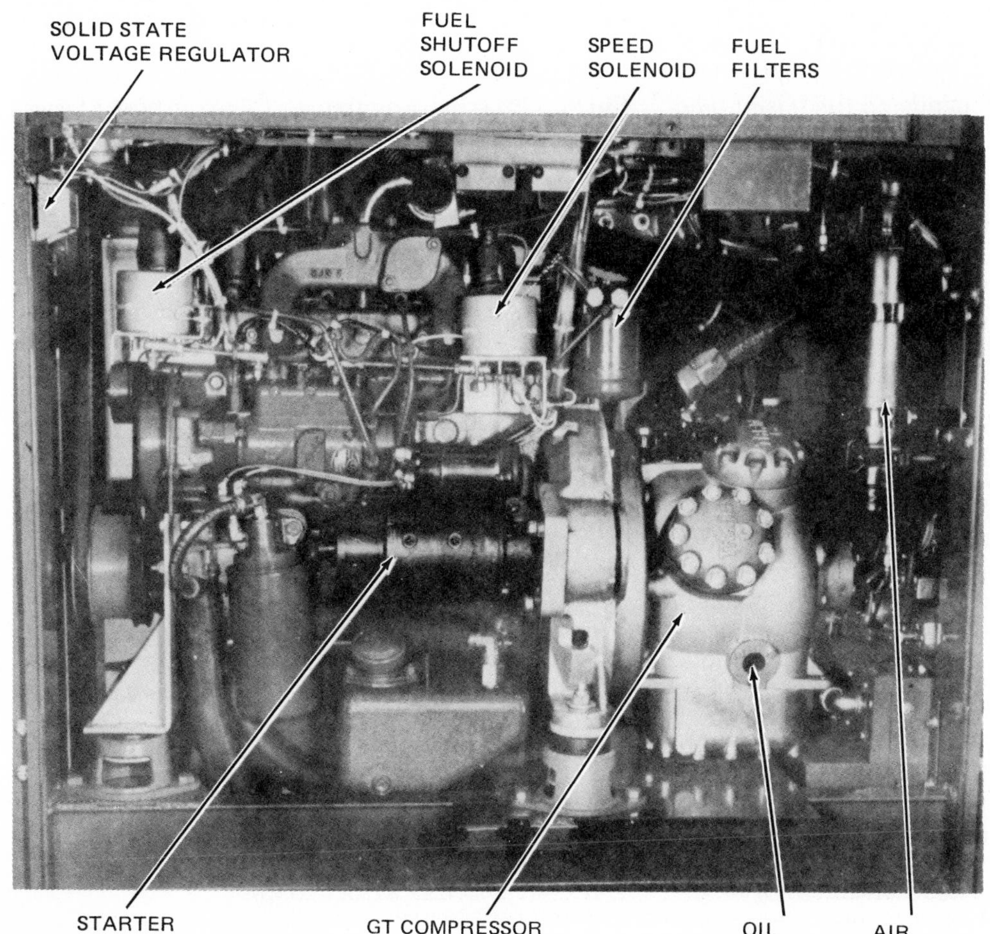

Fig. 16-28 View of a refrigeration engine and compressor assembly.

valves and service valves into the midway position. Start the motor to operate the vacuum pump. If, after 5 min, the low-pressure (left side) vacuum gauge scale reading is not at or near 28 in Hg [71.12 cm Hg], you can assume that the system has a leak. If there does not appear to be a leak, operate the vacuum pump for an additional 20 min. **NOTE** The vacuum gauge reading will vary between 28 and 29.56 in Hg [71.12 and 75.08 cm Hg], depending on the condition of the vacuum pump. After this time, close both manifold hand valves, remove the vacuum pump, and connect the refrigerant supply to the center port. Charge the system as recommended above in the material on adding refrigerant.

TRANSPORT REFRIGERATION

Although the basic transport refrigeration system has many similarities to an air conditioning system, it is also different in a number of ways. For instance, the entire system—that is, the engine, the compressor, and the refrigeration components—are built into one housing which is fastened to the body of the motortruck or trailer (see Fig. 16-28). The cooling capacity refrigeration system (Btu/hr) [kJ/h] is usually greater than that of an air conditioning system because it must affect a much larger area at a much lower temperature. The required cooling capacity is generally between 12,000 Btu/hr [4320 kJ/h] and 140,000 Btu/hr [50,400 kJ/h], with a maximum return air flow to the evaporator of −20°F [−28.8°C] at an ambient temperature of 100°F [37.8°C]. The specification, of course, depends on the design and capacity of the refrigeration system, the body design (particularly with regard to the composition of the material and its thickness), as well as the overall body length of the vehicle and the anticipated frequency of body door opening and closing.

The compressor is driven by either a gas or a diesel water-cooled engine of a power range between 24 and 25 hp [17.9–18.6 kW]. However, some smaller refrigeration systems use small air-cooled engines of a power range between 5 and 15 hp.

The compressors may be of the axial piston type, the reciprocating type, or the two- or four-piston design. The smaller units use the same magnetic clutch as does an air conditioning system. The compressor on larger units pumps continuously at maximum engine speed (which is about 2000 rpm) for maximum set cooling, and when the set cooling temperature is reached the engine automatically is reduced to low-cooling speed until the temperature rises and, once again, additional cooling is required.

To control the confined space temperature, that is, to hold it constant without cycling from cooling to heating, several additional valves are used. **NOTE** On new refrigeration systems, the thermostatic control unit is a solid state design.

The evaporator and condenser are commonly made from stainless steel. The receiver and drier are separate units. Some specially designed units have electric motors to drive the compressor at the loading or parking side.

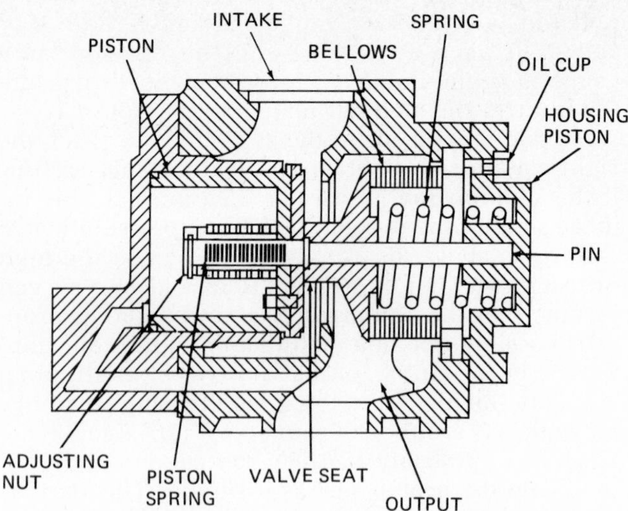

Fig. 16-29 Schematic view of one suction pressure (throttling) valve. (*Thermo King Corporation*)

The engine's starting and charging systems are identical to any other engine electric system. They, too, have oil pressure and cooling temperature gauges but, in addition, some have a cooling level indicator as well as an hourmeter to indicate the engine's cumulative operating time. Safety shutdown devices are also inherent features; should the engine oil pressure fall below the predetermined safe operating pressure, or the coolant temperature exceed the safety level, the engine automatically shuts down.

Suction Pressure Regulators The purpose of these valves is to control the maximum suction pressure of the compressor and thereby prevent overloading of the compressor and engine, or overloading of the electric motor (see Fig. 16-29). Maximum suction pressure could be exceeded when the refrigeration system is being started up (during the pulldown). The suction pressure is set or adjusted to about 15 to 17 psi [103.3 to 117.1 kPa]. However, if the pressure setting is higher, the engine may become

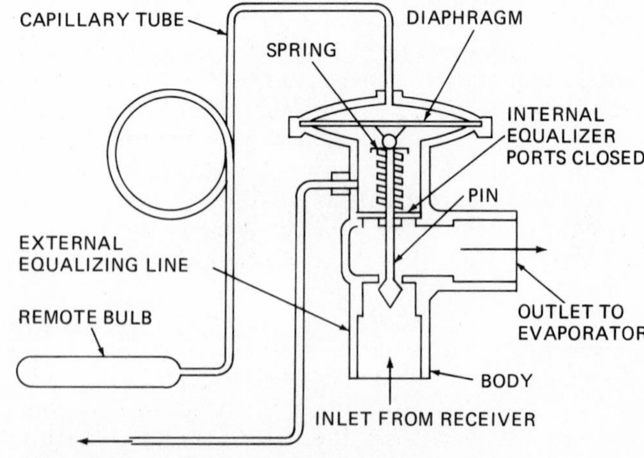

Fig. 16-30 Schematic view of a thermostatic expansion valve. (*Thermo King Corporation*)

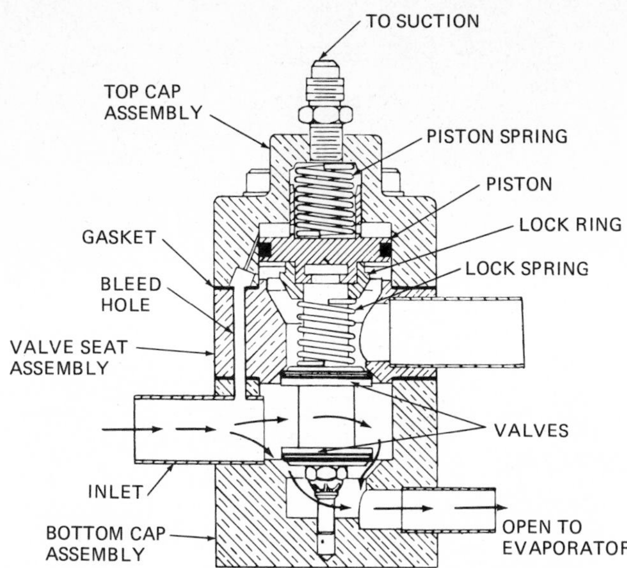

Fig. 16-31 Schematic view of a three-way valve in the HEAT/DEFROST position. (*Thermo King Corporation*)

overloaded, as liquid may enter the compressor. If the pressure setting is too low, the cooling temperature may not be achieved.

A bellows spring tends to push the suction valve open, and the force of the bellows tends to push the valve closed.

NOTE The bellows is a temperature-sensing device which expands as the temperature increases and retracts as it decreases.

When the compressor is operating, the inlet pressure from the evaporator acts on the bellows assembly area against the force of the adjusting spring and bellow. The outlet suction pressure acts on the large piston. This positions the valve so as to create the required suction pressure. **NOTE** The thermostatic expansion valve used on a refrigeration system is slightly different than the one used on an air conditioning system. See Fig. 16-30.

Three-Way Valve System The purpose of the three-way valve, also known as the *defrost* or *heating valve*, is to place the refrigeration system in the heating or cooling cycle. It is a pressure-sensing valve which responds to the actions of the pilot solenoid valve. The solenoid valve either allows the suction pressure to be exerted against the valve piston, or it removes the suction pressure from the piston. The pilot solenoid may be energized by operating the manual switch, or through an air flow sensor switch positioned in front of the evaporator. See Fig. 16-31.

OPERATION Assume the refrigeration system is set at the refrigeration cycle and the air flow through the evaporator coil is unrestricted. The pilot solenoid valve is then disengaged and the suction pressure is removed from the three-way valve piston. The inlet pressure passes through the bypass onto the top of the piston, thereby equalizing the force on the piston, and the spring force then moves the piston down. This opens the top valve and closes the lower valve; the discharge refrigerant from the compressor can now flow to the condensor coil.

If the solenoid valve is energized by placing the manual switch in the HEAT/DEFROST position, or energized through the air flow sensor switch suction, (low) pressure acts on the three-way valve piston. Consequently the discharge (high) pressure forces the piston upward against its spring force, causing the upper valve to close and the lower valve to open, and the discharged refrigerant from the compressor is then directed out of the lower right-hand port, through the heat/defrost coil expansion valve, and into the evaporator coil. This converts the evaporator into a condensor and the condensor into an evaporator, placing the refrigeration system into the heat/defrost cycle.

Reverse-Cycle Valve The reverse-cycle valve serves the same purpose as a three-way valve, that is, it directs the refrigerant flow during the cooling and defrost/heating cycle (see Fig. 16-32). The valve action also is controlled through a pilot solenoid valve; however, the pilot solenoid valve places either the suction pressure or the discharge pressure onto the piston of the reverse-cycle valve. The valve body has four ports which connect the valve with (1) the compressor suction line, (2) the discharge

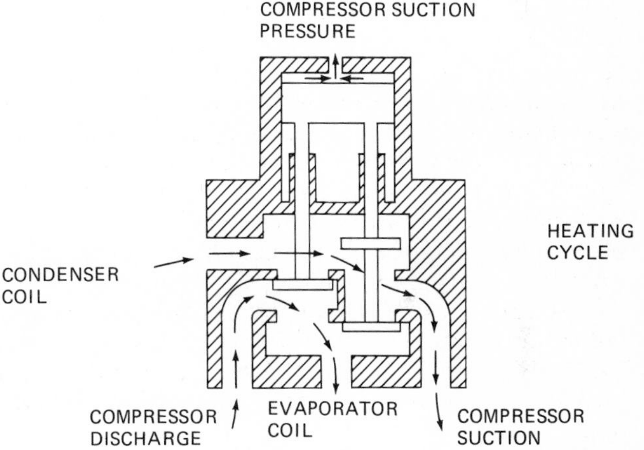

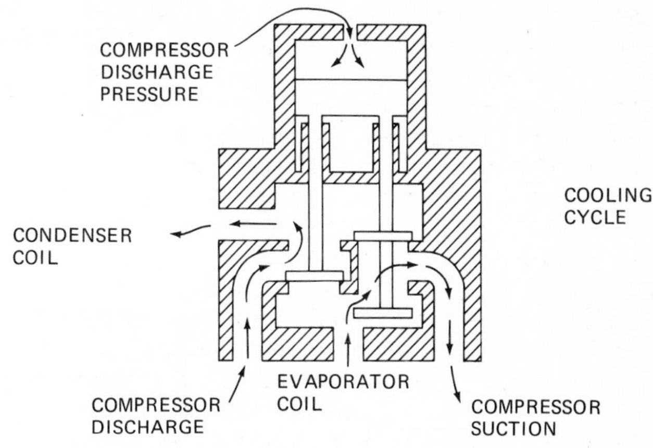

Fig. 16-32 Schematic view of a reverse-cycle valve. (*Thermo King Corporation*)

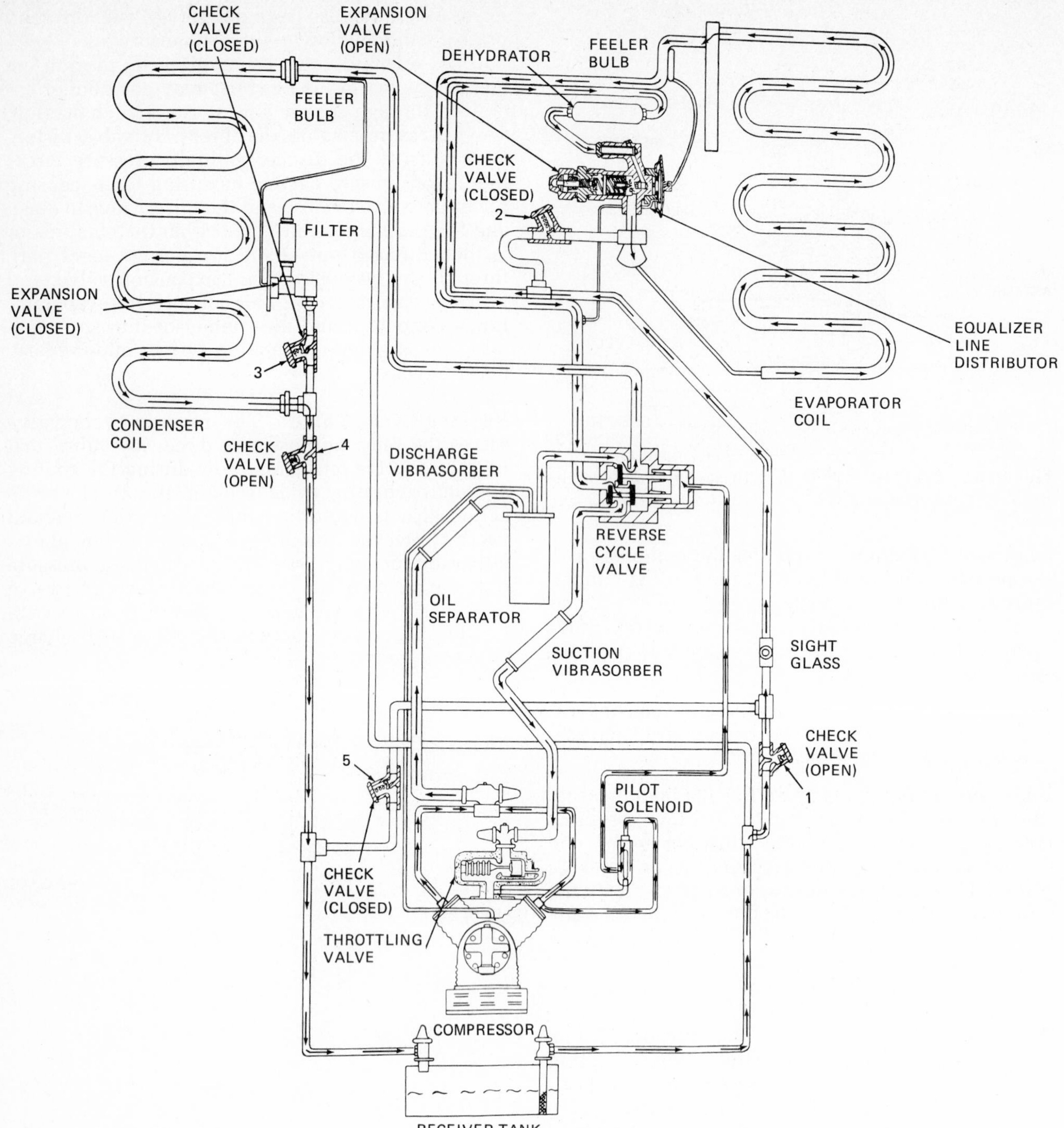

Fig. 16-33 Refrigeration cycle diagram. (*Thermo King Corporation*)

line, (3) the condensor coil, (4) the evaporator coil, and (5) the pilot solenoid valve. In the valve housing are three valves which are opened and closed through the pilot valve or system pressure. **NOTE** The left-hand valve is a dual-purpose valve.

Cooling Cycle The refrigerant is pumped from both sides of the compressor, over the discharge service valve, through the discharge vibrasorber, through the oil separator, and into the reverse-cycling valve. Meanwhile the pilot solenoid valve has placed discharge pressure onto the reverse-cycling valve piston, forcing both valve stems down, thus seating the left- and right-hand valves. Therefore, discharge pressure is directed through the reverse-cycling valve and out of the condenser port, through the condenser, and into the discharge line. It is then directed out of the receiver tank, to the dehydrator (drier) expansion valve-cool, through the evaporator coil, and into the reverse-cycling valve evaporator port. The refrigerant flows past the lower valve and out of the compressor suction port, through the suction vibrasorber, through the suction service valve, and into the left- and right-hand suction ports of the

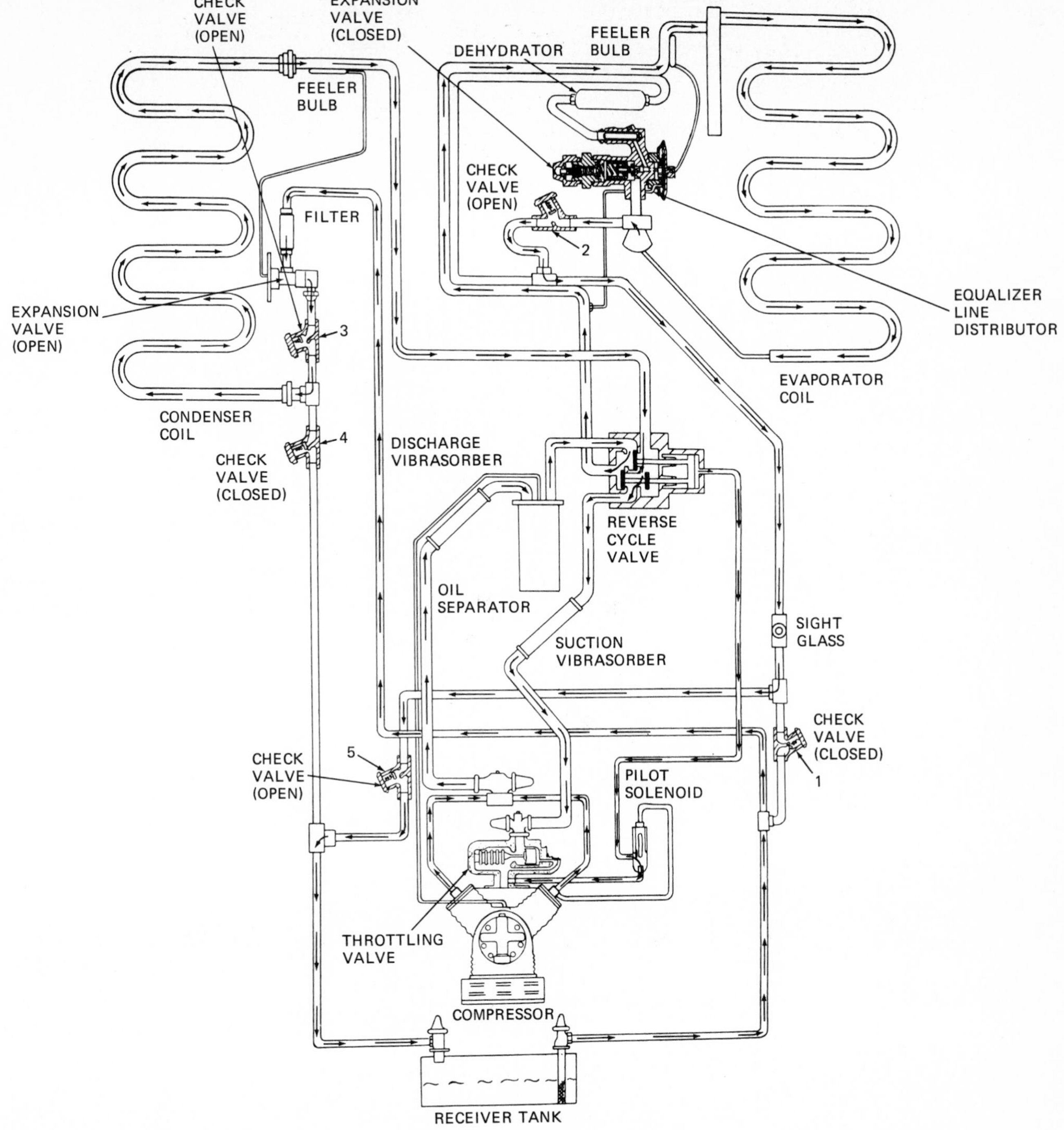

Fig. 16-34 Heating and defrost cycle. (*Thermo King Corporation*)

compressor. Due to the refrigerant flow, check valves 1 and 4 are forced open, and valves 2, 3, and 5 are forced closed. See Fig. 16-33.

Heat/Defrost Cycle When the air flow through the evaporator is restricted due to ice buildup on its core or the manual switch is placed in the heat cycle to melt the ice buildup from the evaporator core, the pilot solenoid is energized. This reduces the discharge pressure to suction pressure, which in turn lifts the reverse-cycling valve piston upward. The refrigerant now flows through the discharge service valve, through the discharge vibrasorber and the oil separator, and into the recycling valve compressor discharge port. The pressure forces the recycling valves upward, opening the flow to the evaporator port and closing off the flow to the condenser coil. This converts the evaporator coil to a heat-dissipating unit and converts the condenser to a heat-absorbing unit because of the reverse flow of the refrigerant.

Refrigerant now flows from the reverse-recycling valve and through the evaporator coil, forcing check valves 2 and 5 to open and valve 1 to close. It then

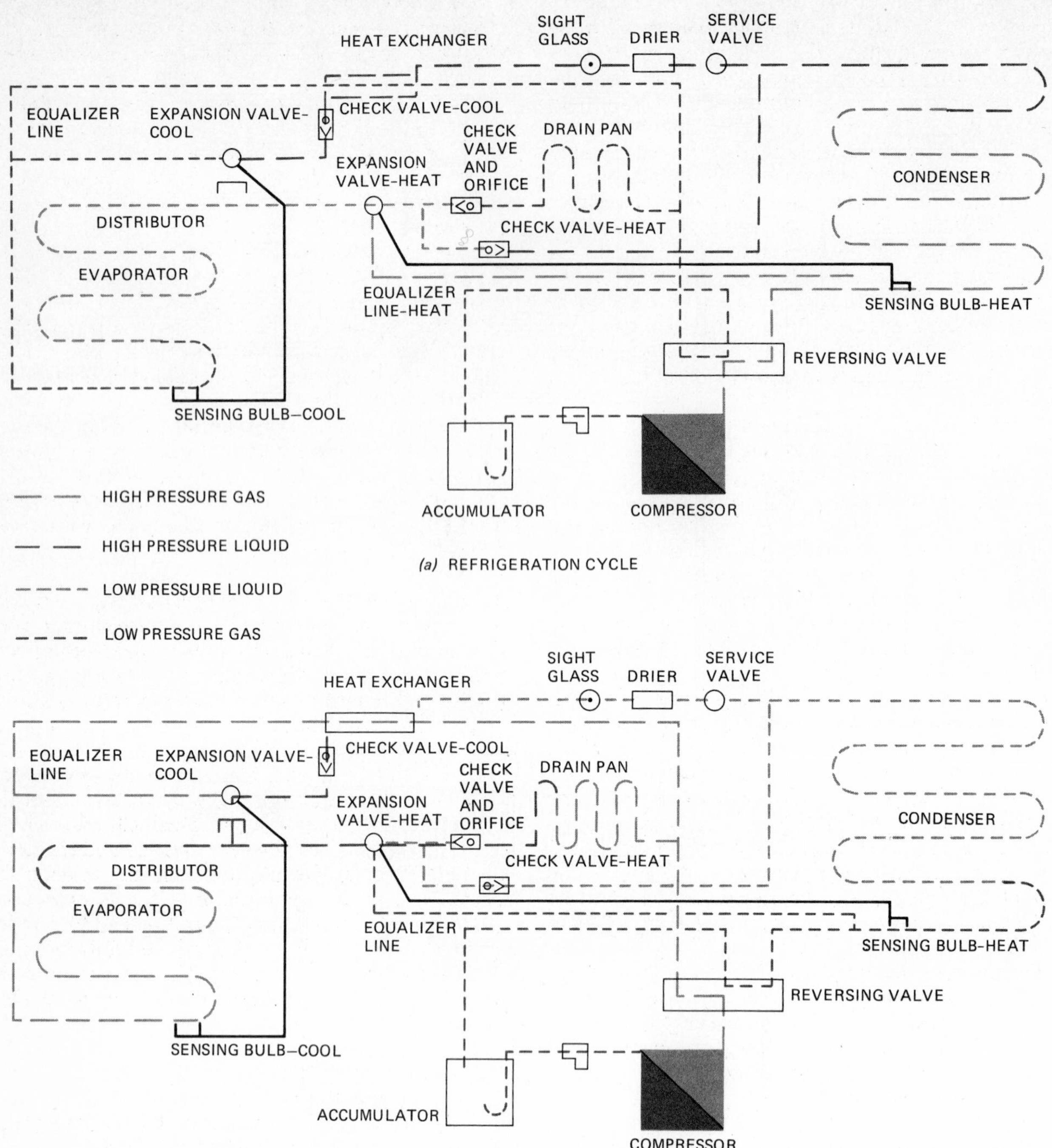

Fig. 16-35 (*a*) Refrigeration (cooling) cycle; (*b*) heating cycle. (*The Trane Company*)

flows out of the receiver, through the reverse expansion valve, through check valve and the condenser coil, and into the reverse-cycling valve, forcing the right-hand valve upward. This directs the flow out of the compressor suction port, through the suction vibrasorber, the suction-service valve, and the throttling valve, and into both suction sides of the compressor. **NOTE** The flow of the refrigerant forces check valves 1 and 4 to close. Check valve 1 then blocks the flow to the sight glass and valve 4 blocks the flow to the receiver. The condenser expansion valve bulb attached to the condenser senses the low temperature. When the system is set for the refrigeration cycle, the condenser expansion valve closes as soon as it senses the higher temperature. See Fig. 16-34.

Cooling/Heating Cycle for Temperature Control Another refrigerant system is shown in Fig. 16-35*a*. When this system is in the cooling cycle, the check valve (heat solenoid) is energized, consequently closing its check valve, and the check valve-cool is de-energized, thus opening the check valve. The PL-1 cool (pilot light) glows, the temperature controller energizes the high-speed engine solenoid, and the engine operates at high-speed cooling (see

Fig. 16-36). The refrigerant is pumped over the reversing valve, through the condenser, the service valve, the drier, the sight glass and around the heat exchanger, through the check valve-cool, and through the expansion valve-cool. The expansion valve responds to the sensing bulb-cool (attached to the outlet end of the evaporator), allowing refrigerant to enter the system. The superheated vapor leaves the evaporator, passes through the heat exchanger, flows through the reversing valve into the accumulator, and reenters the compressor over the service valve. After the temperature within the space reaches the temperature controller preset setting, the controller responds by disengaging the high-speed solenoid, and the engine then operates on low-speed cooling.

If under this condition the temperature decreases below that at which it is set at the controller, the check valve-cool solenoid then energizes and closes the check valve, and the check valve-heat is deenergized, thus opening the valve (Fig. 16-35*b* and 16-36). This causes the refrigerant flow to reverse, the cool pilot light to go out, and the heat pilot light to light. The refrigerant then flows from the compressor to the reversing valve (here the flow is reversed), through the heat exchanger, through the evaporator (which now assumes the function of the condenser), and into the expansion valve-heat. This valve has responded to the sensing bulb attached to the condenser. The refrigerant now flows over the open check valve-heat and into the condenser, which now functions as the evaporator. From the condenser, the superheated vapor flows over the reversing valve, to and through the accumulator, and then over the suction service valve into the suction port of the compressor. As the space temperature increases, the temperature controller responds and switches to the cooling cycle.

To speed up the heating cycle, the operator can override the low engine speed by closing the high heat switch (SW-6), which energizes the high-speed solenoid. This moves the engine governor into high speed, causing the engine and compressor to operate at rated speed. See Fig. 16-36.

DEFROST The operator has two defrost options—manual and automatic. When the manual/automatic switch (SW5) (see Fig. 16-36) is placed into the MANUAL position, the defrost relay is energized and the cool and heat pilot light will go out. Current then flows to the temperature controller, and thence to the check valve-heat solenoid and check valve-cool solenoid, closing both valves. Current flows to the defrost pilot light (indicating defrosting cycle) and to the damper solenoid, closing the damper door. This prevents hot air from entering the cooled area, and it remains cool during the defrost cycle.

The electric action places the refrigerant system into the heat cycle; however, the check valve-heat is closed and the refrigerant (at a high temperature and high pressure) is directed from the expansion valve-heat through the check valve and orifice, through the defrost coil, and back to the evaporator. When the defrost timer opens the circuit, the defrost cycle is interrupted and the temperature controller takes effect and again controls the temperature within the space.

When the manual/automatic defrost switch is placed in the AUTOMATIC position, no electric action takes place. However, as soon as the (defrost) air switch located at the evaporator core closes owing to restricted airflow to the evaporator, the defrost relay is actuated and the defrost light lights. The damper solenoid becomes energized and closes the damper door, and the check valve-heat and check valve-cool solenoids are energized. This places the refrigerant system into the heat cycle and the refrigerant then flows through the check valve/orifice, through the defrost coil, and back to the evaporator, but not through the condenser.

The defrost cycle is interrupted and the temperature controller takes over to control the air temperature within the space when either the air flow through the evaporator becomes unrestricted (opened) or when the defrost air switch or the timer opens the defrost relay circuit.

Refrigeration System Troubleshooting On the whole, a refrigeration system is subject to the same type of failure problems as an air conditioning control system. When the confined space temperature cannot be brought down to the temperature controller setting, even though the ambient temperature and operating conditions are normal, the following checks should be made. First, check the engine performance, the condition of the drive belts, and the general condition of the compressor. Check the body of the motortruck or trailer for damage and the doors for tight fit or proper closure. Ask the driver if the load is too great spacewise and if it is precooled. Ask if there is room at the top of the load to provide air flow, or if the contents are stacked tightly on top of one another so as to prevent air flow around the load. Next, check the refrigeration system for the following:

1. Level of refrigerant
2. The presence of air
3. Cleanliness of the condenser and evaporator coil
4. Twisted or damaged refrigerant lines
5. Excessive oil circulation
6. The voltage of the various switches and solenoids

If none of these checks indicate the reason for lack of temperature control, install the test manifold within the system and make a performance test. The various combinations of low- and high-pressure readings at the low- and high-pressure gauges will reveal the same type of trouble areas as outlined above in the material on testing and servicing air conditioning systems. However, in addition, if the low-pressure gauge has a high pressure, it could possibly be caused by a faulty (stuck open) pilot solenoid valve, or the throttle valve may be faulty and therefore allowing liquid refrigerant to enter the compressor. Suppose the low-pressure gauge (vacuum scale) indicates that the pressure is slightly

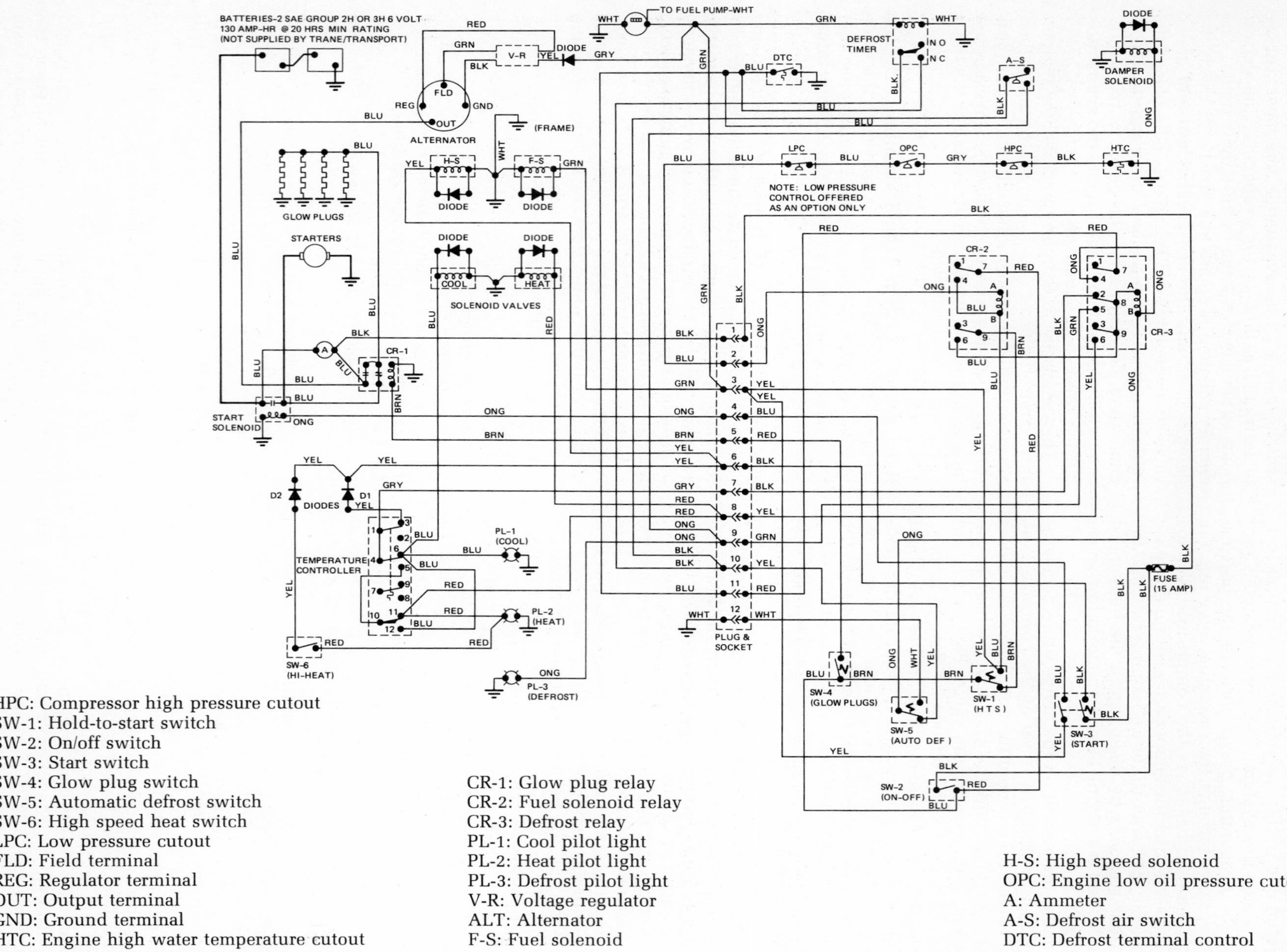

HPC: Compressor high pressure cutout
SW-1: Hold-to-start switch
SW-2: On/off switch
SW-3: Start switch
SW-4: Glow plug switch
SW-5: Automatic defrost switch
SW-6: High speed heat switch
LPC: Low pressure cutout
FLD: Field terminal
REG: Regulator terminal
OUT: Output terminal
GND: Ground terminal
HTC: Engine high water temperature cutout

CR-1: Glow plug relay
CR-2: Fuel solenoid relay
CR-3: Defrost relay
PL-1: Cool pilot light
PL-2: Heat pilot light
PL-3: Defrost pilot light
V-R: Voltage regulator
ALT: Alternator
F-S: Fuel solenoid

H-S: High speed solenoid
OPC: Engine low oil pressure cutout
A: Ammeter
A-S: Defrost air switch
DTC: Defrost terminal control

Fig. 16-36 Electric system diagram of a refrigeration system. (*The Trane Company*)

lower than specified, for example, say the gauge reads 0.6 in Hg [1.5 cm Hg] and the refrigerant temperature should be −20°F [−28.8°C]. This would give a confined space temperature of about −20°F + 15°F = −5°F [−20.6°C]. If the space temperature is higher, the evaporator shutter may be (stuck) closed. If the unit is not defrosting, it may be that the evaporator shutter is (stuck) open, the defrost check valve is (stuck) closed, or there may be an electric failure.

The evacuation of air and moisture from the system should be performed in two independent steps, first, by purging the low-pressure side, and then by purging the high-pressure side. This is also recommended when charging the system.

Review Questions

1. List the major components of an air conditioning system.
2. Define the term "latent heat" ("hidden heat").
3. By which three methods is heat transferred?
4. Explain the pumping principle of a double-acting axial compressor.
5. What is the purpose of (*a*) an evaporator and (*b*) a condenser?
6. Explain the operation of a thermostatic expansion valve.
7. What is the simplest method to control the temperature within the drive compartment?
8. What purpose do the high- and low-pressure switches serve?
9. List nine reasons why the driver compartment may have insufficient heat or poor defrosting.
10. List seven reasons why the air conditioning system could have a low cooling effect, or very little cooling effect.
11. Explain how to (*a*) connect the test instruments to the air conditioning system and (*b*) use them to make a performance test.
12. List the precautions you must take when bleeding the air conditioning system.
13. What are the major differences between an air conditioning system and a transport refrigeration system?
14. Name three valves that could be used to cycle the refrigeration system from cool to heat, or vice versa.
15. Outline the principle used to convert a refrigeration system from the cool to the heat cycle, or vice versa.
16. What is the purpose of the evaporator shutter door(s)?
17. Outline two methods by which the refrigeration system can be placed into the defrost cycle.
18. Under what conditions, during a performance test, would the low- and high-pressure system gauges show a lower pressure than specified.

Conversion Tables

Well over 95% of the world's population already uses metric units of measurement or is converting to them. The tremendous advantage of the metric system is its simplicity and its universality: All relationships between the various units of the metric system work in powers of 10, and unified symbols are used for each unit instead of many different abbreviations.

However, North America still relies primarily on the United States Customary system of measurement, and it is the primary system used in this textbook. To assist you when you must work with both systems, these conversion charts are supplied. They will provide you with a fast and simple means of converting USCS to metric units, and vice versa.

For example, if you want to know the displacement in liters or cubic centimeters of a diesel engine having a displacement of 600 in³ (cubic inches), select the capacity and volume conversion table. Refer to the in³ entry in the left-hand column. The comparable amount in liters (l) and in cubic centimeters (cm³) is shown to the right. Since 1 in³ equals 16.39 cm³, 600 in³ equals 600 × 16.39, or 9834 cm³. Since 1 in³ is also equal to 0.0164 l, 600 in³ equals 600 × 0.0164, or 9.84 l.

Area The metric units of area are based on the square meter (m²). Other units are created by multiplying or dividing by a factor of 10.

AREA

	in²	ft²	yd²	mm²	cm²	dm²	m²
1 in² =	—	0.0069		645.2	6.452	0.06452	0.00064
1 ft² =	144	—	0.1111	92,903	929	9.29	0.0929
1 yd² =	1296	9	—	836,100	8361	83.61	0.8361
1 mi² =		27,878,400					2,589,998
1 mm² =	0.0015			—	0.01	0.0001	0.000001
1 cm² =	0.155	0.0017		100	—	0.01	0.0001
1 dm² =	15.5	0.1076	0.01196	10,000	100	—	0.01
1 m² =	1550	10.76	1.196	1,000,000	10,000	100	—

Capacity The metric units of capacity are based on the liter (l). Other units are created by multiplying or dividing by a factor of 10.

Volume The metric units of volume are based on the cubic meter (m³). Other units are created by multiplying or dividing by a factor of 10.

CAPACITY AND VOLUME

	in³	ft³	U.S. qt	U.S. gal	Imp. qt	Imp. gal	cm³	dm³	m³	l
1 in³ =	—		0.01732		0.01442		16.39	0.01639		0.0164
1 ft³ =	1728	—	29.92	7.481	24.92	6.229		28.32	0.02832	28.32
1 yd³ =	46,656	27	807.9	202	672.8	168.2		764.6	0.7646	764.6
1 U.S. qt =	57.75	0.03342	—	0.25	0.8327	0.2082	946.4	0.9464		0.946
1 U.S. gal =	231	0.1337	4	—	3.331	0.8327	3785	3.785	0.003785	3.785
1 Imp. qt. =	69.36	0.04014	1.201	0.3002	—	0.25	1136	1.136		1.136
1 Imp. gal =	277.4	0.1605	4.804	1.201	4	—	4546	4.546	0.004546	4.546
1 cm³ =	0.06102	0.003	0.105	0.0264	0.088	0.022	—	0.001	0.000001	0.001
1 dm³ =	61.02	0.03531	1.057	0.2642	0.88	0.22	1000	—	0.001	1
1 m³ =	61,023	35.31	1057	264.2	880	220		1000	—	1000
1 l =	61.02	0.03531	1.057	0.2642	0.88	0.22	1000	1.0	0.001	—

Energy The metric unit of energy is the newton-meter (N·m) or joule (J). One joule is the amount of work done when a force of one newton moves an object a distance of one meter (or 1 J = 1 N·m).

ENERGY

	J	N·m	Btu	ft·lb
1 J =	—	1.0	0.00094	0.7376
1 N·m =	1.0	—	0.00094	0.7376
1 Btu =	1055.01	1055.01	—	778.3

FORCE The metric unit of force is the newton (N). It is defined as the force needed to move a mass of one kilogram a distance of one meter. It also can be defined as the force which, when applied to an object with a mass of one kilogram, accelerates it at a rate of one meter per second per second (1 m/s²). The force of the earth's gravity acting on a mass of one kilogram = 9.81 N, so 1 kg = 9.81 N.

1 kg = 9.81 N
1 lb = 4.448 N
1 oz = 0.278 N
1 N = 0.101 kg = 0.224 lb = 0.138 oz

Length The metric units of length are based on the meter (m). Other units are created by multiplying or dividing by a factor of 10.

LENGTH

	in	ft	yd	mi (statute)	nmi	mm	cm	m	km	μm
1 in =	—	0.08333	0.02778			25.4	2.54	0.0254		25,400
1 ft =	12	—	0.3333	0.00019	0.00016	304.8	30.48	0.30488		
1 yd =	36	3	—	0.00057	0.00048	914.4	91.44	0.9144		
1 mi (statute)	63,360	5280	1760	—	0.8684			1609.3	1.609	
1 nmi =	72,960	6080	2027	1.152	—			1853.3	1.853	
1 mm =	0.03937	0.003281				—	0.1	0.001		1000
1 cm =	0.3937	0.03281	0.01094			10	—	100		10,000
1 m =	39.37	3.281	1.094	0.00062	0.00053	1000	100	—	0.001	
1 km =	39,370	3281	1093.6	0.6214	0.5396	10^6	100,000	1000	—	
1 μm =	0.000039					0.01	0.0001	0.000001		—

Mass The metric units of mass are based on the kilogram (kg), which is defined as the mass of one liter of water at 4°C [39° F]. Other units are created by multiplying or dividing by a factor of 10.

MASS

	oz	lb	g	kg
1 oz =	—	0.0625	28.35	0.02835
1 lb =	16	—	453.59	0.45359
1 g =	0.03527		—	0.001
1 kg =	35.27	2.2046	1000	—

Power The metric unit of power is the watt (W). This is the power required to move a weight of one newton a distance of one meter in a time of one second (1 W = 1 N·m/s).

POWER

	hp	hp (metric)	ft · lb/s	kg · m/s	kW	W	Btu/min
1 hp =	—	1.014	550	76.04	0.746	746	42.4
1 hp (metric) =	0.986	—	542.5	75.00	0.736	736	41.8
1 ft · lb/s =			—	0.30488		0.0226	0.001285
1 kg · m/s =			3.281	—		0.0741	0.0042
1 kW =	1.341	1.360	737.28	102.00	—	1000	56.8
1 W =	0.00134	0.00136	0.737	0.102	0.001	—	
1 Btu/min =	0.0236	0.0239	12.96	3.939	0.0176	17.6	—

Pressure The metric unit of pressure is the pascal (Pa). One pascal is produced when a force of one newton is applied to an area of one square meter.

Pressure (Pa) = force/area = N/m^2

PRESSURE

	inH_2O	cmH_2O	inHg	cmHg	psi	kg/cm^2	atm	kPa
1 inH_2O =	—	2.54	0.0735	1.866	0.0361	0.0025	0.0024	0.248
1 inHg =	13.6	34.544	—	2.54	0.491	0.0345	0.0334	3.386
1 psi =	27.7	70.104	2.036	5.171	—	0.0703	0.068	6.89
1 kg/cm^2 =	393.73	1000.0	28.96	73.55	14.22	—	0.9678	37.97
1 atm =	407.19	1033.0	29.92	75.96	14.70	1.033	—	101.28
1 kPa =	4.01	10.18	0.295	0.750	0.145	0.026	0.0098	—

The boiling point of water varies with atmospheric pressure, which varies with altitude as follows:

ATMOSPHERIC PRESSURE AT VARIOUS ALTITUDES VERSUS THE BOILING POINT OF WATER

Altitude		Atmospheric pressure			Boiling point of water	
ft	m	psi	inHg	kPa	°F	°C
Sea level		14.69	29.92	101.28	212	100
1000	304.8	14.16	28.86	97.56	210.1	99
2000	609.6	13.66	27.82	94.11	208.3	98
3000	914.4	13.16	26.81	90.67	206.5	97
4000	1219.4	12.68	25.84	87.36	204.6	95.9
5000	1524.0	12.22	24.89	84.19	202.8	94.9
6000	1828.8	11.77	23.98	81.09	201.0	94.1
7000	2133.6	11.33	23.09	78.06	199.3	93.0
8000	2438.4	10.91	22.22	75.16	197.4	91.9
9000	2743.2	10.50	21.38	72.34	195.7	91
10,000	3048.0	10.10	20.58	69.58	194.0	90

Temperature The metric unit of temperature is the degree Celsius. Use the following formulas to convert from degrees Celsius to degrees Fahrenheit, and vice versa:

$$°F = 1.8C + 32$$
$$°C = (F - 32) \div 1.8$$

Example 1 Convert 0 and 100°C to degrees Fahrenheit.

$$1.8\,(0°) + 32 = 32°F$$
$$1.8\,(100°) + 32 = 212°F$$

Example 2 Convert 32 and 212°F to degrees Celsius.

$$(32° - 32) \div 1.8 = 0°C$$
$$(212° - 32) \div 1.8 = 100°C$$

In most cases, however, you will find it simpler to refer to a conversion chart, such as the one on the following page, for your answer.

TEMPERATURE CONVERSION

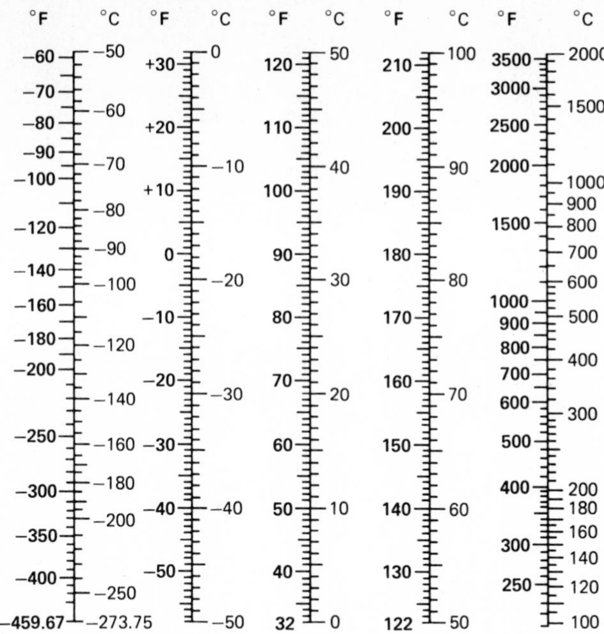

Torque The metric unit of torque is the newton-meter (N · m). This measurement is replacing the kilogram-meter (kg · m), which you may still encounter in your work.

TORQUE

	lb·ft	kg·m	N·m
1 lb·ft =	—	0.1383	1.355
1 kg·m =	7.233	—	9.80
1 N·m =	0.738	7.233	—

Work Work is related to energy and is measured in the same unit, the newton meter (N·m).

Index